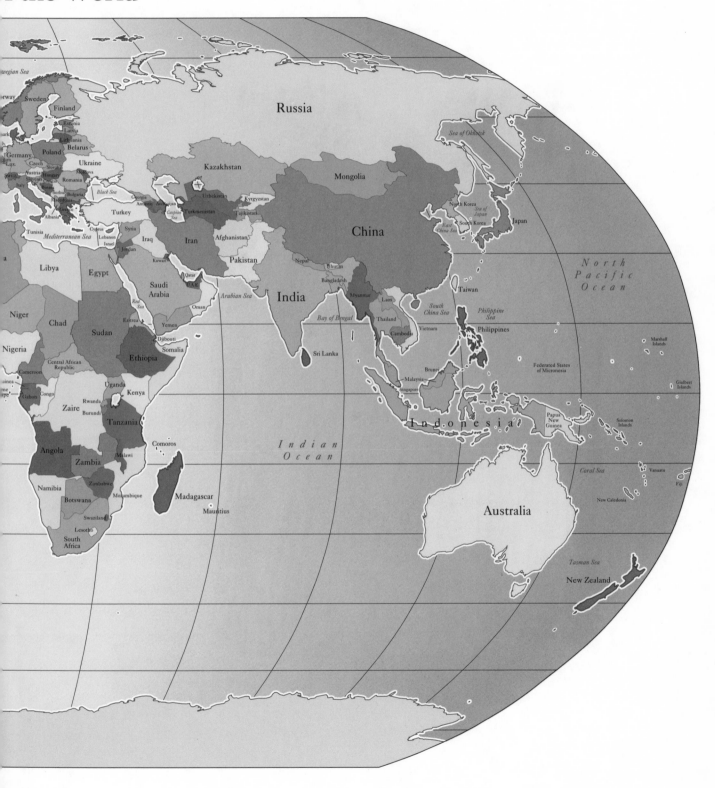

ENCYCLOPEDIA OF U.S. FOREIGN RELATIONS

ENCYCLOPEDIA OF
U.S. FOREIGN RELATIONS

SENIOR EDITORS

Bruce W. Jentleson   Thomas G. Paterson

PREPARED UNDER THE AUSPICES OF THE
Council on Foreign Relations

SENIOR CONSULTING EDITOR

Nicholas X. Rizopoulos

VOLUME 4

Oxford University Press
New York Oxford
1997

OXFORD UNIVERSITY PRESS

Oxford   New York
Athens   Auckland   Bangkok   Bogotá   Bombay   Buenos Aires
Calcutta   Cape Town   Dar es Salaam   Delhi   Florence   Hong Kong
Istanbul   Karachi   Kuala Lumpur   Madras   Madrid   Melbourne
Mexico City   Nairobi   Paris   Singapore   Taipei   Tokyo   Toronto

and associated companies in
Berlin   Ibadan

Published by Oxford University Press, Inc.,
198 Madison Avenue, New York, New York 10016

Oxford is a registered trademark of Oxford University Press

Library of Congress Cataloging-in-Publication Data
Encyclopedia of U.S. foreign relations / senior editors, Bruce W.
Jentleson, Thomas G. Paterson.
p. cm.
Includes bibliographical references and index.
1. United States—Foreign relations—Encyclopedias. 2. United
States—Relations—Encyclopedias. I. Jentleson, Bruce W., 1951-.
II. Paterson, Thomas G., 1941-.
E183.7.E53   1997   96-8159   327.73—dc20   CIP
ISBN 0-19-511055-2 (4-vol. set)
ISBN 0-19-511059-5 (vol. 4)

Printing (last digit): 9 8 7 6 5 4 3 2 1

Printed in the United States of America
on acid-free paper

REISCHAUER, EDWIN OLDFATHER

(*b.* 15 October 1910; *d.* 1 September 1990)

Ambassador to Japan (1961–1966). Born in Tokyo, the son of U.S. missionaries, Reischauer grew up fluent in Japanese and respectful of Japanese culture. Earning a Ph.D. at Harvard University in 1939, Reischauer became one of the foremost U.S. scholars of East Asian history. His professional career balanced academic and government service in a lifelong attempt to increase U.S. knowledge and understanding of Japan. During World War II, Reischauer served in both the Department of State and the army before returning to teaching at Harvard University in 1946. After helping establish one of the first U.S. centers for East Asian studies there, Reischauer was appointed ambassador to Japan in 1961. As ambassador he advocated the creation of an equal partnership to replace the 1950s view that Japan was America's junior partner. Confronted with escalating U.S. intervention in Vietnam and emerging Japanese-American trade tensions, Reischauer argued that both nations should discuss these conflicts in an atmosphere of respect and mutual accommodation. During his tenure the United States and Japan avoided open conflict, but relations deteriorated in the late 1960s and early 1970s. Reischauer returned to Harvard in 1966 and subsequently wrote his memoirs.

BARNEY J. RICKMAN III

See also International Trade and Commerce; Japan

FURTHER READING

Fairbank, John K., Edwin O. Reischauer, and Albert M. Craig. *East Asia: Tradition and Transformation*. Boston, 1989.

Reischauer, Edwin O. *My Life Between Japan and America*. New York, 1986.

———. *The Japanese Today: Change and Continuity*. Cambridge, Mass., 1988.

———. *Japan: The Story of a Nation*, 4th ed. New York, 1991.

REPARATIONS

Payment in goods or money by one country to another in compensation for injuries inflicted in war. From the dawn of civilization the victor on the battlefield has frequently extracted an indemnity from the defeated. With the rise of articulate public opinion in the nineteenth century, governments felt obliged to provide a moral justification for such impositions. The second reich of Otto von Bismarck set a precedent by collecting 5 billion francs from France ($1 = 5.18 francs) after the Franco-Prussian War of 1870–1871.

World War I caused more devastation than any previous conflict in human history. When the guns fell silent in 1918 the question remained of who would pay for the lives and property destroyed. Article 231 of the Treaty of Versailles required Germany to accept responsibility for "all the loss and damage to which the Allied and Associated governments and their nationals have been subjected as a consequence of the war imposed upon them by the aggression of Germany and her allies."

Germany, however, obviously could not be required to shoulder a burden beyond its capacity to pay. At the Paris Peace Conference of 1919 the United States and its European Allies failed to agree on that capacity or on the magnitude of the levy that remained compatible with social stability in the fledgling Weimar Republic. The chief American experts, Norman Davis and Thomas W. Lamont, suggested a maximum charge of 60 billion gold marks ($1 = 4.2 gold marks) in hard currency and a like amount in German marks. The British and French negotiators held out for substantially more. Faced with deadlock, the peace conference created a Reparation Commission and delegated to that body the task of ascertaining Germany's actual liability by May 1921. President Woodrow Wilson agreed to include veterans' pensions, but that affected only the distribution and not the total amount of the projected bill.

As a result of the U.S. Senate's failure to ratify the peace treaty, the United States withdrew from the Reparation Commission. Henceforth the United States maintained only "observers." In May 1921 the commission set the total German responsibility at 132 billion gold marks. That levy, however, included less than met the eye. The commission specified that 50 billion marks of "A" and "B" bonds would be payable at 5 percent interest over thirty-seven years. The balance of 82 billion gold marks in "C" bonds would bear no interest and would become payable only when the commission determined that Weimar government could afford to pay. The "C" bonds actually figured as an international "funny money" that the Europeans hoped could eventually be set off against Allied war debts to America. The U.S. government resented the transparent attempt to link debts and repa-

1

rations. The United States had lent over $10 billion to their Allies during the war and Americans felt strongly about prompt repayment.

In 1922 the U.S. Congress created the World War Foreign Debt Commission and summoned the Allies to fund their borrowings. Great Britain in particular continued to insist on a set-off of debts against reparations. In the Balfour Note (1922) the British stated that they would collect from their debtors only what proved necessary to pay Washington. Under mounting pressure, the Europeans all funded their war debts at concessionary rates—with substantial forgiveness of the interest due—between 1923 and 1926. Nevertheless, Americans and Europeans continued to hold divergent views about the justice of such payments and the propriety of linking debts and reparations.

Reparations remained the chief problem in international economic diplomacy until the Great Depression. Germany destroyed its own currency rather than raise the taxes necessary to pay, lurched from one partial moratorium to another, and finally defaulted altogether in January 1923. The French and Belgians sent troops to occupy the Ruhr—the industrial heartland of Germany. The Germans organized "passive resistance" to the occupation. After the protagonists exhausted themselves in the Ruhr struggle, the United States proposed another investigation of German capacity to pay. A committee of private experts, headed by the Chicago banker Charles G. Dawes, elaborated a plan for German currency stabilization and rescheduled the reparations debt. Under the 1924 Dawes Plan Germany received protection against destabilizing transfers. Reparations increased gradually to 2.5 billion Reichsmarks, or 3.1 percent of national income, in 1929.

Germany, however, resented even the reduced levy as an emblem of national humiliation. It paid not from current production, but solely from the product of international loans. In 1929 a new expert committee, under General Electric Company executive Owen D. Young, was charged with arranging a final liquidation of the war debt and reduced the annuity due by another 20 percent. No nation expressed full satisfaction with the Young Plan. Resentment ran high in the United States, where Secretary of the Treasury Ogden Mills complained that Young had "tied debts and reparations together" and "written the principles of the Balfour Note" into his report.

The Young Plan lasted less than two years. As the Depression deepened, President Herbert Hoover proposed a one-year moratorium on remittance of debts and reparations. Reparation payments never resumed. At Lausanne in 1932 the Allies canceled them altogether, subject to a final token payment that Germany never made. The Allies subsequently defaulted on their war debts and years of mutual recrimination followed. In the end, Germany transferred 16.8 billion marks in reparations, but at the same time received 44.7 billion in speculative mark purchases and loans on which it subsequently defaulted. Few outside the sphere of high finance understood the technical mechanics of those transfers. Ultimately, the United States in effect paid the interwar "reparations" to Germany.

When World War II ended with Germany's unconditional surrender (May 1945), the four victors—the United States, Great Britain, the Soviet Union, and France—established separate occupation regimes in their respective zones. Under Soviet pressure at the Yalta Conference, the United States and Great Britain initially had agreed to use the figure of $20 billion as a basis for discussion of the new German reparations obligation. Half of that sum was earmarked for the Soviet Union. The Soviets took possession of dismantled German machinery and other property and also designated special factories to produce exclusively for them. In addition to retaining the services of 4 million prisoners of war, they also demanded forced labor from Germans living in their occupation zone. Owing to the huge unmet needs of their domestic economy, however, the Soviets remained dissatisfied and complained that they were denied promised reparations from the western zones. This acrimonious issue was one of several that led to the breakdown of East-West comity and the onset of the Cold War. Washington policymakers quickly grew skeptical of the political and economic feasibility of large-scale reparations. After mid-1946 they became convinced that, unless they allowed the western zones of Germany to invest their surplus at home, the country would become a giant soup kitchen, with the U.S. taxpayer obliged to furnish the soup. Under "Operation Paperclip," U.S. and British forces carried out industrial espionage and seized useful patents in chemicals, machine tools, and other high-tech industries, but those undertakings remained narrowly focused. The United States did not exact reparations from Japan.

Since the 1940s a number of nations have laid claim to reparation for various sorts of transgressions. The German Federal Republic voluntarily paid reparations to Israel for the sufferings visited on individual Jews by the Nazi predecessor regime. The United States paid compensation when it inadvertently shot down an Iranian civilian airliner. Nevertheless, the principle of reparation for damages is not firmly established in international law. The United Nations considered imposing a reparations obligation on Iraq after the 1991 Gulf War, but no concrete plan for collection emerged.

STEPHEN A. SCHUKER

See also Davis, Norman Hezekiah; Dawes Plan; Germany; Versailles Treaty of 1919; War Debt of World War I; World War II

FURTHER READING

Cairncross, Alec. *The Price of War: British Policy on German Reparations, 1941–1949.* Oxford, 1986.

Gimbel, John. *Science, Technology, and Reparations: Exploitation and Plunder in Postwar Germany.* Stanford, Calif., 1990.

Kent, Bruce. *The Spoils of War: The Politics, Economics, and Diplomacy of Reparations, 1918–1932.* Oxford, 1989.

McNeil, William C. *American Money and the Weimar Republic: Economics and Politics on the Eve of the Great Depression.* New York, 1986.

Schuker, Stephen A. *American "Reparations" to Germany, 1919–1933: Implications for the Third-World Debt Crisis.* Princeton Studies in International Finance, no. 61. Princeton, N.J., 1988.

Schuker, Stephen A. *The End of French Predominance in Europe: The Financial Crisis of 1924 and the Adoption of the Dawes Plan.* Chapel Hill, N.C., 1976.

Weill-Raynal, Etienne. *Les Réparations allemandes et al France,* 3 vols. Paris, 1947.

REPUBLICAN PARTY

One of the two major parties in U.S. politics almost since its founding over the slavery crisis in the mid-1850s, at which time it displaced the previously powerful Whig party. Like all major American parties, and U.S. politics in general, the Republican Party (also known by the nickname G.O.P. or Grand Old Party) usually has been more concerned with domestic than with foreign policy. At times, however, as in the 1890s and the 1940s, differences over foreign policy have contributed to divisions within the party. At other times, as in the 1950s and the 1980s, international concerns have played a major part in shaping the party's ideological direction.

The immediate cause of the Republican Party's formation was protest in all the Northern states against the passage of the Kansas-Nebraska Act in 1854, opening the western territories to slavery. The roots of the party, however, went deep in American history. The antislavery Liberty and Free-Soil Parties had run presidential candidates in the 1840s, attracting enough votes in 1844 and 1848 to tip the balance between the contending major parties, the Democrats and the Whigs, but failing to carry any states. By the 1850s antislavery strategists had come to recognize that they needed a more broadly based set of issues to have a chance at national victory. "An Anti-Slavery man per se cannot be elected," wrote one of their leaders, Horace Greeley, editor of the *New York Tribune*, "but a Tariff, River-and-Harbor, Pacific Railroad, Free-Homestead man may succeed although he is Anti-Slavery." Recruits for the new party were made available by the disintegration after 1852 of the Whig Party, first over the nativist hysteria that exploded in national politics in the mid-1850s, and then, more decisively, over slavery. Since the 1830s, the Whigs had represented the more conservative strain in U.S. politics on economic and moral issues that earlier had been expressed by the Federalists. Those who were conservative on these issues and were not pro-slavery were the natural base for a new major party. The new party, formed more or less spontaneously at public meetings throughout the Northeast and Midwest to protest the Kansas-Nebraska Act, took the name Republican, in part to express its adherents' belief in ordered liberty, in part to help bring over Democrats who traced their origins to Thomas Jefferson's old Republican Party, and in part to attract the crucial bloc of naturalized German-American voters who associated the title with the popular Republicaner Party they had known in German politics. One of the issues taken up by the new party to broaden its base was the protective tariff, widely supported in the industrial cities and towns and coal fields of the Northeast. According to Andrew Curtin, Republican candidate for governor of Pennsylvania in 1860, voters in his state were "pining for protectionism."

The Republicans lost narrowly in 1856 with their first presidential candidate, John Charles Frémont, the "pathfinder" of the West; but when the Democrats split over the slavery issue in 1860, the new Republican Party won the presidency with Abraham Lincoln of Illinois as their candidate. Republicans simultaneously won majorities in both houses of Congress and elected governors in most Northern states. Although the Republicans had promised only to halt extension of slavery rather than to abolish it in states where it already existed, Lincoln's election was viewed in the South as threatening the continuation of slavery and thirteen Southern states seceded from the Union. Lincoln ordered military action to prevent secession and the Civil War followed. In addition to conducting the war, the Lincoln administration and Republican majorities in Congress pushed through a broad program of economic and social legislation, much of which had a profound impact on the development of the nation: the Homestead Act of 1862, which made public land in the West available free to farmers who promised to develop it; the Thirteenth Amendment, which abolished slavery; the Agricultural College (Morrill) Act of 1862, which provided federal assistance for creation of state agricultural and vocational colleges, the foundation of most future state universities; a substantial increase in the tariff; the creation of a national banking system; the chartering of the Union Pacific and Central Pacific railroads, which soon linked the East and West Coasts; and establishment of the Immigration Bureau to attract labor from Europe.

After the Union victory in the Civil War in 1865, the Republican Party briefly divided into two factions. Following Lincoln's assassination, the moderate faction was led by his successor Andrew Johnson, a one-time Democratic senator from Tennessee who sought to reintegrate the South and restore its social structure on much the same basis that had existed before the war, except for the elimination of slavery. A radical faction, however, led by Senator Charles Sumner and Representative Thaddeus Stevens, and dominant Republicans in Congress, aimed to fundamentally restructure the South on the basis of full and equal political and economic rights for the formerly enslaved African Americans, a policy known as Reconstruction. The radicals swept the 1866 midterm congressional elections and, after a series of political clashes with them, Johnson narrowly escaped removal by impeachment in 1868. That same year, General Ulysses S. Grant, the victorious commander of the Union armies during the Civil War, was elected president. A great general, Grant was not an astute political leader. He gave the radical Republicans in congress control of national policy, a power they were largely to maintain for the next sixteen years. Republican supremacy in national politics was based on an efficient federal government patronage machine as well as on loyalty felt by many in the Northeast and West to the party that had "saved the Union." Except for the two separate administrations of Grover Cleveland (1885–1889; 1893–1897), the Republicans held the White House until 1912, despite scandals in the Grant administration and some of its successors. Radical Reconstruction ended after 1876, when Republican national leaders agreed to the restoration of Democratic white supremacist state administrations in the South in exchange for Democratic acceptance of the victory of the Republican candidate, Rutherford B. Hayes, in that year's disputed presidential election.

For some years after Reconstruction ended, the chief substantive difference between the major parties was over the protective tariff: the Republicans generally supported it as an aid to industrial growth, while the Democrats opposed it as a burden on consumers and agriculture. In other aspects of foreign policy, Republican administrations during the period embarked on numerous enterprises to add new territories and enlarge U.S. international influence. In 1867, Secretary of State William H. Seward, who had been Lincoln's principal rival for the Republican presidential nomination in 1860, achieved purchase of the vast northern territory of Alaska from Russia for $7.2 million. President Grant's effort to take over Santo Domingo (now the Dominican Republic) was thwarted, but President Hayes succeeded in establishing U.S. sovereignty over part of the Solomon Islands in the Pacific. Republican efforts to acquire the Hawai'ian Islands, stalled by the Cleveland administrations, finally bore fruit when Hawai'i was annexed in 1898 under the Republican administration of William McKinley. James G. Blaine of Maine, a major Republican leader and unsuccessful presidential aspirant for three decades, as secretary of state in 1889 launched the Pan-American Union to coordinate relations between the United States and the nations of Latin America.

The Progressive Era

During the 1880s and early 1890s, neither major party was able to secure clear dominance in national politics. Severe economic depression during Cleveland's second term, however, opened the way for the election of President William McKinley in 1896, and the restoration of the Republicans as the normal majority party. McKinley represented a faction within the G.O.P. that favored concentration on domestic economic growth and shrank from extensive foreign involvements. Other Republicans, including Theodore Roosevelt of New York and Senators Henry Cabot Lodge of Massachusetts and Albert Beveridge of Indiana, proposed a far more active role for the United States in world affairs, particularly through expansion of American naval power in the Caribbean and the Pacific, as called for by the strategic doctrines of Captain (later Admiral) Alfred Mahan. Widely reported atrocities by the Spanish colonial government in Cuba, where a struggle for independence had erupted, gave the expansionists their chance. In 1898, after the battleship *Maine* blew up in a Cuban harbor, McKinley reluctantly asked for a declaration of war against Spain. As a result of the Spanish-American War, quickly and easily won by the United States, Cuba was granted independence and the United States acquired Puerto Rico, Guam, and the Philippine Islands. Isolationists resisted major U.S. military involvement outside of North America. In particular, a bipartisan group including conservative Republicans like Speaker of the House Thomas B. Reed of Maine and Senator George Hoar of Massachusetts, as well as many Democrats, opposed acquisition of the distant Philippines. The peace treaty was approved by the Senate in 1899 by only a single vote.

The war had the incidental effect of making something of a national hero of Roosevelt, who led his "Rough Riders" in action (on foot) in Cuba. A former assistant secretary of the navy, he was elected governor of New York and then, in 1900, McKinley's vice president. McKinley's assassination in 1901 elevated the energetic Roosevelt to the presidency, putting the expansionist internationalists in the driver's seat in both the national administration and the Republican Party. As president, Roosevelt generally proceeded with caution, applying his admonition to "speak softly but carry a big stick." His principal foreign policy initiative was to foment a revolution in the part of Colombia occupying the Isthmus of Panama, securing Panamanian independence and gaining treaty rights enabling the United States to begin construction of the Panama Canal. He also sent troops into Santo Domingo to collect debts owed to foreign powers and mediated the peace negotiation that ended the Russo-Japanese War in 1904, for which he was awarded the Nobel Peace Prize.

Roosevelt drew support for his domestic program of economic and social reform on the Republican faction known as the Progressives, but he also maintained friendly relations with conservative "Old Guard" Republican leaders such as Speaker of the House Joseph Cannon of Illinois and Senate Majority Leader Nelson Aldrich of Rhode Island. On foreign policy, the Progressives were divided. Some, including Roosevelt and Beveridge, promoted a policy of vigorous internationalism; but others, such as Senator Robert M. LaFollette of Wisconsin and Representative (later Senator) George Norris of Nebraska, favored benign isolationism, arguing that foreign involvements would undermine domestic reform.

Under Roosevelt's chosen successor, William Howard Taft of Ohio (1908–1912), antagonism between Progressive and Old Guard Republicans became intense, leading to a revolt in the House of Representatives in 1910 in which Norris led a bipartisan coalition of Progressives and Democrats to undercut Cannon's power as Speaker. As the 1912 presidential election approached, LaFollette announced that he would challenge Taft for the Republican nomination. Roosevelt, who had become increasingly critical of the Taft administration, entered the fray, pushing LaFollette aside, and taking up the Progressive mantle against his old friend, Taft. After Taft was narrowly renominated at the tumultuous Republican national convention in Chicago, Roosevelt agreed to bolt the Republican Party and lead a Progressive "Bull Moose" third-party ticket in the November election. The split in the Republican Party resulted in the election of Woodrow Wilson, the Democratic candidate, as president, and large Democratic majorities in both houses of Congress. The Wilson administration, while embarking on its own domestic reform program, was confronted in 1914 with the outbreak of general war in Europe. This resulted in realignments within the Republican party. Both Roosevelt and Lodge, now leaders among conservative Senate Republicans, criticized what they regarded as the timidity of Wilson's policy of neutrality between the European combatants. Progressive isolationists, including LaFollette and Norris, who had supported Wilson's domestic reforms, on the other hand, attacked what they perceived as the administration's tilt toward the Allied powers, particularly Great Britain. After Wilson's reelection in 1916, in part on his claim that he "kept us out of war," relations between the United States and Germany swiftly deteriorated. In April 1917, Wilson asked for a declaration of war against Germany and Congress approved it. In the Senate, LaFollette, two other Progressive Republicans, and three Democrats voted against the declaration; in the House, thirty-five Republicans (mostly Progressives), eighteen Democrats, and one Socialist opposed it.

During and after America's participation in the First World War, Wilson became identified as the champion of a benevolent internationalism, aimed at "making the world safe for democracy." In this he was criticized not only by the isolationists but also by more tough-minded internationalists like Roosevelt, returned to the Republican fold in 1916, and Lodge, who argued that America's role in world affairs should be determined by a more narrowly defined concept of national interest. When Wilson returned from the Paris Peace Conference in 1919 with a treaty that included his proposed League of Nations, he faced opposition from both wings of the Republican party, which had won congressional majorities in the 1918 midterm elections. Roosevelt, who had seemed the likely Republican candidate for president in 1920, died in his sleep at the beginning of 1919; but Lodge, now chairman of the Senate Foreign Relations Committee, whose internationalism was yielding precedence to his nationalism, marshaled a majority of Senate Republicans to approve participation by the United States in the League only on condition of reservations that he claimed would protect American sovereignty. Isolationist Progressive Republican senators, including LaFollette, Norris, and Hiram Johnson of California, opposed the League under any circumstances, and the Wilson loyalists joined the isolationist Republicans to reject the Versailles treaty.

Isolationism

Although many prominent Republicans, including former President Taft, supported the League, the landslide victory of the Republican ticket in the 1920 election was interpreted as a public endorsement of America's nonparticipation. The new Republican president, Warren G. Harding of Ohio, called for a return to "normalcy," which seemed to include reduction of involvement by the United States in world affairs. The Republican administrations of the 1920s (led by Presidents Harding, Calvin Coolidge, and Herbert Hoover) promoted a series of international efforts to achieve world disarmament.

They also approved repeated increases in tariff rates, climaxed by the highly protectionist Smoot-Hawley Act of 1930. Severe economic depression returned the Democrats to power under the leadership of Franklin D. Roosevelt in 1933. The Roosevelt administration soon faced the rise of totalitarian powers in Europe and Asia. Particularly after the outbreak of the Second World War in 1939, Roosevelt edged cautiously toward support of countries resisting aggression by Germany, Italy, and Japan. In the Senate, these efforts were vigorously resisted by isolationists, who included both liberal Democrats like Burton K. Wheeler of Montana and Progressive Republicans such as Johnson and William Borah of Idaho, and Robert LaFollette, Jr., elected to his father's seat in the Senate from Wisconsin on a third-party Progressive ticket. They were joined by conservative Republicans such as Senators Arthur H. Vandenberg of Michigan and Robert A. Taft of Ohio, son of the former president, whose views were based on national interest concerns rather than domestic altruism. Republican isolationism was particularly strong in the Midwest, where it was championed by the vehemently anti-British Colonel Robert R. McCormick, publisher of the influential *Chicago Tribune*. It was fed not only by the impulse to remain aloof from old world conflicts behind the barriers of two oceans, but also by resistance to U.S. alignment with Great Britain among some German Americans and Irish Americans. Roosevelt's policy of cautiously backing the combatants against Hitler and preparing for war was supported by the internationalist wing of the Republican party, based mainly in the Northeast and given journalistic voice by such publications as the *New York Herald Tribune* and Henry Luce's magazines, *Time*, *Life*, and *Fortune*. Wendell L. Willkie, Roosevelt's unsuccessful Republican opponent for a third term in 1940, had entered national politics under Luce's sponsorship, and generally took an internationalist line, though he tried to placate the isolationists during his campaign.

Japan's attack on Pearl Harbor on 7 December 1941 buried the quarrel between internationalists and isolationists for the duration of the Second World War. After the war, President Harry S. Truman responded to expansionist moves by the Soviet Union with a policy aimed at containing communism all over the globe. Senator Vandenberg, who had spectacularly converted to internationalism during the war, helped to mobilize bi-partisan support for Truman's plan to rebuild Western Europe in order to check communism there. Governor Thomas E. Dewey of New York, the unsuccessful Republican presidential nominee in 1944 and 1948, was also an internationalist, expressing the outlook of financiers, lawyers, and publishers in the party's Eastern establishment. Taft, who dominated congressional Republicans after the party's victory in the 1946 midterm elections, at first unenthusiastically approved parts of the containment policy, but soon reverted to his pre-war isolationism and argued for withdrawal of U.S. forces into a "Fortress America" guarded by nuclear weapons.

After Robert LaFollette, Jr., who had rejoined the Republican Party, was defeated in the 1946 Wisconsin senatorial primary by a returned war veteran, Joseph McCarthy, the old Progressive element in the isolationist wing of the Republican party virtually disappeared. A few years after winning election to the Senate, McCarthy, with Taft's tacit approval, began attacking Truman from the right, charging that the administration was protecting alleged communists who under Roosevelt had influenced formation of foreign policy. The struggle between isolationists and internationalists reached a climax at the 1952 Republican national convention in Chicago where Taft was opposed for the presidential nomination by General

Dwight D. Eisenhower, commander of Allied forces in Europe during the Second World War. The party's heart appeared to belong to Taft. But after twenty years out of power in the executive branch, Republican politicians wanted a winner. Under Dewey's skillful management, deploying Wall Street's economic power, Eisenhower's candidacy rolled to victory on the first ballot. Aided by the unpopularity of the Korean War, which had begun under Truman in 1950, Eisenhower was elected president in November. After Taft's death in 1953, even conservative isolationism largely withered away in the Republican Party if not in the country, supplanted by militant anti-communism. Eisenhower kept the United States firmly involved in world affairs. While accepting a negotiated settlement in Korea, he continued the containment policy based on the Western alliance and the U.S. nuclear deterrent.

Cold War Internationalism

When a new kind of hard-right conservatism developed within the party in the 1960s, it was aggressively anti-communist and pro-interventionist rather than isolationist. Senator Barry Goldwater of Arizona, the principal champion of this new conservatism in domestic policy, went beyond Taft in attacking welfare state liberalism, but in foreign policy he advocated efforts to go beyond containment and roll back the frontiers of communism. A new progressive faction, led by Governor Nelson Rockefeller of New York and largely based on the Eastern financial, legal, and media establishment, criticized Goldwater's foreign policy approach as reckless, but staunchly supported the Cold War containment policy developed under Truman and Eisenhower. In 1964 Goldwater swept over the establishment to win the party's presidential nomination. He went down to landslide defeat in November, but the libertarian philosophy he represented was to reemerge two decades later as a major element in the party's dominant conservatism. The Democratic presidents of the 1960s, John F. Kennedy and Lyndon B. Johnson, pursued the containment policy and gradually introduced and expanded American forces in South Vietnam, in order to defend its pro-Western government against communist insurgents and invaders from North Vietnam. By 1968 the United States was deeply involved in Vietnam, and the war, as well as domestic struggles over civil rights, had divided the Democratic Party. Richard M. Nixon, who had been Eisenhower's vice president and the unsuccessful Republican presidential nominee in 1960, took advantage of the Democratic disunity to win the presidency, promising to end the Vietnam War. He continued it, however, for four more years, seeking a means to withdraw without ceding communist domination in Southeast Asia.

Despite his reputation as a fervent cold warrior, Nixon initiated relations with the People's Republic of China and forged the less confrontational relationship of détente with the Soviet Union. Henry Kissinger, Nixon's influential national security adviser, argued that the United States and the Western alliance should warily accept the Soviet Union and China as partners in preserving peace based on mutual self-interest. In 1972 the Democratic presidential nomination was won by Senator George McGovern of South Dakota, an extreme liberal whose campaign theme, "Come home, America," recalled the old progressive isolationism of the LaFollettes and Norris. Nixon, warning of the dangers of appeasement, rolled to landslide reelection. Two years later, however, the Watergate scandals, growing out of campaign dirty tricks, led to his resignation in the face of impeachment. He was succeeded by former House Minority Leader, Gerald Ford of Michigan, whom Nixon had named as vice president when Spiro Agnew was forced to resign that office because of another, separate scandal. In 1975, Ford terminated U.S. involvement in Vietnam by ordering complete withdrawal, thereby leaving all of former Indo-China to the victorious communists. With the advice of Kissinger, now secretary of state, Ford mixed containment with cautious pursuit of détente with the Soviet Union and China. In 1976 former Governor Ronald Reagan of California, who had inherited the leadership of the Goldwater conservatives, challenged Ford for the Republican presidential nomination, largely on the charge that Ford and Kissinger had gone too far in appeasing the communist powers. Ford narrowly won the nomination after accepting hard-line language demanded by the Reaganites in the foreign policy plank in the platform. Despite the cloud left by Nixon's fall and high unemployment, Ford came surprisingly close to winning the general election against the Democratic nominee, former Governor Jimmy Carter of Georgia. By 1980, conservatism partly descended from Goldwater's campaign had become a major trend. In the 1980 presidential primaries Reagan easily defeated George Bush, who was backed by some of what remained of the party's old moderate establishment. As a gesture to party unity, Reagan took Bush as his running mate. President Carter's standing with the public had been undermined by severe economic problems and the impression—left by such events as the Soviet invasion of Afghanistan and the Iran hostage crisis—that he had allowed the international stature of the United States to erode, and he proved an easy target for the charismatic Reagan. The Republicans not only won the White House but also took control of the Senate for the first time in twenty-six years.

The Reagan Era

As president, Reagan set out to implement the conservative ideology on which he had campaigned. He identified four major policy goals, three of which—a steep reduction of federal taxes, cuts in domestic spending, and moving toward a balanced federal budget—were domestic. The fourth however, had foreign policy implications: a massive defense buildup, restoring cuts made under the Carter administration and going beyond previous levels. Reagan's underlying aim in foreign policy was nothing less than a shift of the world balance of power to favor the United States vis-a-vis the Soviet Union. He characterized the Soviet Union as an "evil empire" and strengthened the nuclear force in Western Europe, to the horror of liberal critics who feared he would precipitate military holocaust. The administration provided support to indigenous anticommunist insurgencies in a number of Third World countries and sought through covert operations to destabilize communist or communist-influenced regimes in Eastern Europe and other parts of the world. In October 1983, Reagan sent U.S. troops to depose a marxist regime in the Caribbean island of Grenada. When the Soviet Union, because of the cost of maintaining the arms race with the United States as well as inherent economic flaws in the communist system, began to falter in the mid-1980s, Reagan proved willing to negotiate with the reformist Soviet leadership led by Mikhail Gorbachev. By the end of his second term, a new relationship had developed between the two superpowers, in which the United States now clearly held the upper hand.

Enormously popular with the public, Reagan easily won a second term, although the Democrats recaptured the Senate in 1986 and controlled the House of Representatives during both of his terms. Throughout his presidency, Reagan maintained remarkable unity within the Republican party; old differences among conservatives, moderates, and progressives were largely submerged, and he attracted the support of a large number of traditionally Democratic voters. In Congress unity on roll call votes in both parties rose to levels not seen since the 1930s, partly because of the polarizing effects of Reagan's policies. He faced considerable opposition from Congress, particularly after the Democrats regained control of the Senate. Congress tried to restrain the administration's penchant for covert operations, and in particular tried to block aid to the Contra insurgency against Nicaragua's Marxist government. The revelation late in 1986 that the administration had sold arms to Iran's Islamic fundamentalist regime in an effort to obtain help in freeing American hostages from Iranian-backed groups in Lebanon, and that part of the proceeds had gone to fund the Contras in Nicaragua in an effort to circumvent the congressional ban on such aid, produced a scandal which at times seemed to assume almost Watergate proportions. But public approval of the administration's record remained sufficiently high to secure the election of Vice President Bush as Reagan's successor in 1988.

Bush's administration witnessed the end of the Cold War and disintegration of the Soviet Union, bringing to ultimate success the containment strategy maintained by all presidents since Truman and applied with particular intensity by Reagan. In 1991 Bush led the nation to war in the Persian Gulf to force the Iraqi government of Saddam Hussein to withdraw from its conquest of the oil-rich emirate of Kuwait, with united congressional support from Republicans, but over the opposition of many Democrats. The speedy success of the campaign brought considerable, but fleeting, popularity. Economic recession and a major tax increase in violation of his chief 1988 campaign promise led to Bush's defeat for reelection in 1992 by his Democratic opponent, Governor Bill Clinton of Arkansas. In the mid-1990s the removal of the Soviet Union as a tangible threat resulted in some revival of isolationist sentiment within the Republican party. In general, however, the party consensus in favor of prudent international involvement, which had begun with Vandenburg and Eisenhower, appeared to hold firm. Clinton's call for congressional approval of the North American Free Trade Agreement (NAFTA), which had been concluded under Bush, was supported by a much higher proportion of Republicans than Democrats. After the 1994 midterm elections in which the Republicans won control of both houses of congress for the first time in forty years, the party seemed inclined to place somewhat greater emphasis on national interest in the conduct of foreign policy but remained committed to an active U.S. role in world affairs.

A. JAMES REICHLEY

See also American Civil War; Arthur, Chester Alan; Blaine, James Gillespie; Bush, George Herbert Walker; Coolidge, Calvin; Eisenhower, Dwight David; Ford, Gerald Rudolph; Goldwater, Barry; Grant, Ulysses Simpson; Harding, Warren; Hoover, Herbert; Hughes, Charles Evans; Isolationism; Johnson, Andrew; La Follette, Robert Marion; Lincoln, Abraham; Lodge, Henry Cabot, Sr.; Luce, Henry Robinson; McKinley, William; McKinley Tariff Act; Open Door Policy; Panama and Panama Canal; Reagan Doctrine; Reagan, Ronald Wilson; Rockefeller, Nelson Aldrich; Roosevelt, Theodore; Root, Elihu; Seward, William Henry; Spanish-American-Cuban-Filipino War, 1898; Sumner, Charles; Taft, Robert A.; Taft, William Howard; Vandenberg, Arthur Hendrick

FURTHER READING

Divine, Robert A. *Foreign Policy and U.S. Presidential Elections, 1940–1964*, 2 vols. New York, 1974.
Epstein, Leon D. *Political Parties in the American Mold.* Madison, Wisc., 1986.
Foner, Eric. *Reconstruction: America's Unfinished Revolution, 1863–1877.* New York, 1988.
Mayer, George H. *The Republican Party, 1854–1964.* New York, 1964.
Moos, Malcolm. *The Republicans.* New York, 1956.
Pomper, Gerald M. *Passions and Interests: Political Party Concepts of American Democracy.* Lawrence, Kans., 1992.
Reichley, A. James. *The Life of the Parties: A History of American Political Parties.* New York, 1992.
Schlesinger, Arthur M., Jr. *The Cycles of American History.* Boston, 1986.
Sundquist, James L. *Dynamics of the Party System: Alignment and Trident Realignment of Political Parties in the United States*, rev. ed. Washington, D.C., 1983.
White, John Kenneth. *The New Politics of Old Values.* Hanover, N. H., 1988.

REVISIONISM

The practice of rewriting history to make a particular point. Sometimes the point is occupational or political: to win academic promotion or enhance one's reputation. Sometimes the point is intellectual: to utilize new evidence to correct previous misconceptions or to test inherited wisdom. Often the point is ideological: to dragoon the historical past into the battles of the political present. To be provocative, which most revisionism intends to be, requires an orthodoxy open to attack. Fawning patriotic accounts of wars often serve to spark revisionist reconsiderations, particularly if the subsequent peace settlements fall short of expectations. Also, political leaders sometimes criticize or revise their predecessors' records for narrow partisan gain. Scholarly revisionism in this country has focused on historical writings that tend to glorify the past, excuse U.S. wrongdoing but heap blame on adversaries, and support official policy.

The first major wave of revisionism in U.S. foreign relations came during the decade after World War I. Skeptics like Harry Elmer Barnes and C. Hartley Grattan contended that the war had not been a struggle to make the world safe for democracy, as Woodrow Wilson had promised, but a contest to protect the profits of munitions-makers and bankers. As the Versailles system broke down completely during the 1930s, revisionism approached the status of a new orthodoxy. Conservatives such as Charles Tansill joined liberal historians such as Charles Beard and Walter Millis to create an atmosphere that tended to confirm the isolationist mood of the Depression decade.

World War II seemed a likely target for a reactive revisionism, especially since it segued into a Cold War in which the United States resuscitated its erstwhile enemies to confront its recent ally. A minor but vitriolic revisionist school did develop around President Franklin D. Roosevelt's actions: "back door" theorists such as Tansill claimed that Roosevelt had allowed, even provoked, the Japanese into war in Asia in order to wage an otherwise unpopular war in Europe. Cold War conservatives charged Roosevelt with selling out Poland and China at the Yalta Conference in order to appease the Soviet Union. But the revisionists on World War II never got very far attacking the fundamental premise that the war was worth fighting; most Americans held to the belief that Adolf Hitler and the Japanese militarists needed to be stopped. And the antirevisionist books of Herbert Feis, William Langer, and S. Everett Gleason challenged the critique of Roosevelt in order to maintain public support for a strong Cold War foreign policy.

The Cold War found its revisionists during the 1960s, at a time when the costs of containing communism, especially in Vietnam, were growing painfully evident. Where the Cold War orthodoxy of the late 1940s and 1950s had seen the superpower confrontation as a case of Soviet aggression catalyzing U.S resistance, the revisionists of the 1960s turned things around or apportioned blame more evenly. Economic revisionists perceived U.S. officials and business executives as demanding a world open to U.S. exports and investments, thus generating endless overseas intervention like that in Southeast Asia. Marxists among these economic revisionists, such as Gabriel Kolko and Harry Magdoff, saw this expansive drive as a necessity of U.S capitalism; liberals like William Appleman Williams judged it a tragic and unnecessary mistake, calling for an "open door" at home. Other Cold War revisionists concentrated on noneconomic issues. Gar Alperovitz founded a school of atomic revisionism by alleging that a primary purpose of dropping atomic bombs on Hiroshima and Nagasaki was to intimidate the Soviet Union. Thomas G. Paterson emphasized the interplay of ideas and interests in a chaotic international system that ensured conflict. Daniel Yergin traced divisions within the American official mind to account for a U.S. hard-line policy.

Like the revisionists of World War I, the Cold War revisionists were sufficiently persuasive to shift mainstream thinking substantially in their direction; partly for this reason, Vietnam War revisionism developed early. Another, more obvious, reason was the failure of the U.S. war effort in Southeast Asia. Moderate revisionists such as Senator J. William Fulbright and historian and presidential adviser Arthur Schlesinger, Jr., accepted the containment premises that guided U.S. intervention in Vietnam, but thought Southeast Asia the wrong place to apply containment. Left revisionists like Richard J. Barnet of the Institute for Policy Studies in Washington, D.C., contended that the premises had been wrong from the start. The Vietnam revisionists were even more successful than the Cold War revisionists in scaling the heights of orthodoxy; by 1979, when the historian Guenther Lewy offered a rousing defense of U.S. actions in Vietnam, it was not unreasonable to consider him (and later similar writers) revisionist from the right.

The end of the Cold War quickly produced a school of U.S triumphalism, which claimed that containment had forced the disintegration of the Soviet Union. Just as quickly it evoked a revisionism. Historian Paul Kennedy, for example, placed the United States in a long line of imperial overreachers that had exhausted themselves at home to extend power abroad. Other critics of the "win" thesis suggested that both sides lost the Cold War, and that advocates of nuclear disarmament, the courageous people of Eastern Europe, Soviet reformers, and European proponents of détente—not U.S. cold warriors—had brought the Cold War to a close. As before, a new orthodoxy had sparked revisionism.

H. WILLIAM BRANDS

See also Beard, Charles Austin; Cold War; Détente; Fulbright, James William; Third World; Vietnam War; Williams, William Appleman

FURTHER READING
Barnet, Richard J. *The Roots of War.* New York, 1972.
Cohen, Warren I. *The American Revisionists: The Lessons of Intervention in World War I.* Chicago, 1967.
Combs, Jerald A. *American Diplomatic History: Two Centuries of Changing Interpretations.* Berkeley, Calif., 1983.
Kennedy, Paul. *The Rise and Fall of the Great Powers.* New York, 1987.
Neu, Charles. "The Changing Interpretative Structure of American Foreign Policy." In *Twentieth-Century American Foreign Policy,* edited by John Braeman et al. Columbus, Ohio, 1971.
Tucker, Robert W. *The Radical Left and American Foreign Policy.* Baltimore, Md., 1971.

REYKJAVÍK SUMMIT
See Reagan, Ronald Wilson

RHEE, SYNGMAN
(*b.* 26 April 1875; *d.* 19 July 1965)

The first president of the Republic of Korea (ROK) who served in that capacity from 1948 to 1960 and forged a career out of manipulating U.S. influence in Asia. He periodically courted or flaunted U.S. authority to secure advantages for his fledgling state. Born in Hwanghae Province, Rhee helped form the Western-oriented Independence Club in 1896 to bolster the autonomy of a fragile Korean monarchy beset by Japanese, Russian, and Chinese predations. Reactionary Korean authorities imprisoned the young activist for seven years during which Rhee endured severe torture and converted to Christianity. Amnesty for political prisoners accompanied the Japanese assimilation of Korea in 1904 and Rhee used his freedom to pursue an education in the United States. He had already studied English in Seoul, Korea.

Rhee received a bachelor's degree from George Washington University (1907), an M.A. from Harvard (1908), and a Ph.D. in theology from Princeton (1910).

Rhee returned to Korea in 1910, but he fled shortly thereafter for conspiring against the Japanese occupation. As an exile in Hawai'i, he managed the Korean Christian Institute and later won election as president of the Korean provisional government from 1920 to 1925. Rhee lobbied intensively for U.S. Department of State recognition of his political legitimacy and he ultimately secured his return to the south of Korea in 1945 through the U.S. military. Immersing himself in Korean politics, Rhee formed the National Society for the Rapid Realization of Korean Independence. Although this endeavor proved unsuccessful, he triumphed in UN-sponsored elections for the Republic of Korea (South Korea) in 1948. Rhee amassed support through ardent anticommunism and a commitment to reunify the Korean peninsula, then divided into South Korea and Kim Il Sung's North Korea.

From 1948 to 1950, Rhee heightened Cold War tensions in Asia with calls for a "march north" to eliminate Kim's Pyongyang regime. Provocative forays by South Korean troops into the north preceded the June 1950 outbreak of the Korean War. Rhee served as a cooperative but vexing U.S. ally. He instituted a program in 1951 to strengthen his officer corps after the discovery of widespread corruption and incompetency. Yet Rhee sabotaged armistice negotiations in June 1953 by releasing some 28,000 North Korean prisoners into his nation's countryside. In August he relented and agreed to seek peace in the face of an enemy offensive and worsening relations with Washington. The subsequent stationing of U.S. troops along the thirty-eighth parallel reflected the desire to restrain the authoritarian Rhee as well as deter North Korean aggression. Rhee directed an increasingly corrupt and inefficient government that proved unable to foster consistent economic growth. A student-led coup in April 1960 overthrew his regime, forcing Rhee into exile in Hawai'i for the remainder of his life.

JEFFREY D. BASS

See also Cold War; Kim Il Sung; Korea; Korean War; Truman Doctrine; Truman, Harry S.

FURTHER READING

Allen, Richard C. *Korea's Syngman Rhee: An Unauthorized Portrait.* Rutland, Vt., 1960.
MacDonald, Donald Stone. *U.S.-Korean Relations from Liberation to Self-Reliance: The Twenty-Year Record.* Boulder, Colo., 1992.
Oliver, Robert T. *Syngman Rhee: The Man Behind the Myth.* New York, 1955.

RHODESIA
See Zimbabwe

RICHARDSON, ELLIOT LEE
(*b.* 20 July 1920)

Secretary of defense (1973), ambassador to Great Britain (1975–1976), and ambassador to the Law of the Sea Conference (1976–1980). Richardson held numerous state and federal offices from the end of World War II to the 1990s. As a liberal Republican internationalist, he helped shape the contours of U.S. foreign policy during the Cold War. His most significant foreign affairs activities occurred from 1969 to 1980. During much of this period Richardson fostered the development of détente with the Soviet Union and encouraged a dialogue between the wealthy countries of the Northern Hemisphere and the impoverished nations south of the equator.

Richardson served in the U.S. Army during World War II and, after the war, clerked for Supreme Court Justice Felix Frankfurter. In 1953 he became an assistant to Massachusetts Republican Senator Leverett Saltonstall, a supporter of the Truman and Eisenhower administrations' Cold War policies. From 1955 to 1968 Richardson held a variety of appointed and elected positions in Washington and Massachusetts. When Richard Nixon won the presidency in 1968, he appointed Richardson undersecretary of state for political affairs, a position he held for a year. During that time he helped Henry Kissinger explore Soviet attitudes toward arms control. From 1970 until 1973 he served as secretary of health, education, and welfare, but he reentered foreign affairs in 1973, when he served briefly as secretary of defense. He helped downsize the military after the Vietnam War.

Nixon fired Richardson as attorney general during the height of the Watergate crisis in 1973, but Richardson returned to take up the post of ambassador to Great Britain under President Gerald Ford. During the Carter administration Richardson became the U.S. ambassador to the Law of the Sea Conference. He spent four years patiently negotiating a treaty that would reconcile the hopes of developing nations to achieve wealth from what the United Nations (UN) characterized as "the common heritage of mankind" and U.S. concerns over the costs of development and limitations on private enterprise. The Law of the Sea Treaty was finally drafted in 1980, but newly inaugurated President Ronald Reagan refused to sign it, arguing that it did not offer sufficient protection to U.S. economic interests.

Richardson practiced international law after 1980. He also served as a U.S. observer of the Philippine elections in 1989, and as the UN observer of the Nicaraguan elections of 1990.

ROBERT D. SCHULZINGER

See also Law of the Sea; Watergate

FURTHER READING

Hollick, Ann L. *U.S. Foreign Policy and the Law of the Sea.* Princeton, N.J., 1981.
Richardson, Elliot L. *The Creative Balance.* New York, 1976.

RIDGWAY, MATTHEW BUNKER

(*b.* 3 March 1895; *d.* 26 July 1993)

U.S. military general who commanded United Nations forces in the Korean War and also received important diplomatic assignments at various stages of his career. Born at Fort Monroe, Virginia, the son of an artillery officer, young Ridgway graduated from West Point in 1917 and was subsequently given military-diplomatic assignments in Nicaragua, Bolivia, Paraguay, China, and the Philippines. He became one of the great battle leaders of World War II, commanding the 82nd Airborne Division through Italy, France, and Germany. Afterwards, he advised the United Nations on plans for a peacekeeping force, then held military-diplomatic posts in the Mediterranean, the Caribbean, and Washington, D.C.

Six months after the beginning of the Korean War, in December 1950, Ridgway was sent to the peninsula where he took command of the Eighth Army retreating under an onslaught of Chinese and North Korean forces. In a counteroffensive, his troops drove the enemy back north of the 38th parallel. When, in April 1951, President Harry S. Truman relieved General Douglas MacArthur, the overall commander in the Far East, for publicly seeking to widen the war into China, Ridgway became MacArthur's successor. With Ridgway's support, truce talks began in July 1951 and led to an armistice two years later.

Ridgway also was commander of Allied occupation forces in Japan when the United States signed a peace treaty and mutual security treaty with that country in 1951. In May 1952 he replaced Dwight D. Eisenhower as supreme commander of Allied Forces in Europe, where he worked to build up the North Atlantic Treaty Organization's multinational forces. In August 1953 President Eisenhower appointed him U.S. Army Chief of Staff, a position he held until June 1955. Ridgway's opposition to reducing the Army in favor of what he considered an imbalanced emphasis on airpower, nuclear weapons, and the new strategic doctrine of "massive retaliation" caused him to clash repeatedly with the president, the secretary of defense, and the chairman of the Joint Chiefs of Staff.

In the mid-1950s Ridgway exerted an important restraining influence during crises over offshore islands in the Taiwan Strait and over French Indochina. In 1954, when French appeals for direct U.S. military intervention in Vietnam found support among senior officials in the administration, Ridgway helped persuade Eisenhower against it, asserting that such a step would drag the United States into a disastrous war. Fourteen years later Ridgway helped convince President Lyndon Johnson to stop increasing U.S. military forces there and to seek a negotiated peace with Hanoi. Ridgway later described the Vietnam War as the "worst blunder ever made in American foreign policy" and maintained that "there was no vital American interest in Indochina."

In retirement, Ridgway wrote his memoirs and worked as an executive at Pittsburgh's Mellon Institute, a military and industry research organization. Upon his death, Ridgway was widely hailed for his field leadership in World War II and the Korean War and for his policy of military restraint in the Eisenhower administration.

JOHN WHITECLAY CHAMBERS II

See also Eisenhower, Dwight David; French Indochina; Japan; Jinmen-Mazu Crises; Johnson, Lyndon Baines; Korean War; MacArthur, Douglas; North Atlantic Treaty Organization; Nuclear Weapons and Strategy; Truman, Harry S.; Vietnam War

FURTHER READING

Blair, Clay. *Ridgway's Paratroopers: The American Airborne in World War II.* Garden City, N.Y.,1985.

Edwards, Paul M. *General Matthew B. Ridgway: An Annotated Bibliography.* Westport, Conn., 1993.

Ridgway, Matthew B., *Soldier: The Memoirs of Matthew B. Ridgway.* New York, 1956.

———. *The Korean War.* Garden City, N.Y., 1967.

RIDGWAY, ROZANNE LEJEANNE

(*b.* 22 August 1935)

Career Foreign Service officer (1957–1989) who became one of the highest-ranking women in the history of the Department of State. As counselor of the Department of State (1980–1981) and assistant secretary of state for European and Canadian Affairs (1985–1989), she received important assignments from the administrations of President Jimmy Carter and Ronald Reagan. Born in St. Paul, Minnesota, Ridgway graduated from Hamline University (1957) and immediately joined the Department of State. As an authority on the disputes over fishing resources on the west coast of South America, she became deputy assistant secretary of state for oceans and fisheries in 1975. She contributed to the establishment of the U.S. 200-mile exclusive economic zone in offshore waters. In 1977 Ridgway became ambassador to Finland, and, in 1980, counselor of the State Department. Ridgway helped prepare U.S. policy positions for the human rights conference in Madrid. During the Reagan administration, Ridgway's experience in the area of oceans and fisheries led to her appointment as a special assistant to the secretary of state. In 1983 she became ambassador to the German Democratic Republic. Two years later Secretary of State George P. Shultz selected Ridgway to serve as the assistant secretary of state for European and Canadian Affairs. She helped prepare briefing statements for President Reagan's summit meeting with Mikhail Gorbachev in 1985. In 1989 Ridgway left government service to become president of the Atlantic Council in Washington, D.C.

CHARLES D. McGRAW

See also Reagan, Ronald Wilson; State, U.S. Department of

FURTHER READING

McGlen, Nancy E., and Meredith Reid Sarkees. *Women in Foreign Policy: The Insiders.* New York, 1993.

Wilson, Joan Hoff. "Conclusion: Of Mice and Men." In *Women and American Foreign Policy: Lobbyists, Critics, and Insiders*, edited by Edward P. Crapol. New York, 1987.

RIO TREATY
(1947)

A regional security pact, officially the American Treaty of Reciprocal Assistance, signed by the United States and twenty Latin American nations on 2 September 1947 at the Inter-American Conference for the Maintenance of Security and Peace held in Rio de Janeiro. This collective security agreement, permitted under article 51 of the United Nations Charter, incorporated the principle that an attack against one was to be considered an attack against all. Signatories would decide by a two-thirds majority what kind of collective action might be taken against aggression, except "that no State shall be required to use armed force without its consent." The treaty continued the inter-American cooperation that had characterized the Good Neighbor Policy. The Rio Treaty was also a Cold War pact aimed at the Soviet Union. In practice, the treaty has been invoked, in conjunction with the consultative organs of the Organization of American States (OAS) to resolve intrahemispheric controversies, such as the dispute between Costa Rica and Nicaragua in 1955 or the Dominican Republic's attack on Venezuelan President Rómulo Betancourt in 1960. When the United States decided that international communism supported by the Soviet Union threatened its hemispheric interests, however, Washington usually bypassed the Rio Treaty and acted unilaterally, as in Guatemala (1954), Cuba (1962), the Dominican Republic (1965), Nicaragua (1981–1986), and Grenada (1983). The United States refuted on several occasions Argentina's contention that British occupation of the Malvinas (Falkland Islands) was an issue under the Rio Treaty.

STEPHEN G. RABE

See also Cold War; Dominican Republic; Falkland Islands; Good Neighbor Policy; Grenada Invasion; Guatemala; Latin America; Organization of American States; United Nations

FURTHER READING

Connell-Smith, Gordon. *The Inter-American System.* London, 1966.

Mecham, J. Lloyd. *The United States and Inter-American Security, 1889–1960.* Austin, Tex., 1961.

Smith, Gaddis. *The Last Years of the Monroe Doctrine, 1945–1993.* New York, 1994.

ROCKEFELLER, NELSON ALDRICH
(*b.* 8 July 1908; *d.* 26 January 1979)

Republican governor of New York (1958–1973) and U.S. vice president (1973–1977). Born in Bar Harbor, Maine, the second son of John D. Rockefeller, Jr. and the grandson of Standard Oil millionaire John D. Rockefeller, Nelson Rockefeller grew up in Manhattan, graduated from Dartmouth College in 1930, and went to work for the family oil business. In 1940 he began a career in public service that spanned almost forty years and included governmental posts under four U.S. presidents, including three years as vice president under Gerald Ford.

Rockefeller was an early advocate of inter-American cooperation, believing that a politically and economically stable Latin America would both strengthen the United States's political security, particularly with regard to the Soviet Union, and provide investment opportunities for U.S. business. Rockefeller's belief in the social responsibilities of ownership led him to initiate an economic assistance program in Venezuela when he served as director from 1935 to 1940 of Creole Petroleum, a Standard Oil affiliate based there. He also urged the U.S. government to encourage and improve its cultural, scientific, and educational relations with the Americas. Backed by his family's money, he founded various private organizations that sought to promote Third World development.

In 1940 President Franklin D. Roosevelt appointed Rockefeller coordinator of the Office of Inter-American Affairs and, in 1944, assistant secretary of state for Latin American affairs. Rockefeller's aggressive lobbying on behalf of Argentina and other formerly pro-fascist governments and his proposed Pan-American alliance alienated a number of senior Democrats and he was dismissed in August 1945. However, he maintained his influence in Latin American affairs by continuing to use family money to fund economic and social development projects.

In 1950 President Harry S. Truman appointed Rockefeller chairman of the Advisory Board on International Development of the Four Point Program. Between 1952 and 1955 he served as chairman of President Eisenhower's Advisory Committee on Government Organization, undersecretary of health, education, and welfare, and special assistant on foreign policy. Throughout the Eisenhower presidency, Rockefeller worked closely with the Central Intelligence Agency (CIA) and William Cameron Townsend, founder of the ultraconservative

Wycliffe Bible Translation movement, to usher in an era of pro-American democracy in Latin America. In 1956 Rockefeller started the Special Studies Project of the Rockefeller Brothers Fund, which brought together a group of prominent leaders and intellectuals, including Henry A. Kissinger, to define U.S. national goals and determine how to achieve them. Kissinger would remain an adviser to Rockefeller and later would be introduced by Rockefeller to Richard M. Nixon.

After defeating incumbent Averell Harriman in 1958, Rockefeller began the first of four consecutive terms as governor of the state of New York. During his tenure, he endeared himself to liberals, making great strides in improving education, health care and other social services, and avidly supporting the arts. But Rockefeller's administrations also were notorious for substantial tax increases and budget deficits, which alienated his party's conservative wing.

Rockefeller viewed the governorship as a stepping stone to the White House, but he failed to defeat Vice President Richard Nixon for the Republican nomination in 1960, and also was unsuccessful at winning his party's nomination in 1964 and 1968. In 1969 President Nixon dispatched Rockefeller on a fact-finding mission to Latin America. The resulting Rockefeller Report portrayed a crisis in the region and made eighty-three specific recommendations for U.S.-Latin American policy. Nixon acted on many of Rockefeller's suggestions.

In December 1973 Rockefeller resigned as governor of New York to chair two commissions: the National Commission on Water Quality and the Commission on Critical Choices for Americans. Beginning on 20 December 1974, Rockefeller served for twenty-five months as President Ford's vice president following the resignation of Nixon amid the Watergate scandal. While vice president he also served as chairman of the President's Commission on the CIA and head of the White House Domestic Council. In 1975 he withdrew his name from consideration as Ford's running mate for the upcoming presidential election. During the administration of Jimmy Carter, Rockefeller advised the Democratic president on the Panama Canal treaties. Rockefeller retired from public life in January 1977 and died of a heart attack in New York on 26 January 1979.

Douglas Brinkley

See also Ford, Gerald Rudolph; Latin America; Oil and Foreign Policy

FURTHER READING

Alsop, Stewart. *Nixon and Rockefeller: A Double Portrait.* Garden City, N.Y., 1960.
Colby, Gerald, and Charlotte Dennett. *Thy Will Be Done; The Conquest of the Amazon: Nelson Rockefeller and Evangelism in the Age of Oil.* New York, 1995.
Collier, Peter, and David Horowitz. *The Rockefellers: An American Dynasty.* New York, 1976.
Connery, Robert H., and Gerald Benjamin. *Rockefeller of New York: Executive Power in the Statehouse.* Ithaca, 1979.
Desmond, James. *Nelson Rockefeller: A Political Biography.* New York, 1964.
Persico, Joseph E. *The Imperial Rockefeller: A Biography of Nelson A. Rockefeller.* New York, 1982.

ROGERS, WILLIAM PIERCE

(*b.* 23 June 1913)

U.S. attorney general (1957–1961) and secretary of state (1969–1973). Born in New York, Rogers earned a law degree (1937) from Cornell University. After service in World War II he served as counsel for several Senate committees and was appointed deputy attorney general (1953–1957) under President Dwight D. Eisenhower, then attorney general in 1957. President Richard M. Nixon appointed Rogers secretary of state in 1969 despite Rogers's limited experience in foreign affairs. Nixon and his national security adviser, Henry Kissinger, however, conducted U.S. foreign policy largely without consulting the secretary. Rogers's primary contribution was an unsuccessful Middle East peace proposal that called for Arab guarantees of Israel's territorial integrity in conjunction with Israel's withdrawal from the occupied territories. The Rogers Plan failed both because of Israeli and Arab intransigence and the bureaucratic stratagems of Kissinger and his supporters within the NSC, who argued against the Rogers Plan. Nixon asked for Rogers's resignation in 1973 and then appointed Kissinger secretary of state. Rogers returned to his law practice, and in 1986 President Ronald Reagan named him head of a commission to study the National Aeronautics and Space Agency in the wake of the Challenger space shuttle explosion.

Shane J. Maddock

See also Middle East; Nixon, Richard Milhous

FURTHER READING

Ambrose, Stephen E. *Nixon: The Triumph of a Politician, 1962–1972.* New York, 1991.
Garthoff, Raymond L. *Détente and Confrontation: American-Soviet Relations from Nixon to Reagan.* Washington D.C., 1985.
Isaacson, Walter. *Kissinger: A Biography.* New York, 1992.

ROGERS ACT

(1924)

A law signed on 24 May 1924 to combine the diplomatic and consular service functions of U.S. legations and embassies by creating the Foreign Service of the United States. Representative John Jacob Rogers, Republican from Massachusetts, and Department of State official Wilbur J. Carr wrote the act and shepherded it into law.

The two were influenced by the progressive campaigns for remaking government, the need for more services that came with the growth in U.S. overseas economic activity, and the increasing complexity of foreign affairs following World War I. They sought to create a more professional and efficient foreign service by ending the existing dual system in which political functions were handled by diplomatic service and legal functions by the consular service. The act intended to establish a Foreign Service staffed by skilled, career-minded professionals from a wide spectrum of U.S. society whose employment and decisions were free from political meddling. The bill received support from business executives, travelers, the public (influenced by supportive magazine articles), Republican and Democratic politicians, Secretary of State Robert Lansing, and President Calvin Coolidge. The act passed unanimously in the Senate and carried a 184 to 27 majority in the House.

The Rogers Act required all applicants for the Foreign Service to pass a rigorous written and oral examination. Appointees then entered a probationary period after which they were assigned a title and one of nine grades. Advancement rested on merit as measured by regular performance reports. Pay scale was higher than for all other federal employees and included a retirement system. While the Rogers Act democratized the Foreign Service and staffed U.S. legations and embassies with more highly trained civil servants, many positions remained political appointments and the elite nature of the Foreign Service was not entirely eliminated. The Foreign Service Act of 1946 modified the Rogers Act by putting in place a new personnel structure, salary and promotion system, and in-service training.

Bruce D. Mactavish

See also Ambassadors and Embassies; Carr, Wilbur John; Diplomatic Method; Foreign Service; State, U.S. Department of

FURTHER READING

Blancke, W. Wendell. *The Foreign Service of the United States.* New York, 1969.

Ilchman, Warren Frederick. *Professional Diplomacy in the United States, 1779–1939: A Study of Administrative History.* Chicago, 1961.

Kennedy, Charles Stuart. *The American Consul: A History of the United States Consular Service, 1776–1914.* New York, 1990.

ROLLBACK AND LIBERATION

A postwar critique of the dominant U.S. policy of containment of communism. During the late 1940s and early 1950s, the call for "rollback" and "liberation" grew in intensity among those who believed that simply "containing" the further spread of communism and Soviet influence and control was not enough. The policy of containment, as it came to be known, accepted Soviet control of Eastern Europe but was opposed to any additional communist encroachment into Europe, Asia, or the Third World. However, as some critics saw it, events such as the Soviet consolidation of power in Eastern Europe, the "fall" of Jiang Jieshi (Chiang Kai-Shek) and the Nationalists in China in 1949, and the North Korean attack on South Korea in 1950 demonstrated that containment was not working. In other words, the United States had won World War II but was losing the postwar peace, and therefore communism needed to be "rolled back" and countries that had fallen to it needed to be "liberated." Moreover, in addition to perceiving that the United States was losing the Cold War abroad, especially in Asia, proponents of a rollback policy believed that the United States was threatened by subversion from within. Thus, there was a need to roll back communism at home as well, a need which McCarthyism sought to fill.

Despite the presence of prominent individuals sympathetic to the view in both administrations, the supporters of rollback and liberation were basically unsuccessful in their efforts to get Presidents Harry S. Truman and Dwight D. Eisenhower to reorient their foreign policies beyond containment. During the Korean War, for example, Secretary of State Dean Acheson urged a full liberation of the Korean peninsula, a policy that Truman briefly embraced until Chinese forces entered the conflict. Secretary of State John Foster Dulles was most prominent in publicly advocating a policy of liberation, especially during the early years of the Eisenhower administration. Dulles's public advocacy, however, proved in many instances to be more rhetoric than doctrine. For example, the outcome of the Korean War was not a liberated peninsula but an armistice sustaining the two separate Korean states, the communist North and the noncommunist South. And the Eisenhower administration failed to respond forcefully to the Soviet suppression of uprisings in Poland and Hungary: in the case of the 1956 Hungarian rebellion, some historians argue that the U.S. rollack and liberation rhetoric actually convinced Hungarians that the United States would intervene on their behalf.

Nonetheless, the political challenge made by those in favor of rollback and liberation had two lasting effects. First, it reinforced perceptions held by U.S. policymakers and the American public that global communism was monolithic, controlled by the Soviet Union, and an ever present threat. Second, foreign policy views that were critical of the containment policy from a liberal-left political perspective, arguing for a more pragmatic or cooperative policy, lost credibility and legitimacy during the Cold War years. In short, the proponents of rollback and liberation contributed to the formation of a hard-line anticommunist consensus on the need to forestall vigorously the expansion of communism throughout the world, leading directly to U.S. involvement in Vietnam.

With the collapse of the anticommunist consensus due to the crises of the Vietnam War and Watergate, the view in favor of rollback and liberation became much less prominent. The election of Ronald Reagan to the presidency, however, led to a revival of rollback and liberation since many members of his administration were sympathetic to this view. This was best embodied by the so-called "Reagan Doctrine," which symbolized the need to roll back communist successes in the Third World, such as in Afghanistan, Angola, and, most importantly, Central America. Developed during Reagan's second term, the Reagan Doctrine emphasized the vigorous support, both covert and overt, of "surrogate" guerilla forces actively engaged in fighting Soviet-backed Marxist-Leninist regimes, with the ultimate goal of rolling back communist expansion in these areas.

Whether the Reagan Doctrine was actually successful in its efforts at rollback and liberation is a matter of some debate. On one hand, by 1989–1990, the pro-Soviet Marxist governments in Afghanistan, Nicaragua, and Cambodia had fallen. And many view the Afghan debacle as a key factor in the fall of the Soviet Union itself. On the other hand, in both Angola and Afghanistan, the forces previously supported by the United States proved to be hardly democratic or even prepared to end the fighting, and brutal warfare continues in both countries. And in El Salvador and Nicaragua, only time will tell how long it will take to reconstruct the economies and political fabric after a decade of internal warfare.

JEREL A. ROSATI

See also Cold War; Containment; Eastern Europe; Korean War; Reagan Doctrine; Vietnam War

FURTHER READING

Melanson, Richard A. *Writing History and Making Policy: The Cold War, Vietnam, and Revisionism.* Lanham, Md., 1983.
Nuechterlein, Donald E. "The Reagan Doctrine in Perspective." *Perspectives on Political Science* (Winter 1990): 43–49.
O'Sullivan, John. "James Burnham and the New World Order." *National Review* (5 November 1990).
Sanders, Jerry A. *Peddlers of Crisis: The Committee on the Present Danger and the Politics of Containment.* Boston, 1983.

ROMANIA

An Eastern European state bordered by the Black Sea, Bulgaria, Yugosalvia, Hungary, and Ukraine. The modern nation of Romania was formed in 1861 from what under the Ottoman Empire (and for centuries before) had been the principalities of Moldavia and Walachia. The next fifty years were highly unstable amidst the end of Ottoman rule, political struggles between pro-democratic and autocratic-monarchical forces, and an ongoing peasant rebellion.

Romania stayed neutral during the first two years of World War I. It joined the Allies in 1916, in large part seeking to gain three provinces of Austria-Hungary (Banat, Bukovina, and Transylvania) that had large ethnic Romanian populations. It received these territories as part of the Paris peace settlement, thus doubling in area and population.

During the early part of World War II, Germany helped Hungary take back northern Transylvania, and the Soviet Union seized parts of Romania's northeastern territory and Bulgaria parts of its southeastern territory. German troops occupied all of Romania in October 1940. Hitler left the cooperative Premier Ion Antonescu in power. In August 1944, with Germany now much weakened, King Michael overthrow Antonescu and brought Romania to the side of the Allies. At the end of the war the parts of Transylvania taken by Hungary, were returned to Romania, but not the territory taken by the Soviet Union and Bulgaria.

The Soviet troops which occupied Romania in 1944 also stayed. Under Soviet protection, the Romanian Communist party came to power. Political opponents were killed and imprisoned and King Michael was forced to abdicate the thrown in 1947. The constitution, adopted in 1948, modeled the government and political system along Stalinist lines.

U.S.-Romanian relations during the communist period were shaped by Romania's relationship to the Soviet Union. Thus, in the late 1940s and 1950s, when Romania was a loyal ally of the USSR, Romanian-U.S. relations were cool. Romania joined the Warsaw Treaty Organization and the Council for Mutual Economic Assistance dominated by the Soviets, and much of its trade was confined to the USSR and its other socialist allies. U.S.-Romanian trade, which had never been of great significance, declined dramatically between 1947 and 1954, both because of U.S. restrictions such as the Export Control Act of 1949 and the creation of the NATO-like COCOM, and because of Soviet efforts to confine trade of East bloc states to each other.

U.S.-Romanian relations began to improve in the early 1960s. Unwilling to follow Khrushchev's plan to foster specialization within the Council on Mutual Economic Assistance (CMEA), which would have forced Romania to concentrate on agriculture, Romanian leaders Gheorghe-Dej and later Nicolae Ceausescu turned to increased trade with the West to balance Romania's economic dependence on the Soviet Union and other socialist states. Although political control remained very tight at home, Romania's foreign policy began to diverge from that of the Soviet Union in some areas. Romania became the first communist country to recognize Israel, and Romanian troops did not take part in the invasion of Czechoslovakia in 1968.

Developments in Romanian foriegn policy in the mid-1960s coincided with a change in U.S. policy toward the communist world. Lyndon Johnson's effort to use trade to influence developments in the region found a ready partner in Romania. In an effort to encourage Romania to become more independent from the Soviet Union, the United States took measures to encourage greater trade with Romania. The U.S.-Romanian agreement of June 1964 eased licensing requirements and established a U.S. trade office in Bucharest. The Export Administration Act of 1969, which reduced controls on exports to communist countries, and other policies adopted during the effort at détente in the late 1960s and early 1970s also had a positive impact on U.S.-Romanian economic relations. President Nixon's 1969 visit to Romania was followed by Ceausescu's visit to Washington in December 1973. In January 1975, the United States granted Romania most-favored-nation status. The authorization of OPIC programs for Romania in 1972 and Romania's joining of the IMF in April 1973 made further credit and financing available to Romania.

Improvements in U.S.-Romanian economic relations were accompanied by continued controversy in the United States due to the highly repressive nature of Ceausescu's regime and concern over Romanian limits on emigration and other human rights issues. In contrast to the situation in Hungary and Poland, increased economic ties between the United States and Romania were not followed by greater contact with Western ideas or citizen exchange. Although Romania maintained its independent foreign policy line, the Ceausescu regime continued to rely heavily on the secret police and repression. Ceausescu also adopted increasingly repressive measures toward the population, particularly women and the large Hungarian minority centered in Transylvania. In 1988, Romania renounced its MFN status in light of the likely success of U.S. opponents of such status for Romania in having it revoked by the U.S. Congress.

U.S.-Romanian relations improved after the violent downfall of the Ceausescu regime in 1989. Romania's MFN status was restored in 1993. Romania also became eligible for a variety of economic assistance programs designed to foster the move to recreate a market economy. In 1993, the United States and Romania signed a bilateral investment treaty and the United States granted investment capital for private sector development through the Enterprise Fund for Romania. However, the slow approach of the country's new leadership to economic reform and the continued difficulties the country is experiencing under the govern-

ment of the National Salvation Front, which includes many functionaries of the old system, have to date been reflected in the caution of U.S. businesses in investing in Romania.

SHARON L. WOLCHIK

See also Eastern Europe; Russia and the Soviet Union; Warsaw Pact; World War I; World War II

FURTHER READING

Jowitt, Kenneth. *Revolutionary Breakthroughs and National Development: The Case of Romania, 1944–1965.* Berkeley, Calif., 1971.

Linden, Ronald H. *Bear and Foxes: The International Relations of the East European States, 1965–1969.* Boulder, Colo., 1979.

Harrington, Joseph F. and Bruce J. Courtney. *Tweaking the Nose of the Russians: Fifty Years of American-Romanian Relations, 1940–1990.* Boulder, Colo., 1991.

ROOSEVELT, ANNA ELEANOR
(*b.* 11 October 1884; *d.* 7 November 1962)

Humanitarian, peace advocate, diplomat, and first lady. She was born in New York City, the niece of President Theodore Roosevelt. Educated at Allenswood, a finishing school outside London, she married her distant cousin Franklin D. Roosevelt in 1905, raised a family of five children, and first participated in national politics when her husband became assistant secretary of the navy (1913–1921). Shattered by her discovery of Franklin's affair with her own social secretary in 1918, Eleanor stayed married but sought a more independent life through friendships with feminist activists. After her husband's affliction with polio in 1921, she became his surrogate in Democratic Party politics, while remaining active in the League of Women Voters, the Women's Trade Union League, and several women's peace organizations. In 1923 she helped administer the Edward Bok Peace Award, a $50,000 prize for the best prescription for "preserving world peace." In contrast to her husband's repudiation of the League of Nations to gain the Democratic presidential nomination in 1932, Eleanor Roosevelt always kept the White House open to pacifists and internationalists.

During some twelve years as first lady, through her massive correspondence, press conferences, lectures, radio addresses, syndicated newspaper columns ("My Day"), and peripatetic travels, including wartime visits to England and the South Pacific, Eleanor often took positions in advance of her husband. "I sometimes acted as a spur, even though the spurring was not always wanted or welcome," she later wrote. Her youthful pacifism evolved into strong antifascism, and she publicly linked white supremacy in the United States to white supremacy in Adolf Hitler's Europe. She worked publicly and privately on behalf of Jewish refugees from Nazism and advocated lifting the arms embargo against republican forces in the Spanish Civil War. Breaking with her protégés in the American Youth Congress, Eleanor supported a military draft, Lend-Lease, and other interventionist measures prior to Pearl Harbor. During the war she championed liberal plans for a postwar world. She found Winston Churchill "loveable & emotional & very human but I don't want him to write the peace or carry it out." At the second Quebec Conference in 1944 she pushed the Morgenthau Plan for harsh treatment of Germany. Eleanor's plans to attend the inaugural meeting of the United Nations (UN) organization were cut short by the president's death in April 1945.

Devoting the remainder of her life to the promotion of human rights issues around the world, Roosevelt was appointed by President Harry S. Truman as a delegate to the United Nations and chaired the commission that produced the UN Declaration on Human Rights, adopted in December 1948. One of the first civilians to visit the concentration camps and interview Holocaust survivors after the war, she was nominated four times for the Nobel Peace Prize, primarily for her humanitarian efforts. She continued to urge East-West dialogue despite the deepening Cold War. Fearful that unilateral action would undermine the U.S. commitment to international organizations, Mrs. Roosevelt opposed the dismantling of both the UN Relief and Rehabilitation Agency (UNRRA) and the Truman Doctrine (in favor of military aid to Greece and Turkey). She supported the Marshall Plan but preferred to administer European recovery through the United Nations. When her UN term ended in 1953, she travelled the world for the American Association for the United Nations, including trips to Russia in 1957 and 1958, as an unofficial ambassador for peace and human dignity. Anticipating the next generation's admonition to think globally and act locally, she emphasized that universal human rights began "in small places, close to home…Unless these rights have meaning there, they have little meaning anywhere." In her last years the energetic septuagenarian taught at Brandeis University, hosted a television program on the "prospects of mankind," returned as a UN delegate under John F. Kennedy, worked on a committee to gain the release of the Bay of Pigs prisoners from Cuba and advocated increased economic aid for the Third World.

J. GARRY CLIFFORD

See also Bay of Pigs Invasion; Churchill, Winston Leonard Spencer; Cold War; Holocaust; Human Rights; Kennedy, John Fitzgerald; League of Nations; Lend-Lease; Marshall Plan; Morgenthau Plan; Peace Movements and Societies, 1914 to Present; Roosevelt, Franklin Delano; Spain; Truman Doctrine; United Nations; United Nations Relief and Rehabilitation Administration

FURTHER READING

Berger, Jason. *A New Deal for the World: Eleanor Roosevelt and American Foreign Policy.* New York, 1981.
Cook, Blanche Wiesen. *Eleanor Roosevelt.* New York, 1992.
Goodwin, Doris Kearns. *No Ordinary Time.* New York, 1994.
Lash, Joseph P. *Eleanor and Franklin.* New York, 1971.
—— *Eleanor: The Years Alone.* New York, 1972.

ROOSEVELT, FRANKLIN DELANO
(*b.* 30 January 1882; *d.* 12 April 1945)

Thirty-second president of the United States. During his twelve years as president (1933–1945) Roosevelt led the United States from political isolationism, to undeclared war against Nazi Germany, and then, after the Japanese attack on Pearl Harbor, 7 December 1941, to full participation and world leadership in World War II. He died four weeks before the surrender of Germany and four months before victory over Japan, but he helped shape the postwar world at a number of wartime summit conferences.

No president had a greater influence on transforming the relationship of the United States to the rest of the world and in expanding the power of the presidency in domestic and foreign affairs. No president attracted, in his lifetime and afterwards, so much adulation and criticism. During his administration the United States not only led the Allied powers to victory over the Axis but also acquired and used more economic and military power than any nation in history. In spite of these achievements, critics variously charged Roosevelt with manipulating Japan into attacking at Pearl Harbor in 1941 in order to bring the United States into war, with being too much under the influence of British Prime Minister Winston Churchill or of undermining the British empire, with permitting the expansion of Soviet communism into the heart of Europe, and with being responsible for the victory of the Communists in China.

Roosevelt remains controversial in part because his inner character and thoughts are as elusive to historians as they were to his contemporaries. He was—to use the characterizations applied to him by various commentators—lion, fox, juggler, magician, heroic champion of freedom, superficial improviser, and sometimes a liar. He seldom committed his thoughts to paper and was not given to intellectual speculation or introspection. He kept no diary and wrote no memoirs.

Roosevelt had little use for theory. He shunned fixed ideological positions and had an aversion to detailed planning for unknown situations. He was a master of improvisation and when the future was opaque, he preferred postponement. He often told successive visitors quite different things. His fondness for rambling anecdotes and personal reminiscence charmed some but irritated those who preferred a structured, formal process of decision-making.

Aware of the role of chance and the unexpected in international affairs, he nevertheless pursued and largely achieved the goal of national security founded on military and economic power and inspired by practical idealism.

Serene assurance was Roosevelt's hallmark in both domestic and international leadership. He never showed a hint of self-doubt or personal tension. No president had a warmer relationship with the press, thanks to his weekly off-the-record news conferences and the good-humored way he appeared to take reporters into his confidence. And no president communicated as effectively with the American people, thanks to his frequent and eloquent radio speeches and "fireside chats" delivered in a deep, beautifully cadenced voice. He had domestic enemies, mostly on the conservative edge of politics, but the majority of the American people trusted and revered him.

A clue to Roosevelt's character and behavior lies in his love and knowledge of the sea. Politics, both at home and abroad, required the capacity to meet ever-changing conditions, tacking to the right and then to the left, turning back if necessary, avoiding placing oneself or the ship in an inescapable condition. But every change of course was related to reaching a definite objective: economic recovery at home and victory over aggressor nations on the world scene. Like a good sea captain, he communicated supreme self-confidence to passengers and crew. He was always optimistic in public and private, probably more optimistic on many issues than he really felt.

Roosevelt, as much as any president in U.S. history, was personally in charge of foreign policy. He did not confide in Secretary of State Cordell Hull and most of the time left the secretary in charge of relatively unimportant issues. The president encouraged U.S. ambassadors abroad to write him directly and privately, employed special agents for specific missions, and conducted his own diplomacy at the highest levels face to face with foreign leaders, most notably Prime Minister Churchill and Soviet leader Joseph Stalin. During the war years Roosevelt relied heavily on Harry Hopkins, a personal aide and advisor in a role reminiscent of President Woodrow Wilson's Colonel Edward M. House and anticipating that of national security adviser of the 1960s and 1970s. Before the outbreak of World War II in 1939, Roosevelt avoided confrontation with Congress over foreign policy; but between 1939 and 1941 he prevailed over congressional isolationists with a policy of aiding victims of German and Japanese aggression. After the United States entered the war, Roosevelt, as commander in chief, did not consult Congress on the intertwined matters of military strategy and foreign policy. His diplomacy and political commitments were secret, for understandable reasons of wartime security. But the secrecy would haunt his memory far into the future.

Early Life

Roosevelt was the only child of James Roosevelt and Sara Delano, wealthy and cosmopolitan New York patricians. Born in Hyde Park, as a child he traveled frequently to Europe with his mother. He liked England, but was less enthusiastic about France and Germany. He was educated at the exclusive Groton School in Massachusetts (where in 1898 he cheered U.S. victory in the war with Spain), Harvard College (class of 1904 and chief editor of the undergraduate newspaper), and Columbia University Law School. He was not interested in the life of a lawyer and spent all his life in politics. He married Eleanor Roosevelt, a distant cousin, in 1905. Although always a democrat, Franklin much admired another cousin, Republican President Theodore Roosevelt. He followed the older man's republican trajectory to a remarkable degree: an apprenticeship in New York state politics; a passion for naval affairs and an admiration for Admiral Alfred Thayer Mahan, theorist and popular writer on the importance of seapower; assistant secretary of the navy; governor of New York; vice-presidential candidate (Theodore was elected in 1900, but Franklin lost in 1920), and president.

Roosevelt found his service as assistant secretary of the navy during the eight years of the Wilson administration a time of unalloyed delight. As a skilled and passionate sailor, he spent as much time as possible on naval vessels and in the company of naval officers. An exuberant and unreflective imperialist, he relished helping supervise the Marine Corps landings at Vera Cruz and Tamico, Mexico, and the occupation of Haiti and the Dominican Republic. Privately he flaunted his own seagoing expertise while making fun of the landlubber secretary of the navy, Josephus Daniels. When the European war broke out in 1914, Roosevelt was unequivocally pro-British and anti-German and privately out of sympathy with the neutral posture of President Wilson. Cousin Theodore's bellicosity was far more to the young man's taste than the president's intellectualism. Roosevelt threw all his energy into preparing the navy for a war he was sure would come. He rejoiced when the United States declared war on Germany in 1917. He then devoted his attention to encouraging the navy to perfect antisubmarine operations against the Germans. His happiest moment was a 1918 trip on a destroyer through the war zone to Europe.

Roosevelt, as a subcabinet officer, had little personal contact with President Wilson and had no role in shaping U.S. war aims and policy at the Paris Peace Conference of 1919. He watched as Wilson suffered a devastating physical collapse in the failed effort to win Senate approval for the treaty containing a commitment to U.S. membership in the League of Nations. At that stage Roosevelt's ideas about the United States' place in the world were superficial.

Roosevelt was the Democratic vice-presidential candidate in 1920, selected for his youth, his name, his athletic good looks, and his energy. Both the Democratic ticket, headed by James M. Cox, and the possibility of U.S. membership in the League of Nations were soundly defeated by Republican Warren G. Harding. Roosevelt, lacking Wilson's obsession for the League, drew a powerful lesson from the older man's fate: it was dangerous to make large international commitments before being absolutely sure of the support of Congress and the public.

In 1921 Roosevelt, while on vacation at the family summer home in Campobello, New Brunswick, Canada, was stricken with poliomyelitis, also called infantile paralysis. He was more seriously crippled than he ever allowed the public to realize, but he rejected his doting mother's wish that he assume the leisure of a country gentleman. During the 1920s, while learning to cope with the permanent damage to his legs inflicted by the disease, Roosevelt maintained his political contacts, and wrote occasionally and blandly on foreign affairs. He played a prominent part in the Democratic convention of 1928 in support of the nomination of New York Governor Al Smith. That year Roosevelt was elected governor of New York while Republican Herbert Hoover easily defeated Smith for president. Roosevelt's popularity as governor and Hoover's failure to cope with the economic depression following the stock market crash of 1929 led to Roosevelt's nomination for president in 1932 and his decisive victory over Hoover. The overriding issue of the campaign was the appalling unemployment everywhere in the nation. Foreign policy played no role in the election.

First Term as President

President Roosevelt was not an isolationist, but in 1933 he was determined not to let any foreign policy issue interfere with his capacity to implement the New Deal, his sweeping and eclectic measures for dealing with the devastating economic conditions in the United States. His inaugural address—famous for the line "the only thing we have to fear is fear itself"—was explicit in saying that he would concentrate on recovery at home and treat international economic issues as secondary. He added, with characteristic vagueness: "In the field of world policy, I would dedicate this nation to the policy of the good neighbor."

Roosevelt immediately declined to commit the United States to an international monetary agreement under discussion at the London economic conference (1933) and instead took the dollar off the gold standard in order to combat deflation. U.S. participation in the London conference had been arranged by the outgoing Hoover administration, but Roosevelt, in a popular phrase of the time, "torpedoed" the conference by sending special emissary Raymond Moley to London to announce that the United States would not agree to any limitation on its own freedom of action in international monetary policy.

Until the late 1930s Roosevelt avoided taking a stance that contained the slightest risk of drawing the United States into armed conflict. For example, he criticized Italy's 1935 war of conquest against Ethiopia but did no more than request that U.S. oil companies hold their exports to Italy to the level of previous years. Roosevelt recognized the doleful strategic implications of Nazi Germany's 1936 reoccupation and remilitarization of the Rhineland, in clear violation of treaty commitments, but he refrained from official condemnation. He privately deplored the plight of the Spanish government in its losing civil war against General Francisco Franco, a fascist supported by Germany and Italy, but he was careful not to risk U.S. involvement in the conflict. The major issue in Asia in 1933 was Japan's aggression against China and annexation of Manchuria as a spurious independent empire, Manchukuo. Roosevelt continued the Hoover administration's policy of refusing to recognize the legality of Japan's conquest, but like Hoover he avoided taking a threatening posture toward Japan.

Roosevelt in his early years as president chose not to risk his political capital combatting the mood of isolationism prevalent in Congress, a mood expressed in the backward-looking neutrality legislation passed in 1935, 1936, and 1937. The legislation barred Americans from lending money or selling munitions to governments at war or engaged in civil war. The laws flowed from two dubious premises: first, that the United States had entered World War I primarily to serve the interest of bankers and munitions makers, the "merchants of death"; and second, that the European balance of power and survival of democratic regimes was not vital concern for the security of the United States. It had the unintended result of favoring aggressors who had prepared in advance for war while depriving the victims of aggression of aid they might otherwise have obtained from the United States. President Roosevelt disagreed with both premises, but in the mid-1930s he let Congress have its way and never contemplated using the veto.

The foreign policy innovations of the first administration were all designed directly or indirectly to improve the U.S. economy. Roosevelt's meeting with Soviet Foreign Minister Maksim Litvinov in November 1933 led to the establishment of diplomatic relations between the United States and the Soviet Union and agreement to settle economic claims of the two countries against each other. Roosevelt's hope that diplomatic relations would be followed by a surge of Russian buying in the United States was disappointed. Conversely, the Soviet expectation of strategic cooperation with the United States against Japan was also unfulfilled.

More successful was the Good Neighbor Policy for Latin America. Twenty years earlier the young Roosevelt had been an enthusiast for U.S. intervention in Mexico, Central America, and the Caribbean. He boasted, with pardonable exaggeration, that he wrote the constitution of Haiti and it was "a pretty good constitution, too." The mature president realized that the habit of U.S. armed intervention and strident assertions of U.S. dominance under the Monroe Doctrine had produced deep resentment in Latin America, were not justified in terms of military security, and were an obstacle to trade. In 1934, under the Good Neighbor Policy, Roosevelt withdrew U.S. forces from Haiti, moved to terminate U.S. supervision of the finances of the Dominican Republic, and relinquished U.S. rights of intervention in Cuba under the Platt Amendment provisions of the Cuban-American Treaty of 1903. The Good Neighbor Policy was dramatically illustrated by Roosevelt's attendance in 1936 of a special inter-American conference in Brazil—the first time an American president had met with Latin American leaders outside the United States. Roosevelt supported and the U.S. Senate unanimously approved the Buenos Aires protocol of 23 December 1936 declaring: "The High Contracting Parties declare inadmissible the intervention of any of them, directly or indirectly, and for whatever reason, in the internal or external affairs of any other of the Parties."

A third early foreign policy innovation was the negotiation of reciprocal trade agreements with every country willing to participate. Roosevelt left the details to Secretary of State Cordell Hull. The agreements, authorized by the Reciprocal Trade Act of 1934 as periodically renewed, made possible the bilateral lowering of tariffs in the interest of higher trade and employment. Hull saw reciprocal trade as fulfillment of the traditional low-tariff traditions of the Democratic party and as a contribution to world peace. He noted later that the United States did not go to war during World War II with any nation with whom a reciprocal trade agreement had been signed. His administration also created the Export-Import Bank to mediate foreign trade.

Roosevelt's Road to World War II

Roosevelt won reelection in 1936, carrying every state save Maine and Vermont. During his second term war broke out or intensified in Asia and Europe and Roosevelt moved cautiously—some would say deviously—to prepare the American public for possible intervention. In response to Japan's resumed attack on China in 1937, Roosevelt in a speech in Chicago (5 October 1937) compared "acts of international aggression" to an epidemic of physical disease requiring "a quarantine of the patients in order to protect the health of the community against the spread of the disease." He apparently was saying that the United States should join other nations in imposing an economic embargo on aggressor nations. But

in the absence of strong public support for the idea, he retreated, refusing to say specifically what he had in mind. But when pressed by reporters to specify exactly what the quarantine metaphor meant—an embargo on trade with Japan, for example—Roosevelt was deliberately vague. He did not want to get ahead of public opinion by advocating anything as provocative as an embargo on trade with Japan. But in 1939 the United States did give Japan notice that it was withdrawing from a trade treaty, thus clearing the way for possible economic sanctions.

Roosevelt was little more than an observer of the British and French policy of appeasement, the effort to prevent war by giving in to the territorial and political demands of German dictator Adolf Hitler, most notably the 1938 demand for the annexation of part of Czechoslovakia to Germany. Roosevelt recognized that Hitler was an evil force and never tried to use his vaunted charm to establish a personal relationship. But the president had no credible inducements to urge the British and French to stand firm.

When Hitler negotiated a nonaggression pact with Stalin and invaded Poland in 1939, the British and French finally abandoned appeasement and declared war on Germany—and soon found themselves desperate. World War II had begun. Roosevelt's contempt for Nazi Germany was open. But in 1939–1940 he was deterred at first from translating contempt into heavy assistance to the nations fighting Germany by the isolationist mood of Congress and the American people, the restrictions of the neutrality legislation in assisting nations at war, and the prospect of the 1940 presidential campaign. He did secure a revision of the neutrality legislation (4 November 1939), permitting belligerents to buy munitions in the United States with cash (no loans) and carry them away in their own ships. The procedure was known as "cash and carry." He also sent a diplomatic confidant, Undersecretary of State Summer Wells, to London, Paris, Rome, and Berlin in February 1940 to find a basis for peace negotiations. His real purpose was to buy time for the British and French to build their military power.

The Wells mission proved futile. Within two weeks of Wells's return (9 April 1940) Hitler launched the lightning attack on western Europe. By the spring of 1940 Nazi Germany had conquered Denmark, Norway, Belgium, and the Netherlands and forced the British army to retreat across the Channel. In June, France surrendered. Half the country was held under direct German occupation and the other, with a capital at Vichy, became a Nazi puppet state. Meanwhile (11 May), Winston Churchill succeeded Neville Chamberlain as British prime minister. Roosevelt and Churchill immediately established the closest working relationship between a U.S. president and a foreign leader in history, a relationship at the core of wartime diplomacy.

The next eighteen months, until December 1941, demonstrated either Roosevelt's mastery of political leadership or the extent of his deviousness, depending on the point of view of the commentator. He told the American people that his primary purpose was to protect the United States from war and he promised during the 1940 presidential campaign, when he was running for an unprecedented third time, that American boys would never again be sent to fight in foreign wars.

For Great Britain to survive Hitler's air attack and the likely German invasion to follow, more was needed than Churchill's inspiring leadership. Churchill asked Roosevelt for substantial help, including the loan of U.S. destroyers to protect supply lines against German U-boats. But Roosevelt delayed for domestic political reasons. He feared that the Republicans might nominate an uncompromising isolationist as presidential candidate. That fear disappeared when the nomination went to Wendell Willkie, a critic of the New Deal domestic programs but no isolationist. Roosevelt in July accepted the Democratic nomination and began to move more boldly. In September he agreed to transfer fifty U.S. destroyers, surplus from World War I, to the British navy in return for ninety-year leases to the United States of sites on British colonial territory for air and naval bases from Newfoundland south to Bermuda and through the Caribbean. The beauty of the destroyers-for-bases deal was that it could be represented to isolationists as a means of defending the Western Hemisphere and thus keeping the United States out of the war while at the same time it sent an unequivocal signal to Germany of Roosevelt's commitment to the survival of Great Britain.

It is impossible to say when Roosevelt reached the conclusion that the United States must enter the war against Germany. Month by month he devoted more of his time to military, especially naval, preparedness. Mentally and psychologically he educated himself for the role of a wartime commander in chief. He once said that if he couldn't be president, he would like to be an admiral. He also was proud of his "map mind." He thought in terms of oceanic distances, sea-lanes, and fortifications. Thus until the United States entered the war he indulged his love of the sea and used his position as commander in chief to spend weeks every year on U.S. warships on long cruises in the Atlantic, the Caribbean, and the Pacific.

By the end of 1940 Great Britain had run out of money with which to make purchases in the United States. Roosevelt's response was to ask Congress to approve the lend-lease program, authorizing him as president to send economic and military aid to any country whose defense he deemed vital to the security of the United States. The lend-lease legislation, designated House Resolution 1776, passed in March 1941. But the British merchant ships carrying the needed supplies fell prey to German submarines. Under Roosevelt's personal direction, the United States moved to secure the North Atlantic sea lanes between America and Great Britain. Greenland and Iceland were declared to be within the Western Hemisphere and thus under the Monroe Doctrine. The United States sent troops to both in 1941. U.S. destroyers accompanied British and Canadian warships in convoying merchant ships and inevitably clashed with German submarines. Roosevelt in the fall of 1941 ordered the U.S. Navy to "shoot on sight." The United States and Germany were in a state of undeclared war, although Roosevelt misrepresented U.S. naval operations as defensive, in response to unprovoked German attack. That came close to lying.

Meanwhile, Roosevelt had encouraged military staff talks between the United States and Great Britain. In August 1941 he boarded the cruiser *Augusta* for a secret naval rendezvous with Churchill in Placenta Bay, on the coast of Newfoundland. The two men and their military advisors planned global strategy, including how best to get aid to the Soviet Union, which, to the surprise of many military authorities, had not crumbled under the surprise German attack of June 1941. They noted the growing threat of Japan's expansion into Southeast Asia. Although there was no formal U.S. commitment, the tenor of conversations left no doubts that the United States would come to Great Britain's aid if Japan attacked.

Roosevelt and Churchill also issued the "Atlantic Charter" at the Newfoundland meeting. It was a deliberately general and idealistic statement of war aims, much less specific than Wilson's Fourteen Points of 1918, affirming their wish for "the final destruction of Nazi tyranny," for the restoration of "sovereign rights and self-government…to those who have been forcibly deprived of them," and for a peaceful world where all people could live under governments of their own choosing with "freedom from fear and want." The fact that the Soviet Union, soon to be a formal ally in the war against Germany, was violating sovereign rights, especially those of Poland, was an issue that would plague Roosevelt and his successors for half a century.

Roosevelt's handling of the confrontation with Japan between 1939 and 1941 failed in its primary objective of restraining Japan's advance without requiring the United States to go to war. Because Roosevelt considered German power the greater threat to the United States, he was open to a temporary settlement provided Japan halted the advance into Southeast Asia. In return Japan could have some of the restrictions lifted from Secretary of State Hull and others not to betray China, to make no concessions on the principle of the Open Door. And in Tokyo the militarists controlling Japan's course were bent on creating a vast empire by force. Roosevelt's inclinations notwithstanding, there was little room for bargaining.

Roosevelt's dilemma was that the United States could neither accept Japan's conquest of China and growing strategic threat to the Philippines and European colonies nor assemble the power necessary for effective deterrence. Roosevelt hoped that escalating economic sanctions, reinforcing U.S. air forces in the Philippines, and stationing the Pacific fleet at Pearl Harbor would deter Japan. His hopes were dashed by the Japanese attack of 7 December 1941.

Some historians and other critics charge that Roosevelt wanted war and deliberately maneuvered the Japanese into firing the first shot as an ensured way of overcoming American isolationism and getting the United States into war with Germany, Japan's ally. The title of Charles C. Tansill's *Back Door to War: The Roosevelt Foreign Policy, 1933–1941* (1952) expressed the essence of this argument. Some adherents of this school claim that Roosevelt knew the Japanese would attack Pearl Harbor and that he deliberately left local forces unwarned and unprepared in order to ensure the success of the attack. There is no credible evidence to support this calumny. A pervasive and understandable U.S. intelligence failure, not sinister and callous willingness on Roosevelt's part to sacrifice U.S. ships and lives, explains Japan's success in launching a surprise attack.

Wartime Alliance Leader

The Japanese attack followed by German and Italian declarations of war against the United States (December 11) removed the domestic political constraints on Roosevelt's foreign policy and left him a free hand to organize the alliance. At the heart of Roosevelt's wartime diplomacy was his almost daily communication with Churchill—usually long messages from Churchill and short replies. Roosevelt also gathered information by letter and personal interview from hundreds of American and foreign officials, and relied for confidential missions on Harry Hopkins and others. Admiral William D. Leahy served as chairman of the Joint Chiefs of Staff and as the president's military advisor. Roosevelt generally ignored the Department of State, even to the point of failing to inform the secretary of important negotiations and agreements.

On the strategic side of wartime foreign policy, three of Roosevelt's decisions are of central importance. The first, overriding the preference of Chief of Staff General George C. Marshall, was to invade North Africa in 1942 rather than attempt an early cross-Channel invasion aimed at the heart of Germany power. North Africa was followed by the invasion of Italy in 1943 and the postponement, as Marshall feared and the British wished, of the cross-Channel operation until 1944. Another broad decision was to send as much military aid as possible to the Soviet Union even if U.S. needs were not met as quickly as the army would have liked. The third decision

was to be faithful to the inter-Allied strategy of defeating Germany first, although that meant devoting fewer resources to the war against Japan than the U.S. Navy wanted and designating almost no resources to China.

Roosevelt's strategic decisions aimed to win the war with the least loss of American lives. He avoided costly premature operations. He relied heavily on U.S. productive power and the use of naval and air power. The United States suffered only 292,131 combat deaths out of 16,353,659 in military service. It is difficult to see how the war could have been won with fewer casualties.

On the political side, Roosevelt sought to minimize conflict with the Soviet Union in order to hasten victory over Germany and to assure the entry of the Soviet Union into the war against Japan. He was aware that Stalin's aims and methods conflicted with the idealistic principles of the Atlantic Charter, but he saw nothing to be gained by challenging the Soviet Union while the war remained to be won. Better to downplay and postpone the problems and hope for some moderation in Soviet behavior after victory. His capacity to charm the press, the public, and other politicians was a secret of his domestic success. He hoped the same techniques would work in diplomacy and tried them on Stalin on the occasions of their two meetings—at Tehran in 1943 and at Yalta in 1945. Roosevelt was disappointed. We cannot know whether he really believed that a smile and a friendly attitude had a better chance of winning cooperation than scowls and threats.

In spite of public rhetoric of U.S.-Soviet fraternal friendship, Roosevelt placed important limits on cooperation. British and U.S. military leadership shared information and coordinated strategy and tactics through the Combined Chiefs of Staff. British forces in Europe fought under an American supreme Allied commander, General Dwight D. Eisenhower. No comparable arrangements exited or were desired with the Soviets.

The limits of cooperation and trust are best illustrated in the development of the atomic bomb to which the United States, in cooperation with the British, devoted every possible scientific and engineering resource lest the Germans acquire the potential weapon first. Roosevelt agreed with Churchill that the Soviets should not be informed in advance of this endeavor, much less invited to participate. They also agreed that the decisions on the use and postwar control of the atomic bombs should be made by Great Britain and the United States. In the autumn of 1944 the Danish nuclear physicist Niels Bohr proposed to Roosevelt and Churchill that the Soviets be brought into the secret as a way of preventing a postwar nuclear arms race. Roosevelt and Churchill explicitly rejected Bohr's proposal and agreed to maintain an Anglo-American monopoly.

Roosevelt believed the German people were in some measure responsible for Hitler's crimes, and not solely victims. Thus, he favored drastic punishment for Germany including permanent partition, demilitarization, and dismantling of heavy industry. Roosevelt expressed outrage against the Holocaust, but his administration was slow to take steps to save Jewish refugees. He had a deep antipathy to the French in general and to General Charles de Gaulle in particular and was reluctant to see France reestablished as a major power. Drawing a conclusion from the aftermath of World War I, he believed the United States would withdraw its forces from Europe within two years of victory over Germany. He did not seem much concerned over the likelihood that the Soviet Union would then fill a European vacuum of power.

Roosevelt believed that the age of colonial empires was over, but he was vague on exactly how decolonization should proceed and transitions to independence achieved. He was fond of the concept of trusteeship, during which one or more major powers would be responsible for governing former colonies and preparing them for independence. He was proud that the United States had promised independence to the Philippines and believed that U.S. rule there should be a model for other colonial devolutions. Churchill resented Roosevelt's unsolicited advice on how to grant independence to India and scoffed at the president's suggestion that the crown colony of Hong Kong be returned to China immediately after the war. Roosevelt's harshest criticism was reserved for French colonialism in Indochina and on several occasions he said the French should not be allowed to return to its colonies there. He mentioned putting Indochina under trusteeship, perhaps with China in charge, in order to prepare the people for independence. He also favored full independence for Arab countries still under French and British control. His solution for Palestine as a homeland for the Jews was a three-headed administration in Jerusalem headed by a Muslim, a Jew, and a Christian. In the last year of his life Roosevelt said less on colonial issues. His influence on the dissolution of empires was, in fact, not great. The weakness of the imperial nations and the nationalistic assertiveness stimulated by the war were working toward an inevitable outcome no matter what the United States did.

Roosevelt noticed, but did not lead, rising American public support for a new collective security organization, the United Nations. He was haunted by the ghost of Woodrow Wilson's mistake in getting ahead of public opinion on the League of Nations, and was determined not to make the same mistake. He favored postwar security maintained by "Four Policeman"—the United States, Great Britain, the Soviet Union, and China—each with responsibility for a geographical sphere, and was opposed to giving any significant influence to small, weak nations. These concepts were ultimately reflected in the Security Council of the United Nations, with veto power on action residing in the council's permanent members (Roosevelt's "four policemen" plus France).

Yalta and the Roosevelt Legacy

The climax of Roosevelt's diplomacy and the last great event of his life was the Yalta conference with Stalin and Churchill in February 1945. The Big Three leaders who had met in 1943 at Tehran gathered in the onetime resort town in the Crimea to celebrate impending victory over Germany and reach what agreements they could on postwar issues. They agreed to the occupation of a defeated Germany divided into Soviet, British, U.S., and French zones. Stalin confirmed that the Soviet Union would enter the war against Japan two or three months after the defeat of Germany, and in a secret deal received Roosevelt's guarantee of a Soviet sphere of influence in Manchuria. The three leaders discussed the structure of the postwar United Nations including the necessity of big-power veto, although they were unclear on precisely what the veto would cover. They issued a benign public statement about the principles to be followed in the liberation of Europe, but privately glossed over the conflict between Soviet and Western differences on what those principles meant, especially as applied to the treatment and boundaries of postwar Poland. They decided that the communist Lublin government in Poland should be reorganized to include noncommunists, but the language of the Yalta accord was so vague as to invite later acrimony.

Roosevelt at Yalta was exhausted and, as it turned out, near death. But his poor health did not affect the outcome of the conference. The agreements with the Soviet Union confirmed what had previously been accepted in general terms. Behind idealistic rhetoric lay Roosevelt's recognition that the Soviets would do what they wished in areas controlled by the Red Army. He was not prepared, nor were the American people, to use the hint of force in order to modify Soviet behavior. Two world wars in a quarter century were enough.

Roosevelt lived less than two months after his return from the Yalta conference. The testimony of people who saw him in the last year of his life, and photographs, document the extent of his physical decline, and raises the question of whether it was irresponsible of him to accept nomination for a fourth term. In his final days Roosevelt exchanged messages with Churchill and Stalin about Soviet complaints and suspicions that Great Britain and the United States were contemplating a separate peace with Germany. In his last message to Churchill he said "I would minimize the general Soviet problem as much as possible." The next day, 12 April, at the "little White House" in Warm Springs, Georgia, he died from a massive cerebral hemorrhage. He had not had the time or inclination to brief the new vice president, Harry S. Truman.

A final unanswerable question is whether events would have unfolded much differently after April 1945 had Roosevelt lived, and specifically would the deterioration of relations between the Soviet Union and the West, leading soon to the Cold War, have been delayed or prevented. Roosevelt would probably have not been as blunt with the Soviets as President Truman was in 1945, but before his death he had ample evidence of the fragility of Soviet pledges to introduce democratic regimes in Eastern Europe. Roosevelt probably would have given Stalin the benefit of the doubt a little longer. He was, after all, a master of postponement. But it is unlikely that the confrontation leading to the Cold War would or could have been prevented altogether.

Roosevelt's critics after the war blamed him for the rise of Soviet power and the spread of Moscow-controlled communism into Eastern Europe. Critics also blamed Roosevelt and his administration for not bringing about a unified anticommunist China under Nationalist leader Jiang Jieshi (Chiang Kai-shek). Defenders, on the other hand, argued that it was beyond the capacity of the United States to defeat Germany without the Soviet alliance, and simultaneously prevent the Soviet Union from seizing its own security zone and imposing its political system behind the Iron Curtain. Roosevelt had no choice but to hope that in victory the worst features of Soviet oppression would abate. The United States, moreover, could not defeat Japan and simultaneously take sides in a Chinese civil war.

GADDIS SMITH

See also Atlantic Charter; Churchill, Winston Leonard Spencer; Cold War; Destroyers-for-Bases Deal; Good Neighbor Policy; Holocaust; Hopkins, Harry Lloyd; Isolationism; Japan; League of Nations; Lend-Lease; Neutrality Acts of the 1930s; Pearl Harbor, Attack on; Presidency; Reciprocal Trade Agreement Act; Russia and the Soviet Union; Stalin, Joseph; World War II; Yalta Conference

FURTHER READING

Burns, James MacGregor. *Roosevelt: The Lion and the Fox.* New York.
Feis, Herbert. *Churchill, Roosevelt, Stalin: The War They Waged and the Peace They Sought.* Princeton, N.J., 1957.
Freidel, Frank. *Franklin D. Roosevelt: A Rendezvous with Destiny.* Boston, 1990.
Dallek, Robert. *Franklin D. Roosevelt and American Foreign Policy, 1932–1945.* New York, 1979.
Kimball, Warren F. *The Juggler: Franklin Roosevelt as Wartime Statesman.* Princeton, N.J., 1991.
Kimball, Warren F., ed. *Churchill & Roosevelt: The Complete Correspondence,* 3 vols. Princeton, N.J., 1984.
Sherwood, Robert E. *Roosevelt and Hopkins.* New York, 1950.
Smith, Gaddis. *American Diplomacy During the Second World War,* 2nd ed. New York, 1985.
Throne, Christopher. *Allies of a Kind: The United States, Britain and the War Against Japan, 1941–1945.* New York, 1978.
Wood, Bryce. *The Making of the Good Neighbor Policy.* New York, 1961.

ROOSEVELT, THEODORE
(*b.* 27 October 1858; *d.* 6 January 1919)

President of the United States (1901–1909), known for his outspoken nationalism and diplomatic skill. He assumed the presidency on 15 September 1901 in Buffalo, New York, moments after William McKinley died from an assassin's bullet fired eight days earlier. Roosevelt's foreign policy philosophy was articulated in his main diplomatic principle that power and responsibility must be combined. The two ingredients, in both his thought and practice, were inseparable and indissoluble. Self-assured, he used moralistic or jingoistic rhetoric with no reflection or hesitation. Cosmopolitan by virtue of his birth to moderate New York wealth, a traveler to Europe in adolescence, fluent in several languages, a reader of many other languages (including Old Norse), possessed of a quick mind and a photographic memory, Theodore Roosevelt was an American internationalist. He fiercely resisted popular sentiment for an isolationist foreign policy. Well-known as a spokesman for U.S. expansionist sentiment and a big navy before he became president, as president Roosevelt instituted a globalist diplomacy that made the United States an active participant in world affairs.

Theodore Roosevelt was born in New York City to Theodore Roosevelt and Martha Bulloch Roosevelt. Theodore was a sickly, asthmatic child with terrible eyesight that went undiagnosed until he was thirteen. Educated at Groton and Harvard (A.B., 1880), Theodore blossomed after his father's death in 1878. In 1882 he published his first book, *The Naval War of 1812*, which he wrote as a Harvard senior, and became, to the astonishment of his family, a professional Republican politician rather than a corporation lawyer. A successful New York state legislator from 1881 to 1884, Roosevelt attracted national attention as a reformer, opposed James G. Blaine's presidential nomination in 1884, and unexpectedly rejected a "mugwump" (a sarcastic term for amateur gentleman reformer) career by reluctantly supporting the losing Republican ticket. His wife Alice died in childbirth and his mother died late in February 1884, but he managed to finish his legislative term. He consoled himself with a visit to the Dakota Territory ranch he had bought in 1883; he then returned to New York only to lose a three-way election for mayor in 1886.

In November of that year he married Edith Kermit Carow and established his family at Sagamore Hill in Oyster Bay, Long Island, before becoming a notable but minor Republican public official. He learned the ways of Washington, D.C. as President Benjamin Harrison's civil service commissioner (1889–1893) and soon returned to New York City as police commissioner (1895–1897). In both roles he displayed a charismatic ability to win public support and attention from the press while exasperating both friends and enemies with his unrelenting moralist rhetoric.

Roosevelt was elected governor of New York in the close election of 1898, decided by state corruption issues and not by his ineffective war hero campaign tactics. In his role as the strong executive and steward of the people, Roosevelt infuriated Senator ("Boss") Thomas Platt as much by his moralist diction as by his executive policies. On most matters Platt and Roosevelt worked well together as accommodationist, professional politicians. Platt maneuvered Roosevelt out of New York state politics into the expected dead end of the national vice presidency, a role Roosevelt resisted but could not politically reject. In 1901 Roosevelt suddenly became president at a time when McKinley had been quietly facing the need for major change in America. The most dramatic differences between the two men were those of style: McKinley favored finessing change; Roosevelt confronted and dramatized change, making himself its agent rather than its messenger.

At the age of forty-three, Roosevelt was the youngest president to take office, a seventh generation urban aristocrat, Harvard graduate, published historian who became president of the American Historical Association in 1912, and a professional natural scientist. Roosevelt had fought in the Spanish-American-Cuban-Filipino War in 1898. Senator Mark Hanna, McKinley's friend and Ohio ally, regarded this unusual new president as a dangerous cowboy. Roosevelt's vigorous style and charismatic political appeal tended to mask the fundamental conservatism of his political career. He feared revolution at home and abroad and believed that moderate change was necessary to forestall a more radical transformation of the United States.

The War of 1898

Roosevelt played a central role in the War of 1898. As McKinley's assistant secretary of the navy (a misleading title since the assistant traditionally ran the office for the politically appointed secretary), he readied the navy for an unprecedented foreign war, maneuvered the appointment of the gifted naval officer George Dewey to be chief of the Pacific Squadron, and, when the war began, volunteered to lead an invasion force to help liberate Cuba from Spanish rule. Secretary of the Navy John Davis Long claimed that Roosevelt was the classic jingo in power. Others, however, applauded Roosevelt as a naval strategist and historian who meticulously followed the U.S. Navy's "War Plan of June, 1896," written during Grover Cleveland's presidency, as a means of diverting Spain's attention and navy to Asia and Europe and thereby preventing its concentration in the Cuban theater. Roosevelt volunteered to fight in Cuba because he

believed that political leaders who favored war should not shrink from fighting in them. With his friend Colonel Leonard Wood, Roosevelt organized the Rough Riders (the first voluntary cavalry regiment), who trained in Tampa and fought in Cuba. Roosevelt led his dismounted troops in the Rough Riders's famous charge at Kettle Hill to help win the battle of San Juan and defeat the Spanish troops defending Santiago de Cuba. Roosevelt was promoted to colonel and assumed command of the Rough Riders.

Roosevelt's appointment and tenure as assistant secretary of the navy were defining moments in his political life. He won the post only after intense political lobbying by his political allies. But Roosevelt's appointment served McKinley's centrist political image, helping to mollify the expansionist jingo wing of the Republican Party while providing the president with an expendable scapegoat if a war went badly.

Europe did not always treat the United States as a serious power during this period. Great Britain linked U.S. concessions in Canada's Alaska boundary dispute to an agreement to end joint isthmian canal rights. The United States insisted on keeping the issues separate, but only hard brinkmanship diplomacy by Roosevelt and some minor last minute compromises ended the acrimonious dispute on 20 October 1903. The Anglo-German–Venezuelan blockade of December 1902–February 1903, which was the most grievous example of European disdain, gave Roosevelt a dramatic and golden opportunity to reaffirm the Monroe Doctrine and the new U.S. naval power.

The Venezuelan issue demonstrated the dual problems of Latin American debt defaults and civil war. Europe was responsible for overlending money to Latin American leaders, who took a relatively small amount of cash up front in return for placing an enormous (and unpayable) debt on their nations' future. European bankers marketed bonds for the total amount of the loans to greedy investors attracted by high interest. By 1900 organized bondholder committees demanded settlements and put pressure on national governments to collect defaulted loans by force. A series of civil wars in the affected Latin American countries created additional claims and made debt default a serious diplomatic crisis in the Caribbean region.

Venezuela's civil wars were costly and led to friction with Trinidad, a nearby British colony. To finance its domestic wars, the Venezuelan government seized property in its significant German settlements and reacted contemptuously to European diplomatic entreaties. In response, Germany and Great Britain wanted to punish Venezuela and increase their Latin American influence. Germany could gain a naval foothold by winning control of a Venezuelan port as part of a debt settlement. Great

Britain, troubled by its costly navy-buildup rivalry with Germany, hoped a joint Venezuelan naval operation would lead to a détente with Germany. Neither European power understood that their plan was unrealistic: even together the two nations lacked the sufficient naval or military forces to subdue a defiant Venezuela.

Six months before the blockade began, Roosevelt assembled the entire U.S. Navy at Culebra, an excellent deep-water harbor just west of Puerto Rico. The navy's mission was twofold: to organize U.S. warships into modern fleets and to be ready to intervene in Venezuela, a policy made clear when Admiral Dewey, an outspoken foe of Germany, was named operations commander. The Europeans attacked Venezuela on 7 December 1902. Venezuelan President Cipriano Castro immediately arrested all Europeans he could find, mobilized an enormous citizen army, and agreed to any arbitration the United States could secure.

Faced with unified U.S.-Venezuelan resistance and the overwhelming U.S. naval superiority over the combined European fleet, the fragile European alliance looked for a way out. On 15 December, British Minister Arthur Balfour publicly accepted the Monroe Doctrine in an address before Parliament. On 17 December the Germans agreed to arbitration. A week earlier Kaiser Wilhelm II had appointed Roosevelt's old friend Hermann (Speck) von Sternburg as the new German minister to Washington, an act that conceded a new diplomatic respect for the United States as an equal power.

The United States had won European acceptance of arbitration as an alternative to gunboat diplomacy. Venezuela could pay only a fraction of the debt and war claims against it. Great Britain, Germany, and Italy argued, as the intervening powers, for priority payment of their claims. The United States, confident that the Hague Permanent Court of Arbitration would not rule in favor of war, was bitterly disappointed when the Russian judge, influenced by the outbreak of the Russo-Japanese War, ruled on 23 February 1904 in favor of the intervening powers. This ruling destroyed the U.S. confidence in Hague Court arbitration proceedings and forced Roosevelt to find a different means of discouraging European interventions in the Caribbean.

The Panama Canal Controversy

The Spanish-American-Cuban-Filipino War of 1898 dramatized the U.S. need for an inter-oceanic canal when the battleship *Oregon* took six months to reach the Cuban war theater from its West Coast base. The Bidlack-Mallarino Treaty of 1848 defined the tripartite relationship between Colombia, Panama, and the United States that endured until Panama's Revolution of 1903. The United States received a vague "right of transit" across the isthmus, designed to bar a British canal and make the United

States the legal protector of a valuable potential route. In return the United States agreed to honor Colombian sovereignty over legally independent Panama, a key provision, since Colombia was too isolated from Panama to police it effectively. The first treaty signed by President Roosevelt in December 1901, Hay-Pauncefote II, ended the 1850 Clayton-Bulwer Treaty's provision for joint Anglo-American control of a canal and opened the way for a U.S. canal. Veteran Colombian diplomat Carlos Martínez Silva understood that the termination of the British presence in Central America ended Colombia's advantage in playing off European and U.S. interests. The United States was now the only major power in the region.

Ferdinand de Lesseps's work on a French Panama Canal, based on his success at Suez, began in 1880 and ended in bankruptcy six years later. When the French canal receiver, Compagnie Nouvelle du Canal de Panama, accepted the American evaluation of French holdings at $40 million (instead of $109 million), President Roosevelt announced in December 1901 that the U.S. Isthmian Canal Commission had reversed its Nicaraguan preference in favor of Panama, citing the cost and technological advantages of a Panama canal's shorter length. Philippe Bunau-Varilla, a French nationalist and canal engineer (and discredited de Lesseps investor), was influential in both the French decision to compromise on the price they would accept for the canal and in the U.S. Senate debate. In a bruising political battle the Senate approved the Spooner Act by a vote of 42–34, in a compromise that called for the canal to be built in Panama but only if a timely diplomatic settlement could be reached with Colombia.

Democratic Senator Mark Hanna had received assurances from Colombia that it would not stand in the way of a normal transfer of the French canal concession to the United States. At this critical point Colombia's Liberal-Conservative battles of over half a century erupted in a brutal, bloody civil war. The War of the Thousand Days disrupted and distorted what had been a routine diplomatic transfer among allies of a venture that would benefit both parties, especially Colombia. As the war became an ugly and costly stalemate, the Colombian desire for an international canal diminished, except as a way of replenishing Colombia's shattered economy.

Only when the main war theater shifted to Panama, where the Liberals threatened to win control of the future canal as well as the revolution itself, did Colombian president José Manuel Marroquín appeal for U.S. intervention. The Roosevelt administration had already responded to revolutionary changes in Colombia by gradually shifting its policy from alliance with Colombia against Panama to a careful ad hoc neutrality. Marroquín, a religious politician, offered the United States a settlement of the paralyzed canal negotiations in return for U.S. intervention against the now winning Liberals in Panama. The U.S.-brokered peace, signed aboard the battleship *Wisconsin* on 21 November 1902, was a major diplomatic agreement. Colombia granted many of the Liberals's war demands and also agreed to settle quickly the stalled canal negotiations. On 17 March 1903 the U.S. Senate approved the Hay-Herrán Convention which called for a $10 million cash payment to Colombia, a $250,000 yearly rental, and a ninety-nine-year renewable lease.

Marroquín, still deeply ambivalent about any canal, reneged on his agreement, using the need for Colombian Senate approval as his reason. Panama was aware of the impending rejection and began its revolutionary separation movement in April 1903. The Colombian Senate, more interested in domestic politics and indifferent to Panama as well as the United States, unanimously rejected the Hay-Herràn Treaty on 12 August. John Bassett Moore, a Columbia University law professor and Department of State adviser, in his influential memorandum of 15 September 1903, made the U.S. legal case that Colombia had breached its obligation in the original 1846 treaty giving the United States the right of transit—for Moore, the right to build a canal. Roosevelt refused to consider negotiating a share of the $40 million paid to the French receivers for the de Lesseps property, already compromised from the original $109 million, because he considered it blackmail and a betrayal of a negotiated convention and of the reassurances the United States had received at the time the *Wisconsin* treaty had settled the Colombian civil war.

Roosevelt planned to ask Congress to approve a unilateral U.S. seizure of the canal area under the Moore Memorandum's reading of the Bidlack-Mallarino Treaty. But U.S. military intelligence, widespread newspaper reports, Bunau-Varilla's own information, and the activities of Panama's revolutionaries in New York convinced him that a revolution without U.S. help was imminent. Roosevelt made known that he would support Panama's independence but would not overtly help a revolution. Panama belonged to Colombia only because the United States enforced Colombia's weak claim to sovereignty. Roosevelt could easily afford to do nothing. Without U.S. support for Colombia, Panama would choose independence. Panama wanted a canal, either as part of Colombia or as an independent state.

The Colombian Senate's rejection effectively encouraged an already separatist-minded Panama to seek its own solution. Marroquín, in a bizarre action, appointed a known Panamanian separatist, José Obaldía, as governor in September 1903. Not surprisingly, Obaldía publicly proclaimed his allegiance to Panama's independence and a canal treaty with the United States. Marroquín's apparent contradictions reflected Colombia's divisions. A new

and international canal symbolized the dilemma that encroaching modernism presented to Bogotá's entrenched parochial society. Marroquín never opposed the canal directly, but he delayed, obfuscated, lied (to his own foreign ministers as well as to the United States), and disrupted diplomatic cable lines that could have facilitated further negotiations. Only a small minority of Colombians opposed or favored a canal; most were indifferent to anything beyond narrow local or regional interests. The idea of a canal or of the developmental trade capitalism it embodied was foreign to the pre-modern Colombian ethos that had endured civil war largely over religious ideology.

Panama's revolution of 3 November 1903 was a bloodless coup led by an elitist junta. The junta had been deceived by Bunau-Varilla into believing that the United States was an active participant rather than a neutral sympathizer. Even though he knew from Bunau-Varilla's public pronouncements that the revolution would occur around the U.S. election day, Roosevelt kept minimal naval forces in the region and gave no new orders. John Hubbard, commander of the gunboat *Nashville* and the most intellectual of the U.S. naval officers in the area, completely understood the dominant U.S. policy of guarded neutrality and continued legal alliance with Colombia. He allowed a small Colombian army ashore on the eve of the revolution.

Panama went ahead independently. Manuel Amador Guerrero proclaimed Panamanian independence and arrested Colombian General Torres. The revolution itself played out tensely in the Colombian siege at Colón where the troops left behind by Torres confronted the forty-seven bluejackets from the *Nashville* in an armed stalemate while the largely French contingent of diplomats and canal workers watched the negotiations. The Colombians, not at all eager to fight, quickly accepted Panama's bribes, which Bunau-Varilla generously funded by loans, and sailed off to paid exile. The French diplomats, previously skeptical of U.S. policy, warmly applauded the nuanced U.S. diplomacy and restraint and credited it with preventing a needless bloodbath over Panama. Their testimony won official French support. Europe and Latin America, whatever their misgivings over U.S. power, wanted a new isthmian canal, and supported the new Republic of Panama, rejecting Marroquín's call to arms against an illegal U.S. invader.

The resultant Hay-Bunau-Varilla Treaty of February 1904 proved a disaster for Panama and also a casualty of domestic turmoil in both Colombia and the United States. Bunau-Varilla cashed in his participation by selling out the Panamanians he ostensibly represented. Secretary of State John Hay, worried by possible Democratic opposition to any treaty and by Democratic Senator John Tyler Morgan's xenophobic opposition to Colombia and

France, wrote the most extreme of Morgan's rejected Hay-Herràn amendments into the new treaty to make it irresistible to a nationalistic U.S. Senate.

The Panama Canal cost $347 million and opened in August 1914 as a technologically advanced lock canal, radically different from de Lesseps' impossible dream of a sea-level Suez Canal built by private funds. Roosevelt regarded his diplomacy over the canal—with Colombia, Europe, and his own Congress—as the most important achievement of his presidency. Recent defenses of Roosevelt's actions cite Panama's unwilling subjection to Colombian rule and profit, and the central role of domestic politics in all of the countries involved. Roosevelt and the French were also influenced by the cultural-economic arguments of French philosopher Henri Saint-Simon's (1760–1825), popular in the nineteenth century, that encouraged improved communications and transportation as universally beneficial. Critics and many historians have agreed with Colombian interpretations that Roosevelt's diplomacy was imperialistic and brutal.

The Russo-Japanese War and the Nobel Peace Prize: 1904–1906

In the Russo-Japanese War of 1904–1905, Roosevelt became a reluctant mediator in order to prevent the war from engulfing the world. Alone among the Western leaders in not assuming Japan's racial inferiority, he supported that country's defensive war against Russian encroachment. Roosevelt feared a European domination of Asia which might exclude U.S. interests. He regarded Japan as America's natural ally to maintain an Asian balance of power that would prevent Europe from extracting further concessions from a weak China, which had lost Hong Kong to Great Britain and Jiaozhou to Germany.

To encourage Japan's leadership of an Asian balance of power Roosevelt's Russo-Japanese War diplomacy encouraged Oriental Japan's victory over European Russia. First, he persuaded Kaiser Wilhelm II of Germany not to enlarge the conflict; then he preserved the newly won Japanese power with the Portsmouth Peace Conference settlement of 1905. The Russo-Japanese War (and its peace) ended Europe's unquestioned world hegemony, now successfully challenged by Japan and the United States, the two new major powers from distant continents.

Russia, an unruly and unpredictable giant under Czar Nicholas II, put increasing pressure on newly modernizing Japan, especially in Korea and Manchuria, sensitive areas for the United States's small but significant East Asian interests. The Japanese attack on the Russian fleet at Port Arthur on 10 February 1904 plunged the United States and Europe into a complex and dangerous diplomatic conflict that symbolized a radically changing world. Roosevelt sent his Boston friend, the capable diplomat

George Lengerke Meyer, to St. Petersburg as ambassador, and sent his confidential messages through the British diplomatic pouch from Berlin to keep them from the czar's curious eyes. Roosevelt also warned the kaiser that the United States would not tolerate a European alliance with Russia against Japan. When Japan won every major military battle, Russia responded by dispatching its Baltic fleet, which the Japanese also sank in the final Battle of Tsushima Strait on 27–29 May 1905.

Although the Japanese appeared to have won the war, Russia still had ample resources to defeat its economically exhausted foe. Japan asked Roosevelt, the only Western leader who appeared to respect Japanese rights, culture, and power, to act as peace mediator.

In early June, Russia and Japan agreed to Roosevelt's peace talks. On 29 July 1905, Secretary of War William Howard Taft signed the secret Taft-Katsura Agreement in which the United States acquiesced to Japan's interest in Korea and Japan acknowledged U.S. interests in the Philippines. The Taft-Katsura Agreement signalled the effective end of the United States's China-first Asian policy implicit in the Open Door Notes of 1899 and 1900. At the Portsmouth Peace Conference (9–29 August 1905), after weeks of unpromising deadlock, the final surprise agreement on 5 September 1905 recognized Japan's dominant rights in Korea and increased its concessions in Manchuria but denied the Japanese claims for a cash indemnity; Russia conceded half of Sakhalin Island. Japan had won a handsome settlement, but its people had been misled into expecting a total political victory and blamed Roosevelt for the compromise. For his diplomatic role at Portsmouth, combined with the Moroccan settlement discussed later, Roosevelt was awarded the 1906 Nobel Peace Prize.

Roosevelt's active diplomacy, carefully shielded from an insular and suspicious Congress, quietly triumphed at the Algerciras, Spain, conference (16 January–7 April 1906) called to determine control of Morocco. While Russia, France's main European ally, was at war with Japan, Wilhelm II seized the opportunity to demand a commercial open door in French-dominated Morocco and thereby threatened to cause a European conflict. German Ambassador Sternburg's ill-considered offer that Germany would abide by Roosevelt's wishes enabled Roosevelt to engineer a settlement that preserved the French status quo (and European peace) while appearing to give the kaiser a public diplomatic victory. Congress approved the Algerciras Convention in December 1906 but pointedly restated its commitment to U.S. non-involvement in Europe.

The Roosevelt Corollary

The Roosevelt Corollary to the Monroe Doctrine formally stated Roosevelt's consistent policy of removing serious European encroachment from the Caribbean, an area that the United States regarded as vital to its strategic interests. Turn-of-the-century Europe was as buffeted by the transition to modernist thought and technology as were the United States and Latin America. New technology, especially in naval weaponry, added to the radical diplomatic challenges of Germany's ambitions for a greater world role. When German Kaiser Wilhelm II replaced Chancellor Otto von Bismarck in 1890, he changed Bismarck's Continental focus and challenged Great Britain's role as the dominant world naval power. Germany's challenge complicated a Caribbean region already shaken by Spain's removal as the dominant (and weak) European power. The United States had to deal with the threat that Great Britain, Germany, and France would try to fill the vacuum from Spain's demise and bring European wars to the New World. Rapidly changing warship technology made strategic planning difficult. Even a concert of Europe (briefly considered on the eve of the Spanish-American-Cuban-Filipino War) was a possibility for the United States to contemplate. Insulating Cuba from European ambitions became the first order of business for McKinley, Secretary of War Elihu Root, and, subsequently President Roosevelt's own foreign policy.

The Platt Amendment, passed by Congress on 2 March 1901, was the foundation of U.S. policy in the Caribbean, a domestic and diplomatic compromise between Cuban annexation and its complete independence. The Platt Amendment was primarily designed to limit European strategic threats to the United States through an unsecured Cuba, which was long perceived as the soft underbelly of the mainland United States. The Platt Amendment gave Cuba political independence while maintaining enough U.S. control over Cuban foreign policy to prevent unacceptable European intrusion. In addition, Guantánamo Bay came under a U.S. lease (1903) as part of the Platt Amendment and this arrangement gave the United States a strategic naval base to control the Caribbean. For a short time the Platt Amendment model of a limited U.S. protectorate seemed attractive to weak Caribbean nations like the Dominican Republic and to the United States. But the promise of ultimate U.S. intervention proved to be a fatal flaw for the Platt Amendment policy. In 1906 Cuba's major political parties wished for and got U.S. intervention rather than share power with the opposition.

By 1905 Roosevelt had already changed U.S. foreign policy. Europe generally approved of the way in which the United States resolved the Panama Canal problem and acquiesced in the face of new U.S. naval strength and firmness. When the dangerous financial crisis in the Dominican Republic deepened into anarchy, Europe looked to the United States for a solution.

The Roosevelt Corollary used blunt language to change the Monroe Doctrine's original position of European nonintervention to the right of intervention by the United States. "Chronic wrongdoing, or an impotence which results in a general loosening of the ties of civilized society, may in America, as elsewhere, ultimately require intervention by some civilized nation, and in the Western Hemisphere the adherence of the Monroe Doctrine, may force the United States, however reluctantly, in flagrant cases of such wrongdoing or impotence, to the exercise of an international police power." Roosevelt's words offended Latin Americans at the same time they reassured Europe. Continuing diplomatic crises in Europe itself and in Asia and Africa made the distant Caribbean too costly for individual European navies to contest. When the United States was ready to accept responsiblity, Europe eagerly concurred. Roosevelt's Corollary expressed his consistent diplomatic philosophy of combining power with responsibility.

In January 1905, after five years of unrelenting civil war had reduced the Dominican Republic to bankruptcy and anarchy, Roosevelt sent Navy Commander Albert C. Dillingham, who was trusted and liked by a majority of Dominican factions, to create an "agreement" for a U.S. protectorate. When Dillingham made concessions to relieve Dominican anxieties, he inadvertently gave the agreement the appearance of a treaty. The U.S. Senate rebelled, fearing that Roosevelt had tried to usurp its treaty power. When the bitter constitutional battle lingered, Roosevelt proclaimed a modus vivendi by executive order on 31 March 1905, establishing a wide-ranging naval and economic protectorate.

Under its terms the United States took control of the twelve Dominican ports and collected the customs revenue (the sole Dominican income), apportioning 45 percent for Dominican government operating expenses and 55 percent in escrow toward settlement of the debt. Roosevelt appointed Johns Hopkins University economist Jacob Hollander as a Treasury special agent. Hollander negotiated with the mostly European creditors for an average 50 percent reduction in return for a quick cash settlement. With the customs houses under U.S. naval protection, the constant revolutions to win control of their money ended. So did the regular European gunboat visits to win further debt concessions. By 1907, when Secretary of State Elihu Root compromised with the Senate over the language of the U.S.-Dominican convention, the immediate Dominican crisis had passed. Although Roosevelt's modus vivendi proved a short-term success, it did not (nor could it) change the basic and continuing instability of Dominican domestic politics.

Roosevelt's Latin American policies were flawed by the ferocity of his diction as well as his paternalistic role as the spokesman of civilization in the New World. Although Roosevelt's policies appear to demonstrate his commitment to using a big stick, his actions may be more benign and idealistic than his words. Roosevelt was an active leader in the Hague world peace movement, which began in 1899 but faltered even before World War I. While a student at Harvard he learned the theories of French naturalist Jean Lamarck (1744–1829), and the principle that changes in environment can change society convinced him that the United States could help Latin America develop effective economic and political institutions. He never wavered in his policy of power coupled with responsibility, even though the power part of the equation offended its recipients more than the responsibility part assured them. There were few direct economic returns from agricultural Latin America beyond the profits already taken from bankers' fees for servicing new debt issues. Roosevelt worked with Mexico's president Porfirio Díaz to settle the long standing U.S.-Mexican Pious land dispute, the first case heard by the new Hague Court of Permanent Arbitration in October 1902. He also worked with Díaz to settle a Central American series of wars, resulting in the *Marblehead* treaty of 27 October 1906 and the eight conventions of the Central American Peace Conference (20 November–14 December 1907) in Washington.

Secretary of State Root's complex diplomatic initiatives for the Third International American Conference (26 July–26 August 1906) were intended to allay Latin American fears of U.S. ambitions and to extend cultural, social, political and economic inter-American relations. When Roosevelt's prized Platt policy fell apart in Cuba, he desperately looked for a way short of intervention to mediate what was almost entirely a Cuban domestic political struggle. Both sides preferred U.S. occupation to a rival Cuban political victory. The United States reluctantly intervened on 28 September 1906, but withdrew on 28 January 1909, a date chosen because it was the birthday of José Martí, the Cuban revolutionary poet and leader who died a martyr in 1895. The fundamental failure in Cuba was caused by a misplaced joint U.S.-Cuban reliance on sugar-based agriculture and export trade. Sugar, overproduced throughout the world in beets and cane, was Cuba's curse and not its salvation. There seemed no attractive alternatives for Cuba than this futile dependence on extractive agriculture export.

Roosevelt's Asian Policy

Roosevelt's East Asian policy, though significant, reflected his consistent belief in the primacy of Europe in U.S. foreign policy. Although he supported the U.S. supression of the Philippine insurrection and the subsequent protectorate status for the Philippines, by 1907 Roosevelt regarded—and regretted—U.S. control of the Philippines as a costly "albatross." The initial U.S. presence represented a desire (encouraged by and shared with the British) to keep the Philippines out of German hands.

German control of the Chinese port of Jiaozhou (December 1897) had encouraged reluctant U.S. support for a war with Spain to circumvent possible (and disastrous) German ambitions closer to the heart of U.S. strategic vital interests. American-German enmity began in the early 1890s when Germany resisted accepting American agricultural exports, especially pork offered at well-below European prices. Germany needed coaling stations, vital in the brief pre-oil warship era. Great Britain and France were amply supplied by their respective empires; the United States and Germany competed for newly strategic islands. When Germany sent a large naval force to Manila Bay just after the American naval victory against Spain, friction between Commodore Dewey and the Germans exacerbated the already strong German-U.S. tensions.

The San Francisco earthquake of 1906 precipitated a serious diplomatic crisis with Japan, which was still ambivalent about Roosevelt's role as peacemaker during the war with Russia. The destruction of San Francisco schools led California to exclude Asian children from the rebuilt school system. Nativism in California had been exacerbated by serious recession and the increasing number of unskilled Japanese immigrants working for low wages. Disputes over emigration already had led to an ineffective Japanese agreement to limit voluntarily emigration (1900), a nativist Japanese and Korean Exclusion League (1905), and a Chinese boycott of American imports in 1905. Japan correctly argued that the San Francisco exclusion practices violated Japan's most-favored-nation status won in the U.S.-Japanese Treaty of 1894.

At a White House meeting in February 1907, Roosevelt convinced the San Francisco school board to rescind segregation in return for limits on Japanese immigration. Roosevelt barred Japanese entry on passports from other countries, such as Canada, or from U.S. protectorates, in an executive order on 14 March 1907, which followed an amendment to the Immigration Act of 1907 on 20 February. Japan formally agreed to this compromise in its "Gentlemen's Agreement" note of 24 February 1907; it barred passports to Japanese laborers and agreed to the U.S. right to bar immigration that circumvented the agreed-upon restrictions.

In a dramatic diplomatic demonstration, Roosevelt sent the Great White Fleet around the world (16 December 1907–22 February 1908), thereby promoting and exhibiting the U.S Navy's sixteen battleships (most of them recent) and the United States's new status as the world's second-ranked naval power (after Great Britain). Almost everyone—the navy, Congress, and the press—doubted the navy's capability and opposed the cruise. When huge crowds turned out in Trinidad (despite British attempts to downplay the visit), followed by an even bigger crowd in Rio de Janeiro, the Department of State was flooded with requests for additional visits. The Japanese, keenly aware of the naval symbolism, graciously invited the advancing fleet to friendly festivities in Yokohama.

The Root-Takahira Agreement of 30 November 1908 was an exchange of notes that formalized and extended the previous Japanese-U.S. understandings. Both nations agreed to support the "existing status quo" in each other's possessions and the Open Door in China. That the Japanese regarded the status quo as recognition of their primacy in Korea and Manchuria has disturbed historians respectful of Open Door ideology more than it did Roosevelt, who accepted Japan as the major Asian power without serious qualms. He was certain that Japanese primacy was preferable to Russian hegemony.

Roosevelt and the Modern Age

In 1912 Roosevelt, denied the Republican presidential nomination, split the Republican party by running as a third-party, Bull Moose Progressive. In a campaign devoted entirely to domestic issues Roosevelt came in second to Governor Woodrow Wilson of New Jersey, who won the presidency with only 42 percent of the popular vote. Roosevelt consistently opposed Wilson's conduct toward the war in Europe, especially his insistence on U.S. neutrality. Roosevelt's disappointment at being overshadowed by another scholar in politics at a time of world crisis added to the bitterness of his words. Roosevelt had proposed a similar idea to Wilson's League of Nations in his Nobel Peace Prize acceptance speech in Oslo in 1910. Although the Republican Party, reunited with Roosevelt in 1916, solidly opposed Wilson's League of Nations, its leaders—Taft, Roosevelt, and Henry Cabot Lodge, the chairman of the Senate Foreign Relations Committee—remained committed internationalists, determined not to allow Wilson the political credit for the peace.

In 1898 the world order created by Spanish Catholic rule in the late-fifteenth century ended dramatically when the Protestant United States forcibly removed the last vestige of Spanish Catholic hegemony in Latin America and Asia. Roosevelt played a central role in the Spanish-American-Cuban-Filipino War and the Russo-Japanese War, the two important smaller world wars that have been overshadowed in the historical literature by the Great War of 1914. The deaths of Queen Victoria and William McKinley in 1901 marked the close of the Victorian era and the opening of a new century and a new modern age.

By assuring the rapid dissemination of new discoveries in science and the arts, the new communications technology led to a cosmopolitan international culture which transcended older national and regional boundaries. Roosevelt was well attuned to this transitional age of modernism and eager to make the United States one of its leaders. During Roosevelt's presidency, the Wright brothers flew the first airplane; Max Planck began his experiments in quantum physics; Einstein discovered relativity; Cézanne, Matisse, and Picasso changed the face and role of art; and novelists as diverse as Henry James, Virginia Woolf, and Marcel Proust radically changed fiction writing. As a leader who understood the growing importance of promoting international culture, Roosevelt was frequently perceived by congressional traditionalists as an agent of change and as a radical.

Roosevelt's adventurous temperament and intellect enabled him to combine nationalism, regionalism, and internationalism in a foreign policy that made the United States the dominant regional power and a significant world power. Even though his hopes for greater economic and political independence for the former Spanish Caribbean colonies failed, he helped (momentarily) to stabilize the region and discourage Europe's ambitions. As a practicing internationalist he played the major role in the Portsmouth (1905), Algerciras (1906), and Central American (1907) peace conferences. His tumultuous relations with Congress reflected the defining conflicts being played out in the United States over the political division of power between the conduct of foreign relations and unfolding domestic reform in the first era in which the strong constitutional powers of the executive became an issue.

RICHARD H. COLLIN

See also Bunau-Varilla, Philippe; Colombia; Cuba; Dominican Republic; Germany; Morocco; Nobel Peace Prize; Open Door Policy; Panama and Panama Canal; Permanent Court of Arbitration (Hague Tribunal); Platt Amendment; Portsmouth, Treaty of; Presidency; Roosevelt Corollary; Root, Elihu; Root-Takahira Agreement; Russo-Japanese War; Spanish-American-Cuban-Filipino War, 1898; Taft-Katsura Agreement; Venezuela

FURTHER READING

Beale, Howard K. *Theodore Roosevelt and the Rise of America to World Power.* Baltimore, Md., 1956.

Blum, John Morton. *The Republican Roosevelt.* New York, 1954.

Burton, David H. *Theodore Roosevelt: Confident Imperialist.* Philadelphia, 1968.

Collin, Richard H. *Theodore Roosevelt, Culture, Diplomacy, and Expansion: A New View of American Imperialism.* Baton Rouge, La., 1985.

———. *Theodore Roosevelt's Caribbean: The Panama Canal, The Monroe Doctrine, and the Latin American Context.* Baton Rouge, La., 1990.

Connif, Michael L. *Panama and the United States: The Forced Alliance.* Athens, Ga.,1991.

Cooper, John Milton. *The Warrior and the Priest.* Cambridge, Mass., 1983.

Darby, Philip. *Three Faces of Imperialism: British and American Approaches to Asia and Africa, 1870–1970.* New Haven, Conn., 1987.

Doyle, Michael W. *Empires*. Ithaca, N.Y., 1986.

Dyer, Thomas G. *Theodore Roosevelt and the Idea of Race*. Baton Rouge, La., 1980.

Esthus, Raymond. *Double Eagle and Rising Sun: The Russians and Japanese at Portsmouth in 1905*. Durham, N.C., 1988.

Gardner, Lloyd, ed., *Redefining the Past: Essays in Diplomatic History in Honor of William Appleman Williams*. Corvallis, Ore., 1986.

Gatewood, Willard B., Jr. *Theodore Roosevelt and the Art of Controversy*. Baton Rouge, La., 1970.

Gould, Lewis L. *The Presidency of Theodore Roosevelt*. Lawrence, Kans., 1991.

Harbaugh, William H. *Power and Responsibility: The Life and Times of Theodore Roosevelt*. New York, 1961.

LaFeber, Walter. *The Panama Canal*. New York, 1989.

———. *The American Search for Opportunity, 1865–1913*, vol. 2 of *The Cambridge History of American Foreign Relations*. New York, 1993.

Marks, Frederick W., III. *Velvet on Iron: The Diplomacy of Theodore Roosevelt*. Lincoln, Neb., 1979.

Morison, E. E., John Blum, and Alfred D. Chandler. *The Letters of Theodore Roosevelt*, 8 vols. Cambridge, Mass., 1951–1954.

Neu, Charles. *An Uncertain Friendship: Theodore Roosevelt and Japan, 1906–1909*. Cambridge, Mass., 1967.

Reckner, James B. *Teddy Roosevelt's Great White Fleet*. Annapolis, Md., 1988.

Sumida, Jon Tetsuro. *In Defense of Naval Supremacy: Finance, Technology, and British Naval Policy, 1889–1914*. Boston, 1989.

Widenor, William C. *Henry Cabot Lodge and the Search for an American Foreign Policy*. Berkeley, Calif., 1980.

ROOSEVELT COROLLARY

A statement by President Theodore Roosevelt extending the Monroe Doctrine to include U.S. policing of disorder in Latin America to prevent European intervention. Roosevelt announced this dramatically new U.S. policy toward Latin America in his annual message to Congress on 4 December 1904. Roosevelt's blunt diction warned that "chronic wrongdoing, or an impotence which results in a general loosening of the ties of civilized society, may in America, as elsewhere, ultimately require intervention by some civilized nation, and in the Western Hemisphere, the adherence of the United States to the Monroe Doctrine may force the United States, however reluctantly, in flagrant cases of such wrongdoing or impotence, to the exercise of an international peace power." Roosevelt's Corollary changed the Monroe Doctrine's original emphasis on European nonintervention in the Western Hemisphere to the United States's assertion of its right to intervene and impose itself as an international police force.

The Roosevelt Corollary offended Latin America by its moralistic language and its paternalistic assumptions. The main target of the new policy, however, was Europe, and the primary U.S. intention was its continued discouragement of further European intervention in the unsettled domestic politics of many of the Caribbean republics. Venezuela and the Dominican Republic were the major trouble spots. After Great Britain, Germany, and Italy imposed a blockade on Venezuela in December 1902, the United States objected to armed European intervention to collect debts and insisted that the dispute be submitted to international arbitration. When the Hague Court in February 1904 granted first priority on Venezuela's assets to the claims of the three intervening powers, the United States was forced to abandon its international arbitration policy.

In early 1905 the worsening financial crisis in the Dominican Republic presented Roosevelt with the best opportunity to put the Roosevelt Corollary into practice. In a state of anarchy for five years following the assassination of dictator Ulises Heureaux, the Dominicans could not pay the interest on their external debt of more than $40 million shared by most of the European powers and the United States. Europe, increasingly preoccupied with conflicts in Europe itself and in the more profitable and accessible colonies in Africa and Asia, was eager to give up the expensive role of debt collector in the Caribbean. Roosevelt's policy of merging power with responsibility, combined with Europe's more immediate concerns raised by the Russo-Japanese War that began in 1904, led to many European governments' encouragement of U.S. leadership in restoring order and arranging for a repayment of the Dominican debt.

Roosevelt tried to settle the Dominican crisis with an unofficial U.S. naval protectorate arrangement. But to the U.S. Senate, Captain Albert C. Dillingham's plan looked too much like a treaty and it refused to go along with an agreement that it feared might limit the Senate's foreign policy powers. Roosevelt countered by establishing a modus vivendi by executive order and on 31 March 1905 the United States took control of the twelve Dominican ports in receivership under a naval protectorate. The navy's intervention eliminated the internal revolutions fought for control of the various customs houses and ended the threat of European intervention. Roosevelt appointed Johns Hopkins University economist Jacob Hollander to negotiate a debt settlement. Customs income collected by the United States was divided, with 55 percent placed in escrow to pay the negotiated debt settlement. In 1907 the debt was settled, the Senate approved a rewritten treaty, and the U.S. protectorate ended. The Dominican results remain mixed. The nation returned to its internal political upheavals and the United States launched new interventions. The Roosevelt Corollary still rankles Latin Americans, Europeans, and U.S. historians with its moralistic and paternalistic prose. Europe, however, was dissuaded from further overt intervention in the Caribbean, the main purpose of the Roosevelt Corollary policy.

RICHARD H. COLLIN

See also Arbitration; Dominican Republic; Latin America; Monroe Doctrine; Roosevelt, Theodore; Venezuela

FURTHER READING

Collin, Richard H. *Theodore Roosevelt's Caribbean: The Panama Canal, The Monroe Doctrine, and the Latin American Context.* Baton Rouge, La., 1990.

Healy, David. *Drive to Hegemony: The United States in the Caribbean, 1898–1917.* Madison, Wis., 1988.

Jessup, Philip C. *Elihu Root,* 2 vols. New York, 1938.

LaFeber, Walter. *Inevitable Revolutions: The United States in Central America,* rev. ed. New York, 1993.

ROOT, ELIHU

(*b.* 15 February 1845; *d.* 7 February 1937)

Republican internationalist who served as secretary of war under Presidents William McKinley and Theodore Roosevelt (1899–1904), Roosevelt's secretary of state (1905–1909), and U.S. Senator from New York (1909–1915). Root was born in Clinton, New York, and graduated from Hamilton College (B.A., 1864) and the University of the City of New York (law degree, 1867), and joined the bar, specializing in corporate law. Active in Republican politics, Root became a close friend of Roosevelt's. As secretary of war, Root devised the Platt Amendment and reorganized the army. The Platt Amendment to the Army Appropriation Bill (2 March 1901) incorporated into the Cuban Constitution of 1901 and the U.S.-Cuban Treaty of 22 May 1903 limited Cuba's freedom in foreign alliances and gave the United States the right to lease land for naval bases and to intervene to preserve Cuban independence. The Cubans protested but Root saw the Platt Amendment as a compromise to avoid total U.S. annexation and yet maintain Cuba's political independence. Root's Army General Staff Corps (1903) modernized and depoliticized the army and the War Department's command structure.

As secretary of state Root worked with Roosevelt in planning the Roosevelt Corollary (first announced in 1904), through which the United States took responsibility for assuring stability in the Western Hemisphere through the use of "international police power." The Roosevelt Corollary to the Monroe Doctrine was essentially a strategic policy to prevent further European gunboat diplomacy in the Caribbean but it also served as a hegemonic instrument to regulate the Americas. It began as a modus vivendi by executive order (31 March 1905), instituting the same naval protectorate over the Dominican Republic that the Senate had refused to approve in Roosevelt's proposed U.S.-Dominican agreement.

The Dominican intervention of 1905 became a model. Root superintended the U.S. negotiations to reduce and refund the Dominican debt and worked closely with the Dominicans to assure their financial security. Root further underscored U.S. sympathy for Latin American independence and development in his 26 July–26 August 1906 mission to the Third International American Conference at Rio de Janeiro, which included a trip with his family to several Latin American nations. Root made friends with Latin American diplomats in Washington and he worked with his friend Andrew Carnegie to arrange for the construction of a Pan-American Union building in Washington, D.C.

Root was successful in easing European tension over the German-French-Moroccan dispute settled at the Algeciras Conference in 1906. He worked with Roosevelt in mediating the Russo-Japanese War, achieving the peace that was signed at Portsmouth, New Hampshire, in 1905. During the Hague Peace Conference's last meeting in 1907, Root tried hard to revive the Hague Peace Movement. He secured a compromise over the California school crisis with Japan, negotiating the Gentlemen's Agreements and the Root-Takahira Agreement of 1908, both granting generous concessions to Japan's power and sensitivity.

Root helped make the consular service a professional diplomatic department in the U.S. foreign service. He also settled the North Atlantic fisheries controversies with Great Britain.

Although the historian Richard Leopold makes a good case for Root as a prototypical conservative, "cosmopolitan" may be a better term. He thought in the same global terms as Roosevelt and understood and encouraged cultural interchange through art. Root supported the preservation of the architecture of the Washington Mall in 1902, and in 1907 the American Academy in Rome, and later served as trustee and vice president of the Metropolitan Museum of Art and as trustee for the Carnegie Corporation. Root saw economic development in terms of mutual international exchange, which he (and President Roosevelt) found compatible with American national interests. In 1912 he was awarded the Nobel Peace Prize for his role in establishing peaceful relations with Latin America and Japan as Roosevelt's secretary of state.

Root served as chairman of the 1912 Republican National Convention and supported President William H. Taft's renomination against his old friend Theodore Roosevelt. As a senator from New York he supported the Allies and criticized President Woodrow Wilson's neutrality policies. After World War I he advocated American membership in the League of Nations but with safeguard reservations unacceptable to Wilson.

Root's later career marked a return to his interest in the arts which he regarded as "rather essential to understanding what I am." He worked for the American Federation of Arts, the New York Public Library, the American School for Classical Studies in Athens, and supported the first major Mexican Art Exhibition in the United States. He also served as an officer of several Andrew Carnegie Corporation philanthropic boards.

RICHARD H. COLLIN

See also Cuba; Dominican Republic; Foreign Service; Gentlemen's Agreements; Japan; League of Nations; Nobel Peace Prize; Pan-Americanism; Philanthropic Foundations; Platt Amendment; Portsmouth, Treaty of; Roosevelt, Theodore; Roosevelt Corollary; Root-Takahira Agreement; World War II

FURTHER READING

Jessup, Philip C. *Elihu Root*, 2 vols. New York, 1938.
Leopold, Richard W. *Elihu Root and the Conservative Tradition.* Boston, 1954.
Toth, Charles W. "Elihu Root." In *An Uncertain Tradition: American Secretaries of State in the Twentieth Century,* edited by Norman A. Graebner. New York, 1961.

ROOT-TAKAHIRA AGREEMENT

An exchange of notes on 30 November 1908 between the U.S. and Japanese governments when Elihu Root was Secretary of State and Kogoro Takahira was the Japanese minister to Washington, that eased tensions. The agreement extended U.S. recognition of Japan's growing influence on the Asian mainland granted in the secret Taft-Katsura Memorandum (1905) and confirmed the Gentlemen's Agreement (1907) limiting emigration of unskilled Japanese laborers, a critical prior Japanese concession.

The notes specified maintaining an undefined "existent status quo" in the Pacific, the Open Door in China, and mutual support for China's independence and integrity. Japan, however, regarded the note as recognition of its primacy in Korea and southern Manchuria. By 1907 President Theodore Roosevelt regarded the Philippines as a liability, impossible to defend against a determined foe. He thus had no problem conciliating Japan and reversing the assumptions of the Open Door Notes of 1899 and 1900 that had ranked China's status as the United States's primary concern in Asia. The United States coupled its conciliatory diplomacy by sending the Great White Fleet around the world, a gesture of power to Japan and to the world that the concessions emanated from strength and not weakness.

RICHARD H. COLLIN

See also China; Gentlemen's Agreements; Japan; Open Door Policy; Roosevelt, Theodore; Taft-Katsura Agreement

FURTHER READING

Esthus, Raymond. *Theodore Roosevelt and Japan.* Seattle, Wash., 1967.
Jessup, Philip. *Elihu Root*, 2 vols. New York, 1938.
Reckner, James R. *Teddy Roosevelt's Great White Fleet.* Annapolis, Md., 1988.

ROSTOW, WALT WHITMAN
(*b.* 7 October 1916)

Economist, foreign policy analyst, and adviser to presidents Dwight D. Eisenhower, John F. Kennedy, and Lyndon B. Johnson. The son of Russian-Jewish immigrants, Rostow was born in New York City, graduated from Yale University, attended Oxford as a Rhodes scholar, and became a professor of economics at the Massachusetts Institute of Technology. Rostow won wide recognition for his writings on Third World economic development, especially his influential book *The Stages of Economic Development: A Non-Communist Manifesto* (1960). He argued that the United States had the capacity and a vital national interest in leading developing nations in Asia, Africa, and Latin America through clear stages of capitalist growth to sustained prosperity and "modernization," thereby enlarging the noncommunist world. Rostow occasionally advised the Eisenhower administration, but achieved his greatest influence as chair of the State Department's Policy Planning Committee (1961–1963) and as national security adviser (1963–1969) during the Kennedy and Johnson presidencies. He advised President Kennedy on foreign economic policy and coined the phrase "development decade" to popularize the administration's ambitious foreign-aid programs. His role in the Vietnam War was especially controversial. In October 1961 he and General Maxwell Taylor led a mission to South Vietnam that recommended increased aid and the dispatch of U.S. combat troops to that country. In Johnson's White House, Rostow became a chief architect of military escalation. Rostow left public office in 1969 and took up a position at the University of Texas, where he continued to write numerous books and articles on economic development, foreign policy, and history.

DENNIS MERRILL

See also Foreign Aid; Johnson, Lyndon Baines; Kennedy, John Fitzgerald; Vietnam War

FURTHER READING

Halberstam, David. *The Best and the Brightest.* New York, 1972.
Merrill, Dennis. *Bread and the Ballot: The United States and India's Economic Development, 1947–1963.* Chapel Hill, N.C., 1990.
Packenham, Robert A. *Liberal America and the Third World: Political Development Ideas in Foreign Aid and Social Science.* Princeton, 1973.
Rostow, Walt Whitman. *The World Economy: History and Prospect.* Austin, 1978.
———. *Eisenhower, Kennedy, and Foreign Aid.* Austin, Tex., 1985.

RUSH-BAGOT AGREEMENT
(1817)

An exchange of diplomatic notes in Washington, D.C., dated 28 and 29 April 1817, between acting U.S. secretary of state Richard Rush and British minister Charles Bagot. Approved a year later by the U.S. Senate and signed by President James Monroe, the agreement demilitarized the Great Lakes and Lake Champlain, thereby helping to ease the age-old fear of invasion of British North America by the United States and vice versa.

When the War of 1812 came to an end with the signing of the Treaty of Ghent in December 1814 and its ratification by the U.S. Senate in February 1815, both Great Britain and the United States had substantial numbers of naval vessels on the Great Lakes and Lake Champlain, and it appeared to the United States that the British were poised to secure naval supremacy. Confronted with the prospect of an expensive arms race, the U.S. government instructed its minister to Great Britain, John Quincy Adams, to propose joint disarmament of the Great Lakes. Adams first advanced the proposal to British Foreign Secretary Lord Robert Stewart Castlereagh in January 1816. Since Adams did not have treaty-making authority, the talks moved to Washington, D.C., where Secretary of State James Monroe discussed the issue with Charles Bagot, the British minister. The two diplomats reached agreement, although Bagot had to await formal approval of the terms from London, by which time Monroe had become president and Rush acting secretary of state. Notes were exchanged between the two in late April 1817. The Senate approved the agreement on 16 April 1818, and after the president's signature the Rush-Bagot Agreement gained treaty status.

In severely restricting the size and number of naval ships on the Great Lakes and Lake Champlain, the two countries provided the first example of reciprocal naval disarmament. Although modified, the pact remains in force, sustaining the practice of an unarmed U.S.-Canadian border. Combined with the subsequent Convention of 1818 with Great Britain, the Rush-Bagot Agreement encouraged the process of Anglo-American reconciliation in the nineteenth century.

THOM M. ARMSTRONG

See also Adams, John Quincy; Castlereagh, Robert Stewart; Monroe, James; War of 1812

FURTHER READING

Bemis, Samuel Flagg. *John Quincy Adams and the Foundations of American Foreign Policy.* New York, 1949.
Hitsman, J. M. *Safeguarding Canada, 1763–1871.* Toronto, 1968.
Perkins, Bradford. *Castlereagh and Adams: England and the United States, 1812–1823.* Berkeley, Calif., 1964.
Powell, John H. *Richard Rush: Republican Diplomat, 1780–1859.* Philadelphia, 1942.

RUSK, DAVID DEAN

(*b.* 9 February 1909; *d.* 21 December 1994)

Secretary of state (1961–1969) who made a public case for U.S. intervention in Vietnam. Born in Cherokee County, Georgia, Rusk's first international experiences came from a Rhodes Scholarship at Oxford and taking university courses in Berlin. After teaching international relations for six years at Mills College in California (while also studying law) he joined the active army in 1940. From 1943 to 1945 Rusk served in Burma and China and at war's end joined the Department of War general staff. He played a role in establishing the 38th parallel as a dividing line between Soviet and U.S. occupation of Korea. Rusk was about to enter a military career when, in 1947, Secretary of State George Marshall invited him to head the Department of State's office of Special Political Affairs. Agreeing with the Department's opposition to the creation of an independent state of Israel in 1948, Rusk loyally defended Harry S. Truman when the president overrode that opposition—the first of many such turns as Rusk followed Marshall's belief that officials should support the president regardless of private disagreements.

In 1948 Rusk directed the Department of State's office of United Nations Affairs. He urged recognizing the United Nation's importance, but (as in the Truman Doctrine debates of 1947), he refused to subordinate U.S. unilateral policies to the international organization. In March 1950, as debate boiled over China policy, Rush volunteered to become assistant secretary of state for Far Eastern Affairs thus earning Dean Acheson's gratitude. During the Korean War, he joined others who urged President Truman to send troops across the 38th parallel. When China intervened massively, Rusk condemned China as a "Slavic Manchukuo"—a puppet of the Soviet Union.

Rusk became president of the Rockefeller Foundation in 1952 and emphasized development projects in Third World countries and investigations of health hazards from nuclear tests. In 1960 he published an essay in *Foreign Affairs* that exalted presidential power in foreign affairs. Senator John F. Kennedy did not know Rusk but he liked the essay, and upon his inauguration Kennedy appointed Rusk secretary of state on the advice of, among others, former Secretary of State Dean Acheson, who recalled Rusk's loyalty and hard-line policies in 1950. Kennedy later criticized the Department's slow responses to White House requests for reports and action, but the two men agreed on issues. Rusk was absolutely loyal to Presidents Kennedy and Lyndon B. Johnson, who later wrote that "the man who has served me most intelligently, faithfully, and nobly" was Rusk.

The secretary tried at times to restrain Kennedy. Rusk privately condemned the Bay of Pigs invasion plans, but publicly defended the administration after the disaster. During the 1961 Berlin confrontation, he deliberately slowed his responses to Kennedy in order to ease the standoff. His views wavered during the Cuban missile crisis of

1962, but at critical moments Rusk helped stop the Pentagon's recommendation to use force. Realizing that Soviet power was overrated, Rusk supported the 1963 nuclear test ban and the movement toward détente in the Cold War. Rusk disliked the dictatorships of Latin America and Africa and pushed for aid to both regions. But in 1961–1962 he helped the Central Intelligence Agency replace leftists in Zaire with U.S.-bribed conservatives. Opposing South Africa's policy of apartheid, Rusk nevertheless was against the imposition of sanctions. In 1965 he suppressed doubts to send troops into the Dominican Republic.

The Vietnam War dominated Rusk's secretaryship. Rusk questioned Kennedy's commitment of combat troops, Johnson's 1965 decisions to escalate U.S. involvement, and the 1965–1967 bombings of North Vietnam. Rusk feared especially a Chinese military response such as that in the Korean War. But neither could Rusk think of losing South Vietnam. Committed to Cold War beliefs, accepting the domino theory, and fearing Chinese and Soviet gains, he supported escalation and ardently defended the Americanization of the war in Vietnam. His public defense helped destroy congressional support for the war, especially as the hatred between Rusk and Senator J. William Fulbright, chairman of the Senate Foreign Relations Committee, became "almost biblical," in one observer's words. After leaving the Department of State in 1969 Rusk taught at the University of Georgia and worked with his son on a memoir, published in 1990.

WALTER LaFEBER

See also Acheson, Dean Gooderham; Bay of Pigs Invasion; Berlin; China; Cold War; Cuban Missile Crisis; Détente; Dominican Republic; Domino Theory; Fulbright, James William; Israel; Johnson, Lyndon Baines; Kennedy, John Fitzgerald; Korean War; Marshall, George Catlett, Jr.; Philanthropic Foundations, Overseas Programs; South Africa; Truman, Harry S.; Vietnam War; Zaire

FURTHER READING

Cohen, Warren I. *Dean Rusk.* Totowa, N.J., 1980.
Rusk, Dean. As told to Richard Rusk. *As I Saw It.* New York, 1990.
Schoenbaum, Thomas J. *Waging Peace and War: Dean Rusk in the Truman, Kennedy, and Johnson Years.* New York, 1988.

RUSSIA AND THE SOVIET UNION

Russia—before 1917 the empire of the Czars, later the Soviet Union (Union of Soviet Socialist Republics, USSR), and now Russia once again—is the largest country in the world, spanning Europe and Asia. U.S.-Russian relations have a long history, including and especially the 1945–1991 period when U.S.-Soviet relations were the central defining feature of U.S. foreign policy.

The Beginnings of Relations: 1763–1867

The United States and Russia first encountered each other during the eighteenth century, when both were peripheral to the heartland of Europe, in culture and economic importance. Thomas Jefferson and Czar Alexander I were both epigones of the French Enlightenment, as were Benjamin Franklin and the Russian political philosopher Alexander Radishchev. Despite such cultural commonalities, these two future powers might have had almost nothing to do with each other, had it not been for the way the international system developed before and during the Napoleonic period, early in the nineteenth century.

The American historian John Gaddis referred to these years as a "heritage of harmony," although he noted that little underpinned the heritage other than their episodic diplomatic hostility to Great Britain. The United States and Russia were as historian Norman Saul wrote, more like "distant friends" in the period prior to the American Civil War. The French writer Alexis de Tocqueville saw Russia and the United States as the heirs of Europe: the United States developing a complex mix of liberty and equality; Russia representing the way of "servitude."

Catherine the Great initially had no strong views about the American Revolution, but her Declaration of Armed Neutrality in 1780 favored the American and French causes, and was directed primarily against the British. During the 1790s, however, her growing fear of all things revolutionary impeded Russian diplomatic recognition of the United States. The two nations did not exchange envoys until 1809.

The cultural impact of the American Revolution in Russia was considerable. The figure of George Washington, regarded as the disinterested Father of Liberty, was of great interest to literary and philosophically minded Russian writers and intellectuals like Alexander Radishchev, Nikolai Novikov, and Nikolai Karamzin.

During the first quarter of the nineteenth century, knowledge of the new American Republic's institutions of government spread in Russia, as elsewhere in Europe. As the Russian government became more conservative and Russian intellectuals more radical, interest in the United States became characteristic of opposition circles, rather than official ones. Some of the Decembrist rebels, who tried to prevent the reactionary Czar Nicholas I from ascending the throne in 1825, were very interested in U.S. Federalism, as demonstrated by their constitutional schemes for Russia's future.

Trade grew considerably between the mid-eighteenth century and the early nineteenth, involving both U.S. staples, such as cotton, rice, coffee, tea, and sugar, and Russian ones including iron, hemp, cloth, and furs. Though U.S. sympathy with the Polish side in the 1830

Russia and the Former Soviet Republics

revolt against Russia delayed matters, a commercial treaty was finally signed in 1832. It did little more than guarantee reciprocity in the conduct of trade between the two nations and grant most-favored-nation status to each. Renewed annually, it lasted until 1911, when it was abrogated by the United States in the furor over the Russian treatment of Jews.

Political relations were similarly low key. At the end of the Napoleonic period, Russia had consolidated its position as one of the European great powers, while the United States was preparing to focus its energies on the North American continent. The United States proclaimed the Monroe Doctrine in 1823, warning the European powers against further colonization in the Western Hemisphere. The fundamental object of the declaration was the possibility of Spanish intervention to resuscitate its decomposing North American empire, but it also was directed against Russia, which was supporting Spain. Neither side wished the situation to deteriorate however, and the "distant friendship" was not seriously affected.

As the second half of the nineteenth century began, both Russia and the United States underwent the ordeal of major reform. In Russia, the emancipation of

the serfs in 1861 led to a series of other reforms. The so-called "Great Reforms" postponed the Imperial regime's day of reckoning, although they could not save it. In the United States, the political battles over slavery led to the Civil War.

The Russian government watched the outbreak of the U.S. Civil War with alarm. Still recovering from its defeat in the Crimean War, Russia was determined to restore its status as a European great power and effectively pursue its rivalry with Great Britain. A divided or permanently enfeebled United States could be of little help as a counterweight to Great Britain and France. So despite its marginal social similarity to the South, the Russian government unhesitatingly supported the North, while Great Britain and France, whose political interests cut the other way, recognized the Confederate States of America.

The Russian government, although periodically displeased with President Abraham Lincoln's conduct of the war, remained unswervingly loyal. Naval visits were exchanged and were well covered by the press.

Russia's sale of Alaska to the United States was no mere by-product of the good feeling of the Civil War years, but had its origins a decade earlier in the troubles

U.S. MINISTERS AND AMBASSADORS TO RUSSIA AND THE SOVIET UNION[1]

MINISTER	PERIOD OF APPOINTMENT	ADMINISTRATION
Francis Dana[2]	1780	
William Short[3]	1808	Jefferson
John Quincy Adams[4]	1809–1814	Madison
James A. Bayard[5]	1815	Madison
William Pinkney	1816–1818	Madison
		Monroe
George Washington Campbell	1818–1820	Monroe
Henry Middleton	1820–1830	Monroe
		Adams
		Jackson
John Randolph[6]	1830	Jackson
James Buchanan	1832–1833	Jackson
Mahlon Dickerson[7]	1834	Jackson
William Wilkins	1834–1835	Jackson
John Randolph Clay	1836–1837	Jackson
		Van Buren
George M. Dallas	1837–1839	Van Buren
Churchill C. Cambreleng	1840–1841	Van Buren
		Harrison
		Tyler
Charles C. Todd	1841–1846	Tyler
		Polk
Ralph I. Ingersoll	1846–1848	Polk
Arthur P. Bagby	1848–1849	Polk Taylor
Neill S. Brown	1850–1853	Fillmore
		Pierce
Thomas H. Seymour	1853	Pierce
		Buchanan
Francis W. Pickens	1858–1860	Buchanan
John Appleton	1860–1861	Buchanan
		Lincoln
Cassius M. Clay	1863–1869	Lincoln
		A. Johnson
		Grant
John L. Dawson[8]		Grant
Henry A. Smythe[9]		Grant
Andrew G. Curtin	1869–1872	Grant
James L. Orr	1872–1873	Grant
Marshall Jewell	1873	Grant
George H. Boker	1875–1878	Grant
		Hayes
Edwin W. Stoughton	1877–1879	Hayes
John W. Foster	1880–1881	Hayes
		Garfield
William H. Hunt	1882–1884	Arthur
Aaron H. Sargent[10]		Arthur
Alphonso Taft	1884–1885	Arthur
Alexander R. Lawton[11]		Arthur
George V. N. Lothrop	1885–1888	Arthur
		Cleveland
Lambert Tree	1888–1889	Cleveland
Allen Thorndike Rice[12]	1889	Cleveland
		Harrison

(table continues on next page)

MINISTER	PERIOD OF APPOINTMENT	ADMINISTRATION
Charles Emory Smith	1890–1892	Harrison
Andrew D. White	1892–1894	Harrison
		Cleveland
Clifton R. Breckinridge	1894–1897	Cleveland

AMBASSADOR

Ethan A. Hitchcock	1897	McKinley
Charlemagne Tower	1899–1902	McKinley
		T. Roosevelt
Robert S. McCormick	1902–1905	T. Roosevelt
George V.L. Meyer	1905–1907	T. Roosevelt
John W. Riddle	1906–1909	T. Roosevelt
		Taft
William Woodville Rockhill	1909–1911	Taft
Curtis Guild	1911–1913	Taft
Henry M. Pindell[13]	1914	Wilson
George T. Marye	1914–1916	Wilson
David R. Francis	1916–1918[14]	Wilson
William Christian Bullitt	1933–1936	F. D. Roosevelt
Joseph E. Davies	1936	F. D. Roosevelt
Laurence A. Steinhardt	1939–1941	F. D. Roosevelt
William H. Standley	1942–1943	F. D. Roosevelt
W. Averell Harriman	1943–1946	F. D. Roosevelt
		Truman
Walter Bedell Smith	1946–1948	Truman
Alan G. Kirk	1949–1951	Truman
George F. Kennan	1952[15]	Truman
Charles E. Bohlen	1953–1957	Eisenhower
Llewellyn E. Thompson	1957–1962	Eisenhower
		Kennedy
Foy D. Kohler	1962–1966	Kennedy
		L. B. Johnson
Llewellyn E. Thompson	1966–1969	L. B. Johnson
Jacob D. Beam	1969–1973[16]	Nixon
Walter J. Stoessel, Jr.	1973–1976	Nixon
		Ford
Malcolm Toon	1976–1977	Carter
Thomas J. Watson, Jr.	1979–1981	Carter
Arthur Adair Hartman	1981–1987	Reagan
Jack F. Matlock, Jr.	1987–1991	Reagan
		Bush
Robert S. Strauss	1991–1993	Bush
Thomas R. Pickering	1993–Present	Clinton

[1] Representatives from Dana to Francis were commissioned to Russia; those from Bullitt to date have been commissioned to the Union of Soviet Socialist Republics.
[2] Proceeded to post, but was not officially received at court; left post, Sept. 1783.
[3] Did not proceed to post, his nomination having been rejected by the Senate while he was en route.
[4] Nomination of 6 Mar 1809 rejected by the Senate; nomination of 26 June 1809 confirmed.
[5] Did not proceed to post.
[6] Proceeded to post, but did not present credentials; left post, 19 Sept. 1830.
[7] Declined appointment.
[8] Not commissioned; nomination rejected by the Senate.
[9] Not commissioned; nomination tabled by the Senate.
[10] Not commissioned; although nomination was confirmed by the Senate.
[11] Not commissioned; nomination withdrawn before the Senate acted upon it.
[12] Took oath of office, but died in the U.S. before proceeding to post.
[13] Declined appointment.
[14] Felix Cole was serving as Chargé d' Affaires ad interim when the Embassy in Russia was closed, 14 Sept. 1919.
[15] The govt. of the Soviet Union declared Kennan persona non grata, 3 Oct. 1952, and he did not return to his post.
[16] Adolph Dubs served as Chargé d' Affaires ad interim, Jan. 1973–Mar. 1974.

Sources: *Principal Officers of the Department of State and United States Chiefs of Missions.* ©1991 by Office of the Historian, Bureau of Public Affairs, Washington, D.C.;
The U.S. Government Manual, Annual. Washington, D.C.

of the Russian American (trading) Company. Operating from Alaska, far from the Russian heartland, the monopolistic company was resistant to reform. Influential Russians thought that in view of the growing determination of the United States to dominate the North American continent it would be better to sell this outpost, rather than to lose it by stages to Yankee interlopers. The sale was thus related in a curious way both to the reforming spirit of Russian liberals in the 1860s and to the growth of American imperial ambition. The treaty was signed at Secretary of State William Seward's house in Washington, D.C.,at the end of March 1867. For slightly more than $7 million, Alaska passed to the United States.

Industrialization, Emigration, Confrontation: 1867–1917

The Russian-U.S. relationship became increasingly important to both parties between the U.S. purchase of Alaska and the Russian Revolution of 1917. Most significantly it gradually became more acrimonious, a process culminating in the abrogation of the Russo-American trade treaty in 1911. At the outbreak of World War I, relations were at an all-time low.

One cluster of issues dividing both governments and peoples centered on how the Russian government treated its own subjects. Once these problems between Russia and the United States began in the 1870s, they would never go away entirely, recurring after the Bolsheviks took power, and again in the 1970s and 1980s. If the Russian (or later, Soviet) government treated its people badly, was it the business of the United States to improve their situation? Should the United States offer the Russians economic inducements to change their behavior? Should it penalize them if they did not?

United States concern focused initially, and periodically thereafter, on the plight of Russia's Jews. In 1881, after the assassination of Alexander II, the "Czar Liberator," pogroms broke out in more than 100 Russian localities. The periodic pogroms that followed accelerated the great wave of East European Jewish emigration to the United States. By 1914 the Jewish population of the United States had grown to about three million, ten times what it was in 1880.

One result of this massive emigration was the involvement of U.S. citizens of Russian birth in commercial relations between the two countries. But since almost all emigration from Russia was illegal under Russian law, when such people returned to Russia on business or family affairs, they were often harassed, expelled, or arrested.

In a more general way, the position of Russian Jews and other national minorities deteriorated after 1881, due to a pronounced increase in officially sanctioned Russification. Though the evidence is sketchy, it may be that the marked anti-Russian shift in American public opinion during the last quarter of the nineteenth century owes even more to these policies than is commonly realized, for the Polish, Finnish, and Baltic immigrants to the United States also brought with them an anti-Russian point of view.

The increasingly negative image of Russia in the United States was also part of a complex process of self-definition, closely connected with the development of mass media and the creation of a national public opinion. By the 1890s, more and more people believed that the role of the United States was in part to be the champion of the downtrodden and oppressed around the world. Points of view generated in centers of media influence, like New York, were picked up by an increasingly large network of newspapers and magazines across the country. To some extent, Americans implicitly began to identify what was good about their country as that which was "not like Russia," the archetypal old regime from which the venturesome fled to the new world.

In 1891 a major famine devastated Russia. The government was unprepared and slow to respond. As a result, private and governmental agencies from abroad tried to pick up the slack. U.S. grain growers and traders were particularly eager to extend food aid. They believed that charity also would bring a payoff, opening the Russian market to further U.S. exports in the future.

But despite the best efforts of the grain interests and the appeals of President Benjamin Harrison, the United States was not willing to provide the shipping to get the grain to Russia, largely because of the way Russia treated its ethnic minorities and political prisoners. The attention of Americans had been drawn to the plight of the latter by *Siberia and the Exile System* (1891), a remarkable exposé by George Kennan, perhaps the United States' first Russian expert and the great-uncle of the future historian and ambassador to the Soviet Union. There were debates in the press and in Congress. Congressmen John Overton Pendleton of West Virginia proclaimed that "friendship between tyranny and liberty; between Asiatic despotism and modern civilization; between the inertia of barbarism and the spirit of progress" was impossible. The vocabulary was strikingly similar to that of the disputes that would rage in the 1970s over whether the Soviet Union should be granted most-favored-nation (MFN) treatment if it refused to allow Jewish emigration.

Kennan had begun his adventurous career in Russia by publishing *Tent Life in Siberia*, an account of the attempt by the Western Union Company to build an above-ground telegraph line to Europe, via Alaska, the Bering Straits, and Siberia between 1865 and 1867. However, Kennan was gradually drawn into the controversy about Russian political prisoners, and he made several trips to Russia in the 1880s. Initially sympathetic to the Russian government he was dramatically won over by the Russian prisoners he encountered in the camps. He found them not to be the slavering, crazed, and hirsute bomb-throwers of the political cartoonists, but liberal-minded, principled defenders of Western values against Czarist oppression.

Precisely how accurate Kennan's portrayals were, especially as they pertain to what the Russian exiles actually stood for, is open to debate. But his depictions of them, both in his astoundingly popular public lectures and in his book, were graphic and riveting. The publication of *Siberia and the Exile System* inaugurated a full century of American interest in and sympathy for Russian political prisoners, which had much in common with the defense of Russian Jewry in the United States. Lobbies with names like "The Friends of Russian Freedom" began to make their appearance toward the end of the 1890s. Many of the founding members were children of leading U.S. abolitionists from the time of the Civil War. Such organizations became a familiar part of the U.S. landscape over much of the century that followed. How much good they ultimately accomplished is not easy to decide.

An early climax in the downhill course of relations came with the infamous 1903 pogrom at Kishinev, the capital of Bessarabia, which was then under Russian control. The attack on the Jews in Kishinev began on 19 April and lasted for two full days. By the time government troops took action to stop the violence, fifty people had died and 100 were severely injured. Five times that number required medical attention. Stores had been pillaged, over 700 houses had been destroyed, and more than 10,000 people became homeless.

This miserable episode caused a sensation in the U.S. press and led to intense pressure by Jewish organizations on Congress and the executive branch. The Russian ambassador in Washington poured oil on the flames by suggesting that the victims were guilty of exploiting their Russian neighbors and deserved what they got.

In addition to the immediate damage done to Russian-U.S. relations, the massacre led to the founding of the American Jewish Committee in 1906, thus adding a sophisticated and well-connected group of participants to the anti-Russian lobbying in Washington. Focusing on the demand that Russia treat all holders of U.S. passports equally, the American Jewish Committee helped keep the issue of Russian anti-Semitism before both Republican and Democrat voters in the election of 1908. The committee went on to play an important role in the campaign that finally forced President William Howard Taft to terminate the commercial treaty of 1832, on the grounds that Russia continued to violate it by discriminating against U.S. citizens because of their religious beliefs. The cause became national in 1911, and by the end of the year overwhelming majorities in both houses of Congress forced the president to act.

A number of critics, Russian and American, pointed out the inherent irony and anomaly of this situation. The United States was as rich in bigotry and racism as Russia. African-Americans had been disenfranchised in the South and the number of lynchings per year was high. In Atlanta, three years after the Kishinev pogrom, more than ten African-Americans were killed and at least 140 were injured in a race riot that a local paper dubbed "an American Kishinev." Anti-Irish and Anti-Catholic feeling was high in many parts of the country; Chinese exclusion laws were still being passed, as the Russian government was quick to point out, and anti-Semitism was common in the United States. None of these factors, however, was an effective counter to the general notion that the American thing to do was to champion people "less fortunate than ourselves."

Official Russia deplored what it regarded as the peculiar and misguided tendency of the United States to construe its national interest in terms of uninformed and moralistic intervention in the internal affairs of another nation. The influential and conservative daily newspaper *Novoe Vremia (New Times)* wrote that the whole affair revealed the degree to which "Jewish bankers have become the real lords of America."

After the turn of the century, a more practical set of issues added to, and blended with, the growing resentment felt on both sides about political prisoners and ethnic issues. The clash of rival imperialisms in the Far East was quickly becoming a bitterly contested and nasty affair. These confrontations helped to realign the European and world order, put new pressures on previously stable relationships, and produced strange bedfellows, sometimes in whirlwind fashion. Great Britain, the United States, Russia, and Japan were among the powers most deeply involved in China, especially in the struggle to control Manchuria and achieve a dominant position in the railroad building going on across the Far East.

The United States enthusiastically supported Japan in its war with Russia. American bankers provided the major loans to Japan, in the belief that Russia represented the major danger to the Open Door Policy. At least one important American banker, Jacob Schiff, supported Japan financially in part because of his ire at Russian anti-Semitism. But despite his own emphatic Russophobia, President Theodore Roosevelt believed that a total Japanese victory was not in the interest of the United States. He therefore moved skillfully and discreetly to bring the two sides together. A treaty signed in Portsmouth, New Hampshire, in the summer of 1905 gave Japan control of southern Manchuria, but left the Russian position in the north substantially intact.

On the eve of World War I, educated Russians and Americans each regarded violence as peculiarly characteristic of the other. Americans saw Russian violence as connected to "feudalism," "barbarous medievalism," or at any rate, something "backward." Russians, on the other hand, saw the United States as the arch-capitalist nation. Both the far Right and the far Left were opposed to industrial capitalism and both extremes were powerful in Russia. The more moderate factions, by contrast, were intrigued by U.S. dynamism and vitality, some of which they hoped could be captured for Russia. They sometimes called the dynamic, modern, industrial American development that fascinated them "Americanism" (*amerikanizm*).

In the post–U.S. Civil War period, Russian intellectuals, publicists, and journalists developed an increasingly negative view of the United States, derived from the writings of a group of politically and socially romantic intellectuals known as the Slavophiles. The first generation, active between the late 1830s and the early 1860s, were civilized aristocrats, instinctively opposed to the industrial modernity they saw emerging in much of Western Europe. Their view of the struggle for Russia's future produced a potentially xenophobic Russian nationalism, which stressed the traditional relations between different classes, but was also hostile to the activist, "Westernizing" Russian state, as it had developed after Peter the Great. In the second half of the nineteenth century, a "Russian socialism" evolved from Slavophile ideas, which stressed the substitution of a nativist, socialist communalism for both bureaucracy and capitalism.

Both conservative and socialist intellectuals in Russia tended to contrast Russian communalism with U.S. individualism; Russian generosity and openness with American guile and mercenary tendencies; Russian rootedness with American rootlessness. American violence was not spontaneous, but systemic: the violence of the assembly line and slaughter house, rather than of the pogrom.

One cannot explain the extreme hostility of early Bolshevik culture to the idea of "America" without understanding how these romantic attitudes became part of the political and intellectual Left, as well as of the Right. They were as characteristic of the Bolshevik Maxim Gorky as of the conservative nationalist Fedor Dostoevsky.

From Revolution to Recognition: 1917–1933

Most Americans greeted the news of the 1917 revolution in Russia with excitement. For Americans, Russian adherence to the Allied position in World War I had been the source of a certain embarrassment. It was harder to understand the struggle as one of democracy versus autocracy when the Russian Empire was a charter member of the democratic side. Now Russia had become democratic too. This change no doubt helps explain the combination of relief and high excitement in the public opinion of Western Europe and the United States between the revolution in March and the Bolshevik seizure of power in November 1917.

George F. Kennan, historian and diplomat, framed his classic interpretations of the encounter between the Americans and the Russians in terms of the collision of two worlds that had almost no understanding of each other and were following totally different paths. The Bolsheviks were driven by an ideology that was notably weak in the United States. Of Marxism's few U.S. adherents, many were foreign born and concentrated in several large cities, especially in New York. Indeed, few Americans knew anything about Russia. There was the now elderly George Kennan, advising President Woodrow Wilson informally about Russia, but much of his information was out-of-date. Samuel Harper, a professor of government at the University of Chicago, was better connected among younger political figures. Archibald Cary Coolidge of Harvard had begun to teach Russian history and had built a great library collection there. But in general, even educated Americans were ill informed about Russia.

Woodrow Wilson viewed World War I in overwhelmingly national terms, as expressed most notably in his "Fourteen Points." The U.S. government's attention, like that of its European counterparts, was entirely fixed on the successful prosecution of the war against Germany.

The Bolsheviks, more or less in power after November 1917, totally rejected the Americans' frame of reference and their middle-class liberal traditions. Bourgeois democracy, to them, was a total sham. Since shortly after the outbreak of war, Vladimir Lenin's goal had been to turn the "imperialist war" into a proletarian revolution; he succeeded in Russia, though not, as he had hoped, in Europe as a whole.

In effect, the two sides failed to find any common ground whatever. The Americans, like their West European allies, made every effort to persuade the Bolsheviks, as they had the ill-fated "provisional government" that preceded them, to fight the war against Germany to the finish.

Lenin, however, had promised his radical supporters to leave the war immediately. He soon proceeded to do so, even at the heavy cost of abandoning much of the western portion of the old Czarist empire to the Germans in the Treaty of Brest-Litovsk, signed in the spring of 1918. Months before that, the French had already proposed to their allies that armed intervention be undertaken in Russia, in the hope of restoring the eastern front against Germany.

The United States and Great Britain initially rebuffed the French, but within a few months they changed their minds. Brest-Litovsk helped convince them that the new Soviet government had become a German satellite. It now appeared that the Germans had substantially strengthened their position in the western front, an idea confirmed by the massive German spring offensive.

The British took the lead, intervening in the Murmansk-Archangel region of northern Russia initially to protect the supplies sent there for the use of the Russian imperial government against the Germans. U.S. involvement consisted at first of a few Marines, supplemented by several battalions of fresh troops under British command. These troops arrived in Murmansk in the fall of 1918. In all, 14,000 U.S. troops were involved in the intervention, in the north and around Vladivostok in the Russian Far East. Additional instances of Allied intervention took place in the Caucasus.

The deepening of the Russian civil war further persuaded allied statesmen that intervention should be pursued more seriously. When the evacuation of 40,000 Czech troops across the trans-Siberian railroad to Vladivostok was interrupted by friction with the Bolshevik authorities, fighting broke out all along the line. The Czechs were the largest, best disciplined and best armed force in Siberia. Their officers were strongly anti-Communist, and they soon became involved in other anti-Bolshevik activities.

The Czechs launched an emotional appeal to Washington for assistance on 2 July 1918 and it was answered by a wave of public support, both for the "heroic" Czechs and the mission to democratize Russia. Their military success triggered further intervention by Allied forces. The Japanese reoccupied Vladivostok, where they were later joined by a U.S. troop contingent of 7,500 that spent most of its time guarding the port. The Americans in Murmansk, however, engaged the Red Army on several occasions and suffered about 150 casualties before they withdrew in mid-1919.

The United States was by and large the most reluctant intervener among the Western powers, but because of the subsequent global rivalry, Soviet scholars generally gave U.S. intervention a retrospective prominence that it did not have at the time. The Soviet view was that the entire intervention had been a desperate Western effort to strangle the infant revolution in its cradle. No one should deny that ideological hostility played a significant role, especially among the French and the British. But Soviet scholarship never adequately took account of the necessity felt among Western leaders of maintaining the Eastern Front against the Germans, at a time when the German war effort did not appear to be anywhere near the end of the road.

In any event, the Allied intervention was a disaster. It was episodic and inadequately planned. It was not sufficiently forceful to overthrow the Bolsheviks, but significant enough to leave a legacy of bitterness and suspicion. It is right to point out that the Soviet government often used the intervention to whip up anti-Western sentiment, but it was the Western governments that put this weapon in their hands.

The impact of the Russian Revolution on rest of the world was profound. Among U.S. intellectuals reactions varied: some were powerfully drawn to the utopian promise of fundamental human transformation pro-claimed by the Revolution's ideology. Louise Bryant, Bessie Beatty, and John Reed, author of *Ten Days that Shook the World*, were only the most prominent radicals of the period who resoundingly applauded the Revolution. Others, like the Russian-American radical Emma Goldman, later repudiated their initial enthusiasm and came to regard the Soviet regime as a new incarnation of age-old Russian tyranny.

Among middle-class U.S. citizens there was much less enthusiasm; and the U.S. labor movement remained notably cool. The first of what were to be periodic "red scares" in the United States occurred in 1919–1920, triggered by postwar labor unrest, fear of bomb-throwing foreigners, and resurgent nativism. This hysterical reaction would not have taken the form that it did without the looming presence of the Russian Revolution. Neither the Palmer raids in Chicago nor the crushing of the Boston police strike and of the "general strike" in Seattle would have unfolded quite the way they did were it not for the much-strengthened fear of radicalism that followed the second phase of the Russian Revolution. President Wilson declared Soviet Russia to be "the negation of everything that is American." In 1920, Attorney General A. Mitchell Palmer, blending foreign and domestic anxieties, captured the prevailing atmosphere of the time most vividly:

> By stealing, murder and lies, Bolshevism has looted Russia not only of its material strength, but of its moral force. A small clique of outcasts from the East Side of New York has attempted this....Because a disreputable alien—Leon Bronstein, the man who now calls himself Trotzky—can inaugurate a reign of terror from his throne room in the Kremlin; because this lowest of all types known to New York can sleep in the Czar's bed, while hundreds of thousands in Russia are without food or shelter....

The general attitude of the Soviet elites toward the United States was equally complex, if not incoherent. The size, power, and economic dynamism of the United States, the inventiveness and ruthlessness of its economic leaders, seemed to epitomize the worst aspects of advanced capitalism. To many Bolsheviks whose socialism contained a great deal of old-fashioned romantic agrarianism, such as Maxim Gorky, who called New York "the city of the yellow devil:" U.S. capitalism was utterly detestable, mechanistic, heartless, shallow, violent, mercenary, and without culture. And yet, even among communists who fundamentally endorsed that view, as did Lenin, there was a fascination with the seemingly endless inventiveness of American industrial culture, with its tremendous technological achievements.

To Lenin, vividly aware of Russia's backwardness, and increasingly anxious about the deformations that Russia's lack of culture might bring, the achievements of capitalist industrialization were very impressive and so very necessary for Russia's future development. And since the United States had become the richest and most advanced of the capitalist nations, a communist revolution would be taking place there in the not-too-distant future. So as Lenin jockeyed for position with the great states of world capitalism, he showed a special interest in the United States that can only partially be explained by his desire to sow discord among these states and buy time for socialist Russia to grow strong. Lenin's sucessor, Joseph Stalin, agreed. The essence of Leninism, he wrote, was "the combination of Russian revolutionary sweep and American efficiency." The attitude of the American political elites toward the new Soviet state was, as historian John Gaddis has pointed out, "based on the assumption, increasingly pervasive in early twentieth-century American diplomacy, that the internal ideological orientation of a state would determine its behavior in the international arena." This was a point of view that helped define U.S. hostility toward the Soviet Union until very recently.

At the same time, U.S. businesses were from early on eager to enter the Russian market, and American humanitarism was notably evident in the famine relief organization directed by Herbert Hoover at the end of World War I. U.S. capital and technical expertise found ways to enter the Soviet Union throughout the 1920s, often through "concessions," like the one that gave rise to Armand Hammer's successful pencil factory. By 1930, U.S. goods constituted 25% of all Soviet imports, a higher percentage than that of any other country.

Nevertheless, political recognition languished, despite these growing economic ties. The refusal of the Soviet government to repay the debts of the Czarist government influenced public opinion, and the Communist International's efforts to subvert American institutions provided U.S. politicians with seemingly unimpeachable reasons for nonrecognition.

Influential private groups like the Roman Catholic Church also were vehement in their opposition. Journals like *The Pilot* and *America* excoriated the murders of prominent Russian and Polish clerics by Soviet thugs. Non-recognition was one of the few international issues on which both the American Federation of Labor and the National Association of Manufacturers solidly agreed. The fortunes of the American Communist Party reflceted this public animosity: membership plummeted from close to 90,000 in 1919 to around 7,000 a decade later.

Given such an array of forces opposed to a formal recognition of Soviet Russia, it may seem extraordinary that it happened as soon as 1933. Part of the explanation is that, during the late 1920s, anti-Soviet sentiment died down among ordinary Americans. The Soviet Union was now much less of a lightning rod for than it had been in the aftermath of the Red Scare. Furthermore, both at home and abroad the Great Depression as well as the increasingly ominous international scene affected public attitudes significantly.

The prospect of dramatically increased trade with the Soviet Union was especially alluring during the Depression years. The Democratic Party under Franklin Roosevelt was more pragmatic about international political and economic issues than its Republican predecessor. Furthermore, the United States was by now the only major nation in the world that still refused to recognize the Soviet Union. Roosevelt regarded nonrecognition as a failed policy, like Prohibition, not as a principled stand. In addition, the rise of German and Japanese militarism subtly diminished the danger the Soviet Union seemed to pose to U.S. interests. Both the United States and the Soviet Union wanted to oppose Japanese expansion in Asia, and the absence of normal diplomatic relations was an embarrassing hindrance.

After Roosevelt entered the White House in early 1933 events moved rapidly. Recognition became official in November of that year, with the Soviet Union pledging to refrain from propagandizing in the United States while also guaranteeing the rights of U.S. citizens in the Soviet Union. The United States seems to have believed this agreement to have meant a reorientation of American Communist Party activity away from the Comintern, an interpretation rejected by the Soviet Union. William C. Bullitt became the first U.S. ambassador fully accredited to the Soviet regime.

Recognition and the Grand Alliance: 1933–1945

Neither the economic nor the foreign policy benefits anticipated by both sides actually materialized. There was some tendency for each to believe that the other had agreed to recognition only under the pressures of circumstance. This was particularly true of the Soviet side. Neither, therefore, was eager to make concessions. Roosevelt knew that U.S. public opinion would not at this point allow him to take vigorous action against Japan in East Asia. But without something more than just moral support for the Soviet Union against Japan, the negotiations on debts and credits went nowhere. After a while, Soviet tensions with Japan eased somewhat and stronger U.S. support seemed even less worth working for. Meanwhile, Communist party propaganda in the United States did not change much, and the volume of trade remained stuck at the 1930 level.

In the intellectual community, however, the situation was very different. With the capitalist world mired in depression, it became much easier for intellectuals in Western Europe and the United States to believe that the Soviet Union's great experiment held vital lessons for their governments and societies. Many radicals from the United States and Europe visited the Soviet Union and most were impressed with what they saw, exhibiting, in some cases, an extraordinary ability to overlook evidence that did not correspond to their ideological longings. Many echoed the famous words of Lincoln Steffens on returning from an earlier visit (1920) to the Soviet Union: "I have been over to the future and it works."

Stalin's utopian economic policies and particularly his purges did trigger a response in the United States, however. After observing the purges in both Germany and the Soviet Union in 1934, an anti-Communist Left, very small at first, began to argue that the Russian Revolution had degenerated into a repressive bureaucratic collectivism that could be compared with Fascist Italy and even National Socialist Germany. The followers of the exiled Leon Trotsky, small in numbers, but disproportionately influential in leftist circles, took this view. Trotsky spoke of "bureaucratic degeneration" and called Stalin "the gravedigger of the revolution."

After 1935, less ideologically minded citizens of the United States also began to see similarities between Soviet Communism and the two Fascist nations, Germany and Italy. They began to use a new term which Trotsky himself ultimately adopted, calling all three "totalitarian" states of a new type, made possible by the technological advances of the twentieth century. Everything about these new autocracies was as centralized as possible. They were militarized and ideologically fanatical, given over to coercion and violence, both internally and externally. Not only was there no possible opposition of any kind to their rule, but they seemed possessed by a utopian determination to make their subjects over "totally" in the image of the ideology of the leader and his elite party.

This comparison of the major "dictatorships" and their contrasting with the "democracies" drew broader support from U.S. public opinion as the 1930s drew to a close. Although some leftist intellectuals (and a few conservatives too) excused, or even supported, the escalation of purging in the Soviet Union, on the whole it made a very bad impression on Americans. With the increased danger of war, the execution of a large part of the Red Army officer corps in 1937 seemed stupid as well as immoral. By the time of the "Winter War" with Finland in 1939 and the division of Poland, large numbers of Americans were prepared to regard the Soviet state as a species of "Red Facism," very much like its German rival to the west. Even many ideologically engaged intellectuals were disillusioned by the events of 1939, beginning with the Molotrov-Ribbentrop Pact, and they formed a crucial part of the anti-Soviet "Cold War Left" that would emerge in the United States after World War II.

The war profoundly changed the arena in which relations between the Soviet Union and United States were to be played out. Symbolic politics and modest economic relations gave way to the epic struggle against Germany, the Grand Alliance, as Churchill called it, and then to the Cold War. At the war's end, the United States and Russia emerged as global rivals, dwarfing the nations of Europe, just as Tocqueville had predicted more than a century earlier.

Between 1941 and 1945, ideological issues receded. Americans are prone to adopt the view that if we are allied with another nation, the people and even their leaders must be good folk, "like us." This was the view that came to dominate the popular media during the war and found notable expression in books like Wendell Wilkie's *One World* and the depiction of the sinister Stalin as a genial "Uncle Joe." This did not happen overnight; it took time for the memory of Soviet actions in 1939 to fade a bit. But the new direction of the war and the creation of the alliance made yesterday seem far away.

Not only the circumstances of the war and the vagaries of U.S. public opinion but President Roosevelt's own views contributed to the improvement in relations. Roosevelt never believed that the Soviet Union should be compared to Nazi Germany as a source of evil in the world. He believed it was a dictatorship with an absurd and repellent ideology, but it was not as violent and dangerous as Germany. And Roosevelt, a great believer in his ability to deal with all kinds of people, believed he could get along with Stalin.

After the passage of Lend-Lease legislation by Congress, the big issue among the Allies became the "second front." Allied action was demanded by the Soviet leadership from the first contacts between Great Britain and the Soviet Union in June, 1941. How soon would the West move? How many divisions would they send? As early as that fall, Stalin was demanding that British prime minister Winston Churchill send thirty divisions either to the Caucasus in the south or to Archangel in the north. Stalin regarded the North African and Italian campaigns as unimportant and kept pressing for a major invasion, preferably through northern France. One may sympathize with Churchill's irritation at Soviet pressure. He could not refrain from telling Stalin that if the Soviet Union had not acquiesced in the fall of France in 1940 there already would be a second front. But one must remember the enormous disparity in casualties: fifty Soviets were being killed fighting the Axis for every U.S. casualty.

Another Soviet war aim that caused trouble later was the demand that Great Britain and the United States recognize the Soviet Union's 1941 frontiers. This meant

Allied agreement that the Soviet Union should retain the territory taken from Finland in the Winter War, as well as agreement to the annexation of the three Baltic states and the acquisition of a large piece of what had been Poland.

The Polish problem was the most acute, and it foreshadowed the whole question of the future of Eastern Europe after the war. The Polish government in exile in London refused to accept the 1941 Russo-Polish border as demanded by the Soviets and held out for the frontier that had existed prior to the Molotov-Ribbentrop Pact. In April 1943, the Soviet government broke off all relations with the London Poles in a dispute over who was responsible for the massacre of around 15,000 Polish officers at Katyn Forest near Smolensk. (In 1990, the government of Mikhail Gorbachev finally admitted what by this time the whole non-Soviet world knew: that the Polish officers had been killed not by the Nazis but by Soviet security forces.)

At the Tehran Conference in November 1943, Churchill proposed a solution to the frontier issue: Poland should simply be moved west. The Soviet Union would keep what it had taken from Poland and Poland would be compensated at German expense. This arrangement bound the contracting parties together against Germany and made the Soviet Union appear as the natural protector of postwar Poland.

At the Yalta Conference in February 1945, Roosevelt and Churchill conceded to the Soviet Union that the Soviet-sponsored and highly unrepresentative "Union of Polish Patriots," rather than the London government-in-exile, would form the nucleus of the postwar Polish regime. Churchill, and in a more complex and ambiguous way Roosevelt, recognized that wherever the Red Army would go, Soviet power would be established. And yet, neither Roosevelt nor Churchill foresaw exactly what the Soviet Union was going to do in its sphere of influence, or how abject the "friendly governments" that Stalin had set up were actually going to be. The Soviet Union also agreed at Yalta to enter the war against Japan after Germany's defeat in return for a series of territorial concessions in East Asia, including Soviet possession of the Kurile Islands and the lower half of Sakhalin Island.

The last of the great wartime conferences took place at Potsdam in August 1945, with President Harry S. Truman now representing the United States. A week later, the United States dropped the first of two atomic bombs on Japan, and the Soviet Union entered the war in the Pacific.

The Cold War: 1946–1986

As World War II was coming to an end, America's Soviet policy was being conducted by a new group of U.S. specialists, trained in Russian language, history, and culture. These men knew the Soviet Union and its people well. Their view of the prospects for good relations between the two giants was well informed, sophisticated, but bleak. Such men as George F. Kennan and Charles Bohlen had been trained, prior to U.S. recognition of the Soviet Union, in the Department of State's Division of Eastern European Affairs, which had been built up in the 1920s and 1930s by its chief, Robert F. Kelley. After an eighteen-month stint in Eastern Europe as vice-consuls, the officers were sent to the seminar in what were then called "Oriental languages" at the Sorbonne in France (or, in Kennan's case, the University of Berlin), and then returned to diplomatic posts in Eastern Europe. There they were expected to perfect their language skills and use their post as a window on the Soviet Union.

Since July 1944, Kennan had served under Ambassador Averell Harriman as minister-counselor in the U.S. embassy in Moscow, in effect the number two person in the embassy on the civilian side. Kennan's grim view of the Soviet Union had been at odds with some of the more optimistic assessments coming from the Roosevelt White House, but it was confirmed by the sharp deterioration in U.S.-Soviet relations in 1946. Soviet forces were reluctant to leave both Iran and Manchuria, confirming the views of those who thought that the Soviet Union would continue to expand until it was confronted by something more than verbal threats.

In February 1946, Stalin made a speech in Moscow that stressed the incompatibility of capitalism and communism and blamed capitalist instability for the outbreak of World War II. A week later came the so-called Gouzenko case, a sensational espionage incident in Canada in which twenty-two people were arrested for stealing nuclear secrets for the Soviets. Leads derived from the case ultimately led to the arrests of Klaus Fuchs in Great Britain and Julius and Ethel Rosenberg in the United States.

A few days later George Kennan sent what became known as his "Long Telegram" analyzing the "sources of Soviet conduct" as internally driven. A thoroughly assimilated ideology, he argued, ensured that the Soviet Union would treat the capitalist world as irredeemably hostile. There was no concession that the United States could make that could lead to a substantive improvement in relations with this latest and most ideological manifestation of Russia's autocratic tradition. This gloomy prognosis received striking confirmation from the former Commissar for Foreign Affairs, Maxim Litvinov, in a remarkable interview with a CBS News correspondent, conducted in June 1946 but not made public until after Litvinov's death in 1951.

Kennan had regarded himself as a voice crying in the wilderness, but Washington was now ready to listen to what he had to say. His telegram provided Secretary of State James F. Byrnes and President Truman with the intellectual rationale for major changes in U.S. policy toward the Soviet Union. An abbreviated version of Kennan's telegram subsequently became famous as the "X" article, published the following year in the journal *Foreign Affairs*.

Early in March 1946, Churchill made his famous "Iron Curtain" speech at Fulton, Missouri. The term made its way into mainstream U.S. political discourse almost immediately. Truman appeared on the rostrum with Churchill, but he moved rather hesitantly toward the policy changes implied by Churchill's speech. Even when Truman fired Secretary of Commerce and Labor Henry Wallace, known for his pro-Soviet views, the president's action seemed an awkward and belated concession, made under pressure, rather than a decisive move toward a new and tougher policy toward Moscow.

The congressional elections of 1946 demonstrated what the polls also had made clear: fear of the Soviet Union's aggressive intent was a prime concern of the U.S. electorate. By defining the issues between the parties as a fight between "Communism," often linked to radicals in the U.S. labor movement, and "Americanism" the Republicans took control of both houses for the first time since 1928.

As viewed from Washington, Soviet pressure became dramatically more apparent during the winter of 1946–1947. The withdrawal of British forces from Greece, whose conservative government was increasingly threatened by a Communist-inspired insurgency seemingly encouraged by Moscow, and continuing Soviet pressure on Turkey gave rise to renewed fears that the Soviet Union was on the march. In a cumulative response to these developments, the President announced his "Truman Doctrine" on 12 March before both houses of Congress. In it he pledged that the United States would help democracies all over the world "maintain their free institutions and their national integrity against aggressive movements that seek to impose on them totalitarian regimes." In June 1947, Secretary of State George C. Marshall proclaimed what became known as the "Marshall Plan" at the Harvard commencement: a pledge to help rebuild the shattered economies of European states, so that their people should not, in despair, turn to Communism or be subverted by some combination of external and internal forces.

The Yalta and Potsdam agreements had stipulated that defeated Germany was to be treated as a single political and economic entity, although it was to be divided into four zones of occupation. As early as the first few months of 1946, it was clear there was going to be trouble about four-power unity. Political parties were quickly reestablished in the Soviet zone. There were two "bourgeois" parties, a Socialist Party, and a very small Communist Party. Early in 1946, it was clear that the two bourgeois parties were to have no influence at all, and in April, the small Communist Party "merged" with the large socialist party to form the Socialist Unity Party, under firm Communist Party control.

The Cold War continued to worsen through the rest of 1947 and into 1948. With the communist coup of February 1948 in Czechoslovakia, Washington's belief in a communist "blueprint" or "master plan" for world conquest grew. There was special concern that the Italian Communist Party, expelled from Italy's coalition government in 1947, might come to power legally in the Italian elections of the following year. However it was narrowly defeated by the Christian Democratic party, supported by substantial covert U.S. aid.

By the spring of 1948, the French had united their zone of occupation in Germany to those of Great Britain and the United States, and it was clear that come kind of West German state was likely to be formed in the near future. It was under these circumstances that the Soviet Union chose to cut off access to West Berlin, isolated deep in the Soviet zone. U.S. General Lucius Clay favored breaking the blockade by force, but he was overruled, and the Berlin airlift followed. These dramatic events marked the end of even a pretense of four-power control, and both West and East German states were established in 1949. Divided Germany became part of a similarly divided Europe. The North Atlantic Treaty, signed in April 1949, led to the establishment of the North Atlantic Treaty Organization (NATO). The Soviet response was the Warsaw Pact, formalized in 1955.

The onset of the Cold War had equally dramatic repercussions at home. The entire center and left of the U.S. political spectrum split into a dominant "Cold War Left," militantly anticommunist and cautious about any shade of radical or utopian thinking and a residual left more accommodating to Soviet interests and points of view. At the same time, conservative Republicans, and some Democrats too, also split into an isolationist wing led by Senator Robert Taft of Ohio, and an internationalist wing, with Senator Arthur Vandenberg of Michigan, a prominent spokesman for a bipartisan policy of confronting communism in Europe and elsewhere. This policy, intimately associated with the name of George F. Kennan, became known, over the course of its evolution, as "containment."

An important aspect of the Cold War experience in the United States (and apparently also in the Soviet Union) was increased ideological militancy. The most extreme manifestation of ideological zealotry was the accusation by Senator Joseph McCarthy that the U.S. government, particularly the Department of State, was riddled with spies. The Korean War and the involvement in it of Chinese Communist leader Mao Zedong and his new revolutionary government also increased tensions between the two power blocs and fueled the military buildup. The application of "brainwashing" techniques by the Chinese Communists and the fantastic charges of U.S. "germ warfare" led to fresh fears of penetration and infiltration of the United States by the sinister, worldwide communist enemy.

The death of Stalin in 1953 and the accession to power of Nikita Khrushchev led to some improvements in U.S.-Soviet relations. Khrushchev broke with Stalin's policy dictum that war between capitalism and communism was inevitable and proclaimed the necessity of "peaceful coexistence." In his famous "Secret Speech" in 1956, Khrushchev undertook the first serious criticisms of Stalin in the Soviet Union since the 1920s. He made serious attempts to move away from the violent and repressive extremes of Stalinism and undertook limited political and economic reform and the rehabilitation of many of Stalin's victims in the purges of the 1930s.

These developments were of the utmost importance to Soviet relations with the United States. On the one hand, they inaugurated a stop-and-start process of reform that ultimately, under Mikhail Gorbachev, would careen out of control and lead to the collapse of the Soviet Union. Just how destabilizing the reform process in the Soviet Union might be was prefigured in the Hungarian Revolution and volatile process of reform in Poland known as the "Polish October," both of which took place in 1956. On the other hand, Khrushchev's reforms made possible a serious dialogue with the noncommunist world, in particular with the United States, about how to achieve greater political stability and "managed competition" in the context of the Cold War.

Subsequently, the humiliating Soviet retreat in the Cuban missile crisis played an important role in Khrushchev's downfall in 1964. Under his successor, Leonid Brezhnev, arms control negotiations resumed in an increasingly regularized format, but against the backdrop of an ambitious, protracted and global Soviet military buildup. The Test Ban Treaty of 1963, achieved by Khrushchev and President John F. Kennedy in the aftermath of the crisis, was an important early milestone in the arms control process.

At the time of Khrushchev's ouster, two of the Soviet Union's major diplomatic objectives were a solution to the "German problem" and a final acceptance by the Western powers of the Soviet Union's postwar borders. The matter of legitimation was extremely important to the Soviet leadership, which no longer regarded itself as a crusader for world revolution, but as having achieved a Communist version of the old Russian Empire. The capitalist world, they insisted, had to acknowledge that achievement.

Much of what the Soviets wanted was achieved by the Helsinki Accords in the 1970s. Nevertheless, while Europe and the United States accepted postwar Soviet borders, the Soviet Union accepted the so-called "Third Basket," a collection of human rights guarantees that supplied to dissidents in the Soviet Union and Eastern Europe a freshly signed document to which they could legitimately appeal.

Brezhnev's military buildup began as a kind of reaction against the relative military weakness of the Soviet Union at the time of the Cuban missile crisis; but it was also an end in itself. The Soviet Union was determined to become a global superpower, to break out of its Eurasian base and cut a more impressive figure in the Third World. The Soviet Union already had a beachhead in Cuba and had long expressed its support for anticolonial and postcolonial "liberation movements." Now it began to move toward active support of such movements in Angola and Mozambique and in the horn of Africa. An important goal of U.S. policy during these years thus became to persuade the Soviet Union to observe a restraint in these adventures comparable to their restraint in the European heartland.

Moscow's global ambitions were to end in an overextension that would play a role in the eventual collapse of the Soviet Union. The culmination of this "imperial overstretch" came in the ill-fated Soviet invasion of Afghanistan in December 1979, an adventure that badly damaged U.S.-Soviet relations, undermined the administration of President Jimmy Carter, and ultimately produced exhaustion and cynicism in the Soviet Union itself. The parallels with the American intervention in Vietnam were numerous and striking.

According to the historian Adam B. Ulam, the involvement of the United States in Vietnam was, from the standpoint of U.S.-Soviet relations, "a momentous blunder." Even more seriously, the Vietnam War shattered the entire domestic context in which U.S. foreign policy had been made since the end of World War II. Together with issues of 1960s radicalism, the war created domestic divisions of a kind not seen in the United States since the 1930s.

As the decade of the 1970s began, the Soviet Union's position in the world seemed more secure than ever. Even Soviet blunders in the Middle East and the U.S. opening to China seemed minor matters. This meant that Brezhnev could enter upon more ambitious negotiations with the United States "from a position of strength." In the geopolitical vocabulary of Soviet strategists, "the correlation of forces" was shifting in their favor. Their military buildup had certainly brought them closer to strategic parity with the United States, and the Soviet Union seemed more stable than the United States—especially after the Watergate crisis and the resignation of President Richard Nixon.

The Soviet leadership was eager to strike a deal with the United States that would ratify this strategic parity and prevent the new United States relationship with

China from developing into a more ambitious anti-Soviet alliance. The United States also was interested in negotiation. President Nixon wanted Soviet help in ending the Vietnam War on relatively favorable terms. He also realized that the U.S. economy was facing difficulties and that the U.S. was overcommitted around the world. A new era of hard choices seemed to lie ahead. Moreover, many European nations, impressed by German Chancellor Willy Brandt's conciliatory Ostpolitik policy toward Eastern Europe, were pressing the United States for a general improvement in East-West relations.

Secretary of State Henry Kissinger and Nixon had adopted broad goals in line with their policy of détente. The key element was to establish a working U.S.-Soviet relationship, undergirded by a broadly based U.S. effort to both entice and pressure the Soviet Union and China into becoming real participants in the international community.

A major element in these potentially far-ranging negotiations was the arms control process between the Soviet Union and the United States that began in 1968 with the Nuclear Non-Proliferation Treaty. The Strategic Arms Limitation Treaty (SALT) process began the following year and lasted, with interruptions and name changes dictated by domestic political considerations, until the Soviet Union ceased to exist.

In entering into a more intimate relationship with the United States, an important risk for the Soviet Union was that the negotiation process might give the United States the idea that it had some real leverage over Soviet domestic policies. Soviet Jews already had been trying in large numbers to emigrate, and they were supported by substantial segments of U.S. public opinion. Responding to these domestic constituencies, Senator Henry Jackson put forward legislation that ultimately became the Jackson-Vanik Amendment. This legislation decreed that nations with "non-market economies" that denied the right of their citizens to emigrate should not be granted "most-favored-nation treatment." It quickly became a major weapon in the hands of many "neo-conservatives," who thought that Kissinger's détente policy had too many carrots and not enough sticks.

Soviet policymakers thus faced a dilemma: they did not want to respond to outsiders meddling in their internal affairs; but they also did not want to put détente at risk. Emboldened by what they perceived as a greater governmental reluctance to crack down hard, Soviet dissidents spoke out more forcefully, often appealing to the human rights provisions of the Helsinki Final Act.

Gorbachev and the End of the Soviet Union

When Ronald Reagan became president in 1980, U.S.-Soviet relations were on a downward spiral. In Poland, General Wójceich Jaruzelski's martial law regime had apparently crushed the Solidarity movement; and the Soviet Union had invaded Afghanistan, where their ultimate intentions were unclear. President Jimmy Carter's foreign policy was regarded by much of U.S. public opinion as having been insufficiently tough, and Ronald Reagan was surrounded by advisers, such as Jeane Kirkpatrick, who were committed to substituting old-fashioned Cold War militancy for a policy of greater accommodation to Soviet interests.

At that same time, the Soviet succession crisis that extended from the old age of Brezhnev through the brief reigns of Yuri Andropov and Konstantin Chernenko became a major factor in bilateral relations, as did Ronald Reagan's determination to introduce the Strategic Defense Initiative (SDI or "Star Wars"). The SDI's ability to protect the United States from Soviet attack was doubted by most knowledgeable scientists, but both Soviet and U.S. leaders could see that it was likely to have remarkable indirect results in stimulating the development of U.S. military technology.

The possibility of a vast new and technologically sophisticated arms race was particularly daunting for the Soviet Union at a time when all its economic problems were accelerating. The institutionalized corruption of Brezhnevian "stability" was also becoming more and more obvious, as was the entrenchment of political immobilism. Relations between the two superpowers remained frigid for several years, and only began to improve again after Gorbachev became general secretary of the Soviet Communist Party in March 1985.

Reagan and Gorbachev met for the first time in Geneva, Switzerland, in November 1986. Even though little was achieved, it was a momentous occasion. Reagan came to believe that he could "do business with Gorbachev," as had Margaret Thatcher of Great Britain earlier. For his part, Gorbachev decided that Reagan was a less formidable opponent than he had feared and that they could get along.

The rapprochement that began in Geneva reinvigorated a trend that had been a principal characteristic of détente: improved relations between the superpowers demanded real Soviet restraint in international affairs. So while Gorbachev concentrated on domestic reform, he pulled back to a greater and greater extent from foreign policy adventurism—withdrawing forces from Afghanistan, decreasing support for the Sandinistas in Nicaragua, and lowering the Soviet profile in Indochina and Africa.

Most important of all, of course, was his decision to allow the Soviet satellite regimes in Eastern Europe much greater independence. It took people in the region some time to realize the opportunity that they had been offered and how isolated the old-line Communist leadership had become. It also took Gorbachev a while to realize that without the threat of invasion by the Red Army, there was no holding the "socialist camp" together.

The role played by the United States in the collapse of the Soviet Union was vitally important but indirect. The global rivalry—political, military, and economic—took its toll on the vastly weaker Soviet economy. Ultimately, the Soviet economy was drawn into the world market, despite its efforts at socialist autarky, with damaging consequences. Gorbachev's decision to undertake extensive domestic reform, with the understanding and support of the West, meant that to intervene aggressively in order to protect traditional Soviet international interests became far more difficult. The vastly ambitious plans of the Brezhnev era atrophied and disappeared, then Stalin's East European Empire, and finally the Soviet Union itself. In the aftermath of the failed coup of August 1991, Boris Yeltsin replaced Gorbachev as Soviet leader. Russia was again a sovereign nation, along with a variety of weaker neighbors whose relation to the old center of their geopolitical world remained to be redefined.

Russia's Agony: 1991–1996

Yeltsin's first struggle was with the gathering chaos of post-Soviet reality. Russia's constitution was authoritarian and jerry-built, vesting large and ill-defined powers in the presidency. Its parliament was increasingly dominated by communists and nationalists. There is virtually no legal system, merely what Russians themselves called "the battle of the laws" in the Russian Republic, the regions, and cities. Privatization began, but in an extremely uneven fashion, much of it entailing the former elite engaging in what was called "nomenklatura privatization," establishing ownership over what, previously, it had merely managed. The country remained in serious financial straits, health and human services declined, organized crime became increasingly threatening, and various regions of the country are politically and economically moving away from the center. And, of course, Russia was still a military superpower, with a large nuclear arsenal. Its political class, particularly top foreign political and military thinkers, cherished the imperial past and spoke of the nations of the former Soviet Union as the "near abroad." Yet, as the conflict in Chechnya demonstrated, the Red Army's ability to make war has drastically declined.

Russia not only still lacks the necessary political, legal, and fiscal institutions to support a stable democratic government, but arguably also lacks a "democratic culture," broadly speaking. In the immediate post-Soviet period, Russians felt humiliated, torn between envy of Western material prosperity and their traditional neo-Slavophile scorn of Western, especially U.S., materialism. Westerners have argued that Westerners must come to accept the reasonableness of markets and political compromise, but

such a radical cultural reorientation was extraordinarily difficult, especially at a time when so many statistical indicators seem headed in the wrong direction. It fell to the United States to deal with this extraordinarily complex and difficult situation, at a time when U.S. citizens were interested overwhelmingly in domestic issues and less interested in financially assisting foreign nations than they have been in many years. Even if they were most disposed to be generous, it was not clear how outsiders could put substantial resources at the service of real reform and greater stability. There was some private investment, to be sure, but many potential investors were too uncertain about the future to commit themselves. Moreover, ultimately the success of political and economic reform lay with the Russians and their leaders.

President Bill Clinton, like President George Bush before him, supported President Yeltsin as the only port in the storm. Even before the disastrous war in Chechnya, or the political challenges posed by the somewhat revitalized communist party in the 1996 presidential election, observers were uneasily aware of the limitations of reliance on Yeltsin. The way to the "common European home" of which Gorbachev spoke poignantly during his period in power would be long and winding.

ABBOTT GLEASON

See also Alaska Purchase; Alexander I, Czar; Angola; Berlin; Bohlen, Charles Eustis; Brezhnev, Leonid Ilyich; China; Cold War; Containment; Cuba; Czech Republic; Détente; Eastern Europe; Gorbachev, Mikhail Sergeevich; Helsinki Accords; Hungary; Kennan, George Frost; Khrushchev, Nikita Sergeyevich; Lenin, Vladimir Ilyich; Monroe Doctrine; North Atlantic Treaty Organization; Russo-Japanese War; Stalin, Joseph; Truman Doctrine; Vietnam War; Warsaw Pact; World War I; World War II; Yeltsin, Boris Nikolayevich

FURTHER READING

Bialer, Seweryn, and Michael Mandelbaum. *Gorbachev's Russia and American Foreign Policy.* Boulder, Colo., 1987.

Dallek, Robert. *The American Style of Foreign Policy.* New York, 1983.

Daniels, Robert V. *Russia. The Roots of Confrontation.* Cambridge, 1985.

Gaddis, John Lewis. *Russia, the Soviet Union and the United States: An Interpretive History.* New York, 1990.

———. *The United States and the Origins of the Cold War 1941–1947.* New York, 1972.

Garrison, Mark, and Abbott Gleason. *Shared Destiny. Fifty Years of Soviet-American Relations.* Boston, 1985.

Garthoff, Raymond. *Détente and Confrontation. American-Soviet Relations from Nixon to Reagan.* Washington, D.C., 1985.

Gorbachev, Mikhail. *Memoirs.* New York, 1996.

Kennan, George F. *Russia and the West Under Lenin and Stalin.* Boston, 1962.

———. *Russia Leaves the War.* Princeton, N.J., 1958.

———. *The Decision to Intervene.* Princeton, N.J., 1958.

LaFeber, Walter. *America, Russia and the Cold War 1945–1990.* New York, 1991.

Paterson, Thomas G., and Robert J. McMahon, eds. *The Origins of the Cold War*. Lexington, Mass., 1991.

Rogger, Hans. *Jewish Policies and Right-Wing Politics in Imperial Russia*. Berkeley/Los Angeles, Calif., 1986.

Ryavec, Karl W. *United States–Soviet Relations*. London, 1989.

Saul, Norman. *Distant Friends*. Lawrence, Kans., 1991.

Simons, Thomas. *The Cold War Is Over?* New York, 1990.

Ulam, Adam B. *Dangerous Relations. The Soviet Union in World Politics, 1970–1982*. New York, 1983.

———. *Expansion and Coexistence. Soviet Foreign Policy 1917–1973*. New York/Washington, D.C., 1975.

RUSSO-JAPANESE WAR

(1904–1905)

A conflict arising from incompatible national ambitions in East Asia. On 8 February 1904, Japan launched a surprise attack on Port Arthur, just south of Dalian near the tip of the Liaodong Peninsula in northeast China. Port Arthur had been the home of Russia's Far Eastern fleet ever since Russia had leased both the port and the peninsula from China in 1898. The Japanese resented those very concessions, which Russia, France, and Germany had denied Japan after the Sino-Japanese War of 1894–1895. Russia's refusal to evacuate Manchuria, which it had occupied during the Boxer Rebellion of 1900, led to the diplomatic breakdown preceding the war.

The attack on Port Arthur was the first in a chain of embarrassing reverses for Czar Nicholas II's military forces. The Japanese navy destroyed the Far Eastern fleet in July 1904, and Port Arthur fell the following January. Russian reverses in Manchuria climaxed in defeat at the massive battle of Mukden in February 1905. Russia ultimately pinned its hopes for victory on the Baltic fleet, which traveled for seven months to reach the Pacific. Along the way the fleet created an international incident by mistakenly firing on British trawlers in the North Sea. The fleet's arduous voyage ended in quick destruction when it encountered Admiral Heihachiro Tōgō's ships at Tsushima Strait in May. With his military setbacks compounded by growing internal upheavals, the czar reluctantly agreed to peace talks proposed by President Theodore Roosevelt.

The United States had initially favored the Japanese in the war but their surprising string of victories threatened to tip the Asian balance of power too far in Tokyo's favor. Roosevelt hoped that a timely peace would preserve the balance and forestall any outcome that could jeopardize Chinese neutrality or territorial integrity. By the time the negotiators convened in August 1905 at Portsmouth, New Hampshire, Japanese forces had taken their first Russian territory, Sakhalin Island. Roosevelt did not attend the negotiations, but he influenced the outcome at crucial points through observers at Portsmouth and U.S. diplomats abroad. The Treaty of Portsmouth ended the Russo-Japanese War in September. Its terms favored Japan, but Russia escaped without having to pay the indemnity its rival originally demanded. Although popular opinion in Russia and Japan blamed Roosevelt for a treaty satisfactory to neither, in the United States and Europe the president was hailed as a statesman of the first order. He won the Nobel Peace Prize in 1906 for helping to bring the war to an end and for his role in the Algeciras Conference, which defused a Franco-German dispute over Morocco.

PAUL R. GRASS

See also Japan; Portsmouth, Treaty of; Roosevelt, Theodore; Russia and the Soviet Union

FURTHER READING

Gould, Lewis L. *The Presidency of Theodore Roosevelt*. Lawrence, Kans., 1991.

Walder, David. *The Short Victorious War: The Russo-Japanese Conflict, 1904–1905*. New York, 1973.

Westwood, J.N. *Russia Against Japan, 1904–1905: A New Look at the Russo-Japanese War*. London, 1986.

RWANDA

A Central African republic bordered by Zaire, Uganda, Tanzania, and Burundi, which achieved its independence on 1 July 1962 and since been rocked by ethnic conflict between Hutus and Tutsis. A German colony in the late nineteenth century (as part of German East Africa), Rwanda became a League of Nations mandate administered by Belgium following World War I (as part of Runada-Urundi), and a trust territory of the United Nations governed by Belgium after World War II. Since independence, U.S. relations with Rwanda have been friendly, consisting primarily of developmental and humanitarian aid to this very poor country through Agency of International Development (AID) programs and the Development Fund for Africa. The death of Rwanda's Hutu president, Juvenal Habyarimana, whose plane was shot down on 7 April 1994, ignited a vicious civil war.

Since the year 1500 the majority Hutu population in Rwanda had been ruled by minority Tutsis. First the Germans, and later the Belgians, maintained this hierarchy during indirect colonial rule. In 1959 the Hutu overthrew the Tutsi monarchy under the guidance of the Party of the Hutu Emancipation Movement (PARMEHUTU), leading more than 160,000 Tutsis to flee to neighboring countries. Inefficiency and corruption within PARMEHUTU, which won the first election in 1962, led to a military coup on 5 July 1963 under the leadership of Major General Juvenal Habyarimana. A new constitution was overwhelmingly approved in 1978, as was Habyarimana's presidency.

In October 1990, however, the Ugandan-based, Tutsi-led Rwandan Patriotic Front (RPF) launched an attack on Rwandan government forces. RPF's early success, and pressure from the outside world, forced Habyarimana to permit the emergence of opposition parties and to share power with Tutsis in an agreement signed 4 August 1993 at Arusha, Tanzania, temporarily ending the civil war. By the Arusha Peace Accord, a prime minister was to share power with the president, five Tutsis were to become cabinet ministers, and the Rwandan National Army was to be composed of forty percent Tutsis. To ensure these agreements the United Nations Assistance Mission for Rwanda (UNAMIR) was established.

Peace crashed along with Habyarimana's plane in April 1994. Habyarimana's death (President Cyprien Ntaryamira of Burundi also died in the crash) set off Hutu death squads and the militia which proceeded to slaughter Tutsis, as well as opposition Hutus, including Prime Minister Agathe Uwilingiyimana. Between 200,000 and 500,000 Tutsis were massacred in what the international community has termed a genocide. Hundreds of thousands of Rwandans fled the country as well, packing into refugee camps in both Zaire and Tanzania, where starvation and disease also took their toll. At the height of the crisis, the United States deployed some 275 marines in neighboring Burundi in readiness to assist the evacuation of approximately 240 U.S. citizens from Rwanda. Both France and Belgium sent in troops as well to protect their nationals. The United Nations responded by sending 5,500 troops in an attempt to protect fleeing Tutsis and opposition Hutus. Between April and October 1994, the United States provided about $200 million in aid. Most of this aid was used to support the estimated 2.6 million refugees and displaced persons from Rwanda in Tanzania, Zaire, Burundi, and Uganda. The United States also took an active role in promoting reconciliation in Rwanda through the Organization of African Unity. Nevertheless, there was extensive and often passionate criticism of the failure of the United States, the United Nations, and others in the international community to take earlier and more decisive action.

The year 1995 witnessed the creation of a coalition government of Tutsis and Hutus in Rwanda which hoped to end the killing, return the refugees, and put on trial those responsible for the genocide. The desire to punish former Hutu leaders and the militia, the *Interahmwe*, which aided in the killing, led to their fleeing to Zaire where they established military bases in preparation to renewing the war. According to Human Rights Watch, China, France, South Africa, and Zaire, have all violated the arms embargo against the Hutus. None of those responsible for the genocide have so far been brought before the International Tribunal on Rwanda. As of March 1996, peace was nowhere near in sight for Rwanda or the millions of refugees still scattered throughout southern and central Africa.

CHRISTOPHER M. PAULIN

See also Africa; Humanitarian Intervention and Relief; Mandates and Trusteeships; Refugees

FURTHER READING

Destexhe, Alain. "The Third Genocide." *Foreign Policy*, 97, (Winter 1994–1995): 3–17.

Echevarria, Vito. "Arms Trade Sparked Refugee Crisis." *New African*, 344, (October 1995): 24–25.

Legum, Colin. "Looming Tragedy." *New African*, 327, (February 1995): 31.

"Refugee Nightmare in Rwanda: The Beginning." *Foreign Policy Bulletin*, vol. 5, 1 (July/August 1994): 34–37.

"Rwanda: Background Notes." *United States Department of State*, February 1989.

Versi, Anver. "Rwanda's Killing Field." *New African*, 320 (June 1994): 11–13.

S

SADAT, ANWAR EL-

(*b.* 25 December 1918; *d.* 6 October 1981)

President of Egypt from 1970 to 1981. Sadat's relationship with the United States evolved from antagonism to strategic partnership, and in the end he advanced the Middle East peace process in cooperation with the United States.

A member of the Free Officers Society that took power in Cairo in 1952, Sadat served dutifully in a variety of posts under Gamal Abdel Nasser. Having been appointed vice president in 1969, Sadat claimed executive authority immediately after Nasser's sudden death in September 1970. Although many Egyptians doubted that Nasser had wanted him as successor, Sadat consolidated his power by claiming a 90 percent majority in a plebiscite held on 15 October 1970 and by crushing a hostile conspiracy of militants in his government in May 1971.

Egypt's ongoing conflict with Israel generated much tension in Sadat's early relationship with the United States. As vice president in 1970, Sadat had opposed Secretary of State William P. Rogers's plan to arrange a cease-fire of the Egyptian-Israeli "war of attrition" along the Suez Canal. In 1971–1972, President Sadat repeatedly threatened to revoke the cease-fire that Nasser had accepted and, using Soviet-supplied weapons, to resume war against Israeli forces occupying the Sinai. Sadat hoped to frighten the Richard M. Nixon administration into pressuring Israel to leave the Sinai.

To Sadat's chagrin, Nixon delivered the military planes that President Lyndon B. Johnson had promised Israel. The U.S. Navy's acquisition of base rights in Greece in 1972 also concerned Sadat. He refused to pledge to seek peace with Israel or negotiate directly with Israel. Israel first had to withdraw from the Sinai, Sadat insisted. He openly relished the prospect that Arab oil-exporting states might inflate the price of oil sold to Western countries.

Sadat and U.S. leaders eventually realized a convoluted rapprochement. It originated in Sadat's decision in July 1972 to expel the 20,000 Soviet military advisers stationed in Egypt because of policy differences and cultural tensions between the advisers and the Egyptian people. U.S. officials were delighted by this development and yet puzzled that Sadat failed first to demand a concession from Washington, such as pressure on Israel to evacuate the Sinai.

Sadat continued to threaten to attack Israeli forces in late 1972 and 1973. Western officials such as Secretary of State Henry Kissinger concluded that the departure of Soviet advisers diminished the chance of an Egyptian attack. Kissinger disparaged Sadat's leadership abilities, calculating that the Israelis would decisively win any battle Sadat provoked, and therefore dismissed Sadat's pronouncements as overzealous rhetoric.

Free from Soviet restraints and mindful of Western indifference, however, Sadat launched a surprise offensive across the Suez Canal on 6 October 1973. Completely surprised by this attack and by a coordinated Syrian foray into Golan, U.S. officials delivered emergency shipments of weapons to Israel to enable it to counterattack (and perhaps to deter Israel from using its nuclear weapons). After Israeli troops crossed the Suez Canal on 16 October and threatened to encircle the Egyptian Third Army, Kissinger actively sought a stalemate to end the war. He denied Sadat's wish for a United Nations cease-fire resolution until Israeli forces had sufficiently neutralized Egypt's military advance. After the United Nations passed the cease-fire resolution on 22 October, Kissinger visited Cairo to convince Sadat to accept it. When Israel briefly violated the cease-fire by resuming operations in Egypt, Sadat protested directly to President Nixon. Kissinger pressured Israel on 27 October to allow Egyptian relief convoys to reach the besieged Third Army.

Sadat had reasons to detest U.S. policy during the Arab-Israeli war. The emergency arms deliveries enabled Israeli troops to breach the canal, and rumors circulated in Cairo that U.S. soldiers even crewed Israeli tanks. Sadat concluded, however, that the arms shipments both reflected Washington's immense power and provided it with leverage over Israel. Thus he welcomed U.S. help in the search for a stable resolution of the conflict with Israel. The Egyptian leader suspended his emotive anti-American, anti-Israeli rhetoric and encouraged his people to accept the existence of Israel.

After the 1973 war Kissinger sought a permanent settlement of the Arab-Israeli conflict. Sadat's unexpected success at crossing the canal earned Kissinger's admiration. In early November he persuaded Sadat to pursue complete disengagement rather than simple removal of Israeli forces and proposed to him a compromise peace involving mutual recognition and Israeli withdrawal from the Sinai. Personal contact produced friendship between the two statesmen. Sadat called Kissinger his friend and brother and declared him the first U.S. official to treat Arab states fairly.

Through Kissinger's diplomatic efforts, Sadat and Israeli officials eventually agreed to major disengagement accords in 1974 and 1975. Sadat expressed his gratitude toward Washington in various ways. He lobbied oil-exporting states to rescind their embargo against the United States and lavishly welcomed Nixon to Egypt in June 1974, when the besieged U.S. president sought to revive his flagging domestic political position by demonstrating his continuing prestige overseas. In 1974, Sadat reopened diplomatic relations with Washington. He met President Gerald R. Ford in June 1975, declaring him a friend. Within days Sadat reopened the Suez Canal as a gesture of amity toward Washington and invited U.S. Navy ships to join the inaugural convoy. Finally, Sadat secretly assured Kissinger that Egypt would not attack Israel even if Syria did.

President Jimmy Carter also embraced Sadat as an agent for peace in the Middle East. In early 1977, Carter appealed to the Egyptian leader to attend a multilateral conference in Geneva to discuss Middle East peace. Carter encouraged the direct Egyptian-Israeli peace negotiations that followed Sadat's stunning November 1977 visit to Jerusalem. When those talks deadlocked, the U.S. president emerged as arbitrator, hosting a summit at Camp David in September 1978 and clinching the March 1979 peace treaty with visits to Cairo and Jerusalem and a signing ceremony in Washington.

Carter rewarded Sadat for his peacemaking role with $1.5 billion in military aid and a pledge of $3.5 billion over four years. After the Iranian Revolution and Soviet invasion of Afghanistan of 1979, Carter viewed Sadat as an ally in the Middle East. Vilified by radical Arab regimes for making peace, Sadat saw the United States as a protector. In December 1979 he offered the Pentagon military base facilities and hinted at his readiness to cooperate in regional defense plans. In 1980, U.S. and Egyptian forces conducted joint maneuvers, U.S. soldiers used Egyptian staging areas for the military rescue mission into Iran, and U.S. surveillance aircraft gained base privileges in Egypt. President Ronald Reagan found Sadat receptive to his anti-Soviet "strategic consensus" strategy, and Sadat guaranteed the U.S. Rapid Deployment Force access to the Ras Banas military base.

Partnership with the United States did not save Sadat from problems such as isolation in the Arab community and economic, political, demographic, and cultural turmoil at home. On 6 October 1981 an Islamic fundamentalist army officer assassinated Sadat as the Egyptian president reviewed a military parade.

PETER L. HAHN

See also Egypt; Israel; Kissinger, Henry Alfred; Middle East; Nasser, Gamal Abdel

FURTHER READING

Hirst, David, and Irene Beeson *Sadat*. London, 1981.
Israeli, Raphael. *Man of Defiance: A Political Biography of Anwar Sadat*. London, 1985.
Lippman, Thomas W. *Egypt after Nasser: Sadat, Peace, and the Mirage of Prosperity*. New York, 1989.

SAINT KITTS AND NEVIS

See Appendix 2

SAINT LAWRENCE SEAWAY

A series of locks and other engineering improvements that allow deep draft ocean-going ships to sail between the Great Lakes and the Atlantic Ocean via the Saint Lawrence River. Opened in 1959, the Seaway superseded a system of small canals going back to the nineteenth century. Although popularly considered a monument to the goodwill between the United States and Canada, the seaway is also an example of the ability of competing economic interests to derail Canadian-U.S. cooperation. After the U.S. Senate defeated the Saint Lawrence Deep Waterway Treaty of 1932, the two sides spent twenty years blaming each other and threatening to build their own waterways. Finally, in August 1954, after the decline of domestic opposition in the United States from power and transportation interests, Ottawa and Washington exchanged diplomatic notes agreeing to joint building of the seaway roughly along the terms of the 1932 accord. The construction of locks, canals, and power plants took four years and cost more than one billion dollars. The result was the creation of North America's "fourth seacoast," major savings in shipping bulk products such as wheat, and some environmental damage, such as the introduction of the zebra mussel to inland waters. Like the Panama Canal, the Saint Lawrence Seaway can no longer accommodate the largest ocean-going ships, but it is still an extremely important artery of international commerce for the middle of the continent.

KURK DORSEY

See also Canada; Shipping Companies

FURTHER READING

Sussman, Gennifer. *The Saint Lawrence Seaway: History and Analysis of a Joint Water Highway*. Washington, D.C., 1978.
Willoughby, William R., *The Saint Lawrence Waterway: A Study in Politics and Diplomacy*. Madison, Wis., 1961.

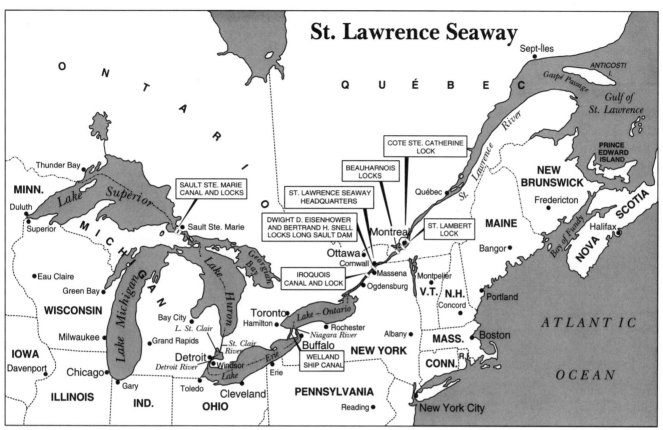

St. Lawrence Seaway

From "St. Lawrence Seaway," C. Celcil Lingard, In *Merit Students Encyclopedia*, Volume 16. ©1991 by Macmillan Educational Company. Reprinted with permission of the publisher.

SAINT LUCIA

See Appendix 2

SAINT PIERRE–MIQUELON AFFAIR

A crisis growing from the December 1941 occupation by forces loyal to Free French leader General Charles de Gaulle of a tiny archipelago, including the islands of Saint Pierre and Miquelon, located off the southern coast of Newfoundland. These strategically important islands had been under French sovereignty since the sixteenth century, but their takeover against the advice of British and Canadian authorities and the violent objections of U.S. Secretary of State Cordell Hull to any challenge to the United States's recognition of Vichy France caused the "Saint Pierre–Miquelon Affair" to become a major incident in wartime Franco-American relations during World War II.

This diplomatic tempest resulted from the Free French desire to gain recognition as the legitimate government of France and the antagonism of Franklin D. Roosevelt's administration toward de Gaulle's movement. When the United States sought to prevent Admiral Emile Muselier from enlisting Saint Pierre and Miquelon in the Free French cause, de Gaulle ordered the armed seizure of the islands. An infuriated Hull demanded that the "so-called Free French" be brought to heel, but President Roosevelt took no action and the islands remained under Free French control. Saint Pierre and Miquelon called into question the continued recognition of Vichy France and set the stage for the problems that were to be encountered during Operation TORCH, the invasion of French North Africa in November 1942. The affair also contributed to Roosevelt's loss of confidence in the political acumen of his secretary of state.

THEODORE A. WILSON

See also de Gaulle, Charles André Joseph Marie; France; Hull, Cordell; Roosevelt, Franklin Delano; World War II

FURTHER READING

Anglin, Douglas S. *The St. Pierre and Miquelon Affair*. Toronto, 1966.
Costigliola, Frank. *France and the United States: The Cold Alliance Since World War II*. New York, 1992.

SAINT VINCENT AND THE GRENADINES

See Appendix 2

SAKHAROV, ANDREI

(*b.* 1921; *d.* 1989)

Soviet physicist who developed the Soviet hydrogen bomb and who later became a human-rights and arms-control activist and Nobel Peace Prize laureate, known for his courageous opposition to the Soviet regime.

Following his work on the hydrogen bomb, in 1955 Sakharov began to oppose nuclear testing. After the Soviet 60-megaton test of 1961, which he deplored, he persuaded Soviet premier Nikita Khrushchev to agree to the Limited Nuclear Test Ban Treaty of 1963. Sakharov's 1968 essay, "Progress, Peaceful Coexistence, and Intellectual Freedom," called for nuclear disarmament, U.S.-Soviet cooperation, and freedom of expression within the Soviet Union. After its publication, Soviet authorities removed him from security-classified work, whereupon he became more active and vocal in defense of human rights and disarmament. Sakharov was awarded the Nobel Peace Prize in 1975 but the Kremlin denied him permission to go to Stockholm to accept it and the KGB, the Soviet state security organization, subjected him to repeated interrogations. In 1977 President Jimmy Carter attempted to intervene on Sakharov's behalf but Soviet leader Leonid Brezhnev criticized Carter for violating Soviet sovereignty. In 1980, following Sakharov's public opposition to the Soviet invasion of Afghanistan, Brezhnev confined him to house arrest in the city of Gorky, where he continued to campaign for human rights. In 1986, a year after to coming to power, Mikhail Gorbachev freed Sakharov, who spent the last three years of his life in the Congress of Peoples Deputies, challenging Gorbachev on disarmament, human rights, and democracy. In the United States and elsewhere, those who believed in effective arms control were encouraged by Sakharov's outspoken bravery.

DAVID W. MCFADDEN

See also Human Rights; Limited Nuclear Test Ban Treaty; Nobel Peace Prize; Nuclear Weapons and Strategy; Russia and the Soviet Union

FURTHER READING

Drell, Sidney D. and Sergei P. Kapitza, eds. *Sakharov Remembered.* New York, 1991.

Sakharov, Andrei. *Memoirs.* Translated by Richard Lourie. New York, 1990.

Sakharov, Andrei. *Moscow and Beyond, 1986 to 1989.* Translated by Antonia Bouis. New York, 1991.

SALISBURY, THIRD MARQUESS OF
Robert Arthur Talbot Gascoyne-Cecil

(*b.* 3 February 1830; *d.* 22 August 1903)

Conservative British prime minister and foreign secretary. He served four times as prime minister between 1885 and 1902, and four times as foreign secretary between 1878 and 1900. A man of wealth and aristocratic lineage, educated at Eton and Oxford, Lord Salisbury opposed radical ideas and was skeptical of democratic institutions. He served as secretary of state for India from 1866 to 1867, resigning in a dispute with the Conservative government's advocacy of parliamentary reform. Although initially distrustful of Conservative leader Benjamin Disraeli, Salisbury eventually became an admirer. Disraeli appointed him foreign secretary in 1878 at the height of a crisis with Russia over the Balkans and the future control of Constantinople. Salisbury's diplomacy brought Russia to the conference table at the Congress of Berlin in mid-June 1878. After Disraeli's death in 1881, Salisbury assumed leadership of the Conservative opposition in the House of Lords and clashed with William Gladstone by opposing home rule for Ireland and advocating an expanded British Empire.

Salisbury's tenures as prime minister often combined the offices of prime minister and foreign secretary. Salisbury managed his governments by granting wide discretion to his ministers and operating a "studiously unobtrusive" Foreign Office. His foreign policies, aimed towards the defense and enlargement of the empire, were pragmatic and cautious. He avoided serious conflicts with the European powers despite continuous imperialistic rivalries. While he sought without success to win the cooperation of the Continental powers in promoting intervention against Turkey to halt the massacre of Armenians, Salisbury generally opposed alliance commitments, believing them dangerous. Although he saw his principles partially abandoned when his government concluded an alliance with Japan in 1902, Salisbury did not back efforts to conclude an alliance with Germany. The partition of Africa occupied much of Salisbury's attention and created serious Anglo-French discord until 1898 when the French accepted Great Britain's dominance on the Nile following the Fashoda Crisis. A traditional imperialist who believed British rule necessary for the advancement of "backward" races, Salisbury imposed rule by force in colonial territories. His governments annexed Burma, strengthened the British hold on the Upper Nile and Zanzibar in Africa, and reconquered the Sudan in 1896.

Salisbury viewed the United States as an emerging economic power, but one with little interest in or capacity for foreign involvements outside the Western Hemisphere. His manner in dealing with U.S. policymakers was condescending but cordial. When President Grover

Cleveland insisted on the immediate recall of Sir Lionel Sackville-West, the British minister to Washington, for a minor indiscretion during the presidential election campaign of 1888, Salisbury signaled his displeasure by refusing to appoint a new minister until Cleveland had left office. In 1890, Salisbury dismissed the claim of Secretary of State James G. Blaine that the Bering Sea was solely under the jurisdiction of the United States and therefore off-limits to Canadian vessels engaged in the pelagic seal fur trade. In 1895, Salisbury calmly waited for four months before responding to Secretary of State Richard Olney's belligerent memorandum asserting that, under the Monroe Doctrine, the British boundary dispute with Venezuela had to be submitted to arbitration. Salisbury's slow response, while his government was preoccupied with the Boers in southern Africa and with Kaiser Wilhelm II in Germany, allowed both sides time for a diplomatic solution. He also supported the Open Door Policy the United States advocated for China. Hampered by various afflictions of old age, Salisbury retired in 1902 after leading his government through the conclusion of the Boer War.

MICHAEL J. DEVINE

See also Africa; Great Britain; Open Door Policy; Sealing; Venezuelan Boundary Dispute

FURTHER READING

Blake, Lord Robert and Hugh Cecil, eds. *Salisbury: The Man and His Policies.* New York, 1987.
Cecil, Lady Gwendolen. *Life of Robert, Marquis of Salisbury,* 4 vols. London, 1921–1932.
Grenville, John A.S. *Lord Salisbury and Foreign Policy: The Close of the Nineteenth Century.* London, 1964.

SALT I AND SALT II

See Strategic Arms Limitation Talks and Agreements

SAMOA

See also Appendix 2

SAMOA, AMERICAN

Five strategically located volcanic islands and two coral atolls in the South Pacific Ocean administered by the U.S. Department of the Interior as an unincorporated territory of the United States. Once an area of intense international rivalry, American Samoa is located some 4,000 miles from San Francisco, about halfway between Hawaii and New Zealand. The capital of Pago Pago, on the largest island of Tutuila, possesses one of the best land-protected, deep-water harbors in the Pacific.

In the early-nineteenth century American whalers and traders plying the waters between California and Australia visited Samoa, and in 1839, during his extensive exploration of the Pacific, Lieutenant Charles Wilkes of the U.S. Navy surveyed the rugged islands. Private U.S. investors gradually expanded their interests in the area. In 1872, U.S. Commander Richard W. Meade and Samoan chiefs signed an agreement that granted the United States the exclusive right to a coaling station at Pago Pago. Six years later, after the end of the divisive Reconstruction era at home and while Great Britain and Germany actively cultivated ties with native Samoan leaders, the U.S. Senate unanimously approved a new but similar treaty. Soon the U.S. Navy deposited hundreds of tons of coal at Pago Pago.

In the 1880s, as the United States was building its steel-hulled New Navy and Pacific commercial steamship lines were expanding, the U.S Department of State warned Great Britain and Germany away from Samoa, arguing that the islands lay along a great commercial route vital to the economic well-being of the United States. The German Foreign Office protested that Washington was treating the Pacific Ocean "as an American lake." In 1889 the foreign scramble for Samoa intensified. International intrigue aggravated factionalism among Samoa's chiefs, and Chancellor Otto von Bismarck insisted on solidifying German interests there. U.S. and German warships menacingly faced each other. Congress appropriated funds to defend U.S. interests militarily, but when a hurricane destroyed the warships, diplomacy gained ascendancy. In the pact of June 1889, Great Britain, Germany, and the United States devised a three-way protectorate that limited Samoa's independence.

Ten years later, after the Spanish-American-Cuban-Filipino War and the U.S. annexation of the Philippines, a new agreement partitioned Samoa. In the December 1899 treaty Germany received the islands of what is today called Western Samoa (seized by New Zealand in 1914 but granted independence in 1962) and the United States received Tutuila, with its coveted harbor of Pago Pago, and adjacent islands. As compensation for renouncing its claims to Samoa, Great Britain obtained the Gilbert Islands and Solomon Islands.

During World War II, Japan threatened but never attacked Samoa. The U.S. Navy administered American Samoa until 1951, when the Department of Interior took over. American Samoa's population of some 55,000 (1995) is primarily Polynesian and its dollar economy relies on exports of canned tuna to the United States. American Samoa receives U.S. foreign aid and sends a nonvoting delegate to the U.S. House of Representatives. More than 85,000 Samoans reside in the United States.

THOMAS G. PATERSON

See also Germany; Great Britain; Pacific Island Nations and U.S. Territories; Shipping Companies; Wilkes, Charles

FURTHER READING

Campbell, Charles S. *The Transformation of American Foreign Relations, 1865–1900*. New York, 1976.
Gray, J. A. C. *Amerika Samoa: A History of American Samoa and its United States Naval Administration*. Annapolis, Md., 1960.
Kennedy, Paul M. *The Samoan Tangle: A Study in Anglo-German Relations*. New York, 1974
Ryden, George H. *The Foreign Policy of the United States in Relation to Samoa*. New Haven, Conn., 1933.

SANCTIONS

See Economic Sanctions

SANDINO, AUGUSTO CÉSAR
(*b.* 1895; *d.* 23 February, 1934)

Leader of anti-U.S. forces in Nicaragua in the early twentieth century. The illegitimate son of a wealthy landowner and his Indian servant, Augusto Sandino worked as a day laborer in several multinational corporations before becoming the leader of a rebel army and Nicaragua's most enduring national hero. An opponent of the U.S. occupation of 1912–1925 and 1926–1933 and the conservative Nicaraguan politicians supported by the U.S. Marines, Sandino alone among all the leaders of rebel armies boldly refused to lay down his arms in the peace brokered by the United States in 1926. During the occupation of 1926–1933, the United States launched a punitive expedition against Sandino's army of "bandits," but failed to capture the popular leader. Assassinated by Anastasio Somoza's National Guard in 1934, Sandino's name and spirit lived on in the Sandinista National Liberation Front, which overthrew the dictatorship of the Somoza dynasty in 1979 and governed Nicaragua until 1990.

LeeAnna Y. Keith

See also Nicaragua

FURTHER READING

Macauley, Neill. *The Sandino Affair.* Chicago, 1967.
Selser, Gregorio. *Sandino.* London, 1981.

SANE

See Peace Movements and Societies, 1914 to Present

SANFORD, HENRY SHELTON
(*b.* 23 June 1823; *d.* 21 May 1891)

U.S. diplomat and business entrepreneur who sought to stimulate U.S. interest in Africa. Born in Woodbury, Connecticut, Sanford travelled extensively in Europe, held temporary posts as attaché to the U.S. minister to Russia (1847) and acting secretary of the U.S. legation in Berlin (1848), and earned a Doctor of Laws degree from the University of Heidelberg in 1849. Bright, ambitious, egotistical, and fluent in several languages, he served as secretary of the U.S. Legation in Paris (1849–1853) and chargé d'affaires on an intern basis for eight months (1853–1854). Sanford's duties in Paris were routine and his tenure uneventful. However, he lived extravagantly and enjoyed Parisian society to the fullest. In 1854 Secretary of State William L. Marcy issued a circular urging, but not requiring, U.S. representatives abroad to dress in a manner reflecting republicanism and simplicity, rather than the traditional ornate diplomatic uniform common in European courts. Sanford responded enthusiastically, donning a black suit at all formal occasions. This put Sanford at odds with John Y. Mason, the Democrat appointed to serve as minister to Paris. While Sanford, a Whig, would have been replaced anyway, he used the disagreement over proper attire to resign in protest and cause a stir in diplomatic circles. As U.S. minister to Belgium (1861–1869) Sanford gained notoriety during the American Civil War for his work in establishing a network of spies throughout Europe to report on and disrupt Confederate diplomatic initiatives and arms purchases. In 1861 he carried an offer of a command in the Union army to the Italian revolutionary leader, Giuseppe Garibaldi. The ill-conceived negotiations failed when the Italian hero demanded supreme command of the Union forces and a declaration that emancipation of slaves would result from a Union victory. Meanwhile, Sanford coordinated pro-Union propaganda efforts in Europe, assisted in arms purchases, and maintained an extensive correspondence with Secretary of State William H. Seward, who had great confidence in Sanford's bold and unorthodox methods, which included hiring private detectives in various foreign capitals. Sanford's energetic activities and his lack of concern for his colleagues' sensibilities earned him the scorn of fellow diplomats, who referred to him as a "Legation on Wheels" and considered him overzealous and vain. After failing to secure an appointment as minister to Spain in 1869, Sanford left the diplomatic service, although he continued unsuccessfully to seek ministerial appointments for the next twenty years. Looking for business opportunities in the southern United States, Sanford became an early developer of the citrus industry.

In 1877, Sanford's efforts to win appointment as minister to Belgium failed when his reputation was tarnished by unproven accusations that he had illegally profited from his diplomatic post during the Civil War. That same year, however, King Leopold of Belgium, seeking to advance his nation's interests in the Congo, secured Sanford's services. Sanford served as a U.S. delegate to Leopold's 1877 Brussels Conference, ostensibly organized to promote scientific exploration, repress the slave trade, and assist philanthropic endeavors. Sanford reported that the conference had initiated a "great work of civilization and humanity." On Leopold's behalf Sanford lobbied the U.S. government to recognize the Association Internationale Africaine, the Belgian leader's mechanism for advancing his imperialist designs in central Africa. In 1884–1885, Sanford attended the Berlin West African Conference as an adviser to the U.S. minister to Germany; he was, in the words of explorer Henry Morton Stanley, "most valuable" in winning U.S. recognition of Leopold's Congo Free State. Hoping to realize fabulous profits in the Congo, Sanford organized the Sanford Exploring Expedition in 1886, but this commercial venture failed when the support promised by King Leopold never materialized. By now completely disillusioned with King Leopold, Sanford played a minor role as an "Additional Delegate" from the United States to the Brussels Antislavery Conference of 1889–1990.

MICHAEL J. DEVINE

See also Africa; American Civil War; Belgium; Seward, William Henry; Zaire

FURTHER READING
Fry, Joseph A. *Henry S. Sanford: Diplomacy and Business in Nineteenth-Century America*. 1982.
Roark, James L. "American Expansionism vs. European Imperialism: Henry Sanford and the Congo Episode, 1883–1885." *Mid-America* 60 (1978): 21–33.

SAN FRANCISCO CONFERENCE
See United Nations

SAN LORENZO EL REAL, TREATY OF
See Pinckney's Treaty

SAN MARINO
See Appendix 2

SÃO TOMÉ AND PRINCIPE
See Appendix 2

SAUDI ARABIA

Kingdom occupying most of the Arabian peninsula, bordered by Jordan, Iraq, Kuwait, the Persian Gulf, Qatar, Oman, Yemen, and the Red Sea. It is an absolute monarchy and the largest country as well as the largest oil producer in the Middle East. Saudi Arabia long has represented a cornerstone of U.S. foreign policy interests in the region. The recorded history of what is now Saudi Arabia goes back many centuries, but its "modern" period may be said to have begun in the sixteenth century, when much of the Arabian peninsula was conquered and made part of the Ottoman empire, although local Arabian chieftains, in particular those belonging to the Saud family, maintained their rule over inland areas. The British established their presence as well on the peninsula in the nineteenth century with protectorates along the southern and eastern coastal areas. Culminating almost thirty years of struggle led by Abd al-Aziz ibn Saud, the unified Kingdom of Saudi Arabia was established in 1932.

Oil and Cold War, 1930s–1980s
While official diplomatic relations with the United States were not established until 1939, it was in 1933 that the first U.S. oil company, Standard Oil of California, was granted rights to explore for and produce oil. The first major oil discovery was made in 1938, although full-scale production would not start until after World War II. A number of other U.S. oil companies also had been granted concessions, and in 1944 they joined together with the Saudi government to form the Arabian-American Oil Company (Aramco). In 1943, in the midst of World War II and at the urging of U.S. petroleum companies doing business in the Persian Gulf region, President Franklin D. Roosevelt declared Saudi Arabia to be a vital interest of the United States. Subsequent to that declaration, the United States sent a military mission to Saudi Arabia which provided training for Saudi forces and assisted in the construction of military facilities within the kingdom. In 1945, King Ibn Saud and President Roosevelt met on a U.S. warship in the Suez Canal to further strengthen the relationship. Concerns regarding the spread of Soviet influence in the region following World War II inspired the expansion of U.S.-Saudi relations during the Cold War period. In an effort to contain Soviet influence in the Middle East, President Harry S. Truman gave Ibn Saud assurances that the United States would protect the territorial integrity and political independence of Saudi Arabia. In 1951, this relationship was cemented with a

mutual defense pact, which stated that the United States would provide military equipment and training to the Saudis, while Saudi Arabia allowed the establishment of a permanent U.S. military mission within its borders. Initially, U.S. aid to Saudi Arabia was on a grant basis. From 1946 to 1962 the U.S. military used the air base at Dhahran, and in 1963 President John F. Kennedy dispatched a squadron of fighters to Saudi Arabia in order to ward off air assaults from Egyptian forces that were involved in the civil war in neighboring Yemen. The Egyptians, who were backing Yemeni republicans, launched the air raids on Saudi territory in an effort to make the Saudis cease their support of Yemeni loyalists.

The U.S.-Saudi relationship remained strong over the next several decades despite difficulties stemming from U.S. support of Israel. The establishment of the state of Israel in 1948 was met with opposition in Riyadh, and the Saudi government refused to officially recognize Israel or engage in relations with it in any way. There also was some anti-Western sentiment within Saudi Arabia, as with the criticism by opponents of the monarchy (under King Saud, following Ibn Saud's death) of the Dhahran air base as a concession to Western domination of the region, causing the United States to terminate some economic aid in 1954. Saudi relations with the United States improved after the United States condemned the Israeli, British, and French attack on Egypt in the Suez crisis of 1956. In 1957 President Dwight D. Eisenhower declared that the United States would extend economic and military assistance, including troops if necessary, to any Middle Eastern state requiring protection against communist threats. This became known as the Eisenhower Doctrine. After initially signing a solidarity agreement with Egyptian president Gamal Abdel Nasser in 1957 (the Cairo Solidarity Agreement), King Saud agreed to renew the lease for the U.S. air base, supported the Eisenhower Doctrine, and undertook to convince other Arab leaders of its usefulness. Following the 1967 Arab-Israeli war, however, the Saudis became increasingly sensitive to U.S.-Israeli ties, and Israeli concerns about U.S.-Saudi ties also mounted. When actual arms sales to the Saudis were proposed, they met with opposition in the U.S. Congress. Thus, several agreements for weapons sales to Saudi Arabia were reduced or canceled during this period—or tied to Israeli military aid—and there was a cooling of relations between the United States and the Saudis.

When the Arab-Israeli war of 1973 broke out and the United States continued its aid to Israel, Saudi Arabia led a movement by all the Arab oil-producing countries to exert political pressure on the West by massive cuts in oil production. Organization of Petroleum Exporting Countries (OPEC) members placed an embargo on the United States and several other Western countries. Although Saudi Arabia was initially at the forefront of organizing the embargo, its role within OPEC was beneficial to U.S. interests. As negotiations between the West and OPEC proceeded, it became clear that the Saudis were a moderating influence on more radical members, such as Libya and Algeria, who sought to cut off all supplies to the West until all their demands were met. At an OPEC meeting in March 1974, Saudi Arabia pressed for a resumption of supplies to the United States and resisted any moves to further increase prices, which had already risen to four times their level before the 1973 war. In negotiations with the West, the Saudis made it clear that the continued supply of oil was dependent not only on a change in policy regarding Israel but also on increased assistance to Saudi efforts to industrialize and diversify their economy. Accordingly, the United States and Saudi Arabia signed an important economic and military agreement in May 1974, which allocated U.S. aid specifically to the modernization and training of Saudi forces.

Improved relations with the United States were nevertheless causing some domestic difficulties for the Saudi government. Following the seizure in 1979 of the Grand Mosque in Mecca by opponents of the Saudi monarchy and subsequent riots by elements of Saudi Arabia's Shi'ite population, the high visibility of U.S.-Saudi relations was lessened. In 1980, however, President Jimmy Carter loaned four AWACS (airborne warning and control system) aircraft and their crews to Saudi Arabia to monitor the Iran-Iraq war. The sale was resisted by some supporters of Israel in the U.S. Congress, and the Saudis saw delays in the transfer as a sign of deteriorating relations with the United States. The transfer of AWACS was finally approved at the urging of the Ronald Reagan administration, albeit by a narrow margin in the U.S. Congress and with many restrictions. In addition, the Saudis assisted the United States in supporting the Afghan rebels in their fight against occupying Soviet forces throughout the 1980s. Still, there was concern in both Riyadh and Washington that close U.S.-Saudi ties would have a destabilizing effect on the Saudi monarchy. In addition, the Saudis continued to feel frustrated by what they saw as U.S. intransigence regarding the Palestinian issue. In a 1978 meeting between President Carter and King Khalid, the king suggested that the United States press Israel to withdraw from territories occupied after the 1967 war, as well as support statehood and resettlement rights for the Palestinians. During this same meeting, the United States expressed concern about increased Soviet ties with the two Yemens. Advanced fighter aircraft were sent to Saudi Arabia in the early 1980s, in part to check the spread of Soviet influence. On another front, two Saudi oil tankers were attacked in May 1984, as Iran and Iraq began air attacks against shipping in the Persian Gulf. That same month, citing concerns about an escalation in the Iran-

Iraq war and threats to the flow of oil, the United States authorized the sale of 400 Stinger anti-aircraft missiles.

The Gulf War and the 1990s

More than ever before, U.S.-Saudi relations were becoming closer in presenting a united front against common foes. And then in August 1990 came the Iraqi invasion of Kuwait. After quickly taking over Kuwait, Iraqi forces appeared to be positioning themselves for an attack on Saudi Arabia itself. The Saudis did not bend to Iraqi intimidation and allowed the Kuwaiti government-in-exile to take up residence in Saudi Arabia. Still, the presence of Iraqi troops in occupied Kuwait loomed as a serious threat. It offered Saddam Hussein new oil reserves, new sources of cash, and a new deep water port. It also allowed Iraqi forces to be in close enough proximity to Saudi Arabia's oil fields so as to be able to intimidate the other Gulf states militarily and politically. In addition, with a quarter of the world's oil reserves under their control, the Iraqis could dominate the world's oil market and more forcefully threaten to raise prices or reduce supplies for either economic or political reasons. This represented a massive shift in the balance of power in the Persian Gulf region, and it was seen as unacceptable by both the Saudis and the United States.

The immediate U.S. response was to begin the massive deployment of forces to Saudi Arabia as part of Operation Desert Shield. In an address to the U.S. Congress in September 1990, President George Bush unequivocally stated that the United States would use force if necessary to protect Saudi Arabian territorial integrity. In addition, the Arab League voted to defend Saudi Arabia. Many countries—Arab, Western, and others—sent troops to Saudi Arabia in what would be a long buildup to the war that began in early 1991. The UN Security Council condemned the Iraqi invasion and supported the creation of a blockade against Iraq and an embargo on its exports and imports. A series of additional resolutions were passed by the United Nations, including one that allowed the use of "all necessary means" to expel Iraqi forces from Kuwait. The air war against Iraq (Operation Desert Storm) began on 17 January 1991, followed by the ground war on 24 February 1991. In response, Iraq attacked Saudi Arabian territory forty-six times with Scud missiles. The United States installed Patriot air defense systems in Saudi Arabia and the Scuds did little military damage. On 29 January 1991, Iraqi forces did successfully take the Saudi border town of Kharfji. The town was soon retaken by Saudi and U.S. forces.

The Gulf War was a watershed event for U.S.-Saudi relations. The United States successfully marshaled and led a twenty-eight-nation coalition against Iraq, and emerged as the post–Cold War world's foremost military power as it shattered the Iraqi forces. In the process, the Iraqi threat to the Saudis had been greatly diminished, and the dynamic of the Arab-Israeli conflict had been substantially altered. Saudi financial support of the Palestinian Liberation Organization (PLO) had been generous, particularly in the 1980s, and their political support of the Palestinian position had been unstinting since the creation of Israel in 1948. The Saudis were shocked, then, when the PLO supported the Iraqis during the war. The Saudis retaliated by expelling Palestinians from their territory and cutting off aid to the PLO. In addition, de facto cooperation between Saudi Arabia and Israel during the war altered the decades-old image of a united Arab front against Israel. After the war, albeit with some reluctance and characteristic caution, the Saudis agreed to participate in the U.S.-initiated Middle East peace conference held in Madrid in October 1991. This was an unprecedented meeting of Israeli and Arab states officials, which launched the peace process that eventually led to the 1993 Israeli-Palestinian Oslo Accord and the 1994 Israel-Jordan peace treaty. Concurrent with the bilateral negotiations between Israel and its immediate neighbors (Syria and Lebanon), multilateral talks were begun with broad Arab participation, including Maghreb states such as Tunisia and Morocco as well as the Gulf states led by Saudi Arabia, on such issues as regional economic development, arms control, and regional security.

As the 1990s unfolded, the U.S.-Saudi relationship remained dominated by security concerns in the Persian Gulf and by economic ties regarding oil supplies from the Saudis and sales of advanced technologies and other major exports from the United States. The war was disastrous for the Saudi economy, its costs estimated at over $60 billion which came on top of a decade-long downturn in world oil prices. Saudi Arabia continues to see the United States as an important market for its oil exports. In the mid-1980s, exports to the United States and Canada had fallen to 6 percent of Saudi exports, down from 15 percent in the early 1980s. By the 1990s, however, a renewed emphasis on the North American market by the Saudis and competitive pricing brought one-third of Saudi exported oil to North America. In the 1990s, the Clinton administration brokered several deals with the Saudis, including the sale of advanced civilian aircraft. Such U.S. sales are seen as important for the U.S. domestic economy, as well as for U.S.-Saudi relations.

While there has been a consistent attempt to strike a balance in U.S.-Saudi relations that does not open the Saudi government up to the charge of being dependent on the United States, the Gulf War bolstered internal opposition to the monarchy. Pressures for domestic reforms mounted after the war, both from middle-class elements who saw the regime as too weak to defend the state and from religious forces who depicted cooperation with the West as an alliance with infidels. Both elements have called for reforms aimed at opening up the political system and increasing the accountability of the monarchy and of its security forces. In 1992, more than one hundred professionals and religious leaders signed a letter demanding the end of governmental corruption and termination of the alliance with the United States. A terrorist bomb attack on the Saudi National Guard training center in 1995 by Islamic opponents, killing five Americans, and a terrorist bomb attack on a U.S. military training center in Saudi Arabia in 1996 underscored the difficulty of striking a balance between close relations with the United States and coping with internal opposition.

The geo-strategic and economic importance of Saudi Arabia to the United States and the importance of the U.S. market and military protection to the Saudis nonetheless ensure that the relationship will continue to be close. It seems likely that only a radical change in the Saudi regime could alter this state of affairs.

JAMES P. KETTERER

See also Gulf War of 1990–1991; Israel; Middle East; Oil and Foreign Policy; Oil and World Politics; Organization of Petroleum Exporting Countries

FURTHER READING

Altorki, Soraya. *Women in Saudi Arabia: Ideology and Behavior Among the Elite*. New York, 1986.
David, Peter. *Triumph in the Desert*. New York, 1991.
Eickelman, Dale F., and James Piscatori. *Muslim Politics*. Princeton, N.J., 1996.
Lacey, Robert. *The Kingdom: Arabia and the House of Saud*. New York, 1982.
Long, David E. *The United States and Saudi Arabia: Ambivalent Allies*. Boulder, Colo., 1989.
Norton, Augustus Richard. "Breaking Through the Wall of Fear." *Current History* (January 1992): 37–41.
Safran, Nadav. *Saudi Arabia: The Ceaseless Quest for Security*. Cambridge, Mass., 1985.
Woodward, Peter. *Oil and Labor in the Middle East: Saudi Arabia and the Oil Boom*. New York, 1988.

SCHMIDT, HELMUT

(*b.* 23 December 1918)

German Social Democratic party leader and chancellor of West Germany from 1974 until 1982. Schmidt had previously served as defense minister and finance minister under Willy Brandt. During this turbulent period in U.S.-German affairs, Schmidt played an important role in shaping the transatlantic debate on security issues and "Ostpolitik." By and large relations between West Germany and the administration of President Gerald Ford were marked by mutual respect and understanding. During the Jimmy Carter administration, however, bilateral affairs were plagued by recurrent communications barriers and poor personal relationships between Schmidt and Carter.

The neutron-weapons controversy was a case in point. Carter first proposed the production and deployment of neutron weapons and then reversed himself in 1978. This about-face damaged U.S.-German relations because a hard-fought consensus to deploy the weapons already had been reached in Bonn and within the North Atlantic Treaty Organization.

In a highly publicized speech at the London-based International Institute for Strategic Studies in 1977, Schmidt drew the attention of senior U.S. officials to the deployment of Soviet intermediate-range nuclear missiles in Eastern Europe, which had created a "Euro-strategic" imbalance that could lead to potential Soviet pressure and nuclear blackmail. Schmidt's initiative and the resulting deliberations within NATO led to the Double Track Decision in December 1979. NATO agreed simultaneously to deploy new intermediate-range nuclear missiles in Europe (mostly in West Germany) to counter Soviet SS-20 missiles and to negotiate with the Soviet Union to remove these weapons on both sides.

The Soviet invasion of Afghanistan in 1979 prompted U.S. economic sanctions and created additional tensions between Washington and Bonn. The Carter administration's confrontational response contrasted with Schmidt's efforts to coordinate a common position within NATO and to keep lines of communication open to the Soviet leadership. Bilateral frictions escalated to a high point just prior to Schmidt's visit to Moscow in 1980. Schmidt was credited for his role as an intermediary, however, when Leonid Brezhnev first signalled his willingness to reenter arms negotiations with the United States during meetings with the German chancellor.

When President Ronald Reagan was inaugurated in 1981, Schmidt lobbied the new administration to take up negotiations with the Kremlin. Although President Reagan stood firm on deployment, in arms negotiations he proposed the zero-zero option: the United States would not deploy any Pershing II or land-based cruise missiles if the Soviet Union agreed to eliminate its medium-range nuclear weapons. Schmidt and his advisers supported these proposals.

By the end of 1982, Schmidt's term ended abruptly due to intense domestic pressures. Despite the advances made in articulating a more assertive foreign policy, Schmidt's influence on U.S. decision-making waned as his domestic support eroded.

BARBARA HEEP-RICHTER

See also Carter, James Earl; North Atlantic Treaty Organization; Nuclear Weapons and Strategy

FURTHER READING

Hanrider, Wolfram F., ed. *Helmut Schmidt: Prospectives on Politics.* Boulder, Colo., 1982.

Heep, Barbara. *Helmut Schmidt und Amerika, Eine Schwierige Partnerschaft.* Bonn, 1990.

Schmidt, Helmut. *Menschen und Maechte.* Berlin, 1987.

SCHUMAN, ROBERT

(*b.* 29 June 1886; *d.* 4 September 1963)

French statesman who helped lay the foundation for European integration after World War II. Born in Luxembourg, Schuman attended the Universities of Bonn, Berlin, and Munich and received his Doctorate in Law from Strasbourg. He served in the French Chamber of Deputies from 1919 through 1962, except during the German occupation, when Gestapo forces arrested and briefly imprisoned him for aiding anti-Nazi refugees. From 1942 until the liberation of France, Schuman served in the French underground and helped found the Mouvement Républicain Populaire (MRP), a Catholic political party. After the war, he returned to the French Assembly as an MRP deputy from Metz. He served twice as finance minister (1945–1948, under the Blum and Ramadier governments) and twice as prime minister (November 1947 through July 1948 and for one week in August 1948). During his tenure as French foreign minister (1948–1952) Schuman became an important architect of the North Atlantic Treaty (1949) and the subsequent North Atlantic Treaty Organization. He was less successful in dealing with the international aspects of France's colonial war in Indochina.

In 1949, Schuman and German Federal Republic chancellor Konrad Adenauer reconciled Franco-German relations for the first time since World War II, then worked with other Continental leaders to produce the first ever European economic union. The "Schuman Plan," drafted by Schuman adviser Jean Monnet and articulated by the French foreign minister on 9 May 1950, called for a unified European coal and steel community as a precursor to a Continental common market. Great Britain rejected the proposal, but France, West Germany, Italy, and the Benelux countries accepted it and on 30 June 1950 they signed a treaty establishing the European Coal and Steel Community. The Treaty of Rome (1957) formalized the founding of a European Economic Community in 1958 and Schuman served as its first president from 1958 to 1960. He remained a member of its Parliamentary Assembly until February 1963.

DEBORAH KISATSKY

See also European Union; French Indochina; Monnet, Jean; North Atlantic Treaty Organization

FURTHER READING

Dell, Edmund. *The Schuman Plan and the British Abdication of Leadership in Europe.* New York, 1995.

Duchêne, François. *Jean Monnet, the First Statesman of Interdependence.* New York, 1994.

Keyserlingk, Robert Wendelin. *Fathers of Europe, Patriots of Peace.* Montreal, 1972.

Monnet, Jean. *Memoirs.* London, 1978.

SCIENCE AND TECHNOLOGY

A broad but important field that has played a significant role in shaping U.S. international relations. The power and prospects of science and technology cut across every national purpose pursued by U.S. foreign policy. In fields such as trade, defense, agriculture, health, environment, and energy, the moving front of technology not only creates new diplomatic opportunities, but also changes the international balance of power and wealth. In the practice of diplomacy itself, advanced tools of transportation and telecommunications not only create new means to assist the conduct of international relations but also often influence the results of negotiations. Even in basic and applied research—for which objectives are set by individual investigators in firms and universities—intergovernmental agreements create frameworks for essential cooperation and transfers of know-how across borders.

Links of foreign policy with scientific and technological enterprises multiplied rapidly over the post–World War II period. But diplomats rarely found the combination comfortable. As former secretary of state Henry Kissinger said, "Technology daily outstrips the ability of our institutions to cope with its fruits. Our political imagination must catch up with our scientific vision." Accordingly, it is important to consider the organization of institutions and decision-making processes. Unless the government has clear and consistent coupling of science and technology with international affairs, choices are not formulated fully and consequences of decisions are not anticipated in a timely way.

Science has always been proud of its internationalist ethos, and U.S. scientists and political leaders since colonial days have been alert to technical progress abroad. Thus this discussion opens with brief historical highlights of the federal government's internationally relevant policies for science beginning in the eighteenth century.

During the nineteenth and twentieth centuries, U.S. research universities emerged as the world's premier research centers and today play a critical role in the movement of knowledge among the nations. During the first half of the twentieth century, scientists and engineers were mobilized in war and then for arms control. Topics for the turn of the century encompass growing concerns about climate change; trends in the worldwide

SELECTED UNITED NATIONS ORGANIZATIONS AND AGENCIES INVOLVED IN SCIENCE AND TECHNOLOGY	
Agency	Year Founded
International Telecommunication Union	1865
International Labor Organization	1919
Food and Agriculture Organization	1945
United Nations Educational, Scientific and Cultural Organization	1946
Inter-Governmental Maritime Consultative Organization	1948
World Health Organization	1948
World Meteorological Organization	1950
International Atomic Energy Agency	1957
United Nations Conference on Trade and Development	1964
United Nations Development Program	1966
United Nations Industrial Development Organization	1967
United Nations Fund for Population Activities	1967
United Nations Environment Program	1973
World Intellectual Property Organization	1974
World Trade Organization	1995

distribution of research funding and personnel; and the hoped-for acceleration of science-led economic development in low income countries. Looking ahead, many twenty-first century challenges lie at the intersection of science and technology with U.S. foreign policy. In the broadest civilian arenas, global collaboration will be needed to cope with population growth and the resulting demands on food, energy, jobs, and economic investment. Diplomacy, furthermore, must reconcile the widely recognized needs for nations simultaneously to compete and to cooperate. For instance, joint actions will be required to fund and manage research in many fields (such as climate change) while nations compete for global markets in the technologically advanced products and services (such as environmental technologies).

Two general distinctions will be useful in approaching this subject. One relates to science vis-à-vis technology. While there is a large overlap between the science-intensive research characteristic of universities, and the technology-oriented and market-driven activities typical of firms, each domain tends to follow independent incentives and directions. U.S. foreign policy has had to cope mostly with technological issues—such as the innovations in weapons or negotiations about intellectual property rights. But the insights of research science also have frequently emerged as driving issues in diplomacy—such as demographic projections of population, macroeconomic estimates of needs for saving and investment, chemical findings about transnational air pollution, and biomedical approaches to improve international public health. Whenever asymmetries occur in the capacity of nations to absorb transfers of technology for economic development—these asymmetries relate to the level of educational and scientific infrastructure of nations—U.S. foreign policy has to deal simultaneously with science and with technology in its relationships, especially with developing countries.

A second distinction concerns "science and technology in policy" vis-à-vis "policy for science and technology." While overlaps occur among the issues in these two categories, foreign policy often turns primarily on "science in policy." For these interactions the challenge is to incorporate pertinent elements, research information, and technical specialists into the formulation and execution of policy regarding such diverse subjects as energy and defense. Of course, such subjects also have powerful political and economic features. For the second category, "policy for science," the challenge is to chart and conduct governmental policies that foster U.S. (and global) progress in science and technology per se. For example, the United States wishes to assure access by U.S. investigators to the oceans and to astronomical research sites throughout the world and then to facilitate sharing related observations by investigators from many nations. Any rapid reconnaissance of this sprawling terrain necessarily must be content with mapping only the broad boundaries and highlighting a few of the prominent hills and valleys.

Historical Highlights

Before the Revolution, the United States sent representatives around the world to skillfully pursue the national

SCIENCE ADVISERS		
ADMINISTRATION	ADVISER	PERIOD OF APPOINTMENT
Eisenhower	James R. Killian, Jr.	1957–1961
Kennedy	Jerome B. Wiesner	1961–1964
L. Johnson	Donald F. Hornig	1964–1969
Nixon	Lee A. Dubridge	1969–1970
	Edward E. David, Jr.	1970–1973
Ford	H. Guyford Stever	1976–1977
Carter	Frank Press	1977–1981
Reagan	George A. Keyworth II	1981–1985
	William R. Graham, Jr.	1986–1989
Bush	D. Allan Bromley	1989–1993
Clinton	John H. Gibbons	1993–Present

Source: U.S. Office of Science and Technology Policy

interest. Often, the tasks involved science. In 1775, for example, Benjamin Franklin was appointed to the Committee of Secret Correspondence, the direct forerunner of the Department of State, and he promoted U.S. interests abroad until 1784. His replacement as minister to Paris was Thomas Jefferson, who later served as the first Secretary of State. Both Franklin and Jefferson were deeply interested in "natural philosophy," as science was then known. Indeed, since Franklin was better known as a scientist than as a statesman, his scientific eminence underlay his success as a diplomat in Paris.

Both Jefferson and Franklin gathered and sent back to the United States a wide variety of information and samples about agriculture, architecture, and modern instruments useful in commerce. Jefferson, in particular, was acutely aware of the international traditions in science. He once noted: "The brotherly spirit of science…unites into one family all its votaries of whatever grade, and however widely dispersed through the different quarters of the globe." Combining this notion with James Madison's remark—"If we are to be one nation in any respect, it clearly ought to be in respect to other nations"—there was from the earliest days of the Republic a convergence of the awareness that the U.S. system could and should tap the many scientific and technological benefits flowing from foreign sources.

Specialized military and engineering prowess was imported during the Revolutionary period. Throughout the early nineteenth century, foreign patents were licensed, and technically gifted immigrants arrived to assist industrialization. Private commercial incentives fueled these technological exchanges. In fact, formal diplomatic initiatives concerning science were comparatively rare. But the United States emerged as a great power in large measure because it saw and seized worldwide opportunities for applying innovations.

The Constitutional recognition of the importance of patents—reflecting principles that respected freedom and offered economic incentives—foreshadows late twentieth century global disputes on intellectual property rights in countries that do not recognize private innovation in this way. The births of institutions such as the Library of Congress and the Weather Bureau show how the federal government laid the foundations for information exchange and for cooperation in weather forecasts—later seen to be among the interests served by U.S. foreign policy.

Many of these institutions and their leaders went on to play key roles in representing the United States in international activities. For example, the Smithsonian Institution, founded in 1846 by the bequest of an Englishman, James Smithson, in order to "increase and diffuse knowledge," has engaged outstanding scientists and administrators across many fields central to U.S. activities in expeditions and surveys around the world. Similarly, the National Academy of Sciences, founded in 1863 and charged with providing expert advice to the Executive branch, experienced enormous growth after World War II; it has been an important scientific resource for international affairs, from agriculture to aviation, more recently encompassing the National Academy of Engineering and the Institute of Medicine.

These nineteenth-century scientific organizations became partners with the Department of State and the Congress. Their capabilities constitute an essential part of the foundation for the conduct of contemporary foreign affairs. Of course, the nineteenth-century rationale for establishing these federal activities did not always emphasize, or even mention, international ramifications. Indeed, today as in the past, the hope for self-sufficiency and national leadership competes with the sometimes painful recognition that not only is science inherently international, but that talent is spread widely throughout the world. As research investments grow rapidly in other nations, international cooperation is not merely desirable, but essential, for achieving U.S. goals.

Military and Nuclear Energy Issues

Since the turn of the twentieth century, military demands often dominated the role of science and technology in international affairs. During World War I, and more prominently in World War II, scientists and engineers were mobilized. Revolutionary changes in weapons, ships, aircraft, and communications became crucial assets for political and diplomatic leaders. Whenever foreign policy aims in war became clearly defined, extraordinary technological means were developed to achieve those aims.

The Manhattan Project, the U.S. government's secret research effort that produced the world's first two atomic bombs, was later regarded as the most visible exemplar of the role of scientists in World War II. Vannevar Bush, chairman of the National Defense Research Committee during the war and a distinguished engineer from MIT, recommended in early 1942 to President Franklin D. Roosevelt that the United States start a project to produce fissionable material. The Army Corps of Engineers under General Leslie Groves quickly organized the complex and far-flung development of atomic weapons. Scientists and engineers from many academic and industrial laboratories were recruited into the effort. Los Alamos, New Mexico, was the location of the major facility that carried out research, design, and assembly of the bombs. This facility was directed by J. Robert Oppenheimer, a theoretical physicist who later headed the Institute for Advanced Study in Princeton. After Enrico Fermi's demonstration in late 1942 at the University of Chicago that a chain reaction with uranium was feasible, the enormous effort proceeded rapidly. By July 1945, President Harry S. Truman was told that initial tests were successful; two bombs were then exploded in Hiroshima and Nagasaki in August 1945, leading to Japan's surrender.

The large post–World War II governmental support for defense research was based upon the public awareness that science and technology had brilliantly served the nation in war and the widely shared belief that the emerging challenge posed by the Soviet Union required a comparable commitment to technology-based defense. Wartime innovations were symbolized not only by the development of nuclear weapons, but also by such advances as radar, proximity fuses, and new aircraft.

Thus the war effort had made a case that scientists and engineers could help meet many national goals. In 1945, when Vannevar Bush submitted his legendary paper on postwar research policies, entitled "Science—the Endless Frontier," the nation welcomed this case and began to pursue a much expanded federal program for science and technology, often led by defense projects.

After World War II, science and technology figured centrally in many components of foreign policy. One consistent goal for over forty years was maintaining technological superiority among the nations of the North Atlantic Treaty Organization (NATO). This was key to the concept of deterrence, protecting against an East-West war by balancing nuclear and other advanced weapons against the larger conventional armies maintained by the Soviet Union and its Warsaw Pact. Another goal was control of those very weapons as initially proposed in the Baruch Plan and later pursued in such U.S.-Soviet nuclear arms control negotiations as the Strategic Arms Limitation Talks (SALT) and Strategic Arms Reduction Treaties (START). Throughout these complex negotiations, scientists and engineers were closely involved with U.S. diplomats.

International institutions were created to control the military use of atomic energy while enhancing civilian applications (the International Atomic Energy Agency), to limit the proliferation of nuclear weapons (Nuclear Non-Proliferation Treaty), and to brake the diffusion of weapons-building information through controls on the export of sensitive components (Coordinating Committee for Multilateral Strategic Export Controls, [COCOM]). Further, extraordinary techniques for intelligence gathering—by satellites and other technical means—were developed to enhance the reliability of estimates of military threats such as intercontinental missiles; the Departments of Defense and State and the Central Intelligence Agency used rapidly advancing technological tools to serve the intelligence needs of foreign policy.

Scientists as Activists and Advisers

Individual scientists and engineers have been prominent in public and private activities related to U.S. foreign policy. Linus Pauling, for example, was awarded not only a Nobel Prize in chemistry for his research but also a Nobel Peace Prize for his efforts to publicize the risks of nuclear war. Informal and nongovernmental exchanges—such as at the meetings of Pugwash, a group started in the 1950s by industrialist Cyrus Eaton—brought together leading scientists from the former Soviet Union and the United States for off-the-record exchanges about deterrence, defense, and arms control in the hope of reducing the potential for conflict and lessening tensions during the Cold War. More formally, distinguished scientists in the White House and Department of Defense brought together senior experts from outside government to assess tradeoffs in the development of new defense systems and to weigh ideas for arms control and disarmament. Such studies became part of the conceptual framework for foreign policy and military strategy, and the external advisers often became members of official negotiating teams. This process began regularly at the White House when MIT's executive James Killian and then Harvard chemist George Kistiakowsky became the first officially designated science advisers to President Dwight D. Eisenhower, and the institutional apparatus was further expanded by MIT electrical engineer Jerome Weisner, science adviser to President John F. Kennedy.

By the early 1960s—as the Soviet space and military programs seemed to carry grave threats to U.S. security—the White House created a new Office of Science and Technology (OST) to help coordinate analyses of strategic issues and recommendations with the National Security Council. The President's Science Advisory Committee (PSAC) included a group of nongovernmental experts who devoted intensive efforts to both military and civilian studies. OST helped with issues of science in domestic and foreign policy as well as policies for defense research and development. Although Presidents Lyndon Johnson, Richard Nixon, Gerald Ford, Jimmy Carter, Ronald Reagan, George Bush, and Bill Clinton used their science advisers in radically different ways—often buffeted by domestic policies and budgetary constraints as well as international trends and crises—by the 1990s the renamed White House Office of Science and Technology Policy (OSTP) had come to play a key role in shaping policies and programs for the integration of science and technology into the context of foreign affairs.

The Assistant to the President for Science and Technology serves as the director of the OSTP, and is informally known as the science adviser. The science adviser helps the president in exchanges with the heads of foreign governments about science and technology initiatives and agreements, especially where U.S. technical leadership is used to achieve broader foreign policy objectives. The science adviser also represents the United States at a wide variety of meetings such as with science ministers of the industrialized countries in the Organization for Economic Cooperation and Development (OECD). International areas of direct concern to the OSTP include: environmental change such as studies of biodiversity; economic growth including assessments of U.S. technological competitiveness in global trade; the management of a growing number of global science "megaprojects" such as multibillion-dollar facilities for high-energy physics and projects of space exploration; science and technology negotiations related to intellectual property rights; the implementation of technology

transfer arrangements with developing countries; and the facilitation of nongovernmental international cooperation involving U.S. universities.

With President Clinton's creation of the National Science and Technology Council (NSTC) in November 1993—which the president chairs and which includes the cabinet heads of most federal agencies—science and technology generally have an even more visible role in international topics. The NSTC's Committee on International Science, Engineering, and Technology (CISET) aims to coordinate all interagency activities that affect overall foreign policy along with the scores of specific international negotiations that depend in part on expertise in science and technology. In parallel, the President's Council of Advisers on Science and Technology (PCAST)—a group of nongovernmental executives from universities, foundations, and firms—provides advice through the science adviser on both domestic and international topics.

Department of State and International Organizations

The Department of State depends heavily upon other federal agencies for technical advice. It is important to recognize the historical evolution of international scientific activities; see chart for several key policy developments since the late 1800s. With the steady diffusion over time of internationally pertinent science and technology-intensive activities throughout the federal government, most executive agencies and congressional committees touch the intersection of science and technology with foreign policy. For example, the Department of Commerce has extensive global exchanges for cooperating in materials research, setting industrial standards, and exploring the oceans. Although the Department of State is a small agency, it has the statutory responsibility for "oversight" of all of these activities. Beginning in 1974, one of the Department of State's thirty or so principal units has been devoted to coordinating the task; this is the Bureau of Oceans and International Environmental and Scientific Affairs, headed by an assistant secretary.

International organizations also depend heavily upon science and technology. Just as it has been difficult to bring coherence to the rapidly expanding number of tasks in U.S. federal agencies conducting international activities—putting the Department of State under heavy pressure—it has been even more difficult to ensure both the quality and the coordination of efforts in the United Nations (UN) and similar intergovernmental organizations. As former secretary of state Cyrus Vance said, "For some time it has been clear that advances in science and technology are outdistancing the capacity of existing international organizations to deal with them." The previous table lists in chronological order, by date of founding, a few of the major UN bodies with activities in science and technology. The United States played a constructive role in giving birth to many of these agencies in the immediate post–World War II era. However, despite the idealism and competence of many UN career civil servants, most observers see substantial deficiencies in international scientific organizations. These deficiencies, including politicization and lack of accountability, deter participation by many U.S. scientists and engineers, produce frustration in the Department of State, and provoke skepticism in Congress about making appropriations to fund U.S. commitments to the agencies. The withdrawal of the United States from UNESCO was an example of how, even when some scientific activities of an international organization are valuable for U.S. foreign policy, the overall character and efficiency of a global institution may be found wanting.

Generally speaking, the highest priority for the United Nations system for several decades has been to accelerate the economic and social development of less developed countries. Science and technology have been among the most critical engines for development—to expand jobs, enhance industrialization, promote trade, and serve a variety of other purposes. At the 1979 United Nations Vienna Conference on Science and Technology for Development, a "program of action" was drawn up. This expensive program, touching most international agencies, aimed to build "indigenous capacity" in science and technology for developing countries. Yet the effectiveness of this program has been uneven at best. Accordingly, many nations concluded during the 1980s and 1990s that dependence upon monolithic intergovernmental agreements and government-to-government transfers of resources is not nearly as effective as greater emphasis on initiatives by the private sector. U.S. diplomacy began to promote economic growth through decentralized patterns of private initiative and trade, and by facilitating agreements between firms, universities, and other nongovernmental organizations.

In the evolution of U.S. foreign assistance—whether through the United Nations or in other ways—policy reviews have often focused efforts on how best to incorporate science and technology in the U.S. linkages. For example, when President Truman announced in 1946 the "Point Four" program to expand bilateral aid to developing countries, technical assistance was a high priority. Almost twenty-five years later, when the Hannah Report in 1969 reviewed the mission and operations of the Agency for International Development, a prominent emphasis was the expansion of technical exchanges between American campuses and other countries. Almost twenty-five years following that review, when the Carnegie Commission on Science, Technology, and Government in 1992 assessed U.S. relationships with developing countries following the end of the Cold War, the principal recommendation for the future was the creation of "partnerships in global development" that would be based largely upon nongovernmental initiatives with U.S. science and technology assets.

Global Issues

U.S. diplomacy influences, both directly and indirectly, the global flows of people and knowledge in science and technology. These flows occur through varied channels including trade, immigration, cultural exchanges, educational activities, links by nongovernmental organizations, and the framework for direct U.S. investment in other countries.

One example is that the United States has become a university for the world. For the roughly one million students who travel abroad to pursue higher education, the United States is by far the preferred destination, attracting over 400,000 foreign students in the early 1990s. For many years, about sixty percent of all Asian and Latin American students who study abroad have come to the United States, and about seventy-five percent of all foreign students in the United States have come from developing or newly industrialized countries. Between the mid-1970s and mid-1990s the number of foreign students in the United States more than doubled. Most foreign students have come for technical training, typically to study engineering and the sciences, with some concentrating on business and management. In this way, although the U.S. government is the primary source of funding for only a small percent of all foreign students, the United States helps build capacity for science and technology in developing countries. Recent trends suggest an inevitable change in this situation as developing nations build their own domestic educational bases. Moreover, there is evidence of increasing appeal of European universities for graduate training.

U.S. foreign policy also increasingly confronts global economic issues that relate to the technological capacity and level of industrialization of other countries. While the distribution of scientific and engineering talent and funds still is disproportionate to the industrial world, the balance is changing as developing countries increase their technological strength. U.S. foreign policy mediates the strains arising from commercial competition as firms strike global alliances and seek to regulate intellectual property rights. In a similar fashion, U.S. diplomacy must reconcile the sometimes conflicting goals of fostering technology-based trade while promoting democracy and respect for human rights; such acute issues were raised during the 1990s in U.S. relations with China and other Asian nations, and the leaders of human rights campaigns often were drawn from the global scientific, engineering, and medical communities.

Public health measures to control the global spread of infectious diseases have demanded active cooperation among governments. Biomedical scientists and public health physicians created U.S. leadership in the successful campaign by the World Health Organization to eradicate smallpox. Similarly, the United States has been among the leaders in promoting vaccination of children around the world, disseminating appropriate means of birth control and family planning, and implementing standards for health and safety for workers. Even on health, however, nations often disagree when intrusive inspections and externally derived standards may be imposed (as on the reporting of AIDS cases) or when national priorities and values conflict with another country's regulations (as in the U.S.-Mexico disputes about workplace health rules).

On environmental matters the United States has faced complex problems in integrating effective foreign policy with science and technology. In 1972, at the time of the United Nations Conference on the Human Environment in Stockholm, the list of environmental issues already had become formidable. Cities around the world, including many in the United States, suffered acute air pollution, and lakes and streams were polluted with waste and choked by lack of oxygen. The Stockholm conference accelerated international action on goals such as controls on dumping of waste at sea, and led to the establishment of the United Nations Environment Program. In 1992, at the time of the United Nations Conference on Environment and Development in Rio de Janeiro, demands for environmental action had expanded. Even stronger tensions, however, had emerged in debates on the reconciliation of environmental protection and economic development. Although the Montreal Protocol of 1987 had begun to eliminate the release of chlorofluorocarbons (CFC's) that cause stratospheric ozone depletion, the so-called "ozone hole" was a symbol for sharply increased public awareness of possibly irreversible effects of industrialization on the environment. Diplomacy about the environment, in short, came to face a new set of issues that demand, on the one hand, global cooperation to foster progress on the frontiers of research in the environmental sciences while, on the other hand, organizing credible assessments from all reliable technical sources to guide policymaking and anchor a credible rationale for enforcement of prudent global environmental agreements. Moreover, international treaties on environmental issues must encompass resolution of conflicts relating economic with environmental choices. Social values and politics must mesh with unfolding scientific observations and the uncertain projections of long-term trends. In many global cross-currents related to science, nongovernmental organizations often have been important for independent analysis and debate, sometimes becoming

thorns in the sides of foreign ministries. The private scientific community has organized mechanisms for orchestrating international cooperation, promoting research, and advising governments and United Nations agencies. One such organization is the International Council of Scientific Unions (ICSU). ICSU was designated as the principal scientific adviser to the United Nations Conference on Environment and Development in Rio de Janeiro in 1992, and has played a comparable role, often informally, in assisting national governments and international entities in pulling together the scientific information bearing on both national policy and intergovernmental agreements.

These illustrations of how science converges with global issues could be multiplied many times. Furthermore, tradeoffs among science-informed options arise not only in negotiations affecting bilateral agreements (between the United States and any individual country), but also in multilateral negotiations within entities such as NATO and the World Trade Organization, and within financial institutions such as the World Bank and the regional development banks whose goals focus largely on economic development. For almost every global issue addressed by U.S. foreign policy, science and technology are among the nation's major instruments for action.

Future Challenges for Policy

During the second half of the twentieth century, science and technology most clearly affected foreign policymaking in issues of national security and in programs related to space and intelligence. Not only did extraordinary technologies shape the possibilities with which policymakers had to contend, but for defense, space, and intelligence, policy dictated the directions and urgency of large investments in research and development. By the mid-1990s, following the break up of the Soviet Union and the subsequent reduction in the overall U.S. defense effort (including research and development), national security policy depended less strongly upon technological advances for Cold War–oriented nuclear deterrence. Instead, the nation confronted a more complex set of potential threats with new priorities for funding science and technology.

For instance, the Department of Defense emphasized so-called "smart weapons" (electronically guided missiles with high accuracy) as it reduced total forces. The Departments of Defense and State also became more concerned with coping with terrorism and exploring the implications of new forms of "information warfare" that could undercut conventional systems for command, control, communications, and intelligence ($C^3 I$). Furthermore, as technological skills diffused around the world, U.S. foreign policy sought new ways to resolve the complex technical issues of how to brake the proliferation of weapons—not only the nuclear, chemical, and biological means of mass destruction, but also short-range and medium-range missiles. Nonproliferation will continue for many years to be a major challenge for science and technology in U.S. foreign policy. This was seen, for instance, in the UN's special inspections of Iraq after the Gulf War of 1990–1991 and in the disagreements with China and Russia about exporting nuclear technology to Asia and the Middle East.

Many less grave challenges arise in bringing science and technology into day-to-day operations of foreign policy. For example, the U.S. government must decide how to support global programs guiding standards for telecommunications and civil aviation (science in policy) and objectives for long-range space research (policy for science). In such cases, usually the technical issues are compounded by choices on funding levels and by the diverse inclinations of countries with respect to the roles and degree of freedom of the private sector in international regimes. Two illustrations help to explain growing challenges to U.S. foreign policy.

The first is "megascience," large research projects involving cooperation by scientists from many nations. "Megascience" denotes certain research fields and projects that require unusual facilities, or orchestrate programs having wide geographical scope, with large funding. Few nations can afford to carry out these projects individually and in any case, most such projects benefit from scientific cooperation; thus, many interested nations, with their scientists, must collaborate. Some such large projects involve "distributed" scientific efforts, the hundreds of observing stations orchestrated around the world to investigate and monitor the weather, including hurricanes, monsoons, and conventional forecasts to aid agriculture, aviation, and the development of large-scale computer models in climatology. Generally, over several decades nations have been successful in cooperation on such dispersed programs. Global change research and the human genome project currently proceed effectively.

In contrast, "centralized" megascience is exemplified by the facilities used in high-energy physics research at a single site to explore the organization of matter and the origin of the universe. Such facilities cost many billions of dollars, and successful examples of cooperation include CERN in Switzerland and Fermilab in Illinois. By the late 1980s, planning and managing the next generation of such centralized efforts had become controversial—both within the global research community as national budgets tightened, and in intergovernmental talks such as those held at the OECD Megascience Forum, started in 1992 as a mechanism to nurture exchanges about long-range coordination of global research priorities. A painful lesson was learned, for example, in the case of the Superconducting Supercollider (SSC) that was originally planned for construction in Texas. The United States began the project as a national initiative; later, as expenses grew, it was not possible to arrange sufficient foreign donors to the program; and deep friction emerged in eleventh-hour financing negotiations with Japan. When the costs rose from $5 billion to more than $10 billion and the congressional stipulation for foreign financial participation was not met while U.S. budget cuts were being imposed, the SSC was canceled in 1993. Future centralized facilities of this character probably will be planned in advance on an international, or perhaps regional, basis. To do so, particularly when jobs and commercial advantages are at stake, diplomatic negotiations will be designed to chart mutually agreeable terms for pooling talent and funds, not only from science-rich and prosperous countries, but also from the increasing number of nations with growing scientific, technological, and economic capacity. Most of these issues in megascience concern policy for science, viewed nationally and globally.

Megascience also raises the "free rider" issue. In international investments for research, some countries gain the benefits of research merely by closely watching and copying the results of the investments by other countries, thus becoming a "free rider" on the global pool of science. Throughout the 1970s and the 1980s, this was a U.S. complaint about Japan, which was evidently gifted at exploiting the results of research in the United States and Europe, while arguably under-investing in basic research in Japan. There will be a continuing temptation for many countries strapped for resources to underemphasize investments in basic science; indeed, individual firms are also vulnerable to this temptation, because a sponsor cannot appropriate all of the benefits. Hence, American foreign policy aims to encourage nations to contribute equitably and proportionately to a global reservoir of research available and helpful to all.

A second challenge for integrating science and technology into U.S. foreign policy—one with strong economic implications—is access to, and protection of, technology. One issue is reciprocity in access to academic and industrial laboratories. Openness in the United States—especially on research-intensive university campuses—creates a situation in which scientists from other nations generally have far easier access to the base of U.S. research than U.S. professionals have to centers abroad. Such asymmetry was especially visible in U.S.-Japan relations during the 1970s and 1980s. Diverse linguistic, nontariff, and other barriers limit participation by U.S. public and private sector experts desiring to visit or work in the laboratories and factories of many countries.

In a sense, the opposite issue to access is the protection of intellectual property rights abroad and the elimination of piracy of copyrighted material, as in computer software and pharmaceuticals. U.S. technology-intensive firms and inventors, and those from most nations, require access to an independent judiciary—and clear lines of legal defense—for assuring returns on their patents and on the sales of commercially valuable technology. This can best be ensured by a combination of informal international scientific exchange with formal cooperation to harmonize the legal frameworks for protecting intellectual property rights across borders. The World Trade Organization, created in 1995, is one of the major forums for negotiations on this subject. Given the many legal and cultural forces influencing sophisticated patterns of access and protection, U.S. foreign economic policy requires strong advice from scientists and engineers in appraising options for such negotiations and enforcing agreements.

Foreign ministries everywhere typically are weak in handling such subjects, and the U.S. Department of State is no exception. For the future, higher level scientific knowledge and expertise will be required for diplomacy to be successful, just as in the past military and technological expertise was essential for charting foreign policy about deterrence and arms control. In parallel, the U.S. government's technically based mission agencies—from the National Science Foundation, Environmental Protection Agency, and the National Institutes of Health to the Departments of Defense, Commerce, Agriculture, and Energy—will have to become more effective in thinking through their priorities for international activities.

RODNEY W. NICHOLS

See also Baruch, Bernard Mannes; Environment; Foreign Aid; International Atomic Energy Agency; Manhattan Project; National Aeronautics and Space Administration; Nuclear Weapons and Strategy; Oppenheimer, Julius Robert; State, U.S. Department of; United Nations

FURTHER READING

Agency for International Development. *Development and the National Interest: U.S. Economic Assistance into the Twenty-First Century.* Washington, D.C., 1989.
Carnegie Commission on Science, Technology, and Government. *Partnerships for Global Development: The Clearing Horizon.* New York, 1992.
———. *Science and Technology in U.S. International Affairs.* New York, 1992.
Committee on International Relations, U.S. House of Representatives. *Science, Technology, and American Diplomacy.* Washington, D.C., 1977.
Dupree, A. Hunter. *Science in the Federal Government: A History.* 1986.
Granger, John V. *Technology and International Relations.* San Francisco, 1979.
Hass, Ernst B. *Scientists and World Order: The Uses of Technical Knowledge in International Organization.* 1977.
Nye, Joseph S., Jr. *Bound to Lead: The Changing Nature of American Power.* New York, 1990.
Skolnikoff, Eugene B. *The Elusive Transformation: Science, Technology, and the Evolution of International Politics.* Princeton, N.J., 1993.
Task Force on Science Policy, Committee on Science and Technology, House of Representatives. *A History of Science Policy in the United States, 1940–1985.* No. 1 of *Science Policy Study Background Report.* Washington, D.C., 1986.
UNESCO, *World Science Report 1996.* Paris, 1996.
U.S. Congress Office of Technology Assessment. *International Partnerships in Large Science Projects.* Washington, D.C., 1995.

SCOWCROFT, BRENT

(*b.* 19 March 1925)

Career military officer who served as national security adviser to Presidents Gerald Ford (1973–1975) and George Bush (1989–1993). The son of a wholesale grocer, Scowcroft was born in Ogden, Utah. After World War II, in which he flew for the Air Force, he received a B.S. degree from the U.S. Military Academy in 1947. He completed his postgraduate education at Georgetown University, then earned advanced degrees (M.A., 1953, and Ph.D., 1967) from Columbia University. He quickly distinguished himself as a scholar in the military, advancing to the rank of Air Force lieutenant general in 1974 and serving on the faculties of the U.S. Air Force Academy in Colorado Springs, the U.S. Military Academy at West Point, and the National War College. His knowledge of both the Serbian and Russian languages was utilized during two years spent as assistant air attache at the U.S. embassy in Belgrade, and his scholarship contributed to the work of the long-range planning division of the office of the deputy chief of staff for plans and operations. As adviser on national security affairs to Presidents Ford and Bush, he was known as an unflappable and dedicated practitioner of realpolitik. "I'm a Mormon. I'm known for loyalty," he is said to have told Henry Kissinger at the outset of their close relationship.

Scowcroft's Columbia doctoral dissertation discussed the relationship between Congress and foreign policy. By the time he became President Richard Nixon's military assistant in 1972, Scowcroft specialized in arms control and defense. During the Ford presidency he served as deputy assistant to the president for national security affairs and then succeeded Henry Kissinger as the assistant to the president for national security affairs. Ford's brief presidency involved Scowcroft in the effort to save South Vietnam during its final days, and in the *S. S. Mayaguez* crisis with the temporary capture of its U.S. crew by Cambodians. In 1975 he accompanied the president to Asia, including the People's Republic of China, to shore up American interests in the region.

During the Democratic interregnum of Jimmy Carter, Scowcroft joined his former superior as a high officer of the foreign policy consulting firm known as Kissinger Associates. (In 1993, after the Bush presidency, he created the Scowcroft Group.) Under Ronald Reagan, he headed the President's Commission on Strategic Forces (Scowcroft Commission), which made recommendations aimed at reducing U.S. vulnerability to a future Pearl Harbor-style first-strike attack. He also served under Senator John Tower of Texas on the President's Special Review Board charged with investigating the Iran-Contra affair. In the first intensive study of the affair, the Tower Commission castigated the Reagan administration for its lack of control over its own National Security Council and for enabling out-of-control advisers to pursue policies that were "directly counter to the Administration's own policies on terrorism, the Iran-Iraq War, and military support for the war." The report, however, failed to uncover any firm evidence of the president's knowledge that funds had been diverted from the arms supply program to aid the anti-leftist Contras in Nicaragua. Following his election to the presidency in 1988, George Bush, who had been impressed by Scowcroft's work while he himself was director of the Central Intelligence Agency and later while vice president under Reagan, reappointed Scowcroft as national security adviser.

Scowcroft, known during the Reagan years as a hardliner on arms control, was nevertheless a critic of the Strategic Defense Initiative program. On general East-West issues, he remained a cautious skeptic toward Mikhail Gorbachev and indeed toward Russia even after the collapse of the Soviet Union. President Bush sent Scowcroft on two secret missions to the Chinese government after the 1989 Tiananmen Square massacre in Beijing. Scowcroft both encouraged keeping diplomatic lines open to Beijing and supported Bush's efforts to work for political liberalization in China. He called the initiative "the president's finest moment." Throughout the Persian Gulf crisis of 1990–1991, Scowcroft sat among Bush's intimate circle of planners and was regarded as a reliable presidential sounding board. After Bush left office, Scowcroft traveled with the former president to Beijing in early 1994 and the two men worked together on a book about U.S. foreign policy toward Eastern Europe.

HERBERT S. PARMET

See also Bush, George Herbert Walker; China; Ford, Gerald Rudolph; Gulf War of 1990–1991; Iran-Contra Affair; Kissinger, Henry Alfred; Mayaguez Incident; Nixon, Richard Milhous; Strategic Defense Initiative

FURTHER READING

Beschloss, Michael R., and Strobe Talbott. *At the Highest Levels.* Boston, 1993.
Cannon, James. *Time and Chance: Gerald Ford's Appointment With History.* New York, 1994.
Duffy, Michael, and Dan Goodgame. *Marching In Place: The Status Quo Presidency of George Bush.* New York, 1992.
Ford, Gerald R. *A Time to Heal.* New York, 1979.
Greene, John Robert. *The Presidency of Gerald R. Ford.* Lawrence, Kans., 1995.

SDI

See Strategic Defense Initiative

SEALING

The act of harvesting seals for their fur or, on occasion, for their meat or blubber. Like other elements of the fur trade, sealing took place on the borders of societies and therefore led to confrontation among competing nations. In the colonial and early republic periods, sealing was a natural extension of whaling, as far-flung New England whalers and merchants took the opportunity to collect sealskins from remote parts of South America, Antarctica, and the North Pacific. In the middle of the nineteenth century, the northern fur seal (*Callorhinus ursinus*), which has home islands, or rookeries, scattered throughout the northern Pacific, became the subject of the most intense hunting.

Beginning in the mid-1880s, U.S. and British diplomats sought to resolve a crisis brought on by pelagic, or open-sea, harvesting of the northern fur seal in the Bering Sea. The British argued that Canadian sealers had an inalienable right to take any animals found in international waters, but the U.S. diplomats countered that the seals belonged to the United States because they were born on the Pribilof Islands, which were U.S. property. After a split decision at the Bering Sea arbitration tribunal in Paris in 1893 satisfied neither side by placing some restrictions on Canadians without accepting the U.S. claim, diplomats from both sides began to move slowly towards a compromise based on scientific understanding. U.S. government scientists demonstrated that pelagic sealers killed large numbers of breeding females, making it impossible for natural reproduction to keep pace with human predation. British and Canadian diplomats, scientists, and sealers were slow to accept this concept, but they eventually had to admit that the evidence was overwhelming.

Matters became more complex when Japanese sealers began to catch seals from the Pribilof herd in the late 1890s. The dispute now became multilateral, with Japan and Russia—owner of the remaining rookery islands—adding their enmity to the Anglo-American confrontation. But the continuing decline of the seals, from two million in 1870 to 150,000 in 1910, along with a warming of U.S.-Canadian relations, made a settlement possible. In 1911 the four nations agreed to the North Pacific Fur

Seal Convention, whereby Canada and Japan agreed to outlaw pelagic sealing in exchange for the establishment of a system of compensation from those nations with seal rookeries. Japan withdrew from the convention in 1941, ostensibly because the seals ate too many fish. After World War II, Japan, Canada, and the United States entered into an agreement similar to the convention of 1911.

The United States is also party to the 1972 Convention for the Conservation of Antarctic Seals, a delayed reaction to decades of damaging sealing activities in the region, which required each nation to pass its own protective legislation.

KURK DORSEY

See also Antarctica; Canada; Fur Trade; Great Britain; Whaling; Wildlife

FURTHER READING

Bailey, Thomas. "The North Pacific Sealing Convention of 1911." *Pacific Historical Review*, 4, March 1935.
Busch, Briton. *The War Against the Seals: A History of the North American Seal Fishery*. Montreal, 1985.
Dorsey, Kurk. "Putting a Ceiling on Sealing: Conservation and Cooperation in the International Arena, 1909–1911." *Environmental History Review*, 15, Fall 1991.

SEATO

See Southeast Asia Treaty Organization

SELF-DETERMINATION

The principle acknowledging the right of a people to organize their own nation and choose their own form of government free of external coercion. Self-determination is an expression of nationalism, independence, and sovereignty. The methods by which peoples have exercised the principle include revolution, secession, plebiscite, and territorial consolidation. Self-determination is implicit in the U.S. Declaration of Independence (1776) and the French Declaration of the Rights of Man (1789), and the new nations born in the nineteenth century from the Spanish Empire proclaimed it. President Woodrow Wilson in particular elevated the principle in his Fourteen Points during the era of World War I. The Versailles Treaty of 1919 honored self-determination when it broke up old empires and created new, independent states—for example, Austria, Czechoslovakia, Finland, Poland, and Yugoslavia. The Atlantic Charter of 1941 endorsed the principle, as did the United Nations Charter of 1945. As the Cold War unfolded after World War II, the United States labeled the Soviet presence in Eastern Europe a violation of self-determination.

As the process of decolonization accelerated after World War II, self-determination became the banner of independence movements in Vietnam, India, and Indonesia, to name but a few. The UN General Assembly approved a vague declaration in 1960 which stated that "all people have the right to self-determination; by virtue of that right they freely determine their political status and freely pursue their economic, social, and cultural development." Who possesses the right is a question that has dogged international relations. Does it apply not only to peoples seeking to end colonial rule but also to peoples—minorities—in sovereign nations? Ethnic-cultural groups (such as Biafrans in Nigeria, French Canadians in Canada, and Bangladeshis in Pakistan) and religious groups (such as Shia in Iraq and Catholics in Northern Ireland) have asserted the right. For the last several decades, radical Palestinian organizations have cited the right of self-determination to justify terrorism in their pursuit of a homeland. By the early 1990s self-determination movements seeking sovereignty bedeviled some sixty countries. The United States has often rhetorically endorsed self-determination but also frequently opposed efforts to achieve it by revolution, secession, or violence. When Yugoslavia splintered in the early 1990s, the United States, to no avail, called for the maintenance of Yugoslavia's territorial integrity and then hesitated to intervene in the many ethnic wars that followed.

THOMAS G. PATERSON

See also Atlantic Charter; Bangladesh; Canada; Colonialism; Fourteen Points; Imperialism; Iraq; Nigeria; Northern Ireland; Terrorism; United Nations; Versailles Treaty of 1919; Wilson, Thomas Woodrow; Yugoslavia

FURTHER READING

Alexander, Yonah, and Robert A. Friedlander, eds. *Self-Determination: National, Regional, and Global Dimensions*. Boulder, Colo., 1980.
Cassese, Antonio. *Self-Determination of Peoples: A Legal Reappraisal*. New York, 1995.
Cobban, Alfred. *The Nation State and National Self-Determination*. New York, 1969.
Gordon, David C. *Self-Determination and History in the Third World*. Princeton, N.J., 1971.
Halperin, Morton H., and David J. Scheffer, eds. *Self-Determination in the New World Order*. Washington, D.C., 1992.

SENEGAL

A republic located in Western Africa, bordering the North Atlantic Ocean between Mauritania, Mali, Guinea, and Guinea-Bissau, Senegal is a largely French-speaking and Muslim nation whose capital is Dakar. Senegal has had a long and relatively important relationship with the United States beginning in the nineteenth century when the United States maintained a consulate on the Island of Gorée. Millions of African Americans can trace their origins to the slave station on that island. Full diplomatic relations between the United States and Senegal began at the time of independence in 1960. Although Senegal has maintained very close ties with France, it has moved closer and closer to the United States over the years. The United States has been a major supplier of foreign assistance ($45 million in 1992), including PL480 food and project support in agriculture, health, and private sector development. Trade between Senegal and the United States has remained rather limited, with the United States accounting for under two percent of Senegal's exports and only about six percent of the country's imports. U.S. direct investment was small ($35 million) but continues to grow. In spite of severe economic difficulties and an inability in the past to conform to International Monetary Fund conditionalities, Senegal, as one of Africa's longest standing democracies, has continued to be the beneficiary of IMF support. Nominally nonaligned for most of its existence, Senegal has played an extremely important role as a leader of African and broader international groups such as the Organization of African Unity (OAU), Economic Community of West African States (ECOWAS), and the Communité Economiqúe du L'Africa de L'ovest (CEAO); more than fifty nations have diplomatic representation in Dakar. Relations with the United States have been close and cordial. Senegal served as an alternative landing site for the National Air and Space Administration space shuttle. At the urging of Washington, Senegal has provided troops to the Economic Community of West Africa's Monitoring Group (ECOMOG) in Liberia and was one of only two sub-Saharan African nations to contribute troops to the allies during the war in the Gulf in the early 1990s.

RICHARD VENGROFF

See also Africa; Gulf War of 1990–1991

FURTHER READING

Villalon, Leonardo. *Islamic Society and State Power in Senegal.* Cambridge, Eng., 1995.

SERBIA

The larger of the two remaining republics in the former Yugoslavia, bounded by Croatia, Hungary, Romania, Bulgaria, Macedonia, Albania, and Bosnia-Herzegovina. Both early in the twentieth century, when already an independent state, and at the century's close, as the dominant republic in the crumbling former Yugoslavia, Serbia has had an impact on international affairs quite disproportionate to its relatively small size.

The medieval Serb state was founded in the twelfth century. Under Stephen Dushan, during the thirteenth century, the empire reached its territorial apogee, expanding into present-day Montenegro and Macedonia, parts of Bosnia, as well as

into northern Greece and western Bulgaria. However, the Battle of Kosovo Field in 1389 marked the end of an independent Serb state, as well as the beginning of five centuries of Turkish rule. In 1804 the Serbs unsuccessfully rebelled against Ottoman rule; in 1815 another insurrection was more successful, paving the way for autonomy, in 1829, and de facto independence in 1856. At the Congress of Berlin in 1878 Serbia was officially recognized as an independent state.

The United States was one of the first countries to extend diplomatic recognition. During the early 1900s Serbia pursued a policy of strengthening its bonds with ethnic Serbs living within the Austro-Hungarian Empire, particularly in Bosnia. The resulting tensions between Austria-Hungary and Serbia, exacerbated by Austria's annexation of Bosnia-Herzegovina in 1908 and Serbia's territorial expansion though its victories in the Balkan War of 1912–1913, culminated in the assassination of Archduke Franz Ferdinand by a Serb nationalist in the Bosnian capital of Sarajevo in 1914, thus triggering World War I. At the Paris Peace Conference President Woodrow Wilson argued that, though the peoples of central and southeast Europe were entitled to self-determination, the proliferation of tiny nation-states was not in the security interests of the "new" Europe. It was felt that a South Slav federation with Serbia and Croatia at its base would provide an effective buffer to prevent renewed domination of the region by an outside power. Thus the Kingdom of Serbs, Croats, and Slovenes was created in 1918; it was renamed Yugoslavia in 1929. The new country began to crumble in the 1930s due to deep-seated animosities between Serbs and Croats. Matters worsened as a result of Yugoslavia's humiliating military collapse in the wake of the German blitzkrieg in April 1941. During World War II, the United States and its Allies provided aid to the partisan forces of Josip Broz Tito, largely controlled by communists, who were fighting a guerrilla war against the Nazis as well as against Serb and Croat nationalists. President Harry Truman supported Tito in his consolidation of the Yugoslav state and especially in his 1948 break with Soviet leader Joseph Stalin as a means of challenging the Soviets and depriving them of a sphere of influence in the Adriatic.

While inter-republic and ethnic tensions in Yugoslavia persisted even during the Tito era, upon Tito's death in 1980 they began to increase significantly. External factors such as the end of the Cold War and the examples of revolution and self-determination being set elsewhere in Eastern Europe produced a mix of permissive and suggestive effects, while recession and other economic problems were further exacerbants. But the key factor was the demagogic exploitation by leaders such as the communist apparatchik Slobodan Milosevic of an antagonistic and virulent form of nationalism that transformed ethnic tensions into ethnic hatreds. Milosevic's first efforts to forge a "greater Serbia" were directed at Kosovo, and in the late 1980s took the form of massive human rights abuses and political repression. Serbia's population overall was about two-thirds ethnic Serbs, eighteen percent Albanians, three and one-half percent Hungarians and a mix of Croats, Muslims, and Montenegrins. Kosovo's population was predominantly Albanian, and for that reason during the Tito era had been given special status as an "autonomous province" within the Serbian republic. Since Kosovo was the ancient center of the Serb empire, it had always infuriated the Serbs that Tito, himself a Croat/Slovene, apparently had tried to deny Serbia its rightful historical heritage. The initial U.S. response to Milosevic's antics was cautious, partly reflecting the George Bush administration's overarching concern with keeping Yugoslavia together and partly reflecting cross-pressures of different coalitions within Congress. In November 1990 a bill did pass Congress (the Nickles-Bentley Amendment) threatening economic sanctions if human rights improvements were not made.

By May 1991, the overall situation in Yugoslavia had drastically deteriorated. The Department of State severely criticized the Serbian elections held in December 1990; sudden changes in election laws prompted a boycott of the elections by the Albanians in Kosovo; and Milosevic's Socialist Party was accused of stealing funds from the Yugoslav treasury, manipulating election procedures in Serbia, and intimidating voters. The Serbian government's harsh crackdown in Kosovo, which included the suspension of its autonomous status, led to the widest outbreak of unrest in Yugoslavia since 1981. Secretary of State James Baker traveled to Belgrade on 21 June 1991 following the annual Conference on Security and Cooperation in Europe (CSCE) summit in Berlin. With less than one week left before Slovenia and Croatia were scheduled officially to announce their secession from Yugoslavia, Baker urged them to reconsider, stating that the United States would not recognize unilateral acts by the two republics. The Bush administration was later accused of having given Milosevic and the Yugoslav National Army (JNA) a "green light" to use force to keep Slovenia and Croatia from seceding; and congressional critics questioned Baker's choice not to use the threat of NATO or U.S. force to prevent the escalation of inter-republican hostilities. The Bush administration, however, argued that the use of force in an attempt to hold a country together when torn by civil war was simply never a credible U.S. option.

In any event, war did break out. The Serb-dominated JNA moved first against Slovenia, but quickly switched its focus to Croatia, with which it shared a border and which had a significant ethnic Serbian population. While the United States held the JNA and the Serbian leadership largely responsible for the resulting bloodshed, it appeared content to allow the European Community

(EC) to assume the lead negotiating role in seeking to stop the war. Once the war had spread to Bosnia-Herzegovina in April 1992, the United States took some more active measures but still did not assert its leadership. After the international recognition of Bosnia-Herzegovina, Serbia and Montenegro formed a new entity and sought unsuccessfully to be officially recognized as the successor state to the former Yugoslavia. The new federal government, formed by Milosevic, consisted of the anticommunist nationalist, Dobrica Cosic, as president, and Milan Panic, a Serbian-born U.S. businessman well known to the U.S. government, as prime minister. To Milosevic's surprise, the two men formed an alliance with the Serbian opposition who were intent on stopping the war in Bosnia. Panic decided to run against Milosevic in the Serbian presidential race called for in December 1992. The Department of State delayed for months the Serbian opposition parties' requests for an exception to the sanctions regime that would provide a television transmitter for independent stations to counteract Milosevic's monopoly of the airwaves. Milosevic won the election handily, and Panic—who had won thirty-six percent of the vote—was forced to resign his post as prime minister.

During the summer of 1992 Bosnian Serb prison camps had been discovered in northern and eastern Bosnia. Photos of these internment camps appeared in several U.S. newspapers and magazines. In the 1992 presidential campaign Bill Clinton argued that the United States should take a harder line with the Serbs. Administration initiatives in the United Nations Security Council to toughen the sanctions against Serbia-Montenegro and to impose a no-fly zone were not adopted until November 1992, following Clinton's victory. On 27 December 1992, less than one month before leaving office, President Bush informed Milosevic that the United States would consider any further attacks on the Albanian minority in Kosovo a direct threat to U.S. national interests. This decision sparked a debate in Washington since Kosovo, unlike Bosnia, was recognized as an integral part of Serbia. Others praised the preventive measure, since a Serb military crackdown in Kosovo could have the potential of escalating the war and involving neighboring countries.

The Clinton administration initially made no significant changes in U.S. policy toward Serbia. Failing to enforce the threats of air attacks on Serb targets which he had made during the campaign, Clinton allowed the UN and EC negotiators to take the lead in resolving the conflict by diplomatic means. However, the United States refused to support the resulting Vance-Owen plan in 1993, on the grounds that it gave insufficient land to the Muslims. The Department of State even accused the Europeans of appeasing the Serbs by offering them an excessively generous territorial settlement. While portraying Milosevic as the principal culprit in the breakup of Yugoslavia, the United States also showed flexibility in using him as a foil to the Bosnian Serbs, led by Radovan Karadzic. Milosevic's dispute with Karadzic concerning the approach to be taken regarding European Union and U.S. peace overtures in 1993 and 1994 proved advantageous to the West in dividing the Serbian leadership. Milosevic, however, tried to play both sides, as for example with his claims to the West of having closed the Serbian-Bosnian border, the reality being a slowing but not cessation of the flow of vital supplies and goods into Bosnian Serb territory.

The fundamental problem in U.S. policy towards Serbia became clear in March 1994 when the Bosnians and Croats decided to cease their own hostilities and form a confederation—in effect creating a union of Bosnian government—and Croatian-controlled lands. Similar demands by the Bosnian Serbs for the right to associate with Serbia were rejected by the international community. Finally, in the Dayton peace talks, initiated by the United States in late 1995 in the wake of the changed military balance against the Serbs following NATO air strikes and the Croatian recapture of the Krajina, the Bosnian Serb leadership agreed to allow Milosevic—instead of Karadzic—to head their delegation and negotiate on their behalf. Milosevic, against the will of some of the Bosnian Serb delegates to the conference, made substantial territorial concessions. In particular, he agreed that Sarajevo should be reunified and governed by the Bosnian Muslims. He also acquiesced to the retention by the Bosnian Federation of the Gorazde enclave, and agreed to a land corridor to connect the enclave to the rest of the Federation-controlled territory. With the implementation of the peace plan and the arrival of NATO troops in Bosnia in December 1995, the UN Security Council agreed to suspend economic sanctions imposed on Serbia and Montenegro; the United States followed suit in January 1996. The suspension of sanctions remained conditional, until the Bosnian elections were held in September 1996, when all but the "outer wall" sanctions, such as official diplomatic recognition, were lifted.

LUKE ZAHNER

See also Austria; Baker, James Addison, III; Bosnia-Herzegovina; Croatia; Human Rights; Hungary; Tito, Josip Broz; World War I; Yugoslavia

FURTHER READING

Cohen, Leonard. *Broken Bonds: The Disintegration of Yugoslavia.* Boulder, Colo., 1993.
Crnobrnja, Mihailo. *The Yugoslav Drama.* Montreal, 1994.
Woodward, Susan. *Balkan Tragedy: Chaos and Disintegration after the Cold War.* Washington, D.C., 1995.
Zimmermann, Warren. "Origins of a Catastrophe." *Foreign Affairs.* January/February 1995.

SEWARD, WILLIAM HENRY

(*b.* 16 May 1801; *d.* 16 October 1872)

U.S. senator (1849–1861) and secretary of state (1861–1869), who managed the North's foreign affairs during the Civil War and set the United States on an expansionist course after the war. Born in Florida, New York, Seward graduated from Union College, practiced law, and was elected the first Whig governor of New York (1838–1842). As a U.S. senator, Seward was the generally acknowledged leader of the Republican Party. His widely disseminated orations included discourses on foreign relations in which the United States appeared as a nation of destiny, whose "mission" was "to renovate the condition of mankind" by extending throughout the world the ideals elucidated in the Declaration of Independence.

In March 1861 Seward became secretary of state in the administration of Abraham Lincoln, who left the conduct of foreign relations almost entirely to him, a practice also adhered to by the next chief executive, Andrew Johnson. Secretary Seward had to contend with a divided Union engulfed in total war and afterward with Johnson, an inept president stridently engaged in a power struggle with hostile partisans in Congress.

Following the outbreak of the American Civil War and the political disintegration of the United States, Seward wrote American diplomats overseas that their responsibility was to help prevent foreign intervention. Seward shared Lincoln's belief that if the American Union was not restored, democracy, the "hope of the world," might be forever doomed. Hence Seward adroitly and vigorously opposed all efforts by Confederate agents operating in Europe to invoke great power intervention for the purpose of assuring the independence of the Confederacy.

It was Seward who in December 1861 contrived a peaceful settlement of the *Trent* affair, one of the most dangerous diplomatic crises in U.S. history. Seward carefully laid the groundwork for a postwar admission of guilt and damages to be paid by the British government, owing to massive depredations against the U.S. merchant marine by Confederate warships such as the *Alabama*, which were built in British shipyards and supplied largely in British ports. Seward's "case," pressed relentlessly for five years, made possible the 1871 Treaty of Washington and the ensuing Geneva arbitration award that resolved the dispute with England over the *Alabama* claims.

Radical abolitionists criticized Seward during the early years of the Civil War for reinforcing Lincoln's determination to place the preservation of the Union ahead of the immediate emancipation of slaves in the South, but it was the secretary of state who quietly negotiated a treaty with Great Britain for the suppression of the African slave trade, initiated diplomatic relations with the black republics of Liberia and Haiti, and, when the opportunity came, gave his support to emancipation both by proclamation and by constitutional amendment.

Among other foreign policy achievements, Seward peaceably pressured the French out of Mexico in 1867 (but with U.S. military power available if necessary), strengthened the U.S. commercial position in Japan, promoted an international postal agreement, supported the completion of the Atlantic cable, established the diplomatic foundations for the eventual settlement of the San Juan boundary dispute, and persuaded the British at last to recognize U.S. naturalization laws. During his tenure as secretary of state, Seward managed to improve the international status of the United States by negotiating more treaties with foreign nations (the most famous for the Alaska Purchase in 1867) than had all his predecessors together.

Some of the initiatives by which Seward sought to advance the commercial hegemony of the United States as a vehicle for spreading democracy abroad failed because they were too visionary or overreaching at the time. His attempts to annex Hawaii, to purchase portions of the Danish West Indies, to construct an interoceanic canal at Panama, to establish intercontinental telegraphic communications through Asia to Europe, to open up trade with China and Korea, to acquire U.S. bases in Iceland, Greenland, and the Caribbean, and to facilitate monetary reform that would make the dollar a basic unit of exchange ended in disappointment, but all later became reality.

Seward's legacy included the preservation of the American Union, the eradication of slavery, and significant diplomatic successes. As a young man he had expressed his conviction "that however birth or language or climate may have made them differ, the nations of the earth are nevertheless one family, and all mankind are brethren." His conception of manifest destiny in foreign relations had been to "assail aristocracy" and spread democracy.

NORMAN B. FERRIS

See also Alabama Claims; Alaska Purchase; American Civil War; Communications Policy; Confederate States of America; Lincoln, Abraham; Manifest Destiny; Mexico; Panama and Panama Canal; Slave Trade and Slavery; Trent Affair

FURTHER READING

Ferris, Norman B. *Desperate Diplomacy: William H. Seward's Foreign Policy, 1861.* Knoxville, Tenn., 1976.
Ferris, Norman B. "William H. Seward and the Faith of a Nation." In *Traditions and Values: American Diplomacy, 1790–1865,* edited by Norman A. Graebner. Lanham, Md., 1985.
Paludin, Phillip Shaw. *The Presidency of Abraham Lincoln.* Lawrence, Kans., 1994.
Seward, Frederick W. *Autobiography of William H. Seward, From 1801 to 1834 with a Memoir of His Life and Selections from His Let-

ters from 1831 to 1846.* New York, 1877.
Seward, Frederick W. *Seward at Washington as Senator and Secretary of State. A Memoir of His Life with Selections from His Letters,* 2 vols. New York, 1891.
Van Deusen, Glyndon. *William Henry Seward.* New York, 1967.

SEYCHELLES

See Appendix 2

SHAH OF IRAN
Mohammad Reza Shah Pahlavi
(*b.* 26 October 1919; *d.* July 1980)

Monarch of Iran from 1941 until 1979, when he was deposed in the Islamic revolution led by Ayatollah Ruhollah Khomeini. From the mid-1950s until the revolution the shah allied his government closely with the United States. His downfall in 1979 ended the close U.S. relationship with Iran and initiated an era of considerable tension between the two countries which continued into the mid-1990s.

The shah's father, Reza Khan (1878–1944), was an army officer from a simple family who helped engineer a coup d'etat in 1921 that enabled him four years later to depose the reigning Qajar dynasty and crown himself shah. The crown prince was sent to Switzerland to study at the age of twelve. He returned to Iran in 1936 and completed his studies at Iran's military academy. He ascended to the Peacock Throne in 1941, after Great Britain and the Soviet Union invaded Iran during World War II to establish a supply corridor to Soviet territory.

During World War II and in the early postwar period the young shah was politically weak and ineffective. This was a period of great flux in Iran, with traditional political forces reasserting their power and new forces emerging to challenge these traditional forces and the authority of the monarch. The first such challenge was posed by the Communist Tudeh (Masses) party, which flourished under Soviet wartime occupation and was probably the most popular political organization in Iran at the end of the war. The Tudeh party helped foment the 1945–1946 Azerbaijan crisis and was seriously weakened when this crisis came to an end. The United States played a key role in resolving this crisis and the shah subsequently looked to the United States for assistance. U.S. officials rebuffed the shah's repeated requests for military and economic aid in the late 1940s, though they slowly increased their involvement in Iran in other ways during this period.

A second challenge to the shah's authority occurred in the early 1950s, when Mohammad Mosaddeq emerged as the leader of a popular political movement that sought to nationalize Iran's British-controlled oil industry and democratize its political system—a goal that inevitably meant reducing the shah's power. Bowing to Mosaddeq's popularity, the shah appointed him prime minister in April 1951. Mosaddeq then nationalized the oil industry and began a protracted campaign to wrest power from the shah and place it in the hands of the Majlis (Parliament) and cabinet. The shah was paralyzed with indecision during Mosaddeq's tenure, refusing to act against him. By early 1953, U.S. officials had concluded that Mosaddeq had created conditions that might lead to a Tudeh takeover. Accordingly, the Central Intelligence Agency engineered a coup that ousted Mosaddeq. The shah reluctantly supported the coup, though he played no direct role in it.

Mosaddeq's challenge to his authority and the crucial U.S. role in deflecting this challenge apparently convinced the shah that he needed to be more forceful and that he would have to rely heavily on U.S. support for several years. He therefore initiated a harsh crackdown on his opponents immediately after the coup, jailing thousands of Mosaddeq supporters and Tudeh members, conducting show trials of Mosaddeq and his top associates, muzzling the press, and rigging the February 1954 elections to pack the Majlis with his supporters. The United States provided the shah with large amounts of economic aid during the post-coup period and undertook a major effort to restructure and modernize his security forces. This assistance enabled the shah to weather this period and created the foundations for the authoritarian regime the shah presided over in the 1960s and 1970s.

By 1957 the shah's grip on power was much stronger, and U.S. officials began to pressure him to carry out reforms to broaden his base of support. The shah therefore eased restrictions on political activity and initiated certain limited socioeconomic reforms. Unrest remained widespread, however, and the more open political environment also produced a flourish of opposition activity and several significant challenges to the shah's authority in the late 1950s and early 1960s. With a strong repressive apparatus now in place the shah was able to suppress these challenges without much difficulty. This period of greater openness came to an end in June 1963, when the security forces attacked large demonstrations organized by followers of Ayatollah Khomeini, killing hundreds. Although the shah expanded his "White Revolution" of socioeconomic reforms substantially in the mid-1960s, he did not implement political reforms again until the late 1970s.

The shah's attitude toward the United States was rather bitter and disillusioned; he blamed the United States for pressuring him to pursue political reform and for having close ties to several of the figures who chal-

lenged him in this period. Moreover, with rapidly growing oil revenue and a strong security apparatus in place, the shah grew less dependent on U.S. support. He therefore began to distance himself from the United States and allowed U.S. aid programs to lapse, was less candid with U.S. officials, and significantly but cautiously improved his relations with the Soviet Union. However, on a number of issues, such as combating Arab radicalism and limiting Soviet influence in the region, he recognized that his interests still largely coincided with the United States, and he continued to cooperate accordingly. The shah therefore transformed Iran in the mid-1960s from a highly dependent, insecure U.S. client to a relatively independent junior partner of the United States. During a 1972 visit to Tehran, President Richard Nixon agreed to sell large amounts of U.S. military equipment to Iran, making Iran a "regional policeman" and a prototype for the Nixon Doctrine. Nevertheless, at the same time the shah was playing a leading role in efforts by the Organization of Petroleum Exporting Countries to raise world oil prices, which culminated in the huge price increases that followed the 1973 Arab-Israeli War.

Within his country the shah's autocratic regime left him aloof and isolated from the Iranian people. Inequality grew sharply, corruption flourished, Western values and culture proliferated, political freedoms were sharply restricted, and billions of dollars were spent on advanced military equipment and other items of dubious practical value. The shah's close relations with the United States, the conservative Arab states, and Israel further stirred discontent and unrest. The first open manifestations of this unrest occurred in the early 1970s, when leftist and Islamic guerrillas began to attack symbols of the shah's regime. The shah responded with severe repression, provoking condemnation from international human rights organizations. The 1973–1974 oil boom compounded these problems, creating an increasingly chaotic and unstable situation. By early 1978 the first signs of revolution had appeared.

President Jimmy Carter had made very ambivalent statements about Iran during his presidential campaign and his first year in office, leaving the shah uncertain about his regime's standing with the United States. Moreover, the shah had secretly been undergoing treatment for lymphatic leukemia since 1974. These factors left him listless and indecisive as the revolution unfolded in 1978, and the autocratic regime deprived the shah of legitimacy and constrained his ability to respond to the growing challenge to his authority. The shah's efforts to quell the revolution were erratic, ranging from conciliatory gestures to harsh repression. He became increasingly withdrawn as the revolution escalated in the fall of 1978, avoiding the public and often failing to respond to the revolutionaries' initiatives. The shah's feebleness emboldened the revolutionary leadership and contributed to the difficulties that faced U.S. officials seeking to respond effectively to the growing crisis. By December 1978 he had resigned himself to defeat, initiating negotiations with moderate opposition figures on the composition of a transition government. He fled into exile on 16 January 1979, leaving Iran to the revolutionaries.

The shah's psychological and physical health deteriorated rapidly while he was in exile. He wrote a book titled *Answer to History*, which blamed the United States for his downfall. He pressured U.S. officials to permit him to enter the United States for medical treatment, precipitating the November 1979 seizure of the U.S. embassy in Tehran. After leaving the United States in December, he lived in Panama for several months and then traveled to Egypt, where he died of cancer in July 1980.

MARK J. GASIOROWSKI

See also Iran; Mosaddeq, Mohammad

FURTHER READING
Alam, Asadollah. *The Shah and I: The Confidential Diaries of Iran's Royal Court*. London, 1992.
Pahlavi, Mohammad Reza Shah. *Mission for My Country*. New York, 1961.
——. *Answer to History*. New York, 1980.
Zonis, Marvin. *Majestic Failure: The Fall of the Shah*. Chicago, 1991.

SHANDONG QUESTION

(1919–1922)

The issue over the sovereignty of the Shandong (Shantung) province in northeast China. Shandong was a German colony from 1899 until the Japanese seized it at the outset of World War I. At the Paris Peace Conference of 1919, President Woodrow Wilson advocated the return of Shandong to China. He saw such a restoration both as China's moral right and in the United States's interest as a way of containing the Japanese in East Asia and protecting the Open Door Policy.

After taking Shandong from Germany, Tokyo forced China to agree by treaty to recognize Japan as the legal successor of the ousted Germans. The British, French, and Russians accepted the legal validity of this arrangement, but Wilson emphatically did not. Wilson invited the Chinese delegates to make their case before the peace conference. He asked that Japan contribute to the new international order by foregoing the fruits of conquest. The Japanese threatened not to sign the Versailles Treaty if they were forced immediately to evacuate Shandong. Wilson compromised and accepted Tokyo's verbal assurances that its troops would be withdrawn in the near future. The Japanese, in turn, signed the peace treaty

and joined the League of Nations. However, many of Wilson's critics believed that this arrangement sacrificed Chinese interests to Japanese expansionism. The unpopular Shandong settlement figured prominently in the U.S. Senate's rejection of the Versailles Treaty. The Japanese proved true to their word and their troops left Shandong in 1922.

HUGH D. PHILLIPS

See also China; Japan; Open Door Policy; Paris Peace Conference of 1919; Versailles Treaty of 1919

FURTHER READING
Fifield, Russell. *Woodrow Wilson and the Far East: The Diplomacy of the Shantung Question*. Hamden, Conn., 1965.
Levin, N. Gordon, Jr. *Woodrow Wilson and World Politics: America's Response to War and Revolution*. London, 1968.

SHANTUNG QUESTION

See Shandong Question

SHERMAN, JOHN

(*b.* 10 May 1823; *d.* 22 October 1900)

Republican senator (1861–1877, 1881–1897) and secretary of state (5 March 1897–27 April 1898). Born in Lancaster, Ohio, he left school at the age of fourteen, found work constructing canal improvements, and read law in an uncle's office. He was the younger brother of Civil War general William Tecumseh Sherman. Admitted to the bar in Ohio in 1844, John became active in Whig politics. Soon afterward he helped organize the national Republican Party and served as chairman of Ohio's first Republican convention in 1855. Sherman served in the U.S. House of Representatives (1855–1861) and then won election to the Senate. During his first tenure in the Senate, he opposed radical reconstruction measures and voted to impeach President Andrew Johnson, although he expressed a personal satisfaction that the impeachment effort failed.

Throughout his long political career Sherman was noted more for his unwavering party loyalty than for consistent personal convictions or principles. President Rutherford B. Hayes appointed Sherman secretary of the Treasury, a post he held from 1877 to 1881. Considered an authority on federal finance, Sherman was responsible for resumption of specie payments in 1879, an achievement that caused gleeful bankers to compare his tenure as secretary of the Treasury with that of Alexander Hamilton. Greenbackers, Silverites, and Populists, on the other hand, viewed him as too sympathetic to capitalist interests. While he was chairman of the Senate Finance

Committee, Sherman's name was attached to the Antitrust and Silver Purchase Acts of 1890, but his support for these measures was lukewarm. Early in his senate career Sherman supported reductions in tariffs, but after 1872, when his party's policies shifted, he consistently voted for protectionist tariffs and opposed reciprocity agreements. Viewing Sherman's inconsistencies, one of his Republican colleagues observed, "If in these thirty years Sherman has had any guiding principles in finance, he has so concealed it that I am ignorant of its form and features!" Meanwhile, mugwumps and liberal reformers viewed Sherman as an unreliable ally of civil-service reform and a crass opportunist. On foreign policy issues, Sherman at first opposed Chinese exclusion but later modified his views; he favored compromise during the Samoan Crisis of 1889, and believed Hawai'i should eventually be annexed as part of California. A Republican loyalist and frequent mediator among various factions within his party, Sherman unsuccessfully sought his party's nomination for the presidency in 1880, 1884, and 1888.

President William McKinley appointed Sherman secretary of state to make available his senate seat for an Ohio political insider, Mark Hanna. But Sherman lacked diplomatic experience and was troubled by poor memory and various afflictions of his advanced age. His opposition to overseas expansion in the Philippines and Caribbean put him out of step with the emphasis of the McKinley administration. And he was not closely involved in the management of important diplomatic issues facing the administration, including Hawai'ian annexation, negotiations with Spain over the Cuban crisis, and the sealing disputes with Canada and Great Britain. Toward the end of his tenure, the assistant secretary of state, William R. Day, a close personal friend of the president, attended cabinet meetings in Sherman's place. When the United States declared war on Spain in April 1898, Sherman resigned from the cabinet in protest, expressed bitterness towards McKinley and Hanna, and publicly stated his anti-expansionist views.

MICHAEL J. DEVINE

See also Hawai'i; McKinley, William; Samoa, American; Sealing; Spanish-American-Cuban-Filipino War, 1898; Tariffs

FURTHER READING

Sears, L. M. "John Sherman." In *American Secretaries of State and Their Diplomacy*, edited by S. F. Bemis. IX, New York, 1929.

Sherman, John. *John Sherman's Recollection of Forty Years in the House, Senate, and Cabinet: An Autobiography*. Chicago, 1895.

Nichols, Jeanette. "Rutherford B. Hayes and John Sherman" *Ohio History* (1961):125–138

Weaver, John B. "John Sherman and the Politics of Change." *Hayes Historical Journal* 6 (1987):7–19

SHIDEHARA, KIJURO

(*b.* 1872; *d.* 10 March 1951)

Japan's ambassador to the United States (1919–1922), minister of foreign affairs (1924–1927; 1929–1931), and prime minister (October 1945–April 1946). Shidehara is best known for his advocacy of "Shidehara diplomacy," an approach to foreign affairs that stressed international cooperation and building strong trade relations. He also played an important role in reforming the Japanese constitution during the U.S. occupation of 1945–1952. Born in Osaka, Shidehara studied law at Tokyo Imperial University. He began his foreign service career in 1896, and because of his educational background and marriage to Iwasaki Masako, daughter of the Mitsubishi chairman, he advanced quickly, serving in posts in Korea, Europe, and the United States.

As ambassador to the United States, Shidehara served as Japan's delegate to the Washington Naval Conference where he reduced tensions with Beijing by returning Shandong Province to China. In 1924 Shidehara joined the cabinet of Prime Minister Kato Takaaki as minister of foreign affairs and promoted Japan's world trade to fuel economic growth at home. Following the ideals of the League of Nations Covenant and the provisions of the Washington conference agreement, he stressed a policy that respected legitimate Chinese demands and cooperation with Great Britain and the United States. However, the Manchurian Incident of September 1931 momentarily derailed Shidehara's career, as more aggressive, expansionist leaders gained control of Japan's foreign policy, forcing out Shidehara and fellow cabinet members. From 1931 to 1945 Shidehara continued to serve in the House of Peers. While differing with the aggressive turn of Japanese politics, he remained largely inactive.

Recognizing his earlier sympathies for the United States and the West, his previous advocacy of peaceful international cooperation, and his long retirement from active politics, U.S. General Douglas MacArthur appointed Shidehara prime minister in October 1945. He served until April 1946. Shidehara helped the career of Yoshida Shigeru (prime minister, 1946–1954) by appointing him foreign minister, and he drafted the address in which Emperor Hirohito renounced his divinity. He also authored Article 9 of the 1947 constitution that prohibits Japan from engaging in war or maintaining military forces. As a founding member of the Japanese Progressive Party, Shidehara won election to the Diet, where he became speaker of the lower house, a post he occupied until his death.

BRUCE D. MACTAVISH

See also Japan; Manchurian Crisis; Washington Conference on the Limitation of Armaments

FURTHER READING

Brown, Sydney. "Shidehara Kijuro: The Diplomacy of the Yen." In *Diplomats in Crises: United States-Chinese-Japanese Relations, 1919–1941.* Richard D. Burns and Edward M. Bennett, eds. Santa Barbara, Calif., 1974.

Buckley, Roger. *U.S.-Japan Alliance Diplomacy, 1945–1990.* Cambridge, Mass., 1992.

Schaller, Michael. *The American Occupation of Japan: Origins of the Cold War in Asia.* New York, 1985.

SHIPPING COMPANIES

Companies that actually operate ships, as distinct from those that merely arrange space for the transport of cargo. U.S. shipping companies operate ships under both U.S. and foreign flags, so-called "flags of convenience." From its leading position after World War II, the U.S.-flag merchant marine has steadily declined to less than 3 percent of the world fleet, placing it below the top ten fleets. Foreign-flag ships owned by U.S. shipping companies, however, constitute another 3 to 4 percent of the world total. The companies and their operations have evolved in response to legislative measures reflecting Congress's concerns since the early part of this century about the role of the U.S. merchant fleet and the anticompetitive practices of the companies.

The most important pieces of shipping legislation are the 1916 Shipping Act with its various amendments, the Merchant Marine Acts of 1920, 1928, 1936, and 1970, and the Shipping Act of 1984. These acts both regulate the competitive behavior of the companies and promote their growth through subsidies and preferred access to cargo. To implement the laws the 1916 Act created the U.S. Shipping Board, replaced in 1936 by the U.S. Maritime Commission, which became part of the Department of Commerce in 1951. In 1961 the regulatory functions were assumed by the newly created, independent Federal Maritime Commission; the promotional functions were vested in the U.S. Maritime Administration (MARAD), which remained in the Department of Commerce.

U.S.-flag merchant ships are owned by private shipping companies as well as the government. Government-owned vessels constitute the National Defense Reserve Fleet (NDRF), which, intended for military and other emergencies, is in a high state of readiness but not normally in active operation. These ships are managed by private shipping companies under five-year contracts with MARAD. The number and names of these management agents change over time because of a competitive bidding process, but all are operators of U.S.-flag vessels. Included are such major foreign trade carriers as American President Lines (APL), Crowley American Transport, Farrell Lines, Keystone Shipping, Lykes Brothers, and OMI Shipping Management.

While there were 148 U.S.-flag operators in 1992, the number varies over time as companies and subsidiaries are created and dissolved in response to current commercial and political imperatives. This also affects the size and composition of the privately owned U.S.-flag fleet, which in 1992 numbered 348 ships. Of these, 50 were on charter to the Military Sealift Command, the mission of which is to meet the armed services' needs for ocean transport in a national emergency; 118 were in trade between the U.S. and foreign countries (foreign trades); 24 traded between foreign countries (cross-trades); and the remainder were in domestic trade, including 65 ships operated by 16 companies on the Great Lakes.

In the scheduled services (liner trades), U.S. shipping companies are world leaders providing "water only" as well as intermodal services for both containerized and noncontainerized (break-bulk) general cargo. Major operators include, in addition to those mentioned above, Sea-Land Service, AFRAM Lines, Waterman Steamship, Navieras de Puerto Rico, and the Sea-Barge Group. In the foreign bulk trades, EXXON and the Keystone Shipping Companies are prominent in oil carriage. OMI Shipping Company and Maritime Overseas Corporation are major carriers of oil and dry bulk cargoes, often reserved for U.S.-flag ships under the Public Law 480 Cargo Preference Program.

The major reason for operating a U.S.-flag fleet is to meet the nation's commercial and defense needs, particularly as stated in the 1936 Merchant Marine Act. The ability to meet these needs has been questioned as the country's ocean-borne foreign commerce has become increasingly dominated by foreign flag operators, and U.S.-flag participation in trade with some countries is dependent on bilateral agreements. To maintain the fleet's viability, maritime support bills are frequently presented in Congress. In 1993 a failed bill proposed a new subsidy package of $1.5 billion over ten years. Absent renewed subsidies, APL and Sea-Land sought and received MARAD's permission in early 1995 to register under a foreign flag (Marshall Islands) some of their newly built ships. In April 1995, Congress began consideration of a subsidy bill submitted by President Bill Clinton's administration.

The interaction between shipping companies and foreign policy is well illustrated in MARAD's conditions for APL and Sea-Land's foreign-flag registration. The ships have to be under "friendly" flags and in an emergency they must be returned to U.S. registry and made available for government service. Another pointed example is the 1987 reflagging of Kuwaiti tankers to the U.S. flag. As the Iran-Iraq War turned toward attacks on tankers in the Persian Gulf, Kuwait asked for U.S. Navy protection of the state-owned Kuwait Oil Tanker Company's (KOTC) tankers. Washington demurred, as legal protection by the

Navy could only be extended to U.S.-flag ships. When the Soviet Union indicated readiness to meet Kuwait's request, however, the United States waived several flag requirements, and nine KOTC ships were put under U.S.-flag in July 1987 to be operated by the Gleneagle Shipping Company, a U.S. subsidiary of the English company, Denholm Shipping.

In general, access for U.S.-flag operators to growing volumes of cargo is dependent on the success of U.S. commercial policies and favorable renegotiations of various bilateral shipping agreements, particularly with China and countries in South America and the former Soviet Union.

BERNHARD J. ABRAHAMSSON

FURTHER READING

Alderton, Patrick M. *Sea Transport: Operation and Economics*. United Kingdom, 1995.

Frankel, Ernst G. *Regulation and Policies of American Shipping*. Boston, 1982.

Kendall, Lane C. *The Business of Shipping*. Centerville, Md., 1986.

U.S. Department of Commerce, Maritime Administration. *Annual Report*. Washington, D.C.

———. *Foreign Flag Merchant Ships Owned by U.S. Parent Companies. Annual Report*. Washington, D.C.

Whitehurst, C.H. *The U.S. Merchant Marine*. Annapolis, Md., 1983.

SHULTZ, GEORGE PRATT

(*b.* 13 December 1920)

Secretary of state (1982–1989) under Ronald Reagan. Born in New York City, Shultz has enjoyed a distinguished career in academe, the corporate world, and government. Shultz, who received a doctorate in industrial economics from the Massachusetts Institute of Technology in 1949, served as secretary of labor, the first director of the Office of Management and Budget, and secretary of the treasury in the Nixon administration. In July 1982 he became secretary of state—his fourth cabinet-level post.

Two central convictions that Shultz brought to the Department of State were that U.S. foreign policy had been floundering since the fall of Vietnam, and that diplomacy needed to be supported by the appropriate use of force. His style, often plodding and always deliberate, stood in marked contrast to the general ideological tenor of the Reagan administration. Shultz respected Reagan, but became nervous about the president's tendency to believe in the "script" of an event or issue as portrayed to the public, rather than in the facts of the matter.

Shultz's diplomatic style appeared to pay off in his achievements as secretary of state. The Intermediate-Range Nuclear Forces (INF) Treaty, signed in Washing-

ton on 7 December 1987, eliminated an entire class of U.S. and Soviet nuclear missiles and provided for unprecedented verification procedures. One year later Shultz announced that the United States would enter into "a substantive dialogue" with the Palestine Liberation Organization (PLO), after the PLO recognized Israel's right to exist and renounced terrorism in all forms.

On other issues, Shultz advocated sending U.S. troops to Beirut as part of a multinational force, against the advice of secretary of defense Caspar Weinberger. An October 1983 terrorist attack against the U.S. marines' barracks in Beirut resulted in the deaths of 239 soldiers. After the tragedy, Shultz did not second-guess the wisdom of deploying U.S. troops in Lebanon, but placed the blame on missed diplomatic opportunities and the tentativeness of the multinational military presence. Shultz strongly advocated the U.S. invasion of Grenada on 25 October 1983 to prevent the taking of U.S. hostages in the wake of the military overthrow and subsequent execution of Prime Minister Maurice Bishop. Shultz believed that the Grenada invasion also put the world on notice that the United States was ready to use force in support of its diplomatic objectives. Shultz strongly supported aid to the Nicaraguan Contra rebels as well as aid to the government of El Salvador, which was facing its own rebellion. Critics argued that U.S. aid to the Contras was in effect creating the civil war in Nicaragua, while aid to El Salvador, whose government had a dismal human rights record, embroiled the United States in a setting too reminiscent of the Vietnam War.

The Iran-Contra scandal cast a glaring light on the conduct of foreign policy under Shultz's direction. Shultz's reputation was enhanced by the knowledge that he had opposed the arms-for-hostages deal, and by his condemnation of the "renegade NSC [National Security Council] staff" during congressional hearings. On the other hand, the scandal revealed what Shultz termed "a kind of guerrilla warfare going on" between himself and members of the NSC and Reagan White House staffs. He and Weinberger repeatedly thought that their opposition had killed the arms deals with Iran. Shultz expressed shock and embarrassment over the extent to which national security advisers Robert McFarlane and John Poindexter and Central Intelligence Agency director William Casey deliberately hid the Iran-Contra operation from him.

Assessments of Shultz's stewardship of U.S. foreign policy invariably are caught up in the debate over the legacy of the Reagan administration. The collapse of communism in Eastern Europe and the Soviet Union, the subsequent agreements to reduce strategic nuclear arsenals, acceleration of the peace process in the Middle East, and the fading—although not necessarily resolved—regional conflicts in Central America, southern Africa, Afghanistan, and elsewhere have been attributed to the Reagan administration. Critics have argued, however, that these changes happened in spite of Reagan's expensive arms buildup and deliberate intensification of the Cold War, and that the ending of the Cold War stemmed more from the reforms launched by Mikhail Gorbachev in Russia than from U.S. steadfastness.

DAVID A. HUBERT

See also Casey, William Joseph; Contras; El Salvador; Grenada Invasion; Intermediate-Range Nuclear Forces Treaty; Iran-Contra Affair; Lebanon; Middle East; Nicaragua; Reagan, Ronald Wilson

FURTHER READING

Beschloss, Michael R., and Strobe Talbott. *At the Highest Levels. The Inside Story of the End of the Cold War.* Boston, 1993.

Hoffmann, Stanley. "Endless Turmoil for How Much Triumph?" *Foreign Policy* 94 (Spring 1994): 148–157.

LaFeber, Walter. "Turmoil and Triumph." *American Historical Review* 98 (October 1993): 1203–1205.

Shultz, George P. *Turmoil and Triumph.* New York, 1993.

Weigel, George. "Shultz, Reagan, and the Revisionists." *Commentary* 96 (August 1993): 50-53.

SHUTTLE DIPLOMACY

See Kissinger, Henry Alfred

SIAM

See Thailand

SIERRA LEONE

Republic located in West Africa, bordering the North Atlantic Ocean between Guinea and Liberia. The dominant ethnic groups in the country are the Mende, Temne, and Krio peoples. Sierra Leone has no one dominant religion with a nearly even split of Christians, Muslims, and practitioners of traditional religions, although Islam is currently the fastest growing religion. Sierra Leone began to take its current shape in the late-eighteenth century when the British established contacts for the purpose of establishing a home for former slaves and eventually for slaves recaptured from slaving vessels.

Sierra Leone gained its independence on 27 April 1961 under the government of the Sierra Leone People's Party (SLPP) which was led by Albert Margai. That same year, Sierra Leone entered into diplomatic relations with the United States. In 1967, the All People's Congress (APC), led by Siaka Stevens, won a general election

but was forced out by a coup. A year later, the APC regained power in a counter-coup and over the next decade and a half Sierra Leone was converted from a multiparty member of the British Commonwealth to a one-party republican state. In 1985, President Stevens resigned and J.S. Momoh was elected president a year later. Although maintaining a one-party system, initially President Momoh made conscious effort to make the government more accessible to the people. President Momoh was removed by a military coup in April 1992. The military government, led by Captain Valentine Strasser, has been faced with civil war, making the plans announced in 1994 for a transition to civilian rule uncertain. Generally speaking, the United States and Sierra Leone have had good relations although Sierra Leone has never been a high priority for the United States.

ANTHONY Q. CHEESEBORO

See also Africa

FURTHER READING

Hayward, Fred, M. "Sierra Leone: State Consolidation, Fragmentation, and Decay," in *Contemporary West African States*, edited by Donal Cruise O'Brien, John Dunn, and Richard Rathbone. Cambridge, Mass., 1989.

Rodney, Walter. *A History of the Upper Guinea Coast 1545–1800.* Oxford, 1970.

SINGAPORE

Located in Southeastern Asia, at the southern tip of the Malay Peninsula, a former British colony and during 1963–1965 part of the Federation of Malaysia, Singapore became an independent republic in 1965. Within a year the United States granted Singapore diplomatic recognition, and since then the U.S.-Singaporean relations have been largely cooperative, although there have been occasional and incidents of tension and potential conflict.

Singapore is unique in being akin to a "city-state." While it consists of over fifty islands, more than ninety percent of its population lives in the capital city of Singapore. Over seventy-five percent of the population are ethnic Chinese, with Malays as the next largest ethnic group (about fifteen percent).

While scarce on natural resources and small in area, Singapore has become one of the world's leading newly industrialized countries. It is the world's second busiest port and a major regional communications and services center. The United States is Singapore's largest trading partner as well as its largest source of foreign investment. Annual per capita income is among the highest in Asia.

The United States provides no bilateral economic assistance to this burgeoning economy, but it does provide a small military training program. Since the United

States lost its access to military bases in the Philippines, Singapore has afforded limited access to air and naval facilities. It also has taken part in joint military exercises with the United States. Singapore also participates in a Five Powers Defense Agreement with Australia, New Zealand, Malaysia, and Great Britain. It also was a founding member of and remains quite active in the Association of Southeast Asian Nations (ASEAN).

In the 1970s and 1980s Singapore was a strong opponent of Vietnam's invasion and occupation of Kampuchea/Cambodia. It even initially went to the extent of supporting the ousted and odious Khmer Rouge. In ensuing years Singapore's backing and financial assistance was a key factor in the success of the efforts by Prince Norodom Sihanouk to organize a united front, and of the peacemaking and peacekeeping initiatives taken under the auspices of the United Nations.

One of the recurring sources of U.S.-Singaporean tensions has been differing interpretations of democracy and standards for human rights. While formally a democracy, Singapore has long been dominated by a single political party, the People's Action Party (PAP). Its leader, Lee Kuan Yew, served as prime minister from independence until 1988 when he stepped down and was replaced by a new PAP leader. Prime Minister Lee often argued that U.S. views on pluralism were more ethnocentric and less universal than often contended, and that strong single-party democracy was more appropriate as an "Asian model." Diplomatic conflicts have ensued, as in 1986 when the Lee government imposed restrictions on *Time*, the *Asian Wall Street Journal*, and two other Western publications in retaliation for their "unfavorable" coverage of Singaporean domestic politics and for consorting with opponents of the government. In 1994 the government insisted, despite Clinton administration protests, on punishing by caning a U.S. teenager accused of having defaced public spaces with graffiti.

MACALISTER BROWN

See also Australia; Cambodia; Human Rights; Malaysia

FURTHER READING

Milne, Robert Stephen and Diane K. Mauzy. *Singapore: The Legacy of Lee Kuan Yew*. Boulder, Colo., 1990.
Warfel, David and Bruce Burton, eds. *The Political Economy of Foreign Policy in Southeast Asia*. New York, 1990.

SINO-JAPANESE WAR

(1894–1895)

A conflict between Japan and China over hegemony in Korea, where Japanese influence had begun to replace Chinese rule. The Japanese forces, with superior organiza-tion, Western military techniques and weapons, and popular support, swiftly defeated the Chinese on land and sea. The 1895 Treaty of Shimonoseki awarded the victor a wide range of concessions, demonstrating to the West both Japan's emergence as an imperialist power and imperial China's ominous vulnerability. From the humiliated Qing (Ch'ing) government Japan extracted the Liaodong (Liaotung) Peninsula, Taiwan, and the Pescadores, as well as most-favored-nation trading privileges and an indemnity of 200 million silver taels (one tael weighing about thirty-seven grams). China also recognized Korea's independence. European powers, particularly Russia, objected to Japanese control of Liaodong. Subsequently they pressed Japan into returning the peninsula to China, which leased it to Russia shortly thereafter in an exchange that embittered the Japanese against the Russians. China's commercial and transportation concessions to continental European powers soon caused fear in Great Britain and the United States that a prostrate China was about to be carved up. In 1899 and 1900 the Open Door Notes (equal trade opportunity and the preservation of China's territorial integrity) sprang from the new environment created by the Sino-Japanese War.

PAUL R. GRASS

See also China; Japan; Korea; Open Door Policy

FURTHER READING

Conroy, Hilary. *The Japanese Seizure of Korea: 1868–1910*. Philadelphia, 1960.
Hunt, Michael. *The Making of a Special Relationship: The United States and China to 1914*. New York, 1983.
Jansen, Marius B. *Japan and China: From War to Peace, 1894–1972*. Chicago, 1975.
Lone, Stewart. *Japan's First Modern War: Army and Society in the Conflict with China, 1894-95*. New York, 1994.

SIOUX WARS

See Native Americans

SLAVE TRADE AND SLAVERY

The first recorded arrival of Africans into the British North American colonies occurred in 1619 when a Dutch armed vessel landed between twenty and thirty Africans into Virginia. It remains unclear whether these Africans, likely seized from a Spanish slaver in the Caribbean, were sold as slaves or indentured servants, but others quickly followed, and by 1660 British and Dutch captains had established a small but thriving slave trade in the British North American colonies. The number of African slaves carried to British North America remained small until the mid-eighteenth century, when the cultivation

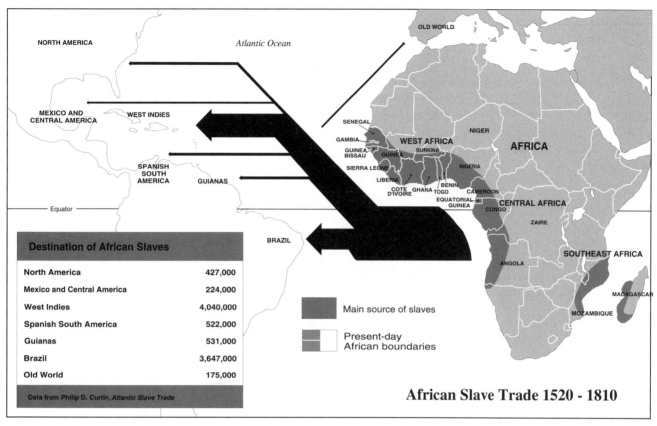

Destination of African Slaves

North America	427,000
Mexico and Central America	224,000
West Indies	4,040,000
Spanish South America	522,000
Guianas	531,000
Brazil	3,647,000
Old World	175,000

Data from Philip D. Curtin, *Atlantic Slave Trade*

Main source of slaves

Present-day
African boundaries

African Slave Trade 1520 - 1810

From *America and Its People*, James Kirby Martin et al., 2nd Edition. ©1993 James Kirby Martin, Randy Roberts, Steven Mintz, Linda O. McMurry, and James H. Jones. Reprinted with permission of Addison-Wesley Educational Publishers, Inc.

of rice, indigo, and tobacco created an increased demand for labor that European indentured servants and convict immigrants could not satisfy. Following the abolition of the Royal African Company monopoly on carrying slaves to North America in 1712, New England and middle colony merchants developed a highly profitable triangular trade carrying rum to Africa, slaves to the West Indies, and sugar and molasses to the northern colonies. By mid-century American merchants began to compete with British merchants in bringing slaves directly to the British North American colonies.

Opposition to the slave trade had existed in the American colonies from its beginning, but no official action was taken against it until 1761, when Quakers succeeded in ending the slave trade in Pennsylvania ports. Perhaps as a consequence of Revolutionary ideology and certainly as the profitability of slavery declined in both the North and South, opposition to the slave trade spread quickly. Between 1778 and 1787, Virginia, Maryland, and North and South Carolina either abolished or severely restricted the slave trade in their ports. Rhode Island, which had profited most from slave trading in the colonial period, closed its ports to slavers in 1787, and Connecticut, New York, Massachusetts, and Pennsylvania shortly followed.

During the War for American Independence, the British Navy temporarily ended the slave trade throughout the United States.

Although the Constitution prohibited Congress from outlawing the slave trade or imposing onerous taxes on imported slaves until 1808, Congress adopted several laws aimed at discouraging Americans from participating in the Atlantic slave trade. In 1794, Congress imposed a $2,000 fine on those outfitting slavers in American ports and threatened the owners of slave ships with the confiscation of their vessels. In anticipation of the ending of the Constitutional ban, in 1807 Congress prepared legislation for 1 January 1808 forbidding foreign trade in slaves, aimed at insuring the gradual extinction of slavery in the United States. In 1820 Congress designated slaving as a form of piracy, a capital offense.

Ironically, in 1793, one year before Congress passed its first act against the slave trade, Eli Whitney invented the cotton gin, which, by facilitating the processing of raw cotton, permitted the massive expansion of cotton agriculture and greatly increased the demand for slaves. Despite stern laws forbidding it, the Atlantic slave trade continued.

It is not known how many African slaves entered the United States illegally between 1808 and 1862, when the traffic to the United States actually ended. Estimates range from only a few to as many as 300,000. Circumstantial evidence suggests that the number was small. Opponents of slavery never made the slave trade a major issue in their campaign to abolish the institution, and the sensation created when new slaves from Africa were discovered indicates that the trade was not a common activity. But the trade did continue, and Americans and others also carried slaves to Cuba and Brazil, probably in greater numbers.

Attempts to suppress the trade continually embroiled the United States in international controversies, particularly with Great Britain, which was fully committed to its suppression. Between 1783 and 1824, there was virtually no international cooperation in combatting the slave trade, in part because no nation would allow another the right to board and search its ships on the high seas. After the War of 1812, still bitter over British impressment, Americans especially opposed British attempts to board and search any ships flying an American flag. In 1818 President James Monroe rejected a proposal from the British foreign secretary, Lord Castlereagh, for a treaty establishing a mutual right of search.

In 1824, however, under pressure from the House of Representatives, Monroe finally consented to mutual search in negotiations with Great Britain. Secretary of State John Quincy Adams consented only after Great Britain agreed to his demand that Great Britain classify slavers as pirates, whose ships could be boarded and searched by all nations. Partisan politics, Southern fears that the agreement might later extend to an attack on slavery itself, and lingering resentment over British naval practices before 1812 led the Senate to defeat the treaty. These elements, and especially Southern sensitivities, reappeared after Adams became president. The Senate defeated another treaty he had negotiated with Colombia that was similar to the British treaty.

Subsequent British attempts to negotiate multilateral agreements to end the African slave trade also failed because of American obstructionism. In 1834 the United States declined to enter into an Anglo-Franco-American Anti–Slave Trade Convention, and in 1841 it rejected an invitation to join Austria, Great Britain, France, and Prussia in a quadruple alliance that would have permitted the search and seizure of all suspected slavers whatever their flag. The U.S. minister in Paris, Lewis Cass, also urged the French to withdraw, and when France agreed to do so the negotiations collapsed.

The lack of multinational agreements and the failure of the United States to maintain a naval squadron in African waters prevented Great Britain and the United States from effectively combating the traffic in slaves. Because specially-built slave ships were fast and able to outrun British and American naval vessels, most escaped capture on the high seas. Furthermore, legal restrictions placed on American navy captains by Southerners and shipowners in slave trafficking protected all but the most incautious slave traders. Aware of weak U.S. policy and the American refusal to permit naval officers of other nations to search American ships, slave traders increasingly sailed under the U.S. flag, much to the embarrassment of the United States and the fury of Northerners.

Frustration of Northern opponents of the slave trade and fears of Southerners, who wanted no impediments, reached a high point in a controversy with Spain between 1839 and 1842. In 1839, fifty-three Africans aboard the *Amistad*, a Spanish intercoastal slaver sailing out of Havana, seized control of the ship, killed the captain and a mate, and put the crew of two overboard, where they presumably perished. Two Spaniards had purchased the Africans, all of whom had been recently transported to Cuba from Africa by Portuguese slave merchants in Havana, and were transporting them to plantations elsewhere on the island. The Africans ordered the Spaniards to sail the ship to Africa. The owners, hoping to be rescued by British cruisers, instead sailed into American waters and eventually brought the ship to Long Island in search of food and water, where an American naval officer captured the ship for salvage. American authorities jailed the forty surviving Africans in Connecticut pending a court decision on their fate.

When the Spanish minister to the United States demanded that the ship and its cargo of slaves be returned to Spain in accord with Pinckney's Treaty of 1795, the U.S. government agreed. But abolitionists and others in the United States protested, and in March 1841, after two years of sometimes bitter litigation, the Supreme Court ultimately decided the slaves were "kidnaped Africans" and freed them.

Anglo-American Controversies

The most important Anglo-American controversy arose in November 1841 when British authorities in Nassau liberated U.S. slaves on the *Creole*, a U.S. intercoastal slaver diverted to the British port after a mutiny on a voyage from Virginia to Louisiana. Following an American protest and demands by slaveholders that the slaves be returned to the United States, a British judge ruled that any slaves entering free British territory were immediately free. A Louisiana court agreed in a case in which the slaveholders had sued their American insurers for compensation. The insurers retained Judah Benjamin, a prominent New Orleans attorney and later secretary of state of the Confederacy, who argued successfully that under international law the British authorities in Nassau could free the slaves. A mixed Anglo-American claims commission voided the Louisiana decision, however, and agreed in 1853 to compensate the American slaveholders.

The commission concluded that Nassau officials had violated international law—Nassau's municipal laws did authorize boarding the U.S. ship.

Growing Anglo-American disputes over the slave trade led to an attempt to resolve the problem during the Webster-Ashburton negotiations of 1842. An effort to get around the search issue by requiring British and American ships to cruise African waters jointly in search of slavers failed when President John Tyler opposed entangling the United States with Great Britain. He also worried about potential Southern opposition to the agreement. Both nations agreed only to maintain an African squadron of at least eighty guns in these waters and to cooperate with each other, a commitment the United States failed to honor. Southerners feared joint success in ending the slave trade would be followed by a British assault on domestic American slavery. Also, the U.S. Navy was not large enough to meet American obligations without a substantial increase in naval appropriations, which Congress was unwilling to grant.

In addition to problems resulting from the failure to develop and implement an effective slave-trade policy, slavery itself directly influenced other aspects of American foreign relations. In 1816, American philanthropists founded the American Colonization Society and sought to erect on the East Coast of Africa a refuge for slaves taken from slave ships and a home for freed American slaves. Two years later, agents of the society arrived in Sierra Leone, a British colony established partly for the same purpose, and explored the coast for a likely settlement. In 1821, Americans forced local African chiefs to sell a coastal area that eventually became Liberia.

The establishment of Liberia embroiled the United States in African affairs, and between 1821 and 1847 the Liberian settlement survived as a client state and protectorate of the United States. Local African leaders, many of whom regularly provided slaves to European and American slave traders, threatened the settlement and initially raided it in search of new slaves. In 1826 Liberians and Americans, including American naval officers and their men, attacked and defeated the local chiefs and won guarantees for the security of the settlement. In 1847, after two decades of relative peace, Liberia declared its independence.

Southerners paid close attention to all international questions that touched upon slavery. Beyond weakening anti–slave trade agreements and frustrating attempts to prosecute slave traders, they also tried to prevent the United States from participating in the Panama Conference of 1826, partly because slavery was on the agenda. They successfully prevented the United States from recognizing the black republics of Haiti and Liberia, and when in 1833 Great Britain abolished slavery in its empire, many Southerners became convinced that Great Britain intended to destroy slavery in the United States as well. These fears contributed to the movement to annex Texas during the next decade.

The initial American movement into Texas had little to do with slavery. In 1821, the Spanish opened Texas to settlement by carefully chosen empresarios, a policy continued by Mexico. By 1835 Americans, most of whom had come from the American South and had carried their slaves with them, dominated the province. Although Mexico abolished slavery in all its territories in 1829, Texans had avoided the law through a variety of ruses. The Mexican-Texan dispute over slavery was one of the issues that led to the Texan rebellion in 1835.

Texas sought annexation to the United States immediately after securing its independence in 1836, but President Martin Van Buren objected, fearing that the annexation of Texas as a slave state would provoke a bitter sectional crisis and lead to a war with Mexico. A second attempt at annexation, however, began in 1843 and succeeded in 1845 after a bitter and divisive battle.

Led by President John Tyler and Texas President Sam Houston, the United States and Texas secretly negotiated a treaty of annexation in 1844. Tyler and many Southerners had been concerned that Great Britain intended to offer debt-ridden Texas a huge loan in exchange for the abolition of slavery. When Secretary of State John C. Calhoun's defense of slavery, and argument that annexation was necessary to preserve the institution in the United States, became public in a diplomatic note to the British minister to the United States, Richard Pakenham, Northern antislavery groups joined abolitionists in charging that the entire movement to annex Texas was a conspiracy by an "aggressive slavocracy" to expand and perpetuate slavery. The treaty was soundly defeated by a partisan vote, but Southern Democrats revived the issue in the election of 1844 by nominating an avowed expansionist, James K. Polk, who ran on a platform calling for the immediate annexation of Texas. Tyler used Polk's election to secure annexation through a joint resolution of Congress, which caused Mexico to sever relations with the United States.

President Polk failed in his attempts to restore relations with Mexico, resolve a number of other issues between the nations, and acquire all or part of the Mexican province of Alta California in 1846, and when fighting erupted between U.S. and Mexican troops in disputed territory along the Texas-Mexican border, war began. Slavery became a central issue to Americans throughout the war. Northern antislavery interests insisted that any land acquired from Mexico as a result of the war had to be free territory; moderates hoped to avoid the slavery question altogether by refusing to accept any Mexican land; Southerners were concerned that extensive acquisitions of Mexican land would bring into the nation a large

Indian, African American, and mixed population along with land unfit for slavery. Expansionists, primarily from the Midwest, sought the acquisition of all of Mexico. The Treaty of Guadalupe-Hidalgo of 1848, ending the war, provided for the acquisition of the northern third of Mexico. As feared, attempts to organize the territory inaugurated a bitter contest between North and South over the expansion of slavery into the new territory.

The sectional conflict following the war with Mexico effectively paralyzed American foreign relations. Southerners opposed the acquisition of Canadian territory and Russian America; Northerners frustrated Southern attempts to purchase Cuba from Spain. Many Southerners regarded the acquisition of Cuba as an essential means of increasing Southern power in both houses of Congress, and in 1854, three American diplomats, led by Pierre Soulé of Louisiana, met in Ostend, Belgium and issued the Ostend Manifesto, which called for seizing the island if Spain refused to sell it. After an uproar in the North, President Franklin Pierce repudiated the document. Subsequently, private armies of filibusters attempted to seize Cuba, revolutionize the island, and annex it to the United States. They failed.

Northern and Southern interests momentarily converged in Central America after the discovery of gold in newly acquired California. Northern entrepreneurs, most notably Cornelius Vanderbilt, sought to secure transit rights and develop rail and canal transportation across Panama and Nicaragua. Southern expansionists saw an opportunity to acquire territory eminently suitable to slavery. With the help of Vanderbilt, an American adventurer, William Walker, seized control of Nicaragua in 1855. To strengthen his position in Central America, he reestablished slavery in the nation, so hoping to win support from Southerners in the United States. The action alienated Northerners, and when Walker came under the influence of Vanderbilt's rivals in New York and thereby lost the wealthy magnate's support, Walker's opponents in Nicaragua and neighboring states were emboldened. In 1857, a Central American army drove him from Nicaragua.

The Civil War Years

Frustrated in attempts to acquire Cuba and Nicaragua, some Southern extremists advocated withdrawing from the American Union and creating an independent Caribbean empire. Counting on support from Great Britain, which would benefit from stability and secure transit between the oceans, Southerners promoted the creation of a new nation encompassing the slave states of the American South, Cuba, the northern provinces of Mexico, and the states of Central America. In 1860, when Abraham Lincoln won election to the presidency on a platform pledging to contain slavery, Southern extremists called for secession. In April 1861, following the secession of several states and the failure of several attempts to resolve the post-election crisis, the Civil War began.

The secession of the Southern states removed slavery as an impediment in American foreign relations. In 1862, the United States formally recognized Haiti and Liberia and negotiated commercial treaties with both nations. Even more significantly, the United States and Great Britain concluded a treaty for the suppression of the slave trade that provided for the mutual right of search and detention off the African and Cuban coasts and established prize courts in Sierra Leone, the Cape of Good Hope, and New York. In 1863 they extended the treaty to include waters around Madagascar, Puerto Rico, and Santo Domingo. After more than a half century, the Atlantic slave trade was finally brought under control. In 1870, both nations agreed to turn suspected slavers of each nation over to cruisers of that nation—American captains brought suspected slavers to Key West and New York.

The slave question preoccupied the diplomacy of the American Civil War, although both the Union and the Confederacy initially insisted that the war was being fought for other reasons. President Lincoln maintained that his sole war aim was to preserve the Union and that the federal government had no intention of interfering with slavery in the states where it existed. Lincoln hoped to maintain the support of border slave states and to strengthen the hands of Southern unionists.

Confederate officials also sought to evade the question of slavery, insisting that the Southern states were merely exercising their right to withdraw from a union that no longer served their interests. Confederates feared that reference to slavery would alienate Great Britain and France, whose sympathy and crucial support they avidly sought.

Lincoln's refusal to confront slavery directly and explicitly deeply concerned Union diplomats in Great Britain and on the Continent, who feared that there was a preponderance of sympathy among ruling groups for the Confederacy and that the working class, which identified with the free North, might not continue its support in the face of extended economic privation caused by the loss of American cotton. These diplomats, many of whom had been active in the antislavery movement, urged Lincoln and Secretary of State William Henry Seward to make the war an antislavery crusade. Many friends of the Union in Great Britain found their pro-Union arguments less and less convincing to their compatriots as the Union refused to attack slavery *per se* and the economic situation in Great Britain worsened.

In 1862, however, following the Battle of Antietam, Lincoln decided to shift the thrust of the war by issuing the preliminary Emancipation Proclamation. He had been waiting for a military triumph so as to avoid the impression that the Union assault on slavery was an act of desperation. Since the Europeans regarded the Battle of Antietam as indecisive, rather than as a Union victory, the stratagem failed; they roundly criticized Lincoln and Seward with attempting to provoke a slave uprising in the South that would lead to a race war. Nevertheless, the fact that a Union victory after the date the Emancipation Proclamation went into effect, 1 January 1863, would mean the end of slavery made it virtually impossible for the British government to support the Confederacy. No other nation in Europe would act without a British initiative.

After 1863, the Confederacy could no longer avoid the slavery question in their contacts with European officials. Confederate agents initially argued that the Emancipation Proclamation did not end slavery in border states loyal to the Union and only pertained to slaves in territory under Confederate control. Confederates thus argued that the inability of the Union to defeat the Confederacy militarily meant that the Emancipation Proclamation was a sham. Unfortunately for the Confederate argument, by mid-1863 the military tide had changed. Union victories at Gettysburg and Vicksburg spelled the end of the Confederacy.

In one last desperate attempt to secure European support in late 1864, Confederate Secretary of State Judah P. Benjamin dispatched Duncan F. Kenner to Europe on a secret mission with the authority to offer Southern emancipation of the slaves in exchange for support. The British and French rejected any such amendment because, at that time, it had become clear that the Southern cause was lost.

The slave trade and slavery thus ceased to be a factor in American foreign relations in the 1860s. Before that time, it hamstrung some policies, promoted others, and generally embarrassed the United States, which otherwise perceived itself as a liberal, progressive model for the rest of the world. But perhaps the most important influence that slavery had on American foreign relations was indirect. Slavery provided the labor for the production of massive quantities of cotton, the export of which fueled the American economy, and both cotton and the income it generated promoted American industrialization. By 1860, the American economy had become national, freed from its dependence on either cotton production or foreign markets for its raw materials. Slavery thus had a profound influence on American economic development, which in turn became increasingly important in American foreign relations throughout the rest of the century.

KINLEY BRAUER

See also Africa; American Civil War; Amistad Affair; Benjamin, Judah Philip; Constitution; Creole Affair; Cuba; Filibusters; International Law; Liberia; Mexico, War with; Ostend Manifesto; Pinckney's Treaty; Webster, Daniel

FURTHER READING

Brauer, Kinley J. "The Slavery Problem in the Diplomacy of the American Civil War." *Pacific Historical Review*, 46 (August 1977): 439-69.

DuBois, W. E. B. *The Suppression of the African Slave-Trade to the United States of America, 1638-1870.* New York, 1896; reissued New York, 1965.

Duignan, Peter, and L. H. Gann. *The United States and Africa: A History.* New York, 1984.

Howard, Warren S. *American Slavers and the Federal Law, 1837–1862.* Berkeley, Calif., 1963.

Jones, Howard. *To the Webster-Ashburton Treaty: A Study in Anglo-American Relations, 1783–1843.* Chapel Hill, N.C., 1977.

———. *Mutiny on the Amistad: The Saga of a Slave Revolt and Its Impact on American Abolition, Law, and Diplomacy.* New York, 1987.

May, Robert E. *The Southern Dream of a Caribbean Empire, 1854–1861.* 2nd ed. Athens, Ga., 1989.

Owsley, Frank L. *King Cotton Diplomacy: Foreign Relations of the Confederate States of America.* 2nd ed. Chicago, 1959.

Pletcher, David M. *The Diplomacy of Annexation; Texas, Oregon, and the Mexican War.* Columbia, Mo., 1973.

Soulsby, Hugh B. *The Right of Search and the Slave Trade in Anglo-American Relations, 1814-1862.* Baltimore, Md., 1933.

SLBM

See Nuclear Weapons and Strategy; Submarine Warfare

SLIDELL, JOHN

(*b.* 1793; d. 29 July 1871)

Pre-Civil War diplomat and Confederate envoy to France. Born in New York City, he moved to New Orleans in 1819. As a Louisiana congressman he was sent in 1845 by President James Polk to Mexico to purchase California and the territory between it and Texas, but failed. In the U.S. Senate from 1853 until 1861, Slidell was a manipulative political intriguer, particularly influential in the administration of James Buchanan, but little interested in foreign affairs. After Louisiana seceded, however, he became Confederate commissioner to France. Traveling to his post on board the British mail steamer *Trent*, Slidell was forcibly abducted, by Captain Charles Wilkes of the U.S.S. *San Jacinto*, and eventually confined in Fort Warren prison. He was released in late 1861 as a result of a strong British protest to the Lincoln administration.

In Paris, Slidell worked to induce the French government to aid the Confederate cause, but Emperor Louis Napoleon, although sympathetic, decided not to act overtly because he could not persuade the British government to join his intervention schemes. Slidell's main achievement in France was raising money for the Southern war effort. Following the South's capitulation, Slidell and his family remained in Europe, where he died six years later.

NORMAN B. FERRIS

See also American Civil War; Confederate States of America; Trent Affair

SLOVIA

See Czech Republic; Appendix 2

SLOVENIA

A central European state that was, until 1991, a constituent republic of the former Yugoslavia, it is bordered by Austria, Hungary, Croatia, the Adriatic Sea, and Italy. Slovenia declared itself an independent state on 25 June 1991. Until the end of World War I, Slovenia formed part of the Habsburg empire, comprising the Austrian Crownlands of Carinthia, Carniola, and Styria. As early as 1848 Slovenes had called for the consolidation of all Slovene-speaking lands into one political and administrative unit. By the late nineteenth century, there were serious moves afoot for the unification of Slovenia with Croatia and Serbia into a South Slav state. By the end of World War I the majority of Slovenes and their leaders favored separation from Austria-Hungary. The Kingdom of Serbs, Croats, and Slovenes was formally proclaimed on 29 October 1918; it was renamed Yugoslavia in 1929. During World War II, Slovenia was occupied by the Axis powers, but in 1946 reemerged as one of the republics in the new communist state of Yugoslavia formed by Josip Broz Tito. Tensions among the constituent republics of the Yugoslav federation started after Tito's death in 1980. Slovenes resented the domineering role played by the Serbian leadership as well as what they felt was the inequity of Belgrade's economic demands upon them. Then, too, external factors, such as the end of the Cold War and the examples of revolution seen elsewhere in Eastern Europe, mounting economic problems, and the intentional cultivation of ethnic animosities by leaders such as Serbian president Slobodan Milosevic, combined to fuel the fires of independence. Slovene leaders also felt they were blessed by geography: they did not share a border with Serbia. In addition, Slovenia had far greater ethnic homogeneity than any other Yugoslav republic (almost 90 percent Slovene).

Secretary of State James Baker visited Belgrade on 21 June 1991 and delivered a speech in support of Yugoslav unity. To this day, critics contend that Baker missed a golden opportunity to give Milosevic and the Yugoslav National Army (JNA) a clear warning against the use of force, and that this was interpreted as a green light by those intent on using force in quelling secessionist moves in the republics. What we do know is that four days after Baker's visit, Slovenia and Croatia declared their independence. The Serbian-controlled Yugoslav army moved immediately against both breakaway republics, but quickly desisted against Slovenia (which was never crucial to the Greater Serbia desired by Milosevic and his cohorts). Initial U.S. policy was not to recognize the independence of any of the constituent republics until a political solution could be found for the entire Yugoslav crisis. Lord Carrington was mandated by the European Community (EC) to concoct such a solution, and the United States decided to take a hands-off approach to the region until his mission had been completed. However, Germany unilaterally recognized Slovenia and Croatia on 17 December 1991, and the EC quickly followed suit. After some delay, the United States recognized Slovenia's independence officially on 7 April 1992.

Many in the U.S. policy community believed that if Slovenia had been willing to remain somehow in the Yugoslav federation awhile longer, some sort of negotiated settlement could have been achieved that might have prevented the general outbreak of hostilities which escalated into the violence that soon led to the brutal war in Croatia and Bosnia-Herzegovina. Be that as it may, once it became clear that the old Yugoslavia was beyond salvation, the Bush administration recognized that of all the constituent republics, Slovenia had the best chance of surviving as an independent state. U.S. dealings with Slovenia then passed through various stages. At first, the country was given only limited attention; Slovenia did not have a separate desk officer at the Department of State until the summer of 1993. Later, once Washington began to take Slovenia more seriously, the goal became to differentiate to the greatest extent possible between it and the other constituent republics of the former Yugoslavia, placing Slovenia within the larger grouping of Central European nations. The United States thus supported the rapid integration of Slovenia into European and Atlantic structures, such as the Organization on Security and Cooperation in Europe (OSCE), and the European Union (EU). Despite the constraints of the U.N. arms embargo, on the territory of the former Yugoslavia (which was lifted in June 1996), the United States and Slovenia have cultivated a relationship in the defense arena. Initiated in November 1993, the bilateral Military to Military Joint Contact Team Program provides advice and assistance on civilian military control, family welfare, military budgeting in a democracy, and other soft areas of defense. (Due to the arms embargo no weapons or intelligence equipment could be included.) Slovenia also became a member of the North Atlantic

Treaty Organization's (NATO's) Partnership for Peace, and has begun to engage in joint exercises dealing with peacekeeping, humanitarian aid, disaster relief, and search and rescue missions.

The economic reforms and liberalization policies taken by Slovene government on the macroeconomic level have met with U.S. approval and encouragement. The country reduced inflation from a high of 32 percent in 1993 to 10 percent in 1995. Slovenia's GDP grew by 5.5 percent, making it the fastest growing economy in East-Central Europe. However, Slovenia's privatization and restructuring of some 2,500 large "socially owned" enterprises has been relatively slow. Management-worker buyouts, the most common method of Slovene privatization, have left few opportunities for foreign investment. Two other barriers to foreign investment are the requirements that any company incorporated in Slovenia must have a managing director or proxy of Slovene nationality, and that neither individuals of foreign nationality nor any foreign registered company can buy land.

Overall, current relations between the United States and Slovenia can be characterized as cooperative and are seen to be improving. Slovenia has been commended for its human rights record and relative freedom of the press. There is some concern in Washington that too many of Slovenia's current leaders belonged to the former communist regime; but this is the case in most of the post-communist Eastern European countries.

AIMEE BRESLOW

See also Croatia; Serbia; Tito, Josip Broz; Yugoslavia

FURTHER READING

Cohen, Leonard J. *Broken Bonds: The Disintegration of Yugoslavia.* Boulder, Colo., 1993.
Glenny, Misha. *The Fall of Yugoslavia: The Third Balkan War.* New York, 1993.
Jansa, Janez. *The Making of the Slovenian State 1988-1992: The Collapse of Yugoslavia.* Ljubljana, 1994.

SMITH, GERARD C.

(*b.* 1914; *d.* 4 July 1994)

Director of the Arms Control and Disarmament and Agency (ACDA) (1969–1973) and arms-control advocate. In 1950, after pursuing a successful law career, he became a special assistant to the Atomic Energy Commission, where he acquired a deep interest in nuclear-arms control. Four years later Smith joined the Department of State, where he served as special assistant for atomic affairs and director of the policy planning staff. From 1961 to 1968 he often advised the administrations of John F. Kennedy and Lyndon B. Johnson on arms-control issues. His chief responsibility as ACDA director was

leading the delegation to the Strategic Arms Limitation Talks (1969–1972), which produced the SALT I agreement in 1972. He later advised President Jimmy Carter on nonproliferation issues. Until his death in 1994 he continued to write and speak about arms control, despite constant attacks from conservative groups.

SHANE J. MADDOCK

See also Arms Control and Disarmament Agency; Strategic Arms Limitation Talks and Agreements

FURTHER READING

Newhouse, John. *War and Peace in the Nuclear Age.* New York, 1989.
Smith, Gerard C. *Doubletalk: The Story of the First Strategic Arms Limitation Talks.* Garden City, N.Y., 1980.
———. *Disarming Diplomat: The Memoirs of Ambassador Gerald C. Smith, Arms Control Negotiator.* Lanham, Md., 1996.
Thompson, Kenneth, ed. *Gerard Smith on Arms Control.* New York, 1987.

SMITH, ROBERT

(*b.* 3 November 1757; *d.* 26 November 1842)

Secretary of the navy (1801–1809), attorney general (1805), and secretary of state (1809–1811). Born in Pennsylvania to parents of Scotch-Irish descent, Smith, a 1781 graduate of the College of New Jersey (now Princeton University), studied law for five years and subsequently established the largest admiralty practice of his day. Prior to holding national office, he served in the Maryland Senate (1793–1795), the Maryland House of Delegates (1796–1800), and the Baltimore city council (1798–1801). Early in his political career Smith was nominally a Federalist, but he gradually shifted his allegiance to Thomas Jefferson and the Republicans. With Jefferson's inauguration as president in 1801, Smith was appointed secretary of the navy in July. He served in this post—and temporarily also as attorney general—for two terms under Jefferson.

The United States was at war with Tripoli when Smith assumed the office of secretary, and throughout his tenure he vigorously fought to prevent the demise of the relatively new Navy Department. In particular, Smith clashed with Secretary of the Treasury Albert Gallatin, whose dual objectives were national debt elimination and economic retrenchment.

As secretary of state under James Madison, Smith presided over the department at a time when the United States confronted the twin crises produced by Great Britain's orders in council and France's decrees, which violated U.S. neutral rights and brought the United States to the brink of war. He negotiated the Erskine Agreement of 1809 with Great Britain, which called for the British to withdraw their orders in council as they applied to the United States, in exchange for the United States lifting the nonintercourse against Great Britain and continuing to enforce it against France. Because he violated his instructions, British Prime Minister David Erskine was subsequently recalled and the agreement was repudiated by the British government.

With respect to U.S. relations with Spain, particularly the long-held goal of acquiring West Florida, the secretary of state demonstrated resolve. Smith supported clandestine operations in Spanish territory designed to exploit Spanish weakness in the area. He agreed with President Madison that the United States should occupy West Florida. In their thinking, the acquisition of the Floridas was a logical step to follow the purchase of the Louisiana Territory.

In March 1811, Secretary of the Treasury Albert Gallatin threatened to resign if Smith were not removed from the cabinet. Having lent his support to an earlier (albeit unsuccessful) scheme to discredit Smith and his brother, Senator Samuel Smith of Maryland, Gallatin was still reeling from recent congressional attacks on administration policies over the rechartering of the Bank of the United States. Fearful of losing Gallatin, anxious to prevent Robert Smith from becoming a serious candidate for high elective office, and hoping to bring James Monroe into his cabinet, Madison fired Smith.

Smith lashed out at Madison and his policies by publishing his *Address to the People of the United States* (1811). He hoped to redeem his reputation and gain satisfaction by toppling the administration, whose policies were unpopular with many Republicans and Federalists alike. Concerned about the possible political fallout for firing Smith, the president determined that a response was required. The poet Joel Barlow, newly appointed minister to France, successfully defended the administration from Smith's charges. Smith never again held high public office. Shortly after his return to Baltimore from Washington, he became president of the Universal Life Insurance Company. In 1813 he was made president of an American Bible Society auxiliary, and in the same year selected to become provost of the University of Maryland. In 1818, he became president of the Maryland Agricultural Society.

THOM M. ARMSTRONG

See also Barbary States; Florida; Gallatin, Albert; Great Britain; Jefferson, Thomas; Madison, James; Neutral Rights; Orders in Council; War of 1812

FURTHER READING

Adams, Henry. *A History of the United States of America During the Administrations of Thomas Jefferson and James Madison,* 9 vols. New York, 1889–1891.
Armstrong, Thom M. *Politics, Diplomacy and Intrigue in the Early Republic: The Cabinet Career of Robert Smith, 1801–1811.* Dubuque, Iowa, 1991.
Cassell, Frank A. *Merchant Congressman in the Young Republic: Samuel Smith of Maryland, 1752–1839.* Madison, Wis.,1971.
Tansill, Charles C. "Robert Smith." In *American Secretaries of State and Their Diplomacy,* 10 vols., edited by Samuel Flagg Bemis. New York, 1928.

SMITH, WALTER BEDELL

(*b.* 5 October 1895; *d.* 9 August 1961)

Career army officer and General Dwight D. Eisenhower's chief of staff (1942–1945), ambassador to the Soviet Union (1946–1949), and director of central intelligence (1950–1953). Smith began as an enlisted man in the Indiana National Guard and distinguished himself before and during World War II as staff officer to Generals George C. Marshall and Dwight D. Eisenhower. After the war he helped implement U.S. Cold War strategy. In 1946, due in part to his wartime experience in negotiating with the Soviets, Smith was named by President Harry S. Truman to be ambassador to the Soviet Union. Smith's tenure in Moscow encompassed the divisive foreign ministers conferences and the Berlin blockade. Suspicious of Soviet intentions, he advocated a firm policy of containment. He left Moscow in 1949. Beginning in 1950 Smith headed the Central Intelligence Agency where the vast administrative skills acquired during his years as a staff officer were put to use. Three years later President Eisenhower appointed Smith undersecretary of state. In that capacity, he headed the U.S. delegation to the 1954 Geneva Conference called to resolve the Indochina problem.

T. MICHAEL RUDDY

See also Berlin; Central Intelligence Agency; Cold War; Containment; French Indochina; Truman, Harry S.; Vietnam

FURTHER READING

Crosswell, Daniel K. R. *The Chief of Staff: The Military Career of General Walter Bedell Smith.* New York, 1991.
Montague, Ludwell L. *General Walter Bedell Smith as Director of Central Intelligence.* University Park, Pa., 1992.
Smith, Walter Bedell. *My Three Years in Moscow.* Philadelphia, Pa., 1950.

SMOOT-HAWLEY TARIFF ACT

See Protectionism; Tariffs

SOLOMON ISLANDS

See Appendix 2

SOLZHENITSYN, ALEKSANDR ISAYEVICH

(*b.* 11 December 1918)

Dissident novelist and Nobel laureate, who ranks as one of Russia's literary giants. His widely read and vividly realistic depictions of the brutality of the Soviet system helped shape U.S. and world perceptions of Soviet communism for decades. Born in Kislovodsk, Russia, and educated in public schools in Rostov-on-Don, he graduated from Rostov University with a degree in mathematics and physics. In 1945 he was arrested for criticizing Joseph Stalin and served eight years at hard labor. Upon his release in 1953 he was resentenced to "perpetual" exile in Kazakhstan but gained his freedom in 1956 as part of Soviet Communist party leader Nikita Khrushchev's program of de-Stalinization. Solzhenitsyn's autobiographical novel of his labor camp experiences, *One Day in the Life of Ivan Denisovich*, was published in 1963 by the literary journal *Novy Mir* with the explicit approval of Khrushchev. Despite the support of editor Aleksandr Tvardovsky and many Soviet writers, Solzhenitsyn failed in his attempt to publish his major work, *The Gulag Archipelago*, in the USSR, but it was eventually published abroad in 1973. In 1969 Solzhenitsyn was expelled from the Soviet Writers Union but received the Nobel Prize for Literature in 1970. As a disturbing force in the era of détente, he was permanently exiled abroad in 1974 and eventually settled in the United States. In the mid-1970s he criticized the policy of détente and what he perceived as the West's culpability in promoting Soviet power. President Gerald Ford refused to meet with Solzhenitsyn in 1974, fearing that he would irritate the Kremlin and jeopardize negotiations over the limitation of strategic arms. Invited to return to the Soviet Union in the late 1980s in Mikhail Gorbachev's era, Solzhenitsyn declined, calling instead for the destruction of communism. His essay, "How to Revitalize Russia," published in *Komsomolskaya Pravda* in 1990, was a clarion call for the revival of Russian nationalism and spirituality and a new union of the Slavic peoples of the USSR. *Lenin in Zurich* (1975) and *August 1914* (1972), later published under the title *The Red Wheel* (1989), attempted a historical reconstruction of the origins of the communist system. Solzhenitsyn returned to a noncommunist Russia in 1994 where he continued his call for spiritual and nationalist renewal but to an often unreceptive public preoccupied with an ongoing economic and political crisis.

DAVID W. MCFADDEN

See also Cold War; Communism; Khrushchev, Nikita Sergeyevich; Russia and the Soviet Union; Stalin, Joseph

FURTHER READING

Remnick, David. "The Exile Returns." *New Yorker* 69 (1994): 64–70, 72–83.

Scammel, Michael, ed. *The Solzhenitsyn Files.* New York, 1995.

Solzhenitsyn, Aleksandr. *The Russian Question.* New York, 1995.

SOMALIA

East African republic bordering the northwestern Indian Ocean, Gulf of Aden, Ethiopia, Djibouti, and Kenya. It was created in 1960 from the British protectorate of Somaliland and the United Nations Trust Territory of Somalia (formerly Italian Somaliland). Somali irredentism and other regional tensions combined with those of the Cold War and the geopolitical significance of the region to create a volatile situation in the Horn of Africa. An armed coup in 1969 produced a new leader in Somalia, Muhammad Siad Barre, who favored the Soviet style of state management in domestic politics, but the Ethiopian revolution in 1974 led gradually to a shift in regional allegiances. Ethiopia began to turn toward the Soviet Union, a development that was mirrored by Somalia's turning back toward the West. In 1977 Ethiopia expelled all U.S. personnel, and a Somali-populated section of Ethiopia, the Ogaden, successfully rebelled amid fierce fighting with unofficial Somalian assistance. Soviet assistance to the Ethiopian regime, which eventually suppressed the rebellion, led Somalia to expel Soviet personnel from its territory. Subsequently, U.S. relations with Somalia improved, including large flows of military aid.

Political infighting gradually deteriorated into a civil war during 1989: it was fed both by unrest caused by the dictatorial rule of Siad Barre and by clashes between rival clans. Siad Barre was overthrown in January 1991, but the internal warfare intensified, causing massive starvation and leaving hundreds of thousands of refugees. The United Nations arranged a cease-fire in February 1992 but it did not hold. Later in the year the UN sent peacekeeping forces but they also were unable to restore order.

In December 1992 President George Bush launched Operation Restore Hope, sending about 27,000 U.S. troops to Somalia to join the UN peacekeepers on what initially was intended as a largely humanitarian mission of providing the security necessary for food supplies to go through and of restoring order generally. While the mission initially proved successful, it did not end satisfactorily. The factional fighting broke out again, leading in early June 1993 to attacks by General Muhammad Farah Aideed and his militia on UN peacekeeping forces. U.S. forces joined the UN-sanctioned effort to capture Aideed, but they also ended up clashing with him, culminating in urban battles on 3–4 October in which eighteen U.S. soldiers were killed and another was dragged through the streets of Mogadishu. Within days President Bill Clinton announced that U.S. troops would be withdrawn by the end of March 1994 (as they were), although the United States would continue to support the peace process in other ways. The Somalia intervention sparked intense debate in the United States not just over this particular issue but more generally about the involvement of U.S. military forces in UN peacekeeping operations.

CATHERINE ELKINS

See also Ethiopia; Humanitarian Intervention and Relief; Russia and the Soviet Union; United Nations

FURTHER READING

Hirsch, John L. and Whert B. Oakley. *Somalia and Operation Restore Hope*. Washington, D.C., 1995.
Lefebvre, Jeffrey Alan. *Arms for the Horn: U.S. Security Policy in Ethiopia and Somalia, 1953–1991*. Pittsburgh, 1991.
Sahnoun, Mohamed. *Somalia: The Missed Opportunities*. Washington, D.C., 1994.
United Nations Blue Book Series, vol. 3, *The United Nations and Somalia, 1992–1996*. New York, 1996.

SOMOZA DEBAYLE, ANASTASIO

(*b.* 5 December 1925; *d.* 17 September 1980)

Dictator and president of Nicaragua (1967–1979). Son of Anastasio Somoza García (dictator-president, 1937–1956), brother of Luis Somoza Debayle (dictator-president or the power behind puppet presidents, 1956–1967), "Tachito" was born in León. His father, founder of the family dynasty, rose to power in the U.S.-organized Guardia Nacional de Nicaragua in the 1920s and 1930s. He established a pattern of currying favor with Washington and individual Americans in order to strengthen his regime. His sons carried on the tradition. Educated at the La Salle Military Academy and the U.S. Military Academy at West Point (1946), Tachito rose rapidly within the Nicaraguan National Guard from second lieutenant (1941) and inspector general (1946) to chief of staff (1949) and the top position of "jefe director" (1956).

Although Luis, who had presided over a period of superficial democratization and modernization, opposed the presidential ambitions of his intemperate younger brother, Tachito extended his family's dynastic rule in 1967 after a bloody campaign period and rigged election. Blocked by the constitution from reelection in 1971, Somoza amended that document to allow himself another year in office. Then, with the support and advice of U.S. Ambassador Turner Shelton, he devised a scheme whereby in 1972 he turned over titular power to a puppet triumvirate while a new constitution was written that allowed his reelection. After another fraudulent election in 1974, he occupied the presidency until July 1979.

Somoza's rule was marked by increasing greed and violence. Following a December 1972 earthquake, which killed more than 10,000 people and destroyed much of the capital city of Managua, Somoza allowed his National Guard to plunder relief supplies. Meanwhile he expanded his control over sectors of the banking, construction, demolition, and concrete industries, to which he then diverted monies from international emergency economic assistance through legal, if unethical, government contracts. By 1979 his real wealth had swelled from a few hundred million dollars to probably more than one billion. As anger over his greed mounted and the country began to unify against him, the dictator increasingly turned to violence to quell his opposition. In his last eighteen months as president, during the "war of liberation," approximately 50,000 people died, most of them unarmed civilians killed by the Guard.

Somoza's formula for rule was simple: first, control the National Guard through direct command, occasional purges, and the condoning of corruption among all ranks; and, second, cultivate the support of the United States through the manipulation of a network of friends in the U.S. Congress and by serving as an unfailing ally in the United Nations and in the fight against communism in Latin America. By the time of his ouster, Somoza's National Guard was the most heavily U.S.-trained military establishment in Latin America. It was not until President Jimmy Carter's administration (1977–1981) that the United States complained of Somoza's violation of the human rights of the Nicaraguan people. Still, Washington maintained diplomatic relations, and it was not until 1978 that military aid was suspended. U.S. approval of a large International Monetary Fund loan actually came barely three months before his downfall.

Internal opposition to Somoza's dictatorial rule spread through most sectors of society and featured two general strikes and many demonstrations in 1978, spontaneous mass insurrections in six cities in September 1978, and, eventually, a carefully coordinated insurrection led by the Sandinista Front for National Liberation in June–July 1979. By then the Carter administration had decided to try to have Somoza replaced—but by a conservative, pro-U.S. regime, not by the nationalistic Sandinistas. Washington's efforts to persuade the Organization of American States (OAS) to help create this outcome failed utterly. Somoza fled on 17 July 1979 and the revolutionaries took control two days later. The exiled dictator was assassinated in a bazooka attack in Asunción, Paraguay, by seven former members of the Argentine People's Revolutionary Army. *Internacionalista* veterans of the war in Nicaragua, the commandos claimed to have decided late in 1979 that "it would be an outrage to permit Somoza to die peacefully in bed."

THOMAS W. WALKER

See also Carter, James Earl; Human Rights; Latin America; Nicaragua

FURTHER READING

Millett, Richard. *The Guardians of the Dynasty: A History of the U.S.-Created Guardia Nacional de Nicaragua and the Somoza Family.* Maryknoll, N.Y., 1977.

Morley, Morris H. *Washington, Somoza, and the Sandinistas: State and Regime in U.S. Policy Toward Nicaragua, 1969–1981.* Cambridge, England, 1994.

SONNENFELDT DOCTRINE

An off-the-record statement made by Department of State counselor Helmut Sonnenfeldt, a close aide to Secretary of State Henry A. Kissinger, at a conference of U.S. ambassadors in London in December 1975 that "it must be our policy to strive for an evolution that makes the relationship between the Eastern Europeans and the Soviet Union an organic one." Sonnenfeldt was alleged to have argued that a more "organic" relationship would provide for greater stability in the region and, as a result, make civil unrest and war less likely. Leaked to the press, Sonnenfeldt's remarks aroused critics who charged that he advocated acceptance of permanent Soviet domination of Eastern Europe.

Sonnenfeldt, Kissinger, and President Gerald Ford denied that a Sonnenfeldt Doctrine ever existed, claiming that Sonnenfeldt's remarks had been distorted and misunderstood. The controversy over the so-called doctrine coincided with a heated debate over the merits of détente or rapprochement with the Soviet Union. Ford's signing of the Conference on Security and Cooperation in Europe Final Act in 1975 (often referred to as the Helsinki Final Act, for the city where it was signed) had ignited charges in some circles that the United States was trying to legitimize Soviet domination of Eastern Europe. Proponents of détente believed that easing tensions between the blocs would avert military conflict between Eastern Europe and Western nations and ameliorate the difficult conditions for people living in Eastern Europe. Critics charged that détente bestowed legitimacy on communist rule and provided the Kremlin and its allies in East European capitals with desperately needed credits and hard currency to retain power and enhance their strategic position in the world.

JEFFREY GEDMIN

See also Cold War; Eastern Europe; Helsinki Accords

FURTHER READING

Gaddis, John Lewis. *Strategies of Containment: A Critical Appraisal of Postwar American National Security Policy.* New York, 1982.

Garthoff, Raymond L. *Détente and Confrontation: American-Soviet Relations from Nixon to Reagan.* Washington, D.C., 1985.

SOROS, GEORGE

(*b.* 12 August 1930)

A phenomenally successful financier of Hungarian birth, George Soros has accumulated great wealth through a series of shrewd investment activities over a generation. His financial empire is dominated by the Quantum Fund, valued at some $11 billion in the mid-1990s. He has parlayed his fortune into a network of foundations around the world, foundations that operate as private foreign policy apparatuses and which, in the final analysis, are accountable to no one but their founder.

In the mid-1980s Soros began providing financial support for Eastern European dissidents challenging local communist regimes. By the late 1980s his efforts to encourage the growth of democratic ideas and institutions worldwide had spawned a network of foundations in some twenty-six countries, the majority in Eastern Europe and the states of the former Soviet Union. These foundations are loosely coordinated under the omnibus Open Society Foundation. Perhaps the most visible manifestation of this effort to encourage his concept of open societies was the founding, in 1990, of the Central European University in Budapest with an initial grant of $230 million. His Moscow-based foundation has been the conduit for some $350 million designated for a variety of cultural, educational, and scientific programs in Russia. He also has utilized his foundations' funds as a means to intervene quite unabashedly in the political affairs of Macedonia, Ukraine, and Albania.

Now a naturalized U.S. citizen, Soros has been supported by the Clinton administration's Department of State in many of his unofficial diplomatic activities. He is well-connected in such centers of foreign policy formulation as the Carnegie Endowment for International Peace and the Council on Foreign Relations. His brand of "entrepreneurial diplomacy" is similar in some respects to that conducted during the Cold War by the Carnegie Corporation and the Ford and Rockefeller Foundations. There are significant differences as well. Soros's ventures into the foreign policy arena come at a time when U.S. foreign policy appears, to many, to lack a focus. He seems to bask in the attention that his sometimes flamboyant activities attract. The overseas programs of the Carnegie Corporation and the Ford and Rockefeller Foundations, on the other hand, traditionally seek to deflect attention from their own involvement. Fortuitously for Soros, his interests have coincided with an effort to encourage greater private sector involvement in foreign policy initiatives. For example, his role was central in keeping the Sarajevo waterworks functioning during the prolonged Serbian siege of that city in the early 1990s. The blurring of the lines between public diplomacy and private influence is further illustrated by his 1994 purchase from the

U.S. government of Radio Free Europe's research institute and the leasing of its archives for fifty years. The reorganized structure will be the Prague-based Open Media Research Institute.

EDWARD H. BERMAN

See also Philanthropic Foundations, Overseas Programs; Radio Free Europe and Radio Liberty

FURTHER READING

Bruck, Connie. "The World According to Soros." *The New Yorker* (23 January 1995): 54–78.

SOUTH AFRICA

A republic of more than 40 million people located at the extreme southern tip of the African continent, and the most prosperous country in Africa. Southern Africa, home to the indigenous Khoisan peoples, was settled in the seventeenth century by the Dutch (Boers, later known as Afrikaners), somewhat earlier by the African peoples, and in the nineteenth century by the British, who consolidated control through the Boer War of 1899–1902.

In 1910 the Union of South Africa was formed as a self-governing dominion within the British Empire. Its constitution gave almost total power to whites. In 1912 black Africans formed the South African Native National Congress to lead their fight for political rights and equality.

Led by Boer general Jan Smuts, South Africa sided with the Allies in World War I. It played an important role, driving the Germans out of Namibia (then called German Southwest Africa) and what is now Tanzania (German East Africa). The League of Nations gave South Africa control over Namibia in 1920. Smuts served as prime minister of South Africa from 1919 to 1924.

Smuts was replaced by J.B.M. Hertzog, a much stronger advocate of Afrikaner nationalism and the founder of the National Party (NP) back in 1912. Under Hertzog, Afrikaans became an official language along with English, and significant independence from Britain was achieved (1931).

With the approach of World War II, South Africans split between the pro-neutrality Hertzog and the pro-British Smuts. Smuts prevailed, becoming prime minister again and bringing South Africa into the war fighting on the side of the Allies in northern Africa, the Horn of Africa, and Europe.

The rise to power of the Afrikaners' National Party in 1948 resulted in the official imposition of the distinctive policies of racial segregation known as *apartheid* (Afrikaans for "separateness,") which eventually led to severe international criticism. In 1961 South Africa became an independent republic and withdrew from the British Commonwealth.

U.S. policy toward South Africa has been shaped by the interplay between American domestic trends, primarily advances by the Civil Rights movement, and the evolution and subsequent demise of apartheid. In the post–World War II era, as attention to racial discrimination in the United States grew and measures such as the Civil Rights Act of 1964 were taken to gradually eliminate it, South Africa's white minority government moved in the other direction, imposing stricter racial discrimination and becoming increasingly oppressive of black political rights. With the advent of a post-apartheid era in South Africa following a negotiated settlement between the white minority and the black majority in 1993, which resulted in successful all-race elections in April 1994, South Africa was set to become one of the most important U.S. allies on the continent.

Despite certain parallels between the colonial, settlement, and frontier experiences of the United States and South Africa, until the twentieth century there were few contacts between the two countries. The United States had few direct interests in southern Africa and, as a British colony, South Africa looked to London throughout the nineteenth century. At the beginning of the twentieth century, close ties began to develop between the nascent Civil Rights movement in the United States and those beginning to struggle for black political rights in South Africa. In the first several decades of the twentieth century, independent black South African churches and leaders of the country's principal liberation movement, the African National Congress (ANC), drew inspiration from such African-American leaders as W. E. B. DuBois, Booker T. Washington, and Marcus Garvey. South African Prime Minister Jan Smuts closely cooperated with the United States to create the United Nations in the immediate postwar period.

The United States and Apartheid

When the National Party won a whites-only election in 1948 on its platform of strict racial segregation and black disenfranchisement, top U.S. decision makers paid little notice. South Africa's white minority government, strongly averse to communism, was ideologically close to the United States as the Cold War developed. Conversely, South Africa—positioned astride critical maritime routes—was strategically important to the United States. Although the United States opposed South Africa's inclusion in the North Atlantic Treaty Organization (NATO), which NP Prime Minister Daniel Malan sought, relations continued to be close and included military cooperation. South African troops participated in the Berlin Airlift (1948–1949) and the U.S.-led coalition in the Korean War (1950–1953).

In 1948, however, South Africa's race policies were raised by India at the United Nations, forcing the United

States to clarify its policy on apartheid. The United States generally argued that apartheid was a matter of "domestic jurisdiction" that remained outside of international authority and abstained on General Assembly resolutions critical of apartheid. In the early 1950s, however, when South Africa refused to allow its occupation of South-West Africa (now Namibia), which it held under a 1920 mandate of the League of Nations, to come under the purview of the Trusteeship Council, the United States became less acquiescent.

Nevertheless, throughout the administration of President Dwight D. Eisenhower the United States abstained from openly criticizing South Africa in the UN, saying only that it regretted certain developments within South Africa, and continued economic and military cooperation. In 1955 and 1957 the two nations signed agreements for cooperation in naval and nuclear energy matters, respectively. Commercial relations continued as before, and U.S. investors increased their holdings in South Africa by nearly $140 million between 1953 and 1960.

As the Civil Rights movement in the United States gained force, policy toward South Africa (and its worsening racial tensions) began to shift as well. The 1954 *Brown* v. *Board of Education* Supreme Court decision, outlawing segregated schools, set the United States on the path toward desegregation and restoration of civil rights to African Americans, even as South Africa was increasingly enacting onerous apartheid laws. Amidst mounting black resistance to apartheid in South Africa, ties between leaders of the U.S. Civil Rights movement and the liberation struggle in South Africa grew stronger. Dr. Martin Luther King, Jr., formulated his strategy of nonviolent protest in part from the concepts of passive resistance of Mohandas Gandhi, the leader of India's successful independence movement who began his career by resisting anti-Indian discrimination in South Africa in 1907. The 1957 bus boycott in Montgomery, Alabama, led by Dr. King, was closely modeled on the 1950–1952 Defiance Campaign led by the ANC in South Africa, and ANC leader Albert Luthuli and Dr. King exchanged correspondence.

In 1958, following the introduction of more draconian segregation laws in South Africa, the United States abandoned its policy of abstention at the UN and, implicitly, the doctrine that apartheid was an issue only within the domestic jurisdiction of South Africa. This move set an important precedent, leading eventually to acceptance in the 1990s by the international community of the principle that certain forms of intervention in the internal affairs of another state were justified if significant human rights or humanitarian concerns were involved.

Events in South Africa in the early 1960s reinforced the changing nature of U.S.–South African bilateral rela-

tions. When South African police killed sixty-nine unarmed antiapartheid protesters in the Sharpeville township in 1960, the United States recalled its ambassador and joined a unanimous vote in the UN Security Council that "deplored the policies and actions of the South African government." U.S. investors also began to disinvest, although as stability returned in the wake of a government crackdown they generally re-invested. By 1962, after the outcry over the Sharpeville massacre subsided, there was a renormalization of relations.

U.S. policy under the administration of President John F. Kennedy shifted further toward condemnation of apartheid. Kennedy's increasing criticism of South Africa was driven by a combination of interest (he sought to woo newly independent African states very critical of South Africa into the pro-Western fold against the Soviets) and morality (he was supportive of the U.S. Civil Rights movement). Although the United States opposed sanctions demanded by African states in the UN General Assembly, Kennedy refused to grant a request by South African prime minister Hendrik Verwoerd—known as the architect of apartheid—to be received at the White House. But the preeminence of Cold War concerns precluded further steps against South Africa, particularly when it came to military and commercial relationships. In 1962 an agreement was reached to set up a U.S. space tracking station on South African soil. Under President Lyndon B. Johnson, anticommunism continued to drive policy, although Johnson also was committed to U.S. civil rights, and South Africa's worsening racial policies were inimical to this general principle. When the U.S. ship *Franklin Delano Roosevelt* docked in Cape Town in 1967, however, a row developed over shore leave for African-American U.S. sailors and naval cooperation came to a halt.

With the election of President Richard Nixon, U.S. policy shifted back toward closer ties. In a comprehensive review, policy was redefined in terms directly related to the pursuit of Cold War objectives. Secretary of State Henry Kissinger declared that white settler states in southern Africa (South Africa, Rhodesia [now Zimbabwe], Angola, and Mozambique) were unlikely to be overthrown. In National Security Study Memorandum 39, the cornerstone of the Nixon Africa policy was set: "Through selective relaxation of our stance toward the white regimes, [we can] encourage some modification in their current racial and colonial policies." Thus, opposition to apartheid would take a backseat to strategic and commercial interests in acknowledgment of South Africa's position as an anti-Soviet ally. Once again the United States abstained on UN resolutions against South Africa and cultivated close military ties.

The year 1976 witnessed significant changes in the political climate of both the United States and South

Africa. With the inauguration of President Jimmy Carter, tensions rose over South African repression of its increasingly restive black majority. Carter was elected with backing from the African-American community, and he expressed strong support for domestic civil rights causes. Carter's broader foreign policy strategy, shifting attention from the Cold War toward a greater attention to human rights, was reflected in his South Africa policy. The appointment of African American Andrew Young as U.S. ambassador to the United Nations symbolized the change in approach; Young hinted that sanctions against South Africa were possible and agreed with the view that the white minority government was illegitimate. A meeting between South African prime minister John Vorster and U.S. vice president Walter Mondale in May 1977 in Vienna was a benchmark in U.S.–South African relations. Mondale delivered a clear and frank message: the United States called for majority rule for Rhodesia, Namibia, and South Africa.

With the murder of black activist Stephen Biko by South African police while in detention in late 1977 and the subsequent crackdown, the United States joined other nations in approving a mandatory UN arms embargo. A defensive South African regime responded sharply, and relations deteriorated further; Vorster waged a reelection campaign on an anti-U.S. platform. Commercial ties continued, but U.S. firms in South Africa came under increasing pressure from the American public to abide by a code of conduct known as the Sullivan Principles, which were drafted in 1977 by the Reverend Leon Sullivan, an African-American clergymen from Philadelphia. The Carter administration embraced the principles, which included nonsegregation in the workplace, equal pay, and equal employment practices, but did not embrace mandatory economic sanctions.

From Constructive Engagement to Sanctions

Carter's defeat and President Ronald Reagan's victory in 1980 led to a shift in U.S. policy back in the direction of cooperation. Even prior to taking office, Reagan's principal adviser on Africa, Chester A. Crocker, outlined a regional policy for southern Africa known as constructive engagement," which emphasized "traditional Cold War concerns along with quiet persuasion in U.S. efforts to stimulate racial reform in South Africa. Crocker, outlining his views in an article in *Foreign Affairs*, noted that the primary U.S. objective in the region should be to confront Soviet influence and secure U.S. economic and security interests.

Constructive engagement had four principal objectives: fostering movement away from apartheid and toward a system of government that included blacks; preserving continued U.S. access to strategic minerals neces-

sary for defense-related industry—especially chromium, platinum-group metals, manganese, and vanadium—that could only be obtained from South Africa or the Soviet Union; securing the strategic Cape sea lanes; and countering the Soviet-Cuban threat in the region, particularly in Angola. Similarly, U.S. firms were encouraged to become "constructively involved" in South Africa by using their influence to improve conditions for blacks.

The United States sought peaceful evolutionary change away from apartheid as well as regional nonaggression pacts between South Africa and its neighbors. One such pact, the 1984 Nkomati Accord with Mozambique, was strongly encouraged by the United States and used to demonstrate the effectiveness of constructive engagement. Limited constitutional reforms were adopted in South Africa in 1984, granting political rights to so-called "Coloreds" (citizens of mixed race) and South Africa's Indian population, but excluding blacks and so ensuring white hegemony.

President P. W. Botha's cautious reform program did not pacify South Africa's restive black majority and inflamed political tensions. In September 1984 a general uprising began. The insurrection and the ruthless response by the South African regime sharpened divisions between the Reagan administration and its critics on the appropriate policy for ending apartheid in South Africa. To the critics, constructive engagement appeared to encourage continued racial dominance. Congressional calls for sanctions began to rise, and legislation imposing economic sanctions, to which the Reagan administration was bitterly opposed, began to move toward enactment. Protest against apartheid in the United States gathered steam, demanding divestment by U.S. firms and economic sanctions. Daily demonstrations and a civil disobedience campaign at the South African embassy in Washington began on Thanksgiving Day, 1984; among the protestors arrested were not only prominent African-American political leaders, but also a broad coalition of civil rights activists and a number of congressmen, mostly Democrats but also some Republicans. The Free South Africa movement was also active on U.S. college campuses, with demonstrations demanding that universities, state and local governments, pension funds, and other public institutions disinvest from companies doing business in South Africa. The movement's cause was aided by graphic, often daily broadcasts of the violent confrontation between blacks and the South African police.

As violence and repression intensified in South Africa in mid-1985, it was clear that sanctions legislation would be enacted by the U.S. Congress, despite Reagan administration objections. In August 1985, following a hard-line speech by the increasingly recalcitrant Botha, U.S. banks, led by Chase Manhattan, refused to roll over short-term loans to South Africa, precipitating a major economic crisis in the country. Aware of the strength of congressional support for sanctions, President Reagan reluctantly imposed by executive order a set of limited economic sanctions against South Africa ending nuclear cooperation and banning most new loans, the export of computers and technology used in implementing apartheid, and later the importation of South African gold coins. Constructive engagement came under continued congressional and public criticism, and the debate over sanctions became highly polarized.

As the insurrection in South Africa grew stronger, pressure mounted in the United States for tougher sanctions than those imposed by Reagan. When a formerly limited state of emergency in South Africa was extended and police repression intensified in 1986, moderate U.S. Senate Republicans, with an eye on upcoming midterm elections in which their continued majority control of the Senate would be challenged, broke with Reagan and backed wide-ranging sanctions. Congress passed the Comprehensive Anti-Apartheid Act (CAAA) just a few weeks before the November elections. When Reagan vetoed the bill, the House of Representatives voted to override, 313 to 83; the Senate concurred, rebuking the president in a 78–21 vote. Sanctions legislation against South Africa was the first override of a presidential veto on a foreign policy issue since the 1973 War Powers Resolution.

The CAAA comprehensively defined an alternative U.S. policy toward South Africa. It contained a detailed set of statements on U.S. policy to end apartheid, imposed wide-ranging economic sanctions, including a ban on new U.S. investments and loans, an extensive trade embargo, and denial of landing rights to South African-flagged air carriers. Moreover, the CAAA required five actions by the South African government before sanctions would be lifted: freeing political prisoners, including ANC leader Nelson Mandela; canceling the state of emergency and legalizing banned political parties such as the ANC; repealing racially discriminatory legislation; granting political freedoms to South African blacks; and entering good faith negotiations with legitimate black political leaders to dismantle apartheid. Unless "substantial progress" was made in South Africa, further sanctions were called for in the law.

Throughout 1987 and 1988 a stalemate ensued in South Africa with further repression and resistance leading to little political change. The United States began to work toward urging negotiation among South Africa's banned and exiled political groups and the white minority government. Secretary of State George Shultz, in a major policy change, received ANC President Oliver Tambo in Washington in 1988. Critics of Reagan administration policy tried to push more extensive sanctions

legislation through Congress but were unsuccessful as doubts were raised about their potential efficacy in ending apartheid.

The sanctions brought a significant diminution in U.S. corporate engagement in South Africa. By 1990 investor watchdog groups reported that only between 120 and 130 U.S. companies remained in South Africa out of the more than 300 present in 1985. Similarly, U.S. direct investment plunged from some $2.3 billion in 1982 to $700 million in 1989. Most universities, pension funds, and institutional investors divested their holdings in South Africa–related stocks, further reinforcing the punitive effect of the CAAA. Some 179 state and local governments also enacted anti-apartheid laws, making South Africa unique as a foreign policy issue in the depth and breadth of its significance in U.S. domestic politics.

The administration of President George Bush sought to defuse the tension between the executive and legislative branches on U.S. South Africa policy. As the political climate in South Africa loosened, especially after the ailing Botha was replaced by a more reform-minded F. W. De Klerk, the Bush administration supported nascent moves toward negotiation away from apartheid. The demise of the Cold War in late 1989 reverberated in southern Africa. The South African government's argument that the ANC was Soviet-inspired now mattered much less from a U.S. perspective, and the settlement of South Africa's occupation of Namibia through U.S.-brokered negotiation created a dramatically new environment in the subcontinent for all parties to the conflict.

The End of Apartheid

In this changed climate, De Klerk took several major steps in early 1990—most significantly releasing Mandela (by then perhaps the world's most celebrated political prisoner), legalizing the ANC and other opposition groups, and calling for negotiations to end apartheid. The Bush administration welcomed the shift and reemphasized to the South African government the benefits of further political reform while maintaining the position that all conditions set out in the CAAA be met before sanctions could be removed.

The Bush administration played a supportive but quiet role in encouraging negotiations. U.S. nongovernmental organizations, such as the Aspen Institute, had been holding regular forums for South African political leaders as a way of facilitating dialogue prior to formal negotiation. As negotiations began in earnest, Bush rewarded De Klerk with a Washington summit in September 1990, in which he lent political support for the transition away from apartheid, and—to De Klerk's delight—termed the process "irreversible" (a term related to conditions for easing CAAA sanctions). This angered some in Congress, for example the Black Caucus, which argued that the white government had not gone far enough to warrant such praise.

The transition from apartheid continued into 1991, with De Klerk's government repealing a number of apartheid laws, releasing political prisoners and allowing the return of exiles, permitting mass protests by blacks, and engaging in negotiation with the ANC over the course of further change. By June 1991, following repeal of apartheid's cornerstone legislation that classified all South Africans by race, President Bush lifted some sanctions, notably the bans on new investment and loans, declaring that all CAAA conditions for their repeal had been met. Bush left in place the mandatory arms embargo, and military-related export controls, as well as prohibitions on Export-Import Bank loans and U.S. support for South African loans at the International Monetary Fund.

Following the lifting of sanctions, and indeed preceding it, U.S. policy had begun to place emphasis on economic and development assistance to South African blacks and training for democracy. Beginning in 1987, $10 million was provided for this purpose, but this amount increased to nearly $40 million in 1991 and increased again to an annual level of about $80 million beginning in 1992. This assistance made South Africa the largest single recipient of U.S. aid in sub-Saharan Africa. Throughout 1991 and 1992, as South Africa's transition grew more turbulent and factional violence persisted, U.S. policy centered around efforts to keep the negotiation process on track and holding out the potential for demonstrative rewards should a settlement be reached. When constitutional negotiations broke down in mid-1992, the administration supported UN efforts to assist in the resumption of talks, and former U.S. secretary of state Cyrus Vance led a UN fact-finding and mediation mission.

When President Bill Clinton assumed office in 1993, one of his first acts of South Africa policy was to call ANC leader Mandela. Although it was feared this reflected a decided tilt in U.S. policy toward the ANC, the Clinton administration generally continued Bush policy to encourage negotiated change. As constitutional negotiations in South Africa continued into 1993, the United States and other Western states were supportive. When right-wing black and white political leaders walked out of talks with the government and ANC in mid-1993, U.S. diplomats worked actively (but unsuccessfully) to mediate. In mid-1993 Clinton presided over a ceremony in Philadelphia that awarded the Freedom Medal to De Klerk and Mandela for their efforts to negotiate peace in South Africa, and the president met with both political leaders (albeit separately) during their U.S. stay.

Agreement between the South African government and ANC on an interim power-sharing constitution in November 1993, ending apartheid, led the United States and other Western powers to welcome South Africa back into the international community. Days after the adoption of the new charter, the U.S. Congress passed legislation that repealed the remaining CAAA sanctions, called on state and local governments to remove punitive laws, made South Africa eligible for most-favored-nation status, and authorized further democracy-building and developmental assistance. The law also encouraged and promoted U.S. trade and investment for South Africa, and targeted black-owned businesses for aid. Just after South Africa's historic pact, U.S. Secretary of Commerce Ron Brown, an African American, led a high-level trade mission to encourage bilateral relations. U.S. nongovernmental organizations were deeply engaged in voter education and election monitoring in South Africa's first all-race elections in April 1994.

Following the election of Mandela as president of South Africa in the 1994 elections, President Clinton announced a new three-year, $600 million aid, trade, and investment package for South Africa, more than doubling the previous annual allocation. The new package meant that South Africa would receive more assistance than all other African countries combined. Announcement of the assistance was carefully planned—after the peaceful days of voting but before the final election results were announced—to show U.S. support for the successful election and the negotiated transfer of power. The assistance package was also an inducement to all parties to accept the outcome. Clinton pledged to lobby leaders of other Western countries for aid to post-apartheid South Africa and to press for favorable terms at the International Monetary Fund and the World Bank. In June 1994 Mandela visited the United States on a state visit, consolidating the new close ties between South Africa and the United States.

By the mid-1990s South Africa was poised to become the most important U.S. political and economic partner in Africa. Indeed, U.S. investments and trade ties burgeoned between 1994 and early 1996. Many policymakers believed that because the United States played an important role in the international community's imposition of sanctions against apartheid, it had a special role in post-apartheid reconstruction. Indeed, the history and diverse racial composition of the U.S. population has made and will continue to make South Africa and its turbulent search for reconciliation and interracial and interethnic cooperation of special concern. As the post-apartheid era dawns in South Africa, U.S. political and commercial ties to South Africa will remain very important—in opposition to the trend with many other African states—precisely because of the role U.S. domestic politics plays in the formulation of our South Africa policy. In 1995, a high-profile U.S.–South Africa Binational Commission was established to further cement the budding alliance between the two states.

TIMOTHY D. SISK

See also Africa; Cold War; Colonialism; Crocker, Chester Arthur; De Klerk, Frederik Willem; DuBois, William Edward Burghardt; Economic Sanctions; Garvey, Marcus Moziah; Mandela, Nelson Rolihlahla; Namibia

FURTHER READING

Arnold, Millard. "Engaging South Africa After Apartheid." *Foreign Policy* 87 (1992): 139-156.
Baker, Pauline H. *The United States and South Africa: The Reagan Years*. New York, 1989.
Borstelmann, Thomas. *Apartheid, Colonialism, and the Cold War: The United States and Southern Africa in the Early Cold War*. New York, 1993.
Coker, Christopher. *The United States and South Africa, 1968–1985: Constructive Engagement and Its Critics*. Durham, N.C., 1986.
Crocker, Chester A. *High Noon in Southern Africa: Making Peace in a Rough Neighborhood*. New York, 1992.
Danaher, Kevin. *The Political Economy of U.S. Policy Toward South Africa*. Boulder, Colo., 1985.
Lulat, Y. G.-M. *U.S. Relations with South Africa: An Annotated Bibliography*. Boulder, Colo., 1991.
Study Commission on U.S. Policy Toward Southern Africa. *South Africa: Time Running Out*. Berkeley, Calif., 1981.

SOUTHEAST ASIA TREATY ORGANIZATION

An alliance created in 1954 between the United States and seven other nations following the defeat of France in Vietnam and intended to contain the further spread of communism in Southeast Asia. The other members were Great Britain, France, Australia, New Zealand, Pakistan, the Philippines, and Thailand. Southeast Asia Treaty Organization (SEATO) members pledged to defend one another as well as other designated nations—South Vietnam, Cambodia, and Laos—against aggression and subversion. In its initial conception, particularly as seen by its principal architect, Secretary of State John Foster Dulles, SEATO was to be the Southeast Asian equivalent of the North Atlantic Treaty Organization. In practice, however, it did not achieve comparable success. For example, only three other SEATO nations—Thailand, New Zealand, and Australia—ever sent troops to fight in Vietnam. The U.S. rapprochement with the People's Republic of China, starting with President Richard M. Nixon's visit to that country in 1971, further reduced the salience of SEATO. In 1977 it was officially dissolved. U.S. defense commitments to the Philippines and Thailand continued, however, based on bilateral agreements. The Association of Southeast Asian Nations, which invited Vietnam to its annual summit for the first time in 1994, helped reassure its member nations with regard to defense as well as economic cooperation.

MACALISTER BROWN

See also Dulles, John Foster; Vietnam War

FURTHER READING

Buszynski, Leszek. *SEATO, The Failure of an Alliance Strategy*. Singapore, 1983.
Wurfel, David, and Bruce Burton, eds. *The Political Economy of Foreign Policy in Southeast Asia*. New York, 1990.

SOVIET UNION

See Russia and the Soviet Union

SPACE POLICY

The space policy of the United States was from the mid-1950s until the end of the Cold War primarily driven by competition with the Soviet Union, the only other country to develop comprehensive capabilities for civilian and national security activities in space. Initially, in the aftermath of the 1957 launch of the first satellite *Sputnik* by the Soviet Union, President Dwight Eisenhower rejected the notion that it was important for the United States to try to match Soviet space "firsts." Instead, he insisted that the goals and content of the U.S. space program should reflect a balanced assessment of U.S. interests. In contrast, his successor, President John Kennedy, in 1961 decided that the United States should enter, and win, the U.S.-USSR "race" for dramatic space achievement. The key marker set for winning this space race was being the first to land a person on the moon. This commitment and its long-lasting impacts shaped U.S. space policy over seven presidential administrations (Kennedy to Bush). However, with the demise of the Soviet Union, this motive force disappeared, and in the first half of the 1990s the United States struggled to develop a consensus in support of new policy directions in space.

Soon after the end of World War II it was clear to careful observers that activities in space would have important national security, political, and scientific implications, but it was not until 1955 that the United States decided to launch an Earth satellite. Although this decision was taken in the context of scientific planning for the 1957–1958 International Geophysical Year, President Eisenhower made it in consultation with his National Security Council. The NSC was involved because of an unchanging reality: space capabilities are "dual use" in character—they can be employed for military as well as civilian purposes. The Eisenhower administration was considering development of reconnaissance satellites, and wanted to ensure that any scientific satellite project would help establish the right of free orbital overflight of any place on Earth on the principle that outer space was beyond any nation-state's jurisdiction. It was the Soviet

Union, not the United States, however, that launched the first scientific satellite, *Sputnik I*, on 4 October 1957. Worldwide reaction to the accomplishment was strongly positive and admiring, and Soviet leaders boasted that the achievement symbolized the superiority of the communist system. Washington's attempts to downplay the political significance of the Soviet feat were unsuccessful, and the Eisenhower administration was forced to develop a rapid U.S. response. After briefly considering putting all U.S. space activities under Department of Defense (DOD) management, Eisenhower decided in March 1958 to separate civilian and military space activities, and to create a new organization, the National Aeronautics and Space Administration (NASA), to manage the civilian effort. Since then, the institutional separation of most civilian and national security space efforts has remained a fundamental principle of U.S. space policy.

In early 1958 the Department of Defense created an Advanced Research Projects Agency (ARPA) to manage military space programs, but this initiative was successfully resisted by the military services, and by 1960 most Department of Defense space activities were under the control of the air force, with the navy and army retaining secondary roles. This remains the case today. Recognizing the extreme secrecy required for the conduct of reconnaissance and other intelligence satellite programs, Eisenhower in 1960 created a separate National Reconnaissance Office (NRO) to manage those programs; so great was the need for secrecy that even the existence of this agency remained classified until 1992. On 26 January 1960, the Eisenhower administration adopted a comprehensive statement, "U.S. Policy on Outer Space," which directed planners to "select from among those current or projected U.S. space activities of intrinsic military, scientific, or technological value, one or more projects which offer demonstrably effective advantage over the Soviets and, so far as is consistent with solid achievements in the overall space program, stress these projects in present and future programming." This well summarized the cautious Eisenhower approach to the space race, an approach soon reversed by President Kennedy, who entered the White House in January 1961.

The Decision to Go to the Moon

On 12 April 1961, the Soviet Union orbited the first human being to go into space, Yury Gagarin. If anything, the reaction to this feat around the world and within the United States was even more intense and positive than the reaction to *Sputnik I*. President Kennedy decided that the United States should enter an all-out space race with the Soviet Union. On 20 April, in a memorandum to Vice President Lyndon Johnson, Kennedy asked for an "overall survey of where we stand in space" and posed the following questions: "Do we have a chance of beating the Soviets by putting a laboratory in space, or by a trip around the moon, or by a rocket to go to the moon and back with a man? Is there any other space program that promises dramatic results in which we could win?" The response to these queries came on 8 May, in a memorandum signed by NASA Administrator James E. Webb and Secretary of Defense Robert S. McNamara, who advised Kennedy that "major successes, such as orbiting a man as the Soviets have just done, lend national prestige even though the scientific, commercial, or military value of the undertaking may by ordinary standards be marginal or economically unjustified. *This nation needs to make a positive decision to pursue space projects aimed at enhancing national prestige.* Our attainments are a major element in the international competition between the Soviet system and our own. The non-military, non-commercial, non-scientific but 'civilian' projects such as lunar and planetary exploration are, in this sense, part of the battle along the fluid front of the Cold War....It is men, not merely machines, in space that captures the imagination of the world." Kennedy accepted their recommendation that the United States commit to sending people to the moon, and on 25 May 1961, speaking before a joint session of Congress, he declared that it was "time for this nation to take a clearly leading role in space achievement." With this announcement, the central role in U.S. space policy of large space projects with human involvement, undertaken primarily for their political benefits, became manifest.

During the 1960s there was indeed a race between the United States and the Soviet Union to be first to send people both around and to the moon. Due to a variety of factors—weak political support in the post-Khrushchev era, bureaucratic rivalries and inefficiencies, and the untimely death in 1966 of its leading space engineer, Sergei Korolev—the Soviet Union squandered its early space lead. In the United States, however, despite changing national priorities and the death of three astronauts in January 1967 during a launch pad test, there was consistent political support for Project Apollo and the effort was in general well-managed by NASA and its contractor team. In December 1968, *Apollo 8* sent its three-person crew into lunar orbit. On 20 July 1969 Neil Armstrong and Buzz Aldrin became the first humans to set foot on a celestial body other than earth. In terms of the objectives set for it eight years earlier, Apollo was a resounding success; the world *was* impressed.

In the years after landing on the moon, debates over whether to undertake other large-scale projects involving humans became a continuing feature of U.S. space policy. Much less policy attention was given to issues of robotic space science and applications programs, which went forward largely on their own momentum, often explicitly with a budget that was an agreed-upon percentage of overall NASA funding. The Kennedy initiative helped shape the institutional evolution of NASA into an organization centered on human spaceflight activities, and this focus in turn shaped public and congressional perception of space policy priorities. As it became clear that the United States would attempt the first lunar landing sometime in mid-1969, White House attention turned to the policies and programs that would constitute the U.S. space effort in the post-Apollo period. There had been little attention to this issue in the final years of the Johnson administration, but one of President Richard M. Nixon's early actions was the creation of a Space Task Group, chaired by Vice President Spiro T. Agnew, to provide "definitive recommendations" on post-Apollo plans. The Task Group submitted its report to the President on 15 September 1969: it recommended an extremely ambitious post-Apollo effort, with the long-range goal of sending humans to Mars before the end of the twentieth century. These visionary proposals were almost totally rejected by the Nixon administration, which was determined to reduce the NASA budget and saw little political advantage for the president in approving ambitious long-range programs which would not be completed until after he left office. On 7 March 1970, Nixon issued a space policy statement in which he noted the need "to define new goals which make sense for the Seventies….Many critical problems here on this planet, it said, "make high priority demands on our attention and our resources. By no means should we allow our space program to stagnate. But—with the entire future and the entire universe before us—we should not try to do everything at once. Our approach to space must be bold—but it must also be balanced."

The Nixon administration did approve one program that had been recommended by the Space Task Group, but only in modified form. This was the development of a partially reusable space transportation system, which became known as the Space Shuttle. President Nixon's decision to go ahead with the Shuttle was, in ways somewhat similar to the Kennedy decision to go to the moon, based on considerations of foreign policy and national pride. On 15 August 1971, the president's close adviser Caspar ("Cap") Weinberger prepared a memorandum for Nixon, suggesting that failure to approve the Shuttle "would be confirming in some respects, a belief that I fear is gaining credence at home and abroad: That our best years are behind us, that we are turning inward, reducing our defense commitments, and voluntarily giving up our superpower status, and our desire to maintain world superiority." In a handwritten notation on the memorandum, Nixon indicated "I agree with Cap." The final decision to approve the Shuttle was made over the 1971–1972 New Year's weekend. In addition to the foreign policy justifications for the program, the White House also was aware that starting the Shuttle would lead to new jobs in states that were key to Nixon's 1972 re-election bid. Meeting with NASA Administrator James Fletcher on 5 January, the day that Shuttle approval was announced, Nixon said, "Even if it were not a good investment, we would have to do it anyway, because [human] space flight is here to stay."

The Shuttle was approved only after its design had been modified so that it could be developed within a very restricted budget and could also meet the requirements set forth by the Department of Defense as a condition for agreeing to launch all military payloads on the Shuttle. The notion that a single U.S. launch system, managed by NASA, could serve both civilian and military needs was a deviation from the policy of separate civilian and military space programs, but NASA needed to launch military payloads to justify Shuttle development in terms of cost-effectiveness. The Shuttle was first launched in April 1981 and, though difficult and expensive to operate, became in the next few years a versatile means of carrying out a wide variety of scientific and engineering activities in space. In addition, it gave the United States crucial experience in the development and use of a first-generation reusable space transportation system. However, the policy of having only a single launch system for providing all U.S. access to space proved deeply flawed; this was most dramatically demonstrated after the January 1986 *Challenger* disaster, in which seven astronauts including a high-school teacher-astronaut were killed, and which grounded the Shuttle fleet for 32 months. After the accident, the Shuttle was taken out of the business of launching commercial communication satellites; this provided a business opportunity for firms eager to offer launch services on a commercial basis using their existing expendable launch vehicles (ELVs). Even before the *Challanger* accident, the Department of Defense had been insisting on the need to maintain an ELV fleet to provide a backup to the Shuttle; after 1986, the Department of Defense began a transition that eventually led to removal of all DOD payloads from the Shuttle. By the early 1990s, civilian and military space efforts were once again almost totally separate.

Military Space Programs

As of the 1990s, the basic policy set out by the Eisenhower administration for the national security uses of space—that space capabilities would be developed and employed when they were the most effective means for carrying out various military objectives—has remained in place. Although there was early consideration of the desirability of deploying weapons systems in space (and even on the moon), it soon became clear that there were no major military advantages to such a move. U.S. policy has therefore consistently aimed at keeping space a weapons-free environment and has viewed military space systems as "force multipliers" for terrestrial military activities. There have been two exceptions to the general policy of keeping space weapons-free. From the earliest days of the space effort, some have argued that it was important for the United States to control access to and use of space, and thus to have the capability to destroy hostile satellites. There have been continuing debates about the wisdom of developing and deploying an anti-satellite system.

In 1983 President Ronald Reagan proposed developing a defense against attacks from strategic missiles. As originally conceived, this proposal, which became known as the Strategic Defense Initiative (SDI), would have involved the space-based deployment of large-scale missile defense capabilities. With the collapse of the Soviet strategic threat, the rationale for space defense shifted to protection against accidental launches or, particularly, launches by Third World countries; the name given to systems designed to meet this objective was Global Protection Against Limited Strikes (GPALS). One issue in the heated debate over a space-based missile defense involved the need to revise the 1972 Anti-Ballistic Missile (ABM) Treaty in order to be able to test such a system. The 1991 Persian Gulf conflict was widely viewed as the first "space war," in the sense that a wide variety of communications, navigation, weather, and observation satellites were centrally used by the U.S.-led coalition forces. In the aftermath of the Gulf War, policymakers focused on making sure space capabilities could be used even more effectively in future conflicts.

The proposals put forth in 1969 by the Space Task Group had called for the simultaneous development of a space station as well as the space shuttle. To those committed to a vision of the future in which a permanent outpost in low-Earth orbit would be a necessary step to the full development of space, and to eventual exploration and settlement beyond Earth's orbit, the decision to develop only the Shuttle merely postponed the day when a space station would also be approved. President Jimmy Carter, however, was not a space enthusiast. He considered cancelling the Shuttle program because of cost overruns and schedule delays, but was persuaded that it was needed to launch the observation satellites needed to verify high-priority arms limitation agreements. Carter approved a policy statement issued on 14 October 1978 that declared that "our space policy will become more evolutionary rather than centering around a single, massive engineering feat." To make the point stronger, and as a response to those who were urging Carter to approve a space station program, the statement added that "it is neither feasible nor necessary to commit the United States to a high-challenge, highly-visible space engineering initiative comparable to *Apollo*."

In 1983, NASA was finally able to gain approval to develop a space station project from President Ronald Reagan. This came in the context of the station's role in assuring continued U.S. space leadership; the president was informed that the Soviet Union had had a modest station program for over a decade, and that it was also important for the United States to develop a capability for long-duration orbital flight. The proposed station was to be a general-purpose space laboratory, so its approval by the Reagan administration did not commit the United States to any particular long-range space policy.

Ronald Reagan was the first president to give focused policy attention to the possibility of significant private-sector activity in space. Even earlier, however, a productive government-industry partnership had led to satellite communications becoming a multi-billion dollar business. Industry developed the technological capabilities (sometimes with government support for research and development), while Washington took the lead in creating the institutional framework for satellite communications. Institutional innovations such as the Communications Satellite Corporation (COMSAT) in 1962 and the International Telecommunications Satellite Organization (INTELSAT) in 1964 were key, as was the 1971 deregulation of the U.S. communications market so that satellites could compete with ground-based systems. The Reagan administration hoped for similar commercial success in remote sensing observation from space, manufacturing materials in the zero-gravity space environment, and in launching private payloads into orbit, but progress in space commercialization has been slow: research results related to materials-processing in space did not show early promise, while markets for Earth observation products were limited. Nevertheless, a commercial space-launch industry did emerge, and by the 1990s was competing with Europe and the non-market economies of China and Russia for its share of the launch market.

The potency of U.S.-USSR competition as a rationale for the U.S. space program began to wane during the Reagan administration. Reagan's final space policy statement on 5 January 1988 noted that "a fundamental objective guiding United States space activities has been, and continues to be, space leadership," but with the end of the Cold War a few years later, the accomplishments of the Soviet space program, which had served as a measuring stick for such leadership, no longer seemed particularly relevant. In 1984, the Congress had required President Reagan to establish a National Commission on Space to propose long-range goals for the U.S. space program. The Commission report, *Pioneering the Space Frontier*, issued in 1986, recommended that the United States "lead the exploration and development of the space frontier, advancing science, technology, enterprise, and building institutions and systems that make accessible vast new resources and support human settlements beyond Earth orbit, from the highlands of the Moon to the plains of Mars." In the wake of the *Challenger* accident, however, the report received little public attention.

Subsequently, however, President George Bush accepted the Commission's concept that space development was justified in its own right, not because of its link to other national interests. On 20 July 1989, the twentieth anniversary of the first lunar landing, Bush proposed a Space Exploration Initiative built around a "long-term, continuing commitment" to human exploration of the solar system, including a "return to the moon, this time to stay," and human missions to Mars. Public and congressional reaction to Bush's proposal was notably lacking in enthusiasm; the combination of deep budget deficits and other competing priorities made it politically unattractive. Within a year it was clear that the United States would not be starting large new programs of space exploration anytime soon. NASA was having trouble launching the space shuttle on a regular basis, the Hubble Space Telescope had been put in orbit with a flawed primary mirror, the space station was behind schedule and over budget, and there was little money available for new space ventures.

In the early 1990s, attention switched from developing new long-term goals and policies to the issue of "fixing NASA." The space agency seemed to have lost its managerial and technical excellence, and there was growing agreement that a period of institutional and program reform would have to precede any new directions in space policy. A new NASA administrator, Daniel Goldin, from 1992 on devoted his energies to reforming NASA's programs and institutional structure. The quest for a sustainable post–Cold War consensus regarding the longer-term relevance of space to the U.S. national interest continued, even as that reconstruction effort went forward.

A New Cooperative Strategy

Although Cold War competition was the dominant force shaping U.S. space policy for the three decades after 1958, international space cooperation has also played an important role. From the U.S. point of view, in addition to maintaining preeminent capabilities, the primary policy objective of such cooperation has been as another means of exercising leadership among the world's space powers. Cooperation was relatively modest during the 1960s; U.S. allies did not have the capabilities to make them major cooperative partners, and the Soviet Union rebuffed most U.S. initiatives. Even after he announced the Apollo program, President Kennedy several times attempted to interest Moscow in cooperating in lunar exploration, but with no success.

When the United States won the race to the moon in 1969, Washington made a policy decision to expand cooperative interactions with both allies and the Soviet Union. Europe was invited to participate in the post-Apollo program of human space flight. After more than two years of contentious negotiations, which focused on the fear of some in the White House that cooperation would result in unwanted technology transfer, the United States and several European countries agreed that Europe would develop a pressurized laboratory, to be known as *Spacelab*, for use with the space shuttle. In 1972 the United States and the Soviet Union agreed to a docking of two spacecraft with crews aboard; the 1975 Apollo-Soyuz "handshake in space" was a potent symbol of the then-dominant policy of U.S.-Soviet détente. This mission was actually intended as a first step in a long-range program of U.S.-Soviet space cooperation, but after 1979, Carter and Reagan administration displeasure with Soviet human rights behavior, and foreign policy issues such as the invasion of Afghanistan and suppression of dissent in Poland, led to the cancellation of further joint activities.

When President Reagan announced approval of space station development in January 1984, he also invited U.S. allies to participate in that undertaking. Ten European nations, Canada, and Japan accepted his invitation; in September 1988 they signed agreements that initiated the largest experiment in peacetime technological collaboration ever undertaken. The partnership was troubled from the start, however, primarily because the program did not have a firm political base in the United States and thus was subject to recurring schedule slippage and design changes. The United States in 1993 made a fundamental shift in its strategy for space cooperation. It in essence proposed merging its future program of human space flight with that of Russia, the successor state to its erstwhile Soviet competitor. Persuading its space station partners to accept Russia as a new partner, the United States reshaped its station plans to give priority to U.S.-Russian collaboration in developing a core station, with the contributions of other partners to be added later. In preparation for collaboration on the station, a number of other cooperative U.S.-Russian missions were planned. This new approach once again linked space activity with central U.S. policy goals in a way that had not been the case since the Kennedy decision to accept the Soviet challenge and use space achievement as a symbol of national vitality. Now space cooperation was viewed as a way of supporting reform in the former Soviet Union, providing productive employment for aerospace engineers and other Russian workers, and encouraging Russian compliance with such agreements as the Missile Technology Control Regime (designed to limit the spread of long- and medium-range missiles by stemming the flow of technology useful for their development to countries that did not possess such a capability).

Since the beginning of the Space Age in 1957, the United States has pursued several general lines of space policy. National security organizations have found space capabilities extremely useful in carrying out their responsibilities, and there has been a steady increase in its military and intelligence uses. Meanwhile, from 1960, when the Eisenhower administration agreed to launch privately-developed communications satellites, to the initiatives of the 1980s and 1990s designed to foster private sector space activities, the government has acted as a partner in the commercialization of space. Civilian space activities have been the source of policy controversies since the mid-1950s. Successive administrations have had different views about U.S.-Soviet competition, ranging from a grudging acceptance of the reality of a space race by the Eisenhower, Nixon, and Carter administrations to acceptance of the rivalry as a central element of space policy by the Kennedy and Reagan administrations. Since the end of the Cold War, administrations have struggled to find a substitute for the space race as the central rationale for U.S. space policy. Enhanced international cooperation has emerged as an important element of a new U.S. space strategy, but by the mid-1990s, a fully articulated U.S. civilian space policy appropriate for the closing years of the twentieth century has yet to emerge.

JOHN M. LOGSDON

See also Cold War; National Aeronautics and Space Administration; Russia and the Soviet Union; Sputnik I; Strategic Defense Initiative

FURTHER READING

Byerly, Radford, ed. *Space Policy Reconsidered.* Boulder, Colo., 1989.
Logsdon, John. *The Decision to Go to the Moon: Project Apollo and the National Interest.* Cambridge, 1970.
Logsdon, John, et al., ed.. *Exploring the Unknown; Selected Documents in the History of the U.S. Civil Space Program.* NASA, Washington, D.C., 1995.
McCurdy, Howard. *The Space Station Decision.* Baltimore, Md., 1990.
McDougall, Walter...*the Heavens and the Earth: a Political History of the Space Age.* New York, 1985.
Stares, Paul. *The Militarization of Space: U.S. Policy, 1945-84.* Ithaca, N.Y., 1985.

SPAIN

Located in southwestern Europe, bordered by the North Atlantic Ocean and the Mediterrean Sea, Portugal, and France. It is the dominant nation on the Iberian Peninsula, one of Europe's great powers in the sixteenth and seventeenth centuries, and, until well into the nineteenth century, ruler of one of the world's great empires, encompassing much of the Americas. The relationship between the United States and Spain has been marked by three general attributes. First, the relationship is a long-standing one, going back to Spain's important role in the birth of the United States. Second, despite the fact that other nations, such as Great Britain, have had a more consistently high-profile relationship with the United States, Spain has been a part of many crucial episodes in U.S. history (independence, the late nineteenth-century move to global prominence, and the geostrategic calculations of the early Cold War). Third, despite Spain's recurrent importance in U.S. foreign relations, the two nations have never developed anything approaching a genuinely mutual friendship, each keeping the other at arm's length. In virtually every instance the relations between the two nations have been utilitarian in character, a series of diplomatic marriages of convenience.

Spain was involved in the American colonies' fight for independence almost from the beginning. In August 1776 the Spanish and French governments established a dummy corporation, Rodrique Hortalez and Company, whose purpose was to funnel military supplies to the rebellious colonies. Despite this early participation, Spanish involvement in U.S. independence was never a simple matter. Spain was far less enthusiastic about the success of the colonies than France. Spain's lack of enthusiasm was a result of a number of its own foreign policy concerns. It was eager to recover control of Gibraltar from Great Britain and was concerned that Great Britain might retaliate by supporting rebellion in the Spanish colonies. By the late eighteenth century the Spanish empire in North America and South America was grotesquely vulnerable. It was vulnerable not only to Spain's rivals (including Great Britain) but also to internal rebellion. Open support for the rebellious British colonies would put Spain in a precarious position. By its actions, it would help champion independence for a subjugated population, while still exerting control over millions.

Thus, neither of the two possible outcomes to the struggle between Great Britain and the colonies was particularly attractive for Spain. One possible outcome was a British victory, which would solidify British control over North America and place Great Britain in a position to challenge Spain's power in the Western Hemisphere. The second possible outcome involved a victory of the colonies over Great Britain, which was by no means an unalloyed advantage for Spain, because a victory by the colonies would be a victory for republicanism, an ideology incompatible with the history and predispositions of the ruling class in Madrid in the late eighteenth century. In addition, a colonial victory would simply replace one New World rival (Great Britain) with another (the United States)—not necessarily a better arrangement.

As a result, Spain was slow to side openly and significantly with the colonies in their struggle for independence. When a formal agreement to support the colonies came (12 April 1779), it came via France with two particularly strict conditions. First, the Spanish laid claim to the territory between the Allegheny Mountains and the Mississippi River. Second, Spain required that the hostilities not cease until it had recovered control of Gibraltar. All this amounted to arm's-length and highly cautious diplomacy. Spain's entry into the war to free the colonies was by way of an agreement with France, not the colonies, and even then only in a very limited manner.

The extent of Spain's reluctance to commit fully to the colonies was illustrated by its treatment of John Jay, the Continental Congress's envoy to Madrid. Jay arrived at his post in 1779 and represented the colonies for two and a half years. During that period Jay was spied upon, regularly snubbed, and in fact was never officially received by the Spanish government. Even after the British surrender at Yorktown in 1781, Spain withheld formal recognition of the United States, continuing to launder its support through France. The Treaty of Paris of 1783, by which Great Britain conceded independence to the United States, was a profound diplomatic trauma for Spain. The United States had pursued, and consummated, the peace agreement with Great Britain essentially independent of France and (particularly) Spain. While not an intentional sellout, the agreement did leave Spain short of its primary European goal in the conflict (the recovery of Gibraltar). The treaty also gave the United States title to the Allegheny-Mississippi territory that Spain had hoped to control. Taken together these provisions set a tone and provided an agenda for future relations.

The period following U.S. independence was one of chronic, if low-level, crisis with Spain. Spain was a chief competitor to the United States in terms of territorial aspirations, and the rivalry focused on two specific areas. The first was the Mississippi River, specifically navigation rights for the United States. The peace agreement with Great Britain gave the United States control of what now is considered to be the Midwest. The profitable functioning of agriculture in this area required free access to the Mississippi, and the Spanish were hesitant to allow U.S. farmers free use of the river. In 1784 the Spanish government closed the river to U.S. commerce; negotiations during the period 1785–1786 failed to produce a solution and the matter festered.

The second territorial area of concern was the boundary between the United States and Spanish Florida. Both of these issues were not settled until a 1795 agreement granted the United States essentially free navigation on the Mississippi River and accepted U.S. claims on the location of the Florida border. Shortly thereafter, the Louisiana Purchase sealed the navigation issue, but Florida remained an irritant in U.S.-Spanish relations well into the nineteenth century. The issue came to a head during the winter of 1817. Responding to a series of incursions, forces under the command of General Andrew Jackson moved into Spanish Florida. The punitive expedition took on the air of a small-scale invasion, enraging the Spanish. Subsequent negotiations resulted in the Adams-Onís Treaty of 22 February 1819. The agreement provided for the transfer of Florida to the United States in exchange for the withdrawal of U.S. claims to Texas and the assumption of financial claims against Spain by U.S. citizens. The agreement was formalized on 22 February 1821.

With the Mississippi River and Florida questions settled, U.S.-Spanish relations became more indirect. For example, the United States began to recognize the independence of former Spanish colonies in the Western Hemisphere in the spring of 1822, reflecting both the reality of the dissolution of the Spanish New World empire and the general sentiment favoring such a dissolution within the United States. The dissolution of the Spanish empire seemed a necessary eventuality for the practical realization of the exclusivist aspirations of the young Republic. The Monroe Doctrine served as a warning to the European powers, particularly Spain, not to try and reverse the tidal wave of decolonization and, by doing so, challenge the future U.S. hegemony in the Hemisphere. By the end of the century, however, the United States and Spain again came into direct conflict, ultimately leading to war. The Spanish-American-Cuban-Filipino War of 1898 was far more complex and substantial than the brief period of open hostilities.

The War of 1898

Two important factors accounted for the outbreak of war. The first was the general move by the United States toward a place in the global balance of power. The nation's geographic, demographic, and economic stature gave it credentials for Great Power status and, in a variety of ways, it was experimenting with such a position. The chief arena for the expansion of U.S. influence was the Western Hemisphere. Excluding Great Britain's control over Canada, the major remaining European imperial power in the Western Hemisphere was Spain. Power politics alone suggested a potential conflict. The second factor involved Spanish policy toward Cuba. In 1895 anti-Spanish elements in Cuba rebelled against Madrid, and the following year the Spanish took vigorous measures against the revolt. While atrocities were committed by both sides, the Spanish atrocities were more widely reported in the U.S. press. The Spanish decision to counter the insurgency by the use of concentration camps led to the death of thousands and the fervent enmity of the U.S. public. That public (aided by a rabidly anti-Spanish press) sided with the rebels, effectively dehumanizing the Spanish and preparing the psychological basis for war.

U.S. president William McKinley was a determined opponent of war, but he was overwhelmed by events. On 15 February 1898 the U.S. battleship *Maine* exploded and sank in Havana's harbor and more than 250 U.S. sailors were killed. On 28 March a naval review board concluded that the explosion was of external origin, popularly assumed to be a Spanish mine. The *Maine* incident fueled the public's ardor for war. The United States issued an ultimatum to Spain on 27 March (to be met before noon on 20 April), requiring that the latter end the concentration camp strategy, accept an armistice with the Cuban insurgents, and recognize Cuban independence. On 9 April Spain partially accepted the U.S. demands, although it refused to budge on the question of Cuban independence. On 11 April President McKinley requested congressional authority to intervene with force in Cuba. The authorization included an explicit rejection of U.S. control of Cuba (the Teller Amendment). Spain took the lead, declaring war on the United States on 23 April. The United States responded two days later.

Despite its brevity (a cease-fire was ordered on 12 August), the 1898 war was a watershed event for both Spain and the United States. For Spain, it was the crushing end of global importance. The war stripped Spain of most of its remaining imperial holdings. The nation's geopolitical concerns contracted to an obsession with holding on to relatively useless territory in North Africa. Once a superpower, Spain by the early twentieth century was not even a major European power. For its part, the United States had embarked on the contrary path. It assumed formal control of Guam, Puerto Rico, and the Philippines, with virtual control over Cuba. This aggrandizement framed the divisive debate over ratifying the 10 December 1898 peace agreement hammered out in Paris. The debate was about more than the treaty; the issue was between those who equated expansion and imperialism with geostrategic power, diplomatic prestige, and economic prosperity and those who opposed expansion and imperialism as mistakes of historical, geostrategic, and moral significance. U.S. insularity died on 6 February 1899 with the Senate's ratification (by a one-vote margin) of the treaty.

Following the conclusion of the war an era of bilateral disengagement began. Spain became an almost purely European power, of concern primarily to Great Britain and France. During the first thirty-five years of the twentieth century, the United States and Spain were relatively uninvolved with one another because they had little to talk about. This disengagement began to change in 1936. In the summer of that year, another in a series of power grabs by the Spanish military turned into a three-year civil war. The war was the defining political event for Spain in the twentieth century. The Spanish Civil War was, at base, a particularly Spanish event. To see the war as merely a dress-rehearsal for World War II, which it admittedly mirrored and presaged, is to miss the war's roots in the Spanish reality of the late 1930s. In addition, the Spanish Civil War had a significant international dimension. Spanish in origin, the conflict was fanned from outside as foreign powers positioned themselves to take advantage of the situation. The contending parties (the Loyalists and Nationalists) sought and received assistance from outside Spain. The Nationalist side was particularly successful, gaining decisive material and manpower support from Nazi Germany and Fascist Italy.

The government of Spain and the Loyalist forces were much less successful in obtaining outside support. The Western democracies, primarily Great Britain and France, feared support of the Republic would bring on a general European war and offered little help. The U.S. public was split on the war. Organized labor, mainline Protestants, the Jewish community, and the political left generally sided with the Republic and pressured President Franklin D. Roosevelt to support the elected government. The political right, the hierarchy of the Catholic church, and committed isolationists pressured the administration to withhold support from the elected government. Although official U.S. policy remained one of nonintervention, thousands of U.S. citizens traveled to Spain to fight on the Loyalist side, in what was called the Abraham Lincoln Brigade. Those efforts notwithstanding, the Republic died on 1 April 1939. General Francisco Franco assumed the positions of president and generalissimo, which he held until his death in 1975.

Spain was destined to pay a price for its connection to and support of the defeated Axis powers in World War II. (Spain had signed the Anti-Comintern Pact on 26 March 1939, consulted with Adolf Hitler and Benito Mussolini, and sent troops to fight alongside the Nazis in Russia). The United States supported sanctions directed against Spain, albeit unenthusiastically. At the 1945 Potsdam summit, President Harry S. Truman charted a compromise course on Spain, positioning the United States between the harsh demands of the Soviet Union for intervention to remove Franco and the more benign stance of Winston Churchill, who rejected any intervention to remove Franco. Nevertheless, on 4 March 1946 the United States joined Great Britain and France in calling for General Franco's ouster as necessary for improved relations. On 1 June 1946 the United Nations branded Spain a threat to world peace. On 9 December the UN banned Spain from participation in that organization, broke diplomatic relations between the UN and Spain, and recommended that member states downgrade diplomatic relations with Spain. The United States supported and complied with these decisions.

The Cold War Years

Although the United States went along with Spain's ostracism, it also sought closer ties for geostrategic concerns. As early as 1947 Franco had floated the idea of a bilateral defense arrangement between Spain and the United States, an idea as politically unfeasible as was Spanish membership in the North Atlantic Treaty Organization (NATO) after its formation in 1949. Prompted by a series of crises during the late 1940s and early 1950s, the United States began to construct a global security network to aid in the policy of containing the Soviet Union. As part of the U.S. response to perceived Soviet aggression, a place was found for Spain in the defense of the West.

During 1950 the ostracism of Spain began to erode (on 4 November the UN voted to void the resolutions that had condemned Spain, barred it from membership in the organization, and recommended the diplomatic boycott). The beginning of the end of the most punitive period of ostracism, which the UN vote signified, was intimately connected to a shift in the global geostrategic situation and, inevitably, a reshuffling of the post–World War agenda in the West—particularly the United States. On the most basic level, continuing the political fights of the 1930s and 1940s was simply anachronistic. Beyond that, the Cold War redefined what was expedient. In 1951 the United States began talks aimed at forging a security relationship with Spain, and on 20 September 1953 that relationship was formalized with the Pact of Madrid, an executive agreement providing the United States access to Spanish territory in return for U.S. financial aid to the Franco regime. On 15 December 1955 Spain joined the UN, although membership in NATO and the European Community (EC) was denied.

The events surrounding the creation of the U.S.-Spanish quasi-alliance helped define the character of the relationship into the 1980s. The Madrid Pact was a purely utilitarian arrangement, a swap of dollars for access to territory. It placed the United States at the center of Spanish foreign and defense policy and (by necessity) made the U.S.-Spanish relationship a key issue in Spain's domestic politics. The issues escalated upon the death of Franco in 1975. Franco's death raised the question as to whether Spanish foreign and defense policies were to be altered. It also began a transformative process by which Spain would ultimately democratize itself. The playing out of that process presented the United States with a series of foreign policy challenges and decisions.

As Spain democratized, the United States pursued various connected policy goals. Most important, Spain could not be permitted to fall into chaos—there could not be a replay of the events of 1936–1939. Such chaos could lead to the establishment of a left-wing regime hostile to U.S. economic and security interests. Backing democratization seemed the best course, although some in Spain thought the U.S. commitment to be tepid. The vague reaction by the United States to the February 1981 right-wing coup attempt, declaring at first that it was an internal Spanish matter, fueled such opinions. Whatever form of government Spain decided on, it was agreed that the country should remain a part of the U.S. defense network. While Spain's value to the United States and the West had fluctuated over the years, it was still an important asset that the United States wanted to retain. If at all possible, Spain was to remain a part of the defense network via inclusion in NATO. The objective military value of such an inclusion was slight. The symbolic value of incorporating a newly democratic Spain into an alliance facing fundamental questions about its viability was enormous. For the United States the optimal scenario was a democratic Spain, center-right in that it would become a member of NATO and maintain a special connection with the United States.

By the early 1980s the United States almost had reached its foreign policy goals regarding Spain. Spanish democratization was a relatively swift and orderly process under the direction of Prime Minister Adolfo Suarez (the constitution was ratified in December 1978). Suarez enjoyed the rock-solid backing of the Spanish king Juan Carlos, a grandson of the last serving Spanish monarch. On 3 July 1976 Juan Carlos, whose dedication to democratization was as firm as it was surprising, plucked Suarez from relative obscurity and placed the 44-year-old in the center of what was to be a defining era for Spain. The early years of the Spanish democracy were dominated by the center-right party (the UCD) headed by Suarez. For its part, the United States was generally satisfied with the UCD's tenure in government, particularly following Suarez's replacement by the far more pro-American Leopoldo Calvo Sotelo in January 1981. Spanish membership in NATO was more problematic.

Following Franco's demise the main impediment to NATO membership was no longer external, because most members of NATO were supportive of Spain's entry. The obstacle was internal. Spain had sought membership in NATO since at least 1957, and the ruling UCD had formally endorsed the idea during an October 1978 party congress. The Suarez government, however, made virtually no move toward securing membership. The reasons for this reticence are many, including the predominance of domestic affairs, a split within the UCD over the actual importance of membership, and the relative lack of pressure put on Spain by NATO members. The split within the party was key, pitting as it did two foreign policy camps against each other. The first camp, of which Suarez was a member, was content to leave Spanish foreign policy alone, to retain the status quo, including nonmembership in NATO. The second camp, labeled the "Atlanticists," saw the membership matter quite differently. For this group, membership in NATO (as well as in other intergovernmental organizations) served two more general purposes. First, membership would help ensnare Spain in a web of democratic nations, a web that would help ensure the success of democracy in Spain. Second, membership would represent the external manifestation of Spain's internal reform and modernization. Calvo Sotelo moved quickly for NATO membership, which came on 30 May 1982.

U.S. satisfaction with Spain's move soon ebbed. On 22 October 1982 the UCD was swept from power by election and replaced by the Spanish Socialist Workers' Party (PSOE). The PSOE was formally committed to withdrawing Spain from NATO (as well as drastically reducing the U.S.-Spanish security relationship). Opposition to membership in NATO had been a central issue in the 1982 campaign, and PSOE leader and new Prime Minister Felipe González Márquez seemed to be unalterably committed to withdrawal. While he had informal contact with the PSOE as early as 1975 (González met briefly with President Jimmy Carter in June 1980), he was not initially comfortable with the party in power and its foreign policy rhetoric. Upon assuming power in December 1982, González froze Spanish incorporation into NATO pending a referendum on the subject promised in the campaign.

Had the promised referendum been held in early 1983 there is little doubt that the outcome would have been a rejection of NATO membership and a defeat for the United States, but the referendum was delayed, in part through U.S. pressure. By the time it was finally held in December 1984, the socialists had made a 180-degree turn on the issue. Shrill opposition had been replaced by a firm commitment to remaining in the alliance. Continued membership in NATO was clearly tied to Spain's admission to the EC, a goal that had been a central Spanish concern since at least February 1962; nations such as Great Britain and Germany made it clear that Spain's withdrawal from NATO would damage Spain's chances for EC membership. Another factor that led to the commitment to NATO membership was that the United States and other NATO members had threatened diplomatic and economic consequences. The ambitious plans that González held for the economic and technological modernization of Spain (bringing it into the global mainstream) required foreign capital and other international assistance. González knew that his own political future was tied to the success of such efforts. By the time the promised referendum on membership was held on 12 March 1986, the PSOE government and Prime Minister González had fought tirelessly and successfully for a pro-membership outcome.

U.S. relations with Spain since the 1986 referendum have been proper if not particularly close. With the end of the Cold War Spain's importance as a military partner declined, and the United States began pursuing a policy of demilitarizing relations by downsizing its forces, a move welcomed by the PSOE government. As long as no contentious issues divide them, the United States and Spain should be able to maintain their diplomatic marriage of convenience well into the future.

SHELDON L. STANTON

See also Adams-Onís Treaty; American Revolution; Colonialism; Cuba; Florida; France; Franco, Francisco; Hearst, William Randolph; Jackson, Andrew; Jay, John; Louisiana Purchase; McKinley, William; North Atlantic Treaty Organization; Philippines; Puerto Rico; Roosevelt, Theodore; Spanish-American-Cuban-Filipino War, 1898; Teller Amendment

FURTHER READING

Cortada, James. *Two Nations Over Time: Spain and the United States, 1776–1976.* Westport, Conn., 1978.

Heiburg, William. *The 16th Nation: Spain's Role in NATO.* Washington, D.C., 1983.

Little, Douglas. *Malevolent Neutrality: The United States and Great Britain and the Origins of the Spanish Civil War.* Ithaca, N.Y., 1985.

Lowi, Theodore. "Bases in Spain." In *American Civil-Military Relations,* edited by Harold Stein. Birmingham, Ala., 1963.

Marias, Julian. "From Spain." In *As Others See Us: The United States Through Foreign Eyes,* edited by Franz Joseph. Princeton, N.J., 1959.

Pike, F. B. "The Background to the Civil War in Spain and the U.S. Response to the War." In *The Spanish Civil War, 1936–1939: American Hemispheric Perspectives,* edited by M. Falcoff. Lincoln, Nebr., 1982.

Pollack, Benny, and Graham Hunter. *The Paradox of Spanish Foreign Policy.* New York, 1987.

Trask, David F. *The War With Spain in 1898.* New York, 1981.

Whitaker, Arthur P. *Spain and Defense of the West.* New York, 1962.

SPANISH-AMERICAN-CUBAN-FILIPINO WAR, 1898

Popularly known as the Spanish-American War (21 April–12 August 1898), a war against Spain, with Cuban and Filipino participation, fought largely in Cuba and the Philippines. U.S. military forces destroyed two Spanish fleets and invaded the Spanish colonial territories of Cuba, Puerto Rico, the Philippine Islands, and Guam. As a result, the United States gained the Philippines and other Spanish possessions in the Pacific, Puerto Rico, and a protectorate over Cuba.

Cuba had long attracted U.S. interest. Its location, ninety miles from Florida and commanding the Gulf of Mexico and the Caribbean Sea, gave the island a strategic importance that grew as the United States became

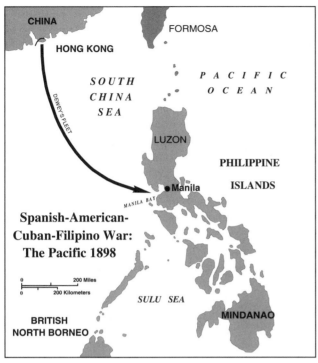

Spanish-American-Cuban-Filipino War: The Pacific 1898

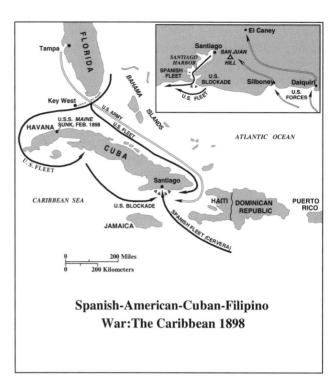

Spanish-American-Cuban-Filipino War: The Caribbean 1898

increasingly interested in a transisthmian canal across Central America and island naval bases. Before the war Americans and Cubans had extensive and growing relationships. Thousands of Cubans lived, worked, and studied in the United States, and U.S. businessmen made large investments in Cuban sugar plantations, mills, railroads, mines, and utilities. The spark that ignited the war came from the Cuban struggle for independence from Spain. During the early 1890s José Martí y Pérez, the leading Cuban insurrectionist, persuaded many Cuban workers and elites to support a revolutionary party directed by a junta in New York City. In February 1895 revolution broke out in Cuba.

The Cuban Revolution

Cuba's leading general, Máximo Gómez y Báez, initiated a strategy of destroying the island's economy by burning sugarcane fields and grinding mills, believing that the Spanish would leave the island when it no longer had economic value. General Antonio Maceo y Grajales, a charismatic Afro-Cuban leader, spread the war from the eastern to the western part of the island. Spain sent General Valeriano Weyler y Nicolau and more than 200,000 soldiers to quell the insurrection. The Spanish succeeded in killing Martí and Maceo in separate battles, but Gómez, aided by General Calixto García Iñiguez, continued to control much of the island's countryside. Weyler's

forces held Cuba's important towns and cities. Unable to engage Gómez's dispersed military forces in decisive pitched battles, Spain attempted to undercut insurgent strength by removing peasant support. Weyler forced several hundred thousand small farmers and agricultural laborers to move from their villages to fortified towns and cities. The Spanish government, however, failed to provide adequate food and sanitation. Disease spread among the relocated Cubans, and the reconcentration sites became death camps. By 1898 more than 200,000 civilians had perished, and many more were at risk. Despite this calamity, Weyler's campaign failed to end the insurrection; at the same time, Gómez's attrition strategy did not force the Spanish to evacuate Cuba.

From the start of the Cuban Revolution, the U.S. public favored Cuban independence over Spanish colonialism. Cuban propagandists and the U.S. sensationalist press stimulated these sentiments. Politicians jockeyed to take advantage of popular sentiment by taking strong pro-Cuban stands, and Congress passed nonbinding resolutions favoring recognition of Cuban belligerency. President Grover Cleveland and Secretary of State Richard Olney ignored congressional and public pressure for U.S. intervention. They refused to recognize or to extend belligerency rights to the Cubans because they did not believe the insurgents had a functioning government and because the Cuban army was intentionally burning U.S. property. Olney also worried that a Cuban victory might end in a racial war if Cuban troops, drawn largely from Afro-Cuban rural laborers, invaded Cuba's urban Creole residential areas. Olney urged Spain to grant self-government to Cuba, and Cleveland offered his good offices to that end. Cleveland also warned Spain that the United States would not wait indefinitely for a military solution; if Spanish sovereignty no longer existed on the island and continued warfare would result in useless destruction, then higher moral obligations would require the United States to intervene.

McKinley and U.S. Victory

When William McKinley became president in March 1897, Congress favored recognizing Cuban belligerency, and the U.S. business community wanted peace in Cuba, which was expected to help revive the U.S. economy. Apprised of the horrors in Cuban reconcentration camps, McKinley demanded that Spain conduct humane warfare or face U.S. intervention. He also offered his good offices to end the Cuban fighting. A new Spanish government, formed during October 1897 by Práxedes Mateo Sagasta, promised to end reconcentration and to provide political and economic autonomy to Cuba. McKinley welcomed Sagasta's initiatives, but the Cuban insurrectionists rejected autonomy, vowing to fight for complete independence.

During 1898 a series of unexpected incidents moved the United States and Spain toward war. On 12 January Spanish army officers in Havana rioted against Cuban autonomy. Although the rioters did not threaten U.S. citizens, McKinley sent the USS *Maine* to Havana harbor as a precautionary measure. On 9 February the *New York Journal* published a letter written by the Spanish minister in Washington, Enrique Dupuy de Lôme, in which he ridiculed McKinley and implied that Sagasta's reforms were insincere. The following week, on 15 February, the *Maine* blew up in Havana harbor, resulting in the death of 266 sailors. Why the ship's powder magazines exploded was a mystery, but many people suspected that Spain was responsible. The McKinley administration ordered a naval inquiry and urged the public to remain calm until the facts became known. While the naval court deliberated, the McKinley administration prepared for war. On 6 March Congress appropriated $50 million for national defense. Eleven days later, Republican Senator Redfield Proctor of Vermont delivered a moving speech in the Senate. Having recently spent two weeks in Cuba, Proctor vividly described the misery and horror of reconcentration camps; his graphic words broadened support for U.S. military intervention, particularly among business and religious groups.

On 24 March the U.S. Naval Court concluded that an external explosion, probably a mine, had ignited the *Maine*'s magazines, but the court had no evidence as to who detonated the mine. (In 1976 Admiral Hyman Rickover and a team of naval engineers concluded that the most probable cause of the explosion was spontaneous combustion in a coal bunker located next to the ship's munitions). The naval court report created intense indignation. Persuaded that Spain was at least indirectly responsible for the *Maine* disaster, many people demanded immediate military intervention to end Spanish rule in Cuba. Legislators mirrored the public mood. House Republicans were especially anxious that McKinley act quickly for fear that Democratic congressmen would seize the issue and use it during the fall election campaign. More than 100 Republican representatives threatened to join the Democrats in voting for war if McKinley did not act forcefully.

Under intense political pressure, McKinley attempted a diplomatic solution. On 27 March he asked Sagasta to conclude a six-month armistice with the insurgents, during which the Spanish and Cubans would seek a political settlement. Washington expected these negotiations to result in Cuban independence. If Spanish-Cuban negotiations failed, McKinley offered to arbitrate a settlement. At the same time, Spain was to carry out its promise to end reconcentration and cooperate with the United States in providing humanitarian relief. Sagasta's response of 31 March only partially met McKinley's demands. He ordered an end to reconcentration in western Cuba and increased aid to the people in the camps, but Spain would not stop fighting unless the Cuban insurgents asked for an armistice. Considering Sagasta's reply unacceptable, McKinley decided to give the Cuban issue to Congress.

With war imminent, Europe's six Great Powers and Pope Leo XIII searched for a peaceful solution. The Europeans urged McKinley to continue negotiations and Sagasta to proclaim an immediate suspension of hostilities. On 9 April the Spanish government authorized suspending hostilities if the insurgents agreed to do so. The McKinley administration pressed the Cuban junta to accept the Spanish offer, but the Cubans believed Spain was attempting to trick the Cuban army into a cease-fire. If hostilities ended, Spanish troops still would be in Cuba, and at the end of six months it would be difficult for the insurgents to resume fighting. The McKinley administration's disagreement with the Cuban junta over Spain's offer soured U.S.-Cuban relations. After the United States entered the war, the McKinley administration rebuffed all attempts by the Cuban junta to establish a working relationship.

In an 11 April message to Congress, McKinley criticized both the Spanish and the Cubans. He denounced Spain for the prolonged war in Cuba, the large loss of Cuban life, and the failure to protect U.S. lives and property, as demonstrated by the *Maine* explosion. The president also faulted the Cubans for the destruction of U.S. property. McKinley opposed recognizing the Republic of Cuba for several reasons: he believed that it existed in name only; he wanted a U.S. Army invading Cuba to be free of any restrictions that might stem from Cuban sovereignty; and he sought to protect the interests of U.S. citizens who had claims originating from Cuban destruction of their property. McKinley concluded his message by asking Congress for authority to use military force to compel both the Spanish and Cubans to stop fighting. Thus, McKinley signaled his intention to shunt aside both the Spanish and the Cubans and to assert U.S. primacy in determining the future of postwar Cuba.

Congress overwhelmingly supported U.S. military intervention in Cuba, even if this meant war with Spain. Legislators, however, were divided over McKinley's refusal to recognize the Cuban Republic. Cuban lobbyists secured the cooperation of Senator Henry M. Teller in proposing a congressional resolution that stated that after the United States pacified the island, it would neither annex nor control Cuba. Without debate and by voice vote Congress accepted the Teller Amendment. After extended debate, the Senate voted 52 to 35 and the House of Representatives 311 to 6 that Cuba was independent; the congressional resolutions authorizing military intervention, however, made no reference to recognition of the Cuban Republic. McKinley signed the resolutions on 21 April, and the next day he ordered a naval blockade of Cuba.

U.S. military victories led to an early peace. The U.S. Navy's strategy, approved by McKinley, was to engage the enemy at vulnerable outposts where military action posed the least risk to U.S. forces. Accordingly, on 1 May Commodore George Dewey sank the decrepit fleet of Admiral Patricio Montojo y Pasare. The U.S. Navy blockaded the port, and on 3 July, when Cervera's ships tried to escape, Rear Admiral William T. Sampson's squadron destroyed Cervera's fleet. During both battles the United States lost no ships and just one seaman.

With superior naval support, the U.S. Army invaded Cuba, Puerto Rico, Luzon in the Philippines, and Guam in the Ladrones (Marianas). Major General William R. Shafter directed 17,000 U.S. troops in an assault on the defenses of Santiago de Cuba, and on 16 July General José Toral surrendered the city to Shafter. Major General Nelson A. Miles invaded and occupied most of Puerto Rico. With Dewey's encouragement and military assistance, Philippine insurgents, led by Emilio Aguinaldo, formed an army that besieged the Spanish forces in Manila. Hours after a cease-fire was signed in Washington, Major General Wesley Merritt lead 11,000 U.S. soldiers in securing Manila. The U.S. Army refused to allow Aguinaldo's soldiers to enter the city, but despite

the U.S. rebuff, Aguinaldo continued to fight Spanish forces located in outposts throughout the archipelago and constructed a government designed to secure Filipino independence.

Peace Treaty

Negotiations for peace began in mid-July, when Sagasta asked McKinley for terms. Although the United States had entered the war to secure Cuba's independence from Spain, the mood of expansion and the course of battle had broadened U.S. goals. McKinley asked Spain to relinquish sovereignty over Cuba and to cede Puerto Rico and Guam to the United States. The Philippines presented a more complicated and difficult problem. During May, after Dewey's naval victory, the McKinley administration had decided to retain a port in the Philippines that was expected to benefit U.S. commerce throughout the Far East. By August the president was leaning toward keeping Manila and sufficient territory around the city to ensure its military security. McKinley and his cabinet, however, were undecided about the future of the rest of the islands. McKinley proposed to Spain that U.S. forces occupy Manila and that peace commissioners meet on 1 October in Paris to draw up a treaty that would settle the disposition of the Philippines. On 12 August 1898 Spain signed a protocol embodying McKinley's terms.

After the war ended U.S. military officers advised McKinley to keep all of the Philippines. General Francis V. Greene, recently returned from the Philippines, reasoned that if Spain retained a portion of the islands, the Spanish and Filipinos would continue to fight and their war might draw in the United States. If Spain left the islands, Greene believed Filipino rule would end in anarchy. He predicted that keeping some of the islands and allowing Germany or Japan to secure the rest could lead to a major war. U.S. Navy Commander Royal B. Bradford, a naval officer assigned to the U.S. peace commissioners in Paris, recommended U.S. annexation of all of Spain's Pacific colonies, and he warned against allowing Germany to secure any of them. During October, in advance of national elections, the president toured the Midwest and found his audiences favorable to acquiring the Philippines. Upon returning to Washington, McKinley asked Spain to cede the entire Philippine archipelago to the United States. The Spanish were willing to relinquish the Philippines, and during the Paris negotiations they had been asking for as much as $400 million. Under cover of an ultimatum, McKinley offered $20 million, and Spain reluctantly accepted. The peace commissioners signed the treaty on 10 December 1898.

President McKinley skillfully managed Senate approval of the Treaty of Paris. Republicans did not have a two-thirds majority in the Senate, and McKinley had to hold Republican legislators together while gaining some Democratic votes. William Jennings Bryan, the defeated 1896 Democratic presidential candidate, encouraged several Democrats to vote for the treaty. Bryan hoped that once peace was secured, Congress would pass legislation favorable to the Philippines. On 6 February 1899 the Senate voted 57 to 27 to accept the treaty; it went into effect on 11 April 1899.

Despite U.S. sympathy for Cuban independence, the United States imposed a military government over the island and later established a protectorate. U.S. hegemonic control was deemed necessary to secure the island against European incursions and to prevent domestic political turbulence. Lacking confidence in Cuban insurgent army officers and the large Afro-Cuban population, the McKinley administration encouraged the development of a Cuban government aligned more closely to island planter and merchant elites. In 1902 Washington and Havana adopted a reciprocal trade treaty, and the following year the United States effected the Platt Amendment which gave the U.S. government the right to intervene in Cuban political affairs. In the Philippines the United States refused to recognize Aguinaldo's government. Fighting broke out between U.S. and Filipino soldiers that led to four years of warfare before the United States defeated the Filipino independence movement. As a result of the Spanish-American-Cuban-Filipino War, the United States eliminated Spain from the Caribbean, took a much larger role in the Pacific and East Asia, and emerged as a world power.

JOHN L. OFFNER

See also Aguinaldo, Emilio; Cuba; Dewey, George; Guam; Hearst, William Randolph; Journalism and Foreign Policy; Maine, USS; McKinley, William; Philippines; Platt Amendment; Puerto Rico; Roosevelt, Theodore; Spain; Teller Amendment

FURTHER READING

Bradford, James C., ed. *Crucible of Empire: The Spanish-American War and Its Aftermath.* Annapolis, Md., 1993.

Linderman, Gerald F. *The Mirror of War: American Society and the Spanish-American War.* Ann Arbor, Mich., 1974.

May, Ernest R. *Imperial Democracy: The Emergence of America as a Great Power.* New York, 1961.

Offner, John L. *An Unwanted War: The Diplomacy of the United States and Spain Over Cuba, 1895–1898.* Chapel Hill, N.C., 1992.

Paterson, Thomas G. "United States Intervention in Cuba, 1898: Interpretations of the Spanish-American-Cuban-Filipino War." *The History Teacher* 29 (May 1996):341–361.

Pérez, Louis A., Jr. *Cuba and the United States: Ties of Singular Intimacy.* Athens, Ga., 1990.

Trask, David F. *The War with Spain in 1898.* New York, 1981.

SPANISH CIVIL WAR

See Spain

SPHERES OF INFLUENCE

Geographic areas dominated by foreign powers without being formally incorporated into their sovereign jurisdiction. The subject peoples are often required to grant the dominant state exclusive commercial rights or are restricted diplomatically and militarily to behavior that it prescribes. Spheres of influence rest on an agreement, or sometimes just a mutual tolerance, between the dominating state and others outside the sphere that the former will have exclusive rights in that area. That agreement can be tacit, as in the formula that British prime minister Winston Churchill proposed to Soviet leader Joseph Stalin to divide influence in the post–World War II Balkans. It can also be laid out in formal declarations, as in the Monroe Doctrine (1823) of the United States and such treaties as the 1907 agreement between Great Britain and Russia to recognize each other's spheres in Persia.

The Soviet Union and the United States were able to avoid war after 1945 by tacitly accepting each other's spheres of influence in Europe. One near exception to this general pattern occurred outside Europe, when in 1962 the Soviets sought to pull Cuba out of the traditional U.S. sphere of military dominance in the Western Hemisphere. In general, proponents of the realist school of international relations and foreign policy have argued that these spheres, along with the superpowers' nuclear weapons, served to promote a long superpower peace by demarcating areas of vital interest, areas in which each state could intervene without fear of direct response by the other. Idealists and some liberals have tended to disagree, arguing that spheres of influence are illegitimate and unnecessary manifestations of big-power imperialism. For this reason, and to avoid political reprisal from Americans of Eastern European descent, U.S. presidents throughout the Cold War would not acknowledge publicly U.S. acquiescence to the Soviet sphere of influence in Eastern Europe. Although the end of the Cold War weakened the U.S. and Russian spheres of influence considerably, Russian leaders began asserting rights to special privileges, including unilateral intervention, in large areas of the former Soviet Union that they called the "near abroad," creating one of the more controversial post–Cold War issues in relations between Russia and the United States.

JOSEPH LEPGOLD

See also Cold War; Monroe Doctrine; Russia and the Soviet Union

FURTHER READING

Bogdan, Coreliu. *Spheres of Influence.* Boulder, Colo., 1988.

Gardner, Lloyd C. *Spheres of Influence: The Great Powers Partition Europe, from Munich to Yalta.* Chicago, 1993.

Rutherford, Geddes W., "Spheres of Influence: An Aspect of Semi-Suzerainty." *American Journal of International Law* 20 (April 1926): 300–325.

SPUTNIK I

The first artificial satellite to orbit the earth, launched by the Soviet Union on 4 October 1957. The satellite created alarm in the United States because the event followed a successful Soviet launch of an intercontinental missile and repeated U.S. failures of rocket and missile tests. It appeared that the United States had fallen behind the Soviet Union militarily and technologically. The post-Sputnik panic fueled the arms race, increased Cold War tensions, set back negotiations for a nuclear test ban treaty, and permitted Democratic politicians to manipulate fears of a "missile gap." President Dwight D. Eisenhower attempted to downplay *Sputnik*, but he accelerated U.S. space and missile programs and initiated federal funding of education as a national security measure. The United States successfully launched its own satellite, *Explorer 1*, on 31 January 1958.

SHANE J. MADDOCK

See also Eisenhower, Dwight David; Space Policy

FURTHER READING

Bulkeley, Rip. *The Sputniks Crisis and Early United States Space Policy*. Bloomington, Ind., 1991.
Divine, Robert A. *The Sputnik Challenge*. New York, 1993.
McDougall, Walter A. *The Heavens and the Earth: A Political History of the Space Age*. New York, 1985.

SRI LANKA

An island nation located southeast of India, across the Palk Straight in the Indian Ocean, that changed its name from Ceylon to Sri Lanka ("Resplendent Island") in 1972. U.S. interaction with Sri Lanka has been principally a derivative of relations with India. U.S. missionary and commercial contacts developed in the early nineteenth century when Ceylon was part of British India (annexed by the British in 1815). U.S. diplomatic ties with Ceylon began in 1850 when the United States designated a commercial agent, an office that in 1900 was elevated to a consul and eventually to that of an embassy, after Ceylon attained independence in 1948. An overriding concern of Ceylon was avoiding domination by India. After an alliance with Great Britain from 1948 to 1956, Ceylon adopted a policy of nonalignment but pursued cordial relations with and economic assistance from the major powers. The United States, while being careful to avoid antagonizing India, most notably over the contentious issue of the demands of peoples of south Indian origin for an independent state within Sri Lanka, played a reasonably effective balancing role and thus helped to assure Sri Lanka's continued economic cultural orientation toward the West. The United States has had virtually no policy toward the violent civil war—ethnic conflict between Tamils and Sinhalese, and among intraethnic factions—that has plagued Sri Lanka since the mid-1980s.

GARY R. HESS

See also Great Britain; India; Nonaligned Movement

FURTHER READING

Cohen, Stephen Philip, ed. *The Security of South Asia: American and Asian Perspectives*. Urbana, Ill., 1987.
Goonetileke, H. A. I., ed. *Images of Sri Lanka Through American Eyes: Travellers in Ceylon in the 19th and 20th Centuries*. Colombo, Sri Lanka, 1976.

STALIN, JOSEPH VISSARIONOVICH

(*b.* 21 December 1879; *d.* 5 March 1953)

Ruler of Soviet Russia as head of the Communist party and government; generalissimo of the Soviet armed forces during World War II; and virtual dictator from 1924 until his death. Stalin was born in Gori, Georgia, the son of a shoemaker, and was educated at Tiflis Orthodox Theological Seminary, from which he was expelled in 1899 for his radical activities. An obscure and little-known Bolshevik during the early phase of the Revolution, Stalin (his real name was Dzhugashvili, which he had changed to Stalin—"man of steel"—shortly before the outbreak of World War I) first came to prominence as co-editor of *Pravda* (1917) and then as commissar for nationalities in 1919. He ordered the brutal crackdown on Georgia's Menshevik government and the forced incorporation of it and other republics into the new Union of Soviet Socialist Republics (USSR) in 1923. Toward the end of his life, Vladimir Lenin warned his colleagues about Stalin, who by then had played an important role in the Civil War and been elected general secretary of the Central committee of the party, calling him "rude" and "intolerable as general secretary." But Stalin used his position in the party to outmaneuver his principal rivals, Nikolai Bukharin and Leon Trotsky, following Lenin's death in 1924, and he was able to assume supreme power by the end of the decade. Stalin forced the collectivization of agriculture and ruthlessly persecuted the kulaks while discarding Lenin's New Economic Policy. A brutal reign of terror followed during the 1930s whose aim was the elimination of all real (or imagined) opposition forces—be they peasants, workers, intellectuals, military officers, or former colleagues.

Stalin welcomed the increasing U.S. trade and investment in Soviet Russia in the 1920s, led by Henry Ford and W. Averell Harriman. He pursued an initially cautious policy toward the United States, sending Foreign Minister Maxim Litvinov to Washington to negotiate a recognition agreement with Franklin D. Roosevelt in 1933 by which both countries hoped to restrain Japanese aggression in Manchuria and Asia and improve trade prospects between the two countries. But disillusionment on both sides resulted from unwillingness of either to cement a military alliance, and the suspicion, led by U.S. ambassador William C. Bullitt, that the Soviets were slow to fulfill their pledges to repay the czarist debt or restrain foreign communists from revolutionary propaganda. Initial U.S. interest and curiosity regarding the Soviet planned economy (and the involvement of thousands of U.S. technicians and workers in building it) soured in the late 1930s as deaths and arrests in the Stalin-directed Great Terror became known. Stalin reversed Litvinov's attempts to build collective security in Europe against Adolf Hitler by appointing Vyacheslav Molotov as foreign minister and signing a non-aggression pact with Hitler in August 1939, by which the Soviet Union pledged neutrality in the expected European war, and in turn received a free hand in the Baltic states and eastern Poland. The pact alarmed the United States, but after the outbreak of war, Roosevelt assured Stalin through the Welles-Oumansky negotiations in 1940 that the United States would assist the USSR if Hitler attacked the country.

The German invasion of the USSR in June 1941 prompted FDR's extension of Lend-Lease assistance to Stalin's beleaguered nation. The declaration of the United Nations in January 1942 brought Great Britain, the United States, and the USSR into an alliance, pledging military unity until total German surrender. U.S.-Soviet relations in the Grand Alliance became severely frayed. The three allies disagreed over the timing and conditions for a second front in Western Europe, the treatment of Germany after the war, reconstruction assistance, and the composition of governments in Poland and elsewhere in Eastern Europe. Stalin was a tough, crafty alliance partner who admired U.S. technology and military power but distrusted FDR's idealism. Stalin worked to create and protect a Soviet "buffer zone" against Western Europe such as in his famous October 1944 "percentages agreement" with Churchill for the division of spheres of influence in the Balkans. Churchill acknowledged Stalin's fidelity to this agreement; but even before the end of the war, U.S. public opinion was beginning to condemn Stalin's seeming expansionism and the agreements reached at the Yalta Conference for Soviet entry into the war against Japan in exchange for territory in the Far East, for the reorganization of the communist-dominated Polish government, as well as for many disturbing Soviet statements on both security and self-determination issues in Eastern Europe, and future occupation zones for Germany: all of which served both as the last agreements of the Grand Alliance and the beginning of what became a slide into mutual hostility and Cold War.

When Roosevelt died in April 1945 Stalin proceeded at first to try to maintain good relations with his successor, Harry S. Truman. Their first meeting, and the last wartime conference at Potsdam (July), proved difficult, and no long-term agreements on reparations and the shape of Europe after the war were reached. Potsdam would prove to be the last summit meeting until 1955. The development of the U.S. atomic bomb, U.S. foreign aid to noncommunist Europe, the U.S. domination of postwar global financial institutions, and the strengthening of the Red Army's occupation of Eastern Europe brought the United States and the Soviet Union to the brink of open conflict by 1947. Stalin feared a revived, rearmed Germany; never felt compensated for tremendous Soviet losses on the eastern front; and charged Truman with both "atomic" and "dollar" diplomacy. Stalin's support for Kim Il Sung's attempt to unify the Korean peninsula in June 1950 sparked U.S. and then Chinese military intervention and led to the Korean War stalemate. Stalin died under suspicious circumstances in 1953; his death precipitated both a struggle for power and a brief but inconsequential thaw in the Cold War.

Americans have continued to hold Stalin principally responsible for the Cold War; and he remains a monstrous figure in world history (often compared to Hitler). Radical reassessments of the full scope of his reign and his relationship to the West have only begun with the recent opening of Russian archives.

DAVID W. McFADDEN

See also Bullitt, William Christian; Churchill, Winston Leonard Spencer; Cold War; Harriman, William Averell; Hitler, Adolf; Korean War; Lend-Lease; Lenin, Vladimir Ilyich; Molotov, Vyacheslav Mikhailovich; Potsdam Conference; Roosevelt, Franklin Delano; Russia and the Soviet Union; Truman, Harry S.; World War II; Yalta Conference

FURTHER READING

Bennett, Edward M. *Franklin D. Roosevelt and the Search for Security: American-Soviet Relations, 1933–1939.* Wilmington, Del., 1985.

———. *Franklin D. Roosevelt and the Search for Victory: American-Soviet Relations, 1939–1945.* Wilmington, Del., 1990.

Clemens, Diane S. *Yalta.* New York, 1970.

Helloway, David. *Stalin and the Bomb.* New Haven, Conn., 1994.

Hochschild, Adam. *The Unquiet Ghost: Russians Remember Stalin.* New York, 1995.

Mastny, Vojtech. *Russia's Road to the Cold War: Diplomacy, Strategy and the Politics of Communism, 1941–1975.* New York, 1979.

Paterson, Thomas G. *On Every Front: The Making and Unmaking of the Cold War,* revised edition. New York, 1992.

Taubman, William. *Stalin's American Policy.* New York, 1983.

Tucker, Robert C. *Stalin in Power: The Revolution from Above, 1928–1941.* New York, 1992.

Volkogonov, Dmitri. *Stalin: Triumph and Tragedy,* edited and translated by Harold Shukman. New York, 1991.

START

See Strategic Arms Reduction Treaties

STAR WARS

See Strategic Defense Initiative

STATE, U.S. DEPARTMENT OF

The oldest cabinet-level department of the executive branch of the U.S. federal government and one of the smallest. The ministry of foreign affairs of the United States, the Department of State is the organization through which the president directs the foreign policy of the nation. The secretary of state heads the department and, until the Presidential Succession Act of 1947, was third in the line of presidential succession. He now ranks just after the vice president, speaker of the House, and president *pro tempore* of the Senate.

The secretary presides over a modest bureaucracy, which in the mid-1990s numbered approximately 10,000 within the United States (mostly in Washington) and another 7,000 overseas. This total includes approximately 8,000 Foreign Service officers and staff personnel. The Foreign Service staffs about 262 overseas missions. This number has fluctuated since 1988 as budget restrictions have led to post closings, while the breakup of the Soviet Union and other political changes in the early 1990s have required the creation of new missions. The Department of State's budget for 1995 was approximately $4.7 billion.

The Department of State and its overseas posts constitute by far the largest diplomatic establishment of any nation in the world. Through the secretary, deputy secretary, four undersecretaries, six regional and fourteen functional bureaus, diplomatic exchanges with U.S. missions abroad are conducted. The department communicates with these posts by classified and unclassified radio telegraph, unclassified and classified diplomatic pouches and, increasingly, by telephone, fax machines, and direct satellite systems.

The secretary of state, through the Board of the Foreign Service and the director general of the Foreign Service, also manages the Foreign Service of the United States. The Foreign Service is the functional civilian equivalent of the career military personnel in the armed services. It staffs overseas embassies and consulates, provides substantial leadership in departmental positions, and seconds personnel to other government departments.

The Department of State is the formal manager of U.S. relations with other countries, but it competes with other government departments and agencies; this has been particularly true in the post–World War II period. The department has statutory responsibility for foreign affairs, but this role has been eroded in practice by the president's national security adviser and other large bureaucracies with foreign affairs responsibilities, particularly the Department of Defense (DOD), the Central Intelligence Agency (CIA), and the Commerce Department, as well as to a lesser degree the United States Information Agency (USIA), the Agency for International Development (AID), and the Arms Control and Disarmament Agency (ACDA). In addition the secretary of state is a statutory member of the National Security Council.

The constitutional authority for directing foreign relations derives from Article II of the U.S. Constitution, which asserts the primacy of the federal government in foreign affairs and specifically authorizes the president to receive ambassadors. This constitutional language has consistently been interpreted to mean that the president is the chief point of official contact between the United States and other national governments and supranational entities. This authorization includes the power to extend or withhold or suspend diplomatic relations. Article II, section 2, in addition to making the president commander in chief of the armed forces, authorizes him to make treaties (with the advice and consent of the Senate) and to appoint "Ambassadors, other public Ministers, and consuls."

While these provisions place the conduct of foreign relations with the executive branch, other powers conferred on Congress—to declare war, appropriate funds, advise and consent on treaties—give Congress significant ability to influence foreign policy. The balance between the executive branch and Congress has shifted with events and attitudes over time. From World War II to the early 1970s during the heady days of the Cold War, the executive branch predominated. After the Vietnam War and the Watergate scandal, Congress reasserted itself by passing the War Powers Act and investigating the CIA. The Department of State frequently bears the burden of this tension and conflict, suffering criticism when U.S. foreign policies go awry.

On the other hand, many individual Department of State and Foreign Service officers are highly respected for their expertise and experience—by Congress, informational organizations such as the Council on Foreign Relations, and the general public. The role of the secretary of state is the principal determinant of the department's prestige. In this respect, the best secretaries of state have been those who have had both close personal relations and dominant influence with the presidents they served. Since World War II, George Marshall, Dean Acheson, John Foster Dulles, Henry Kissinger, George Shultz (prior to the Iran-Contra affair in 1986), and James Baker all had major impact on their presidents. Some, notably Kissinger and Baker, did not make full use of the department's capabilities. They preferred to operate through a small group of confidants who were placed in strategically important positions within the bureaucracy.   Some secretaries had limited ties and influence with their presidents, but used and strength-

SECRETARIES OF STATE

ADMINISTRATION	SECRETARY	PERIOD OF APPOINTMENT
Washington	Thomas Jefferson	1790–1793
	Edmund Randolph	1794–1795
	Timothy Pickering	1795–1800
J. Adams		
	John Marshall	1800–1801
Jefferson	James Madison	1801–1809
Madison	Robert Smith	1809–1811
	James Monroe	1811–1817
	John Quincy Adams	1817–1825
J. Q. Adams	Henry Clay	1825–1829
Jackson	Martin Van Buren	1829–1831
	Edward Livingston	1831–1833
	Louis McLane	1833–1834
	John Forsyth	1834–1841
Van Buren		
W. H. Harrison	Daniel Webster	1841–1843
Tyler		
	Abel P. Upshur	1843–1844
	John C. Calhoun	1844–1845
Polk	James Buchanan	1845–1849
Taylor	John M. Clayton	1849–1850
Fillmore		
	Daniel Webster	1850–1852
	Edward Everett	1852–1853
Pierce	William L. Marcy	1853–1857
Buchanan	Lewis Cass	1857–1860
	Jeremiah S. Black	1860–1861
Lincoln	William H. Seward	1861–1869
A. Johnson		
Grant	Elihu B. Washburne	1869
	Hamilton Fish	1869–1877
Hayes	William M. Evarts	1877–1881
Garfield	James G. Blaine	1881
Arthur		
	Frederick T. Frelinghuysen	1881–1885
Cleveland	Thomas F. Bayard	1885–1889
B. Harrison	James G. Blaine	1889–1892
	John W. Foster	1892–1893
Cleveland	Walter Q. Gresham	1893–1895
	Richard Olney	1895–1897
McKinley	John Sherman	1897–1898
	William R. Day	1898
	John M. Hay	1898–1905
T. Roosevelt		
	Elihu Root	1905–1909
	Robert Bacon	1909

(table continues on next page)

ADMINISTRATION	SECRETARY	PERIOD OF APPOINTMENT
Taft	Philander C. Knox	1909–1913
Wilson	William Jennings Bryan	1913–1915
	Robert Lansing	1915–1920
	Bainbridge Colby	1920–1921
Harding	Charles Evans Hughes	1921–1925
Coolidge		
	Frank B. Kellogg	1925–1929
Hoover	Henry L. Stimson	1929–1933
F. Roosevelt	Cordell Hull	1933–1944
	Edward R. Stettinius, Jr.	1944–1945
Truman		
	James F. Byrnes	1945–1947
	George C. Marshall	1947–1949
	Dean Acheson	1949–1953
Eisenhower	John Foster Dulles	1953–1959
	Christian A. Herter	1959–1961
Kennedy	Dean Rusk	1961–1969
L. Johnson		
Nixon	William P. Rogers	1969–1973
	Henry A. Kissinger	1973–1977
Ford		
Carter	Cyrus R. Vance	1977–1980
	Edmund S. Muskie	1980–1981
Reagan	Alexander M. Haig, Jr.	1981–1982
	George P. Shultz	1982–1989
Bush	James A. Baker III	1989–1992
	Lawrence Eagleburger	1992–1993
Clinton	Warren W. Christopher	1993–Present

Source: U.S. Department of State

ened the department just the same. Dean Rusk, Cyrus Vance, and Shultz (after 1986) fit this mold. Warren Christopher used the Department and maintained President Bill Clinton's ear, but did not prove to be a strong secretary on policy questions. Another arrangement bears heavily on the institutional position of the Department of State in contemporary foreign policy decision-making. The 1947 National Security Act, which established the Department of Defense and the CIA, also created the National Security Council (NSC), composed of senior members of the government, and broadened to include others for specific sessions. The assistant to the president for national security affairs directs the NSC and plays a key foreign policy role because he has both the most direct access to the president and heads the small but influential NSC staff within the Executive Office of the President. This organizational structure created another potential layer between the secretary of state and the president.

From 1947 to 1961, the president's national security adviser served primarily as a manager, coordinating the work of the cabinet departments and ensuring that issues got to the president as the president wanted. This "traffic cop" model was best represented by Robert Cutler under President Dwight D. Eisenhower, and to an extent by Brent Scowcroft under President George Bush. Beginning in 1961 with President John F. Kennedy's administration, several national security advisers used their staff coordinating power to promote policies they advocated or supported. McGeorge Bundy and W.W. Rostow under Presidents Kennedy and Lyndon Johnson both played activist roles. Later, Kissinger and Zbigniew Brzezinski, under Presidents Richard Nixon and Jimmy Carter respectively, were so aggressive in performing their duties that they were widely believed to have undermined Secretaries of State William P. Rogers and Vance. In the Clinton administration, Anthony Lake resembled Scowcroft more than the activists.

In many respects, the Department of State's focus is the general "national interest," in its more abstract and least particular sense, in contrast to the more group-specific interests in departments like Agriculture, Commerce, or Defense. But the Department of State also operates without a permanent, committed constituency to support it in intragovernmental struggles. Farmers will support the Department of Agriculture in public and congressional debate, but only a relatively small group of academics, business leaders, financiers, involved state and local officials, and a few attentive citizens follow foreign affairs closely. Even then, on any given issue, there are large segments which, while attentive, will oppose the department's position. The Department of State grew gradually from modest beginnings only as the country's involvement abroad expanded. It did not even become a substantial organizational force within the U.S. government until the twentieth century and reached its current position only when the United States became a superpower following World War II.

Creation and Growth: 1775–1867

Active U.S. diplomacy preceded the creation of the Department of State. In September 1776 the Continental Congress posted Benjamin Franklin to Paris as the head of a three-person committee to persuade the French to support the U.S. independence movement. Franklin was then appointed minister to France in September 1778, becoming the first U.S. minister to be received by a foreign power when he presented his credentials on 23 March 1779.

The Continental Congress established a Committee of Secret Correspondence as early as 1775 to communicate with sympathizers abroad, but it had a highly limited mandate and never came together as an organization. The Department of State as an organized entity traces its roots to the Department of Foreign Affairs established by the Congress on 10 January 1781. Robert R. Livingston of New York served as the new nation's first secretary of foreign affairs (1781–1783), with a staff of three and an overseas component of ten. Like many of his successors, Livingston had limited scope and little freedom of action because neither his duties nor the department's powers were well defined.

His successor, John Jay (1784–1790), experienced much the same difficulty as his predecessor with too little power and insufficient freedom of action. In fact, Jay's criticism of the fledgling department's weakness at the Constitutional Convention of 1787 led to the changes incorporated in the new Constitution of 1789. That same year, Representative James Madison (a future secretary of state) wrote the legislation creating the new department. Signed on 15 September 1789 by President George Washington, it named the new foreign affairs organiza-

tion the "Department of State," and also gave it some domestic responsibilities in the area of archives, laws and commissions, pardons, and copyrights. (The department shed most of these responsibilities in the late nineteenth century, today retaining only certain record-keeping responsibilities for foreign affairs.) Thomas Jefferson took up his post as secretary of state on 22 March 1790, becoming the first cabinet appointee in the new U.S. federal government.

The new department began with a minuscule staff—a chief clerk, three other clerks, one translator, and a messenger—and a total budget of $57,000. The department expanded slowly, reaching twenty-three domestic employees in 1830, compared to only ten in 1790, and with 156 individuals serving abroad in 1830, up from twenty in 1790. Expenditures grew to $432,200 in 1830.

The policy of "as little political connection abroad as possible" laid down by President Washington in his Farewell Address in 1796, coupled with the United States' focus on its own growth, caused less attention to be devoted to foreign affairs after the War of 1812, and most of that (such as the annexation of Florida) was directed from the White House. This also reflected the growing suspicion of all things foreign that began to characterize the U.S. view of the world then and has continued throughout its history. This orientation, coupled with the new democratic ideology and disdain for the ways of traditional diplomacy, gradually led to a chronic underfunding of foreign affairs efforts. This penury showed immediately in the personnel policies of the new department. Diplomats could not serve as consuls and vice versa. (Consuls focus on visa and citizen protection issues, while diplomats deal mostly with political and economic issues.) Salaries were inadequate for diplomats, and consular officers had to live off their commissions. There was no exchange between those serving at home and those serving abroad, and some stayed abroad for years at a time. Departmental employees eventually came under the Civil Service Act of 1883, but those serving abroad were not covered by a merit and tenure system until 1905. Several professionals in the late nineteenth century were able to develop special diplomatic skills and knowledge. Still, the spoils system, which gave diplomatic and consular appointments to political contributors or loyal followers, remained in effect until the Rogers Act of 1924 laid the foundation for the modern career Foreign Service.

U.S diplomats and the Department of State performed effectively in the early part of the nineteenth century largely because of unusually capable secretaries of state who possessed substantial political skills. Six of them—Jefferson, Madison, James Monroe, John Quincy Adams, Martin Van Buren, and James Buchanan—became presidents. Two others—Henry Clay and Daniel

Webster—were political heavyweights and presidential candidates. The United States had some important successes in this period. Treaties normalized relations with Great Britain and Spain; the Louisiana Purchase guaranteed U.S. westward expansion; the War of 1812 was brought to a successful closure; Florida was annexed in 1819; and a firm border with Spanish America was set. The department, including the secretary of state, played important roles in all of these events. In 1823, Secretary Adams, in fact, articulated the Monroe Doctrine (named for his president), which warned European and other nations that the United States would regard their involvement in Latin America as an "unfriendly disposition."

From 1823 until the end of the Civil War, the United States devoted itself to western expansion and nation building. From a domestic staff of twenty-three and a budget of $432,200 in 1830, the department grew to a staff of forty-two and a budget of $1,700,000 in 1870. Foreign staff expanded from 176 in 1830 to 869 in 1870, and the number of posts grew from fifteen diplomatic and 141 consular in 1830 to thirty-six diplomatic and 318 consular in 1870. This expansion reflected primarily the growth of U.S. commerce, not political involvement abroad, with the exception of the War with Mexico in the 1840s. Such policy direction as there was came primarily from the political arena with little help from the department until Secretary William H. Seward's eight-year tenure (1861–1869). The first important reorganization of the department took place in 1833 when Secretary of State Louis McLane, recognizing that the department remained overworked, underpaid, and poorly organized, developed the basic concept of today's extensive and complex bureau system by creating seven bureaus. The two most important were the Diplomatic and Consular Bureaus. Each had worldwide responsibilities, the first for diplomatic activities and correspondence, the second for consular affairs. The remaining five bureaus were named Translation; Archives, Laws and Commissions; Pardons, Remissions, Copyrights and Library; Disbursing and Superintending, all of which reflected administrative functions and domestic activities later transferred elsewhere. In addition, Congress approved the first assistant secretary position for the department (a second was added in 1866), and McLane gave the chief clerk broad administrative responsibilities for day-to-day operation of the department. Overall personnel policies remained much the same during the mid-nineteenth century except for reforms initiated in 1856 by Congress. Salaries were increased from $10,000 to $17,500 for ministers (large for the time, but they remained at those levels until 1946). Stipends were now given to consuls, who turned consular service fees directly over to the treasury, and the department developed written regulations for the foreign services. The 1856 Act provided badly needed improvement, but it stopped short of professionalizing the services. The 1856 Act also centralized the passport function in the Department of State. Until this time, mayors, governors, and other local officials could issue them, and the U.S. government did not require its citizens to carry passports except in wartime. By 1914, all U.S. travelers abroad were required to carry passports.

Despite the slow pace of professionalization, U.S. diplomacy continued to be successful in extending the doctrine of Manifest Destiny. Disputes over fisheries and trade with Great Britain were successfully resolved by a series of treaties in the 1840s and 1850s. The department's chief clerk, Nicholas Trist, proved again the diplomatic adage "it is easier to get forgiveness than permission" when he went to Mexico with General Winfield Scott's army, ignored Washington orders recalling him, and negotiated the Treaty of Guadaloupe-Hidalgo in 1848, granting extensive territory to the United States. During the Civil War, Secretary of State William Seward and the department, working closely with President Abraham Lincoln, prevailed upon the European states not to recognize the Confederacy. Seward concluded his stewardship of the Department of State by negotiating the purchase of Alaska from Russia in 1867, extending U.S security control to the Pacific edge of the continent.

Rise to Preeminence: 1867–1947

With the end of the Civil War and the purchase of Alaska, the United States emerged more powerful than ever and enjoyed virtual immunity from serious international complications for the next fifty years. This condition, along with the country's continuing settlement of the west and a prevailing xenophobia both in the press and in Congress, meant that the conduct of U.S. diplomacy changed only slowly until the turn of the century. In 1870, Secretary of State Hamilton Fish undertook the second major reorganization of the department, expanding the bureau system created in 1833. This reorganization lasted for thirty-nine years. He created two diplomatic and two consular bureaus. The first of each supervised U.S. relations with Europe, China, and Japan; the second diplomatic and consular bureaus dealt with the rest of the world—Latin America, Russia, Hawai'i, and Africa. This permitted the beginning of specialization in regional areas and in functional capability. Five other bureaus were established: Law, Accounts, Statistics, Passport, and Chief Clerk's Bureau. This latter entity became the forerunner of today's Management Bureau and the modern Executive Secretariat, instituted by Secretary of State Edward Stettinius in 1944 and fully developed and used by Marshall in 1947. The department also acquired new quarters, replacing those it long held in the Washington City Orphan Asylum. In 1875, the department began moving into the State, War and Navy Build-

DEPARTMENT OF STATE

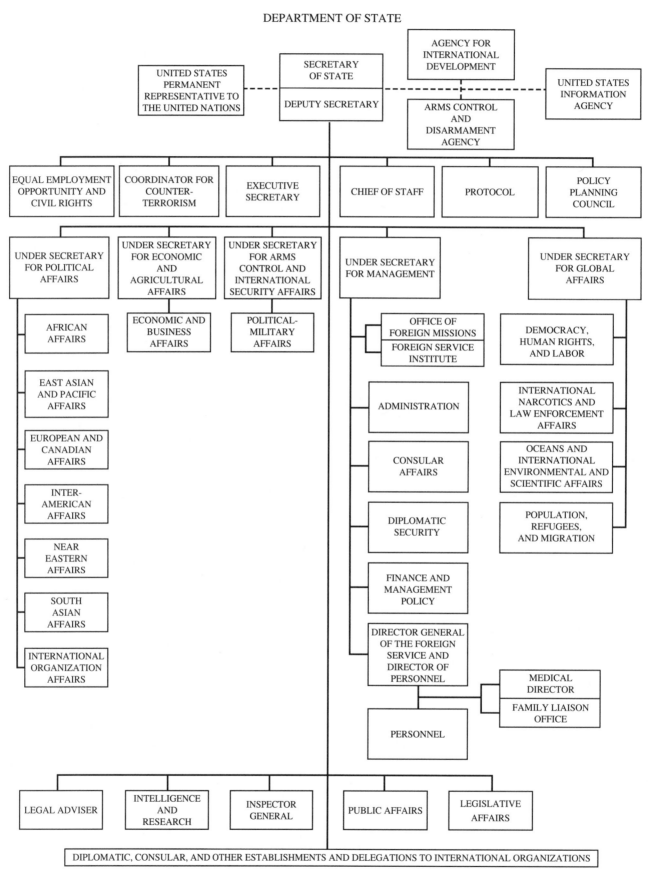

Source: *The U.S. Government Manual, Annual.* Washington, D.C.

ing next to the White House (now the Old Executive Office Building). Completed in 1888, the building was an impressive modern structure that improved the department's prestige in Washington. The department remained there, assuming exclusive occupancy in 1930, until it moved in 1947 to a new structure in the Foggy Bottom area of Washington. Following the expansion of that building in 1957, most of the department moved there. By the 1990s, more than 75 percent of the department's offices were located at "Main State"; the rest used eleven other annexes in the area.

Reflecting its increasing interest in international matters and its growing power, the United States in 1893 finally named ambassadors to the principal foreign missions. Until this time, minister had been the senior diplomatic rank abroad, but now ambassadors were named to Great Britain, France, Germany, and Italy. (That list gradually expanded; in 1947, all heads of mission to Latin America carried the ambassadorial title.) In the 1960s, President Kennedy decided to send ambassadors rather than ministers to all newly independent countries. During this time, the department's overall growth was quite modest. From 1870 to 1900, the number of diplomatic posts abroad grew only from thirty-six to forty-one, and consular posts remained at 318. Departmental domestic personnel increased from sixty-five to ninety-one, and those in foreign service from 804 to 1,137.

The nation's continuing focus on internal growth fostered a certain insularity in U. S. diplomats and departmental civil servants. Chronic problems of the department continued: employees at home and abroad were seriously underpaid; appointments were subject to the spoils system; and no merit and tenure legislation was enacted. Most diplomats therefore had to be persons of independent means. The vast majority of those were wealthy easterners—which only reinforced suspicions of the department and raised questions of the representativeness of U.S. diplomatic personnel (which continue to this day). As a result, the department and its employees abroad felt beleaguered and remained attached to the formalities of traditional diplomatic practice. This either amused or annoyed most of their fellow citizens. Scholars, foreshadowing contemporary criticism of the department, saw it as old-fashioned and obsessed with formalistic diplomatic method, slow to change its practices even to assimilate such inventions of the day as the telephone and the typewriter. Nevertheless, events conspired to move the department away from the familiar position it had held since the War of 1812. The 1898 war with Spain caused the United States to shift away from its traditional nonengagement when it ejected the Spanish from Cuba and took over conquered colonial possessions—Puerto Rico, the Philippines, and Guam—from Spain. These new responsibilities broadened U.S. horizons, made it an imperial power, making it clear not only to its own citizens, but to others as well, that the United States now had nearly all the characteristics of a great power: size, population, economic resources, military power (notably a new navy), and potential.

From 1899 until World War I, the United States greatly enlarged its international role. Secretary of State John Hay's 1899–1900 proposals for an "Open Door" policy, which provided unrestricted access for all nations to China's markets and commitment to the territorial and political integrity of China, directed new attention to the Far East. Similarly, a more activist role in policing Latin American countries, announced by President Theodore Roosevelt in the 1904 corollary to the Monroe Doctrine, led to more U.S. intervention in the Western Hemisphere and a greater role for the department. By 1910 the department had jumped from ninety-one employees to 234, then expanded further as a result of World War I to 708 in 1920. Overseas personnel, however, dropped from 1,137 in 1900 to 1,043 in 1910, and to 514 in 1920. There would not be such a surge in personnel until World War II produced an increase from 1,128 departmental employees in 1940 to 3,767 in 1945 and a postwar high of 8,606. Overseas employment went from 840 in 1940 to 7,710 in 1950, before dropping back. In both cases, the apparent drop after 1950 was more than made up by the expansion of personnel in other agencies, especially the United States Information Agency (USIA) and the Agency for International Development (AID).

Anticipation of this growth began in 1909 with the third reorganization of the department, which led to an expansion of its functions. Assistant Secretary of State Francis M. Huntington directed the effort, aided substantially by Wilbur J. Carr, known as the "Father of the Foreign Service," who directed the Consular Bureau from 1909 to 1924, and was assistant secretary from 1924 to 1937. The 1909 reforms created for the first time geographic bureaus to deal with four regions—Western Europe, the Near East, the Far East, and Latin America. Other bureaus also were created to handle new functional responsibilities—a Bureau of Trade Relations, and the Division of Information, a forerunner of USIA. For the first time, a number of talented officers from the foreign service were brought back to staff the geographic bureaus, adding real expertise and hands-on experience.

The department's growth accompanied a strong, sustained movement toward a fully professionalized and a truly "democratic" foreign service. President Grover Cleveland had taken the first steps in 1885 when he required entrance into the Consular Service by competitive examination. In 1905, President Theodore Roosevelt established a competitive exam system and the first merit system for all diplomatic and consular positions except those of minister and ambassador. The following year, a position classification system emerged for consular offices, followed in 1909 by the creation of a Board of

Examiners to administer both written and oral examinations to diplomatic candidates. In 1915 legislation passed to permit assignment of diplomatic and consular officers to functional positions in addition to specific jobs. This change permitted assignment by administrative transfer rather than successive presidential appointments, and greatly increased the department's flexibility.

The department's workload grew dramatically just before and during World War I. Expenditures increased from $4.9 million in 1910 to $13.6 million in 1920. The war and subsequent peace negotiations brought diplomacy back into the popular consciousness for the first time since the days of the Revolution. Ironically, the department lost policymaking influence during this same period. The principal reason was that President Woodrow Wilson and his secretaries of state never established a close working relationship. The president's confidant, Colonel Edward M. House, emerged as Wilson's special agent; the same situation pertained in World War II, when President Franklin D. Roosevelt and Secretary Cordell Hull remained rather distant and Roosevelt used Harry Hopkins in a role similar to House's. More important, in both world wars the Department of State found itself insufficiently organized to exercise leadership in the vastly expanded milieu of wartime governance. Wartime mobilization meant that the Departments of War, the Navy, and the Treasury, and special agencies for war production, played increasingly important roles. Secretary of State Robert Lansing recognized this and in 1920 called for "complete repair and reorganization" of the United States' machinery of foreign relations. He appealed to Congress to further modernize, democratize, and professionalize the department and the foreign service, and to clarify the relationship between the department to other agencies. Congress responded with the 1924 Rogers Act, which significantly strengthened the department's foreign operations, creating the Foreign Service of the United States of America. This new entity combined the foreign and consular services into one organization, provided for rotation at posts, home leave, and representational expenses (these were not actually paid until 1931, and have consistently remained at very low levels). The act also permitted career officers to remain in the service after tours as chiefs of mission. Earlier, officers had been required to resign upon accepting a presidential appointment, with no guarantee of reappointment. While the new legislation provided a way to drop individuals who had outlived their usefulness, this policy also led to the loss of substantial skill and expertise at senior levels. The 1931 Moses-Linthcum Act added fairer promotion practices, better salaries, annual and sick leave, and an improved retirement system. Government budgetary reductions during the 1930s Depression reduced some of these benefits, but the basic structure remained in place.

Despite the general recognition that a major reform of the Department of State itself was overdue, the department undertook no such structural or personnel reorganization in the interwar years. The secretary retained both policy and administrative responsibility, with an undersecretary (converted to deputy secretary in the early 1970s) to provide help as requested. Senior positions remained few, but a fifth geographic bureau was added. A new Division of Publications emerged in 1921 to handle informational work, including the archival series *Foreign Relations of the United States*. A Division of International Conferences was developed in 1929 to cope with expanded multilateral diplomacy. In 1938 a Division of Cultural Relations began dealing with the emerging field of cultural diplomacy, and the first Division of Communications now organized modern telecommunications support.

During World War II the Department of State expanded operations in many areas, particularly in the economic field. Departmental officials helped set up several wartime agencies, particularly those that planned ahead for reconstruction of war-devastated countries, but Roosevelt often ignored the department's advice on day-to-day policymaking. In fact, the only area of postwar policy the department influenced was in the preparation of future postwar international organizations. Given Hull's poor relationship with the president and the quickly visible deficiencies of the department's organization for wartime, the Department of State played only a small role in shaping grand wartime strategy. The work it did was often left unread.

The promotion of Edward Stettinius to secretary late in 1944 enabled him to carry out plans he had made a year earlier, after being named undersecretary, subjecting the department to its fourth major reorganization. This time the secretary's Order 1301, issued in December 1944, specifically set out to cure ills many others had previously observed: lack of sufficient staff support, unsound division of responsibilities, inadequate information gathering, and ineffective long-range planning.

The department now grouped similar functions in the same office, and placed offices under an undersecretary, or one of six assistant secretaries. A Staff Committee consisting of the secretary and his principal deputies became the managerial group, a Coordinating Committee pulled the various threads of policy together, and a Joint Secretariat became the far more complex descendant of the 1870 Chief Clerk's Bureau. A Policy Committee and Committee on Postwar Problems also came into being, becoming precursors to the contemporary Policy Planning Staff established in 1947.

Stettinius also improved the status of several functional units so as to strengthen coordination of activities that overlapped the traditional geographic bureaus. Trade

Relations, Cultural Relations, and Public Information moved up from division to bureau status. Stettinius's successor James Byrnes continued to strengthen the department's coordinating capabilities. In September 1945, a portion of the wartime Office of Strategic Services (OSS) was brought into the Department of State as the Interim Research and Intelligence Service, predecessor organization to today's Bureau of Intelligence and Research.

Economic functions were pulled together under an undersecretary for economic affairs in mid-1946. This new senior position gave the assistant secretary for economic affairs more high-level clout, and the pair teamed up to supervise economic reporting and develop relations with the new international economic institutions such as the International Bank for Reconstruction and Development (World Bank) and the International Monetary Fund (IMF). A new Bureau of International Organization Affairs supervised this area, as well as matters relating to the newly created United Nations (UN).

The Foreign Service Act of 1946 substantially strengthened and built upon the 1924 Rogers Act. A director general of the Foreign Service was created, along with a Foreign Service Board, and the competitive examinations were also improved. The act also increased personnel flexibility by making permanent the concept of the Foreign Service Reserve Corps. The Foreign Service Reserve (FSR) was developed during the war to manage the burgeoning need for specialists such as lawyers, doctors, economists, and intelligence analysts. It has been maintained since that time as a way for bringing in specialists for either full-time or part-time service. In the years immediately following World War II many retained that status long enough to serve out full careers. Others transferred to the regular Foreign Service. The 1946 act also converted the Foreign Service School, which offered language training and some professional courses, into a full-fledged Foreign Service Institute (FSI). This institution provided advanced training in subjects of particular importance and in short supply elsewhere, specifically languages, area studies, and subjects such as economics and consular affairs. In the 1990s, the FSI was expanded and given its own campus, becoming the National Foreign Affairs Training Center in Arlington, Virginia.

By early 1947, the Department of State had completed this phase of its internal reforms, which marked the transition between the old Department of State and Foreign Service and the new—bigger, more complex, far more bureaucratized, and much more involved in dealing with key national and international issues.

United States as Global Leader: Since 1947

As the department moved to Foggy Bottom, the United States made striking advances in its global posture. The United States had not retreated as far into itself as it had after World War I, in part because it was much more involved in World War II, the consensus which created the UN in 1945 quickly broke down, and efforts to cooperate with the Soviet Union failed, virtually pushing the country into a leadership role. The Truman Doctrine, the Rio Pact, the Marshall Plan, and the North Atlantic Treaty Organization (NATO) were major U.S. initiatives designed to contain what the United States perceived as Soviet and Soviet-sponsored expansionist threats in areas the United States deemed of great importance to its own security.

The Cold War had begun. One of the United States' leading Soviet experts, Foreign Service officer George F. Kennan, laid out the doctrine of containment in his now-famous "X" article in *Foreign Affairs* magazine, heralding the "golden age" of the Department of State, a ten-year period in which the department played a key role in developing and implementing policies that shaped the postwar world. On the darker side, suspicion of Department of State personnel also emerged. In response to Cold War concerns that a few U.S. diplomats may have been abetting Moscow, President Harry S. Truman instituted a loyalty review program in 1947. In 1950, Wisconsin Senator Joseph McCarthy blamed "traitors" in the Department of State for such misfortunes as the "loss" of China to the communists and Soviet acquisition of the atomic bomb. McCarthy initiated a vendetta against the Department of State by publicly claiming that 205 "card-carrying communists" were employed within its ranks. McCarthy's allegations were never proved, and the senator himself was eventually censured by the Senate over this and other ideologically driven witchhunts. In the hysteria that followed McCarthy's outbursts, however, some department officers were dismissed by Secretaries Dean Acheson and John Foster Dulles, including veteran ambassador Joseph Davies and China expert John Stewart Service, who were forced out of the Foreign Service with their reputations severely damaged. (Service was later reinstated by the federal courts with full back pay and damages.) This confusing of dissent with disloyalty and the general atmosphere of fear, intimidation, and outrage that reigned at the time stifled the expression of minority opinions and adversely affected objective reporting from within the department for many years.

Some scholars also have noted that the loss of a generation of Far Eastern specialists, including the nation's most capable China experts, crippled the department's Far Eastern Bureau and indirectly led to serious mistakes in Vietnam a decade later. Moreover, many talented young people choose not to enter the Foreign Service because of perceived public hostility. This feeling slowly died out, only to revive in 1968–1975, when internal dissent regarding the Vietnam War was widely publicized. This time, however, no one was dismissed;

and indeed Secretary Dean Rusk established dissent procedures which have evolved in ways that offer some protection.

Wielding the reorganized Department of State, three secretaries of state who maintained very close relations with their presidents—George Marshall, Dean Acheson, and John Foster Dulles—dominated foreign policymaking in the late 1940s and 1950s in a way seldom seen before or since. As the United States grew more powerful and expanded its overseas commitments, a consensus grew around a more activist policy than ever before in U.S. history outside of wartime. As long as this consensus prevailed—it began to break down during the Vietnam War in the late 1960s—the Department of State maintained its prestige and leading role.

A more activist U.S. foreign policy, however, required more organizational changes that reshaped the department's operating milieu. Along the way, additional bureaucratic actors challenged the department for influence. The National Security Act of 1947, as noted earlier, folded the armed services into a single gigantic organization, the Department of Defense (DOD); created the nation's first peacetime intelligence agency, the CIA; and set up the National Security Council (NSC) and the NSC staff. In time, each of these invaded the Department of State's "turf." State, NSC, and DOD became the main points in what often has been a triangular struggle for power. Particularly challenging was the DOD under a strong secretary such as Robert McNamara in the 1960s. The Department of State's ability to contend successfully in such a tussle depended on the power, intimacy, and influence of the secretary's relationship with the president as well as the department's bureaucratic capability to act promptly in response to world events and perceived presidential needs. Most of the responses involving direct allocation of budgetary resources, however, were set up outside the Department of State. The DOD managed the disbursement of direct military assistance. The Economic Cooperation Administration was developed in the 1950s to disburse Marshall Plan economic aid to Europe and to provide other assistance worldwide, including economic aid labeled "Defense Support Assistance." President Kennedy reorganized U.S. assistance, in 1961 creating the United States Agency for International Development (USAID), which remains in place today. The USIA was created in 1953 with the transfer of the information function from the Department of State in response to a recommendation of the 1949 Hoover Commission on governmental organization and the desire to counter Soviet propaganda more effectively. In 1978, the Department of State's Bureau of Cultural affairs was transferred to the USIA. In 1961 President Kennedy specifically created the Peace Corps outside the Department of State and independent of other foreign aid agencies. Today, the Peace Corps continues to work principally in poor countries. Kennedy also established the Arms Control and Disarmament Agency (ACDA) to study arms control questions and conduct arms control negotiations. This agency came into its own when in the early 1970s the Strategic Arms Limitation Agreements (SALT I and SALT II) and then in the 1980s the agreement through the Strategic Arms Reduction Talks (START I and START II) were negotiated with the Soviet Union and the agency supervised the SALT II negotiations in the late 1970s.

The Departments of Commerce, Agriculture, Labor, and the Treasury also have substantial interests abroad. Labor works primarily through the AFL-CIO, but jointly supervises embassy labor attachés. Agriculture has had its own small separate foreign service for over fifty years, and Treasury has sent attachés abroad for nearly seventy years. Until 1980, the Foreign Service performed commercial functions in embassies and consulates. In the late 1970s, Secretary of State Vance went against prevailing opinion in the career service and agreed to transfer the commercial function to the Department of Commerce, as well as those officers who wished to transfer into the Foreign Commercial Service (FCS). Many chose to do so, and formed the nucleus of the FCS for several years.

As foreign economic policy steadily became more important in the 1970s and 1980s, other challengers to the Department of State's primacy emerged. In the early 1960s, President Kennedy created the U.S. Trade Representative (USTR), a presidential assistant at the ambassadorial level, but that individual really did not play a key foreign economic role until Robert Strauss held the position in Jimmy Carter's administration, from 1977 to 1981. Trade issues with Japan, among others, as well as major multilateral negotiations within the General Agreement on Tariffs and Trade (GATT) structure moved to the fore in the 1980s and early 1990s; the Office of the USTR in the White House became the coordinating center for foreign economic policy. Mickey Kanter, the Bill Clinton administration's USTR, has played a prominent role in dealing with virtually all major international economic issues.

Thus, while in theory all agencies get their "foreign policy guidance" from the secretary of state, only USIA, AID, and ACDA are bound to do so by law, and only a powerful secretary of state who is close to the president can enforce this state of affairs. In 1930, with very few exceptions, those working for the U.S. government abroad were concentrated in the Department of State or the Foreign Service, yet by the 1970s, the Department of State's 12,848 domestic and foreign employees represented only between 10 and 15 percent of those working on foreign issues. That percentage has declined even more since the 1970s as the United States found more to do abroad and successive budget cuts shrank the Department of State's exposure overseas. Other organizations picked up the slack—along with greater influence in policymaking. Not only the Department of State, but the rest of the executive branch, has had to adjust to more congressional influence and activity. Foreign issues became more politically sensitive, and international problems demanded more resources. Congress used its power over the purse—as well as the more traditional Senate prerogatives with respect to treaties and appointments—to influence and shape foreign assistance legislation and budgets. The Department of State acquired its first assistant secretary of congressional relations in 1949, and the new Bureau of Congressional Relations quickly grew in size to manage departmental dealings with Congress. Congress began to interest itself in several areas on a more regular basis. Under pressure from constituents, Congress began to deal with immigration law more openly. The 1965 Immigration Act abolished earlier quotas, and opened the way for Asian and Latin American immigration on a larger and much more sustained scale than ever before. This policy put pressure not only on the Department of State's Consular Bureau, but on the U.S. Immigration and Naturalization Service (INS) which controls the internal administration of noncitizens.

Congress's policy disputes with the executive branch reached their peak during the Vietnam War. They centered not just on the war itself, but on the powers of the presidency. This led to passage of the 1973 War Powers Resolution, which attempted to prescribe conditions under which the president can commit U.S. troops to combat and reporting requirements for doing so. President Nixon vetoed the bill, but his veto was overridden.

Reorganization and Reform

Since the end of World War II, the needs of the Department of State have been frequently analyzed. Twenty-one studies of the department were made from 1947 to 1993, by groups ranging from citizens' committees to groups from within the department itself.

The 1949 Hoover Commission recommended measures to break down the distinctions between Foreign Service officers and the civil servants who staffed the department. In 1954, Secretary Dulles asked Brown University President Henry M. Wriston to study the department and recommend measures to improve poor morale, poor management, inequalities between different categories of employees, and the irregular intake of Foreign Service officers.

Wriston recommended that most civil service employees be integrated into the Foreign Service and, in turn, that Foreign Service employees be brought back to serve in positions in the department. Several years of "Wristonization" followed, changes that doubled the size of

the Foreign Service and saw 1,500 Foreign Service officers pass through department positions by mid-1959. Neither Foreign nor Civil Service officers were happy about this, but most outsiders and many within believed that some integration was good, and that more exposure of Foreign Service officers to Washington was a healthy prescription. Behind the reorganization and reform efforts since the 1950s has been the lingering belief, spurred on by internal debate, that the department is incapable of managing the nation's foreign policy, or possibly even itself. Debate within the Kennedy administration after the Bay of Pigs fiasco led to several changes. One important step was the creation of a twenty-four-hour Operations Center as part of the Department of State's Executive Secretariat, which took over the task of alerting senior Department of State officers, the White House, and other government departments to fast-breaking developments.

The Operations Center was one effort to break the logjam caused by seven separate layers of bureaucracy that Secretary Rusk identified in 1962 as handling traffic between himself and action officers. Another such effort was the establishment of a Politico-Military Bureau at the Department of State and of a counterpart bureau at the DOD called International Security Affairs. When the United States engaged more heavily in Vietnam a few years later, "Pol/Mil" assisted the Department of State to shift gears to deal with Vietnam and related issues. The Bay of Pigs episode also led to recommendations by former General Maxwell Taylor that a coordinating mechanism be developed that would have interdepartmental groups at each level in Washington to correspond to the integrated Country Teams in embassies. Abroad, ambassadors already had authority over all nonmilitary activities, provided by a letter originally issued to them by President Kennedy (and renewed in more or less the same form by every president since). The result was National Security Action Memorandum (NSAM) 341 issued in March 1966. It set up interdepartmental groups at all levels, beginning with the Senior Interdepartmental Group (SIG) chaired by the undersecretary (after 1970, called deputy secretary) of state and composed of his counterparts from DOD, CIA, USIA, the Joint Chiefs of Staff, and other agencies as required. At the assistant secretary level, Interdepartmental Regional Groups (IRGs) were established, again with the State officer as chair. Similar groups, supervised by the IRGs, were organized on an *ad hoc* basis at working levels as needed. Early SIG/IRG operations were intermittently successful and slowly superseded earlier mechanisms (some in place since the wartime years of the 1940s) as the primary working form of interagency coordination. The principle of interdepartmental coordination stuck, and the system has continued in more or less the same form from 1966 on. Usually a representative of the NSC chairs the IRG groups (the Clinton administration practice), though the Department of State chaired them initially and has done so in other administrations. In any case, the department has used the evolved SIG/IRG system to help ensure the impressive intragovernmental coordination responsible for U.S. diplomatic success in the 1990–1991 Gulf War.

Creation of the SIG/IRG system stimulated wider agitation on other issues. A group of "Young Turks" took over the governing board of the American Foreign Service Association (AFSA), the professional association for the Foreign Service that in the early 1970s became the Foreign Service's bargaining agent under the Labor Relations Act. The AFSA board promptly organized a Committee on Career Principles, which produced a 1968 study, *Toward a Modern Diplomacy*. This study criticized the department's management weakness, urged that the foreign affairs organization of the government be tightened and further integrated, insisted that new technology be brought into the department as quickly as possible, and suggested that intragovernmental coordination could be significantly improved if Foreign Service personnel were seconded for assignments to other agencies both to broaden their own horizons and to help integrate interagency operations.

Prodded by the Foreign Service and by concern voiced in Congress, the department undertook a massive internal review in 1970 under the leadership of Undersecretary Elliot Richardson and Deputy Undersecretary William B. Macomber, Jr. The report, *Diplomacy for the '70s*, concluded that the Department of State lacked the skills and modern managerial methods for efficient operations. Traditional diplomatic skills were not enough; they required a new breed of "diplomat-manager," and a more dynamic, aggressive style of leadership to make the new SIG/IRG system function effectively. Brilliant traditional reporting officers were not enough; the new breed must be able to run a cultural program or an AID program. The department adopted most of the 500-plus recommendations. The major personnel change saw establishment of a "cone" system for Foreign Service officers, which encouraged functional specialization in either political, economic, administrative, or consular work. Not everyone rejoiced at this recasting of an age-old debate between specialists and generalists. Traditionalists insisted that a diplomat must rely on experience and the intuition it generates. Others believed the future belonged to well-trained specialists. Many grudgingly acknowledged that both are required, and hoped that the best generalists might develop enough specific knowledge to turn them into effective managers and that the best specialists might expand their interests over time rather than narrow them.

The 1970 reforms strengthened the career services, but only peripherally addressed an important source of tension: the relationship between career officer and political appointees. There were always two kinds of political appointees: the distinguished person of affairs who had established competence in another area, and the high-stakes political contributor who knew little about the country where he or she was going. Even career officers acknowledged the positive contributions of those in the "distinguished" category, but most believed the Foreign Service had enough talent to increase the percentage of career officers in senior jobs. Proponents of senior career appointments cite the contribution of career officers to U.S. post–World War II policy. They note further that the overwhelming majority of other major powers draw their ambassadorial and other senior appointments from career ranks, and that the second-ranking individual in most major foreign ministries is a senior career official. Politicians and others who oppose limiting political appointments argue that the department as well as the Foreign Service needs periodic infusions of outside talent to avoid encrustation, and that presidents have the right and the need to appoint key officials they personally trust. Career supporters point to excellent examples of career officers who have served their presidents well: Kennan, Loy Henderson, Charles Bohlen, and Robert Murphy in the 1940s and 1950s, and more recently David Newsom, Richard Murphy, and Lawrence Eagleburger in the 1970s and 1980s. Those arguing for "political" appointments noted the contributions made by Harvard professor Edwin Reischauer as ambassador to Japan, lawyer David Bruce as ambassador to Great Britain, former Princeton President Robert Goheen as ambassador to India, and former Senate Majority Leader Mike Mansfield as ambassador to Japan. While many noncareer ambassadors have had disastrous tenures, not every career officer has done well either. The political reality of the need for presidential control suggests the persistence of "politicals."

In a troubling development, however, even career appointments became more political after the basic U.S. foreign policy consensus fractured during the Vietnam War. Career officers simply rotated to new posts if the incoming administration disliked the policies with which they had been identified previously. When the Jimmy Carter administration took office in 1977, however, it dismissed and retired several career officials who had directed U.S. policy in Southeast Asia and Vietnam. The incoming Ronald Reagan team in 1981 followed the same policy, sidelining career officers who had administered Carter's controversial Central American policies. The change from Republican George Bush to Democrat Bill Clinton in 1993 saw this practice dwindle; but there is nothing to prevent it from occurring again.

The 1980 Foreign Service Act moved to reduce senior careerists' staying power. It created a "Senior Foreign Service," which increased the number of supergrade-equivalent positions for the Foreign Service, but also limited the tenure and tightened the promotion rules of those affected. Since 1950, career officers have held about two-thirds of ambassadorial appointments. The career percentage tends to go down at the beginning of an administration and to rise at the end.

Diplomats also feel the problem of terrorism, which grew sharply during the 1970s and 1980s, the most serious example being when Iran held over fifty U.S. diplomats hostage for 444 days, from 1979 to 1981. Assassinations and aircraft hijackings have left the concept of diplomatic immunity in shreds. The Department of State reacted by tightening security and embarking on a campaign to strengthen security protection at over 100 U.S. missions abroad.

Organizational Challenge in the 1990s

Increasing complexity and growing challenge mark the Department of State's environment in the 1990s. Beginning in the 1970s, the traditional distinction between domestic and international affairs began to break down. Compared with the years before World War II, the department has become involved in a much greater range of issues as the United States expanded its international engagement. Organizationally, this challenge was met by growth and acquisition of new functions: information, cultural affairs, intelligence, and research. More bureaus were added after the mid-1970s to deal with human rights; refugee programs; narcotics; communication and information policy; oceans, international environment, and science; diplomatic security; and space arms negotiations.

Increasingly in the late 1980s and 1990s, the U.S. federal government was not the only U.S. institution to conduct foreign affairs. States and cities had their own foreign relations, even their own offices abroad. In 1989, Kentucky took a direct yen loan from Japan, and Illinois gave $100 million in aid to Poland. Atlanta had twenty overseas offices. The activities of these entities and groups range from economic contracting abroad to running immigration posts. The Department of State created a three-person unit in the Bureau of Public Affairs to monitor these intergovernmental relations, although it had no control and little effective influence over them. In a crisis, state and city officials might consult the Department of State, but felt little obligation to do so.

As U.S. citizens gained more experience in dealing with foreign cultures, as many have over the past fifty years, they were loath to take the word of federal officials. Some even said that this weakened the argument for a specialized career service. Today, a businessperson or a Drug Enforcement Agency (DEA) officer might know as much about politics and financial affairs in Colombia or Bolivia as a traditional diplomat. Several state governors have led independent trade missions abroad and built a reservoir of their own contacts in key countries.

In sum, the foreign affairs function is not as centralized as it once was. Since 1991, the United States has struggled to redefine its basic approach to a world in which economic markets were becoming one and communication had become more swift and secure while telecommunications have not made diplomacy obsolete but radio communications, television, telephone, the photocopier, the fax machine, and electronic mail have nonetheless changed the general patterns of all our lives, including those of diplomats. These developments also made it extremely difficult to keep secrets. Worldwide television news deeply influenced public and elite perceptions of international issues, often dictating which problems would be attended to and which not.

A number of contemporary issues increasingly involved transnational problems that cannot be dealt with successfully either unilaterally or bilaterally. Problems such as environmental pollution, destruction of rainforests, international drug trafficking, the spread of AIDS, and worldwide shortages of water and energy could neither be ignored nor solved in the old narrow diplomatic framework. Interdependence, a concept that began to gain ground in the early 1970s, emerged as a fact of life. Interdependence also highlighted the growing importance of international organizations and nongovernmental organizations. In addition to U.N.-related groups such as the World Health Organization (WHO), the International Atomic Energy Agency, and the International Labor Organization, such nongovernmental organizations as Amnesty International, CARE, and Catholic Relief Services, came to play important roles across national borders. The Department of State's organizational struggle continues to develop links with these latter groups.

The department has struggled to adapt its personnel systems to equal opportunity and diversity concerns. Two class action lawsuits were filed alleging discrimination by gender (Palmer et al., filed 1976) and race (Thomas et al., filed 1986). Under a 1994 consent decree, the department admitted to gender discrimination in the 1976–1983 period in the Palmer case (discussions continue for the post-1984 period). In the Thomas case, litigation was suspended in 1993 in order to begin settlement talks that in March 1995 produced an agreement on minority promotions and recruitment. The director general of the Foreign Service began to review all recruitment and promotion policies, and major departmental efforts got under way to strengthen representation while maintaining a merit promotion system. Successive secretaries of state have grappled with all of these problems and how to address them. Both political and career department senior leadership have sought to find time between major policy decisions and other responsibilities to shape the department so that it could identify issues, put them before senior political leadership, and then develop responses, policies, and strategies, and carry them out. The department had neither the organization nor the resources to deal with these problems by itself, and even with the increased interagency coordination, many doubt whether the department is adequately anticipating and planning for the profound changes of the post–Cold War world.

In 1992–1993, the department again put together a task force composed of Foreign and Civil Service officers and outside experts. It produced a report, *A New Model for Managing Foreign Affairs*, urging a thorough reorganization of the internal structure of the department and the merger of the arms control function into the Department of State, discontinuing ACDA. It sought to link policy formulation to resource control and asserted that the NSC should be reshaped to be the catalyst and point of coordination for this effort. The report pictured three roles for the Department of State: "policy formulation across the range of international issues, implementation or conduct of foreign relations, and coordination of major overseas programs and activities of the government." It called for improved dialogue between the executive branch and Congress. Internally, it sought restructuring of the department's bureaus by function under an expanded team of five undersecretaries to cover economics and the environment, global issues and programs, international security, regional and multilateral diplomacy, and strategic management and program support. If fully implemented, these structural changes would be as significant a reorganization as the post–World War II reshaping of the department. No changes could fully resolve some dilemmas, such as political versus career staffing, equal personnel opportunity, suspicion of the department for involvement with foreigners, conflicts with other departments, or conflicts with the legislative branch. Most thoughtful diplomats and policymakers realize this even as they mutter about it and understand that the department can never fully escape its public scapegoat role without unlikely major structural changes being made in the U.S. government and an equally unlikely change of heart in the U.S. Congress and the public.

JOHN D. STEMPEL

See also Agency for International Development; Ambassadors and Embassies; Arms Control and Disarmament Agency; Bureaucracy; Central Intelligence Agency; Congress; Constitution; Diplomatic Method; Foreign Service; Immigration; McCarthyism; National Security Act; Nongovernmental Organizations; Passports and Visas; Peace Corps; Presidency; Rogers Act; United States Information Agency; War Powers Resolution

FURTHER READING

Campbell, John Franklin. *The Foreign Affairs Fudge Factory*. New York, 1971.

Destler, I. M., Leslie H. Gelb, and Anthony Lake. *The Unmaking of American Foreign Policy*. New York,1984.

Diplomacy for the '70's: A Program of Management Reform for the Department of State. Department of State Publication 8551. Washington, D.C., 1970.

Fry, Earl, Stan A. Taylor, and Robert S. Woods. *America the Vincible: U.S. Foreign Policy for the Twenty-First Century*. Englewood Cliffs, N.J., 1994.

Goehlert, R. V., and Ed Hoffmeister. *The Department of State and American Diplomacy*. New York, 1986.

Henkin, Louis. *Foreign Affairs and the Constitution*. Mineola, N.Y., 1972.

Ilchman, Warren F. *Professional Diplomacy in the United States, 1779–1939*. Chicago, 1961.

Kennedy, Charles S. *The American Consul*. Westport, Conn., 1980.

Newsom, David D. *Diplomacy and the American Democracy*. Bloomington, Ind., 1988.

Schulzinger, Robert D. *The Making of the American Diplomatic Mind*. Middletown, 1975.

State 2000: A New Model for Managing Foreign Affairs. Washington: U.S. Department of State Publication 10029. Washington, D.C., 1992.

Stearns, Monteagle. *Talking to Strangers: Improving American Diplomacy at Home and Abroad*. Princeton, N.J., 1996.

Steinbrunner, John D., ed. *Restructuring American Foreign Policy*. Washington, D.C., 1989.

Stuart, Graham H. *The Department of State: A History of Its Organization, Procedure and Personnel*. New York, 1949.

Trask, David F. *A Short History of the U.S. Department of State, 1781-1981*. Washington, D.C., 1981.

STATUS OF FORCES AGREEMENTS

Formal treaties between the United States (in diplomatic parlance, the "sending state") and a nation where it bases military forces (the "host nation" or the "territorial state"). A status of forces agreement (or, by its diplomatic acronym, SOFA) specifies the conditions under which the host nation assumes jurisdiction to prosecute U.S. military personnel for criminal offenses.

Under traditional international law, military personnel stationed abroad are considered to be representatives of U.S. sovereign power and thus cloaked with "sovereign immunity" from host nation criminal prosecutions. Like diplomats, they can be declared persona non grata and expelled, but not punished, by the host nation. The traditional international law approach grated on the political sensitivities of both the United States and foreign host nations, particularly those of the North Atlantic Treaty Organization (NATO). Expelling offenders, or leaving their prosecution to U.S. authorities, was untenable to allied host nations. On the other hand, a blanket abdication of jurisdiction by the U.S. military to host nation criminal courts was seen as damaging to the military mission. The diplomatically fashioned middle ground is the SOFA.

The archetype of the post–World War II SOFA is the NATO SOFA, which was concluded in 1951. Like most SOFAs, it sets up two different concepts of jurisdiction: (1) "exclusive" jurisdiction by which each nation retains the right to try foreign military personnel for offenses which are unique to its own laws, and (2) "concurrent" jurisdiction which apportions primary jurisdiction to one nation or the other (usually according to the nationality of the victim) where offenses violate the laws of both nations.

SOFAs apply only to criminal offenses. U.S. military personnel normally are subject to the civil jurisdiction of host nation courts. Dependents of U.S. service personnel are generally subject to host nation civil and criminal jurisdiction. SOFA treaties usually provide for basic due process standards as a condition of host nation jurisdiction, but they still occasionally generate criticism, litigation, and political controversy when U.S. military personnel are committed to foreign jurisdictions for trial on criminal charges.

In the 1990s both Congress and the executive branch have SOFAs under review because of likely post-Cold War revisions in U.S. overseas force deployments, as well as increased emphasis on nontraditional military roles and missions such as peacekeeping and humanitarian intervention.

WILLIAM T. WARNER

See also Extraterritoriality; International Law; North Atlantic Treaty Organization; Overseas Military Bases

FURTHER READING
Kramer, Donald T. "Criminal Jurisdiction of Courts of Foreign Nations Over American Armed Forces Stationed Abroad." *American Law Reports, Federal* 17 and supplement (1987 and 1994): 725–758.
Teagarden, Martin. "Status of Forces Agreements." *Air Force Law Review* 26 (1987): 21.

STETTINIUS, EDWARD REILLY, JR.
(*b.* 22 October 1900; *d.* 31 October 1949)

Secretary of state (1944–1945), who helped found the United Nations (UN). President Franklin D. Roosevelt named Stettinius secretary of state soon after the November 1944 election. The long-time secretary, Cordell Hull, was ill, and he had agreed to remain in office only until after the election. If not for Hull's declining health, Stettinius never would have become secretary at such an important juncture.

Born in Chicago, Stettinius grew up in the wealthy home of his father, a partner in J. P. Morgan & Company who served President Woodrow Wilson as assistant secretary of war during World War I. Young Stettinius attended the University of Virginia; an indifferent student, he failed in five years to earn a degree. His father's contacts proved invaluable, however, and Stettinius soon became a vice president of General Motors. In 1934 he joined United States Steel Corporation as chairman of finance and in four years he became chairman of the board of directors.

Although identified with big business, Stettinius held liberal views, and he publicly supported Franklin Roosevelt. In return, the president appointed him to various advisory commissions during the New Deal. After war erupted in Europe, Roosevelt named him director of Lend-Lease, where he proved to be an able and efficient administrator; in 1943 Stettinius became undersecretary of state, in which office he spent his efforts reorganizing the department. In 1944, at the Dumbarton Oaks Conference, Stettinius helped shape what in 1945 became the United Nations Organization.

As Secretary Hull's health declined, Stettinius became the logical choice for secretary of state. The appointment also sent another message: Roosevelt himself would dictate war and postwar policy toward the Allies. Stettinius advised the president at the Yalta Conference in February 1945, but his most important role came later that spring at the San Francisco Conference which established the United Nations. There, Soviet-American differences emerged over veto powers for members of the Security Council. The Soviet Union demanded the power to veto discussion of any topic that came before the General Assembly. The United States refused to accept any such curtailing of free speech at the new international organization; Stettinius insisted that council members could veto only UN actions. After Stettinius's genial and skillful negotiations, the Soviets agreed to the U.S. position.

At the conclusion of the conference, the new president, Harry S. Truman, accepted Stettinius's resignation and appointed James F. Byrnes secretary of state. But Truman also acknowledged Stettinius's previous work and later in 1945 appointed him the first U.S. ambassador to the UN.

TERRY H. ANDERSON

See also Dumbarton Oaks Conference; Lend-Lease; State, U.S. Department of; United Nations

FURTHER READING
Campbell, Thomas M., and George C. Herring, eds. *The Diaries of Edward R. Stettinius, Jr.* New York, 1975.
Walker, Richard L. *E. R. Stettinius, Jr.*, vol. 14 of *The American Secretaries of State and Their Diplomacy.* New York, 1965.

STEVENSON, ADLAI EWING II

(*b.* 5 February 1900; *d.* 14 July 1965)

Democratic presidential candidate, statesman, and U.S. ambassador to the United Nations (1961–1965). Born in Los Angeles, California, Stevenson graduated from Princeton and earned a law degree at Northwestern University. He served in the New Deal in the 1930s and in the Departments of Navy and State during World War II. In 1948 he became governor of Illinois. Stevenson became the Democratic Party's so-called liberal conscience during the Eisenhower years, making unsuccessful presidential bids in 1952 and 1956. He also traveled widely, for example to the Middle East in 1953 and to Latin America in 1960. Seeking a more flexible stance against Soviet expansionism, he advocated an equal partnership with U.S. allies, an end to the military draft and nuclear testing, and greater sensitivity toward Arab rights.

Sympathetic to some of these goals, President John F. Kennedy appointed Stevenson ambassador to the United Nations. Stevenson grew unhappy, however, that the president seldom consulted him. At the United Nations, Stevenson pressed for disarmament, tried to persuade Presidents Kennedy and Lyndon B. Johnson to seat the People's Republic of China, dramatically presented evidence of the secret installation of Soviet missile bases in Cuba in October 1962, and declared himself willing to await a Soviet confession of the missile emplacement until "hell freezes over." But, typically consistent with his moderate internationalism, Stevenson urged negotiation rather than confrontation during the missile crisis. Witty and eloquent, an inspiration to young liberals, and a dedicated public servant, Stevenson nonetheless eventually fell out of favor with Kennedy and some of his advisers, who thought Stevenson "soft."

THOMAS W. ZEILER

See also China; Cuban Missile Crisis; United Nations

FURTHER READING

Johnson, Walter, ed. *The Papers of Adlai E. Stevenson*, 8 vols. Boston, 1972–1979.

McKeever, Porter. *Adlai Stevenson: His Life and Legacy*. New York, 1989.

Morton, John Bartlow. *Adlai Stevenson and the World*. Garden City, N.Y., 1978.

STILWELL, JOSEPH

(*b.* 19 March 1883; *d.* 12 October 1946)

Commander of U.S. forces in China, Burma, and India (1942–1944), this career military officer (West Point, 1904) was long associated with U.S. policy toward China. A gifted linguist, he became the U.S. Army's first language officer in China (1920–1923). Subsequent service as executive officer of the Fifteenth Infantry in Tianjin (1926–1929) and as U.S. military attaché (1935–1939) gave Stilwell intimate knowledge of China during the Kuomintang rise to national power and the ensuing Japanese aggression. He did not hide his low opinion of leader Jiang Jieshi (Chiang Kai-shek) or his conviction that Chinese soldiers, properly trained, fed, led, and equipped, could fight effectively. A close relationship with General George C. Marshall at the Fort Benning Infantry School in the early 1930s eventually led to Stilwell's appointment as commanding general of U.S. forces in China, Burma, and India in early 1942. His mission was to organize Chinese divisions, reopen a supply route through Burma to Chongqing with British help, and thus make China the staging point for the final invasion of Japan. Allied priorities in other theaters and Jiang's reluctance to use Chinese troops in Burma soon thwarted Stilwell's strategy. In 1943, moreover, President Franklin D. Roosevelt adopted the proposal of "Flying Tiger" General Claire Lee Chennault to fight the Japanese almost exclusively with air power. As Stilwell predicted, the Japanese launched a massive counterattack that nearly overran all U.S. air bases. Roosevelt thereupon demanded that Stilwell be given unrestricted command of all forces, Chinese and foreign, in China. When Jiang balked, fearing U.S. contacts with Chinese communist forces, Roosevelt sent an ultimatum. "I handed this little bundle of paprika to the Peanut," Stilwell noted in his diary on 19 September 1944. "The harpoon hit the little bugger in the solar plexus, and went right through him." The humiliated Chinese leader had his revenge a month later when Stilwell was replaced by General Albert C. Wedemeyer. "Vinegar Joe's" death from cancer in October 1946 came just as the final phase of the civil war between the Communists and Nationalists was beginning in earnest—an ironic epitaph to the limits of U.S. influence on Chinese affairs.

J. GARRY CLIFFORD

See also China; Jiang Jieshi; World War II

FURTHER READING

Romanus, Charles F. *Stilwell's Mission to China*. Washington, D.C., 1953.

———, and Riley Suderland. *Stilwell's Command Problems*. Washington, D.C., 1956.

Schaller, Michael. *The U.S. Crusade in China, 1938–1945*. New York, 1979.

Tuchman, Barbara W. *Stilwell and the American Experience in China, 1911–1945*. New York, 1970.

White, Theodore H., ed. *The Stilwell Papers*. New York, 1948.

STIMSON, HENRY LEWIS

(*b.* 21 September 1867; *d.* 20 October 1950)

Longtime public servant who served both as secretary of war (1911–1913 and 1940–1945) and secretary of state

(1929–1933). Born in New York City, Stimson was initially educated at home by his father, an eminent surgeon who had studied in Paris under the scientist Louis Pasteur. The young Stimson attended Phillips Academy at Andover (1880–1883), and afterward Yale (A.B. 1888), Harvard (M.A. 1889), and the Harvard Law School (1889–1890). At Harvard he studied philosophy and history, developed a flair for broad-ranged analysis, and connected his legal training to contemporary public issues. A first-rate lawyer, he entered the New York firm of Root and Clarke in 1891 and came under the tutelage of the senior partner Elihu Root, later secretary of war and secretary of state under William McKinley and Theodore Roosevelt. Himself secretary of war under President William H. Taft from 1911 to 1913, Stimson backed chief of staff General Leonard Wood in his wish to expand the power of the army's general staff over its bureau chiefs. An ardent interventionist and graduate of the Plattsburg training camps, Stimson served as a colonel of field artillery during World War I.

After the war, and while maintaining his lucrative law practice, he undertook a special mission to Nicaragua for President Calvin Coolidge in 1927. U.S. Marines had installed themselves as a legation guard in 1912, and after momentarily departing in 1925, were sent back in large numbers to protect the Nicaraguan government against revolutionary opponents. In the Peace of Tipitapa (May 1927), Stimson arranged a truce between the government and revolutionaries that allowed for later elections. He also created a U.S.-trained national guard to perpetuate the domestic order imposed by the marines. His tenure as governor general of the Philippines (1928–1929) was notable for close personal relations with Filipino leaders, increased cooperation with the Philippines legislature, and modest economic reforms.

As secretary of state under President Herbert Hoover (1929–1933), Stimson found himself in substantial disagreement with his chief. The differences stemmed in part from Stimson's failure to see the political side of issues, even more so because his own considerable wealth insulated him against the dire economic problems requiring Hoover's attention during the Great Depression. Most important, he and Hoover disagreed over what means the United States should employ to maintain world peace. During the London Naval Conference in 1930, in an attempt to gain French acquiescence in limiting cruisers, destroyers, and submarines, Stimson proposed an agreement for consultation in the event of international crisis. The French seemed willing to agree if, perhaps, they might thereby obtain more U.S. cooperation in Europe. Hoover responded unsympathetically, however, and the project collapsed. More important differences arose following the occupation of Manchuria by the Japanese army in 1931–1932 and Japan's subsequent

withdrawal from the League of Nations. Displaying what Hoover called Stimson's "combat psychology," Stimson wanted to restrain the Japanese by encouraging the League of Nations to impose economic sanctions. Hoover vetoed sanctions, likening them to "sticking pins in tigers." The tepid U.S. response came in the so-called Stimson Doctrine of 7 January 1932, in which the United States refused to recognize any territorial gains that violated existing treaties. When the Japanese defiantly reconstituted Manchuria as the puppet state of Manchukuo, Stimson remarked that he had only "spears of straw and swords of ice to work with." When aggression continued to gain the upper hand in Europe and Asia after 1933, Stimson and Hoover took opposite sides in the ensuing isolationist-interventionist debates, Stimson favoring interventionism.

In June 1940 President Franklin D. Roosevelt appointed Stimson and Frank Knox, both Republicans, to head the Departments of War and the Navy. An outspoken advocate of preparedness and aid to the Allies, the aging secretary oversaw creation of the huge U.S. Army and Air Force that eventually defeated Germany, Italy, and Japan. He pushed for economic embargoes against Japan before Pearl Harbor. He advocated an early cross-Channel invasion of France in 1942 to keep Russia in the war. With "the door that was always open" between their adjoining offices, Stimson ensured harmonious civil-military relations with army chief of staff General George C. Marshall. As President Harry S. Truman's senior adviser on the military use of atomic energy, Stimson made the deciding recommendation to drop the atomic bombs on Japan in August 1945. "My chief purpose was to end the war in victory with the least possible cost in the lives of the men in the armies I had helped to raise," he later wrote. In his last cabinet meeting in September 1945, Stimson advocated a direct approach to the Soviet Union to reach agreement on the international control of nuclear weapons. After retirement, he collaborated with McGeorge Bundy in writing his memoirs, *In Active Service in Peace and War* (1947), and supported the Cold War policies of his wartime associates.

J. Garry Clifford

See also Cold War; Hiroshima and Nagasaki Bombings of 1945; Hoover, Herbert; Japan; League of Nations; London Naval Conferences of 1930 and 1935–1936; Manchurian Crisis; Nicaragua; Philippines; Root, Elihu; World War II

FURTHER READING

Current, Richard N. *Secretary Stimson: A Study in Statecraft.* Brunswick, N.J., 1954.
Ferrell, Robert H. *American Diplomacy in the Great Depression: Hoover-Stimson Foreign Policy, 1929–1933.* New Haven, Conn., 1957.

Hodgson, Godfrey. *The Colonel: The Life and Times of Henry L. Stimson.* New York, 1990.
Morison, Elting E. *Turmoil and Tradition: A Study of the Life and Times of Henry L. Stimson.* Boston, 1960.

STIMSON DOCTRINE

See Manchurian Crisis; Stimson, Henry Lewis

STOCKHOLM CONFERENCE

See United Nations Conference on the Human Environment, Stockholm

STRAIGHT, WILLARD DICKERMAN

(*b.* 31 January 1880; *d.* 1 December 1918)

Diplomat, financier, and publicist on Asian affairs. Born in Oswego, New York, he became fluent in Chinese and Japanese while his father was a missionary stationed in Asia. After graduating from Cornell Univerisity in 1901, Straight returned to East Asia to work, first in the Chinese Customs Services and then as a journalist during the Russo-Japanese War. He subsequently served at U.S. consular posts in Korea, Cuba, and China. He deplored U.S. acquiescence in Japan's annexation of Korea. From November 1908 to June 1909 he headed the Department of State's Division of Far Eastern Affairs. A principal architect of "dollar diplomacy," the encouragement of U.S. investment for profit and as an instrument of political stabilization, Straight sought to implement this policy in and out of government. After leaving the Department of State in 1909 he worked simultaneously for U.S. banking interests in Asia and to expand U.S. influence and protect the Chinese government. After dollar diplomacy collapsed in China in 1911, he represented U.S. financial interests through the J.P. Morgan banking concern and American International Corporation. While preparing to serve as secretary of the U.S. peace commission at the Paris Peace Conference, Straight died of pneumonia in Paris.

JANET M. MANSON

See also China; Dollar Diplomacy; Japan

FURTHER READING
Cohen, Warren I. *America's Response to China: A History of Sino-American Relations.* New York, 1990.
Croly, Herbert D. *Willard Straight.* 1924.
Kahn, Helen Dodson. "Willard D. Straight and the Great Game of Empire." In *Makers of American Diplomacy: From Benjamin Franklin to Henry Kissinger,* edited by Frank J. Merli and Theodore A. Wilson. New York, 1974.

STRATEGIC AIR COMMAND

The U.S. Air Force branch charged with long-range offensive operations, primarily during the Cold War with carrying out a nuclear attack against the Soviet Union in the event of a general war. SAC controlled both the air force's strategic-bomber force as well as its intercontinental ballistic missiles from its headquarters at Offutt Air Force Base in Nebraska. It was established as one of three branches of the army air force in 1946, and continued after 1947 when the air force became an independent service. The other two divisions of the air force were the Tactical Air Command, charged with direct support of ground-combat operations, and the Air Defense Command, charged with the defense of the United States against air attack.

Given the centrality of its mission to the air force during the Cold War, SAC became the largest and most prestigious of the three commands, because of the general commitment within the air force to the proposition that air power was likely to be the most decisive weapon in any future war, especially one fought with nuclear weapons. This implied that strategic bombardment was the most important mission of the air force, and, indeed, of the military services in general. The paradox of deterring a nuclear war by planning to fight it, exemplified by SAC's motto "peace is our profession," as well as SAC's attitude toward the importance of its mission were satirized in the 1963 film *Dr. Strangelove, or, How I Learned to Stop Worrying and Love the Bomb,* based on the book of the same title by Peter George.

With the end of the Cold War, the centrality of strategic air power to the mission of the air force declined. In an effort to adjust to the changed world situation, the air force was reorganized in 1992, and the Strategic Air Command was abolished.

BENJAMIN FORDHAM

See also Defense, U.S. Department of; National Security and National Defense; Nuclear Weapons and Strategy

FURTHER READING
Ball, Desmond. *Politics and Force Levels: The Strategic Missile Program of the Kennedy Administration.* Berkeley, Calif., 1980.
Borowski, Harry R. *A Hollow Threat: Strategic Air Power and Containment Before Korea.* Westport, Conn., 1982.

STRATEGIC ARMS LIMITATION TALKS AND AGREEMENTS

Soviet-U.S. negotiations culminating in agreements in 1972 and 1979 to limit strategic nuclear weapons. During the first part of the twentieth century, large warships were commonly believed to be the defining characteristic of a great power. Following the United States' use of nuclear weapons on Hiroshima and Nagasaki in 1945, nuclear weapons became the "capital weapon" of the last half of the twentieth century. In 1946, the United States and the Soviet Union presented proposals to the United Nations for nuclear disarmament, but these proposals—the Baruch and Gromyko plans—were not accepted for various reasons.

In the absence of nuclear disarmament, the United States and the USSR came to rely on nuclear deterrence as the means of convincing the other side not to use nuclear weapons. For deterrence to work, both sides needed to possess the ability to inflict unacceptable damage on the other side; consequently, the United States and the Soviet Union built and deployed increasingly destructive and sophisticated nuclear weapons throughout the Cold War.

U.S. nuclear-tipped missiles were placed in Europe. The Soviet Union sent missiles and nuclear weapons clandestinely to Cuba in 1962, an action that, when discovered by U.S. surveillance, catalyzed the most serious crisis of the entire Cold War. As a result of the crisis, President John F. Kennedy and Premier Nikita Khrushchev concluded that nuclear war was not simply a hypothetical possibility; it could really happen. In the months following the resolution of the Cuban missile crisis, two agreements were signed to lessen the danger of nuclear war: the "Hot Line" Agreement and the Limited Nuclear Test Ban Treaty (1963).

Vietnam soon dominated the attention of U.S. policymakers. Nonetheless, in 1966 the U.S. government sought to open negotiations with the USSR with the intent of limiting strategic nuclear arms. Only after the People's Republic of China exploded its first thermonuclear weapon in 1967 did the Soviet government respond positively to the American invitation. Soviet Premier Alexey Kosygin visited the United States in June 1967 and met with President Lyndon Johnson in Glassboro, New Jersey, to discuss offensive and defensive weapons systems. Johnson and Kosygin failed, however, to place any limits on these arms, and the United States began to deploy "multiple, independently targetable reentry vehicles" (MIRVs) three months after the Glassboro summit meeting. MIRVs were significant because, in effect, they were a force multiplier. Prior to deployment of MIRVs (and a related technology called "multiple reentry vehicles"), one missile carried one warhead. Once MIRVs were deployed, one missile could carry up to thirty warheads, each programmed to hit a different target.

In July 1968, the Non-Proliferation Treaty (NPT) was signed; states which did not possess nuclear weapons pledged not to acquire them, while the states that possessed nuclear weapons, including the United States and the USSR, promised to "pursue negotiations in good faith on effective measures relating to cessation of the nuclear arms race at an early date...." Perhaps related to this obligation, in 1968 the United States and the Soviet Union agreed to begin formal discussions to limit strategic nuclear weapons. The Soviet and Warsaw Pact invasion of Czechoslovakia in August 1968, however, caused the United States to postpone the opening of these negotiations.

SALT I

When Richard Nixon became president in January 1969, he ordered a comprehensive review of U.S. strategic nuclear programs, thus delaying U.S.-Soviet negotiations designed to limit strategic nuclear weapons until November of that year. SALT (Strategic Arms Limitation Talks) negotiations were conducted in alternate sessions in Helsinki, Finland, and Vienna, Austria.

The U.S. delegation was headed by the director of the Arms Control and Disarmament Agency, Gerard C. Smith, and consisted of representatives of the Departments of State and Defense, the Central Intelligence Agency, the Joint Chiefs of Staff, and the National Security Council. Although the U.S. delegation was formally responsible for the negotiations, Dr. Henry A. Kissinger, who at the time of the SALT I negotiations was President Nixon's assistant for national security affairs, conducted secret, "back-channel" negotiations with the Soviet ambassador in Washington, D.C., Anatoly Dobrynin.

The task facing the SALT I negotiators was difficult because the American and Soviet nuclear arsenals differed significantly. After thirty months of negotiations, the two sides did reach two agreements, which together were known as the "SALT I" agreements: one limiting defensive weapons and the other restricting offensive systems.

President Nixon traveled to Moscow in May 1972 and signed with Soviet Leader Leonid Brezhnev a number of agreements in several different functional issue areas. The most important of these agreements was undoubtedly the Anti-Ballistic Missile (ABM) Treaty, which allowed the United States and the Soviet Union to deploy no more than 100 ABM launchers at each of two sites. In essence, the two signatories agreed to forgo effective defense of their respective homelands, and consequently the ABM Treaty was cited as the most important arms-control agreement since the 1921 Washington Naval Treaty.

The treaty called for the establishment of a U.S.-Soviet "Standing Consultative Commission" in order to "promote the objectives and implementation of the provisions of the treaty," and to deal with questions concerning compliance with the treaty. The U.S. Senate approved the treaty by a vote of 88 to 2.

At the time that the agreement was signed, the United States had 1,054 operational ICBMs and 656 SLBMs deployed, while the USSR had 1,618 ICBMs and 740 SLBMs deployed. By reducing their number of deployed ICBMs to 1,000 (U.S.) and 1,409 (USSR), the United States would be allowed to deployed a maximum of 710 SLBMs and the USSR would be allowed 950 SLBMs. The USSR was allowed to build and deploy 308 modern, large ("heavy") ICBMs. The main reason given by Nixon and Kissinger for the unequal numbers of missiles was that the U.S. capacity to "MIRV" its missiles meant actual parity in the number of deliverable bombs.

Because of the belief that submarine-launched ballistic missiles (SLBMs) were less vulnerable to preemptive attack and destruction and therefore more stabilizing than land-based missiles, each signatory could deploy additional SLBMs by dismantling ICBMs. If all of their old ICBMs were dismantled, the United States could deploy up to 710 SLBMs on forty-four submarines, and the USSR could build up to 950 SLBMs on sixty-two submarines. When the U.S. Congress passed the law that established the Arms Control and Disarmament Agency in 1961, it stipulated that any agreement concerning limitations of U.S. weapons must be submitted to both houses of Congress for majority approval before it could become law and be implemented. As a result, the Interim Agreement was submitted to the House of Representatives and the Senate. During the congressional debate, Senator Henry Jackson, Democrat from Washington state, introduced an amendment to the Interim Agreement that any future arms control agreement "not limit the United States to levels of intercontinental strategic forces inferior to the limits for the Soviet Union." The Senate passed the Jackson Amendment by a vote of 55 to 35 and, thus reassured, the Interim Agreement by a vote of 88 to 2.

SALT II

Several months following the approval of the SALT I agreements, U.S. and Soviet delegations resumed their negotiations to limit further strategic nuclear weapons. This second phase of negotiations, known as "SALT II," lasted from November 1972 to the signing of the SALT II treaty in June 1979. The SALT I agreements had taken two and a half years to negotiate; the SALT II treaty took almost seven years, because contentious Soviet-U.S. political relations and the increasing complexity of limiting advanced technology slowed the process.

President Nixon initiated the SALT II negotiations and supported them until his resignation from the presidency in August 1974. Nixon's successor, Gerald R. Ford, also supported the negotiations and met with Brezhnev in Vladivostok on 23 and 24 November to conclude an "agreement in principle," which did not legally bind the two signatories, but did provide an objective for the negotiators. The "Vladivostok Accord" stipulated that each side should be limited to a total of 2,400 strategic nuclear vehicles (ICBMs, SLBMs plus long-range bombers) and, of this total, 1,320 could be equipped with MIRVed warheads.

The attempts of weapons designers, engineers, and scientists to develop weapons was followed by the attempt of diplomats and political leaders to limit these weapons. New technologies and weapons complicated the negotiators' task. The USSR, for example, began to deploy a new bomber, the Tupolov (TU) 22M, also known in the West by its NATO code name, the "Backfire" bomber. American scientists were working on a new large ICBM called the "Missile Experimental" (MX) and several different versions of cruise missiles, which were subsonic, air-breathing, long-range missiles capable of highly accurate targeting. The 1976 presidential campaign introduced further complexities into the SALT II negotiations. Candidates Ronald Reagan, Henry Jackson, George Wallace, and Jimmy Carter criticized the Ford administration for its support of détente with the Soviet Union, which, of course, included a denunciation of SALT, the centerpiece of détente.

When Carter came into office in January 1977, he had high hopes for achieving significant limitations on conventional and nuclear weapons. Carter sent his new Secretary of State, Cyrus Vance, to Moscow to present a new proposal for deep cuts in the levels that had been tentatively agreed to in Vladivostok by President Ford in 1974. Because of Carter's emphasis on human rights and the way in which he publicized the deep cuts proposal even before it was presented to the Soviets, Russian leaders reacted quickly and negatively to the new initiative. But within several months Soviet and U.S. negotiators were meeting again.

Several foreign policy issues overshadowed SALT in importance. In September 1977, President Carter signed the Panama Canal treaties, and after expending significant political capital, was able to win ratification by one vote. Also in mid-to-late 1977, the Cuban government, with the assistance of the Soviets, deployed Cuban troops in the Horn of Africa. Secretary of State Vance and National Security Affairs Adviser Zbigniew Brzezinski disagreed about the importance of this deployment. In particular, Vance believed that progress on SALT II should not be linked to Cuban and Soviet activities in Africa, whereas Brzezinski insisted that they be linked. The China issue also divided the two foreign policy officials. In December 1978 when Vance was out of town, Brzezinski (with the approval of President Carter) announced that the United States and the People's Republic of China were going to establish full diplomatic relations. This decision greatly concerned Soviet leaders and slowed the conclusion of the SALT II treaty.

After almost seven years of negotiations, the SALT II treaty was signed in Vienna on 18 June 1979. The treaty

SUMMARY OF MAJOR SALT PROPOSALS AND AGREEMENTS

	SALT I INTERIM AGREEMENT (MAY 1972) U.S./USSR	VLADIVOSTOK ACCORDS (NOVEMBER 1974)	MOSCOW COMPREHENSIVE PROPOSAL (MARCH 1977)	SALT II AGREEMENT (JUNE 1979)
ICBMS	1000/1409			2,400–2,250
SLBMS	710/950	2400 (total SNLVS)	1,800–2,000	(by 12/31/81)
Long-range Bombers	*			
MIRVED Launchers	*	1320	1,100–1,200	1,200 for ICBM and SLBM, 1,320 including ALCM
MIRVED ICBMS	*	*	550	820
MLBMS**	308	308	150	308
ALCM	*	(dispute over whether included under SNLV ceiling)	2,500-km range limit	2,500-km range limit during 3-yr. protocol < 500-km range not to count as MIRVED launchers
GLCM/SLCM	*	*	2,500-km range limit	600-km range limit
Backfire Bomber	*	(dispute over whether included under SNLV ceiling)	"strict limit" on deployment to intercontinental range	statement to accompany agreement
Land-Mobile ICBMS	U.S. Unilateral Statement Favoring Ban	*	0	protocol includes prohibition on testing.
"New" ICBMS and SLBMS	*	*	ban on new ICBMS only	one new ICBM allowed
Ballistic-Missile Flight-Test	*	*	6 per year for ICBMS 6 per year for SLBMS	
Limits on MIRVS				10 for ICBMS/ASBMS 14 for SLBMS

*not included
**USSR only

GLOSSARY

ALCM	air-launched cruise missile
ASBM	air-to-surface ballistic missile
GLCM	ground-launched cruise missile
ICBM	(land-based) intercontinental ballistic missile
MARV	maneuverable reentry vehicle
MIRV	multiple, independently-targeted reentry vehicle
MLBM	(Soviet SS-9/SS-18 type)
MLVM	modern large ballistic missile
SLBM	submarine-launched ballistic missile
SLCM	sea-launched cruise missile
SNLV	strategic nuclear launch vehicle (missiles plus long-range bombers)

Source *The Dynamics of Domestic Politics of Arms Control: The Salt II Treaty Ratification Debate*, Dan Caldwell. ©1991 by the University of South Carolina Press. Reprinted with permission of the University of South Carolina Press.

consisted of three parts: a treaty, a protocol and a statement of principles. The treaty, scheduled to remain in effect from the time it entered into force until 31 December 1985, contained nineteen articles and was seventy-eight pages long. It placed a limit of 2,400 (to be lowered to 2,250 by the end of 1981) on the number of strategic nuclear launch vehicles held by each side. Within this ceiling, no more than 1,320 ICBMs, SLBMs, and heavy bombers could be equipped with multiple independently targetable reentry vehicles or long-range cruise missiles. Within this sub-limit, no more than 1,200 ICBMs, SLBMs, or ASBMs could be MIRVed, and within this sub-limit, no more than 820 ICBMs could be MIRVed. In addition to these overall limits, the treaty contained the following additional limitations:

Ceilings on the launch weight and throw weight of light and heavy ICBMs;

A limit on the testing and deployment of one new type of ICBM;

A freeze on the number of reentry vehicles on certain types of ICBMs: a limit of 10 reentry vehicles on the one new type of ICBM permitted for each side, a limit of 14 reentry vehicles on SLBMs, and a limit of 10 reentry vehicles on air-to-surface ballistic missiles (ASBM);

A ban on the testing and deployment of air-launched cruise missiles with ranges greater than 600 kilometers on aircraft other than those counted as heavy bombers;

A ban on the construction of additional fixed ICBM launchers and on any increase in the number of fixed heavy ICBM launchers, which limited the USSR to 308 modern large ballistic missiles and the United States to zero;

A ban on heavy mobile ICBMs, heavy SLBMs and heavy ASBMs;

A ban on certain types of strategic offensive weapons not yet deployed by either side, such as ballistic missiles with ranges greater than 600 kilometers on surface ships;

An agreement to exchange data on a regular basis on the numbers of weapons deployed and limited by the treaty;

Advance notification of certain ICBM test launches; and,

A ban on ICBM systems with a capacity to reload quickly.

The second part of the SALT II agreement consisted of a protocol, scheduled to remain in effect until the end of 1981, that banned the flight testing and deployment of ICBMs from mobile launch platforms; prohibited the deployment of land-based or sea-based cruise missiles with a range of greater than 600 kilometers; and banned the testing and deployment of air-to-surface ballistic missiles.

The third part of the SALT II agreement consisted of a joint statement of principles to guide the next round of SALT negotiations.

The Soviet backfire bomber had been one of the major points of contention in the SALT II negotiations. Although limitations on the backfire were not formally part of the SALT II agreement, in a letter to President Carter accompanying the agreement, Brezhnev committed his country to produce no more than thirty planes per year and to limit the upgrading of the capabilities of the backfire. The Department of State noted that these commitments had the same legal force as the rest of the SALT II agreement and if the Soviet Union were to violate these commitments, the United States could withdraw from the treaty.

After President Carter submitted the treaty to the Senate for its advice and consent, a heated battle ensued. Three different Senate committees (Foreign Relations, Armed Services, and Select Intelligence) held hearings on the treaty. The Foreign Relations Committee by a vote of nine to six recommended that the treaty be ratified. The Armed Services Committee adopted a report highly critical of the treaty. The Intelligence Committee concluded that the treaty was "adequately verifiable."

By late August 1979, it appeared that the treaty would be ratified. In the last few days of August, however, Senator Frank Church announced that a Soviet "combat brigade" had been discovered in Cuba. Church, chairman of the Foreign Relations Committee, noted that "there is no likelihood whatever that the Senate will ratify the SALT treaty as long as Soviet combat troops are in Cuba." This imbroglio delayed consideration of the treaty, and in November a second international event intervened to complicate ratification. A group of Iranian "students" took over the U.S. embassy in Tehran and seized Americans as hostages. The hostage crisis raised questions in the minds of many Americans about the foreign policy competence of the Carter administration. Finally, in late December 1979, Soviet forces invaded Afghanistan. This event caused President Carter to withdraw the SALT II treaty from the Senate.

The SALT II treaty was never ratified; however, both the United States and the Soviet Union abided by its provisions for a number of years. Once elected president, Ronald Reagan, who had been very critical of the treaty, continued to observe its terms until late in his administration. Reagan developed a new approach to limiting strategic nuclear weapons which he called the Strategic Arms Reduction Talks (START). These negotiations, which eventually culminated in two START treaties, were the descendants of the SALT process that had begun in 1969.

DAN CALDWELL

See also Arms Control and Disarmament Agency; Baruch, Bernard Mannes; Brezhnev, Leonid Ilyich; Carter, James Earl; Hot Line Agreements; Johnson, Lyndon Baines;

Kissinger, Henry Alfred; Limited Nuclear Test Ban Treaty; Nixon, Richard Milhous; Nuclear Nonproliferation; Nuclear Weapons and Strategy; Realism; Smith, Gerard C.; Strategic Arms Reduction Treaties

FURTHER READING

Brzezinski, Zbigniew. *Power and Principle: Memoirs of the National Security Adviser 1977–1981.* New York, 1983.

Caldwell, Dan. *The Dynamics of Domestic Politics and Arms Control: The SALT II Treaty Ratification Debate.* Columbia, S.C., 1991.

Carter, Jimmy. *Keeping Faith: Memoirs of a President.* New York, 1982. Re-issued Fayetteville, Ark., 1995.

Dobrynin, Anatoly. *In Confidence: Moscow's Ambassador to America's Six Cold War Presidents.* New York, 1995.

Kissinger, Henry. *White House Years.* Boston, 1979.

Newhouse, John. *Cold Dawn: The Story of SALT.* New York, 1973. Reissued Washington, D.C., 1989.

Nixon, Richard M. *RN: The Memoirs of Richard Nixon.* New York, 1978.

Smith, Gerard C. *Doubletalk: The Story of the First Strategic Arms Limitation Talks.* New York, 1980.

Talbott, Strobe. *Endgame: The Inside Story of SALT II.* New York, 1980.

Vance, Cyrus R. *Hard Choices: Critical Years in America's Foreign Policy.* New York, 1983.

STRATEGIC ARMS REDUCTION TREATIES

Two agreements designed to reduce the numbers of long-range nuclear weapons in the arsenals of the United States and the Soviet Union. Negotiations to limit these types of weapons had begun in 1969 and culminated in the SALT I agreements of 1972 and the SALT II treaty of 1979. Negotiations to reduce the number of strategic weapons were continued under President Ronald Reagan, but no agreements on long-range weapons were concluded.

In July 1991, President George Bush and Soviet president Mikhail Gorbachev concluded the first Strategic Arms Reduction Treaty (START I), which called for a one-third reduction in the number of nuclear warheads and bombs held by the United States and the USSR. When the Soviet Union disintegrated in December 1991, the status of the START I treaty became uncertain because long-range nuclear weapons were stationed in four of the former Soviet republics: Russia, Ukraine, Belorussia, and Kazakhstan. The three non-Russian states agreed to ratify both the START I treaty and the nonproliferation treaty, and either to destroy or turn over their nuclear weapons to Russia by 1999. Belorussia and Kazakhstan complied quickly. In early 1994, following an agreement brokered by the Clinton administration and in part financed by a U.S. assistance program, Ukraine began sending its strategic nuclear weapons to Russia for dismantling and destruction. In November 1994, Ukraine ratified the nonproliferation treaty, opening the way for the two START treaties to enter force in December 1994.

In January 1993, President Bush and Russian president Boris Yeltsin signed the second Strategic Arms Reduction Treaty (START II), which called for further reductions of fifty percent in the levels of weapons called for in the START I treaty. When the START II treaty is implemented, the United States and Russia will be left with between 3,000 and 3,500 strategic nuclear weapons. On 26 January 1996, the U.S. Senate overwhelmingly approved a resolution of ratification of the START II Treaty by a vote of 87 to 4. Prior to entering into force, the treaty must be approved by both bodies of the Russian Parliament: the Council of Federation (the upper house) and the Duma (the lower house). The re-election of Yeltsin to a second presidential term in July 1996 increased the possibility of ratification of the treaty by the Russian government.

DAN CALDWELL

See also Gorbachev, Mikhail Sergeevich; Nuclear Nonproliferation; Nuclear Weapons and Strategy; Reagan, Ronald Wilson; Russia and the Soviet Union; Strategic Arms Limitation Talks and Agreements; Ukraine

FURTHER READING

Beschloss, Michael R., and Strobe Talbott. *At the Highest Levels: The Inside Story of the End of the Cold War.* Boston, 1993.

Lepingwell, John W. R. "START II and the Politics of Arms Control in Russia." *International Security* 20 (Fall 1995): 63–91.

U.S. Arms Control and Disarmament Agency. *Arms Control and Disarmament Agreements: The Treaty between the United States of America and the Union of the Soviet Socialist Republics on the Reduction and Limitation of Strategic Offensive Arms.* Washington D.C., 1991.

STRATEGIC DEFENSE INITIATIVE

President Ronald Reagan's idea to develop active space-based defenses against nuclear attack. Dramatically announced by Reagan during a televised address on defense policy on 23 March 1983, Strategic Defense Initiative (SDI) became the rubric for a variety of projects, some already underway, others newly initiated. To coordinate the projects, the Strategic Defense Initiative Office (SDIO) was created in the Department of Defense, with additional support from the Department of Energy. Assigned special priority, SDI became the Pentagon's single most expensive research and development program.

In appealing for public approval, President Reagan expressed the hope that SDI would make nuclear weapons "impotent and obsolete" and replace reliance on "mutual assured destruction" with a new concept called "assured survival." Although, in his address, he

STRATEGIC ARMS REDUCTION TREATIES

START I
(signed July 31, 1991)

Maximum number of Strategic Nuclear Launch Vehicles (ICBMs, SLBMs, and long-range bombers)		1,600
Maximum accountable warheads		6,000
- Of these, the maximum number allowed to be deployed on ballistic missiles		4,900
Maximum number of air-launched cruise missiles (ALCMs) permitted on each long-range bomber	US:	20
	Russia:	16
Maximum number of modern, large ballistic ("heavy") missiles	US:	0
	Russia:	154
- Of these, the maximum number of warheads allowed to be deployed on each		10
Maximum number of warheads allowed to be deployed on mobile ICBMs		1,110
Maximum aggregate ballistic missile throw-weight on mobile ICBMs (in metric tons)		3,600
Maximum number of non-deployed mobile ICBMs		250
Maximum number of non-deployed ICBM launchers		110

START II
(signed January 3, 1993)

	Phase I[1]	Phase II[2]
Maximum number of deployed warheads	3,800-4,250	3,000-3,500
- Of these, maximum number to be deployed on SLBMs	2,160	1,700-1,750
- Of these, maximum number to be deployed on MIRVed ICBMs	1,200	
- Of these, maximum number to be deployed on SS-18 (Russia only)	650	

Ban on testing and deployment of land-based MIRVed missiles.

Provisions concerning the Russian modern, large ballistic missiles (SS-18):

- 90 silos may be converted to launch smaller SS-25 ICBMs
- 64 silos must be destroyed
- All non-deployed SS-18 ICBMs and their launch canisters must be destroyed

A maximum of 100 long-range ("heavy") bombers may be exempted from START II limits.

[1]Phase I of the treaty must be completed seven years after the entry into force of the START II Treaty.
[2]Phase II of the treaty must be completed no later than January 1, 2003, or no later than December 31, 2000, if the US and Russia reach a formal agreement within one year after START II enters into force committing the US to help finance the elimination of strategic offensive arms in Russia.

claimed to have the endorsement of the Joint Chiefs of Staff, he had in fact only discussed such a project with the chiefs in very general terms. Nor had he raised the question in advance with the members of his cabinet, his science adviser, and the civilians in charge of advanced weapons development in the Department of Defense, probably because he anticipated a negative reaction. Instead, he relied on the encouragement of an informal "kitchen cabinet" of old friends, aided by a few technological enthusiasts, among whom the most prominent were the physicist Edward Teller and his protégé at the Lawrence Livermore National Laboratory, Lowell Wood.

Supporters of SDI had differing priorities. Lieutenant General (USA retired) Daniel O. Graham's Washington-based "High Frontier" lobby urged near-term deployment of a space-based defense using off-the-shelf kinetic energy weapons (rocket-driven projectiles) so as to seize the "high ground" of space before the Soviets. A Department of Defense–appointed technical committee recommended investigating the feasibility of a "layered" ground-based and space-based defense employing sensors, battle management satellites, and both kinetic energy and more exotic directed-energy weapons (including chemically-fueled and other lasers). Teller, who thought space-based weapons too vulnerable to countermeasures, favored the use of ground-based Anti-Ballistic Missiles (ABMs) and of the proposed X-ray laser, to be "popped up" from submarines close enough to Soviet launch sites to destroy missiles in boost phase. The projected space deployments inspired journalists to dub the program "Star Wars" after a popular Hollywood film.

The rationales offered on behalf of SDI also were varied. General James A. Abrahamson, SDIO's first director, saw both near-term and long-term benefits. It would provide cost-effective technologies capable of nullifying the Soviet offensive threat to the survival of U.S. retaliatory forces, serve as a hedge against a potential Soviet break-out from the ABM Treaty to deploy a national ground-based defense, and determine whether an effective multilayered defense might be developed for future deployment. It also might help, he thought, to persuade the Soviet leaders to accept a more stable strategic posture in which both sides would rely primarily on defensive capabilities. Some strategic supporters favored the program because it could provide "intermediate" tactical defenses useful against theater attack. Tactical ABMs, they argued, would make NATO's pledge to defend Western Europe more credible by eliminating the need to respond to a major Soviet attack in Europe, either conventional or nuclear, with a nuclear attack upon the Soviet Union. Others thought that the superpowers were in an unannounced race to militarize space, and that whichever side succeeded first would gain at least temporary military superiority. Robert C. McFarlane, who headed the small sub-group within the National Security Council that drafted the announcement, asserted that SDI had been given a radical goal in order to "stress the Soviet system." McFarlane subsequently credited SDI with significantly contributing to the Soviet Union's willingness to negotiate arms control and to the collapse of Soviet communism.

The program aroused criticism on legal, technical, economic, and political grounds. Those who had served as U.S. negotiators of the 1972 ABM Treaty disputed the claim of the Department of State's legal adviser that a "legally correct" interpretation of the treaty permitted testing of technologies not contemplated when the treaty was signed, agreeing instead with the Soviet view that the treaty banned all testing of ABMs in space, including those weapons anticipated by SDI. Most technical experts doubted that any conceivable shield would be robust or reliable enough to absorb a massive attack, especially since the system could not be tested in advance but would have to work perfectly the first time it

would be needed. They also argued that it would be vulnerable to less expensive countermeasures and could be evaded by low-trajectory and air-breathing delivery systems. Several years into the program, an ad hoc committee of the American Physical Society was allowed to examine the results of research on directed-energy technologies and concluded that an informed decision as to whether any of these technologies would yield effective and "survivable" weapons would not be possible for at least another decade. NATO Allies complained that SDI would be destabilizing because it would induce the Soviets to add offensive capacity and rule out further progress in arms control. Arms control advocates denounced it as a brazen political hoax, aimed at stealing the peace issue from the nuclear freeze campaign in order to quell opposition to a military buildup. Many critics argued that SDI would only extend the arms race into space, at enormous cost, without diminishing the need to rely on deterrence by nuclear retaliation, merely repeating the folly of previous "last moves" in the arms race. In response to McFarlane's claim, critics argued that the downfall of the Soviet Union derived primarily from internal factors and that SDI may actually have delayed the Soviet decision to accept arms reductions by enabling the Soviet military to cite it as fresh evidence of a relentless American drive for strategic superiority.

Reagan's reelection in 1984, by a convincing margin and after a campaign in which SDI had been hotly debated, served to override opposition; but, as the technical prospects remained unpromising and the national debt rose alarmingly, skeptics in Congress sought to restrain SDI's budget, which totaled $4 billion a year until fiscal 1990, when support sank to $3 billion. The SDIO tried to stave off looming demise by proposing early deployment of a "Phase I" system, but Congress balked at the projected cost. The new willingness of the Soviet leadership under President Mikhail Gorbachev to negotiate arms reduction made early deployment seem altogether inadvisable.

Iraq's use of Scud missiles in the Persian Gulf War of 1990–1991, against U.S. forces based in Saudi Arabia and in attacks on cities in Israel, reinforced support previously expressed in Congress, notably by Senator Samuel Nunn, Democrat of Georgia, chairman of the Senate Armed Services Committee, for ground-based defenses capable of intercepting a small salvo of ICBMs, whether deliberately or accidentally launched, and of tactical ABMs to protect against short-range missiles. During the Bush administration, then, SDI was reoriented to stress reactivation, as early as 2001, of the 100 single-warhead ABMs previously deployed in North Dakota and allowed under the ABM Treaty. (If the treaty were renegotiated or renounced, five more ABM batteries would be deployed at other sites, providing a large enough "footprint" to protect much of continental United States from a small attack.) Emphasis also was placed on developing ground-based tactical Theater High-Altitude Area Defense (THAAD).

In May 1993, the Clinton administration's first secretary of defense, Les Aspin, declared the "Star Wars" era at an end. He changed the name of the SDIO to the "Ballistic Missile Defense Organization" (BMDO) and demoted it in the Pentagon hierarchy. The SDIO had reported directly to the secretary of defense; the BMDO was to report to the undersecretary for acquisition and technology. At the same time, Aspin lowered the agency's budgetary expectations. His predecessor, Dick Cheney, had requested $6.8 billion in 1994 to support near-term development and deployment of ballistic missile defenses. Aspin proposed a $3.8 billion budget for 1994 to be used first of all to acquire systems capable of intercepting short-range missiles, not ICBMs. As a secondary priority, the agency would supervise continued research on ground-based and space-based ballistic missile defenses—including "brilliant eyes" (space sensors to track missiles) and "brilliant pebbles"—small, relatively cheap pods containing kinetic-energy weapons, each equipped with sensors, guidance, and propellant, to be permanently orbited in large numbers so as to be available for boost-phase interception virtually anywhere, any time.

Thus, a decade after Reagan's announcement and after the expenditure of some $30 billion, the program survived, but without its original grandiose design, its high profile, or the central place it had in strategic and foreign policy considerations under Ronald Reagan. Whether active defenses are actually deployed in the future will depend, as in the past, not only on technological feasibility, but also on threat perceptions, estimates of the effectiveness of techniques of evasion, and willingness to bear the high costs of promised but uncertain benefits.

SANFORD LAKOFF

See also Antiballistic Missile Treaty; Cold War; Gulf War of 1990–1991; Nuclear Weapons and Strategy; Reagan, Ronald Wilson; Teller, Edward

FURTHER READING

Boffey, Philip M., ed. *Claiming the Heavens: the New York Times Complete Guide to the Star Wars Debate.* New York, 1988.
Broad, Wiiliam J. *Teller's War: The Top-Secret Story Behind the Star Wars Deception.* New York, 1992.
Brown, Harold, ed. *The Strategic Defense Initiative: Shield or Snare?* Boulder, Colo., 1987.
Daalder, Ivo H. *The SDI Challenge to Europe.* Cambridge, Mass., 1987.
Hoffman, Fred S., Albert Wohlstetter, and David S. Yost, eds. *Swords and Shields: NATO, The USSR, and New Choices for Long-Range Offense and Defense.* Lexington, Mass., 1987.
Lakoff, Sanford, and Herbert F. York. *A Shield in Space? Technology, Politics, and the Strategic Defense Initiative.* Berkeley, Calif., 1989.
Lakoff, Sanford, and Randy Willoughby, eds. *Strategic Defense and the Western Alliance.* Lexington, Mass., 1987.
Payne, Keith B., John Kohout, and Willis Stanley. *Missile Defense in the 21st Century: Protection Against Limited Threats, Including Lessons from the Gulf War.* Boulder, Colo., 1991.

STRAUSS, LEWIS

(*b.* 31 January 1896; *d.* 21 January 1974)

Investment banker, conservative Republican, and an important architect of U.S. nuclear energy and weapons policies. Strauss was born in Charleston, West Virginia. In 1917 he volunteered to work without pay for Herbert Hoover, then chairman of the Food Administration. Despite the limitation of just a high school education, Strauss rose quickly to private secretary, a position that allowed him to be helpful to powerful people such as Felix Warburg, who was leading the Joint Distribution Committee's efforts to save Eastern European Jewry from the ravages of World War I. In 1919, Warburg rewarded Strauss with a job at his investment banking firm, Kuhn, Loeb & Company, a position that quickly made Strauss a wealthy man.

A longtime member of the naval reserves, Strauss rose to the rank of admiral during World War II, serving first with the Bureau of Ordnance and then as special assistant to fellow investment banker Secretary of the Navy James Forrestal. It was during the last year of the war, as a member of Forrestal's staff, that Strauss became involved with atomic energy planning and research. Though opposed to the use of atomic weapons on Hiroshima and Nagasaki, he nevertheless became a relentless advocate of a nuclear weapons buildup against the Soviet Union.

In 1948 President Harry S. Truman appointed Strauss a commissioner to the newly formed Atomic Energy Commission (AEC). Until he resigned in 1950, Strauss fought doggedly for more and bigger atomic weapons, increased efforts to detect Soviet nuclear tests, stricter security measures, and corporate control over the nuclear power industry. In August 1949, in response to the Soviet Union's development of atomic weapons, Strauss became the Truman administration's most aggressive advocate for a crash program to develop the hydrogen bomb.

In 1953, with Dwight D. Eisenhower's election to the presidency, Strauss returned to the AEC as chairman, determined to pursue the policies he had earlier advocated. Discounting the effects of radioactive fallout, he aggressively increased atmospheric nuclear testing with devastating consequences for many people in both the Pacific and the American West. Long suspicious of the liberal politics of physicist J. Robert Oppenheimer, "father of the atomic bomb"—but in 1949 an opponent of the hydrogen bomb program—Strauss encouraged, supported, and directed the successful effort of conservatives throughout the government to destroy Oppenheimer's influence. His victory over Oppenheimer in 1954 led in 1958 to an ironic and bitter end to his government career when liberals in Congress blocked his confirmation as secretary of commerce.

MARTIN J. SHERWIN

See also Atomic Energy Commission; Hydrogen Bomb; Nuclear Weapons and Strategy

FURTHER READING

Pfau, Richard. *No Sacrifice Too Great: The Life of Lewis L. Strauss.* Charlottesville, Va., 1984.
Stern, Philip M. *The Oppenheimer Case: Security on Trial.* New York, 1969.
Strauss, Lewis L. *Men and Decisions.* New York, 1962.

STRAUSS, ROBERT

(*b.* 19 October 1918)

Influential political consultant, special adviser to President Jimmy Carter, and ambassador to the Soviet Union and Russia (1991–1992). Born in Lockhart, Texas, he began practicing law in 1941. He first came to national prominence as a political campaign manager and fundraiser for the Democratic Party during the 1968 presidential race. After Carter's election in 1976, Strauss became special representative for trade negotiations and later acted as the president's personal representative in the second round of Middle East peace talks in 1979. After Carter's defeat in the 1980 election he returned to his prominent Washington law practice. Strauss reentered the diplomatic arena in 1991 as President George Bush's ambassador to the Soviet Union, and he continued as ambassador to Russia after the Soviet Union's collapse, a post he relinquished in November 1992. Thereafter he lobbied for aid to Russia and for increased U.S. investment in Russian industries.

SHANE J. MADDOCK

See also Carter, James Earl; Russia and the Soviet Union

FURTHER READING

Beschloss, Michael R., and Strobe Talbott. *At the Highest Levels: The Inside Story of the End of the Cold War.* Boston, 1993.
Smith, Gaddis. *Morality, Reason, and Power: American Diplomacy in the Carter Years.* New York, 1986.

STRONG, JOSIAH

(*b.* 19 January 1847; *d.* 28 April 1916)

Congregational minister, social gospel reformer, and enthusiast for U.S. expansion, whose ideas reached a wide audience. Born in Illinois and later active in Ohio, Strong won instant national prominence with the publication in 1885 of his first book, *Our Country.* Strong's primary concern was to inspire a sense of Christian social responsibility at home. In a chapter on "The Anglo-Saxon and the World's Future," however, he celebrated the spread of British and U.S. political and religious influence around the globe. He extolled U.S. citizens as superior Anglo-Saxons and wrote that the world would soon "enter upon a new stage of its history—*the final competition of the races, for which the Anglo-Saxon is being schooled*…this power race will move down upon Mexico, Central, and South America, out upon the islands of the sea, over upon Africa and beyond. And can anyone doubt that the result…will be the 'survival of the fittest'?" Strong worked to collect funds for Christian missionary activities abroad as part of his objective to spread U.S. civilization overseas.

The presence of Darwinistic thinking in *Our Country* reflects the ideology of the times. Although some historians have stressed his expansionist views, Strong's contemporaries reacted primarily to his views on domestic affairs. A number of commentators nonetheless continue to highlight a small part of his writing to characterize and criticize the nature of American imperialism.

GADDIS SMITH

See also Missionaries; Race and Racism

FURTHER READING

Field, James A., Jr. "American Imperialism: The Worst Chapter in Almost Any Book." *American Historical Review* 83 (June 1978): 844–83.
Mueller, Dorothea R. "Josiah Strong and American Nationalism: A Reevaluation." *Journal of American History* 53 (December 1966): 487–503.
Strong, Josiah. *Expansion under New World-Conditions.* Edited by Ralph E. Weber. New York, 1971.

STUART, JOHN LEIGHTON

(*b.* 24 June 1876; *d.* 18 September 1962)

Missionary educator and U.S. ambassador to China (1946–1949). Born in Hangzhou, China, the son of Southern Presbyterian missionaries, Stuart was educated at Hampden-Sydney College in Virginia. Ordained in the Southern Presbyterian Church, he returned in 1904 to China as a missionary. In 1919 Stuart was named president of Yenching University in Beijing, which under his direction became China's most distinguished Protestant educational institution. Many future leaders, Nationalists as well as Communists, were students there. The founding of Harvard-Yenching Institute in 1928 spurred the study of China in the United States.

When Japan encroached upon China in the 1930s, Stuart used every means at his disposal to encourage U.S. assistance to China, backing Stanley K. Hornbeck of the Department of State in his hardline strategy toward Japan. After the Japanese occupation of northern and coastal China in 1937, Stuart acted as an intermediary, carrying various Japanese peace proposals to the Nationalists in Chongqing. After the Japanese attack on Pearl Harbor in December 1941, Stuart was subject to house arrest for the duration of the war.

In July 1946, President Harry S. Truman named Stuart ambassador to China, at the instigation of General George C. Marshall. The general was in China to facilitate the nation's peaceful unification and thus avoid a debilitating civil war between the Nationalists and the Communists. Marshall hoped that Stuart would persuade Jiang Jieshi (Chiang Kai-shek) to compromise. During the prolonged negotiations, in which Stuart played a direct role, the missionary's sympathy for Jiang became obvious. By mid-1946, however, little hope remained that full-scale civil war could be avoided. When Marshall returned to the United States to become secretary of state, he retained Stuart as ambassador.

Through 1947 and most of 1948 Stuart pressed Washington to expand its aid to Jiang's Nationalist government. Marshall had become convinced, however, that corruption and misrule so characterized the Nationalist regime that such assistance would be squandered. In late 1948, when Stuart foresaw Nationalist defeat, he unsuccessfully urged Washington to work for a coalition government of Nationalists and Communists. In May 1949, Communist armies swept across the Yangtze River. Stuart remained in Nanjing, hoping to initiate contact with the Communist leadership, which, in turn, assigned Huang Hua, a Yenching graduate, to deal with Stuart. On June 28, Huang told Stuart that Mao Zedong and Zhou Enlai would welcome his informal visit to Beijing. On 1 July, however, Secretary of State Dean Acheson instructed Stuart that his proposed trip had been considered at the "highest level" and was to be canceled. There was to be no early accommodation with the Chinese Communists. In August 1949 Stuart returned to the United States and soon suffered a stroke, which kept him bedridden until his death in 1962.

EDMUND S. WEHRLE

See also Acheson, Dean Gooderham; Hornbeck, Stanley Kuhl; Jiang Jieshi; Marshall, George Catlett, Jr.; Missionaries; Sino-Japanese War; Truman, Harry S.

FURTHER READING

Brewer, John C., and Kenneth W. Rea, eds. *The Forgotten Ambassador: The Reports of John Leighton Stuart, 1946–1949*. Boulder, Colo., 1981.
Shaw, Yu-ming. *An American Missionary in China: John Leighton Stuart and Chinese-American Relations*. Cambridge, Mass., 1992.
Stuart, John Leighton. *Fifty Years in China: The Memoirs of John Leighton Stuart, Missionary and Ambassador*. New York, 1954.

SUBMARINE-LAUNCHED BALLISTIC MISSILE

See Nuclear Weapons and Strategy; Submarine Warfare

SUBMARINE WARFARE

Naval action in which manned submersible craft are used. The practice can be traced back at least to the Revolutionary War. Connecticut inventor David Bushnell's one-person, hand-powered submersible *Turtle* conducted an unsuccessful attack on a British warship in New York Harbor in 1776. By the mid-nineteenth century two distinct forms of undersea weapons had evolved: unmanned systems, initially called "torpedoes" but later "mines," and manned systems called "submarines." The term "submarine warfare" generically can refer to either, but in common usage has come to refer only to conflict involving manned submersibles.

Submarine warfare has often and substantially intersected with U.S. foreign relations. The Confederacy turned to submarines in a desperate attempt to break the Union blockade of southern ports during the Civil War (1861–1865). The German submarine campaign against Allied commerce during World War I (1914–1918) drove President Woodrow Wilson to resist the German policy diplomatically for two years and finally to ask Congress to declare war on Germany in April 1917. The German submarine campaign against Allied and neutral commerce during World War II (1939–1945) provided an excuse for President Franklin D. Roosevelt to issue "shoot-on-sight" orders to U.S. antisubmarine patrols months before the formal declaration of war by Germany on the United States in December 1941. The U.S. campaign of unrestricted submarine warfare against Japanese commerce initiated immediately after the attack on Pearl Harbor in December 1941 played a major role in the defeat of Japan and marked a complete change in U.S. policy from that of World War I. During the Cold War (1945–1989) Soviet and U.S. submarines became a key factor in the global balance of power, first in regard to the attack and defense of the North Atlantic Treaty Organization's (NATO's) vital North Atlantic sea lanes and after 1959 both as platforms for submarine-launched ballistic missiles (SLBMs) and as primary hunters of those platforms. U.S. submarines also made an early post–Cold War combat appearance on the international stage when they launched cruise missiles with conventional warheads against Iraq during Operation Desert Storm and its aftermath (1991–1994).

The Confederate States of America, unable to match the overwhelmingly superior maritime resources of the Union, quickly recognized that qualitative superiority resulting from technological innovation was its only hope of breaking the blockade of southern ports proclaimed by the Union in April 1861. Over the next four years the Confederate Navy pioneered the development of the ironclad surface warship, the mine, and the submarine, all in a vain attempt to counteract the quantitative Federal advantage. Attacks by Confederate submarines damaged several blockading ships, but their only sinking was that of the U.S.S. *Housatonic* off Charleston by the C.S.S. *Hunley* in 1864.

More aggressive development of the submarine by the South might have broken the blockade and taken the Confederacy nearer to independence, but the South lacked the maritime engineers and industrial capability to develop and construct an effective submarine force while meeting other demands on its resources. The *Hunley* and her sister ships were improvised out of desperation. The forced pace of development ensured that far more Southern submariners than Union blockaders died as necessity pushed the Confederacy to deploy in combat a weapons system that remained experimental. The results were a few Union casualties and a hint of the future, but the blockade itself was never jeopardized.

Despite the steady development of technology between 1865 and 1914, few naval or political leaders regarded the submarine as useful for anything but coastal defense as World War I began. International conferences at The Hague (1899 and 1907) and London (1908–1909) had considered various aspects of war at sea in great detail but had ignored the possibility of submarine attacks on merchant vessels. In Great Britain a retired First Sea Lord, Admiral Sir John Fisher, raised this concern privately within the Admiralty, pointing out Great Britain's vulnerability to such operations, but his warnings were dismissed by First Lord of the Admiralty Winston Churchill. The contempt of senior naval officers in all nations for the possibilities of undersea warfare was epitomized in 1913 by the British admiral who, informed during war games that his flagship had been torpedoed by a submarine, signaled an obscenity to its commander while continuing to steam full speed ahead.

World War I

The U.S. government shared this dismissive attitude. As a result, it had submarines to defend U.S. coastlines but no established policy toward submarine warfare directed against commerce when Germany announced on 4 February 1915 that its submarines would attack Allied merchant shipping in a war zone around Great Britain. President Woodrow Wilson, on 10 February, after only pro forma consultation with the Departments of the State and the Navy, nevertheless sent Berlin an ultimatum. The document stated that the United States would hold Germany to "a strict accountability" for any damage to U.S. ships, lives, or property from submarine attacks in violation of international law as his government defined it.

In essence, Wilson insisted that Germany conduct all warfare against commerce, surface or submarine, according to the rules adopted during the sailing-ship era. Attacks without warning would not be tolerated. A submarine was obligated to visit and search the merchant vessel in order to determine if it carried contraband or was otherwise liable to capture. The submarine could sink the prize only after its passengers and crew, and especially any passengers of neutral citizenship, had been removed to safety. Because a submarine that surfaced to conduct such an inspection might be rammed or sunk by concealed guns, and because even the largest submarine could hardly take on board any substantial number of prisoners, Wilson in effect was stating that the United States would not permit any submarine attacks against Allied merchant shipping because such attacks might endanger U.S. lives or property.

The key test of U.S. resolve to resist the new German policy came on 7 May 1915, when a U-boat sank the British liner *Lusitania*, on a voyage from New York to Liverpool, off the Irish coast. More than a thousand lives were lost, 128 of them American. The ship was a Royal Navy auxiliary, sailing under Admiralty orders to ram enemy submarines on sight and carrying American-made munitions to the British army. The Germans claimed that the *Lusitania* had been armed, although both the British and American governments denied that charge. Wilson demanded that Germany apologize for its illegal act, pay an indemnity for the lost U.S. lives, and refrain from any actions in violation of existing international law as he defined it. Secretary of State William Jennings Bryan, who believed the president's stance to be justified neither as law nor as policy, resigned in June 1915 rather than sign the ultimatum. After a long debate, Berlin agreed to pay the indemnity and rein in its submarine commanders.

The *Lusitania* incident set the tone for the next two years. Wilson insisted that Germany abandon its most effective naval weapon, submarine attacks against Allied commerce; the Germans attempted to conduct as effective a submarine campaign as possible without driving the United States into the war. A modus vivendi seemed possible at times. In 1915 Washington proposed that Germany abandon submarine warfare in return for lifting

Great Britain's blockade of foodstuffs. A year later Secretary of State Robert Lansing seemed willing to admit the German contentions that armed Allied merchant ships could legitimately be attacked without warning and that it was the obligation of a neutral country to keep its citizens off such ships. Ultimately, however, for leaders in both nations, the issue went beyond such technicalities of international law. Wilson, for reasons of politics and national security, was not prepared to modify substantially his initial rejection of submarine warfare against commerce. The German government, motivated by similar considerations, was unwilling to lose the war as the price for peace with the United States.

On 9 January 1917 Berlin's patience ran out. Germany initiated unrestricted submarine warfare, a policy of sinking all Allied and neutral merchant ships in Allied waters, effective 1 February. Wilson asked Congress on 2 April to declare war on Germany. He explained that the U.S. would fight for many reasons, but he identified German submarine attacks on commerce in violation of neutral rights as the primary *casus belli*. By the armistice on 11 November 1918 German U-boats had sunk more than 12,000,000 Gross Register Tons (GRT) of Allied and neutral shipping, approximately 7,000,000 after the United States entered into the war.

The near-success of the German campaign made the submarine a focus of naval attention throughout the interwar period. At the Washington Conference on Limitation of Naval Armaments (1921–1922), the British government suggested a permanent ban on submarines and pressed to outlaw submarine warfare against commerce. The U.S. Navy, its eyes already on the value of submarine commerce raiding in a possible war with Japan, was ambivalent, and French determination to retain full use of the submarine for a possible future war against Great Britain effectively killed the British proposal. The London Naval Disarmament Conference (1930) established a submarine tonnage limit of 52,700 tons for the U.S., British, and Japanese navies, a limit Great Britain agreed to extend to the German navy by a separate treaty in 1935. Despite much talk, many treaties, and considerable war planning, however, the military value and legal status of the submarine remained in dispute when World War II began in 1939.

During the interwar period many U.S. citizens became convinced that Bryan had been correct when he argued after the *Lusitania* sinking that Wilson's insistence on maintaining eighteenth-century maritime rights in the face of twentieth-century technology had not served the national interest. U.S. intervention in World War I had therefore been a mistake. Because of this widespread view, the Congress passed a series of neutrality acts during the 1930s that attempted to prevent future entanglements by extending de facto legitimacy to submarine warfare against commerce. The laws forbade both entry of U.S. merchant ships into war zones and travel by U.S. citizens on belligerent ships.

World War II

President Franklin D. Roosevelt accepted these limitations reluctantly, but he did not challenge them when war broke out again in Europe. Instead, he set out to aid the Allies and to involve the United States in the war against Nazi Germany by other means. The U.S. Navy initiated antisubmarine patrols to protect the neutrality of the American continents in September 1939, at first for a distance of 300 miles from the coast. Early in 1941 FDR extended his definition of the Americas to include Greenland and then Iceland. U.S. destroyers patrolled the northwest Atlantic, escorting convoys to Iceland and notifying British forces of U-boat locations. Inevitably clashes developed, despite Adolf Hitler's orders for his commanders to avoid provocation, beginning with the U.S.S. *Greer* and the *U-652* on 4 September. For the next three months the two navies fought a bloody undeclared war, with submarines and destroyers attacking each other on sight and the Germans sinking U.S. as well as Allied ships without warning.

The United States and Germany continued to fight their undeclared conflict in the North Atlantic, and only Pearl Harbor induced Berlin to make the war official. The German U-boats ultimately would sink almost 15,000,000 GRTs of Allied and neutral shipping, for a loss of 781 submarines. Final U.S. abandonment of Wilsonian definitions of maritime law came after Germany's surrender, with the dropping of war crimes charges based on the waging of unrestricted submarine warfare against German submarine force commander Admiral Karl Doenitz. By 1945 the United States not only recognized such warfare as legitimate, but had itself mounted the most successful submarine campaign in history against Japan.

Although the U.S. Navy had been ambivalent about Wilson's rejection of submarine warfare against commerce during World War I and about the British proposal to outlaw such warfare in 1921, strategic planning during the interwar period had convinced naval strategists that Japan was uniquely vulnerable to submarine blockade. Long before the Neutrality Acts of the mid-1930s established that a neutral United States would not challenge belligerent use of submarines against commerce, naval planners targeted the Japanese merchant marine as a special objective of the U.S. submarine force in any future conflict.

These plans went into operation immediately following the attack on Pearl Harbor, on orders of the chief of naval operations. Over the next four years U.S. submarines sank tankers, passenger liners, freighters, ferries, fishing vessels, and every other enemy commercial vessel they could destroy. The Japanese high command considered this policy barbaric and made no attempt to deploy its own submarines against U.S. commerce. Japan lost the war, in large measure because U.S. submarines strangled the imperial supply lines carrying oil, rice, rubber, and other vital raw materials from Southeast Asia to Japan. The Japanese merchant fleet began the war with approximately 6,000,000 GRTs of shipping; over the next four years U.S. submarines sank 5,300,000 GRTs with a loss of fifty-two U.S. subs. The U.S. Navy ironically accomplished what its Confederate, imperial German, and Nazi enemies had been unable to do: win a decisive victory by submarine warfare.

The Cold War and After

The end of World War II and the beginning of the Cold War (1945–1989) changed the role of the submarine from combatant to deterrent but did not reduce its importance. The demonstrated vulnerability of NATO's transatlantic supply lines and the availability of captured German technology such as the snorkel led the Soviet Union to make a substantial investment in submarines after 1945. The U.S. Navy and its NATO Allies responded by developing hunter-killer teams to protect their precious convoys, teams that by the late 1950s were spearheaded by U.S. nuclear attack submarines developed by Admiral Hyman Rickover. The Soviets quickly deployed nuclear attack submarines of their own, further escalating the arms race but maintaining a balance of power.

Another, far more dangerous escalation began in 1959, when the United States commissioned the U.S.S. *George Washington*, a nuclear submarine carrying sixteen *Polaris* missiles with 1,500-mile range and thermonuclear warheads. For the next thirty years the United States and the Soviet Union would develop and deploy ever bigger submarines carrying longer range missiles with more destructive warheads. Both sides also would develop and deploy ever more silent and deadly attack submarines to hunt and kill the SLBM platforms. By 1982 SLBMs would account for over half of the total U.S. warheads available for a nuclear exchange. The SLBM became the third element, along with manned bombers and land-based intercontinental ballistic missiles, of the strategic "triad" on which U.S. and Soviet strategic arms control negotiators based their calculations for SALT I (1972), the Vladivostok agreements (1974), and other accords.

Despite the enormous U.S. and Soviet investment in submarines after 1945, the ships remained in the role of mutual deterrent throughout the Cold War. During the Cuban Missile Crisis (1962) U.S. anti-submarine forces harassed Soviet subs far more aggressively than President John Kennedy authorized, but the patience and professionalism of the Soviet commanders prevented a clash.

Submarines from the two nations have collided during exercises, but the frequency, seriousness, and number of lives lost in these "accidents" remain highly classified.

U.S. submarines resumed their combat role, however, by launching *Tomahawk* cruise missiles at Iraq during Operation Desert Storm and its aftermath (1991–1994). This ability to approach an enemy coast undetected and to strike with conventionally armed cruise missiles against heavily defended targets with minimal warning and remarkable accuracy indicates that the importance of "submarine warfare" to U.S. foreign relations is likely to continue well into the twenty-first century.

JOHN W. COOGAN

See also American Civil War; Cold War; Cuban Missile Crisis; Gulf War of 1990–1991; Nuclear Weapons and Strategy; Strategic Arms Limitation Talks and Agreements; Washington Conference on the Limitation of Armaments; World War I; World War II

FURTHER READING
Arnett, Eric H. *Sea-Launched Cruise Missiles and U.S. Security*. New York, 1991.
Birnbaum, Karl E. *Peace Moves and U-Boat Warfare*. Stockholm, 1958.
Devlin, Patrick B. *Too Proud to Fight: Woodrow Wilson's Neutrality*. New York, 1975.
Doerries, Reinhard R. *Imperial Challenge*. Translated by Christa D. Shannon. Chapel Hill, N.C., 1989.
Grunawalt, Richard J., editor. *The Law of Naval Warfare: Targeting Enemy Merchant Shipping*. Newport, R.I., 1993.
Manson, Janet M. *Diplomatic Ramifications of Unrestricted Submarine Warfare, 1939–1941*. New York, 1990.
Morison, Samuel Eliot. *History of United States Naval Operations in World War II*. Vol. 1, *Battle of the Atlantic*; Vol. 4, *Coral Sea, Midway, and Submarine Actions*. Boston, 1975.
Roland, Alex. *Underwater Warfare in the Age of Sail*. Bloomington, Ind., 1978.
Spinardi, Graham. *From Polaris to Trident*. New York, 1994.

SUDAN

Republic located in northeast Africa, bordering on the Red Sea, Ethiopia, Kenya, Uganda, Zaire, Central African Republic, Chad, Libya, and Egypt. Relations between the United States and Sudan, the largest country in Africa, have been largely shaped by that country's internal conflicts. Great Britain's rule, from 1898 through 1955, exacerbated differences between the northern and southern regions of the country; these differences have persisted and periodically have destabilized Sudanese governments. Since 1983 the country has been torn by a brutal civil war, in which the northern Muslims have sought to force Islam and Islamic law on the southern, heavily Christian population.

Sudan broke off diplomatic relations with the United States after the 1967 Arab-Israeli war, and turned increasingly to socialist and communist countries for aid and assistance. Ties with the United States were reestablished in 1971, and the relationship warmed considerably during the following decade. A coup in 1985, however, created a radical new Sudanese government that emphasized non-alignment over Western connections. The Khartoum government came to be dominated by Hasan al-Turabi, leader of the National Islamic Front. Under Al-Turabi Sudan allied itself with Iran and other radical states and movements, and was widely believed to have become a principal supporter of terrorism. In 1993 the Clinton administration put Sudan on the U.S. sanctions list for state sponsors of terrorism. While U.S. policy recognized Sudan's strategic importance, friendlier relations must await greater political stability and more substantial democratization efforts.

CATHERINE ELKINS

See also Africa; Middle East; Terrorism

FURTHER READING

Khalid, M. *Nimeiri and the Revolution of Dis-May*. London, 1985.
Sylvester, Anthony. *Sudan under Nimieri*. London, 1977.
Woodward, Peter. *Sudan, 1898-1989: The Unstable State*. Boulder, Colo., 1989.

SUEZ CRISIS

A defining moment of the Cold War and of Western relations with the Middle East. The Suez crisis of 1956 revealed the inability of Great Britain and France to function as independent actors, and the tenuousness of London's rule over its empire. In the aftermath of the crisis the United States acknowledged that it had no alternative but to take a leading, exposed role in Middle Eastern affairs. The Soviet Union demonstrated its intention to make the Middle East a key battleground in the bipolar struggle for global influence. Both Egypt and Israel proved their autonomy and their ability to bedevil the plans of larger nations. The Suez crisis also illustrated the strengths and weaknesses of economic diplomacy.

Origins: Great Britain, the United States, and the Aswan Dam

At the end of the Second World War the British government had no intention of renouncing its empire. Indian independence, which came in 1947, seemed a separate act, which, rather than presaging a continued trend, deepened the focus of the British foreign office on the Middle East, a crucial source of oil as well as an important strategic location. When the British government agreed in October 1954 to evacuate the massive Suez Canal base, Foreign Minister Anthony Eden assumed that this concession would lead to improved relations

with the Egyptian government led by Gamal Abdel Nasser, a thirty-six-year-old former army officer.

In order to woo Nasser, in 1955 the British government, together with private British and German firms, proposed to build a high dam at Aswan for the Egyptian government. This construction project had become a top priority for Nasser, who sought new sources for irrigation and hydroelectric power. But the continued British financial plight made it impossible for London to fund this undertaking on its own. By the end of World War II Great Britain had become virtually bankrupt and British solvency always remained questionable. Eden, now prime minister, and his foreign secretary Harold Macmillan, decided to approach the only source of the available money, the United States, both directly and through the World Bank, the Bretton Woods institution designed to sponsor large capital construction projects.

President Dwight D. Eisenhower, Secretary of State John Foster Dulles, and Secretary of the Treasury George Humphrey initially demonstrated little enthusiasm. Opinion in Washington suddenly changed in September 1955 when Nasser announced that the Soviet Union through Czechoslovakia had agreed to provide MiG fighters, Ilyushin bombers, and Stalin tanks in exchange for Egyptian cotton. This transaction marked the first entry of the Soviet Union into Middle Eastern affairs and alarmed London and Washington. Now funding the dam became a chief priority, an "essential move in the game," as Macmillan put it.

On 16 December 1955, the U.S. and British governments, together with the World Bank, presented formal financing offers to the Egyptian government. The road to improved relations with Nasser, and by extension to the rest of the Arab world, seemed assured. Yet within three months the picture had altered. Cairo's "Voice of the Arabs" radio station, which broadcast propaganda against continued British colonial rule, enraged Eden; the prime minister also blamed Nasser for the firing by Jordan's King Hussein of General Sir John Glubb (Glubb Pasha), the British head of the Jordanian army. Eisenhower and Dulles deeply resented Nasser's rejection of the Anglo-American attempt to achieve a settlement of the Arab-Israeli conflict, which had dominated regional politics during the eight years since Israeli independence. Furthermore, Eisenhower believed that "the Arabs, absorbing major consignments of arms from the Soviets, are growing more arrogant daily and disregarding the interests of Western Europe and of the United States in the Middle East region." The American and British governments decided to withdraw the financing for the dam. Dulles, rather tactlessly, announced this decision to Egyptian Ambassador Ahmed Hussein on 19 July 1956, confident that Nasser could not effectively retaliate against the West.

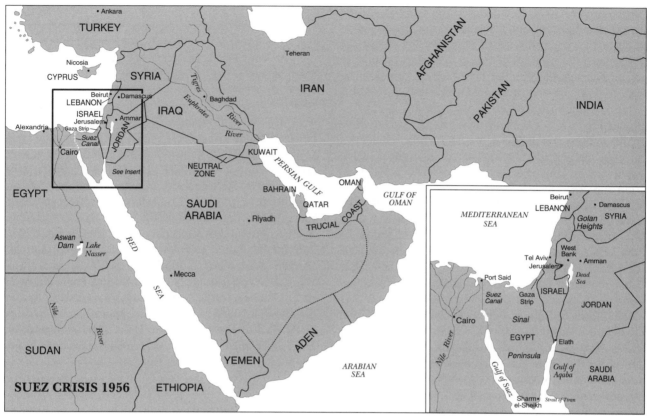

From: *The Course of American Diplomacy,* Howard Jones, Volume II. ©1992, by The McGraw-Hill Companies. Reprinted with permission of The McGraw-Hill Companies.

Egypt's Nationalization of the Suez Canal

One week later, to the surprise of the world, Nasser wreaked his revenge by nationalizing the Suez Canal. Long a symbol of empire, the Suez Canal provided a route for British imperial trade as well as a passageway for 70 percent of Western Europe's oil. The Suez Canal Company was Egyptian-chartered, but the British government owned 44 percent of the shares and French investors controlled many of the remaining shares. Its employment and management policies reflected nineteenth-century colonial practices. Nationalizing the Canal and the Canal Company shares was a move totally supported by the Egyptian people and bore no risk of an immediate military response since the last British troops had left Egypt on 18 June 1956.

Eden's first reaction to the nationalization was to attempt to seize the Canal back by military force. French officials concurred because Nasser had encouraged rebels in Algeria. The French government, led by Prime Minister Guy Mollet and Foreign Minister Christian Pineau, erroneously believed that if Great Britain and France defeated Nasser, the Algerian rebellion would collapse. The American government viewed this belliger-

ence with apprehension. Dulles soon journeyed to London to try to convince British and French leaders first to exhaust all diplomatic channels. As a result, the Western Allies agreed to convene a conference in London to discuss Nasser's seizure of the Canal. The three sponsoring governments sent invitations to major trading nations as well as to all signatories of the Convention of 1888, which governed the Canal's operation. Dulles insisted that all discussions be based on the convention lest a precedent be set that would permit Panama to seek international discussions about the American-owned and -run canal in Latin America. The Soviet Union, as the successor state to Russia, which had signed the convention, received an invitation and attended the conference, while Egypt refused to send a representative. The conclave convened on 16 August with delegates voting 18 to 4 in favor of a resolution calling on Nasser to transfer control of the Canal to an international authority. Sir Robert Menzies, prime minister of Australia, journeyed to Egypt to receive Nasser's rejection in person.

Upon returning from London, Dulles met with Eisenhower on 30 August. At this point they decided definitely against the use of force because, in the president's words, "this was not the issue upon which to try to downgrade

Nasser." With Great Britain and France increasing the tempo of military planning, Dulles scrambled for a way to distract these traditional allies, in the belief that the passage of time would remove the incentive for military action. His solution was the Suez Canal Users Association (SCUA). From beginning to end the plan, which called for European navigation pilots to be stationed on either end of the Canal, made no sense. However, it postponed military action because the British and French governments agreed to participate in a second London conference in the hope that acquiescence now would bring U.S. assistance later. On 14 September the European pilots who had remained at work walked off, to be replaced by recruits from Egypt and Eastern European countries. If the Western pilot boycott had closed down the Canal, it would have provided the only possible legal argument for Western intervention. But even though the Canal remained open to traffic, Anglo-French military planning continued nonetheless.

The British military plan, known as Musketeer Revise, adopted by the British cabinet's Egypt committee on 14 September, had four parts: (1) the neutralization of the Egyptian Air Force by air strikes over three days; (2) aerial disruption of Egyptian morale and Egypt's economy; (3) psychological warfare; and (4) a military landing at Port Said. As they secretly refined their planning, the British and French governments asked that the Security Council consider the Canal seizure. This démarche represented a failure for U.S. diplomatic efforts. Since the crisis began, Dulles had resisted any mention of the United Nations, again fearing supplying a precedent for Panama.

The Security Council began discussing the issue on 5 October and after a week had agreed with Egypt on "Six Principles" as a basis for negotiations. These included free and open transit through the Canal, respect for Egypt's sovereignty, and nonpolitical operation of the Canal. During these meetings Dulles took the opportunity to warn the British and French foreign ministers explicitly against the use of force. Instead, Great Britain and France continued their planning with an unlikely ally—Israel. Prime Minister David Ben-Gurion and Foreign Secretary Golda Meir had become increasingly alarmed at the potential effect of Soviet arms on the Middle Eastern balance of power. The general consensus in the Jewish state held that it would be better if a new round in the Arab-Israeli confrontation, basically a foregone conclusion, came sooner rather than later. Throughout the 1950s France was Israel's closest ally and most reliable military supplier. For this reason the Israeli government could not easily ignore the French request that it participate in the Anglo-French military action. Israeli leaders, however, worried that Israel would bear the brunt of any Egyptian military response.

The presence of Great Britain in the conspiracy further increased Israel's fears. Great Britain had governed Palestine under a League of Nations mandate since the end of World War I. In February 1947 it had renounced the mandate and asked the United Nations to determine the fate of the territory. The world body's decision in favor of partition between Jewish and Arab states met with disfavor in London, a displeasure which was signified by the British government's decision not to contribute to a smooth transition. Jewish bitterness against Great Britain was equalled by British furor at the terrorist war waged by the Irgun and Stern terrorist groups against the British army in Palestine. Israel was the last nation the Eden government would have chosen as an ally, but France continued to act as middleman during September and into October 1956. As a result, Ben-Gurion, his French counterpart, and British Foreign Secretary Selwyn Lloyd surreptitiously met in Sèvres, France from 22 to 24 October. In the secret Sèvres protocol they agreed on an initial Israeli strike against Egypt to be followed by an Anglo-French ultimatum to Israel and Egypt to cease fighting. Thereafter British and French forces would follow the script of Musketeer Revise.

The Attack on Egypt

Precisely on schedule Israeli forces on 29 October launched an attack on Egypt. The Eisenhower administration, left in the dark by its allies, was shocked. U.S. alarm turned to fury when officials learned that Great Britain had colluded with France and Israel. This reaction arose from several factors. That America's closest ally could have double-crossed the administration played a large role in the American response as did the ramshackle structure of the military plan. The timing contributed to Washington's reaction. Dulles had repeatedly warned British officials to take no action before the U.S. presidential election, scheduled for 6 November. The juxtaposition of the Suez invasion with the Hungarian crisis, however, was the most important determinant of the livid American response. The Soviet decision to crush brutally the Hungarian government left the administration militarily impotent. Its only recourse was to expose and publicize Moscow's actions to the world at large. Instead Soviet diplomats had a field day denouncing Anglo-French imperialists.

Blocked by British and French vetoes in the Security Council, the United States turned to the General Assembly. On 1 November Dulles recommended an imposed cease-fire which would be supervised by a United Nations military force (UNEF). Five days later, after the Anglo-French expeditionary force finally had landed in Egypt, the British government reluctantly acquiesced. Eden and his colleagues had agreed because the British pound had come under severe strain and the Cabinet knew American assistance could only come with a cease-fire. Yet British leaders still misunderstood the U.S. position. They assumed that the cease-fire would provide a figleaf for a European victory. During November they learned to their amazement that the U.S. government required a true Anglo-French withdrawal before extending any aid. For Great Britain, the double-barreled pressure of no aid for the pound/no oil for Western Europe proved overwhelming. Throughout the twentieth century British governments had made the maintenance of a strong pound, which served as an international trading and reserve currency, a central part of British foreign policy. That being the case, the Eden government could not withstand U.S. economic pressure. On 3 December British officials finally satisfied administration members that Great Britain and France would depart expeditiously. Thereafter U.S. aid flowed generously.

British and French forces sailed from Egypt on 22 December. Israeli troops, having trounced their Egyptian adversaries, remained in Sharm al-Sheikh near the the Straits of Tiran in the Gulf of Aqaba and Gaza. The Egyptian government had used its ability to block the strategic waterway to harass and obstruct Israeli shipping from the port of Eilat while also insisting that Israeli shipping be barred from using the Suez Canal. Gaza had been the location of terrorist strikes against the Jewish state which the Israeli government had answered with raids of its own. Not surprisingly then, the Ben-Gurion government was not eager to relinquish conquered territory.

Aftermath and Consequences

But removing these troops became a top Eisenhower administration priority. At the same time U.S. officials prepared a new Middle Eastern démarche. Having previously been content to stand behind and also hide behind British initiatives, U.S. diplomats after the Suez Crisis became convinced that the time had come for a major U.S move. They believed that the harsh U.S. stance against its traditional allies had bolstered the reputation of the United States in the region. To capitalize on this supposed rise in status, the president on 5 January 1957 sent to Congress a plan which would come to be known as the Eisenhower Doctrine. It called for an appropriation of $200 million for American economic and military assistance in the Middle East to "any nation or group of nations which desires such aid," and asked for advance authorization to deploy U.S. troops "to secure and protect the territorial integrity and political independence of nations requesting such aid, against overt armed aggression from any nation controlled by International Communism."

As Congress discussed the new Middle East initiative, the administration continued to pressure Israel to withdraw its troops from Sharm al-Sheikh and Gaza. Under the threat of U.S. and United Nations economic sanctions, Israeli foreign minister Golda Meir on 1 March announced her government's acquiescence. Economic action in this case had not proved determinative. Rather, U.S. economic pressure had served as the symbol of potential U.S. ostracism. As Dulles told U.S. ambassador to the United Nations Henry Cabot Lodge, Israeli officials did "not want to antagonize the Eisenhower administration for four years. That is more important than any sanctions." At the same time the United States had offered to Israel an aide-mémoire recognizing the international status of the Straits of Tiran, and France had given a similar guarantee with respect to Gaza. Stationing UNEF forces in both areas provided further reassurance. The combination of the carrot and the stick had been successful.

Dulles had proclaimed his United Nations speech of 1 November 1956 the finest moment of his career. However, in retrospect, the Suez crisis revealed disastrous diplomatic miscalculations on the part of all three Western nations. The British government went to war in order to assert its hegemony in the Middle East. Inexplicably, it did not first assure itself of U.S. support, although Great Britain could sustain neither its financial nor its foreign policy unaided. France, having encouraged Great Britain in this misguided policy, shared the humiliation of withdrawal, which further undermined the standing of both countries in the region. While Paris could withstand economic pressure, it had no choice but to withdraw its troops once London had decided to do so.

The United States first erroneously assumed that it could abruptly withdraw the financing offer for the Aswan High Dam without fear of engendering Egyptian retaliation. It then compounded its error by betting that humiliating its erstwhile allies would bolster its own prestige within the emerging developing world. Of the great powers, only the Soviet Union benefited from the crisis. Supplying arms to Nasser had upset the Middle Eastern balance of power and put the West on the defensive. Moscow's threat on 5 November to rain down rockets on London and Paris should Western troops not evacuate Egypt, while without substantive effect, further increased Soviet credit with Arab nations, as did the Soviet offer to fund the Aswan High Dam.

Israel and Egypt also emerged from the Suez crisis with enhanced reputations. Western observers and Arabs alike had viewed the Israeli victory in the 1948 war for independence as a fluke. The smashing success of Israeli forces permanently quashed that assumption. Israel easily surmounted the threat of U.S. and United Nations sanctions. The Eisenhower administration indeed rewarded Israel for its territorial withdrawal by providing written recognition of the international status of the Straits of Tiran and by demonstrating an enhanced sense of responsibility for the Jewish state. The stationing of UNEF forces in Gaza and at Sharm al-Sheikh near the Straits of Tiran bought Israeli governments ten years to nurture development within the security of quiet borders.

Notwithstanding the Egyptian defeat, the Suez crisis strengthened Nasser's position. The British and French withdrawal gave to the Egyptian president an aura of strength. That Egypt retained control over the Suez Canal increased Nasser's prestige in the region, especially among the poorest citizens of the Middle East. Nasserism remained a force to be reckoned with until Nasser's death in 1970. Egypt easily survived economic sanctions imposed by Great Britain, France, and the United States at the end of July 1956. In part, Egypt's poverty rendered it immune to economic pressure. Furthermore, communist bloc nations and others provided Egypt with such funds as it required. Finally, the cause for which Egypt had been punished was one of great importance to the Egyptian government and people.

Only Great Britain, which had placed financial policy at the center of its foreign policy, proved vulnerable to economic weapons. Thereafter British leaders made sure never to stray far from American strategy. The United States found itself immersed in Middle East diplomacy and, at least to its initial dismay, increasingly tied to Israel. The Middle East changed from an imperial playground to a Cold War battleground.

DIANE B. KUNZ

See also Cold War; Economic Sanctions; Eden, Robert Anthony; Eisenhower, Dwight David; France; Great Britain; International Bank for Reconstruction and Development; Macmillan, Maurice Harold; Middle East; Nasser, Gamal Abdel; Palestine (to 1948)

FURTHER READING

Kunz, Diane B. *The Economic Diplomacy of the Suez Crisis*. Chapel Hill, N.C., 1991.

Kyle, Keith. *Suez*. London, 1991.

Louis, Wm. R., and Roger Owen, eds. *Suez 1956: The Crisis and its Consequences*. Oxford, 1989.

Schoenbaum, David. *The United States and the State of Israel*. New York, 1993.

Troen, Selwyn I., and Moshe Shemesh, eds. *The Suez-Sinai Crisis 1956—Retrospective and Reappraisal*. New York, 1990.

SUKARNO

(*b*. 6 June 1901; *d*. 21 June 1970)

Indonesian nationalist leader and president (1949–1966). Born in Java, educated as an engineer, Sukarno (who, like many Javanese, went by a single name) devoted much of his early adulthood to struggling against Dutch colonial rule. He welcomed Japanese forces as liberators in March 1942 and worked closely with the occupation government. Upon Japan's defeat in August 1945, he proclaimed Indonesian independence from the Netherlands. He spent the next four years fighting to compel the Dutch to accept his proclamation; they finally did in December 1949.

As the first president of the Indonesian republic, Sukarno adopted a position of nonalignment between the superpowers. Initially this posture merely annoyed U.S. officials, who in fact had helped persuade the Dutch to drop their efforts to hold on to Indonesia. When Sukarno hosted the 1955 Bandung Conference of Asian and African states, the Eisenhower administration discounted its significance. Gradually, however, Sukarno's increasing reliance on the powerful Indonesian Communist Party (PKI) generated concern in Washington that Indonesia might follow China into the communist camp. The Central Intelligence Agency lent support to Sukarno's rivals; in 1958 the U.S. agency backed a revolt in Sumatra against Sukarno's government.

When the revolt failed, Washington reversed course and tried to repair relations with Jakarta. The Kennedy administration boosted aid to Indonesia. At the same time, though, military attachés of the U.S. embassy cultivated connections to the Indonesian military, whose leaders despised the communists and distrusted Sukarno. The Pentagon brought promising Indonesian officers to the United States for training.

Tension between Washington and Jakarta again escalated after Sukarno in 1963 announced a "confrontation" with Malaysia, which Sukarno deemed a stalking horse for continued Western imperialism. Closer ties between Indonesia and China prompted additional worries in Washington and cutbacks in U.S. aid. Johnson administration officials quietly hinted to the Indonesian military that the United States would not object to Sukarno's overthrow.

Such hints doubtless encouraged the Indonesian officers, but it took the assassination of several generals in a 1965 PKI-inspired coup attempt to impel them to action. General (later President) Suharto led a purge of the PKI in which literally hundreds of thousands of communists and their alleged sympathizers were murdered. Meanwhile, Suharto eased Sukarno aside, divesting him of effective presidential power in March 1966 and the rest of his official authority in May 1967. As Presidents Lyndon B. Johnson and then Richard M. Nixon rewarded Suharto's actions with new aid, Sukarno languished under house arrest until his death.

H. WILLIAM BRANDS

See also Central Intelligence Agency; China; Indonesia; Nonaligned Movement

FURTHER READING

Brands, H. W. "The Limits of Manipulation: How the United States Didn't Topple Sukarno." *Journal of American History* 76 (December 1989): 785–808.

Legge, J.D. *Sukarno: A Political Biography.* New York, 1972.

Penders, C.L.M. *The Life and Times of Sukarno.* Kuala Lumpur, 1974.

SULLIVAN PRINCIPLES

See South Africa

SUMNER, CHARLES

(*b.* 6 January 1811; *d.* 11 March 1874)

Chairman of the Senate Foreign Relations Committee (1861–1871). Born in Boston, he failed to establish a successful law practice, despite having graduated from Harvard Law School. During travels in Europe between 1837 and 1841 he became acquainted with eminent political and literary figures, especially in Great Britain. Returning home, he devoted most of his time to the antislavery movement, and he opposed the war with Mexico.

Elected to the U.S. Senate from Massachusetts in 1851, Sumner was detested in the South as a symbol of radical abolitionism. At the outset of the Civil War, having begun an eleven-year tenure as chairman of the Foreign Relations Committee, he began a relentless campaign to oust the secretary of state, William Seward, from Abraham Lincoln's cabinet, so that he or another radical Republican could occupy the office. Believing that his own opinions should be decisive in the foreign relations of the Lincoln administration, Sumner regularly urged them upon the president. He cultivated a friendship with Mrs. Lincoln, denounced Seward to foreign diplomats and journalists, and employed spies in the Department of State to keep himself informed of the secretary's every move. Lincoln, however, refused to dismiss Seward, nor to allow Sumner to undermine the secretary's foreign policy. During the *Trent* affair, for example, Lincoln adopted Seward's solution to the imbroglio with Great Britain, deciding that Sumner's call for foreign arbitration would not meet with British approval. Although some scholars have claimed that Sumner played a decisive role in averting armed conflict with Great Britain during the American Civil War, Sumner's role was actually minor.

Perhaps Sumner's most important foreign relations service was his support of the Alaska Purchase treaty negotiated by Seward in 1867. Sumner's opposition could have dealt a mortal blow to that initiative. Sumner's obstruction of bills and appointments favored by President Ulysses Grant, including Grant's efforts to annex the Dominican Republic, led to his ouster as chairman of the Foreign Relations Committee not long before his death.

NORMAN B. FERRIS

See also Alaska Purchase; American Civil War; Lincoln, Abraham; Seward, William Henry; Slave Trade and Slavery; *Trent* Affair

FURTHER READING

Donald, David. *Charles Sumner and the Coming of the Civil War.* New York, 1960.

———. *Charles Sumner and the Rights of Man.* New York, 1970.

SUN YAT-SEN

See Sun Zhongshan

SUN ZHONGSHAN

(*b.* 1866; *d.* 12 March 1925)

The leader of the 1911 revolution in China that overthrew the Manchu regime and the imperial system and established the Republic of China. Educated in Hawai'i and Japan, Christian, English-speaking, and a physician of Western medicine, Sun Zhongshan (Sun Yat-sen) became a professional revolutionary early in life and advocated anti-imperialism, national economic development, and republicanism. Having lived in the San Francisco and New York areas as well as in London, he was well known and popular among overseas Chinese and had many supporters in the West. Sun was China's first president and a founder of the Nationalist Party, the Guomindang (Kuomintang). Chinese of all political persuasions have revered him as the father of modern China, even though his actual accomplishments failed to equal his ambitions and he died a frustrated man. Although he admired the United States and tried to win its support for his activities, he was disappointed that Washington kept its distance from him.

GORDON H. CHANG

See also China

FURTHER READING

Fairbank, John K. *The United States and China,* 4th ed. Cambridge, Mass., 1983.

Schiffrin, Harold Z. *Sun Yat-sen and the Origins of the Chinese Revolution.* Berkeley, Calif., 1968.

SUPREME COURT AND THE JUDICIARY

The judiciary is one of three branches of the federal government, and though it remains "the least dangerous branch," the cases decided by the federal courts have not only shaped life in the United States itself but often enough the conduct of U.S. foreign relations as well.

The Constitution gives the federal courts jurisdiction to decide designated categories of cases, many of which affect U.S. foreign relations, such as cases involving ambassadors and some cases involving foreign states or foreign nationals. The law which the courts apply includes treaties with foreign governments and principles of customary international law, as well as U.S. law regulating commerce with foreign nations and other "foreign relations law." For two hundred years, as the place of the judiciary was developed and refined, the courts promulgated judicial policy and legal doctrines that, in respect of foreign relations, give extraordinary weight to the "public interest" and call for unusual deference to the political branches.

The U.S. Constitution distributes the authority of the federal government among three branches of government. Legislative powers are vested in Congress, executive power is granted to the president, and "judicial power of the United States shall be vested in one supreme Court, and in such inferior Courts as the Congress may from time to time ordain and establish" (Art. III, Sect. 1).

The Federal Courts and Their Jurisdiction

Congress established the Supreme Court at the nation's beginnings, and has maintained it throughout U.S. national history. At the end of the twentieth century, the "inferior courts" authorized by the Constitution consist principally of a network of district courts having original jurisdiction (to decide cases that originate there, not on appeal from other courts), and a layer of courts of appeals that review decisions of the district courts, whose judgments are subject to review by the Supreme Court. Under its general legislative powers, Congress also has created courts of special original jurisdiction, some of which have importance for U.S. foreign relations, such as the U.S. Court of Federal Claims and the Court of International Trade, and special appellate courts such as the Court of Tax Appeals and the U.S. Court of Appeals for the Federal Circuit. Congress also has established administrative courts, "quasi-judicial" tribunals for administrative agencies, such as the Immigration and Naturalization Service and the Federal Trade Commission.

According to the Constitution, federal judicial power extends to any case or controversy arising under the Constitution, laws, or treaties of the United States; to cases defined by particular subject matter, such as those affecting foreign diplomats, or cases of admiralty and maritime jurisdiction; to controversies between enumerated parties such as controversies to which the United States is a party; controversies between states, between citizens of different states ("diversity jurisdiction"), or between a citizen and a foreign national (Art. III, Sect. 2). A federal court can decide only cases and controversies that are within the judicial power of the United States, and, with one exception which the Constitution itself mandates—the limited original jurisdiction of the Supreme Court—only if Congress has conferred jurisdiction on the court to decide such a case or controversy.

Congress has given the lower courts general "federal question" jurisdiction, that is, jurisdiction of "civil actions arising under the Constitution, laws, or treaties of the United States" (28 U.S.C. § 1331), and criminal jurisdiction of "all offenses against the laws of the United States" (18 U.S.C. § 3231), as well as special jurisdiction of particular cases, such as civil suits or criminal proceedings under Civil Rights Acts for violation of individual rights (see 28 U.S.C. § 1343, 42 U.S.C. §§ 1981 et seq., 18 U.S.C. §§ 241 et seq.). The federal courts also have jurisdiction over controversies between citizens of different states, or between a citizen of a state and a foreign state or a foreign national ("diversity of citizenship" jurisdiction) if the amount in controversy exceeds $50,000 (see 28 U.S.C. § 1332). In such cases the federal courts apply the law of the state in which the court sits (Erie Railroad Co. v. Tompkins, 304 U.S. 64 (1938)). The Supreme Court, too, exercises appellate jurisdiction only if Congress has authorized it. Since 1987, almost all the Supreme Court's appellate jurisdiction is discretionary. Petitioners must ask the Court to "grant certiorari" and review the case. The Court reviews and grants certiorari in only about 150 cases out of thousands of petitions each year; in the mid-1990s, the Court has heard fewer than 100 cases each term.

Federal courts are subject to the constitutional limitations governing every branch of the U.S. government, notably the Bill of Rights, as well as to limitations applying to the courts in particular. The Supreme Court as well as the general federal courts can exercise jurisdiction only over "cases or controversies," authentic cases brought by persons who have "standing." Persons can sue only to vindicate their own legal interests and to seek a remedy only for their own injuries, not for general grievances or—ordinarily—for injuries to third parties. A person cannot sue as a citizen to challenge a governmental action on the ground that it is a breach of the Constitutional "social contract," that it violates some Constitutional provision in which the citizen has only an undifferentiated political interest as a citizen. In only a very limited category of cases can persons assert their financial interests as federal taxpayers to object to a federal expenditure of funds. (Flast v. Cohen, 392 U.S. 83 (1968)). A state cannot challenge a federal act solely on the ground that it usurps powers not delegated to the United States and reserved to the states (Amendment X). Congress and the president cannot sue each other for alleged violation of the separation of powers. But individual members of Congress have brought suit to protect their personal interests as members of Congress, such as the effectiveness of their vote.

Ordinarily, a proceeding does not present a case or controversy if the issue has become "moot" (that is, if the controversy has been otherwise resolved), or if a case is not yet "ripe" or sufficiently "concrete"—technical conceptions which the Supreme Court has developed and refined. The requirement of "case or controversy" precludes the federal courts from giving advisory opinions.

The Supreme Court also has decided that federal courts should avoid hearing some issues from considerations of "prudence," in the public interest generally, or in the interest of the judicial function—for example, because the litigants are not well suited to bring a particular claim, or because it would be best not to adjudicate an issue at the particular time or in particular context.

The courts have identified a special principle of limitation, the "political question doctrine." Certain issues are "political" only, and not justiciable. Principally, the courts will not review issues which the Constitution, as interpreted, vests final, unreviewable authority in another branch of government, such as impeachment proceedings (see *Nixon v. U.S., 506 U.S. 113 S.Ct. 732 (1993)*), or a determination by either house of Congress as to whether one of its members meets the necessary constitutional qualifications for holding office (Art. I, Sect. 5).

But the Court has also defined "political questions" more broadly.

Prominent on the surface of any case held to involve a political question is found a textually demonstrable constitutional commitment to a coordinate political department; or a lack of judicially discoverable and manageable standards for resolving it; or the impossibility of deciding without an initial policy determination of a kind clearly for nonjudicial discretion; or the impossibility of a court's undertaking independent resolution without expressing lack of the respect due coordinate branches of government; or an unusual need for unquestioning adherence to a political decision already made; or the potentiality of embarrassment from multifarious pronouncements by various departments on one question. *(Baker v. Carr, 369 U.S. 186, at 217 (1962)).*

Contrary to common impression, the Supreme Court has held very few questions to be nonjusticiable political questions. Sometimes, however, courts loosely declare a question to be "political" in a different sense: in rejecting a challenge to an action of Congress (or of the executive), the courts may conclude that the action challenged is within the Constitutional authority of Congress (or the executive), but may add that the wisdom or desirability of the action is "political," for the political branches to decide, and the courts have no authority to review it.

The Federal Judiciary and the Separation of Powers

The Constitution does not express a commitment to the "separation of powers," and does not declare the three branches of government to be "separate." In fact, some of their powers are not separate but intermingled to achieve "checks and balances"—for example, the president's power to veto legislation, or the requirement of Senate consent to presidential treaties or appointments. But separation of powers was a principle of good government in the ideology of the framers of the Constitution, and some commitment to separation is reflected in the fact that the powers of the government of the United States are defined under three headings (legislative, executive, judicial) and distributed among three branches. In any event, separation is established as a cardinal principle of U.S. constitutional jurisprudence, prohibiting usurpation by one branch of functions allocated to another, or interference by one branch with the authority of another, or even undue delegation of authority by one branch to another.

The principle of separation of powers applies to the judiciary as well as to the other branches. Separation of powers has been held to imply that Congress cannot impose on federal judges duties not of a judicial character. (See *Hayburn's case, 2 Dall. (2 U.S.) 409 (1792)*; also *Morrison v. Olson, 487 U.S. 654 (1988); Mistretta v. United States, 488 U.S. 361 (1989))*. The terms of service of federal judges and their compensation are fixed by Congress, but the Constitution protects their independence—a special aspect of separation of powers—by guaranteeing them life tenure ("they shall hold their office during good behaviour") as well as "compensation, which shall not be diminished during their continuance in office" (Art. III, Sect. 1). But judges, like other officials, are subject to removal from office by impeachment (by the House of Representatives, Art. I, Sect. 5) and conviction (by the Senate, Art. I, Sect. 6) for treason, bribery or other "high Crimes and Misdemeanors." (Art. II, Sect. 4).

Separation of powers is not seen as violated by judicial lawmaking. Courts inevitably make law when they construe the Constitution and when they interpret acts of Congress. Courts make law by authority delegated to them by Congress. Courts make law on their own authority when they develop doctrine for their own guidance, as in the prudential grounds for avoiding adjudication or the Act of State doctrine.

The principle of separation of powers has not prevented the development of "judicial review," a major contribution by the Supreme Court to the ideology of constitutionalism which has been emulated around the world. In 1803, in the case of *Marbury v. Madison, 5 U.S. (1 Cranch)*

137 (1803), Chief Justice John Marshall asserted the authority (and the duty) of a court in the United States, in deciding a case before it, to refuse to give effect to a statutory provision which the court determines to be beyond the power of Congress under the Constitution. From that date, courts have exercised authority to review the constitutionality of acts of the political branches (or of the states) when necessary to decide a case before them. In time, the Supreme Court declared and established "judicial supremacy": judicial interpretation of the Constitution is not only binding on the parties in the case before them, but is final and binding thereafter on the political branches of the federal government and on the states. A hundred and fifty years later the Court said that *Marbury* had declared that "the federal judiciary is supreme in the exposition of the law of the Constitution, and that principle has ever since been respected by this Court and the Country as a permanent and indispensable feature of our Constitutional system." *(Cooper* v. *Aaron, 358 U.S. 1, 17 (1958))*.

The power of judicial review has given the Supreme Court a dual character. On one hand it is the highest court of review of alleged error in cases appealed from the lower federal courts, and of federal questions decided by state courts. The Supreme Court is also a constitutional court, interpreting the Constitution, monitoring its application by the political branches (and by the states), and nullifying acts that it determines to be unconstitutional. Lower federal courts, and state courts of all levels, also exercise such functions of constitutional review, subject to review by the U.S. Supreme Court.

Judicial review has inspired a jurisprudence of its own, particularly in the application of the Bill of Rights. In general, individual rights protected by the Constitution are not absolute, and often bow to the public interest. But, the Supreme Court has decided, freedoms protected by the First Amendment—religion, speech, press, assembly—and rights of privacy and autonomy in intimate matters, enjoy extraordinary protection, and invasions of such rights will be strictly scrutinized by the courts and will be upheld only for compelling public interests. Similarly, distinctions and classifications based on race are suspect, must be strictly scrutinized, and can be justified only by compelling public interest. Distinctions based on gender are also looked at skeptically and are sustained only for important public interests.

State courts are established, and their jurisdiction defined, by state legislatures pursuant to authority conferred by state constitutions. In establishing the lower federal judiciary and conferring jurisdiction upon it, Congress assumed, generally, that the state courts would remain available to decide federal questions.

Unless Congress determines otherwise, cases arising under the U.S. Constitution or under laws or treaties of the United States may be adjudicated by state courts, and Congress has provided for Supreme Court review of final decisions on federal questions by the highest state court that has jurisdiction of the matter. But Supreme Court review of state court decisions is available only when the requirements of a case or controversy are satisfied. Congress has authorized parties to request removal from the state to the federal courts many categories of cases involving federal questions *(28 U.S.C. §§ 1441 et seq.)*.

The Courts and Foreign Affairs

Nothing in the U.S. Constitution suggests a special role for the courts regarding foreign affairs, or special treatment by the courts of matters relating to or impinging on foreign affairs. But the judicial power of the United States as defined in Article III of the Constitution, and the authority of the federal courts as determined by Congress, have applications that impinge importantly on U.S. foreign relations. Notably, the federal courts exercise jurisdiction over cases arising under treaties of the United States or under international law. Cases arising under domestic U.S. law include those arising under acts of Congress that regulate foreign commerce and other foreign intercourse; acts under Congress's war powers and its foreign affairs power; and exercises of presidential foreign affairs power that may have the character of law. Constitutional as well as prudential limitations on the exercise of jurisdiction by the courts have important, sometimes different, applications and implications for foreign affairs. The consequences for the courts of the separation of powers, and the exercise of judicial review, also are similar as well as different in foreign or in domestic matters.

Most important, perhaps, has been the Court's authority to determine what the Constitution means and the special Constitutional doctrines that the Supreme Court has developed in matters relating to foreign affairs.

In regard to foreign affairs (as to internal matters), the Supreme Court's reading of the Constitution is authoritative and final, and binding on the political branches. The Court has read the Constitution to give full power to the federal government in foreign affairs and large powers to each of the political branches.

For purposes relating to foreign affairs, the Court's reading of the Constitution also has had a special character. The Supreme Court has felt free to read the Constitution's text liberally. It has inferred additional power for the federal government and for each of its three branches from opaque text and ambiguous, undefined terms (for example, "The Executive Power" Art. II, Sect. 1) and from the structure of the Constitution. It has not hesitated to find in the Constitution what the framers might have intended and should have put there (but did not). Radically, uniquely, the Supreme Court has looked for federal power in foreign affairs outside the Constitution.

In no case has the Supreme Court held any action of Congress or of the president relating to foreign affairs to be beyond the powers of the federal government under the U.S. Constitution. The Court's large readings of the power of Congress to regulate interstate commerce *(U.S. v. Darby, 312 U.S. 100 (1941))*, apply as well to commerce with foreign nations. The power of Congress to declare war has been construed to include the power to decide whether the United States shall go to war, engage in limited war, or remain at peace; the power to prepare for war and to establish national programs and prescribe policies that might defend against war or prevent war; the power to do what is necessary to wage war successfully; the power to address the consequences of war. The courts have allowed Congress to read its power to tax and spend for the general welfare broadly, to include, for example, power to spend for foreign aid. The courts also have read liberally the authority explicitly given to the president— the power to appoint and to receive ambassadors, to make treaties (with the advice and consent of the Senate), to execute the laws, and to act on the implications of his designation as commander in chief. They have taken seriously the characterization of "the very delicate, plenary and exclusive power of the president as the sole organ of the federal government in the field of international relations" *(U.S. v. Curtiss-Wright Export Corp., 299 U.S. 304 at 320)*. In all, the courts have recognized a broad presidential "foreign affairs power," which includes authority to make executive agreements other than treaties, whether by authorization from Congress or (sometimes) on the president's own authority. (See *Dames & Moore v. Regan, 453 U.S. 654 (1981); U.S. v. Belmont, 301 U.S. 324 (1937)*).

The Supreme Court achieved perhaps the most radical expansion of the authority of the U.S. government in foreign affairs not by interpretation of explicit Constitutional text but by resort to extra-Constitutional authority. In *U.S. v. Curtiss-Wright Export Corp.*, the Supreme Court declared that the cardinal Constitutional principle of "enumerated powers"—that the federal government has only the powers delegated to it—applies only to domestic matters; that in regard to foreign affairs, the powers of the federal government derive not only from the Constitution but from U.S. national sovereignty. Thus the federal government has all the foreign affairs powers that other nations have under international law.

From the theory of *Curtiss-Wright* (and perhaps also by large interpretations of the foreign commerce and the war powers), the Court has found powers in the federal government not expressly listed in the Constitution: a power to act outside the United States (for example, to govern territories acquired in war), and to regulate the activities of U.S. citizens abroad. (See *American Ins. Co. v. Canter, 26 U.S. (1 Pet.) 516 (1828); The Insular Cases, Downes v.* *Bidwell, 182 U.S. 244 (1901); Blackmer v. United States, 284 U.S. 421 (1932)*, and other cases cited and discussed in *U.S. v. Verdugo-Urquidez, 494 U.S. 259, 268 (1990)*. The Court also has found a plenary power in the federal government to regulate immigration as well as the status and interests of aliens in the United States. The Court has continued to rule that Congressional immigration policy is subject to virtually no constitutional restraints *(The Chinese Exclusion Case, 130 U.S. 581 (1889))*. When last the Court spoke on the matter it held that even aliens lawfully and long resident in the United States could be deported for any reason or no reason *(Galvan v. Press, 347 US 522, 531 (1954);* see also *Shaughnessy v. U.S. ex rel. Mezei, 345 U.S. 206 (1953))*. Whether those cases would be followed today is not certain, and the extent to which such governmental powers to act abroad, or to regulate immigration and the rights of aliens in the United States, are constrained by the provisions of the Bill of Rights, remains a matter of some dispute (see *U.S. v. Verdugo-Urquidez, 494 U.S. 259 (1990))*.

The Court's declaration that the foreign affairs power is extraConstitutional continues to be debated, but its conclusion that the federal government has full authority in foreign affairs (to the total exclusion of the states) has not been disputed. In addition to explicit limitations on the states not to make treaties or go to war, and other restrictions in Art. I, Sect. 10 of the Constitution, the Court has read the grant of power to Congress to regulate foreign commerce as prohibiting state burdens on foreign commerce. And, in general, states cannot interfere in U.S. foreign affairs or impinge on national foreign policy *(Zschernig v. Miller, 389 U.S. 429 (1968))*.

Separation of Powers in Foreign Affairs

In principle, separation of powers applies to foreign as well as to domestic affairs. Each branch has only the powers allocated to it, and separation precludes usurpation by one branch of the authority of another. Presumably, the separation of powers principles that govern interbranch disputes in a domestic context—as when the Court struck down Congress's use of the legislative veto to control executive action *(I.N.S. v. Chadha, 462 U.S. 919 (1983))*, or a Congressional claim to appoint members of a commission *(Buckley v. Valeo, 424 U.S. 1 (1976))*—hold as well in foreign affairs.

The special Constitutional (or extraConstitutional) character of foreign affairs is reflected also in the distribution of authority between Congress and the president. In foreign as in domestic affairs, Congress legislates and the president "shall take care that the laws are faithfully executed," Art. 2). But some foreign affairs powers explicitly allocated in the Constitution do not conform to a "legislative-executive" division. The treaty-making power, for example, is often lawmaking in character and purpose, but it is exercised by the president (though he requires the consent of the Senate). The power to declare war is not strictly of a legislative character but is exercised by Congress.

In foreign affairs, the Court has not been disposed to find limitations on the power of the two political branches when they act together or when they concur. The Court has found virtually no limitation on the powers of Congress to delegate authority to the president in foreign affairs. The Court found support for the president's power to conclude the hostages agreement with Iran in long Congressional acquiescence in the practice of settling claims by executive agreement (without Senate consent or Congressional approval) (*Dames & Moore* v. *Regan*).

The chronic Constitutional issues of foreign affairs arise from competition for power between the president and Congress. In a famous essay on the powers of the president in relation to those of Congress, Justice Robert Jackson said: "When the president acts in absence of either a Congressional grant or denial of authority, he can only rely upon his own independent powers, but there is a zone of twilight in which he and Congress may have concurrent authority, or in which its distribution is uncertain." (*Youngstown Sheet & Tube Co.* v. *Sawyer, 343 U.S. 579, 637 (1952).*)

Foreign affairs have provided the principal issues of power in that "twilight zone." The courts have done little to resolve them. In part that may be because the requirement of "standing" and other "case or controversy" implications of Article III, mean that the courts cannot hear political disputes where no personal interests are asserted, and commonly no one has standing to challenge much of what the president and Congress do in foreign affairs. Congress as a body cannot bring the president to court, and the courts have held that individual members of Congress, often those most immediately interested in challenging a presidential action, do not have standing to do so unless their Congressional votes have in effect been nullified. Some courts, and some justices of the Supreme Court, also have invoked the political question doctrine to remove themselves from interbranch disputes, leaving the dispute to be resolved by the political branches or to remain unresolved. Examples include *Goldwater* v. *Carter, 444 U.S. 996 (1979)*, the attempt by members of Congress to challenge President Carter's termination of the Defense Treaty with the Republic of China (Taiwan); and several lower court cases arising out of the Vietnam War, such as *Mora* v. *McNamara, 387 F.2d 862 (D.C.Cir.), cert. denied, 389 U.S. 934 (1967)*.

The Constitutional separation of powers also has served, in significant measure, to immunize executive foreign policy and conduct of foreign relations from judicial scrutiny and influence. Separation of the judiciary has isolated and insulated the courts from foreign policy and from foreign affairs in significant respects. The federal judiciary is populated by members of the legal profession, few of whom acquire sophisticated familiarity with foreign affairs. The life of a federal judge is busy and lonely, and the mores of the judiciary discourage contact and familiarity with foreign policy and foreign affairs. Movement between the judiciary and the foreign policy establishment is rare; only a few of the justices of the Supreme Court have been president (Taft), or secretary of state (John Jay, John Marshall, William Day, Charles Evans Hughes), or legislators, officials or public citizens with special foreign affairs experience (Sutherland, Burton, Murphy; earlier, Ellsworth, Clifford, Waite, L.Q.C. Lamar). Federal judges have life tenure and only a few have strayed from the judiciary for foreign affairs assignments (Fuller, the first Harlan, Byrnes, Robert Jackson). A judiciary that is politically and culturally removed from foreign affairs is inclined to self-restraint, and disposed to develop doctrines of deference to "the experts," meaning the executive branch.

Major theoretical issues of Constitutional authority in foreign affairs remain unresolved. The courts have not determined whether the provision vesting "the Executive power" in the president is an additional grant of power, or only a heading for the specific executive powers that follow. The Supreme Court has not indicated how the powers of the United States inherent in its sovereignty are divided between Congress and the president, and has referred to both "the Foreign Affairs Power" of Congress and "the Foreign Affairs Power" of the president. Nor have the courts resolved the issues of Justice Jackson's "twilight zone," where the distribution of power is uncertain or concurrent: which powers are in that zone; which of these powers belong to one branch or the other, and if so to which; which powers are concurrent, and which branch prevails in case of conflict. The courts have not decided chronic issues as to claims of executive privilege to withhold information even from Congress.

In particular, the courts have done little to resolve the two-century-old controversy regarding the respective authority of Congress and the president as to war and peace. The Supreme Court has held that Congress has power to decide for war or peace, to do whatever is necessary to wage war successfully, to legislate to address the consequences of war, and to regulate as well as to spend to prepare for the common defense (*Ex parte Milligan, 31 U.S. (4 Wall.) 2 (1866); the Prize Cases, 67 U.S. (2 Black) 635 (1862); Woods* v. *Miller Co., 333 U.S. 138 (1948)*). The Supreme Court has found large presidential authority as commander in chief during wars declared, authorized, or ratified by Congress, including authority to intern persons of Japanese ancestry during World War II (see *Kore-*

matsu). But the courts have avoided deciding whether the president has authority to deploy U.S. forces in foreign hostilities in the absence of authorization by Congress. The many attempts to litigate the president's authority to pursue the Vietnam War did not succeed, some lower courts declaring that the war had been authorized by Congress (in the Tonkin Gulf Resolution), other courts declaring the issue "political" and not justiciable. (The Supreme Court refused to review those cases.) On the other hand, the Court denied President Harry S. Truman authority as commander in chief to seize steel mills to maintain production of steel necessary for prosecuting the Korean War.

The courts have not considered objections to the War Powers Resolution (1973), the constitutionality of which has been challenged by every president since its adoption, nor have there been judicial interpretations of the confusing provisions of that highly controversial legislation. The courts have not decided whether the president may put the United States at war pursuant to a resolution of the United Nations Security Council and the UN Charter (a treaty of the United States) without authorization from Congress, as President George Bush claimed in respect of the Persian Gulf War (1991), and as President Bill Clinton claimed in planning action in Haiti (1994). (In both cases the president in fact sought authorization from Congress.) But one district court denied in principle the president's authority to go to war without authorization from Congress *(Dellums v. Bush, 752 F.Supp. 1141 (D.D.C. 1990))*.

In foreign as in domestic affairs, the courts generally apply law made by others: the Constitution; acts of Congress; principles of international law; provisions of U.S. treaties; executive orders and actions that have legal character. To be sure, the courts make law even when they apply the law deriving from those other sources—when they interpret the Constitution, an act of Congress, or a treaty, or when they determine the existence or content of a principle of customary international law. But in foreign affairs (as elsewhere) the courts also have made and declared law on their own authority, especially for their own guidance. The Supreme Court has decided to permit the trial in U.S. courts of an individual abducted from another country *(U.S. v. Alvarez-Machain, 112 S.Ct. 2188 (1992))*. The Court has developed a doctrine requiring courts not to sit in judgment on the acts of a foreign state applied in its own territory.

The Bill of Rights and Foreign Affairs

In the jurisprudence of constitutional rights, even "fundamental freedoms" are not absolute, and must be balanced against important public interests. Where foreign affairs are concerned, the judiciary tends to give even greater weight to the public interest, and accords even greater deference to the views of the political branches as to what the public interest requires. Even in the face of individual rights entitled to extraordinary protection, the courts have commonly upheld governmental action to maintain national security, support friendly diplomatic relations, or wage war successfully. The courts have not seen fit to distinguish between national security and general "foreign policy" interests of the United States (see, for instance, *Haig v. Agee, 453 U.S. 280 (1981)*). The Supreme Court has accepted far-reaching invasions of private rights, such as the internment of citizens of Japanese descent during the World War II *(Korematsu v. United States, 323 U.S. 214 (1944))*. The courts have upheld foreign affairs decisions that affected individual property rights, such as the Iran hostage settlement *(Dames Moore v. Regan)*. They also have accepted questionable executive interpretations of acts of Congress that have foreign policy implications, such as restrictions on travel abroad.

The courts have interpreted the Constitution as protecting rights of aliens as well as of United States citizens. Nonetheless, Congress may deport even longtime law-abiding resident aliens with little or no interference from the judiciary, but discrimination against aliens by the states is prima facie a denial of equal protection of the laws (Amendment XIV) and aliens ordinarily form a "suspect classification" for purposes of determining the standard of judicial scrutiny.

The right to travel, generally recognized as a fundamental right within the United States, is more readily outweighed by foreign affairs interests when an individual seeks to travel abroad. Thus, a passport to travel abroad may be revoked if the individual's foreign activities are adjudged to be a threat to "national security or foreign policy" *(Haig v. Agee, 453 U.S. 280 (1980))*, or if the denial of a passport is designed to bar travel to a particular country, part of a general national policy towards that country *(Zemel v. Rusk, 381 U.S. 1 (1965))*.

The freedom of expression and of the press are fundamental liberties which usually rank above claims of important public interest, but even these freedoms commonly bow before public foreign affairs interests. The Supreme Court upheld limitations on freedom of expression by war-related legislation during and after World War I *(Abrams v. U.S., 250 U.S. 616 (1919); Schenck v. U.S. 249 U.S. 47 (1919))*, and the courts continued to defer to the judgment of the political branches even after first amendment protections expanded and flourished following World War II. The courts have not precluded punishment for violations—by speech or publication—of military censorship or other security regulations, or by symbolic speech such as burning a draft card in protest against the Vietnam War *(U.S. v. O'Brien, 391 U.S. 367 (1968))*. The Supreme Court upheld the enforcement of a contract to obtain advance review of publication by a former agent of the Central Intelligence Agency *(Snepp* v. *United States, 444 U.S. 507 (1980))*. The government did not have to grant a visa to allow an alien excludable under U.S. law to come speak in the United States, although U.S. nationals claimed a right under the First Amendment to hear the speaker's views *(Kleindienst* v. *Mandell, 408 U.S. 753 (1972))*. But the Court invalidated a provision in the District of Columbia Code prohibiting picketing near foreign embassies *(Boos* v. *Barry, 485 U.S. 312 (1988))*.

In one major instance the Supreme Court refused to defer to the executive branch. The Court refused to enjoin publication of the "Pentagon Papers" because the executive branch had failed to overcome the heavy presumption against prior restraint by proving that immediate and irreparable harm to national security would result from publication of the classified materials *(New York Times Co.* v. *United States, 403 U.S. 713 (1971))*. But some justices suggested that an injunction might have issued if it had been authorized by Congress, and some seemed prepared to uphold laws against such publication if enforced by criminal sanctions after publication (rather than by restraining publication in advance by judicial injunction).

The Supreme Court also has suggested that the executive is privileged not to disclose high-level communications involving military, diplomatic, or national security matters even when required for the administration of justice *(U.S.* v. *Nixon, 418 U.S. 683 (1974)*.

Federal Jurisdiction and Foreign Affairs

Federal courts address foreign affairs issues that fall within their jurisdiction. The jurisdiction of the general courts includes some cases of special significance for foreign affairs. For example, some circuit courts of appeals review decisions of local courts in territories with which the United States has special relations, such as Guam or the Northern Mariana Islands. Federal courts of special jurisdiction also consider foreign affairs matters; for example, the U.S. Court of Federal Claims has jurisdiction over claims that the U.S. government has taken property by international agreement without paying just compensation. When the Supreme Court upheld the president's power to conclude an agreement to resolve the hostage crisis with Iran (1979–1980), by which the United States agreed to suspend private lawsuits against Iran and to transfer those claims to arbitration before a special claims tribunal, the Court noted that the suspension of individual claims might constitute a taking of property for which the litigants could claim compensation in the Court of Federal Claims *(Dames & Moore)*.

Another court of special jurisdiction, the Court of International Trade (replacing the former Customs Court), has exclusive jurisdiction over a range of tariff, customs, and trade matters *(28 U.S.C. §§ 1581 et seq.)*. Appeal from both the U.S. Federal Court of Claims and the Court of International Trade (as well as from final decisions of the International Trade Commission) is to a special appellate court, the Court of Appeals for the Federal Circuit *(28 U.S.C. § 1295)*.

The constitutional and statutory law governing the courts in foreign affairs is the same as that in domestic affairs. Many foreign affairs cases fall into one or more of the jurisdictional categories of the courts. Cases arising under the Constitution include those challenging the constitutionality of an act of Congress, or actions of the president or of the states, affecting U.S. foreign affairs. Cases arising under the laws of the United States may involve the interpretation or application of laws of Congress that relate to U.S. foreign affairs, such as laws that regulate commerce with foreign states; or that exercise the power of Congress to declare war and wage war successfully; or the power of Congress to regulate the value of foreign coin; or the power of Congress to define and punish piracies and felonies committed on the high seas and offenses against the law of nations. (Even cases arising under laws that seem strictly domestic may impinge on the foreign relations of the United States, for example, when law is applied to actions, interests, or property of foreign nationals in the United States, or of U.S. nationals in foreign countries.) Cases arising under the laws of the United States include cases arising under international law. The judicial power of the United States and the jurisdiction of the federal courts extend to cases arising under U.S. treaties.

The jurisdiction of the federal courts also includes cases or controversies between designated parties that may be of particular foreign policy significance. It extends to "all cases affecting ambassadors, other public ministers and consuls," and to controversies "between a state [of the United States], or the Citizens thereof, and foreign states, citizens or subjects" (Art. 3, Sect. 2(1)). (The Eleventh Amendment to the Constitution subsequently provided that the judicial power does not extend to suits brought against one of the states by a citizen or subject of a foreign state.) The Constitution gives the Supreme Court original jurisdiction over cases affecting ambassadors and other ministers as well as cases to which a state is a party, including those between a state and foreign states or foreign citizens or subjects. But the Court has allowed Congress to give original jurisdiction over cases affecting ambassadors and other ministers to the district courts as well *(Börs* v. *Preston, 111 U.S. 252 (1884))*.

The courts of the United States are open to suits by foreign governments recognized by the United States, and to suits by foreign nationals, as well as to suits against foreign states, officials, diplomats, or nationals where they do not enjoy immunity from suit under international law or under the laws of the United States.

The doctrines which the courts have developed to limit adjudication—requirements of case or controversy, standing, ripeness, concreteness, "nonmootness," justiciability (nonpolitical questions)—might apply with greater force or frequency in matters relating to foreign affairs. Thus, a question is more likely to be deemed a "political question" and nonjusticiable if it relates to an exercise of power by the political branches in foreign affairs. If a challenged act is found to be within the plenary authority of the political branches, a court may be more disposed to conclude that it lacks standards for resolving the issue, or that there is an unusual need to adhere to a political decision and to avoid "multifarious pronouncements by various departments" *(Baker* v. *Carr).*

Sovereign and Diplomatic Immunity

Foreign affairs provide additional limitations on the exercise of jurisdiction, some required by international law and some of the courts' own making.

The courts, both federal and state, must respect the privileges and immunities of foreign states; of accredited foreign diplomats and consular personnel; of public international organizations (such as the United Nations); of foreign-country representatives to the UN and to other intergovernmental organizations; and of officials of such organizations, to the extent provided by international law, treaties, or laws of the United States (unless such immunity has been effectively waived). At one time, the courts determined claims of immunity wholly by reference to customary international law. Later, the courts accepted also, and felt bound by, "suggestions" of immunity by the executive branch. Since 1976, the immunity of foreign states has been governed by federal law—the Foreign Sovereign Immunities Act—which applies international law as the United States sees it. Basically, that Act gives foreign states immunity in suits arising out of acts of a governmental character but not those of a commercial character or those arising out of torts committed in the United States (see *28 U.S.C. §§ 1330, 1602 et seq., Restatement [Third] of the Foreign Relations Law of the United States, §§ 451–60).*

The immunity of accredited diplomats and consuls is also governed by international law, which has been codified by treaties to which the United States is party. The privileges and immunities of the United Nations, of member representatives to the UN, or of the secretary general and other UN officials, are governed by the UN Charter and by the Headquarters Agreement between the United States and the United Nations (an international agreement equivalent to a treaty), and by the

International Organizations Immunities Act (an act of Congress, *22 U.S.C. §§ 288 et seq.).* In general, accredited diplomats, member representatives to the UN, and the UN secretary general enjoy full immunity from the jurisdiction of the courts. Consuls and UN officials enjoy only "line of official duty" immunity.

The immunity of a foreign state from the jurisdiction of the courts is required by international law as well as by Congress's Foreign Sovereign Immunities Act. In addition, the courts, on their own authority and initiative, have developed a policy of deference to foreign states, the Act of State Doctrine. Under that doctrine, federal and state courts in the United States will not sit in judgment on the acts of a foreign state carried on within its own territory, and will give effect to such acts *(Banco Nacional de Cuba* v. *Sabbatino, 376 U.S. 398 (1964)).* That doctrine is an expression of judicial self-restraint reflecting the courts' doubts about their competence in matters involving the foreign relations of the United States. The doctrine also reflects the principle of separation of powers, and "expresses the strong sense of the judicial branch that its engagement in the task of passing on the validity of foreign acts of state may hinder rather than further this country's pursuit of goals both for itself and for the community of nations as a whole in the international sphere." *(Sabbatino, 376 U.S. 398, at 423.)*

Since the doctrine is made by judges and for the courts' own guidance, the courts have felt free to determine its scope and to develop exceptions. The courts have had to decide which official foreign action or involvement constitutes an "act" of the foreign "state"; what "sitting in judgment" on that act implies; what "giving effect" to the act requires. The courts will give effect to such a foreign act even if the act is contrary to international law. But some lower courts have suggested an exception to the doctrine when the foreign act is inconsistent with the foreign state's obligations under a treaty with the United States *(Kalamazoo Spice Extraction Co.* v. *Government of Socialist Ethiopia, 729 F.2d 422 (6th Cir. 1984);* compare *Restatement (Third) of Foreign Relations Law of the United States § 443).* Courts also have carved an exception to the doctrine in cases under the Alien Tort Claims Act. They have given judgment in suits against foreign officials for torture and other gross violations of human rights, because they were disposed to assume that the foreign government did not countenance such actions, and they were therefore not acts of the foreign state for purposes of the Act of State Doctrine. Congress also enacted an exception to the doctrine, directing the courts not to give effect to a foreign act that expropriates property of U.S. nationals without the compensation required by international law *(The Second Hickenlooper Amendment, 22 U.S.C. § 2370(e)(2) (1970)).*

U.S. Courts and International Law

From the beginnings of U.S. history, the Supreme Court has declared that the United States became amenable to international law when it became a nation, and international law—both treaties and customary law—was law of the United States to be applied by courts of appropriate jurisdiction in cases before them *(The Paquete Habana, 175 U.S. 677 (1900))*. The interpretation of a treaty for purposes of U.S. law is a traditional judicial function; the judiciary will give weight to executive interpretation, but such interpretation will not necessarily be determinative (see *Perkins* v. *Elg, 307 U.S. 325 (1939))*.

Judicial application of customary international law has raised complex issues. For a long time, international law was applied by both state and federal courts independently, and after *Erie* v. *Tompkins*, some thought that international law was part of the common law and therefore of state law, and that a federal court was bound to follow determinations of international law by the highest court of the state in which the federal court sat. In *Sabbatino*, the Supreme Court declared that international law (as well as the Act of State Doctrine) was federal law, and state courts were bound by determinations of the law by the Supreme Court of the United States *(376 U.S. at 425)*. For purposes of U.S. law, judicial determinations of international law and judicial interpretation of U.S. treaties are binding also on the executive and on Congress. However, the president might decide to denounce a treaty, and Congress could legislate contrary to U.S. obligations under a treaty or under international law. The courts will not give effect to a treaty that is no longer in effect under international law; they will not apply a treaty in the face of a subsequent act of Congress *(Whitney* v. *Robertson)*.

The courts have determined the place of treaties and of international law in the hierarchy of U.S. law. The Supreme Court has decided that a treaty can be given effect as U.S. law only to the extent that it is not inconsistent with the Constitution *(Reid* v. *Covert, 354 U.S. 1 (1957))*. The Court also would probably hold that a principle of customary international law cannot be given effect as law in the United States if it is inconsistent with the Constitution.

So, too, the Court has read the Supremacy Clause of the Constitution (art. 6) as declaring the equal status in U.S. law of treaties and acts of Congress, so that in case of inconsistency between treaty and statute, the later will prevail *(Whitney* v. *Robertson, 124 U.S. 190, 194 (1888))*. Again, the Court might well hold that international law has status equal to that of a statute so that when they conflict, the later in time will prevail. Some commentators have expressed doubt that a principle of international law should be given effect in the face of an earlier act of Congress.

The Supreme Court has distinguished between treaties that are self-executing and those that require implementation, ordinarily by act of Congress. Presumably, only a self-executing treaty is automatically law of the land. Whether a treaty is self-executing is ordinarily determined by whether the undertaking is of a character that can be given effect by the courts without an intervening action by Congress or the president. For example, a treaty promising that the United States will pay money requires Congress to appropriate the money; it is not a promise that the courts can carry out or enforce. In recent years the president and the Senate have begun to declare human rights treaties non–self-executing even though they could be given effect by the courts without Congressional implementation (see, for example, the declaration attached by the United States to its ratifications of the International Covenant on Civil and Political Rights, the Convention on the Elimination of All Forms of Racial Discrimination, and the Convention Against Torture and Other Cruel, Inhuman, or Degrading Treatment or Punishment). The Supreme Court has not considered whether such declarations must be honored by the courts, or whether, perhaps, the courts are constitutionally obliged to give effect to the treaty as U.S. law without awaiting implementation.

Customary international law, like treaties, is also law of the land to be applied by the courts. The courts have applied customary international law, for example, in recognizing and giving effect to state sovereign immunity and to the immunity of diplomats or consuls, either upon claim by the foreign state or diplomat or when suggested on their behalf by the U.S. Department of Justice. (See, for example, *The Schooner Exchange* v. *McFaddon, 11 U.S. (7 Cranch.) 116 (1812); Ex parte Peru, 318 U.S. 578 (1943).)* In recent years, U.S. courts have been called upon to apply the customary international law of human rights. By the Alien Tort Claims Act *(28 U.S.C. § 1350)*, for example, Congress gave federal courts jurisdiction over suits by foreign nationals in tort for violation of a U.S. treaty or the Law of Nations. Several courts have interpreted that act as providing relief to aliens claiming a remedy for torture or extra-judicial killings and disappearances, as violations of the customary international law of human rights. *(Filartiga* v. *Pena-Irala, 630 F.2d 876 (2d Cir. 1980).)*

The customary law of human rights also has been invoked in U.S. courts on behalf of aliens not lawfully admitted to the United States, where U.S. constitutional safeguards were held inapplicable or insufficient (see the discussion of Congress's plenary power over immigration, above). Such aliens have had some limited success arguing that customary international law bars their indefinite detention. (See, for example, *Rodriguez-Fernandez* v. *Wilkinson, 505 F. Supp. 787 (D. Kan. 1980),* affirmed, *654*

F.2d 1382 (10th Cir. 1981).) However, a different U.S. court refused to enjoin executive officials from detaining such aliens even if the detention violated customary international human rights law (see *Garcia-Mir* v. *Meese, 788 F.2d 1446 (11th Cir. 1986), cert. denied, 479 U.S. 889 (1986)*).

Judicial supremacy in interpreting and monitoring compliance with the Constitution by the political branches and by the states, applies to foreign as well as to domestic affairs. In principle, all the issues raised by judicial review—doctrines of interpretation, judicial self-restraint or activism—apply to both. The jurisprudence of judicial review as it relates to individual rights—preferred freedoms, suspect classifications, levels of judicial scrutiny, the weight of public interest required to outweigh an individual right—apply as well in foreign affairs, in principle.

In practice, however, judicial review looks different and has a different effect in foreign affairs. The courts have developed an attitude, approaching a doctrine, of greater deference to the political branches in regard to foreign affairs, and greater self-restraint by the courts when asked to invalidate political action. They are disposed to accept determinations by the political branches as to the scope of their constitutional authority, or executive interpretations of legislative authorization or delegation. The courts give special weight to executive determinations of international law and to executive interpretations of treaties, as well as executive (administrative) determinations of fact, for example in the application of the Protocol on Refugees (a treaty of the United States) and of foreign affairs legislation. In balancing the public interest against individual rights, the courts give great weight to executive determinations of the requirements of "national interest." During the Cold War, for instance, courts were particularly deferential to executive assertions of the demands of national security.

State Courts and Foreign Affairs

Issues affecting U.S. foreign affairs may arise in state courts as well as in federal courts, but a decision of a foreign affairs question by the highest court of a state that has jurisdiction over the matter is subject to review by the U.S. Supreme Court. Like other federal questions, cases involving foreign affairs brought in a state court may be removed to a lower federal court.

Foreign affairs are national. Like the U.S. Constitution, U.S. laws relating to foreign affairs, U.S. treaties, and customary international law, are supreme and binding on the states. (Art. VI, the "Supremacy Clause.") Supreme Court interpretations of U.S. foreign affairs law, of treaties of the United States, and Supreme Court determinations of international law, are binding on the states and on state courts.

Courts in the United States are not major contributors to the formation or formulation of U.S. foreign policy, nor are they direct participants in the conduct of foreign relations. Courts decide only cases or controversies that come before them, and most issues of U.S. foreign policy escape them. Some issues the courts avoid. The courts have not resolved chronic issues of separation of powers in foreign affairs between Congress and the president — distribution of power in "the twilight zone," the locus of war powers, executive privilege. When the courts hear an important foreign affairs case, they tend to defer to the political branches—as they did when they upheld the internment of Japanese Americans during World War II. Some courts abstained, while some deferred to the executive, on issues arising out of the Vietnam War. The courts did not uphold challenges to executive abduction abroad or to the interdiction of refugees on the high seas. (See *Alvarez-Machain* v. *U.S., 504 U.S. 655 (1992); Sale* v. *Haitian Centers Council, Inc., 113 Sup.Ct. 2549 (1993)*.)

But foreign affairs are governed by the Constitution, and the Constitution is what the judges say it is, in foreign as in domestic matters. The judges have helped establish that foreign affairs are national affairs (from which the states are excluded), and the judges invalidate undue state burdens on commerce with foreign nations. In principle, the courts determine the Constitutional authority of the branches of the federal government (including their own). In principle, the courts are responsible to assure that U.S. officials respect private rights under the Constitution and laws, in foreign as in domestic matters. Constitutional issues apart, U.S. courts impinge on foreign affairs when they enforce rights under treaties and international law, and international arbitral awards; when they decide cases involving foreign governments, foreign citizens, or foreign companies; when they adjudicate transnational property rights, rights under contracts involving foreign nationals, or family disputes involving foreign citizens and foreign law; and when they provide some remedies for some violations of international human rights by foreign officials.

In all, courts help maintain the rule of law in respect of transnational matters in the United States, and contribute to the rule of law in international life.

Louis Henkin

See also Chadha Decision; Congress; Constitution; Curtiss-Wright Case; International Law; Presidency

FURTHER READING

American Law Institute. *Restatement of the Law (Third), The Foreign Relations Law of the United States.* Philadelphia, Pa., 1987.
Ely, John H. *War and Responsibility.* Anniston, N.J., 1993.
Frankfurter and Landis. *The Business of the Supreme Court.* 1928.
Glennon. *Constitutional Diplomacy.* 1990.
Henkin, Louis, Glennon, Rogers, eds. *Foreign Affairs and the U.S. Constitution.* 1990.

———. "International Law as Law in the United States." *82 Michigan Law Review* 1555 (1984).

———. *Constitutionalism, Democracy, and Foreign Affairs.* New York, 1990.

Henkin, Louis. *Foreign Affairs and the Constitution.* 2nd ed. 1996.

———. "The Constitution and U.S. Sovereignty: A Century of Chinese Exclusion and its Progeny." *100 Harvard Law Review* 853 (1987).

Jackson, R. H. *The Struggle for Judicial Supremacy.* 1941.

Koh, Harold H. *The National Security Constitution: Sharing Power after the Iran-Contra Affair.* New Haven, Conn., 1990.

Wright, Miller, and Cooper. *Federal Practice and Procedure,* 2nd ed. 1988.

SURINAME

See Appendix 2

SUSSEX

See World War I

SWAZILAND

A southeastern African kingdom located between Mozambique and South Africa, which became independent in 1967 and is primarily inhabited by Nguni and Sotho speaking peoples. The nation of Swaziland has its origins in the *mfecane*, a series of migrations and conflicts that racked southern and central Africa during the late eighteenth and early nineteenth centuries. The founder of Swaziland was King Sobhuza; he led Nguni speaking people into the area from what is now South Africa after suffering defeats in battles with other Nguni speaking people. With the expansion of Boers and British into eastern South Africa in the late nineteenth century, the Swazi kingdom came under increasing pressure. Swazi policy of avoiding armed confrontation with whites allowed the kingdom to maintain at least some of its territory. In 1906, Swaziland became a High Commissioner Territory and was assigned a British Commissioner. Like Botswana and Lesotho, the country was left out of the Union of South Africa when the latter was formed in 1910. From 1906 to 1966, Swaziland's government was under direct white oversight in the form of high commissioners or advisory boards. In 1968, Swaziland gained complete independence, with its traditional monarchy intact, while remaining a member of the British Commonwealth. Although formal relations were not established until 1974, interaction between Swaziland and the United States dates from 1968 when study grants were made available to Swazi students through the U.S. Coun-

cil of International Programs. After diplomatic recognition, the United States was most active through the AID program which supported the government's Rural Development Areas Program to diversify Swaziland's economy. Swaziland has a primarily agricultural economy which exports items such as corn, livestock, sugar cane, and cotton. Most of the industrial goods produced in Swaziland are also of agricultural origin, including processed meat and sugar.

Since its independence, Swaziland has had to undertake a pro-Western approach that favored the United States largely because of its proximity to South Africa. The large number of Swazi workers in South Africa also has had a mediating effect on Swaziland's policies. Despite Swaziland's overall weak position, its border with Mozambique did present some problems to South Africa as African National Congress (ANC) activity against the South African government increased in the late 1970s.

ANTHONY Q. CHEESEBORO

See also Africa; South Africa

FURTHER READING

Omer-Cooper, J.D. *History of Southern Africa.* London, 1994.

Harris, Betty J. *Political Economy of the Southern African Periphery.* London, 1993.

SWEDEN

A Nordic kingdom bordering the Baltic Sea between Norway and Finland that generally has maintained friendly relations with the United States despite occasional disputes and tensions—especially during World War II and at the height of the Cold War. Relations between the United States and Sweden initially developed out of contacts between Ambassador Gustav Philip Creutz and Benjamin Franklin in Paris during the American Revolution. Sweden's neutrality in the conflict, however, precluded official relations until a peace agreement was reached. In February 1783, Franklin and Creutz inaugurated relations on behalf of their respective governments by signing a Treaty of Amity and Commerce, which articulated a policy for the free shipment of goods between the two countries. This treaty was the United States' first with a non-belligerent state.

Adequate diplomatic relations did not come about until 1810 when the first U.S. citizen was appointed vice-consul in Göteborg. Over the course of the nineteenth century, Sweden and the United States expanded their relationship through increased trade, a shared commitment to stay out of European wars, and increased Swedish immigration. Swedish settlement of North America had actually begun in 1638 in Delaware, and it was these early Swedes who introduced the log cabin to the American colonial landscape. Significant numbers of Swedish immigrants did not settle, however, until after the American Revolution. In the 1830s and 1840s, Swedes, along with Danes, Finns and Norwegians, moved to the farmlands of the Ohio and upper–Mississippi River valleys and the Great Lakes region. By the late nineteenth century, Swedes were part of the one million Scandinavian immigrants to the United States, settling mainly in the northern parts of the country. By 1920, there were well over 600,000 Swedish-born and first-generation Swedish Americans in this region alone.

During the first years of World War I, the United States and Sweden worked at parallel purposes, strongly advocating the right of neutrals to ship goods freely. Sweden's proximity to the belligerent nations of Europe greatly hindered its trade, however, and the Swedish government's efforts to secure stronger diplomatic support from the U.S. government came to naught. Once the United States entered the war, it sided with Great Britain in criticizing Sweden for being too benevolent toward Germany and for allowing coded German cables to be sent through Swedish telegraph lines across the Atlantic Ocean.

During World War II Sweden continued to observe strict neutrality, but the war was brought to its doorstep as all of its Scandinavian neighbors were either occupied by or allied with Nazi Germany. In order to prevent provoking retaliatory measures from Germany, Sweden maintained its trade with the Third Reich, including vital industrial products, and allowed German troops to pass through Swedish territory, which brought diplomatic pressure to bear from the United States and the Allies.

At the onset of the Cold War, Sweden was determined to remain nonaligned, rejecting a defense arrangement with the United States through NATO, although its own plans for an alliance among Nordic countries failed to materialize. Despite its nonaligned status, Sweden was a vital component of U.S. strategic planning in Northern Europe as the U.S. foreign policy establishment realized the possible threat to NATO allies Norway and Denmark if Sweden's independence was compromised. Some U.S. government officials criticized Sweden as a "neutralist free rider," however, because it indirectly derived security from NATO without sharing the burdens of military obligation and cooperation with the United States regarding the Soviet Union.

Tensions mounted during the Vietnam War when Stockholm's severe criticism of the war irritated the U.S. government. When the U.S. ambassador to Sweden Jerome H. Holland returned to the United States in August 1972, Washington did not appoint a successor. In the meantime, Swedish prime minister Olof Palme kept up his attacks against U.S. policy in Vietnam and denounced the Christmas bombing of Cambodia in December 1972 as an "outrage," comparing it to fascist massacres of the 1930s and 1940s. The Swedish ambassador in Washington, Hubert De Besche, was transferred the following January, and the U.S. government requested that his replacement be delayed. Full diplomatic relations were not restored until April 1974. Even then, the two countries continued to clash on a number of issues, including North-South economic and political relations.

Cooperation resumed in the 1980s and 1990s over defense matters as Soviet submarine activity in Swedish territorial waters aroused suspicion in Stockholm. In 1987, at Washington's behest, Swedish companies stopped exporting sensitive Western technology to Warsaw Pact countries. In return, the United States dropped its requirement that Swedish companies be licensed to export technology originating in the United States. In a marked departure from its neutral stance, Sweden became a participant in NATO's Partnership for Peace program in 1994. Swedish troops, stationed in Bosnia-Herzegovina initially under the United Nations peacekeeping force, became an integral part of NATO's Implementation Force (IFOR) in the U.S. sector in December 1995, coming under direct U.S. command.

DAVID P. AUGUSTYN

See also Neutral Rights; Vietnam War

FURTHER READING

Lindmark, Sture, and Tore Tallroth, eds. *Swedes Looking West, Aspects on Swedish-American Relations.* Stockholm, 1983.
Scott, Franklin D. *Scandinavia.* Cambridge, 1975.
Solheim, Bruce Olav. *The Nordic Nexus: A Lesson in Peaceful Security.* Westport, Conn., 1984.
Sundelius, Bengt, ed. *Foreign Policies of Northern Europe.* Boulder, Colo., 1982.

SWITZERLAND

Located in mountainous Central Europe, surrounded by France, Italy, Austria, and Germany, a nation long known for its ability to preserve its neutrality in the face of major European conflict. The Swiss capital is Geneva. Official diplomatic contacts between the United States and Switzerland began in July 1822 when the U.S. government authorized the Swiss consul in New York to perform his duties. The wars of the Napoleonic Era had prompted a wave of Swiss emigration to the United States, and with the restoration of the Swiss confederation under the federal pact (*Bundesvertrag*) of 1815, the Swiss desired to establish a consulate in the United States to protect the business interests, persons, and property of Swiss immigrants and merchants. The United States, however, delayed opening a consulate in Switzerland until 1830.

During the first part of the nineteenth century, Switzerland, which was then the only republic in Europe, looked to the United States for moral support while, in turn, Switzerland provided the United States with a hope for democratic progress on the Continent. After a brief war broke out in 1847 between Protestant and Catholic cantons (states of the Swiss Confederation), an unprecedented wave of emigration to the United States took place. After the resolution of the conflict in 1848, the new government relied upon the U.S. Constitution for reorganizing the political structure of the new Helvetic Republic. Formal diplomatic relations between the two countries commenced on 12 July 1850. A "Convention of Friendship, Reciprocal Establishments, Commerce and the Surrender of Fugitive Criminals" was ratified in 1855 and still forms the basis of U.S.-Swiss relations.

In 1856–1857 U.S. Minister Theodore S. Fay, with the tacit approval of the secretary of state, played a crucial mediating role between Switzerland and Prussia, following an insurrection by Prussian loyalists in Neuchâtel, a former Prussian principality, which brought the two countries to the brink of war. Accepted as a disinterested and skillful diplomat, Fay traveled to both Bern and Berlin, speaking to the federal council and to the Prussian king, softening the positions of both. Fay also is credited with influencing internal Swiss policies regarding the right of residence of Jews. With consummate diplomatic skill he objected to the policy of seven of the seventeen Swiss cantons absolutely restricting Jewish residence. Fay's "Israeli note" refuted the justifications given for such policies in 1859 and was published by the federal council. The Swiss president reported to Fay that public opinion favored the abolition of such restrictions. Eventually, in the revised constitution of 1874, explicit guarantees of religious freedom in Switzerland were included.

On the other hand, U.S.-Swiss relations became strained in the twentieth century over issues of international obligations versus the right to neutrality. The United States and Switzerland began both world wars as neutrals, but eventually the United States joined both times in the hostilities. Following World War I, and although neutrals were excluded from the Paris Peace Conference of 1919, Switzerland became one of the original members of the League of Nations. At the insistence of President Woodrow Wilson the seat of the League was established in Geneva. In partial recognition of its traditional neutrality, Switzerland was exempted from participating in the League's potential military activities, but not from economic sanctions. Eventually, the disintegration of the League during the 1930s induced the Swiss to abandon collective security and to revert to their former position of absolute neutrality.

During World War II, the Swiss were pressured by the Allies to compromise their neutrality. Given Switzerland's unique geographic vulnerability, completely surrounded by hostile Axis powers, the Swiss resisted such pressures with varying degrees of success, fearing that otherwise their country would certainly become a theater of war. By 1943, the Swiss had agreed to restrict trade with Germany in order to escape Allied blacklisting and postwar sanctions, but stubbornly refused to reduce trade to zero levels. Continued U.S. pressure to decrease German rail transshipment through Switzerland hurt U.S.-Swiss relations far into the postwar period. However, Switzerland did its best to ensure the welfare of American prisoners of war (POWs) held by both Germany and Japan. Using diplomatic means and also acting through the Geneva-based International Commission of the Red Cross (founded in 1864), the Swiss sought the enforcement of Geneva Convention standards for POWs.

Because the Swiss economy emerged from World War II in good condition, Switzerland did not request or receive U.S. Marshall Plan aid. In fact, the Swiss agreed to liquidate German assets in Switzerland and share the proceeds with the devastated European countries. Also, while a staunch supporter of liberal trading principles espoused by the United States, Switzerland did not initially join the International Monetary Fund (IMF) or the General Agreement on Tariffs and Trade (GATT). Considerations of neutrality led Switzerland to prefer membership in the European Free Trade Association (EFTA) over the European Economic Community (EEC). It eventually joined the GATT as a full member in 1966 and the IMF in 1982. Neutrality also dictated that Switzerland not join the United Nations although, ironically, the European headquarters of the UN are located in Geneva.

During the Cold War, the Swiss, while remaining inveterate anticommunists, nevertheless, fought to maintain their neutrality, again despite U.S. pressure over economic issues. For example, in 1951 the United States imposed an embargo on exports to Eastern Europe and insisted that Switzerland be subjected to monitoring by the Group of Consultants and the Coordinating Committee (COCOM). Moreover, the United States threatened Switzerland with heavy economic sanctions, leading Switzerland to accede to U.S. pressure. Conversely, it was with great reticence that Switzerland maintained its diplomatic relationships with communist countries. Only as late as 1970 did it finally agree to diplomatic recognition of the German Democratic Republic, North Vietnam and North Korea.

In military matters during the Cold War, Switzerland maintained its militia as the pillar of its security played next to no role in arms control debates, and recognizing the need for the NATO alliance. The Swiss did sign the Nuclear Non-Proliferation Treaty (NPT) in 1969, although domestic debate delayed its ratification for eight years. Switzerland also joined the Conference on Security and Cooperation in Europe (CSCE), coordinating its policies with those of other neutral and non-aligned countries.

REBECCA BRITTON

See also International Red Cross and Red Crescent Movement; League of Nations; Marshall Plan; Nuclear Nonproliferation; World War I; World War II

FURTHER READING
Meier, Heinz K. *The United States and Switzerland in the Nineteenth Century.* The Hague, 1963.
———. *Friendship Under Stress; U.S.-Swiss Relations, 1900–1950.* Bern, 1970.
Milivojevic, Marko and Pierre Maurer, eds. *Swiss Neutrality and Security: Armed Forces, National Defense, and Foreign Policy.* New York, 1990.

SYRIA

A Middle Eastern republic, bordering the Mediterranean Sea, Turkey, Iraq, Jordan, Israel, and Lebanon. A successor state to the Ottoman Empire, Syria was ruled by France from 1918 until World War II. In April 1946, assisted by British and U.S. pressure on France, Syria became an independent republic.

Initial contacts between what became Syria and the United States took place in the mid-nineteenth century, when U.S. missionaries set up several influential institutions there, most notably the American University of Beirut.

Syrian political relations with the United States since independence have ranged from cool to hostile, and can be divided into three eras. During the first of these periods, from Syrian independence in 1946 until Damascus turned to the Soviets in 1956, Washington exerted limited influence in Syria and the two countries enjoyed decent relations. This calm period began to decline in 1954 when the Ba'th Party, a radical pan-Arabist and anti-American group, became a powerful force. In February 1956, the second era began with the signing of a Czech arms deal by Damascus, which led to a deterioration of relations with Washington. From then until 1989, Syrian authorities aligned increasingly with Moscow against Washington. Milestones included the 1958 union with Egypt (the United Arab Republic) and its dissolution in 1961; the arch-leftist regime of 1966–1970; and the 1980 Treaty of Friendship and Cooperation with the Soviet Union. Active Syrian involvement in the Arab-Israeli wars of 1967 and 1973 caused relations with Washington to worsen.

President Hafiz al-Assad (1970–) improved ties to the United States, most notably by working with Henry Kissinger to sign a disengagement agreement with Israel in 1974; this agreement left Israel in control of the Golan Heights, which had been seized from Syria in 1967. The gradual Syrian conquest of Lebanon then caused U.S.-Syrian relations to worsen again, with the nadir occurring in December 1983, when American naval fighters attacked Syrian positions in Lebanon. Tensions between the two countries continued, primarily due to a surreptitious but evident Syrian role in the seizure of American hostages in Lebanon during the decade 1982–1992.

The fall of Romania's Nicolae Ceausescu in December 1989 marked the beginning of the third era, for this event made Assad aware of the fragility of Soviet backing and prompted him to make amends with the United States. His opportunity came in August 1990, when Saddam Hussein invaded Kuwait; joining the U.S.-led coalition against Iraq placed Damascus for the first time in a time of crisis on the same side as Washington.

Assad's desire for improved relations with the United States also prompted him to join the U.S.-organized Middle East peace process in October 1991 and to take some small steps to open the country. Still, Assad made no fundamental changes and achieved little progress toward peace with Israel, despite intense efforts by the Clinton administration. Working closely with Israel's Labor government, the president and secretary of state helped the two states reach the outlines of a compromise solution. But two problems arose and prevented a deal. First, Asad did not accept a compromise, insisting on his terms in almost every key area. Second, skeptics in Israel and the United States found the American-sponsored approach to Syria too accommodating of Assad, especially given his continued support for terrorism and for groups opposed to the peace process. The election of a Likud government in May 1996 then led to a fundamental reassessment of the negotiations.

Thus, bilateral ties with the United States in late 1996 had more or less returned to where they began decades earlier—cool but engaged.

DANIEL PIPES

See also Egypt; Iran-Iraq War; Israel; Lebanon; Middle East

FURTHER READING
Lesch, David W. *Syria and the United States: Eisenhower's Cold War in the Middle East.* Boulder, Colo., 1992.
Ma'oz, Moshe. *Syria and Israel: From War to Peacemaking.* Oxford, 1995.
Pipes, Daniel. *Syria Beyond the Peace Process.* Washington, D.C., 1996.
Saunders, Bonnie F. *The United States and Arab Nationalism: The Syrian Case, 1953–1960.* Westport, Conn., 1996.

T

TAFT, ROBERT A.

(*b.* 8 September 1889; *d.* 31 July 1953)

Anti-interventionist senator from Ohio who was the son of the 27th U.S. president. A graduate of Princeton University and Harvard Law School, Taft worked for U.S. Food Administrator Herbert Hoover during World War I and served in the Ohio legislature before winning election to the U.S. Senate in 1938. A thoughtful conservative and master parliamentarian who earned the sobriquet "Mr. Republican," Taft voted against Selective Service and Lend-Lease, and criticized President Franklin D. Roosevelt's alleged usurpation of executive powers prior to the Japanese bombing of Pearl Harbor. After World War II he condemned the Nuremberg war crimes trials for violating "that fundamental principle…that a man cannot be tried under an ex-post facto statute." An "Asia Firster," Taft rejected bipartisanship in the Cold War because he did not accept President Harry S. Truman's emphasis on containing communist expansion in Western Europe. Although he supported the Truman Doctrine for Greece and Turkey, he opposed the Marshall Plan as too expensive and voted against the North Atlantic Treaty. He thereafter consistently sought to limit U.S. military commitment to NATO. A strong backer of U.S. military action in Korea, Taft nonetheless decried Truman's failure to ask Congress for a declaration of war.

Taft sought the Republican nomination for president in 1952 but lost to Dwight D. Eisenhower, the favorite of the Eastern internationalist wing of the party. Taft anticipated a basic theme of Dwight D. Eisenhower's policies, however, by warning that excessive military and foreign expenditures in peacetime might turn the United States into a "garrison state." An avid Republican partisan, Taft gave initial approval to Senator Joseph McCarthy's investigations of communist subversion. During the Vietnam era, a new generation remembered Taft's opposition to the draft, his demands for greater congressional influence in the making of foreign policy, and his criticism of U.S. interventionism abroad.

J. GARRY CLIFFORD

See also Containment; Korean War; Lend-Lease; Marshall Plan; McCarthyism; North Atlantic Treaty Organization; Nuremberg, International Tribunal at; Truman Doctrine

FURTHER READING

Doenecke, Justic D. *Not to the Swift: The Old Isolationists in the Cold War Era*. Lewisburg, Pa., 1979.
Paterson, Thomas G., ed. *Cold War Critics*. Chicago, 1971.
Patterson, James T. *Mr. Republican*. Boston, 1972.
Radosh, Ronald. *Prophets on the Right*. New York, 1974.

TAFT, WILLIAM HOWARD

(*b.* 15 September 1857; *d.* 8 March 1930)

Secretary of war (1904–1908) and 27th president of the United States (1909–1913). Born in Cincinnati, Ohio, Taft graduated from Yale in 1878 and Cincinnati Law School two years later. After serving as a judge in Ohio, he was appointed president of the Second Philippine Commission in 1900 and went to the Philippines to direct U.S. administration of the archipelago; he became its governor-general, and ultimately proved to be an efficient colonial official.

Taft's success in the Philippines led to his designation as secretary of war in 1904. President Theodore Roosevelt entrusted Taft with important responsibilities in foreign affairs, including supervising the building of the Panama Canal, assuming control of Cuba as its provisional governor in 1906, and serving as the administration's roving ambassador to the world. He undertook missions to Asia in 1905 and 1907, and during the former trip, signed the secret Taft-Katsura Agreement with Japan; in this agreement, the United States accepted Japanese control of Korea while Japan promised to maintain a hands-off policy in the Philippines.

As Roosevelt's hand-picked successor to the presidency in 1908, Taft shared his predecessor's view of the U.S. role in the world. Taft sought above all else to promote market expansionism and to increase American investments abroad; his stratagem to use dollars instead of war to promote order in politically unstable nations, primarily in the Caribbean, became known as "dollar diplomacy." He resorted to direct military intervention in 1912, however, in both Cuba and Nicaragua. In Asia, he saw dollar diplomacy as the best way to limit Japanese expansion, maintain Chinese independence, and promote U.S. trade and investments. Taft's pressure on China did secure American participation in railroad consortia, but in general his attempts to expand U.S. economic interests in Asia, primarily the injection of U.S. capital into China, fell far short of his goals, while damaging U.S. relations with Japan and Russia. Both nations remained adamant in their intentions of unilaterally exploiting their respective spheres of influence in China; thus they resisted U.S. efforts to achieve the "open door" for American investors.

After his electoral defeat for a second term as president, Taft became professor of constitutional law at Yale (1913–1921). He supported the United States' entrance into World War I and later campaigned actively for U.S. membership in the League of Nations. From 1921 to 1930, he served as Chief Justice of the U.S. Supreme Court, a position better suited to his cautious and reactive temperament than the presidency.

Taft does not rank as a great world leader. Far more so than Theodore Roosevelt, he based his foreign policies on an assumed mutuality of interests of the public and private spheres, a presumption that also characterized the four presidential administrations that followed Taft's.

JOHN M. CRAIG

See also Dollar Diplomacy; Knox, Philander Chase; League of Nations; Panama and Panama Canal; Philippines; Taft-Katsura Agreement

FURTHER READING
Minger, Ralph Eldin. *William Howard Taft and United States Foreign Policy: The Apprenticeship Years, 1900-1908*. Urbana, Ill., 1975.
Scholes, Walter V., and Marie V. Scholes. *The Foreign Policies of the Taft Administration*. Columbia, Mo., 1970.

TAFT-KATSURA AGREEMENT
(1905)

An official memorandum that affirmed U.S. recognition of Japan's dominance in Korea, in return for a Japanese pledge not to challenge U.S. control over the Philippines. In July 1905, as part of President Theodore Roosevelt's plan to bring about a peaceful settlement of the Russo-Japanese War, Secretary of War William Howard Taft went to Tokyo and initiated secret discussions with Japan's prime minister, Taro Katsura. With considerable candor, Taft and Katsura exchanged views regarding the two nations' mutual desire for peace in Asia. Katsura promised noninterference in the Philippines, and Taft assured his host that the United States would permit Japan a free hand in Korea. The Taft-Katsura agreement of July 29 became the basis of the Root-Takahira agreement of 1908, which reaffirmed the commitment of the U.S. and Japan to respect one another's territorial possessions, while additionally pledging the two nations to uphold the territorial integrity of China and to maintain the open door there. Together, the two agreements reflected Roosevelt's desire for a balance of power in Asia

that would be based upon the mutual interests of those nations most committed to the concept of the open door—the United States, Japan, and Great Britain.

JOHN M. CRAIG

See also Japan; Roosevelt, Theodore; Root-Takahira Agreement; Taft, William Howard

FURTHER READING
Marks, Frederick W., III. *Velvet on Iron: The Diplomacy of Theodore Roosevelt*. Lincoln, Nebr., 1979.
Esthus, Raymond. *Double Eagle and Rising Sun: The Russians and Japanese at Portsmouth in 1908*. Durham, N.C., 1988.
Minger, Ralph Eldin. *William Howard Taft and United States Foreign Policy: The Apprenticeship Years, 1900-1908*. Urbana, Ill., 1975.

TAIWAN

Island located in the Western Pacific, off the southeastern coast of China between Japan and the Philippines. After the communist victory in China in 1949, the U.S.-supported Chinese Nationalist government of Jiang Jieshi (Chiang Kai-shek) retreated to the offshore island of Taiwan. For a time, the United States cut its aid to the Nationalists and seemed prepared to accept a Communist takeover of the island. The start of the Korean War changed U.S. policy, however, leading to renewed U.S. support for the Nationalists on Taiwan. U.S. officials now saw Taiwan as a strategic asset, an "unsinkable aircraft carrier" in the chain of defenses the United States was building to contain the spread of communism in Asia. A well-publicized debate between General Douglas MacArthur and the Truman administration regarding the possible utility of Jiang's forces in the war against the Chinese Communists in Korea was an important factor behind President Harry Truman's eventual dismissal of MacArthur.

The potential for military conflict between Chinese Communist and Chinese Nationalist forces in the Taiwan Strait during the 1950s precipitated a renewed debate over the extent of the U.S. defense commitment to Jiang's Nationalists. Congressional ratification in 1955 of the U.S. Security Treaty with the Nationalist government was accompanied by the passage of the "Formosa Resolution," which attempted to define U.S. commitment to defend Taiwan and related territories, including Jinmen (Quemoy) and Mazu (Matsu), the small islands near the mainland coast that were still held by the Nationalists.

U.S. frustration with the protracted conflict in Vietnam during the late 1960s prompted the Nixon administration to reassess its 20-year-old policy of containment. The Sino-Soviet split in the 1960s, President Nixon's opening to Beijing in 1972, and the major pullback of U.S. forces in Vietnam and Asia in the late 1960s and early 1970s changed the United States' view of the mainland government. Relations with Beijing were now seen more as a strategic asset in the U.S. struggle against the Soviet Union. The issue was no longer how the United States could work with Jiang's Nationalists to block the expansion of the common enemy, Communist China. Instead, the issue became—and remains—how to find a proper balance between improving relations with the People's Republic of China (PRC) on the mainland, a strategically important new friend, and maintaining good relations with the Nationalists on Taiwan.

Initially the United States kept official relations with Taiwan and even tried to preserve Taiwan's seat in the UN, but the capital city of Taipei was expelled and Beijing seated in late 1971. The issue crystallized in 1979 when the Carter administration broke official ties with Taiwan as a precondition for establishing diplomatic relations with the PRC. The policy shift culminated in the passage in early 1979 of the Taiwan Relations Act (TRA), Public Law 96-8. The law reduced U.S. ties with Taiwan to an unofficial status overseen by an ostensibly unofficial entity, the American Institute in Taiwan. Congress extensively amended the draft law submitted by the Carter administration to strengthen language underlining the continued U.S. interest in the stability, economic prosperity, and security of the people on Taiwan. In particular, the act promised continued U.S. shipments of military equipment for Taiwan's defense against possible military action by the mainland.

The governments in both Beijing and Taipei have claimed that they represent all of China, including Taiwan. Both have long contended that diplomatic recognition of one foreclosed recognition of the other. In a U.S.-PRC joint communique in December 1978, the United States recognized the government of the People's Republic of China as the sole legal government of China and acknowledged the Chinese position that there is but one China, and Taiwan is part of China. The joint communique also stated that "within this context, the people of the United States will maintain cultural, commercial, and other unofficial relations with the people of Taiwan." In a unilateral statement released on 16 December 1978 (issued concurrently with the Joint Communiqué on the Establishment of Diplomatic Relations between the United States and the PRC), the United States declared that it continues to have an interest in the peaceful resolution of the Taiwan issue and expects that the Taiwan issue will be settled peacefully by the Chinese themselves.

Thus, while the Chinese Nationalists focused their attention on Taiwan, they insisted that they govern the island as part of their mandate as the legitimate government of all of China. They called their government the Republic of China (ROC). On 1 January 1979, the United States notified Taiwan authorities of intent to terminate the 1954 U.S.-ROC Mutual Defense Treaty effective 1 January 1980.

Since derecognition, the United States, in accordance with the TRA, has continued the sale of selected defensive military equipment and defense technology to Taiwan. These sales often have prompted strong objections from the PRC. On 17 August 1982, a U.S.-PRC joint communiqué committed the PRC to strive for a peaceful solution to the Taiwan question, while the United States stated that, "It does not seek to carry out a long-term policy of arms sales to Taiwan, that its arms sales to Taiwan will not exceed, either in qualitative or quantitative terms, the level of those supplied in recent years since the establishment of diplomatic relations between the United States and China, and that it intends to reduce gradually its sales of arms to Taiwan."

U.S. government arms sales to Taiwan slowly declined, but remained over $600 million a year. Taiwan's 1992 purchase of 150 F-16 aircraft (worth $5.9 billion) represented an exception to this trend. U.S. transfers of military-related technology allowed Taiwan to develop advanced fighter aircraft and other military equipment to defend the island.

Commercial ties between the United States and Taiwan have expanded since the 1979 derecognition. Taiwan continues to enjoy Export-Import Bank financing, Overseas Private Investment Corporation (OPIC) guarantees, most-favored-nation status, and ready access to U.S. markets. For several years, Taiwan was the largest beneficiary of the U.S. Generalized System of Preference (GSP) program. In 1988 Taiwan "graduated" from the GSP program. Because of rapid advances in Taiwan's economic growth, the U.S. Agency for International Development (AID) mission in Taiwan closed in 1965; more than $1.7 billion in U.S. economic aid was provided between 1949 and 1965.

In the 1990s, the United States remained Taiwan's main foreign investor and trading partner. U.S. markets received about twenty-five percent of Taiwan's exports. The United States supplied a much smaller percentage of Taiwan's imports. Overall, the imbalance in U.S. trade with Taiwan led to an $8.85 billion U.S. trade deficit in 1993—the third largest for the United States after Japan and China. Taiwan-manufactured electronic goods, textiles, and other consumer products made up the bulk of Taiwan exports to the United States, while Taiwan imports from the United States consisted primarily of agricultural products, industrial raw materials, and capital equipment. Taiwan's recent high level of foreign exchange reserves ($80 billion) and its ambitious $300 billion, six-year development program for the 1990s also attracted strong U.S. attention.

Taiwan's economic development contributed to continued political stability on the island. Taiwan's per capita income was over $10,000 per year. The economy distributed wealth in a relatively balanced way that gave all major sectors in society an important stake in continued economic progress. The benefits of economic prosperity tended to offset the political costs of opposition to the forty years of authoritarian, one-party rule by the Chinese Nationalists. The Nationalists have continued to follow the political legacy of Jiang Jieshi, who died in 1975.

American officials long criticized the perceived excesses of the Nationalists' authoritarian rule and pressed for increased political liberalization that would allow the more than eighty-five percent of the population whose roots on the island predate 1949 to have a greater role in running their own affairs. Americans broadly supported the considerable progress toward democracy Taiwan made since martial law was lifted in 1987.

The switch in U.S. recognition and the 1982 communiqué on arms sales to Taiwan did not remove the so-called Taiwan issue in U.S.-PRC relations. For many years U.S. policy toward Taiwan and the mainland represented a three-sided, zero-sum game among U.S., PRC, and Chinese Nationalist leaders. U.S. policymakers could assume that improvements in U.S. relations with Beijing would be viewed negatively by the Chinese Nationalists in Taipei, and improvements in U.S. relations with Taipei would be seen negatively in Beijing. The Chinese Communists in Beijing and Chinese Nationalists in Taipei, though no longer actively fighting militarily, were engaged in a protracted political struggle in which relations with the United States were a key point of contention.

The ending of martial law in Taiwan in 1987 and subsequent rapid political liberalization in Taiwan changed this equation substantially in several ways. Chinese Nationalist leaders no longer seek to tightly limit unofficial contacts with the PRC, resulting in more than 10 million visits from Taiwan to the mainland since 1987. Taiwan's annual trade with the mainland in 1995 was worth over $20 billion. Its cumulative investment was estimated by the PRC at $25 billion at the end of 1995. The Taipei leadership also no longer appears as unified as in the past in support of a one-China policy. Political liberalization has allowed the emergence of a viable opposition party, the Democratic Progressive Party (DPP), which publicly supports Taiwan self-determination. Generational and other changes have given rise to a Chinese Nationalist leadership whose roots are in Taiwan, in comparison to earlier Nationalist leaders, like Jiang Jieshi, whose roots were on the mainland. The new generation of Nationalist leaders is thought to be more ambivalent about the goal of China reunification and more concerned with nurturing progress on Taiwan.

Prompted partly by domestic political pressures in newly democratizing Taiwan, Nationalist leaders in the mid-1990s further modified adherence to a one China policy while seeking greater international recognition. Both trends met strong opposition from Beijing. When Taiwan president Lee Teng-hui visited Cornell University in the United States in June, 1995, Beijing responded with military exercises including ballistic missile tests directed at Taiwan while excoriating Lee Teng-hui for allegedly seeking Taiwan independence. Beijing's campaign of military actions to intimidate Taiwan continued in an effort to influence the outcomes of the December 1995 legislative elections in Taiwan and the first direct election of the president there in March 1996. The U.S. government weighed in during February and March 1996 with sharp criticism of Beijing's "reckless" behavior and deployment of two aircraft carrier battle groups to the Taiwan area. Tensions subsided following Lee Teng-hui's election as Taiwan president in March 1996.

ROBERT G. SUTTER

See also China; Jiang Jieshi; Jinmen-Mazu Crises

FURTHER READING

Clough, Ralph N. *Island China.* Cambridge, Mass., 1978.
Gold, Thomas B. *State and Society in the Taiwan Miracle.* Armonk, N.Y., 1986.
Myers, Ramon H., ed. *A Unique Relationship: The United States and the Republic of China Under the Taiwan Relations Act.* Stanford, Calif., 1989.
Sutter, Robert G. *Taiwan: Entering the 21st Century.* Lanham, Md., 1988.
Sutter, Robert G. and William Johnson, eds. *Taiwan in World Affairs.* Boulder, Colo., 1994.
Tien, Hung-mao. *The Great Transition: Political and Social Change in the Republic of China.* Stanford, Calif., 1989.

TAJIKISTAN

See Appendix 2

TALLEYRAND, CHARLES MAURICE
Comte de Talleyrand-Perigord

(*b.* 2 February 1754; *d.* 17 May 1838)

Legendary French statesman and diplomat, simultaneously admired and vilified for his brilliance, wit, cynicism, and opportunism. Talleyrand, a member of the high nobility, began his career as an abbot and became bishop of Autun in 1789. He was active in the first phase of the French Revolution, during which he helped prepare the elections to the States General in 1787 and called for a new constitution that would provide representative government for France and an end to the financial privileges of the clergy and nobility. The revolution soon turned more radical, however, and in 1792 the government denounced Talleyrand for his secret correspondence with Louis XVI. Talleyrand fled to the United States in January 1794, returning to Paris only after the fall of Robespierre. The Directory (1795–1799) appointed him foreign minister in September 1797, a post at which he also served under Napoleon from 1799 to 1807.

Talleyrand viewed U.S. commercial concessions to Great Britain in Jay's Treaty (1794) as contrary to the Franco-American Treaty of Amity and Commerce (1778), and thus a threat to French maritime interests. In retaliation, he inaugurated a limited naval war on U.S. commerce. When President John Adams sent a three-person mission to Paris in 1797 to settle the dispute, Talleyrand met with them privately but refused official recognition of their mission (and their instructions to negotiate a new treaty). In what came to be known as the XYZ Affair, he demanded through three unofficial agents (called X, Y, and Z), a bribe of $250,000, a "loan" of several million dollars, and an apology for Adams's critical remarks about revolutionary France. The commissioners refused these demands and went home. Talleyrand now realized that he had overestimated pro-French sentiment in the United States. He worried that as a result of the "quasi-war" on the high seas the United States not only might form an alliance with Great Britain, but also might invade Spain's colonies in the Americas and destroy French plans to reacquire the Louisiana territory from Spain.

Talleyrand soon reversed French policy and informed the Adams administration that a new U.S. minister to France would be welcomed with the respect due a great nation. Adams accepted Talleyrand's overture in order to prevent a full-scale war and sent a new three-person commission to France. Under Talleyrand's guidance, the two nations negotiated the Treaty of Mortefontaine (Convention of 1800), under which the United States agreed to give up claims against France for attacks on its shipping in return for suspension of the Franco-American Alliance of 1778.

After having reacquired Louisiana for France from Spain in the Treaty of San Ildefonso (1800), Talleyrand was stunned when Napoleon in turn sold it to the United States in 1803. When asked by U.S. negotiators how far the purchase extended, he made his famous reply: "You have made a noble bargain for yourselves, and I suppose you will make the most of it."

Talleyrand's diplomatic career continued intermittently during the next 30 years. While serving as foreign minister under Napoleon, he negotiated the Treaty of Amiens with England in 1802, briefly restoring peace to Europe after six years of war. He left office in 1807 over disagreements with Napoleon's excessive expansionist ambitions, and later opposed the invasion of Russia. After France's military defeat by the Quadruple Alliance (April 1814), Talleyrand supported the return of the

Bourbon monarchy and returned briefly to the foreign ministry under Louis XVIII. His skillful diplomacy succeeded in giving France an effective voice in the treaty settlement arrived at the Congress of Vienna (1814–1815), where his diplomatic talents shone at their brightest. Although very much a conservative, and a proponent of the principle of legitimacy, Talleyrand did not get along either with Louis or with his successor, the reactionary Charles X, and he turned mostly to private pursuits between 1815 and 1829. He aided the Revolution of 1830, which brought Louis-Philippe to the throne. Talleyrand served the July Monarchy as ambassador to Great Britain (1830–1834).

REBECCA G. GOODMAN

See also Adams, John; Convention of 1800; France; Jay's Treaty; XYZ Affair

FURTHER READING

Cooper, Duff. *Talleyrand.* New York, 1986.
DeConde, Alexander. *The Quasi-War.* New York, 1966.
Elkins, Stanley, and Eric McKitrick. *The Age of Federalism: The Early American Republic, 1788-1800.* New York, 1993.
Kissinger, H.A. *A World Restored: Mettenreich, Castlereagh, and the Problems of Peace 1812–1822.* 1957.
Morlot, Georges-Albert. *Talleyrand: une Mystification Historique.* Paris, France, 1991.

TANZANIA, UNITED REPUBLIC OF

Located in Eastern Africa, bordering the Indian Ocean, Mozambique, Malawi, Zambia, Zaire, Burundi, Rwanda, Uganda, and Kenya, and thus at a crossroads between East and South Africa. This region, especially along its coast, was at the center of an ancient Swahili culture dating back to the first century A.D. After 1800, Arab planters and traders, headquartered at Zanzibar, spearheaded a major expansion into Tanzania and other parts of East Africa prior to the arrival of European settlers.

In the modern colonial era Tanzania consisted of two territories: the island protectorate of Zanzibar, which was controlled by the British, and the mainland colony of Tanganyika, which was held by the Germans prior to World War I. After the war, both territories came under British administration. In 1954, the Tanganyika National Union, an African political party, was formed. Its leader was Julius Nyerere, the man who would become Tanzania's first president. Like Kwame Nkrumah in Ghana, Nyerere was a strong proponent of Pan-Africanism; even before Tanganyika gained its independence, Nyerere sought to unify it with the other major territories in East Africa such as Uganda and Kenya.

Nyerere's Pan-African ambitions brought him to the attention of the United States prior to Tanganyika actually gaining its independence in 1961. As early as 1957, the

U.S. consul wrote to the Department of State that Tanganyika was pressing toward independence but he doubted the capacity of the Tanganyikans to govern themselves due the relatively short time that the territory had been under British administration.

Despite U.S. reservations, Tanganyika did gain its independence in 1961 and the country was recognized by the United States that same year. Zanzibar, the smaller portion of what was to become Tanzania, gained its independence in December 1963 under the leadership of an Arab government led by Ali Muhsin. In early 1963, John Okello led a revolt that wiped out the Arab government, and a Swahili-dominated government led by Abeid Karume soon took over. By April 1964 Zanzibar and Tanganyika had effected a unification creating the country of Tanzania.

President Nyerere, like Nkrumah and others of his generation, was a staunch advocate of Third World nonalignment. By June 1964, Tanzania had experienced the first of several early diplomatic confrontations with the United States. In neighboring Congo (Zaire), the Belgian and U.S. governments actively worked to support the government of Moise Tshombe after the withdrawal of UN troops. This action was vigorously criticized by President Nyerere. Later that year, Tanzanian diplomats claimed to have uncovered a plot against Nyerere. The U.S. ambassador strongly denied the accusations and later produced evidence supporting his case. President Nyerere, however, would offer only a tepid public apology. Finally, in early 1965, Tanzanian officials intercepted a conversation in which U.S. officials in Tanzania spoke of bringing "big guns" to Zanzibar on its anniversary.

Tanzania's problems with the West were not limited to the United States. Between 1965 and 1967, Tanzania would suffer serious strains in its relationships with Great Britain and Germany as well. These developments eventually pushed Tanzania closer to the Eastern Bloc and toward the pursuit of "African socialism," which Nyerere construed as a combination of extensive nationalization of the economy with the creation of "Ujamaa," or collectivist villages and farms in the countryside, and a highly antarkik trade policy. The United States opposed Nyerere's African socialism by blocking some of its applications for World Bank loans.

A key factor in the improvement of U.S.-Tanzanian relations in the late 1970s was Tanzania's calculation that an "enemy of my enemy is my friend" as it applied to Uganda and its ruler Idi Amin. In 1978 a border dispute set off major fighting in which Tanzanian troops joined forces with Ugandans opposed to Amin, defeated his army, and overthrew him.

President Nyerere retired from power in 1985 and was succeeded by Ali Hassan Mwinyi. With some changes, such as the introduction of multiparty politics, President Mwinyi has followed much the same policies as his predecessor.

Anthony Q. Cheeseboro

See also Africa; Nonaligned Movement; Uganda

FURTHER READING

Havenik, Kjell. *Tanzania: The Limits to Development from Above.* Uppsala, Sweden, 1993.

Mittelman, James, H. *Underdevelopment and the Transition to Socialism: Mozambique and Tanzania.* New York, 1981.

Pratt, Cranford. *The Critical Phase in Tanzania 1945-1968: Nyerere and the Emergence of a Socialist Strategy.* Cambridge, Mass., 1976.

Yeager, Rodger. *Tanzania: An African Experiment.* Boulder, Colo., 1983; 1991.

TARIFFS

Duties or taxes levied by a governing authority on imported (or less frequently, exported) goods to protect domestic production and raise revenue. There are different types of tariffs. One type is the specific duty, which is a fixed surcharge calculated on the physical amount of a product, such as 10 cents per pound on steel tubing. Another type is the *ad valorem* duty, which is a fixed percentage tax based on the value of the imported product. The term tariff can be used to refer to the duty applied to a particular product, such as a tariff of seven and a half percent on dried packaged pasta; or, it can refer to the entire tariff schedule of a country, such as the U.S. Tariff of 1816. In the latter case the reference would be to an official list that defines and classifies imported products, and indicates the specific or *ad valorem* duty to be paid on each product.

Specific duties are straightforward and are easy for a nation's customs service to collect. However, in times of inflation they fall behind prices and must be continually revised if they are to serve any purpose. Furthermore, they are not easily compared from one product to the next, and make it more difficult for trade negotiators to evaluate tariff levels in one country against those in another. To avoid these problems, nations have turned increasingly to *ad valorem* tariffs. The latter are more complicated than specific duties, since a value must first be determined for each product as the basis for the application of a percentage duty. Normally customs officers will accept the transaction value declared by an importer, although they can independently value goods if the circumstances appear uncertain.

Tariffs and their administration by governments have a history stretching back to ancient times. The precursor of the tariff is the toll, which was haphazardly imposed on travelers and traders by any governing authority that had the power to enforce them. Tariffs were a more sophisticated version of the toll, and they were arranged in schedules and administered in a systematic fashion by government bureaucracies.

Tariffs, both on exported and imported goods, were originally used as sources of revenue for political authorities. By the beginning of the eighteenth century import duties were the primary source of revenue for the countries of Europe. The importance of the revenue effect of tariffs continued until the twentieth century; for example, following the Civil War in the United States, the import duties on foreign spirits alone accounted for almost half of the total receipts of the U.S. federal treasury.

Tariffs had another important function in that they protected domestic producers from foreign competition. The advent of income and sales taxes meant that the revenue effects of tariffs receded in importance, while the protective effects of these duties became more prominent politically. With the exception of a brief period of free trade led by Great Britain and followed by France and Germany in the mid-nineteenth century, increasing tariff protectionsim remained the standard policy of most nations into the middle of the twentieth century.

Today, tariffs are retained by countries mainly for the protection they afford to domestic producers. However, in modern commercial relations tariffs are one of many policy tools—along with quotas, subsidies, health or sanitary requirements, or other regulations—that governments use to ensure that domestic producers have preferential access to the nation's domestic market. Unlike subsidies or domestic regulations, tariffs are transparent and their effects are relatively easily assessed; and unlike quotas which establish quantitative limits on imports, tariffs do not limit imports directly but operate within the price system to raise the price of imports. For these reasons, tariffs are generally regarded as doing less damage to free markets than other forms of trade restrictions.

The protection of domestic producers through tariffs is undertaken for a variety of political reasons. Tariffs have historically been used as a part of a policy of mercantilism, in which nations seek a surplus of exports over imports in order to enhance national wealth and power. Tariffs may also be used simply to protect an industry that is unable to compete successfully with foreign competition, specifically to protect the jobs or wages of labor, or to protect the profits of management. Tariffs can foster the development of "infant industries," and they can maintain or promote self-reliance in times of crisis by protecting industries crucial to national defense or security. Tariffs also can be used as an industrial policy to draw foreign investment into a country, because when tariffs are high, overseas producers cannot export and instead are motivated to access foreign markets through building branch plants in lieu of trade.

The effect of tariff protectionism is best evaluated in comparison to its antithesis, namely free trade. Free trade is a concept that nowhere has been expressed in its pure form, although it has been approximated in various degrees and at different times. The theory behind free trade is that given unrestricted opportunities to trade abroad, a division of labor resulting in specialization, efficiency, and exchange will maximize the welfare of nations participating in that trade. Such a system will give all producers access to larger markets than they would have under a system of protectionism, and hence they will be able to achieve economies of scale allowing them to produce and sell at lower costs. The effect of a free trade system for participating countries is that producers have access to more consumers, and consumers can buy from the producers offering the lowest priced and/or best quality goods. Higher real national product and lower prices for goods ensure mutual gain, and a higher aggregate standard of living for the countries concerned.

In contrast to free trade, tariffs have harmful effects on the general welfare of a country. Tariffs generally ensure that markets remain small, which reduces economies of scale and causes production costs to remain high leading to higher prices for consumers. Countries that use tariffs to protect inefficient domestic firms from foreign competition lose the advantage of buying from efficient foreign firms, and they lose again by buying from domestic firms that operate at high costs serving relatively small domestic markets. The latter argument is particularly compelling in the modern economy, since international competition in some industries like automobiles is so keen that firms need to access a global market in order to survive.

In the case of tariffs used to promote an infant industry, the higher costs created for consumers may be justifiable provided that as the industry matures its costs decline and it is able to offer products at a price competitive with foreign producers. However, experience has shown that industries that reach maturity under a high-tariff regime do not easily lose their dependence on tariff protection, and continue to be unable to meet foreign competition. The conclusion is that tariffs are an inefficient tool of economic and development policy despite the fact that they have been used by all countries at one time or another.

Given that tariffs are inefficient and costly, the question arises as to why they are so prevalent in economic life. This question has long frustrated economists, who have noted the discrepancy between the benefits of free trade in theory, and the persistence of tariffs and other protectionism in practice. The reason for this discrepancy was neatly explained some time ago by Vilfredo Pareto, who observed that individuals will work much harder to achieve a large gain than they will to avert a small loss. He then reasoned that "a protectionist measure provides large benefits to a small number of people, and causes a very great number of consumers a small loss, [which] makes it easier to put a protectionist measure into practice."

The existence of tariffs is explained more by politics than economics, especially the politics of interest group demands on government. Pareto's rule has been the basis for the existence of special-interest protectionism ever since the establishment of democratic government. The fact is that free trade helps everyone a little, but tariffs (and other forms of protection) help a few people a lot, hence there has always been and always will be the incentive for special interests to pressure government for protectionist policies.

Tariffs in U.S. History

Throughout U.S. history tariffs have fluctuated in terms of variety, purpose, and levels of protection. The first U.S. tariff bill was introduced in 1789. Both in intention and effect a means of generating government revenue, the Tariff Act of 1789 was also seen by its creators as a method of providing protection for domestic producers. The U.S. tariff policy remained largely unchanged for the next twenty-five years, undergoing only minor alterations to increase government revenues or to renew temporary laws that were due to expire. The one notable exception was a doubling of duties on imports for the duration of the War of 1812 in order to gain revenues for the war effort against the British.

Following the war, nationalism and demands for protection from various "infant industries" that had grown during the war led to the Tariff of 1816. The Tariff of 1816 was the first U.S. tariff created primarily for the purpose of protecting domestic industry, with revenue generation as only a secondary goal. It imposed duties that were lower than what had prevailed during the war, but higher than the prewar duties. Various tariffs were imposed during the 1820s, often amidst much fractious debate which pitted states producing wool, glass, hemp, iron, and lead against those which were most dependent upon imports or were involved in the merchant marine business. Most notable among these was the Tariff Act of 1828, which represented the high point for pre-Civil War tariff levels. The Tariff Act of 1828 came to be referred to as the "Tariff of Abominations" as it seemed to please virtually no one, and especially exasperated the southern states.

Tariff levels were lowered in the Compromise Tariff of 1833, then raised again in the 1842 Tariff, and then lowered again in the Walker Act of 1846. Prosperity in the following decade saw the conclusion of the United States' first reciprocity agreement with another country (Canada) in 1854, and tariffs were substantially reduced in the Tariff Act of 1857. The Morrill Tariff of 1861, and its revisions in 1862, 1864, 1867, and 1869 set tariffs at

heights unprecedented in U.S. history. In spite of minor revisions in subsequent years, tariff levels remained for the most part unchanged until 1890 when, under McKinley, tariff protectionism was further increased. The Dingley Tariff of 1897 saw the highest duties ever passed and the protectionist trend continued in the Payne-Aldrich Tariffs of 1909.

The Underwood Act of 1913 brought, for the first time since the tariffs of 1846 and 1857, real reductions in tariff levels. Following World War I, agricultural producers and a new generation of infant industries were demanding protection, a demand which was satisfied first by the Emergency Tariff of 1921, and then with more permanent intentions by the Fordney-McCumber Tariff Act of 1922.

With the advent of the Great Depression, the demands for greater protection from domestic industries increased, resulting in the Smoot-Hawley Tariff Act of 1930. The Smoot-Hawley tariff raised U.S. tariffs to record high levels, but did not represent any fundamental change in U.S. trade policy. Rather, it was merely another step in a long march of increased protectionism in the United States and the world in general. It was, however, a decisive step that caused other nations to retaliate. In response to Smoot-Hawley, other countries increased their own levels of protection, and, notably, Great Britain in 1931 ended its long-held free trade policy. The result was a downward spiral of protectionism leading to a collapse of the international trade system. Although exact estimates vary, it is certain that all countries raised tariffs markedly in 1930–1931, trebling them in some cases. Over the years 1929–1934 world trade underwent a decline of sixty-six percent.

The U.S. Constitution gives Congress the power to regulate commerce, and consequently tariff levels are established by congressional legislation. However, the Smoot-Hawley Tariff Act was widely regarded as being created by congressional committees that were not well versed in the details of tariff administration. The issues and the tariff bill proved to be too complex for Congress to manage effectively. Special interest lobbyists, however, understood their concerns quite well and were able to present convincing cases to Congress, with the result that protection was freely given to those groups that requested it. Congress's inability to come to terms with the issues at hand, the activities of special interest lobbies, and the natural protectionist sympathies of the time led to an extreme result. It could be fairly said of the Smoot-Hawley tariff that both the president and the congressional leadership had lost control over trade policy.

Tariffs were lowered again as a result of the Reciprocal Trade Agreements Act of 1934 (RTAA). The RTAA, although basically only an amendment to the Smoot-Hawley Act, was a watershed in U.S. and international trade policy. It transferred tariff-setting policy from the Congress to the president, enabling him to, in the course of trade negotiations with other countries, decrease (or increase) tariffs from Smoot-Hawley levels by up to fifty percent. This act was created because, although Congress had the authority to regulate commerce, it had proved itself unable to resist the demands of constituents for protection, whereas the presidency was better able to structure itself bureaucratically for dealing with tariff questions. The act was a milestone in international economic relations because of its implicit acceptance that tariffs should not be set by a state unilaterally, but instead should be set bilaterally through negotiated agreements. The U.S. government sought reciprocal trade agreements with as many other countries as possible, concluding twenty-one agreements and making reductions in approximately a thousand duties by 1939. Eleven more agreements were reached during World War II. The liberalization resulting from the RTAA did increase trade flows. But more significantly, the act served as a model for other nations, with the result that international commercial policy underwent a revolution of sorts. The RTAA also made the important contribution of giving nations experience in trade liberalization which was put to use after the war in the creation of the General Agreement on Tariffs and Trade (GATT).

Tariffs in the Postwar Period

The protectionism of the 1930s was nothing new in a qualitative sense. Protectionism had always been the norm in economic relations between states. However, the unprecedented levels of protectionism and the shock of the Depression and subsequent world war it helped bring on led the general public to question the conventional wisdom of protectionism. By the mid-1950s liberal trade had supplanted protectionism as the orthodox ideological position. The swell of support for liberal trade in the post-war era was expressed through negotiated trade liberalization agreements under the auspices of GATT.

The GATT was created in 1947 as a contract of trading rules to support the reduction of tariffs, and was to be incorporated into a new international trade authority called the International Trade Organization (ITO). The ITO was stillborn due to its rejection by the U.S. Congress. Unlike the GATT, which was a temporary and minimal instrument, the ITO was designed as an international organization that could have exercised far-reaching powers to influence the commercial policies of its member states. U.S. legislators objected to these powers because they allegedly compromised Congress's constitutional mandate to regulate international commerce. Despite the failure of the ITO, the GATT survived, and it encouraged countries to make their trade policies through negotiation with other countries.

The GATT incorporated the bilateral negotiation process established by the RTAA, and simply multilateralized it. However, this change was not accomplished in one step. The early GATT negotiations to reduce tariffs were multilateral in name, but in fact the real action occurred bilaterally between trading partners that served as principal suppliers or consumers of each other's products. Negotiations were conducted on the basis of reciprocity, and then bilateral agreements were multilateralized through the Most-Favored-Nation (MFN) principle. The MFN principle meant that nations agreed to extend to all countries the tariff reductions that they granted to their most favored partner. This principle reduced trade discrimination between countries, and was instrumental in promoting a more liberal approach to trade policy.

The GATT permitted an exception to MFN treatment, the immediate purpose of which was to provide for closer economic relations among the formerly belligerent countries of Western Europe. This exception is contained in Article XXIV, and it permits GATT contracting parties to form free trade areas or customs unions, even though these regional arrangements might be a source of discrimination in GATT trading relations. In free trade areas, participating nations remove trade restrictions (especially tariffs) on trade within the area, but retain their own tariffs on goods from other countries. In a customs union, members remove restrictions internally, and also establish a common external tariff on goods from outside the union. The European Common Market—precursor to the modern European Union (EU)—was first established as a customs union in 1958.

The GATT succeeded in establishing multilateral trade rules in those areas where contracting parties were in agreement, but the regime suffered from numerous exceptions. One area was agriculture, where the United States in 1955 received a waiver for agricultural policies that were inconsistent with GATT rules, and which implicitly served as an excuse for the greater excesses of the Europeans in later years under the Common Agricultural Policy of the EU. Another area of exceptions was textiles, where, under the umbrella of general agreements beginning with the Long-Term Arrangement on Cotton Textiles of 1962, large importing countries like the United States applied an extensive system of quotas to textile and clothing products mainly from developing countries. These exceptions point out that the long process of liberalizing international trade has been uneven, and has had numerous setbacks.

Since its inception in 1947, the GATT has held eight multilateral negotiations, and each has promoted a lowering of tariff levels. Further reductions have been stimulated by regional trade agreements, such as the U.S.-Canada Free Trade Agreement (FTA) or the North American Free Trade Agreement (NAFTA). Tariffs continue to be important instruments in the trade policies of most developing countries, which have pursued less liberal policies than developed countries during the last several decades. However, for industrialized countries, the negotiations in GATT and elsewhere have largely eliminated tariffs as a serious impediment to international commerce. This represents a remarkable accomplishment for the liberal approach to international economic relations between nations.

On 1 January 1995, the World Trade Organization (WTO) succeeded the GATT, following the conclusion of the lengthy Uruguay Round trade negotiation. The Uruguay Round achieved high-level results on tariff liberalization, and more importantly, it incorporated agreements on textiles and agriculture that had long been excluded from GATT disciplines. The mechanism of incorporation was a process called "tariffication," whereby the protection stemming from quotas or other devices was converted to tariffs, in preparation for subsequent negotiated reductions. The creation of the WTO represents an important turning point in the establishment of multilateral trade rules, and its operation will further reduce the impact of tariffs and other forms of protection on world trade.

GILBERT R. WINHAM

See also Free Trade; General Agreement on Tariffs and Trade; Most-Favored-Nation Principle; Reciprocal Trade Agreement Act

FURTHER READING

Bhagwati, Jagdish. *Protectionism.* Cambridge, Mass., 1988.
Low, Patrick. *Trading Free: The GATT and U.S. Trade Policy.* New York, 1992.
Michaely, Michael. *Theory of Commercial Policy: Trade and Protection.* Chicago, 1977.
Preeg, Ernest H. *Traders and Diplomats: An Analysis of the Kennedy Round under the General Agreement on Tariffs and Trade.* Washington, D.C., 1970.
Ratner, Sidney. *The Tariff in American History.* New York, 1972.
Samuelson, Paul A. *Economics,* 14th ed. New York, 1992.
Winham, Gilbert R. *The Evolution of International Trade Agreements.* Toronto, 1992.

TAYLOR, MAXWELL DAVENPORT

(*b.* 26 August 1901; *d.* 19 April 1987)

One of the last "soldier-statesmen" of World War II and one of the first "war managers" of the Cold War, General Maxwell Taylor became a chief military participant in the political decision-making of the Vietnam War.

Born in Missouri, Taylor graduated from West Point in 1922 and later served as its superintendent (1945–1949). He commanded the 101st Airborne Division during the Normandy landings (1944), played an important role in the occupation of postwar Germany, and, as Army Chief of Staff (1955–1959), struggled against a budget-cutting President Dwight Eisenhower. His account of his frustrations, *The Uncertain Trumpet* (1959), attracted the attention of Senator John F. Kennedy, who, as president, named him his Military Adviser (1961–1962) and Chairman of the Joint Chiefs of Staff (1962–1964). President Lyndon Johnson first appointed him Ambassador to Vietnam (1964–1965) and then retained him as a Special Consultant on Vietnam (1965–1969).

At the beginning of the Vietnam War, Taylor favored a strong U.S. military presence, though he played an equivocal role in the 1963 coup against South Vietnamese President Ngo Dinh Diem. As ambassador to South Vietnam, however, he was instrumental in the ouster of General Nguyen Khanh (1964). During the initial U.S. ground troop deployment decisions of 1965, Taylor unsuccessfully argued for an emphasis on bombing rather than on sending combat troops. But, by the Tet Offensive (1968), Johnson was ready for different advice, and Taylor was one of the "wise men" who convinced him to deescalate.

TIMOTHY J. LOMPERIS

See also Kennedy, John Fitzgerald; Tet Offensive; Vietnam War

FURTHER READING

Kinnard, Douglas. *The Certain Trumpet: Maxwell Taylor and the American Experience in Vietnam.* Washington, D.C., 1991.

TAYLOR, ZACHARY

(*b.* 24 November 1784; *d.* 9 July 1850)

Twelfth president of the United States (1849–1850). Born in Montebello, Virginia, Taylor became a career soldier whose military service included participation in the War of 1812, the Black Hawk War, and the Seminole Wars, where he acquired the nickname "Old Rough and Ready." At the outset of the War with Mexico in 1846, he defeated larger forces at Palo Alto, Resaca de la Palma, and Monterrey. In February 1847, Taylor's dramatic defense at Buena Vista against General Santa Anna resulted in victory when the Mexican commander retreated from the battlefield. Taylor's military record in the War with Mexico earned him the Whig Party nomination and election to the presidency in 1848.

Lacking experience in foreign affairs, Taylor's uncompromising positions produced crises with France (by encouraging Secretary of State John Middleton Clayton's disregard for diplomatic protocol in the Poussin Affair concerning the *Eugenie* claims), Portugal (*General Armstrong* claims), and Spain (demand for the release of a captured filibuster expedition against Cuba). Fearful of

the potential negative consequences of the lingering spirit of Manifest Destiny upon the debate over the extension of slavery and Anglo-American relations, Taylor
opposed the annexation of Cuba and Canada. His desire
to maintain harmonious Anglo-American relations also
contributed to the negotiation of the Clayton-Bulwer
Treaty of 1850. In this agreement, Great Britain and the
United States, attempting to settle conflicting interests
in Central America, pledged not to "occupy, fortify, or
colonize, or assume or exercise dominion over Nicaragua,
Costa Rica, the Mosquito Coast, or any part of Central
America." They also agreed on joint control and protection of any isthmian canal. Taylor died in office in the
midst of the great sectional crisis of 1850.

DEAN FAFOUTIS

See also Clayton, John Middleton; Filibusters; Mexico,
war With; Young America

FURTHER READING

Bauer, Karl Jack. *Zachary Taylor: Soldier, Planter, Statesman of the Old
    Southwest.* Baton Rouge, La., 1985.
Hamilton, Holman. *Zachary Taylor.* 2 vols. Indianapolis, Ind.,
    1941–1951.
Smith, Elbert. *The Presidencies of Zachary Taylor and Millard Fill-
    more.* Lawrence, Kans., 1988.

TECHNICAL COOPERATION ADMINISTRATION

See Point Four

TECHNOLOGY TRANSFER

The United States, a technological leader in the post-
World War II era, has both encouraged and inhibited
technology transfer as an instrument of foreign policy,
often with significant effects on other countries and on
U.S. relations with these countries.

Technology transfer refers to the diffusion of technology—whether as a product or in disembodied form—from
one individual to another, from one corporation to another, from one government to another, or among these or
other actors. Technology transfer is a foreign affairs matter
when technology flows cross national boundaries. The
mechanisms for such transfers are several, including publications, private licensing arrangements, sales of equipment or intellectual property, transfers of a turnkey plant,
education of foreign students, inter-governmental agreements of cooperation, industrial espionage, and many
more. In many instances, transnational corporations are
important conduits for the transfer of technology.

While private actors often carry out technology transfer, policy makers influence the pattern of international
technology transfer by setting and shaping the political,
legal, and regulatory framework in which it occurs. As
part of its foreign policy, the United States has both promoted technology transfer to garner political influence
and international prestige (President Eisenhower's
"Atoms-for-Peace" program, for example) and to strength-
en allies by decreasing their dependency on or vulnerability to a common adversary, and restricted technology
flows ("technology denial") to weaken, punish, deter, or
otherwise influence adversaries. Technology denial based
on the nature of the technologies themselves as enhancing an adversary's military capabilities are generally
referred to as "national security" controls, while those
intended more to influence the target's behavior or policies are considered "foreign policy" controls.

During the Cold War, the main thrust of U.S. technology transfer policy was the creation of national and international institutions to control the transfer of technology
to the Soviet Union and its military and ideological allies.
New legislation was developed (the Export Control Act
of 1949) and new institutions created (COCOM, the
Coordinating Committee for Multilateral Export Controls which included the NATO countries plus others) to
serve these ends. Technology transfer policies in this area
became known as "economic warfare" and "the strategic
embargo." Simultaneously and in complementary fashion, the United States also promoted technology transfer
to such key allies as Western Europe and Japan.

Declining American economic and technological
supremacy, growing allied and U.S. business dissatisfaction with the economic costs of an expansive embargo,
and an emerging spirit of détente led Congress and
COCOM to liberalize technology transfer controls in the
1970s. Under the new guidelines, technology transfer
controls governed only products and technologies that
contributed significantly to a potential enemy's military
capability and that were unavailable from other sources.
Preserving the West's technological superiority over the
East in defense-related technologies, rather than economic warfare per se, became the goal of U.S. and
COCOM technology transfer policy. Still, during the
1970s and 1980s, the strategy of containment remained
the guiding principle of technology transfer policy, albeit
with limited recognition of the importance of expanding
nonstrategic trade.

The U.S. government also selectively used alternating
strategies of technology transfer and technology denial to
influence countries in desired ways. The Nixon administration thought that the liberalization of trade and technology transfer controls ("carrots") could engender
desired foreign policy outcomes in the Soviet Union.
Senator Henry Jackson (using the so-called Jackson-
Vanik Amendment) sought to withhold trade and technology transfer and use the "stick" by requiring more

desirable Soviet domestic policies (particularly, freer immigration) before liberalizing trade and technology transfer policies. The Carter administration advocated a policy of "economic diplomacy," designed to generate through "carrots" and "sticks," more desirable foreign and domestic policies in the Soviet Union. The debate in these instances centered on two competing visions of the role of technology transfer in superpower relations. One school of thought adopted a liberal notion of building linkages with adversaries through mutually rewarding commercial exchange in the hope that economic cooperation would moderate foreign policy behavior. Critics, however, argued that expanded trade and technology was harmful to Western interests. They maintained that even technology with an exclusively civilian purpose could "free resources" in the Soviet economy, thereby supporting its military activities. American ambivalence over the role of technology transfer, mutual suspicion, and heavy-handed attempts to extract political concessions limited the effectiveness of these efforts.

Worsening U.S.-Soviet relations in the 1980s brought an end to most of these initiatives. During that decade, the United States tightened national security technology transfer controls to the East, reinforcing the arms race but also placing a costly regulatory burden on U.S. exporters and straining relations with some COCOM allies. One exception to this trend was the liberalization of technology restrictions to the People's Republic of China, as part of the normalization of U.S.-China relations and the playing out of the "strategic triangle" competition.

In addition to national security motivations for technology transfer limitations, the United States has used technology controls to further other foreign policy interests. Thus, American policymakers targeted technology controls against certain communist and non-communist countries for reasons ranging from human rights (Cuba) to terrorism (Libya) to regional stability (Iran). Unlike most national security controls on technology, which were regulated by the COCOM mechanism to coordinate restrictions with the practices of U.S. allies, foreign policy controls on technology were often unilateral. This important difference was often the source of protracted and heated domestic debate about the cost and effectiveness of such restrictions and the cause of diplomatic imbroglios with allies that resisted U.S. extraterritorial application of its controls on actors or goods abroad. The dispute between the United States and its NATO allies over the export of construction equipment for the Soviet gas pipeline in the 1980s was the most notable example.

Traditionally, the United States has been reluctant to restrict or promote technology transfer simply to further commercial and economic goals. Preferring to allow market forces to determine trade and technological relations, the United States has not used commercial technology and industrial policies to influence political or economic goals with other countries. When the United States has attempted to do so, for example, the effort to restrict the transfer of aerospace technology to Japan (the FSX case), its actions threatened longstanding U.S.-Japanese defense cooperation. That case points to a possible redefinition of the role of technology transfer in U.S. national security. Many in Congress and in the executive branch questioned the longstanding assumption that technological openness necessarily serves U.S. interests and asked whether the technological bases of national security now require government protection and limitations on technology transfer to economic competitors.

The most striking feature in the making of U.S. technology transfer policy is the diffusion of authority across executive bureaus and the uneven allocation of authority between the executive and the Congress. At one point, more than a dozen agencies administered some aspect of U.S. technology transfer policy. Traditionally, the White House and the departments of Commerce, State, Defense, and Energy were key players. Each agency brought a unique perspective to the issue area. These multiple perspectives and participants often made the coordination of U.S. technology transfer difficult. Perhaps because of the perceived importance of technology transfer to national security and the complexity of this policy area, the President and executive agencies have shown substantial policy autonomy vis-a-vis Congress, despite repeated congressional efforts to improve interagency coordination and limit the commercial costs of technology controls. In this respect, technology transfer policy often differs from U.S. trade policy where Congress plays a more determinative role.

The end of the Cold War represented a watershed in U.S. technology transfer policy. By the late 1980s, four changes in the international system challenged the traditional directions in U.S. technology transfer policy.

The foremost change was the end of geopolitical and ideological hostility between East and West of the prior forty years. The basic Western security concern of a sudden Soviet attack on Western Europe or the more diffuse concern of a Soviet policy of radical activism in the Third World dissolved. Instead, the residual concern from the East became economic decline and political instability that could create regional conflicts and encourage the outflow of military technologies from this region to other areas of instability. The United States and its allies now found themselves aiding former Soviet defense industries albeit to convert to commercial and civilian production. Until the final conversion of these industries to civilian projects, Soviet successor states face near-term economic pressures to export weapons and dangerous technologies to earn foreign exchange.

Second, revolutions in Central and Eastern Europe and the dissolution of the Soviet Union led to the need for U.S. and Western economic and technological assistance—an affirmative technology transfer to former adversaries to help replace command economies with market systems. Certain technologies, for example, telecommunications and personal computers, are particularly important in promoting democratic pluralism and contributing to the creation of modern financial markets. With the end of the Cold War, the general sense was that the greatest potential security threat from the East would be the failure of economic and political reforms and the regional instability that would ensue.

Third, U.S. economic and technological competitiveness increasingly depends on open international flows of technology. U.S. technological supremacy is no longer a given, and policymakers can no longer slight the competitive costs of technology controls. Because technological progress essential to both national security and economic health are driven by civilian applications, not defense procurement, what is controlled or licensed as strategic technology must now reflect the importance of a healthy commercial sector to U.S. security by allowing domestic firms to compete on even footing in international markets and encouraging firms to cooperate in arrangements that enhance U.S. technological resources.

Finally, nuclear, chemical and biological weapons, and missile technology have proliferated throughout the developing world. Countries acquiring these dangerous technologies include several in unstable regions or known terrorist states. Although nonproliferation technology controls have a long history, the end of the Cold War and a hot war in the Persian Gulf (the 1990–1991 war against Iraq) accentuated the problem of regional instability and proliferation as a fundamental security and arms control issue facing the United States in the post-Cold War era. In this changed environment, the effectiveness of U.S. technology transfer will be measured by how well it serves several divergent goals: promoting modernization and democracy in former rival states of the East, enhancing American competitiveness; and slowing the proliferation of dangerous technologies to nations and regions that threaten regional or international stability.

Along with other post-World War II economic policies, technology controls directed toward the containment of communist capabilities and influence may have contributed to the West's substantial qualitative lead times in defense-related technologies. With the fall of communism—first in Central and Eastern Europe and then the Soviet Union—a case can be made that containment policies, including technology transfer controls, played a role in the downfall of America's chief ideological and military rival, the Soviet Union. The argument is simple:

denying militarily important technology to the East forced the Soviets to divert resources into efforts to develop such technology indigenously or procure it through illegal means and, thus, contributed to policies that ultimately crippled their internal economic strength and political legitimacy. The inability of the Soviet Union to compete economically and technologically with the West eventually loosened its grip on its internal and external empires.

Because no one can know what the course of communism would have been absent such policies, this argument is also ultimately unprovable. To what degree technology controls contributed to this end and at what costs to the United States and its allies are matters of continuing debate. Some judge technology transfer policy as an important pillar of American and Western Cold War strategy. Those in the public or private sector, more intimately aware of the economic consequences of technology controls have often questioned the effectiveness of the policy or noted that technology controls retarded the advancement of technology and economic development of both the sender and target states. In addition to the economic costs of technology transfer controls to the United States, the policy of technology restrictions also created periodic tensions between the United States and the other COCOM members. All in all, taking stock of Cold War national security technology transfer controls, most conclude that they were a qualified success in serving a broader strategy of containment, but with declining American economic and technological supremacy in the 1970s and 1980s, their associated economic and political cost had become increasingly difficult to bear.

Whatever its past successes, the end of the Cold War presents a fundamentally different economic and security environment and new challenges for the use of technology transfer policy, and has created new standards for assessing their effectiveness. To meet these new challenges the United States has re-oriented its technology transfer policies in several ways. To confront the threat of proliferation, the United States has strengthened its technology controls to regions of proliferation concern and fostered the development of multilateral institutions such as the Nuclear Suppliers Group (for nuclear-related technology), the Australia Group (for chemical and biological weapons technology), and the Missile Technology Control Regime (for missile systems technology) to coordinate multilateral technology controls. Member states in each of these regimes include the most advanced industrial states (including some former Cold War rivals), the member countries that have achieved general consensus over the technologies to control, and the potential countries or regions of concern. To strengthen U.S. competitiveness, requirements for licensing technology transfer for U.S. exporters have been liberalized for most destinations and permissible thresholds of exportable technologies have been raised. The government also is considering innovative ways to enhance, rather than impede, U.S. technological competitiveness. Finally, to strengthen nascent efforts to establish market economies and democratic governments in Central and Eastern Europe and the former Soviet Union, the United States has encouraged technology transfer provided the recipient guarantees its peaceful use and agrees not to re-transfer the item to a third party in a region of instability. The United States also has assisted other countries to establish their own technology transfer systems and encouraged new governments to join the emerging multilateral nonproliferation regimes.

GARY K BERTSCH
WILLIAM J. LONG

See also Atoms for Peace; Chemical Weapons; Cold War; Coordinating Committee For Multilateral Export Controls; Export Controls

FURTHER READING

Bertsch, Gary K., ed. *Controlling East-West Trade and Technology Transfer: Power, Politics, and Policy.* Durham, N.C., 1988.

Bertsch, Gary K., Richard T. Cupitt, and Steven Elliott-Gower, eds. *International Cooperation on Nonproliferation Export Controls.* Ann Arbor, Mich., 1994.

Jentleson, Bruce W. *Pipeline Politics: The Complex Political Economy of East-West Energy Trade.* Ithaca, N.Y., 1986.

Long, William J. *U.S. Export Control Policy: Executive Autonomy Versus Congressional Reform.* New York, 1989.

Mastanduno, Michael. *Economic Containment: COCOM and the Politics of East-West Trade.* Ithaca, N.Y., 1992.

Nau, Henry R. *Technology Transfer and U.S. Foreign Policy.* New York, 1976.

TECUMSEH

See Native Americans

TELECOMMUNICATION COMPANIES

Telephone, cable, and satellite service providers have helped bring the world closer together. Transportation systems were once at the heart of the global industrial economy. Communications networks are the key to growth and job production in the emerging world information economy. Not surprisingly, countries and their communications firms are scrambling to be winners in the telecommunications arena. As a result, the structure of the telecommunications industry is in flux, as established equipment and service companies reinvent themselves in the face of competition from new entrants into their markets. Regulatory changes engulfed the world's telecommunications industry after the United States broke up AT&T in 1984. Many countries experimented with competition, corporatization, privatization, and liberalization in various parts of their communications sectors. Technological advances also transformed the industry. The microprocessor and cheap memory revolutionized the communications industry in the 1980s. In the 1990s the networking of computers to form a global information infrastructure proceeded.

On the high end of the equipment market, the tremendous cost of developing new equipment meant that only a few firms could capture enough business to survive the shakeout of the 1980s. Seven firms persisted: AT&T Technologies (now spun off as Lucent), Northern Telecom (Canada), Alcatel (France), Siemens (Germany), L.M. Ericsson (Sweden), NEC (Japan), and Fujitsu (Japan). At the lower end, the market for terminal equipment, including handsets, modems, and data terminals, became a fast-changing commodity market. Other dynamic equipment makers focused on building the components needed to integrate the new information infrastructure. Companies like Hughes (satellites) and Cisco Systems (routers) are thriving.

On the service side, the Telecommunications Act of 1996, the most comprehensive reformulation of U.S. communications regulations in more than six decades, promised to unleash greater cross-sector competition. To encourage growth, innovation, and competition, the United States obliterated almost all boundaries separating local and long-distance, cable and telephone, and wireline and cellular services. Service providers now may provide content and broadcasters, while studios and other content providers may provide telephone services. To illustrate, AT&T now may offer local telephone service again and Bell South may compete with AT&T, MCI, and Sprint to provide long-distance service. Time Warner, TCI, or even power companies may provide local telephone services. And, once again, the regulatory changes that started in the United States are likely to spill over to other countries.

Overseas, after 1984, many industrialized countries, including the United Kingdom, Australia, Canada, Sweden, New Zealand, and Japan, promoted competition and change. But entrenched monopolists such as France Telecom and Singapore Telecom resisted most attempts to introduce competition into their core telephone businesses. Nonetheless, the trend among industrial countries is toward greater liberalization and competition. The fifteen member countries of the European Union, for example, were scheduled to allow competition in basic communications by 1998. Simultaneously, many key developing countries including Mexico, Chile, Thailand, Hong Kong, and Hungary have liberalized their markets and allowed foreign firms to participate in them. However, many poor countries—except China—still use their telecommunications companies to generate foreign exchange that is diverted to purposes other than investing in a new infrastructure. As a result the teledensity gap between middle-income and poor countries is widening and unless investment increases substantially, most poor countries will miss out on the information age. U.S. foreign policymakers negotiated bilateral and multilateral agreements to promote market access for U.S. equipment makers and service providers.

The United States also is willing to open its markets further to foreign firms from countries that welcome U.S. firms. Improving market access for value-added communications and information services was high on the agenda of the North American Free Trade Agreement, and the focus of attention during the Uruguay Round of multilateral trade negotiations. These two negotiations resulted in significant liberalization in the provision of value-added services. Negotiations to promote competition in basic telecommunications services under the auspices of the World Trade Organization are scheduled to conclude in early 1997. In the late 1980s U.S. policymakers began to focus on the accounts among telephone companies internationally. Because it is usually less expensive to call from the United States to other countries than vice versa and because many more calls are made from the United States to other countries than vice versa, U.S. international service providers must compensate foreign authorities for the imbalance. By the 1990s the Federal Communications Commission, the U.S. Trade Representative, and other government agencies became concerned when the U.S. settlement deficit exceeded $3 billion. To reduce this deficit the United States supports renegotiating accounting rates among international carriers and may reconsider the entire accounting rate system. Beginning in 1993, the Clinton Administration pressed for the development of a national and a global information infrastructure. Nobody can predict with certainty which firms will triumph and which will fail, but, as the Internet and World Wide Web mania shows, there will be significant opportunities for many firms, from many sectors and many countries, to shape global communications and the evolution of global networks.

JONATHAN D. ARONSON

See also Communications Policy; North American Free Trade Agreement

FURTHER READING

Brock, Gerald W. *Telecommunications Policy for the Information Age: From Monopoly to Competition.* Cambridge, Mass., 1994.

Drake, William J., ed. *The New Information Infrastructure: Strategies for U.S. Policy.* New York, 1995.

Wellenius, Bjorn, and Peter Stern, eds. *Implementing Reforms in the Telecommunications Sector: Lessons from Experience.* Washington, D.C., 1994.

TELECOMMUNICATIONS

See Communications Policy; Telecommunications Companies

TELEVISION AND FOREIGN POLICY

Television has been important to U.S. foreign policy in two rather distinct ways. First, it has, since the 1950s, become the way most U.S. citizens obtain information about the outside world. And second, television has itself become a tool and an issue in foreign policymaking.

As to the first point, television has been much more graphic as a medium of information than either newspapers or radio. As such, it may have seriously influenced not only what U.S. voters know about a foreign country, but also how much they were affected, be it by guerrilla ambushes of Vietnam, famine in Ethiopia, or a massacre in Beijing. If television in the United States had been treated as a state monopoly, this might have provided incumbent administrations with a dangerous tool. Happily, television has mostly been a private operation in the United States, like radio and the newspapers. At the minimum, this has assured a choice of viewpoints, as for decades there were three major television networks in the United States, and as these now have been supplemented by private cable services, as well as by public broadcasting stations. Still, the owners of the various private television networks, in competing for audiences for their commercial advertising, could thus be accused of seeking to entertain, more than to inform, in their news broadcasts; of choosing more coverage for a news story when graphic film footage is available and less coverage when it is not. Americans may thus have reacted more to the famines in Ethiopia and Somalia, because the cameras were present, than to similar famines in the Sudan, where they were absent. And the United States was more hostile to the 1989 shootings of pro-democracy demonstrators in Beijing, because these could be seen on television, than to similar shootings in Burma in the same year, where more people where killed but no television cameras were on hand.

In any area of voter choice, and on foreign policy issues in particular, there have to be serious worries if the choice is based not on what information is delivered, but on how it is delivered. Right-wing critics sometimes accuse all of the media, printed as well as electronic, of having a liberal bias. Actually, the electronic medium may impose a somewhat different bias—toward short attention spans, artificial drama, and emotion over reflection.

As modern cable and satellite technology has offered the typical U.S. home many more television channels in the 1980s and 1990s, it has been possible for some channels, for example those of PBS (Public Broadcasting System), to cover the news in more depth, and for other cable channels to specialize in round-the-clock news coverage, most particularly CNN (Cable News Network). Yet CNN, in the process of offering real-time coverage of world news, can also be accused of seeking to win audiences by dwelling on the more exciting and graphic events, and of thus going into less depth on the pertinent details of the news. Even the best of the television services, for example C-SPAN, which alternates between live coverage of the Senate and the House of Representatives and panel discussions and academic seminars, may not match what was previously achieved, in sophistication and depth, by the print media.

A different development is only partially the result of television technology: the major television networks, together with CNN, will now regularly carry live coverage and interviews from the side opposing the United States in any given war; for example reporting from Baghdad during the U.S. air raids of Desert Storm, from Port au Prince as the United States was about to invade Haiti, and earlier from Hanoi during the Vietnam War. Two worrisome possibilities are worth mentioning in this context. Americans might become too fascinated by the coverage of such a high-tech, seemingly made-for-TV war. Conversely, the inherent nature of a televised war might be made to seem graphically more horrible, in ways that distort priorities. Some analysts have thus attributed the United States' loss of support for the Vietnam War to the fact that television had made it a "living room war," causing every American, whether or not he or she had a son in the jungles of Southeast Asia, to feel more directly the agonies and apparent setbacks of that conflict. Military experts interpreted the communist Tet Offensive of 1968 as a defeat for the Vietcong. But the television spectacle of the U.S. Embassy in Saigon being under attack conveyed just the opposite image to Americans at home. Arabs and other terrorists seizing hostages in the 1970s and 1980s were similarly exploiting the particular pain caused by live television coverage of their victims' plight; television increased the terrorists' leverage, and decreased the responsible governments' ability to act.

Turning to the second way in which television now plays an increased role in international relations, the trans-boundary evolution of this medium, as a means of transmitting information, and/or as a form of entertainment, has been much more contentious than most Americans realize. With U.S. television programs repeatedly becoming the most popular entertainment product in many corners of the world, with U.S. news programs leaking across borders and now raining down from satellites, even the most open and democratic foreign countries might be concerned about this development on grounds of protecting their own national culture. And the governments which are not so open or democratic, which have something to hide, naturally fear the intrusion of U.S. network news telecasts, or something as pervasive as CNN.

One thus often saw the Soviet Union presenting resolutions at the United Nations in the late stages of the Cold War, calling for a ban on any international television transmissions which had not been approved by the government of the territory receiving such signals. Yet the U.S. government and U.S. television networks were also troubled to find many other nations—in the Third World, and even the democracies of Scandinavia—demanding that television not be so freely allowed to cross borders, because it was not just a flow of information, but also a possibly addictive cultural consumer good. Examples abound. For decades, Canadians have primarily watched the television programs beamed across the border from the United States, with Canadian academic and cultural leaders becoming genuinely concerned lest this further erode Canadian identity. More significantly, East Germans, during the same decades, were able to watch the evening news on West German television. If one marvelled that these East Germans never became completely adjusted to communist rule, as the fall of the Berlin Wall dramatically showed in 1989, the trans-boundary flow of television signals clearly played an important role here. Similarly, Estonians (who can understand Finnish) were continually getting the latest news from Finnish television, while also watching Helsinki's entertainment programs, which were often simply U.S. programs dubbed into the local language. Any free rendition of world news certainly contributed to undermining communist rule, as did the "background" in U.S. television programs, portraying "the American way of life."

Most Americans are unaware how popular soap operas, westerns, and other television series have become around the world. The U.S. government officials charged with dealing with such issues, as for example in the USIA (United States Information Agency), have largely welcomed such flows of television signals (even if they would prefer that the most popular program were to be something less demeaning to U.S. character than "Dallas"), because television could reinforce the radio outreach attempted over these decades by the Voice of America (VOA), by Radio Liberty and Radio Free Europe (RFE). But television is a cultural commodity as well as the free flow of information. Hollywood may have been a powerful weapon in the Cold War, but Hollywood also has wanted to earn revenues for its products, rather than having them consumed free. The United States thus has fought continuously against the right of other countries to jam radio broadcasts or to jam television broadcasts; it also has litigated to make local governments around the Caribbean shut down any unlicensed hotels or cable operators receiving and showing the signals of such pay-television operators as Home Box Office (HBO).

The "cultural commodity" factor is also illustrated in the concern the U.S. government itself now attaches to the "intellectual property" element in Hollywood productions, and in the reluctance of West European authorities (illustrated well in the General Agreement on Tariffs and Trade negotiations) to have their populations watch too many hours of U.S.-produced television. (When U.S. culture is fed into foreign homes via television, the people who are unsympathetic to it refer to it instead as "cultural imperialism.") In any event, as new technologies, including satellite transmissions, video cassette recorders (VCRs), and cable systems make television signals ever easier to tune across borders, the net of such impact is likely to keep increasing.

GEORGE H. QUESTER

See also Cable News Network; Gulf War of 1990–1991; Journalism and Foreign Policy; Vietnam War

FURTHER READING

Epstein, Edward Jay. *News from Nowhere.* New York, 1973.
Gunster, Jonathan F. *The United States and the Debate on the World "Information Order."* Washington, D.C., 1979.
Larson, James F. *Global Television and Foreign Policy.* New York, 1988.
McNeil, Robert. *The People Machine: The Influence of Television on American Politics.* New York, 1972.
McPhail, Thomas L. *Electronic Colonialism: The Future of International Broadcasting and Communication.* Beverly Hills, Calif., 1981.
Quester, George H. *The International Politics of Television.* Lexington, Mass., 1990.
Ranney, Austin. *Channels of Power.* New York, 1983.
Tunstall, Jeremy. *The Media Are American.* New York, 1977.
Winn, Marie. *The Plug-In Drug.* New York, 1977.

TELLER, EDWARD

(*b.* 15 January 1908)

American physicist born in Hungary. Teller was educated in Germany and came to the United States in 1935 as one of the many Jewish scientists fleeing the Nazi terror in Europe. (He was naturalized in 1941.) He is best known for his contributions to the development of nuclear weapons and nuclear strategy, and for his zeal in selling his often highly personal views on nuclear and other security issues to political authorities.

Teller was one of the earliest scientists to join the secret atomic bomb project at Los Alamos (the Manhattan Project) during World War II. He continued to work on nuclear weapons and related technology throughout his life. In 1951, while working at Los Alamos, he came up with the long-sought "breakthrough" to the design of a practical hydrogen bomb. This invention earned him the well-known sobriquet "Father of the Hydrogen Bomb." Shortly thereafter, expressing great personal dissatisfaction with the way things were going at the Los Alamos laboratory, Teller joined Ernest O. Lawrence in establishing a second American nuclear weapons laboratory at Livermore, California, where he remained for the rest of his career. He also was a professor of physics at the University of California, Berkeley, from 1953 to 1975.

In the 1950s, Teller became deeply involved in the security hearings which eventually declared his wartime boss, J. Robert Oppenheimer, to be a security risk. As one of the few scientists to testify against Oppenheimer at the hearings that led to that conclusion, Teller's testimony was considered to have been highly damaging.

Throughout the 1960s and 1970s, Teller campaigned diligently against arms control negotiations with the Soviets, claiming that whatever the United States might accomplish in the negotiations would inevitably undermine national security. In the early 1980s he was a key figure in persuading President Ronald Reagan that a highly effective system for defense against long-range ballistic missiles armed with nuclear warheads could be built at a reasonable cost in the near future. That enterprise, officially called the Strategic Defense Initiative but widely known as "Star Wars," secured public support, especially in conservative circles, in large part because of Teller's advocacy.

HERBERT F. YORK

See also Manhattan Project; National Security and National Defense; Nuclear Weapons and Strategy; Oppenheimer, Julius Robert; Reagan, Ronald Wilson; Strategic Defense Initiative

FURTHER READING

Blumberg, Stanley and Gwinn Owens. *Energy and Conflict: The Life and Times of Edward Teller.* New York, 1976.
York, Herbert. *The Advisers: Oppenheimer, Teller, and the Superbomb.* San Francisco, Calif., 1976.

TELLER AMENDMENT

(April 1898)

A congressional joint resolution against U.S. annexation of Cuba. On the eve of the Spanish-American-Cuban-Filipino War, Cuban lobbyists sought a congressional declaration opposing annexation to the United States. They persuaded Senator Henry M. Teller, Silver Republican of Colorado, to sponsor an amendment to a set of congressional military resolutions. The amendment stated that the United States had no intention of exercising "sovereignty, jurisdiction, or control" over Cuba, and after pacifying the island, the United States would "leave the government and control of [Cuba] to its people." Although Teller favored expansionism and believed Cuba would eventually become American, he opposed forcible annexation. Most legislators viewed the amendment as an expression of the nation's non-acquisitive intent as it entered the war. The Senate adopted the amendment (1898) by voice vote, and House members made no objection to it. President William McKinley accepted Teller's amendment because he did not want to acquire the island. Earlier, McKinley had considered purchasing Cuba, but he had concluded that many senators would resist annexation. Some senators objected to adding people of different cultural and racial makeup while others considered Cuban sugar production as threatening constituent agricultural interests. Despite the Teller Amendment, after the war the United States controlled Cuba through a military occupation that led to the Platt Amendment.

JOHN L. OFFNER

See also Cuba; Platt Amendment; Spanish-American-Cuban-Filipino War, 1898

FURTHER READING

Foner, Philip S. *The Spanish-Cuban-American War and the Birth of American Imperialism, 1895–1902.* 2 vols. New York: 1972.
Healy, David F. *The United States in Cuba, 1898–1902.* Madison, Wis., 1963.
Offner, John L. *An Unwanted War: The Diplomacy of the United States and Spain over Cuba, 1895–1898.* Chapel Hill, N.C., 1992.

TENG HSIAO-PING

See Deng Xiaoping

TERRORISM

The deliberate and systematic use (or threatened use) of unsanctioned violence to further political objectives through intimidation or coercion of target groups that normally extend beyond the immediate victims. Terrorism's ancestry can be traced back to the first-century Jewish sects, the Zealots and Sicarii. The terms "terrorism" and "terrorist" are of more modern origin, having first come into use during the French Revolution to describe in part the violent means employed by the Jacobin government from May 1793 to July 1794.

No universally accepted definition of terrorism exists. The difficulty in defining terrorism arises in part from the debate over whether to take political objectives into consideration. In the words of Yassir Arafat: "Nobody is a terrorist who stands for a just cause." This normative approach would make the distinction between 'freedom fighter' and 'terrorist' one of ends rather than means, and consequently reduces the term "terrorist" to a pejorative label for one's enemies. Attempts to include the tactics employed by colonial, racist, or totalitarian states to control their populations also have clouded the debate on terrorism. Terrorism is essentially a psychological tactic employing fear and publicity as its two most important elements. Its victims are not the objective but rather the means by which to instill fear among a wider audience.

Terrorism exploded onto the international scene in the late 1960s and quickly became part of the international political agenda. In Latin America Che Guevara's death in 1967 marked the defeat of rural guerrilla warfare in Venezuela, Bolivia, and Peru and the shifting of emphasis to urban terrorism. By 1970 the Uruguayan Tupamaros, the Brazilian National Liberation Alliance, and the Argentine People's Revolutionary Army all had launched campaigns of urban terrorism. In the United States, Japan, and Europe the social turmoil of the 1960s and the failure of the New Left led to the formation of ideological terrorist groups or the adoption of terrorist tactics by existing ones. Groups such as the Weather Underground, an offshoot of the Students for a Democratic Society (SDS), appeared in the United States, and the Japanese Red Army evolved from the Zenga Kuren student group. Andreas Baader and Ulricke Meinhof created the German Red Army Faction in 1968. Italy's Red Brigades evolved in 1970 from an established political party, the Metropolitan Political Collective.

Many existing nationalist and ethnic groups also adopted terrorist tactics at this time. The Provisional Wing of the Irish Republican Army turned to terrorism in 1967, followed by the Protestant Ulster Defense Organization. The Spanish Basque Nation and Liberty (ETA) began its terrorist campaign in 1968. In the Middle East the trigger was the defeat of the Arab states in 1967 by Israel during the Six-Day War, which led the Palestine Liberation Organization (PLO) to select Yassir Arafat as its chief and to turn to terrorism to publicize its cause and to keep Palestine an issue on the world agenda.

U.S. Policy in the 1970s and 1980s

The United States first became involved in a major incident of international terrorism on 6 September 1970, when members of the Popular Front for the Liberation of Palestine (PFLP) hijacked aircraft belonging to TWA, Swissair, and British Air and forced them to fly to Dawson Field in Jordan. In negotiations complicated by an ongoing civil war between Jordan's King Hussein and Palestinians residing in Jordan, President Richard Nixon and National Security Adviser Henry Kissinger persuaded the other countries involved (Britain, West Germany, Switzerland, the Netherlands, and Israel) to maintain a united front and not seek separate deals with the terrorists. According to Kissinger, the key in securing the release of the hostages without undermining King Hussein lay in demonstrating determination to the terrorists without adopting an attitude of impotent scolding.

Apart from this incident, the formulation of a counterterrorism policy initially was left to the Department of States geographic bureaus on the assumption that terrorism was no more than a manifestation of local problems. As the number of international terrorist incidents mounted, policymakers learned that terrorism was a distinct problem and that an effective counterterrorism policy required coordination between domestic law enforcement agencies and foreign policy, national defense, and intelligence agencies. The first steps toward achieving policy coherence were taken in 1972 in the aftermath of the attack by Arafat's Black September organization on Israeli athletes at the Munich Olympics, when Nixon established a cabinet-level committee for combating terrorism, chaired by the secretary of state. This committee supervised an Interagency Working Group that grew from a dozen to over thirty agencies by the end of the decade. The Department of State created the Office for Combating Terrorism to coordinate counter terrorism foreign policy.

Black September struck again in March 1973, seizing both the incoming U.S. ambassador to the Sudan, Cleo Noel, and the departing chargé d'affaires, George More, at a reception at the Saudi Embassy in Khartoum. After Nixon announced at a press conference that the United States would not make concessions to the terrorists' demands, Black September murdered both men. Nixon's public response represented a departure from the low-key diplomacy that had contributed to the successful resolution of the earlier air hijacking incident and may have convinced the terrorists that there was no possibility for fruitful negotiations. The president's decision not to negotiate, however, was widely regarded as correct and has become one of three cornerstones of U.S. counterterrorism policy. The others are to seek international support to isolate and pressure terrorist-sponsoring states and to work with other countries to develop practical measures to counter terrorism.

Although every subsequent administration has reaffirmed these principles, President Gerald Ford departed from the policy of no concessions in September 1976 when Croatian terrorists hijacked TWA flight 355 over New York and demanded that their cause be publicized in Britain, France, and the United States. The hijackers landed in France and, when the French refused to allow their aircraft to proceed to Croatia, they were persuaded to surrender peacefully after learning that Ford had met their demands. The incident was too brief (two days), the demands were too moderate, and the group was too inconsequential for Ford's action to overturn the precedent set by Nixon.

The hijacking had little impact on ongoing U.S. efforts to combat the sauve qui peut attitude of some countries as they attempted to escape terrorism through concessions, such as occurred in October 1973 when Black September induced West Germany to release the three surviving terrorists from the Munich Olympics by hijacking a Lufthansa aircraft. To build a consensus, the United States pressed for international agreements on fighting terrorism. Initial agreements included: the 1970 Hague Convention on Aircraft Hijacking, the 1971 Montreal Convention on Aircraft Sabotage, the 1975 Convention on Prevention and Punishment of Internationally Protected Persons, and the 1979 Convention on the Taking of Hostages. Members of the G-7 (Canada, France, West Germany, Great Britain, Japan, Italy, and the United States) used their annual meetings to establish common policies on terrorism, issuing joint declarations to highlight their unity. The declaration made at the 1978 Bonn Summit, for example, called upon member countries to terminate civilian airline service to any country failing to prosecute or extradite a hijacker. These early agreements were especially significant because antiterrorism resolutions in the United Nations (UN) were stalled by debate over the definition of terrorism and Third World efforts to include language that exempted "freedom fighters." The General Assembly's first resolution unequivocally condemning terrorism was not passed until December 1985.

The Jimmy Carter administration transferred the responsibility for counterterrorism from the cabinet to the National Security Council and, following a 1977 review of U.S. policy procedures, pioneered the "lead agency concept" for managing terrorist incidents. Under this system, responsibility for coordination of the U.S. response to incidents abroad rests with the Department of State, response to domestic incidents with the Department of Justice (FBI), and response to incidents aboard aircraft with the Federal Aviation Administration (FAA). To give the United States a counterterrorist capability, Carter ordered the formation of Delta Force in 1977. Delta Force's failure to rescue the U.S. hostages held in Iran cost the U.S. eight lives and considerable prestige, but should not obscure the fact that Carter's threat of military retaliation was one factor in preventing the trial for espionage of the U.S. hostages held by Iran.

The great ordeal of the Carter presidency was the crisis with Iran that unfolded as the shah fell and U.S. diplomats were held hostage for 444 days. Seized 4 November 1979 ostensibly in retaliation against the U.S. for admitting the shah for medical treatment, the hostages were actually being manipulated by Iranian militants to maneuver their own government into a more anti-American position. Until their domestic agenda had been achieved with the election of a more radical parliament and until the Iran-Iraq War, which began in September 1980, gave Iran an immediate need for money and an end to her diplomatic isolation, negotiations for the hostages' release were futile. Carter's belief that the crisis would be quickly ended and his deep emotional involvement led him to remain in Washington until it was resolved. This decision in effect made him a hostage of the hostages. Then Deputy Secretary of State Warren Christopher later concluded that Carter would have been better advised to have distanced himself from the situation.

The Reagan Years

According to Australian criminologist Grant Wardlaw, the key to formulating counterterrorist policy is a balanced appreciation of the threat and a judicious response. From its inception the Ronald Reagan administration had great difficulty in achieving such balance. President Reagan himself escalated both the rhetoric and the public's expectations when on 28 January 1981 he used the return of the hostages released by Iran to announce that his policy on terrorism would be one of "swift and effective retribution." One manifestation of this policy was expressed in National Security Directive (NSDD) 138, which described terrorism by any person or group as a threat to national security and authorized the use of military force against terrorists. In reality the administration was seldom able to act because it was unable to reconcile deep divisions between advocates of strong retaliation led by Secretary of State Shultz and those of restraint led by Secretary of Defense Weinberger.

One initial reason for the attention the Reagan administration paid to terrorism lay in the suspicion that the Soviet Union was supporting a "terrorist network" engaged in undermining Western governments. The Soviets never made a secret of their assistance to revolutionary movements, many of which did engage in terrorism. The Soviets, for example, trained, funded, and equipped PLO guerrilla fighters. Their East Bloc partners permitted safehouses for and the transit of terrorist teams; Poland and East Germany even allowed Abu Nidal to operate businesses openly. Although Bulgarian intelligence's involvement in the attempted assassination of Pope John Paul II was not proved in court, the evidence of complicity was substantial. Yet the administration was never able to obtain support within the intelligence community for the conclusion that the Soviet Union directly trained or supported terrorists. Its efforts to promote international condemnation of Soviet activities were undercut by, among other factors, perceptions abroad that the United States was engaged in supporting terrorism in Latin America through its backing of the Nicaraguan Contras.

By contrast, the United States made a clearer case against the state-sponsored terrorism frequently practiced by Libya, Syria, Iraq, and Iran, for whom terrorism was an attractive weapon because it was far less expensive than conventional warfare and less likely to provoke a military response. These states used terrorists to eliminate dissidents, to fight a war by proxy with Israel, to control the Palestinian movement, to derail the Middle East peace process, to extort economic or other concessions, and to undermine Western influence in Lebanon. In response the United States tried to raise the cost to the state using terrorism as a weapon. Congress took the initiative, passing Section 6(j) of the Export Administration Act of 1979, which required the administration to identify and place economic sanctions on countries that have repeatedly provided support for international terrorism. The so-called "terrorism list," designated eight nations as terrorism sponsors: Cuba, Iran, Iraq, Libya, North Korea, Sudan, Syria, and the former South-Yemen. Diplomatic and economic pressure on these states has produced limited successes. Iraq in 1983 and Syria in 1987 both expelled the Abu Nidal group in response to western diplomatic and economic pressure, although both also continued to support other terrorist groups. The inflexibility of the "list" approach, however, highlights the potential contradiction between a long-term counterterrorist strategy on the one hand and the need to respond to individual incidents and to other dimensions of bilateral relationships on the other. The premature removal of Iraq from the list in order to permit U.S. assistance during Iraq's war with Iran was one instance of this difficulty; another was the necessity of allying with Syria, which was on the list, during the Gulf War against Iraq.

Iran, through its association with the Islamic revolutionary terrorism that emerged in the late 1970s, arguably has been the most successful terrorist state-sponsor. These terrorists were predominantly Shia Muslims principally from Lebanon and the Gulf States who were recruited, trained, supported, and directed by Iran. For them the United States, as the principal supporter of the region's moderate Arab states (and of Israel) and as a major opponent of Iran, was one of the Great Satans (the former Soviet Union was the other). Among other incidents, Iranian-sponsored terrorists were responsible for the 1983 bombings of the U.S. and French embassies in Kuwait. Included in the seventeen persons arrested for these attacks was the Lebanese brother-in-law of Imad Mughniyah, the person responsible for holding the foreign hostages in Lebanon. Indeed, Lebanon remains their great center of strength. There Iranian Revolutionary Guards (IRG) from their headquarters in the Bekaa Valley gave the Shia movement Hizballah (The Party of God) a terrorist dimension.

In Lebanon direct confrontation with the United States came in the aftermath of the Israeli invasion in 1982, which was undertaken to destroy the PLO infrastructure there. Following the evacuation of PLO fighters under a UN guarantee, Christian Phalange militiamen murdered hundreds of Palestinian civilians in the Sabra and Shatila refugee camps, while the Israeli army stood by. In reaction to this outrage, U.S. Marines were redeployed to Beirut as part of an international peacekeeping force. At the same time the United States sought to reestablish the authority of the Lebanese state by rebuilding its armed forces and assisting them militarily, which was seen by Muslims as support for Israel and the Christian factions that controlled the army. In retaliation, suicide truck bombers first struck the U.S. embassy in Beirut on 18 April 1983 and then attacked the headquarters of the French and U.S. military contingents on 23 October. Convinced that Hizballah was behind the attacks, France launched an air strike against the IRG headquarters. U.S. aircraft were to have participated, but the Reagan Administration split over whether the available evidence was sufficiently conclusive to justify an attack. Following the subsequent bombing of the relocated U.S. embassy on 20 September 1984, reconnaissance photographs clearly indicated that the suicide driver had practiced on an obstacle course set-up at the IRG headquarters. Yet the administration again did not retaliate.

In Lebanon the Reagan administration failed to make good on its pledge of swift and effective retribution: at first because insufficient intelligence was available to meet its standard of irrefutable evidence; and later, when such evidence seemingly was available, because the administration remained divided between restraint and retaliation. Elsewhere, it did employ the military option successfully. In 1985 U.S. fighters diverted to Italy the aircraft carrying Mohammed Abbas, mastermind of the hijacking of the cruiseship *Achille Lauro*. The following year aircraft attacked Libya in retaliation for Qaddafi's role in the bombing of La Belle Disco in West Berlin. The results, however, were mixed. When, to preserve its good relations with the PLO, Italy chose to release rather than prosecute or extradite Abbas, close ties to a NATO ally induced the U.S. to mute its protests. The attack on Libya temporarily dissuaded Qaddafi from undertaking further terrorist attacks, and fear that the U.S. would repeat its earlier military response helped induce the Europeans and Japanese to join more readily in the imposition of sanctions. Both operations produced tensions within NATO. The Italian government fell as a result of the *Achille Lauro* incident and British Prime Minister Margaret Thatcher was strongly attacked in Parliament for allowing U.S. aircraft based in Britain to participate in the bombing of Libya.

By the time of the second embassy bombing in Lebanon, in September 1984, Hizballah had broadened its offensive through the kidnapping of foreigners. The Iran-Contra affair originated in Reagan's emotional involvement with these hostages. His deep concern led the White House to agree to an Israeli initiative involving the clandestine sale of arms to Iran and to persevere in that undertaking against the opposition of both Shultz and Weinberger in the expectation it would encourage Iranian moderates and secure the hostages' release. Although Iran ultimately received over 2,000 TOW missiles as well as spare parts for other weapons, only three hostages were released and Hizballah soon took others to replace them. The initiative also failed to moderate the hard-line attitude of Iran, and its exposure in a Beirut newspaper led to the greatest crisis of the Reagan presidency and undermined the credibility of U.S. counterterrorism policy.

While the secret negotiations with Iran were in progress, Vice-President Bush was conducting a high-profile review of counterterrorism policy. The subsequent revelation of the Iran-Contra affair made the vice-president's task force's endorsement of a no-concessions policy appear hypocritical, but its practical recommendations for increased international cooperation in law enforcement, improved protection for U.S. diplomatic facilities, enhanced intelligence capabilities, and legislative initiatives were not seriously affected. The United States already was participating at the working-group level with the Trevi Group (created in 1976 by the European Community to foster counterterrorism cooperation), and had negotiated mutual assistance treaties that enabled law enforcement officers to obtain evidence in another country. Through the Anti-Terrorist Assistance Program (ATAP), which was approved in 1983, the United States was providing aid with the physical security and crisis management aspects of counterterrorism. Other non-ATAP assistance programs, however, ran into difficulties. In El Salvador, government personnel who had received U.S. training in counterinsurgency formed Death Squads to terrorize political opponents.

U.S. interests abroad have always been favored targets for terrorists. By 1980 approximately one-third of all terrorist attacks were targeted directly at U.S. personnel or installations. In response the Department of State undertook a multibillion dollar security enhancement program to improve physical security and created the Diplomatic Security Bureau. Success in reducing terrorist attacks against diplomatic targets came only at a price; as "official America" became more difficult to attack, terrorists compensated by turning their attention to corporate America. The U.S. government has a moral and, following the bombing of Pan Am Flight 103 in December 1988 (which killed 270 persons including 189 Americans) a legal obligation to provide warnings and advice to its citizens abroad. The FAA furnishes airlines with Aviation Security Bulletins; the State Department promotes coordination on security through the American Private Sector Overseas Advisory Council (ASAC) and provides advisories to the general public.

The Reagan administration also took action to curtail the support for international terrorism at home. The training and equipping of terrorists in the United States, such as Sikh militants, was both legal and unregulated until the International Traffic in Arms Regulations were expanded in January 1985. U.S. courts blocked the extradition of Irish Republican Army (IRA) members accused of violent crimes, including murder, because their actions were viewed as political crimes until Congress amended the law in 1985. The Federal Bureau of Investigation (FBI) lacked authority and U.S. courts lacked jurisdiction in cases involving the murder of private citizens overseas until a 1985 law made such terrorism a federal crime. Using this authority in 1987 FBI agents seized Fawaz Younis and brought him to the U.S. where he was tried and convicted for the 1985 hijacking of a Royal Jordanian Airlines flight in which United States citizens were involved.

U.S. Policy in the 1990s

When President George Bush took office he inherited two ongoing terrorist-related problems: the remaining hostages in Lebanon and the bombing of Pan Am Flight 103. In April 1990 the hostage captors demanded that President Bush send Assistant Secretary of State John Kelly to Damascus to negotiate the release of a hostage. Bush's refusal signaled that hostages could no longer be used to manipulate the U.S. government and thereby reduced their value to the captors, facilitating their ultimate release. During the lengthy investigation of the Pan Am disaster, Syria and Iran were prime suspects. Although there was insufficient evidence to link them directly to the crime, relatives of the victims and President Bush's own Commission on Aviation Security recommended that he make the state-sponsors of terrorism pay a price. By refusing to take precipitate action, however, Bush later was able to draw Syria into the alliance against Saddam Hussein following the Iraqi invasion of Kuwait. His prudence was justified when by November 1991 investigators had uncovered sufficient evidence to indict two Libyan intelligence officers for the bombing. Later, during the Kuwait crisis, when Saddam Hussein held thousands of foreign hostages, which he referred to as "human shields," Bush again decided that the hostages would not affect U.S. policy. By distancing himself from the emotional dimension of terrorism and refraining from building unreasonable public expectations in all three incidents, he was able to return to the low-key approach of the Nixon administration.

President Bill Clinton continued this proportional response to terrorism when the World Trade Center in New York City was bombed in February 1993. His response was equally measured following the shooting of three U.S. diplomats in Karachi, Pakistan, two years later. Both incidents seemed to be the work of a new breed of Islamic revolutionary terrorists who emerged as a legacy of the Afghan War.

Afghanistan remains as a major training ground; nearly all of the competing Afghan factions are associated with the camps which train terrorists of many nations. Their "graduates" have been involved in incidents on four continents, ranging from the WTC bombing to the attempted assassination of Egyptian President Hosni Mubarak in Ethiopia in 1995. As their relationship to state-sponsors are much more tenuous, these terrorists are both more unpredictable and less susceptible to control through diplomatic pressure. Although the U.S. did strike Baghdad with cruise missiles in retaliation for Saddam's attempt to assassinate former President Bush during his 1993 visit to Kuwait, U.S. reaction has been directed predominately toward intelligence and law enforcement. U.S. law enforcement officials scored major successes with the prosecution of the WTC bombers and the apprehension and extradition of alleged WTC bombing mastermind, Ramsi Yousef, from Pakistan in 1995.

Terrorism also was used to strike at the 1993 Israel-PLO peace accords, one of the cornerstones of U.S. foreign policy. In attempts to derail the resulting peace process, an Israeli terrorist assassinated Israeli Prime Minister Rabin and the Palestinian Islamic Jihad and Hamas organizations unleashed campaigns of suicide bombings inside Israel. President Clinton responded by calling the first ever anti-terrorist summit at Sharm el-Sheikh in Egypt in 1996 and by promising financial aid to Israel and others fighting terrorism. A significant boost to the peace process came when the PLO removed the demand for the destruction of Israel from its charter. But even this was not enough to quell Israeli fears, and in the subsequent general election the more cautious Likud party under hard-line advocate Benjamin Netanyahu narrowly defeated the Labor party led by Rabin's successor as Prime Minister, Shimon Peres.

Domestically, the Clinton administration has attempted to stop the flow of funds from U.S. sources to terrorist groups. The IRA is probably the best known instance, but Hizballah and Hamas also raise and receive funds from U.S. sources. In response to the damage done to the peace process by terrorist attacks, Clinton froze the assets of thirty Arab and Israeli groups and individuals throughout the U.S. Legislative proposals to make fundraising for these groups illegal, to make terrorism a Federal crime, and to make the deportation or exclusion of suspected terrorists easier initially stalled as a result of opposition by human rights advocates, a reflection of the ongoing difficulty democratic governments have reconciling individual liberty with the fight against terrorism. The balance shifted dramatically, however, in 1995 as a result of the Oklahoma City bombing. Although the work of domestic terrorists, it revived fears of foreign terrorist attacks and contributed to passage of the Anti-Terrorist and Effective Death Penalty Act of 1996. This act restricts foreign assistance to governments that provide assistance to countries that are not "cooperating fully" with U.S. anti-terrorist efforts; makes deportation of terrorist suspects easier; and allocates $1 billion over five years to fight terrorism.

Since its dramatic appearance, contemporary terrorism has ebbed and flowed, but it remains a cheap, low-risk alternative to conventional means of influence. Iran, principally but not solely through Hizballah surrogates, remains the most active state-sponsor. In addition new forms have arisen, such as narco-terrorism, the association of terrorists with drug traffickers, and the autonomous Islamic terrorism spawned by the Afghan War. This new breed of terrorists has shown a willingness to inflict massive casualties, yet it is still in its capacity to provoke panic and overreaction rather than in the destruction it causes that terrorism's enduring threat lies.

KENNETH A. DUNCAN

See also Bush, George Herbert Walker; Carter, James Earl; Iran; Iran-Contra Affair; Lebanon; Middle East; Narcotics, International; Palestine Liberation Organization; Pan Am Flight 103; Reagan, Ronald Wilson

FURTHER READING

Adams, James. *The Financing of Terror*. New York, 1986.
Christopher, Warren, ed. *American Hostages in Iran: The Conduct of a Crisis*. New Haven, Conn., 1985.
Congressional Research Service. *International Terrorism: A Compilation of Major Laws, Treaties, Agreements, and Executive Documents*, a report prepared for the U.S. House of Representatives Committee on Foreign Affairs by the Library of Congress. Washington, D.C., 1994.
Crenshaw, Martha, ed. *Terrorism in Context*. Philadelphia, 1995.
Jenkins, Brian. *International Terrorism: The Other World War*. Santa Monica, Calif., 1985.
Kegley, Charles Jr., ed. *International Terrorism: Characteristics, Causes, Controls*. New York, 1990.
Laqueur, Walter. *The Age of Terrorism*. New York, 1987.
Long, David E. *The Anatomy of Terrorism*. New York, 1990.
Martin, David C., and John Walcott. *Best Laid Plans: The Inside Story of America's War Against Terrorism*. New York, 1988.
Rapoport, David C. ed. *Inside Terrorist Organizations*. New York, 1988.
Reich, Walter, ed. *Origins of Terrorism: Psychologies, Ideologies, Theologies, States of Mind*. New York, 1990.
Simon, Jeffrey D. *The Terrorist Trap: America's Experience with Terrorism*. Bloomington, Ind., 1994.
United States Department of State. *Patterns of Global Terrorism*, an annual report submitted to Congress in compliance with Title 22 USC, Section 2656(f).

TEST BAN TREATY

See Limited Nuclear Test Ban Treaty

TET OFFENSIVE

The massive attack in January 1968 against major urban areas in South Vietnam by Vietcong forces directed by North Vietnamese leaders. (For Vietnamese, Tet is the traditional lunar new year holiday.) Considered by many analysts to be the turning point of the Vietnam War, the assault simultaneously hit virtually every provincial capital and district town in South Vietnam. Designed to be the final blow in a revolutionary overthrow of the South Vietnamese government, an "atom bomb of people's war," the offensive was launched to force the United States to negotiate the withdrawal of U.S. forces, numbering half a million at the time. While U.S. and South Vietnamese forces beat back the offensive, and communist forces by far suffered the greatest casualties, the political effects of Tet ranked as a defeat for the United States and a victory for the communists of North Vietnam and their allies in the South, the Vietcong.

When U.S. ground combat troops first went to Vietnam in March 1965, U.S. strategy was one of attrition—to wear down enemy forces through a "graduated escalation" that would eventually achieve a "crossover point" whereby the rate of communist casualties would exceed their rate of new replacements. The Tet Offensive seemed to expose dramatically the futility of this strategy. The offensive itself began with countrywide attacks on 30 and 31 January by an initial communist force of more than 80,000, which penetrated both the capital city of Saigon and the former Imperial capital of Hue. Hue was held for three weeks. By 31 March, the Vietcong had been expelled from areas it had seized during Tet. Tens of thousands of soldiers and civilians died, and more than a million became refugees. In this carnage, the southern communist guerrilla forces (Vietcong) were nearly annihilated. After Tet, the communist war effort continued, ultimately to victory in 1975, with the fighting done mostly by regular military units from North Vietnam.

Despite this communist military defeat, the Tet Offensive made a shambles of U.S. war policy and of President Lyndon Johnson's political fortunes. Public support of Johnson's handling of the war plummeted to twenty-six percent. 1968 was also an election year, and antiwar candidate Senator Eugene McCarthy garnered forty-two percent of the vote against Johnson in the New Hampshire primary held on 12 March. McCarthy's unexpectedly strong showing was in large part a negative public reaction to Tet; before Tet, Johnson administration officials had spoken optimistically about making progress in Vietnam. A credibility gap opened wide after Tet. Senator Robert F. Kennedy also became more outspoken against Johnson's war policies and soon joined the race for the Democratic nomination for president. Some have argued that media coverage of Tet was distorted; others have interpreted the military outcome as less politically important than the impact of the U.S. public's seeing so graphically on television the intensity of the fighting and the extent of the communist challenge. Some observers scored the administration for an "intelligence gap," a failure to detect communist planning for the offensive. An outside group of foreign policy experts, called the Wise Men, counseled the president to cut his losses and seek an honorable path for the withdrawal of U.S. forces. The president announced on 31 March that he would de-escalate the war (he had not accepted General William Westmoreland's request for 200,000 more troops) and seek a negotiated settlement. Johnson also stunned the nation when he said that he would not seek reelection. In the end, Tet was a military victory and a political defeat for the United States, but a military defeat and a political victory for the Vietnamese communists.

TIMOTHY J. LOMPERIS

See also Johnson, Lyndon Baines; Kennedy, Robert Francis; McCarthy, Eugene Joseph; Public Opinion; Vietnam; Vietnam War

FURTHER READING

Braestrup, Peter. *Big Story!* 2 vols. Boulder, Colo., 1977.
Brodie, Bernard. "The Tet Offensive." In *Decisive Battles of the Twentieth Century*, edited by Noble Frankland and Christopher Dowling. London, 1976.
Oberdorfer, Don. *Tet!* New York, 1971.
Spector, Ronald H. *After Tet: The Bloodiest Year in Vietnam.* New York, 1993.
Turner, Kathleen. *Lyndon Johnson's Dual War: Vietnam and the Press.* Chicago, 1985.
Wirtz, James J. *The Tet Offensive: Intelligence Failure in War.* Ithaca, N.Y., 1991.

TEXAS

See Mexico, War with

THAILAND

A constitutional monarchy located in Southeast Asia bordering Laos, Cambodia, Myanmar (formerly Burma), and the Gulf of Thailand. The kingdom of Thailand (until 1939 known as Siam) has enjoyed U.S. diplomatic recognition since the 1830s. Unlike many of its neighbors, Siam managed to avert European colonization. Its kings did make extensive economic concessions to the European powers, and they maintained generally good relations, including sending some Thai troops to fight with Great Britain and France in World War I. During World War II, Japanese occupation faces pushed Thailand into a nominal alliance with Tokyo, which Thai underground leaders repudiated at the war's end. Relations with the United States then grew closer as communism made advances in China and Indochina. In 1954 Thailand became a charter member of the Southeast Asian Treaty Organization (SEATO), the regional anti-communist alliance built up by the United States, following the French collapse in Vietnam. The United States utilized air and naval bases in Thailand during its war in Vietnam, and the Thais contributed special ground forces, an arrangement quite profitable to the Thai economy. After the communists seized power in all of Indochina in 1975 more than 300,000 Laotians fled to Thailand, and as many Cambodians followed in 1979. Thailand did not grant them permanent asylum; the United Nations subsidized interim camps, third country resettlement, and voluntary repatriation.

SEATO disbanded in 1977 but a joint U.S. Military Advisory Group (JUSMAG) concerned with military training and arms procurement remained in Bangkok. This also was a period of recurring domestic instability, including bloody clashes between conservative groups and radical students and rule by a military junta from 1976 to 1979. While there was greater stability in the 1980s, the early 1990s once again were marked by violent unrest and military intervention. The United States has usually protested against the military coups and violations of human rights, but has stopped well short of breaking existing cooperative relationships. Thai military elements also have appeared in the 1990s to deal secretly along the Cambodian border with the infamous Khmer Rouge, both for private commercial gain and to maintain a potential counterweight to any Vietnamese presence in Cambodia.

Over the years, U.S.-Thai economic relations have been both mutually beneficial and at times quite contentious. U.S. assistance has focused on road construction, agricultural commodity sales, import preferences, investment guarantees, military equipment grants and sales, and narcotics interdiction and substitution crops in border areas near Laos and Myanmar. Friction has arisen over U.S. insistence on a number of economic issues, particularly the protection of intellectual property rights, and rights for workers. Thailand is a member of the Association of Southeast Asian Nations (ASEAN) and the Asia-Pacific Economic Cooperation (APEC).

MACALISTER BROWN

See also Cambodia; Laos; Myanmar; Southeast Asia Treaty Organization; Vietnam

FURTHER READING

LePoer, Barbara Leitch, ed. *Thailand, a Country Study*. Washington, D.C., 1989.

Muscat, Robert J. *Thailand and the United States: Development, Security and Foreign Aid*. New York, 1990.

THANT, U

(*b.* 22 January 1909; *d.* 25 November 1974)

Burmese diplomat and educator who served as the third secretary-general of the United Nations (1961–1971). Born in Pantanow, he was educated at University College in Rangoon and worked as a teacher and journalist. Thant gained international prominence as Burma's permanent representative at the United Nations (UN) in the late 1950s, when he emerged as a leader of Asian and African countries in the General Assembly. When Secretary-General Dag Hammarsköld died in a plane crash in September 1961, a standoff developed between the United States and the Soviet Union over a replacement. Thant emerged as a compromise candidate and was sworn in as acting secretary-general in November 1961. A year later, the Security Council confirmed him for a full five-year term.

Thant faced a range of crises deriving from the Cold War, Arab-Israeli tension in the Middle East, and decolonization. He inherited the tenuous UN peacekeeping operation in the Congo, composed of a multinational military force, and worked to fulfill the UN's goals of preventing civil war in and dismemberment of that country. During his tenure, the number of developing countries in the United Nations increased dramatically, giving them unprecedented strength in the General Assembly.

In October 1962, Thant played an active role in the Cuban missile crisis. He used his friendly relations with John F. Kennedy and Nikita Khrushchev, as well as his reputation for impartiality, to maintain avenues of communication and reduce tension between the superpowers. Thant traveled to Havana, Cuba, to discuss the crisis with Fidel Castro. Throughout the 1960s, Thant quietly sought to instigate peace talks between the United States and North Vietnam, but neither side accepted his terms.

Thant's most controversial actions occurred in May 1967 in the midst of a showdown between Egypt and Israel. Egyptian President Gamal Abdel Nasser had demanded the withdrawal of the UN emergency force that separated Israeli and Egyptian forces in the Sinai. With advice from Ralph Bunche, the undersecretary-general for political affairs, Thant acceded after Nasser promised not to attack Israel. Fearful of Nasser's motives, Israel launched a preemptive strike on 5 June 1967, starting the Six Day War. After his second term as secretary-general ended in 1971, Thant retired to the suburbs of New York. He was succeeded as secretary-general by Kurt Waldheim.

KURK DORSEY

See also Bunche, Ralph Johnson; Cold War; Congo; Cuban Missile Crisis; Egypt; Israel; Middle East; Nasser, Gamal Abdel; United Nations; Vietnam War

FURTHER READING

Nassif, Ramses. *U Thant in New York, 1961–1971*. New York, 1988.

Thant, U. *View from the UN: The Memoirs of U Thant*. New York, 1978.

THATCHER, MARGARET HILDA
Baroness Thatcher

(*b.* 13 October 1925)

Prime Minister of Great Britain (1979–1990), she reestablished strong and amicable U.S.-British relations, and forged with President Ronald Reagan a formidable partnership of conservative leaders.

Thatcher, born Margaret Roberts and educated at Kesteven & Grantham Girls School and at Oxford, passed her bar exams in 1953 as a tax barrister. Elected Member of Parliament for Finchley as a Conservative in 1959, Thatcher became parliamentary secretary at the Ministry of Pensions during Harold Macmillan's premiership in 1961, and later, in 1970, served as Secretary of State for Education and Science in Edward Heath's government.

In 1974 Harold Wilson's Labour Party defeated the Conservatives. In the realignment that followed in 1975, Thatcher suprisingly emerged as Tory leader; revitalized the party; and led it to victory in 1979. Ronald Reagan's presidential victory in 1980 initiated eight years of close U.S.-British relations largely based on Reagan's and Thatcher's ideological compatibility and commonality of views on economic issues.

There were tangible mutual benefits in this friendship. In 1980, to American satisfaction, the British led the European Economic Community (EEC) in imposing heavy sanctions on Iran during the hostage crisis. In mid-July, Reagan supplied Great Britain with Trident missile equipment. By 2 April 1982, U.S.-British relations faced a grave test after the Argentine invasion of the Falkland Islands (Malvinas). Washington risked offending its Latin American friends in supporting Great Britain with intelligence assistance and military equipment in its massive military operation. In 1986, Thatcher in turn permitted British-based U.S. aircraft to bomb Libya, while other European powers shunned the Americans.

The Reagan-Thatcher years also witnessed some major disagreements. Thatcher disapproved of the 1983

U.S. effort to topple the left-wing government of Grenada; Grenada was a member of the British Commonwealth. Furthermore, in 1983, Thatcher spoke of a rapprochement between East and West, later informing the United States that both Great Britain and Europe would rather abandon their strong ties with Washington than abandon the Siberian pipeline being built by the Soviets to supply Europe with gas. In October 1986, Thatcher was shut out of the Reykjavik Summit as Reagan and the Soviet leader, Mikhail Gorbachev, discussed the removal of all intermediate-range nuclear missiles from Europe. Thatcher later convinced the Reagan administration not to base the idea of nuclear deterrence entirely upon the hoped-for success of SDI, the so-called Star Wars project. While believing in arms control, Thatcher asserted that the world would be far more dangerous without nuclear weapons. Ironically, the "Iron Lady" (a nickname Thatcher earned by being unapologetically anti-communist) was also the first Western leader to meet with Gorbachev, just before he became the new leader of the Soviet Union, and her favorable assessment—"someone you can do business with"—had a major impact on his subsequent career.

In the Middle East, Thatcher basically toed the U.S. line through the Iran-Iraq War and the 1982 Israeli invasion of Lebanon. But in 1987, Great Britain aligned with the European Community in calling for the Palestinians to be involved in all future Arab-Israeli peace talks.

The end of the Cold War coincided with growing economic difficulties in Great Britain. In November 1990, a crisis within the British Cabinet forced Thatcher reluctantly to step down as prime minister. She was succeeded by John Major, and was soon thereafter given a life peerage by Queen Elizabeth, whose relations with the first ever woman prime minister had been noticeably cool throughout.

CHRISTOPHER M. PAULIN

See also Falkland Islands; Gorbachev, Mikhail Sergeevich; Great Britain; Grenada Invasion; Iran; Libya; Middle East; Reagan, Ronald Wilson; Strategic Defense Initiative

FURTHER READING
Bartlett, C.J. *'The Special Relationship:' A Political History of Anglo-American Relations Since 1945.* London, 1992.
Thatcher, Margaret. *The Downing Street Years.* London, 1994.
Young, Hugo. *The Iron Lady.* New York, 1989.

THIEU, NGUYEN VAN

(*b.* 5 April 1923)

The longest ruling and last president of the Republic of South Vietnam (1965–1975). Though a more effective leader than his chief predecessor, Ngo Dinh Diem, Thieu bore a heavy responsibility for his country's collapse following the communist offensive of 1975.

Thieu owed his position to his service as a line officer with combat experience. He graduated from the Vietnamese Military Academy in 1949 and fought against the Vietminh. Under President Diem (1955–1963), he held three separate divisional commands, but his artillery brigade led the pivotal attack on the presidential palace in the 1963 coup against Diem. By 1965 he had maneuvered himself into power and won the presidential election of 1967. He was re-elected in 1971 after forcing his rivals out of the race.

Though Thieu implemented comprehensive land reforms in 1970 and broadened the appeal of his regime to both the Buddhist majority and the minority sects of the Mekong Delta, he remained intolerant of political opposition. Indeed, although he bitterly protested the terms of the Paris Peace Agreement of 1973 that left 150,000 North Vietnamese troops in the south, he was in a stronger military and political position than that of any of his predecessors. In two short years, however, he squandered these advantages by opting for a military policy that overextended his forces while suppressing dissent in ways that alienated the U.S. Congress to the point where it sharply curtailed further economic and military assistance to the Saigon government. When communist forces, emboldened by this disaffection, launched a new offensive in March 1975, Thieu so bungled his troop deployments that a sharp communist attack turned into a complete rout of his army. With the collapse of the army's final stand in Xuan Loc on 20 April 1975, Thieu fled the country. In the mid-1990s he was living in Great Britain, shunning all contact with Americans.

TIMOTHY J. LOMPERIS

See also Diem, Ngo Dinh; Vietnam; Vietnam War

FURTHER READING
Bui Diem with David Chanoff. *In the Jaws of History.* Boston, 1987.

THINK TANKS

Nongovernmental, nonprofit organizations that carry out research and analysis on public policy issues. By the mid-1990s several hundred of these organizations existed in the United States, ranging in size from the RAND Corporation, with an annual budget of more than $100 million and more than one thousand employees, to tiny organizations with staffs of fewer than ten persons. A number of think tanks have international issues and foreign and defense policy as their primary or exclusive focus, while others mix domestic and foreign policy research.

Think tanks differ in many ways, including the type and level of expertise of their staffs, the types of studies they produce, and the ways that they interact with policymakers. Early foreign policy think tanks, such as the Carnegie Endowment for International Peace (founded in 1910) and the Hoover Institution on War, Revolution, and Peace (founded in 1919), sought to document the causes of war and increase international awareness among a U.S. elite and citizenry that retained strong isolationist tendencies. Other organizations, such as the Brookings Institution (founded in 1927), initially sought to improve the management practices of government, although over time Brookings studies increasingly focused on substantive issues of domestic and foreign policy.

The RAND Corporation (formally incorporated in 1948) and the Hudson Institute (founded in 1961) are the most prominent examples of a second generation of think tanks that do much of their work in the form of contracted research reports for government agencies, especially the Department of Defense. These institutions often employ an eclectic group of experts including mathematicians, physicists, engineers, and operations researchers, as well as specialists in the social sciences. A third generation of think tanks has grown up since the 1960s. Many of these organizations, such as the left-oriented Institute for Policy Studies (founded in 1963), the conservative Heritage Foundation (founded in 1973), and the libertarian Cato Institute (founded in 1977) assume strong ideological stances. Other institutions have sought to find niches in the crowded "marketplace of ideas" by specializing in particular regions or policy problems, such as the Overseas Development Council (founded in 1969), the Washington Institute for Near East Policy (founded in 1985), Institute for International Economics (founded in 1981), and the Worldwatch Institute (founded in 1974).

Policy expertise flows from think tanks into the policy process in a variety of ways. In addition to the traditional mechanisms of public education through books and articles in scholarly and popular journals and contracted reports to government agencies, think-tank expertise may enter the policy process through testimony before congressional committees, interviews and commentaries in newspapers, and appearances on television news and "talk" shows by their scholars and fellows. Think tanks also serve as sources of personnel to the executive branch's appointive policy positions. Many staff members of the Heritage Foundation, for example, became officials in the Reagan administrations during the 1980s. In addition, some think tanks publish brief analyses of current legislation before Congress. Still others, including the Center for Strategic and International Studies (founded in 1962), sponsor conferences, study groups, and other forums in which policymakers interact directly with researchers and with each other. To improve access to policymakers, most think tanks with a strong foreign policy focus are based in Washington, D.C. There are important exceptions, such as RAND and the Hoover Institution, both of whose headquarters are located in California.

The end of the Cold War has created important challenges for think tanks. Institutions that depend heavily on contract revenue from a declining defense budget faced funding cuts. Future intellectual challenges for think tanks include the need to increase staff expertise in geographic regions and policy problems (notably the environment, international trade, and peacekeeping) that were under-studied while policymakers' and researchers' attention was focused on superpower conflict, and the need to develop new approaches to better understand the world's problems and guide U.S. foreign policy in the post–Cold War era.

R. KENT WEAVER

See also Carnegie Endowment for International Peace; Cold War; Heritage Foundation

FURTHER READING

Ricci, David M. *The Transformation of American Politics: The New Washington and the Rise of Think Tanks.* New Haven, Conn., 1995.
Roberts, Brad, Stanton H. Burnett, and Murray Weidenbaum. "Think Tanks in a New World," *Washington Quarterly,* 16 (Winter 1993): 169–182.
Smith, Bruce. *The RAND Corporation: Case Study of a Nonprofit Advisory Corporation.* Cambridge, Mass., 1966.
Smith, James Allen. *The Idea Brokers: Think Tanks and the Rise of the New Policy Elite.* New York, 1991.
Weiss, Carol. *Organizations for Policy Analysis: Helping Government Think.* Newbury Park, Calif., 1992.

THIRD WORLD

A term used to describe countries emerging from the process of decolonization. The term "Third World" entered the U.S. foreign policy lexicon in the years following World War II. Coined by France in the early 1950s, the concept was used at a conference of twenty-nine nonaligned countries in Bandung, Indonesia, in 1955. As used by the nonaligned countries, the term was meant to distinguish the developing nations of Asia, Africa, and Latin America from the "First World," or Western industrialized countries, and those of the "Second World," or Eastern socialist bloc. The expression soon came to be used interchangeably with such terms as the "South," a reference to the fact that nearly all developing countries lie south of the equator. More problematic and a source of resentment on the part of the Third World was the use of such phrases as "less developed countries" (LDCs) and "underdeveloped countries," because they implied that the appropriate standard of comparison and modernity was that of the "North," or Western industrialized nations.

During the 1950s and 1960s organizations such as the Nonaligned Movement and the Group of 77 (G-77) served to bring together the developing countries and provided a forum in which Third World elites could discuss their countries' interests, which ranged from decolonization to issues of economic cooperation. Entities such as G-77 also served as a vehicle for the world's developing countries to press for economic concessions from the industrialized West. Initially composed of seventy-seven members, the G-77 was formed to represent Third World countries during the first United Nations Conference on Trade and Development (UNCTAD) in 1964. UNCTAD, which became a permanent organization within the United Nations, was itself the product of lobbying on the part of Third World states. Their efforts had received support from the Soviet Union, particularly since the latter saw the Western bloc, not itself, as the target of complaints and demands for economic redress on the part of the developing countries. The Third World's actions in this arena culminated in its call during the 1970s for a New International Economic Order (NIEO) meant to restructure the international economic system in such a manner as to produce greater economic equality. Significantly for the eventual collapse of the Third World's economic agenda, among the few countries in the UN General Assembly that voted against a charter incorporating most of the NIEO platform were Western economic powers, such as the United States and West Germany.

Despite these points of contention with the West, during the Cold War years the majority of Third World states were committed to the principle of nonalignment with either the United States or the Soviet Union. This stance permitted a number of Third World countries to be the beneficiaries of foreign economic and military aid extended by both the superpowers in an effort to secure their support. Some of these countries, however, among them Afghanistan, Angola, and Vietnam, also served as the fields on which strategic and military elements of the bipolar confrontation were played out.

The approximately 170 countries that made up the Third World in the mid-1990s contained more than three-fourths of the world's population but accounted for less than one-fifth of the global gross national product. Many of these nations feared that with the end of the Cold War they would find themselves increasingly marginalized in the international arena. Both foreign aid trends and public opinion polls in the United States that indicated declining support for assistance to the Third World seemed to support that view. Nevertheless, a number of developments in the 1990s in the Third World

indicated the likelihood of a continued U.S. foreign policy focus on these countries. These developments included the growing military capacity of some nations, as well as the spread of terrorist movements and drug trafficking organizations in Third World countries, all of which had the capacity to affect U.S. security interests. The economic performance of the Third World and its ability to pay its debts was also a concern because of the potential for conflict within increasingly impoverished countries and because U.S. trade with many of these countries was of growing importance to the U.S. economy.

CAROLINE A. HARTZELL

See also Africa; Foreign Aid; Latin America; New International Economic Order; Nonaligned Movement; United Nations Conference on Trade and Development

FURTHER READING

Atlantic Working Group on the United States and Developing Countries. *The United States and the Developing Countries.* Boulder, Colo., 1977.

Berg, Robert J., and David F. Gordon, eds. *Cooperation for International Development: The United States and the Third World in the 1990s.* Boulder, Colo., 1989.

Haq, Mahbub ul. *The Poverty Curtain: Choices for the Third World.* New York, 1976.

Slater, Robert O., Barry M. Schutz, and Steven R. Dorr, eds. *Global Transformation and the Third World.* Boulder, Colo., 1993.

THIRD WORLD DEBT

Third World debt emerged as a major foreign policy challenge to the United States during the decade of the 1980s, following a financial collapse in nearby Mexico in 1982. Mexico's crisis triggered a wave of near defaults in more than three dozen other nations across Latin America, Asia, and Africa—the regions which, after the start of the Cold War, had come to be known as the Third World—threatening bankruptcy for many international lenders and chaos in global financial markets. For the United States, the world's leading monetary power, this was a challenge that simply could not be ignored.

Economically less developed nations had long relied upon foreign borrowing to underwrite domestic development aspirations. And even prior to the 1980s it was not uncommon for some countries to experience occasional difficulties in servicing external obligations. Earlier debt problems, however, had been relatively few in number and small in magnitude. Large-scale lending to a wide range of developing nations did not really take off until after the first oil shock in 1973. By 1982 aggregate Third World debt had risen to more than $750 billion, including some $450 billion owed to commercial banks. Latin America alone accounted for half the total. Mexico, along with Brazil, ranked as the leading borrower in the Third World.

INTERNATIONAL DEBT OF DEVELOPING AND TRANSITION ECONOMIES, 1980, 1985, 1990, AND 1995 (US$ BILLIONS)				
	1980	**1985**	**1990**	**1995 (p)**
All countries	572.3	990.7	1,510.0	2,067.7
Africa, South of the Sahara	56.2	98.8	190.3	223.3
East Asia and the Pacific	88.6	166.2	271.1	472.8
Europe and Central Asia	80.7	157.7	262.1	379.8
Latin America and the Caribbean	242.2	390.1	476.7	607.2
North Africa and the Middle East	66.3	109.6	180.8	217.0
South Asia	38.2	68.3	128.4	167.6

(p) Preliminary

Source: World Bank

Washington's policy response to the debt crisis, under the presidencies of Ronald Reagan and George Bush, reflected security as well as commercial interests. Of most immediate concern were the risks to U.S. banks, which in the previous decade had become dangerously over-exposed to Third World borrowers, especially in Latin America. Beyond that was the potential for serious disorder in Mexico, our large southern neighbor, or elsewhere in the Third World, where growth had suddenly ground to a halt. Washington's goals, therefore, were twofold—to avert a U.S. banking crisis while preserving economic and political stability in debtor countries. Policy evolved through three distinct phases before the challenge was considered safely resolved.

During the first phase, which lasted until 1985, central emphasis was on rescheduling obligations to ease severe cash-flow strains. In return, debtors were expected to comply with strict domestic austerity programs while maintaining interest payments to creditors. The premise of the policy was that borrowers' illiquidity and stalled development were essentially transitory; their longer-term ability to service debt remained sound. All they needed was sufficient time for internal policy adjustments to rekindle growth, which in turn would gradually shrink debt burdens and restore external creditworthiness. In fact, however, even the most determined debtors found it difficult to escape recession or attract new foreign financing.

Accordingly, in 1985 policy shifted to the so-called Baker Plan, named after Treasury secretary James Baker, calling for massive new lending by banks and international institutions to support debtor growth. Creditor response was unenthusiastic, however, and stagnation persisted in most countries. Increasingly, it became evident that in many cases debt-service capacity had indeed been impaired and that growth would not be restored without a significant reduction of outstanding obligations. During Mexico's presidential election in 1988, successful candidate Carlos Salinas de Gotari openly called for debt relief.

Washington's response, in early 1989, was a call by Nicholas Brady, Baker's successor at the Treasury, for a negotiated reduction of debtor liabilities. In subsequent years, beginning with Mexico, agreements were reached under the Brady Plan with virtually all major borrowers to write down a significant portion of debt burdens. By the time President George Bush left office, the Third World debt crisis was generally regarded as effectively resolved. Although development remained fragile in many countries, neither a banking crisis nor debtor instability had been allowed to impair fundamental U.S. interests.

BENJAMIN J. COHEN

FURTHER READING

Cline, William R. *International Debt Reexamined*. Washington: Institute for International Economics, 1994.

Kuczynski, Pedro-Pablo. *Latin American Debt*. Baltimore: Johns Hopkins University Press, 1988.

Lissakers, Karin. *Banks, Borrowers, and the Establishment: A Revisionist Account of the International Debt Crisis*. New York: Basic Books, 1991.

THOMPSON, LLEWELLYN E., JR.

(*b.* 24 August 1904; *d.* 6 February 1972)

A career diplomat who specialized in Soviet affairs and twice served as ambassador to the Soviet Union (1957–1962; 1966–1969). Born and raised in Las Animas, Colorado, Thompson joined the Foreign Service in 1929 and served in it until his death. A perceptive judge of foreign affairs, he worked in various posts in Europe, including high commissioner, and then ambassador, to Austria in the 1950s. As ambassador to the Soviet Union and ambassador-at-large (1962–1966), he was also involved in such seminal Cold War events as various summit meetings, Soviet Premier Nikita Khrushchev's visit to the United States in 1959, the Cuban Missile Crisis, the Berlin Crisis, and negotiations for the Limited Nuclear Test Ban Treaty of 1963. A respected member of the Executive Committee during the missile crisis, Thompson urged a firm stand against Khrushchev but advised President John F. Kennedy to avoid air strikes and take the less confrontational approach of a blockade of Cuba. Intimate with many top Soviet leaders, Thompson was a superlative behind-the-scenes negotiator who won accolades at home and abroad for his nondoctrinaire approach to superpower relations.

THOMAS W. ZEILER

See also Austria; Berlin; Cuban Missile Crisis; Limited Nuclear Test Ban Treaty; Russia and the Soviet Union

FURTHER READING

Burke, Lee H. *Ambassador at Large: Diplomat Extraordinary.* The Hague, 1972.
Frankel, Benjamin, ed. *The Cold War, 1945–1991: Leaders and Other Important Figures in the United States and Western Europe.* Detroit, Mich., 1992.

TIANANMEN SQUARE MASSACRE
See China

TIANJIN, TREATIES OF
See Opium Wars

TIPPECANOE, BATTLE OF
See Native Americans

TITO
Josip Broz
(*b.* 7 May 1892; *d.* 4 May 1980)

Leader of Yugoslavia, 1945–1980. Marshall Tito, as he was best known in the West, was born Josip Broz in Kumrovec, Croatia, to a Croat father and a Slovene mother. He first joined the Communist party in 1919 in Siberia, where he served with the Red Army in the Russian civil war; then returned home to Zagreb, Croatia, in 1920 to the newly founded Kingdom of Serbs, Croats, and Slovenes, and became a union organizer and an

active member of the Yugoslav Communist party. In August 1928 Tito was arrested for illegal activities and, in a highly publicized Zagreb trial, received a five-year prison sentence. Upon his release in 1934, he rose quickly in the party's underground hierarchy and was made secretary-general of the Communist party of Yugoslavia in 1937. Tito came to the forefront of Yugoslav politics during World War II as the leader of the partisan resistance that based its defense on an all-Yugoslav platform, fighting both the Nazi occupiers and the domestic Chetnik resistance that was set on returning the monarchy to power after expelling the fascists. Western (especially British) support was instrumental to his victory. In 1944, Tito convinced the Allies to recognize the military and political institutions put in place by the Yugoslav communists, and they agreed not to take military action on Yugoslav soil without Tito's permission. The communists assumed full power in Yugoslavia by late 1945, and from that time until his death Tito dominated every aspect of Yugoslav politics as a virtual dictator.

Tito's leadership evolved into a political dogma called "Titoism," which pervaded the social, political, and economic aspects of Yugoslav life. Titoism was based on a troika of principles: a version of recent Yugoslav history reflecting in large measure the partisans' mythology, nonalignment, and workers' self-management. Among the new communist states of Eastern Europe, only Tito was able to achieve total control of his own state, creating both an impressive military force and a political organization both of which were responsive solely to his own leadership. Initially, the United States took a cautious approach toward Tito's 1948 break with the Soviets—not least because of his previous support of the Greek communist insurgency. National security reports to President Harry S. Truman emphasized that Tito remained a staunch Marxist-Leninist, committed to communist expansionism and embracing the rhetoric of anti-imperialist, anti-Western doctrines. Nevertheless, Tito's success in leaving the Soviet orbit set a historic precedent, which the United States believed would heavily influence Russia's relations with its other neighbors. Even more tangibly, it deprived the Soviets of important strategic assets and balanced communist gains elsewhere. After his break with Stalin, Tito set out to create an entirely new image—both in internal and external affairs—for Yugoslavia. In 1949 Stalin launched a political, psychological, and economic attack against Yugoslavia, which included leaving Yugoslavia out of the new, Soviet-dominated Council for Mutual Economic Assistance (CMEA). At this point Tito began to discuss opening trade relations with the West, while emphasizing that he would not permit any kind of interference in internal Yugoslav political affairs. Essentially, the West accepted Tito's conditions; nevertheless, the United States successfully used economic incentives as a bargaining tool to pressure Tito into abandoning fully his assistance to the Greek guerrillas. In December 1949, U.S. backing helped Yugoslavia to win a seat on the United Nations Security Council in the face of Soviet protests. The United States also relaxed export controls in favor of Yugoslavia and agreed to furnish all goods that were in short supply as long as they posed no threat to international security. Next, the prohibition on munitions and goods used to make them was removed. This aid was crucial in keeping the Tito regime afloat despite continuing Soviet pressures and in discouraging any Soviet inclination to invade Yugoslavia. Truman and Secretary of State Dean Acheson fought relentlessly against congressional opposition to obtain aid for Yugoslavia, justifying it as a way of maintaining U.S. bargaining power in the region. By 1952 they felt sure that they had carried Tito over the roughest spots in securing his independence from the Soviet bloc.

In 1953, the death of Stalin actually caused a positive shift in Soviet policy towards Tito. The United States was not too worried about the implications of this rapprochement: they reasoned that with Western economic and military assistance Tito was faring better than he ever could have through his old association with the Soviet Union, and with no immediate threat to his personal power. The United States chose to stress the value and importance of the Balkan Pact of Mutual Defense, a treaty of friendship and collaboration among North Atlantic Treaty Organization (NATO) members Greece and Turkey, and Yugoslavia, signed in August 1954. Clearly, as long as Yugoslavia was not a member of NATO, the Pact would be one of the major means for Tito to enhance his prestige and respectability both abroad and at home while gaining a certain degree of indirect participation in NATO planning. In fact, the hopes of the Pact were not achieved—Yugoslavia was never successfully drawn into the Western defense system, and its relations with Greece and Turkey deteriorated.

By 1954, Moscow, under Nikita Khrushchev, had resumed trade with Belgrade and relaxed military and political pressures; the Soviet party line on Tito shifted from criticism and condemnation to praise and admiration. The United States responded with greater support for Yugoslav independence from the Soviet bloc. As a result, Tito became less fearful of a Soviet attack. He thus gave only qualified endorsement to the Soviet intervention in Poland and Hungary in 1956. On the other hand, in the mid-1950s Tito became the godfather of the anticolonial, anti-imperialist nonalignment movement. This concept served multiple purposes in the external politics of Yugoslavia. First, it sharply distinguished Yugoslavia from the Warsaw Pact countries. Second, it was designed to be equidistant between the Western and communist blocs—albeit nominally tilted toward the Soviet side. And finally, it helped to unify Yugoslavia, underlining a specific Yugoslav orientation while deemphasizing issues of ethnicity and nationality within the federation of constituent republics.

In 1961 President John F. Kennedy appointed George Kennan as ambassador to Yugoslavia. Kennan became an active supporter of Titoism. He strongly resisted U.S. congressional presence, supported by anti-Tito Yugoslav immigrants in the United States, to cut off aid to Yugoslavia because its nonaligned stand in part reflected Soviet views. Kennan argued that Yugoslavia provided an effective barrier to the Warsaw Pact and strengthened NATO's southern front. Kennan resigned when lobbyists were able to convince the U.S. legislature to reverse a number of aid packages. But before his departure from Belgrade, Kennan worked out terms directly with Tito under which U.S. assistance was restored in exchange for assurances of continued Yugoslav political and military independence. In 1968 USSR-Yugoslav relations again deteriorated when Tito strongly criticized the Soviet intervention in Czechoslovakia as an attack against the independence of a socialist country, which he saw as implicitly opening the way to an attack on Yugoslavia itself. Tito used this episode as an excuse for revamping the Yugoslav defense doctrines and forging even better relations with the United States. Washington was receptive; President Richard Nixon visited Yugoslavia in September 1970, and Tito paid his first ceremonial visit to the United States in October–November 1971.

Major developments within Yugoslavia between 1965 and 1972 reflected the results of Tito's decentralization of economic and political power and the consequent rise of nationalist passions within the individual republics. Tito moved forward by purging all those who threatened him: the old-guard conservatives from middle and lower level party positions in 1969; then top Croatian leaders on charges of "nationalism" in December 1971; finally, in September 1972, Tito swept his broom over the entire party, condemning a new "pseudo-liberalism" within the Serbian leadership. Tito also used a new constitution to further decentralize and liberalize Yugoslavia's economy, extending the system of self-management, while implementing a rotating and collective presidency (with himself as chairman). This presidential system was widely viewed as a means to preclude the rise of any strong and competing leaders. When Tito's grave illness was announced on 11 September 1976, the possibility of Soviet intervention in a post-Tito Yugoslavia again became a primary U.S. concern. But there was little the West could do if Tito chose to encourage closer ties to the Soviet Union by peaceful means.

Tito remained in power until his death on 4 May 1980. Representatives from 122 countries attended his funeral. His successful challenge to the Soviet Empire was lauded, as was his forceful leadership that had united Yugoslavia into a seemingly stable federation. Yet ten years later, none of the pillars of Titoism had survived. Tito's purging of talented and dynamic leaders in the early 1970s and the subsequent restocking of the party leadership with weak and colorless figures greatly aided nationalist politicians such as Slobodan Milosevic and Franjo Tudjman in their rise to power in the early 1990s. While Tito was able to hold Yugoslavia together as a non-aligned nation during his lifetime, he did not leave in place effective institutional mechanisms that could overcome serious differences and historic enmities among the country's ethnic groups.

MARGUERITE GALATY

See also Eastern Europe; Kennan, George Frost; Non-aligned Movement; North Atlantic Treaty Organization; Russia and the Soviet Union; Stalin, Joseph; Yugoslavia

FURTHER READING
Beloff, Nora. *Tito's Flawed Legacy: Yugoslavia & the West Since 1939.* Boulder, Colo., 1985.
Djilas, Milovan. *Tito: The Story from the Inside.* London, 1981.
Johnson, A. Ross. "Yugoslavia: In the Twilight of Tito." In *The Washington Papers*, vol. 2. London, 1974.
Pavlowitch, Stevan K. *Tito: Yugoslavia's Great Dictator—A Reassessment.* London, 1992.

TLATELOLCO TREATY

See Nuclear Nonproliferation

TOGO

See Appendix 2

TOJO, HIDEKI

(*b.* 30 December 1884; *d.* 23 December 1948)

A career Japanese army officer, Hideki Tojo served as vice-minister of war (1938–1939), minister of war (1940–1941), and prime minister (1941–1944) and was directly responsible for some of the key decisions that caused the Japan-U.S. war. A proponent of Japanese imperialism, Tojo argued that Japan's security required control of Manchuria and North China. Japan invaded Manchuria (1931) and moved into North China, acts that started the Sino-Japanese war (1937). The United States opposed Japanese expansionism through an escalating series of economic sanctions. Although Tojo did not actually want war with the United States, during 1941 he blocked any proposed compromise solutions that would have required Japan's withdrawal from China. Faced with

declining oil stocks, Tojo—having succeeded Prince Konoye as prime minister—decided in November 1941 that Japan had no choice but to proceed with the surprise attack at Pearl Harbor. Tojo resigned after Japan's defeat at Saipan (1944). Following the Japanese surrender, Tojo was arrested, tried, and executed as a war criminal.

BARNEY J. RICKMAN III

See also Japan; Pearl Harbor, Attack on

FURTHER READING
Browne, Courtney. *Tojo: The Last Banzai.* New York, 1967.
Butow, Robert J.C. *Tojo and the Coming of the War.* Princeton, N.J., 1961.
Iriye, Akira. *The Origins of the Second World War in Asia and the Pacific.* New York, 1993.

TOKYO ROUND

See General Agreement on Tariffs and Trade

TONKIN GULF RESOLUTION

See Vietnam War

TORQUAY ROUND

See General Agreement on Tariffs and Trade

TOURISM

The word "tourism"—traveling for pleasure, the largest industry in the world—originated in the eighteenth century to describe the activities of young male British aristocrats who were being educated for careers in politics, government, and the diplomatic service. In order to round out their studies, they embarked upon a customary three-year grand tour of the European continent, returning home only after their cultural education had been completed. Traveling for pleasure implies four basic elements: transience, leisure, privilege, and being away from home. Although tourism is most often thought of exclusively as leisure travel, it encompasses business related travel as well.

The World Travel and Tourism Council (WTTC) is a global coalition of chief executive officers from all sectors of the industry, including transportation, accommodation, catering, recreational, cultural, and travel services. Their 1993 report, *Travel and Tourism in the World Economy*, suggests that by virtually any economic measure, including gross output, value-added, capital investment, employment, and tax contributions, tourism is the largest industry in the world. It accounts for $3.4 trillion in gross national product; 204 million jobs; 10.7 percent of global capital investment; 11 percent of worldwide consumer spending; and almost 12 percent of indirect corporate taxes. Once the exclusive province of the wealthy, tourism or travel abroad has become common for most of the world's middle-class population. In fact, tourism has become the largest commodity in international trade for many nations. For example, the U.S. Bureau of Economic Analysis reported in 1995 that the total direct and indirect impact of travel in the United States exceeded $740 billion in expenditures and $210.5 billion in earnings, and employed over 10 million people.

The role of governments in international travel includes diplomatic recognition and reciprocal relations between countries, bilateral agreements on commerce and trade, air transportation agreements, and other international regulations. Before citizens of one nation can cross the border of another country, there must first be established a diplomatic agreement that permits such travel between the two countries. Government agreements, moreover, can serve to either encourage or discourage the flow of travelers. Also, revenues from tourism are viewed either as an import or an export, and trade issues are frequently at the heart of government policy.

There are numerous international and intergovernmental bodies involved in worldwide tourism policies. The United States has primarily been active in three: the Organization of American States (OAS) Tourism Development Program, the Organization for Economic Cooperation and Development (OECD) Tourism Committee, and the World Tourism Organization (WTO). The mission of the OAS Tourism Development Program, formed in 1970, is to assist tourism authorities of member states in developing, promoting, and regulating their tourism sectors. The OECD Tourism Committee, organized in 1965, is concerned with tourism policy and international tourism trends of member nations. The WTO, established in 1975 and located in Madrid, Spain, is an official consultive organization to the United Nations and is the only international organization that represents all countries and official government tourist interests. The WTO provides a clearinghouse for the collection, analysis, and dissemination of technical tourism information; a multinational approach to international discussion and negotiations on tourism matters; and international conferences, seminars, and training focusing on the reduction of barriers to international tourism.

The extent and impact of international tourism is difficult to measure because there is a basic inconsistency in the data gathered by different nations. Of the 166 countries that report annual tourism statistics, four have no measures of international visitors, thirteen cannot provide international tourism receipt information, forty-six do not even estimate international tourism expenditures, and more than one-half have no measures of international departures. In order to standardize the collection of tourism data by nations, the WTO cosponsored a conference in 1991 which had three primary aims: the development of a uniform and integrated definition and classification system of tourism statistics; the implementation of a strict methodology for determining the economic impact of tourism; and the establishment of a coherent work program between governments and the tourism industry for the collection of tourism data. Two years later, the United Nations accepted the report of the WTO and adopted its recommendations relating to the collection of tourism statistics. One significant resolution passed by the WTO conference was the recommendation that tourism be defined as "the activities of people traveling for leisure, business or other purposes to places outside their usual environment, and staying for no more than one consecutive year, and whose main purpose of travel is other than the exercise of an activity remunerated from within the place visited."

The U.S. National Tourism Policy Act was enacted in 1981 with the main purpose of optimizing the contribution of the tourism and recreation industries to economic prosperity, full employment, and the international balance of payments of the United States. U.S. as well as other developed countries' social and economic trends favor long-term growth in both domestic and international travel demand. Greater leisure time, increased disposable income, higher levels of education, and a heightened awareness of other countries and peoples are significant factors influencing the growing market for travel and tourism.

WILLIAM F. THEOBALD

See also Passports and Visas

FURTHER READING

Feifer, Maxine. *Tourism in History: From Imperial Rome to the Present.* New York, 1985.

Hawkins, Donald E., and J. R. Brent Richie, eds. *World Travel and Tourism Review: Indicators, Trends and Forecasts.* Wallingford, England, 1991.

Theobald, William F., ed. *Global Tourism: The Next Decade.* Oxford, 1994.

World Tourism Organization *Compendium of Tourism Statistics.* Annual. Madrid, 1980-1995.

TOUSSAINT-L'OUVERTURE, FRANÇOIS-DOMINIQUE
(*b.* 1743; *d.* 7 April 1803)

Leader of a slave revolt against French rule in Haiti (1791) and the fight for Haitian independence (1801). At the time of the French Revolution, Saint Domingue (present-day Haiti) was the richest of the French colonies in the West Indies with more than 3,000 coffee, sugar, and cocoa plantations operated by slaves. The slave system was especially brutal because most owners of the plantations did not live on the island and felt it cheaper to work slaves to death and replace them than to treat them well. In 1791 a massive slave revolt broke out. Although born a slave, Toussaint-L'Ouverture rose in power as administrator of a plantation, where he learned French and gained self-confidence, wealth, and prestige. In the fall of 1791 he joined the revolt and quickly became the leader of the rebels with the goal of establishing self-government and perhaps independence. After war broke out between France and Great Britain in 1793, he maneuvered skillfully through the international turbulence. Toussaint planned to continue the plantation economy to provide revenue for the rebellion and to destroy the idea of black incompetence. Great Britain opened commercial relationships with the rebels, as did the United States.

A turning point came in 1801 with Napoleon Bonaparte's decision to reestablish French control on the island during the temporary peace with Great Britain (Treaty of Amiens) and build a new empire in North America based in Louisiana (acquired in 1800 from Spain). To accomplish this objective it was necessary first to defeat Toussaint. Napoleon sent an army that inflicted heavy casualties, but yellow fever and the continued resistance of the former slaves decimated the French. Indeed, one of the reasons for Napoleon's decision to sell the vast Louisiana Territory to the United States in 1803 was the disruption of his imperial dream by the failure to suppress the rebellion. Toussaint was seized by the French through trickery in 1802 and taken to France, where he died in prison. The Saint Domingue rebels declared independence on 31 December 1803, but President Thomas Jefferson refused to recognize Haiti lest it set an example for slaves in the southern United States.

RONALD L. HATZENBUEHLER

See also Amiens, Treaty of; Haiti; Louisiana Purchase; Napoleon Bonaparte

FURTHER READING

DeConde, Alexander. *This Affair of Louisiana.* New York, 1976.

James, C. L. R. *The Black Jacobins: Toussaint L'Ouverture and the San Domingo Revolution,* 2nd rev. ed. New York, 1963.

Tyson, George F., Jr., ed. *Toussaint L'Ouverture.* Englewood Cliffs, N.J., 1978.

TOWER COMMISSION

See Iran-Contra Affair

TRADE AGREEMENTS ACT

See Reciprocal Trade Agreements Act

TRADE REPRESENTATIVES

See United States Trade Representative

TRADING WITH THE ENEMY ACT

A law passed on 6 October 1917 that progressively gave the president extensive powers, through the 1970s, to regulate the United States' international and domestic finances during national emergencies. Because such emergencies were broadly defined, this wide-ranging measure often dealt with enemies and economic crises at home. Presidents had authority to prohibit manipulation of currency and gold assets, bank payments, foreign exchange transactions and licenses, exports, and the transfer of property to a hostile country. During World War I, the act strangled the economics of the Central Powers by placing an embargo on U.S. exports to them and to neutral nations from which they normally obtained badly needed supplies. Amended several times afterward by Congress and by executive orders, the act helped combat some of the ill effects of the Great Depression. Franklin D. Roosevelt drew on its authority to limit currency exchanges, for instance, and thus legally undergird the bank holiday in 1933. During World War II, the act froze Axis financial assets, while at home it sanctioned consumer credit controls. During the Cold War, presidents became even more reliant on this law. In the foreign policy arena, they instituted export controls against such communist enemies as North Korea, Cuba, Vietnam, and Cambodia while occasionally easing restrictions for humanitarian reasons. At home, the Nixon administration resorted to the act in such supposed emergencies as a post office strike and a balance-of-payments crisis. The potential for the abuse of executive power, and the aftershock of Watergate, prompted Congress in 1977 to overhaul the Trading with the Enemy Act by the International Emergency Economic Powers Act (IEEPA). This law provided a precise definition of a national emergency, restricting presidential authority to times of war formally declared by Congress (although the War Powers Resolution undermined this constraint). President George Bush employed the revised law by declaring a national emergency in the Persian Gulf in August 1990. He then seized Iraqi assets and coordinated sanctions with the United Nations in ensuing the Gulf War.

THOMAS W. ZEILER

See also Blockade; Cold War; Economic Sanctions; Export Controls; World War I; World War II

FURTHER READING

Domke, Martin. *Trading with the Enemy in World War II.* New York, 1943.

Long, William J. *U.S. Export Control Policy: Executive Autonomy vs. Congressional Reform.* New York, 1989.

U.S. Congress. Senate Subcommittee on International Trade and Commerce of the Committee on International Relations. *Trading With the Enemy Act.* Committee Print. 94th Cong., 2d sess., 1976.

TRANSCONTINENTAL TREATY OF 1819

See Adams-Onís Treaty

TREASURY, U.S. DEPARTMENT OF

The country's finance ministry, with primary responsibility for formulating and recommending domestic and international financial, economic, and tax policies, as well as managing the public debt. The department's international policy responsibilities have, in a manner of speaking, made it into the de facto accountant of U.S. foreign policy. Treasury participates in the entire range of U.S. foreign economic decision-making with an eye to gauging the impact of potential policy actions on both the domestic U.S. economy and on the nation's balance-of-payments position.

The Treasury Department enjoyed a relatively rapid growth in its influence on U.S. external relations during the early 1960s. Prior to this period, its greatest impact on twentieth-century U.S. international economic policy occurred in 1944, when Treasury Secretary Harry Dexter White spoke for the U.S. government during the Bretton Woods conference, which designed the international financial system implemented after World War II ended. The department subsequently dominated U.S. activities in the International Monetary Fund (IMF) and the World Bank, but played only a marginal role in foreign-aid allocations and a minimal role in trade relations—both of which were subordinated to national security priorities in the immediate post–World War II era.

The Treasury Department's enhanced role in contemporary U.S. external economic relations has mainly been the outgrowth of three important trends which became increasingly visible beginning in the 1960s.

First, the rapid acceleration of international economic interdependence has meant that the performance of the domestic economy—the major concern of all finance ministers—has been increasingly affected by the external sector. Like other nominally domestic departments, Treasury could therefore point to jurisdictional interests in a growing number of international economic issues.

Second, the decline in relative U.S. domestic economic strength and the deterioration of the U.S. international balance-of-payments position following European and Japanese recovery from World War II brought about economic problems that caused a fundamental shift in U.S.

priorities. Domestic economic and political considerations began to push ahead of national security objectives as the principal criteria for making decisions on foreign economic policy.

Third, the tendency for recent presidents has been to look to the Secretary of the Treasury as the country's senior economic policy official and therefore as the head of the senior White House coordinating group on domestic and international economic policies. Secretary of the Treasury John Connally (1971–1972) was virtually single-handedly in charge of U.S. international economic policy in the critical weeks following President Richard Nixon's announcement of the New Economic Policy initiatives in August 1971. The early part of James Baker's stint as Secretary of the Treasury (1985–1988) was marked by major international financial and trade policy initiatives to reduce the overvaluation of the dollar and bring its exchange rate more into line with U.S. international competitiveness.

Like finance ministries everywhere, the Treasury Department has the undisputed lead role in formulating and administering international monetary policy (which encompasses exchange rate management, balance-of-payments programs, U.S. participation in the IMF, and international monetary reform proposals), international financial policies dealing with private international capital flows, U.S. participation in multilateral development banks (such as the World Bank and the Inter-American Development Bank), relief of Third World debt (two major U.S. debt-relief initiatives were the Baker and the Brady Plans, named after two Treasury secretaries), and tax policies affecting overseas U.S. citizens as well as foreign companies operating in the United States. The department has also taken the lead in the intensified efforts begun in the 1980s by the Group of Seven (G-7) industrialized countries to enhance the coordination of monetary and fiscal policies. These efforts are mostly undertaken to encourage growth, restrain inflation, or promote exchange-rate stability.

A critical catalyst that served to catapult the Treasury into a position of primary influence on U.S. foreign relations was the steady persistence of the U.S. balance-of-payments deficits (the country was spending more abroad than it was earning from overseas), which began in the 1950s. European countries with balance-of-payments surpluses started in the late 1950s to pressure the United States to reduce its net dollar outflow. Tensions in international monetary relations became progressively worse in the latter half of the 1960s, when the size of the U.S. deficits grew dramatically larger. Throughout the 1960s and early 1970s (prior to the adoption in 1973 of floating exchange rates), the Treasury Department was the lead agency in implementing a wide-ranging series of measures designed to reduce the size of these balance-

SECRETARIES OF THE TREASURY

ADMINISTRATION	SECRETARY	PERIOD OF APPOINTMENT
Washington	Alexander Hamilton	1789-1795
	Oliver Wolcott	1795-1800
J. Adams		
	Samuel Dexter	1800-1801
Jefferson		
	Albert Gallatin	1801-1813
Madison		
	George W. Campbell	1814
	Alexander J. Dallas	1814-1816
	William H. Crawford	1816-1825
Monroe		
J.Q. Adams	Richard Rush	1825-1829
Jackson	Samuel D. Ingham	1829-1831
	Louis McLane	1831-1833
	William J. Duane	1833
	Roger B. Taney	1833-1834
	Levi Woodbury	1834-1841
Van Buren		
W. H. Harrison	Thomas Ewing	1841
Tyler		
	Walter Forward	1841-1843
	John C. Spencer	1843-1844
	George M. Bibb	1844-1845
Polk	Robert J. Walker	1845-1849
Taylor	William M. Meredith	1849-1850
Fillmore	Thomas Corwin	1850-1853
Pierce	James Guthrie	1853-1857
Buchanan	Howell Cobb	1857-1860
	Philip F. Thomas	1860-1861
	John A. Dix	1861
Lincoln	Salmon P. Chase	1861-1864
	William P. Fessenden	1864-1865
	Hugh McCullough	1865-1869
A. Johnson		
Grant	George S. Boutwell	1869-1873
	William A. Richardson	1873-1874
	Benjamin H. Bristow	1874-1876
	Lot M. Morrill	1876-1877
Hayes	John Sherman	1877–1881
Garfield	William Windom	1881
Arthur	Charles J. Folger	1881–1884
	Walter Q. Gresham	1884
	Hugh McCulloch	1884–1885
Cleveland	Daniel Manning	1885–1887
	Charles S. Fairchild	1887–1889
B. Harrison	William Windom	1889–1891
	Charles Foster	1891–1893
Cleveland	John G. Carlisle	1893–1897

(table continues on next page)

ADMINISTRATION	SECRETARY	PERIOD OF APPOINTMENT
McKinley	Lyman J. Gage	1897–1902
T. Roosevelt		
	L.M. Shaw	1902–1907
	George B. Cortelyou	1907–1909
Taft	Franklin MacVeagh	1909–1913
Wilson	W. G. McAdoo	1913–1918
	Carter Glass	1918–1920
	David F. Houston	1920–1921
Harding	Andrew W. Mellon	1921–1932
Coolidge		
Hoover		
	Ogden L. Mills	1932–1933
F. Roosevelt	William H. Woodin	1933–1934
	Henry Morganthau, Jr.	1934–1945
Truman	Fred M. Vinson	1945–1946
	John W. Snyder	1946–1953
Eisenhower	George M. Humphrey	1953–1957
	Robert B. Anderson	1957–1961
Kennedy	C. Douglas Dillon	1961–1965
L. Johnson		
	Henry H. Fowler	1965–1968
	Joseph W. Barr	1968–1969
Nixon	David M. Kennedy	1969–1970
	John B. Connally	1971–1972
	George P. Shultz	1972–1974
	William E. Simon	1974–1977
Ford		
Carter	W. Michael Blumenthal	1977–1979
	G. William Miller	1979–1981
Reagan	Donald T. Regan	1981–1985
	James A. Baker III	1985–1988
	Nicholas F. Brady	1988–1993
Bush		
Clinton	Lloyd Bentsen	1993–1995
	Robert E. Rubin	1995–Present

Source: U.S. Department of the Treasury

of-payments deficits. These measures included reductions of overseas spending by U.S. government agencies, businesses, and even American tourists. Foreign aid outlays were tied to purchases of U.S. goods and services; dependents of military personnel stationed overseas were encouraged to return home; governments of wealthy allies were asked to pay more of the costs of U.S. bases overseas; and capital controls were imposed (temporarily) on dollar outflows from domestic corporations and banks.

The United States' failure to return to balance-of-payments equilibrium despite these measures had a profound impact on the world economy. Eventually, the dollar had to be devalued on two occasions—but to little avail. The international financial community's impatience at the slow improvement in the U.S. balance-of-payments position caused such massive selling of dollars in the early spring of 1973 that the Bretton Woods System of fixed exchange rates collapsed, and the world suddenly shifted to a floating exchange rate system. Under such a system, it is the Treasury Department that determines on a day-to-day basis whether to intervene in the foreign exchange markets in an effort either to restrain an increase (appreciation) in the dollar's value in terms of other currencies or to restrain a decline (depreciation) in the dollar's value. Treasury also determines when broader policy changes and international collaboration are needed to offset longer-term upward or downward pressures on the dollar in the foreign exchange markets.

When the once-large U.S. merchandise trade surplus began to decline in the late 1960s, trade policy became an active sector of the Treasury's interest. Because of its domestic orientation and larger concerns with both maximizing U.S. international competitiveness and minimizing internal price increases, the department has usually advocated liberal trade policies in interagency trade councils. Unhappy with the Treasury Department's allegedly relaxed administration of the U.S. antidumping and countervailing duty statutes, which protect American companies from unfair foreign competition, President Jimmy Carter's administration in 1980 transferred this operational authority to the Commerce Department. Treasury, however, has retained the chair of the interagency Committee on Foreign Investment in the United States, the group that implements the Exon-Florio amendment by reviewing foreign acquisitions of companies in the United States to ensure that national security is not adversely affected.

The Treasury and State Departments are the only agencies in the executive branch that are actively involved in every phase of U.S. external economic relations. Their different "constituencies" have led to several major disagreements on international economic policy. For example, in the North-South dialogue of the 1970s, the Department of State showed a predisposition to accommodate some of the economic demands of the less-developed countries (LDCs), while the Treasury adamantly opposed virtually all of these demands on the grounds that they violated free market principles and, therefore, desirable economic policies as well.

Organizationally, Treasury's international policy activities are headed by the Under Secretary for International Affairs, a post created in 1989 to enhance the prestige and power of a position that previously had been at the assistant secretary level. Staff activities are concentrated in the Office of International Affairs (OIA), which consists of some 150 trained economists, one of the largest bodies of international economic expertise in the U.S. government. The OIA is composed of eighteen offices (as of early 1994) reporting to deputy assistant secretaries with responsibilities in international monetary affairs; international development and debt policy; trade and investment policy; Middle East and energy policy; Eastern Europe and the former Soviet Union; and the developing nations. The OIA also assigns financial attachés to U.S. embassies in ten economically important countries.

Several other divisions of Treasury have an occasionally significant effect on U.S. foreign relations. For example, the Customs Service determines classification of goods for the purpose of determining what level of tariffs should be imposed. The Office of Foreign Assets Control is charged with seizing the financial assets and property of foreign countries subject to such sanctions.

STEPHEN D. COHEN

See also Baker, James; Balance of Power and Balance of Trade; Brady Plan; Bretton Woods System; Group of Seven; International Debt; International Monetary Fund; International Trade and Commerce

FURTHER READING

Cohen, Stephen D. *The Making of United States International Economic Policy*, 4th ed. New York, 1994.

Destler, I. M., and C. Randall Henning. *Dollar Politics: Exchange Rate Policymaking in the United States*. Washington, D.C., 1989.

Volker, Paul, and Toyoo Gyohten. *Changing Fortunes—The World's Money and the Threat to American Leadership*. New York, 1992.

TRENT AFFAIR

An Anglo-American crisis sparked by the U.S. capture of two Confederate States of America diplomats from a British ship on 8 November 1861. To win European recognition and disavowal of the Union blockade, President Jefferson Davis of the Confederacy dispatched James Mason of Virginia as minister to Great Britain and John Slidell of Louisiana as minister to France. In mid-October 1861 the two emissaries slipped through the blockade at Charleston and headed for Havana, Cuba, where they transferred to the British steamship *Trent*. They expected to board another steamer at Saint Thomas and then pass on to Europe under neutral colors. Captain Charles Wilkes of the USS *San Jacinto* saw the *Trent* in the Bahama Channel. On 8 November, without orders from Washington, Wilkes fired two warning shots across its bow and signaled it to stop. A boarding party then seized Mason and Slidell as the "embodiment of dispatches" (contraband) and therefore traitors to the United States. Wilkes allowed the *Trent* to resume its voyage to Great Britain, but he took the two captives and their two secretaries to Virginia. The prisoners were then sent to Fort Warren in Boston.

Northerners at first rejoiced at the news, boasting that Wilkes not only had avenged the Union disaster at Bull Run the previous July but had righted a long succession of British wrongs at sea. Yet Wilkes's rash and unauthorized action caused great trouble. Had he searched the *Trent*, he might have discovered that Mason and the British commander had hidden the Confederate mail packet; had the mail been discovered, the British vessel would have lost its neutral status and become subject to capture and adjudication before a prize court.

In Great Britain, the *Trent* affair was considered a flagrant violation of national honor. Indeed, the fiery prime minister, Lord Palmerston, opened an emergency cabinet meeting with a near call to arms: "I don't know whether you are going to stand this, but I'll be damned if I do!" The following day the cabinet recommended that its minister in Washington, Lord Lyons, make three demands: reparations, the immediate release of Mason and Slidell, and a formal apology "for the insult offered to the British flag." In an ominous series of moves, the British government put the navy on alert, readied military supply operations, and sent to Canada 11,000 troops, who left Great Britain to the sound of a band playing "Dixie."

Great Britain's harsh words might have brought the nations to war had it not been for the timely intervention of a problem in communications. The Atlantic cable was malfunctioning, and it took nearly two weeks for news to travel between Great Britain and the United States. As a result, the British note did not arrive in Washington until a month after Americans learned of the *Trent*. These delays had the fortuitous effect of allowing emotions to cool.

In the meantime, Prince Albert, Queen Victoria's consort, searched for a way out of the crisis. Opposing war, he rose from his sickbed to tone down the British ultimatum: Lyons was to ask about the *Trent* matter and seek reparations. He also was to accept an explanation rather than demand an apology. Most important, the United States should have a face-saving way out of the crisis by being able to reply that Wilkes had acted without government orders, "or, if he did, that he misapprehended them." When the revised instructions reached Lyons, he was "to abstain from anything like menace" when seeking the envoys' release and "to be rather easy about the apology."

On 19 December Secretary of State William Seward received the note from Lyons and delivered it to President Abraham Lincoln for a decision. The first public outburst of satisfaction over Wilkes's actions had quieted into sober reflection, and many influential Northerners who had pondered the possibility of war now called on the administration to release Mason and Slidell and grant reparations and an apology. In addition, leaders in France, Italy, Prussia, Denmark, and Russia recognized that the *Trent* precedent would endanger all vessels at sea and condemned the U.S. action. The Union minister in London, Charles Francis Adams, assured Washington that Palmerston's ministry would not retreat from its demands. Lincoln consulted his cabinet and then summed up the administration's position when he commented, "One war at a time."

In late December 1861, Seward presented a White House note to Lyons, and then released it to the press. The United States, Seward cleverly explained to the American people, had won a major diplomatic victory because Great Britain had finally recognized the neutral rights that the United States had fought for during the War of 1812. He declared that Wilkes had acted correctly in searching the *Trent*, but he then added an argument not substantiated in international law: the seizure of Mason and Slidell, Seward asserted, was justified because "persons, as well as property, may become contraband." The administration would nonetheless surrender the men, who were, after all, of "comparative unimportance."

The outcome of the *Trent* affair also signaled the warning that the Palmerston ministry intended to remain neutral, a stand that actually satisfied neither the Confederacy nor the Union. According to the Confederate agent in Great Britain, Henry Hotze, the *Trent* crisis had actually hurt the Southern cause by permitting the British government to claim a major diplomatic victory and thus become less subject to popular pressure in favor of intervention. Adams cautiously offered the same observation. The British ministry, he wrote Seward, had gained a much stronger position at home; thus it was critical that the Union avoid raising any issue that might provide Great Britain with a pretext to exploit the American domestic crisis.

HOWARD JONES

See also Adams, Charles Francis; American Civil War; Confederate States of America; Great Britain; Impressment; Lincoln, Abraham; Palmerston, Henry John Temple; Seward, William; Slidell, John; Wilkes, Charles

FURTHER READING

Ferris, Norman B. *The Trent Affair: A Diplomatic Crisis.* Knoxville, Tenn., 1977.
Jones, Howard. *Union in Peril: The Crisis over British Intervention in the Civil War.* Chapel Hill, N.C., 1992.
Warren, Gordon H. *Fountain of Discontent: The Trent Affair and Freedom of the Seas.* Boston, Mass., 1981.

TRIESTE

A major deep-water seaport on the northeastern shore of the Adriatic Sea, the northwestern coast of the Istrian Peninsula, and today the capital of the Italian province of Friuli-Venezia-Giulia. Trieste (and its surrounding area) has been the focus of boundary disputes between Italy and Yugoslavia during the better part of the twentieth century. Although the area had been under the political control of the duke of Austria (and later of the Habsburg Empire) since the fourteenth century, Italian nationalists claimed it as part of "Italia irredenta" (unredeemed Italy) after the 1860s. Italian culture dominated the city itself, but Slavs populated the countryside. At the outbreak of World War I, Italy, officially a member of the Triple Alliance, demanded additional territory, including Trieste, from Vienna in exchange for maintaining neutrality during the war. But concessions from the Austro-Hungarian government, acting under German pressure, came too late. On 26 April 1915, Italy signed the secret Treaty of London with the Allied Powers, who were ready to meet most of Italy's irredentist demands in order to secure a declaration of war against its former allies.

President Woodrow Wilson ostensibly refused to recognize the validity of the Treaty of London at the Paris

Peace Conference, but he condeded to Italy's acquisition of Trieste. In 1919 Italy received almost all the territory promised in the Treaty of London, despite counterclaims by the newly created Kingdom of Serbs, Croats, and Slovenes (renamed Yugoslavia in 1929). During the interwar years, the Fascist government implemented a thorough Italianization of the area, angering the Slavic inhabitants. As a result of the Axis invasion of Yugoslavia, Trieste remained a battleground until May 1945, when both British troops and Yugoslav forces accepted the surrender of the defending German soldiers.

After World War II, Yugoslavia, now communist and supported by the Soviet Union, again demanded Trieste and its coastal region. Washington interpreted the claims as another example of Soviet expansionism. In June 1945, Josip Broz Tito, the communist leader of Yugoslavia, accepted the Anglo-American proposal to partition the region into two temporary zones of military occupation. Anglo-American forces occupied the city of Trieste and the more heavily populated Zone A; Yugoslavs controlled the more rural, southern Zone B. The peace treaty with Italy in 1947 created the Free Territory of Trieste but failed to establish a functioning government. Great Britain, France, and the United States then proposed that the Free Territory be given to Italy on the basis of self-determination. Yugoslavia's break with the Soviet Union in 1948 largely diminished American interest in the region. On 5 October 1954 representatives from Great Britain, the United States, Italy, and Yugoslavia agreed to a permanent partition of the Free Territory according to which Italy regained sole control of the city of Trieste and the immediate environs. Yugoslavia maintained possession of the territory that had been Zone B.

CAROL A. JACKSON

See also Italy; World War I; World War II; Yugoslavia

FURTHER READING

Hughes, H. Stuart. *The United States and Italy.* 3d ed. Cambridge, Mass., 1979.
Novak, Bogdan C. *Trieste, 1941–1954: The Ethnic, Political, and Ideological Struggle.* Chicago, 1970.
Rabel, Roberto G. *Between East and West: Trieste, the United States, and the Cold War, 1941–1954.* Durham, N.C., 1988.

TRILATERAL COMMISSION

Private organization founded in 1973 in New York City by David Rockefeller, chairman of the board of directors of Chase Manhattan Bank, to encourage closer cooperation among the democratic industrialized countries of North America, Western Europe, and Japan; to analyze major issues facing these countries; and to develop policy proposals. Much of the commission's focus is on the promotion of world trade and international monetary stability.

Financial support for the Trilateral Commission is provided primarily by major foundations and corporations. Drawn from fifteen countries (Canada, United States, Belgium, Denmark, France, Germany, Ireland, Italy, Luxembourg, Netherlands, Norway, Portugal, Spain, United Kingdom, and Japan), membership is quite exclusive, consisting of several hundred prominent individuals with backgrounds in academia, business, labor, the media, and politics. The Trilateral Commission has three headquarters—New York, Paris, and Tokyo—each with a small, full-time staff. It normally meets once a year, rotating sessions between the trilateral regions. The Trilateral Commission constitutes a significant group of influential American opinion leaders, liberals as well as conservatives from both major political parties, who also have been heavily recruited into governmental policymaking positions. Thus, many top-level appointees in the administration of President Jimmy Carter, including Zbigniew Brzezinski, National Security Adviser; Cyrus Vance, Secretary of State; Harold Brown, Secretary of Defense; Michael Blumenthal, Secretary of the Treasury; and Warren Christopher, Deputy Secretary of State, were members of the Trilateral Commission. Carter was also a member. Given its exclusive membership and private activities, both the political right and political left have accused the Trilateral Commission of being part of a formidable "internationalist" power elite that dominates U.S. foreign policy.

JEREL A. ROSATI

See also Carter, James Earl; Public Opinion; Rockefeller, Nelson Aldrich

FURTHER READING

Roberts, Brad. "The Enigmatic Trilateral Commission." *Millennium: Journal of International Studies* 11 (Autumn 1982): 185–202.
Sklar, Holly, ed. *Trilateralism: The Trilateral Commission and Elite Planning for World Management.* Boston, 1980.

TRINIDAD AND TOBAGO

Two islands located in the extreme southeastern Caribbean Sea, off the northeastern coast of Venezuela, that formed a nation on 31 August 1962 when they achieved independence from Great Britain. Columbus claimed these islands for Spain in 1498 during his third voyage. In 1802, Spain ceded Trinidad to Great Britain, which had conquered it in 1797; and in 1814, Great Britain acquired Tobago after two centuries of imperial struggles. In 1889 the two islands became a single colonial unit. Today Trinidad and Tobago is a republic governed under a parliamentary system. An elected president is head of state and the major political parties are the People's National Movement (PNM) and the National Alliance for Reconstruction (NAR). Full diplomatic relations have been maintained with the United States since independence, as has United Nations (UN) membership, and active participation in the British Commonwealth of Nations. Trinidad and Tobago joined the Organization of American States (OAS) in 1967, and helped found the Caribbean Community and Common Market (CARICOM) in 1973.

Trinidad and Tobago's independence movement leaders, particularly Eric Williams (PNM), advanced their cause by mobilizing dissatisfaction with the U.S. presence, since World War II, at the military base in Chaguaramas (the base closed in 1967). But since independence, the island nation's generally pro-Western policies have, for the most part, resulted in cordial diplomatic relations with the United States. But close links with Cuba, China, and, before its demise, the Soviet Union, have also shown signs of an independent foreign policy. Trinidad and Tobago stridently criticized the U.S.-led invasion of Grenada in 1983, and became increasingly uneasy with the military orientation of U.S. activities in the Caribbean during Ronald Reagan's administration, which in 1985 oversaw the establishment of a U.S.-financed regional security system that incorporated a number of smaller Caribbean nations (Antigua and Barbuda, Barbados, Dominica, Grenada, St. Kitts-Nevis, St. Lucia, and St. Vincent and the Grenadines).

Security concerns within Trinidad and Tobago, following an attempted coup by Muslim rebels in 1990, helped improve relations with the United States. In 1994, Trinidad and Tobago backed the U.S.-led, UN-sanctioned invasion of Haiti to oust the military dictatorship and install the democratically elected President Jean-Bertrand Aristide. That same year Trinidad and Tobago led the call among CARICOM nations for participation in the North American Free Trade Agreement (NAFTA).

RODERICK A. MCDONALD

See also Grenada Invasion; Haiti; Nonaligned Movement; North American Free Trade Agreement; Organization of American States; Reagan, Ronald Wilson

FURTHER READING

Brereton, Bridget. *A History of Modern Trinidad, 1783–1862.* Kingston, Jamaica, 1981.

Meditz, Sandra W., and Dennis M. Hanratty, eds. *Islands of the Commonwealth Caribbean: A Regional Study.* Washington, D.C., 1989.

Ryan, Selwyn, ed. *Trinidad and Tobago: The Independence Experience, 1962–1987.* St. Augustine, Trinidad, 1988.

Country Profile: Trinidad and Tobago, Guyana, Suriname, Netherlands Antilles and Aruba, Windward, and Leeward Islands. London, quarterly.

TRIST, NICHOLAS PHILIP

(*b.* 2 June 1800; *d.* 11 February 1874)

Diplomat who negotiated the treaty ending the war with Mexico. Born in Charlottesville, Virginia, Trist studied

briefly at the U.S. Military Academy and then read law in the law office of Thomas Jefferson. Henry Clay, as secretary of state, offered him a clerkship in his department, largely to help Trist's debt-ridden mother. Trist continued in that post after Andrew Jackson assumed the presidency in 1829, and, for a time, served as President Jackson's private secretary. Between 1833 and 1841, he worked as U.S. consul in Havana, Cuba. His recall in 1841 resulted more from partisan politics than from charges of impropriety (such as participation in the slave trade) that a congressional investigation in 1840 failed to sustain. In 1845 President James K. Polk appointed Trist chief clerk in the Department of State.

The war with Mexico created for Trist a unique venture in public service. In mid-April 1847 the president, in an effort to end an unpopular war, instructed Trist to join General Winfield Scott's army in central Mexico and attempt to open negotiations with the Mexican government. In his baggage were detailed instructions to secure a boundary line along the Rio Grande to New Mexico, then west to California, with frontage on the Pacific Ocean to include the bay of San Diego. Trist negotiated an armistice in August that produced a Mexican offer of San Francisco, but not San Diego. When President Polk received the Mexican proposal, he recalled Trist without naming a successor. In late November, Mexican officials promised Trist a suitable treaty if he would disregard his instructions and remain in Mexico. During January 1848, Trist negotiated the Treaty of Guadalupe Hidalgo, which brought New Mexico and California, with San Diego, into the United States. Despite Trist's success in establishing a treaty, Polk refused to see him or compensate him for his expenses in Mexico. Failing in a career at law, Trist repeatedly sought refuge in an appointment to public office. Although a Southerner, he opposed secession, voted for Abraham Lincoln, and finally, in 1870, received an appointment from Republican President Ulysses S. Grant as postmaster at Alexandria, Virginia.

NORMAN A. GRAEBNER

See also Cuba; Mexico, War with; Polk, James Knox

FURTHER READING

Graebner, Norman A. *Empire on the Pacific: A Study in American Continental Expansion.* New York, 1955.

Klein, Julius. *The Making of the Treaty of Guadalupe Hidalgo on February 2, 1848.* Berkeley, Calif., 1905.

TRUDEAU, PIERRE ELLIOTT

(*b.* 18 October 1919)

Prime minister of Canada (1968–1979 and 1980–1984). The son of a wealthy Montreal businessman, Trudeau was educated at College Saint-Jean-de-Brebeuf, University of Montreal, Harvard University, and the London

School of Economics. In the 1950s he was a leading civil libertarian in his native province of Quebec, and the founder and publisher of a liberal intellectual magazine, *Cité Libre*. In the early 1960s, Trudeau became increasingly concerned about the rise of separatist nationalism in Quebec, joined the federal Liberal Party, and was elected to the federal parliament in 1965. He became minister of justice in 1967 and was elected party leader and prime minister in 1968.

Trudeau's principal interest was the retention of Quebec in the Canadian federation; all other issues, such as Canadian-U.S. relations, were secondary to this consideration. Initially, Trudeau took little interest in the United States, its politics, its economy, or its culture and was neither pro- nor anti-American in his personal attitudes. In 1968–1969, Trudeau questioned whether Canada should remain a member of the North Atlantic Treaty Organization (NATO), which he regarded as anachronistic, but he first carefully checked out U.S. attitudes with President Richard Nixon. In the end, Trudeau accepted that Canada should remain in NATO, but with a diminished contribution.

On strategic issues there was no particular friction during Trudeau's tenure with either the Nixon, Gerald Ford, or Jimmy Carter administrations: Ronald Reagan was a different matter. Trudeau's time in office witnessed a considerable growth in Canadian nationalist sentiment. Coupled with the energy crises of the 1970s and early 1980s this development encouraged the Canadian government to reverse its long-standing preference for unlimited oil and gas exports to the United States in 1972, and to limit such outflows in the future. In 1980 the Trudeau government introduced its National Energy Program, which attempted to assert Canadian control and Canadian ownership in the oil and gas industry. Unpopular in western Canada, this policy also became extremely unpopular with the Reagan administration. Together with Trudeau's presumed notions of "equivalence" in assessing the United States and the Soviet Union as rival superpowers, this policy shift led to a chill in Canadian-U.S. relations. Trudeau's National Energy Program, premised on oil prices rising, proved an expensive failure when instead prices fell. Its failure helped lead to Canadian acceptance of free trade with the United States, later in the decade, through the North American Free Trade Agreement (NAFTA). Trudeau helped design his country's new constitution in 1982, which gave Canada complete independence from Great Britain. He resigned as prime minister and returned to private life in June 1984; but he has remained an active and controversial public figure in Canadian political life.

Robert Bothwell

See also Canada; North American Free Trade Agreement; Oil and Foreign Policy; Reagan, Ronald Wilson

FURTHER READING

Bothwell, Robert. *Canada and the United States*. New York, 1992.
Granatstein, Jack, and Robert Bothwell. *Pirouette*. Toronto, 1990.
Trudeau, Pierre Elliott. *Memoirs*. Toronto, 1993.

TRUJILLO MOLINA, RAFAEL LEÓNIDAS

(*b.* 24 October 1891; *d.* 30 May 1961)

Strong, often brutal, and corrupt dictator who ruled the Dominican Republic from 1930 until his assassination in 1961. Born into a lower class family, Trujillo became an officer in the Dominican Constabulary, the new Dominican military forces created and trained by the U.S. Marines during the U.S. occupation of the Dominican Republic. During the occupation years, 1916–1924, Trujillo fought against the Dominican guerrillas who opposed the U.S. intervention. At the end of the occupation in 1924, Horacio Vásquez was elected president and Trujillo began serving as chief of the National Army. In 1930, Trujillo participated in the overthrow of Vásquez and assumed the presidency.

Trujillo's regime was marked by totalitarianism in a context of economic progress. His rule rested on extreme coercion of the opposition and intolerance towards dissent. The political party which he created in 1931 included hundreds of so-called inspectors, whose main task was to gather information on dissenters. He also forced intellectuals to support his regime and did not hesitate to repress them even beyond Dominican borders, as was the case with Jesús de Galíndez, a Spanish journalist openly critical of Trujillo's rule who was kidnapped in New York City in 1956 and never heard from again.

Convinced that his country, which shares the island of Hispaniola with Haiti, was becoming Haitianized, in October 1937 Trujillo ordered the massacre of thousands of Haitians who resided along the Dominican-Haitian border. This bloody episode, which resulted in the execution of at least 12,000 Haitians, produced an international outcry. President Franklin D. Roosevelt temporarily withdrew U.S. support from the dictatorship to protest its genocidal actions. A few years later, during World War II, Trujillo's standing with the Roosevelt administration improved because he cooperated with President Roosevelt's requests that the Dominican Republic harbor Jewish immigrants escaping Nazism. The Dominican Republic declared war on Germany and Japan in December 1941.

From the onset of his rule Trujillo amassed an enormous personal fortune estimated in 1961 at more than $500 million, gained from large-scale corruption and monopolistic control of many of the country's economic activities. Thus, national prosperity and Trujillo's own economic gain became inseparably intertwined. During the postwar years and in light of the new international alignments of the Cold War era, Trujillo once again sought to manipulate international circumstances to his advantage. At first, during 1944–1946, he allowed communist organizations to operate freely in the Dominican Republic, and he dispatched an ambassador to Moscow. Sensing the increasing polarization of the early years of the Cold War, in October 1946 he began a program of repression against Dominican communists and declared himself to be the American champion of anticommunism. The caudillo's dictatorial rule reached its peak in 1955–1956, when he organized a grandiose International Fair to showcase the material accomplishments of his regime.

In June 1959 nearly 200 Dominican exiles, backed by Cuba's Fidel Castro and Venezuela's President Rómulo Betancourt, invaded the Dominican Republic from Cuba in an abortive attempt to overthrow Trujillo. Trujillo soon launched an even more brutal persecution of Dominican dissidents, which led the Dominican Catholic Church to withdraw its earlier support from Trujillo's regime. Trujillo became increasingly isolated and vulnerable as he faced growing international opposition. In August 1960 the Organization of American States (OAS) imposed economic sanctions against the Dominican Republic in response to Trujillo's role in planning an assassination attempt against Betancourt.

The administrations of Dwight D. Eisenhower and John F. Kennedy wanted the help of Latin American countries in overthrowing Castro's regime. But Betancourt, the Costa Rican leader José Figueres, and other democratic leaders also demanded an end to Trujillo's dictatorship. The United States began to work toward Trujillo's removal. The Eisenhower administration supported the OAS, economic sanctions, and the Kennedy administration authorized the Central Intelligence Agency to deliver arms and ammunition to a group of discontented Dominicans, who killed Trujillo on 30 May 1961 in the outskirts of Santo Domingo City. The Kennedy administration assisted the Trujillo family to leave the country in November 1961.

JAIME DOMÍNGUEZ

See also Betancourt, Rómulo; Castro, Fidel; Dominican Republic; Haiti; Johnson, Lyndon Baines; Organization of American States

FURTHER READING

Calder, Bruce J. *The Impact of Intervention: The Dominican Republic during the U.S. Occupation of 1916–1924.* Austin, Tex., 1984.

Crassweller, Robert D. *Trujillo: The Life and Times of a Caribbean Dictator.* New York, 1966.

Gleijeses, Piero. *The Dominican Crisis: The 1965 Constitutionalist Revolt and American Intervention.* Baltimore, Md., 1978.

Welles, Sumner. *Naboth's Vineyard: The Dominican Republic, 1844–1924.* 2 vols. New York, 1928.

Wiarda, Howard J. *Dictatorship and Development: The Methods of Control in Trujillo's Dominican Republic.* Gainesville, Fla., 1968.

TRUMAN, HARRY S.

(*b.* 8 May 1884; *d.* 26 December 1972)

Thirty-third president of the United States (1945–1953) noted for launching Cold War policies directed at the containment of the Soviet Union. Born in Lamar, Missouri, Truman grew up in Independence. After high school, he worked at clerical jobs for five years, and then operated his family's farm in Grandview. He enlisted in the army when the United States entered World War I in 1917, and rose to the rank of Captain, bravely commanding his "Battery D" troops in France. After the war, he married his childhood sweetheart, Elizabeth ("Bess") Virginia Wallace, and opened a Kansas City haberdashery, which failed in 1922. Elected judge of the eastern district of Jackson County, Truman lost his reelection bid in 1924, sold automobile club memberships, and then won two terms as presiding judge of Jackson County, where he oversaw public construction and maintained judicious relations with Thomas J. Pendergast's powerful, but corrupt, Kansas City Democratic political machine.

Elected to the U.S. Senate in 1934, Truman became a loyal supporter of President Franklin D. Roosevelt's New Deal. Truman won reelection in 1940, and during 1941–1944 he headed a special Senate committee investigating wartime military spending. Truman was the compromise Democratic candidate for vice president in 1944—between Henry Wallace on the left and James F. Byrnes on the right. Upon Roosevelt's death on 12 April 1945, Vice President Truman became president.

Truman profoundly shaped U.S. foreign policy during the next eight years, establishing the containment doctrine as the basis of the United States's Cold War posture. When he left the White House, nonetheless, his public standing was extremely low, due largely to perceived Soviet, or communist, advances in Eastern Europe and China, the bitter Korean War stalemate, and McCarthyite allegations of communist subversion in government. A decade later, however, historians classified Truman as a "near great" president whose administration had reconstructed Western Europe and Japan, resisted communism in Greece and Korea, and created the North Atlantic Treaty Organization (NATO). Popular writers hailed the "plain speaking" Truman as the allegory of American life—a person who overcame adversity from childhood through the presidency—and Democratic and Republican presidents alike have claimed to be latter-day Trumans. In the early 1990s, many commentators credited him with forging the foreign policy that ultimately brought about the demise of the Soviet Union and European communism and ended the Cold War.

This popular bipartisan acclaim, however, contends with scholarly assessments that explore the way in which Truman's parochial and nationalist background, and combative personality, infused his diplomacy and policymaking and intensified the postwar Soviet-U.S. conflict. For example, young Truman's poor eyesight and extended illness alienated him from his peers and his feisty father, and may have fostered ambivalence toward powerful men. He deferred to senior officials such as W. Averell Harriman, ambassador to Moscow, and to Secretaries of State George C. Marshall and Dean G. Acheson, but impetuously denounced the Department of State's "striped pants boys," the military's "brass hats" and "prima donnas," political "fakirs" [sic] such as Theodore and Franklin Roosevelt, and he labelled foreign leaders, including Russia's Joseph Stalin and France's Charles de Gaulle, as a "son of a bitch."

Truman's need to demonstrate his authority led him to upbraid Soviet Foreign Minister Vyacheslav Molotov in April 1945 for Russia's alleged failure to keep its agreements, and to admonish Secretary of State James F. Byrnes in December 1945 for negotiating too independently with the Russians. Truman also naively likened Stalin to Pendergast, and then felt slighted that the Soviet leader might have broken his word, or "contract," over Poland, Iran, or Germany.

Truman's self-tutelage in history, derived largely from romantic biographies, increased his knowledge of the globe but provided little sense of nuance. He believed that current events had precise historical analogues. Thus the new president would be "amazed" that the accords Roosevelt, Stalin, and Winston Churchill signed at the Yalta Conference in February 1945 were so "hazy" and fraught with "new meaning" at every reading. Truman's heavy reliance on the "lessons of history" led him to apply inexact analogies about appeasement of Germany and Japan in the 1930s to postwar disputes with the Soviet Union, while his youthful Bible reading instilled stern belief that "punishment always followed transgression," a maxim that guided his diplomacy toward North Korea and the People's Republic of China. Finally, Truman's early writings disdained non-Americans ("Chink doctor," "dago," "Jew clerk," "bohunks," and "Rooshans'"), and later he questioned the loyalty of "hyphenate" Americans.

Truman did identify with Woodrow Wilson's League of Nations, and as a senator he voted to revise U.S. neutrality laws to permit sale of war materials to opponents of Nazi Germany, and to provide Lend Lease aid for Great Britain and the Soviet Union. "I am no appeaser," he declared.

His internationalism relied heavily on military preparedness. He deplored disarmament, pacifists, and "disloyal inhabitants," and too quickly blamed international conflict on "outlaws," "savages," and "totalitarians." Germany's attack on the Soviet Union in 1941 led to his hasty remark that the two powers should be allowed to destroy one another. But he opposed Hitler's winning, and he inveighed against the "twin blights of atheism and communism." Although he strongly supported the fledgling United Nations, Truman in 1945 was less an incipient internationalist than a parochial nationalist, who feared that enemies at home and abroad would thwart America's mission ("the Lord's will") to "win the peace" on its own terms.

Truman publicly praised President Roosevelt but disliked his predecessor's conduct of foreign policy. Roosevelt acted as his own secretary of state and relied heavily on personal diplomacy, compromise, and vague agreements to resolve difficult problems. Truman depended on his secretary of state to formulate policy, keep him well informed, and present important decisions for his confirmation. Secretary of State Byrnes lost his job for not consulting closely about his diplomacy, whereas Secretary of State George C. Marshall and Dean Acheson carefully sought Truman's approval of their undertakings. Truman also preferred quick, unambiguous, and firm decisions, which sometimes led him to define complex problems in oversimplified terms that obstructed artful compromises.

U.S. officials in 1945 sought to create a postwar international order based on the principles of representative government, equal access for all nations to the world's trade and raw materials, and no territorial changes without consent of the peoples involved. Soviet leaders emphasized their nation's need for security, and recovery from wartime devastation. They sought to establish "friendly" governments (or a sphere of influence) on their borders, to extract reparations from wartime enemies, and to regain former territories of pre-1917 Tsarist Russia.

The Origins of the Cold War

Truman negotiated at the Postdam Conference in July 1945, but he was determined to advance U.S. interests: "win, lose or draw—and we must win." He called the atomic bomb his "ace in the hole," and believed that it would induce the Russians to accept U.S. plans for postwar Germany, which included restoring significant economic production before assessing reparations payments. When Stalin balked, Truman insisted that each power take reparations from its own occupation zone. This precluded Russian access to Ruhr industry, and augured that Germany would be divided between East and West. Military and political considerations influenced the president's decision to use atomic bombs against Japan. Atomic action would end the war swiftly and save lives. But the president also believed that the bombs would cause Japan to "fold up" before the Russians entered the Pacific war, thereby minimizing their advance into Manchuria and assuring the United States of exclusive occupation control of Japan.

Truman backed Secretary Byrnes's hardline, or "bomb in his pocket," diplomacy at the foreign ministers' conference in September. Truman viewed the United States as the world's "trustee" for atomic power, and thought that America's technological genius assured its supremacy. The president also dressed down Byrnes for allegedly appeasing Russia in negotiating compromise accords in Moscow in December 1945 on Eastern Europe, Asia, and atomic power. The Soviets understood only an "iron fist," Truman said, and he was tired of "babying" them. He approved the Baruch Plan for international control of atomic energy and weapons because it would deny weapons to the Soviets and preserve indirect U.S. control.

In early 1946, Truman initiated his "get tough" policy. This included strong protests against Soviet troops in Iran and thwarting the Soviet Union's claim to share control of the strategic Turkish Straits. The United States soon began limited military aid to Iran, and to Turkey, which military planners envisioned as a base for major military operations against the USSR. The president deemed war unlikely, but he strongly agreed with the September 1946 report of White House aides Clark Clifford and George Elsey which charged that the Soviet Union intended global conquest by military power and political subversion.

Great Britain's decision to halt aid to Greece led the president to announce his Truman Doctrine to Congress on 12 March 1947. He called for $400 million in military and economic aid to Greece and to Turkey, and stressed that failure to help "free peoples" resist totalitarianism would permit Soviet, or communist, influence to spread across Europe and Asia. The Truman Doctrine established precedent for repeated U.S. intervention in foreign crises and became the guide to the U.S. policy of containment in the Cold War.

Truman next sanctioned Secretary Marshall's 5 June 1947 address which invited Europe to propose an economic recovery program underwritten by U.S. aid. The Truman administration skillfully built public political support for vast European aid, and persuaded France to agree to include Western Germany by promising to keep U.S. occupation troops there and to create an international authority to supervise German industry. Meanwhile, Soviet pressure on Eastern Europe, and a Communist coup d'etat in Czechoslovakia in February 1948, inspired Truman to blame the USSR for the Cold War, and to call for greater military preparedness. Congress promptly funded the European Recovery Program (ERP), which provided $13 billion in ERP aid during 1948–1952. This assistance helped to spur West European recovery and political stability, reintegrate western Germany and assuage France, and foster U.S. foreign trade and investment.

Truman next met the challenge of Stalin's June 1948 blockade of the Western powers' ground access to occu-

pied Berlin, whereby the Soviets sought to forestall creation of a sovereign West German state. The president, who probably overestimated Soviet designs on all of Germany, refused to withdraw from Berlin or to challenge the blockade militarily. Instead, he firmly supported the Berlin airlift and counter-blockade of eastern Germany. Truman also sent B-29 bombers to Europe, although these aircraft were not modified to carry atomic bombs, and he repeatedly refused to transfer presidential control of atomic weapons to the military. Eventually, the president's steadfast moderation forced Stalin to agree to a diplomatic end to the Berlin blockade in May 1949.

At the same time, the United States joined with eleven European nations to form its first peacetime alliance, the North Atlantic Treaty Organization (NATO), and promoted formation in September 1949 of the Federal Republic of Germany, which joined NATO in 1955. The Soviet Union, meanwhile, fostered the German Democratic Republic, which joined its Warsaw Pact in 1956.

U.S. containment policy probably sustained the postwar division of Europe, but the president could, and did, claim that it bolstered Western Europe's political and economic revitalization and averted war. Truman's similar strategy for Asia, however, succeeded only in Japan. There U.S. unilateral occupation policies fostered parliamentary government, economic productivity, and then sovereignty in 1952—under the "umbrella" of U.S. forces stationed in Japan and on Okinawa. With respect to China and Korea, containment evolved into "rollback," or "liberation," with drastic consequences.

Truman initially shied away from taking sides in the postwar conflict in China between Jiang Jieshi's (Chiang Kai-shek's) Nationalist regime, which the president regarded as the world's "rottenest" government, and Mao Zedong's Chinese Communist Party (CCP), which he derided as "bandits" and a "cutthroat organization." But Truman could not perceive China's civil war apart from the Soviet-U.S Cold War. He sent General George C. Marshall to mediate in China in late 1945, but ensured the failure of that mission by pledging not to halt military aid to the Nationalists even if they proved to be uncompromising in negotiations. Most important, Truman approved the Department of State's White Paper of August 1949. This weighty document sought to fend off charges that U.S. policymakers had "lost" China by detailing past U.S. aid to the Nationalist regime and describing that regime's extensive flaws. But the White Paper also challenged the CCP's legitimacy to govern, and called on the Chinese people to throw off their communist "yoke," and not to serve Soviet interests. In the summer of 1949 the president rebuffed overtures from the emergent People's Republic of China (PRC) and refused to extend diplomatic recognition. He denied the PRC's presumptive right to rule Taiwan, from where the Guomindang regime, with

U.S. aid, continued its economic warfare and a blockade against the PRC. In sum, Truman set the matrix for long-term, hostile U.S. policy toward the PRC well before the direct Sino-U.S. conflict in Korea.

The Korean War and Truman's Record Assessed

In June 1950, Truman attributed North Korea's attack on South Korea not to a civil war between two rival regimes in a divided country, but to Soviet intent to "swallow up one piece of Asia after another." The president quickly gained United Nations (UN) sanction to restore peace in South Korea. His swift decision to commit U.S. forces to the conflict was intended to preserve South Korea's independence and maintain U.S. credibility around the world. But he did not wait to gain Congress's approval to use U.S. troops, and his dispatch of the Seventh Fleet to the Taiwan Straits signalled renewed U.S. involvement in China's civil war, although Truman saw the fleet both protecting Taiwan and blocking a reckless move from Taiwan against the mainland.

Truman read Korea as a major issue of American security and world peace. His decision, taken in September 1950, to send General MacArthur's U.S./UN forces north of the 38th parallel—the boundary between North and South Korea—to unify the nation by military means, changed the original political objectives of the war. Containment now became "rollback," or "liberation."

The president ignored diplomatic advice that he had given General MacArthur too much latitude to advance his forces north toward the Manchurian border, and that the PRC and Soviet Union would view creation of an anti-communist state in North Korea as a security threat. Further, he disregarded as "blackmail" PRC warnings in October that they would enter the war.

PRC intervention in Korea in November 1950 forced America's bitter retreat southward, while Truman's hasty remark that use of the atomic bomb was always under consideration caused British leaders to fly to Washington to preclude atomic war. When Prime Minister Clement Attlee insisted that PRC leaders could be Marxist and nationalist, and "not bow to Stalin," Truman insisted that China's new leaders were "fully tied" to the USSR.

The president refused to compromise with the PRC: no negotiations prior to a cease-fire; no diplomatic recognition, nor a seat in the UN; and continued U.S. aid to the Guomindang on Taiwan. Further, America's insistence that the UN brand the PRC an "aggressor" in February 1951 precluded an early settlement. Finally, General MacArthur's provocative demand that the PRC surrender to him or face destruction, and public release of his statement that "there is no substitute for victory," led Truman to fire his larger-than-life commander in April 1951. This was a politically courageous act, although MacArthur's insubordinate behav-ior was not the sole cause of the crisis. The president, who always dealt cautiously with MacArthur, should have issued more specific directives to his commander, and the two men shared similar Korean War goals until the president realized in the winter of 1951 that he had to extricate the United States from the costly conflict.

Still, Truman's diplomacy obstructed a formal armistice. First, he refused, for ideological and political reasons, the standard military practice (and the Geneva Convention of 1949, to which his administration adhered) of compulsory exchange of all prisoners of war (POWs). Thus, Truman insisted on voluntary POW exchanges only, and the fighting in Korea continued until his successor, President Dwight Eisenhower, effected a compromise in June 1953 whereby a neutral nations' commission took custody of POWs reluctant to be repatriated, and the boundary between North and South Korea was restored near the 38th parallel.

Truman's decision to intervene in the Korean War preserved South Korea's independence and enhanced the UN's collective security prestige. Truman also set the stage for long-term political and military commitments to South Korea and the Chinese Nationalists on Taiwan, and to France to wage war in Indochina, while relations between the United States and the PRC were embittered for a generation. Further, the Truman administration's military budget nearly quadrupled between 1950 and 1953, the president's domestic Fair Deal program lay in shambles, and McCarthyism was rampant nationally. Truman departed the presidency with the United States standing on a Cold War footing at home and abroad.

President Truman provided strong leadership for U.S. foreign policy, although neither the Cold War nor the forty years of peace between the superpowers can be attributed to one leader or nation. World War II created complex problems that generated an inescapable Soviet-U.S. conflict. Truman's policymaking inevitably would reflect his determination, and that of his senior diplomatic-military advisers, to avert "appeasement" in the face of Stalin's harsh realpolitik, and to establish maximal U.S. national security.

Truman insisted that the United States not forgo postwar responsibility to create a peaceful and prosperous world order. He firmly fostered foreign aid and military commitment to promote political-economic reconstruction and security in Western Europe and Japan. Moreover, even during the heat of the Berlin crisis, the president, who wrote that two world wars were "enough for anybody," resisted military conflict. After he recognized his own "overreach" during the Korean War, he mustered political courage to fire his imperious military commander and to seek return to the political status quo.

From the Postdam Conference through the Korean War, however, Truman's policies contributed to the growing Cold War and increasing militarization of U.S. foreign policy. His diplomacy was that of a man of limited vision, often unable to see beyond his immediate decision or visualize alternatives. He had a penchant for simplistic historical analogies and, as a British diplomat wrote in 1947, the president often showed "staggering disregard" for the implications of his statements. Despite his pride in his knowledge of the past, he lacked insight into the history unfolding around him.

Most significantly, Truman assumed that America's moral-industrial-military superiority assured that he could order the world on U.S. terms. He disregarded contrary views, impugned his critics' loyalty, and often did not grasp the basis for the positions taken by other nations or leaders. His insisted that Stalin had broken his agreements, and attributed conflict with the Soviets to sinister designs. He blamed civil wars on Soviet, or PRC, machinations, rather than on indigenous political rivalries or anti-colonial struggles. The president remained convinced, as he wrote in his undelivered Farewell Address, that "Russia was at the root" of every problem in France and Italy, Iran, Greece and Turkey, and China, and he boasted that "Trumanism" had saved these countries from Soviet invasion and had "knocked the socks off the communists" in Korea and elsewhere.

Truman left the presidency in January 1953, and retired to Independence. He largely spent his time working on his memoirs, and overseeing construction of the Harry S. Truman Library, which became an important research repository. The former president worked in his office there, and received many visitors, until his health failed in the late 1960s. Since his death Truman's popularity has soared among the general public and among historians, in polls about presidents. He has been admired for his bold Cold War policies, common-folk style, and decisiveness. Critical scholars, however, have depicted Truman as a parochial nationalist in a cosmopolitan world of atomic power, superpower rivalry, and revolutionary upheaval. According to them, he lacked qualities of presidential leadership and oversimplified complex issues, while his get-tough style caused him to miss opportunities of initiating any serious attempts at détente with the Soviet Union.

ARNOLD A. OFFNER

See also Anti-Communism; Berlin; Byrnes, James F.; Cold War; Containment; Germany; Korean War; Marshall Plan; McCarthyism; North Atlantic Treaty Organization; Nuclear Weapons and Strategy; Postdam Conference; Presidency; Russia and the Soviet Union; Truman Doctrine; Yalta Conference

FURTHER READING

Donovan, Robert J. *Conflict and Crisis: The Presidency of Harry S. Truman, 1945–1948.* New York, 1977.

———. *Tumultuous Years: The Presidency of Harry S. Truman, 1949–1953.* New York, 1982.

Ferrell, Robert H. *Harry S. Truman: A Life.* Columbia, Mo., 1994.

Hamby, Alonzo L. *Man of the People: A Life of Harry S. Truman.* New York, 1995.

Lacey, Michael, ed. *The Truman Presidency.* New York, 1989.

Larson, Deborah Welch. *Origins of Containment: A Psychological Explanation.* Princeton, N.J., 1985.

Leffler, Melvyn. *Preponderance of Power: National Security, the Truman Administration, and the Cold War.* Stanford, Calif., 1992.

McCoy, Donald R. *The Presidency of Harry S Truman.* Lawrence, Kans., 1984.

McCullough, David. *Truman.* New York, 1992.

Paterson, Thomas G. *On Every Front: The Making and Unmaking of the Cold War.* New York, 1992.

Pemberton, William E. *Harry S. Truman: Fair Dealer and Cold Warrior.* Boston, 1989.

Truman, Harry S. *Year of Decisions.* Garden City, N.Y., 1955.

———. *Years of Trial and Hope.* Garden City, N.Y., 1956.

Yergin, Daniel. *Shattered Peace: the Origins of the Cold War and the National Security State.* Rev. ed. Boston, 1990.

TRUMAN DOCTRINE

A statement on 12 March 1947 calling for the containment of communism, including President Harry S. Truman's request to Congress to provide $400 million in military and economic aid, and to send civilian and military advisers, to Greece and to Turkey. In his statement, a major departure from U.S. foreign policy, the president insisted that this peacetime step was necessary to prevent totalitarian regimes from imposing their will upon other nations, thereby undermining world peace and U.S. security. Defense of Greece and Turkey, he said, was necessary to preserve order in the Middle East and freedom in Europe. American newspapers and public opinion quickly hailed the Truman Doctrine, and Congress passed the proposed legislation in early May 1947.

Truman subsequently claimed that his doctrine marked a "turning point" in U.S. foreign policy, which now held that its security was at stake wherever "aggression" threatened peace. Administration officials, and later historians, argued that U.S. national interest required sustaining noncommunist governments in the strategically vital eastern Mediterranean. They further posited that if the Greek communist insurgents, controlling a good part of northern Greece in early 1947, had defeated the royalist Athens government, the Soviet Union might have been tempted to challenge Western power in the Mediterranean as a whole and to seek to control the region's critical waterways and vast oil reserves.

Many other scholars, and contemporary critics such as Walter Lippmann, judged that the Truman Doctrine produced unwarranted U.S. intervention into Greece's civil war with little regard for the indigenous causes of that conflict (as well as an unwarranted haste in blaming

Moscow for the activities of the Greek communist party). The doctrine became a central element in Cold War mentality, and spurred an overblown campaign to contain the Soviet Union and world communism, which were too readily blamed for nearly every international or civil conflict. Critics of the Truman Doctrine also said that its sweeping rhetoric exceeded the administrations's intentions and capabilities, failed to distinguish between the United States' vital and peripheral interests, and fueled an anticommunist crusade that led to indiscriminate U.S. intervention in crises from the Caribbean to Southeast Asia as well as in the Middle East and the Persian Gulf. J. William Fulbright, chairman of the Senate Foreign Relations Committee during the 1960s, asserted in 1972 that almost every American foreign policy mistake of the previous quarter century derived from the Truman Doctrine.

Background: Greece and Turkey

Truman's decision to intervene in Greece and Turkey in 1947 had precursors. The president long believed that the Soviet Union intended to dominate Iran and Turkey. In September 1946 White House aides Clark Clifford and George Elsey compiled a lengthy report charging that the Soviet Union intended to establish "puppet" regimes in Greece and Turkey. The report reflected the administration's strong consensus that Soviet foreign policy was aggressive, expansionist, and unlimited. But U.S. officials also believed that their recent "get tough" policy was paying dividends, especially in persuading the Soviets to withdraw their troops from Iran (stationed there during World War II). Truman also forced the Russians to relent on their long-standing claim to share control of the Turkish Straits—pathway for attacks on Russia during both world wars—by sending a U.S. task force to the Mediterranean in August 1946. Soon thereafter, the United States sent limited military aid to Iran and Turkey.

The Truman administration also closely watched Greece, which had been under British political tutelage since its liberation in the fall of 1944 from German occupation. By 1947, however, Greece was locked in a bitter civil war. On one side stood the Athens government, which had emerged in 1946, following parliamentary elections boycotted by the left, and was composed of extremely conservative and largely royalist factions dependent on British aid to maintain their power. On the other side was the "Democratic Army"—successor to the wartime National Liberation Front (EAM), and its military arm, the National Popular Liberation Army (ELAS). Greek communists had originally organized EAM-ELAS, which led the wartime resistance to the Nazis, became a broadly based leftist-republican coalition with a populist program, and unsuccessfully fought the British-backed government in Athens in December 1944. By late 1946

the Democratic Army had gained aid and sanctuary for its forces in the north chiefly from Yugoslavia, less so from Bulgaria and Albania; but not from the Soviet Union.

U.S. diplomats claimed, however, that Greek communists were tied to Moscow, which intended to use its Balkan "satellites" to dominate Greece, Turkey, and the eastern Mediterranean. As Undersecretary of State Dean Acheson said, Greek "capitulation" to the Soviets would lead to the loss of the Middle East and its oil, North Africa, and probably Europe and Asia. But until early 1947 the United States had given only minimal aid to Greece because Truman administration officials recognized that the Athens regime was politically and economically bankrupt.

Washington felt the need to react, however, when the British government, on 21 February 1947, announced that its own desperate economic straits required that its aid to Greece cease on 31 March. Truman and Secretary of State George C. Marshall immediately approved a State-War-Navy department proposal to step into the British breach. The president, confronting a Republican-led Congress bent on budget cuts and lower taxes, insisted on informing House and Senate leaders of his intention to intervene.

At their famous White House meeting on 27 February, administration officials spoke in apocalyptic terms. Marshall insisted that only the United States could prevent the Soviets from first dominating Greece and then "Europe, the Middle East, and Asia"; and Acheson warned that a communist "infection" in Greece would spread from Europe to Africa, and to Asia, and that the choice was between U.S. democracy or Soviet dictatorship. Arthur Vandenberg, Republican chairman of the Senate Foreign Relations Committee, responded for his stunned colleagues, saying that if the president would say as much—"scare hell out of the country"—Congress would have to support him.

The Speech and Its Implementation

The president's aides readily crafted a statement proclaiming that the United States was obligated to help "free peoples maintain their free institutions" against aggressive movements that sought to impose "totalitarian regimes" upon them. They brushed off caveats that such "sweeping" language, or "flamboyant anti-communism," might open the United States to endless requests for military assistance from other nations, and that recent Russian behavior did not justify this "all-out" speech. As Clifford insisted, the speech was intended to be the "opening gun" in a campaign to persuade the public that "the war was not over by any means," while Truman told his Cabinet that "this is only the beginning. It means [the] U.S. going into European politics. It means the greatest selling job ever facing a President."

The "selling job" meant that Acheson would excise from the speech references to Greece's strategic location, to Middle East resources, and to conflict between free enterprise and state-directed economies. There was no mention of the complex background of the Greek civil war or of the Russo-Turkish dispute over the Straits. Nor was anything said about the authoritarian nature of the Greek and Turkish governments, or that more than two-thirds of the proposed aid would be military. Further, despite strong objections from George F. Kennan, the State Department's senior Soviet expert, that Turkey had no indigenous communist problem, and that the Soviet Union might regard military aid to a nation on its border as provocative, Turkey was quietly "slipped into the oven with Greece," as one official noted. Finally, because U.S. officials wished to act unilaterally, reference to the United Nations was limited to noting that it was not able to offer immediate aid to either Greece or Turkey.

President Truman, in his epoch-making speech to a joint session of Congress, stressed America's need to help "free peoples" resist totalitarianism. He insisted that every nation had to choose between "alternative ways of life"—majority will and free institutions, or forcibly imposed minority will, terror, and oppression. U.S. policy had "to support free peoples who are resisting attempted subjugation by armed minorities or by outside pressures." Failure to aid "democratic" Greece and Turkey would have drastic effects, reaching east and west, and endanger world peace as well as U.S. security.

In testimony to Congress, officials melded strategic concerns with their emergent "domino" theory. They warned that Soviet control of the Turkish Straits would "cut the world in half," and permit a Soviet advance from the Persian Gulf and the Suez Canal across India to China. Similarly, the United States had to contain the Soviets, while congressional leaders concluded that it was equally impossible to "desert" the president without destroying the United States' world influence. Congress imposed only one restraint, namely Vandenberg's amendment that American aid would cease if the United Nations deemed it unnecessary. But this was "window dressing," Acheson recalled, because of the United States' influence over UN voting. The Senate passed the Greek-Turkish aid bill on 22 April by a vote of 67 to 23; the House followed on 8 May by a vote of 287 to 107; and Truman signed the revised conference bill into law on 22 May. Meanwhile, a special UN committee investigating the conflict in Greece concluded that it derived from domestic causes and Balkan national rivalries, but not—as the Truman Doctrine had made it seem—from Russian efforts to impose communism and dominate the Mediterranean.

U.S. aid to Greece, beginning in summer 1947, seemed at first only to spur the Athens regime to greater repression, which U.S. officials largely ignored for the next two years. Meanwhile, the American Mission for Aid to Greece (AMAG) gradually took control over the Greek govern-

ment's major political and economic functions, and insisted on imposing a "crushing defeat" and "unconditional surrender" on the rebel forces. The United States utilized increased Truman Doctrine appropriations to enlarge the Greek Army to a peak of more than 250,000 by November 1948 against 25,000 for the Democratic Army, at a cost of $500 million, a far greater sum than the communist Balkan nations' aid to the Democratic Army. U.S. military officials also organized and advised the Greek Army, at the highest levels and in combat, and Britain was pressed to retain its remaining 5,000 troops in Greece.

U.S. support ultimately enabled the Greek government to prevail over the insurgents. But victory was also achieved because Joseph Stalin, who had never aided the Greek communist leaders, reacted mildly to the Truman Doctrine, and did not challenge Anglo-U.S. influence in Greece. In early 1948, Stalin pressed Marshall Josip Broz Tito of Yugoslavia to halt his aid to the Greek rebels. When Tito refused, Stalin expelled Yugoslavia from the recently formed Communist Information Bureau (Cominform) and withdrew Russian advisers from Belgrade. Continued Soviet pressure, combined with Yugoslavia's need for U.S. economic assistance, and the Greek communists' loyalty to Stalin over Tito (because of the latter's ideological independence), led Yugoslavia's leader to halt aid and to close his nation's borders to the Greek rebels in July 1949. Greece's civil war ended that October, with 158,000 dead, more than 800,000 refugees, and the nation's economy and social structure devastated.

Meanwhile, the United States expended several hundred million dollars of increased Truman Doctrine aid to modernize Turkey's armed forces, first to resist a Soviet assault—although none was foreseen—through the Straits or the Black Sea; later, to halt a Russian attack on Iran or the Persian Gulf; and finally, to develop air capacity, including America's use of its own B-29s, to bomb (if need be) Soviet oil resources in the Caucasus and in Romania. In 1952 Greece and Turkey were admitted to the fledgling North Atlantic Treaty Organization (NATO).

Opinion about the Truman Doctrine remains sharply divided. Some historians still emphasize that in 1947 the United States had to assume Britain's role in the Mediterranean, and that U.S. national security managers had to oppose any prospect of a Greek communist victory because this might have led to a Stalinist regime that would have imperilled Western security. The Truman administration, moreover, did not intend to police the world or to militarize U.S. foreign policy; this came only later as a result of the Korean War.

Other analysts emphasize the Truman Doctrine's negative long-term consequences. First, the Truman administration's rhetorical division of the world into "free" versus "totalitarian" states, and gross exaggeration of the Soviet behavior toward Greece and Turkey, created an "ideological straitjacket" for American foreign policy, heightened East-West bloc tension, and signalled a turn away from diplomacy to resolve disputes with the Russians. Second, Congress gave the president almost carte blanche to wage a Cold War and to intervene in another nation's civil war, undermining the constitutional checks-and-balances system between executive and legislative branches, thus contributing to the emergence of an "imperial presidency." Third, at least initially, American policy did not address the deeper causes of the Greek civil war; instead, it substituted a military solution for genuine reform of the political-economic order—dating back to the Metaxas dictatorship (1936–1941)—that had engendered the conflict.

The Truman Doctrine also established the "model" aid program for later interventions, including assisting France in 1950 to wage war in Indochina. Most notably, Truman's response that year to the outbreak of war in Korea was marked by his view that "this is the Greece of the Far East. If we are tough enough now, there won't be another step." Such thinking inclined Americans to blame primarily the Soviet Union, or the People's Republic of China, for wars often rooted, in large part, in domestic or anticolonial causes. As Walter Lippmann warned in his book *The Cold War* (1947), the Truman Doctrine also invited authoritarian regimes to raise an anticommunist banner in order to attract U.S. aid. The Truman Doctrine's virulent anticommunism and emphasis on military containment became hallmarks of U.S. Cold War foreign policy.

ARNOLD A. OFFNER

See also Acheson, Dean Gooderham; Clifford, Clark McAdams; Cold War; Containment; Domino Theory; Greece; Kennan, George Frost; Lippmann, Walter; Marshall, George Catlett, Jr.; Truman, Harry S.; Turkey

FURTHER READING

Freeland, Richard M. *The Truman Doctrine and the Origins of McCarthyism: Foreign Policy, Domestic Politics, and Internal Security, 1946-1948.* New York, 1974.

Iatrides, John O. *Revolt in Athens: The Greek Communist 'Second Round,' 1944-1945.* 1972.

Jones, Howard. *"A New Kind of War": America's Global Strategy and the Truman Doctrine in Greece.* New York, 1989.

Jones, Joseph M. *The Fifteen Weeks (February 21-June 5, 1947).* New York, 1955.

Kuniholm, Bruce R. *The Origins of the Cold War in the Near East: Great Power Conflicts and Diplomacy in Iran, Turkey, and Greece.* Princeton, N.J., 1979.

Leffler, Melvyn P. *A Preponderance of Power: National Security, the Truman Administration, and the Cold War.* Stanford, Calif., 1992.

Pollard, Richard A. *Economic Security and the Origins of the Cold War, 1945-1950.* New York, 1985.

U.S. Senate Committee on Foreign Relations. *Legislative Origins of the Truman Doctrine, Hearings Held in Executive Session, a Bill to Provide for Assistance to Greece and Turkey,* on S. 938, Eightieth Cong., 1st Sess. Washington, D.C., 1973.

Wittner, Lawrence S. *American Intervention in Greece, 1943-1949.* New York, 1982.

TRUSTEESHIPS

See Mandates and Trusteeships

TRUST TERRITORY OF THE PACIFIC ISLANDS

See Mandates and Trusteeships; Pacific Island Nations and U.S. Territories

TUNISIA

Located in North Africa across from the Strait of Sicily, between Algeria and Libya, an Arab republic, rich in mineral resources, that has taken moderate positions on most regional and international issues. During World War II, in November 1942, American and other Allied troops landed in the French province of Algeria and pushed on to Tunis, where Axis forces surrendered in May 1943 after bloody fighting. A French protectorate from 1883 to 1956, Tunisia generally still maintains cordial relations with France and other European nations. Periodic attempts to improve relations with its neighbors and other Arab states have not caused these Western ties to deteriorate significantly; Tunisia's pro-Western reputation even survived its allowing the Palestine Liberation Organization (PLO) to maintain headquarters near Tunis following the PLO's ejection from Beirut, Lebanon, in 1982. The United States thus continued to provide some economic assistance and military training programs to Tunisia, and worked very closely with the Tunisian government when the dialogue with the PLO was opened in December 1988. Tunisia later played a key role, as a member of the "steering group," in initiating the multilateral talks on the Middle East peace process at the 1991 Madrid Conference.

Tunisia was ruled from the time it gained independence in 1957 until 1987 by President Habib Bourguiba. Since 1987, the United States has supported Tunisia's steps toward political liberalization. Potential danger to these ongoing ties exist, however, because of growing tensions between reformers and Islamic fundamentalists in Tunisia, and over human rights issues that have arisen in that context.

CATHERINE ELKINS

See also Africa; Middle East; Palestine Liberation Organization

FURTHER READING

Lacroix-Riz, Annie. *Les Protectorats d'Afrique du Nord, entre la France et Washington, Maroc et Tunisie.* Paris, 1988.

Parker, Richard S. *North Africa.* 1984.

Zartman, I. William, ed. *Tunisia: The Political Economy of Reform.* Boulder, Colo., 1991.

TURKEY

A republic located both in Europe and in Asia Minor, the heart of what used to be the Ottoman Empire. Turkey is bordered by Greece and the Aegean Sea in the west; by the Black Sea in the north; by the former Soviet Union, Armenia, and Iran in the east; and by Iraq, Syria, and the Mediterranean Sea in the south. Although commercial relations between the United States and the Ottoman Empire began in the eighteenth century, formal treaty arrangements were not established until May 1830. These arrangements guaranteed most-favored-nation privileges and extended to the United States additional privileges, known as the "capitulations," which exempted U.S. nationals from control by Ottoman courts and from all taxes except those on commerce. Until World War I, relations revolved around commerce and, more importantly, missionary work. At the outbreak of war, U.S. missionaries operating in territory that later became the present-day Turkish Republic supervised 426 schools with 25,000 students—almost exclusively Christian and mostly Armenian.

World Wars I and II

During World War I, the Ottoman Empire abrogated the capitulatory regime and in November 1914 entered the war on the side of the Central Powers. Subsequently, Turkey's ruthless repression of its Armenian population—a significant element of whom, seeking an independent state, had joined the resistance against the government and assisted the Russian cause against Turkey, largely in the Caucasus region—complicated U.S.-Turkish relations. Some scholars have charged that Armenians were the victims of genocide, while others have compared the situation in Eastern Turkey to Lebanon in recent times, emphasizing the wider context in which continuous intercommunal warfare was perpetrated by irregular forces (many of whom were of Kurdish ethnicity) and complicated by disease, famine, suffering, and massacres throughout the region. While the Armenian issue complicated relations between the United States and Turkey, it did not disrupt diplomatic relations, which were broken only in April 1917 after the United States entered the war; but the two countries did not, however, engage in hostilities.

By war's end, the Anatolian heartland had lost approximately twenty percent of its population of 12 million (a figure that does not include Armenians who were either killed—estimates range from 600,000 to 1.5 million—or deported). The heartland's partition, moreover, was prefigured by four wartime secret treaties, some of whose stipulations were embodied in the punitive Treaty of Sèvres (1920) that was imposed on the sultan. The Allies, who could not agree among themselves on the

supervision of areas previously assigned to Russia in the secret agreements, encouraged the United States to take part in the partition. Prodded by advocates of the Armenian cause, the Wilson administration considered taking responsibility for an Armenian mandate under League of Nations auspices, but the idea was decisively rejected by the U.S. Senate. By then, the occupation of Turkish territories in Anatolia by the British, French, Italians, and, subsequently, the Greeks, had aroused the Turkish nationalist spirit, which under the aegis of Mustafa Kemal (later, Atatürk) rallied supporters to the nationalist cause. The Turkish nationalists proceeded to secure their eastern front against the Armenians, compose their differences with the Soviet regime, reach agreements with the French and Italians, and drive the Greeks out of Asia Minor. They then concluded an armistice with the British, abolished the sultanate, and in July 1923 signed the Treaty of Lausanne (which undid the Treaty of Sèvres and gave Turkey international legitimacy as a sovereign, independent state). In October 1923 Turkey was proclaimed a republic.

Kemal Atatürk recognized the necessity of remodeling not only government and society, but the Turks' sense of identity as well. As a soldier Atatürk had saved the country and won its acceptance by Europe; as a statesman, he renounced foreign ambitions and ideologies which smacked of internationalism (Pan-Turkism and Pan-Islamic ideologies) and limited his aspirations to the reconstruction of Turkish national territory. He now undertook far-reaching reforms, including secularization of the state; the adoption of new civil, criminal, and commercial codes; the adoption of a Latinized alphabet; and the political emancipation of women. These reforms helped transform the structure of Turkish society, reorient it toward the West, and lay the groundwork for a modern, democratic, secular nation.

As World War II approached, the problem for Atatürk's successor, İsmet İnönü, was to understand the complex international situation and avoid the hasty strategy of World War I that had proven so devastating. These tasks were made more difficult during World War II by Russia and Germany's contemplation of a division of interests in the Near East at Turkey's expense, and Russia and Great Britain's interest in pushing Turkey into the war in order to force Germany to redeploy her armies. İnönü was successful in maintaining Turkey's neutrality until February 1945 when, in order to ensure Turkish participation in the San Francisco Conference, Turkey declared war on Germany and Japan.

The Cold War

At the end of World War II, Stalin's attempts to acquire control of the Turkish Straits, support Georgian and Armenian irredentism in Kars and Ardahan, and put pressure on Turkey to accommodate Soviet desires had a profound effect on Turkish-American relations. Prior to this time, Turkey had been virtually outside of U.S. cognizance and within Great Britain's sphere of influence. In the centuries before World War II, it was the British who, protecting their line of communications, had sought to limit Russia's historical aspirations toward Turkey and Iran. The United States as yet had no strategic interests in Turkey and had not even reestablished diplomatic relations until 1927—after the Senate, divided by partisan politics and influenced by pro-Armenian pressure groups, had rejected the Treaty of Lausanne. The British Empire, however, was no longer able to support Turkish resistance to a growing Russian threat. Given its predominance and broadened responsibilities after World War II, the United States now assumed the role. During a crisis over Turkey in August 1946, President Harry S. Truman made what he considered to be his most important decision since the decision to bomb Hiroshima a year before: that it was in the vital interest of the United States that the Soviet Union not be allowed to obtain control over Turkey—either by force or the threat of force—and that the United States would resist with all means at its disposal any Soviet aggression.

Truman's key decision resulted in the reformulation of U.S. policies not only toward Turkey, but toward Iran and Greece as well. It led to the establishment of what later became the U.S. Sixth Fleet and, in the wake of Great Britain's withdrawal from the region, to a clear recognition within the highest circles of the U.S. government that the United States had undertaken an unprecedented commitment to maintain the balance of power in the Near East. U.S. policy was publicly articulated by the president on 12 March 1947, in what became known as the Truman Doctrine. The president's specific aim was to gain congressional approval for a $400 million appropriation to aid Greece and Turkey, although the real impetus was provided by the civil war in Greece and Great Britain's inability to continue propping up the conservative Athens government. The president's speech was seen by the administration to be a turning point—a signal to proceed in Europe, where the Greek-Turkish Aid Program served as a model for the Marshall Plan. Turkey next sought formal guarantees of its security, but the United States turned its attention first to the problem of restoring the balance of power in Europe through the Marshall Plan (the economic component) and then through the North Atlantic Treaty Organization (the military component).

Among the factors that increased Turkey's strategic importance to the West at this time was the fact that the Middle East was supplying three-quarters of all European oil requirements and contained resources that dwarfed those of the rest of the world. Soviet denial of Middle East oil, it was recognized, would seriously jeopardize the European Recovery Plan. Turkey was seen as the strongest anticommunist country on the periphery of the Soviet Union, the only country in the Eastern Mediterranean capable of providing substantial military resistance to the Soviets. As such, Turkey constituted a deterrent to Soviet aggression and provided something of a protective screen to the entire region; loss of Turkey to the Soviet Union would give the Soviets a valuable strategic position in the region. An alliance between the United States and Turkey, on the other hand, was increasingly desirable. If Bulgaria attacked Greece, Turkey would not oppose Bulgaria unless intervention were dictated by the requirements of a larger security framework that included the United States. If the Soviets attacked Iran, and Turkey remained neutral, the Soviet right flank would be protected. Oil interests in the Gulf, meanwhile, would be vulnerable, and European economic vitality would be threatened.

Within the U.S. military, meanwhile, although the Middle East was seen as "vital" to the defense of the United States and Turkey was recognized as playing a crucial role in that defense, the armed services fought among themselves over the interpretation of the term "vital" because it affected their respective military missions and the size of defense appropriations. In this debate, top officials in the Air Force and the Navy argued that Turkey's role in international security was inseparably linked to the balance of power in Europe and therefore deserved support. These officials were pitted against the army chief of staff, who saw Turkey as linked primarily to the balance of power in the Middle East (which he saw as a British responsibility) and who felt that the United States should concentrate on maintaining the balance of power in Europe (where the Army had a dominant role). NSC-68 (a short-hand designation for National Security Council Paper No. 68), which was implemented after the Korean War began, endorsed the idea of perimeter defense and, coupled with massive increases in defense appropriations, made distinctions between peripheral and vital interests unnecessary. As a result, categorical definitions of Turkey as either a Middle Eastern or as a European country were no longer relevant; it became possible to recognize and support its unique geopolitical position in the defense of both regions.

In the interim, Turkey committed a combat brigade to the war in Korea, where its performance was characterized by General Douglas MacArthur as "bravest of the brave." In the course of the war, 29,882 Turks served in this brigade; 717 were killed and 2,256 were wounded in action. This commitment (suggested by the U.S. ambassador in Turkey) was motivated by a desire for admission to NATO and for a security guarantee from the U.S.—just as Turkey's abandonment of one-party rule in the early postwar years was motivated in part by a desire to underscore the country's allegiance to the West. After the commencement of the Korean War, the United States recognized that if it wanted to obtain Turkey's full cooperation in regional security issues (for example, in Iran or the Balkans), or to assure its cobelligerence in the event of an attack on Europe, it would need to give Turkey a security commitment. Such a commitment also was necessary to secure access to Turkey's valuable bases and to close the Bosporus Straits. Without a security commitment from the United States, there was concern that Turkey would drift toward neutrality. These were some of the reasons why President Truman decided in May 1951 that the United States should endorse the inclusion of Turkey as a full member of NATO. In February 1952 Turkey (along with Greece) was formally admitted to full membership in NATO. The United States felt that it needed this commitment, as did the Turks, whom experience had taught the value of a credible deterrent.

Under the administration of President Dwight D. Eisenhower, the assumptions that undergirded Turkey's accession to NATO were reinforced and Turkey's role in the defense of the West was strengthened. In 1955 Turkey joined the Western-sponsored Baghdad Pact (subsequently renamed the Central Treaty Organization). High-altitude U-2s were stationed at İncirlik Air Base near Adana beginning in 1956 and important electronic installations for gaining information from the Soviet Union were set up along the Black Sea. In accordance with an agreement reached in 1957, the United States stationed U.S. strike aircraft equipped with tactical nuclear weapons in Turkey and was granted extensive military facilities, which strengthened its potential to mount effective air strikes against the Soviet Union. In 1958 Turkish bases were used by U.S. forces as a staging area for the crisis in Lebanon. Over time, installations in Turkey would serve many additional functions: electromagnetic monitoring, forward basing, radio navigation, seismographic detection, contingency storage of war reserve material (ammunition and fuel for the Sixth Fleet), radar warning, space monitoring, and early warning sites. Sites in Turkey, which became even more critical after the fall of the shah of Iran in 1979, for a time provided up to twenty-five percent of NATO's hard intelligence about Soviet strategic nuclear activities. Even in the early years, military assistance to Turkey was substantial and during the Eisenhower administration averaged approximately $200 million a year.

When *Sputnik* dramatized the Soviet long-range missile threat to the United States in October 1957, the United States led a NATO decision to deploy missiles and stocks of nuclear warheads on the Continent in order to respond to a perceived loss of confidence in the U.S. commitment to Europe. As a consequence, the United States and Turkey reached agreement in October 1959 to deploy a squadron of Jupiter missiles in Turkey. The mis-

siles were not installed until the autumn of 1961, apparently became operational in July 1962, and were formally handed over to the Turks only on 22 October 1962, in the midst of the Cuban missile crisis. A decision to use the missiles required agreement between Turkey, which owned the missiles, and the United States, which retained custody of the warheads.

During the Cuban missile crisis, when the missiles in Turkey became a major issue, the United States secretly agreed to remove them. To the extent that the Jupiters invited attack and were obsolete by the time they were installed—and to the extent that assurances regarding their removal were consistent with strategic plans, improved Turkey's security, and strengthened deterrence—the decision was a wise one. In the aftermath of the Cuban missile crisis, Ankara's importance in U.S. nuclear strategies diminished, thus removing an impediment to Turkey's better relations with Moscow. Following the 1960 revolution, and under a more permissive constitution, Turks began to question more freely traditional assumptions about foreign policy in general and their relations with the United States in particular. Subsequent revelations that a "deal" had been made for Turkey's missiles took time to surface and ultimately only contributed to, rather than caused, the erosion of Turkey's faith in the NATO alliance.

The Cyprus Issue and Economic Relations

Relations between the United States and Turkey were seriously affected for the first time in the alliance after intercommunal violence erupted in Cyprus (independent since 1960) in late 1963 and Greek Cypriot terrorists, aspiring to *enosis* (union) with Greece, attempted to intimidate the Turkish Cypriot minority. Official records indicate that during the 1963–1964 crisis, 364 Turkish Cypriots (and 174 Greek Cypriots) were killed, and approximately 25,000 Turkish Cypriots became refugees. In Turkish eyes, one of the culprits in the Cyprus crisis was President Lyndon B. Johnson, who warned in a June 1964 letter to Prime Minister İnönü that Turkey (which was entitled under the 1959 Treaty of Guarantee to assist the Turkish Cypriot community, and which had begun preparations for a landing in Cyprus) should not use any U.S.-supplied equipment to invade Cyprus. Johnson's letter also called into question U.S. obligations under NATO if Turkey took a step that resulted in Soviet intervention. After the Cyprus crisis of 1963–1964, U.S.-Turkish relations were less tied to the axioms—and enforced solidarity—of the early postwar years.

While the Turks continued to distrust the Soviets, Ankara's policies clearly became more flexible. Improvement in Turco-Soviet relations, beginning in the 1960s, was marked by economic assistance from the Soviet Union, complementing a diminishing level of grant assistance from the United States, which was increasingly mired in the war in Vietnam. The new balance in Turkish policy can best be understood through comparison with earlier events. For example, during the war in Lebanon in 1958 the United States had used Turkish bases to support its intervention. Following events of the early 1960s, the Turks were more guarded about unquestioned support for U.S. policies or unrestricted U.S. use of Turkish facilities for non-NATO contingencies. In 1965 Turkey chose not to participate in the U.S.-sponsored proposal for a multilateral nuclear force in Europe. During the 1967 and 1973 Arab-Israeli Wars, the United States was allowed to use communication stations in Turkey, but was not allowed to use Turkish bases for direct combat or logistical support. The United States was, however, allowed to use Turkish bases for the evacuation of U.S. citizens during the Jordanian Civil War in 1970 and the Iranian Revolution in 1979.

A new Cyprus crisis, meanwhile, arose in July 1974—sparked by an assassination attempt against President Makarios, orchestrated by the military dictatorship in Athens—and again tested mutual U.S.-Turkish obligations and responsibilities. The crisis, it should be noted, was ongoing and had earlier flared up in November 1967 when Turkish Cypriot villagers were massacred and Turkey again had pondered intervention. The 1974 crisis, however, was far more costly. Following Turkey's military intervention, Greek/Greek Cypriot casualties were estimated at 6,000 and Turkish/Turkish Cypriot casualties at 3,500, including 1,500 dead. Most of the 180,000 Greek Cypriots in the north fled or moved south, while the majority of the 40,000 Turkish Cypriots in the south eventually moved to the north. Initially, Ankara was responding to a coup in Nicosia that was backed by the military dictatorship in Athens and led by Nikos Sampson, a terrorist bent on union with Greece who had led one of the Greek Cypriot private armies in 1963–1964. Turkish forces occupied the northern part of the island to protect the Turkish minority. A second Turkish action in August—to consolidate vulnerable positions, according to the Turks; to expand and consolidate their base, according to the Greeks—precipitated a U.S. congressional embargo on transfers of military equipment to Turkey (effective February 1975), and resulted in a subsequent decision in Ankara to suspend U.S. operations at military installations in Turkey (as of July 1975). These developments made explicit what had been implicit until then: that U.S. access to facilities in Turkey was directly related to U.S. decisions on military assistance. Blunt assessments of the problem called into question fundamental assumptions on both sides, and forced discussion over the merits of continuing the special relationship (which began to improve after the embargo was lifted in September 1978 and arms shipments were resumed in February 1979). A Defense and Economic Cooperation Agreement (DECA) negotiated in 1980 now forms the basis for the U.S.-Turkish military relationship.

In the 1960s, meanwhile, Turkey's economic relations with the European Economic Community (EEC as it was then known)—and particularly with Germany—markedly improved. The "Ankara Agreement" of 1963 associated Turkey with the EEC, while a supplementary agreement in 1971 provided for a transitional stage toward full integration in the EEC (subsequently the European Community, or EC, and eventually the European Union, or EU). Europe's economic growth created a demand for Turkish labor, eased unemployment in Turkey, and—through remittances from Turkish workers—eased foreign exchange shortages and balance of payments deficits.

The oil crises of 1973–1974 and 1978–1979, however, combined with Turkey's lack of developed indigenous energy resources, caused Turkey's oil bill to rise from $124 million in 1972 to $3.86 billion by 1980. High oil bills and a recession in Europe (which led to the halt of Turkey's labor migration) led Turkey to drain its foreign exchange reserves, rely on state-owned economic enterprises as a short-term solution to job creation, and borrow on the short-term credit market—a set of policies that contributed to a vicious cycle of hyperinflation, stagnation, and huge balance of payments deficits that ultimately proved unsustainable.

Relations between Ankara and Moscow, meanwhile, continued to improve. By 1978, the Soviet Union was aiding forty-four different development projects in Turkey, and by the end of the decade Turkey received more Soviet economic assistance than any non-communist state except India and Afghanistan. If Prime Minister Ecevit could declare in May 1978 that Turkey felt no threat from the Soviet Union, however, that statement required qualification, particularly in December 1979 after the Soviet invasion of Afghanistan (which worried the Turks far more than the fall of the shah of Iran).

Additional cause for concern grew out of political and economic problems and endemic civil violence. By September 1980 an average of over twenty politically motivated murders were being committed in Turkey every day, and more than 13,000 people had been killed or wounded over the previous two years (numbers differ depending on the definition of the motives involved). Two-fifths of Turkey's work force were unemployed, and the rate of inflation had reached 128 percent.

In September 1980, as the economic and political situation grew worse and the death toll by terrorist attacks reached twenty-eight per day, General Kenan Evren, former commanding officer of the Turkish brigade that had fought valiantly in Korea and chief of staff of the armed forces, announced that the military leadership, acting in its traditional capacity as guardian of the state, was taking over control of the government. The sense of relief with which Turks greeted the restoration of order seemed virtually unanimous.

1980s–1990s

During the first administration of President Ronald Reagan, relations between the United States and Turkey improved markedly, as the East-West conflict raised the specter of a new Cold War and appropriations for Turkey's defense needs correspondingly increased. Even under conservative estimates, U.S. assistance to Turkey in its various forms throughout the 1980s amounted to well over $1 billion a year (if one includes concessional loans and grants, U.S. military construction funds, navy ship transfers, Defense Industrial Cooperation industrial machinery; and the U.S. share of international programs and loans such as NATO Infrastructure, NATO Airborne Warning and Control Systems (AWACS), World Bank project loans, United Nations Development Program funds, and Dependable Undertaking Funds). But perceptions of the international balance of power began to change during the second Reagan administration, and during the administration of President George Bush appropriations for Turkey's defense needs, while still significant, became less urgent to the United States.

In Turkey, meanwhile, anger over congressional debate on the so-called "Armenian resolution," which proposed a day of commemoration for the alleged genocide of 1.5 million Armenians by the Ottoman Empire, exacerbated U.S.-Turkish relations. The source of Turkish concern, aside from a belief that judgments on the matter were best left to historians, was a concern that the resolution, if passed by the U.S. Congress, would give a fillip to Armenian terrorists—who in earlier years had targeted and assassinated Turkish diplomats—and lend legitimacy to future claims by Armenians for compensation and territory in Turkey. U.S. port visits and training missions were halted, restrictions were put on the modernization of facilities, and meetings on military cooperation were suspended. The U.S.-Turkish relationship itself was called into question until the resolution was narrowly defeated in early 1990—on the eve of the Gulf War and as the Cold War was drawing to a close.

The bottom line in the U.S.-Turkish relationship during the Cold War was that, when U.S.-Soviet relations were troubled, relations between the United States and Turkey were generally good. Good relations were founded on U.S. military and economic assistance as well as a U.S. guarantee of Turkey's security—a guarantee that served as a deterrent against a Soviet attack—in exchange for the use of Turkish facilities and bases, and an important Turkish role in the defense of the West. But as U.S.-Soviet relations improved, the U.S.-Turkish relationship became more troubled as first one and then another party raised questions about the relationship and challenged the other's notion of their reciprocal obligations.

If Turkey's security relationship with the United States was solidly grounded in mutual interests, its economic relationship with the West, while increasingly significant in terms of trade, nevertheless ran into serious obstacles as Turkey sought integration into the world economy. The process of overcoming these obstacles began in 1980, before the military coup, when the government of Süleyman Demirel began to address some of Turkey's serious economic problems by introducing the first of a series of broad-based economic stabilization measures. Placing great reliance on market forces, subsequent Turkish governments (the military government ended in 1983) sought to eliminate subsidies to inefficient public-sector enterprises, curtail imports, increase exports by devaluing the lira, cut oil consumption, introduce a tight monetary policy to limit inflation, and remove barriers to foreign investment. Over time, some of these economic measures, while not uniformly successful, would begin to turn around Turkey's economy. In the 1980s, Turkey's exports rose from $2.9 billion to $11.7 billion.

In 1987, meanwhile, Turkey applied for admission to the EC. With the decline of the Soviet Union, the EC began to give priority to economic and political concerns over NATO's military priorities, with the result that it was less responsive than it otherwise would have been to the Turks' application. The Turks, in turn, began to look to other mechanisms—and in particular to the Black Sea Economic Cooperation initiative—to help modernize their country, although they recognized that it could not replace the EC.

Specific concerns addressed by the EC Commission in its 1989 decision to postpone consideration of Turkey's application were Turkey's size, population, and substantially lower level of development than the European average. Purchasing power in Turkey was one-third that of the EC average, and the country suffered from high inflation rates and high unemployment. More than 50 percent of the labor force in Turkey was employed in agriculture, and the Community was concerned about the access of Turkish labor to the EC labor market at a time when unemployment was a problem for the twelve associated economies.

While the Turks saw the lack of a commitment to Turkey's entry as the denial of a right that it had earned through its commitment to the NATO alliance and a rejection of Turkey's commitment to Europe, they were not surprised. The Turkish government, trying to cast the best possible light on the situation, emphasized the report's affirmation of Turkey's qualification to become a full member and its call for a customs union between Turkey and the EC by 1995. Membership in the EC, Turks believed, would guarantee the continued Westernization of their country and cement its identity in Europe. Rejection of Turkey's membership, President Özal warned in the years before his death in April 1993, would push Turkey away from Europe and encourage the spread of religious fundamentalism throughout the region. Islamic fundamentalists had never captured more than ten percent of the vote in Turkey until that time, but their cause clearly would be fueled by such rejection. The run-up to the elections in Turkey, on 24 December 1995, raised precisely this concern in the EC (where Prime Minister Çiller issued some of the same warnings as Özal) and contributed to the European Parliament's decision on 13 December 1995 to admit Turkey to the customs union (Turkey formally joined the customs union on 1 January 1996). Even so, the pro-Islamic Welfare Party captured twenty-one and four-tenths percent of the vote (and 158 seats in the recently expanded 550-seat parliament). The next two highest vote-getters—the center-right Motherland (nineteen and six-tenths percent and 133 seats) and True Path (nineteen and two-tenths percent and 135 seats) Parties—were close behind.

Some of the Welfare Party's support could be explained as a protest against the corruption and ineptitude of Turkey's traditional parties (which were heavily involved in patronage) and also as a response to the Welfare Party's capacity to deliver services on the municipal level, where migrants from rural areas responded favorably to its well-organized efforts. While secularists generally regard the Welfare Party as a threat to the nationalist-oriented secular political order established by Kemal Atatürk, some see it as a safety valve for concerns that otherwise might follow a more subversive course. They also see the public expression of pro-Islamic sentiment, under secular control, as a source of support for that order—at least to the extent that it meets an inner need for meaning not satisfied by Turkey's political culture. The limits of the Welfare Party's influence were suggested by its inability to form a coalition government in early 1996 (potential coalition partners were wary of giving it control of important ministries) and the advent in March 1996 of a shaky center-right coalition government under the True Path and Motherland parties. The collapse of that government (because of personality clashes and corruption charges), however, eventually resulted in the formation of an even shakier coalition under the Welfare and True Path parties in July 1996. The government seemed less an indication of a major sea change in Turkish politics and more the result of a deal between True Path Party leader Tansu Çiller, who was determined to be a part of any government (and hence to avoid prosecution for alleged corruption), and Welfare Party leader Necmettin Erbakan, who was willing to tone down his pro-Islamic, anti-Western rhetoric and, at least rhetorically, pay obeisance to Turkey's secular political system.

On the geopolitical level, meanwhile, while reduction of the Soviet military threat to Europe diminished Turkey's importance in NATO, the Gulf War underscored Turkey's continuing (although changing) strategic importance to the West. Turkey's contribution to the anti-Iraq coalition included closing the Iraqi oil pipeline; allowing the allied coalition access to its military bases, from which Iraqi targets were bombed; and deploying the Turkish Army along the Iraqi border, which forced Iraq to deploy its troops to the north and raised the prospect of a two-front war. Turkey's borders with both Iran and Iraq enhanced its relative influence in the Persian Gulf region, where the end of the Cold War created an environment that was less stable.

In the aftermath of the Gulf War, the United States, in conjunction with coalition forces, launched Operation Provide Comfort, an enormous relief effort to provide humanitarian aid to Kurdish refugees through bases in eastern Turkey and to protect them from Iraqi reprisals. The Turks supported this humanitarian goal and continued to renew the mandate for Poised Hammer, the military arm of Provide Comfort, to operate out of İncirlik. While helping to deter Saddam Hussein, however, the safe haven in Iraq has allowed Kurdish nationalists to establish the rough framework for an autonomous government under Masoud Barzani's Kurdistan Democratic Party (KDP) and Jalal Talabani's Patriotic Union of Kurdistan (PUK). The Turkish fear is that autonomy will be a steppingstone to independence and lead not only to the disintegration of Iraq, but (serious tribal differences notwithstanding) an irredentist nationalist movement seeking to incorporate the more than 20 million Kurds of Iraq, Iran, Turkey, and Syria, thereby threatening the territorial integrity of the Turkish state.

The new international environment that Turkey confronts is much more complicated and very different from that which it faced during the Cold War era, when the legacy of Atatürk reigned supreme. From the beginning of the modern Turkish state, eliminating ethnic differences by fiat was a means to an end: creating the cohesion necessary for the state's survival. Such cohesion, fostered through both persuasion and repression, helped to create a national identity that enabled Turkey to withstand threats to its territorial integrity and sovereignty in the years following Lausanne and throughout the Cold War.

In recent years Turkey has come into its own as a regional power. More secure about its identity, it has begun to confront some of the existential problems that were submerged in the process of nation-building and to reconcile itself with its past. Where the immediate threat to Turkey's existence during the Cold War was geopolitical, those most prominent in the post-Cold War era are fundamentally different: cross-cutting forces that can cross borders and divide nations—Islam, pan-Turkism, and Kurdish separatism and nationalism.

The emergence of Turkic-speaking republics in the Trans-Caucasus and Central Asia has reinvigorated Turkey's interest in the world's Turkic-speaking population, which by different estimates includes between 120 to 180 million people in a region that stretches from Albania to China. The emergence of those republics, following the EC's decision to postpone Turkey's application for membership, perhaps understandably generated compensatory rhetoric about Turkey's regaining its historic mission as a great power through its connection to the East. But Turkish leaders (former President Özal's initial rhetoric notwithstanding) have been careful to deny Pan-Turkish aspirations—which have always had limited support in Turkey—and instead emphasize commonalities of civilization, culture, language, and belief, and a shared interest in democracy and a market economy. Much of the initial euphoria over the connection with the Central Asian regimes, moreover, has subsided as pragmatic concerns have underscored Turkey's limited means and Russia's continuing influence in the "near abroad."

The Kurdish Question

The Kurdish question, unlike those posed by Islam or Pan-Turkism, has not evoked prudent policies from Turkey's leadership and has become Turkey's most profound problem. The French nation-state concept, on which Atatürk modeled the Turkish state, based citizenship on individual identity (as opposed to either ethnic or religious identity). As a result, legal status was not given to ethnic minorities (although it was to religious minorities, such as the Greek Orthodox, Armenians, and Jews), and the dictates of nation-building made Kurds, like the rest of Turkey's many ethnic minorities, all Turks by decree. Given the problem of creating a new identity for a multi-ethnic population, and the fact that at the time ethnicity was seen as less crucial to one's identity than religion, which Atatürk sought to replace, he opted for subsuming the population under the rubric "Turk." While the political community "imagined" by Atatürk became a reality for most Turkish citizens (including many assimilated Kurds, some of whom served and continue to serve in parliament—estimates generally range from 80 to 100, although one estimate widely cited in 1995 was that 136 of 450 deputies were of at least partial Kurdish ethnicity), it did not work for all Kurds. Observers have noted that in the civil service, the armed forces, and the professions, there is no discrimination against people of Kurdish origin—provided that they are content to call themselves "Turks." While Turkey is by far the most democratic state in which Kurds live in the Middle East, it is culturally the most repressive. As a result, while assimilation has worked for many, for many others it has worked imperfectly or not at all, and Turkey's Kurdish problem is the result.

Turks widely acknowledge that they know little about the Kurds. Even defining who is and who is not a Kurd is not an easy matter. If a citizen of Turkey had one grandparent who was a Kurd—as was the case with President Özal, one of at least three Turkish presidents with Kurdish ancestry—does that make him Turkish, Kurdish, or both?

It is widely believed that at least half of Turkey's estimated 12 million Kurds (statistics in Turkey are unreliable) live outside the southeastern region (commonly referred to as "Kurdistan" in the West), and that millions of Kurds live in Turkey's major western cities. This development makes the radical solution of a separate state in the southeast for the Kurds—advocated by the terrorist Kurdish Workers Party (PKK)—a solution that will solve neither Turkey's Kurdish problem (the government would still have the problem of governing at least 6 million Kurds in western Turkey), nor the problems of the Kurdish population in the southeast (a vast majority of whom, according to a widely discussed study by Professor Doğu Ergil, oppose a separate state and prefer a solution within the boundaries of the Turkish Republic that includes a recognition of Kurdish cultural identity and a reformed political and legal structure). Only one-third of those interviewed in the study had a relative linked with the PKK (there was no indication of how close the relative might be). Interestingly, only forty percent of this subgroup thought that the PKK's main aim was to establish a separate state—conflicting statements by the PKK leadership may be responsible for confusion about its goals. Even so, fully seventy-five percent of this subgroup opposed the establishment of a separate state.

Turkish governments, aware of what they must do to improve their human rights record and institutionalize democracy if Turkey is to be accepted as a member of the European Union (EU), have been increasingly sensitive to the minority rights of Kurds. They have made belated and halting attempts to recognize the cultural identity of Kurds and have continued to plow billions of dollars into the Southeast Anatolia Project, which promises to meet half of their energy needs and raise the standard of living in southeastern Turkey. But Abdullah Öcalan, the Syrian-based leader of the PKK who trains his guerrillas in Lebanon's Bekaa Valley (controlled by Syria), has been waging an all-out war against the central government and has provoked a virtual civil war in the southeast. His methods have been condemned by both Barzani and Talabani (who require the Turkish government's support to preserve their lifeline). The KDP and PUK, in addition to fighting each other, have occasionally fought against the PKK in northern Iraq.

Öcalan's goals, while difficult to pin down, have ranged from separatism to federalism with a heavy overlay of Marxism. In March 1993 he declared a unilateral cease-fire, which was broken after two months when the PKK attacked and killed 33 unarmed and newly discharged soldiers on a bus stopped at a roadblock. In December 1995 he declared another unilateral cease-fire; he has continued to threaten since then, however, not only Turkey, but the United States and Germany as well. Germany's Chancellor Helmut Kohl and Foreign Minister Klaus Kinkel, for example, have received death threats from the PKK, and Öcalan has said that he could have bombs detonated all over Germany if Bonn did not end its military support of Turkey.

Under former Prime Minister Tansu Çiller, meanwhile, the government gave a free hand to the military, which is determined to crush the growing separatist movement by military means. In March 1995, Turkey sent 35,000 troops into northern Iraq to root out guerrillas and destroy the PKK's camps, facilities, and weapons caches. One analyst has summed up the perspective of the Turkish right and the military in opposing even cultural rights for the Kurds by describing the slippery slope they envision: cultural rights will lead to political rights, to federation, to statehood, and finally to union with adjacent Kurds. The result of this vision, and the tenaciousness with which it is held, is evident in the statistics cited below. To counter the PKK's harsh tactics, the military, too, has used harsh tactics. The collateral damage has killed innocent victims and gained the PKK growing sympathy among a minority of Turkey's Kurdish population—as well as among the many thousands of Kurdish Turks working in Germany. According to one thoughtful observer, while the Kurdish people initially despised the PKK as a student movement, and later supported it out of fear, they have begun to sympathize with it in reaction to human rights violations by the government, and now are giving it more support.

In 1993 alone the death toll of the undeclared war between Turkey and the PKK was over 4,000; the cost to Ankara was estimated at $7 billion for the same year. The numbers were even higher in 1994, and costs continued to escalate as the number of security personnel engaged by the government more than doubled—according to one estimate they approached 500,000. In 1995 a total of 3,521 people were killed in 4,058 incidents involving not only the PKK but extreme leftist organizations and radical Islamic elements as well. According to Turkish government figures, the PKK has 5,000 militants and a militia of 50,000 to 60,000. The PKK claims 30,000 full-time guerrillas.

Some analysts have argued that the government's failure to establish a political middle ground between the PKK and the state has been critical in the PKK's growth. This continues to be the case and no imaginative approaches are in sight—as evidenced by the fate of the pro-Kurdish Democracy Party, eight of whose members had their legislative immunity removed in 1994; they were subsequently arrested, charged with being members of an outlawed armed organization, and convicted. In October 1995 the Court of Appeals upheld the prison sentences passed on six of the politicians and ordered the retrial of the other two. More recently, during the 24 December 1995 general elections, the pro-Kurdish People's Democracy Party (HADEP) received a big percentage of the votes in southeastern provinces with a predominantly Kurdish population (forty-six and seven-tenths percent of the votes in Diyarbakir and fifty-four and three-tenths percent in Hakkari), but failed to get any substantial votes in the west—in part, perhaps, because migrants had not registered in voter lists, but also because Kurds in the west had more faith and greater investment than Kurds in the east in alternative political parties and were less subject to PKK pressure. Although there may have been a pool of as many as five million eligible Kurdish voters, HADEP received only one million, two hundred thousand votes, or four and two-tenths percent of the total votes.

PKK terrorism and the Turkish government's efforts to confront it, meanwhile, have caused many casualties—not just in terms of body counts, but in terms of the abuse of human rights and press censorship and has created serious differences between Turkey and Europe (the administration of President Bill Clinton has been critical, but more understanding, while Congress, responding to the influence of Greek, Armenian and, more recently, Kurdish lobbies, has been less so). According to Yavuz Önen, the chairman of Turkey's Human Rights Foundation, 192 citizens, including thirty-seven children, died as a result of PKK attacks against innocent civilians in 1994; leftist groups killed another twenty-six. In 1995, the numbers grew, although that judgment depends on one's sources. According to the respected Turkish *Daily News*, 433 civilians (as well as an additional 481 soldiers) were killed by the PKK (which suffered 2,554 dead) in 1995. Amnesty International has documented at least seventy civilians and prisoners killed by armed PKK members in 1995—most of the victims were Kurdish teachers and villagers (mostly government-armed village guards) and their extended families, including women and children.

In the course of living under emergency rule, Önen asserts, over 1,000 villages were emptied and burned; two to three million people moved away from their homes; and more than 4,000 people were killed. The Ministry of Foreign Affairs has been very critical of the evidence on which the Human Rights Foundation has based their findings, and the government is investigating the Foundation's allegations. In May 1996, the Committee to Protect Journalists ranked then Turkish Prime Minister Mesut Yılmaz fourth on its list of ten worst enemies of the press and documented fifty-one cases of Turkish journalists in jail at the end of 1995. Turkish sources assert that most journalists in jail are militants of various terrorist organizations using their journalist identities as cover. In July 1994, for example, thirty-five of seventy-eight journalists in prison had worked for the pro-Kurdish daily Özgür *Gündem*. The celebrated writer Orhan Pamuk, who has been very critical of the government, also has observed the pro-Kurdish newspapers have been unabashed in their support of the PKK, touting its military victories and publishing the number of soldiers killed. The pro-

Kurdish daily *Özgür Ülke* even published articles by Öcalan himself under the pen name Ali Firat. Sources for other statistics, however, are indisputable and come from the government itself. According to Justice Minister Firuz Çilingiroğlu, for example, in 1994 there were 768 torture cases initiated against 1,375 people, with convictions in 224 cases.

Beyond questions of fact, defenders of the Turkish government's harsh measures argue that critics have been insufficiently appreciative of the threat the PKK poses to the Turkish state. It is easy to be critical of human rights abuses, they point out, when one lives in a homogeneous society that is not threatened from within or without. The Turks, on the other hand, in confronting the Kurdish problem, face a challenge to the very identity and territorial integrity of the state. The challenge is compounded by vestigial feudal structures in the southeast, where class, religious, and cultural differences not only divide the country but cut across international boundaries. By March 1995, the number of "unsolved murders" or "mystery killings" in Turkey over the previous five years had reached 1,271, with suspects including the PKK, Islamic terrorist organizations such as Hezbollah, security organizations within the Turkish state itself, and foreign-based organizations in Iran, Iraq, and Syria. Wars in the Balkans and the Caucasus (where Russia has not abided by the Conventional Forces in Europe Agreement), not to mention long-term differences with Greece over Cyprus and the Aegean, compound Turkey's security problems. Turks, moreover, resent gratuitous advice, especially when it is uninformed about their problems' complexities; such advice to them smacks of the capitulations, in which minorities in Turkey became a means of foreign interference in Turkish affairs that eventually contributed to the downfall of the Ottoman Empire. They worry that such interference (some of which is prompted by ethnic lobbies with an axe to grind in the United States and Europe) could cause the demise of the Turkish state. They point to Israel's recent difficulties in dealing with terrorist organizations such as Hamas, which is supported by some of the same states (Syria and Iran) that support the PKK.

In spite of the difficulties discussed above, it is important to point out that, while situated in what is commonly recognized as "a very rough neighborhood," Turkey is a secular, democratic state. The statistics and reports about its problems and shortcomings mentioned here, moreover, have come from the Turkish press which, with the enormous exception of the Kurdish question, is still relatively free. Outspoken intellectuals such as Yaşar Kemal and Orhan Pamuk continue to speak out. Politicians such as Cem Boyner, academics such as Doğu Ergil, and Muslim intellectuals such as Ismail Nacar continue to seek ways to promote a solution to Turkey's most serious problem. Trends suggest that if in the past the

basis for Turkey's relationship with the United States was geopolitical, with common values being important but of secondary concern, the relationship in the future will increasingly reverse the priority of these two factors. Turkey's strategic ties with the West will continue to be important (former Assistant Secretary of State Richard Holbrooke characterized Turkey in 1995 as the new "front-line state of Europe"). But its economic ties (in 1995 Secretary of Commerce Ron Brown characterized it as one of the world's ten "Big Emerging Markets") are growing in importance; and as Turkey continues to make progress in becoming a working democracy, its common values with the West, which are fundamental, will assume an even greater importance.

BRUCE R. KUNIHOLM

See also Armenia; Cold War; Cyprus; Greece; Gulf War of 1990–1991; Iran; Iraq; Kurds; Middle East; North Atlantic Treaty Organization; Truman Doctrine; World War I

FURTHER READING
Andrews, Peter Alford. *Ethnic Groups in the Republic of Turkey.* Wiesbaden, 1989.
Kinros, Lord [Patrick Balfour]. *Atatürk: The Rebirth of a Nation.* London, 1964.
Dyer, Gwynne. "Turkish 'Falsifiers' and Armenian 'Deceivers': Historiography and the Armenian Massacres." In *Middle East Studies* 12 (1976): 99–107.
Hale, William. *Turkish Politics and the Military.* London, 1994.
Heper, Metin, and Jacob M. Landau, eds. *Political Parties and Democracy in Turkey.* London, 1991.
İmset, İsmet. *The PKK: A Report on Separatist Violence in Turkey (1973–1992).* Ankara, 1992.
Kuniholm, Bruce. *The Origins of the Cold War in the Near East: Great Power Conflict and Diplomacy in Iran, Turkey, and Greece.* Revised Edition. Princeton, N.J., 1994.
Mango, Andrew. *Turkey: The Challenge of a New Role.* Westport, Conn., 1994.
McDowall, David. *A Modern History of the Kurds.* London, 1996.
Tapper, Richard, ed. *Islam in Modern Turkey: Religion, Politics, and Literature in a Secular State.* London, 1991.
Zürcher, Erik J. *Turkey: A Modern History.* London, 1993.

TURKMENISTAN
See Appendix 2

TURNER, FREDERICK JACKSON
(*b.* 14 November 1861; *d.* 14 March 1932)

Eminent American historian who formulated the "frontier thesis" at the 1893 meeting of the American Historical Association in Chicago. Turner was born in Wisconsin and received his Ph.D. from the Johns Hopkins University (1890). Responding to the 1890 census that suggested that the frontier had disappeared, the University of Wisconsin (1888–1910) historian claimed that the United States' economic success, political democracy, and vigorous individualism had been based on the "magic fountain" of an expanding frontier and westward expansion. Turner's thesis on the vital connection between expansion and American democracy, and his corresponding argument that the frontier's disappearance necessitated "a vigorous foreign policy" and "the extension of U.S. influence to outlying islands and adjoining countries," helped shape the foreign policy views of many U.S. leaders, including Presidents Theodore Roosevelt and Woodrow Wilson. In 1910 Turner moved to Harvard University, and in 1933 he posthumously won the Pulitzer Prize for *The Significance of Sections in American History.*

EDWARD P. CRAPOL

See also Continental Expansion; Roosevelt, Theodore; Wilson, Thomas Woodrow

FURTHER READING

Billington, Ray Allen. *Frederick Jackson Turner: Historian, Scholar, Teacher.* New York, 1973.
Turner, Frederick Jackson. *The Frontier in American History.* New York, 1920.
——— . *The Rise of the New West.* New York, 1906.

TURNER, STANSFIELD

(*b.* 1 December 1923)

Director of the Central Intelligence Agency (CIA) in the administration of President Jimmy Carter. Illinois-born, Stansfield Turner graduated from the U.S. Naval Academy in 1946 and attended Oxford University as a Rhodes Scholar. Rising to the rank of admiral (1955–1975), Turner commanded a mine-sweeper, a destroyer, a guided-missile cruiser, a carrier task group, and the Second Fleet, protecting NATO's southern flank. He also served as president of the Naval War College (1972–1974). President Jimmy Carter named him director of the CIA, a position he held throughout Carter's administration (1977–1981). As director, Turner sought improvements in worldwide intelligence collection—through the use of advanced satellites and other technical means—while downgrading covert activities. After leaving the government, he became a lecturer, writer, and television commentator on intelligence issues, counter-terrorism, military strategy, and foreign affairs. A dominant theme in his commentary has been the need to improve intelligence collection for use against terrorist groups, especially by means of traditional espionage methods.

LOCH K. JOHNSON

See also Carter, James Earl; Central Intelligence Agency; Intelligence

FURTHER READING

Johnson, Loch K. *America's Secret Power: The CIA in a Democratic Society.* New York, 1989.
Turner, Stansfield. *Secrecy and Democracy: The CIA in Transition.* Boston, 1985.
——— . *Terrorism and Democracy.* Boston, 1991.

TYLER, JOHN

(*b.* 29 March 1790; *d.* 18 January 1862)

Tenth president of the United States (1841–1845). A member of a politically prominent Virginia family, Tyler was a member of Congress (1817–1821), governor of Virginia (1825–1827), and a U.S. Senator (1827–1836). A Whig who opposed the slave trade but believed slavery should be protected in the states where it was legal, Tyler was his party's vice presidential candidate on the winning ticket headed by William Henry Harrison. When President Harrison died within a month of the inauguration, Tyler became president and insisted that he serve in the fullest sense, not merely act, as president.

His foreign policy agenda was neither narrowly pro-slavery nor exclusively tied to the South's ascendancy in the Union. Tyler was a disciple of James Madison and Thomas Jefferson and believed that territorial and commercial expansion would allay sectional tensions, preserve the Union, and promote national power. Under the guidance of his first secretary of state, Daniel Webster, Tyler settled the Maine boundary dispute and preserved peace with Great Britain through the Webster-Ashburton Treaty. Tyler brought Hawai'i into America's sphere of influence, and he secured the nation's first treaty with China (Treaty of Wangxia [Wanghu]) in 1844. Tyler also settled the Seminole War in Florida and gained congressional approval of Texas's annexation by joint resolution, thus setting the United States on a course toward war with Mexico over the territory.

EDWARD P. CRAPOL

See also China; Hawai'i; Mexico, War with; Slave Trade and Slavery; Wangxia, Treaty of; Webster-Ashburton Treaty

FURTHER READING

Chitwood, Oliver Perry. *John Tyler, Champion of the Old South.* New York, 1939.
Hietala, Thomas R. *Manifest Design: Anxious Aggrandizement in Late Jacksonian America.* Ithaca, N.Y., 1985.
Seager, Robert, Jr. *And Tyler Too: A Biography of John and Julia Gardiner Tyler.* New York, 1963.
Tyler, Lyon G. *The Letters and Times of the Tylers.* 3 vols. New York, 1970.

U

UGANDA

Located in Eastern Africa, bordering Kenya, Sudan, Zaire, Burundi, and Rwanda. Uganda offers no intrinsic geopolitical or commercial interests to the United States. However, this is not to suggest that there has been no U.S. involvement in Ugandan affairs since that country's independence from the United Kingdom on 9 October 1962. Indeed, the history of relations between the United States and Uganda has been a mix of conflict and cooperation.

During its first decade of independence under Milton Obote, Uganda's official foreign policy was one of non-alignment. Nevertheless it did maintain close relations with Great Britain, often supported Western policy vis-á-vis the Soviet bloc, and made the United States its second largest trading partner. Yet Obote also interpreted nonalignment to mean "anti-imperialist" attacks on certain U.S. and other Western policies in the Third World, particularly the U.S. intervention in Vietnam.

Previously a pillar of the Obote regime, on 25 January 1971 Major General Idi Amin staged a coup d'etat to forestall his imminent arrest for financial irregularities relating to defense spending, unauthorized aid to the Anya Nya rebels of southern Sudan after the Obote regime had upgraded relations with the government of Jaffar Numayri in Khartoum, and an impending investigation of Amin's role in the murder of his sole rival in the Ugandan military, Brigadier Acap Oboya. After his assumption to power, Amin discarded both the policies of nonalignment and socialism.

The new Ugandan regime established relations with South Africa, significantly improved relations with Israel, and expelled Soviet advisors. Amin's reorientation of Ugandan foreign policy, placing Kampala firmly in the Western camp, led to the Nixon administration's quick recognition of the new regime. By 1973, the United States had replaced Great Britain as Kampala's foremost commercial interest. This warming of official U.S.-Ugandan relations did not last long, however. As Amin sought to raise Uganda's profile in the international community, he established close ties not only with staunch U.S. allies in the Muslim world like Saudi Arabia, but also with U.S. antagonists such as Libya and the Palestinian Liberation Organization, which both had military advisors operating with the Ugandan military as early as February 1972.

Amin's increasingly belligerent foreign policy, coupled with egregious human rights violations within Uganda, forced the United States to take the extraordinary step of closing its Kampala embassy in November 1973. The Nixon administration reportedly was also irritated with Amin's repeated telegrams to the president regarding Watergate. This break in diplomatic relations did not affect commercial relations and the United States continued to import Ugandan coffee, and U.S. firms proceeded to furnish aircraft to the Ugandan armed forces and intelligence services. Despite the deterioration in U.S.-Ugandan relations, the Nixon, Ford, and Carter administrations pursued this policy in an effort to challenge increased Soviet activity in East Africa. Commercial relations remained intact until October 1978 when the U.S. Congress initiated a trade embargo against Uganda to punish Amin for his association with terrorist organizations and for the brutal excesses of the regime. By mid-1978 it had become apparent that hundreds of thousands of Ugandans had been murdered by organs of the Amin regime. At the end of Amin's eight-year reign, approximately 300,000 Ugandans had lost their lives to political violence.

In 1978 Amin's grip on Uganda began to weaken. When vice-president Mustafa Adrisi was seriously injured in a mysterious car accident, troops dissatisfied with Amin and loyal to Adrisi began to mutiny. Declaring that his arch-rival Julius Nyerre, president of Tanzania, was responsible for the unrest, Amin's military invaded Tanzania and annexed a section of that country's territory. Nyerre counterattacked with his own military and an amalgam of Ugandan military officers in exile under the banner of the Uganda National Liberation Army (UNLA). The UNLA took Kampala in April 1979 and Amin was forced to flee to Jeddah, Saudi Arabia. The United States played no role in Amin's departure from Uganda but welcomed the coup due to Amin's increasingly friendly relations with Libya and the Soviet Union.

Immediately following Amin's overthrow, the Carter administration restored official relations between the two capitals and, in a humanitarian gesture, Washington provided emergency financial assistance to the interim government of Godfrey Binaisa. The Binaisa government lasted only eleven months until the return of Milton Obote in May 1980. Shunning his previous preference for nonalignment, Obote declared a pro-Western foreign policy. Consequently, Washington increased agricultural assistance to Kampala. During the early 1980s routine economic development assistance and trade relations underpinned stable relations between Washington and Kampala. However, the continuing struggle between the Obote regime and the antigovernment forces of the National Resistance Movement (NRM) began to strain U.S.-Ugandan relations in July 1984. At that time, the U.S. Department of State sharply criticized the Obote government for the massacre of between 100,000 and 200,000 Ugandans in the Lowero Triangle region of the country (central Uganda).

Obote was overthrown in 1985 by General Tito Lutwa Okello, who established a military government. The Okello regime, however, did not last long. Okello's coup d'etat had so weakened the institutions of the Ugandan state that even the military government was unable to withstand the consistent NRM assault. After barely six months in power, the Okello regime was deposed and NRM leader Yoweri Museveni claimed the presidency on 29 January 1986. Upon assumption of power, the Museveni government articulated a foreign policy that emphasized pan-African cooperation in foreign affairs and economic relations. In practice this policy involved supporting initiatives that would establish closer commercial and developmental relations in eastern and southern Africa. The Museveni government placed great importance on the role of such regional institutions as the Preferential Trade Area for Eastern and Southern Africa in fostering economic cooperation and development. Nevertheless, the bulk of Uganda's trade remained directed toward the United States and Western Europe.

The United States welcomed the return of stability to Uganda provided by Museveni and the NRM with first the resumption of and then incremental increases in Washington's aid program. The NRM government successfully stabilized Uganda's political environment, and in 1995 the government introduced a new constitution. That same year Ugandans voted in their first presidential and parliamentary elections.

In the mid-1990s Uganda remained by all measures one of the poorest countries in the world, but U.S. economic development aid made a considerable impact on the country's macroeconomic health. For example, in 1993–1994 the Ugandan economy grew at 4.5 percent, somewhat slower than the 7.1 percent registered for 1992–1993, but still healthy. With U.S. encouragement, the Ugandan government freed prices and the exchange rate, removed nontariff barriers to trade, lowered import tariffs, implemented a new investment code, and reformed import procedures. According to a 1996 report by the United States Agency for International Development (AID), Uganda's transition to a free enterprise constitutional democracy was almost complete. The Clinton administration set out a number of economic development–related objectives for Uganda in the last half of the 1990s in an effort to consolidate and build on Kampala's progress in the early part of the decade. AID was charged with helping to increase agricultural productivity and income in rural Uganda. Also on Washington's list of priorities was increasing the quality and efficiency of Uganda's educational infrastructure. In addition, AID worked to improve the life expectancy of the Ugandan population, which ranked the lowest in the world at 37 years and with the continuing HIV crisis was expected to fall to $31\frac{1}{2}$ years by 2010. Finally, AID endeavored to rehabilitate Uganda's environment and biodiversity in targeted areas in an effort to attract tourism to the country.

In the latter half of the 1990s, however, Washington's interests in Uganda may no longer be confined to issues relating to economic development and humanitarian relief. In sharp comparison to the Cold War period, during which Uganda was insignificant to U.S. efforts in challenging Soviet influence in sub-Saharan Africa, Uganda may indeed retain an important role in U.S. Africa policy. Relations between the United States and Sudan deteriorated in the mid-1990s due to the Bashir regime's support for international terrorism. Consequently, some U.S. officials and observers suggested that Uganda, along with other states bordering Sudan, should become Washington's partners as regional counterweights to Khartoum.

STEVEN A. COOK

See also Africa; Tanzania, United Republic of

FURTHER READING
Byrnes, Rita M., ed. *Uganda: A Country Study*. Washington, D.C., 1992.
Hansen, Holger Bernt, and Michael Twaddle, eds. *Uganda Now: Between Decay and Development*. London, 1988.
Jorgensen, Jan Jelmert. *Uganda: A Modern History*. New York, 1981.
Omara-Otunnu, Ami. *Politics and the Military in Uganda, 1890–1985*. New York, 1987.
United States House of Representatives. *Hearings on United States-Uganda Relations*. 95th Cong., 2nd sess. Washington, D.C., 1978.

UKRAINE

Located in Eastern Europe, bordering the Black Sea, Moldova, Romania, Hungary, Slovakia, Poland, Belarus, and Russia, the second largest country after Russia, in all of Europe. Direct U.S. foreign relations with Ukraine were virtually nonexistent both before and during Ukraine's incorporation into the Soviet Union. Ukraine regained its independence with its Declaration of State Sovereignty 16 July 1991; its Declaration of Independence 24 August 1991; and overwhelmingly passed its Independence Referendum on 1 December 1991. The

United States recognized Ukrainian independence on 25 December 1991, and established open and formal diplomatic relations on 23 January 1992. Two months later President George Bush appointed Roman Popadiuk as the first U.S. ambassador to Ukraine.

From 1991 to 1993, the United States pursued a "denuclearize Ukraine first" approach, and to this end established a policy of withholding any significant aid to Ukraine unless it relinquished its nuclear arsenal. In December 1991, Ukraine announced it would remove all its tactical nuclear weapons to Russia for destruction by 1 July 1992. Ukraine halted the shipments in March 1992, claiming Russia was not destroying the transferred weapons. The shipments resumed after the United States intervened and pressured Ukraine to continue the transfer. Ukraine completed the removal of all tactical nuclear weapons two months prior to the promised July withdrawal. The United States and Ukraine, along with Belarus, Kazakhstan, and Russia signed onto the Lisbon Protocol on 22 May 1992, making each country individually a party to the START I Treaty. The United States desired the Verkhovna Rada (Ukrainian parliament) to ratify START I and accede to the Non-Proliferation Treaty (NPT) as soon as possible. This policy resonated well with Ukraine's executive branch but failed to gain the cooperation of the Rada. The Rada insisted on first gaining certain security guarantees and financial assistance for weapons removal and economic stabilization programs, fearing that without the weapons their territorial integrity might be threatened.

In December 1992 and again a few months later, the United States promised $175 million in Nunn-Lugar funds for weapons dismantlement if the Rada would ratify START I and accede to the NPT. Ukraine, however, estimated its weapons dismantlement costs would run to $3.8 billion and their country would need more substantial assistance. On 3 March 1993, U.S. policymakers pressured the International Monetary Fund (IMF) to withhold $1.1 billion in pending loans unless Ukraine managed to curb its spiraling inflation.

In 1993, U.S. policy towards Ukraine noticeably shifted from pressuring Ukraine into desired behavior, to a two-track approach of moving Ukraine towards denuclearization, while simultaneously assisting their country in building democratic and economic stability. Strobe Talbott, then coordinator of U.S. policy towards the Former Soviet Union (FSU), visited Kiev in 1993 to announce that Washington wanted to "turn over a new leaf in its relations with Kiev," and offered U.S. assistance as mediator in Ukraine's greatest security concern: Ukrainian-Russian disputes.

On 18 November 1993 the Ukrainian Rada ratified START I with thirteen conditions, effectively rejecting Article 5 of the Lisbon Protocol that had committed Ukraine to acceding to the NPT. It took the United States to break the triangular nuclear stalemate that had evolved between the United States, Ukraine, and Russia. Extending to Ukraine an understanding of its security needs, the United States promised to confirm its obligations under the Conference for Security and Cooperation in Europe (CSCE) respecting their "independence, sovereignty, and existing borders," while also promising to refrain from using force, threat of force, and economic pressure to gain political ends at the expense of Ukraine's sovereignty. The United States further confirmed its obligations under the NPT to demand immediate action by the United Nations Security Council (UNSC) should Ukraine be threatened or attacked with nuclear weapons. The United States made these promises contingent upon Ukraine acceding to the NPT.

This new "carrot-and-stick" approach proved advantageous to U.S. security interests in the region when on 14 January 1994, President Clinton successfully brokered the Trilateral Agreement between the United States, Ukraine, and Russia, providing for the transfer of nearly two hundred Ukrainian nuclear warheads to Russia for dismantlement, Russia returning nuclear fuel rods to Ukraine, and the United States providing $60 million to carry out the agreement. The Trilateral Agreement further served as the nuclear watershed allowing the Rada to ratify START I on 3 February 1994, with the previously imposed conditions removed.

The United States also spearheaded NATO's Partnership for Peace Initiative (PFP) aimed at slowly opening NATO's doors to East European membership. Ukraine signed the agreement to join the PFP on 8 February 1994. Warm relations continuing to grow, Ukrainian President Kravchuk came to Washington, D.C., 4 March 1994 where President Clinton pledged the United States would double its aid package to Ukraine that year to $700 million. The aid was in recognition of Ukraine fulfilling its promise to eliminate 176 long-range missiles and 1,800 nuclear warheads. President Clinton stated, "Ukraine can play a great stabilizing role in the future," and strongly reaffirmed U.S. support for Ukraine's "independence, sovereignty, and territory." Two days later the first trainload of nuclear warheads from Ukraine arrived in Russia for dismantlement. Finally ending the nuclear tango between Ukraine and the United States, Ukraine acceded to the NPT in November 1994.

While the nuclear debate has been at the forefront of U.S. relations with Ukraine, the United States also has sought to prevent military threats, encourage the growth of democracy and economic reform, and has sought to promote regional stability in its policy towards Ukraine. To this end, Ukraine received Overseas Private Investment Company (OPIC) investment guarantees in May 1992; was extended Most-Favored-Nation trading status on 22 June 1992; saw the arrival of the first fifty Peace Corps volunteers in November 1992; received a $30 million pledge to improve safety at Ukraine's nuclear power plants; and had U.S. investors in Ukraine financially assisted by the Export-Import Bank.

NATALIE MELNYCZUK

See also International Monetary Fund; Nuclear Nonproliferation; Russia and the Soviet Union; Strategic Arms Reduction Treaties

FURTHER READING

Woehrel, Steven. *Ukraine.* U.S. Library of Congress, Congressional Research Service: Washington, D.C., January, 1994.

Woolf, Amy F., and Theodore W. Galdi. *Nuclear Weapons in the Former Soviet Union: Location, Command, and Control.* U.S. Library of Congress, Congressional Research Service: Washington, D.C., December, 1993.

UN

See United Nations

UNCONDITIONAL SURRENDER

The concept of a defeated war power surrendering to the victor absolutely and without negotiated conditions was specifically applicable to the losing side in World War II. Every international war in American history prior to World War II ended with a negotiated settlement. In each case the defeated power conceded territory or accepted some restrictions on its status in order to bring the war to an end. But the losing government itself remained in power. For example, Great Britain in 1783 had to recognize the independence of the United States within certain territorial boundaries. Mexico in 1848 had to relinquish territory to the United States but received monetary compensation. Spain in 1899 had to grant independence to Cuba and cede Puerto Rico and the Philippines to the United States. Germany in 1918 at the end of World War I accepted an armistice on condition that the peace settlement be consistent with President Woodrow Wilson's Fourteen Points and related conditions.

But afterwards many Germans, above all Adolf Hitler, claimed that the conditions offered had been violated in the Versailles Peace Treaty of 1919 and that Germany had been tricked and betrayed into relinquishing the power to continue the war. Hitler, coming to power in 1933, freed Germany from the restrictions of the 1919 settlement and then started World War II. President Franklin D. Roosevelt and his advisers in World War II were determined that this time Germany would not be able to claim that the conditions of peace had been violated. This time there would be unconditional surrender.

Lessons of the past mingled with a fear in 1942–1943 that the Soviet Union might make a separate peace with Germany. By pledging unconditional surrender, the United States and Great Britain could reassure the Soviets that there was no chance of their being left to fight alone. Thus at the conference at Casablanca, Morocco, on 24 January 1943, Roosevelt, supported by British Prime Minister Winston S. Churchill, called for "unconditional surrender by Germany, Italy, and Japan. That…does not mean the destruction of the population of Germany, Italy, or Japan, but it does mean the destruction of the philosophies in those countries which are based on conquest and the subjugation of other people."

When Italy surrendered in September 1943 its government, having ousted Benito Mussolini, was permitted to continue in existence, and the Italian people as a whole were treated with sympathy. In May 1945 Germany did surrender unconditionally and had to accept several years of military occupation. Whether Japan should be offered, as a condition, the right to maintain the institution of the emperor was sharply debated within the United States in the summer of 1945. Only after the atomic bombs were dropped on Japan in August 1945 were the Japanese told the emperor could remain but under the control of the victors. Otherwise, the surrender of Japan of 2 September 1945 was unconditional.

A strong argument against unconditional surrender as a general policy, advanced during World War II and since, is that it deprives the enemy of hope and thereby prolongs war. It also saddles the victor with the expense and responsibility of governing the defeated nation for as long as it takes to create a new regime. Critics also argue that unconditional surrender overlooks the possibility that today's enemy may be tomorrow's ally.

In the Korean War the U.S. government briefly contemplated imposing unconditional surrender on North Korea in order to force the unification of North and South, but after the militarily punishing intervention of the People's Republic of China, the United States realized that the costs and risks of such an objective were too high. The war between the United States and North Vietnam ended with the negotiated Paris Accords of 1973, not with surrender. The Gulf War of 1990–1991 led to the defeat of Saddam Hussein's Iraq, the expulsion of Iraq from Kuwait, and other restrictions imposed by the victors—but not to unconditional surrender.

GADDIS SMITH

See also Churchill, Winston Leonard Spencer; Germany; Great Britain; Japan; Roosevelt, Franklin Delano; World War II

FURTHER READING

Armstrong, Anne. *Unconditional Surrender: the Impact of the Casablanca Policy upon World War.* New Brunswick, 1961. Reissued Westport, Conn., 1974.

Kecskemeti, Paul. *Strategic Surrender: the Politics of Victory and Defeat.* Stanford, Calif., 1958. Reissued New York, 1964.

O'Connor, Raymond G. *Diplomacy for Victory: FDR and Unconditional Surrender.* New York, 1971.

UNCTAD

See United Nations Conference on Trade and Development

UNDERWOOD ACT

See Tariffs

UNITED ARAB EMIRATES

A federation of seven Arab sheikdoms, located in southeast Arabia on the southern end of the Persian Gulf and the Gulf of Oman, which possesses 10 percent of the world's proven oil reserves. The seven emirates are Abu Dhabi, Aiman, Dubai, Fujairah, Ras Al-Khaimah, Sharjah, and Umm Al-Qaiwain. Since proclaiming its independence from Great Britain on 2 August 1971, the UAE—headed by the ruler of Abu Dhubai, which is the largest and most populous of the seven emirates—has generally maintained friendly political and close economic ties with the United States. Washington opened an embassy in Abu Dhabi in May 1972 and a full-time U.S. ambassador presented his credentials to the UAE two years later. By the early 1990s, the United States had become one of the UAE's major trading partners. Nevertheless, diplomatic relations between the United States and the UAE have suffered occasional strains. After the British withdrawal in 1971, Washington kept silent when its client across the Gulf, the shah of Iran, occupied three small, strategically located islands (the Greater and Lesser Tunbs and Abu Musa) belonging to the sheikdom of Sharjah. Abu Dhabi participated in the 1973–1974 Arab oil embargo against the United States because of Washington's support for Israel during the October 1973 Arab-Israeli War. The UAE also broke relations with Cairo after Egypt signed the Camp David-brokered peace treaty with Israel in 1979. During the Iran-Iraq War, the UAE was one of the few Arab states that maintained stable relations with Tehran, which had broken diplomatic relations with the United States. Unlike neighboring Oman, the UAE did not sign on to the Carter Doctrine and throughout the 1980s refused to cooperate militarily with the United States.

In the 1990s, however, the UAE sought to nurture close security relations with Washington. Iraqi accusations that the UAE and Kuwait were violating OPEC oil quotas, prompted a change in UAE policy. In July 1990, alarmed by Iraq's increasingly aggressive stance, the UAE agreed to conduct a joint military exercise in the Gulf with U.S. forces. After Iraq's invasion of Kuwait in August and during the Desert Shield and Desert Storm operations, the UAE actively assisted U.S. and allied military operations by offering military facilities to Coalition forces, provided $1 billion in war assistance, and contributed combat forces to the 10,000 frontline troops provided by the Gulf Cooperation Council (GCC). After Iraq's eviction from Kuwait, the UAE continued to grant the United States access to military facilities. Washington, in turn, sold to the UAE substantial amounts of sophisticated military equipment, including HAWK missiles. By the mid-1990s, the UAE had come to favor a high-profile U.S. military presence in the Gulf owing to its fear of direct aggression by Iraq, or domination by Iran which has refused to recognize Sharjah's shared sovereignty over the three Gulf islands. At the end of 1995, the Clinton administration began discussions with the UAE about propositioning a third heavy brigade of guard forces to support those already accepted by Kuwait and Qatar.

JEFFREY A. LEFEBVRE

See also Carter Doctrine; Gulf War of 1990–1991; Iran; Iran-Iraq War; Iraq; Oil and Foreign Policy

FURTHER READING

Cordesman, Anthony. *The Gulf and the West: Strategic Relations and Military Realities.* Boulder, Colo., 1988.

Gause, F. Gregory. *Oil Monarchies: Domestic and Security Challenges in the Arab Gulf States.* New York, 1994.

Graz, Liesl. *The Turbulent Gulf.* London, 1992.

Kelly, John Barrett. *Arabia, the Gulf, and the West.* New York, 1980.

Twinam, Joseph Wright. *The Gulf, Cooperation, and the Council: An American Perspective.* Washington, D.C., 1992.

UNITED KINGDOM

See Great Britain

UNITED NATIONS

An international organization of sovereign nations founded in 1945, with its main headquarters in New York. According to its charter, the United Nations's (UN) purposes include maintaining international peace and security; developing friendly relations among nations; achieving international cooperation concerning economic, social, cultural, and humanitarian problems; and promoting respect for human rights and fundamental freedoms for all. The UN's mandate is vast; it covers all subjects of international relations. Membership is open to all "peace-loving states" that accept the obligations of the UN Charter and that are judged by the organization to be able and willing to fulfill these obligations.

Although an overwhelming majority of Americans have consistently favored U.S. membership in the United Nations, the functions that the United Nations should perform have often been a matter of debate and some of its activities have been sharply criticized.

Origins

The UN was created at the United Nations Conference on International Organization (UNCIO) which met in San Francisco from 25 April to 26 June 1945 and concluded with the signing of the Charter. The UN Charter entered into force on 24 October 1945 when it had been ratified by the five states that were designated as permanent members of the Security Council—China, France, the Union of Soviet Socialist Republics, the United Kingdom, and the United States—and a majority of the other forty-six original signatories of the charter.

The origins of the United Nations, however, can be traced to the Atlantic Charter, a declaration that President Franklin Delano Roosevelt and Prime Minister Winston S. Churchill issued in August 1941 outlining the principles that they felt should undergird the postwar international order. When the governments of the United States, China, the Soviet Union, the United Kingdom, and twenty-two other countries signed the Declaration of the United Nations on 1 January 1942, support for these principles was broadened. Although it was not foreseen at the time, the name of the declaration would be transferred to the new organization.

The United States played a preeminent role in the development of the UN. Within the U.S. Department of State, planning for the creation of a broadly based, general international organization began in June 1942. The Advisory Committee on Post-War Planning, which had been established in April of that year, created the Special Subcommittee on International Organization, chaired by Sumner Welles. This subcommittee reviewed the past experience of international organizations and began drafting documents for a new one. A proposal was completed by March 1943. Secretary of State Cordell Hull began informal conversations with individual members of Congress in the Spring of 1943. Assuring congressional support was particularly important in view of the Senate's refusal to give its advice and consent to the ratification of the League of Nations Covenant. The results of the advisory committee's work on international organizations to that point were reported to the president in June 1943.

One of the first questions that had been addressed was whether efforts should be devoted to reviving the League of Nations or creating a new international organization. Continuing the League of Nations was widely seen as undesirable. The League was associated with the failure to stop the collapse of the world economy in the 1930s and to prevent the outbreak of World War II. Moreover, neither the United States nor the Soviet Union were members of the League, and the participation of both states was regarded as essential to the success of a post-World War II organization. The United States never joined the League, and although the Soviet Union joined in 1934, it was expelled in 1939 after its attack on Poland. Nevertheless, the planners drew heavily on the League experience, and the mandate and structure of the United Nations closely resemble the League's. Carrying the linkage further, when the League was dissolved in April 1946, its assets, including the Palais des Nations—the League's headquarters in Geneva—were transferred to the UN.

Deliberations within the Advisory Committee continued, and by August 1943 a draft UN Charter had been prepared. Consultations with members of Congress also continued, and the groundwork was laid for U.S. participation in a broadly based, general international organization. In September 1943, a group of Republican leaders meeting on Mackinaw Island, Michigan assured bipartisan support by endorsing U.S. participation in a postwar international organization, and later that month the House of Representatives adopted a resolution introduced by Senator J. William Fulbright favoring the creation of an international organization and the participation of the United States in such an organization. On 30 October 1943, at the meeting of the Allied foreign ministers in Moscow, Secretary Hull obtained the agreement of the foreign ministers of China, the USSR, and the United Kingdom to jointly sign on behalf of their governments a U.S. draft on general security that declared the following:

> That they recognize the necessity of establishing at the earliest practicable date a general international organization, based on the principle of the sovereign equality of all peace-loving states, and open to membership by all such states, large and small, for the maintenance of international peace and security.

With this declaration and commitment as a springboard, planning within the United States and among the Allies intensified.

When there were disagreements among the Allies, the United States's position almost always prevailed. The United States felt that the new international organization should have a broad mandate that would include taking action to promote international cooperation to solve economic, social, and humanitarian problems and to encour-

U.S. AMBASSADORS TO THE UNITED NATIONS

Ambassador	Period of Appointment	Administration
Edward R. Stettinius, Jr.	1945–1946[1]	Truman
Warren R. Austin	1947[2]–1953	Truman
Henry Cabot Lodge, Jr.	1953–1960	Eisenhower
James J. Wadsworth	1960–1961	Eisenhower
Adlai E. Stevenson	1961–1965	Kennedy
		L. Johnson
Arthur J. Goldberg	1965–1968	L. Johnson
George W. Ball	1968	L. Johnson
James Russell Wiggins	1968–1969	L. Johnson
Charles W. Yost	1969–1971	Nixon
George Bush	1971–1973	Nixon
John A. Scali	1973–1975	Nixon
		Ford
Daniel P. Moynihan	1975–1976	Ford
William W. Scranton	1976–1977	Ford
Andrew J. Young	1977–1979	Carter
Donald F. McHenry	1979–1981	Carter
Jeane J. Kirkpatrick	1981–1985	Reagan
Vernon A. Walters	1985–1989	Reagan
		Bush
Thomas R. Pickering	1989–1992	Bush
Edward J. Perkins	1992–1993	Bush
Madeleine K. Albright	1993–Present	Clinton

[1]Attended the first meeting of the Security Council at London on this date; in lieu of a letter of credence, submitted to the Acting Secretary-General of the United Nations a copy of his letter of designation dated 21 Dec. 1945.
[2]Letter of credence sent by telegram to the Secretariat of the United Nations on this date.

Sources: *Principal Officers of the Department of State and United States Chiefs of Missions.* ©1991 by Office of the Historian, Bureau of Public Affairs, Washington, D.C.; *The U.S. Government Manual*, Annual. Washington, D.C.

age respect for human rights. The U.S. position was grounded in the belief that healthy economic and social conditions were essential to the maintenance of peace; that the runaway inflation in Germany had contributed to the rise of Adolf Hitler; and that any government that violated human rights as that of Nazi Germany did would be a threat to international peace. The Soviet Union preferred that the UN's mandate should be narrowly confined to security issues, but ultimately acquiesced to the American view. In early 1943, Prime Minister Churchill indicated that he favored establishing several regional organizations that would function under some world institution. Although President Roosevelt may have favored a regional approach for a while, in the end the United States pushed for and won acceptance of a worldwide approach, primarily because U.S. planners believed that this approach was the one most likely to assure U.S. participation in the new organization.

The planning culminated in the Dumbarton Oaks Conversations, which were held from 21 August through 7 October 1944, and which included the United States, the United Kingdom, the Soviet Union, and China. The U.S. "Tentative Proposals for a General International Organization" provided the basic framework for the discussions. On the final day of the conversations the four governments approved the "Proposals for the Establishment of a General International Organization."

The Dumbarton Oaks proposals had various gaps. Among these was how voting should be conducted in the Security Council. At the Yalta Conference in February 1945, President Roosevelt proposed that unanimity among the five permanent members be required for decisions on all non-procedural issues. This so-called Yalta formula was accepted by Prime Minister Churchill and Marshall Joseph Stalin and incorporated in the Dumbarton Oaks proposals. At Yalta the three governments also

---

SECRETARIES GENERAL
OF THE UNITED NATIONS

Secretary General	Nation	Dates
Trygve Lie	Norway	1946–1952
Dag Hammarskjöld	Sweden	1953–1961
U Thant	Burma	1961–1971
Kurt Waldheim	Austria	1972–1981
Javier Pérez de Cuéllar	Peru	1982–1991
Boutros Boutros-Ghali	Egypt	1992–Present

Source: *The U.S. Government Manual*

---

agreed to convene the United Nations Conference on International Organization and to invite China and France to join them in sponsoring the conference. During the San Francisco conference the Dumbarton Oaks proposals were modified primarily in response to the pressure from smaller countries that argued that they should have greater scope and authority in the United Nations, but the basic features of the proposals remained intact.

Nor has the UN Charter changed very much since it entered into force in 1945. Only two of the articles have been amended, those specifying the size of the Security Council and the Economic and Social Council. The Security Council was increased from eleven to fifteen members, and the Economic and Social Council from eighteen to twenty-seven and then fifty-four members. Both articles were amended in response to the most significant change in the UN, the increase in its membership from the original fifty-one members to more than 180 in the 1990s. This change has dramatically altered the character and functioning of the United Nations.

Structure

The UN Charter created a structurally complex organization. There are six principal organs: the General Assembly; the Security Council; the Economic and Social Council; the Trusteeship Council; the International Court of Justice; and the Secretariat. In addition, the charter permits the establishment of subsidiary organs, and it requires that the various specialized agencies, established by intergovernmental agreement and having responsibilities in economic, social, cultural, health, and related fields "shall be brought into relationship with the United Nations...." Over time, the UN's structure has expanded so that in the 1990s the United Nations system—as the ensemble of organizations came to be called—consisted of fifteen specialized agencies, two autonomous affiliated organizations, fifteen organizations created by and reporting to the General Assembly, six functional and five regional commissions, and some sev-

enty-five special committees. The International Atomic Energy Agency is an affiliated organization. The Food and Agricultural Organization, the International Labor Organization, the International Monetary Fund, the United Nations Educational, Cultural, and Scientific Organization, the World Bank Group, and the World Health Organization are major specialized agencies.

The General Assembly is at the hub of the UN system. It consists of all members of the UN, and it "may discuss any questions or any matters within the scope of the present charter or relating to the powers and functions of any organs provided for in the present charter...." Senator Arthur H. Vandenberg of Michigan, who played a crucial role at San Francisco in inserting and preserving this broad mandate, foresaw that it would enable the General Assembly to become the "town meeting of the world." Senator Vandenberg's vision has been amply fulfilled, the General Assembly's agendas provide a nearly complete catalog to the issues of post–World War II international relations.

The General Assembly can initiate studies and make recommendations. It receives and considers reports from other organs, approves the budget of the organization, apportions the expenses of the organization among the members, and elects members of other bodies. Each member state has one vote and may have up to five representatives in the assembly.

Decisions in the General Assembly on "important questions," require a two-thirds majority of the members that are present and voting. These questions include recommendations relating to peace and security, specified elections of other bodies, the admission of new members, suspensions of the privileges of membership, and expulsion. Decisions on "other questions" require only a majority of members present and voting. This includes deciding whether additional categories of questions should require a two-thirds majority.

The General Assembly meets annually. Sessions normally start the third Tuesday in September and end in mid- to late- December. Special sessions are convoked by the secretary-general at the request of the Security Council or a majority of the UN's members. By 1994 the assembly had held nine emergency sessions and eighteen special sessions.

The Security Council has primary responsibility for the UN's functions with respect to the maintenance of peace and security. In recognition of this, the General Assembly may not make recommendations with regard to disputes or situations that the Security Council is considering unless the Council requests it to take action.

The Security Council consists of fifteen members, the five permanent members designated in the charter—China, France, the Russian Federation (as the successor to the USSR), the United Kingdom, and the United

States—and ten members elected by the General Assembly for two-year terms. Decisions on "procedural matters" require nine affirmative votes, and decisions on "other matters" require nine affirmative votes including the concurring votes of the permanent members. The question of whether or not a decision concerns a procedural matter is regarded as an important issue and is thus subject to the veto.

The Security Council may investigate disputes, or situations that may give rise to disputes and may recommend methods or procedures of adjustment. The Security Council "shall determine the existence of any threat to the peace, breach of the peace, or act of aggression and shall make recommendations, or decide what measures shall be taken…to maintain or restore international peace and security." The council can order the severance of diplomatic relations and economic sanctions, and it can authorize the use of military force. According to the charter, the Security Council's decisions are binding on all UN member states.

The UN's structure differs from the League's in the clear primacy given to the Security Council with respect to the maintenance of peace and security; the League Covenant was less clear on this point. It also differs in allowing majority voting decisions in the League Assembly and Council required the agreement of all members represented at the meeting.

The UN's Economic and Social Council is also a structural innovation in relation to the League. Consisting of fifty-four members elected by the General Assembly for three-year terms, it is responsible for stimulating and coordinating the economic, social, and humanitarian work of the UN and its specialized agencies and affiliated bodies.

The Trusteeship Council was created to oversee the administration of the trust territories. By 1994, with the termination of all eleven trust territories, its responsibilities had vanished.

The International Court of Justice (ICJ) is the principal judicial organ of the United Nations. Its statute was based on that of the League of Nations Permanent Court of International Justice and is an integral part of the UN Charter. The court consists of fifteen members elected by absolute majorities in the General Assembly and the Security Council for nine-year terms from a list nominated by national groups in the Permanent Court of Arbitration or if such groups do not exist national bodies functioning under the same procedures. A third of the membership of the court is elected every three years.

All members of the UN are automatically parties to the statute of the ICJ. The General Assembly and the Security Council may request advisory opinions on any legal question from the ICJ. The court may hear cases that parties refer to it, on issues for which it is given jurisdiction under the UN Charter or other treaties or conventions that are in force. In addition, states may accept the compulsory jurisdiction of the court with respect to specified legal issues. As of 1994, fewer than sixty states had accepted the compulsory jurisdiction of the court. The United States accepted compulsory jurisdiction in 1946 but withdrew its acceptance in 1986.

The Secretariat administers the UN's programs. It is headed by the secretary-general, who is elected by the General Assembly on the recommendation of the Security Council. The secretary-general is the UN's chief administrative officer. Under Article 99 of the Charter, "the secretary-general may bring to the attention of the Security Council any matter which in his opinion may threaten the maintenance of international peace and security." The secretary-general must make an annual report to the General Assembly on the work of the organization. In the 1990s some 29,000 international civil servants served under the secretary-general's direction at the UN headquarters in New York, the UN offices in Geneva and Vienna, and elsewhere throughout the world.

Political Dynamics of UN Decision-Making

The General Assembly, the Security Council, and the secretary-general have been the UN's dominant components. Interactions among these three principal organs and actions within the assembly and the council have defined the UN's history and role in international affairs. These interactions and actions have both reflected and shaped the broad currents of the post World War II era. From the UN's first days, issues linked with the Cold War, such as Iran and Korea, were notable themes. By the mid-1960s, issues that had North-South dimensions, especially decolonization and development, became at least equally salient. Gradually, such global issues as those involving population, food and hunger, the environment, refugees, and human rights gained in prominence.

During the Cold War, decisions in the Security Council were frequently blocked because of the requirement that the permanent members concur. Almost all issues found the United States and its allies on the opposite side from the Soviet Union and its allies. This not only obstructed actions relating to the maintenance of international peace and security but also other actions where the Security Council had a role, such as the admission of new members and the election of the secretary-general.

The paralysis of the Security Council gave added impetus to the inevitable pressure brought by smaller states to increase the role of the General Assembly. The United States contributed to this pressure. In 1950, when the Soviet Union vetoed a recommendation that Trygve Lie be reappointed as secretary-general, the United States backed the extension of his term of office for three years by a General Assembly decision. That same year, when another Soviet veto precluded Security Council action with respect to the prosecution of the Korean War, the United States successfully proposed that the General Assembly adopt the "Uniting for Peace Resolution." This resolution specified procedures under which the assembly could make recommendations to member states with respect to the use of armed force to restore international peace and security even though the issue was on the agenda of the Security Council.

From the first session in 1946 through the sessions in the early 1960s, the United States had considerable enthusiasm for the General Assembly and provided important leadership for it. At first, the United States could generally count on a two-thirds majority backing positions it favored, and on roll call votes it voted with the majority more than half of the time. When mustering a majority became more problematic because of the expansion of the UN's membership and the radicalization of many developing countries, the United States could at least usually find a blocking third to prevent the assembly from taking actions that it opposed, but this capacity too eroded with membership expansion.

In 1960, seventeen states were admitted to the UN, all but one from Africa. Prior to this, the UN's membership had included only five African states, Ethiopia, and South Africa, which were among the original fifty-one members, Morocco and Tunisia, which had been admitted in 1956, and Ghana, which had been admitted in 1957. With the decolonization of Africa, African states came to be the largest single group of UN members. In 1964 African, Asian, and Latin American states joined together to form the Group of Seventy-Seven, which became the UN's preeminent caucus. The Group of Seventy-Seven eventually came to include more than 120 states. Since 1964, the states participating in the Group of Seventy-Seven have comprised more than a two-thirds majority of the UN's members. By the 1970s, cohesion among the Group of Seventy-Seven had increased so that the members were voting identically on more than seventy percent of the roll call votes in each assembly session. The Group of Seventy-Seven had effective control of the Assembly.

When Nikita S. Khrushchev headed his country's delegation to the General Assembly in 1960, he pursued initiatives designed to make the USSR the leader of the non-Western majority in the UN, but the delegates of the developing countries insisted on recasting his initiatives in their own terms. During the quarter of a century from 1964 through the 1980s, the Soviet Union and the Group of Seventy-Seven frequently pursued similar aims in the United Nations, but most of the time, it was the Soviet Union that supported the Group of Seventy-Seven rather than the opposite. The Seventy-Seven could, however,

regularly count on the support of the Soviet Union and its allies in the Warsaw Treaty Organization and the Council for Mutual Economic Assistance.

As the Group of Seventy-Seven asserted its views on issues relating to the world economy, the Arab-Israeli conflict, and South Africa, the United States increasingly found itself in a minority position within the assembly. Starting in the mid-1960s, it voted with the winning side on less than fifty percent of the roll call votes in the General Assembly, and in some sessions the proportion fell to less than twenty percent. Daniel Patrick Moynihan, who was the U.S. Ambassador and Permanent Representative to the UN for eight months in 1975 and 1976 described his experiences in a book evocatively entitled *A Dangerous Place*. In February 1975, prior to his appointment, he had proposed in an article published in *Commentary* that the United States should go into opposition in the United Nations, that the United States should devote itself not to efforts to placate the majority but rather to confrontationally asserting the values of liberty, a strategy he energetically pursued after his appointment. When Andrew Young became U.S. ambassador and permanent representative to the United Nations in the Carter administration, the United States again sought to cooperate with the assembly majority, but without notable success, and when Jeane Kirkpatrick took over as the Reagan administration's UN ambassador and permanent representative, the U.S. posture again became that of confrontation.

This time the confrontation escalated beyond verbal assaults. In 1985 the United States withdrew from a UN specialized agency, the United Nations Educational, Scientific, and Cultural Organization (UNESCO) because of disagreements with the character, direction, and management of the organization's activities. Unlike its previous withdrawal in 1977 from another specialized agency, the International Labor Organization, which seemed certain to be reversed and was in 1980, the withdrawal from UNESCO seemed likely to be longer lasting and has been. The United Kingdom and Singapore followed the United States and also withdrew from UNESCO. The U.S. withdrawal from UNESCO was clearly intended to issue a broader warning. In 1985 the United States began to refuse to pay a significant portion of its assessed contribution to the UN. The U.S. action contributed to the UN system's serious financial difficulties—difficulties, however, that had multiple causes including nonpayment of contributions by other states and substantial inefficiencies. The UN system's financial difficulties continued into the 1990s even after the United States formally reversed its position and accepted the obligation of paying its assessments.

A Soviet step touched off a shift in the political dynamics of decision-making processes in the United Nations. On 17 September 1987, Mikhail Gorbachev published an article in *Pravda* and *Izvestia* that expressed a very different view of the UN from that which the USSR had taken. He argued that modern technology provided unprecedented opportunities to meet human needs but also "put into question the very immortality of the human race." He called upon the UN to take action to protect human rights and ecological security. He stressed that the UN's peacekeeping role should be expanded. He argued for enhanced authority and powers for the UN secretary-general, and maintained that there should be greater reliance on the International Court of Justice.

Soviet behavior in the UN began to give substance to Gorbachev's rhetoric. In an address to the UN General Assembly in December 1988, Gorbachev declared "that the 'use or threat of force' could no longer be an 'instrument of foreign policy.'" He pledged to shift the USSR's military doctrine to a purely defensive stance and to cut half a million Soviet troops as well as many tanks, artillery pieces, and war planes in Eastern Europe. The shift in Soviet policy meant that it was at least conceivable that the UN could play a larger role in international security affairs and the Security Council could function as had been envisaged at San Francisco.

At first the United States was skeptical, but as Soviet behavior increasingly evidenced willingness to cooperate within the UN, the United States began to think more seriously about the possibilities that the UN offered in international security issues. The shift in Soviet and U.S. policies lead to a revitalization of the Security Council. From 1988 through 1994, the Security Council authorized twenty peacekeeping operations, whereas in the preceding thirty-three years it had authorized only eleven. The shift also facilitated the UN's playing a larger role in security issues in other ways; for instance, by helping to resolve the Iran-Iraq War and bring about the Soviet withdrawal from Afghanistan.

In the media's coverage of the UN, attention to the Security Council's activity supplanted that given to the General Assembly's bombast. Moreover, divisions within the assembly began to shift. With the fall of communism in Eastern Europe, the Soviet voting bloc collapsed. As a consequence of the changed Soviet policy, the Soviet Union, and then its successor the Russian Federation, could no longer be counted on to automatically support the Group of Seventy-Seven. As more and more states chose to organize their economies on the basis of market principles and private property, less and less support could be garnered for the collectivist solutions that the assembly proposed in its quest for a New International Economic Order in the 1970s. And as South Africa ended apartheid and held elections with universal participation and as historic steps were taken toward the solution of the Arab-Israeli conflict, the salience of these issues that had frequently consumed the assembly diminished. Nevertheless, in the early 1990s, in roll call votes in the General Assembly the United States continued to find itself in a minority, voting with the winning side less than 25 percent of the time.

As of the mid-1990s, new alignments had yet to emerge in the General Assembly. It was clear that no resolution on an "important" issue could be adopted without broad support in the Group of Seventy-Seven. It was also clear that the United States was uniquely positioned to exercise leadership in the assembly and the Security Council. Its assessed contribution, which was set at twenty-five percent of the UN's regular budget in 1972, was more than twice the next largest, that of Japan, and the United States contributed an even higher proportion to the UN's peacekeeping operations, although increasingly Americans contested this. Because of the importance of its financial contribution for the UN to take significant action, at the least U.S. consent is required. But the United States and the developing country majority continued to be at odds on many issues, as the roll call voting indicates. Thus the assembly often acted more like a pressure group against the United States than a planning or legislative body including the United States.

Secretaries-general also have been important factors in the political dynamics of the United Nations. As of 1994, there had been six UN secretaries-general: Trygve Lie, 1946–1953; Dag Hammarskjöld, 1953–1961; U Thant, 1961–1971; Kurt Waldheim, 1972–1982; Javier Pérez de Cuéllar, 1982–1991; and, Boutros Boutros-Ghali, 1992–present. The secretary-general is the principal factor in UN decision-making that is not tied to particular national interests. His is, as Javier Perez de Cuellar so aptly said in a lecture at Oxford University in 1986, the sole voice able to speak freely for the interests of the UN Charter and the world. All have sought to be mediators in international conflicts, and all have sought to provide leadership for the United Nations, albeit with varying degrees of success.

The personal abilities, interests, and talents of the secretary-general have been very important in determining the role that he has played and the influence that he has had, but the possibilities that have been open to the UN secretary-general have depended very much upon the broad configuration of international relations. Success in the role of secretary-general has depended upon retaining the confidence of the majority within the General Assembly, especially the Group of Seventy-Seven, and the permanent members of the Security Council, especially the United States.

Both Dag Hammarskjöld and Boutros Boutros-Ghali have played particularly prominent roles in UN decision-making, frequently seeking to seize the initiative in issues involving international peace and security. Both held office at times of great fluidity in international relations, Hammarskjöld at the height of decolonization in Africa and Boutros-Ghali during the emergence of the post-Cold War world order. Both sought to define an expanded UN role in world affairs.

Maintaining International Peace and Security

Maintaining international peace and security is the United Nations most important task. In accepting the UN Charter member states accept the obligation in Article 2 to:...refrain in their international relations from the threat or use of force against the territorial integrity or political independence of any state, or in any other manner inconsistent with the Purposes of the United Nations.

In effect, the charter sought to rule out the use of military force in international relations, and in Chapter VII it gave the Security Council authority to enforce this prohibition. The Security Council's authority extends both to actions by UN members and states that are not members.

According to Article 43 of the charter, member states were to sign agreements under which they would make specified military forces available to the United Nations; the Security Council then could deploy these forces to back its decisions to maintain or restore international peace and security. Intensive negotiations were held in the early years of the United Nations to achieve these agreements, but the negotiations failed. No agreements have been signed under Article 43 of the charter. The United Nations has not had any military forces permanently at its disposal; all military forces deployed under UN auspices have been made available through ad hoc voluntary contributions.

Despite the lack of Article 43 agreements, on two occasions enforcement operations have been undertaken under the auspices of the United Nations. The first was in June 1950, when military forces of the Democratic Republic of Korea (North Korea) invaded the territory of the Republic of Korea (South Korea), and the second was when Iraq invaded Kuwait in August 1990. In both instances, the Security Council first condemned the invasion, and then authorized member states take steps to repel the invasion. The fact that the Soviet Union was not participating in UN bodies because of its boycott over the issue of Chinese representation made it possible for the UN to act in 1950. In 1990, the Soviet Union was fully part of the consensus against the Iraqi invasion. In both instances the United States took the lead, deployed substantial numbers of its own military forces, enlisted the support of other UN members, and organized coalitions. In both instances the goal of the operation came to be the restoration of the status quo ante bellum, although in both there were arguments for more far-

reaching goals, particularly changing the regime of the state that had initiated the invasion.

Why enforcement actions were taken under UN auspices in these two instances and not in the other interstate wars that have taken place since 1945 is to be explained largely by the fact that the United States took the leadership, both within the United Nations, by mustering a majority for action, and in the field, by supplying the bulk of the troops. In both instances, the U.S. government felt that U.S. national interests were directly threatened.

The fact that enforcement actions were not taken in other interstate wars does not mean that the United Nations was not involved. Almost always, the UN adopted resolutions calling for cease-fires, as it did in the Iran-Iraq War. Sometimes, as in the Soviet invasion of Afghanistan, the UN became involved in mediation efforts. Frequently it called for an embargo on the shipment of military supplies to the combatants.

On occasion, the UN deployed military forces, although in a very special and limited way. The classic formula was developed in the 1956 Suez crisis, when in October, Great Britain, France, and Israel attacked Egypt. First the UN General Assembly ordered a cease-fire and the withdrawal of troops to positions behind established armistice lines; British and French vetoes had blocked Security Council action. The General Assembly then decided to create a United Nations Emergency Force (UNEF) that would supervise the implementation of the cease-fire by interposing itself between the belligerent parties. Conceptually, UNEF was an elaboration and expansion of truce supervision and observation efforts that the UN had deployed since the late 1940s, but it was larger by an order of magnitude and had more extensive responsibilities. UNEF was comprised of military forces from countries such as Canada, Columbia, Norway, Pakistan, and Sweden that were not permanent members of the Security Council. It was deployed on the territory of a country only with that country's consent, thus it was only deployed on the Egyptian side of the line. At peak strength, UNEF numbered no more than 6,000 lightly armed personnel. Its function was not to enforce a solution, but rather to forestall the re-ignition of hostilities. More broadly, its purpose was to prevent the geographical spread and escalation of hostilities and to forestall superpower intervention. The United Nations Emergency Force was quickly labeled a "peacekeeping" operation, in contrast to its position in the Korean and Kuwait Wars. UNEF became a model for UN involvement in interstate conflicts through the mid-1980s.

In the late 1980s and 1990s, however, the UN was confronted with and sought to address new sets of issues, those involved in intrastate conflicts stemming from ideological, ethnic, and other divisions. The UN had had a taste of these issues during the 1960s in its involvement in the Congo when its military operation there, The United Nations Operation in the Congo (ONUC after the French title *Organisation des Nations Unies au Congo*) had to deal first with reconstituting the instruments of civil authority and then with the attempted secession of the province of Katanga. The Congo operation showed that in such circumstances it is almost impossible for UN actions not to support or be perceived as supporting one side or the other. When the UN becomes linked actually or perceptually to one side in a conflict, the risk to UN personnel rises dramatically. The Congo episode also showed that such operations are costly and difficult to end because it is hard to define clear, obtainable goals. When ONUC forces were at their peak strength in the first four years, the cost was about $100 million per year; the annual cost of UNEF forces had been less than $20 million. ONUC was widely perceived as siding with the aims of Joseph Mobuto and the West.

The Congo experience was a foretaste of what happened in the 1990s as the United Nations became deeply involved in intra-state conflicts, most notably in the former Yugoslavia, Somalia, Rwanda, and Haiti. As of January 1994, seventeen UN operations involving a total of more than 70,000 personnel were in the field at an annual cost of about $3.2 billion, and during the course of the year, the UN authorized actions that would lead to a UN presence in Haiti. Some of the operations were traditional peacekeeping forces, but others undertook new missions. Generally, the mandate of these forces was initially defined as that of providing humanitarian assistance, but there were constant pressures to expand this mandate, first to ensure that humanitarian assistance could be delivered, then to prevent atrocities and serious violations of human rights and to promote democracy.

UN Secretary-General Boutros Boutros-Ghali was among the foremost advocates of an expanded role for the UN. In a report that he prepared in 1992 for the Security Council, *An Agenda for Peace*, he argued that the changed character of international affairs demanded that the UN undertake new and more ambitious roles, and he set out a plan for equipping the UN to do this. He suggested that the UN could engage in peacemaking and peacebuilding as well as peacekeeping. Though these terms were never precisely defined, it was clear that they would involve using military force to bring about, enforce, and preserve order and a political settlement. Initially, the Clinton administration strongly encouraged and supported the secretary-general. For a while, consideration of practical issues such as how the UN could have assured immediate access to military forces and funding for peacemaking and peacebuilding operations dominated the discussion of the secretary-general's suggestions and the UN's activities in the field.

Soon, however, it became clear that much more fundamental issues were at stake. Military calamities in Soma-

lia and highly visible costs in human lives and lack of success in bringing about a settlement in Yugoslavia provoked public—and in the United States, congressional—involvement in what became a highly controversial debate. It became clear that if the UN were to deploy military forces or authorize their deployment for something beyond efforts to repulse visible aggression as in Korea or Kuwait or traditional peacekeeping operations, several issues would have to be settled. There would have to be agreement on the purposes of the operation, achievable goals would have to be defined, and clear understandings would have to be reached concerning the command of the forces. The debate revealed an absence of consensus on all of these issues. Various political leaders and observers argued that the UN should support organized groups seeking national self-determination or the installation or restoration of democratic regimes. Others argued that these goals were too broad and vague and that to follow them would involve the United Nations in endless ambiguous and controversial situations. In the United States, as a consequence of the Somalia debacle and the Yugoslav imbroglio, a substantial body of opinion came to be strongly opposed to U.S. forces serving under any non-U.S. commander and wanted to reduce and limit U.S. financial contributions to UN military operations. It was apparent that it would be some time before consensus could be achieved on these basic issues.

The UN's contribution to international peace and security has been considerably broader than the relatively limited number of actions that have been taken under Chapter VII of the charter. Over the first half-century of its existence. the United Nations refined the norm concerning the non-use of military force outlined in Article II of the charter. It also defined criteria for determining the legitimacy of the territorial borders of states: national-self-determination became the touchstone. Achieving consensus on these norms not only provided a basis for UN action, it also provided guidelines for states to orient their actions. The declining incidence of interstate war is perhaps a hopeful sign that norms defined in the UN can, over time, win acceptance and affect the behavior of states.

Beyond formulating norms to guide its own actions and those of states, the UN also has undertaken many functions. It has provided a framework for the negotiation of arms control agreements, among the most important, the 1968 Treaty on the Non-Proliferation of Nuclear Weapons, the 1975 Biological and Toxin Weapons Convention, and the 1992 Convention on the Prohibition of the Development, Production, Stockpiling, and Use of Chemical Weapons.

Have the UN's activities contributed to peace? It has been argued that certain UN activities have exacerbated conflicts, especially the General Assembly's often one-sided resolutions on the Arab-Israeli conflict and apartheid in South Africa. In both instances because there was such strong feeling within the assembly that the side it favored had greater claims for justice, the assembly's actions were primarily oriented toward affecting the outcome rather than dampening the conflict. It also has been argued that some of the UN's peacekeeping operations have prolonged conflicts by creating conditions that allowed the parties to disputes to avoid the painful adjustments that would be required for settlements. There is, however, broad agreement among scholars and policymakers that the UN's activities on balance have made a substantial contribution to peace.

Economic and Environmental Issues

As was foreseen from the very beginning, the United Nations' engagement with economic issues has been highly decentralized. Many of the most important activities have been conducted by specialized and affiliated agencies, such as the International Monetary Fund (IMF), the International Bank for Reconstruction and Development (World Bank), and the World Trade Organization (WTO) and its predecessor, the General Agreement on Tariffs and Trade (GATT).

During the Cold War period, the effects of the UN's structural decentralization were magnified by the fact that the Soviet Union and—until 1980—China, did not belong to the IMF, the World Bank, or GATT and attacked these agencies as instruments of imperialism. During this period the Soviet Union and the Group of Seventy-Seven attempted to have the UN itself take over the functions of these agencies and pushed the General Assembly to create the United Nations Conference on Trade and Development (UNCTAD), an organization that they hoped would supplant GATT. The Soviet Union and the Group of Seventy-Seven argued that the IMF, the World Bank, and GATT gave too much stress to private property and market principles; these states preferred greater governmental intervention in economic affairs. By the 1990s, however, this debate was passé, China and Russia were members of the IMF and the World Bank, and both sought membership in the WTO. The decentralization remained, but its only dimension was functional—the ideological overlay had disappeared.

Some planners for the United Nations had hoped that the Economic and Social Council (ECOSOC) would provide broad, general direction for the world economy, but this hope has proved a chimera. Even with eighteen members, ECOSOC was too large, and when its size was increased to twenty-seven and then fifty-four it became a mini-General Assembly. Council members have more frequently been represented by diplomatists rather than economic policymakers. The open, public nature of ECOSOC meetings has discouraged frank discussion.

Nor has ECOSOC been an effective mechanism for coordinating the economic activities of the UN system. The specialized and affiliated agencies have had too much constitutional and budgetary autonomy for ECOSOC significantly to affect their policymaking.

ECOSOC has been primarily a debating forum, a place where arguments that later would be heard in the General Assembly were rehearsed. Economic debates in ECOSOC and the General Assembly have focused largely on North-South issues. Matters concerning the economic policies of the high-income countries are treated elsewhere, in the Organization for Economic Cooperation and Development (OECD), in the IMF, or in the summit meetings of the Group of Seven industrialized countries. The dominant theme of the UN debates has been the necessity of accelerating the economic development of developing countries. While all UN members have subscribed to this objective, the extent of agreement on the measures that should be employed to gain it has varied.

In the 1950s and early 1960s, there appeared to be substantial agreement. The UN created the United Nations Development Program (UNDP) to provide technical assistance to developing countries, declared the 1960s the first development decade, and set targets for both growth and for the transfer of resources from high- to low- income countries. In practice, however, most donor countries proved unwilling or unable to meet the targets for transfer of resources.

In the 1970s, the rhetorical agreement on measures dissipated. The Group of Seventy-Seven became confrontational and rammed through the General Assembly several resolutions demanding a New International Economic Order (NIEO). Displacing or radically altering the IMF, the World Bank, and GATT was a central feature of the NIEO program. Under NIEO, the transfer of resources to developing countries would be greatly increased, automatic, and unconditional. The resources available to the UNDP, IMF, and the World Bank depend on voluntary decisions by donor governments and assistance from the IMF and the World Bank is conditional upon recipients meeting performance criteria. The early successes of the Organization of Petroleum Exporting Countries (OPEC) in increasing the price of petroleum apparently led developing country representatives to believe that the Group of Seventy-Seven's bargaining power was sufficient to extract concessions from the high-income countries.

As time progressed, OPEC's strength waned for both political and economic reasons. In the 1980s the pressure and enthusiasm for NIEO diminished dramatically. By the mid-1990s the confrontation in the UN on economic development issues had eased greatly, and most resolutions in ECOSOC and the General Assembly were adopted without a vote. But the resolutions were lackluster, they contained neither fresh insights for development strategies nor much hope for rapid improvement among the poorest countries. By the 1990s it was evident that some developing countries, especially in East Asia, were achieving phenomenal rates of economic growth, while others, particularly in Africa, were growing only slowly or were stagnating. Differential economic performances diminished the ability of the Group of Seventy-Seven to agree on broad, general programs or appeals.

The debates in the UN on economic issues, despite the oscillation between consensus and confrontation and whether the tone has been optimistic or pessimistic, have made it impossible for the world community to gloss over or ignore poverty, and they have continuously held up the hope of eliminating poverty.

Underlying the debates on economic issues in the United Nations, there has been much important and significant but unheralded work. The UN's statistical work is among the most important. The UN and its functional and regional commissions and the specialized agencies have collected and disseminated a vast array of statistical data. They first established common criteria and standards for the collection of data, then trained national statisticians in the techniques of collection and handling of data, compiled the data, when necessary transformed it into common measures, and finally set up mechanisms for regularly publishing and disseminating it. Since the mid-1960s, the data provided by the UN system has made it possible to monitor the progress of the entire world economy. The information that this monitoring has provided has been essential to the formulation of national and international policies. The debates in the UN could not have occurred, or at least would not have taken the form that they have, had it not been for the data that the UN system produced.

The technical assistance provided by the specialized agencies, the UNDP, and other organizations created by the General Assembly, particularly the United Nations Population Fund, also has been a useful though untouted contribution of the UN system. This technical assistance has helped enhance the administrative and managerial capacity of developing countries.

Finally, the United Nations has convened large public conferences on special topics of particular relevance to the world economy. The topics include the application of science and technology for the benefit of less developed countries; the environment; food; new sources of energy; peaceful uses of atomic energy; population; problems of the least developed countries; and water. These conferences generally conclude with the adoption of action plans, but their most important effect probably has been that of calling attention to and mobilizing concern for the problems involved.

The conferences on the environment will undoubtedly have had the greatest consequences. In 1972 the UN convened in Stockholm the United Nations Conference on the Human Environment. The conference adopted a far-reaching Declaration on the Human Environment, and it set in motion processes that have profoundly affected national and international policies and the United Nations. The establishment of the United Nations Environment Programme (UNEP) in 1973 was one important consequence of the Stockholm conference. Its function is to be a catalytic force, working with other elements of the UN system and other national and international governmental and nongovernmental organizations to promote concern for the environment and action to protect it. With its secretariat located in Nairobi, Kenya, UNEP is the only UN program with headquarters in a developing country.

In the decade after the Stockholm conference more than 100 countries established environmental protection agencies. Awareness that environmental degradation could hamper economic development, despoil living conditions, and even threaten life increased sharply. Increasingly there was agreement that strategies for environmental protection and economic development had to be linked, and the developing countries—which contain four-fifths of the world's population and by their sheer numbers will eventually comprise the largest share of the world economy—had to be involved, which is why having UNEP headquartered in a developing country was symbolically so important.

In 1983 the General Assembly decided to create a World Commission on Environment and Development. The task of the commission was "to propose long-term environmental strategies for achieving sustainable development by the year 2000 and beyond." The commission was headed by Gro Harlem Brundtland, leader of the Labour Party and sometime Prime Minister of Norway. In its report, *Our Common Future*, the commission called attention to the growing number of possibly life-threatening environmental hazards and argued that poverty had to be eliminated: that a world in which poverty was endemic would "…always be prone to ecological and other catastrophes." The commission called for a new era of economic growth and put forward the concept of sustainable development as the guiding principle for this new era:

> "…sustainable development is not a fixed state of harmony, but rather a process of change in which the exploitation of resources, the direction of investments, the orientation of technological development, and institutional change are made consistent with future as well as present needs."

Our Common Future was released in April 1987 and presented to the forty-second General Assembly that fall. It rapidly became a focal point for discussion within the United Nations, the UN's member states, and the world community.

In 1989, the General Assembly decided to convene in 1992 the United Nations Conference on Environment and Development (UNCED). UNCED, or the Earth Summit, met in Rio de Janeiro, Brazil from 3 June through 14 June 1992. It was the largest conference that the UN has ever held. One hundred and seventy-two states, 8,000 delegates, 3,000 representatives of non-governmental organizations, and 9,000 representatives of the media attended. UNCED adopted the Rio Declaration on Environment and Development, which endorsed and amplified the concept of sustainable development; Agenda 21, a comprehensive action plan of more than 600 pages; the Framework Convention on Climate Change; the Convention on Biodiversity; and, the Statement of Principles on Forests.

In 1993 the UN General Assembly created the Commission on Sustainable Development, which was charged with monitoring progress toward obtaining the goals set forth in Rio. When both the Climate Change Convention and the Biodiversity Convention came into effect in 1994, additional monitoring bodies became active. This meant that several institutions were in place to check on the implementation of the obligations specified in these treaties.

By the mid-1990s, sustainable development had become the leitmotif for United Nations activities relating to economic and environmental issues. The two topics had become firmly joined. The institutions and instruments for progress toward the goal of sustainable development were in place. How well these would be used remained to be seen.

Social Welfare, Refugees, and Human Rights

The United Nations has continued activities that the League of Nations had undertaken with respect to social welfare and refugees. Its major innovation—as was mandated in the charter—has been its extensive involvement in issues relating to human rights. The UN immediately took steps to insure that the activities that the League had undertaken with respect to the control of narcotic drugs, the protection of women and children, and the outlawing of slavery would be continued, and these activities have been an important part of the UN's work. At the same time, the specialized agencies with mandates in this area launched their activities: the International Labour Organization; the United Nations Educational, Scientific, and Cultural Organization; and the World Health Organization, and these activities too have been continued and expanded. Given the role of these agencies, the UN's work in the social welfare field has been as decentralized as its economic activities.

As it became apparent that situations in the post–World War II order would continue to produce refugees, it became more and more clear that some instrumentalities beyond those temporary agencies that had been created during World War II and its immediate aftermath would be required. In 1949 the UN established the United Nations Relief and Works Agency for Palestine Refugees in the Near East (UNRWA) to provide assistance for the then 750,000 Palestinians who had become refugees as a consequence of the 1948 Arab-Israeli War. As of the mid-1990s, UNRWA was providing a variety of services to 2.5 million Palestinian refugees and their descendants in the Middle East. About a third of these lived in UNRWA refugee camps.

In 1950 the United Nations created the office of the high commissioner for refugees (UNHCR), who is elected by the General Assembly on the nomination of the secretary-general. The high commission's mandate is to provide international protection for refugees and to facilitate their voluntary repatriation or assimilation within new national communities. The UNHCR's programs are financed by voluntary contributions, primarily from governments. As of the mid-1990s, the UNHCR's annual budget exceeded one billion dollars, and in the former Yugoslavia alone the UNHCR was assisting more than three million people. The total world refugee population exceeded eighteen million people.

The UN also launched its ambitious program in human rights in the immediate post–World War II period. At its first session, the Economic and Social Council established a Commission on Human Rights. Mrs. Franklin D. Roosevelt was elected chairman of the commission. The commission undertook the preparation of two documents, a declaration of general principles and a legally binding convention. The Universal Declaration of Human Rights was completed by June 1948 and was approved by the Third General Assembly on 10 December 1948 by a vote of forty-eight to zero, with eight abstentions (Byelorussia, Czechoslovakia, Poland, Saudi Arabia, the Ukraine, the Union of South Africa, the Soviet Union, and Yugoslavia) and two absences (Honduras and Yemen). The Universal Declaration of Human Rights has become a common standard against which the performance of all governments is measured. It contains all of the rights and freedoms that were developed in the classic statements such as the French Declaration of the Rights of Man and the U.S. Bill of Rights.

The UN has prepared several other declarations and many legally binding conventions. Among the more important conventions are Convention on the Prevention and the Punishment of the Crime of Genocide, 1948; the International Covenant on Civil and Political Rights, 1966; the International Covenant on Economic and Social Rights, 1966; the Convention on the Political Rights of Women, 1953; the International Convention on the Elimination of All Forms of Racial Discrimination, 1966; the Convention on the Elimination of All Forms of Discrimination against Women; the Convention on the Rights of the Child, 1989; and the Convention against Torture and Other Cruel, Inhuman, or Degrading Treatment or Punishment, 1984. For all of these conventions, mechanisms have been established to monitor progress in their implementation. Usually this is done by examining and commenting on reports, but under certain conditions complaints about violations are examined.

As of the mid-1990s, all of these treaties were in effect, and several had been ratified by 100 or more states. The United States, however, despite its leadership in the human rights field in the early days of the UN, had only ratified two of them: The Convention on the Prevention and Punishment of the Crime of Genocide and the International Covenant on Civil and Political Rights. The United States is skeptical that group rights, such as that of national self-determination should be included along with individual rights in legally binding conventions, as they are in the two covenants. Nor does the United States accept the notion that economic and social rights can be treated in the same way as civil and political rights. More generally, the United States seems reluctant to accept any obligation that would allow external sources to comment on the exercise of civil and political rights within the country. On the other hand, many countries sign and ratify conventions regardless of whether or not they intend to or are capable of complying with them. Promoting compliance with the UN's conventions is one of the organization's major tasks.

The United Nations also has done several other things to encourage progress in the realization of human rights and to discourage violations. It has provided technical assistance. The General Assembly has adopted resolutions condemning what it considers particularly egregious violations in such countries as Afghanistan, Cuba, El Salvador, Equatorial Guinea, Iran, Iraq, Myanmar (Burma), Haiti, and South Africa, and it has appointed working groups and reporters to investigate conditions and report regularly. It has convened conferences, for instance the World Conference on Human Rights in Vienna in 1993, and in 1993 the United Nations General Assembly decided to create the post of high commissioner for human rights.

The high commissioner, who has the rank of under-secretary-general, is the highest UN official with princi-

pal responsibility for human rights and is the focal point for the UN's activities.

In its human rights activities, the UN has given highest priority to the establishment of human equality and the elimination of discrimination. Racial discrimination received greatest attention, then gender discrimination. The United Nations has always been concerned with children, as was evidenced by the early creation of the United Nations Children's Fund and its continuing vitality. In the early days of the United Nations, it was mainly Western states that stressed civil and political rights, but starting in the 1980s more and more states came to argue for the importance of these rights. More and more states came to see that freedom of expression and association, free elections, and other basic democratic rights were essential not only in their own right but also as instruments for achieving many other goals, among them non-violence, economic growth, and environmental protection.

The United Nations and the Future

The United Nations has never played the central role in international affairs that many of its founders hoped it would. During the Cold War, the UN's inability to do more was frequently ascribed to the paralysis in the Security Council caused by the Soviet-U.S. conflict and the way this conflict provoked tensions that permeated the UN's other organs. Since the end of the Cold War, the UN has become more active. Yet it has continued to fall short of the ambitious visions that were held for it in 1945, raising the question of whether more fundamental issues than the Cold War are at stake.

The underlying reality is that the shift from a global system based on the Westphalian principle of the supremacy of sovereign states, making them the only significant actors in international affairs, to an order in which a collective body like the UN could play a central role would require fundamental shifts in governmental and popular attitudes. For an international institution to play a more central role, there would have to be more agreement on the principles that should guide the conduct of governments and individuals. A world community does not yet exist, though through its efforts to formulate and publicize norms, the UN may be contributing to the formation of a world community. The broad acceptance of the norm against inter-state violence; national self-determination; the principle of sustainable development; and the standards embedded in the Universal Declaration of Human Rights indicate that there may have been some progress. As a nascent world community develops, the UN's role in world affairs could grow.

Even to maintain the role that it had in the mid-1990s, however, it was clear the UN would have to become more efficient and to adapt so that its structure and mandate were appropriate for the emerging realities of the twenty-first century. The five permanent members of the Security Council were no longer the only states that conceivably qualified for that status, Germany, Japan, and India were all plausible candidates. The charter focused on interstate conflicts, but intrastate conflicts had become prevalent and certainly were threatening. How global economic development should be approached was an open and unsettled question. Throughout its history the UN has adapted to changing international conditions, but more rapid and fundamental changes may be required.

HAROLD K. JACOBSON

See also Atlantic Charter; China; Churchill, Winston Leonard Spencer; Communism; Geneva Conventions; Genocide Convention; Group of Seven; Haiti; Hammarskjöld, Dag Hjalmar Agne Carl; International Joint Commission; International Law; Kirkpatrick, Jeane Duane; Korean War; Law of the Sea; League of Nations; Lie, Trygve; Moynihan, Daniel Patrick; Nuclear Nonproliferation; Rio Treaty; Roosevelt, Franklin Delano; Russia and the Soviet Union; Stalin, Joseph; Thant, U; Third World; United Nations Conference on the Human Environment, Stockholm; United Nations Conference on Trade and Development; United Nations Environment Program; United Nations Relief and Rehabilitation Administration; Waldheim, Kurt; Walters, Vernon Anthony; World War II

FURTHER READING

Issues Before the United Nations. United Nations Association of the United States of America. Latham, Md. (Annual).

Abi-Saab, Georges. *The United Nations Operation in the Congo, 1960–1964.* Oxford, 1978.

Alger, Chadwick F., Gene M. Lyons, and John E. Trent, eds. *The United Nations System: The Politics of Member States.* Tokyo, New York, Paris, 1995.

Beschloss, Michael R., and Strobe Talbott. *At the Highest Level: The Inside Story of the End of the Cold War.* Boston, Mass., 1993.

Brownlie, Ian. *Basic Documents on Human Rights.* 3rd ed. Oxford, 1992.

Coate, Roger A. *U.S. Policy and the Future of the United Nations.* New York, 1995.

Damrosch, Lori Fisher, ed. *Enforcing Restraint: Collective Intervention in Internal Conflicts.* New York, 1993.

Diehl, Paul F. *International Peace Keeping.* Baltimore, Md., 1993.

Gerson, Allan. *The Kirkpatrick Mission: Diplomacy Without Apology, America at the United Nations, 1981–1985.* New York, 1991.

Krasner, Stephen D. *Structural Conflict: The Third World Against Global Liberalism.* Berkeley, Calif., 1985.

Lefever, Ernest, W. *Uncertain Mandate: Politics of the U.N. Congo Operation.* Baltimore, Md., 1976.

Meisler, Stanley. *United Nations: The First Fifty Years.* New York, 1995.

Robinson, Nicholas A., ed. *Agenda 21: Earth's Action Plan.* New York, 1993.

Urquhart, Brian. *Hammarskjöld.* New York, 1972.

Wainhouse, David W. *International Peacekeeping at the Crossroads.* Baltimore, Md., 1973.

UNITED NATIONS CONFERENCE ON ENVIRONMENT AND DEVELOPMENT

See Earth Summit, Rio de Janeiro

UNITED NATIONS CONFERENCE ON LAW OF THE SEA

See Law of the Sea

UNITED NATIONS CONFERENCE ON THE HUMAN ENVIRONMENT, STOCKHOLM

(1972)

A major landmark in the international community's recognition of, and response to, environmental degradation due to human activities. The conference, held in Sweden on 5–16 June 1972, and attended by 112 nations, served as the culmination of evolving awareness about the subject, buttressed by private organizational efforts to manage the environment. The U.S. government played a major role in initiating the conference. The major institutional outcome was the establishment of the United Nations Environment Program (UNEP). The normative effect was the formal recognition by governments of the preservation of "nature" as a central objective of public policy. The record of private environmental organizations dates back to the turn of the century. However, the most significant effort took place during the post–World War II period, most notably since the 1960s. Nature conservation movements, in conjunction with the increasingly political attention paid to environmental concerns, led to the consolidation of diverse views on environment, which, in turn, set the stage for the debates at Stockholm. In general, industrial countries, including the United States, emphasized regulation and pollution control; developing countries stressed the prevalence of pollution due to poverty and to the vicious cycle of underdevelopment. The scientific community introduced the evidence of interconnections between natural and social systems, supporting the growing arguments that human beings were influencing natural ecological balances in adverse ways. The conference founded the Global Environmental Monitoring System (GEMS), the International Register of Potentially Toxic Chemicals (IRPTC), and the International Referral System for Sources of Environmental Information (INFOTERRA). Several notable conventions on environmental management were finalized thereafter. The Stockholm Conference served as a point of no return: the international community had formally recognized the salience of environmental issues and put in place the organizational mechanisms for monitoring and, potentially, for management. The Stockholm Declaration on the Human Environment and the Declaration of Principles became the foundation for work that subsequently culminated in the United Nations Conference on Environment and Development, or Earth Summit, held at Rio de Janeiro in 1992.

NAZLI CHOUCRI

See also Earth Summit, Rio de Janeiro; Environment; United Nations; United Nations Environment Program

FURTHER READING

Tolba, Mostafa K., Osama A. El-Kholy, E. El-Hinnawi, M. W. Holdgate, D. F. McMichael, and R. E. Munn. *The World Environment 1972–1992: Two Decades of Challenge.* London, 1992.

UNITED NATIONS CONFERENCE ON TRADE AND DEVELOPMENT

Convened by the UN General Assembly in 1964, it subsequently became a permanent organ of the United Nations reporting to the Economic and Social Council (ECOSOC). United Nations Conference on Trade and Development (UNCTAD) originated out of the concerns of newly independent, developing countries that the major international economic institutions, specifically the World Bank, the International Monetary Fund, and the General Agreement on Tariffs and Trade (GATT) were not giving adequate attention to their needs and were dominated by the industrialized countries. UNCTAD has sought to establish principles and policies for trade and aid designed to accelerate self-sustaining growth in developing countries. In the 1970s, it was a primary locus for North-South conflict over the proposed New International Economic Order (NIEO) and a major cause of U.S. dissatisfaction with the UN.

The Conference itself meets every four years, while its Trade and Development Board, the permanent governing organ, meets annually. The professional staff has played a key role in shaping UNCTAD's work. The institution's dynamics have been shaped by a pattern of group bargaining, prompted both by the size of its membership (166 in 1994) and the high degree of unity among the developing countries of the Group of 77 (G-77), which today numbers over 120 developing countries. The Western, industrialized countries formed "Group B," while the former socialist countries and China alone formed the two remaining groups. Structurally, UNCTAD has been comprised of several standing committees and working groups. The former deal with commodities, economic cooperation among developing countries, invisibles and financing related to trade, manufactures, preferences, shipping, and transfer of technology. The latter include groups on least-developed countries, international ship-

ping legislation, the International Trade Center, and restrictive practices.

Although, as part of the NIEO, UNCTAD sought operational responsibility for transfer of technology and commodities in the 1970s, it has functioned primarily as a forum of debate, negotiation, and legitimation of new norms in the international trade and aid systems. Its record over thirty years includes few substantial achievements. The quadrennial conferences have seldom been judged successful, resulting in doubts about the institution's future. The role of UNCTAD's professional staff in providing analyses and recommendations for the Group of 77 and of its secretary-general as the proponent of G-77 views, has historically linked the organization closely to the G-77. UNCTAD's first secretary-general, Raul Prebisch, was responsible for the structuralist analysis of North-South relations that formed the basis of the organization's doctrine. The staff's importance is magnified by the limited expertise within many developing countries' governments.

In many respects, UNCTAD's formation was the developing world's response to the GATT-based international trading system that was perceived as benefiting only the developed, industrialized nations. In place of GATT's norm of nondiscrimination, UNCTAD sought preferences; in place of free market approaches, it sought redistribution of wealth and benefits in favor of the poorer nations. In place of decision-making processes that gave the wealthiest nations greater weight, the developing countries sought to create in UNCTAD a body to decide trade and development matters on the basis of one-state-one-vote. It has been a vehicle, therefore, for the developing countries to seek greater power, status, and role in international economic decision-making, as well as new rules.

UNCTAD never succeeded in replacing the GATT. In fact, since the early 1980s, increasing numbers of developing countries have joined the GATT. Yet, UNCTAD did lead to changes in the GATT, specifically the addition in 1965 of a new section (Part IV) on trade and development. And, UNCTAD and the GATT have jointly operated the International Trade Center in Geneva, a body that aids developing countries in training personnel in general marketing and export promotion techniques.

UNCTAD has sought over the years to realize the goals of the United Nations Development Decade, the NIEO, and the principles laid out in the Charter of Economic Rights and Duties of States. Key areas of concern have included favorable trade policies, technology transfer, increased economic assistance particularly to least developed countries, technical assistance and economic diversification programs, and commodity agreements.

The New Delhi Conference (1968) secured agreement in principle on a generalized system of preferences

(GSP) to promote developing country exports through preferential access to developed country markets and non-reciprocity. Yet, the specific terms of preferences (scope, timing, and duration), were left to individual developed country governments (or, in the case of the European Community, the members as a group) to implement. And, a "graduation clause" was added to the GATT articles to establish the principle that countries' preferential treatment would end when they reached higher levels of development. In addition, many products were excluded, and there was no general agreement on which countries should be included.

The North-South Confrontation

At the height of the North-South confrontation in the 1970s, UNCTAD was given a mandate by the UN General Assembly to negotiate an Integrated Programme of Commodities (IPC), something on which it had already worked. The G-77 and UNCTAD staff hoped to use the proposed IPC to accelerate development and the transfer of resources by negotiating international commodity agreements for key raw material exports and establishing a common fund to stabilize prices through a buffer stocks program.

The focus on commodities was designed to address a key area of developing country trade: raw material exports. Structuralist analyses of economic dependency had historically singled out the terms of commodity trade as indicative of the exploitation of poor countries. According to such analyses, relative to the manufactured products the developing countries imported from the industrialized countries, their raw material exports had suffered a decline in terms of trade over time. In addition, many developing countries that export one or a few commodities to a limited number of markets find those products subject to fluctuating demand and prices they do not control, as well as competition from synthetics. Usually they lack the resources to diversify production, or even to stockpile. Commodity trade also has historically been controlled by a few, large multinational corporations. Added to the equation in the 1970s were two key variables: the twenty-year decline in real value of export earnings for many commodities and the emergence of the Organization of Petroleum Exporting Countries (OPEC) as a powerful actor.

The sense that control of raw materials could be a major source of power was palpable in the mid-1970s and the willingness of some OPEC members to support the NIEO agenda appeared to strengthen the Group of 77's bargaining position. The Club of Rome's work on limits to growth generated fears of resource scarcities among developed countries that aided the G-77's assertiveness. OPEC's success in controlling oil supplies and raising prices heightened many developed countries' sense of

vulnerability. Adverse economic developments in both developed and developing countries thus suggested the possibility of negotiating new terms of trade for commodities.

The IPC negotiations were unsuccessful, however. Discussions were marked by radical, ideological rhetoric and confrontation. The G-77 and UNCTAD staff pressed for broad agreement in the interests of maintaining unity among the developing countries whose stake in commodity trade varied widely. They did little to persuade the developed countries or promote compromise. The developed countries, led by the United States, distrusted the developing countries and feared that concessions would only lead to more demands. Although interested in improving markets and even providing compensatory financing for commodities, they advocated a case-by-case approach and sought to avoid IPC becoming a vehicle for resource transfer, an aid program. The United States preferred stalemate in the IPC negotiations to any agreement that reflected G-77 principles; the G-77 itself accepted stalemate in hopes of larger, future gains. Three years of negotiation (1974–1977) yielded no progress. Instead, individual agreements have been negotiated for a few commodities, but only the agreements for rubber and tropical timber are the direct result of UNCTAD's efforts. The proposed common fund was never fully accepted, although it eventually did become operational albeit at a low level of funding and without U.S. representation.

UNCTAD also has sought to address monetary and financial issues. At one point, it urged the IMF to allocate reserves directly to the central banks of various developing countries. It sought to soften the terms of economic assistance and multilateral lending and to eliminate the practice of linking aid to purchases of goods and services in the donor nations. In 1978, the Trade and Development Board recommended the retroactive adjustment of the terms of official development assistance debts, essentially asking creditor nations to dismiss much of the debt owed by developing nations. The South's success in getting the IMF to create and expand its Compensatory Financing Facility to compensate developing countries for falling commodity prices and export earnings, as well as permit members to borrow in excess of their regular quota limits under such circumstances, represented further achievement, but not one directly attributable to UNCTAD.

UNCTAD staff has conducted pioneering work on addressing the situation of the world's least-developed countries. In 1979, UNCTAD established a Substantial New Programme of Action for these countries. The Programme's main objectives included: to promote structural changes necessary to overcome their extreme economic difficulties; to provide minimum living standards for the poor that meet international standards; to identify and support major investment priorities and initiatives; to contain as far as possible the effects of natural disasters. Landocked and island developing countries have drawn particular attention from UNCTAD. It has established special funds to facilitate transit-transport infrastructures for the former and inter-island transport systems for the latter. UNCTAD's efforts also secured special favorable treatment for the least-developed countries in the GATT Tokyo Round negotiations (1975–1979).

Another key objective is linked to UNCTAD's efforts to enhance mutual self-help among developing countries. A Committee on Economic Cooperation Among Developing Countries was established in 1976 to serve as a forum in which to discuss the potential for an expansion of trade among developing countries and to devise strategies for greater collective self-reliance.

Finally, UNCTAD has worked to promote the transfer of technical knowledge by advocating changes in national laws and international agreements governing the intellectual property system. It has been active in working for an international code of conduct to end restrictive business practices and provide an international framework for the transfer, acquisition, and development of technology between developed and developing countries.

Although the South continued to use UNCTAD as a forum to call for a NIEO in the 1980s, the collapse of commodity power, the erosion of G-77 solidarity, the debt crisis, and their weakened economic position led many countries to adopt more pragmatic strategies. UNCTAD meetings produced little more than empty dialogue.

In the late 1990s, UNCTAD's future is again in doubt. At the 1992 conference in Cartagena, the G-77's unity had disappeared. The Latin American states were moving closer to the United States, thanks at least in part to the "Initiative for the Americas" and negotiations for the North American Free Trade Agreement. The newly industrializing countries of East and Southeast Asia as well as the South Asian states found little in common with either the Latin Americans or Africans. Only the African states clung to the NIEO agenda. The end of the Cold War had marginalized the South's importance as an area of superpower competition. The North had succeeded in defeating or ignoring many of the South's proposed programs. The potential transformation of the international trading system through the creation of the World Trade Organization (WTO) in late 1994 will doubtless lead to further questions about the future of UNCTAD.

MARGARET P. KARNS

See also General Agreement on Tariffs and Trade; Generalized System of Preferences; New International Economic Order; Third World Debt; United Nations; World Trade Organization

FURTHER READING

Bhagwati, Jagdish N. *The New International Economic Order: The North-South Debate.* Cambridge, Mass., 1977.

Bhattacharya, Anindya K. "The Influence of the International Secretariat: UNCTAD and Generalized Tariff Preferences," *International Organization* 30: 1 (Winter 1976), 75–90.

Cordovez, Diego. "The Making of UNCTAD: Institutional Background and Legislative History," *Journal of World Trade Law* 1 (May-June 1967), 243–328.

Gosovic, Branislav. *UNCTAD: Conflict and Compromise.* Leiden, Neth., 1972.

Murphy, Craig N. *The Emergence of the NIEO Ideology.* Boulder, Colo., 1984.

Nye, Gerald. "UNCTAD: Poor Nations' Pressure Group." In *The Anatomy of Influence: Decision-making in an International Organization.* Robert W. Cox and Harold K. Jacobson, eds. New Haven, Conn., 1974.

Rothstein, Robert L. *Global Bargaining: UNCTAD and the Quest for a New International Economic Order.* Princeton, N.J., 1979.

Williams, Marc. *Third World Cooperation: The Group of 77 in UNCTAD.* New York, 1991.

UNITED NATIONS ENVIRONMENT PROGRAM

Established in 1973 as an outcome of the United Nations Conference on the Human Environment held at Stockholm in 1972. The program, headquartered in Nairobi, Kenya, represents a formal institutional commitment by the international community to establish an organization with catalytic responsibilities for environmental management. The United States helped initiate the program and continues to support it. Its mandate is to stimulate and organize environmental actions for the international community as a whole, including but not limited to the United Nations system. Since its inception, the United Nations Environment Program (UNEP) was shaped by the thinking of the scientific community and by environmental problems of an increasingly visible nature and by public demands for viable modes of environmental management. Responsibility for governance lies with the governing council, which reports to the United Nations Economic and Social Commission (ECOSOC) and the UN General Assembly. UNEP serves as the secretariat for the Committee of International Development Institutions on the Environment (CIDIE) and for the UN Designated Officials on Environmental Matters (DOEM). UNEP's core priorities include follow-up on the action plan of Stockholm, promotion of international environmental law, most notably through "soft law," referring primarily to emergent norms and customs, and articulation of general principles in support of environmental management. UNEP has had considerable success in several areas. These include expansion of the Regional Seas Program and the adoption of a set of regionally specific action plans, promotion of and support for the adoption of the Vienna Convention for the Protection of the Ozone Layer (1985) and the Montreal Protocol on Substances that Deplete the Ozone Layer (1987), and successful diplomacy leading to the adoption of the Convention on Biological Diversity (1992). Innovative work on cleaner industrial production and efforts to upgrade the environmental assessment and management capabilities of developing countries are noteworthy. UNEP has increasingly become the environmental conscience of the international community. Its primary link is to government agencies responsible for environment, traditionally "weak" ministries in that they do not have strong financial resources; however, these have become stronger, buttressed by access to the scientific and technical skills of UNEP or routed through UNEP's professional networks at both national and international levels.

NAZLI CHOUCRI

See also Biodiversity Treaty; Environment; Montreal Protocol; United Nations Conference on the Human Environment, Stockholm

FURTHER READING

Thacher, Peter S. "Multilateral Cooperation and Global Change." *Journal of International Affairs* 44 (2) (Winter 1991).

United Nations. *Report of the United Nations Conference on the Human Environment, Stockholm, June 5–6, 1972.* New York, 1973.

UNITED NATIONS RELIEF AND REHABILITATION ADMINISTRATION

Since World War II, a number of organizations have been created to aid persons displaced by war, famine, and political upheaval. The UN Relief and Rehabilitation Administration (UNRRA) was the first of these organizations and operated from 9 November 1943 to 30 June 1947, expending almost $4 billion. UNRRA provided temporary care for wartime refugees and helped between nine million and fourteen million return to their homes. (Estimates of the numbers vary.) More than one million additional persons remained, however, and sought resettlement rather than repatriation.

To address the needs for resettlement, the UN General Assembly created the International Refugee Organization (IRO) in 1946. Many of the remaining World War II refugees seeking resettlement came from Eastern Europe, and hence, IRO came under criticism from the Soviet Union and Eastern European states. IRO was replaced by the Convention on Refugees in 1951 and the Office of the UN High Commissioner for Refugees (UNHCR). The creation of the state of Israel in 1948 prompted the creation in 1949 of yet another organization, the United Nations Relief and Works Agency for Palestine Refugees in the Near East (UNRWA), to care

for the displaced Arab community.

The United States, along with Western European governments, has generally promoted international refugee policy and the concept of "non-refoulement." The latter means that a refugee may not be returned to the country of origin if there is risk of persecution or death. The United States also has supported the principle in the Universal Declaration of Human Rights that everyone has a right to leave their country. Other countries have not necessarily accepted these principles, nor shown much interest in international assistance to refugees, as evidenced in the fact that only some ninety UN members in the 1990s adhere to the Convention on Refugees.

The evolution and expansion of international organizations dealing with refugees is indicative of how limited the conception of refugee affairs was in 1943 when UNRRA's mandate was to care for and repatriate persons displaced by World War II. Few would have anticipated that in the absence of a major war the numbers of refugees fifty years later would exceed those of the 1940s. Indeed, in 1993, the UN High Commissioner for Refugees estimated the number of refugees worldwide at more than 20 million people. The majority of these refugees are the product of ethnic violence and civil strife.

MARGARET P. KARNS

See also Refugees; United Nations

FURTHER READING

Gordenker, Leon. *Refugees in International Politics.* London, 1987.

Holborn, Louise W. *Refugees: A Problem of Our Time.* Metuchen, N.J., 1975.

Woodbridge, George. *UNRRA: The History of the United Nations Relief and Rehabilitation Agency.* New York, 1950.

UNITED STATES INFORMATION AGENCY

An independent executive government agency responsible for public diplomacy or overseas propaganda. It maintains 209 overseas posts in 144 countries, where it is known as the U.S. Information Service (USIS), and employs about nine thousand people, most of whom work abroad. Its 1993 budget was $1.2 billion, which increased rapidly during the Reagan administration. Although unknown to most people in the United States, USIA/USIS is highly visible and well known overseas. It was founded in 1953 to consolidate activities ("Voice of America" and various information centers) begun during World War II. By law, USIA materials may not be distributed in the United States, but overseas facilities are open to U.S. citizens. The Voice of America (VOA) radio programs can be heard in the United States with a shortwave radio receiver.

Major USIA responsibilities include public relations for U.S. embassies and diplomatic missions; operation of the Voice of America and a limited television service called Worldnet; administration of government-sponsored educational and cultural exchanges, including the Fulbright program; operation of 160 overseas cultural centers or libraries, many of which offer English classes and counseling for students who want to study in the United States; publication of thirteen magazines and commercial bulletins in twenty languages and a global news service in five languages. USIA was given responsibility for administering various special programs to promote democratic development in Central and Eastern Europe after the collapse of communism.

Unlike most other national public diplomacy agencies, USIA combines policy-oriented information activities with generally nonpolitical cultural and educational programs. Some argue that the former tend to taint the latter and prefer the separation of nonpolitical organizations—such as the British Council and BBC World Service—from government information activities.

In 1993 President Bill Clinton appointed Joseph S. Duffey, former chancellor of the University of Massachusetts and president of American University, as director of USIA. The Clinton administration proposed consolidating Radio Free Europe and Radio Liberty, which are funded and administered by the U.S. Board for International Broadcasting, with VOA. Another legislative proposal called for the establishment of a new Asian Democracy Radio (or Radio Free Asia) to be administered by USIA. The Clinton administration fought efforts, in 1996, by Senator Jesse Helms to fold USIA into the Department of State.

ROBERT L. STEVENSON

See also Foreign Broadcast Information Service; Radio Free Europe and Radio Liberty; Voice of America

FURTHER READING
Bogart, Leo. *Cool Words, Cold War: A New Look at USIA'a Premises of Propagnada.* Washington, D.C., 1995.

UNITED STATES INTERNATIONAL TRADE COMMISSION
See Tariffs

UNITED STATES TARIFF COMMISSION
See Tariffs

UNITED STATES TRADE REPRESENTATIVE

The Office of the United States Trade Representative (USTR) has the primary responsibility for the formulation and administration of U.S. trade policy. USTR is the U.S. government's chief negotiator for all trade agreements and its representative in major international trade organizations. It took a leading role in the Kennedy, Tokyo, and Uruguay Rounds of multilateral trade negotiations, as well as free trade agreements with Canada, Mexico, and Israel. A relatively small agency (with about 150 full-time professionals) operating within the executive office of the president, the office is headed by the United States trade representative, a cabinet-rank official with the title of ambassador who is directly responsible to the president and to the Congress.

The USTR is not an autonomous actor conducting U.S. trade policy. Rather, it serves to coordinate a process that respects the policy jurisdiction and utilizes the staff expertise of several departments and agencies, principally the Departments of Agriculture, Commerce, Labor, State, and Treasury. Responsibility for administering U.S. trade agreements and enforcing U.S. trade laws remain primarily with the Departments of Agriculture, Commerce, and Treasury.

As in many bureaucratic structures, the real degree of power exerted over trade policy by the office is heavily influenced by the intellectual and negotiating skills, closeness to the president, and stature of the individual serving as USTR.

Timing and circumstance also have determined the legacy of individual USTRs. For example, William Eberle did a skillful job of generating broad support for passage of the essentially liberal trade-oriented Trade Act of 1974 at a time when protectionist sentiment was extremely strong. Robert Strauss gained a reputation as a master dealmaker in the late 1970s for guiding the Tokyo Round of negotiations to a successful conclusion, and for securing a series of trade liberalization measures from Japan. Carla Hills, the USTR in the final years of the Bush administration, and Mickey Kantor, who served under President Clinton, share credit for the successful conclusion of the Uruguay Round of trade negotiations and for bringing to fruition the North American Free Trade Agreement (NAFTA).

Evolution and Authority

The USTR—originally called the Special Representative for Trade Negotiations—was created by Congress under the Trade Expansion Act of 1962. Some key legislators, like House Ways and Means chair Wilbur Mills, objected to continued Department of State had leadership of U.S. delegations to multilateral trade talks. State held princi-

U.S. TRADE REPRESENTATIVES

Name	Dates	Administration
Christian A. Herter	1963–1966	Kennedy
		L.B. Johnson
William Matson Roth	1967–1969	L.B. Johnson
		Nixon
Carl J. Gilbert	1969–1971	Nixon
William D. Eberle	1971–1974	Nixon
		Ford
Frederick B. Dent	1975–1977	Ford
		Carter
Robert S. Strauss	1977–1979	Carter
Reubin O'D. Askew	1979–1980	Carter
William Emerson Brock, III	1981–1985	Reagan
Clayton Yeutter	1985–1989	Reagan
Carla Anderson Hills	1989–1993	Bush
Michael Kantor	1993–Present	Clinton

Source: The U.S. Government Manual

pal responsibility for negotiating trade barrier reductions under the Trade Agreements Program since its inception in 1934. However, some members of Congress believed that the department was too accommodating to the demands and sensitivities of other countries and too little concerned with domestic interests. This was deemed unacceptable in the early 1960s, when the West European and Japanese economies had recovered sufficiently from World War II to become world-class competitors. As a precondition for delegating tariff reduction authority to the president for what became the Kennedy Round of trade negotiations, Congress legislated a transfer of trade negotiating leadership to a presumably more hard-line negotiator—a congressionally created, independent White House agency with direct presidential access.

The authority and staff size of the USTR were increased in the office's 1980 reorganization, which also established its current name. The reorganization also originated in the Congress, which criticized the old system as excessively decentralized and inefficient. Since then, the office has taken the lead role in providing guidance to the president on a broad range of trade policy issues: 1) expansion of exports; 2) matters concerning the General Agreement on Tariffs and Trade (GATT), and its successor, the World Trade Organization (WTO); 3) guidelines for overall U.S. trade policy with regard to unfair trade practices; 4) bilateral trade and commodity issues; 5) energy-related trade issues; 6) trade-related foreign direct investment matters; and 7) policy research.

Organization and Coordinating Functions

The USTR is assisted by three deputies, one of whom serves in Geneva as U.S. representative to the WTO.

The working level is dominated by about fifteen assistant USTRs heading offices divided among regional areas and functional issues such as: WTO affairs; industry; services, investment, and science and technology; agriculture; intellectual property and the environment; textiles; and private sector liaison.

The USTR chairs a network of permanent interagency trade policy committees designed to account for a range of official views and to develop consensus within the executive branch on trade matters. In theory, USTR chairs the cabinet-level Trade Policy Committee, but this was moribund from the 1980s through the mid-1900s—its duties absorbed by the senior White House economic policy coordinating group (variously called the Economic Policy Group and the National Economic Council). The Trade Policy Review Group, which functions at the undersecretary or assistant secretary level, is composed of ten cabinet departments and several White House offices. A third level of the coordinating process consists of the same agencies meeting at the office director level in the Trade Policy Staff Committee. Given its extensive workload, the Trade Policy Staff Committee is subdivided into more than 60 subcommittees and task forces. As chair of coordinating committees, USTR schedules meetings, plans agendas, and manages the paper flow, as well as taking an advocacy role in trying to influence policy substance.

The USTR office also supervises liaison with the private sector advisory committees that counsel the government on trade policy, as well as on objectives and strategies in specific trade negotiations.

About a thousand private sector experts from industry, agriculture, labor, environmental groups, and consumer interests participated (as of 1994) in thirty-eight different advisory groups operating on three tiers. At the apex of the system is a diverse group of senior individuals who compose the Advisory Committee for Trade Policy and Negotiations. Seven more narrowly focused groups make up the second level and deal with agriculture, defense, industry, investment, labor, services, and state and local government issues. Finally, thirty committees deal with specialized technical and sectoral issues in industry and agriculture. These groups have an informal veto over U.S. trade policy since Congress is unlikely to approve legislation strongly opposed by the appointed representatives of the private sector.

The Office of the USTR continues to enjoy a special status on Capitol Hill, in part because it is Congress's offspring and in part because it has maintained its original mandate to balance domestic and international priorities in trade. While the USTR's primary function may be negotiating trade liberalization agreements, it has never acquired a reputation as a knee-jerk free trader, because it still occasionally sides with departmental advocates of protectionism in specific import policy decisions.

Although the USTR usually enjoys an excellent rapport with Congress, it is by no means the only voice of the trade policy domain in the executive branch. It does not have jurisdiction over a number of key operational programs, such as export promotion or imposition of import barriers to protect domestic producers. Also, cabinet departments (usually Agriculture, Commerce, and State) consistently assert jurisdictional leadership over new trade issues, either because their constituencies are affected or because the USTR lacks relevant personnel. Finally, the political savvy of the USTR and their personal relationship with the president help determine the office's real power. For these reasons, some U.S. trade policy analysts still advocate broadening USTR's power by expanding its authority and resources, and elevating it to departmental status.

STEPHEN D. COHEN

FURTHER READING

Cohen, Stephen D. *The Making of United States International Economic Policy,* fourth edition. New York, 1994.
Destler, I. M. *American Trade Politics,* second edition. Washington, 1992.
Lewis, Charles. *Office of the United States Trade Representatives: America's Frontline Trade Officials.* Washington, D.C., 1990.
U.S. Trade Representative. *1996 Trade Policy Agenda and 1995 Annual Report.* Washington, D.C., 1996.

UNITED STATES V. CURTISS-WRIGHT EXPORT CORPORATION

See Curtiss-Wright Case

UNIVERSAL DECLARATION OF HUMAN RIGHTS

See Human Rights

UNRRA

See United Nations Relief and Rehabilitation Administration

UPSHUR, ABEL PARKER

(*b.* 17 June 1790; *d.* 28 February 1844)

Secretary of state (1843–1844). An aristocratic planter, slaveholder, and judge from Virginia's eastern shore, he served as secretary of state during John Tyler's one-term presidency of 1841–1845. Although an adroit diplomatist, a persuasive lobbyist, and an accomplished manipulator of public opinion, Upshur had few diplomatic achievements. His major foreign policy initiatives, the annexation of Texas and the resolution of the Oregon controversy, were brought to fruition by his successors at the Department of State after he was killed during an accidental explosion on the warship *Princeton* in the Potomac River. Upshur was a leading representative of the Old South: he believed expansion offered the only hope for his region and for the preservation of slavery.

EDWARD P. CRAPOL

See also Tyler, John

FURTHER READING

Freehling, William W. *The Road to Disunion: Secessionists at Bay, 1776–1854.* New York, 1990.
Hall, Claude H. *Abel Parker Upshur, Conservative Virginia, 1790-1844.* Madison, Wis., 1964.

URUGUAY

South American republic, bordering the South Atlantic Ocean between Argentina and Brazil. The United States initiated full diplomatic relations with Uruguay in 1867, forty-two years after the territory declared its independence from Spain. U.S. diplomats have sought Uruguayan cooperation in their efforts to dampen conflicts in the region, particularly between Uruguay's two giant neighbors. The rivalries between the two, which date back to competition between the colonial governments of Spain and Portugal, nonetheless led Argentina and Brazil to make frequent use of Uruguay's territory and internal political differences in pursuing their own confrontations.

During World War I, Uruguay at first declared neutrality but then sided with the United States against Germany. During World War II, the United States built naval and air bases in Uruguay and provided loans and military assistance, even though Uruguay did not declare war against the Axis until February 1945. After the war, Uruguay joined the Rio Pact (1947).

While the U.S. relationship with Uruguay has been largely cooperative, sharp disagreements have arisen in recent decades. In 1962 Uruguay was the only member of the Organization of American States to vote against a quarantine of Cuba during the missile crisis on that island. Uruguay suspended relations with Cuba in 1974, after a military-backed government took power in a 1973 coup. Despite this cooperation with U.S. efforts to isolate Cuba, President Jimmy Carter ordered sharp cuts in U.S. military and economic aid to Uruguay's military government in protest against persistent human rights violations by the military. After an elected civilian government was re-established in 1985, it reinstated relations with Cuba.

U.S.-based banks held much of the $6.5 billion in foreign debt that the military government accumulated during its years in power. Officials of the United States encouraged the subsequent civilian governments to renegotiate the loans and to introduce economic reforms and fiscal austerity, using modest foreign aid and conditions attached to loans from multilateral financial institutions as tools to promote reform policies. Uruguayan officials, however, scaled back their reform proposals when they faced widespread public opposition. In the 1990s Uruguay shifted the emphasis of its foreign economic relations away from the United States and toward its neighbors, joining the Southern Cone Common Market with Argentina, Brazil and Paraguay.

CHRISTOPHER WELNA

See also Cuban Missile Crisis; Human Rights; Latin America

FURTHER READING

Drummond, Kitty Lomax. *Relations between Uruguay and the United States.* Durham, N.C., 1936.
Fernandez, Ariosto. *Primeras relaciones politicas y sociales entre la republica oriental de Uruguay y los Estados Unidos de America.* Montevideo, 1958.
Haedo, Eduardo Victor. *El Uruguay y la politica internacional del Rio de la Plata.* Buenos Aires, 1973.
Pomer, Leon. *Conflictos en la Cuenca del Plata en el siglo XIX.* Buenos Aires, 1984.
Whitaker, Arthur P. *The United States and the Southern Cone.* 1976.

URUGUAY ROUND

See General Agreement on Tariffs and Trade

USIA

See United States Information Agency

USSR

See Russia and the Soviet Union

USTR

See United States Trade Representative

U-2 INCIDENT

A Soviet-American dispute arising from the Soviet downing of a U.S. spy plane. On 1 May 1960, two weeks before a four-power summit conference to discuss the future of Berlin—an irritant to the Soviets in that tens of thousands of Germans from the Soviet-controlled sector of East Berlin fled to the Western sectors of the city every year—an American U-2 spy plane piloted by Francis Gary Powers was brought down by Soviet air defenses using SA-2 missiles near Sverdlovsk (now Ekaterinburg) in Central Russia.

Recent documents available from Russian archives and oral testimony from former Soviet leaders suggests that the Soviets may have had second thoughts about the upcoming Paris summit meeting. In the months before the scheduled summit, Nikita Khrushchev was being pressured by Soviet hard-liners to back away from détente. In the West, except for President Dwight D. Eisenhower, there also was little enthusiasm for the summit. On 9 April 1960, a U-2 overflight, tracked and identified by Soviet radar, put Khrushchev's hard-line coterie in a position to force Khrushchev to abandon détente. In this context, the flight of 1 May, piloted by Gary Powers, may have been less the immediate cause and more a kind of a fillip to a decision that had been taken weeks earlier by Khrushchev and his closest confederates.

In any case, once the spy plane went down, with its pilot captured alive, Eisenhower would not pay Khrushchev's price for salvaging the conference by disavowing the U-2 overflight or apologizing. The conference broke up. With the demise of the summit, hope faded that Eisenhower might be able to settle with the Soviets some of the great issues of the Cold War in the time that was left to him in office.

Questions remain about the incident. First, before any of the spring 1960 flights, Eisenhower fretted over the diplomatic implications of the overflights in general and, in particular, the possibility of a U-2 inadvertently coming down in Soviet territory. As far back as October 1959, Khrushchev had asked Eisenhower to do nothing that would compromise the summit and was "beside himself" at the continuing overflights. Eisenhower did not think the risk in terms of the U.S. position in the world was worth the information gleaned from these missions. Given Eisenhower's record of concern, what prompted the president, just days before a summit that he had vested so many hopes in, to approve yet another flight that would carry it along a much longer flight pattern than the earlier 9 April flight? Second, Central Intelligence Agency (CIA) Director John McCone once suggested that Powers had deliberately guided his plane down into Soviet territory. What prompted these assessments? Third, Eisenhower apparently believed that much of the fault for the disruption of the Paris summit lay with then CIA Director Allen Dulles, and that Dulles withheld information on the program and on events that led up to the U-2. Were the president's suspicions and anger warranted? Why would Dulles hide information from Eisenhower? Fourth, why was there such an apparent urgency to retrieve Powers from a Soviet prison? Powers was a highly paid journeyman civilian pilot ($30,000 per year). Presumably his salary was to compensate for the risk. Yet Powers was exchanged for Colonel Rudolph Abel, one of the most important Soviet spies the United States ever captured. Why was such an apparently asymmetric trade pursued with such vigor? Fifth, why was Powers given a job with the CIA on his return and awarded the Intelligence Star—the CIA's highest decoration—for behavior that seemed to be a breach of every injunction of intelligence service, especially "deniability"?

Some suspicions raised by scholars could lead to a conclusion that the U-2 misadventure of May 1960 reflected a deliberate CIA strategy to torpedo the Paris summit. But Powers's unwillingness to commit suicide, his conspicuously identifiable paraphernalia, and the trade of Powers for Abel, most conventional historical accounts indicate, are explicable in terms of the routines of the Cold War national-security bureaucracies of both superpowers.

The many lingering questions about this incident may be beyond answering because of Powers's 1977 death in a civilian helicopter crash. Powers's second wife apparently felt Powers was a plot victim, a second time, and this time fatally, when a helicopter he piloted for a television station apparently ran out of fuel and crashed.

U-2 overflights put the lie to the charges against the Eisenhower administration that it had permitted a "bomber gap" and a "missile gap" in the Soviet's favor by demonstrating through photo reconnaissance that Soviet missile production was far below initial U.S. intelligence projection. But the May 1960 U-2 incident exacted serious costs. The "hard-line" Chinese position in international affairs was reinforced as against the accommodationist line that Khrushchev had been promoting. And Khrushchev's own pro-détente efforts were undermined within the Soviet ruling elite. Moreover, as a result of capturing Powers and his high-altitude camera, intact, the Soviets learned the extent of American knowledge about their failure to produce a meaningful number of advanced, nuclear-capable rockets; hence, as a consequence of the U-2 incident, the Soviets accelerated their production of intercontinental missiles.

Thus, it can also be argued that the "Spirit of Camp David," promoted by Eisenhower and Khrushchev in 1959, evanesced in the aftermath of the U-2 downing. Finally, there was an eventual penalty to the CIA's reputation for reliable advice and operational competence—a slide that accelerated after the failure of the Bay of Pigs expedition against Cuba in early 1961.

JAMES NATHAN

See also Berlin; Cold War; Eisenhower, Dwight David; Intelligence; Khrushchev, Nikita Sergeyevich

FURTHER READING
Richelson, Jeffrey T. *A Century of Spies: Intelligence in the Twentieth Century.* New York, 1995.

UZBEKISTAN
See Appendix 2

V

VAN BUREN, MARTIN

(*b.* 5 December 1782; *d.* 24 July 1862)

Secretary of state (1829–1831), vice president (1833–1837), and eighth president of the United States (1837–1841). Descended from an old Dutch New York family, Van Buren earned the nickname "the Red Fox of Kinderhook" for his reddish hair and his political acumen. In 1828 his development of a coalition of northern and southern Democrats helped elect Andrew Jackson president. Van Buren served as Jackson's secretary of state from 1829 until April 1831, when he resigned in the cabinet crisis precipitated by the Peggy Eaton scandal. During his tenure Van Buren dealt with the reopening of trade with the British West Indies, the French spoliations issue, the Maine-New Brunswick boundary dispute, and the Texas question. Jackson named Van Buren minister to Great Britain as a recess appointment. He had already taken up residence in London when the Senate rejected his appointment. Van Buren then ran for vice president in 1832 as Jackson's running mate.

Van Buren himself was elected president in 1836. Diplomatic issues during his administration included the still-unresolved Maine-New Brunswick boundary controversy with Great Britain and the *Caroline* Affair involving Canadian rebels. In each of these foreign policy crises, Van Buren acted cautiously and responsibly, which undoubtedly cost him political support in the states along the Canadian border. Texas proved to be the most volatile foreign policy issue of Van Buren's administration. After the revolution of 1836, Texans sought annexation to the United States. Van Buren rebuffed their efforts because annexation threatened to aggravate the slavery issue (by admitting another slave state to the Union) and further strain relations with Mexico.

Van Buren was defeated for the presidency in 1840 by the Whig candidate William Henry Harrison, primarily because of hard economic times arising from the Panic of 1837. Van Buren hoped to retake the presidency in 1844 but was denied the Democratic nomination because of a dispute over Texas. During the campaign that led up to the Democratic convention, Van Buren had sent a letter opposing annexation to a member of Congress from Mississippi, William H. Hammet. Proannexation Democrats turned against him, and the nomination and the presidency went instead to James Knox Polk. Four years later

Van Buren accepted the nomination of the Free Soil party but failed again in his bid to win the presidency. Retiring to New York, Van Buren composed an autobiography and his political memoirs.

KENNETH R. STEVENS

See also Canada; Caroline Affair; Jackson, Andrew; Mexico, War with

FURTHER READING

Bassett, John Spencer. "Martin Van Buren, Secretary of State, March 6, 1829, to April 23, 1831." In *The American Secretaries of State and their Diplomacy*, vol. 4, edited by Samuel Flagg Bemis. New York, 1927–1929.

Cole, Donald B. *Martin Van Buren and the American Political System.* Princeton, N.J., 1984.

Niven, John. *Martin Van Buren: The Romantic Age of American Politics.* New York, 1983.

VANCE, CYRUS ROBERTS

(*b.* 27 March 1917)

Secretary of state (1977–1980). Born in Clarksburg, West Virginia, Vance grew up in Bronxville, New York. He graduated from Yale College (1939) and Yale Law School (1942). After serving in the navy during World War II, Vance was admitted to the New York bar in 1947 and practiced law at Simpson, Thatcher, and Bartlett. While serving as general counsel to the Senate Preparedness Investigation Committee in 1958, Vance came to the attention of Senate Majority Leader Lyndon B. Johnson. He became secretary of the army in 1962 and was then appointed deputy secretary of defense in 1964 by President Johnson, who called on Vance to defuse a wide variety of crises: riots in Panama over the sovereignty of the Panama Canal (1964); rebellion in the Dominican Republic (1965); the Greek-Turkish dispute over Cyprus (1967); and the seizure of the U.S. intelligence ship *Pueblo* by North Korea (1968). From May 1968 to January 1969 he assisted W. Averell Harriman, the U.S. representative, at the Vietnam peace talks in Paris. He then resumed his law practice.

Vance returned to Washington in 1977 as secretary of state under President Jimmy Carter and demonstrated a deep commitment to nuclear arms control as well as a reluctance to threaten or use armed force to achieve U.S. foreign policy goals. His strength lay in his proverbial honesty and patient negotiating skills. Suspicious of grand theories of strategy and geopolitics, Vance often clashed with National Security Adviser Zbigniew Brzezinski. For example, Vance thought the United States should move cautiously toward normalizing relations with the People's Republic of China to avoid the appearance of ganging up against the Soviet Union, lest an alarmed Kremlin back away from progress on the limitation of nuclear arms, a matter Vance considered of the highest priority. Brzezinski, on the other hand, urged a strategic relationship with China precisely in order to unsettle the Kremlin. Vance wanted the United States to maintain a low profile with regard to the war in the Horn of Africa between Ethiopia and Somalia over the Ogaden region; Brzezinski saw that struggle as a test of the relative influence of the Soviet Union and the United States. The United States accordingly sided with and provided arms for Somalia. On the question of the faltering regime of the shah of Iran, Vance supported those who believed the shah should meet dissent with genuine reform; Brzezinski argued for urging the shah to employ all force necessary to put down the incipient rebellion. In April 1980 Vance resigned as secretary of state in principled protest over the attempt by the United States to rescue by military force the U.S. hostages held in Iran since November 1979. He returned to law practice in New York and published his memoirs, *Hard Choices* (1983).

In October 1991 United Nations Secretary-General Boutros Boutros-Ghali appointed Vance cochairperson of the Steering Committee of the International Conference on the Former Yugoslavia. In this capacity Vance helped produce the Vance-Owen peace plan for Bosnia, a controversial scheme that President Bill Clinton's administration found largely unacceptable. Vance retired from this position in May 1993, but he continued in his capacity as special mediator in the ongoing contretemps between Greece and the former Yugoslav Republic of Macedonia.

RICHARD A. MELANSON

See also Bosnia-Herzegovina; Brzezinski, Zbigniew Kasimierz; Carter, James Earl; Cyprus; Dominican Republic; Iran; Johnson, Lyndon Baines; Panama and Panama Canal; Pueblo Incident; Somalia

FURTHER READING

Smith, Gaddis. *Morality, Reason and Power: American Diplomacy in the Carter Years*. New York, 1986.

Talbott, Strobe. "The Ultimate Troubleshooter." *Time* (9 March 1992).

Vance, Cyrus. *Hard Choices: Critical Years in America's Foreign Policy*. New York, 1983.

VANDENBERG, ARTHUR HENDRICK

(*b.* 22 March 1884; *d.* 18 April 1951)

Pre–World War II isolationist senator and postwar bipartisan advocate of containment policies (1928–1951). Son of a Grand Rapids, Michigan, harnessmaker ruined in the "Democratic" Panic of 1893, Vandenberg swore allegiance to the Republican party from an early age. A high school orator who took second place in the state competition with a speech advocating U.S. participation in the Hague Peace Conference of 1899, Vandenberg entered the University of Michigan with hopes of becoming a lawyer, politician, or diplomat. Forced to leave after one year for financial reasons, he took a job in 1902 as a reporter at the *Grand Rapids Herald*. Rising to the position of editorial writer and, eventually, publisher of the *Herald*, Vandenberg supported the interventionist foreign policies of his boyhood idol Theodore Roosevelt. When Democrat Woodrow Wilson intervened in Latin America, however, Vandenberg called the action ill-advised "missionary diplomacy." He generally supported Wilson's neutrality policies prior to U.S. entry into World War I and enthusiastically endorsed Wilson's Fourteen Points. During the fight over ratification of the Treaty of Versailles, however, he shifted to a "reservationist" position, holding that U.S. membership in the League of Nations must not interfere with the Monroe Doctrine.

In the 1920s Vandenberg moved from the progressive to the conservative side of the Republican party. In 1928 he was appointed to fill an unexpired term as senator from Michigan. From the start a bombastic "Young Turk," he immediately sought membership on the Foreign Relations Committee. He decisively won election to the Senate in his own right that same year. A protégé of Senator William Borah, Vandenberg came to see himself in the 1930s as successor to Henry Cabot Lodge as leader of Republican senators on foreign policy issues. A cosponsor of the Nye Committee investigations of munitions makers and their influence on the U.S. decision to enter World War I, Vandenberg reflected the isolationism of his midwestern constituents. He helped pass the Neutrality Acts of the 1930s and fought President Franklin D. Roosevelt's efforts to aid the Allied powers through the Lend-Lease Act.

The Japanese attack in December 1941 on Pearl Harbor, as he later put it, "ended isolation for any realist." Vandenberg underwent another conversion, this time to proponent of international collective security. He urged bipartisan support for U.S. membership in the United Nations, served as a delegate to the 1945 San Francisco Conference, and ushered ratification of the UN charter through the Senate. Reflecting his earlier attitudes on the League of Nations Covenant, Vandenberg made certain that UN membership would not preclude regional alliances.

Emerging from World War II as the chief Republican foreign policy spokesman, Vandenberg insisted upon being included in postwar diplomacy, although his role was more that of a watchdog than a policymaker. Officials in the administration of President Harry S. Truman did not hold him in high regard, but they nonetheless worked hard to court him. Vandenberg accompanied Secretary of State James F. Byrnes to the Big Four foreign ministers conferences in Paris and New York and served as a delegate to the first two UN General Assembly sessions. As chairman of the Foreign Relations Committee from 1947 to 1949, he reformed its procedures and worked for passage of Truman Doctrine aid to Greece and Turkey and the Marshall Plan. His 1948 Vandenberg Resolution paved the way for approval of the North Atlantic Treaty Organization (NATO) treaty.

An ardent cold warrior, Vandenberg urged bipartisanship on foreign policy issues, while jealously guarding congressional prerogatives. He avoided the extremism of colleagues such as Senator Joseph McCarthy, who attacked the Truman administration for "losing" China to communism. Albeit reluctantly, he accepted Truman's decision in 1950 to send troops to Korea without a declaration of war. Vandenberg died as bipartisan support for that "police action" waned.

ROBERT L. MESSER

See also Bipartisanship; Borah, William Edgar; Cold War; Collective Security; Fourteen Points; Hague Peace Conferences; Isolationism; League of Nations; Lend-Lease; Lodge, Henry Cabot, Jr.; Marshall Plan; North Atlantic Treaty Organization; Nye, Gerald Prentice; Truman Doctrine; United Nations; Wilson, Thomas Woodrow

FURTHER READING

Hill, Thomas M. "Senator Arthur H. Vandenberg, The Politics of Bipartisanship, and the Origins of the Anti-Soviet Consensus, 1941–1946." *World Affairs* 138 (1975–1976): 219–241.
Tompkins, C. David. *Senator Arthur H. Vandenberg: The Evolution of a Modern Republican, 1884–1945.* East Lansing, Mich., 1970.
Vandenberg, Arthur H., Jr., ed. *The Private Papers of Senator Vandenberg.* Boston, 1952.

VANDENBERG RESOLUTION

See Vandenberg, Arthur Hendrick

VANDERBILT, CORNELIUS

(*b.* 27 May 1794; *d.* 4 January 1877)

One of the great industrialists and tycoons of the nineteenth century. Born on Staten Island, New York, Vanderbilt entered the transportation industry at age sixteen and bought his first steamship in 1829. He devoted much of his prodigious energy to building steamship lines, railroads, and a legendary personal fortune. One business venture, however, drew him into the arena of international politics and intrigue. Vanderbilt's efforts to secure and maintain exclusive rights to interoceanic transport through Nicaragua in the 1850s influenced U.S. relations with that Central American nation.

The California gold rush sparked Vanderbilt's interest in developing a canal or a land-and-water route through Nicaragua that would link the Atlantic and the Pacific oceans. Vanderbilt envied the success of the established route through Panama and was determined to establish a competitive alternative along Nicaragua's San Juan River and Lake Nicaragua. Ascending the often treacherous San Juan by means of ropes and pulleys, Vanderbilt established a passage that was 600 miles shorter and several days faster than the Panamanian route. Vanderbilt's Accessory Transit Company (ATC), chartered in Nicaragua in 1852, enjoyed exclusive rights to the new route. Events in Nicaragua and on Wall Street conspired to deny Vanderbilt the fruits of his ingenuity. Two of his associates, Charles Morgan and Cornelius Garrison, who had been unsuccessful in their efforts to wrest control of the ATC from Vanderbilt by acquiring company stock, attempted to do so by force in Nicaragua. They provided support, including Vanderbilt steamers, to an insurgency in Nicaragua that was led by the Nashville-born filibuster William Walker. The financiers convinced Walker to rescind the ATC's charter and to grant to their company exclusive rights to the trans-Nicaragua route. When the Department of State rebuffed Vanderbilt's requests for intervention to restore his rights to the passage, Vanderbilt decided to follow Morgan and Garrison's example and take the law into his own hands. An expeditionary force financed by Vanderbilt and launched from Costa Rica toppled Walker's government in 1857. The new government, restored to Nicaraguans for reasons having nothing to do with respect for sovereignty, reaffirmed Vanderbilt's monopoly on transportation across the isthmus.

LEEANNA Y. KEITH

See also Nicaragua; Walker, William

VANUATU

See Appendix 2

VATICAN

An enclave in Rome, the last remnant of the independent Papal States, that is today the seat of the papacy, and the center of the Roman Catholic Church. Well into the twentieth century, concern for the separation of church and state joined with religious prejudice to convince much of the U.S. public that diplomatic relations with the papacy were neither constitutional nor desirable. Policymakers, however, often recognized that national interests required closer relations with the Vatican. The tension between domestic political concerns and diplomatic imperatives accounts for the episodic nature of U.S.-Vatican relations, with contacts intensifying at times of crisis and lapsing in times of tranquility. When President James K. Polk recognized the Papal States in 1848, his stated reasons were that diplomatic relations would benefit U.S. commerce and encourage the liberal reforms of the newly elected pope, Pius IX. Since trade with the Papal States was negligible (and was bound to remain so) and since Polk's democratic idealism did not extend to recognizing more liberal regimes such as the short-lived Venetian Republic, the president was probably more prone to cultivate the papacy at a time when his administration was annexing vast Mexican territories with largely Catholic populations. Subsequently, relations slipped into torpor, only to be resuscitated during the Civil War when North and South competed for papal sympathy. The Vatican's tacit support of the North did not deter Congress from refusing in 1867 to fund the U.S. legation in the Papal States. Ostensibly a reaction to alleged restrictions on Protestant worship in Rome, the vote in fact reflected an alliance between Republicans eager to embarrass President Andrew Johnson and supporters of Italian unification critical of the pope's resistance to such unification.

In 1902 William Howard Taft, then governor of the Philippines, led a mission to the Vatican in a futile attempt to settle church-state difficulties in the newly annexed Philippines. To deflect Protestant opposition to contacts with the Vatican, President Theodore Roosevelt described the mission as a business matter without diplomatic character. During World War I, Pope Benedict XV tried to interest Washington in mediating the conflict, but all approaches were deflected by Woodrow Wilson, who considered the papacy a bulwark of the discredited old order and denied it any role in ending the war or planning the peace. Contacts were more cooperative during World War II. Convinced that Allied interests required friendly relations with the Vatican, Franklin D. Roosevelt risked the ire of Protestant groups by appointing Myron C. Taylor as his personal representative to Pope Pius XII. Although the Taylor mission fell short of formal relations, the United States consulted with the Vatican on such matters as Italian belligerency, the bombing of Rome, and the shape of postwar Europe. After the war, anticommunism produced a community of interests, although direct contacts lapsed after Taylor resigned in 1950 and President Harry S. Truman, bowing to Protestant opposition, abandoned his plan to appoint General Mark Clark as ambassador to the Vatican. The tacit alliance unravelled during the Vietnam War: Popes John XXIII (1958–1963) and Paul VI (1963–1978) preferred themes of peace and international cooperation to those of containment and superpower rivalry. Perceiving that papal sympathies could no longer be taken for granted, but wary of domestic opinion, in 1970 President

Richard M. Nixon reestablished the office of personal representative to the pope, and his successors continued the practice.

Relations intensified in the 1980s when the conservative administration of Ronald Reagan and the conservative pontificate of John Paul II (formerly Karol Cardinal Wojtyla of Poland) recognized a mutual interest in undermining communist influence in Eastern Europe and Central America. This coincidence of interests was most apparent in Poland, where the United States and the Vatican collaborated in a clandestine campaign to weaken the communist regime and support the Solidarity movement after the declaration of martial law in 1981. In 1984, Reagan elevated U.S. representation at the Vatican to an embassy and appointed William Wilson as the first American ambassador to the Vatican since 1867. Domestic opposition was muted, suggesting that religious passions had finally given way to national interest as the principal determinant of U.S.-Vatican relations.

DAVID ALVAREZ

See also Poland; Polk, James Knox

FURTHER READING

Alvarez, David. "Purely a Business Matter: The Taft Mission to the Vatican." *Diplomatic History* 16 (Summer 1992): 357–369.

Fogarty, Gerald P. "The United States and the Vatican, 1939–1984." In *Papal Diplomacy in the Modern Age*, Peter C. Kent and John F. Pollard, editors. New York, 1994.

Stock, Leo F., ed. *United States Ministers to the Papal States: Instructions and Despatches, 1848–1868.* Washington, D.C., 1933.

VENEZUELA

Located in northern South America, bordering the Caribbean Sea, Colombia, Guyana, and Brazil, it is the sixth-largest republic in South America. The United States has enjoyed a peaceful and prosperous relationship with Venezuela, benefiting in particular from Venezuela's permission to exploit its vast petroleum reserves. Venezuela has been a reliable ally of the United States, deferring to U.S. hemispheric and global leadership, although in the 1970s and 1980s relations were strained. U.S.-Venezuelan relations were unremarkable during the nineteenth century. The two nations established commercial and diplomatic relations in the 1830s, after Venezuela gained its independence. Because both nations focused on internal development and because Venezuela showed little economic promise, contacts between the two young nations were routine. Bilateral trade averaged less than $10 million a year, and U.S. direct investments amounted to less than $1 million.

Two watersheds in U.S. diplomatic history involved Venezuela—the Venezuela-British Guiana boundary dispute (1895) and the Anglo-German-Italian naval blockade of the Venezuelan coast (1902). Both confrontations were part of the U.S. drive for hegemony in the Western Hemisphere; neither incident specifically concerned U.S.-Venezuelan issues. Exercising that domination, the United States encouraged the overthrow of President Cipriano Castro (1899–1908), who mocked foreign powers and refused to pay Venezuela's international debts. A U.S. naval show of force helped Juan Vicente Gómez (1908–1935) consolidate his regime.

Eager in the post–World War I period for new sources of energy, the United States turned to Venezuela, which had begun to show potential for petroleum development. With the vigorous diplomatic assistance of the Department of State and the connivance of Gómez, U.S. oil companies by 1929 transformed Venezuela into one of the world's leading producers of oil. U.S. direct investments steadily grew to $2.7 billion by 1970, the largest U.S. investment in a Latin American country. Exporters counted Venezuela among the best markets for U.S. goods in the world. U.S.-Venezuelan disputes have predictably centered on the issue of oil. Venezuelan nationalists sought to increase oil income with the Oil Law of 1943, which gave Venezuela a fifty-fifty split of the oil companies' profits. Venezuela nationalized the foreign oil industry in 1976, although U.S. oil companies remained active through service contracts. Venezuela was one of the founding members of the Organization of Petroleum Exporting Countries (OPEC) in 1960. The United States accepted these developments, because Venezuela adhered to free trade and investment principles and opposed using oil as a diplomatic weapon against the United States.

Venezuela followed the U.S. lead during World Wars I and II as well as during the Cold War. General Marcos Pérez Jiménez (1950–1958) was a staunch anticommunist with whom the United States was closely allied. In 1958 he was forced into exile, and democracy was restored with the election as president of Rómulo Betancourt. Betancourt played a key role in supporting the U.S. effort to isolate Fidel Castro's Cuba from the inter-American community, in large part because of Castro's attempt to subvert the Betancourt regime. The administration of President John F. Kennedy tried to make Venezuela one of the models for the Alliance for Progress, pumping in large amounts of foreign aid and hailing it as an example of the democratic reformist alternative to the Castro-communist model.

In the 1970s and 1980s U.S.-Venezuelan relations were more mixed. On the one hand, Venezuela could be relied on to expand rapidly its oil production so as to help ameliorate the shortages and disruptions in world oil markets caused by the 1967 and 1973 Arab-Israeli wars. On the other hand, Venezuela played a key role in urging OPEC to quadruple world oil prices in 1973 and to be active in

the oil politics of the ensuing decade. Under Presidents Rafael Caldera and Carlos Andrés Pérez, Venezuela was a leader throughout the 1970s of the "South" in the North-South conflicts over a new international economic order. In the 1980s Venezuela largely opposed U.S. support of the Nicaraguan Contras and was a member of the Contadora Group in its effort to bring about a peace settlement.

In the late 1980s and early 1990s Venezuela experienced mounting economic problems and political instability. The administrations of Presidents George Bush and Bill Clinton sought to help by agreeing to restructure some of Venezuela's massive international debt. Charges of rampant corruption against President Pérez (who had been reelected in 1988) and his cohorts further destabilized Venezuelan politics. In late 1993 the Clinton administration worked through both public and private channels to help turn back an incipient coup attempt. In December 1993 Rafael Caldera was returned to the presidency for a five-year term. President Caldera proved incapable of halting his nation's economic slide. Desperate for capital, the government encouraged foreign oil companies to reinvest in Venezuela. In 1995–1996, U.S. oil companies eagerly accepted the offer to work again in the number one petroleum supplier for the United States.

STEPHEN G. RABE

See also Alliance for Progress; Betancourt, Rómulo; Contadora Group; Latin America; Oil and Foreign Policy; Organization of Petroleum Exporting Countries

FURTHER READING

Ewell, Judith. *Venezuela and the United States: From Monroe's Hemisphere to Petroleum's Empire.* Athens, Georgia, 1996.
Liss, Sheldon B. *Diplomacy and Dependency: Venezuela, the United States, and the Americas.* Salisbury, N.C., 1978.
Rabe, Stephen G. *The Road to OPEC.* Austin, Tex., 1982.

VENEZUELAN BOUNDARY DISPUTE
(1895–1896)

A diplomatic flare-up between the United States and Great Britain concerning a boundary dispute between Venezuela and British Guiana. The brash insistence of the U.S. government that the Monroe Doctrine gave it the right to intervene in the dispute led briefly to the possibility of war between the United States and Great Britain. The British yielded, because of larger global strategic interests, thereby giving a boost to U.S. assertiveness.

For many years the boundary line between Venezuela and British Guiana had been in dispute. Great Britain had refused to permit arbitration of all territory east of a line drawn by British explorer and surveyor Sir Robert H. Schomburgk in the early 1840s, land that included a

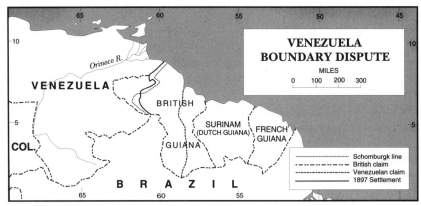

From *American Diplomacy: A History*, Robert H. Ferrell, 3rd Edition. ©1975, 1969, 1959 by W. W. Norton & Company, Inc., renewed ©1987 by Robert H. Ferrell. Reprinted with permission of W. W. Norton & Company

small area at the mouth of the Orinoco River. Conversely, Venezuela claimed that the Essequibo River was its true boundary. The presence of British settlers and the discovery of the largest gold nugget ever found raised the stakes. President Grover Cleveland's administration feared that Venezuela might find itself goaded into war with Great Britain. Were the British to gain additional territory from the conflict, the United States might find itself forced to enter the struggle to back up its insistence that new or expanded European colonies in the Western Hemisphere would not be tolerated.

The pro-Venezuelan lobbying of William L. Scruggs, former U.S. minister at Caracas; House and Senate resolutions endorsing arbitration; and Venezuela's arrest of eight British officials near the Uruan River in April 1895 forced Washington's hand. Secretary of State Richard Olney mistakenly believed the Essequibo to be Venezuela's true boundary. On 20 July 1895 he dispatched to Great Britain what Cleveland called a "twenty-inch gun." Olney's note accused the British of putting Venezuela "under virtual duress," thereby creating a condition that the United States, whose own "honor" and "interests" were involved, could not "regard with indifference." The Monroe Doctrine, he said, required the United States "to treat as an injury to itself the forcible assumption by an European power over an American state." He demanded that Great Britain submit all contested boundaries, not simply territory west of the Schomburgk line, to "impartial arbitration." "The United States is practically sovereign on this continent," he continued, "and its fiat is law upon the subjects to which it confines its interposition." He went on to say that 3,000 miles of ocean "make any permanent political union between an European and an American state unnatural and inexpedient."

On 26 November 1895, Lord Salisbury, British prime minister and foreign secretary, replied that Great Britain's union with such countries as Canada, Jamaica, and Guiana was natural and that the entire British Empire was prepared to maintain this relationship. Fearing a precedent that might be extended to other British possessions, Salisbury denied the right of the United States to insist on arbitration, insisted in turn that British territorial claims were moderate, and accused Venezuela of refusing any reasonable settlement. Although his nation, he said, was ready to arbitrate genuinely disputed territory, it would never accept the "transfer of large numbers of British subjects, who have for many years enjoyed the settled rule of a British colony, [to a country] whose political system is subject to frequent disturbance, and whose institutions as yet too often afford very inadequate protection to life and property." Claiming that the Monroe Doctrine had no application to the Venezuela controversy, Salisbury denied that it was the equivalent of international law. Salisbury also challenged the U.S. claim to own a legitimate interest in every frontier dispute that might arise in the Western Hemisphere.

To Cleveland, the Monroe Doctrine, international morality, and U.S. influence in Latin America were all at stake. Moreover, he genuinely believed in the Venezuelan case. On 17 December 1895 he asked Congress to establish a commission to investigate the contested boundary. If the British appropriated lands that the commission found belonged to Venezuela, he said, the United States would consider the move "willful aggression" on its "rights and interests" and would resist "by every means in its power." Five days later the Senate voted for the needed funds, and on 4 January 1896 the commission began its work. A brief scare resulted, during which Salisbury privately claimed to see war with the United States as "a distinct possibility in the not distant future." Great Britain, however, realized that other problems, particularly with Germany, left it militarily unprepared in North America. Conversely, the United States possessed no warship equal to a single battleship of the British Flying Squadron. Consequently, both sides quickly sought détente.

After complicated negotiations were concluded on 12 November 1896, Salisbury agreed to a five-member arbitration tribunal, composed of two British and two U.S. jurists, plus one from a third nation. Making a major concession, Olney permitted British settlements of fifty years' standing to be excluded from adjudication. In negotiating with Great Britain, Olney acted as if he held power of attorney for Venezuela. In fact, he did not consult Venezuela and abandoned certain Venezuelan claims on his own authority. Caracas was furious, but, lacking leverage, bowed to the inevitable. On 3 October 1899 Venezuela received all territory west of the Schomburgk line plus the pivotal Point Barima at the mouth of the Orinoco. British Guiana received nine-tenths of the disputed land. The details of the outcome, however, were less significant than the manner by which the crisis illuminated continuing U.S. predominance in the Western Hemisphere.

JUSTUS D. DOENECKE

See also Cleveland, Stephen Grover; Great Britain; Olney, Richard; Venezuela

FURTHER READING

Eggert, Gerald G. *Richard Olney*. University Park, Pa., 1974.
Grenville, John A. S., and George Berkeley Young. *Politics, Strategy, and American Diplomacy*. New Haven, Conn., 1966.
May, Ernest R. *Imperial Democracy*. New York, 1961.

VERACRUZ INCIDENT

See Mexico

VERGENNES, DUC DE
Charles Gravier de Vergennes

(*b.* 28 December 1719; *d.* 13 February 1787)

French foreign minister who aided the American colonies in their war of independence against Great Britain. Born in Dijon, France, to a family of government officials, Vergennes began his diplomatic career as secretary to an uncle in the diplomatic corps and served as ambassador to Constantinople and Sweden. Vergennes was appointed foreign minister by King Louis XVI in 1774 and served in that capacity until his death. Vergennes's goal was to restore France to its preeminence in Europe after its defeat by Great Britain in the Seven Years' War (1756–1763). To this end he advocated "secret help" to British North America in its revolt against imperial authority. He believed that Great Britain's loss of the American colonies would undermine its imperial and commercial power and block any further expansion of its influence in Europe. Despite the extensive secret military aid provided by France, however, the rebellion seemed doomed until October 1777, when the Ameri-

cans won the Battle of Saratoga in upstate New York. Then, under Vergennes's guidance, France in February 1778 signed two treaties with the Americans. A commercial treaty formally recognized the independence of the United States and a treaty of alliance pledged both nations to continue the struggle against Great Britain until American independence was "formally or tacitly assured." Neither country was to make peace "without the formal consent of the other," and each guaranteed the other's possessions in North America "forever."

The alliance led to war between France and Great Britain in June 1778. Vergennes wanted France's ally Spain to join the war against England. The Spanish government, however, fearful that the American example would lead to revolt in its own empire, agreed to join the conflict only after France accepted its demand for the restoration of Gibraltar to Spanish control (Convention of Aranjuez, 12 April 1779). Thus, American independence was indirectly tied to the Franco-Spanish agreement.

Three years later, the Continental Congress instructed the American negotiators—Benjamin Franklin, John Jay, and John Adams—to follow any advice offered by the French as they began negotiations for the desired peace treaty with Great Britain. Franklin tried to work with Vergennes, but Jay resented Vergennes's lack of concern about immediate recognition of American independence by the British and his resistance to establishing the western boundary of the United States at the Mississippi River. As a result, Jay decided to negotiate without Vergennes's advice, a position supported enthusiastically by Adams and reluctantly by Franklin. The three men signed a separate preliminary peace treaty with Great Britain in November 1782. Vergennes pragmatically accepted the agreement both as a means of ending a war that had become too costly and as a way of abandoning his commitment to obtain Gibraltar for Spain. France signed the Treaty of Paris with Great Britain on 3 September 1783.

While Vergennes had helped to secure the dismemberment of the first British Empire, in the long run his policy proved a financial and political blunder. A vast (and profitable) trade with the United States never materialized; and military expenditures incurred during the American Revolution brought the old regime in France to the brink of bankruptcy. But his policy did make possible the creation of the United States.

REBECCA G. GOODMAN

See also Adams, John; American Revolution; Beaumarchais, Pierre Augustin Caron de; France; Franklin, Benjamin; Jay, John

FURTHER READING

Bemis, Samuel F. *The Diplomacy of the American Revolution*, 4th ed. New York, 1955.

Murphy, Orville T. *Charles Gravier, Comte de Vergennes*. Albany, N.Y., 1982.

Price, Munro. *Preserving the Monarchy: the Comte de Vergennes, 1774–1787*. New York, 1995.

Stinchcombe, William C. *The American Revolution and the French Alliance*. Syracuse, N.Y., 1969.

VERIFICATION

The process and means by which parties to an agreement are able to determine with confidence that other parties are abiding by the terms of the agreement. Its principal applications in U.S. foreign policy have been in arms control agreements, especially U.S.-Soviet ones during the Cold War, and for enforcing multilateral agreements to prevent the spread of weapons of mass destruction, such as the Nuclear Nonproliferation Treaty of 1987. Verification is a process involving both technology and intelligence. Monitoring and evaluation are required to establish compliance with an agreement. Monitoring refers to the collection and analysis of data by government intelligence agencies. Evaluation is the decision-making component of the verification process and involves assessing the significance of a suspected violation and determining what response should be taken, if any.

Cooperative methods and procedures of verification include exchanges of information on military doctrine, on-site inspections (OSI), funneling weapons and delivery systems through monitored checkpoints, and monitoring devices placed at or near sites. Verification methods and procedures that do not depend on cooperation are intelligence-gathering channels, such as agents, emigrant and defector interviews, communication intercepts, and information leaks, and national technical means (NTM), such as reconnaissance satellites, strategic intelligence aircraft, ground stations for signals intelligence, and ocean surface and subsurface intelligence collection systems. Of all the verification procedures, on-site inspections have been the most controversial.

U.S. concern over verification can be traced to the outbreak of World War II, which was seen, in part, as the result of flaws in such interwar arms control agreements as the Washington Naval Treaty of 1922 and Anglo-German Naval Agreement of 1935 that omitted verification procedures. The relative ease of monitoring naval-building programs had reduced the threat of covert noncompliance, but in the nuclear age the dangers of noncompliance intensified. The weapons involved were capable of inflicting devastating damage even in small numbers. Few in the United States doubted the Soviets would violate any accord if it served their cause. Based on pre–World War II experiences with treaty noncompliance, distrustful perceptions of the Soviet adversary, and the destructive capability of nuclear weapons, verification of compliance became a prerequisite for arms control agreements.

Early U.S. arms control proposals reflected this concern with verification. In the Baruch Plan of 1946, the United States offered to relinquish its nuclear monopoly to international control, but only if the organization could conduct unimpeded inspections of the Soviet Union and other states suspected of developing nuclear weapons, and if it could enforce strong sanctions against violators. President Dwight D. Eisenhower's Open Skies proposal of 1955 was conceived as another way to permit the United States and Soviet Union to inspect each other's military establishments. The Comprehensive Test Ban Treaty negotiations of the late 1950s and early 1960s included elaborate U.S. proposals for on-site monitoring. The advent of space satellites surmounted some of the early obstacles verification posed to arms control. Space satellites offered two advantages: they were too remote to be seen as intrusive, and their surveillance could not be prevented or tampered with. With the Soviet launch in 1957 of the first satellite to transgress national boundaries in space, few objections could be raised to others following suit. The 1963 Limited Test Ban Treaty (LTBT) arose from earlier, more modest technological developments. In 1947 the United States had begun to deploy a network of ground detection stations and radioactive debris-collecting aircraft, the Atomic Energy Detection System, designed to monitor and gather intelligence on Soviet nuclear testing. The existence of a readily available, effective, and nonintrusive system eased agreement on the LTBT.

By the late 1960s advances in monitoring technology, particularly satellites, led to further strategic arms control negotiations. The Antiballistic Missile (ABM) Treaty and the Strategic Arms Limitation Interim Agreement of 1972 (SALT I) were shaped by surveillance capabilities and set important verification precedents. The agreements were weapon-specific, they recognized the role of NTM for monitoring and the principle of noninterference with NTM, and they created an ongoing forum for resolving compliance issues—the Standing Consultative Commission. President Richard M. Nixon's administration, in its efforts to build support in Congress and public approval for these arms control agreements, played down potential postagreement problems with verification. While helpful in the short term, this magnified the political damage wreaked by the verification issue when it eventually did surface. Questions about Soviet compliance began to emerge in the spring of 1975, providing ammunition for arms control critics. Soviet actions were not clear violations, nor did they directly affect the strategic balance (with the possible exception of conversion of SS-11 intercontinental ballistic missiles to more capable SS-19s). The tendency, however, of the Soviets to exploit ambiguities without clearly violating agreements disillusioned many in the United States and heightened the political significance of compliance issues. Verification, critical in advancing public opinion of arms control, was also instrumental in turning public opinion against it. The sense that verification issues had never been effectively addressed by SALT I further complicated the debate over the Strategic Arms Limitation Talks of 1979–1980. Doubts triggered by the loss of key U.S. monitoring sites in Iran in the months prior to signing the agreement further fueled this debate.

Under President Ronald Reagan, critics of arms control ascended to positions of power and made verification the paramount arms control issue. In the first Reagan administration (1981–1985) charges of Soviet violations of past arms control agreements were the principal reason for not proceeding with new agreements. A number of charges of Soviet violations surfaced between 1981 and 1983, and in 1984, in response to a congressional mandate, the Reagan administration produced its first report on Soviet compliance with arms control. A large phased-array radar at Krasnoyarsk, discussed in the report, became central to the compliance debate because the radar was such a clear and obvious violation of the ABM Treaty. While the violations explored in these compliance reports were important, the difficulties of defining clear-cut violations also became evident. Arms control proponents were concerned that demands for resolution of past verification issues and for more effective procedures to avoid past mistakes would hamstring future negotiations. Arms control negotiations with the Soviet Union continued amid this intensifying debate over verification. In the second Reagan administration, with the rise of Mikhail Gorbachev as the new leader of the Soviet Union and the subsequent improvement in U.S.-Soviet relations, U.S. policy shifted from stressing verification as a basis for opposing arms control agreements to resolving verification issues in order to conclude arms control agreements. "Trust, but verify," was Reagan's famous phrase.

The Intermediate Range Nuclear Forces (INF) Treaty signed in 1987 broke new ground. For years the United States had insisted that OSI were necessary for monitoring. The INF Treaty went further than any previous U.S.-Soviet arms control agreement in providing for highly intrusive monitoring provisions, that is, several layers of OSI and a cooperative measure requiring the Soviets to open six SS-25 intercontinental ballistic missile garages per year for viewing by U.S. NTM. The INF Treaty set new standards of rigor for verification, although their transferability to other agreements has been questionable. INF has been relatively easy to verify because the treaty combined total elimination of a class of weapons with a ban on testing to contribute to the weapons' degradation over time. Verifying mobile and cruise missiles, when they are not banned but permitted in reduced numbers, has been far more difficult.

With the end of the Cold War, the pace of arms control negotiations increased. The Conventional Forces in Europe (CFE) Treaty was signed in 1990, Strategic Arms Reduction Talks (START) were completed in the summer of 1991, and the Chemical Weapons Convention (CWC) in 1993. CFE relies on a complex web of verification measures that include NTM, data exchanges, and OSI at declared and nondeclared sites. Despite more cooperation, verification problems still arose, particularly in the removal of treaty-limited equipment out of the CFE zone and its redeployment by Russia in and around the former Soviet states of its "near abroad," and in the redesignation of some divisions as naval infantry in order to exclude them from the army-based CFE mandate. START, unlike INF, did not eliminate strategic systems or testing, so opportunities to store covert systems remained. START verification procedures included elaborate data exchanges, OSI, and an agreement to ban encryption of telemetry during missile tests.

The CWC has established a verification regime that differs from previously negotiated treaties. It called for routine intrusive on-site inspections of declared government installations (for example, production, storage, and destruction facilities) and private industry, and also for short-notice challenge inspections of undeclared facilities to investigate concerns about compliance. The CWC attempted to balance the need to verify compliance with the right of a member state to protect sensitive commercial information. Critics of the CWC have argued that the treaty is only minimally verifiable, owing to the lack of technical means to detect suspicious sites, secret stockpiles, and the potential diversion from civilian to military purposes of common commercial chemicals.

Similar problems of distinguishing between civilian and military applications have created verification problems for implementing certain provisions of the Nuclear Nonproliferation Treaty (NPT) of 1968. Nuclear reactors and related processes, including enrichment technology and chemical separations facilities, have both civilian and military applications. The International Atomic Energy Agency (IAEA), established in 1957, has monitored compliance with NPT based on carefully detailed provisions for inspections laid out in the treaty. The IAEA safeguards to prevent transfers of targeted technologies and diversions of nuclear materials from civilian to military purposes have proven insufficient, in part because the IAEA was not charged with inspecting military facilities. The verification regime has succeeded in deterring many countries from using civilian nuclear energy programs to advance military purposes. Cases like Iraq in the 1980s and North Korea in the 1990s nevertheless revealed that the inspection system alone was insufficient and needed to be supplemented with effective national intelligence means.

Post–Cold War arms control agreements have heavily emphasized OSI, imposing a large financial and administrative burden on bureaucracies responsible for verification. In addition, the sheer number of new arms control agreements that have been negotiated since the end of the Cold War has raised two new verification problems: the lack of adequate scrutiny each treaty can feasibly receive by an overstressed bureaucracy and the task of finding sufficient numbers of properly trained inspectors to meet OSI demands. The importance of verification, however, has remained the same.

EMILY O. GOLDMAN

See also Antiballistic Missile Treaty; Chemical Weapons; Conventional Armed Forces in Europe, Treaty on; Intermediate-Range Nuclear Forces Treaty; International Atomic Energy Agency; Limited Nuclear Test Ban Treaty; Nuclear Nonproliferation; Nuclear Weapons and Strategy; Open Skies; Strategic Arms Limitation Talks and Agreements; Strategic Arms Reduction Treaties

FURTHER READING

Krepon, Michael, and Mary Umberger, ed. *Verification and Compliance*. Cambridge, Mass., 1988.
Potter, William C., ed. *Verification and Arms Control*. Lexington, Mass., 1985.
Roberts, Brad, ed. *Ratifying the Chemical Weapons Convention*. Washington, D.C., 1994.
Scribner, Richard A., Theodore J. Ralston, and William D. Metz. *The Verification Challenge*. Boston, 1985.
Tower, John G., James Brown, and William K. Cheek, eds. *Verification*. Washington, 1992.

VERSAILLES TREATY OF 1919

The international agreement that marked the formal end of World War I, punished defeated Germany, and created the League of Nations. A German delegation of two, headed by Matthias Erzberger, leader of the Catholic Center Party, signed the treaty in the Hall of Mirrors at the Palace of Versailles on 28 June 1919. This was five years to the day that the Austrian heir to the throne, Archduke Franz Ferdinand and his wife were assassinated in Sarajevo, Bosnia, the incident that sparked the "July Crisis," which in turn led to the outbreak of the war six weeks later.

In all, thirty-two nations signed the Versailles treaty. The U.S. Senate, after much debate, rejected the treaty one year later. The treaty emerged from tortuous negotiations held at the Paris Peace Conference (January to June 1919). Bolshevik Russia and Germany (as well as its allies) were excluded from these negotiations. President Woodrow Wilson, who headed the U.S. delegation to Paris and emerged as the chief advocate of a new world order in the Council of Ten and in the Council of Four (where, in the company of the British, French, and Italian prime ministers, the most important "executive" decisions were taken), found that the representatives of victorious Great Britain and France were bent on exacting huge indemnities from Germany in the form of reparations for war damages. The Italians, in turn, were determined to satisfy their own irredentist ambitions at the expense of their neighbors, demanding the annexation to Italy of part of Yugoslavia's northern Adriatic coast and the German-speaking Trentino region in Austria's South Tyrol.

For five months Wilson maneuvered through this minefield of competing ambitions. At the outset, he secured approval of his aim to make the League of Nations Covenant, establishing the world's first international peacekeeping organization, an integral part of the treaty with Germany. Approval of the League Covenant from unsympathetic allies, however, required compromises that galled Wilson, one of which was Germany's exclusion from League membership.

The conference negotiators completed the draft of the peace treaty in early May 1919 and asked the German government to send a delegation to Paris, allowing the Germans only six weeks to consider the document. When the German delegates reviewed the 400-article, 260-page treaty, they naturally feared an extremely hostile public reaction back in Germany. They objected especially to the "war guilt" clause (Article 231), which blamed Germany and its allies exclusively for starting the war. While the German delegation accepted its country's obligation to pay reparations, it sought unsuccessfully to put a $25 billion cap on projected cash payments. In the end, the British and French ordered the German delegates to sign the treaty or face renewed military action. Four separate treaties with Germany's wartime allies were negotiated and signed over the course of the following fourteen months: at Saint-Germain with Austria, and Neuilly with Bulgaria, both in 1919; and, in the following year, at Trianon with Bulgaria, and Sèvres with Turkey.

In addition to extracting reparations in cash (the final sum of $33 billion was set in 1921) and in kind (mostly raw materials) as well as the "war guilt clause," Germany would have to endure a fifteen-year foreign occupation of its Rhineland province as well as of the coal-mining areas along the Saar River. The treaty stripped Germany of its army, navy, and air force, and of its eastern territories, most of which went to newly independent Poland (Posan and West Prussia), while France regained Alsace-Lorraine, and Belgium three small enclaves. Danzig (Gdansk), predominately German in population, was declared a "Free City" under the League's jurisdiction. Germany also lost its overseas colonies which, under the League Covenant, were henceforth to be administered through the new mandate system. As one of the war's putative victims, Japan "inherited" Germany's leasehold on the Shandong (Shantung) province in China.

Five months of exhausting negotiations in Paris took a serious toll on President Wilson's health, just when the fiercest struggle still lay ahead: the U.S. Senate would have to pass the treaty, which included the League Covenant. The chairman of the Senate Foreign Relations Committee (where Wilson first submitted the treaty for consideration on 10 July 1919), Republican Senator Henry Cabot Lodge, was a personal enemy of Wilson. Of the forty-nine Republican senators in Congress, moreover, twelve declared themselves to be "irreconcilables," or diehard opponents of the League in any form, though not of the Versailles treaty as a whole. The remaining thirty-seven Republican senators, led by Lodge, considered themselves "reservationists." They objected primarily to Article 10 of the League Covenant, which obligated League members to come to each other's defense in case of an attack from the outside. Wilson made most Democratic senators toe his line and support the treaty without any reservations.

Wilson and his defenders, including former President William Howard Taft, tried to persuade the Senate and the American public that Article 10 was merely a "moral" obligation that did not compromise the nation's sovereignty. Wilson already had seen to it at Paris that the thirteen-member League of Nations Commission, which voted to approve the covenant on 13 February, accept minor amendments to ease U.S. fears of binding foreign entanglements. These concessions, however, did not satisfy the League's opponents. Lodge's fourteen reservationists in effect disabled Article 10. The treaty, even with the reservationists, failed to secure the necessary two-thirds majority when the Senate first put it to a vote on 19 November (38–53), following Wilson's exhaustive cross-country speaking tour, which covered close to 10,000 miles between 4 and 25 September, when the president suffered the first in a series of incapacitating strokes.

On 19 March 1920 another Senate vote on the treaty, this time without the reservationists, produced the same result (35–49). The rejection of the Versailles Treaty placed the United States in the odd position of being the only victorious power that remained technically at war with Germany; not until 1921, during Warren G. Harding's administration, did the United States sign a separate peace with Germany. More ominously perhaps, the U.S. Senate's rejection of the Versailles Treaty simultaneously scuttled France's attempt to obtain tangible security assurances by means of a formal Franco-Anglo-American treaty of guarantee. The French proposal was intended specifically to protect France against any future German aggression, and its passage depended on U.S. approval of the Versailles treaty itself.

Excluded from League membership (until 1926) and forced to pay huge reparations, the large majority of Germans became united in their opposition to the treaty in ways which ultimately benefited its most outspoken critic, Adolf Hitler. Soon after becoming chancellor in 1933, Hitler repudiated the treaty's reparations provisions and disarmament restrictions.

The Versailles Treaty officially came into force on 10 January 1920, after its formal ratification by Germany, Great Britain, France, Italy, and Japan.

SINA DUBOVOY

See also Dawes Plan; Germany; League of Nations; Paris Peace Conference of 1919; Reparations; United Nations; Wilson, Thomas Woodrow; World War I

FURTHER READING
Ambrosius, Lloyd E. *Woodrow Wilson and the American Diplomatic Tradition: The Treaty Fight in Perspective.* Cambridge, 1987.
Bailey, Thomas A. *Woodrow Wilson and the Great Betrayal.* New York, 1945.
———. *Woodrow Wilson and the Lost Peace.* Chicago, 1944.
Hoover, Herbert. *The Ordeal of Woodrow Wilson.* Baltimore, Md., 1992 [reprint of 1958 edition].
Keynes, John M. *The Economic Consequences of the Peace.* New York, 1920.
Mantoux, Etienne. *The Carthaginian Peace: or The Economic Consequences of Mr. Keynes.* New York, 1978 [reprint of 1946 edition].
Margulies, Herbert F. *The Mild Reservationists and the League of Nations Controversy in the Senate.* Columbia, Mo., 1989.
Stone, Ralph A. *The Irreconcilables: the Fight Against the League of Nations.* Lexington, Ky., 1970.
Sharp, Alan. *The Versailles Settlement: Peacemaking in Paris, 1919.* New York, 1991.

VETERANS OF FOREIGN WARS

An organization of U.S. military personnel who have served overseas. Founded in 1899 in Columbus, Ohio, by veterans of the Spanish-American-Cuban-Filipino War as the American Veterans of Foreign Service, it merged in 1903 with the National Society of the Army of the Philippines; in 1914 it renamed itself the Veterans of Foreign Wars. The VFW has some 2,000,000 members and is headquartered in Washington, D.C. With a staff of 290 people, an annual budget of $22 million, and more than 10,000 local posts, the VFW actively lobbies the government and courts public opinion in support of the needs of veterans and their dependents. For many years the VFW advocated conservative ideals, including ensuring national security through maximum military strength and promoting "Americanism" through education in patriotism and service in local communities. In recent years, however, the VFW's ideological stance has become somewhat less conservative—a trend coinciding with the increased prominence of Vietnam-era veterans in the organization's membership and leadership.

JEREL A. ROSATI

See also Cold War; Public Opinion

FURTHER READING

Lamb, David. "Recruits Put New Face on VFW, Legion." *Los Angeles Times* (2 November 1987).
Severo, Richard, and Lewis Milford. *The Wages of War: When America's Soldiers Came Home—From Valley Forge to Vietnam.* New York, 1989.

VIETNAM

Located in southeastern Asia, bordering the Gulf of Tonkin, the South China Sea, Cambodia, Laos, and China. Contacts between the United States and the Kingdom of Vietnam began in the early nineteenth century, when the U.S. merchant Edmund Roberts attempted unsuccessfully to negotiate a commercial treaty between the two countries. The talks were broken off by the Vietnamese, however, when Roberts refused to perform the kowtow. When the Vietnamese Empire was attacked by the French during the 1880s, U.S. Minister to China John Russell Young offered to mediate the conflict, but Paris rejected the offer. After the French conquest, which placed Vietnam with Laos and Cambodia in a larger territorial unit called the Union of Indochina, the United States established a consular office in Saigon to handle the limited degree of trade and tourist travel between the two countries. Trade increased during the 1930s, however, as the United States began to import natural rubber from southern Indochina. By 1939 over twelve percent of Indochina's exports were destined for the United States. Japanese military occupation of the area in 1940 was a major factor in sparking the Pacific War.

During World War II, President Franklin D. Roosevelt expressed the hope that Vietnam could be placed under a United Nations trusteeship after the restoration of peace in preparation for eventual independence. But Cold War concerns soon began to intervene. After the surrender of Japan, the Truman administration decided to recognize the restoration of French sovereignty, despite an appeal by President Ho Chi Minh for diplomatic recognition of his new communist-dominated Democratic Republic of Vietnam (DRV), which had been created in Hanoi shortly after the end of the war.

When war broke out between the French and Ho Chi Minh's military forces (called the Vietminh) in December 1946, the United States did not initially intervene. But the fall of Nationalist China at the end of the decade intensified fears in Washington of the spread of a red tide throughout Asia, and in February 1950 the United States granted formal diplomatic recognition to the Associated State of Vietnam, a puppet state created by the French to present the Vietnamese people with an alternative to Ho Chi Minh. During the next four years, the level of U.S. military and economic assistance to the French increased steadily until it accounted for nearly two-thirds of the entire French cost of the war.

Facing a disastrous military defeat in the battle of Dien Bien Phu in early 1954, Paris turned to Washington for increased military assistance. President Eisenhower refused to approve a French request for U.S. bomb strikes to relieve Vietminh pressure on the beleaguered military base, but he sought to build a multinational alliance to stave off a communist victory throughout Indochina. The French, however, rejected the proposal and decided to negotiate a settlement.

At the Geneva Conference in July 1954, Vietnam was divided into two separate regroupment zones, with a communist administration in the north and a non-communist one in the south. Although the accords had called for national elections in 1956 to reunite the country under a single government, Ngo Dinh Diem, prime minister of the new Republic of Vietnam (RVN) in Saigon, refused to hold such elections. The Eisenhower administration, which had opposed the settlement at Geneva, supported Diem's decision, and began to provide military and economic assistance to the RVN in an effort to prevent a possible communist takeover of the south. Diem, however, quickly ran into difficulties, alienating large segments of the population with his authoritarian policies. Encouraged by growing popular discontent, revolutionary elements began to promote guerrilla activities to overthrow the Saigon regime, supported by the DRV in Hanoi.

By 1961 the insurgents—popularly labeled the Viet Cong (Vietnamese Communists)—represented a serious threat to the survival of the RVN. In response, President John F. Kennedy increased the number of U.S. advisers in the south. But the insurgents continued to expand their control over the countryside, and in early November 1963 dissident elements in the South Vietnamese army, with Washington's approval, overthrew Ngo Dinh Diem and installed a new military regime in Saigon.

After the assassination of President Kennedy three weeks later, his successor Lyndon Baines Johnson accelerated U.S. support for the RVN, but conditions continued to deteriorate, and in 1965 his administration introduced U.S. combat units in an effort to avert a collapse of the southern regime. During the next three years, the level of U.S. troop strength increased to over half a million, and the cost of the war rose to over $20 billion annually. Hanoi responded to the U.S. military escalation by infiltrating thousands of its own ground troops into the south.

As the war appeared to reach a stalemate, public support for the war effort declined in the United States, and after the Tet Offensive in early 1968 Johnson signaled his willingness to pursue a negotiated settlement. Beginning in 1969, the Nixon administration began to reduce U.S. troops in the south, and the final units departed as a result of the Paris Agreement, signed in January 1973.

After the communist seizure of the south in 1975, the United States held discussions with the newly united Socialist Republic of Vietnam (SRV) to open diplomatic relations, but talks were derailed by Hanoi's demands for war reparations and Washington's demand for a full accounting of all U.S. citizens captured or killed in Vietnam during the war. After Vietnam invaded neighboring Cambodia in December 1978, the United States joined other nations in imposing an economic embargo on trade with the SRV. During the late 1980s, however, talks between the two countries took place to resolve the dispute. At a conference in Paris in 1991, Hanoi agreed to pull its remaining occupation troops out of Cambodia and promised to cooperate with the United States in locating the remains of U.S. soldiers missing in action (MIAs) during the Vietnam War. In January 1994, the Clinton administration ended the U.S. embargo on trade with Vietnam, and formal diplomatic relations between the two countries were established in July 1995. As commercial and tourist contacts increased, the wounds of war gradually began to heal.

WILLIAM J. DUIKER

See also Johnson, Lyndon Baines; Nixon, Richard Milhous; Vietnam War

FUTHER READING

Duiker, William J. *Vietnam: Revolution in Transition.* Second edition. Boulder, Colo., 1995.
Gibbons, William Conrad. *The U.S. Government and the Vietnam War,* 3 vols. Princeton, N.J., 1986.
Herring, George C. *LBJ and Vietnam.* Austin, Tex., 1994.
Karnow, Stanley. *Vietnam: A History.* 2nd ed. New York, N.Y., 1991.

VIETNAM WAR

A conflict in Southeast Asia involving South Vietnamese government forces, backed by the United States, and communist guerrilla forces, backed by North Vietnam. In May 1950, a month before the outbreak of hostilities in Korea, Secretary of State Dean Acheson announced the first increment of U.S. aid to the French in their Indochina war against the Vietnamese nationalists and communists led by Ho Chi Minh. The bitter recriminations in the United States over "who lost China?" produced a compelling domestic incentive for the Harry S. Truman administration to do what it could to prevent a commu-

nist victory in Vietnam or anywhere else in Indochina. The loss of Southeast Asia was defined as threatening the security of the United States and the collectivity of Free World nations. The sovereignties of Vietnam as well as other Southeast Asian countries were valued not for their own merit, but rather as a test of U.S. global position and credibility—a perception that would have a profound impact on the nature of the decision to intervene. Vietnam, or more specifically not losing Vietnam, became an increasingly important component in U.S. global objectives. In December 1950 the United States joined France, Vietnam, Cambodia, and Laos in signing a Mutual Defense Assistance Agreement. The United States agreed to provide military supplies and equipment through a U.S. military advisory group. This small contingent of U.S. advisers provided limited logistical services; all supplies and equipment were dispensed through the French Expeditionary Corps. Year by year, U.S. aid to the French military effort mounted: from $130 million in 1950 to $800 million in 1953, amounting to more than three-fourths of the cost of the French war effort.

As a consequence of the ultimate stalemate in the Korean War, the U.S. domestic political climate became profoundly antagonistic to the further use of U.S. troops on the Asian mainland. Nevertheless, President Dwight D. Eisenhower and his associates were as convinced as the Truman administration had been of Indochina's strategic importance. What inhibited the new president from pressing the French to grant independence to the Indochinese was the fear that the war-weary French would simply withdraw, removing the "cork in the bottle," which in the U.S. view would allow communist forces to spread throughout Southeast Asia, if not farther. Moreover, there was concern that if the United States pressed the French to alter their Indochina policy, they might thwart U.S. policy in Europe by failing to ratify the European Defense Community (EDC) Treaty and thus block the administration's preferred means of bringing about German rearmament.

In May 1953, the French government appointed General Henri Navarre commander in Vietnam and charged him with mounting a major new offensive against the Viet Minh, Ho Chi Minh's forces. The Navarre Plan called for a significant infusion of Vietnamese recruits and French regulars into the anticommunist military force and a change in strategy to large-force actions that would inflict major casualties on the Viet Minh. One of Navarre's first moves, late in 1953, was to dispatch a major French unit of crack troops to Dien Bien Phu, the juncture of a number of roads in northwestern Indochina about 100 miles from the Chinese border. He viewed the site, a valley surrounded by a thousand foothills, as ideal to trap the Viet Minh into engaging in a bloody assault.

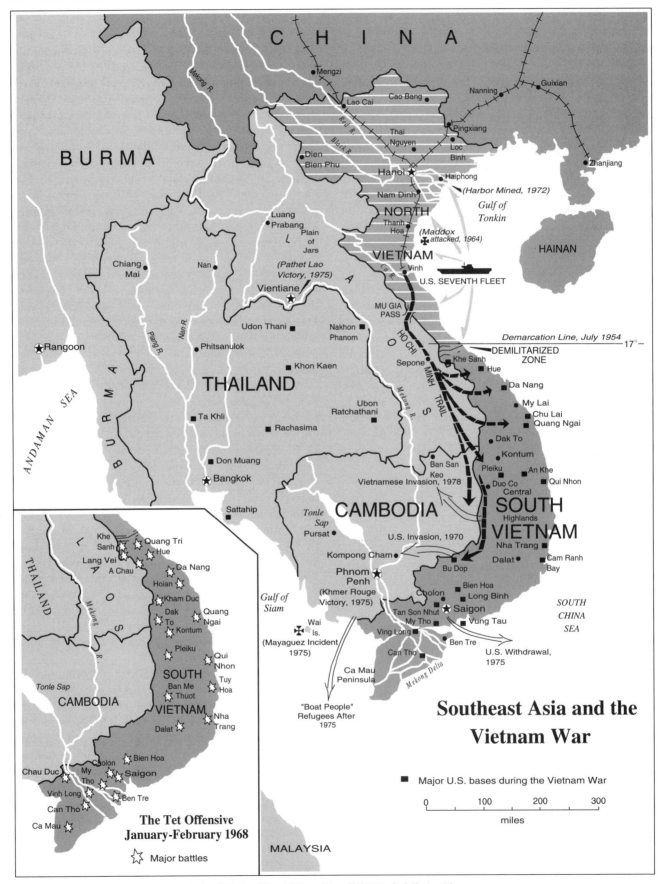

Southeast Asia and the Vietnam War

The Tet Offensive
January-February 1968

☆ Major battles

■ Major U.S. bases during the Vietnam War

0   100   200   300
miles

Navarre had barely fortified Dien Bien Phu when the Viet Minh took the bait, but moved in with such force that they made Dien Bien Phu a trap for the French. By early January 1954, Eisenhower and his advisers recognized that the situation in Dien Bien Phu was serious and that a French defeat might topple the new French government of Joseph Laniel, lead the French to sue for peace, and probably also lead to a French government that would reject EDC. From January through early April, the administration grappled with the crisis produced by the siege of Dien Bien Phu. In doing so it explored two broad policy options: a surgical air strike and the formation of a multinational coalition to resist the Communist advance. Meanwhile, it played an intricate game of coordination and accommodation with domestic political leaders and the French. Yet, given the opportunity to assist France by intervening militarily, President Eisenhower decided not to enter a French colonial war that the United States had backed with funds but no military commitment.

On 7 May 1954, the French forces were defeated at Dien Bien Phu. Shortly thereafter the Geneva Conference was held bringing together representatives of South and North Vietnam, the other emerging Indochinese states of Laos and Cambodia, and the major powers of France, Britain, the United States, the Soviet Union, and the People's Republic of China. The Geneva Accords, formally known as the "Final Declaration of the Geneva Conference on the Problem of Restoring Peace in Indochina," primarily settled military and not political issues in provisionally dividing Vietnam at the seventeenth parallel pending free unifying elections in the North and South that were to have been held by July 1956. Neither the United States nor the South Vietnamese government signed the Accords, although the United States issued a declaration committing itself to refrain from using force to disturb the cease-fire and stating that it would view any aggression as a serious threat to international peace and security. The Accords also affirmed the independence and neutrality of Cambodia and Laos.

Three months following Dien Bien Phu, President Eisenhower convened his National Security Council (NSC) in order to review U.S. policy in Asia. The president was already on record claiming that "strategically South Vietnam's capture by the Communists would bring their power several hundred miles into a hitherto free region. The remaining countries in Southeast Asia would be menaced by a great flanking movement. The freedom of twelve million people would be lost immediately and that of 150 million others in adjacent lands would be seriously endangered. The loss of South Vietnam would have grave consequences for us and for freedom." Eisenhower also had articulated the line of reasoning that came to be known as the "domino theory," that the "fall" of

one state to communism would lead to the next and the next being "knocked over." Not losing Southeast Asia thus became the goal of the United States in the region. The NSC meeting resulted in one of the most important early decisions of the United States' initial involvement: the United States replaced France as the direct supplier of financial and military assistance to South Vietnam. In September 1954 the United States, the United Kingdom, France, Australia, New Zealand, Thailand, Pakistan, and the Philippines signed the Southeast Asia Collective Defense Treaty (which created the Southeast Asia Treaty Organization, or SEATO). Each of the signatories accepted an obligation to assist one another against "aggression by means of armed attack"; South Vietnam, Laos and Cambodia were protocol states to SEATO. Where SEATO involved multilateral relations, the United States solidified its commitment in several bilateral agreements with South Vietnam and also began sending military personnel for purposes of training South Vietnamese Armed Forces and mobile civil guard.

The Diem Regime

In a letter to the president of South Vietnam, Ngo Dinh Diem, President Eisenhower was exceedingly clear: "I am, accordingly, instructing the American Ambassador to Vietnam to examine with you in your capacity as chief of Government, how an intelligent program of American aid given directly to your Government can serve to assist Vietnam in its present hour of trial, provided that your Government is prepared to give assurances as to the standards of performance it would be able to maintain in the event such aid were supplied. The purpose of this offer is to assist the government of Vietnam in developing and maintaining a strong, viable state, capable of resisting attempted subversion or aggression through military means." The U.S. Operations Mission was established in 1955 as an adjunct to the U.S. embassy. The mission was charged with channeling advice and financial support to help Diem solve South Vietnam's economic problems. In 1955 alone, the United States provided over $322 million in economic aid and played a major role in establishing the National Bank of Vietnam. Along with such overt programs, the United States also initiated a great deal of covert activity, much of it under the direction of Colonel Edward G. Lansdale.

Diem, who had been groomed for power by the United States, initially appeared to make successful strides in rehabilitating the economy of South Vietnam, but for a number of reasons failed to gain broad popular support. In consolidating power, Diem's regime became increasingly repressive. Diem, whose authoritarian techniques included the abolition of all opposing political parties, strictly enforced press censorship, and brutal repression of the Buddhists, destroyed the chance to build a democratic nationalism as a counterbalance to Vietnamese communism. By 1959 the North Vietnamese communist government, with its capital in Hanoi, committed its political and military apparatus in the south to the struggle for unification. Thousands of trained military leaders were sent into the south for purposes of overthrowing the Diem government. These cadres worked with procommunist individuals and groups in the south to provide the core for the Viet Cong (VC) military. Infiltration into the south increased substantially in 1959 and, on 10 September 1960, guidelines were established for what would become the National Front for the Liberation of South Vietnam.

Vietnam loomed as a test of the John F. Kennedy administration's inaugural commitment "to pay any price, to bear any burden, in the defense of freedom." By October 1961 mounting VC pressure led President Diem to request military support from the United States—specifically, ground troops to bolster the South Vietnamese army. Before acting on this request, Kennedy dispatched General Maxwell Taylor and Walt Rostow (deputy special assistant to the president for national security affairs) to Vietnam to investigate the question of U.S. troop requirements. Following two weeks of survey work, Taylor confirmed the gloomy military situation. Taylor recommended that an eight-thousand-man logistical task force of engineers, medics, and infantry be sent to the south for purposes of base security. The task force would operate under the guise of providing such humanitarian effort as flood relief operations in the delta, but would really serve as a "visible symbol of the seriousness of American intentions." General Taylor believed that these troops might be forced to engage in combat to protect themselves or their working parties. "As a general reserve, they might be thrown into action (with U.S. agreement) against large, formed guerrilla bands which have abandoned the forests for attacks on major targets." Taylor was unperturbed about "the risks of backing into a major Asian war," which he acknowledged were "present" but "not impressive."

The object of U.S. policy was still to do all that was possible without use of combat forces. This approach was most evident in the Kennedy administration's embrace of the doctrine of counterinsurgency—which involved a range of overt and covert activities by special forces, psychological warfare, intelligence collection, technical assistance, propaganda campaigns, and others. Covert operations in Vietnam now assumed a new level of intensity. Unmarked U.S. bombers operating under the code name "Operation Farmgate," for example, began attacks on enemy rearbase and infrastructure targets. The United States continued to have a great deal of trouble dealing with its local ally. Diem's government had evolved into a family oligarchy that governed through force and repression. Opposition mounted from a wide range of

political, social, and religious groups. Protests raged, including quite dramatic ones such as self-immolations by Buddhist monks. On 1 November 1963, Diem was removed from office and murdered in the back of a U.S.-built personnel carrier. The coup was planned and implemented by South Vietnamese military officers, but U.S. Ambassador Henry Cabot Lodge and the Central Intelligence Agency (CIA) were certainly involved. Kennedy, given the opportunity to instruct Lodge that the coup be stopped, issued no such orders.

Diem's death was followed by a period of great instability in Saigon, but it was also a period of great hope. The removal of Diem initially was viewed by many Vietnamese as a positive step toward the goal of building democratic institutions in Vietnam, but a period of recurring military coups ensued, dashing any such hopes. South Vietnam without Diem was even more unstable, no more democratic, and still a weak fighting force.

Johnson Americanizes the War

Three weeks after Diem's murder, Kennedy was assassinated in Dallas. For both domestic political and foreign military reasons, his successor, President Lyndon B. Johnson, assumed office with the belief that the United States had to ensure the stability and security of South Vietnam. Momentum now was building in favor of action that might change the disintegrating political conditions in South Vietnam. The Joint Chiefs of Staff prepared a contingency bombing program of graduated military pressure against North Vietnam and covert operations along the North Vietnamese coast. These operations included U.S. patrol boat missions against North Vietnamese coastal installations. The U.S. Navy also began De Soto patrols by sending destroyers up the Gulf of Tonkin for intelligence-gathering purposes. On 2 August 1964, the destroyer *Maddox* was returning from one of these electronic espionage missions when North Vietnamese torpedo boats fired on her. Rather than withdrawing U.S. ships from the danger zone, the president ordered another destroyer, the *C. Turner Joy*, to join the *Maddox* in the Gulf of Tonkin. On 4 August both the *Maddox* and the *C. Turner Joy* reportedly came under attack. The president later met with congressional leaders and sought assurance that his action would be supported. On 10 August 1964, Congress passed the Southeast Asia Resolution, also known as the Tonkin Gulf Resolution, which authorized Johnson "to take all necessary measures to repel any armed attack against the forces of the United States and to prevent further aggression." With the 1964 presidential election against Republican conservative Barry Goldwater less than three months away, however, President Johnson had no desire to be portrayed as planning for war. Instead, he left the rhetoric of war to Goldwater and the planning with his military advisers. "Peace candidate" Johnson won the election in a landslide.

Instability in the capital city of Saigon played right into the communists' goal of overthrowing the government in the South. By late 1964, the VC were increasing their terrorist attacks on U.S. installations. The bombing of U.S. Army barracks at Pleiku triggered a sequence of events that quickly led to placing U.S. combat forces on the ground in South Vietnam. Eight Americans were killed and over one hundred wounded in the attack. On 7 February 1965, the day after the VC attack at Pleiku, Johnson issued a prophetic public statement: "We have no choice now but to clear the decks and make absolutely clear our continued determination to back South Vietnam in its fight to maintain its independence." In response to the attack at Pleiku, Johnson announced the deployment to South Vietnam of a HAWK air defense battalion and rather casually observed that "other reinforcements, in units and individuals, may follow." These reinforcements, sent within the next month, consisted of fully equipped ground combat units to protect air bases and proved to be the first step in a U.S. commitment to a ground war in Vietnam. Within hours of the attack, Johnson ordered Flaming Dart reprisal air attacks against preselected North Vietnamese targets. Flaming Dart did not deter the enemy and on 10 February the VC struck again by attacking a hotel at Qui Nhon, a coastal city eighty-five miles east of Pleiku. Twenty-three members of the 140th Maintenance Detachment of an Army aircraft repair unit were killed, and about the same number wounded. This time the U.S. response would not be characterized at tit-for-tat. On 13 February 1965, President Johnson authorized Rolling Thunder, the systematic and expanding bombing campaign against North Vietnamese targets. As suggested by the operation's code name, the bombing would come and go, at first mostly south of the 20th parallel, but soon moving with increasing frequency over all of North Vietnam; by 1967–1968, the Hanoi-Haiphong region became the focus of Rolling Thunder attacks.

As the pace of the air war quickened, the decision to introduce U.S. combat forces simultaneously evolved. General William Westmoreland soon requested that two battalion landing teams of Marines—3,500 men—be assigned to guard the key air base at Da Nang. The initial decision to intervene received extraordinarily favorable public response and was also praised on Capitol Hill. Within two weeks of the marines' arrival at Da Nang, U.S. Army Chief of Staff Harold K. Johnson requested an additional deployment of three divisions to Vietnam. At a 1 April 1965 National Security Council meeting, LBJ approved two additional division deployments (as well as 20,000 support troops) and extended their role beyond mere base security. This appears to be the "break point";

the United States had moved from Rolling Thunder air strikes to passive base defense to aggressive base defense. Only a general combat role remained.

Throughout June and July of 1965 the question of "Americanizing" the war was at the center of all foreign policy discussions. Under Secretary of State George Ball first attempted to influence Johnson's future ability to control events. In a 18 June memo he titled "Keeping the Power of Decision in the South Vietnam Crisis," Ball argued that the United States was on the threshold of a new war. "In raising our commitment from 50,000 to 100,000 or more men and deploying most of the increment in combat roles we were beginning a new war—the United States directly against the VC. The president's most difficult continuing problem in South Vietnam is to prevent 'things' from getting into the saddle—or, in other words, to keep control of policy and prevent the momentum of events from taking command." The president needed to understand the effect of losing control: "Perhaps the large-scale introduction of U.S. forces with their concentrated fire power will force Hanoi and the VC to the decision we are seeking. On the other hand, we may not be able to fight the war successfully enough—even with 500,000 Americans in South Vietnam we must have more evidence than we now have that our troops will not bog down in the jungles and rice paddies—while we slowly blow the country to pieces." Ball tried to review the French experience for Johnson, reminding the president that "the French fought a war in Vietnam, and were finally defeated—after seven years of bloody struggle and when they still had 250,000 combat-hardened veterans in the field, supported by an army of 205,000 South Vietnamese. To be sure, the French were fighting a colonial war while we are fighting to stop aggression. But when we have put enough Americans on the ground in South Vietnam to give the appearance of a white man's war, the distinction as to our ultimate purpose will have less and less practical effect."

Ball's arguments had little influence on policymakers. On 26 June, Secretary of Defense Robert McNamara circulated his "Program of Expanded Military and Political Moves with Respect to Vietnam." McNamara recognized that the VC were clearly winning the war and "the tide almost certainly cannot begin to turn in less than a few months and may not for a year or more; the was is one of attrition and will be a long one." McNamara defined winning as "to create conditions for a favorable settlement by demonstrating to the VC/DRV that the odds are against their winning. Under present conditions, however, the chances of achieving this objective are small—and the VC are winning now—largely because the ratio of guerrilla to anti-guerrilla forces is unfavorable to the government." Secretary McNamara developed three options for the president: (1) cut U.S. losses and withdraw with the best conditions that can be arranged; (2) continue at about the present level, with U.S. forces limited to about 75,000, holding on and playing for the breaks while recognizing that the U.S. position will probably grow weaker; (3) expand substantially the U.S. military pressure against the VC in the South and the North Vietnamese in the North.

McNamara unequivocally supported the third option—a series of expanded military moves as prerequisites for a negotiated settlement on U.S. terms. The secretary recommended that the US/GVN ground strength be increased to whatever force levels were necessary to show the VC that they "cannot win."

On 7 July 1965, General Westmoreland ("acutely aware of the gravity of my conclusions") informed Washington that South Vietnam would fall unless the United States committed forty-four battalions to Southeast Asia (at the time there were approximately 75,000 U.S. troops in Vietnam). The increases brought U.S. and third-country troop levels to forty-four battalions and were accomplished by a call-up of 100,000 reserves. McNamara's military recommendations also included a quarantine of the movement of all war supplies into North Vietnam, the mining of North Vietnam's (DRV) harbors, the destruction of all railway and highway bridges linking China to North Vietnam, armed reconnaissance of communication lines from China, destruction of all war-making supplies inside North Vietnam, and destruction of all airfields and SAM sites. Johnson also heard from his secretary of state, Dean Rusk. In a rare personal memorandum to the president, on 1 July, Rusk argued that "the central objective of the United States in South Vietnam must be to insure that North Vietnam not succeed in taking over or determining the future of South Vietnam by force, i.e., again defined as denial. We must accomplish this objective without a general war if possible." The war aim of the United States was not and could not be concerned with hypothetical issues such as what the South Vietnamese people would do if left alone: "The sole basis for employing U.S. forces is the aggression from the North." If this aggression was removed, the U.S. forces would also leave. Rusk rejected Ball's position by casting the issue within a much broader context with significant consequences. "There can be no serious debate about the fact that we have a commitment to assist the South Vietnamese to resist aggression from the North....The integrity of the U.S. commitment is the principal pillar of peace throughout the world. If that commitment becomes unreliable, the communist world would draw conclusions that would lead to our ruin and almost certainly to a catastrophic war."

President Johnson now decided to send Secretary McNamara to Vietnam ostensibly to meet with General Westmoreland and ascertain force requirements. McNamara's trip received much public attention and the presi-

dent's public statement hinted at the possibility of major escalation. On the second day of McNamara's visit to Saigon, he received a back-channel cable of the utmost importance from his deputy, Cyrus Vance. "Yesterday I met three times with highest authority [President Johnson] on actions associated with 34 battalion plan," the cable read. (The remaining ten battalions of the forty-four battalion request were to come from Korea and Australia.) Vance went on to summarize what Johnson had told him (this is perhaps the most significant declassified document currently available to scholars):

1. It is his current intention to proceed with 34 battalion plan.

2. It is impossible for him to submit supplementary budget request of more than $300-$400 million to Congress before next January.

3. If larger request is made to Congress, he believes this will kill domestic legislative program.

4. We should be prepared to explain to the Congress that we have adequate authority and funds, by use of deficit financing, $700 million supplemental [appropriation] and possible small current supplemental to finance recommended operations until next January, when we will be able to come up with clear and precise figures as to what is required.

I asked highest authority whether request for legislation authorizing call-up of reserves and extension of tours of duty would be acceptable in the light of his comments concerning domestic program, and he said that it would.

I pointed out that we would have great difficulties with Senator Stennis concerning this course of action. He said that he recognized that but we would just have to bull it through. He requested that I talk to Senator Russell Monday and I will.

Johnson had made his decision to Americanize the war. On McNamara's return to Washington on 20 July he presented the president with a report warning of the imminent collapse of South Vietnam. McNamara elaborated and defended an option of "expand[ing] promptly and substantially the U.S. military pressure...while launching a vigorous effort on the political side...." McNamara called for approval of Westmoreland's request for 100,000 more U.S. troops, which would bring the U.S. troop level up to thirty-four battalions (175,000 troops), or forty-four battalions (200,000) if "third country" troops (principally Korean) proved unavailable. He indicated that a twenty-seven-battalion second-phase increase of 100,000 more men might be needed by early 1966, with further increments thereafter. McNamara also urged the president to ask Congress to permit calling up 235,000 reservists to active service and to provide a supplemental appropriation to cover the increased costs of the war.

The McNamara proposal became the focal point of extensive White House deliberations over the next few days. At both the NSC meeting of 21 July and the Joint Chiefs meeting of 22 July, Johnson provided ample evidence of his awareness that an upper-limit deployment might very well be in the range of 600,000 men. At one meeting he turned to McNamara and asked "Now let Bob tell us why we need to risk those 600,000 lives." The president's military advisers emphasized that it would take hundreds of thousands of men and several years to achieve military goals. The Joint Chiefs urged Johnson to call up the Reserves and the National Guard and seek public support on national security grounds. But Johnson decided that there would be no public announcement of a change in policy. Johnson also rejected National Security Advisor McGeorge Bundy's proposal that he go before a joint session of Congress or make his statement in a fireside address. Instead, he simply called a midday press conference. The content as well as the forum of Johnson's message downplayed its significance. The expected call-up of the reserves and request for new funds was absent. As if to downplay Vietnam, Johnson also used the afternoon news conference to announce John Chancellor's nomination as head of the United States Information Agency (USIA) and Abe Fortas as associate justice of the Supreme Court. Joint Chiefs Chairman General Earle Wheeler cabled General Westmoreland and informed him that McNamara's recommendation for troop increases had been approved and would be announced the next day. In announcing the troop increase, Johnson did not fully reveal the levels he had now authorized—175,000 to 200,000. Instead, he noted only the immediate force increment—fighting strength would grow from 75,000 to 125,000. Nor did he tell the U.S. people that just a few days earlier, Clark Clifford had warned against any substantial buildup of U.S. ground troops. "This could be a quagmire," warned the president's trusted friend. "It could turn into an open-ended commitment on our part that would take more and more ground troops, without a realistic hope of ultimate victory." Instead, Johnson chose to deceive the U.S. people with respect to the goals of increased military involvement and their anticipated costs. "Additional forces will be needed later, and they will be sent as requested," Johnson observed at his afternoon press conference. His seemingly passing remark correctly indicated that the U.S. commitment had become open-ended: "I have asked the Commanding General, General Westmoreland, what more he needs to meet this mounting aggression. He has told me. We will meet his needs."

Johnson traveled to Honolulu in February 1966, seven months after the fateful decision, for a first-hand assessment on the war's progress from General Westmoreland and to secure additional commitments for political reform from South Vietnam's President Nguyen Cao Ky. At Honolulu, Johnson heard that the July deployments had staved off defeat in the South, but additional troops would now be needed to take the military initiative. Johnson agreed to another dramatic increase in U.S. troop strength from the 184,000 currently deployed to 429,000 by the end of the year. In exchange for the increase, Johnson utilized his favorite exhortation, that Westmoreland "nail the coonskin to the wall" by reaching the crossover point by December 1966. Nailing the coonskin proved to be elusive. U.S. policy was directed at a war of attrition. The promised light at the end of the tunnel in Vietnam was to be achieved primarily by inflicting losses on the enemy forces. Johnson and his advisers expected the enemy to seek negotiations when this crossover point was reached. Johnson administration officials became fixated on statistics. They employed such terms as kill-rations, body counts, defectors, order of battle, weapons-loss ratios, bombing, pacification, died-of-wounds, and population-control data in order to show that progress was being made. The computers could always demonstrate such progress; statistically the United States could always win the war.

At Johnson's behest Secretary McNamara visited Vietnam in October 1966. It had been twelve months since McNamara's last visit—a period during which U.S. troop deployments had more than doubled. Signs of an inconclusive military stalemate were already evident. Military defeat had been prevented, but little progress had been made in rooting out communist forces and destroying their infrastructure. Moreover, while unremitting but selective application of air and naval power had inflicted serious damage to war-supporting targets in North Vietnam, it had not reduced Hanoi's capacity to support or direct military operations in the South. The introduction of over two hundred thousand ground forces had not moved the United States any closer to its political objectives.

On 14 October 1966, Secretary McNamara wrote Johnson that despite significant increases in U.S. troop deployments and in the intensity of targets in the bombing campaign, Hanoi "knows we can't achieve our goals. The prognosis is bad in that the war cannot be brought to a satisfactory conclusion within the next two years." The U.S. military escalation had blunted communist military initiatives, but had not diminished the enemy's will to continue. "Any military victory in South Vietnam the VC may have had in mind eighteen months ago has been thwarted by our emergency deployments and actions. And our program of bombing the North has exacted a price. My concern continues, however, in other respects. This is because I see no reasonable way to bring the war to an end soon."

The public's perception of the war, particularly the lack of military progress, was creating additional burdens for the administration. Nothing symbolized the potential bankruptcy of a guns-and-butter policy more than the outbreak of racial violence throughout the urban United States during the summer of 1967. In the words of Senator J. William Fulbright, Chairman of the Senate Foreign Relations Committee, the Great Society had become a "sick society." The president's political coalition in Congress and credibility with the general public began unraveling. The president's overall job rating, as reported in the Gallup poll, dropped from 47 percent in mid-July to 39 percent in early August. His job rating on Vietnam showed 54 percent disapproval, an all-time high disapproval rating.

During a 29 September 1967 address to the National Legislative Conference in San Antonio, Texas, Johnson sought a way out by restating his administration's position on negotiations and the conditions under which he would agree to halt bombing in North Vietnam. The president certainly hoped to find the right lever that might bring both sides to the conference table before the 1968 presidential election. Johnson now made public his proposal to North Vietnam for peace: "The United States is willing to stop all aerial and naval bombardment of North Vietnam when this will lead promptly to productive discussion. We, of course, assume that while discussions proceed, North Vietnam would not take advantage of the bombing cessation or limitation." The San Antonio formula represented a modification in the Johnson administration's demand that Hanoi halt infiltration into the South as a precondition for a bombing halt. Now, all Hanoi had to do was show an interest in productive discussions and the bombing would be halted. The president was almost desperately looking for a way out, but Ho Chi Minh had nothing to gain by negotiating with a U.S. president facing reelection. Knowing that Johnson had more to lose, Ho rejected the San Antonio proposal. On 29 November 1967, after almost seven years as secretary of defense, Robert McNamara resigned. His stated reason was to accept a new challenge as president of the World Bank. But it was clear then, and it would become even clearer years later, that in his own way he was a casualty of the war.

During the early morning hours of 31 January 1968 (the Vietnamese New Year, Tet) approximately 80,000 North Vietnamese regulars and guerrillas attacked more than 100 cities throughout South Vietnam. Tet involved enemy attacks on thirty-five of forty-four province capitals, thirty-six district towns, and many villages and hamlets. For weeks prior to the offensive, enemy forces had been infiltrating into Saigon in civilian clothes in preparation for a well-planned campaign of terror. The goal was to achieve a popular uprising against the GVN and to show the U.S. public that the very notion of security in the South was null and void. From a military point of view, the VC suffered a major defeat at Tet. Over half of their committed force was lost and perhaps a quarter of their whole regular force. Moreover, the communists failed to bring about the diversion of U.S. forces from Khe Sahn or elsewhere. Nevertheless, as reported by the U.S. news media, the psychological impact of Tet had a demoralizing effect on the U.S. public. The enemy had demonstrated a capability to enter and attack cities and towns and had employed terrorism for doing vast damage. The Tet offensive set in motion a remarkable sequence of events that included a 1 February cable from General Wheeler to Admiral Ulysses S. Grant Sharp, Jr., and General Westmoreland raising the possibility "whether tactical nuclear weapons should be used if the situation in Khe Sahn should become that desperate." While Wheeler considered that eventuality unlikely, he requested a list of susceptible targets in the areas "which lend themselves to nuclear strikes, whether some contingency nuclear planning would be in order, and what you would consider to be some of the more significant pros and cons of using TAC [tactical] nukes in such a contingency." Westmoreland responded, "The use of tactical weapons should not be required in the present situation." However, should the situation change, "I visualize that either tactical nuclear weapons or chemical agents would be active candidates for employment." During an emotional 16 February news conference, Johnson vehemently denied that nuclear weapons had even been considered, adding even more fuel to the credibility gap fire.

Tet revealed that despite over 525,000 men, billions of dollars, and extensive bombing, the United States had not stopped the enemy from replacing his forces. The intensity of the war and the capacity to sustain it were controlled not by the United States' superior technology, but by the enemy. In effect, the United States faced stalemate in Vietnam. General Westmoreland again needed more troops and requested an additional 206,000 from the president. The reinforcements would bring the total U.S. military commitment in ground forces to three-quarters of a million—yet the United States was no closer to achieving its political objective than at the outset of Americanization in 1965. It was becoming increasingly evident that no amount of military power would bring North Vietnam to the conference table.

On 27 February 1968 General Wheeler sent Johnson a major report on military requirements in Vietnam. The report was based on three days of conferences with Westmoreland and the senior U.S. commander in each of the four Corps areas. The president appointed his new secretary of defense, Clark Clifford, to head a task force to evaluate General Westmoreland's request. The president's initial instructions to Clifford were "give me the lesser of evils." Clifford questioned the Joint Chiefs and those advisers who knew the most about Vietnam. Johnson received the Clifford task-force report on 4 March. The report recommended meeting Westmoreland's immediate military requirements by deploying 22,000 additional personnel (approximately 60 percent of which would be combat and three tactical fighter squadrons). The task force also recommended approval of a 262,000 Reserve call-up in order to help replenish the strategic Reserve levels. It was quite possible that an additional 200,000 U.S. troops, or double or triple that quantity, would not be enough to accomplish U.S. objectives. Upon receiving the Clifford task-force report, Johnson convened a meeting of his principal foreign-policy advisers. Now, for the first time, the president heard Clifford outline the problems he faced. "Your senior advisers have conferred on this matter at very great length. There is a deep-seated concern by your advisers. There is a concern that if we say yea, and step with the addition of 206,000 more men that we might continue down the road as we have been without accomplishing our purpose—which is for a viable South Vietnam which can live in peace. We are not convinced that our present policy will bring us to that objective." Clifford emphasized that the 206,000 request was not just another call for more troops. The new request brought the president to the clearly defined watershed of going down the same road of "more troops, more guns, more planes, more ships?" And, "do you go on killing more Viet Cong and more Vietnamese and killing more Viet Cong and more North Vietnamese?" Clifford now shattered any illusions the president might have held with respect to military progress. "There are grave doubts that we have made the type of progress we had hoped to have made by this time. As we build up our forces, they build up theirs. We continue to fight at a higher level of intensity. Even were we to meet this full request of 206,000 men, and the pattern continues as it has, it is likely that by March he [General Westmoreland] may want another 200,000 to 300,000 men with no end in sight. The reserve forces in North Vietnam are a case for concern as well. They have a very substantial population from which to draw. They have no trouble whatever organizing, equipping, and training their forces." Clifford's next words must have convinced Johnson that the United States needed to disengage from Vietnam. "We seem to have a sinkhole. We put in more—they match it. I see more and more fighting with more and more casualties on the U.S. side and no end in sight to the action." It was also evident that U.S. public opinion would no longer accept a long drawn-out military campaign with high casualties. By March 196, the Gallup Poll reported that 49 percent of the U.S. population believed the United States was wrong to have gotten involved militarily in Vietnam. While seven out of ten of those calling themselves doves thought the country was wrong to ever have gotten involved, four in ten who considered themselves to be hawks thought so as well.

On 31 March 1968, Johnson announced a partial suspension of the bombing against North Vietnam, but he warned that if Hanoi did not demonstrate similar restraint the bombing would be accelerated. In Johnson's words, "there is no need to delay talks that could bring an end to this long and this bloody war. Tonight, I review the offer I made last August—to stop the bombardment of North Vietnam. We ask that talks begin promptly, that they be serious talks on the substance of peace. We assume that during those talks Hanoi will not take advantage of our restraint. We are prepared to move immediately toward peace through negotiations. So tonight, in the hope that this action will lead to early talks, I am taking the first step to de-escalate the conflict. We are reducing—substantially reducing—the present level of hostilities. And we are doing so unilaterally, and at once." The president then stunned the nation by announcing, "I shall not seek, and I will not accept, the nomination of my party for another term as your president." The leader who committed forces abroad thereby removed himself from the disengagement process. The battle over disengagement and its meaning would not preoccupy domestic political debate in the United States.

Nixon, Kissinger, Ford, and the End of the War

Ending the war honorably became a major issue in the 1968 presidential campaign. Republican candidate Richard Nixon stressed that the road to a negotiated peace ran through Moscow, not necessarily Hanoi. In seeking broad political accommodation—détente—with the Soviet Union, Nixon hoped that leaders in the Kremlin would exert pressure on their ideological allies in Hanoi to negotiate an end to the conflict. Toward the end of the campaign Nixon claimed to possess a secret plan to end the war that he would unveil following the election. Once in office, however, Nixon presented no such plan, although it was clear to the new president that the United States could no longer support an open-ended commitment in Southeast Asia. He and National Security Adviser Henry Kissinger wanted to end the war on terms acceptable to U.S. honor and prestige. On 10 April 1969 the administration issued NSAM 36, directing Secretary of Defense Melvin Laird to prepare "a specific timetable for Vietnamizing the war." Vietnamization was a two-pronged effort involving unilateral withdrawal of U.S. troops from South Vietnam while simultaneously turning over greater military responsibilities to South

Vietnamese forces. All previous U.S. withdrawal plans had been based on a reduction in enemy forces. Vietnamization was premised on the realization that there would be no imminent political settlement involving voluntary reduction in enemy forces.

Whereas Johnson established the preeminence of an independent and stable noncommunist government in South Vietnam, Nixon redefined the political objective to a U.S. withdrawal that did not abandon South Vietnam to a quick defeat. But Nixon was also determined not to be sucked into Hanoi's diplomatic sidesteps. He would not repeat Johnson's mistakes. Nixon chose to back up diplomatic initiatives with the most massive bombings of the war. Beginning in March 1969 the United States, under the code name MENU, secretly began bombing Viet Cong and North Vietnamese Army (NVA) sanctuaries in Cambodia. In May 1970, the air strikes on Cambodia moved from covert to open support of ground operations against the North Vietnamese. The secret bombing of Cambodia would later be one of five proposed Articles of Impeachment against Nixon.

On 8 May 1969, Hanoi announced its own ten-point proposal for ending the war, the centerpiece of which was a complete U.S. withdrawal and abolition of the government of South Vietnam. On 14 May 1969, in a nationally televised speech, Nixon answered Hanoi's proposal with an eight-point plan for peace that called for the simultaneous withdrawal of U.S. and communist forces (a major concession by the United States from its previously stipulated requirement of six months). The United States was also willing to accept participation of the communist National Liberation Front (NLF) in the political life of the South with free supervised elections. The 14 May speech shocked the South Vietnamese allies who now feared they would be abandoned by the new administration's need to extricate itself from Vietnam. Meeting on Midway Island, Nixon and South Vietnam's President Nguyen Thieu agreed that, under Vietnamization, 25,000 U.S. troops would be withdrawn immediately and a steady exodus would follow. The Midway meetings revealed schisms between the United States and its Vietnamese allies. Thieu came to Midway committed to four "no's." (1) no recognition of the enemy; (2) no neutralization of South Vietnam; (3) no coalition government, and (4) no surrender of territory to the enemy. According to South Vietnamese Ambassador Bui Diem, "Nixon and Thieu played political poker [at Midway Island]. Thieu tried to get as much as he could without giving way to a plan for total U.S. withdrawal. He hoped for a gradual American withdrawal that would end with a residual U.S. force in South Vietnam. Visualizing a Korean-type solution with the demilitarized zone as a buffer between North and South Vietnam, Thieu hoped that two divisions of American troops, about 40,000 men, would be stationed there to act as a deterrent to a North Vietnamese invasion." Nixon left the Midway meeting jubilant. U.S. troops were to start withdrawing from Vietnam and, of special significance, Nixon had received Thieu's acquiescence for starting secret talks between Hanoi and the United States. Thieu soon learned that the United States would formulate a negotiating strategy that did not include consultation with its Vietnamese allies. U.S. withdrawal and South Vietnam's survival became two separate ends for the allies. Vietnamization ultimately proved counterproductive to what Nixon sought politically from negotiations; the more U.S. troops departed without any progress in negotiations, the less incentive Hanoi had to reach any agreement at all. Conversely, the more the United States diminished its military presence, the more intensely Nixon sought a negotiated settlement. The lack of linkages between the objectives of disengagement and Vietnamization wrought other serious consequences. Congressional opposition increased and the antiwar movement began organizing a series of demonstrations across the United States. In a secret letter to Ho Chi Minh, Nixon warned that if no progress in negotiations occurred by 1 November 1969, he would resort to "measures of great consequence and force." On 15 August 1969, Ho rejected all of Nixon's conditions and insisted that peace would come only when the United States removed all its troops from Vietnam and disassociated itself from the Thieu government.

In 1970 Nixon made perhaps the most controversial decision of his presidency: he sent U.S. forces into Cambodia to shore up the Lon Nol regime with hopes of keeping Cambodia out of communist control. Nixon saw this action as one of those decisive moments in the Cold War, when the will and character of the U.S. people and their leaders were being tested by events and by their enemies. As Nixon told the nation during an evening broadcast, "I would rather be a one-term president than be a two-term president at the cost of seeing America…accept the first defeat in its sound 190-years' history." In vintage Cold War hyperbole: "If, when the chips are down, the world's most powerful nation acts like a pitiful, helpless giant, the forces of totalitarianism and anarchy will threaten free nations and free institutions throughout the world." While such rhetoric rang true with the "silent majority," the political opposition to the war grew and intensified. Antiwar demonstrations spread across the nation's college campuses, and hundreds of thousands of protesters marched on Washington. Congressional opposition also increased and a number of legislative measures seeking to end the war were introduced. In reaction to the U.S. action into Cambodia, the NLF and North Vietnamese delegates walked out of the Paris negotiations. When Nixon (trying to placate public opinion and defying his field commander's wishes) announced that another 150,000 troops would soon be out of Vietnam, Hanoi hardened its resolve not to negotiate; the talks remained deadlocked. With little room to maneuver politically, Nixon, much like Johnson, found that military action provided his only base for seeking to maintain credibility—he approved ground operations into Laos to destroy enemy logistics systems.

By 1971 U.S. annual battle deaths in Vietnam since the Americanization of the war in 1965 were at an all-time low (1,380); yet the military intensity of the war was at an all-time high. The North Vietnamese were using the Paris talks as another mode of fighting. "The war had now entered what communist theoreticians called 'dahn va dam, dam va dahn,'—fighting and talking, talking and fighting." In the spring of 1971, Henry Kissinger began secret talks with Xuan Thuy and Le Duc Tho in Paris (later described as "walks in the night" by Thieu). Kissinger first offered a seven-point peace plan that contained two very important concessions: in exchange for the return of all POWs, a date (31 December 1971) would be set for the complete withdrawal of U.S. forces, and for the first time the United States would not insist that the North do the same. Mutual withdrawal was replaced only by the insistence that the North cease its infiltration. The proposal also separated the military issue from political issues. Under these terms, there could be a negotiated cease-fire without settling the major political question: what kind of government South Vietnam would have in the postwar period.

In March 1972 North Vietnam initiated a massive conventional invasion of South Vietnam spearheaded by over 120,000 North Vietnamese troops that crossed the demilitarized zone (DMZ) in the Central Highlands and also the Cambodian border. The attack caught U.S. intelligence by surprise and for a moment it looked like Saigon might fall. Nixon responded with force. "The bastards have never been bombed like they're going to be bombed this time," he promised. At the time of the attack, Nixon had been preparing for a scheduled summit meeting in Moscow to discuss strategic arms limitations. Divisions within the Nixon administration now manifested themselves. Secretary of Defense Laird and Secretary of State Rogers warned that the bombing program, tagged Linebacker, would ruin the summit; but when Commanding General Creighton Abrams cabled Nixon that "the whole thing may be lost," the president approved the mining of Haiphong, a naval blockade, and the B-52 Linebacker air campaign. According to Nixon, "If we were to lose Vietnam there would have been no respect for the American president...because we had the power and didn't use it...we must be credible." Nixon gambled that the Soviets would not risk détente over Vietnam. Moreover, if South Vietnam fell, détente would be lost anyway since the North's offensive would be spearheaded by Soviet military equipment. Nixon would hardly be in a politically acceptable position for welcoming a thaw in superpower relations.

The dramatic escalation in the bombing program evoked only mild criticism from Moscow and China, neither of which was willing to risk rapprochement for its ally in Hanoi. The North's casualties from its offensive were staggering; it lost more than one half of the two hundred thousand troops it committed. It would take two or three years to replace these forces and Hanoi's leaders now wanted to end the fighting part of the war. Several weeks prior to the scheduled summit, Kissinger met secretly with Soviet leader Leonid Brezhnev and offered major concessions to North Vietnam: the United States would accept a cease-fire in place, in exchange, for the removal of only North Vietnamese forces that had entered South Vietnam since the 31 March offensive (which meant that 20,000 could stay).

The Moscow summit was held in May 1972; Nixon and Brezhnev signed the Strategic Arms Limitation Talks (SALT) treaty as well as a new Berlin treaty. In September 1972, Kissinger and Tho began another series of meetings in Paris, which resulted in a two-track agreement that separated military from political issues—again deferring for the future the question of who would rule South Vietnam. The negotiations produced a tentative agreement, but the terms proved unacceptable to Thieu. Under the proposed treaty: Hanoi agreed to allow Thieu to remain in power in exchange for a grant of political status in South Vietnam to the PRG-Provisional Revolutionary Government; all Prisoners of War (POWs) would be returned within sixty days of cease-fire; the United States would withdraw its remaining troops from the South; all NVA troops currently in the South would be permitted to remain (Washington's greatest concession); a tripartite commission would be created to supervise elections and administer the agreement; and all decisions of the commission would have to be unanimous—giving each delegate an absolute veto. Nixon was apparently swayed by Thieu's fierce lobbying that the proposed Kissinger-Tho pact was tantamount to selling out the government of South Vietnam. Thieu would accept nothing less than the removal of all North Vietnamese troops in exchange for a role for the NLF (now the Provisional Revolution Group) in the Saigon government. Kissinger later described this as a "Greek tragedy...the imperatives on him [Thieu] were almost diametrically opposite of ours."

A week before the 1972 presidential election, Kissinger stated that "peace is at hand," but the talks again stalled and Nixon turned to "jugular diplomacy." Nixon decided that no treaty would be signed until after the November 1972 election when his position would be strengthened by what most observers expected to be an overwhelming election victory over Democratic challenger and antiwar leader George McGovern. Reelected by just such a landslide, Nixon moved swiftly against North Vietnam. During the Christmas 1972 period the United States initiated the most intensive and devastating air attacks of the war, "dropping more than 36,000 tons of bombs and exceeding the tonnage during the entire period from 1969 to 1971...the destruction in parts of Hanoi and Haiphong was heavy, and as many as 1,600 civilians were killed." The bombing certainly gave the North Vietnamese reason to resume negotiations; on 28 December Hanoi consented to negotiations and on 29 December the bombing stopped. The Accord signed in Paris was not much different from the one drafted the previous October. The agreement settled only one real issue: U.S. involvement, not who would rule South Vietnam. Nixon had threatened Thieu with cutting off all aid if he did not go along, but gave Thieu written assurances that if North Vietnam violated the peace, the United States would not abandon South Vietnam. The president promised "swift and severe retaliatory actions" if the North moved against South Vietnam. Thieu told his cabinet: "The United States leaves us without any alternative except that if we sign, and will continue and there is a pledge of retaliation if the agreements are violated....Kissinger treats both Vietnams as adversaries. He considers himself as an outsider in these negotiations and does not distinguish between South Vietnam, as an ally, and North Vietnam, as an enemy. The Americans let the war become their war; when they liked the war they carried it forward. Then they want to stop it, they impose on both sides to stop it. When the Americans wanted to enter, we had no choice, and now here they are ready to leave, we have no choice."

Few of the provisions from the Accords were ever carried out. The North concluded that diplomacy, rather than military means, would be the way to rid their country of a U.S. military presence—even if it meant accepting the temporary existence of a government in South Vietnam. As North Vietnam Colonel Bao noted: "Hundreds of billions of dollars and a half-million United States troops have failed to subdue the Vietnamese people; $300 million more to Saigon can in no way change the situation." Indeed, between 1973-1975 Hanoi pressed forward in its goal of overthrowing the South. On 25 March 1975, Thieu wrote President Gerald Ford, "Hanoi's intention to use the Paris Agreement for a military takeover of South Vietnam was well known to us at the very time of negotiating the Paris Agreement. You may recall that we signed it, not because we naively believed in the enemy's good will, but because we trusted America's solemn commitment to safeguard the peace in Vietnam."

Legacies

There may be no phrase more overused in foreign policy discussions and analyses since the 1960s than "the lessons of Vietnam." Nonetheless, exactly what those lessons are, have been, and continue to be, hotly debated. The debate has been played out in the larger field of U.S. politics, splitting the Democratic Party for more than two decades and fueling the political appeal of Ronald Reagan. It has framed U.S. policy toward a number of other countries and conflicts, most notably Central America in the late 1970s–1980s. And it has come back time and again to heated arguments about the Vietnam War itself, as scholars and former policymakers have continued to reflect, lecture, and write about it. Former Defense Secretary Robert S. McNamara, in his 1995 book, *In Retrospect,* broke his own long silence on the subject with the provocative admission that while "we acted according to what we thought were the principles and traditions of this nation...we were wrong, terribly wrong." It's doubtful, however, that even McNamara will have the final word on a subject as irresistibly compelling as the Vietnam War.

LARRY BERMAN

See also Ball, George Wildman; Cambodia; Cold War; Containment; Diem, Ngo Dinh; Dien Bien Phu; Domino Theory; Eisenhower, Dwight David; Ford, Gerald Rudolph, Jr.; Guerrilla Warfare; Ho Chi Minh; Johnson, Lyndon Baines; Kennedy, John Fitzgerald; Kissinger, Henry Alfred; Lansdale, Edward Geary; Laos; McNamara, Robert Strange; Pentagon Papers; Rostow, Walt Whitman; Rusk, David Dean; Southeast Asia Treaty Organization; Taylor, Maxwell Davenport; Tet Offensive; Thieu, Nguyen Van; Truman, Harry S.; Westmoreland, William

FURTHER READING

Berman, Larry. *Planning A Tragedy: The Americanization of the Vietnam War.* New York, 1982.
———. *Lyndon Johnson's War: The Road to Stalemate in Vietnam.* New York, 1990.
Clodfelter, Mark. *The Limits of Air Power: The American Bombing of North Vietnam.* New York, 1989.
Gardner, Lloyd. *Approaching Vietnam.* New York, 1988.
Gelb, Leslie H., and Richard K. Betts. *The Irony of Vietnam: The System Worked.* Washington, D.C., 1979.
Gibbons, William Conrad. *The U.S. Government and the Vietnam War: Executive and Legislators Roles and Relationships.* Princeton, N.J., 1984–1989.
Halberstam, David. *The Best and the Brightest.* New York, 1972.
———. *The Making of a Quagmire.* New York, 1965.
Hallin, Daniel. *The Uncensored War: The Media and Vietnam.* Berkeley, Calif., 1989.
Herring, George. *America's Longest War: The United States and Vietnam 1950–1975.* 3rd ed. New York, 1996.
Kahin, George McT. *Intervention: How America Became Involved in Vietnam.* New York, 1986.

Karnow, Stanley. *Vietnam: A History.* New York, 1983.

Kissinger, Henry. *Diplomacy.* New York, 1994.

McNamara, Robert. *In Retrospect: The Tragedy and Lessons of Vietnam.* New York, 1995.

The Pentagon Papers: The Defense Department History of United States Decisionmaking on Vietnam. Senator Gravel ed. 5 vols. 1971.

Sheehan, Neil. *A Bright Shining Lie: John Paul Vann and America in Vietnam.* New York, 1988.

Young, Marilyn B. *The Vietnam Wars, 1945–1990.* New York, 1991.

VILLA, PANCHO

(*b.* 4 October 1877; *d.* 20 July 1923)

Mexican revolutionary leader. Born Doroteo Arango, he changed his name to Francisco Villa (and came to be known as Pancho) during the fifteen years he lived as a bandit in the mountains, where he fled at age sixteen after killing a man who had attacked his sister. In 1910 Villa joined Francisco Madero's effort to overthrow the Mexican dictator Porfirio Díaz. When General Victoriano Huerta in turn overthrew President Madero in 1913, Villa joined an uprising, led by General Venustiano Carranza, against Huerta. After Huerta's defeat, Villa joined the peasant leader General Emiliano Zapata in the war against Carranza; they seized Mexico City in November 1914 but were soon driven out. When Carranza entered Mexico City in February 1915, Villa was forced to retreat to his base in the state of Chihuahua. A brilliant tactician, the roguish and often brutal Villa inspired his troops, made up of peons and poor ranchers from northern Mexico, and led them effectively in mobile and fluid guerrilla and light cavalry war. At the peak of his power, Villa commanded 100,000 troops.

In 1914 and 1915 President Woodrow Wilson's administration supported Villa because he seemed the warlord most likely to cooperate with U.S. efforts to hold down anti-American forces within the revolutionary forces; unlike Carranza, for example, Villa welcomed the U.S. military seizure of Veracruz in 1914, which weakened Huerta. Villa tried to embroil the U.S. and Mexican governments in war in order to improve his political standing in Mexico; he would become a hero by fighting the United States. On 10 January 1916, Villa's forces killed sixteen U.S. engineers on their way to reopen a mine in the northern state of Sonora, and on 9 March several hundred Villistas attacked the town of Columbus, New Mexico. Against the Mexican government's wishes, President Wilson ordered General John Pershing and 6,000 troops into northern Mexico to capture Villa. Villa fought on, launching raids into Texas. U.S. and Mexican troops also clashed, as the Mexican government sought to limit the scope of the U.S. intrusion. U.S. forces never captured Villa.

As World War I intensified and President Wilson contemplated U.S. entry into the war, he recalled the U.S. troops from Mexico; the last U.S. soldier left Mexico in February 1917. The Pershing expedition had failed. Villa fought on for years as a local guerrilla, until his death six years later.

JORGE I. DOMÍNGUEZ

See also Díaz (Jose de la Cruz), Porfirio; Huerta, Victoriano; Mexico; Pershing, John

FURTHER READING

Clendenen, Clarence Clemens. *The United States and Pancho Villa: A Study in Unconventional Diplomacy.* Ithaca, N.Y., 1961.

Katz, Friedrich. *The Secret War in Mexico: Europe, the United States, and the Mexican Revolution.* Chicago, 1981.

VIRGIN ISLANDS

A group of islands located in the Eastern Caribbean Sea, east of Puerto Rico. The United States purchased the islands of Saint Croix, Saint John, and Saint Thomas, together with fifty islets and cays, from Denmark in 1917 for $25 million. The U.S. Navy had long sought the islands as a naval base from which the sea lanes leading between the Panama Canal and southern U.S. ports and Europe could be protected or even controlled. Denmark had concluded that the islands could not be defended by the Danish navy, but earlier efforts to arrange their purchase had failed. In 1867 the Senate refused to ratify a treaty that would have paid $7.5 million, and in 1902 Denmark rejected a treaty for just $5 million. During World War II, fears that Germany, which owned shipping properties in Saint Thomas, might take over the islands and use them in their war effort against the Allies convinced all parties finally to agree to the sale.

Until 1931 the U.S. Department of the Navy administered the islands as an unincorporated territory, maintaining Danish governmental institutions under an appointed governor and conferring U.S. citizenship to most of the islanders. Since 1931 the Department of the Interior has administered the islands and, under a series of acts of Congress, considerable self-government has been instituted. As a territory, the U.S. Virgin Islands send a nonvoting delegate to the U.S. House of Representatives. Because of the economic benefits of territorial status, demands for autonomy have been minimal. Without a self-supporting economy, the approximately 100,000 residents of the islands are economically dependent on the United States and have received millions of dollars in assistance since they were purchased. Tourism is the principal industry, and U.S. tax incentives have encouraged the development of oil refining as well. Despite their dependence on financial aid, the islands have a higher per capita income than do citizens of most independent Caribbean states. Immigrants from other Caribbean islands, arriving in search of jobs and higher living standards, have pushed population growth and generated friction with native inhabitants.

CHRISTOPHER WELNA

See also Danish West Indies, Acquisition of; Denmark; World War I

FURTHER READING

Boyer, William W. *America's Virgin Islands: A History of Human Rights and Wrongs.* Durham, N.C., 1983.

Tansill, Charles C. *The Purchase of the Danish West Indies.* Westport, Conn., 1968.

VISAS

See Passports and Visas

VLADIVOSTOK ACCORD

See Strategic Arms Limitation Talks and Agreements

VOA

See Voice of America

VOICE OF AMERICA

The international radio broadcast service of the United States Information Agency. Voice of America (VOA) provides world news as well as reports on U.S. policies and American society. VOA went on the air on 24 February 1942, broadcasting to Germany, and has broadcast continuously ever since. In 1993–1994 VOA broadcast nearly 1,000 hours of programming weekly in forty-six languages and prepared programming for distribution to local stations in two additional languages. Total programming available for local stations totaled 2,500 hours per week. VOA estimates its direct weekly audience at about 100 million listeners. The size of the additional audience for local station programming is unknown. VOA's operating budget for 1993 was an estimated $250 million, with an additional $100 million for capital expenditures. In 1996 VOA broadcast 840 hours a week in six languages. Its operating budget for the 1996–1997 year was $125 million, a significant reduction from previous years. It maintained twenty-five news bureaus throughout the world and broadcast from sites in California, Ohio, North Carolina, and Florida and from thirteen overseas relays. VOA's traditional emphasis on short wave—special frequencies whose signals reach listeners thousands of miles from the transmitter—has shifted toward newer technologies, including standard, medium-wave transmitters, especially in former communist areas; cable radio; collaboration with local broadcasters; and the possibility of direct broadcast from satellites.

VOA is the world's most extensive international broadcaster in terms of languages and hours and one of a handful of U.S. government-financed services with a global reach. Its main competitor is the British Broadcasting Corporation, which has a comparable audience but generally enjoys a higher reputation for independence from government influence and thus possesses greater worldwide credibility. VOA's services include Radio Martí, which was established in 1983 at the insistence of Cuban Americans to broadcast television programs to Cuba, and VOA Europe, a popular music service started in 1985 and aimed at young listeners that is heard in 406 cities and regions in thirty countries. VOA should not be confused with Radio Free Europe and Radio Liberty (RFE/RL), which were established after World War II as journalistic watchdogs, albeit in exile, of communist central Europe and the Soviet Union. In 1993 President Bill Clinton proposed the merger of RFE/RL with VOA and drastically cut their budgets. The RFE/RL headquarters was transferred from Munich to Prague; RFE Hungarian service went off the air in November 1993.

ROBERT L. STEVENSON

See also Communications Policy; Foreign Broadcast Information Service; Radio Free Europe and Radio Liberty; Radio Martí; United States Information Agency

FURTHER READING

Shulman, Holly Cowan. *The Voice of America: Propaganda and Democracy, 1941–1945.* Madison, Wis., 1990.

Sorensen, Thomas C. *The Word War: The Story of American Propaganda.* New York, 1968.

W

WALDHEIM, KURT

(*b.* 21 December 1918)

Diplomat and president of Austria, who served as the fourth secretary-general of the United Nations (1972–1981). Born in Saint Andra-Wordern, near Vienna, and trained as a lawyer, he entered the Austrian diplomatic service after World War II and held many positions, including permanent representative to the United Nations (1962–1968, 1969–1972) and foreign minister (1968–1969). Like his predecessors as secretary-general, Waldheim was a compromise candidate chosen more for his lack of enemies than for his strengths. The Soviets supported him because they believed him to be pliable, while the U.S. government tolerated him for being no threat to its foreign policy goals.

As secretary-general, Waldheim had few notable successes or failures. He undertook few initiatives and was generally content to maintain the status quo at the United Nations. Eager to avoid offending member governments, he did little to address crises such as the Vietnam War or the Yom Kippur War of October 1973 in the Middle East. The increasing power of Third World nations in the General Assembly—displayed in 1975 with Resolution 3379, equating Zionism with racism—combined with Waldheim's caution to erode the already weak U.S. public support for the United Nations. In 1980, he traveled to Tehran to negotiate for the release of the U.S. hostages held by Iranian militants, but with no success. In response to this effort, and because they saw no better alternative, U.S. officials supported Waldheim for a third term in 1981. Only the veto of the Peoples Republic of China, based on its desire for a secretary-general from the developing world, prevented his re-election.

In 1986, the Austrian press publicized documents showing that Waldheim, as a lieutenant serving with the German army in the Balkans in 1943 and 1944, had participated, at least indirectly, in war-crime activities in Yugoslavia and Greece. Waldheim, who up to this point had clearly dissimulated facts about his early life, could not deny his affiliation with the Nazi Party or his service in the German army; but he did continue to portray his wartime service as unremarkable. The revelations not only discredited the United Nations further, but also sparked speculation that the permanent members of the Security Council had known of Waldheim's compromised past. Nevertheless, Waldheim won election to the presidency of Austria in 1986, a position he held until 1992.

KURK DORSEY

See also Austria; Cold War; Holocaust; Middle East; United Nations; Vietnam War

FURTHER READING

Finger, Seymour M., and Arnold A. Saltzman. *Bending With the Winds: Kurt Waldheim and the United Nations.* New York, 1990.
Hazzard, Shirley. *Countenance of Truth: The United Nations and the Waldheim Case.* New York, 1989.
Waldheim, Kurt. *In the Eye of the Storm.* Bethesda, Md., 1986.

WALESA, LECH

(*b.* 29 September 1943)

Polish labor leader, activist, and statesman who challenged Soviet authority and in the process helped to put an end to the Cold War and to communist domination of Eastern Europe. Walesa was an electrician and member of underground free-trade union circles banned in communist Poland. He burst into prominence in 1980 as leader of the Lenin Shipyard strike in Gdansk that gave rise to the Solidarity movement. He chaired Solidarity during its initial phase of legal coexistence with the communist authorities, pursuing a moderate policy of urging democratic reforms while restraining Solidarity militants. The United States encouraged Solidarity, and the Carter administration exerted diplomatic pressure to discourage Soviet military intervention in Poland. After the Warsaw regime suppressed the union by martial law in 1981, Walesa was imprisoned for a year. The resort to martial law excited vigorous public and official protest in the United States. The Reagan administration imposed sanctions on Poland and the Soviet Union in reprisal, and Solidarity received covert aid from American sources. Upon his release from prison, Walesa resumed leadership of the outlawed Solidarity, receiving the Nobel Peace Prize in 1983 in the name of the proscribed union. He headed the opposition coalition that reached the "round table" power-sharing agreement with the government in 1989, restoring Solidarity and holding elections that precipitated the sudden dissolution of the communist order in Poland. Increasingly estranged from his former Solidarity associates on political and personal grounds, Walesa was elected president of the newly democratic Polish Republic in 1990, advocating a speedy and thorough break with the communist past. As president, he called for greater American economic, military, and political assistance to Poland, stressing the need for prompt admission of his country into the NATO alliance. Despite presiding over a robust Polish economic recovery, he was frequently criticized for being erratic, autocratic, and lacking in attributes essential to high office, and failed to win re-election in 1995. Nevertheless, he retained durable prestige as one of the principal figures in the democratic transformation of central Europe at the end of the Cold War.

NEAL PEASE

See also Cold War; Eastern Europe; Nobel Peace Prize; Poland; Russia and the Soviet Union

FURTHER READING

Ash, Timothy Garton. *The Polish Revolution: Solidarity*. New York, 1985.
Walesa, Lech. *A Way of Hope: An Autobiography*. New York, 1987.
———. *The Struggle and the Triumph*. Translated by Franklin Philip. New York, 1992.

WALKER, WILLIAM

(*b.* 8 May 1824; *d.* 12 September 1860)

Perhaps the best known filibuster and adventurer in United States history. Walker was a romantic figure often described as an advocate of slavery expansion and remembered by some Nicaraguans as the leader of the United States's first intervention in their country.

Born in Nashville, Tennessee, Walker trained as a physician but did not practice; he read law and was admitted to the bar in Louisiana but had little success as a lawyer; and he worked as a journalist, serving as an editor of the New Orleans *Daily Crescent*, a paper that interestingly editorialized against filibustering in Cuba.

The restless Walker later moved to California, where journalism and law engaged his time until ideas of colonizing the Mexican state of Sonora attracted his attention. His foray (1853–1854) into Lower California, creating a new republic to which he announced the annexation of Sonora and declared himself president, was a disaster.

Walker's adventure into Mexico, following annexation of Texas and the acquisition of Mexican territory by the United States, moved nervous central American states to closer cooperation with England. The Central American transit route along Nicaragua's San Juan River and through Lake Nicaragua attracted world attention bringing Cornelius Vanderbilt's Accessory Transit Company and many U.S. citizens to a badly divided and war-torn Nicaragua. In the fractional strife of the mid-1850s the Nicaraguan Liberals (Democrats) hoped to retrieve the advantage over their rival Conservatives (Legitimists) by appealing for aid in the United States. One such appeal for armed colonists came to William Walker who prepared a filibustering expedition. His "American Phalanx" of fifty-eight men arrived in Nicaragua on 16 June 1855, where almost immediately Walker revealed his independence of Liberal dominance. After capturing Granada, the Conservative stronghold, Walker became practically the master of Nicaragua; he soon became commander-in-chief of the Nicaraguan army and was the dominant figure in a newly-organized government. In an election held on 29 June 1856, Walker became president, envisioning a new federal republic of Central American states and Cuba, with slavery reestablished and himself as supreme leader. In his adventurous rise Walker made important enemies; he sided with competitors of Vanderbilt for control of the transit company, while his Nicaraguan opponents gained allies in other Central American republics. Cut off from supplies and recruits (Vanderbilt's doing), hit by disease and desertions, and facing a hostile Central American coalition, Walker surrendered to Commander Charles H. Davis of the U.S. Navy, at Rivas, Nicaragua, on 1 May 1857.

Twice more Walker attempted filibustering expeditions. One, at Greytown on Nicaragua's east coast in November 1857, was foiled by a U.S. naval officer before Walker could go inland. A second in August–September 1860, was stopped when a British naval officer accepted Walker's surrender on the Honduran coast. Turned over to Honduran authorities, Walker was shot by a firing squad on 12 September 1860, and buried in Honduras.

WILLIAM KAMMAN

See also Honduras; Nicaragua

FURTHER READING

Carr, Albert Z. *The World and William Walker*. New York, 1963.
Greene, Laurence. *The Filibuster: The Career of William Walker*. Indianapolis, Ind., 1937 (repr. 1974).
Scroggs, William O. *Filibusters and Financiers: The Story of William Walker and His Associates*. New York, 1916 (repr. 1969).

WALLACE, HENRY AGARD

(*b.* 7 October 1888; *d.* 18 November 1965)

Vice president of the United States between 1941 and 1945. Throughout his long career as an agricultural leader and government official, Henry A. Wallace never held a post that dealt primarily with foreign affairs. He was neither a key policymaker nor an influential adviser on major foreign policy decisions. Nonetheless, he became a highly visible and passionate spokesman on foreign affairs, especially during World War II and the early Cold War years. His views aroused bitter opposition by 1948 and relegated him to the fringes of American politics. Wallace's critique of American Cold War assumptions and of the Truman administration has received a more favorable assessment from recent scholars than it received from his contemporaries.

Wallace's views on foreign policy were derived from his midwestern background. Born on a farm near Orient, Iowa, he graduated from Iowa State College, where he excelled in subjects relating to agriculture and genetics. As editor of his family's highly-regarded farm journal, *Wallaces' Farmer*, his evolving views on foreign policy issues such as tariffs, war debt reduction, and U.S. investment abroad reflected his interest in promoting the welfare of farmers. By the early 1930s they also reflected his unorthodox religious beliefs, which included a prominent strain of mysticism. Although he favored a policy of isolationism during the 1920s, both economic and religious considerations eventually led him to the firm conviction that international cooperation was the best route to world peace and prosperity.

Wallace left Iowa and went to Washington in 1933 as Franklin D. Roosevelt's secretary of agriculture. He used his position to speak out for reducing trade barriers, improved relations with Latin America, and, as war in Europe and Asia approached, a strong stand against fascist aggression. As Roosevelt's vice president between 1941 and 1945, Wallace received a great deal of attention by calling for a "century of the common man." He made goodwill trips to Latin America, Soviet Asia, and China that reinforced his belief in the need for American leadership to attain international cooperation and global prosperity in the postwar era. While liberals hailed his vision of the postwar world, critics derided Wallace's ideas by calling them "globaloney." Wallace rebutted his opponents by labeling them "American fascists." Democratic Party regulars were so worried that Wallace's leftist views would jeopardize the ticket in the 1944 election that they persuaded Roosevelt to dump him as his running mate. It was a bitter blow for Wallace, but Roosevelt rewarded his continuing loyalty by naming him secretary of commerce.

As relations between the United States and the Soviet Union progressively deteriorated in 1945 and 1946, Wallace became increasingly outspoken in criticizing the policies of the Truman administration. As the administration moved toward a "get-tough" posture toward the Soviets, he insisted that economic assistance to Soviet Russia and negotiations on nuclear weapons could ease tensions and provide the basis for mutual understanding. He favored accepting the reality of a Soviet sphere of influence in eastern Europe. After Wallace aired some of his views publicly in September 1946, Truman dismissed him from the cabinet. Wallace served for a time as editor

of the *New Republic* and then, in December 1947, announced that he would run as an independent candidate for president.

Wallace attacked Truman's foreign policies as dangerously provocative to the Soviets. He denounced U.S. actions that he believed corrupted the ideals for which the war had been fought, betrayed the legacy of Roosevelt, undercut the United Nations, and destroyed hopes for a "century of the common man." Truman, he asserted, had become the unwitting tool of American Fascists. Wallace's campaign for president was a disaster. As a part of his campaign strategy, Truman made a deliberate effort to tar Wallace as a Soviet pawn. Tagged a spokesman for communist dictators in a political atmosphere increasingly intolerant of dissent, Wallace suffered vocal and sometimes physical attacks. The number of votes he received in the election was small—only about two percent of the total. After the election Wallace retired from public life and returned to agricultural and scientific pursuits. He died in relative obscurity on 18 November 1965.

J. SAMUEL WALKER

See also Cold War; Truman, Harry S.

FURTHER READING

Blum, John Morton editor. *The Price of Vision: The Diary of Henry A. Wallace, 1942–1946.* Boston, 1973.
Walker, J. Samuel. *Henry A. Wallace and American Foreign Policy.* Westport, Conn., 1976.
Wallace, Henry A. *New Frontiers.* New York, 1934.
———. *Toward World Peace.* New York, 1948.
White, Graham, and John Maze. *Henry A. Wallace: His Search for a New World Order.* Chapel Hill, N.C., 1995.

WALTERS, VERNON ANTHONY

(*b.* 3 January 1917)

Army officer, multi-lingual interpreter, presidential aide, and diplomat, Vernon A. Walters was born in New York City. After attending Stonyhurst College in England from 1928 to 1934, he returned home to work as an insurance adjuster in his father's firm. In 1941, Walters enlisted in the army. His ability to speak seven languages, including French, Italian, Spanish, and German, led to Walters's rapid promotion. He established close ties with members of the Brazilian expeditionary force in Italy in 1944. After World War II, he remained in military service and served as a translator for President Harry S. Truman. In 1956, Walters became staff assistant to President Dwight D. Eisenhower. He acted as Vice President Richard M. Nixon's interpreter during Nixon's ill-fated tour of Latin America in 1958, when angry Venezuelans attacked the vice president's motorcade.

In 1962, Walters became the U.S. military attaché in Brazil. His association with General Castelo Branco led to accusations of complicity in the overthrow of Brazilian President João Goulart in 1964. In 1967, Walters went to the Paris embassy as the senior military attaché. He arranged for Henry Kissinger's secret passage into Paris to participate in negotiations to end the Vietnam War. President Nixon appointed Walters as deputy director of the Central Intelligence Agency in 1972. Although he initially aided H.R. Haldeman's attempt to halt the FBI investigation of Watergate, Walters subsequently threatened to resign if Haldeman's obstructionist activities continued. Walters received a commendation from the CIA for resisting efforts by the White House to use the agency in the Watergate cover-up. At the rank of lieutenant general, he resigned from the U.S. army in 1976 and wrote his memoirs. Walters's ideological compatibility with Ronald Reagan led to his appointment as an ambassador-at-large in 1981. Walters worked to improve U.S. relations with Latin American military dictatorships, and in 1985 he succeeded Jeane J. Kirkpatrick as the U.S. permanent representative to the United Nations. From 1989 to 1991, Walters served as ambassador to the Federal Republic of Germany.

CHARLES D. MCGRAW

See also Nixon, Richard Milhous; Reagan, Ronald Wilson

FURTHER READING

Moritz, Charles, editor. "Walters, Vernon A." *Current Biography Yearbook 1988*. (New York, 1988): 594–597.
Walters, Vernon A. *Silent Missions*. Garden City, N.Y.: Doubleday, 1978.

WANGXIA, TREATY OF

The first treaty between the United States and China, signed in the village of Wangxia (Wanghia) on 3 July 1844. This important accord placed American relations with China on a legal and predictable basis and led to increased economic and cultural contacts between the two countries. Americans had been trading on an informal basis with China since the famous voyage of the U.S. ship *Empress of China* in 1784–1785, but the Treaty of Nanjing (Nanking) imposed on China by the British in 1842 after their victory in the Opium War made a diplomatic mission to China necessary. By the terms of their agreement with Great Britain, the Chinese had abolished the monopolistic co-hong trading system, opened five ports to British trade and residence (Canton, Amoy, Ningbo, Fuzhou, and Shanghai), established regular commercial duties, and ceded Hong Kong. These concessions, however, applied only to the British, and it remained an open question whether any of them would be shared by other nations. President John Tyler chose Caleb Cushing as U.S. commissioner to China and Secre-

tary of State Daniel Webster instructed him on 8 May 1843 "to secure the entry of American ships and cargoes" into the treaty ports "on terms as favorable as those which are enjoyed by English merchants."

In his negotiations with Imperial Commissioner Qiying (Ch'i ying), Cushing, assisted by the American missionaries Elijah Bridgman, Peter Parker, and Samuel Wells Williams, achieved that primary goal of U.S. foreign policy and much more. Cushing's treaty went beyond that of Nanjing by specifically giving Americans the right to establish cemeteries, churches, and hospitals in the five port cities, and it also explicitly granted extraterritorial rights to American citizens residing in China. In addition, a most-favored-nation clause ensured that any new concessions obtained from China by other countries automatically would accrue to the United States. The treaty gained the unanimous approval of the U.S. Senate in 1845.

Although some scholars have criticized the Treaty of Wangxia as a "hitchhiking" or "piggybacking" form of imperialism, others have noted that the United States did not use force to wrest concessions from the Chinese. Nor did the United States seek territorial gains from them—such as an American Hong Kong. By placing relations between the two countries on a more stable basis, the Wangxia accord contributed to a substantial increase in trade between the two countries and a larger missionary presence in China.

KENNETH E. SHEWMAKER

See also China; Cushing, Caleb; Extraterritoriality; Hong Kong; Missionaries; Most-Favored-Nation Principle; Opium Wars; Tyler, John; Webster, Daniel

FURTHER READING

Gulick, Edward V. *Peter Parker and the Opening of China*. Cambridge, Mass., 1973.
Welch, Richard E., Jr. "Caleb Cushing's Chinese Mission and the Treaty of Wanghia: A Review." *Oregon Historical Quarterly* 68(1957): 328–57.
Dudden, Arthur Power. *The American Pacific: From the Old China Trade to the Present*. New York, 1992.

WAR, U.S. DEPARTMENT OF

Cabinet-level department formally created by the new constitutional government of the United States by an enactment dated 7 August 1789. The legislation gave the department executive responsibility under the president as commander in chief for administering and guiding an army or armies raised by Congress under the terms of the Constitution. This was in most respects a continuation of arrangements starting with the outbreak of the Revolutionary War for managing the ground forces of the young republic, with the important change that the Boards and

War Office which had been improvised since 1781 had been mainly or entirely within the legislative branch whereas the new Department of War was firmly within the executive branch. In 1949 the Department of War was consolidated with the Department of the Navy and other defense-related offices into the newly created Department of Defense.

Congress, when it first constituted the Department of War, also launched its long tradition of economizing with the military establishment when no enemy or hostilities were immediately visible. The original legislation made no provision for staff agencies or bureaus, which instead were created ad hoc under the orders of commanding generals in the field. The War of 1812, however, demonstrated that this haphazard system left much to be desired. Secretary of War John C. Calhoun, appointed by President James Monroe in 1817, used his seven-year tenure to create and polish a regularized coherent structure for the internal management of a staff system. Calhoun's design, except for the expansion and supplemental modifications during the Civil War, endured largely without change for more than seventy-five years.

The end of the century, however, brought the Spanish-American-Cuban-Filipino War. The U.S. military establishment, including the navy as well as the army, clearly needed organizational reform. The internal staff agencies and bureaus within both the ground and sea services had each become inward-looking and ossified. The army's primary combat branches—infantry, cavalry (later armor), and artillery—saw each other as competitive rivals rather than cooperative partners in a shared enterprise, and did not effectively communicate with each other. Three navy bureaus—hulls, engineering, and ordnance—were each responsible for designing different components of new warships, but they scarcely shared plans.

Ferment for change was influenced partly by similar ferment in European military establishments. Led by President Theodore Roosevelt and his Secretary of War Elihu Root, the new U.S. thinking produced three consolidations. First, in 1900, the secretary of the navy created a committee of virtually retired senior admirals, called the General Board, charged with generating some limited degree of coordination among the bureaus by advising him on such issues as he and they might deem appropriate for their consideration. It was a step ahead, but a weak one.

Second, in 1903, the secretary of war introduced the army's General Staff system, based on a philosophy of military organization considerably different than what one could see in the navy, but nevertheless charged with coordinative advisory and planning duties for the secretary of war somewhat similar to the navy's General Board. The General Staff was a bureaucratically complex management unit, hierarchically structured with specified responsibilities, and manned with officers at different rank levels, compared to the loosely assembled old admirals on the navy committee.

Third, also in 1903, the White House and Congress agreed to create a highest-level uniformed committee named the Joint Army-Navy Board, formed from equal numbers of senior generals and admirals representing both services—the first attempt to generate any coordination or even effective communication between these wholly separate organizations. The Joint Board, forerunner of the Joint Chiefs of Staff system that emerged almost forty years later during World War II, was charged with achieving some coherent cooperation between ground and sea forces, especially in the drafting of war plans for foreseeable contingencies.

The General Staff concept included a General Staff Corps to coordinate all branches of the army under a senior general with the title chief of staff, who reported directly to the civilian secretary of war. At the same time, the position of commanding general of the army was abolished. Organizational management was coming to be seen as a top priority on a par with combat leadership, although this perspective generated continuing debate and acrimony both within and outside the Department of War.

For a decade after 1903, the new General Staff worked on recommendations for a complete reorganization of the army that was carried out in 1913. This called for a major general as chief of staff, supported by twenty-eight younger officers given this short-term assignment as a way to broaden an understanding of general staff duties throughout the service. But this arrangement, whatever it might have achieved as a peacetime mode, soon was perceived by almost all involved government and military officials and knowledgeable outside observers to be seriously defective if the United States were to enter World War I. Precisely how to fix the problem, however, generated many not entirely compatible ideas, illustrating the ancient dilemma as to the best way to organize a military establishment in peacetime in contrast to wartime, and how to shift smoothly from one mode to the other.

The National Defense Act of 1916 improvised answers for some of these questions by creating a new assistant secretary of war with radical new powers to procure war munitions and to speed industrial mobilization. The chief of staff was given substantial new powers and support personnel, and this officer gradually came to be perceived both inside and outside the department as the senior and most distinguished general on active duty. On the other hand, the general's post was with the secretary of war at department headquarters, and some senior officers believed that the army's top uniformed official should be based with troops in the field, not in a bureaucratic office in Washington. These tradinationalists needed some time to accept the idea that the chief of staff was their top-ranking colleague.

SECRETARIES OF WAR

ADMINISTRATION	SECRETARY	PERIOD OF APPOINTMENT
Washington	Henry Knox	1789–1794
	Timothy Pickering	1795–1796
Adams	James McHenry	1796–1800
J. Adams	Samuel Dexter	1800–1801
Jefferson	Henry Dearborn	1801–1809
Madison	William Eustis	1809–1812
	John Armstrong	1813–1814
	James Monroe	1814–1815
	William H. Crawford	1815–1817
	George Graham	1817
	John C. Calhoun	1817–1825
J.Q. Adams	James Barbour	1825–1828
	Peter B. Porter	1828–1829
Jackson	John H. Eaton	1829–1831
	Lewis Cass	1831–1837
	Benjamin Butler	1837
Van Buren	Joel R. Poinsett	1837–1841
W.H. Harrison	John Bell	1841
Tyler		
	John C. Spencer	1841–1843
	James M. Porter	1843–1844
	William Wilkins	1844–1845
Taylor	George W. Crawford	1849–1850
Filmore		
	Charles M. Conrad	1850–1853
Pierce	Jefferson Davis	1853–1857
Buchanan	John B. Floyd	1857–1861
	Joseph Holt	1861
Lincoln	Simon Cameron	1861–1862
	Edwin M. Stanton	1862–1867
A. Johnson	Ulysses S. Grant	1867–1868
	Lorenzo Thomas	1868
	John M. Schofield	1868–1869
	John A. Rawlins	1869
Grant	William T. Sherman	1869
	William W. Belknap	1869–1876
	Alphonso Taft	1876
	James D. Cameron	1876–1877
Hayes	George W. McCrary	1877–1879
	Alexander Ramsey	1879–1881
Garfield	Robert T. Lincoln	1881–1885
Arthur		
Cleveland	William C. Endicott	1885–1889
B. Harrison	Redfield Proctor	1889–1891
	Stephen B. Elkins	1891–1893
Cleveland	Daniel S. Lamont	1893–1897

(table continues on next page)

ADMINISTRATION	SECRETARY	PERIOD OF APPOINTMENT
McKinley	Russell A. Alger	1897–1899
	Elihu Root	1899–1904
T. Roosevelt		
	William Howard Taft	1904–1908
	Luke E. Wright	1908–1909
Taft	Jacob M. Dickinson	1909–1911
	Henry L. Stimson	1911–1913
Wilson	Lindley M. Garrison	1913–1916
	Newton D. Baker	1916–1921
Harding	John W. Weeks	1921–1925
Coolidge		
	Dwight F. Davis	1925–1929
Hoover	James W. Good	1929
	Patrick J. Hurley	1929–1933
F. Roosevelt	George H. Dern	1933–1936
	Harry H. Woodring	1936–1940
	Henry L. Stimson	1940–1945
Truman	Robert P. Patterson	1945–1947
	Kenneth C. Royall	1947

Source: National Archives

This kind of issue was illustrated during World War I by President Woodrow Wilson's decision in his role as commander in chief to base appointments of combat generals for duty on advice received from the civilian secretary of war and the uniformed chief of staff—an idea implemented for the first time when President Wilson put General John J. Pershing in charge of the American Expeditionary Force sent to Europe after the United States entered the war in April 1917. Differences of opinion within the army and among interested outside parties over the process and criteria for promoting individuals to general officer ranks generated continuing acrimony.

President Theodore Roosevelt in 1906, for example, promoted Pershing straight from captain to brigadier general over the heads of 862 officers who outranked Pershing. After U.S. entry into World War I, Congress restored the active ranks of three-star lieutenant general and four-star general, advancing Pershing to the four-star major general level. From President Wilson down, the senior figures on the army side of the defense establishment put themselves and their officers at General Pershing's service, making Pershing the de facto top defense figure. Subsequent presidents serving as commander in chief have similarly tended to defer in full support of the generals picked to head war efforts in the field.

The other side of the dilemma reappeared after the war; arrangements apparently suitable for peacetime were inadequate for wartime, and arrangements improvised for wartime later seemed inappropriate for peacetime. New legislation enacted in June 1920 provided a streamlined Chief of Staff organization empowered narrowly to coordinate, plan for, direct, and supervise all aspects of all components of the army. For these purposes, the General Staff was divided into five primary divisions (G-1 for Personnel, G-2 for Intelligence, G-3 for Organization and Training, G-4 for Supply, and G-5 for Operations) and seven secondary divisions (for auxiliary functions such as budget preparation, legislative liaison, and an inspector general's office).

An essentially new element was introduced by the accelerating avalanche of technological advances starting with the invention of the airplane during the period 1895–1905, ultimately including submarines, later radar and sonar, nuclear weapons, long-range missiles, computers, medical breakthroughs, and whatever further innovations may lie ahead. The first of these major technological innovations, the airplane, was the most confounding, because it called into question almost all axioms of military strategy, tactics, and doctrine. Used in combat for the first time in World War I, fixed-wing self-propelled aircraft were at the heart of massive debates raging in Washington and elsewhere throughout the 1920s.

This debate had different outcomes in the Departments of War and the Department of the Navy. Navy authorities gradually decided that aviation was an important new asset extending and supplementing traditional naval roles and missions, and that it should therefore remain organic to and within the navy. In the Department of War, however, dissidents led by Brigadier General Billy Mitchell believed that appropriately designed aircraft represented a fundamentally new and virtually all-purpose war-fighting capability. They agitated for aviation forces to be removed not only from the army's Signal Corps, where they had originally been lodged, but removed almost entirely from the army as a whole. The dissidents slowly won their case, at least in organizational terms. In 1927 the Joint Army-Navy Board assigned aviation roles and missions in such a manner that autonomy for the army fliers was all but mandated. The Army Air Corps Act of 1935 substantially strengthened this mandate. By the time the United States entered World War II, the Air Corps fought as if it were fully autonomous from the Department of War, with its own chief of staff and related structures parallel to army organizational components, even with its own "pink pants" variations on army uniforms.

In yet another manifestation of the cyclic dilemma, on 28 February 1942, three months after U.S. entry into World War II, the secretary of war issued orders for sweeping changes throughout the Department of War and the army. The secretary and his advisers viewed existing arrangements as far too cumbersome to manage and lead the massive national wartime mobilization and combat around the globe. The urgent new objectives were unified planning, swift decision-making, and immediate decentralized implementation, alongside coordination of all components.

The wartime/peacetime cycle of reorganization after World War II was different from previous ones in that this time a majority of senior officials believed the United States would remain significantly involved in international politics. The organizational changes were the most sweeping structural reforms in the history of the U.S. defense establishment (and the foreign affairs establishment more generally). The National Security Act of 1947 converted the Army Air Corps into the U.S. Air Force, a totally separate third armed service within a new Department of the Air Force, but at the same time submerged it along with the Department of the Army (no longer the Department of War) and the Department of the Navy under the new all-embracing Secretary of Defense. This new super official gained the cabinet status that had previously belonged to the separate service secretaries, who in turn became essentially specialized assistants to the Secretary of Defense. But each service secretary continued to head a civilian bureaucracy that sat on top of a military bureaucracy still led by a uniformed service chief: chief of staff of the army, chief of naval operation, and chief of staff for the air force. Although the Marine Corps remained an organic part of the navy, the comman-

dant—as the Marines' number one officer is known—was gradually given separate status as a full-fledged member of the Joint Chiefs of Staff. The 1949 amendments to the 1947 legislation gave the secretary of defense a vast Department of Defense with which to manage this sprawling organizational terrain. The position of secretary of defense was further strengthened by 1953 and 1958 amendments and by subsequent executive orders and legislation.

In sum, the pattern of consolidation and centralization evident in almost all Department of War organizational reforms from the 1820s through World War II ultimately became a movement that absorbed and downgraded the department itself as an autonomous entity. The successor Army Department after 1947 became a faint shadow of the old Department of War.

VINCENT DAVIS

See also Calhoun, John Caldwell; Defense, U.S. Department of; Joint Chiefs of Staff; National Security Act; Navy, U.S. Department of; Root, Elihu

FURTHER READING

Davis, Vincent. *Postwar Defense Policy and the U.S. Navy, 1943-1946.* Chapel Hill, N.C.; 1966.
Emme, Eugene M., ed. *The Impact of Air Power.* Princeton, N.J., 1959.
Huntington, Samuel P. *The Soldier and the State.* Cambridge, Mass., 1959.
Janowitz, Morris. *The Professional Soldier.* Glencoe, Ill., 1960.
Milett, Allan R.. *The General.* Westport, Conn., 1975.
Millis, Walter, Harvey C. Mansfield, and Harold Stein. *Arms and the State.* New York, 1958.
Morton, Louis. "War Plan ORANGE: Evolution of a Strategy." *World Politics.* January 1959.

WAR DEBT OF WORLD WAR I

At the end of World War I, both victorious and vanquished countries shared a heavy financial burden in the form of debt and reparations. The United States emerged from the war a net creditor to European allies to the tune of nearly $12 billion. By 1922, due to a combination of unwise policy choices on the part of European governments and sluggish growth worldwide, most debtors were threatening default. They appealed for debt forgiveness on political grounds as part of the U.S. contribution to the successful war effort. Debtors also argued that only with debt forgiveness could European economies recover quickly enough to avert social upheaval.

President Calvin Coolidge was unsympathetic to these appeals. He pointed out that the debts were legal in every respect, and that large-scale forgiveness would undermine the integrity of international banking. He stressed that repayment was not only necessary but feasi-

TOTAL PRINCIPAL AND INTEREST TO BE PAID TO THE UNITED STATES BY 15 WAR DEBTORS (AS OF 1931)
(in dollars)

Country	Principal	Interest	Total	Average Interest Rate (Approximate) Over the Whole Period of Payments (percent)
Austria	24,614,885.00	——	24,614,885.00	——
Belgium	417,780,000.00	310,050,500.00	727,830,500.00	1.8
Czechoslovakia	115,000,000.00	197,811,433.88[a]	312,811,433.88	3.3
Esthonia	13,830,000.00	23,877,645.76[a]	37,707,645.76	3.3
Finland	9,000,000.00	12,695,055.00	21,695,055.00	3.3
France	4,025,000,000.00	2,822,674,104.17	6,847,674,104.17	1.6
Great Britain	4,600,000,000.00	6,505,965,000.00	11,105,965,000.00	3.3
Greece	32,467,000.00	5,623,760.00	38,090,760.00	0.3
Hungary	1,939,000.00	2,815,431.42[a]	4,754,431.42	3.3
Italy	2,042,000,000.00	365,677,500.00	2,407,677,500.00	0.4
Latvia	5,775,000.00	10,015,523.13[a]	15,790,523.13	3.3
Lithuania	6,030,000.00	9,039,541.57[a]	15,069,541.57	3.3
Poland	178,560,000.00	303,114,781.29[a]	481,674,781.29	3.3
Rumania	44,590,000.00	77,916,260.05[a]	122,506,260.05	3.3
Yugoslavia	62,850,000.00	32,327,635.00	95,177,635.00	1.0
Total	11,579,435,885.00	10,679,604,171.27	22,259,040,056.27	2.1

[a]Includes deferred payments, later funded into principal

From *War Debts and World Prosperity*, Harold G. Moulton, and Leo Pasvolsky. ©1932 by the Brookings Institution. Reprinted with permission of the Brookings Institution, Washington, D.C.

ble, since most debts were based on a sixty-year schedule, and Germany was to pay large reparations which covered the burden of allied debt. He also dismissed forgiving debts as a U.S. contribution to the war since this would simply shift the burden from irresponsible European governments to the American taxpayer. To demonstrate his determination, he established a War Debt Commission which focused on rescheduling but not forgiving debt. He also proposed exchanging territory for debt—Britain's Caribbean protectorates for its debts to the United States.

In 1922, Germany defaulted on its war reparations and forced the United States into a more conciliatory approach to all allied debt. The Dawes and Young plans provided forgiveness for much of Germany's war debt and established programs to facilitate U.S. private investment in debtor nations. All of France's pre-war debt was forgiven. In all, the United States collected a mere $2.6 billion of the $13 billion total as every debtor (save Finland) defaulted by 1932. In the final analysis, while Coolidge and his successor may have been right had circumstances

been more normal, the hard line the United States took on war debt forgiveness was one of many contributing factors to the collapse of Europe in the 1930's and its degeneration into Fascism and war.

KENDALL W. STILES

See also World War I; World War II; Reparations

FURTHER READING
Gerould, James T., and Laura S. Turnbull, eds. *Interallied Debts and Revision of the Debt Settlements.* New York, 1928.

WAR HAWKS

Democratic-Republicans in the twelfth Congress who promoted war against Great Britain in 1811–1812. Although scholars differ over who deserves to be called a War Hawk, the traditional list consists of about a dozen members of Congress, mainly ardent young patriots from the South and West who could not remember the horrors of the Revolutionary War and thus were willing to risk another war to vindicate the nation's rights. The list included Henry Clay and Richard M. Johnson of Kentucky; Felix Grundy of Tennessee; Langdon Cheves, William Lowndes, John C. Calhoun, and David R. Williams of South Carolina; George M. Troup of Georgia; Peter B. Porter of New York; and John A. Harper of New Hampshire. Clay was the leading War Hawk. As speaker of the House, he packed key committees, interpreted the rules, and directed debate, thereby ensuring that the War Hawks dominated as they pressed their case against Great Britain. Most of the War Hawks favored war because they had become disillusioned with the restrictive system of economic sanctions adopted between 1806 and 1811. The War Hawks hoped that war would vindicate the nation's independence by forcing the British to give up the Orders in Council and impressment. They also hoped that war would unify the Republican Party and silence the Federalist opposition. The War Hawks demonstrated considerable talent and quickly won the respect of other Republicans and of many Federalists as well. Their role in bringing on the War of 1812 was crucial.

DONALD R. HICKEY

See also Calhoun, John Caldwell; Clay, Henry; Reparations; War of 1812

FURTHER READING

Brown, Roger H. *The Republic in Peril: 1812*. New York, 1971.
Fritz, Harry W. "The War Hawks of 1812." *Capitol Studies* 5 (Spring 1977): 25–42.
Horsman, Reginald. "Who Were the War Hawks." *Indiana Magazine of History* 60 (June 1964): 121–136.

WARNKE, PAUL CULLITON

(*b.* 31 January 1920)

Lawyer, Defense Department official in the 1960s, and arms-control negotiator in the 1970s. Born in Massachusetts, he received a B.A. from Yale University (1941) and a law degree from Columbia University (1948). After working in a distinguished law firm in Washington D.C., he joined the administration of President Lyndon Johnson as general counsel for the Department of Defense (1966–1967) and as assistant secretary of defense for international security affairs (1967–1969) during the turbulent years of the Vietnam War.

During the Cold War era, Warnke became part of an informal network of prominent individuals from government, academia, and law who shared an anticommunist consensus and served in high-level policymaking positions within the executive branch. However, like many other establishment figures during the Johnson era, Warnke turned increasingly against the Vietnam War and

the containment policy upon which it was based. Warnke grew skeptical of the utility of military force in a world of growing complexity and interdependence where the threat of Soviet communism had declined. Instead, he emphasized the need for détente with the Soviet Union, greater multilateral cooperation among allies, and the pursuit of arms control to promote global stability and peace.

In 1972, he became a foreign policy adviser to George McGovern, the Democratic nominee for president. In 1973 Warnke became a member of the Trilateral Commission where he met a young governor from Georgia, Jimmy Carter. In 1977 President Carter nominated Warnke as both director of the Arms Control and Disarmament Agency and chief U.S. arms control negotiator for the Strategic Arms Limitation Talks (SALT).

Warnke's nomination to these positions generated a storm of controversy in Congress as conservatives accused Warnke of holding excessively "dovish" views on defense issues. Among those opposed to the Warnke nomination was the Coalition for a Democratic Majority, a group of conservative Democrats which claimed that Warnke favored unilateral disarmament. Despite this opposition, the senate confirmed Warnke's appointment to both positions. Although his efforts contributed to the conclusion of the SALT II treaty with the Soviet Union in June of 1978, Warnke saw his handiwork withdrawn from Senate consideration by Carter in January 1980, shortly after the Soviet invasion of Afghanistan.

Since returning to private practice after leaving the Carter administration in 1978, Warnke has remained an active participant in public affairs and has continued to espouse the principles of liberal internationalism.

JEREL A. ROSATI

See also Arms Control and Disarmament Agency; Carter, James Earl; Nuclear Waepons and Strategy; Strategic Arms Limitation Talks and Agreements

FURTHER READING

Hodgson, Godfrey. "The Establishment." *Foreign Policy* 10 (Spring 1973): 3–40.

WAR OF 1812

(18 June 1812–17 February 1815)

The second and last war between the United States and Great Britain. Deeply divided and woefully unprepared for war, the United States was unable to conduct effective operations. Only Great Britain's unwillingness to prolong the war in order to inflict a punitive peace saved the young republic from possible dismemberment.

Sources of Conflict and Reasons for War

The War of 1812 grew out of the Napoleonic Wars. Great Britain and France were at war almost continuously from 1793 to 1815. Both nations encroached upon U.S. neutral rights, but Great Britain's control of the seas made its encroachments more serious and more galling. The leading causes of the War of 1812 were the Orders in Council—British decrees that regulated U.S. trade with Europe—and impressment, the British practice of removing seamen (many of whom were deserters from the British navy) from U.S. merchant ships.

A host of lesser issues also contributed to Anglo-American tension prior to 1812. Among these were British violations of U.S. territorial waters (which by common agreement extended three miles out to sea); British enforcement of the Rule of 1756, a maritime doctrine that restricted U.S. trade between France's European ports and with France's overseas colonies; British abuses of naval blockades (which had to be properly announced and adequately enforced to be legal); British insistence on a broad definition of contraband (which included naval stores and sometimes even food and money); and British interference with Native Americans in the Northwest Territory (which most people in the United States believed had caused the Indian war that erupted there in 1811).

The United States had an opportunity to resolve some of these issues in the Monroe-Pinckney Treaty of 1806, but President Thomas Jefferson refused to submit this agreement to the Senate because it did not provide for an end to impressment. Instead, hoping to win greater concessions, the United States adopted a series of economic sanctions. Known as the restrictive system, these measures, which were aimed primarily at Great Britain and secondarily at France, rested on the assumption that the European powers and their West Indian colonies were dependent upon the United States, both as a source for food and other raw materials and as a market for their finished products.

The first trade restriction adopted by the United States was the partial Non-importation Act in 1806, which barred a select list of British manufactured goods from the U.S. market. This was a limited measure designed to warn the British of what to expect if they did not respect U.S. rights. The law was suspended during the Monroe-Pinckney negotiations and did not go into effect until late 1807. At that time the United States also adopted the Embargo, a far-reaching and controversial nonexportation law that prohibited all U.S. merchant ships and goods from leaving port. Although there were loopholes in the embargo, it led to a sharp reduction in U.S. trade, causing an economic depression and the loss of customs revenue.

In 1809 the United States repealed the Non-importation Act and the Embargo and substituted the Non-intercourse Act, which reopened U.S. trade with the rest of the world but continued to prohibit all trade with Great Britain, France, and their colonies. In 1810 the United States replaced this measure with Macon's Bill No. 2, which restored trade with both belligerents but promised to reimpose U.S. nonimportation against either nation if the other suspended its restrictions on neutral trade. Hoping to embroil the United States with Great Britain, France made a promise (never fulfilled) to rescind the Continental Decrees. When Great Britain refused to follow suit by suspending the Orders in Council, the president issued a proclamation, which was backed by the Non-importation Act of 1811, barring all British imports from the United States.

When the restrictive system failed to win any concessions from Great Britain, a group of about a dozen "War Hawks," led by Speaker of the House Henry Clay, pushed James Madison, the nation's cautious president, and a reluctant Congress into the War of 1812. The congressional vote, 79–49 in the House of Representatives and 19–13 in the Senate, was the closest vote on any declaration of war in U.S. history. Most members of Congress from Pennsylvania and the South and West voted for war, while most from the North and East voted against it. But the sectional breakdown was really a reflection of party strength: eighty percent of the Democratic-Republicans voted for war (93–23), while all the Federalists voted against it (39–0).

The Democratic-Republicans went to war for a variety of diplomatic, ideological, territorial, and political reasons. In addition to forcing the British to show greater respect for U.S. rights on the high seas, they hoped to vindicate U.S. independence, preserve republican institutions, unify their party, and silence the opposition. They were willing to go to war with Great Britain unprepared and against significant opposition (mainly from the Federalists) because they believed that if the British did not cave in, the conquest of Canada would be (in the words of Jefferson) "a mere matter of marching." Once Canada was conquered, it could be held for ransom on the maritime issues or annexed. Either way the United States would benefit.

The Federalists, on the other hand, opposed the war because they considered it unwise and unjust. They had no desire to see the nation line up with France against England or to support a war designed to further the interests of the Democratic-Republican Party and silence the opposition. Nor were they willing to support a war of conquest against Canada. "Canada has issued no Orders in Council," said Federalist Congressman Samuel Taggart of Massachusetts. "She has not impressed our seamen, taken our ships, confiscated our property, nor in any

The War of 1812

NEWFOUNDLAND

Grand Banks

St. Lawrence R.

NEW
BRUNSWICK

St John R.

Quebec

NOVA SCOTIA

LOWER
CANADA

MAINE
(MASS.)

Halifax

UPPER
CANADA

Montreal

L. Superior

Plattsburg ☆ *L. Champlain*

VT.

N.H.

L. Huron

York ☆ *L. Ontario*

Albany

MICH.
TERR.

Queenston ☆

Ft. Niagra

MASS.

L. Michigan

Detroit

The Thames ☆

Ft. Erie

N.Y.

R.I.
Hartford

CONN.

L. Erie

New York

Ft. Dearborn ☆

PENN.

N.J.

IND.
TERR.

OHIO

Pittsburgh

DEL.

ILLINOIS

☆ Baltimore

TERR.

☆ Tippecanoe (1811)

Washington, D.C.

MD.

Ohio R.

VIRGINIA

Chesapeake Bay

KENTUCKY

Mississippi R.

TENNESSEE

NORTH
CAROLINA

SOUTH
CAROLINA

Bermuda
Islands

MISSISSIPPI

☆ Horseshoe Bend

TERRITORY

GEORGIA

ATLANTIC

OCEAN

☆ Major battles

Mobile

☆ Pensacola

LOUISIANA

☆ New Orleans

FLORIDA

(Sp.)

Jamaica

Antilles

Kingston

Barbados

From *The Course of American Diplomacy,* Howard Jones. Volume I. ©1992 by The McGraw-Hill Companies. Reprinted with permission of the McGraw-Hill Companies.

other respect treated us ill. All the crime alleged against Canada or the Canadians, is that, without any act of their own, they are connected with, and under the protection of a nation that has injured us on the ocean." The Federalists also believed that Great Britain would never surrender its maritime rights, and that the war would boomerang on the United States. "Whether we consider our agriculture, our commerce, our monied system, or our internal safety," declared the Alexandria *Gazette,* "nothing but disaster can result from it."

Peace Negotiations in 1812–1813

Many Democratic-Republicans hoped that the declaration of war itself would shock the British into concessions. That President Madison shared this view is suggested by the haste with which he sent out peace feelers. Five days after the declaration of war, Madison invited the departing British minister, Augustus J. Foster, to the White House to outline U.S. terms. Expressing a desire to avoid "any serious collision," the president told Foster

**Vote in the House of Representatives
on the Declaration of War
in 1812**

ATLANTIC

OCEAN

Yeas   Nays

Not Voting   Unsettled, etc.

Votes not shown:
(general ticket): N. H., 2 nays; N.J., 2 yeas
(districts): Pa., 2 yeas

(Based upon Paullin and Wright, Atlas of the Historical
Geography of the United States, plate 113-A)

GULF OF MEXICO

From *A Short History of American Foreign Policy and Diplomace*, Samuel Flagg Bemis. Henry Holt, 1959.

that the British could restore peace by giving up the Orders in Council and impressment. Foster had no authority to negotiate on these matters, but he was expected to transmit the offer to his superiors in London.

The United States also pursued peace through Jonathan Russell, the U.S. chargé d'affaires in London. On 26 June, barely a week after the declaration of war, the Madison administration authorized Russell to open negotiations for an armistice. The British would have to give up the Orders in Council and impressment, but in return the United States promised to bar all British seamen from U.S. ships.

By the time Russell made this offer in late August, the British had already repealed the Orders in Council. The British government had long undermined its own system for restricting trade with the Continent by issuing special licenses, and in response to growing criticism at home and abroad the government decided in June of 1812 to scrap the Orders. Although the announcement was made shortly before the U.S. declaration or war, slow communication in the age of sail prevented the news from reaching the United States until July. By then the die for war had been cast, but impressment was now the only issue that stood in the way of peace.

The British, however, showed no interest in Russell's offer. Having made a concession on the Orders in Council, they were in no mood to give up impressment, especially since they believed that their naval power rested on continuing the practice. They were convinced, moreover, that the repeal of the Orders would lead to peace once the news reached the United States. Hence they instructed Sir John Borlase Warren, their naval commander on the American station, in Halifax, Nova Scotia, to work for a cease-fire. Foster, who had heard of the repeal of the Orders after leaving the United States, was already trying to arrange a cease-fire. At his suggestion, British officials in Canada signed an armistice with U.S. General Henry Dearborn. Washington, however, repudiated this agreement because it did not provide for an end to impressment. Hence the negotiations in 1812 ended in failure even though both sides sought peace.

In March of 1813, Andrei Dashkov, the Russian minister in Washington, invited the United States to take part in a new round of negotiations under the auspices of his government. The Russians had several reasons for acting. Aside from any prestige they might garner by brokering a peace, they wanted Great Britain, their most important ally, to concentrate all of its resources on the war in Europe against Napoleon. In addition, the United States played a major role in supplying tropical produce from the West Indies to Russian ports in the Baltic. This traffic had come to an abrupt halt with the outbreak of the U.S.-British war, and only the restoration of peace would reopen the trade.

The Madison administration welcomed the Russian offer. Not only did Russia champion neutral rights, but the U.S. campaign against Canada had failed in 1812. One U.S. Army had surrendered at Detroit, a second had been defeated on the Niagara frontier, and a third had made little more than a demonstration on the Saint Lawrence frontier before retreating to the United States. In addition, Federalist opposition to the war remained adamant, and the nation's financial situation was deteriorating. Finally, Napoleon's retreat from Russia in the fall of 1812 had greatly strengthened Great Britain's hand on the Continent. If Great Britain prevailed in Europe, the United States might find itself facing the full weight of British military force. To avoid this possibility, U.S. officials hoped to liquidate the war in the New World while Great Britain was still tied up in the Old.

Without waiting to hear Great Britain's response, Madison dispatched three peace commissioners to Europe. Albert Gallatin, the secretary of the treasury, was chosen to head the mission. He was joined by John

Quincy Adams, the U.S. minister in Saint Petersburg, and James A. Bayard, a moderate Delaware Federalist and U.S. senator. The Senate rejected Gallatin's nomination because he was still a member of the cabinet, but by this time he was already in Europe. The instructions the commissioners carried with them called for a broad range of British concessions, but only an end to impressment was deemed essential to a settlement.

The British, however, rejected the Russian proposal. They had no desire (as Lord Castlereagh, the British foreign secretary, put it) to allow the United States "to mix directly or indirectly Her Maritime Interests with those of another State," and certainly not with those of a great inland power that favored a broad definition of neutral rights.

The British then made a counteroffer to demonstrate their peaceful intentions. After raising the possibility of direct negotiations through several other channels, Castlereagh sent a message to the United States in November of 1813 proposing such discussions. Castlereagh strongly implied, however, that the British would not give up impressment.

President Madison accepted Castlereagh's offer. The campaign against Canada in 1813 had been only a little more successful than the year before. Commodore Oliver H. Perry's spectacular victory on Lake Erie in September had enabled William Henry Harrison to defeat a combined force of British and Native Americans in the Battle of the Thames, thus reestablishing U.S. control over the Northwest Territory. However, British forces captured U.S. bases and torched U.S. towns on the Niagara frontier and rebuffed two invading U.S. Armies on the Saint Lawrence front. Moreover, Napoleon had been defeated in the Battle of Leipzig in October 1813, which foreshadowed his surrender and abdication the following spring.

Madison appointed four men to serve on the new peace commission. Adams was chosen to head the mission. The other members were Bayard, Kentucky War Hawk Henry Clay, and diplomat Jonathan Russell, who had conducted the early armistice negotiations in London. Three weeks later, when Madison learned that Gallatin was still in Europe, his name was added to the list. This time the president mollified the Senate by appointing a new secretary of the treasury. This move assured Senate approval for Gallatin's nomination. The U.S. delegation was exceptionally strong. All except Russell had distinguished themselves in public life, and Adams and Clay still had long and important careers ahead of them.

Great Britain, on the other hand, had to rely on second-rate negotiators because its top officials were busy preparing for the Congress of Vienna, which was charged with forging a general European peace. The British peace mission was headed by Dr. William Adams, an admiralty lawyer selected because U.S. diplomats were known to favor legal arguments. Also on the commission were Lord Gambier, a veteran naval officer who was expected to look after Britain's maritime rights, and Henry Goulburn, an undersecretary in the colonial office who was supposed to protect Britain's interests in Canada. Goulburn was the most ambitious and energetic of the three, and he took charge of the negotiations.

Peace Negotiations in 1814–1815

The negotiations were originally planned for Göteborg, Sweden, but after peace was restored on the Continent in the spring of 1814, Ghent, Belgium, was substituted because it afforded quicker access to both capitals. The negotiations lasted from 8 August 1814 to 24 December 1815—far longer than anyone expected. The talks were held behind closed doors. Although President Madison kept the people of the United States informed, British officials remained silent. This forced the British press to speculate blindly or to rely on U.S. sources for information on the progress of the negotiations. Throughout the negotiations, the U.S. delegation showed greater skill, which forced the British government to keep its envoys on an especially tight leash.

When the negotiations began, the U.S. envoys were still bound to insist on an end to impressment. Six months earlier Secretary of State James Monroe had written that even if the war in Europe ended, the British still had to give up impressment. "This degrading practice," he said, "must cease, our flag must protect the crew, or the United States cannot consider themselves an independent Nation."

Like other U.S. diplomats in an era before rapid communication, the envoys at Ghent were prepared to violate their instructions if necessary. As Clay put it, with the war in Europe over, the U.S. position on impressment had become "a mere theoretic pretension," and if "interests of our country demanded of me the personal risk of a violation of instruction I should not hesitate to incur it." The envoys never had to take this risk because in June 1814 the administration decided to drop its demands on impressment. The news reached the U.S. delegation just as the negotiations were getting under way. Although publicly Democratic-Republican leaders justified their decision by claiming that the end of the European war had brought an end to impressment, privately they conceded that Napoleon's defeat had killed any chance of winning British concessions on the issue.

With impressment out of the way, the envoys were able to focus on other issues, and in the first two weeks of the negotiations the British presented their terms, which reflected their ascendancy in the war. As a sine qua non for peace, the British insisted that the western Native Americans be included in the settlement and that a permanent barrier or reservation be established for them in the Old Northwest. In addition, they demanded U.S. territory in northern Maine (to facilitate overland traffic between Quebec and Halifax) and in present-day Minnesota (to assure access to the Mississippi River). They also called on the United States to demilitarize the Great Lakes—removing all warships from those waters and all fortifications from the shores. Finally, the British declared that, without an equivalent, they would not renew the U.S. right to fish in Canadian waters and to dry fish on Canadian shores. These terms rested upon several considerations, but uppermost was Great Britain's desire to provide better security for Canada and its Native American allies.

In making their demand for a Native American barrier, the British envoys exceeded their instructions in two ways. First, they presented the Indian reservation as a sine qua non, though officials in London saw the barrier as simply one possible means of protecting the Native Americans. Second, even though the British government was only interested in preventing people in the United States from purchasing land in the barrier, the British envoys demanded that the United States refrain from acquiring territory "by purchase or otherwise." This would prevent the United States from acquiring lands inside the barrier by conquest in "defensive" wars. The U.S. envoys, who were not authorized to discuss the surrender of any territory or to make any other major concessions, flatly rejected the British terms. The Native American barrier was particularly objectionable. It undermined U.S. sovereignty, ran counter to a tradition of national control over the Native Americans, and threatened the westward movement. Adams told Goulburn that to condemn such a vast expanse of territory "to perpetual barrenness and solitude [so] that a few hundred savages might find wild beasts to hunt upon it, was a species of game law that a nation descended from Britons would never endure." U.S. stubbornness on this issue convinced Goulburn that the United States was determined "to extirpate the Indians and appropriate their territory."

Convinced that the prospects for peace were remote, the U.S. delegation sent a truce ship home to notify the administration. In mid-October, President Madison sent copies of the envoys' dispatches to Congress. Several days later he also gave Congress the instructions that had authorized the envoys to drop the impressment issue. These documents were published to show the world, and particularly the Federalists, how reasonable the administration was and how unreasonable the British had become. Publication of these documents had the dual effect of generating support for the war at home and embarrassing British officials abroad. With the talks apparently stalled, the mood of the U.S. envoys darkened. Only Clay retained even a shred of hope for peace. An inveterate gambler who sometimes stayed up all night playing cards, Clay thought the British might be bluffing, and he was right. Unwilling to end the negotiations, the British gradually retreated from their demands. Instead of an Indian barrier, they agreed to settle for a pledge to restore the Native Americans to their status as of 1811. This stipulation was too vague to be meaningful. For all practical purposes, the British had abandoned their Native American allies.

Having retreated from their initial terms, the British offered a new basis for peace in October 1814, the principle of *uti possidetis*, which meant that each side would retain whatever territory it held at war's end. If this offer were accepted, the British would gain eastern Maine, Mackinac, and Fort Niagara, while the United States would get Fort Malden and Fort Erie. The British suggested that the agreement be "subject to such modifications as mutual convenience may be found to require." Their hope was to retain northern Maine as well as Mackinac and Fort Niagara, but to trade the rest of eastern Maine for forts Malden and Erie. The British gave little thought to the possibility of retaining New Orleans because by this time their projected campaign against the Crescent City had assumed only minor importance in their overall strategy for ending the war.

When it became evident that the United States would not agree to *uti possidetis*, the British dropped this demand just as they had their others. After more than two decades of almost continuous warfare, the British people longed for peace, and the shrill attacks against the United States in the British press had given way to protests over war taxes. In addition, British officials had become disillusioned with the lack of military progress in the war. Reports that British troops had occupied eastern Maine in July of 1814 and captured and burned Washington, D.C., in August had raised their hopes. However, news soon followed that one British army had retreated from Baltimore, Maryland, when the Royal Navy could not silence the protecting guns of Fort McHenry, and that another British force had withdrawn from Plattsburgh, New York, when Commodore Thomas MacDonough defeated a British squadron on nearby Lake Champlain.

The military failures in 1814 suggested that another campaign would be necessary if the British were to exact any concessions. Another year of fighting was expected to cost 10 million British pounds and was likely to weaken Great Britain's position in Europe. The allies at Vienna were already feuding among themselves, and British officials wondered how quickly they could recall troops from the United States. To buttress their position at home and in the field, British officials asked the Duke of Wellington to take charge of the war with the United States. The "Iron Duke" agreed but refused to leave Europe until the spring or to guarantees success. What

the British needed, he said, was "not a general, or general officers, and troops, but naval superiority on the Lakes." Without this, there was little hope of success. Given the existing military circumstances, Wellington concluded, "you have no right…to demand any concession of territory from America." British officials used Wellington's opinion to justify jettisoning their last territorial demands. The only important issues that remained unsettled were the status of U.S. fishing rights in Canadian waters and British navigation rights on the Mississippi River. Since both rights were guaranteed by the Peace of Paris in 1783, they were likely to stand or fall together. These rights caused a deeper division in the U.S. delegation than any other issue. Clay, representing western interests, wanted to close the Mississippi to the British, while Adams, representing Massachusetts fisherman, insisted on retaining the fisheries. In the end, both issues were left out of the treaty. A tacit admission that both rights continued, this was a victory for Adams.

The Treaty of Ghent

The U.S. and British envoys spent close to a month hammering out a treaty. Their handiwork, completed on 24 December 1814, is known as the Treaty of Ghent or the Peace of Christmas Eve. The treaty mentioned none of the maritime issues that had caused the war nor any of the British demands made earlier in the negotiations. It simply restored the prewar status quo. Each side agreed to evacuate all enemy territory, though the British were allowed to retain several islands in Passamaquoddy Bay (between Maine and New Brunswick) until their ownership was determined. Each side also agreed to make peace with the Native Americans and to work toward stamping out the slave trade. In addition, the treaty established three commissions to fix portions of the U.S.-Canadian boundary and to establish the rightful owner of the Passamaquoddy Islands.

On three earlier occasions—in connection with Jay's Treaty in 1794, a boundary convention in 1803, and the Monroe-Pinckney Treaty in 1806—the United States had insisted on modifications after its envoys had signed an agreement. This time the British would settle for nothing less than unconditional ratification. They also wanted hostilities to end not when the treaty was signed (which was customary) but only after ratifications had been exchanged. Such a provision would entail a delay if the British instrument of ratification (a copy of the treaty, signed by the king) were lost at sea. Hence the envoys agreed that hostilities would cease when both sides had ratified the agreement. The treaty, however, would not be binding until the exchange of ratifications.

On 2 January 1815, Henry Carroll, Clay's personal secretary, boarded the ship *Favourite* in London to take a copy of the treaty to the United States. He was joined by

Anthony Baker, who carried a copy of the British instrument of ratification. The ship reached New York harbor around 8:00 P.M. on 11 January 1815. Carroll made no secret of his mission. Word quickly spread that peace was at hand, and soon the entire nation was celebrating.

If the United States refused to ratify the treaty, the British were prepared to offer a separate peace to Federalist New England, which had aired its hostility to the administration and the war in the Hartford Convention. But no such step was necessary. News of the treaty reached the nation's capital on 13 February and an official copy arrived the following day. Madison submitted the treaty to the Senate on 15 February, and the next day the Senate voted unanimously (35–0) to approve it. Madison gave his own approval later that day, thus completing the ratification process. Since the British had already ratified the pact, this marked the end of hostilities. The war formally came to an end at 11:00 P.M. on 17 February when Monroe exchanged ratifications with Baker, who had arrived in Washington earlier that evening.

Although the United States had won none of its major aims in the war of 1812, President Madison sent a message to Congress announcing the end of the war and congratulating the U.S. people on their success. All across the country Democratic-Republican orators and editors echoed the president's cry. Although the British had surrendered none of their maritime rights and Canada remained in their hands, Democratic-Republicans seized upon General Andrew Jackson's lopsided victory over an invading British force in the Battle of New Orleans (which was actually fought two weeks after the peace treaty had been signed) to insist that the war was a success. The United States, in fact, could not claim to have won the war. But because of the clear-headed determination of its envoys at Ghent, the nation could at least argue that it had won the peace.

The War of 1812 legitimized the United States as a nation and compelled the Great Powers of Europe to treat the young republic with greater respect. It also promoted U.S. nationalism and contributed to the heady expansionism that characterized the nation's foreign policy for the rest of the century. In addition, it broke the power of the western tribes and put an end to foreign interference with Native Americans. The war also destroyed the Federalist Party, whose opposition had been very popular during the conflict but not afterwards. Finally, the war experience reinforced the legacy of anglophobia left by the Revolution that was later buttressed by Irish immigrants.

DONALD R. HICKEY

See also Adams, John Quincy; Blockade; Canada; Castlereagh, Second Viscount; Clay, Henry; Economic Sanctions; Gallatin, Albert; Ghent, Treaty of; Great Britain; Hartford Convention; Impressment; International Trade and Commerce; Madison, James; Monroe, James; Monroe-Pinckney Treaty; Napoleonic Wars; Native Americans; Orders in Council; War Hawks

FURTHER READING

Adams, Henry. *History of the United States During the Administration of Jefferson and Madison*, 9 vols. New York, 1889–1891.
Brown, Roger H. *The Republic in Peril: 1812*. New York, 1964.
Carr, James A. "The Battle of New Orleans and the Treaty of Ghent." *Diplomatic History* 3 (1979): 273–82.
Engelman, Fred L. *The Peace of Christmas Eve*. New York, 1962.
Hickey, Donald R. *The War of 1812: A Forgotten Conflict*. Urbana, Ill. 1989.
Horsman, Reginald. *The Causes of the War of 1812*. Philadelphia, Pa., 1962.
Mahon, John E. *The War of 1812*. Gainesville, Fla., 1972.
Perkins, Bradford. *Castlereagh and Adams: England and the United States, 1812–1823*. Berkeley, Calif., 1964.
———. *Prologue to War: England and the United States, 1805–1812*. Berkeley, Calif., 1961.
Stuart, Reginald C. *United States Expansionism and British North America, 1775–1871*. Chapel Hill, N.C., 1988.
Updyke, Frank A. *The Diplomacy of the War of 1812*. Baltimore, Md., 1915.

WAR POWERS RESOLUTION

A legislative effort to force the president to recognize a congressional role in determining whether military force should be used in foreign policy. From its passage the resolution has been challenged on constitutional grounds. In addition, implementation of the resolution raises important questions of institutional balance between the executive and legislative branches. Although several proposals for revision of the resolution have been offered, none have been adopted. The resolution remained a source of continuing contention between the president and the Congress, irrespective of whether the same or different parties controlled the two ends of Pennsylvania Avenue.

Background

As the U.S. electorate became disillusioned with the conflict in Vietnam, several members of Congress undertook efforts to impose limitations on the ability of a president to commit U.S. forces to major military operations without congressional approval. Those members rejected the traditional willingness of Congress to subordinate itself to the executive branch in all questions involving foreign relations. They contended that Congress should have the power to both authorize and constrain presidential uses of military force if the legislature is to play its proper constitutional role.

Members of Congress argued that the constitution expressly granted the power to declare war to the Congress. In addition, the Congress, through its power to approve all executive branch expenditures, could cut off funds to conduct military action. Based on these arguments, legislation was introduced to limit President Richard Nixon's authority to conduct the conflict in Vietnam. The executive branch opposed this legislation, maintaining that Congress had authorized military operations in Vietnam when it approved the Tonkin Gulf resolution passed by the House and the Senate on 7 August 1964. Some members of Congress proposed legislative measures intended to limit presidential pursuit of military action in Vietnam. In almost every case, these initiatives failed to gain adequate support. Both members of Congress and private individuals challenged executive branch military action in the federal courts on both constitutional and statutory grounds. When the executive branch resisted the litigation while continuing to conduct military operations, the courts avoided definitive rulings through resort to the political question doctrine and other legal theories that allowed judicial deference when the legislative and executive branches were in political conflict. This judicial abstention allowed the executive branch to conduct operations in Vietnam without any effective constraint imposed by Congress.

President Nixon withdrew American forces from Vietnam by the end of March 1973. However, members of Congress continued to pursue mechanisms for limiting executive action that involved significant commitments of military forces to combat. Eventually, Congress passed the War Powers Resolution over President Nixon's veto.

In recommending the War Powers Resolution for passage, the House Committee on Foreign Affairs stated that its objective was "to reaffirm the constitutionally given authority of the Congress to declare war." Although the committee was mindful of the need for the executive to respond to sudden attacks, the committee was convinced that "such extraordinary circumstances" did not raise the central difficulty of "the commitment of U.S. military forces exclusively by the president (purportedly under his authority as commander in chief) without congressional approval or adequate consultation with the Congress."

The War Powers Resolution imposes three principal requirements on the president in situations where U.S. forces are likely to become involved in substantial hostilities: consultation prior to commitment of U.S. forces, reporting after the commitment of those forces, and termination of unauthorized hostilities after sixty days.

In introductory language, the War Powers Resolution states that the purpose of Congress is "to fulfill the intent of the framers of the constitution of the United States and insure that the collective judgement of both the Congress and the president will apply to the introduction of United States armed forces into hostilities...and to the continued use of such forces in hostilities." After citing the constitutional language granting to Congress the power to declare war, the resolution states that the president's power to introduce troops into hostilities is limited to situations involving "(1) a declaration of war, (2) specific statutory authorization, or (3) a national emergency created by attack upon the United States, its territories or possessions, or its armed forces."

In Section 3 of the resolution, the Congress imposes its requirement that the president shall consult the legislative branch prior to the introduction of U.S. forces "into hostilities or into situations where imminent involvement in hostilities is clearly indicated by the circumstances" whenever possible. Whether or not prior consultation is possible, regular consultation is mandated until the forces are removed from the situation.

Section 4 of the resolution contains those provisions intended to trigger the substantive constraints of the resolution. Unless war is formally declared, the president is required to submit a report to Congress within forty-eight hours of the occurrence of: (1) the involvement of U.S. forces in actual hostilities or situations where hostilities are imminent; (2) the entry of combat-equipped U.S. forces into the territory, airspace, or waters of a foreign state for any purpose other than training, supply, replacement, or repair; or (3) the additional deployment of forces in a manner that "substantially" enlarges the U.S. contingent equipped for combat in a foreign nation.

Under Section 5, the president must terminate any deployment of U.S. armed forces that is subject to these reporting requirements within sixty days unless Congress authorizes the commitment by a declaration of war or a specific enactment. An additional thirty days may be added if required for the safe withdrawal of the troops. In effect, the lack of congressional action approving a commitment of U.S. forces to hostilities requires the president to terminate that commitment. Congress also provided that it could at any time, by concurrent resolution, require the president to remove any U.S. forces engaged in hostilities in areas outside the territorial jurisdiction of the United States unless there had been a declaration of war. Congress adopted expedited procedures to avoid potential problems flowing from the possible inability of standard legislative procedure to allow timely action in the face of a crisis requiring response under a short deadline.

Authority to commit U.S forces to hostilities is not to be inferred from any provision of an existing or subsequently enacted statute or ratified treaty unless both Houses have specifically empowered the commitment through legislation which expressly affirms that the enactment is intended to constitute specific statutory authorization within the meaning of the War Powers Resolution.

When Congress passed the resolution, President Nixon exercised his constitutional veto power, notifying

Congress that he would not sign the bill into law. Congress subsequently passed the bill again, overriding Nixon's veto.

Constitutional Issues

Since its passage in 1973, the legislative and executive branches have held conflicting positions on the legality and the legitimacy of the resolution. Some of the central arguments were stated by President Nixon in his veto message returning the War Powers Resolution to Congress. From the presidential perspective, the resolution imposed restrictions "...which are both unconstitutional and dangerous to the best interests of our Nation." He stated that the resolution would seriously undermine this nation's ability to act decisively and convincingly in times of crisis. As a result, the confidence of our allies in our ability to assist them could be diminished and the respect of our adversaries for our deterrent posture would decline. A permanent and substantial element of unpredictability would be injected into the world's assessment of American behavior, further increasing the likelihood of miscalculation and war.

While only President Ronald Reagan has joined in the explicit rejection of the resolution as unconstitutional, several administrations have questioned either the constitutional balance struck by the resolution, or the adequacy of the legislative procedures included in the resolution. However, even while claiming not to be legally bound by the resolution, subsequent administrations have consistently complied with the reporting requirements, although couched in terms of being "consistent with" rather than "under the authority of" the War Powers Resolution.

Most of the legal scholarship considering the War Powers Resolution has been devoted to the question of its constitutionality. The Supreme Court declared the legislative veto to be unconstitutional, casting fatal doubt on the use of a joint resolution to require disengagement of troops from hostilities. After the decision in *Immigration and Naturalization Service v. Chadha*, any resolution requiring the withdrawal of troops must be through a concurrent resolution and thus subject to presidential veto.

Until recently, federal courts have avoided ruling on the question of the scope of the congressional war power by relying on the "political question" doctrine. However, one lower federal court has affirmed the congressional war power as a potential basis for injunctive relief against the president under the proper circumstances. Regardless of the ultimate answer to these judicial questions, the executive branch may seek to avoid compliance through political arguments based on these constitutional doubts.

Institutional Concerns

The provisions of the War Powers Resolution were intended to redress a perceived imbalance between the Congress and the president with regard to warmaking. Some critics suggest that Congress may have created a new imbalance, depriving the president of the capacity to respond to those international emergencies that face contemporary global powers. Others have suggested that the debates surrounding the making of a commitment of troops to hostilities could highlight to the world doubts and disunity about U.S. policy. Further, some have contended that Congress has neither the ability nor the desire to track events on the international scene in a way that would allow quick decision in an emergency.

On the other hand, proponents of congressional participation in warmaking decisions have argued that the resolution can give a presumption of legitimacy to rapid, limited-duration military interventions unilaterally initiated by the executive branch. The resolution requires termination of any covered deployment within sixty days after a report is required unless Congress authorizes the deployment. The president may extend the deployment for another thirty days if immediate withdrawal is not possible. The resolution could be read as providing a ninety-day "window" for unconstrained use of military force by the executive. Commentators have argued that the existence of the resolution may lead the executive branch to opt for quick and intense actions that can be completed before any termination resolution can be passed. Longer action may be "stage-managed" in order to show progress when a six-month report falls due. Finally, termination debates may generate political polarization rather than reasoned decision.

Serious difficulties have been encountered in executive branch attempts to comply with the consultation requirements of the resolution. On occasion, the appropriate members of Congress have been scattered over the globe when reporting was required. Some presidents have found that compliance with the prior consultation requirements threatened military secrecy. President Reagan, for example, did not notify Congress about the bombing of Tripoli until the attack was about to reach its target. In general, the Congress has failed to establish an internal structure geared toward the timely handling of the consultation requirements it has imposed on the executive branch.

The worst problems of the resolution have surrounded the time limitations mandated for deployments. Even though the resolution appears to provide the mechanism, Congress has not forced the termination of any presidential deployment of forces. Because of a drafting error, presidents have succeeded in providing ambiguously designated reports to Congress, placing an unwanted burden upon the legislative branch for triggering the resolution's time limits. In fact, legislative action to trigger the termination time period during a crisis has proven to be an impracticable undertaking. When confronted with deployments that threatened to extend beyond the time limit, the Congress has failed to confront the executive either by triggering the reporting time limit or by attempting to force disengagement. Congress faces such difficulties under the current resolution that it may never play the required role in limiting the use of force.

Proposals for Amendment

Because of the difficulties encountered, several useful suggestions have been offered for either revising or replacing the resolution. First, more precise definition of those "hostilities" that would trigger the resolution's time limitation would minimize contention between the branches about the applicability of that requirement. Second, the ambiguous distinctions between "hostilities" and other circumstances that activate consultation requirements should be eliminated. Third, the resolution should be amended to provide specific identification of the members of Congress to whom reports should be directed. That identification could facilitate prior consultation on deployments.

Other proposed revisions rest on different constitutional grounds. Because no funds may be expended unless authorized by Congress, the legislative branch may prohibit executive expenditures related to military operations. Several scholars have suggested that the resolution should be amended to prohibit the expenditure of funds for military deployments into hostilities unless Congress has authorized the expenditure. Exceptions could be made for actual or imminent attack on U.S. territory or forces, or for rescue of U.S. nationals. Reliance on the power of the purse offers much greater probability of enabling successful congressional limitation of executive branch deployments of military force.

Until Congress undertakes effective revision of the War Powers Resolution, controversial military operations undertaken by the president will be debated on two disparate grounds. On one hand, public commentators will appropriately discuss whether the executive policy is appropriate under the circumstances and whether the relevant constitutional powers have been properly exercised by the branches of government. At the same time, legislators and legal scholars will engage in a distracting debate over whether the president has complied with the specific terms of the resolution. While the constitutional and political debates will play an appropriate role in providing direction to the choices in foreign affairs, debate of the resolution is most likely to be debilitating and distracting, providing an obstacle to the creation of a consensus on decisions on the most critical of public issues: war and peace.

EDWIN M. SMITH

See also Congress; Constitution; Presidency; Vietnam War

FURTHER READING

The War Powers Resolution, P.L. No. 88–408, H. J. Res. 1145, 78 Stat. 384 (1964).

Immigration and Naturalization Service v. Chadha, 426 U.S. 919 (1983).

Biden, Joseph S., Jr., and John B. Ritch III. "Commentary: The War Power at a Constitutional Impasse: A 'Joint Decision' Solution." *Georgetown Law Journal*, 1988.

Glennon, Michael J. *Constitutional Diplomacy*. Princeton, N.J., 1990.

Koh, Harold Hongju. *The National Security Constitution: Sharing Power After the Iran-Contra Affair*. New Haven, Conn., 1990.

WARSAW PACT

(1955–1991)

Known officially as the Warsaw Treaty Organization (WTO), a military and political organization dominated by the Soviet Union during the Cold War. The WTO's original members were Albania, Bulgaria, Czechoslovakia, East Germany, Hungary, Poland, Romania, and the Soviet Union. The Warsaw Treaty was signed on 14 May 1955, six years after the formation of the North Atlantic Treaty Organization (NATO) but only nine days after the ratification of West Germany's entry into NATO. All the member states of the pact had previously been bound to the Soviet Union by bilateral ties, but Moscow sought a political organization to counter the enlarged Western alliance. Moreover, civil disorders in East Germany in June 1953 had exposed fissures in the Soviet sphere of influence.

After the Hungarian uprising in October of 1956, Moscow centralized decision-making in the pact, but the pact continued to show strains. Albania withdrew from military operations in 1961, because it backed China in the Sino-Soviet split, and withdrew formally from the pact in 1968. Soviet troops withdrew from Romania in 1958, and Romania did not take full part in WTO exercises or permit foreign troops to transit its territory. Although the 1968 invasion of Czechoslovakia was nominally a WTO operation (East Germany, Poland, Hungary, and others sent troops), the decision to invade was made by Moscow, which bypassed the organization's Political Consultative Committee.

In the 1980s, the Warsaw Pact was further weakened by Polish resistance to Soviet influence, and by the economic stagnation that beset the Soviet Union's Eastern European and East German allies. East Germany left the pact in September 1990, two weeks before unification with Western Germany. At the October 1990 Military Council meeting, Czechoslovakia, Hungary, and Poland rejected participation in future military exercises. The military structure was officially disbanded in March 1991, and the political organization was dissolved in July of that year.

STEPHEN D. WRAGE

See also Cold War; Czech Republic; Russia and the Soviet Union

FURTHER READING

Fodor, Neil. *The Warsaw Treaty Organization: A Political and Organizational Analysis.* New York, 1990.

Holden, Gerard. *The Warsaw Pact: Soviet Security and Bloc Politics.* London, 1989.

WASHINGTON, BOOKER T.

(*b.* 5 April 1856; *d.* 14 November 1915)

Prominent and influential African-American leader. He founded the Tuskegee Institute in Alabama in 1881 and gained national attention with his heralded and controversial Atlanta Exposition Address of 1895, in which he advocated accommodation between the races in the South. Washington's international interest and influence were varied but generally procapitalist and supportive of European and U.S. expansionism. He was instrumental in organizing a Pan-African conference in 1899, and provided personnel from Tuskegee Institute to aid colonial economic and agricultural development in German Togo, British Nigeria, and the Belgian Congo. Washington influenced the African policy of the Theodore Roosevelt and William Howard Taft administrations, supported sanctions against the Belgian Congo in 1904 (because of mistreatment of workers in the rubber trade), and brokered economic support and U.S. protection for Liberia in 1908. Washington also hosted the first International Meeting on the Negro at Tuskegee in 1912, endorsed U.S. intervention in Haiti in 1915, and fostered educational ties between the United States and Africa. The Booker T. Washington Institute, established in Liberia in 1929, was based on Washington's educational and political philosophy.

DONALD SPIVEY
JOYCE HANSON

See also Africa; Liberia

FURTHER READING

Harlan, Louis R. *Booker T. Washington: The Wizard of Tuskegee, 1901–1915.* New York, 1983.

———, and Raymond W. Smocks, eds. *The Booker T. Washington Papers,* 11 vols. Urbana, Ill., 1972.

Meier, August. *Negro Thought in America, 1880–1915.* 4th ed. Ann Arbor, Mich., 1988.

Spivey, Donald S. *Schooling for the New Slavery: Black Industrial Education, 1868–1915.* Westport, Conn., 1978.

WASHINGTON, GEORGE

(*b.* 22 February 1732; *d.* 14 December 1799)

Commander in chief of the Continental Army during the American Revolution, presiding officer of the Constitutional Convention of 1787, and first president of the United States (1789–1797), whose foreign policy was marked by efforts to protect U.S. interests and independence during years of war in Europe. Perhaps no individual has been more venerated in U.S. history than George Washington, oftentimes dubbed the "father of his country." Washington played a unique and pivotal role in helping create the new nation and then guiding it through its formative years. Though not possessing the intellectual brilliance of Thomas Jefferson, James Madison, or Alexander Hamilton, Washington nevertheless displayed considerable leadership ability and commanded loyalty, whether on the battlefield or in the political arena. A man of moderation and common sense, he committed himself to the republican ideal, helping to secure the foundations of representative government in the world of monarchy. A man of character, not tempted by the lure of power and wealth, he left an indelible imprint on the office of the presidency and foreign policy, establishing influential precedents. Although he left office in 1797 amid controversy and political discord, his death two years later prompted national mourning, which set in motion some of the mythmaking and folklore that have surrounded his historical reputation ever since. Seeking to provide the young nation with models to emulate, writers such as "Parson" Mason Weems took liberty with the truth and penned idealized stories of Washington, portraying him as the most noble and virtuous of all Americans. For example, few gradeschool children have not been exposed to Weem's parable of Washington cutting down the cherry tree.

Early Years

George Washington was born in Westmoreland County, Virginia, and grew up in a society where prestige and affluence were associated with ownership of land. Having little formal education, Washington embarked upon a career as a land surveyor at the age of fifteen. His experiences in the wilderness while surveying and traveling instilled in him appreciation for the West, and revealed to him the possibilities for land acquisition. In 1752, following his brother Lawrence's death, Washington inherited Mount Vernon, which was then a considerable estate along the Potomac River. Although not a particularly wealthy man at the time, his subsequent marriage to the widow Martha Dandridge Custis in 1757 brought with it an additional estate of 15,000 acres and 150 slaves. At first, Washington concentrated on the raising of tobacco, but due to the perceived negative effects of British laws, he gradually turned to the manufacturing of goods he had previously imported, namely cloth. Other economic activities at Mount Vernon included a fishery on the Potomac, crops, and a grist mill. Fish, wheat, and flour were then exported to the West Indies.

Commissioned as a major in the colonial militia, Washington went into the Ohio River Valley in 1753 under Governor Robert Dinwiddie's orders to assert Great Britain's claims against France to that territory. Washington's encounters with the French in 1754 contributed to the outbreak of the French and Indian War (1754–1763). Appointed to the rank of colonel in command of Virginian troops during the war, he failed to receive a regular commission in the British army, most likely due to the overall low esteem of American colonials held by British regulars. Consequently, he did not play a major leadership role in the military campaigns of the war. Disappointed in not receiving a regular command and critical of British conduct during the war, Washington weakened his ties with the mother country. In late 1758, he resigned his commission and returned to civilian life at Mount Vernon.

From 1759 to 1774, Washington played a major role in colonial politics while serving in the Virginia House of Burgesses. His growing interests in western land speculation, which he hoped would enhance his growing wealth and social standing, put him at odds with British policy, particularly the Proclamation of 1763 and the Quebec Act of 1774. As a member of the House of Burgesses, Washington also opposed the Stamp Act, Townshend Duties, and the Coercive Acts that Great Britain imposed on the colonies. He was elected a delegate to the First Continental Congress which met in Philadelphia in September 1774. When hostilities erupted between Great Britain and the colonies in April and May 1775, the Second Continental Congress on 15 June selected Washington to be commander in chief of the newly formed Continental Army, for which he declined pay. Branded a traitor by King George III's Royal Proclamation of Rebellion, Washington, earlier than many Americans, concluded that independence from Great Britain should be the colonies' goal.

As a military commander, Washington held together a disparate, ill-trained army through very difficult times. His first military success was forcing the British to evacuate Boston in March 1776. When he subsequently could not defend New York City, and after sustaining a series of minor defeats, he withdrew to New Jersey. With his main army reduced to 3,000 men, and morale at its lowest point, he boosted the army's sagging spirits by achieving success at Trenton and Princeton in December 1776 and January 1777, respectively. These victories were followed by defeats at Brandywine and Germantown, and the fall of Philadelphia to the British. American spirits were revived with the surrender of British General John Burgoyne to American General Horatio Gates at Saratoga on 17 October 1777.

Gates's victory, and Washington's defeats, gave rise to a scheme among some delegates in Congress to replace Washington with Gates. This plot was thwarted, however, and Washington retained his command. Although the Continental army endured enormous hardships during the winter of 1777–1778 while at Valley Forge, Pennsylvania, it was revitalized by a season of drilling and the consummation of the Franco-American alliance. Washington resumed the struggle, making good use of French troops and especially the French navy, which he believed essential for victory. Although recognizing that French assistance was vital, Washington nevertheless sought to prevent the French from becoming the dominant partner of the alliance. His fear of foreign entanglements carried into the presidency.

Aware that the British had shifted their primary war effort to the south, Washington planned in 1781 to march from New York to Virginia, and to use the French fleet to prevent the escape and rescue of a large British force then in Virginia under General Lord Charles Cornwallis. On 19 October, 7,000 British troops surrendered to the combined American and French armies at Yorktown, thus precipitating the diplomatic negotiations that brought an end to the war. Washington's effective use of French resources was critical to the successful outcome of the war. His ability and diplomatic tact were greatly appreciated by the French allies, and played a key role in helping to hold together the military alliance.

During the winter of 1782–1783, while the army was encamped along the Hudson River, some of the officers, upset over Congress's failure to keep its promise with respect to pay, threatened to march on Philadelphia. Because of the respect he commanded among his men, Washington was able to dissuade the officers from their predetermined course by a carefully crafted speech which he delivered on 15 March 1783. If he had wanted, Washington could have marched on Philadelphia and, with the backing of the army, established himself as head of government. Regardless of the seemingly legitimate complaints the army had with the government, Washington performed an altruistic service for the fledgling nation by helping to establish the principle in the United States that the armed forces were subject to civilian control. With the conclusion of the American Revolution following the Paris Treaty of Peace of 1783, the general resigned his commission on 4 December 1783 and returned to his beloved Mount Vernon.

Retirement from public service, however, did not last long. In the years immediately following the Revolution, domestic and foreign troubles alarmed Washington. The Articles of Confederation, with its emphasis on decentralized government, seemed inadequate to meet the needs of the new nation. The government's inability to raise money, suppress insurrections, provide for defense against European powers, handle conflicts with Native Americans on the frontier, and other weaknesses convinced many Americans, including Washington, that a stronger central government had become essential. The former general thus agreed to serve as a delegate from Virginia to the Constitutional Convention which met in Philadelphia from May through September 1787. Given his stature and reputation, he was chosen president of the convention. In subsequent debates surrounding ratification, Washington, along with James Madison, used his influence in Virginia to secure that state's ratification of the Constitution as a new instrument of government. Following the Constitution's implementation, Washington was the unanimous choice of electors to be the first president. He was sworn in on 30 April 1789 in New York City.

The Washington Presidency and the French Revolution

The Organic Act of 1789 created five executive departments in the new government. The first secretary of the treasury was Alexander Hamilton. Thomas Jefferson, who had served as the United States's first minister to France for five years, became secretary of state. General Henry Knox became head of the department of war. The two lesser offices of attorney general and postmaster general were filled by Edmund Randolph and Samuel Osgood, respectively. Although the Constitution did not refer to a cabinet, Washington nevertheless established the precedent of conferring with his political officers for advice. Even though the Constitution had entrusted to the presidency the greatest responsibility for the conduct of foreign affairs, it did not spell out the exact process. Washington thus established the practice whereby executive department officials negotiated treaties with foreign governments. As required by the Constitution, the Senate then considered treaties for approval or rejection.

Washington's cabinet contained two of the most brilliant and influential men in the nation's history, Hamilton and Jefferson. The president had asked Hamilton as secretary of the treasury to devise an economic plan for the young nation that would pay off foreign and domestic debts and put the country on a course toward solvency and greatness. A superb administrator, Hamilton did as the president requested and presented his financial plan to Congress in a series of reports in early 1790. On financial matters, Washington generally agreed with the views of his secretary of the treasury. The central government needed the fiscal ability to pay off its debts, collect taxes, and contend with foreign and domestic crises; furthermore, manufacturing industries should be encouraged as a way of reducing dependence on European imports. For Hamilton, political stability required fiscal policies that would benefit the socially and economically advantaged, thus tying their loyalty to the new government. Jefferson, James Madison, and other liberals viewed the role of government as much more limited in scope, for they believed that policies should not be pursued that gave advantages to wealthy creditors at the expense of agricultural debtors. Furthermore, they believed government power should be limited or else individual liberties could be threatened. In no small way, these differences in philosophy, as well as the particulars of Hamilton's plan, contributed to the development of political parties in the United States: the Federalists who supported Hamilton's policies and the Democratic-Republicans (or Republicans) who were more in keeping with the views of Jefferson and Madison.

In addition to the different views surrounding Hamilton's plan, philosophy of government, and vision for the United States, the outbreak of the French Revolution and events related to it also contributed significantly to the origins of political parties. Not only were U.S. domestic politics greatly influenced by foreign policy. To Hamiltonians the perceived excesses of the French Revolution, such as the execution of King Louis XVI in 1793, were to be deplored. Mob rule, as Hamilton and his supporters saw it, had replaced legitimate rulers. To Jefferson and his followers, a country like France could not be transformed "from despotism to liberty in a feather bed," even if it entailed the deaths of several thousand aristocrats. Such a position was anathema to Hamiltonians. They saw Great Britain as the last hope for stability and order, particularly after France declared war on Great Britain in February 1793 and thrust the major powers of Europe into world wars that would last for more than two decades.

For Washington, who had been overwhelmingly reelected president in 1792, the French Revolution and the wars that followed presented him with his most mettlesome foreign policy problems. What would happen if France called on the United States to adhere to its treaties with France? Hamilton advised the president that the treaties were no longer binding because they had been made with the government of Louis XVI, which no longer existed. Jeffersonians, however, argued that the treaties had been signed with the French nation and thus remained in force. Although Washington sided with his secretary of state, he sought to avoid the obvious pitfall that might occur should the young republic be dragged into this European conflagration, and he pursued a neutral course. On 22 April 1793 the president, in issuing his Neutrality States, required that they should "with sincerity and good faith adopt and pursue a conduct friendly and impartial toward the belligerent powers...."

Although events linked to the French Revolution would eventually pose the greatest challenge to Washington's government, the first diplomatic crisis he faced as president originated over the Nootka Sound, situated on the west coast of Vancouver Island in present-day British Columbia. During the summer of 1789 several British trading ships, attempting to establish a trading post, were seized by Spanish authorities who claimed the territory for Spain and placed it off limits to foreigners. If war erupted, Hamilton, who possessed pro-British sentiments, was willing to let the British cross U.S. soil from Canada to strike at Spanish territories in Louisiana and Florida. Jefferson, distrustful of the British, cautioned against granting this permission. The crisis of 1789–1790 did not lead to war, and the president did not have to choose which of his advisers' advice to accept, largely because of changing circumstances in Europe. Netherthless, the incident illustrated Great Britain's desire to avoid further possible conflict with the United States. Some British officials feared that if war had broken out the United States may have used the occasion to rectify perceived past injustices, such as continued British retention of forts in the Northwest, in violation of the Treaty of 1783, as well as to avenge British failure to negotiate a trade treaty with the United States.

Far more important than the Nootka Sound crisis as a catalyst for change in Anglo-American relations was the U.S. threat of economic retaliation against Great Britain as a way of forcing a change in British policies toward the United States. With the support of Madison and other friends in Congress, Jefferson used his influence to secure the introduction of several bills in early 1791 that would have imposed discriminatory duties on British goods and severely threatened Great Britain's important commerce with the United States. Hamilton blocked Jefferson's plan out of fear that such measures would endanger the secretary of the treasury's financial schemes, which were predicated upon revenues from trade with Great Britain, and to further the political goal of establishing a stronger central government more along the lines of the British.

Although Jefferson's recommendations failed to get passed by Congress, the mere threat of U.S. retaliatory measures, along with the growing strength of Jeffersonians in the government, convinced the British of the need to alter policy toward the United States. The first step was the establishment of diplomatic relations for the first time since the end of the American Revolution. In October 1791, George Hammond arrived in Philadelphia as the first British minister duly accredited to the United States, with instructions to counter anti-British measures related to trade. Little improvement in Anglo-American relations was made, however, since Hammond possessed only limited powers, and because Jefferson's bargaining position was seriously undermined by the machinations of Hamilton, who secretly informed Hammond that Jefferson's views, which tended to be pro-French and anti-British, did not necessarily reflect the sentiments of Washington and the administration. Thus the urgency for the British to make concessions was mitigated.

Hamilton's Influence

Hamilton was able to exert considerable influence over foreign policy because of the close personal relationship he had with President Washington, dating back to their wartime service together. Not only did Jefferson resent Hamilton's high-handed interference in his departmental affairs, but the secretary of state, whose political and constitutional views differed greatly with those of Hamilton, felt more and more out of step with the administration each passing year. His disagreements with Hamilton contributed to the emergence of two political parties. The Republicans agreed with Jefferson and Madison and opposed such government policies as the perceived anti-French, pro-British foreign policy, support for a national bank, loose interpretation of the Constitution, pro-creditor fiscal policies, and the generally favorable view of a strong central government. The other political party, the Federalists, usually sided with Hamilton and supported the administration's positions. In this era when the prevailing notion was one of noblesse oblige—the idea that the betters of society through their collective wisdom made decisions, leaving little room for dissent—Washington lamented the development of political decisions. So disenchanted did Jefferson become with Hamilton and the administration's policies, that he determined by late 1793 to resign, which he did (over Washington's entreaties) on the very last day of the year. When Jefferson departed as secretary of state, the president was hard-pressed to find a suitable replacement. Although Madison was his first choice, Washington knew that Jefferson's closest friend would not accept for the very reasons that Jefferson was leaving. In the end, the president settled on Edmund Randolph, a fellow Virginian and attorney general in Washington's administration, for lack of a better candidate.

In the months that had preceded Jefferson's resignation, the debate over U.S. policy toward France grew more strident. In April 1792, France had gone to war with Prussia and Austria. French revolutionaries known as the Girondins, who were anxious to bring "liberty, equality, and fraternity" to the rest of Europe, welcomed this war. As Prussian and Austrian armies invaded France, and rumors of the treasonable behavior of Louis XVI circulated, the Legislative Assembly called for new elections and a convention once again to revise the constitution. Shortly after the national convention convened in September 1792, French armies routed the invaders and the convention's first act was to declare France a republic. In January 1793, Louis was tried for treason and beheaded. This event shocked all of Europe, as well as conservatives in the United States such as Hamilton. Great Britain, Holland, Sardinia, and Spain joined Austria and Prussia in war against France. Civil war loomed in France as bitter factional disputes broke out within the convention. Girondins were challenged by a new faction, known as Jacobins, who relied upon the Paris crowds for much of their power, while the Girondins tended to be identified with the provinces. The Jacobins gained control, and the Revolution became more radical, during the ensuing "Reign of Terror," whereby anyone suspected of disloyalty to the Revolution was executed. In the meantime, France mobilized to defend itself against the massed armies of Europe, and succeeded in taking the offensive.

Edmond Genêt, the representative of Girondin leaders of revolutionary France, arrived in the United States on 8 April 1793 and was warmly received. His activities, however, soon caused the Washington administration to turn cool toward him. Determined to test Washington's neutrality policy, Genêt and Hamilton clashed almost from the very beginning over the terms of the 1778 treaty, which Genêt argued allowed for the outfitting of French privateers in U.S. ports for the ultimate purpose of preying upon British merchant ships. Having arrived in the United States with little money with which to hire privateers, Genêt was instructed to ask for complete repayment of the debt that was owed to France for loans incurred during the American Revolution. The money would be used to recruit Americans and to pay for Genêt's privateering schemes against British shipping, as well as for the food supplies he purchased and sent to France and the French West Indies. Hamilton opposed payment, and the president agreed with him. They also considered the outfitting of French privateers to be a violation of U.S. neutrality. Although Jefferson was sympathetic to the Frenchmans' position, even he knew that the United States must prevent the French from using its ports for hostile activities.

Believing that the majority of U.S. citizens did not side with the Washington government's seemingly pro-British and anti-French policy, the impulsive French minister determined to appeal over the head of the revered Washington to effect a change in official policy. Even Jefferson tried to restrain Genêt, but to no avail. In July 1793 the issue became explosive when Genêt outfitted a captured British ship French privateers had renamed The *Petit Démocrate*, and then sent it to sea in clear defiance of U.S. policy. In attempting to appeal to the people over the president, Genêt doomed himself. Even the Republicans, who were previously predisposed toward him, deserted Genêt.

In a special message to Congress, the president condemned Genêt's actions, which he said tended "to involve us in war abroad and discord and anarchy at home." He was careful to distinguish between the actions of an errant diplomat and the friendly nation which had sent him. Washington demanded Genêt's recall, and in February 1794, Joseph Fauchet arrived in Philadelphia as Genêt's successor. Realizing that a change of government had brought the Jacobins to power and that his return home would no doubt result in the loss of his head, Genêt applied for, and was granted, political asylum by the Washington administration. Although he may indeed have been a "burned-out comet," as Hamilton called Genêt, the president had no wish to see him martyred, and thus did not force him to return home.

While Genêt was busily angering the U.S. government by his actions, the U.S. minister in France, Gouverneur Morris, was at odds with the French government. Opposed to the French Revolution, Morris had done his best to save the head of Louis XVI from the death-dealing guillotine, even helping to draft a plan to rescue him from imprisonment. The U.S. legation also became a haven for French aristocrats seeking asylum from French Republican officials. Morris's bias became obvious in the reports he sent home. A personal friend of Washington, Morris frequently circumvented the secretary of state, writing directly to the president. With good cause, Jefferson claimed that Morris "kept the president's mind constantly poisoned with his forebodings."

When Washington asked for Genêt's recall, the Jacobin government retaliated by demanding Morris's and requested a replacement who was more supportive of France's revolution. Because Federalist John Jay was then on his way to England, prompting French fear of an Anglo-American rapprochement at the expense of the 1778 Franco-American treaty, Washington named a well-known, committed Jeffersonian, James Monroe of Virginia, as Morris's successor in order to allay French fears.

Relations with Great Britain, Jay's Treaty, and Pinckney's Treaty

The year 1794 was a momentous one for the young republic. It witnessed efforts at rapprochement with England which culminated in Jay's Treaty, further spoiling relations with France. Foreign policy became central to U.S. domestic politics, solidifying the political parties. Although Hamilton and the Federalists wanted to avoid war with Great Britain at almost any cost, the continuing intransigent position of Great Britain, coupled with its haughtiness, made war a distinct possibility between the two nations. As U.S. ships sailed into the Caribbean to take advantage of newly opened commerce with French ports, the British attempted to throttle this trade with a series of orders in council that began in June 1793. Proclaiming that trade not allowed in peace could not become legal in war, the British enforced their policy known as the Rule of 1756. Its effect was to prevent a great deal of U.S. trade with French colonies. British warships confiscated U.S. ships and cargoes, and further insulted U.S. honor by impressing American seamen into the Royal Navy. With no U.S. Navy to enforce the principle of "free ships make free goods," which was a part of the 1778 commercial treaty with France, the Washington administration was in a quandary: risk war with Great Britain, or risk war with France for not enforcing the commercial provisions of the Franco-American treaty.

Anglo-American problems in the Caribbean were compounded by the U.S. perception that Great Britain also was largely responsible for troubles in the Northwest. These difficulties stemmed from the president's efforts to break Native American resistance to white settlement along the frontier. Two expeditions sent against the Native Americans, in 1790 and 1791, had failed. From the British viewpoint, Americans threatened British influence and trade with the Native Americans south of the treaty line of 1783. Out of self-interest the British offered to mediate, suggesting that the Americans agree to a "neutral, Indian barrier state" in the Northwest that would serve as a buffer with Canada, and thus protect that region from U.S. expansionists and perhaps preserve the lucrative fur trade. As predisposed as the Hamiltonians may have been to Great Britain, even they could not countenance such an offer.

In his third attempt to resolve Native American problems in the Northwest, Washington dispatched General "Mad" Anthony Wayne to the Ohio River Valley during the winter of 1793. The British saw this move as a threat to Canada, as well as to their remaining forts in the Northwest. Anglo-American relations were further strained when, in February 1794, Lord Dorchester, governor-general of Canada, told a delegation of Indians that they would be able to regain some of their lands, since war between the United States and Great Britain would certainly break out within a year. He then sent troops to occupy Fort Miami, some sixty miles southwest of Detroit, in what was clearly U.S. territory. So, by early 1794, the failure of the United States to secure a commercial treaty with Great Britain, the unresolved problems associated with the Treaty of 1783, spoliation claims for confiscated ships and cargoes, and Native American troubles in the Northwest brought the two nations to the brink of war.

In response to public clamor, Jeffersonians in Congress introduced anti-British legislation. A nonintercourse bill against Great Britain did not pass in the Senate because Vice President John Adams cast the tie-breaking "no" vote. However, as Americans drilled for war, certain factors arose that stalled the drift toward war. Whereas the French could have exploited the growing anti-British sentiment, they instead seized U.S. ships sailing to England, justifying this move by complaints that the Federalists were not doing what they could to enforce the free ships-free goods provisions of the commercial treaty with France. This action simply alienated U.S. mercantile and shipping interests.

In the midst of the growing demand for war with Great Britain, the British shrewdly modified their policy of seizing U.S. ships in the Caribbean, at least temporarily, and even offered to pay for some of them. Furthermore, despite the possible threat to U.S. commerce, trade with Great Britain remained much more lucrative than that with France. In the final analysis, British officials recognized that Washington's administration sincerely desired to avert hostilities with Great Britain and favored good relations. Because Federalists controlled the executive branch of the government, as well as the Senate, Washington could send a special envoy to London to resolve outstanding issues and prevent war. Although Hamilton was the first choice of Federalists to undertake this mission, his unpopularity with Republicans prevented his selection. Instead, the president selected the Chief Justice of the United States, John Jay of New York. Washington chose a man with considerable diplomatic experience. Because Jay was a committed Federalist known to favor England, Republicans feared that he would sell out to Great Britain. Though given discretionary power because of his distance from home, Jay received instructions not to sign any document that was contrary to the United States's agreements with France.

The one bargaining chip for Jay was the possibility that if the British proved intractable, he could negotiate with Danish and Swedish ministers in London about joining a group of neutrals being formed to resist Great Britain's high-handed maritime practices. Unfortunately for Jay, Hamilton again interceded in foreign affairs by secretly informing British Minister Hammond that the United States would not join the armed neutrality, since the Washington administration had every intention of avoiding European entanglements. This deliberate act by Hamilton was a gross betrayal of duty by an official of the U.S. government. As a direct consequence, Great Britain knew it had nothing to fear if it refused the United States's wishes.

Jay signed a treaty with Great Britain on 19 November 1794. The British had, for the first time, signed a commercial treaty with the United States, even if limited in scope. The only immediate concession in the treaty was the British promise to evacuate the northwest forts, but this was something they had already agreed to do under the Treaty of Paris of 1783. The issue of the northeastern boundary, pre-Revolutionary War debts, and spoliation claims for British maritime seizures were referred to an arbitration commission for resolution. Another provision included some softening of the U.S. position on the principle of free ships make free goods.

Aware that the treaty would be unpopular with many Americans, especially those who perceived it as a pro-British move and a betrayal of the French alliance, the

Senate voted to keep the treaty's provisions secret during its debate. Neither Washington nor Hamilton, who had left government by this time to practice law in New York City, thought the treaty ideal. It did, however, temporarily reduce the likelihood of a drift toward war with Great Britain, secure British withdrawal from American territory in the Northwest, and keep open trade with Great Britain, thus providing the government with vital revenues received through the imposition of import duties. The former secretary of the treasury recommended that the Senate approve the treaty, and after two weeks of debate, Federalists in the Senate pushed the treaty through on 24 June 1795, by the bare minimum, two-thirds vote of 20 to 10.

When terms of the treaty leaked out, many Americans and the French expressed outrage. Jay was vilified and burned in effigy. Hamilton, who attempted to speak in support of the treaty, was stoned from the platform in New York. Edmund Randolph was the only member of the cabinet who opposed the treaty's ratification, and he became the victim of Hamiltonian schemes to discredit him. A moderate Republican at best, Randolph's opposition to the treaty had to do with the specific terms of the agreement, which he viewed as a failure for both U.S. diplomacy and for himself personally in his capacity as secretary of state. He subsequently resigned his position as secretary of state and was replaced by Timothy Pickering.

After much deliberation, and with ambivalent feelings, the president decided to sign the treaty. With serious political divisions developing within the nation, disputes with Native Americans in the West, a hostile Spain on the U.S. southwestern border, and Hamilton's financial plan threatened, he calculated that going to war with England could have doomed the young republic. Having failed to prevent approval of the treaty in the Senate, pro-French Republicans sought to garner enough votes in the House of Representatives to defeat the appropriations necessary for implementing the treaty.

For two months the debate raged in the House, intensified by the president's refusal to provide the House with documents related to the treaty which that body had requested. In refusing the House request, the president argued that the Constitution gave to the president and the Senate the power to negotiate treaties, not to the House. While debate continued, both the British and French ministers lobbied for and against the treaty, respectively. In the end, however, Washington's support saved the treaty. The House approved the money by a three-vote margin on 30 April 1796.

Washington's courageous decision to proceed with the treaty proved wise. But he did set himself up for severe criticism by some of the very people who had revered him, as well as by the French, who saw the treaty as a betrayal—if not in a technical sense, at least in spirit—

and a pro-British move. Jefferson wrote privately, "Curse on his virtues; they have undone the country." The president, Jefferson continued, was among those "who have had their heads shorn by the harlot England." The treaty did, however, postpone war with Great Britain, which, because of the strong sentiments in the country at the time, could have split the Union. Jay's Treaty also brought about the complete fulfillment by the British of the provisions contained in the Treaty of 1783. Deserted by their British friends, the Native Americans in the Northwest were forced by General Wayne, after the U.S. victory at the Battle of Fallen Timbers, to come to terms with the U.S. government in the subsequent Treaty of Fort Greenville on 3 August 1795.

One of the most important indirect consequences of Jay's Treaty was Pinckney's Treaty with Spain of 1795. The Spanish feared a U.S. or Anglo-American attack on their colonies in North America, and in the treaty conceded almost everything the United States wanted and Spain had resisted for twelve years, including the free navigation of the Mississippi with the right of deposit at New Orleans for three years, subject to renewal. Furthermore, Spain agreed not to incite Native Americans along the United States's southwest border, which was then the 31st parallel. Unlike the unpopular Jay's Treaty, the Senate unanimously approved the popular Pinckney's Treaty in March 1796. For the first time since the Treaty of Paris of 1783, U.S. territory was free from foreign control largely because of the Jay and Pinkney Treaties.

Despite the foreign policy accomplishments of the Washington administration, relations with France continued to deteriorate. Whereas Morris had alienated the French by his antirevolutionary attitudes, his successor as U.S. minister of France, James Monroe, overplayed his pro-French role, placing Washington in an embarrassing position at a time when he was attempting to pursue a policy of neutrality. In a speech before the French National Convention, Monroe implied sympathy for France in its war against England, angering Federalists at home. He made so many guarantees to the French with respect to Jay's Treaty that when its details became known, the French reacted with anger, and Monroe lost credibility. Convinced that the Federalist administration was indeed pro-British and turning its back on its old ally, the French government decreed on 2 July 1796 that it would treat neutrals as they allowed Great Britain to treat them, which meant that France would renew the seizure of U.S. merchant vessels. When Monroe attempted to comfort the French by suggesting that Federalists such as Washington and Adams would be thrown out in the next election, the president ordered his recall. The Directory, the new French government, stated that it would not receive another U.S. minister plenipotentiary until its grievances were addressed.

Angered by U.S. actions, the French embarked upon a policy of intervention in U.S. politics, first when they actively sought to defeat Jay's Treaty and later in their efforts to influence the outcome of the 1796 elections. They also formulated a plan for the reestablishment of a French empire in North America, with the prospect of making the United States a client state.

Washington's Farewell

Although Washington had originally planned to retire from politics at the end of his first term in early 1793, he had stayed on for a second term because friends persuaded him that the critical state of foreign affairs required his remaining at the helm. By 1796 the pressures of foreign affairs, and the abuse to which he was subjected by Republicans and the French alike, convinced him that the time had come to seek the calm of his beloved Mount Vernon. After Washington had confided his intentions to Hamilton, the former secretary of the treasury asked the aging president to delay his farewell statement until three months prior to the actual gathering of electors to cast votes for the next president. His valedictory, much of which had been written by Madison, was to have been delivered in 1792. Washington revised the statement due to the growth of "party disputes" and the tensions over foreign policy. Hamilton, hoping to swing the 1796 election to the Federalists, helped revise the draft of Washington's Farewell Address. Although the outgoing president was offering sage advice for the nation, the address also counted as a partisan Federalist campaign statement and was delivered in written form in a newspaper on 17 September 1796.

In the opening of the address Washington announced his intention to retire from politics and not stand as a candidate for a third term as president, thereby establishing a precedent so strong that no American ran for a third term until Franklin D. Roosevelt did so in 1940. Washington then emphasized what he saw as the evils of political party development, which, he wrote, "opens the door to foreign influence and corruption." No one could mistake what he was saying. Fauchet had tried to prevent the ratification of Jay's Treaty, and his successor, Pierre Adet, had subsidized the press and worked through Jeffersonian Republican societies in an attempt to prevent the House of Representatives from appropriating the necessary funds. Having failed to accomplish these objectives, the French had sought Washington's defeat for reelection in 1796, favoring instead the pro-French Jefferson. Even after Washington's withdrawal from reelection consideration, Adet continued to work against Federalist Adams and for Republican Jefferson.

The retiring president then directed his remarks to the question of formal entanglements with foreign governments. With the French alliance clearly in mind, he stated that, "It is our true policy to steer clear of permanent alliances with any portion of the foreign world...[and] we may safely trust to temporary alliances for extraordinary emergencies." Little did the retiring president know that his words regarding permanent alliances would leave such a powerful imprint on policymakers and the public as they did for generations to come. His recommendation became the cornerstone of U.S. "isolationist" sentiment for approximately 150 years. It was not that Washington believed the United States should remain wholly aloof from European affairs, but that he believed it could not permit European agents and intrigue to influence the affairs of the country.

Although Federalists praised the address, Republicans justifiably perceived it as political propaganda. Nor was it calculated to restore friendship with France. During the subsequent campaign, Federalists portrayed themselves as the patriotic party of Washington and Adams, and against Adet and the Republicans. Since the framers of the Constitution had not anticipated—and would have deplored—political party development, no thought was given to the prospect that men representing different political groups could end up in the same administration as president and vice president. Since the method of voting prior to the Twelfth Amendment failed to provide separate ballots for the two offices, when the votes were counted, Adams became president and Jefferson became vice president, having received the second highest number of votes cast.

In Washington's last weeks as president, Franco-American relations had so plummeted that war seemed a genuine possibility. In the Caribbean, U.S. shipping was subject French decrees. Two days prior to Washington's leaving the presidency in 1797, the French government announced that it would seize U.S. ships and treat as pirates those found guilty of serving the British. Arguing that Jay's Treaty undermined the commercial treaty of 1778, the French announced that they would no more recognize the principle of free ships–free goods. In essence, the limited maritime encounter known as the Quasi-War had commenced.

Although content to be out of the political arena, Washington rose to the call of duty once more when war with France threatened in 1798. He agreed to come out of retirement and assume command of a proposed army, with Hamilton to be second in command, although such an army never actually materialized. In December 1799, after a brief illness, Washington died and was buried in a vault on the grounds of Mount Vernon.

In the years since Washington's death, contemporaries and historians alike have evaluated his record. He was elevated to near-god status by such contemporaries as John Marshall and Parson Mason Weems, who wrote glowing and uncritical biographies, in many ways robbing

Washington of his human qualities, thus causing his life and influence on U.S. history to be oversimplified. Blurring fact and fiction, subsequent generations of Americans have found it difficult to think of Washington as a man who also had his faults. His enormously important role in U.S. history has not been fully understood or appreciated. Some later historians, reacting perhaps negatively to the hagiographic portrayals of the man, have tended to downplay him, attributing to Hamilton, Jefferson, and Madison the genius they believe that Washington lacked, and thus perhaps crediting to them a greater role than they actually deserved in establishing the republic. Such analyses and depictions of Washington do not do him justice. In many ways, what Washington did not do may be as important as what he did. He did not succumb to the temptation to be a military dictator, nor did he seek to create a hereditary monarchy. He did not rush into war with Great Britain, France, or Spain, trying diplomacy instead. His example of serving for only two terms is an illustration of the man's character in not coveting power. Although a patrician by U.S. standards, he feared the prospect of setting the precedent of a lifetime presidency. He genuinely believed in American exceptionalism, that the United States held a special role among the nations of the world, and that "the preservation of the sacred fire of liberty and the destiny of the republican model of government are...deeply, perhaps finally, staked on the experiment entrusted to the hands of the American people." He was committed to sustaining the republican experiment, believing that if he contributed to that experiment's demise, then his name would stand only as an "awful monument."

THOM M. ARMSTRONG

See also American Revolution; Articles of Confederation; France; Great Britain; Constitution; Hamilton, Alexander; Jefferson, Thomas; Gouverneur, Morris; Madison, James; Neutral Rights; Nootka Sound Affair; Jay's Treaty; Pinckney's Treaty; French Revolution; French and Indian War; Monroe, James; Orders in Council; Canada; Native Americans; Fur Treaty; Jay, John; Pickering, Timothy; Washington's Farewell Address

FURTHER READING

Abott, W.W., et al., eds. *The Papers of George Washington*, 24 vols. Charlottesville, Va., 1983–1996.

Alden, John R. *George Washington: A Biography*. Baton Rouge, La., 1984.

Bowman, Albert Hall. *The Struggle for Neutrality: Franco-American Diplomacy During the Federalist Era*. Knoxville, Tenn., 1974.

Brookhiser, Richard. *Founding Father: Rediscovering George Washington*. New York, 1996.

Cunliffe, Marcus. *George Washington: Man and Monument*. Boston, 1958.

DeConde, Alexander. *Entangling Alliance: Politics and Diplomacy under George Washington*. Durham, N.C., 1958.

Fitzpatrick, John C., ed. *Writings of George Washington*, 39 vols. 1931–1944. Reprint Westport, Conn., 1970.

Flexner, James T. *George Washington*, 4 vols. Boston, 1965–1972.

Freeman, Douglas Southall. *George Washington*, 7 vols. New York, 1948–1957.

McDonald, Forrest. *The Presidency of George Washington*. Lawrence, Kans., 1974.

Miller, John C. *The Federalist Era. 1789–1801*. New York, 1960.

Morgan, Edmund S. *The Genius of George Washington*. New York, 1980.

Phelps, Glenn A. *George Washington and American Constitutionalism*. Lawrence, Kans., 1993.

Schwartz, Barry. *George Washington: The Making of an American Symbol*. New York, 1987.

Sears, Louis M. *George Washington and the French Revolution*. 1960. Reprint Westport, Conn., 1973.

Sharp, James Roger. *American Politics in the Early Republic: The New Nation in Crisis*. New Haven, Conn., 1993.

Smith, Richard Norton. *Patriarch: George Washington and the New American Nation*. New York, 1993.

WASHINGTON, TREATY OF

See Alabama Claims

WASHINGTON CONFERENCE ON THE LIMITATION OF ARMAMENTS

The Washington Conference on the Limitation of Armaments, held in 1921–1922, produced three major treaties intended to curtail a naval arms race and stabilize the political situation in the Far East. The leading naval powers of the day, Great Britain, the United States, Japan, France, and Italy, agreed in the Five Power Treaty to limit their navies on the basis of ratios of total battleship tonnage. The Four Power Treaty established spheres of influence in the Pacific and conceded Japanese hegemony in the western part in exchange for Japan's assent to an inferior battleship ratio. The Nine Power Treaty enshrined the Open Door Policy in China, but was a weak attempt to promote China's territorial and administrative integrity at the expense of Great Power interests. Though initially diffusing tensions among Great Britain, the United States, and Japan, the treaties began to collapse in the late 1920s when the Japanese abandoned cooperation with the West to respond unilaterally to the Nationalist unification of China and when German rearmament prompted the French to resume unrestricted naval construction.

EMILY O. GOLDMAN

See also China; Japan; Open Door Policy; Spheres of Influence

FURTHER READING

Buckley, Thomas H. *The United States and the Washington Conference, 1921-1922*. Knoxville, Tenn., 1970.

Goldman, Emily O. *Sunken Treaties: Naval Arms Control Between the Wars*. University Park, Pa., 1994.

Sprout, Harold, and Margaret Sprout. *Toward a New Order of Sea Power: American Naval Policy and the World Scene 1918-1922*. Princeton, N.J., 1940.

WASHINGTON NAVAL CONFERENCE

See Washington Conference on the Limitation of Armaments

WASHINGTON'S FAREWELL ADDRESS

The retirement statement on 17 September 1796 of President George Washington, who sought through this document to state enduring foreign policy principles and to influence the 1796 elections in favor of the Federalists. Tired after many years of public service, apprehensive about the development of partisan politics, fearful that the ongoing formal alliance with France would entangle the young United States in war, and increasingly buffeted by personal and political attacks, President Washington once again sought to return to his beloved Mount Vernon estate and the country life of a Virginia planter. He had completed nearly two terms as the nation's chief executive, and now sought a way of informing the country that he would not be a candidate for a third term as president.

Although he had previously planned to give a speech, Washington decided instead to offer a written announcement to one of his favorite newspapers, Philadelphia's *Daily American Advertiser*. The original draft had been written by James Madison as a valedictory to the country, but the revised draft reflected overwhelmingly the influence of the Federalist partisan, Alexander Hamilton. More than simply a statement to the American people announcing Washington's retirement from politics, the Farewell Address afforded him the occasion to warn the nation against foreign, primarily French, intrigues, and to swing the election to the Federalists and John Adams.

The president's last two years in office were extremely unpleasant, particularly because of criticism he had borne over Jay's Treaty. With England having joined a European coalition in war against revolutionary France in 1793, Republicans condemned what they saw as a pro-British move at the expense of the United States's alliance with France of 1778. Two French diplomats, Joseph Fauchet and Pierre Adet, intervened in American politics by attempting to rally Americans against the treaty. Unsuccessful at preventing the treaty's ratification and implementation, Adet worked to prevent Washington's reelection in 1796, and to promote the candidacy of Thomas Jefferson, who was pro-French.

In his Farewell Address, Washington warned against the evil of partisan spirit that "opens the door to foreign influence and corruption." With France specifically in mind, the outgoing president justified his neutrality policy during the Anglo-French war by arguing that "It is our true policy to steer clear of permanent alliances with any portion of the foreign world...." However, he did leave open the option that "we may safely trust to temporary alliances for extraordinary emergencies."

Timed to influence the outcome of the upcoming election, the Farewell Address clearly represented a partisan Federalist campaign statement. Though hard-pressed to come up with an alternative candidate to replace Washington, Federalists ultimately backed Vice President John Adams. Republicans, supported by Adet, went to work for Jefferson. Federalists shrewdly portrayed themselves as the party of patriotism, while depicting Jefferson as leader of the party that was being duped by a foreign power, the very kind of danger about which Washington had warned in his Farewell Address. Adams narrowly defeated Jefferson.

Although the Farewell Address further intensified political partisanship in the country, its longest lasting influence was in the area of foreign affairs. Little did the retiring president know that his words regarding "permanent alliances" would leave such a powerful imprint for generations to come. His recommendation became the cornerstone of American "isolationist" sentiment for approximately 150 years.

THOM M. ARMSTRONG

See also Adams, John; France; Hamilton, Alexander; Isolationism; Jay's Treaty; Jefferson, Thomas; Madison, James; Washington, George

FURTHER READING

Bemis, Samuel Flagg. "Washington's Farewell Address: A Foreign Policy of Independence." *American Historical Review* 39 (1934): 250–268.

DeConde, Alexander. *Entangling Alliance: Politics and Diplomacy Under George Washington*. Durham, N.C., 1958.

———. "Washington's Farewell, the French Alliance, and the Election of 1796." *Mississippi Valley Historical Review* 48 (1957): 641–658.

Gilbert, Felix. *To the Farewell Address*. Princeton, N.J., 1961.

Kaufman, Burton I., ed. *Washington's Farewell Address: The View from the 20th Century*. Chicago, 1969.

WATERGATE

(1972–1974)

A scandal that triggered a constitutional crisis, led to the resignation of Richard M. Nixon as president of the United States, and in some ways altered the direction of U.S. foreign policy. Watergate represented a complex set of interrelated events. The break-in at the headquarters of the Democratic National Committee at the Watergate office complex in Washington, D.C. on the night of 17–18 June 1972 by five Cuban-American employees of the Committee to Reelect the President (CREEP), several of whom had previously worked for the Central Intelligence Agency, led to the disclosure of efforts by Nixon and his subordinates to disrupt the activities of their domestic political adversaries. Much of this campaign of "dirty tricks" stemmed from the Nixon administration's desire to confound opponents of its conduct of foreign policy, especially toward Vietnam. Several of the Watergate burglars had been employed by White House counselor John Ehrlichman in the summer of 1971 to spy on Daniel Ellsberg after this former Department of Defense official released copies of the secret "Pentagon Papers" to the *New York Times*. In the two years after the Watergate break-in, investigations by journalists and congressional committees revealed that Nixon had participated directly in efforts to conceal White House involvement and had tried to mislead official investigators. Nixon's obstruction of justice became one of three articles of impeachment approved by the House Committee on the Judiciary in July 1974. Nixon resigned on 9 August of that year rather than face almost certain conviction by the senate in an impeachment trial.

Watergate disrupted the Nixon administration's foreign policies. As Nixon became more deeply enmeshed in Watergate, progress stalled on détente between the United States and the Soviet Union. Watergate also restricted U.S. freedom of action during the October 1973 Middle Eastern war. Congress passed the War Powers Resolution, which sharply contradicted Nixon's attempts to send troops into foreign combat, in November 1973, shortly after some of the most damaging revelations of presidential malfeasance were made public. Partly as a result of Watergate, the United States did not provide South Vietnam with all the military assistance it expected after the signing of the Paris Peace Agreement of 1973. In general, the Watergate crisis exacerbated further the increasing distrust between the executive and legislative branches.

ROBERT D. SCHULZINGER

See also Congress; Nixon, Richard Milhous; Presidency

FURTHER READING

Ambrose, Stephen E. *Nixon*. 3 vol. New York, 1987–1991.
Kutler, Stanley I. *The Wars of Watergate*. New York, 1990.

WEBB-POMERENE ACT
(1918)

Before the United States entered World War I, European adversaries of Germany attempted to expand their well-established industrial and financial conglomerates in order to isolate Germany economically. The United States feared that it would be excluded from European markets at a time when its industry was becoming very competitive. U.S. laws, including particularly the Sherman Antitrust Act, had prohibited U.S. firms from creating conglomerates of their own, and many U.S. manufacturers thought that European plans demanded a response.

In 1916, the newly-formed Federal Trade Commission called for a suspension of antitrust law in the case of U.S. firms trading and operating overseas. It envisioned the creation of U.S. conglomerates and spheres of overseas operation capable of competing with the largest international companies. A series of laws—including the Clayton Act of 1916, the Webb-Pomerene Act of 1918, and the Edge Act of 1919—were passed as a result of this report. Altogether, they allowed for the first massive wave of direct U.S. foreign investment and cartel behavior, a pattern which became typical of U.S. international business after World War II.

The Webb-Pomerene Act provided for companies engaged in similar activities to collaborate in entering foreign markets through joint ventures, coordinated pricing, and cooperative marketing strategies. Companies could, for example, agree to divide up foreign markets and set artificially high prices without fear of antitrust prosecution at home. While ostensibly aimed at smaller companies, the law was of greatest benefit to larger corporations like U.S. Steel and General Electric, who moved overseas with a vengeance. U.S. firms were ultimately able to create "little U.S.As" overseas, complete with industrial, financial, and research services at their disposal.

By 1939, the Department of Justice believed U.S. business connections abroad undermined U.S. security as World War II got underway. After the war, economists criticized Webb-Pomerene as a relic of 1930s-style American protectionism and urged its repeal. In the mid-1990s, echoes of Webb-Pomerene calls for greater collaboration between business and government in order to counteract the strength of "Japan, Inc."

KENDALL W. STILES

See also Multinational Corporations

FURTHER READING

Parrini, Carl P. *Heir to Empire: United States Economic Diplomacy, 1916–1923*. Pittsburgh, Pa., 1969.

WEBSTER, DANIEL
(*b.* 18 January 1782; *d.* 24 October 1852)

Senator from Massachusetts (1827–1841 and 1845–1850) and two-term secretary of state (1841–1843, 1850–1852).

Born in Salisbury, New Hampshire, he graduated from Dartmouth College in 1801 and was admitted to the bar in 1805. As a member of Congress from New Hampshire (1813–1817), he opposed the War of 1812, even to the point of voting against taxes to support it. He became a leading constitutional lawyer and served again in the U.S. House of Representatives from Massachusetts (1823–1827). As a senator and member of the Whig party, Webster became a noted orator against sectionalism and states' rights arguments.

Under three presidents (William Henry Harrison, John Tyler, and Millard Fillmore), Webster became the dominant voice in the formulation of American foreign policy. In 1841, Webster made an enduring contribution to international law when he fashioned the doctrine of self-defense in connection with the *Caroline* affair. Perhaps his greatest achievement came in 1842 with the Webster-Ashburton Treaty. This agreement not only promoted peace with Great Britain and possibly averted a third Anglo-American war, but it also contained a provision for U.S. and British warships to cooperate in suppressing the African slave trade. It also contained an extradition article that became the model for subsequent treaties. In a precedent-setting directive of 2 February 1842, Webster extended the protection of the federal government to U.S. missionaries evangelizing in foreign lands. On 30 December of that year he also extended the principles of the Monroe Doctrine to the Hawai'ian Islands in what came to be known as the "Tyler Doctrine." On 8 May 1843 Webster concluded his first term as secretary of state by writing instructions to Caleb Cushing that led to the Treaty of Wangxia (Wanghia).

In his second term as secretary of state, Webster primarily focused on domestic affairs. To gain acceptance of the Compromise of 1850 as a final resolution of regional differences between the North and the South, he used foreign relations to promote national unity. The provocative Hülsemann letter of 21 December 1850, trumpeting U.S. support for Hungarians seeking freedom from Austria and boastfully contrasting American greatness with the insignificance of the Austrian empire, is the classic manifestation of Webster's manipulation of the politics of foreign policy. In 1851, he secured the release of more than 150 American filibusters captured in Narciso Lopez's ill-fated expedition against Cuba by graciously apologizing to the Spanish government. In 1851–1852 he continued the strategy of commercial expansion in the Pacific and East Asia, which he had devised in the 1840s, by forcefully reiterating the Tyler Doctrine and initiating the 1853 mission of Commodore Matthew C. Perry to Japan. This expedition completed what Webster called the "last link" in a "great chain" of global maritime navigation. Finally, Webster contributed to improvements in the Department of State by issuing reports in 1852 that led to the creation of the position of assistant secretary of

state in 1853 and to the adoption of a graduated scale of diplomatic salaries in 1855. During both of his terms as secretary of state, Webster's approach to international politics was that of a calculating nationalist who emphasized commercial expansion and internal unity.

KENNETH E. SHEWMAKER

See also Caroline Affair; Cuba; Cushing, Caleb; Filibusters; Hawai'i; International Law; Missionaries; Monroe Doctrine; Perry, Matthew Calbraith; Slave Trade and Slavery; Tyler, John; Wangxia, Treaty of; Webster-Ashburton Treaty

FURTHER READING

Jones, Howard. *To the Webster-Ashburton Treaty: A Study in Anglo-American Relations, 1783-1843.* Chapel Hill, N.C, 1977.

———. "Daniel Webster: The Diplomatist." In *Daniel Webster: "The Completest Man,"* edited by Kenneth E. Shewmaker, Hanover, N.H, 1990.

Shewmaker, Kenneth E., et al., eds. *The Papers of Daniel Webster, Diplomatic Papers.* 2 vols. Hanover, N.H, 1983-87.

WEBSTER-ASHBURTON TREATY

The Anglo-American agreement signed on 9 August 1842 that resolved most differences between Great Britain and the United States and paved the way for a long-lasting rapprochement. Daniel Webster and British special envoy Lord Ashburton (Alexander Baring) approved this important international agreement. The Webster-Ashburton Treaty ended a dangerous dispute over the northeastern boundary between British Canada and the United States, settled most of the other issues between Great Britain and the United States, improved relations with the country that had the greatest capacity to injure the United States economically and militarily, and may have averted a third Anglo-American war.

In addition to drawing the line between Maine and New Brunswick (Canada), the Webster-Ashburton Treaty established an international boundary along the northwestern frontier up to the Lake of the Woods. While Webster conceded 7,000 of the 12,000 miles in dispute in the northeast, Ashburton relinquished the Indian stream country at the head of the Connecticut River in New Hampshire, Fort Montgomery on Lake Champlain, which mistakenly had been erected on Canadian soil, and 6,500 square miles in the northwest. Great Britain and the United States also agreed to a convention in which both countries promised to maintain independent naval forces off the west coast of Africa which would cooperate in suppressing the African slave trade. Article 10, which remained in force until 1935, became the model for extradition treaties between the United States and other countries. It provided for the extradition of individuals charged with such non-political

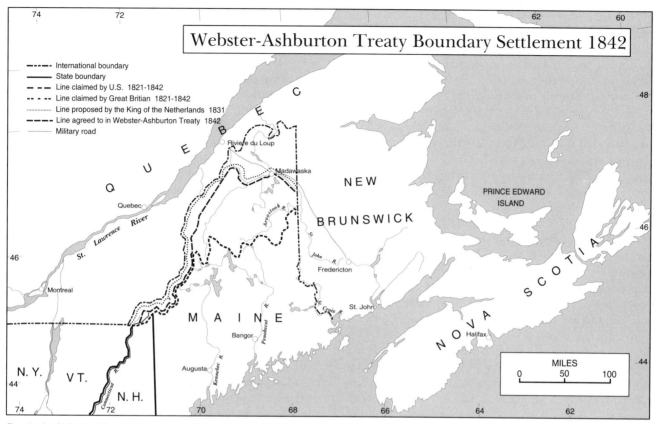

Webster-Ashburton Treaty Boundary Settlement 1842

International boundary
State boundary
Line claimed by U.S. 1821–1842
Line claimed by Great Britian 1821–1842
Line proposed by the King of the Netherlands 1831
Line agreed to in Webster-Ashburton Treaty 1842
Military road

crimes as forgery and murder. In supplemental correspondence accompanying the treaty, Ashburton and Webster finessed the *Caroline* and *Creole* disputes. The former stemmed from the destruction of a U.S. vessel and killing of a U.S. citizen by Canadian troops at Schlosser, New York in 1837, and the latter erupted from the freeing, by British authorities at Nassau in the Bahamas, of American slaves who had mutinied in 1841. Webster also appended to the treaty a letter protesting strongly the British practice of impressment. While the document did not resolve that issue, it helped win domestic acceptance of the agreement by appealing to national pride. Because Ashburton's instructions did not allow him to compromise on the Oregon Question, Webster did not achieve his stated goal of resolving all of the differences between the two countries. Aside from Oregon, however, the Webster-Ashburton Treaty left little for Great Britain and the United States to quarrel about.

As the only international agreement in U.S. history in which the United States conceded a substantial amount of territory that it claimed as its own, about 5,000 square miles in the northeast, the Webster-Ashburton Treaty drew criticism from expansionists. Webster also sparked controversy for using funds from the secret service account to finance a propaganda campaign to gain domestic approval of the accord. Webster himself, however, believed that in advancing the cause of international peace he had registered his greatest achievement as secretary of state.

KENNETH E. SHEWMAKER

See also Ashburton, Alexander Baring; Canada; Caroline Affair; Creole Affair; Extradition; Great Britain; Impressment; Oregon Question; Slave Trade and Slavery; Webster, Daniel

FURTHER READING

Jones, Howard. *To the Webster-Ashburton Treaty: A Study in Anglo-American Relations, 1783–1843*. Chapel Hill, N.C., 1973.

Merk, Frederick. *Fruits of Propaganda in the Tyler Administration*. Cambridge, Mass., 1971.

Shewmaker, Kenneth E., ed. *The Papers of Daniel Webster: Diplomatic Papers, Vol. 1, 1841–1843*. Hanover, N.H. and London, England, 1983.

WEINBERGER, CASPAR WILLARD

(*b.* 18 August 1917)

Secretary of defense, 1981–1987, during the nation's largest peacetime military buildup and the beginning of the end of the Cold War.

Born in San Francisco, Weinberger was graduated from Harvard College and Harvard Law School. During World War II, he served on General Douglas MacArthur's intelligence staff. Returning to California, he became active in the bar and Republican state politics. As governor, Ronald Reagan appointed him state finance director in 1968. Beginning in 1970, Weinberger served in the Nixon administration, mainly as budget director (where his budget slashing earned him the nickname "Cap the Knife").

As Pentagon chief in the 1980s, Weinberger played a major role in shaping the Reagan administration's hardline approach to the Soviet Union. In addition to presiding over a $2 trillion military buildup, he was a leading champion of the administration's Strategic Defense Initiative, a proposed, futuristic, space-based weapons system.

Weinberger's positions involved him in endless wrangling with Reagan's secretary of state, George Shultz. But this was not a simply hawk vs. dove split. While the defense chief did resist any efforts to cut the military budget and was more suspicious of arms-control negotiations than Shultz, he was notably more cautious than the secretary of state about the use of American military power in regional wars and in retaliation against terrorist attacks.

Weinberger opposed Shultz on the desirability of using U.S. forces to respond to Middle East terrorism. He also argued against the deployment of a Marine "peacekeeping" force in Lebanon as well as the use of U.S. forces in Central America. Although Weinberger supported the invasion of Grenada and the navy's presence in the Persian Gulf during the Iran-Iraq War, he (and Shultz) argued against the Iran arms-for-hostages initiative proposed by CIA director William Casey. In 1992 a special prosecutor obtained an indictment against Weinberger for lying to Congress in denying any knowledge of the arms-for-hostages plan involved in the Iran-Contra affair, but he was pardoned before trial by President George Bush.

The feud between Weinberger and Shultz reflected personal and policy differences in the administration. Reagan often relied on Weinberger, a continuing hardliner against the Soviet Union, to counter Shultz's more moderate views. The President's tendency to side with one and then the other of these men helped account for some of the Reagan administration's erratic lurches in foreign policy.

JOHN WHITECLAY CHAMBERS II

See also Defense, U.S. Department of; Reagan, Ronald Wilson

FURTHER READING

Weinberger, Caspar W. *Fighting for Peace: Seven Critical Years in the Pentagon.* New York, 1990.

WELLES, BENJAMIN SUMNER

(*b.* 14 October 1892; *d.* 1961)

Best known as a close foreign policy adviser to President Franklin Roosevelt and an ardent advocate of internationalism in the 1940s, Welles's influence in some areas exceeded that of Secretary of State Cordell Hull, and he played an especially key role in U.S.–Latin American policy. His greatest achievement was most likely his help in drafting the Atlantic Charter in 1941, which laid the foundation for the postwar economic and political order evident in the United Nations Organization and the Bretton Woods System.

Welles was a Groton schoolmate of Roosevelt's and went on to complete degrees at Harvard, Columbia and Brown. He entered diplomatic service in 1915, serving as secretary of the U.S. embassy in Tokyo, Japan, until 1917, when he took a similar position in Buenos Aires, Argentina (1917–1919), thus beginning his specialization on Latin American issues. In 1920–1921 he served as assistant chief in the State Department's Latin American Affairs Division; in 1921–1922 he became its chief. In 1922 he was sent to the Dominican Republic, in 1924 to Honduras, and in 1929 to the Dominican Republic again to assist in economic and political negotiations to stabilize those nations. In early 1933 Welles became assistant secretary of state. As the principal U.S. policy-maker on hemispheric issues, Welles advanced the cause of the Good Neighbor policy which envisioned a new, more respectful relationship between the United States and Latin America. But, during the brief stint as Ambassador to Cuba in 1933–1934, he plotted to overthrow reigning dictator Gerardo Machado—a move which led to the emergence, first, of a short-lived nationalist regime under Ramón Grace San Martín and, finally, a military government under Fulgencio Batista. Welles did not hesitate to wield U.S. power both in the form of an aggressive diplomacy and deployment of warships along the coastline. In 1937 Welles became undersecretary of state for Latin American affairs.

In early 1941, one of Welles's rivals, former ambassador to the Soviet Union William Bullitt, told President Roosevelt that Welles had publicly made homosexual approaches to porters on a train trip, and that he should be fired from the Department of State. U.S. leaders had been aware of Welles's homosexuality, but Roosevelt resisted discharging his close friend. Welles was fired in 1943, however, after a serious dispute with Secretary Hull. Welles went on to write significant treatises on international issues, notably *Where Are We Heading?* in 1946 and *Seven Decisions That Shaped History* in 1951.

KENDALL W. STILES

See also Atlantic Charter; Bretton Woods; Cuba; Good Neighbor Policy; Hull, Cordell

FURTHER READING

Gellman, Irwin F. *Secret Affairs: Franklin Roosevelt, Cordell Hull, and Sumner Welles.* Baltimore, Md., 1995.

Welles, Sumner. *Naboth's Vineyard*. New York, 1928.
———. *Seven Decisions That Shaped History*. New York, 1951.
———. *Where Are We Heading?* New York, 1946.

WEST FLORIDA CONTROVERSY

See Florida

WESTMORELAND, WILLIAM

(*b*. 26 March 1914)

A native of Spartanburg, South Carolina, William Westmoreland's career in the U.S. Army (1936–1972) spanned three major wars: World War II, Korea, and Vietnam. Indeed, as the ramrod backed commander of U.S. forces in Vietnam (1964–1968), he personified the war.

Westmoreland ("Westy" to his friends) graduated from West Point in 1936 and was commissioned in artillery. The North Africa campaign (1942–1943) against German General Erwin Rommel introduced him to war. He served with General George Patton in Sicily, and he was later awarded the Legion of Honor for his heroism at D-Day. It was the Korean War, however, that left an indelible impression on him. As a brigadier general in command of an airborne division, he saw entire U.S. units buckle under communist assault. His most visible postwar assignment came in 1962 as superintendent at West Point. President Lyndon Johnson personally appointed Westmoreland, a classic conventional soldier with a reassuring southern accent, to be his commander in Vietnam.

A master of organization and logistics, he supervised a troop buildup that rose from 16,000 advisers to an expeditionary corps of over one-half million soldiers. Though optimistic in public, Westmoreland knew it was going to be a long war and worried about domestic support. Restricted to waging war in South Vietnam, he adopted a strategy of attrition to break the will of his communist adversaries. Despite inflicting heavy losses on enemy forces from 1965 to 1967, the country-wide communist Tet Offensive of early 1968, which was in fact beaten back, bankrupted this strategy. Johnson withdrew from the presidential race in March, and Westmoreland was brought home in July to become the Army Chief of Staff, a post he held until his retirement in 1972.

In 1976 he published his memoir, *A Soldier Reports*, a tightly-reasoned defense of his war strategy. Nevertheless, the political nuances of this Asian revolution eluded both his analysis and military command. His long held desire to carry the war into North Vietnam proper was never acceptable to President Johnson and his key advisers, who worried about such a move triggering an intervention from China. Ten years after writing his memoir,

he was accused by a CBS television documentary of deliberately undercounting and covering up the true size of communist forces prior to the Tet Offensive of 1968. Many in the foreign policy community came to his defense, and, in a libel suit against CBS, the network publicly apologized to the general, even though it was not required to pay him any damages.

TIMOTHY J. LOMPERIS

See also Tet Offensive; Vietnam War

FURTHER READING

Adler, Renata. *Reckless Disregard: Westmoreland vs. CBS*. New York, 1986.
Westmoreland, Gen. William C. *A Soldier Reports*. New York, 1976.

WHALING

The harvesting of whales for their blubber, oil, or meat. From the earliest days of colonization, Americans have pursued whales on the high seas, joining in a worldwide hunt that steadily drove the great sea mammals toward extinction. Sailing from towns such as New Bedford, Massachusetts, whalers helped to explore remote parts of the world and chart the oceans for future traders. They also brought back raw materials that were used for food and industry. For most of their history, however, whalers faced no regulations, and they systematically overhunted the areas where whales congregated. By the early-twentieth century, many species were in decline, as was the whaling industry itself.

Led by Norway and Great Britain, twenty nations— including the United States—concerned about declining whale populations met in Geneva in 1931 and produced the Convention for the Regulation of Whaling. Responding to the unsustainable killing of female whales, the diplomats agreed to limit killing to adult males. They also prohibited killing of right whales, which had been hunted into commercial extinction, and encouraged all participants to reduce waste. In order to improve scientific understanding, whaling nations had to submit all relevant data to a central authority in Oslo. This convention had little effect because there was no incentive to protect whales, enforcement was difficult, and the whales' wide-ranging aquatic habits made them difficult to study.

In 1937, the United States and eight other whaling nations reconvened in London and signed the Agreement for the Regulation of Whaling, which put some teeth into the 1931 agreement. New rules included a ban on catching grey whales, which were nearly extinct, minimum size limits for all of the baleen whales, a limited open season, and zones where whaling would be prohibited. With the exception of the Soviet Union, ostracized because of Western loathing of communism, most of the whaling nations participated, but the outbreak of the war prevented any assessment of the success of the regulations.

After World War II, whaling returned to the diplomatic agenda, and this time the United States took the lead. Conservation was still a consideration, but now the budding Cold War influenced U.S. policy. U.S. leaders saw whaling as a means to feed Japan, which the United States had occupied after the war. In a protocol signed in late 1945, the Western Allies created the now infamous blue whale unit system, which was supposed to place a global bag limit on whaling. Under this scheme, one blue whale was equal to two fin whales, two and a half humpbacks, or six sei whales. Despite the evidence that the whales were endangered, diplomats set the total blue whale unit quota for 1946 at 16,000.

U.S. diplomats also began work on the International Convention for the Regulation of Whaling, which fifteen nations signed in December 1946. This treaty established the largely ineffective International Whaling Commission (IWC), which proved ineffective in regulating the industry. The IWC charter allows any nation that votes against a regulation to exempt itself from that rule. With such weak protection, the decline of world whale populations and whale harvest continued. Beginning in the 1970s, the environmental movement brought pressure on the IWC to halt whaling, and the United States took the lead in persuading Japan, Norway, Iceland, and the Soviet Union to restrict their whaling activities. In 1986 the IWC finally instituted a moratorium on whaling, but Japan, Norway, and Russia still occasionally catch whales, claiming a need for scientific research.

KURK DORSEY

See also Fisheries; Fur Trade; Sealing; Wildlife

FURTHER READING

Francis, Daniel. *A History of World Whaling.* New York, 1990.
Starbuck, Alexander. *History of the American Whale Fishery.* Secaucus, N.J., 1989.

WHITE, HARRY DEXTER

(*b.* 9 October 1892; *d.* 16 August 1948)

U.S. specialist on international economic policy who helped organize the International Monetary Fund (IMF) and the International Bank for Reconstruction and Development (IBRD or World Bank). Born in Boston, White trained as an economist at Stanford and Harvard. In 1934, a year before receiving his Ph.D. from Harvard, he took a position with the Department of the Treasury, becoming the Director of Monetary Research and, in 1942, assistant secretary of treasury. A staunch supporter of international cooperation, he worked with the British

government to construct a postwar international financial and monetary system, establishing the IMF. White also drafted much of "the Morgenthau Plan," a U.S. policy to deindustrialize postwar Germany. Suffering from a heart condition, he left the government in 1947. In 1948, before the U.S. House of Representatives Committee on Un-American Activities, former communists Elizabeth Bentley and Whittaker Chambers accused White of being an "elite" spy, who had been specially recruited to infiltrate the New Deal administration of President Franklin Roosevelt. White died of a heart attack while vehemently denying the charges. Although never proved or disproved, allegations of White's role as a communist agent have persisted to this day.

JAMES L. GORMLEY

See also International Bank for Reconstruction and Development; International Monetary Fund; Morgenthau Plan

FURTHER READING

Rees, David. *Harry Dexter White: A Study in Paradox.* New York, 1974.
White, Harry Dexter. *The French International Accounts, 1880-1913.* Boston, 1933.

WHO

See World Health Organization

WILDLIFE

Includes all nondomesticated animals, and the subject of diplomacy when species of interest to U.S. citizens have become endangered, usually because economic activity threatens them. This article focuses on those species that generally have not been thought of as commodities, namely birds and land mammals, as opposed to fish and aquatic mammals, such as whales and seals, which have often been the object of intense human exploitation. The Department of State usually has taken an active role in protecting wildlife only when the species in question have economic importance. On occasion the business community has opposed initiatives which it perceives as threatening, but the main obstacle to focusing on wildlife has been a perception among diplomats that environmental diplomacy is not a matter of national security. Therefore, the scope and results of wildlife treaties have often depended on the input of private citizens and government scientists. Groups such as the National Audubon Society and Greenpeace have played an active and consistent role in promoting international wildlife protection.

Although U.S. diplomats have been subject to pressure from domestic interest groups on wildlife issues, the content and fate of many of these treaties also have been linked to greater trends in U.S. foreign policy. It has been much easier to craft wildlife protection treaties with a friendly neighbor, such as Canada, than with a frequent rival, such as Mexico. Wildlife treaties have been a part of concerted efforts to improve relations with other countries, such as the Good Neighbor Policy with Latin America and the pursuit of détente with the Soviet Union. Although wildlife protection, or environmental protection in general, has never been a central goal of U.S. diplomacy, U.S. diplomats have been willing to advance the issue so long as it does not hinder basic foreign policy objectives.

There have been two basic types of wildlife protection treaties. In the first group are those that involve just a few countries dealing with a limited problem. Since the nation's founding, the United States has signed agreements with its neighbors regarding fisheries, northern fur seals, migratory birds, polar bears, and caribou. The second group includes multilateral conventions that deal with large-scale problems of habitat preservation or endangered-species protection. The United States has not uniformly supported such treaties, although it generally has promoted them. The small-scale treaties are more manageable for all involved parties, but they are by nature incapable of handling global environmental problems.

One common thread linking all of the treaties has been the need to regulate international common property. Because human borders bisect the natural migration routes and ranges of so many species, it is rare that a valuable species remains entirely under the jurisdiction of one country. Species that live in many nations or in international waters cannot be the property of any one state but are in practice the shared property of those who exploit them. Such an arrangement encourages destructive competition. The citizens of every nation that has access to a common stock of valuable species have no reason to show forbearance in their harvesting of those animals, because any animal left behind by one person will be taken by another. Unless all parties agree to a common set of restrictions, the species in question will be driven to extinction by unfettered competition.

One of the great challenges for diplomats and treaty advocates has been to reconcile the impulse to guard the national interest with the necessity of yielding sovereignty over an internal natural resource. But successful conservation of transboundary wildlife requires that all participating parties surrender some freedom of action, either through agreeing to pass legislation or by joining an international regulatory agency. When cooperation and trust are not present, the resulting treaty is usually weak and the regulatory agency powerless.

Migratory Birds

The first U.S. wildlife agreement came out of an attempt by Progressive Era conservationists to circumvent the states' rights principles of the Constitution. Spurred by a decline in native birds throughout North America, conservationists created a federal law in 1913 that limited migratory birdhunting to certain times and species, especially ducks, geese, and some shorebirds. Fearing that the Supreme Court would strike down the law because of its restriction of state power, conservationists in Canada and the United States led a drive that resulted in the Migratory Bird Treaty of 1916. Because Canada already had adequate bird protection laws and U.S. sentiment favored similar laws, the treaty was as much a legal maneuver as an attempt to change national behavior. In 1920, in Missouri v. Holland, the Supreme Court upheld the treaty and its enabling legislation as legitimate acts of the federal government.

At almost every point along the way, conservationists and scientists took the lead in negotiating the agreement and creating public pressure on the government to expedite the treaty's progress. The terms created a framework within which the Canadian and U.S. governments had to operate, thus allowing some flexibility while maintaining the goal of bird protection. Because there was no strong opposition based on economics, conservationists were able to dominate the government's position on the treaty and subsequent legislation. It should be noted that the treaty failed to protect predators, piscivores, and many seedeaters, because at the time conservationists had a limited concept of which species were valuable.

At the same time that they were working on the bird treaty with Canada, U.S. conservationists called for similar treaties with Latin American countries, based on the knowledge that many "American" birds wintered south of the Rio Grande River. After years of fruitless negotiations, U.S. and Mexican diplomats and scientists finally worked out the Convention for the Protection of Migratory Birds and Game Mammals in 1936, helped partially by the Good Neighbor Policy and the intercession of the popular ambassador Josephus Daniels. Like the 1916 treaty, this agreement basically provided a list of protected species with general rules on how to protect them. It was an advance only in that it included a few more species and extended protection for them into Mexico. In 1972 the two nations signed an addendum that expanded the number of species protected by the treaty.

The twenty-year gap between the Canadian and Mexican bird treaties demonstrated the importance of trust in negotiating wildlife protection treaties. In the 1910s, U.S. and Canadian diplomats allowed government scientists and respected conservationists to work out the migratory bird treaty because they could foresee no negative consequences of doing so. The subsequent agreement broke new ground in diplomacy. At the same time, U.S. diplomats became reluctant to sanction discussions with Mexico that might imply diplomatic recognition at a time when the Mexican Revolution had led to a severing of ties between Mexico and the United States, and U.S. scientists believed that no Latin American country was ready to enforce a migratory bird law. For their part, Mexican diplomats viewed the migratory bird treaty as a bargaining chip to gain concessions on fishing disputes. When the two sides finally came to terms they did little more than recapitulate the 1916 treaty.

In 1940 the United States led the Pan-American Union (later the Organization of American States) into the Convention on Nature Protection and Wild Life Preservation in the Western Hemisphere. This agreement expanded on the bird treaties by allowing each signatory nation to list plant and animal species that were in need of special protection. In addition, the treaty required each of the nineteen signatory nations to set aside areas equivalent to national parks, national forests, and wildlife refuges. U.S. scientists and conservationists played a leading role in writing and lobbying for the treaty, which was an attempt to export U.S. conservation standards to all of the hemisphere in one step.

The Western Hemisphere Convention was the first modern wildlife protection treaty in that it included the ecological concept of habitat protection. The great weakness of the first two migratory bird treaties was the exclusive focus on regulating hunting. Around 1900 some scientists concluded that hunting laws were irrelevant so long as people were free to cut down forests and drain wetlands. By the 1920s they also recognized that birds needed habitat at the southern end of their migratory routes, as well as important stopover points along the way. Through the 1940 agreement, U.S. conservationists tried to use this combined knowledge to preserve wide swaths of habitat as well as regulate hunting.

The recognition that an "American" bird might spend months in Mexico, Venezuela, or Argentina forced diplomats, scientists, and conservationists to build a broad, hemispheric agreement. Although the Pan-American Union was the official sponsor, the United States determined the terms of the convention and took the necessary steps to bring in most of the member states. This strong U.S. leadership—which stemmed both from the obvious balance of power in the hemisphere and the relative beneficence of the Good Neighbor Policy—was necessary to prevent dissent that might have weakened the terms of the treaty.

Environmentalism and Multilateral Treaties

After World War II it became impossible for one nation to forge such a wide-ranging treaty. Multilateral treaties are the best way to force uniformity of protective regulations around the globe, but multilateral negotiations often yield poor compromises. It is likely that scientists from many countries will not be able to agree with certainty on the data, let alone the best set of regulations. Political differences alone will cause more disharmony, and economic competition can drive wedges between traditional allies. Especially after decolonization created dozens of new states, which often had fundamental disagreements with the Western democracies, major multilateral negotiations developed into clashes between blocs.

The yielding of sovereignty over domestic policy has been a central point of contention between the blocs. As wildlife protection has become more closely tied to politics and economics, the ability of scientists and environmentalists to shape the agreements has lessened. Business leaders in the industrialized countries have been more likely to see threats to their interests in far-reaching multilateral treaties than in the more conservative treaties of the pre-1940 era. Developing countries have feared that the industrialized countries will place the burden of environmental protection on them without providing economic compensation. In addition, the Cold War made East-West cooperation difficult even when Soviet and U.S. scientists agreed on the need for collaboration.

Taking advantage of détente, the rapidly growing environmental movement made itself felt in a number of treaties early in the 1970s. The first Earth Day, a celebration of the biosphere on 25 April 1970, indicated that environmentalist ideas had become widespread and a challenge to the superpowers' ideologies. Like their conservationist predecessors from the Progressive Era, environmentalists became masters at mobilizing public support and lobbying governments. While conservationists worked with and were often part of the government, environmentalists usually have been in conflict with the government. This tension has often made domestic negotiations as critical as international ones.

The United Nations (UN) played an important role in facilitating the multilateral conferences to protect wildlife. It was perhaps the only international organization with the credibility and capability to bring a wide array of governments into one forum. Like the rest of the world, the United Nations focused on the environment in the late 1960s and early 1970s. At the UN Conference on the Human Environment, held in Stockholm, Sweden, in the summer of 1972, delegates took steps to protect the environment and raise awareness around the world about threats to the biosphere. Out of this conference came the UN Environment Program (UNEP), which has subsequently taken on administrative roles for many efforts to protect wildlife. In addition, the conferees established broad principles for governments to follow in protecting endangered species.

The first post–Earth Day wildlife treaty was the Convention on Wetlands of International Importance Especially as Waterfowl Habitat, signed at Ramsar, Iran, on 2 February 1971. Known as the Ramsar Agreement, it combined the best elements of previous bird protection efforts with the worst features of multilateral conventions. The terms of the treaty required each signatory nation to designate at least one wetland as a Ramsar site, based on its value to the global environment, especially migratory waterfowl. The agreement also emphasized that each nation retained sovereignty over its Ramsar sites, including the right to reduce or eliminate them. Therefore, the treaty was more of a litmus test for a government's environmental rhetoric than a major step forward. The United States withheld its accession to the treaty until 1985.

The Convention for the Protection of the World Cultural and Natural Heritage of 23 November 1972 expanded and improved upon the core idea of the Ramsar Agreement. Like the wetlands accord, this convention required each signatory power to designate areas of global importance—including habitat for endangered species—that required protection. The negotiators recognized that many nations need an incentive to withhold such sites from economic development, and they established a fund that countries could tap to finance their protective efforts. In practice, the wealthy Western nations that pushed an environmentalist agenda were obliged to help the poorer nations that contained many of the relevant treasures.

Following up on the heritage agreement, the United States helped lead the Convention on International Trade in Endangered Species of Wild Fauna and Flora (CITES), signed on 3 March 1973 in Washington, which was the first treaty to grow directly from the Stockholm conference. In an unusual development, the U.S. delegation joined with those from the developing world to ban both the export and import of species threatened by international trade. The treaty was the logical extension of the three Endangered Species Acts that the U.S. Congress had passed unanimously between 1966 and 1973. The U.S. public had grown increasingly disgusted by the sight of rare animals killed for their fur or for the reputed medicinal qualities of various organs. In a reversal of the lesson from 1940, environmentalists realized that saving habitat was useless if the reserves became hunting grounds for the unscrupulous.

Signatory nations—125 as of 1994—agreed that trade in any recognizable part of an endangered species would require the approval of the designated management agencies and scientific agencies in countries on either side of the trade. Responsibility for overseeing CITES lies in the hands of UNEP. The negotiators established three lists: the first included endangered species that could not be used for commercial purposes; the second consisted of threatened species that could only be traded so long as scientists certified that the population was ecologically stable; and the third allowed individual nations to declare species as protected and in need of international cooperation. By attacking both the supply and demand of the endangered-species trade, as well as providing for a long list of protected species, the convention was an important step towards adequate protection of the earth's wildlife. As long as some people are willing to pay any price for certain rare items, trade will continue, but CITES makes it very difficult.

Regional Wildlife Protection

After the spate of global protection treaties that attacked the most basic problems of species extinction and habitat loss, the United States returned to agreements that addressed specific local issues. In March 1972, Japan and the United States agreed to the Convention for the Protection of Migratory Birds and Birds in Danger of Extinction, and Their Environment. This agreement not only fulfilled the Progressive Era dream that the sea birds of the Pacific would receive protection, but it also included endangered species endemic to the small islands of the ocean.

In November 1973, Denmark, Norway, the Soviet Union, Canada, and the United States created the Agreement on the Conservation of Polar Bears. Facing growing habitat disruption and increased hunting for trophies and fur, the bears were heading towards extinction. The five nations that held parts of the polar bear's range agreed that they had a duty to protect Arctic flora and fauna, and the means of doing so was to set aside ecosystems with the bears in mind. The treaty dictated that management of the reserves had to be based on the best scientific evidence. In addition, the treaty banned the killing of bears except for scientific or traditional uses.

In November 1976 the Soviet Union and the United States signed the Convention for the Conservation of Migratory Birds and Their Environment. This agreement was the most rigorous of the four migratory bird treaties in that it required both nations to continue scientific research, urged habitat protection, and contained broad criteria for listing species. The treaty required the two nations to cooperate in their scientific endeavors, including banding studies. Although détente made the treaty possible, the two nations agreed that the best remedy for species decline was substantial national effort, even though international cooperation was sometimes necessary.

The Agreement on the Conservation of the Porcupine Caribou Herd of July 1987 between Canada and the United States was designed to address the steady decline of an important species in the far reaches of the North

American Arctic. This particular herd follows an annual migration route that takes it through northeastern Alaska and northwestern Canada. Economic development of the region, including exploration for fossil fuels, threatened to disrupt the ancient and biologically dictated patterns of migration. Reflecting a conflict between the antiregulatory attitude of President Ronald Reagan and scientific evidence that the herd was being damaged, the treaty called on both nations to take action based on ecological principles while at the same time acknowledging the rights of landowners. The treaty also established a scientific panel that could make suggestions, although either party could reject the recommendations. On the surface the treaty was visionary in its emphasis on ecology and the precedent of settling a relatively minor problem through international cooperation, but in reality it obliged neither side to take any protective action.

Biodiversity

In the 1980s environmentalists and scientists began to call more attention to the importance of maintaining biodiversity, that is, protecting a wide range of species. They pointed out that scientists had identified very few of the total number of species in the world, and they expressed concern that people had become too obsessed with flashy endangered species such as bald eagles. Instead, they called on the global community to take steps to preserve vast stretches of habitat as the best means to protect the biological diversity of the earth. Biodiversity was valuable, they argued, for many reasons. People placed aesthetic and cultural value in knowing that wild animals still roamed. It was very likely that some species could provide cures for medical problems, such as cancer. And most importantly, biodiversity protected the health of the biosphere, upon which all humans relied.

Out of this pressure came the biodiversity agreement from the June 1992 UN Conference on the Environment and Development, commonly known as the Earth Summit, in Rio de Janeiro, Brazil. Signatory nations committed themselves to protect biodiversity and to manage the use of the protected species' genetic material in research and product development. President George Bush refused to sign because business leaders and some administration officials argued that the agreement's clauses governing biotechnology and the disbursement of funds for protective work were economic liabilities and infringements on U.S. sovereignty and did nothing to advance the worthy goal of protecting wildlife. The administration supported the clauses that mandated protection of endangered species, but it refused to agree with the argument of developing countries that they deserved certain economic concessions in exchange for strengthening environmental laws. Environmentalists charged that President Bush's decision indicated the abdication of international leadership. In April 1993, President Bill Clinton signed the biodiversity accord after working out an interpretive statement with business and environmental leaders.

The impasse at Rio suggested that wildlife protection diplomacy had changed dramatically over eighty years. As the issues became more global and the crises more challenging, groups of scientists and conservationists could no longer quietly develop and implement adequate international protective regulations. Conflicts over the use of common-property resources became more politicized and the rapid increase in the number of countries made negotiations more difficult. Nonetheless, wildlife protection, as part of a growing environmental awareness, has developed into an important part of foreign policy of the United States.

KURK DORSEY

See also Biodiversity Treaty; Earth Summit; Environment; Fisheries; Fur Trade; Law of the Sea; Sealing; United Nations Conference on the Human Environment, Stockholm; Whaling

FURTHER READING

Caldwell, Lynton Keith. *International Environmental Policy: Emergence and Dimensions*, 2d ed. Durham, N.C., 1990.
Dorsey, Kurk. "Scientists, Citizens, and Statesmen: U.S.-Canadian Wildlife Protection Treaties in the Progressive Era," in *Diplomatic History*, 1995.
Hayden, Sherman Strong. *The International Protection of Wildlife*. New York, 1942.
Lyster, Simon. *International Wildlife Law: An Analysis of International Treaties Concerned with the Conservation of Wildlife*. Cambridge, 1985.
Sand, Peter, ed. *The Effectiveness of International Environmental Agreements: A Survey of Existing Legal Instruments*. Cambridge, 1992.

WILKES, CHARLES

(*b.* 3 April 1798; *d.* 8 February 1877)

Famed explorer of the U.S. Navy in the 1830s and 1840s, who became a notorious Civil War figure after capturing Confederate envoys James Mason and John Slidell from a British mail boat in 1861. Wilkes stands as a transitional figure in U.S. naval history. Born in New York City, he commanded the first U.S. expedition that circled the globe (1838–1842), which augmented national interest in the Oregon Territory and California, strengthened trade throughout the Pacific, and also contributed significantly to scientific knowledge on several levels including hydrography, anthropology, geology, and cartography. A stern taskmaster whose attitudes and shipboard behavior reflected "Old Navy" values, he figured prominently in the shift of the navy from wood and sail to iron, steel, and steam. During his lifetime he demonstrated support for naval science, technological efficiency, intraservice reform, and modernized strategy during wartime.

GEOFFREY S. SMITH

See also California; Oregon Question; Trent Affair

FURTHER READING

Morgan, William James, et al., eds. *Autobiography of Rear Admiral Charles Wilkes, United States Navy, 1798-1877.* Washington, Naval History Center, 1978.

Smith, Geoffrey S. "Charles Wilkes: The Naval Officer as Explorer and Diplomat." In *Captains of the Old Steam Navy: Makers of the American Naval Tradition, 1840-1880.* Editor James C. Bradford. Annapolis, Md., 1986.

Stanton, William. *The Great United States Exploring Expedition of 1838-1842.* Berkeley, Calif., 1975.

WILLIAMS, WILLIAM APPLEMAN

(*b.* 12 June 1921; *d.* 5 March, 1990)

A radical historian whose emphasis on the economic foundations of U.S. foreign relations significantly influenced American historiography. Born in Iowa, Williams graduated from the U.S. Naval Academy (1944), was wounded in the Pacific theater, recuperated in Texas, and there joined the Civil Rights movement: "I consciously became a radical" wanting "structural change as opposed to secondary reform." Studying under Fred Harvey Harrington at the University of Wisconsin, Williams's doctoral dissertation became the book *American-Russian Relations, 1781–1947* (1952), that traced the Cold War's roots to the nineteenth century and questioned the containment theory. At the University of Oregon (1952–1956), he compiled an innovative anthology of documents and essays, *The Shaping of American Diplomacy* (1956, 1962, 1970), which led to the *Tragedy of American Diplomacy* (1959, 1962, 1972), his most influential work. Published after his 1957 return to Wisconsin, *Tragedy* traced late-nineteenth century U.S. imperialism that culminated in an open door policy that led the United States into revolutions, wars, and the Cold War. The *Contours of American History* (1961) reschematized post-1700 history by tracing it through three capitalist stages. The *Roots of the Modern American Empire* (1969) analyzed the persuasive role of agrarian ideology in shaping post-1865 expansion. Later books, essays, and the 1986 Bancroft Lecture at the U.S. Naval Academy critically dissected contemporary problems by placing them in larger historical contexts. Harrington, Williams, and their many students became known as "the Wisconsin school of diplomatic history" for their emphasis on U.S. expansionism and economic causes. In 1968 Williams moved to Oregon State University. His 1980 Organization of American Historians Presidential Address praised Henry Adams's and George Ken-

nan's conservatism for realizing the limits of U.S. power. Williams sparked considerable debate. His critics lamented the lack of extensive footnoting in his most influential work and claimed he underplayed noneconomic factors. But through his passionate commitment to "history as a way of learning," courage for questioning conventional wisdom, emphasis on the contradictions between beliefs in self-determination and expansionism, and placing economic motives at the center of America's worldview, Williams reshaped the writing of diplomatic history.

WALTER LAFEBER

FURTHER READING

Buhle, Paul M. and Edward Rice-Maximin. *William Appleman Williams: The Tragedy of Empire.* New York, 1995.

Gardner, Lloyd C, ed. *Redefining the Past; Essays in Diplomatic History in Honor of William Appleman Williams.* Corvallis, Ore., 1986.

Williams, William Appleman. *A William Appleman Williams Reader: Selections From His Major Historical Writings.* Edited with an Introduction and Notes by Henry W. Berger. Chicago, 1992.

WILLKIE, WENDELL LEWIS

(*b.* 18 February 1892; *d.* 8 October 1944)

Politician, advocate of internationalism, opponent of the New Deal, and failed presidential candidate. Born in Indiana, this lawyer and public utilities executive unexpectedly won the Republican presidential nomination in 1940. A former Wilsonian Democrat who had opposed President Franklin Delano Roosevelt's public power policies, Willkie's advocacy of aid to Great Britain after the fall of France in 1940 gained him the support of Republican internationalists. His backing of the selective service system for the military and the Destroyers-Bases Deal enabled Roosevelt to effect both measures during the campaign without fear of political reprisal. After his electoral defeat, Willkie sought national unity by visiting Great Britain in early 1941, testifying in favor of Lend-Lease aid, and urging all-out U.S. assistance to the Allies. His visits to England, the Middle East, the Soviet Union, and China in 1941–1942—in part as the president's personal representative—led to the publication of the popular book *One World* (1943), which urged postwar international cooperation. Willkie's crusade to convert the Republican Party from isolationism to internationalism was curtailed by his defeat in the 1944 primaries and his premature death that fall at age 52.

J. GARRY CLIFFORD

See also World War II

FURTHER READING

Madison, James, ed. *Wendell Willkie: Hoosier Internationalist.* Bloomington, Ind., 1992.

Neal, Steve. *Dark Horse: A Biography of Wendell Willkie.* Garden City, N.Y., 1984.

WILMOT PROVISO

See Mexico, War with

WILSON, THOMAS WOODROW

(*b.* 28 December 1856; *d.* 3 February 1924)

The twenty-eighth president of the United States (1913–1921) whose strong-willed personality and ideas dominated his era and especially the World War I years. His controversial plans for the postwar period aroused a major debate about the future course of U.S. foreign relations. Born in Staunton, Virginia, Thomas Woodrow Wilson grew up in Augusta, Georgia; Columbia, South Carolina; and Wilmington, North Carolina. His father, a prominent Presbyterian clergyman, moved from church to church. Wilson was educated at Davidson College (1873–1874), Princeton (B.A., 1879), University of Virginia Law School (1879–1880), and Johns Hopkins University (Ph.D. in history and political science, 1885). His first book, *Congressional Government* (1885), was accepted as his doctoral dissertation.

Between 1885 and 1902 Wilson taught at Bryn Mawr College, Wesleyan University, and Princeton. Elected president of Princeton in 1902, he led successful campaigns to modernize the curriculum and improve teaching but clashed with powerful alumni over a proposal to replace privately owned eating clubs with residential colleges. He lost that struggle and was also defeated in a disagreement with Dean Andrew Fleming West over the location of a new graduate school. Some historians, thinking of the later fight over the ratification of the Treaty of Versailles, which ended World War I, have suggested that these early struggles revealed a self-defeating pattern in Wilson's behavior in which he would stake out an extreme position and risk losing everything rather than accept compromise. By 1910 Wilson had become deeply frustrated with his role at Princeton and seized an opportunity to run for governor of New Jersey. His victory and subsequent success as a reformer led to the Democratic presidential nomination in 1912. He won the presidency in November 1912, defeating the Republican incumbent, William Howard Taft, and the Progressive Party candidate, Theodore Roosevelt.

During the 1912 campaign, Wilson concentrated on domestic issues and made passage of progressive reforms the major focus of his first years in office. He advocated the application of Christian moral principles to foreign policy and the promotion of democracy abroad. Although he demanded that U.S. businesses treat their foreign and domestic customers fairly, the Democrats were not antibusiness. The administration supported the overseas expansion of U.S. trade and investments, provided businessmen adhered to the same moral standards abroad that Wilson expected them to follow at home.

The administration's moral tone in foreign policy became evident in promising independence to the Philippines (an American colony since 1898); Secretary of State William Jennings Bryan's negotiating a series of bilateral treaties providing that the signatories would submit all disputes to international investigation before going to war; repealing a law that exempted U.S. coastal shippers from tolls in the nearly completed Panama Canal—a law that the British argued was in conflict with the 1902 Hay-Pauncefote Treaty; proposing a pan-American nonaggression treaty; and offering to apologize to Colombia for the U.S. role in the Panamanian revolution of 1903.

Wilson sometimes seemed cold and imperious to the diplomats and politicians who met him in person. So sure that his analysis of problems was correct, so confident that his policies were virtuous, he often expressed contempt for people who disagreed with him. French Premier Georges Clemenceau, who negotiated with Wilson in Paris in 1919, declared that the president thought of himself as Jesus Christ, handing down God's will to lesser mortals. Yet Wilson had a gift for capturing the U.S. public's mood, articulating the people's ideals brilliantly and inspiring them to support domestic reforms and, for a moment at least, to imagine a new world role. And in private, with his few close friends, his first wife, and his three daughters, he could be wonderfully warm, singing with family members around the piano or convulsing them with his deadly mimicry of opponents' idiosyncrasies.

Wilson's sense that he and his nation were instruments of a divine plan to promote democracy around the world was sharpened by his consciousness that his health was fragile. In his youth he suffered from a series of debilitating intestinal disorders, and as an adult from high blood pressure and (apparently) a series of minor strokes that left him with impaired vision in one eye and recurrent paralysis of his right arm. Wilson, never patient with opponents, became even less willing to soothe and humor others as his health declined.

Early Foreign Policy Issues

To encourage democracy in China, where a weak republic had been created in February 1912, Wilson announced on 1 April 1913 that the United States would be the first nation to recognize the new government. He also withdrew U.S. support from an international consortium of bankers that the Taft administration had assembled to make loans to the Chinese government, arguing that the arrangement was imperialistic. By 1916, however, he decided that Taft had been right in believing that U.S. membership in the consortium might moderate the behavior of other nations. In 1918 the administration urged U.S. bankers to join a second consortium.

U.S. attempts to strengthen China angered the Japanese, who had imperial ambitions there. So did behavior toward Asians in the United States. Asian immigration had been limited since the nineteenth century, but in 1913 California passed a new law banning land ownership by Asian aliens. Wilson could not stop the state's action but agreed to sign a new treaty with Japan preventing other states from doing the same in the future. The treaty proposal died in 1914 after Japan joined the war against Germany in order to seize German holdings in China and the Pacific. Wilson opposed but could not prevent this act, and in November 1917 the Lansing-Ishii Agreement recognized that Japan had "special interests in China, particularly in that part to which her possessions are contiguous." One of the president's most conspicuous failures at the Paris peace conference, at the end of World War I, was his inability to secure Japanese agreement to return to China the territory Japan had seized from Germany. U.S. liberals, who had expected the peace to bring full sovereignty to China, bitterly attacked the treaty's recognition of Japan's conquests in China's Shandong province.

The Mexican Revolution quickly became a major problem for the Wilson administration. After a long period of dictatorial rule, Mexicans overthrew Porfirio Díaz's government in 1910 and installed a new, more democratic government. It lasted only until February 1913, when Victoriano Huerta seized power in a military coup. Wilson, believing that the new regime did not have the support of the Mexican people, refused to recognize it. He could not prevent recognition by other nations, however, nor could he persuade Huerta to resign.

Mexican rebels calling themselves "Constitutionalists" caught Wilson's attention at the end of 1913 and, to help them, he lifted an arms embargo early in 1914 that had been imposed by Taft. On 21 April 1914, he used the excuse of the temporary arrest of some U.S. sailors by Huerta's troops to justify seizing the port of Veracruz. Wilson hoped that this limited intervention would cut Huerta's supply lines and force his resignation. It threatened instead to unite all Mexican factions against the United States. Mediation by Argentina, Brazil, and Chile did not solve the conflict, but rebel victories drove Huerta into exile in July 1914. American forces withdrew from Veracruz on 23 November.

Civil war among the rebel factions followed Huerta's departure. On 19 October 1915, Wilson extended de facto recognition to the faction led by Venustiano Carranza as the most likely to be able to govern Mexico. Carranza's defeated rival, Pancho Villa, vowed vengeance against the United States. Early in 1916 his followers murdered fifteen U.S. mining engineers in Mexico and

then raided Columbus, New Mexico, killing sixteen more Americans. Over Carranza's protests, on 16 March Wilson sent General John J. Pershing and 6,000 U.S. soldiers to pursue Villa in northern Mexico. Republicans and the U.S. press urged full-scale intervention, while Mexican nationalists demanded that Carranza repel the U.S. invasion. U.S. and Mexican government forces skirmished on 12 April and 21 June, leaving forty Mexicans and fourteen Americans dead, and twenty-three Americans prisoners.

Wilson, facing a growing crisis with Germany, did not want war with Mexico. He mobilized forces along the border but did not send them across. Carranza released the prisoners and proposed direct negotiations. The talks, in the autumn of 1916, made little progress, but the president withdrew Pershing's force in early February 1917, soon after the United States broke off diplomatic relations with Germany. On 24 February the British turned over to the Department of State the intercepted Zimmermann Telegram proposing a German-Mexican alliance in the event of war between the United States and Germany. When the Mexican government publicly rejected this proposal, Wilson extended full recognition to the Carranza regime, despite the promulgation of a new constitution which authorized seizure and redistribution of foreign-owned lands and the nationalization of subsurface mineral rights. Thereafter, Wilson rejected all pressures for further military intervention in Mexico and insisted that the Mexican people had the right to self-determination, even if that meant some economic losses for the United States.

In the Caribbean, Wilson's policy was less restrained. In Haiti and the Dominican Republic, continued political and economic instability prompted his intervention. A fear that some European nation might use the unpaid debts of these countries as an excuse to demand the cession of a base that could dominate the approaches to the new Panama Canal reinforced the president's humanitarian concerns. After diplomatic efforts at political and economic stabilization failed, Wilson authorized military intervention in Haiti in March 1915, and in the Dominican Republic in May 1916. U.S. military governments ran Haiti until 1934 and the Dominican Republic until 1922. While the occupiers temporarily raised living standards and improved the infrastructure, nationalists hated being governed by a foreign military. Nor did either regime succeed in implanting a lasting commitment to democracy.

Elsewhere in the hemisphere, the Wilson administration purchased the Virgin Islands from Denmark on 4 August 1916, for $25 million; intervened briefly and nonviolently in Cuba in 1917 and 1921 to discourage revolutionary activities; and maintained a force of 100 Marines in Nicaragua as a warning against political violence. The adminstration's main concern in Nicaragua was to protect

U.S. access to a possible canal route. The Bryan-Chamorro Treaty, signed on 5 August 1914, gave the United States an option on the canal route in return for a $3 million payment. Opposition from Nicaragua's neighbors and from anti-imperialists in the United States delayed ratification in the U.S. Senate until 1916.

World War I

The beginning of World War I in August 1914 drew the United States deeply into European affairs and ultimately into the war itself. During the nearly three years of U.S. neutrality, Wilson attempted to protect the country's neutral rights and to mediate the conflict. Both efforts eventually failed.

Neutrality was gradually undermined by emotional ties many members of the administration felt toward the British and French, and by economic commitments resulting from growing loans to and trade with the Allies. German atrocities in Belgium and a general German disdain for U.S. statements on neutral rights and human rights also caused many Americans to become highly critical of Germany. But most of all, neutrality was challenged by the beginning of German submarine warfare in February 1915. Had Wilson been willing to keep U.S. ships and passengers out of the war zone, as Secretary of State William Jennings Bryan recommended, there would have been little problem, but the president believed the United States must defend its right to trade with the nations at war. If the United States yielded to German intimidation, he believed, it would in effect be siding with the Central Powers against the Allies.

A series of minor incidents during the spring of 1915 showed the administration's uncertainty about its policy, but the sinking of the British passenger liner *Lusitania* on 7 May, with the deaths of 128 Americans, led Wilson to act. He demanded that German submarines obey traditional international rules that guaranteed the safety of passengers and crews of unarmed merchant vessels. If that could not be done, said Wilson, the Germans must stop using submarines. Secretary Bryan was so sure the president's hard line would lead to war that he resigned on 8 June. In his place Wilson appointed Robert Lansing, expecting to handle most important diplomatic issues himself and intending to use Lansing mostly to draft despatches and conduct routine business. Lansing's pro-Allied sentiments seemed to have no more effect on the president than did the even more extreme pro-Allied views of U.S. Ambassador Walter Hines Page in London.

Wilson always realized that an aggressive defense of neutral rights might cause the war he wanted to avoid. The best way to keep the United States out was to bring the war to an end. Just before the Germans announced their submarine policy in early 1915 Wilson sent Colonel Edward M. House to Europe to explore the possibility of a compromise peace. The fact that Wilson asked House, his closest friend—but a private citizen—on whom he had often called upon for advice, to undertake this delicate mission demonstrated the importance the president attached to this initiative. Wilson chose House because he was confident that the Texan understood his wishes and would convey them to the belligerents delicately and discreetly. House basked in his role as the personal emissary of the president, but his mission proved unsuccessful.

Tensions between Germany and the United States increased on 19 August 1915, when the British liner *Arabic* was torpedoed, taking the lives of two more Americans. This attack occurred despite secret orders that had been issued to German commanders to avoid attacks on passenger vessels, and in September the German government acknowledged those orders publicly and apologized for the sinking of the *Arabic*.

Wilson believed the "*Arabic* pledge" was only a stopgap. In December 1915 he sent House back to Europe in pursuit of peace. House had decided that an Allied defeat would be contrary to U.S. interests, so he proposed to British Foreign Secretary Sir Edward Grey that the Allies agree to attend a peace conference and promised that if the Germans refused, the United States would enter the war on the Allied side. Wilson later endorsed a weakened version of the House-Grey Memorandum of February 1916, without the unequivocal promise that the United States would go to war, but the Allies never invoked it. Both sets of belligerents still believed that they could win and neither wanted negotiations.

On 24 March 1916, a German submarine torpedoed the French steamer *Sussex*, injuring several Americans. When Wilson threatened to break off diplomatic relations, German army and civilian leaders who thought submarine warfare had been ineffective secured from their government the "*Sussex* pledge" that submarines would not attack merchant vessels without warning. Wilson, now running for reelection, claimed that summer and autumn that his neutrality policy had proven successful. "He kept us out of war" became an effective campaign slogan that contributed to his narrow victory in November over Republican Charles Evans Hughes.

Wilson understood, however, that his ability to preserve honorable neutrality was fading. A year earlier he had proposed a modest increase in armaments to strengthen U.S. defenses, and in May 1916 he publicly suggested that the United States abandon its traditional isolationism after the war and join an association of nations that would maintain the peace collectively. But none of those steps guaranteed that the United States would avoid the European conflict.

In December 1916 Wilson tried again to bring the belligerents to the peace table, sending identical notes to all the warring nations asking them to state their peace terms. He hoped that public opinion would compel them to offer moderate terms so he might find a compromise. The results were so disappointing that on 22 January 1917 Wilson took a more audacious step, proposing his own peace plan. In his "peace without victory" speech, he staked out a new global role for the United States, offering a settlement that would guarantee all nations security, freedom to trade, and equality under the protection of an international organization of which the United States would be a member.

The speech came too late. The Germans, who had been building up their submarine fleet, had already decided to risk everything on a last effort to crush their enemies. Instead of replying to the president's offer, they announced that, beginning on 1 February 1917, German submarines would sink any ship, belligerent or neutral, that entered the war zone around the British Isles. Wilson immediately broke off diplomatic relations with Germany—but still hoped, somehow, to avoid war.

During February and March, Wilson experimented with arming merchant vessels for self-defense and searched for a way out of the crisis. The Zimmermann Telegram, in which Germany proposed an alliance with Mexico and Japan, intercepted and given to the United States by the British on 24 February, provided further evidence of German hostility. By the beginning of April, Wilson had concluded that war was inescapable. On 2 April 1917 he delivered his war message to a special joint session of Congress. The time had come, he said, not only to defend U.S. rights on the seas, but to make the world "safe for democracy."

Organizing the U.S. economy to wage a world war proved a more formidable task than Wilson at first recognized. The administration tried to disrupt civilian life as little as possible, never appointed a single economic coordinator with power to supervise all phases of production and distribution, and relied on a hodge-podge of special agencies to promote voluntary cooperation among producers, shippers, and manufacturers. For the relatively short period the United States was in the war energetic volunteers such as Bernard Baruch in the War Industries Board and Herbert Hoover in the Food Administration used a combination of patriotic appeals and guaranteed profits to secure the supplies and food needed to support the American Expeditionary Force and help the Allies. That this ill-planned system was able to raise and sustain an effective fighting force was a testimony to the huge power of the U.S. economy. The wartime experience suggested what broadened governmental supervision over the economy might achieve, but Wilson and his advisers had no desire to make the system permanent. At war's end, they quickly terminated the special agencies and canceled extraordinary powers.

For the most part, Wilson delegated wartime military and economic supervision to subordinates. He saw his main role as articulating for the peoples of the world a vision of a postwar order that would be fairer and more stable than that of the nineteenth century. It would mean replacing aggression, secret bargains among governments, and the amoral pursuit of narrow national interests with international moral standards comparable to those taught by Christianity.

On 8 January 1918, in what came to be known as the "Fourteen Points" address, Wilson explained to Congress and the world that he hoped the new world order would end secret deals through "open diplomacy," remove economic barriers to international trade, reduce armaments, begin the abolition of colonialism, restore the independence of nations conquered during the war and free those peoples who had long been ruled by outsiders, and establish an "association of nations."

The Paris Peace Conference

Wilson knew that securing a peace based on the Fourteen Points would not be easy, so he took the unprecedented step of leading the U.S. delegation to the Paris peace conference himself. He did not name a senator or a prominent Republican to the delegation. In November 1918, just before he left, voters in the congressional elections rejected his appeal for a Democratic Party–controlled Congress and elected Republican majorities to both houses. Wilson arrived in Europe in December to the cheers of millions but found that the Allied leaders, like the voters at home, did not share his enthusiasm for a "peace without victory."

During six months of hard bargaining, Wilson won the creation of the League of Nations, secured the application of the principle of self-determination in the breakup of the Austro-Hungarian Empire, and established a mandate system that was supposed to supervise the gradual liquidation of colonialism. But he failed to convince the French that their security interests would be satisfied by the League rather than by occupying portions of Germany; he could not persuade the Italians and the Japanese to give up territories they had been promised in secret wartime treaties; he was unable to get the conferees even to talk about disarmament or the lifting of trade barriers; he conceded to Japan control of Shandong province in China; and he acquiesced in the ill-fated Greek expedition to (and occupation of) western Asia Minor as well as in the decision to exclude the leaders of Bolshevik Russia from the peace conference.

In fact, rather than welcoming revolutionary Russia into the new world system, in July 1918 Wilson had reluctantly joined the British, French, Japanese, and other allies in sending troops into north Russia and Siberia. The proclaimed purpose of the intervention—in the north—was to prevent stores of arms from falling into German hands, and—in the east—to help 70,000 Czech soldiers interned in Russia to escape to fight on the Western Front. Wilson agreed to participate because he feared the real goal of his allies was to dominate Russia, and he hoped that U.S. participation in the invasion would give him influence to support Russian self-determination. His personal aversion to Bolshevism also made it easier for him to accept intervention.

Wilson's claim that his peace plan represented the true desires of the world's peoples had been undermined by elections in France and Britain that endorsed policies of revenge and conquest, and by the congressional elections in the United States that gave the Republicans a majority in the Senate that had to approve the peace treaty. During a trip back to Washington from Paris in March the president met with Senate leaders who told him the treaty could not pass without changes to protect U.S. sovereignty. To get the changes the senators demanded, he had to make further concessions to the European leaders, agreeing to try the German Kaiser for war crimes, conceding to France the right to occupy the west bank of the Rhine River for fifteen years, and allowing territorial concessions to the Italians that violated the principle of self-determination. Thus when he joined Allied and German representatives in a ceremony to sign the treaty on 28 June 1919, in the Hall of Mirrors of the palace at Versailles, Wilson was all too aware that the peace fell short of the goals he had set in the Fourteen Points speech. He hoped that the League of Nations would be able to correct the mistakes and omissions.

Debate over the Treaty in the United States

Wilson returned to the United States on 8 July and presented the treaty to the Senate two days later. In his speech he urged the senators to accept the duty of world leadership, but it became obvious that most Republicans and some Democrats did not endorse Wilson's formula for exercising that leadership. Some criticized specific parts of the treaty such as its failure to force the Japanese out of China or the British out of Ireland. Others feared that membership in the League of Nations under the collective security provision of Article 10 might make the United States go to war against its will. Still others thought the treaty had departed too far from the idealism of the Fourteen Points. Many said they would not vote for the treaty without the adoption of amendments or reservations. Wilson, galled especially by the criticisms of an old foe, Republican Senator Henry Cabot Lodge, now chairman of the Senate Foreign Relations Committee, rejected all compromise.

Wilson lobbied hard with senators on behalf of the treaty, but by the end of the summer he realized he would probably lose. In an effort to revive wartime idealism and arouse public pressure for a favorable vote in the Senate, he left Washington on 3 September for a speaking trip through the West. A few days later, on 12 September, the Senate Foreign Relations Committee heard the testimony of William Bullitt, a young member of the U.S. delegation in Paris who had become a bitter critic of Wilson for his failure to secure all of the Fourteen Points in the peace treaty. Although Bullitt's opinions were not in themselves important, his testimony that Secretary of State Lansing "considered many parts of the treaty thoroughly bad" dealt a serious blow to the ratification cause. Lansing, who had earlier testified that he had so little to do with the negotiation of the treaty that he had not even known until he arrived in Paris of a secret agreement between Japan and Great Britain for the division of Germany's Pacific islands, issued only an evasive and tepid repudiation of Bullitt's statement.

Wilson, alarmed at the apparent crumbling of support for the treaty even within his own administration, pushed his frail, exhausted body through thirty-five speeches in twenty-nine cities during the next three weeks. His arguments were not always logically compelling, but, speaking to large and enthusiastic crowds, he seemed to be winning supporters. Then, on 25 September 1919, after a speech at Pueblo, Colorado, he collapsed and was rushed back to Washington. A few days later, on 2 October, he suffered a massive paralytic stroke followed by a urinary blockage and high fever that nearly killed him.

Although Wilson received the best available medical treatment for his stroke and seemed conscious and alert throughout his ordeal, he should have been removed from office. For more than a month after the attack the president was unable to see anyone other than his wife and doctors and was incapable of dealing with any public business. Not until the first months of 1920 did he begin to resume some control over policy, and even then others handled most matters.

Wilson's wife, Edith Bolling Galt, whom he had married in December 1915 after the death of his first wife, Ellen, in August 1914, conspired with his personal physician, Admiral Cary T. Grayson, to conceal the seriousness of his condition from the country and even his cabinet members. Mrs. Wilson persuaded the doctors, who were misled by the patient's seeming lucidity, that depriving Wilson of his public duties would rob him of a reason for recovery. When Secretary Lansing suggested removing Wilson from office and replacing him with Vice President Thomas R. Marshall, Lansing was eventually fired. Colonel House, who would surely have seen how his friend had deteriorated, had been cut off from all contact with Wilson after a series of disagreements with the president in Paris.

Neither Edith Wilson nor the president's physicians understood that Wilson was suffering from what modern neurologists call a "focal psychosyndrome." Although he appeared rational, he had little control over his emotions and suffered from impaired judgment. By early 1920, as this condition worsened, traits of stubbornness and self-righteousness became exaggerated, and Wilson's ability to comprehend and react to the realities of the external world was largely destroyed.

In autumn 1919 the president's disability prevented him from leading the campaign for ratification of the Treaty of Versailles. His wife's fear that bad news would endanger his life kept from him reports on the strength of the opposition. Without his leadership, the fight for unconditional approval of the treaty collapsed, but he saw no need for compromise, although it appeared to his friends that modest concessions might save the day. On 19 November 1919, the Senate rejected both the unmodified treaty Wilson demanded, and the reservations Republican leaders proposed. When the treaty came up for a second vote on 19 March 1920, Wilson, in the grip of his illness, rejected all suggestions for compromise, and the second vote confirmed the Senate's rejection of the treaty.

Historians differ over the importance of Wilson's health to the treaty fight. Certainly advocates of unconditional ratification lost their strongest champion when he fell seriously ill, but focus on the president's health may divert attention from important questions about the treaty that divided the nation. Lodge was right to point out that Wilson never adequately explained what U.S. obligations would be if a nation defied the League of Nations and began a war. Wilson implied that mere existence of the league would prevent wars, but the return of isolationist sentiment in the United States in the 1920s suggests that Lodge may have been correct when he argued that Americans were unwilling to use their army and navy to enforce league decrees.

Despite two negative votes in the Senate, Wilson still believed that ordinary Americans wanted the treaty approved, and in spring 1920 he considered running for a third term to seek their support. Dr. Grayson reluctantly informed party leaders that the president's health would not permit such a campaign, and the Democrats instead nominated Governor James M. Cox of Ohio. Cox dutifully supported the treaty and was soundly defeated by Republican Warren G. Harding. A month later Wilson won the Nobel Peace Prize, but because of his illness he could not go to Stockholm to accept the honor in person. On 4 March 1921, Wilson's term ended, and he retired to a spacious house on S Street in Washington. There he and Edith lived quietly until his death on 3 February 1924.

Wilson's influence on American foreign policy may have been greater after his death than in his lifetime. Isolationist authors and politicians in the 1930s condemned him for taking the United States into World War I, disparaged his idealism, and rejoiced that the United States had not joined an ineffective League of Nations. But when World War II began, many Americans remembered Wilson's vision and wondered if aggression could have been stopped and war prevented had the United States accepted the responsibility Wilson had urged in the era of World War I. After the United States entered World War II and leaders began planning for the next peace, they were determined to avoid Wilson's political mistakes but to redeem his memory with the establishment of the United Nations and permanent U.S. participation in collective-security arrangements.

During the Cold War between the Soviet Union and the United States and its allies, Wilson's ideas were dismissed by self-styled "realists" as naive, neglectful of the value of military force and the willingness to use it to advance the nation's power and security. Two generations of academics and policy advisers, most prominently George F. Kennan and Henry A. Kissinger, made their reputations by deploring Wilsonian moralism while advocating policy based on careful analysis of the national interest expressed in terms of power. With the end of the Cold War, the problems of the world seemed reminiscent of those Wilson faced—ethnic rivalries, the collapse of a powerful empire (Germany and Austria-Hungary then, the Soviet Union in the 1980s), and uncertainty over the role of the United States. Although there were important differences between the two eras, Wilson's ideas and experience received renewed interest and respect among experts. "In his vision of the future needs of world society," wrote George Kennan in 1989, "I now see Wilson as ahead of any other statesman of his time."

KENDRICK A. CLEMENTS

See also Baruch, Bernard Mannes; Bryan, William Jennings; China; Clemenceau, George; Cold War; Collective Security; Cuba; Díaz (José de la Cruz), Porfirio; Dominican Republic; Fourteen Points; Germany; Grey, Edward; Haiti; Harding, Warren; Hoover, Herbert; House, Edward Mandell; Huerta, Victoriano; Isolationism; Japan; Kennan, George Frost; Kissinger, Henry Alfred; Lansing-Ishii Agreement; Lansing, Robert; League of Nations; Lodge, Henry Cabot; Lusitania; Mandates and Trusteeships; Mexico; Neutral Rights; Nicaragua; Nobel Peace Prize; Panama and Panama Canal; Paris Peace Conference of 1919; Pershing, John; Realism; Recognition; Russia and the Soviet Union; Self-Determination; Taft, William Howard; Versailles Treaty of 1919; Villa, Pancho; Virgin Islands; United Nations; World War I; Zimmermann Telegram

FURTHER READING

Ambrosius, Lloyd. *Wilsonian Statecraft: Theory and Practice of Liberal Internationalism During World War I*. Wilmington, Del., 1991.

Baker, Ray Stannard. *Woodrow Wilson, Life and Letters*, 8 vols. Garden City, N.Y., 1927–39.

Calhoun, Frederick S. *Power and Principle: Armed Intervention in Wilsonian Foreign Policy*. Kent, Ohio, 1986.

Clements, Kendrick A. *The Presidency of Woodrow Wilson*. Lawrence, Kans., 1992.

Conye, G. R. *Woodrow Wilson: British Perspectives, 1912–1922*. New York, 1992.

Cooper, John Milton, Jr. *The Warrior and the Priest: Woodrow Wilson and Theodore Roosevelt*. Cambridge, Mass. 1983.

Heckscher, August. *Woodrow Wilson*. New York, 1991.

Knock, Thomas J. *To End All Wars: Woodrow Wilson and the Quest for a New World Order*. New York, 1992.

Levin, N. Gordon. *Woodrow Wilson and World Politics: America's Response to War and Revolution*. New York, 1968.

Link, Arthur S. *Wilson*, 5 vols. Princeton, N.J., 1947–65.

———. *Woodrow Wilson: Revolution, War, and Peace*. Arlington Heights, Ill., 1979.

Link, Arthur S., ed. *Woodrow Wilson and a Revolutionary World, 1913–1921*. Chapel Hill, N.C., 1982.

———., et al., eds. *The Papers of Woodrow Wilson*, 69 vols. Princeton, N.J. 1966–1993.

Park, Bert E. *Ailing, Aging, Addicted: Studies of Compromised Leadership*. Lexington, Ky., 1993.

Schild, Georg. *Between Ideology and Realpolitik: Woodrow Wilson and the Russian Revolution, 1917–1921*. Westport, Conn., 1995.

Schulte Nordholt, J. W. *Woodrow Wilson: A Life for World Peace*. Berkeley, Calif., 1991.

Smith, Tony. *America's Mission: The United States and the Worldwide Struggle for Democracy in the Twentieth Century*. Princeton, N.J., 1994.

Walworth, Arthur. *Woodrow Wilson*, 2 vols., 3rd ed. New York, 1978.

Weinstein, Edwin. *Woodrow Wilson: A Medical and Psychological Biography*. Princeton, N.J., 1981.

WOMEN, WAR, PEACE, AND FOREIGN RELATIONS

Throughout history, war has been the purview of men. This general principle holds from the Greek *polis*, through the ancient empires, the feudal principalities, early European monarchical regimes, up to and including the modern nation-state. With few exceptions, men have been the combatants in war as well as the policymakers who debated and declared war. Although largely excluded from combat, women have nonetheless played important roles as both supporters and critics in time of war and have, therefore, influenced the formulation of military and foreign policy.

The fact that a nation's leaders could count on the compliance if not the enthusiastic support of women when the country entered a war helped to give a war effort legitimacy and sustainability. Modern warfare pursued by nation-states is especially dependent upon "civilian" morale and patience. As noncombatants, women could either undermine or bolster a war effort depending upon their dissent from, or consent to, a major war effort. The mobilization of an entire people for a war effort, deeded to the West by the French Revolution, has played a major role in subsequent wars, particularly the total wars of the twentieth century.

Although women of the United States have been spared the worst depredations of wartime destruction, save primarily for women of the Confederacy during the Civil War, women often have been noncombatant casualties of wars. Thus, the women of Europe, both East and West, as well as women in post–World War II anticolonial wars, have been placed in harm's way, either as victims of so-called "collateral damage," or as direct targets of strategic, saturation bombing. Here the bombing of German and Japanese cities during World War II, as well as Nazi efforts to exterminate Jewish and Slavic men, women, and children, are the most dramatic examples. The post-Yugoslavian conflict in the Balkans in the early 1990s, where the war aims of one group, the Bosnian Serbs, sought the destruction or displacement of another group, the Bosnian Muslim population, offered stark evidence of the use of rape as an explicit military strategy.

Despite their official exclusion from combat and the highest echelons of foreign policymaking throughout American history, women have made major contributions to war efforts. Although they have supported America's wars, at vital points and to a significant degree, they also have been opponents of war and "militarism" in foreign policy. For example, in 1914, the National American Women's Suffrage Association informed President Woodrow Wilson that its two million members were prepared to engage in the war effort should the United States enter the fray. The association listed a variety of home-front and service efforts in its list of contributions. At the same time, a Women's Peace Party appeared and, by 1915, burgeoned into 165 nationwide groups boasting a total membership of 40,000 women. Participants included such notable public figures as the reformer Jane Addams. U.S. delegates attended a Women's Congress at the Hague in 1915, calling for continuous arbitration of the conflict and a negotiated settlement short of unconditional surrender that, they argued, would lead to a bitter peace. The Women's Peace Party was a forerunner to the Women's International League for Peace and Freedom, an avowedly nonviolent peace group formed after World War I that has supported many post–World War II struggles for national liberation, despite its nonviolent leanings.

During the Cold War, thousands of women rallied to the antinuclear cause through well-publicized "peace encampments" and through more traditional means of political mobilization and persuasion, including petitions, mass marches, and the formation of groups aimed at educating women about peace and security issues. Opinion surveys consistently showed a greater reluctance on the part of women to support force as a means to settle international conflict, as well. Especially in the 1960s and 1970s on such issues as military conscription, amnesty of Vietnam era draft resisters, the arms budget, and Vietnam withdrawal, a gender gap emerged, with women less supportive of increased military expenditure and preparedness and men more likely to support such efforts.

In the 1990s, a division developed within women's rights groups and feminist ranks on the so-called "right to fight" issue and the "combat exclusion rule." The growth of female participation in the U.S. military armed forces was impressive. By mid-1948, in the era when there were Women's Auxiliaries to the major branches of the Armed Services, about one and four-tenths percent of the armed services were female. With the abolition of Women's Auxiliaries and the creation of the All Volunteer Force in 1973, attempts were launched to integrate women into the regular army. By 1995, the percentage of women serving had risen to about twelve percent of the overall total. In the aftermath of the 1991 Persian Gulf War, more barriers to women's participation in combat fell. In March 1994, the navy began integrating women into its combat fleet. The air force and navy opened the door for female combat pilots in 1994. The prohibitions that remain are few, and they pertain to ground combat units and special forces.

Although these changes have been celebrated by such mainstream organizations as the National Organization for Women, many other women, especially pacifist feminists representing a "different voice," question the absorption of women into the military. They believe that a feminist vision of a more just and pacific social order is at odds with the extension of full-fledged military careers and responsibilities to women. They see this trend toward women in the military as a process of cooptation rather than progress. Within the ranks of policymakers, women are growing more visible as diplomats, security analysts, and strategic experts. As of 1995, no women had served as either Secretary of State or Secretary of Defense, but the numbers of women obtaining posts in the Pentagon and the Department of State showed a gradual, but continuous, upward trajectory.

As the ranks of women in the U.S. House of Representatives and the Senate increased, women of a variety of points of view on foreign policy matters took their place on major committees concerned with foreign affairs. Although it remained the case that women were most likely to be associated with "domestic concerns," one area in which bipartisan female commitment was evident was in the broad arena of "human rights." Because so many aspects of women's lives were constructed in and through the language of human rights, both within the United States and throughout the world, influential and activist women, whether in government, international human rights organizations, or scholarship,

favored putting some teeth into the commitment of the international community to the human rights effort. These women advocated strengthening America's determination to protest violations of human rights, including particular crimes of violence against women, and backing up this protest with American diplomatic and, perhaps, military clout. Women in policy positions, however, were as divided as women in general on those circumstances that warrant commitment of American soldiers to duty and danger in order to advance a humanitarian agenda.

JEAN BETHKE ELSHTAIN

See also Addams, Jane; Human Rights; Peace Movements and Societies to 1914; Peace Movements and Societies 1914 to Present; Rankin, Jeanette; State, U.S. Department of

FURTHER READING

Beckman, Peter R., and Francine D'Amico. *Women, Gender, and World Politics.* Westport, Conn., 1994.
Booth, Ken, and Steve Smith. *International Relations Theory Today.* Cambridge, Mass., 1995.
Campbell, D'Ann. *Women at War with America.* Cambridge, Mass., 1984.
Crapol, Edward, ed. *Women and American Foreign Policy.* Wilmington, Del., 2nd ed. 1992.
Elshtain, Jean Bethke. *Women and War.* 2nd ed. Chicago, 1995.
McGlen, Nancy F., and Meredith Reid Sarkees. *The Status of Women in Foreign Policy.* New York, 1995.
Peterson, V. Spike. *Gendered States. Feminist Revisions of International Relations Theory.* Boulder, Colo., 1994.

WOMEN'S INTERNATIONAL LEAGUE FOR PEACE AND FREEDOM

See Peace Movements and Societies, 1914 to Present

WORLD BANK

See International Bank for Reconstruction and Development

WORLD COURT

See Permanent Court of International Justice

WORLD HEALTH ORGANIZATION

A specialized United Nations agency established in 1948 with a mandate to promote "the highest level of health" for "all peoples." Most countries, including the United States, are members of the World Health Organization (WHO), which is based in Geneva, Switzerland and has six regional headquarters: Washington, D.C.; Copenhagen, Denmark; Brazzaville, Congo; Alexandria, Egypt; New Delhi, India; and Manila, the Philippines. The United States has traditionally supplied the largest share (twenty-five percent or about $100 million in 1995) of WHO's regular budget and the largest amount of voluntary contributions (twenty-eight percent or some $65 million in 1993). Voluntary funds are designated for specific projects such as the Global Program on AIDS (Acquired Immune Deficiency Syndrome). The elimination of the deadly disease smallpox, which WHO began to fight in 1955 and had fully eradicated by 1980, ranks as the organization's greatest success.

WHO works to combat tuberculosis, malaria, cholera, diarrhea, venereal disease, AIDS, cancer, and other killing and maiming diseases by serving as a clearinghouse for health information, promoting research, setting sanitary standards, training health personnel, initiating mass vaccination programs, and providing technical advice to governments undertaking national health plans, especially in developing nations. WHO has emphasized prevention through the immunization of children. The American Medical Association has cooperated with WHO to gather and disseminate information on clinical medicine.

Successor to the Office International d'Hygiène Publique (founded in 1907) and the Health Organization of the League of Nations (established in 1923), WHO took over some of the health functions of the United Nations Relief and Rehabilitation Administration, which dissolved in 1947. The World Health Assembly, in which each WHO member has one vote, sets WHO policies, and the Secretariat of some 4,000 staff members conducts agency activities. WHO acts through and must rely on host governments since WHO representatives are attached to national ministries of health. WHO entered Russia in the early 1990s after the breakup of the Soviet Union to advise on health programs, and was one of the first agencies to enter Cambodia in 1992 to rebuild that nation's war-wrecked health system. In 1995 WHO despatched experts to Zaire to combat an outbreak of Ebola virus.

In the 1990s, WHO came under increasing criticism as the United States often clashed with the organization. WHO has long faced budgetary problems because of unpaid contributions, especially from the Soviet successor states. In 1985, the United States, apparently influenced by large pharmaceutical companies, withheld its contribution to the regular budget to protest a WHO program which urged governments to identify lists of essential drugs and to develop local capacities to produce them. Critics in the mid-1990s have charged that WHO lacked efficient management, a coherent strategy, and fiscal accountability (hints of scandal surfaced in 1993). Because WHO is decentralized and dedicated to the "full menu" of health issues, critics also have charged that its overlapping activities are uncoordinated and spread too thinly. WHO has largely adhered to a disease-specific approach, giving less attention to mental and social dimensions of health, such as poverty, inadequate education, and environmental spoilation. Finally, WHO's representatives can implement policy only if recipient countries cooperate, and many have chosen to emphasize the purchase of military equipment over the launching of health projects.

The agency has had to endure the vagaries of world politics. In 1981, when the World Health Assembly issued a code on breast milk substitutes that favored the breast feeding of babies, the United States was the only country to vote against the measure. The Reagan administration argued that the code impeded world trade. WHO's Brazzaville office, responsible for activities in Africa, became inoperative in the early 1990s when civil war wracked the Congo. In 1993, the United States opposed but failed to defeat a World Health Assembly resolution requesting the International Court of Justice to study the legality of the use of nuclear weapons in time of war because of their health effects. Because of the political sensitivity of such issues as family planning, WHO has sometimes shied away from leadership. Despite its differences with WHO, the United States has long valued the organization's many efforts that have saved countless lives. In response to criticism, WHO in 1995 trimmed its headquarters staff, issued a report declaring poverty the largest single cause of death, disease, and suffering, and anncoued plans to issue a new global health charter in 1997.

THOMAS G. PATERSON

See also Acquired Immune Deficiency Syndrome (AIDS) Pandemic; Reagan, Ronald Wilson; United Nations

FURTHER READING

Godlee, Fiona. "The World Health Organization," *British Medical Journal*, series of articles beginning vol. 309, 26 November 1994.

Hoole, Franics W. *Politics and Budgeting in the World Health Organization.* Bloomington, Ind., 1976.

Siddiqi, Javid. *World Health and World Politics: The World Heath Organization and the UN System.* Columbia, S.C., 1994.

Tarimo, E., and A. Cresse, eds. *Achieving Health for All by the Year 2000: Midway Reports of Country Experiences.* Geneva, 1990.

U.S. Department of State. *United States Participation in the United Nations.* Washington, D.C.; annual.

World Health Organization. *The Work of WHO.* Semiannual. Geneva, 1950-present.

World Health Organization. *The World Health Report.* Annual. Geneva, 1950-present.

WORLD TRADE ORGANIZATION

Following the worldwide ratification of the Uruguay Round trade agreement, the World Trade Organization

(WTO) was born 1 January 1995. As the formal institutional framework for the multilateral trading system, the WTO performs three major functions: to serve as the repository for the rules of international trade, to provide the central forum for future multilateral negotiations aimed at further reductions in trade barriers, and to furnish facilities wherein member countries can seek impartial, third party resolutions of trade disputes among themselves. The WTO effectively absorbed and expanded upon the General Agreement on Tariffs and Trade (GATT) which has been in force since 1948. WTO membership is open to existing GATT members who accept the Uruguay Round agreement in its entirety. Other countries will need to have membership applications approved by a two-thirds vote of WTO members.

An international trade organization with expanded powers was necessitated by several agreements in the Uruguay Round going beyond the GATT's limited jurisdiction which covered only trade in goods. In the first instance, the WTO encompassed the legally distinct "GATT 1994" which in turn is comprised of the old GATT Articles of Agreement plus the modifications to and enhancements of the Articles (mainly trade-related investment measures) agreed to in the Uruguay Round. In addition, the new organization was given authority to implement and administer the breakthrough Uruguay Round agreements covering services, trade-related intellectual property rights, the more elaborate and more easily enforced Dispute Settlement Understanding, and the Trade Policy Review Mechanism which will regularly evaluate member countries' trade performances.

Organizationally, the WTO consists of a Ministerial Conference which meets at least once every two years, a Senior Council, and a Secretariat. All important decisions are taken by consensus whenever possible, continuing a practice employed in the GATT. Rules on majority voting are contained in the agreement, and they could theoretically be utilized if it proved impossible to reach consensus on a given matter. With its broader membership, explicit legal status, and a charter sufficiently flexible that it can expand to incorporate new trade agreements on emerging issues such as the environment, the WTO creates an enhanced institutional dimension of global trade cooperation. It has the potential to become a major international economic organization whose influence is on the same level as the International Monetary Fund (IMF) and the World Bank.

The effects of the new WTO on U.S. national interests is subject to a continuing review. Passage by the U.S. Congress in late 1994 of the Uruguay Round legislation containing the WTO provisions was not assured until President Bill Clinton and incoming Senate Majority leader Republican Robert Dole of Kansas reached a last-minute compromise. The compromise was designed to resolve the domestic political dispute concerning the effect WTO membership would have on U.S. sovereignty and commercial interests. Political opponents of the WTO expressed concern that it might gradually adopt a decision-making process based on majority voting, a scenario that warns of the United States being outvoted by smaller economies with different interests. Critics also painted a picture of diminished sovereignty resulting from the possibility of the United States losing dispute settlement cases and facing unpleasant choices, such as obeying the rulings of unelected international civil servants or having to pay compensation to the country winning the judgment. Accordingly, agreement was reached on supplemental legislation that would establish a WTO Dispute Settlement Review Commission, to be comprised of federal appellate judges, to determine if settlement decisions adverse to the United States were soundly based. The supplemental legislation also identifies circumstances in which members of Congress could introduce a joint resolution calling on the president to commence U.S. withdrawal from the organization.

STEPHEN D. COHEN

See also General Agreement on Tariffs and Trade

FURTHER READING

Jeffrey J. Schott. *The Uruguay Round: An Assessment.* Washington, D.C., 1994.
U.S. Congress, General Accounting Office, *Uruguay Round Final Act Should Produce Overall U.S. Economic Gains.* July, 1994.

WORLD WAR I

The war of 1914–1918 which the United States joined as a belligerent in April 1917 and which further elevated the United States to world power status. On 28 June 1914, a nineteen-year-old Bosnian Serb nationalist, Gavrilo Princip, shot and killed the heir to the Austro-Hungarian throne, Archduke Francis Ferdinand, and his wife Sophie, as their motorcade paused after a wrong turn in downtown Sarajevo. The Austrian government responded to the assassination by demanding that Serbia suppress all Slavic nationalist organizations and permit Austria-Hungary to help investigate the murder. Serbia complied in part with the ultimatum but began to mobilize for war. Germany feared that Serbia would be supported by Russia and promised to back Austria. On 28 July Austria declared war on Serbia, and on 1 August Germany declared war on Russia, following that step two days later with a declaration of war on France. On 4 August Great Britain declared war on Germany as German armies moved into neutral Belgium on their way to attack France. In the following months and years the war became worldwide as the Ottoman Empire (October

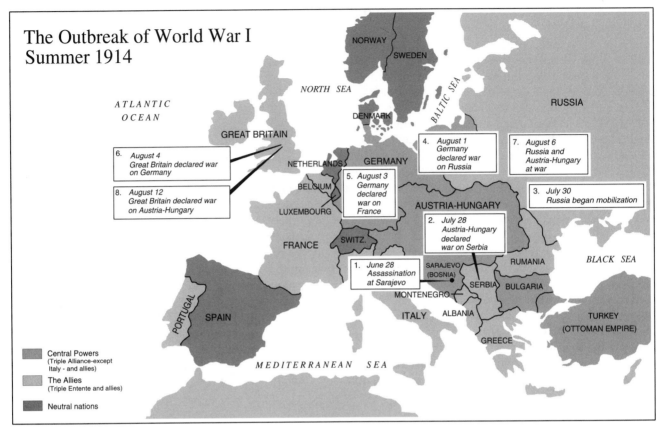

The Outbreak of World War I
Summer 1914

6. *August 4*
Great Britain declared war on Germany

8. *August 12*
Great Britain declared war on Austria-Hungary

4. *August 1*
Germany declared war on Russia

7. *August 6*
Russia and Austria-Hungary at war

5. *August 3*
Germany declared war on France

3. *July 30*
Russia began mobilization

2. *July 28*
Austria-Hungary declared war on Serbia

1. *June 28*
Assassination at Sarajevo

Central Powers
(Triple Alliance-except
Italy - and allies)

The Allies
(Triple Entente and allies)

Neutral nations

1914) and Bulgaria (1915) came in on the side of the Central Powers (Germany and Austria-Hungary), and Japan, Italy (1915), Romania (1916), Portugal (1916), Greece (1917), and the United States (1917) entered on the side of the Allies (Great Britain, France, Serbia, and Russia). In the Middle East and Africa the war extended among the colonies and dependencies of the warring nations.

The forces that led to war in the summer of 1914 had been developing at least since 1870. The Industrial Revolution, beginning first in Great Britain and carrying that nation to political and economic power in the first half of the century, had swept eastward across Europe and westward across the United States in the second half of the 1800s. By the last quarter of the century British factories were less modern than those of Germany and the United States, and British individualism seemed old-fashioned beside the great industrial combinations arising elsewhere. In 1865 Germans were producing less than half as much steel as the British, but by 1900 the German Empire was making more steel than Great Britain. Unification (in 1871) accelerated Germany's drive to secure markets and sources of raw materials, arousing the fear and hostility of the French and British and accentuating competition for colonies in Africa and Asia.

Industrialization and the rapid advance of science and technology also had important military implications by

making possible the development of devastating new weapons and the arming of huge conscript armies. General staffs based on the Prussian model were organized to direct these vast forces, and their rigid war plans shaped and limited the decisions of political leaders. And yet an ambitious autocrat like Germany's Kaiser Wilhelm II could set off unpredictable military events, such as the Anglo-German naval race, which strained relations between those states to the breaking point.

In the United States and Western Europe industrialization had been accompanied by increases in the political power of the middle class and, in some cases, erosion of a monarch's power and the development of a siege mentality among landed aristocracies. To a greater or lesser degree these states adopted public education, tax reforms, and political democracy that enabled their governments both to promote economic growth and to soften some of its harshest impacts on workers. In the Russian, Austro-Hungarian, and Ottoman Empires, however, neither industrialization nor political change had proceeded as far. Royal dynasties remained firmly in control, while around them moved military and bureaucratic groups who represented agricultural interests and were cool to industrial development. Even without the stress of war these empires faced increasing economic crisis, yet none of their leaders dared move toward change because all three had large, increasingly restless minority populations.

Germany, situated between the Eastern empires and the Western democracies, shared characteristics of both. The country had a powerful industrial economy, a strong middle class, and a parliamentary system with a broader franchise than in Great Britain; but Kaiser Wilhelm II appointed the chancellor and retained control over all executive decisions throughout his reign (1888–1918). The powerful Prussian landed gentry vigorously supported his autocratic rule. On the crucial decisions of war and peace the German people, and even the nobility, exercised little influence.

Yet if Germany and the Eastern empires were less democratic than the Western nations, even in the West the dislocations and disruptions of industrialization had produced unresolved tensions and problems. Throughout Europe industrial development accompanied by a rise in class consciousness and the development of labor and socialist organizations often challenged the whole basis of capitalism. Having failed to cure the glaring inequities of capitalism before the war, there was little reason to believe that governments would be more successful during a period of crisis.

Nationalism, one of the great ideologies of the nineteenth century, was another major cause of the war. France, humiliated and sheared of its border provinces of Alsace and Lorraine following the Franco-Prussian War of 1870–1871, sought revenge, and Franco-German tensions heightened after tense confrontations over Morocco in 1905 and 1911. In the Balkans, the ongoing competition for influence between Austria-Hungary and the Russian Empire, the rise of pan-Slavism and other competing national ambitions, produced an explosive situation. Austria precipitated a crisis in 1908 by annexing Bosnia-Herzegovina, a province of the crumbling Ottoman Empire which Serbia also coveted. Russia favored Serbia but backed down when Germany supported the Austrians. Four years later, in 1912–1913, further instability arose when Serbia, Greece, Bulgaria, and Montenegro seized the last Ottoman holdings in the Balkans and then quarreled among themselves over the spoils. Once again, Austria intervened, negotiating the Treaty of London in 1913 to create an independent Albania and to prevent Serbia from annexing the area, thus infuriating the Serbians and their Russian allies. In all of these cases, ethnic loyalties and national ambitions made compromises and rational decisions nearly impossible.

The War in Europe and on the Seas

By June 1914 the opposing armies were prepared, the war plans of the great powers were set, and the willingness of governments to seek compromise was exhausted. Germany's role became crucial. Terrified of a two-front war in which France would be on the west and Russia on the east, German military leaders adopted the Schlieffen Plan which called for a quick and massive offensive against France through neutral Belgium. They hoped to win a war by defeating France while the Russians were still mobilizing. Thus when Austria precipitated a crisis by its ultimatum to Serbia, the Germans dared not wait.

At first the war went according to the German plan. By the end of August German armies had swept through Belgium and were at the Marne River within twenty miles of Paris. But the Belgians and a small British expeditionary force proved surprisingly tough, and at the last minute the French threw everything they had into a desperate attempt to stop the enemy. At the first Battle of the Marne (September 1914) the Allies halted the German attack, but their efforts to outflank the enemy failed. As winter approached, the two sides dug in, building a system of fortifications and trenches that defined a relatively static front for the next four years.

In the East the Russians mobilized more quickly than the Germans expected and launched an offensive that pushed into East Prussia in August of 1914, forcing the Germans to draw troops away from the Western Front. At the Battle of Tannenberg, German General Paul von Hindenburg won a major victory, driving the Russian forces back into Russia; but the Germans could not win the war in the east. Each summer great waves of Russian soldiers again poured west, only to be driven back at huge cost by better armed German forces. The struggle, surging back and forth across the grasslands and forests of eastern Europe, exhausted both sides.

Elsewhere, the war also settled into a deadly stalemate. In the South, Italy entered in 1915 on the Allied side in hopes of seizing territory from Austria, but the Austrians, with German support, were able to stabilize that front. The Ottoman Empire declared war on Russia in October 1914 and prevented the Allies from supplying the Russians through the Black Sea. A huge British, Australian, and New Zealander attempt to reopen the route failed after a summer-long battle on Turkey's Gallipoli Peninsula in 1915. And the vaunted German Navy emerged from its ports only once, to fight a two-day battle off the coast of Jutland on 31 May–1 June 1916. Outnumbered, the Germans then returned to port never to sail again, although they had inflicted severe losses on the superior British fleet.

The first phase of the war, which had been characterized by illusions about decisive victory and a brief conflict, ended. During the next two years (1915–1917) the slaughter continued on a terrifying scale, especially in the trenches of the western front, with Great Britain, France, and Austria-Hungary suffering more than a million casualties each, and the Russians and Germans losing almost two million men each. But all of this bloodshed produced no victor and did not seem even to create a decisive advantage for one side over the other. Increasingly desperate, each belligerent sought new ways to strike at the enemy.

As early as August 1914 the Germans had begun to mine the English Channel, and on 29 October the British announced that goods consigned to Germany on neutral ships would be seized as contraband unless proven otherwise. A few days later, on 3 November, the British declared the entire North Sea a military area and proceeded to mine it extensively. Germany retaliated early in 1915 with an announcement that submarine warfare against belligerent vessels would begin in a war zone around the British Isles on 4 February.

The purpose of the belligerents's actions was to cut off their enemies' trade and starve them into defeat. The blockades and counter-blockades had an immediate impact on the neutral nations such as the United States. Although President Woodrow Wilson shared the conviction of most Americans that the United States should remain neutral during the war, the fact that the economy was in recession when the war began placed him under heavy pressure to maximize trade with the belligerents. They, in particular the Allies, welcomed U.S. trade, but each side was eager to deny that trade to its enemy.

When the war began, Wilson immediately issued an official proclamation of neutrality and then bent over backward to enforce its spirit as well as its letter. A striking example of his attitude was his decision to approve a recommendation by Secretary of State William Jennings Bryan that private loans to the belligerents should be discouraged by the Department of State. Although this action was slightly unneutral in that it limited Allied purchases and thus deprived them of some of their advantage based upon their control of the seas, Wilson believed it was justified to prevent U.S. economic entanglement with the belligerents.

If that was his goal, he failed to achieve it. The need to facilitate trade with loans and credits led the administration to abandon the prohibition in the spring of 1915. U.S. trade with the Allies increased rapidly from $825 million in 1914 to $3.2 billion in 1916, while that with the Central Powers dropped from $169 million to just over $1 million in the same period. Their huge purchases in the United States proved vitally important to the Allies, and a stimulus to the U.S. economy. During the autumn of 1914 and the early spring of 1915, the American government protested against British restrictions on neutral trade but stopped short of threatening to cut off the trade as the administration of Thomas Jefferson had done during the Napoleonic Wars. British Foreign Secretary Sir Edward Grey played the United States beautifully, letting it jump and splash and then reeling it in slowly and carefully. Thus the British cooled U.S. anger with legal debate, cited Civil War precedents to prove the propriety of their actions, and pacified shippers by paying for

cargoes they seized. In the end, satisfied that claims for losses could be adjudicated after the war, the U.S. government bowed to the reality of the British blockade.

The German counter-blockade that began in 1915 was a different matter. Although the Germans had too few submarines (fewer than thirty in early 1915) to pose a major danger to shipping in the war zone, the submarine posed a significantly different threat. Slow, fragile submarines simply could not provide for the safety of passengers and crews of the ships they attacked because to protect themselves they had to fire their torpedoes while submerged. If the Allies seized property, the Germans promised to destroy both property and life. It did the Germans no good to argue that the Allied blockade illegally starved their civilian population. On 10 February 1915, the United States declared that Germany would be held to "strict accountability" for losses of American lives or property.

The German declaration of submarine warfare played into the hands of British propagandists, who were already deluging the United States with exaggerated or fictitious stories of German atrocities. The German invasion of neutral Belgium offended Americans, but British propagandists also invented tales of crucified Canadians, German soap factories using human corpses, and Belgian babies with their hands cut off. What was more, the British controlled the trans-Atlantic cables, and U.S. newsmen soon learned that stories had to take the Allied point of view if they were going to get through. By contrast, German propaganda was clumsy and ineffective. In the end, however, propaganda was a less important force in shaping either U.S. public opinion or the actions of the administration than the things Germany actually did.

Secretary of State William Jennings Bryan recommended that Americans keep out of the war zone, but the president, believing that the United States could not bow to German intimidation and perhaps hoping they would back down, rejected the suggestion. In March and April one American died in the torpedoing of a British liner, the *Falaba*, and three more were killed in an attack on a U.S. tanker, the *Gulflight*. The administration was divided about how to respond to these events until 7 May 1915, when the British liner *Lusitania* was torpedoed off the Irish coast, with the loss of 1,198 people, including 128 Americans.

Americans expressed outrage over this slaughter. It seemed cold and deliberate, especially since the German embassy had published an advertisement warning against entering the war zone on the morning of the very day the *Lusitania* sailed. In the East, some newspapers called for a declaration of war, but elsewhere a commitment to neutrality remained strong. Wilson spoke for these people when he said in a speech at Philadelphia that "there is such a thing as a nation being so right that it does not need to convince others by force that it is right." At the same time, however, the president was determined to assert U.S. rights vigorously. In a sharp note on 13 May he demanded that the German government disavow the sinking and pay reparations. When the Germans replied with an argument that the sinking was justified because the *Lusitania* was carrying small arms ammunition, Wilson drafted a second protest, renewing his earlier demands and adding that German submarines must adhere to traditional rules protecting lives and property. Secretary Bryan, having failed to persuade Wilson to send a simultaneous protest to the British about their violations of neutral rights, and believing that Wilson's second note would lead to a rupture of relations with Germany and war, resigned from the cabinet on 8 June 1915.

Bryan's resignation created an impression that the administration was divided on the *Lusitania* issue and encouraged the Germans to stall. Not until February 1916 did they grudgingly offer to pay reparations for American deaths, but in the meantime they tried to avert similar disasters. On 6 June 1915, the German government secretly ordered submarine commanders not to attack passenger liners. The policy worked until 19 August 1915, when a U-boat sank the British passenger ship, *Arabic*, with the loss of two Americans. German ambassador Count Bernstorff was so alarmed at the anger that swept the United States that he announced, on 1 September, that submarines would no longer sink liners without warning and without providing for the safety of noncombatants. This revelation of the secret orders earned Bernstorff a rebuke from his government, but the "*Arabic* pledge" reduced tension and postponed a crisis.

The other agents of the Central Powers in the United States were not as clever as Bernstorff. One of them, an espionage agent named Dr. Heinrich Albert, left a briefcase full of documents detailing German plans to sabotage U.S. munitions factories on a New York streetcar. The Austrian ambassador, Dr. Constantin Dumba, was ordered out of the country after secret papers regarding his efforts to foment strikes in munitions factories fell into British hands. Two German military attachés, Captains Karl Boy-Ed and Franz von Papen, were also expelled for plotting sabotage.

Yet none of this evidence of German hostility fundamentally shook Americans's desires to remain neutral. To the contrary, early in 1916 anti-interventionists in Congress, fearing that more sinkings might lead Wilson to ask for a declaration of war, introduced the Gore and McLemore Resolutions. The resolutions, strongly backed by former Secretary of State Bryan, would have prohibited the issuance of passports to Americans traveling on belligerent-owned vessels. Wilson, however, denounced the resolution. To the chairman of the Senate Committee on Foreign Relations he wrote, "Once accept a single abatement of right, and many other humiliations would certainly follow, and the whole fine fabric of international law might crumble...."

With the president's help, opponents of the resolutions killed them, but scarcely had they done so when a French passenger ship, the *Sussex*, was torpedoed in the English Channel on 24 March 1916. No Americans died, but several were injured. U.S. anger at this violation of the *Arabic* pledge became compounded when the German government at first denied responsibility for the attack. On 18 April 1916, Secretary of State Robert Lansing (Bryan's successor) sent to Berlin a blunt note demanding that Germany give up "its present methods of submarine warfare against passenger and freight-carrying vessels" or the United States would break off diplomatic relations.

By this time the Germans had fifty-two submarines, of which no more than eighteen could be on station at any one time. The German government was not yet convinced that submarine warfare could be decisive, especially if it resulted in the United States entering the war. On 4 May 1916, the Germans announced that no more merchant or passenger vessels would be sunk without warning and without providing for the safety of the passengers and crew. In return, the Germans demanded that the United States force the British to loosen their blockade on foodstuffs. Wilson chose to accept the "*Sussex* Pledge" but to ignore the condition, thus leaving the Germans free to return to submarine warfare in the future, if they were willing to face a rupture of relations with the United States.

The *Sussex* Pledge came just in time to help Wilson in his campaign for reelection. He claimed that his policy protected U.S. interests and "kept us out of war." But the president had been aware since the beginning of the war that assertions of neutral rights and threats gave no guarantee that the United States would not be drawn into war. The only real hope lay in finding a way to bring the war itself to an end.

In this effort Wilson relied on his closest friend and confidential adviser, Colonel Edward M. House. When the war began, House was in Europe on a private and unsuccessful mission to explore the possibility of reducing tension among the European power blocs. He returned to Europe in early 1915 to sound out the belligerents on U.S. mediation, and early in 1916 he went to London yet again. Although none of his previous trips had been productive because neither side was willing to settle for less than victory, House now believed that he might have found a device for getting peace talks started. In conversations with Sir Edward Grey he suggested that the United States call a peace conference. If the Germans refused to attend, the United States would probably enter the war on the Allied side. On 22 February 1916, House and Grey signed a memorandum including this proposal.

House and Wilson of course knew that they could not guarantee a declaration of war, particularly in light of the congressional mood revealed in the debate over the Gore-McLemore Resolutions. The administration's intentions have been the topic of disagreement among historians, who contend either that the agreement meant that House and Wilson had abandoned neutrality and intended to get the nation into war on the Allied side at the first opportunity, or that it was a desperate stratagem to avoid U.S. involvement by offering enough to get the Allies, then in a disadvantageous military position, to agree to a peace conference.

As it turned out, the House-Grey Memorandum was never invoked. The Allies still hoped for a knockout blow, and they did not want to be inhibited at a peace conference by U.S. idealism. The *Sussex* crisis convinced them that the Germans would soon drag the United States into the war without the Allies having to make any embarrassing commitments. The possibility that Wilson would try to bring the United States into the war rapidly disappeared when Mexican rebel Pancho Villa's forces raided Columbus, New Mexico, on 9 March 1916, leading to the despatch of most of the U.S. Army into northern Mexico in a futile pursuit of Villa. Also in April the British alienated much of U.S. public opinion by ruthlessly suppressing the Irish "Easter Rising." On 27 May 1916, in a speech to the League to Enforce Peace, Wilson made it clear that he did not intend to let the Allies dictate selfish peace terms. The United States, he said, would commit itself to join a postwar association of nations designed to replace alliances and balances of power with a concert of power that would assure a fair settlement of all issues.

During the summer of 1916, as he ran for reelection, Wilson reaffirmed his commitment to neutrality. When the British published a "blacklist" of U.S. firms suspected of aiding the Central Powers and with which British subjects were forbidden to deal, the president asked and received from Congress power to retaliate with economic measures. He also secured passage of the Naval Act of 1916, which authorized more money for naval construction than had ever been spent in peacetime. "Let us build a navy bigger than [Britain's]," said Wilson, "and do what we please." In the East, voters, no longer sure that the president could assure peace with honor, gave majorities to Republican Charles Evans Hughes, but Wilson carried the South and West and narrowly won the presidential election.

Following the election, Wilson decided to try a new approach to securing peace. He drafted identical notes to the belligerents, asking them to state their peace terms.

He hoped that in this public forum they would moderate their demands and create a basis for compromise. On 12 December 1916, before he sent his notes, the Germans suddenly announced their willingness to negotiate. Wilson went ahead anyway, but the Allies were offended at what they thought was German-American collusion and outraged by Wilson's statement that "the objects...of the belligerents on both sides...are virtually the same...." To Allied leaders, their purposes were honorable and defensive. Those of the Central Powers they believed to be aggressive and dishonorable. As House had warned Wilson, it would have been wiser to stress the battlefield stalemate as the reason for holding a peace conference rather than equating the war aims of the two sides.

After the failure of his December initiative, Wilson proposed his own peace terms. On 22 January 1917, in an address to the Senate, he outlined what he called a "peace without victory" which would reestablish the prewar status quo and create a league of nations to resolve conflicts peacefully. His proposal came too late. On 9 January, at a conference of military and civilian officials, the German kaiser had accepted the navy's recommendation that all-out submarine attacks could win the war. With 103 submarines built, German naval officials argued that they could destroy nearly forty percent of Allied merchant shipping within five months and that they could terrorize the neutrals into avoiding the war zone. They also agrued that even if the United States declared war, it could not mobilize fast enough to make any difference in the European front. On 31 January 1917, Germany announced the beginning of unrestricted submarine warfare.

On 3 February, Wilson addressed a joint session of Congress to announce the severance of diplomatic relations with Germany. He did not ask for a declaration of war, and on 26 February he proposed instead that Congress authorize the arming of U.S. merchant vessels. The House quickly passed the legislation, but in the Senate, peace sentiment remained strong, and a minority ("a little band of willful men," as Wilson called them) filibustered the measure to death in the last hours of the congressional session. Even the publication of the intercepted Zimmermann Telegram—in which Germany proposed an alliance with Mexico and Japan in the event of war and offered Mexico the possibility of regaining some of its old territory in the American west and southwest—could not break the filibuster, although it did confirm for most Americans Germany's hostile intent.

On 12 March 1917, an unexpected revolution in Russia led to the abdication of the czar and the beginning of apparent efforts to establish a democratic government. It was now possible to argue that the Allies were all democracies, while the Central Powers were all absolutist governments. But of greater importance than this ideological affinity was the news of German submarines sinking three U.S. ships, the *City of Memphis, Illinois,* and *Vigilancia,* with heavy loss of life, on 18 March. As Wilson would admit in his war message, it was now obvious that "armed neutrality...is impracticable."

The United States Enters the War

When Wilson appeared before Congress on 2 April to ask for a declaration of war, he advanced two major arguments. The first was that German attacks on U.S. neutrality necessitated war. The second and more important argument was that only by entering the war could the United States assure itself of a dominant role in the peacemaking after the conflict. Previously Wilson had hoped to stand above the fray, offering from a disinterested position suggestions that might commend themselves to the exhausted belligerents. He had decided, however, that this course had failed. The only hope for averting future wars even more terrible than the present one was for the United States to take a role that allowed it to dictate the terms of peace, to create "such a concert of free peoples as shall bring peace and safety to all nations and make the world itself at last free." On Good Friday, 6 April 1917, Congress voted to declare war on Germany, in the House by a vote of 373 to 50 and in the Senate by 82 to 6. In hope of splitting the Central Powers, the United States did not declare war on Austria-Hungary until 7 December 1917, and although it severed relations with the Ottoman Empire, it never declared war.

The significant number of votes against the declaration of war in both houses of Congress highlighted a major problem faced by the administration. With one in every seven Americans of foreign birth, ethnic tensions and national loyalties might well undermine the war effort. A strong socialist movement which had commanded nearly a million votes in the 1912 presidential election was united in its opposition to the war, and in Oklahoma, 450 tenant farmers were arrested for attempting to march on Washington to impede the induction of men into the army (the Green Corn Rebellion). Wilson and his advisers feared that a divided nation could not fight the war effectively.

To promote national unity, Wilson established a Committee on Public Information headed by George Creel, a respected journalist. The CPI, or Creel Committee, recruited journalists, artists, movie directors, actors, writers, and scholars to sell the war to Americans and to popularize U.S. goals abroad. Books, pamphlets, movies, and thousands of volunteers interpreted the war for U.S. audiences in clear, simple terms of right against wrong. Overseas, the Creel Committee provided copy to local newspapers in their own languages, blanketed both Allied and enemy countries with copies of Wilson's speeches setting out his liberal war aims, and turned the president into an international hero. As a propaganda agency at home and abroad the CPI was far more effective than the belligerents had been in the United States before the war. But by depicting issues simplistically as right against wrong, the agency in the long run undermined Wilson's hope of achieving a stable, rational peace based upon accommodation and compromise.

From division and discord at the beginning of the war, the pendulum quickly swung toward enforced conformity. Wilson gave Postmaster General Albert Burleson and successive Attorneys General Thomas W. Gregory and A. Mitchell Palmer a free hand to control sedition, espionage, and dissent, and they exercised their powers with enthusiasm. Under the Espionage Act (May 1917), the Trading with the Enemy Act (1917), the Alien Act (1918), and the Sedition Act (1918) the government arrested, imprisoned, or deported several thousand dissenters. State and local governments, as well as private vigilante groups, took up the crusade, and in many places even such inoffensive acts as teaching the German language or playing German music were banned. Although some administration officials courageously defied the national hysteria, and the National Civil Liberties Union, founded in 1917, made a vigorous defense of freedom of speech, the administration's treatment of civil rights was one of the worst blots on its record.

For some conservatives, the war offered an excuse to attack any sort of radicalism, whether or not it had anything to do with the war. The Industrial Workers of the World was a particular target of public and private harassment. By the end of the war a panic about all forms of radicalism had been created which led directly to the great "Red Scare" of 1919.

Probably the major reason for the administration's insensitivity to civil liberties during the war was, ironically, its conviction that the United States must not follow the European path toward centralized government control. Instead, Wilson and his advisers depended upon a voluntary system of cooperation that could be dismantled once the emergency was over. Yet the task became stupendous, and despite Wilson's conversion to the idea of "preparedness" in late 1915, virtually nothing had been done by April 1917 to prepare for war. For the year and a half the United States was in the war, the ideal of volunteerism clashed with the necessities of efficiency, production, planning, and control. With the administration making every effort to arouse patriotism and stimulate voluntary cooperation, super-patriotic extremists found a congenial atmosphere.

Typical of the strained compromises found by the administration between these disparate concepts was the draft law. Memories of riots and widespread evasion of the Civil War draft law made discussion of a conscript system political dynamite in 1915 and 1916. The administration realized that some sort of a draft was essential, but its bill, introduced in April 1917, tried to straddle the issue. The system was to be called "selective service," not the draft. In an effort to preserve the fiction that the task was merely to choose among a whole nation of eager volunteers, the process was administered by local boards chosen from community leaders. Administration leaders awaited with apprehension the first day of registration, on 5 June 1917, but all went well. Ten million men between the ages of twenty-one and thirty-five registered, and by war's end over twenty-four million had signed up. After physical examinations and deferments, nearly six and a half million men were eligible for service, and 2.7 million were inducted. In addition, just over 2 million more volunteered. Although there were some evasions and desertions, the speed and success of the U.S. military mobilization astonished friends and enemies alike. Within about a year, the United States had multiplied its armed forces twenty-fold, to nearly five million, of whom more than two million were actually in Europe.

Housing, feeding, training, arming, supplying, and transporting this new fighting force taxed the volunteerist philosophy to its limits. In May 1917 Secretary of War, Newton Baker, created a Cantonment Division that spent nearly $200 million building thirty-two camps to house 1.3 million men. Most astonishing of all was that camps to house the first 400,000 men were built from scratch within three months. To supply the recruits Baker abandoned the practice of advertising for bids and purchased whatever could be found on the open market. He armed the soldiers the same way, giving them a hodgepodge of weapons bought wherever they could be found or secured from the Allies. When moving men, raw materials, food, and supplies across the country overtaxed the inefficient railroad system, the administration nationalized the railroads and placed them under a Railroad Administration for the duration of the conflict.

Getting the soldiers to France once they were trained was an even greater task. Despite Wilson's 1916 promise to build a fleet second to none, the navy had only about 65,000 men and 300 ships when the war began. A U.S. merchant marine hardly existed. Worse, the German submarine campaign worked. British naval commanders admitted secretly to U.S. officials that shipping losses had been so great in early 1917 that they did not believe they could hold out more than four months. Although they doubted it would work, the British agreed to try out a convoy system, and the U.S. government created a United States Shipping Board to build and operate a huge fleet of merchant vessels. In addition, the United States confiscated German ships previously interned in U.S. ports. The convoy system proved to be a spectacular success, reducing sinkings by two-thirds by November, but even so, by year's end, only 175,000 American sol-

diers had reached France. The shipping shortage was so severe that draft calls had to be cut back because there was no place for the new men to go. In 1918, the British solved the problem by turning practically every ship they could find into a troop transport, leaving themselves desperately short of food and supplies in the process.

The year 1917 was a bleak one for the Allies on the battlefields as well as at sea. In the South the Italians were badly defeated at Caporetto, and in the French Army two-thirds of the divisions suffered incidents of "collective disorder" or mutiny as the soldiers lost faith in their leaders and their cause. In Russia the government and army crumbled because of the Bolshevik Revolution in November.

Knowing that the United States would be arriving in force by the summer of 1918, the Germans risked everything on a last great offensive that spring. The Allies implored General John J. Pershing, commander of the American Expeditionary Force, to let them integrate the few U.S. units then in France into existing Allied units, but Pershing and Wilson refused, except in dire emergencies. The United States believed that only a massive and fresh U.S. Army, thrown suddenly against the enemy, would break the stalemate, and they were determined to grasp the diplomatic advantage that a decisive U.S. intervention would give at the peace conference. The United States's separate status was symbolized by its insistence upon being an "Associated" and not an "Allied" nation. The knowledge that the Yanks were coming encouraged the British and French to make one last stand against the Germans, and on the German side the expectation of overwhelming U.S. intervention was dispiriting. Actual U.S. military participation in stopping the German offensive turned out to be relatively minor. Although American artillery men and Marines fought heroically at Cantigny and Belleau Wood, it was not until July and August that large numbers of U.S. soldiers went into action in the Allied counteroffensive that ended the war. When the war ended in an armistice on 11 November 1918, the Americans had fought bravely and had contributed significantly to shortening the conflict, but the British and French resented U.S. claims that their role entitled them to dictate peace terms. Two-and-a-half million British and French soldiers had died; the United States had lost only 116,000.

Perhaps the most important U.S. contribution to the war was financial. Immediately after the U.S. declaration of war, the British sent a mission to Washington headed by the new foreign secretary, Arthur James Balfour. Although he ostensibly led a purchasing mission, Balfour's more important purpose was to reveal to the United States how desperate the Allies's financial situation had become. Over the next several months the U.S. government extended $10 billion in loans to the British and

French, though not without some suspicion that the United States was being bilked.

Aside from seeking money, the Allies also looked to the United States to supply food, weapons, and the myriad kinds of manufactured goods essential to keeping the war going. In August 1916 Congress had created a Council of National Defense made up of the secretaries of war, navy, interior, agriculture, commerce, and labor to promote "the coordination of industries and resources for the national security and welfare," but the council proved ineffective. After the United States declaration of war in April 1917 the various military services' procurement agencies competed with each other, with Allied purchasing agents, and with civilian purchasers for scarce goods. No one had authority to order factories to shift over to war production, or to plan and coordinate the allocation of raw materials or transportation. No one had adequate authority to settle labor conflicts or to organize food production. Reluctant to enlarge the government bureaucracy and naively hopeful that volunteer "Dollar a Year" experts from industry could mobilize the economy, Wilson was slow to recognize that nothing worked as he expected.

In March 1918, after a disastrous winter of transportation breakdowns, fuel shortages, and industrial chaos, Wilson appointed Bernard M. Baruch chairman of the War Industries Board, an agency designed to coordinate procurement and purchasing activities, and to mobilize industry efficiently. Baruch had little real power, but he proved a genius at manipulating businessmen and government officials. To deal with a labor crisis which had produced over four thousand strikes in 1917, Wilson created a National War Labor Board headed by Frank P. Walsh and former President William Howard Taft. The NWLB also had little power, but its chairs were adept at persuading workers and businessmen that they should accept its compromises. Meanwhile, in August 1917 the president appointed Herbert Hoover as Food Administrator and entrusted him with the task of increasing production and encouraging conservation of agricultural products. Hoover launched a vigorous propaganda campaign to encourage food conservation, but his greatest efforts were directed toward increasing production by guaranteeing farmers high prices both at home and from the Allies, to whom the American government loaned money to buy American products. In addition, Harry A. Garfield in the Fuel Administration and William G. McAdoo in the Railroad Administration were able to bring order to those two crucial areas of the wartime economy.

At best, the administration's economic mobilization program was a patchwork of overlapping and often competing organizations. It seemed to rely on patriotic appeals to voluntary cooperation by private citizens, businesses, and labor, but what really made it work was the power of money. Guaranteed prices to farmers and manufacturers, high wages for workers, and assured profits for the railroad companies made them all eager to cooperate with the government. As a result of the war's costs and the administration's generous policies, the federal budget went from $1 billion in 1916 to $19 billion in 1919, and the national debt from $1 billion in 1915 to $24 billion by 1920. The new federal income tax, legalized by constitutional amendment in 1913, and corporate taxes paid for about a third of the war costs. The rest was borrowed from the American people. Four "Liberty Loans" and a 1919 "Victory Loan" raised $21.4 billion and gave some sixty million Americans a direct, personal stake in the outcome of the war. Because of its generous incentives to secure voluntary cooperation with the war effort, it cost the United States $10 million more per day to fight the war than any other belligerent.

The war was also costly to U.S. interests in another way. In Asia, Japan took advantage of its 1902 alliance with Great Britain to declare war on Germany and to seize German holdings in China. U.S. efforts to block this encroachment on the "Open Door Policy" failed, and in 1915 the Japanese further outraged the United States by delivering a list of "Twenty-One Demands" to China that were intended to make China a Japanese colony. Although Anglo-American pressure succeeded in thwarting this imperialistic move, when the United States entered the war in 1917 the Japanese government realized that the United States was no longer in a position to defend China diplomatically. In the Lansing-Ishii Agreement of November 1917 Japan secured U.S. agreement to the principle that "territorial propinquity creates special relations between countries" and used that ambiguous phrase to justify further demands on the Chinese. The resultant ill will created between the United States and Japan lingered into the 1920s and 1930s.

In the meantime, a second Russian Revolution in November 1917 (known in Russia as the October Revolution because of differences between the Russian and Western calendars) brought to power a much more radical regime under Vladimir Lenin and Leon Trotsky. The Bolsheviks quickly proposed a general peace on the basis of "the liberation of all colonies; the liberation of all dependent, oppressed, and non-sovereign peoples;" published secret treaties that revealed the less-than-noble war aims of the Allies; and set out to negotiate a separate settlement with Germany. Russia and Germany signed such an agreement at Brest-Litovsk on 3 March 1918. Russian peace moves terrified Allied leaders, who had nightmares about hordes of German troops, freed from the Eastern Front, overrunning Allied lines in France and Belgium. Using every argument at their command, they urged the United States to join them in intervening in the Russian civil war with the goal of putting in power a government that would reestablish the Eastern Front.

President Wilson, who had most probably known of the Allies's secret treaties since April or May 1917, was suspicious of Allied motives in proposing intervention in Russia and unconvinced that military intervention could reverse the Revolution. He was, however, deeply concerned that what he referred to as Lenin's "crude formula" of "no annexations, no contributions, no punitive indemnities" might seduce exhausted belligerents into making a "premature peace...before autocracy has been taught its final and convincing lesson." To counter that danger, on 8 January 1918, he went before Congress to offer his own vision of a peace program that might at once reclaim leadership from the Bolsheviks, assure the enemy that if they surrendered they would not be destroyed, and lay down principles to guide the negotiation of a peace treaty of reconciliation and justice.

The Fourteen Points, Armistice, and Peace Conference

In the Fourteen Points speech of 8 January, and in a series of subsequent statements, Wilson presented an analysis of what he believed caused the war, and what could be done to prevent future wars. Believing that the network of military alliances had made prewar conflicts insoluble, he advocated an end to secret agreements. Concluding that arms races had contributed to war, he proposed arms reduction and guarantees of freedom of the seas. With the understanding that economic competition had escalated prewar tensions, he urged the removal of economic barriers among nations and the gradual elimination of the colonial system; and recognizing that war had distorted the map of Europe, he demanded the evacuation of all occupied territory.

To remove the ethnic and nationalistic tensions that had been an immediate cause of war, he urged self-determination for "well-defined national aspirations." To oversee the peace and manage future conflicts he suggested the creation of an international collective security organization.

Although Wilson's Fourteen Points had huge appeal among the peoples of both the Allies and the Central Powers, neither set of leaders was ready to make peace in the late winter of 1918. The Germans were readying a last, great offensive on the Western Front, while the Allies were fantasizing about reestablishing the Eastern Front through intervention in Russia, while gambling that that, plus the arrival of U.S. troops, would give them victory. By autumn these last hopes had crumbled into smoke and death. Although the Germans did indeed make significant breakthroughs in March and April, they did not have the men and supplies to follow up their initial successes, and they could not stop the Allied counterattacks in August. In September the Central Powers began to collapse as Austria-Hungary proposed peace negotiations on

16 September and Bulgaria signed a surrender on 29 September. On the Allied side, heavy losses, sinking morale, and economic exhaustion made it impossible to carry the war into Germany. Allied intervention in Russia, to which Wilson reluctantly agreed in July, not only failed to achieve a reestablishment of the Eastern Front, but was swallowed up by the vast spaces and harsh climate. And to complete the ruin, a terrible influenza epidemic, the greatest plague since the Black Death, swept the world, killing twenty million people the next year and devastating both armies and civilian workforces.

In October 1918 German military leaders, recognizing the imminence of collapse and invasion, demanded that the government sue for peace on the basis of Wilson's Fourteen Points. Suspecting that the British and French would be far less generous than the United States, the German government sent a request for an armistice to Washington on 6 October. If Germany had intended to divide its enemies and buy time to regroup, it was disappointed. Wilson replied that he would not even discuss an armistice with the kaiser. Faced with a military mutiny and a possible civilian revolution, the kaiser replaced his wartime leaders with opposition socialists and liberals. He then abdicated and fled to Holland on 9 November. In the meantime, the Ottoman Empire signed an armistice with the British on 31 October, and Austria-Hungary signed one with the Italians on 3 November.

The German offer to sign an armistice on the basis of the Fourteen Points provided a foretaste of the peace negotiations. Neither the British nor the French reacted enthusiastically about the Fourteen Points, which seemed likely to deprive them of the spoils of victory. Before they would agree to the German proposal, the British rejected the point regarding freedom of the seas and the French insisted that there must be no limit on reparations payments required from Germany. Moreover, the Allies insisted that the borders defined in the ceasefire must be set by the military, and they made sure that those lines put Alsace-Lorraine, the Saar coal basin, the west bank of the Rhine River and the bridges over it under French control. In the east, armistice terms expanded the boundaries of the newly independent Poland and Czechoslovakia at Germany's expense. Colonel House, negotiating the armistice terms for Wilson, could not budge the Allies from these positions, even when he hinted that the United States might be compelled to make a separate peace. At 11:00 A.M. on 11 November 1918, the armistice was signed in a railway carriage at Compiègne in France.

Wilson and House may not have realized the extent to which the armistice terms would determine the final shape of the peace, but certainly they did not delude themselves in believing that a peace based on the Fourteen Points would be easy. In preparation for the struggle over the peace treaty, Wilson made two controversial and possibly mistaken decisions in the autumn of 1918. He decided to lead the U.S. delegation to the Paris Peace Conference, and he intervened in the mid-term congressional election campaign, urging voters to give him Democratic majorities in the Congress that would have to approve the peace treaty. In both cases he tied the future of his peace program to his personal prestige, and in both cases he lost. The voters returned Republican majorities in both houses of Congress, and in Europe Wilson was in due course forced to accept a peace treaty that departed in significant ways from the Fourteen Points. Although historians still debate whether the outcome in each case might have been even worse for Wilson without his personal involvement, it is obvious that in neither case did he achieve the clear victory for which he was hoping.

Wilson arrived in France on 13 December 1918. He brought with him nearly 1,300 civilian and military members of the American Mission to Negotiate Peace, including members of The Inquiry, a group of experts he had appointed in late 1917 to study in detail the issues that would come before the peace conference. But it was Wilson that millions of Frenchmen, Italians, and Britons turned out to see when the president was carried in triumphal procession through the streets of Paris, Rome, and London, and it was upon Wilson that the main burden of defending the Fourteen Points fell when the conference opened in January 1919.

The history of the peace conference was divided into four periods. The first, from the opening on 12 January until 14 February 1919, was dominated by Wilson's total obsession with hammering out a draft of the Covenant of the League of Nations. The second, from 14 February to 14 March, was the period during which Wilson returned to the United States to confront the ominous rumblings of opposition, while British Prime Minister David Lloyd George dealt with pressing domestic issues in Great Britain, and French Premier Georges Clemenceau recovered from the nearly fatal assassination attempt by an anarchist. During the absence of these three principals, their subordinates continued discussion of economic and territorial terms.

Upon Wilson's return to Paris on 14 March, the third period of the conference began. To placate his critics at home, the president asked the Allies to accept amendments to the League Covenant protecting national sovereignty by excluding from the purview of the League such issues as immigration, tariffs, and the Monroe Doctrine. In return, the Europeans demanded concessions on territorial and economic issues, and Wilson had no choice but to compromise. Where the Fourteen Points had implied the need for a comprehensive colonial settlement, Wilson had to accept a League of Nations mandate system that

covered only Germany's colonies and placed them under the supervision of the victorious Allies, who promised vaguely to ready the colonies gradually for self-government. Where the Fourteen (and subsequent additional) Points had promised a nonpunitive peace, Wilson had to agree that Germany's reparations bill would be set in the future by an international commission, and that the total would be inflated by the inclusion of pensions as well as direct war damages. Where Wilson had intended that Germany would be reintegrated quickly into Europe and the League, he was forced to accept a French occupation of the Rhineland and Saar basin for at least fifteen years and German exclusion from the League. The French agreed to this arrangement only because the British and Americans signed a supplementary treaty promising to come to France's defense if necessary.

Elsewhere, Wilson was forced to accept territorial settlements in northern Italy and western Poland and Czechoslovakia that openly violated the concept of national self-determination, as did the treaty's recognition of continued Japanese control over the Shandong province of China. The president believed that his beloved League of Nations would be able to rectify some of these injustices after the passions of war had cooled, and he argued that the peace was better than it would have been without his influence, but critics have often concluded that all he managed to achieve was a peace that was neither generous enough to win German goodwill nor harsh enough to prevent Germany from seeking revenge twenty years later.

The fourth period of the peace conference began when the terms of the proposed treaty were handed to the Germans on 7 May 1919. In this period the Germans were permitted to propose changes in the document, and Lloyd George, with British public opinion now softening toward Germany, led an effort to moderate the peace terms. He proposed a reduction in German reparations, a change in the Polish-German border in Germany's favor, a plebiscite to determine the future of Upper Silesia instead of simply turning it over to Poland, a reduction in the period of Allied occupation of the Rhineland, and the immediate admission of Germany to the League. The other Allies did not accept all of these changes, but the treaty that German delegates signed on 28 June 1919, in the Hall of Mirrors of the Treaty of Versailles, was less harsh than the document they had first read on 7 May. Treaties with Austria (10 September 1919) and with Hungary (4 June 1920) closely followed the Versailles settlement, while others with Bulgaria (27 November 1919) and Turkey (10 August 1920) did not have even the imperfect Wilsonian shape of the Versailles agreement and did not involve the United States.

In his speech presenting the Treaty of Versailles to the Senate on 10 July, Wilson challenged the nation to accept "yet higher levels of service and achievement." He admitted that the agreement was imperfect, but he insisted that the creation of the League alone was a gain of such importance to world peace that the United States could not afford to reject the opportunity.

Those who listened to Wilson that July evening did so with widely mixed reactions. A majority agreed with him and seemed prepared to take up the challenge, although with differing degrees of enthusiasm. A small minority were head-in-the-sand isolationists unwilling to have the United States accept any international obligations. And between these two groups was a diverse set of senators who believed, as Majority Leader Henry Cabot Lodge put it, that "we must do our share to carry out the peace as we have done our share to win the war." The senators were not sure that the treaty Wilson was presenting was the best way to achieve that end. Some of them were disillusioned Wilsonians, who believed that the president had made too many compromises in Paris and had accepted a punitive and dangerous treaty. Some, like Lodge, were realists who believed that the peacekeeping machinery of the League would not work unless the United States was constantly ready to put its armed forces at the call of the international body.

Through the summer of 1919 the debate raged about whether the United States should accept the Treaty of Versailles and become a member of the League of Nations. By August, Wilson realized that it was unlikely he would be able to secure the two-thirds majority he needed to secure Senate approval. He decided to take his case to the people, hoping to generate a wave of public opinion that would sway the Senate. On 3 September, he set out on a three-week speaking tour of the western United States, where much of the opposition to the treaty was concentrated. During the next twenty-two days he delivered thirty-seven major speeches and dozens of minor ones to increasingly enthusiastic audiences. By late September it appeared he succeeded in arousing the public support he wanted, but on 25 September, after a speech at Pueblo, Colorado, he collapsed and was rushed back to Washington. There, on 2 October, he suffered a massive paralytic stroke.

Wilson's illness made him incapable of closely following the treaty fight or any other government business, and it also made him inflexible, intolerant, and petty. Whether he would have found an acceptable compromise with critics of the treaty if he had been well is impossible to say, but certainly his illness deprived treaty supporters of leadership in the crucial weeks before the vote. On 19 November, and again on 19 March 1920, the Senate rejected the treaty. Not until more than twenty years after Wilson's death would the United States take its place in another international organization, the United Nations.

Although Wilson and many other Americans were deeply disappointed at the United States's failure to accept the Treaty of Versailles and join the League of Nations, the United States gained more than it lost from the war. In comparison to the estimated nine million soldiers killed in the war, American losses of only 116,000 were light indeed. No battles were fought on U.S. soil, and although some U.S. ships were sunk by U-boats, the United States came out of the war with sixty percent more merchant tonnage than it had when it entered. The war promoted industrial and scientific development and encouraged the standardization and mass production of many items, including consumer goods, which were never in short supply in the United States. Farmers enjoyed unprecedented prosperity with guaranteed domestic and foreign markets. Organized labor grew steadily, and desirable jobs opened for the first time to African Americans and women. Social reformers were pleased with the wartime adoption of prohibition and suffrage for women, and with campaigns against prostitution, at least in the areas around military camps.

In addition to the enormous benefits the war brought the United States at home, it also made America a world power, even if Americans were reluctant to accept all the implications of their new status. During the course of the war the United States changed a net foreign debt of $3.7 billion into a credit of the same amount, not counting the $10 billion loaned by the government to the European Allies. American overseas investments doubled, from $3.5 billion in 1914 to $7 billion in 1919, while European investments in the United States were nearly halved. By the mid-1920s U.S. trade with Asia had doubled over pre-war figures, and exports to Latin America had increased by twenty percent, with U.S. firms becoming the largest suppliers of foreign goods to Latin America by 1929. U.S. oil companies began to gain a foothold in the Middle East, and in the world's financial and trade circles Americans replaced the British as dominant figures.

The U.S. government played a somewhat ambivalent role in this economic expansion. "When the war is over," said Wilson, "we can force [the Allies] to our way of thinking, because by that time they will, among other things, be financially in our hands...," but the administration did not use U.S. economic might ruthlessly, either for political or economic ends. Loans to the Allies were kept as small as possible and not tied to specific political conditions, and the administration muzzled the ambitious chairman of the United States Shipping Board, Edward N. Hurley, who wanted to use the growing U.S. merchant marine to take over the British carrying-trade while British ships were forced to transport American goods and soldiers to Europe. Although Wilson wanted to be able to exercise economic influence over the Allies at the peace conference, he was equally afraid of a large, permanent governmental role in the economy. When the war ended, the wartime federal bureaucracy was dismantled and with it went much of the president's economic leverage at Paris. In the end some of the war's economic gains, like political influence, proved ephemeral, yet no one outside the United States doubted that America would be a decisive factor in future world developments. For the first time the nation's industrial capacity had been translated into global power, and the temptation to use that strength in the future would be irresistible.

KENDRICK A. CLEMENTS

See also Austria; Balfour, Arthur James; Bernstoff, Johann Heinrich, Graf von; Bosnia-Herzegovina; Bryan, William Jennings; China; Clemenceau, Georges; Committee on Public Information; Fourteen Points; France; Freedom of the Seas; Germany; Great Britain; Grey, Edward; House, Edward Mandell; Japan; Lansing-Ishii Agreement; League of Nations; Lloyd George, David; Lodge, Henry Cabot, Sr.; Lusitania; Morocco; Napoleonic Wars; Neutral Rights; Open Door Policy; Pershing, John; Russia and the Soviet Union; Serbia; Submarine Warfare; Versailles Treaty of 1919; Villa, Pancho; Wilhelm II, Kaiser; Wilson, Thomas Woodrow; Zimmermann Telegram

FURTHER READING

Berghahn, Volker R. *Germany and the Approach of War in 1914,* second ed. New York, 1993.

Coffman, Edward M. *The War to End All Wars: The American Military Experience in World War I.* New York, [Oxford], 1968.

Cooper, John Milton, Jr. *Pivotal Decades: The United States, 1900-1920.* New York, 1990.

Devlin, Patrick. *Too Proud to Fight: Woodrow Wilson's Neutrality.* New York, 1974.

Ferrell, Robert. *Woodrow Wilson and World War I, 1917-1921.* New York, 1985.

Goldstein, Erik. *Winning the Peace: British Diplomatic Strategy, Peace Planning, and the Paris Peace Conference, 1916-1920.* New York, 1991.

Kennedy, David M. *Over Here: The First World War and American Society.* New York, 1980.

Knock, Thomas. *To End All Wars: Woodrow Wilson and the Quest for a New World Order.* New York, 1992.

Link, Arthur S. *Wilson,* 5 vols. Princeton, N.J., 1947–1965.

May, Ernest R. *The World War and American Isolation, 1914–1917.* Cambridge, Mass., 1959.

Schwabe, Klaus. *Woodrow Wilson, Revolutionary Germany, and Peacemaking, 1918-1919: Missionary Diplomacy and the Realities of Power.* Chapel Hill, N.C., 1985.

Stevenson, David. *French War Aims against Germany, 1914–1919.* New York, 1982.

Trask, David. *The AEF and Coalition Warmaking.* Lawrence, Kans., 1993.

Vaughn, Stephen. *Holding Fast the Inner Lines: Democracy, Nationalism, and the Committee on Public Information.* Chapel Hill, N.C., 1980.

Walworth, Arthur. *Wilson and His Peacemakers: American Diplomacy at the Paris Peace Conference, 1919.* New York, 1986.

Winter, J. M. *The Experience of World War I.* New York, 1989.

WORLD WAR II

World War II officially began with the German invasion of Poland (1 September 1939), although Japan had been waging aggressive war against China intermittently since 1931. Between 1939 and the start of formal U.S. belligerency following the surprise Japanese attack on Pearl Harbor (7 December 1941) the United States government was a neutral sympathizing with and giving some assistance to the victims of German and Japanese aggression. During the twenty-seven months of neutrality President Franklin D. Roosevelt confronted a divided public opinion and Congress. He wanted to do everything possible to tip the balance against Germany and Japan, but he was constrained by domestic opposition to intervention, simplistically labeled isolationism. Facing a presidential election in November 1940, he was particularly concerned not to be seen as leading the country into war and thereby losing to a Republican opponent of intervention. After the surrender of France to Germany in June 1940 the survival of Great Britain was in doubt. Roosevelt moved more energetically to win support for aid to the British; in September he announced that the United States would supply surplus naval destroyers to Great Britain in return for naval and air bases on British islands in the western hemisphere. Meanwhile, Japan and Germany signed an alliance designed to intimidate the United States into keeping out of the war and Japan moved beyond China into Southeast Asia.

After his reelection in 1940 Roosevelt had more freedom to act. He asked and won congressional authorization, under the Lend-Lease legislation of March 1941, to provide material assistance including weapons to any nation whose security he determined was vital to the security of the United States. Calling on Americans to turn the country into the "arsenal of democracy," he directed a flow of aid to Great Britain and, after Germany invaded Russia, to the Soviet Union. During this time the United States maintained technical diplomatic relations with Nazi Germany, but made no effort to negotiate with Adolf Hitler.

The United States did conduct a long but unimportant diplomatic exchange with Japan aimed at persuading it to withdraw from China and abandon dreams of conquest. The Japanese government, however, would not compromise on its goal of establishing hegemony over a "greater East Asia coprosperity sphere" and that meant control of China and the resources of Southeast Asia. Faced with Japanese intransigence, the United States applied ever tighter economic sanctions against Japan, beginning with strategic materials and culminating in July 1941 with a total freeze on exports. Faced with what appeared as U.S. determination to strangle their country, Japanese leaders began in 1941 planning for an attack on

The Allies Push Japan Back
1942-1945

Japanese -held areas

Limit of Japanese conquest

the American fleet. When that attack came at Pearl Harbor, and Germany and Italy declared war on the United States four days later, the period of wartime diplomacy began and continued to the surrender of Japan on 2 September 1945.

During those forty-five months the United States held together an alliance with Great Britain and the Soviet Union, achieved the surrender of Italy, Germany, and Japan, and designed institutions and procedures for the postwar era. In the process the United States became the

world's dominant industrial, agricultural, transportation, and military power. U.S. political interests and influence expanded to every part of the world. The other great powers of the prewar period, with the exception of the Soviet Union, either were reduced in status even in victory or were defeated and occupied. The foundations of European empires in Africa, the Middle East, and Asia were undermined beyond the possibility of recovery. The Soviet Union, despite suffering huge casualties and material damage, emerged from the war relatively more

THE SECOND WORLD WAR IN EUROPE

- Hitler's Greater Germany
- Allied with Germany
- Occupied by Germany and its allies
- Grand Alliance
- Neutral nations
- ✕ Major battles

From *A History of Western Society*, McKay, Hill, and Bucker, Volume II, 4th Edition. ©1991 by Houghton Mifflin Company.
Reprinted with permission of Houghton Mifflin Company.

powerful than before, with political control over Europe as far west as the center of Germany and enhanced influence in Asia.

President Roosevelt, British Prime Minister Winston Churchill, and Soviet leader Joseph Stalin dominated wartime diplomacy, making key decisions, corresponding directly with each other, and meeting at summit conferences. Because of wartime conditions, their meetings and most of their decisions were secret. Churchill was the most mobile and he met often with Roosevelt or Stal-

in one-on-one. The three came together twice: at Tehran, Iran, in late 1943, and at Yalta, in the Soviet Union, in February 1945.

The Importance of U.S. Power

The United States faced a daunting military task in December 1941. Japan for the moment controlled the Pacific and was about to overrun the Philippines, Singapore, Malaya, and the Netherlands East Indies. Australia was threatened. Great Britain, having narrowly avoided invasion by Hitler's forces in 1940, was fighting hard in North Africa in a desperate attempt to defend Egypt, the Suez Canal, and the Middle East. The Soviet Union had stopped Hitler's armies on the outskirts of Moscow, but whether the Germans would prevail in a new offensive in the summer of 1942 remained an open question. On the Atlantic, German U-boats were decimating U.S. and British shipping, including oil tankers torpedoed within sight of beaches along the American seaboard. But if the German and Japanese thrusts could be stopped, and if the Allied coalition could be held together, the ultimate outcome would be decided by the greater population, resources, and military potential of the United States and its associates. The first "if" depended on military action and the second on diplomacy. The two became linked.

The central fact behind the military campaigns and the pursuit of political objectives was the astounding weight of U.S. power, which stemmed from a combination of fortunate geographical position, the rich natural resources of the continental United States, advanced technology, sound military leadership, and the effective mobilization of the population in the war effort.

The United States was the only power in the war not to suffer military attack on its industrial base. The Japanese, after attacking Pearl Harbor in Hawai'i, limited their subsequent operations against the United States to the central and western Pacific. German submarines did sink ships within sight of the Atlantic coast in 1942, but the idea that German bombers might strike U.S. cities seemed a fantasy. In an era before intercontinental missiles, the great oceans provided protection. Furthermore, the nation's industrial capacity, in virtual hibernation during the depression, stood posed for extraordinary expansion. The unemployed found jobs, women joined the industrial workforce, and productivity soared even as millions served in the armed forces. The United States' natural resources and imports from Latin America met the needs for a war economy: food, petroleum, coal, iron and other metals, lumber, and textiles.

Using the world's best industrial agricultural technology, the U.S. economy fed, housed, and clothed the population; equipped the armed forces; supplied the Allies with essential military and economic aid through the lend-lease program; and built the ships necessary for adding reach to strength. U.S. military and economic power flowed to corners of the world where it had never been to a significant degree: to the heart of Europe, to North Africa and the Middle East, to all of Asia, to the southern Pacific. Power created influence and interests not only for the duration of the war but also for the distant future.

The war profoundly altered the ways in which Americans thought about the nation's place in the world. Before Pearl Harbor, isolationist arguments had many adherents in Congress and among leaders of public opinion. Both halves of the Monroe Doctrine were regularly invoked as sacred scripture: the rest of the world must keep its hands off the western hemisphere and the United States must abstain from involvement in European politics and war. Isolationists argued that the United States could and should live prosperously with its own resources, and began a defensive shield. No other nation could hurt it. But to throw American lives and fortunes into the interminable conflicts of Europe and Asia would weaken the nation, threaten democratic freedoms, and serve no useful purpose for the world, they claimed.

The Japanese attack of 7 December 1941 silenced some isolationists and converted others to the belief that the United States would have to win the war and lead the world afterwards in keeping the peace. Prewar believers in an active role for the United States became confirmed in their instincts and welcomed the converts. While Roosevelt focused on summit diplomacy and generals and admirals planned operations, thousands of Americans at home wrote, spoke, and planned for the postwar world with a United Nations organization redeeming the failed promise of the League of Nations. In 1943 both the Senate (Connally resolution) and the House of Representatives (Fulbright resolution) voted in favor of U.S. membership in an international collective security organization. The United States, it was said, had something seldom accorded an individual, much less a nation: a second chance to do the right thing. Meanwhile, there was a war to be fought and won.

War Aims and the Atlantic Charter

The United States responded to the Japanese attack with a formal declaration of war against Japan by a vote in both houses of Congress on 8 December 1941. Three days later, on 11 December, Germany and Italy, Japan's allies, declared war on the United States. With Congress and public opinion now united in a war effort, President Roosevelt proceeded to supervise and often personally conduct the negotiations with the Allies necessary for effective military operations. The president avoided announcing detailed objectives for the postwar period. His public declarations emphasized American commitment to "four essential human freedoms…everywhere in the world": freedom of speech, freedom of religion, freedom from want, and freedom from fear, meaning international security against aggression (first enunciated in his January 1941 annual message to Congress). Another statement of U.S. objectives flowed from the Atlantic Charter, originally a joint statement by Roosevelt and Prime Minister Churchill issued in August 1941 and reaffirmed in the "United Nations Declaration" signed by the governments at war with members of the Tripartite (Axis) pact on 1 January 1942 (the United States, Great

WORLD WAR II CONFERENCES

CONFERENCE	DATE	PARTICIPANTS	RESULTS
Argentia, Newfoundland	August 9–12, 1941	Roosevelt, Churchill	Atlantic Charter
Washington, D.C.	December 22, 1941–January 14, 1942	Roosevelt, Churchill	Combined Chiefs of Staff; priority in war effort against Germany; United Nations Declaration
Washington, D.C.	June 19–25, 1942	Roosevelt, Churchill	North African campaign strategy
Moscow, USSR	August 12–15, 1942	Churchill, Stalin, Harriman	Postponement of second front
Casablanca, Morocco	January 14–24, 1943	Roosevelt, Churchill	Unconditional surrender announcement; campaign against Sicily and Italy
Washington, D.C.	May 12–15, 1943	Roosevelt, Churchill	Schedule for cross–channel landing set as May 1, 1944
Quebec, Canada	August 14–24, 1943	Roosevelt, Churchill	Confirmation of cross–channel; landing (OVERLOAD)
Moscow, USSR	October 19–30, 1943	Hull, Eden, Molotov	Postwar international organization to be formed; Russian promise to enter the war against Japan after Germany's defeat; establishment of European Advisory Commission
UNRRA, Washington, D.C.	November 9, 1943	44 nations	Creation of UNRRA
Cairo, Egypt	November 22–26, 1943	Roosevelt, Churchill, Jiang	Postwar Asia: China to recover lost lands; Korea to be independent; Japan to be stripped of Pacific Islands
Teheran, Iran	November 27 – December 1, 1943	Roosevelt, Churchill, Stalin	Agreement on cross–channel landing and international organizations; Soviet reaffirmation of intent to enter the war against Japan
Bretton Woods, New Hampshire	July 1–22, 1944	44 nations	Creation of World Bank and International Monetary Fund
Dumbarton Oaks, Washington, D.C.	August 21– October 7, 1944	U.S., Britain, USSR, China	United Nations Organization
Quebec, Canada	September 11–16, 1944	Roosevelt, Churchill	"Morgenthau Plan" for Germany
Moscow, USSR	October 9–18, 1944	Churchill, Stalin	Spheres of influence in Balkans (percentage scheme)
Yalta, USSR	February 4–11, 1945	Roosevelt, Churchill, Stalin	Polish government structure, elections, and boundaries; United Nations; German reparations; USSR pledge t o declare war against Japan and to recognize Jiang's government; some Japanese territories to USSR
San Francisco, California	April 25– June 26, 1945	50 nations	United Nations Organization Charter
Potsdam (Berlin), Germany	July 17– August 2, 1945	Truman, Churchill/Attlee, Stalin	German reconstruction and reparations; Potsdam Declarationto Japan; Council of Foreign Ministers established

From *American Foreign Relations*, Thomas G. Paterson, J. Garry Clifford, Kenneth J. Hagan, Volume II. © 1995 by D.C. Heath and Company. Reprinted with permission of Houghton Mifflin Company.

Britain, the Soviet Union, China, and twenty-two other nations).

The declaration was an executive agreement, signed on the authority of the president of the United States, and not a treaty submitted to the Senate for approval. But it was the documentary basis for the wartime alliance. The signatories pledged to employ all their military and economic resources for the defeat of those members of the Tripartite Pact with which they were at war (the Soviet Union was not at war with Japan) and "not to make a separate armistice or peace with the enemies."

By embracing the Atlantic Charter, the united nations declared that territorial changes should take place only with "the freely expressed wishes of the people concerned," that all people had the right to chose their form of government, and that "sovereign rights and self government" should be "restored to those who have been forcible deprived of them." The Charter also called for economic cooperation, the disarmament of aggressor nations, and the eventual establishment of a "permanent system of general security." The central problem with the Atlantic Charter was that millions of people under British and Soviet control did not enjoy a choice in the form of government under which they lived and many had been forcibly deprived of sovereignty and self-government. If the Atlantic Charter applied to allies as well as to the enemy, how could the alliance be kept together? That question ran like a bright thread through the fabric of wartime diplomacy. President Roosevelt sought to avoid grappling with this troublesome question while concentrating on cooperation for victory.

The only large region of the world to pose no serious problem during the war was Latin America, and it attracted little high-level attention. The United States worked successfully to persuade the Latin American republics to extirpate Nazi and Japanese influence, to make raw materials fully available, and to declare war against the Axis powers. German U-boats, after inflicting terrible damage in 1942, were largely driven from the Caribbean in 1943. Oil, metals, and food products flowed north and on to Europe. Every republic eventually broke relations and eventually declared war on the Axis. Brazil contributed an army division to the fighting in Italy and made bases available to the United States to support lines of communication to North Africa. The only irritant was the persistent pro-German bias of Argentina. The United States wanted to impose punitive economic sanctions, but refrained because of Great Britain's dependence on Argentina beef. Argentina declared war on Germany in the spring of 1945 in order to be eligible for membership in the United Nations (UN).

Toward the end of the war Latin American governments worried that the United States would become so involved with the UN and world affairs that Latin America would be forgotten. In order to meet this concern, the United States agreed to the Chapultepec conference in Mexico City in February 1945. By signing the resulting Act of Chapultepec the United States committed itself to joining a future hemispheric collective defense treaty.

The most frustrating Allied relationship for the United States was with China. Although the U.S. refusal to acquiesce in the Japanese conquest of China was the principal reason for the war in the Pacific, there was very little the United States could do to help China directly. Japanese armed forces blocked seaborne supplies and only a trickle of matériel could be sent by air from India. Furthermore, the government of Generalissimo Jiang Jieshi (Chiang Kai-Shek) was corrupt, inefficient, and concerned as much with preserving its position for a postwar showdown with the Chinese Communists as it was with fighting the Japanese.

Summit Diplomacy

Secretary of State Cordell Hull and the career Foreign Service of the Department of State, often ignored by President Roosevelt even in peacetime, played a minor role in wartime diplomacy. Roosevelt relied heavily on Harry Hopkins, an intimate adviser of absolute loyalty who had an extraordinary talent for cutting through red tape. He became the president's alter ego and personal envoy. Averell Harriman, lend-lease administrator and ambassador to the Soviet Union (1943–1946), emerged as another important advisor and trusted diplomat. Admiral William D. Leahy, former chief of naval operations and ambassador to Vichy France, served as the president's personal chief of staff and chairman of the embryonic Joint Chiefs of Staff. Leahy regulated the flow of military information to the president and after Roosevelt's death provided continuity for President Harry S. Truman.

In World War I, President Wilson stayed in the United States until opening stages of the Paris Peace Conference of 1919 and received no heads of government in Washington. But in World War II, summit conferences provided the organizing framework of diplomacy from the outset. Roosevelt and Prime Minister Churchill had already met in August 1941 on shipboard in Newfoundland. Churchill came to the United States in December 1941 immediately after Pearl Harbor. He returned four times during the war and hardly a day passed without his sending Roosevelt at least one long message. Roosevelt gave short, prompt replies. In addition Churchill and Roosevelt met twice in Quebec, Canada; at Casablanca, Morocco; at Cairo, Egypt; at Malta; and at the major summits with Stalin at Tehran and Yalta. The final Big Three summit, attended by Roosevelt's successor, Truman, was at the Berlin suburb of Potsdam in July 1945.

The only occasion on which Secretary of State Hull played an important role was the foreign ministers' (U.S.,

British, and Soviet) conference held in Moscow in October 1943. That conference decided on the restoration of Austria, annexed by Germany in 1938, to its previous borders and independent status. Also, the Soviet government gave a conditional promise to enter the war against Japan and adhered, much to Hull's delight, to a vague declaration in favor of establishing a general international security organization.

The allies also held specialized conferences of "working level" officials convened to deal with postwar arrangements on relief, food, aviation, the international economy, and collective security. The most important were the Dumbarton Oaks conference in Washington to develop a preliminary draft of the UN charter and the Bretton Woods conference in New Hampshire on postwar international economic institutions—the International Monetary Fund (IMF) and the International Bank for Reconstruction and Development (World Bank)—designed to promote growth and prevent the destructive competition characteristic of the prewar years.

British and U.S. officials shared plans, intelligence information, and resources. They worked on joint boards that dealt with food, shipping, industrial production, and new weapons including the atomic bomb. Their intelligence services shared plans and secret intercepts. The Combined Chiefs of Staff, a military body with high-level representation from both countries, conferred regularly in Washington. These activities not only facilitated the day-to-day running of the war, but also provided experience for a generation of Americans who would rise to high foreign policy positions in the next decades, the years of the Cold War. There were no comparable connections with the Soviets or any other ally.

Problems in Soviet-American Relations

The United States and the Soviet Union had little in common except Germany as an enemy. Notwithstanding transparent wartime rhetoric about partnership in the cause of freedom, they were deeply divided by the hostile ideologies of liberal democracy and totalitarian democracy. Before the German attack on the Soviet Union in June 1941 most Americans had looked on the Soviet Union and communism as evils quite comparable to Hitler's regime. The Nazi-Soviet Non-Aggression Pact of August 1939 confirmed this view. But Roosevelt, noting the likelihood that Hitler might turn on the Soviet Union, sent warnings to Stalin and tried to keep the way open for collaboration. Hitler did attack the Soviet Union in June 1941.

But how long would and could the Soviet Union avoid defeat? Roosevelt and his advisors recalled that in World War I, Russia had made a separate peace with Germany and that Stalin and Hitler were partners in aggression between 1939–1941. Might Stalin turn his coat yet again?

It was imperative to do everything possible to keep the Soviet Union in the war. But the gap between what was possible and what the Soviets demanded was great. Wartime diplomacy dealt largely with efforts to conceal or close that gap.

The Soviet Union sought three commitments from the United States and Great Britain: military equipment without limit, a treaty recognizing Soviet boundaries as they had existed before the German invasion of June 1941, and the immediate establishment of a second front. Roosevelt ordered that high priority be accorded to the Soviet need for weapons and supplies, to be shipped as grant-aid under the Lend-Lease program with no detailed accounting or commitments required of the Soviets in return. The U.S. military thought the priority too high and feared interruption of the rapid development of its forces. Also, much of the aid fell victim to German U-boats preying on the convoys across the Atlantic into north Russia. The United States supplied all that it could—$11.1 billion by war's end, second only to the $31.6 billion received by the British Empire—but it was never enough to satisfy Soviet requests, improve the general tone of the relationship, or earn any thanks.

The Soviet demand for recognition of postwar territorial and political objectives proved an international and U.S. domestic political landmine. During the period of the Nazi-Soviet Non-Aggression pact (1939–1941) the Soviets annexed the independent states of Latvia, Estonia, and Lithuania and the eastern third of Poland, and made war on Finland to acquire territory on the Soviet border. From Moscow's point of view the annexed territory was vital to the state's security, a buffer against some future attack from the west. Stalin insisted that the Soviet Union could accept nothing less than the boundaries and arrangements prevailing on the eve of the German attack in June 1941. He wanted the United States and Great Britain to sign a treaty recognizing Soviet claims. Public acceptance of Soviet demands would have caused an outcry in the United States over the betrayal of the ideals of the Atlantic Charter. Confrontation with the Soviet Union would have threatened the alliance and victory itself. President Roosevelt thus refused formal support for Soviet objectives while he tried to keep the issue from coming to a head either at home or between the United States and the Soviet Union.

The problem of a second front stood as the central military issue of the war and it led inevitably to profound questions about the political future of Europe, especially the place of Germany. Roosevelt unwisely promised Soviet Foreign Minister V. M. Molotov in May 1942 that there would be a second front before the end of the year. When that front turned out to be in North Africa, not France, the Soviets complained bitterly and they continued to complain, and to suggest that the delay was part of a deliberate effort to let Russians do the dying, until the D-day invasion of Normandy in June 1944. The sour memory of the controversy lingered for decades.

Prime Minister Churchill and the British military insisted on the need to postpone the second front as long as possible. The British wished to avoid the hideous casualties incurred in the trench warfare of World War I and to contain the drain on their small population, dwindling resources, and worldwide commitments. The favored British strategy was to concentrate on bombing Germany while launching peripheral attacks through Italy and the Balkans with no cross-Channel attack until Germany was almost powerless to resist—perhaps, at best, in 1944 or 1945.

General George C. Marshall, the American chief of staff, and his planning staff wanted to unleash U.S. power in a frontal attack as soon as possible, even in 1942. They underestimated the difficulties and exaggerated the degree to which the British were motivated by the desire to retain political influence in the Mediterranean. Roosevelt, on the other hand, was swayed by Churchill's arguments and ordered the North Africa landings of November 1942 instead of preparations for an early cross-Channel attack. The Germans were driven from North Africa within a few months and the next step followed logically: the Allied invasion of Sicily and mainland Italy. The Italian government surrendered but German resistance remained fierce all along the Italian peninsula. And there was no second front in France in 1943.

Unconditional Surrender and the Future of Germany

The delay in meeting Soviet expectations led Roosevelt to look for another way to reassure Stalin of Anglo-American good faith. He chose the policy of unconditional surrender. At a conference in Casablanca, Morocco, in January 1943 Roosevelt and Churchill declared that the total destruction of the military power of Germany, Japan, and Italy was an absolute necessity, requiring "unconditional surrender." This, they said, "does not mean the destruction of the population of Germany, Italy, or Japan, but it does mean the destruction of the philosophies in those countries which are based on conquest and the subjugation of other people." Roosevelt hoped the declaration would remove any suspicion in Moscow that the United States and Great Britain might make a separate peace and thereby use German power against the Soviet Union. Churchill did not think there was much risk of a separate Soviet-German peace.

Unconditional surrender also reflected the memory of Roosevelt and his advisors of how the Germans believed they had been offered a lenient negotiated peace in 1918 and then had been betrayed by the "dictate" of the Versailles treaty of 1919. Hitler had exploited this grievance in his rise to power. This time there would be no misunderstanding. The Germans would know they were defeated. They policy subsequently was criticized for discouraging any resistance to Hitler within Germany and leading the Germans to fight on beyond all limits of rationality.

There was deep disagreement and uncertainty within the U.S. government and among the Allies over objectives for postwar Germany. The Allied governments agreed that Nazism had to be eliminated from Germany. In the Moscow declaration of 1 November 1943 the United States, Great Britain, and the Soviet Union decided that major German war criminals would be punished. At Nuremberg in 1945–1946 an international tribunal sentenced twelve Nazi leaders to death, and seven to prison. Three were acquitted.

It was much more difficult, however, to decide on the fate of an entire nation. President Roosevelt believed in punishing the entire German nation through the permanent partition of the country and the imposition of a harsh standard of living, comparable to that imposed by the Nazis on conquered areas. But the British preferred to maintain a unified Germany and the Soviets, after some ambiguity, shifted in that direction. At the Tehran conference in 1943, Roosevelt, Churchill, and Stalin agreed that all of Germany would be placed under military occupation with a zone for each of the three victors. At Yalta in February 1945 the conferees agreed that the French could have an occupation zone, carved from the U.S.-British zones, with a four-power control council providing coordination for all of Germany. Berlin, located in the middle of the Soviet zone, would be under four-power occupation, a microcosm of Germany as a whole. The British and U.S. wartime failure to get clear written rights over transportation lines into Berlin would lead to difficulty in 1948 when the Soviets imposed a blockade against the western zones of the city. The issue of partition or dismemberment was left open. Roosevelt favored dividing Germany into five or more parts. Churchill was opposed and looked forward to a time when a reformed Germany would play a constructive role in international politics. Stalin's attitude seemed to vacillate.

Meanwhile, Americans who would be responsible for governing part of occupied Germany began planning. The first objective of the civil affairs branch of the army was to minimize the burden of occupation. That meant using Germans as far as possible for routine civilian activities such as running municipal services and providing enough food so that the population did not rise up in desperation. In the summer of 1944 an aide to Secretary of the Treasury Henry Morgenthau complained about the leniency of a draft army plan. Morgenthau agreed and went to Roosevelt. The result was the brief ascendancy of the Morgenthau Plan for the permanent elimination of

German heavy industry. At the second Quebec conference in October, Churchill, seeking a large postwar loan from the United States, reluctantly accepted the Morgenthau Plan. Germany would be reduced to "a country primarily agricultural and pastoral in its character."

Secretary of War Henry L. Stimson and his assistant John J. McCloy were appalled by the Morgenthau Plan. They believed that the German people and the nation were potentially a constructive force for the future of Europe. War criminals should be severely punished, but not the people as a whole. German economic revival was essential both for the overall well-being of Europe and as a source of stability against the spread of "chaos," a codeword for communism. Secretary of State Hull was also opposed, in part because the Department of State had been excluded from a policy role. Roosevelt and Churchill, under pressure, retreated from the Morgenthau Plan. American policy thereafter evolved through several drafts of Joint Chiefs of Staff Directive 1067 (JCS 1067) stressing denazification, demilitarization, democratization, and limited deindustrialization.

At Yalta the Big Three leaders agreed in principle that Germany should pay reparations in kind. But the British and the Americans both remembered the disastrous impact of World War I reparations on political and economic stability and did not want to be saddled with occupying a country so stripped of resources that the people could not support themselves. The United States, said American officials, would end up paying the bill for keeping Germans alive. The Soviets, stressing their heavy losses, proposed that the total amount of reparations be $20 billion with half for the Soviet Union. Roosevelt agreed that this number should be the basis for discussion. The British were opposed to setting any number prematurely.

After the war the United States was reluctant to bear the extra costs of occupying its zone of Germany because reparations were being shipped to the Soviet Union. The Soviets drew heavily from their zone of occupation, including the use of forced labor, but argued that they were denied promised levels of reparations from the western zones. The issue blended with the question of U.S. postwar economic aid for the Soviet Union, which had requested a loan for reconstruction. Secretary Morgenthau had favored a $10 billion low-interest loan, but in the end nothing was forthcoming, in part because of deepening disputes over heavy-handed Soviet policies in Eastern Europe.

Italy as Co-Belligerent

The treatment accorded Italy, Germany's European junior partner, was markedly different. The U.S. government and people never regarded Italy as a dangerous, implacable enemy in the same class as Germany and Japan. Italian dictator Benito Mussolini had conquered Ethiopia in the 1930s, had invaded southern France in June 1940 when the Germans were about to enter Paris, had invaded Greece in October 1940, and had declared war on the United States in December 1941. But many Americans still regarded Mussolini as a posturing buffoon, Italian military forces as supremely inept, and the Italian people as inherently warm-hearted, lacking the perceived German or Japanese capacity for brutality, more victims than villains. The presence of a large Italian-American population in the United States, people with considerable political influence, contributed to this rather benign view.

The policy of unconditional surrender was thus not applied to Italy. U.S. and British forces landed in Sicily on 9 July 1943 and on 25 July, Mussolini was ousted by a pro-surrender group headed by Marshal Pietro Badoglio (Mussolini fled north to German-controlled Italy). On 8 September, with the invasion of mainland Italy under way, the United States and Great Britain agreed to an armistice with the new Italian government. Italy's armed forces surrendered unconditionally. The victors promised the Italian people humane treatment, and recognized the interim, supervised authority of the Badoglio regime. The Allies accepted Italy as a co-belligerent in the war against Germany on 13 October.

Italy's withdrawal from the war led to contention among the Americans, British, and Soviets. The Soviets did not participate in the negotiations for Italy's surrender although Stalin was informed at every stage. He nonetheless grew resentful and suspicious of a separate peace. Moscow pressed for the establishment of a tripartite political-military commission to exercise overall authority in Italy with the Soviet Union as an equal member. The United States rejected the Soviet proposal in favor of an Advisory Council for Italy, a powerless entity which did no more than its name suggested. In short, the Soviet Union had no more direct influence over Italian affairs. Stalin later justified Soviet control over Eastern European countries by citing the Italian model.

A second issue was what kind of government Italy should have. The British favored maintaining the monarchy under King Victor Emmanuel III and favored stability over the elimination of fascist elements. The United States, on the other hand, insisted that the king abdicate (he did in April 1944), and that liberal, antifascist leaders be added to the Italian government. Both the Americans and the British, however, sought to contain the political influence of Italian communists.

Difficulties with France

America's wartime relations with France were difficult and ill-tempered on both sides. During the first phase, lasting until November 1942, the United States maintained diplomatic relations with the Vichy government of

France in spite of its collaboration with Nazi Germany and the antidemocratic character of Vichy leaders. Although American liberals deplored this contact with evil, the Roosevelt administration justified the arrangement on the pragmatic grounds that it provided a listening post in Europe for U.S. diplomats, gave access for intelligence agents in North Africa masquerading as consular officers, and kept open some possibility of persuading Vichy to distance itself from Nazi Germany.

The Vichy regime severed diplomatic relations when the United States invaded North Africa in 1942, but contact with Vichy leadership continued in North Africa. It happened that Admiral Jean Darlan, commander of Vichy forces, was in Algiers when the invasion began. General Dwight D. Eisenhower, commanding the Allied invasion, made a deal to recognize Darlan as the political leader of French North Africa in return for his ordering French troops not to resist the Americans and British. The deal saved many lives, but the public outcry against colluding with a collaborator of the Nazis was vehement. If we deal with Darlan in French territory, will we deal with Hermann Goering in Germany? asked one critic. Roosevelt's embarrassment was somewhat reduced when Darlan was assassinated on Christmas eve by a French monarchist.

The second phase, overlapping with the first, consisted of political warfare between the United States and General Charles de Gaulle, the self-proclaimed leader of the Free French movement and intended savior of France. Roosevelt and Secretary of State Hull detested the imperious de Gaulle and considered him a potential military despot. They were determined that he not be imposed on the French people. The United States refused until 1944 to recognize de Gaulle's authority and tried to have him replaced. But de Gaulle, enjoying British support, consistently outmaneuvered the United States and demonstrated that he did have broad support in France itself.

The third phase, following the Allied landings in Normandy in June 1944, saw the United States reluctantly recognizing that de Gaulle did exercise de facto authority in France. From then until the end of the war there were repeated squabbles but Roosevelt and then Truman moved toward supporting the reconstruction of France as a European power. The principal symbol of the change was that the United States agreed to an occupation zone for France in Germany and accepted France as a permanent member of the Security Council in the forthcoming United Nations. Roosevelt also abandoned his opposition to the restoration of French rule in Indochina.

The Fate of Poland

The powerful advance of the Red Army across eastern Europe after mid-1943 and the cross-Channel invasion of June 1944 brought victory over Germany into view, and forced the Americans and the British to confront the problem of Soviet war aims, above all in Poland. Roosevelt, at his first meeting with Stalin at Tehran in December 1943, sought to avoid a showdown on the future boundaries and political character of Poland by telling Stalin that a powerful Polish-American voting bloc kept him from taking a public stand. He had the 1944 presidential election to worry about. Roosevelt also tried to keep the anti-Soviet leaders of the Polish government in exile in London at arm's length. When the Germans announced in 1943 that they had discovered buried in a forest in Katyn, Poland, the bodies of thousands of Polish officers murdered by the Soviets in 1940, the United States preferred to call the charges propaganda and not ask embarrassing questions. But Moscow broke diplomatic relations with the Polish government in exile when the Poles asked for an investigation of Katyn by the International Red Cross. The Soviets soon organized the nucleus of a communist Polish government, known initially as the Lublin committee. (In 1991 the Soviet government admitted that the Polish officers at Katyn had been killed on Stalin's orders).

The tragic climax of the dilemma between theoretical commitment to Polish independence and the need to maintain good relations with the Soviet Union came in the summer of 1944 as the advancing Red Army reached the outskirts of Warsaw, the Polish capital. Expecting momentary liberation, the Polish underground in the city attacked the German occupiers. But Soviet forces stopped advancing while the Germans killed the Poles. Roosevelt refused to demand that the Soviets either advance or else let the Americans and British drop weapons to the resisting forces with planes that would go on for refueling behind Soviet lines. After the Germans had eliminated the Warsaw resisters, the Soviet advance resumed and soon captured the city. Stalin said that the Red Army had been following a schedule dictated by military considerations. Many in the west, and especially among the Polish exile community, believed the Soviets had deliberately let the Germans dispose of courageous Poles who would have subsequently resisted the imposition of communism.

The two large questions for the future of Poland were boundaries and the nature of a postwar government. Roosevelt and Churchill accepted the Soviet demand that Poland's boundary be moved about two hundred miles to the west, losing a third of its pre-1939 territory to the Soviet Union and gaining another third from pre-1939 Germany. The political outcome also followed Soviet plans, sweetened only by a pledge made at the Yalta conference of February 1945 that the Soviet-sponsored provisional government, which had evolved from the Lublin committee, would be reorganized with the addition of some members of the Polish government in London. The Yalta accord on Poland also called for "free and unfettered elections" as soon as possible. Free elections were never held as long as the Soviet Union remained in control of Poland.

The future of the rest of central and eastern Europe did not attract American attention to the same degree as Poland. The Czechoslovak government in exile had no quarrel with Moscow and in December 1943 signed a mutual defense treaty with the Soviet Union. Greece and Yugoslavia were primarily British concerns. Hungary, Bulgaria, and Romania were Nazi satellites and lay directly in the path of the advancing Red Army. The United States avoided overtures from various shadowy and anti-Soviet groups in those countries. The most dramatic diplomatic exchange took place in Moscow in October 1944 when Churchill proposed that, during the process of liberation, Russia would have ninety percent influence over Romania and seventy-five percent over Bulgaria, Great Britain (in accord with the United States) would have ninety percent control of Greece, while Hungary and Yugoslavia would be divided equally. Stalin agreed. Roosevelt learned of this sketchy spheres-of-influence agreement, but did not embrace it. At Yalta the Big Three leaders issued a public declaration on liberated Europe endorsing the principles of the Atlantic charter. But in reality Soviet control was nearly total in the areas occupied by the Red army. British and U.S. representatives on various control councils were ignored.

Growing American Interests in the Middle East

The interests and influence of the United States in the Middle East grew steadily during the war. In principle the U.S. government recognized the primary responsibility of the British for the region. In practice Americans dealing with the Middle East often criticized and were suspicious of the British. Anglo-American rivalry and friction had three principal sources. The first was oil. Americans became convinced during the war that the petroleum reserves within the United States would be inadequate for future security. Americans in government and in the oil industry believed that the future of the United States depended on secure access to the oil of the Middle East, especially on expanding and protecting the recently attained American position in Saudi Arabia. In order to bolster the American position the United States extended lend-lease aid to Saudi Arabia, although the country was not threatened by German attack.

American suspicion of British colonialism and the idealistic image of the United States was a second and less specific source of friction. Many Americans on the scene, whether in Egypt or Iran, saw their British counterparts as arrogant colonialists of the old school, contemptuous

of other people. The United States, these Americans believed, had the best interests of all people at heart and stood ready to help economic aid and training.

The third and most intractable source of difficulty was the question of a homeland for the Jewish people in the British mandate of Palestine. The British during World War I issued the Balfour Declaration promising such a homeland, provided the rights of the existing Arab population in Palestine were respected. Between the wars, as Jewish population in Palestine grew slowly, Arab opposition increased. In 1939 the British, fearing that the Arabs might join forces with Hitler, promised to accept Jewish immigration of up to 75,000 until 1944 and then cut it off altogether except with Arab approval. The 1939 promise was a death knell for the Balfour Declaration and seemed to doom all hope of an independent Jewish state. The Department of State wished to keep out of the controversy, but the political support in the United States for an independent Jewish state mounted throughout the war.

The Holocaust, Hitler's campaign to exterminate the Jews, gave grim urgency to the question of a Jewish state, but the Department of State discouraged its officials from reporting the substantial evidence of what was taking place. Also, the U.S. military in 1944 rejected suggestions that the railway lines carrying Jews to their deaths at Auschwitz should be bombed. Better, it was said, to concentrate on targets of direct military significance and save Jews by defeating Germany as soon as possible.

On Arab-Jewish questions President Roosevelt tried to please both sides. He received prominent Jewish leaders in the White House, but also met King Ibn Saud of Saudi Arabia in February 1945 and commented afterward that he had learned more about the problem of Arabs and Jews from five minutes' conversation with the king than in all previous years. Hardly an encouraging remark from the Jewish point of view. After Roosevelt's death President Truman pressed Britain to open the doors to Jewish immigration to Palestine and plunged into the diplomacy that contributed eventually to the independent state of Israel.

During the war the United States became deeply involved in Iran for the first time. In 1942 the Soviets in the north and the British in the south put that country under protective occupation in order to exclude the Germans, safeguard oil, and keep open an avenue for sending supplies to Russia—with a pledge to withdraw the troops within six months of the end of the war. The supplies came principally from the United States together with military engineers to maintain the railroad north into Russia. The United States also provided Iran with lend-lease aid and sent advisers to train the national police and modernize government administration. British officials on the spot correctly thought the Americans were trying to undercut their influence and grab a share of the oil monopolized by the Anglo-Persian Oil company.

Americans did have their eyes on oil, but they also saw themselves as anti-imperialist friends of Iran, protection against the selfish designs of both the British and the Soviets. On 1 December 1943 at the Tehran conference, Roosevelt, Churchill, and Stalin issued a declaration of support for the "independence, sovereignty and territorial integrity of Iran." But what that promise would mean in practice and whether Soviet and British troops would withdraw at the end of the war as promised remained unanswered questions.

China: The Mythical Great Power

Roosevelt declared that China was one of the "four policemen" allied against the aggressors and destined to share responsibility for a stable postwar world. He pretended to ignore the incompetence of the Chinese government or the unresolved but temporarily suspended civil war between the government and the Chinese Communists led by Mao Zedong. The fiction of China as a great power irritated Churchill, fooled only the uninformed, and was of little help to China. The immediate problem—providing China with the resources to drive back the Japanese—was insoluble. In 1942 the barrier of the Himalaya mountains and Japanese occupation of coastal China and Southeast Asia prevented supplying China by land. A largely symbolic airlift did carry small quantities of arms "over the Hump" from northeast India to Jiang Jieshi's forces in Chungking. The China theater could not be effectively supplied without drawing away forces that were doing real damage to the enemy. For example, growing American sea power encouraged a maritime strategy in the war with Japan: attacking merchant shipping with submarines, building predominance in the air, moving from island to island ever closer to Japan.

The longer-term problem was the character of the Nationalist government of China, headed by Generalissimo Jiang. This regime was unstable, rife with corruption, and preoccupied with the latent civil war against Mao's Communists. Jiang assumed, correctly enough, that Japan would eventually be defeated by the United States. He therefore preferred to husband his resources for the internal conflict and not dissipate them fighting Japan. There was nothing the United States could do for China except give advice, encouragement, and a large loan that benefited the private fortunes of individual officers without increasing China's effectiveness in the war. The advice was delivered through General Joseph W. Stilwell, a sarcastic and acerbic man who made no effort to conceal his contempt for Jiang while serving simultaneously as head of U.S. forces in China, chief of the military aid program, and chief of staff to Jiang. Roosevelt did invite Jiang to a summit at Cairo, Egypt, in November 1943. Churchill also attended and joined in a declaration that "all the territories Japan has stolen from the Chinese, such as Manchuria, Formosa, and the

Pescadores, shall the Chinese, shall be restored to the Republic of China."

Jiang finally secured General Stilwell's recall in 1944, but a succession of visiting U.S. dignitaries failed to bring about any reforms in Jiang's regime. As victory in the war against Japan neared, the question of U.S. relations with the Chinese Communists came to the fore. The United States overcame Jiang's objections and established a military-diplomatic liaison mission to Mao's forces in northwest China. The Communists impressed members of the mission as dedicated, effective in fighting the Japanese, and popular among the peasants. By 1944 Americans dealing with China were sharply divided between those who advocated direct aid to the Communists and those who wanted U.S. support concentrated on Jiang. Diplomats with first-hand knowledge believed the Communists could well prevail in China in the long run and that it was in the interests of the United States to establish good relations with them, perhaps even favor them over the corrupt Nationalists. Actual policy set in Washington was to continue to support Jiang as the leader of China, but urge him to seek a peaceful settlement with the Communists while instituting democratic reforms and ending corruption in his own government.

The most controversial action in regard to China was the secret Yalta agreement that provided for a Soviet declaration of war against Japan two or three months after the end of the war in Europe, in return for the reestablishment of the "preeminent interests" once enjoyed by Russia in Manchuria and Chinese recognition of Soviet control over Outer Mongolia. The United States had been pressing the Soviet Union to declare war on Japan since 1943 in the belief that only thus could China be liberated and Japan defeated without the use of U.S. troops on a large scale and with heavy casualties. Jiang was not informed of this deal, but President Roosevelt agreed to get Jiang's concurrence. This was secret diplomacy with a vengeance.

Stalin did agree to conclude an alliance with the Nationalist government of China for the purpose of assisting in the defeat of Japan. The alliance was signed in August 1945 at the time of the Soviet Union's entry into the war with Japan. The alliance, however, did not prevent the Soviets from turning captured Japanese weapons over to the Chinese Communists. At the same time, the U.S. transported Nationalist troops north toward the area of Communist concentration. The stage was set for the resumption of full civil war.

The Atomic Bomb and the Defeat of Japan

The Soviet Union declared war on Japan on 8 August 1945, precisely three months after the end of the war in Europe. But by that time U.S. officials no longer needed or wanted Soviet help, a shift in attitude connected to the development of the atomic bomb dropped on

Hiroshima and Nagasaki. The nuclear arms race actually began in 1939 when German physicists published articles on the theoretical possibility of nuclear explosions. President Roosevelt, responding to an appeal from Albert Einstein, committed U.S. resources to scientific work on the subject. By 1942 the early effort had grown into the gigantic Manhattan project, in partnership with Great Britain and Canada but kept secret form the Soviets (although they knew about it from their spies). Niels Bohr, Danish nuclear physicist and a participant in the development of the bomb, suggested to Roosevelt and Churchill in 1944 that the Soviets should be informed in order to lay a solid groundwork for postwar international control of the terrible weapon. Roosevelt and Churchill, meeting at Hyde Park, New York, in September, rejected the idea, opting for continued secrecy and agreeing that the bomb might, "after mature consideration, be used against the Japanese."

By May 1945 the scientists on the Manhattan project reported that atomic bombs would soon be ready. A few suggested that rather than use the bomb against a Japanese city there should be a demonstration with international observers at some uninhabited site, giving Japan a warning and an opportunity to surrender. A special committee convened by Secretary of War Stimson rejected this proposal, because it was not convinced a demonstration would be persuasive and there were no bombs to spare. The committee approved of plans to drop the first available bomb on a center of Japanese war production surrounded by workers' homes.

The fist test atomic explosion at Alamogordo, New Mexico, was detonated 16 July, 1945. Days later Truman and Churchill, with Jiang's concurrence, issued the Potsdam Declaration calling on Japan to surrender in order to avoid "the utter destruction of the Japanese homeland." The declaration did not hint at the existence of the atomic bomb nor did it say that Japan could retain the institution of the emperor, an issue on which U.S. officials were sharply divided. By this time U.S. bombers were dropping explosive and incendiary bombs on Japan with devasting impact. Japan's navy and merchant marine had virtually ceased to exist. In desperation Japan indicated through several diplomatic back channels that it wanted a negotiated surrender. A Japanese effort to enlist the good offices of the Soviet Union was rebuffed in Moscow and scorned in Washington.

On 6 August the first bomb was dropped on Hiroshima; on 8 August the Soviet Union declared war and sent an army into Manchuria; on 9 August the second bomb was dropped on Nagasaki. The next day the Japanese government offered to surrender on condition that Emperor Hirohito be permitted to retain the throne. The United States agreed and the fighting ended on 15 August. The formal surrender took place on the deck of the American battleship *Missouri* on 2 September.

A grim set of questions has since 1945 dogged the decision to use atomic bombs when Japan was already so close to defeat. Was Japan only the victim while the real target had been the Soviet Union, in the sense that the U.S. bombs would compel Moscow to cooperate on a range of contentious issues in Europe and limit Soviet influence in Asia? Was the destruction of Hiroshima and Nagasaki the last chapter of World War II and justifiable as a means of preventing the many thousands of American and even the Japanese casualties that would have accompanied an invasion? Or were the bombs an opening chapter in the Cold War? Or both? The predominant motivation for President Truman and his advisers was to end the war as quickly as possible and thereby save American lives. On the other hand, Truman did feel that possession of the bomb put the United States in a stronger diplomatic position in relation to the Soviet Union.

Another line of questions raises the question of racism: was it easier for the United States to use atomic bombs because the Japanese were not white Europeans? Unquestionably American popular opinion during the war viewed the Japanese as dangerous by virtue of race: untrustworthy, arrogant, cruel, fanatical by nature. The nature of the attack on Pearl Harbor confirmed the stereotype. Japanese propaganda in turn depicted Americans as racially inferior. Combat between the two was marked by atrocities on both sides, truly "war without mercy."

Although the bombs probably would have been dropped even if U.S. relations with the Soviet Union had been as placid, as, say, relations with Canada, the United States rejected the Soviet claim for a share in the occupation of Japan. In contrast to Germany, Japan was fully disarmed and occupied as a single zone under U.S. control with General Douglas MacArthur as supreme commander. The goal of occupation was the democratization of the county under the guidance of U.S. officials so that Japan would never "again become a menace to the United States or to the peace and security of the world." Representatives of other Allies had seats on a meaningless advisory commission.

Planning the United Nations

Roosevelt was personally cautious about committing the United States to a future international security organization. He remembered how Woodrow Wilson had been politically destroyed by the issue of U.S. membership in the League of Nations, and his personal inclinations were for security maintained by agreement among the United States, Great Britain, the Soviet Union, and China—"the four policemen" each with responsibility for a sphere of influence. But Secretary of State Hull, an enthusiastic Wilsonian, and public opinion were far more supportive of a new and better League of Nations than was Roosevelt himself. The president, therefore, let Hull and a team of specialists in the Department of State led by Leo Pasvolsky develop plans for what would become the United Nations. In September and October 1944 the United States hosted a conference at Dumbarton Oaks, an estate in Washington, D.C., for the British, Soviets, and Chinese to review draft plans.

At the Yalta conference Roosevelt, Churchill, and Stalin dealt with the veto question. All were agreed that the permanent members of the Security Council should have the right to veto any proposed action. Roosevelt was no more willing than Stalin to have the national interest infringed by majority vote. But Roosevelt argued that procedural issues should be decided by majority vote (ultimately defined as nine out of fifteen) and that parties to a dispute should not be allowed to block discussion or efforts at peaceful settlement. Stalin wanted an absolute veto on everything, including whether an issue would even be discussed. But he accepted the U.S. position as did the British. The result appeared as Article 27 of the Charter.

Membership in the General Assembly was a second issue. The British Dominions and India would have membership and votes based on the argument that they were functionally independent. So are the separate Soviet republics, said the Russians. Stalin asked for sixteen votes—one for each republic and one for the USSR itself. These votes, the Soviets implied, would be fair in light of the control allegedly exercised by the United States over Latin American governments. After some bargaining, Roosevelt conceded three seats: one for Ukraine, one for Byelorussia, and one for the USSR—with the United States reserving the right to claim additional votes if it proved politically necessary. The issue was more symbolic than substantive, since the General Assembly was only a forum for the expression of opinion, not a body with power to make anything happen.

In May 1945 in San Francisco the conference to perfect the Charter convened. A major unresolved issue was whether the United Nations would have original and exclusive jurisdiction over every threat to peace everywhere in the world or whether regional pacts could be formed to handle problems in defined areas, thereby excluding the United Nations and the possibility of interference with a regional decision by a veto-wielding permanent member of the Security Council. U.S. planners were passionately committed to the United Nations as a universal organization; they condemned the idea of regional pacts as opening the way to old-fashioned spheres of influence. But the universalists were defeated within the American delegation by defenders of hemispheric regionalism under the Monroe Doctrine and by the preference of most Latin American governments for keeping out European political influence. The result was Articles 51 through 54, authorizing action by regional organizations as long as it was consistent with the principles of the United Nations.

Decolonization

Decolonization was one of the greatest consequences of World War II. In 1939 Britain controlled most of the Middle East and ruled India, Burma, Malaya, much of Africa, and dozens of islands in the Caribbean. France had a large share of Africa, a dominant position in Syria and Lebanon, and French Indochina in Southeast Asia. Portugal had Angola and Mozambique. Belgium had the largest African colony, the Congo (later Zaire), and Ruanda-Urundi (later Rwanda and Burundi). The Netherlands had the Netherlands East Indies (subsequently Indonesia); Japan and Korea, Formosa occupation. Italy had Libya, Ethiopia, and a section of East Africa. The United States still maintained the Philippines as a colony.

By 1945 the colonial systems were irrevocably weakened and would soon crumble altogether. U.S. wartime diplomacy contributed to this result, although the most important factor was the military defeat of the colonial powers. President Roosevelt believed that Japan had exploited the weakness of European colonialism in Asia and that future world security required the dissolution of empires. For many Americans, if not for the British and French, this applied universally, not just to peoples subjugated by the Axis.

The dissolution of the Japanese empire in China was easy to implement. Providing for Korea and French Indochina was more difficult. The United States paid little attention during the war to the future of Korea other than to promise in the Cairo Declaration of 1943 that Japan would be expelled and the country would become independent "in due course." The Department of State deliberately kept its distance from Syngman Rhee, a right-wing Korean politician living in exile in the United States and eager to become head of the liberated country. With the sudden defeat of Japan and the advance of Soviet troops through Manchuria toward Korea, the United States had to do something. The United States proposed and Moscow accepted a line of convenience dividing Korea in half along the 38th parallel. American forces would take the surrender of Japanese forces in the south and Soviet troops would do so in the north. The two sides would cooperate, treat the country as an economic unit, and prepare for the reestablishment of a single independent country. Such hopes went unfulfilled.

Roosevelt said the French had exploited the people of Indochina for a century and should not be allowed to return. But by late 1944, with victory over Japan certain and his mind on other things, he lost his anticolonial fervor and permitted U.S. policy to shift toward supporting France's return. A U.S. Office of Strategic Services (OSS) team, imbued with earlier Rooseveltian anticolonialism, arrived in northern Indochina in the summer of 1945. The group met and encouraged Ho Chi Minh, the leader of the Communist independence movement. But Washington refused to back up this local initiative.

Roosevelt also had strong views on the need for Great Britain to grant immediate independence to India. His suggestions and the dispatching of U.S. diplomats to India were deeply resented by Churchill as ignorant meddling. Churchill also dismissed Roosevelt's recommendation that the British return Hong Kong to China immediately after the war. The United States, however, was but a minor contributor to a tide too powerful for Churchill to stem. In India as elsewhere the anticolonialism of the United States facilitated but did not cause the end of empires.

From Roosevelt to Truman

Roosevelt died on 12 April 1945. The new president, Truman, had been vice president only since January. He took office with no experience in diplomacy and no more knowledge than that available to a careful reader of the press. For example, he did not know of the secret agreements at Yalta or of the project to develop the atomic bomb. Historians have long debated whether the sudden change of leadership from Roosevelt to Truman had a decisive impact on the course of U.S. foreign policy and specifically on the deterioration of relations with the Soviet Union. Some argue that Truman's blunt, impatient manner foreclosed any chance of accommodation and made the Cold War inevitable. Others say that Roosevelt was about to deal more sternly with the Soviet Union for violating the principles of the Atlantic Charter.

We cannot know how Roosevelt would have behaved had he lived, but Truman did transform the style of foreign policy to an extraordinary degree. Roosevelt thrived on ambiguity and was a master of creative procrastination. Truman wanted certainty and made quick decisions. Roosevelt kept the strands of policy in his own hands and concealed his thoughts. Truman stated bluntly what he thought and delegated authority, mostly to individuals who disagreed with Roosevelt's nonconfrontational approach to Moscow. Meanwhile, an ill Harry Hopkins, Roosevelt's one close confidant, made one trip for Truman and came home to die. With him died a believer in the possibility of getting along with the Soviets. Henry Morganthau, also a believer in cooperation, lost influence and resigned.

Roosevelt was a cosmopolitan of enormous self-confidence. Truman had a Midwesterner's distrust of foreigners. The result was that U.S. policy under Truman became blunt and impatient. The emphasis shifted from minimizing difficulties with the Soviet Union to finding ways of putting pressure on Moscow. Thus in May 1945 Truman lectured Soviet Foreign Minister Molotov about Poland. "I have never been talked to like this in my life," said the Russian. "Carry out your agreements and you won't get talked to like that," Truman replied.

The last wartime summit conference brought Truman, Churchill, and Stalin together at Potsdam in July 1945. The allies were no longer united in a common cause and their discussions solved few problems while illuminating many differences. Midway through the conference the results of the British election were announced: Churchill and the Conservatives had been defeated by the Labour Party. Churchill's place was assumed by the new prime minister, Clement Attlee.

When word reached Truman of the successful test detonation of the atomic bomb in New Mexico on 16 July, he approached his negotiations with more confidence—which is not to say that he was ready to threaten the Soviets with the new weapon. The Potsdam conference ended on 1 August. One month later Japan formally surrendered and the war was over. U.S. power was at its zenith.

GADDIS SMITH

See also Atlantic Charter; China; Churchill, Winston Leonard Spencer; de Gaulle, Charles André Joseph Marie; Germany; Great Britain; Hiroshima and Nagasaki Bombings of 1945; Holocaust; Hull, Cordell; Iran; Italy; Japan; Jiang Jieshi; Lend-Lease; Manhattan Project; Middle East; Morgenthau Plan; Nuremberg, International Military Tribunal at; Palestine (to 1948); Poland; Potsdam Conference; Roosevelt, Franklin Delano; Russia and the Soviet Union; Saudi Arabia; Stalin, Joseph; Truman, Harry S.; United Nations; Yalta Conference

FURTHER READING

Akira, Iriye. *Power and Culture*. Cambridge, Mass., 1980.
Dallek, Robert. *Franklin D. Roosevelt and American Foreign Policy, 1932-1945*. New York, 1979.
Dower, John. *War Without Mercy*. New York, 1986.
Dozer, Donald. *Are We Good Neighbors?* Gainesville, Fla., 1959.
Feis, Herbert. *Churchill, Roosevelt, Stalin: The War They Waged and the Peace They Sought*. Princeton, N.J., 1957.
Feis, Hebert. *Between War and Peace: the Potsdam Conference*. Princeton, N.J., 1960.
Feis, Hebert. *Japan Subdued: The Atomic Bomb and the End of the War in the Pacific*. Princeton, N.J., 1961.
Kimball, Warren F, ed. *Churchill & Roosevelt: The Complete Correspondence*. 3 vols. Princeton, N.J., 1984.
Kimball, Warren F. *The Juggle*. Princeton N.J., 1991.
Matloff, Maurice, and Edwin M. Snell. *Strategic Planning for Coalition Warfare*. Washington, D.C., 1953.
Schuller, Michael. *The U.S. Crusade in China, 1938-1945*. 1978.
Sherwin, Martin J. *A World Destroyed: The Atomic Bomb and the Grand Alliance*. New York, 1975.
Smith, Gaddis. *American Diplomacy During the Second World War*. 2d ed., 1985.
Thorne, Christopher. *Allies of a Kind: The United States, Britain and the War Against Japan, 1941-1945*. New York, 1978.
Truchman, Barbara W. *Stilwell and the American Experience in China, 1911-1945*. New York, 1970.
Wyman, David. *The Abandonment of the Jews*. 1984.

WTO

See World Trade Organization

X-Y

"X" ARTICLE

See Kennan, George Frost

XYZ AFFAIR

Diplomatic incident in 1797–1798 in which French agents sought under-the-table monies from American representatives before opening official negotiations meant to restore amicable diplomatic relations between France and the United States. News of the attempted shakedown and its rejection by the American envoys unleashed patriotic fervor that caused a war spirit to sweep the United States. When John Adams became president in March 1797, he inherited a dangerous diplomatic imbroglio with France. Incensed with the Anglo-American rapprochement resulting from Jay's Treaty (1795) and angered by the commercial activities of U.S. vessels in the West Indies, France had seized hundreds of American ships in the Caribbean and refused to receive President George Washington's latest diplomatic representative, Charles Cotesworth Pinckey. Adam's first priority was a peaceful solution of these problems; in addition, the president desired termination of the 1778 French Alliance. Thus three commissioners were sent to Paris: Elbridge Gerry, a trusted friend of Adams from Massachusetts; John Marshall, a prominent Virginia Federalist; and Pinckney, the conservative South Carolinian rebuffed in Paris. The commissioners attempted to commence official negotiations in mid-October 1797, but were confronted by agents of Charles Maurice de Talleyrand, the French foreign minister, who first requested money in the form of a loan. The suggestion of a bribe did not actually disturb the U.S. representatives, although legend has it that Pinckney excalimed, "No, no, not a sixpence." But they believed that such a *douceur* should come at the end of negotiations, and thus they rejected the demand. The three diplomats remained in Paris, unsuccessfully trying to strike a bargain while they bickered among themselves. Meanwhile, information about the October incident slowly made its way to Philadelphia, the U.S. capital at that time.

Pressed to divulge details about Franco-American relations, Adams became concerned about the commissioner's safety. Hence he directed that Talleyrand's agents be simply designated by the initials X, Y, and Z in any published reports. In the event, the April 1798 release of Gerry's, Marshall's, and Pinckney's communications with the French government, in popular parlance the XYZ dispatches, pushed the country to the brink of hostilities with its former ally in a confrontation known as the Quasi-War, with friendly relations finally restored only in late 1800 through the Treaty of Mortefontaine.

CLIFFORD L. EGAN

See also Adams, John; American Revolution; France; Jay's Treaty; Marshall, John; Talleyrand, Charles Maurice

FURTHER READING

Bowman, Albert Hall. *The Struggle for Neutrality: Franco-American Diplomacy During the Federalist Era.* Knoxville: University of Tennessee Press, 1974.
DeConde, Alexander. *The Quasi-War: The Politics and Diplomacy of the Undeclared War with France, 1797–1801.* New York, 1966.
Stinchcombe, William C., *The XYZ Affair.* Westport, Conn., 1980.

YALTA CONFERENCE
(4–11 February 1945)

The second of the wartime meetings of President Franklin D. Roosevelt, Prime Minister Winston S. Churchill, and Marshal Joseph Stalin of the Soviet Union, held in the Russian resort city in the Crimea. The fact that Roosevelt and Churchill traveled long distances in dangerous circumstances to meet on Soviet territory was a concession to Stalin's insistence that he could not meet outside of Russia. Germany's last effort to thwart the Allied advance in the West, the Battle of the Bulge, had failed. Soviet forces were near the German frontier in the East. Japan still occupied most of China and was putting up lethal resistance to the U.S. advance across the Pacific.

With victory over Germany in sight, the leaders of the three major Allies agreed on the entry of the Soviet Union into the war against Japan, for which the Soviets would be rewarded with a sphere of influence in Manchuria. The Allied leaders continued their planning for the joint occupation of Germany and punishment of Nazi leaders, while leaving open the possibility of permanent partition of the country. They also outlined the future of Poland on terms favorable to the Soviet Union (the communist Lublin government to be reorganized to include non-communists); issued a declaration calling for free elections in liberated

Europe; and confirmed that the power of decision in the future United Nations would be in the hands of the great powers sitting as permanent members of the Security Council and holding a veto on decisions.

The U.S. conferees at Yalta believed that the meeting augured well for postwar cooperation and Roosevelt gave the American people an optimistic report. But the pleasant atmosphere of the conference faded quickly as acrimonious diplomatic exchanges multiplied with the Soviet government over its intentions in Poland and more generally over questions of political freedom in areas liberated by the Russians.

Roosevelt, who died two months after the conference, did not live to see Yalta transformed from a symbol of victorious Allied cooperation to an accusatory synonym for appeasement of communism in the vocabulary of his Republican critics. His posthumous defenders argued that the reality of Soviet military power meant that Stalin would impose his will on territory he controlled and that there was no practical way Roosevelt could stop him. President Harry S. Truman and Americans in general believed that the Soviets had violated their Yalta commitments to democracy and free elections in Eastern Europe. But it was also the case that words like "democracy" had a very different meaning in Moscow and that the Soviets lived up to the agreements as they interpreted them.

During the Cold War "Yalta" became an explosive word in U.S. politics, linked to attacks on Democrats for being "soft" on communism and having "lost" China and "betrayed" the people and nations imprisoned behind the Iron Curtain. The accusations took little account of the historical context of 1945, but they did contribute to the Republican victory in the 1952 election.

GADDIS SMITH

See also Churchill, Winston Leonard Spencer; Roosevelt, Franklin Delano; Stalin, Joseph; World War II

FURTHER READING

Buhite, Russell D. *Decision at Yalta: An Appraisal of Summit Diplomacy*. Wilmington, Del., 1986.
Clemens, Diane. *Yalta*. New York, 1970.
Feis, Herbert. *Churchill Roosevelt Stalin: The War They Waged and the Peace They Sought*. Princeton, N.J., 1957.
Snell, John L. *The Meaning of Yalta*. Baton Rouge, La., 1956.
Theoharis, Athan. *The Yalta Myths: An Issue in U.S. Politics, 1945–1955*. Columbia, Mo., 1970.

YELTSIN, BORIS NIKOLAYEVICH

(*b.* 1 February 1931)

The Russian leader who disbanded the Union of Soviet Socialist Republics and who governed Russia in the early years of the post–Cold War era. A party functionary of thirty years' standing, Boris Yeltsin moved to Moscow in 1985 at Secretary-General Mikhail Gorbachev's request. Over time, his public criticism of party elitism, corruption, and slowness of reform led to his ouster from Gorbachev's inner circle. Yeltsin nonetheless became one of the most popular Soviet politicians. Elected over party opposition to the Supreme Soviet and in 1990 as president of the Russian Republic, Yeltsin resigned from the Communist Party and campaigned for faster national reforms and for increased autonomy for the Soviet Republics.

Yeltsin risked his life in support of Gorbachev's constitutional authority during a conservative coup attempt in August 1991, although at the time he was Gorbachev's primary liberal critic. After the Soviet Union's dissolution and Gorbachev's resignation in December 1991, Yeltsin became the first democratically elected president of Russia, the chief spokesman for the successor Commonwealth of Independent States, and, in Western eyes, the symbol of Russian reform.

U.S. policy makers had originally looked askance at Yeltsin's loud, unpolished, Khrushchev-like personality and at the threat his vocal criticism posed to Gorbachev. In the wake of the August 1991 coup attempt, Yeltsin's image in the West improved dramatically. Following Gorbachev's resignation, U.S. citizens saw Yeltsin as their best hope for Russia's continuing nuclear disarmament and economic liberalization, as well as for the containment of resurgent right-wing Russian nationalism.

But Yeltsin faced mounting Russian opposition. The speed with which he pushed economic reform and military demobilization, the consequent inflation and dislocation, corruption within his government, and the rapid drop in Russia's international prestige set many Russians against him. When Yeltsin imposed emergency economic measures and proposed a new constitution which would grant the presidency greater powers, opponents in the People's Congress voted instead to curb his powers and challenged the constitutionality of his actions under the existing constitution. In the fall of 1993 the confrontation reached a climax when television audiences around the world watched Russian Army tanks, loyal to Yeltsin, taking aim at the White House, the Parliament building from which two years earlier Yeltsin had defended Gorbachev against the attempted military coup. Dissident legislators, barricaded in the White House, were forcibly subdued. Although Yeltsin retained his presidency, late in 1993 nationalists, communists, and other oppositionists significantly outpolled his own reform party in Russia's first truly democratic parliamentary elections.

During the elections the U.S. government openly sided with Yeltsin. President George Bush had visited Moscow in December 1992. President Bill Clinton met with Yeltsin in Vancouver, Canada, in April 1993 and traveled to Moscow in January 1994. Both presidents tried to bolster

Yeltsin's position by promises of financial assistance.

Still fighting for his political life, Yeltsin in 1994 replaced radical reformers with more moderate economic advisers. He also moved to reassert Russia's diplomatic autonomy. In the Bosnian crisis, for example, Russia refused to follow the United States and Western Europe in their blanket condemnation of the Serbs.

Dismayed both by the December 1993 election of hawkish Russian nationalists such as Vladimir Zhirinovsky and by the government's response to the uprising in Chechnya, the U.S. government accepted Yeltsin's move to the right as regrettable but still preferable to his replacement by extreme nationalists or hard-core communists. By 1996, and amidst serious problems with his health, Yeltsin's approval rating in Russia had dropped below twenty percent. Nevertheless, he won his bid for re-election in June and July 1996, defeating the candidate of the revanchist Communist party, Gannady Zyuganov.

LINDA KILLEN

See also Bosnia-Herzegovina; Gorbachev, Mikhail Sergeevich; Russia and the Soviet Union

FURTHER READING

Buzgalin, A. V. *Bloody October in Moscow: Political Repression in the Name of Reform.* Translated by Renfrey Clarke. New York, 1994.
Morrison, John. *Boris Yeltsin.* New York, 1991.
Yeltsin, Boris N. *Against the Grain.* Translated by Michael Glenny. New York, 1990.
———. *The Struggle for Russia.* Translated by C. A. Fitzgerald. New York, 1994.

YEMEN

Located on the southern coast of the Arabian Peninsula, bordered principally by Saudi Arabia and the Gulf of Aden, and formed in May 1990 by the merger of the Yemen Arab Republic (North Yemen) and the People's Democratic Republic of Yemen (South Yemen). Yemen has been of peripheral and occasional interest to U.S. policy makers. The American approach to events in Yemen has been heavily influenced by Saudi Arabia, which considers Yemen to be part of its sphere of influence.

One notable occasion when Saudi and U.S. perspectives on Yemen differed was in the early 1960s. An Arab nationalist military regime overthrew the centuries-old monarchy in North Yemen in September 1962. The new rulers called upon Egypt for support, and Egyptian President Gamal Abdul Nasser dispatched forces to bolster the revolutionaries. Tribal partisans of the deposed imam took up arms against the new government and received substantial support from Saudi Arabia. The United States, which during the Kennedy Administration sought to improve relations with Nasser, recognized the new Yemeni government over the objections of the Saudis and

of the British, who saw the Egyptian presence in North Yemen as a threat to their protectorate in South Yemen. The civil war in North Yemen ended in 1970 with a compromise that maintained the republican form of the state but integrated many royalist supporters into the government. Between 1970 and 1990 North Yemen's foreign policy was usually aligned with that of Saudi Arabia. In 1967 the British withdrew from South Yemen. A Marxist faction of the South Yemeni independence movement came to power and allied with the Soviet Union.

Yemen next played a role in U.S. foreign policy in 1979, when the two Yemeni states engaged in a brief border war. The Soviet-allied Southerners got the better of the fighting. The Carter Administration, which had just seen a major American ally, the shah of Iran, toppled by a popular revolution, was anxious to reassure the Saudis of continued U.S. support. The United States sent emergency military aid to North Yemen and deployed naval forces off the coast. The war ended with an agreement by the two Yemeni states to unify, a popular goal on both sides of the Yemeni border, but no practical steps were taken to merge the two states.

The collapse of the Soviet empire in 1989 had a profound effect on South Yemeni leaders, who had grown increasingly dependent upon support from Moscow. They revived the issue of unity with the North, and accepted a subordinate position in the united state formed in May 1990. The United States recognized the new Republic of Yemen immediately, but was soon embroiled in a diplomatic confrontation with it. Yemen refused to support the deployment of U.S. forces to the Persian Gulf after the Iraqi invasion of Kuwait in August 1990. The Yemeni position was of greater importance than its intrinsic power merited because Yemen held the Arab seat in the U.N. Security Council at that time. With the end of the crisis, tensions between Yemen and the United States dissipated. In 1994 leaders of the former South Yemeni state attempted to secede and re-establish South Yemeni independence, igniting a brief civil war. The Southerners were supported by Saudi Arabia, but the United States refused to recognize the secessionist regime.

F. GREGORY GAUSE III

See also Gulf War of 1990–1991; Middle East; Saudi Arabia

YOM KIPPUR WAR
See Egypt; Israel; Middle East

YOSHIDA, SHIGERU
(*b.* 22 September 1878; *d.* 20 October 1967)

The key Japanese politician who fostered a U.S.-Japan alliance after World War II. Educated first in the traditional Confucian system, Yoshida graduated from the elite Peers School in Japan before attending the Law School of Tokyo Imperial University. Yoshida then entered the Foreign Ministry in 1906, where over a thirty-three-year career in diplomacy he became a consistent advocate of Japanese cooperation with Great Britain and the United States. Although Yoshida supported Japanese hegemony in Asia, he vocally opposed the Japanese military's campaign to subdue China (1937–1941) because it produced Japanese-Western conflict. Outspoken and autocratic, Yoshida reached the apex of his diplomatic career with his appointment as Ambassador to Great Britain (1936–1939). During World War II, Yoshida joined a conservative group that tried to persuade the Emperor to negotiate an early end to the war. The group's initiative failed, and Yoshida was briefly imprisoned for his activities.

After Japan's defeat and occupation by the United States in 1945, Yoshida served twice as Prime Minister (1946–1947, 1948–1954). Yoshida's relationship with General Douglas MacArthur, the top U.S. official in Japan, was strained. The prime minister labored to limit many of the early U.S. attempts to "democratize" Japan. A fervent social and political conservative, Yoshida had no desire to fully implement the early U.S. reforms to strengthen labor unions while weakening the large business conglomerates. Yoshida, however, supported U.S. efforts after 1948 to rebuild Japan into a strong anti-communist ally. Yoshida signed the Peace Treaty of September 1951 that ended the occupation and a separate mutual security pact that permitted U.S. military bases in Japan. Acceding to U.S. pressure in the face of considerable opposition within his country, Yoshida slowly began to rearm Japan. He created a National Police Reserve in 1950, which was later renamed the Self Defense Forces. The prime minister also refused to recognize the People's Republic of China, and he accepted the U.S. rationale for nuclear tests in the Pacific despite the contamination of a Japanese fishing boat, the *Fukuryu Maru* (Lucky Dragon) in 1954 by radioactive fallout from an American hydrogen bomb explosion. Helped by U.S. military spending in Japan during the Korean War (1950–1954), Yoshida focused on the development of an export-oriented Japanese economy in the 1950s. Forced to resign in 1954 because of a government scandal in the shipping industry, the retired Yoshida wrote books and remained Japan's best known political figure.

BARNEY J. RICKMAN III

See also China; Japan; MacArthur, Douglas

FURTHER READING

Dower, John W. *Empire and Aftermath: Yoshida Shigeru and the Japanese Experience, 1878-1954.* Cambridge, Mass., 1979.

Pyle, Kenneth B. *The Japanese Question: Power and Purpose in a New Era.* Washington, D.C., 1992.

Yoshida, Shigeru. *The Yoshida Memoirs: The Story of Japan in Crisis.* Translated by Kenichi Yoshida. Boston, 1962.

Yoshida, Shigeru. *Japan's Decisive Century, 1867-1967.* New York, 1967.

YOUNG, ANDREW JACKSON, JR.
(*b.* 12 March 1932)

Civil rights leader, member of Congress, U.S. ambassador to the United Nations, and mayor of Atlanta (1982–1989). A member of a prominent New Orleans African-American family, he graduated from Howard University in 1951 and from Hartford Theological Seminary in 1955. He was then ordained a minister in the United Church of Christ.

Young worked as a pastor from 1955 to 1957 in churches in southwestern Georgia and central Alabama, where he helped organize voter registration drives and first met Martin Luther King, Jr. He moved to New York City in 1957 to work for the National Council of Churches. In 1961 he joined the Southern Christian Leadership Conference (SCLC) and in 1964 succeeded Wyatt Walker as SCLC's executive director, becoming, along with Ralph Abernathy, one of King's two closest assistants.

Young resigned from SCLC in 1970 to run unsuccessfully for the U.S. Congress from Atlanta. He ran again in 1972 and won, making him and Barbara Jordan of Texas the first two black Americans to be elected to Congress from the Deep South since Reconstruction. He resigned from Congress in January 1977 to become President Jimmy Carter's ambassador to the United Nations, the first African American to hold the position.

Because of Young's well-known interest in Africa, his appointment to the UN signaled a dramatic change from the Cold War preoccupations of previous administrations. Young made clear that the Carter administration would pay attention to the Third World, and especially Africa, for its own sake. He served as the administration's point man on southern African policy, arguing that the remaining white minority regimes were the Soviets' greatest asset in the region and that the creation of a color-blind democracy would eliminate African interest in seeking help from the Soviet Union or Cuba. His insistence that racism rather than communism ranked as the greatest threat to the stability of the region was a novel interpretation of foreign affairs by an American diplomat of such prominence.

Young's willingness to question Cold War assumptions made him unpopular with more fervent anticommunists. His critics questioned his vociferous and uninhibited style as a spokesperson for U.S. foreign policy, asserting that he too often criticized allies and friends. As the Carter administration moved sharply to the right in its foreign policy in 1978 and 1979, Young's consistent liberalism and relative disinterest in the supposed Soviet threat seemed out of favor in Washington. In July 1979 he met informally and privately with Zehdi Labib, the Palestine Liberation Organization's (PLO) UN observer, in apparent violation of the long-standing U.S. policy of not negotiating with the PLO until it had acknowledged Israel's right to exist as a nation. When word of this meeting leaked to the public, arousing a storm of criticism in the Department of State and among supporters of Israel, Young was forced to resign. It was later revealed that other U.S. diplomats, with presidential approval, had been meeting secretly with PLO representatives.

THOMAS BORSTELMANN

See also Africa; Carter, James Earl; Palestine Liberation Organization; United Nations

FURTHER READING

Gardner, Carl. *Andrew Young: A Biography.* New York, 1978.
Peake, Thomas R. *Keeping the Dream Alive: A History of the Southern Christian Leadership Conference from King to the Nineteen-Eighties.* New York, 1987.
Smith, Gaddis. *Morality, Reason, and Power: American Diplomacy in the Carter Years.* New York, 1986.

YOUNG AMERICA

A nationalistic movement within the Democratic party from the late 1840s to the mid-1850s that declared a belief in the perfection of U.S. democratic and republican government. Seeking to spread its example, advocates of Young America demanded vigorous pursuit of ideological and territorial expansion. Led by George Sanders, editor of the *Democratic Review*, and Senator Stephen A. Douglas of Illinois, other prominent spokesmen of the movement included Senators Pierre Soulé of Louisiana, Isaac P. Walker of Wisconsin, James Shields of Illinois, and Robert J. Walker of Mississippi; Representatives William H. Polk of Tennessee and Edward C. Marshall of California; journalist Edwin De Leon (who first defined the aims of Young America in 1845); and financiers George Law and August Belmont.

In encouraging ideological expansion, Young America urged an interventionist role to support republican movements abroad. To assist the spread of republicanism following the European revolutions of 1848–1849, the movement demanded and secured, from the administration of Democratic president Franklin Pierce, diplomatic appointments for Young America leaders. Sanders became consul at London, Soulé minister to Spain, De Leon minister to Egypt, and Belmont minister at The Hague. In promoting republicanism abroad Young America most vociferously backed the Hungarian revolutionary Lajos Kossuth.

Young America also espoused territorial expansion under the banner of Manifest Destiny, especially the annexing of territory populated by culturally and racially different peoples. The movement thus envisioned the creation of a continental union that included all of North and Central America. Such expectations led advocates of Young America to denounce Great Britain for obstructing U.S. expansion (by controlling Canada); for opposing America's efforts to acquire Cuba (by such means as the Ostend Manifesto); and for establishing a protectorate over the Mosquito Coast and occupying the Bay Islands and Belize, actions which the movement considered a violation of the Clayton-Bulwer Treaty of 1850. The only territorial acquisition by the United States during this period, however, was the Gadsden Purchase from Mexico in 1853, in which the United States received the southernmost portion of the New Mexico territory for purposes of railroad construction.

Young America proved unsuccessful in accomplishing its goals for several reasons. First, the movement was discredited politically by its failed campaign to promote Douglas for the presidency in 1852 and by its inability to unite in favor of any Democratic party presidential candidate in 1856. Second, Young America diplomats were thwarted in their efforts to achieve any of the movement's interventionist aims—by both the rise of Know-Nothing nativism and the strength of traditional isolationism in determining the conduct of U.S. foreign policy. Finally, the movement failed to realize expansionist schemes in Cuba and Central America, where Narciso López and William Walker, respectively, carried out unsuccessful filibustering expeditions. Public interest in territorial expansion had gradually faded as the divisive issue of the extension of slavery into the territories came to dominate U.S. politics in the 1850s.

DEAN FAFOUTIS

See also Clayton, John Middleton; Cuba; Democratic Party; Filibusters; Gadsden Purchase; Honduras; Hungary; Isolationism; Manifest Destiny; Nicaragua; Ostend Manifesto; Pierce, Franklin; Walker, William

FURTHER READING

Curti, Merle. "Young America." *American Historical Review* 32 (1926): 34–55.
Danbom, David B. "The Young America Movement." *Journal of the Illinois State Historical Society* 67 (1974): 294–306.
Spencer, Donald S. *Louis Kossuth and Young America.* Columbia, Mo., 1977.
Weinberg, Albert K. *Manifest Destiny.* Baltimore, 1935.

YOUNG PLAN
See Reparations

YUGOSLAVIA

Until the early 1990s, a federation of six socialist republics, itself a successor to the Kingdom of Serbs, Croats, and Slovenes established in 1918 (and renamed Yugoslavia in 1929). Since 1992, present-day "Yugoslavia" has consisted only of the former constitutient republics of Serbia and Montenegro.

Yugoslavia literally means "land of the southern Slavs." From its creation following World War I until its destruction in the years following the Cold War, it was a multi-ethnic state, situated in the northwestern part of the Balkan peninsula with a long coastline bordering on the Adriatic Sea. Its population included Serbs as the largest ethnic group (thirty-six percent in the 1981 census), Croats (twenty percent), Muslims (nine percent), Slovenes (eight percent), Montenegrins (three percent), Macedonians (six percent), as well as some non-Slavic groups such as Albanians (eight percent), and Hungarians. In terms of religious affiliation, the breakdown was about forty percent Eastern Orthodox, thirty percent Roman Catholic, and twelve percent Muslim.

Historically a region controlled by more powerful outsiders, including the Ottoman and Austro-Hungarian Empires, during World War I the majority of southern Slav peoples—with the exception of the Bulgarians—advanced the idea of forming a unitary state under the aegis of the Serbian monarchy. Fears of future domination by Italy, which was awarded land in Dalmatia and Istria by the Allies in the secret London Treaty of 1915, led to the formation of the London-based Yugoslav Committee to promote the creation of an independent southern Slav nation. In the Corfu Declaration of 1917 a single, democratic, constitutional, parliamentary state, under the Karadjordjevic dynasty, was proposed by Serbian and Croat political leaders—with Serbia, already independent since 1878, clearly aiming at regional hegemony.

When Austria-Hungary collapsed in late 1918, the National Council of Slovenes, Croats, and Serbs became the de facto government of the new nation. In May 1919 the Paris Peace Conference recognized the Kingdom of Serbs, Croats, and Slovenes as including Serbia, Croatia, Slovenia, Montenegro, and Bosnia-Hercegovina. The United States was the first Great Power to recognize it formally. The young kingdom became a charter member of the League of Nations and signed mutual defense treaties with neighboring states.

The future Yugoslavia was set up as a constitutional monarchy under King Peter I of Serbia. Peter died in 1921 and his son Alexander succeeded him. In 1929, while changing the name of the Kingdom to Yugoslavia, Alexander also sought to impose greater unity and uniformity, to abolish the constitution, and to establish a royal dictatorship. He banned political parties, imposed new administrative divisions (which ignored historical ethnic boundaries), and sought to force a single official language upon all citizens. Alexander was assassinated in 1934 by Croatian nationalists, who had all along objected to Serbian predominance, and was succeeded by the young Peter II.

At the outset of World War II, under Alexander's cousin, the Regent Prince Paul, the Yugoslav government first sided with Germany and Italy. In the spring of 1941 the Yugoslav army rebelled and overthrew Paul. The United States offered assistance under the Lend-Lease program, but within weeks the German army invaded Yugoslavia, overran the country, and partitioned it among Germany, Italy, Hungary, and Bulgaria. However, the United States never officially recognized this dismemberment. In Croatia a fascist (Ustasha) puppet regime was established. In due course, several resistance movements emerged and united in the Antifascist Council for the Liberation of Yugoslavia (AVNOJ); they were militarily supported by Great Britain and the United States, most energetically following the Allied invasion of Italy. The two principal resistance groups were the Communist-controlled partisans, led by Josip Broz Tito, and the Chetniks, who wanted to restore the monarchy. The Allies initially favored the Chetniks, but at the December 1943 Tehran conference, Franklin Roosevelt and Winston Churchill—with Joseph Stalin's support—decided to switch their allegiance almost entirely to Tito's partisans, who were proving far more effective in combating the Axis occupation forces. The United States, however, maintained for a while longer a military mission with Mihajlovic, the Chetnik leader. Aided by Soviet troops, it was the Communist partisans who liberated Belgrade in 1944. By the end of the war, Tito and the Communists were in full control of the country and—by November 1945—of the government.

Despite tensions over Tito's claims to the Italian city of Trieste, resolved only in 1954, Yugoslavia was restored to its pre-World War II status with Western approval, transformed now into a federative Socialist republic with a strong central government and a Soviet-style constitution. Until 1949, however, U.S. and Yugoslav relations were relatively cool. In addition to the growing East-West polarization, the United States was upset by Yugoslavia's hard-line role in international forums, its destablizing involvement in Albanian affairs, and its support of the communist guerrillas in the Greek civil war.

When Tito broke with Stalin in 1948, U.S. and Western attitudes and priorities changed dramatically. Although Yugoslavia did not become fully pro-Western, its example in resisting the Soviet Union was seen as quite a valuable asset to the West's overall containment strategy. In 1949 the United States backed Yugoslav efforts to win a temporary seat on the United Nations Security Council. Trade was expanded, including the lifting of some export controls on munitions and related production equipment. In 1951 the Harry Truman administration persuaded Congress to provide Yugoslavia with military and economic aid, even though it was still officially in the communist camp. This aid was crucial in Tito's ability to survive politically and economically—given the ban on trade with Yugoslavia imposed by Stalin on all Soviet bloc countries as well as other efforts to destabilize the Titoist regime—as well as in developing an economic system based on greater decentralization and worker self-management, a far cry from orthodox Marxist-Leninist models.

Following Stalin's death in 1953, Khrushchev made amicable overtures to Tito, including proposals to expand trade and reduce political tension. By 1955 Yugoslavia and the Soviet Union had formally re-established relations; Tito even gave a qualified endorsement to the Soviet invasion of Hungary in 1956, making the argument that it was necessary to preserve the Hungarian Communist Party. More broadly, Tito coalesced with Third World leaders, such as Indonesia's Sukarno and India's Jawaharlal Nehru, in an attempt to forge the nonaligned movement as a "third force" in global politics. This caused strains in Yugoslavia's relations with the United States as the nonaligned movement's positions increasingly found themselves at odds with U.S. interests and policies (especially toward Israel and the Middle East). The Soviet invasion of Czechoslovakia in 1968, however, was not supported by Tito; and the resulting downturn in Yugoslav-Soviet relations was sufficient to inspire President Richard Nixon to exchange official visits with Tito in 1970 and 1971. On the other hand, issues such as U.S. opposition to the socialist government of Salvador Allende in Chile and Tito's siding with the Soviets in the 1973 Arab-Israeli war caused further strains between Washington and Belgrade.

The beginning of the 1970s saw a sharp increase in nationalist rumblings in most Yugoslav republics. Party leaders began calling for constitutional changes to give the individual republics greater independence. In 1974, a new constitution—with an almost confederal character—was adopted to placate these national sentiments. Following Tito's death in 1980, the strains proved worse than anticipated. The collective presidency survived through the 1980s, but the inter-ethnic and inter-republic conflicts intensified and spread. Severe recession and high inflation added to the problem. So too did the demagogic exploitation of nationalist sentiments and fears by leaders such as Serbia's Slobodan Milosevic, who openly touted a "Greater Serbia" even at the risk of provoking civil strife in Kosovo and Bosnia.

Communist party power began to decline in 1989. The prime minister, Ante Markovic, introduced economic austerity measures backed by the International Monetary Fund, and promised multi-party elections for the national legislature. Meanwhile, in the two wealthiest republics, Slovenia and Croatia, political forces supporting secession from a Serb-dominated Yugoslav federation gradually got the upper hand. When Serbia refused to endorse the non-communist and Croatian Stipe Mesic, due to become president of Yugoslavia under the system of rotating leadership, Yugoslavia found itself with no head of state and, effectively, the constitution collapsed.

In 1991 Slovenia, Croatia, and Macedonia declared their independence from Yugoslavia. In 1992 Bosnia and Herzegovina followed suit. Serbia fought brutally to resist these moves—and ostensibly to protect the rights of Serb minorities in Bosnia and Croatia—in wars that became Europe's worst since World War II. Serbia also insisted on the legitimacy of its claim, along with Montenegro, to the right to the name of Yugoslavia and the privileges that came with that, such as the Yugoslav seat in the United Nations. The official U.S. position has been that Yugoslavia had dissolved and that none of the successor republics represented its continuity. The UN also rejected Serbia's claim, and went so far as to expel Yugoslavia from the General Assembly upon revelations of the Serbs' "ethnic cleansing" and death camps. De facto, Yugoslavia thus ceased to exist by late 1995, replaced by separate republics in the land of the southern Slavs—with unsettled borders and a precarious cease-fire on the warring parties, largely brokered by the United States and temporarily supervised by NATO forces.

MARTIN ROSSMANN

See also Bosnia-Herzegovina; Cold War; Croatia; Russia and the Soviet Union; Serbia; Slovenia; Tito

FURTHER READING

Banac, Ivo. *The National Question in Yugoslavia: Origins, History, Politics.* Ithaca, N.Y., 1984.

Hopner, Jacob B. *Yugoslavia in Crisis.* New York, 1962.

Milivojevic, Marko, et al. *Yugoslavia's Security Dilemmas.* Oxford, 1988.

Ramet, Pedro, ed. *Yugoslavia in the 1980s.* Boulder, Colo., 1985.

Rieff, David. *SlaughterHouse: Bosnia and the Failure of the West.* New York, 1995.

Singleton, Fred. *A Short History of the Yugoslav Peoples.* Cambridge, Mass., 1985.

Wolff, Robert Lee. *The Balkans in Our Time.* New York, 1967.

Woodward, Susan L. *Balkan Tragedy: Chaos and Dissolution After the Cold War.* Washington, D.C., 1995.

Z

ZAIRE

Located in the heart of Central Africa, once known as the Belgian Congo, and approximately the size of the United States east of the Mississippi River, Zaire has an estimated population of 45 million, with its capital at Kinshasa (formerly Léopoldville). Rich in strategic minerals including copper, cobalt, tin, gold, uranium, diamonds, and oil, Zaire is also considered to possess the world's greatest hydroelectric power potential. Once abundant in timber and agricultural products, and a natural breadbasket for the entire region, its forests have been seriously depleted and Zaire has become a net importer of food.

Zaire, first discovered by the West through Portuguese explorers in the fifteenth century, was a land of Bantu peoples preyed upon by Afro-Arab slave traders. Its name derives from the Portuguese approximation of the Kikongo word for river. Its vast terrain became the personal property of King Leopold II of Belgium in 1885, as the "Congo Free State" sanctioned by the Berlin Conference that year.

In 1908, the Belgian government assumed responsibility for colonial administration of the Congo, extracting natural resources, including coffee and rubber, for the metropole but providing few benefits to the indigenous population in such sectors as health, higher education, civil liberties, and economic opportunity. Political parties and labor unions were officially sanctioned only a year before a wave of independence swept over many sub-Saharan colonies. (Among these was the small and neighboring former French colony now called Republic of the Congo, not to be confused with the former Belgian Congo or present-day Zaire.)

From independence and throughout the Cold War, U.S. interests in the Congo (the name change to Zaire did not occur until 1971) were, in general: to secure a peaceful, orderly transition from colonial rule to a stable and lasting form of independence under democratic institutions; to deny this nation, and through it, the smaller surrounding states, to Soviet influence; to maintain access to its mineral wealth for the United States and the West; and to at least acquiesce in Belgium's special position based on its former role.

On 30 June 1960 an unruly but voluntary transfer of power occurred from a young King Baudouin of Belgium to the Congo's first president, Joseph Kasavubu, and his left-leaning, erratic prime minister Patrice Lumumba. For the next five years, unrest and bloody attempts at secession based in the diamond region of South Kasai, mineral-rich Elizabethville (now Lubumbashi), and Stanleyville (now Kisangani); violent coups and counter-coups; the presence of United Nations peacekeeping forces in large numbers; and the effects of an intense struggle between the United States and the Soviet Union for influence in the region all became the daily burdens of many of the Congolese people.

When, one month after independence, provincial President Moise Tshombe declared the Katanga (now Shaba) province independent, thereby threatening the integrity of the country, President Dwight D. Eisenhower dispatched the carrier USS *Wasp* to the waters off the Congo's small coastline, supported a UN Security Council resolution to deploy international military assistance to Congolese forces, and provided U.S. airlift to UN forces destined for Elizabethville.

Lumumba, however, also requested military and technical assistance from the Soviet Union and bloc countries, establishing the Cold War context of U.S.-Congolese relations at the outset. Soviet Premier Nikita S. Khrushchev was taking a strong interest in Africa, encouraged by developments in such radicalized new states as Ghana under Kwame Nkrumah, Guinea under Sékou Touré, and the United Arab Republic under Gamal Abdel Nasser.

While in New York City to participate in the pivotal UN Congo debates during the fall of 1960, Khrushchev startled the world and created an enduring image of Soviet bravado by banging his shoe on a desk for the cameras. The UN's central role in this early peacemaking operation was further dramatized by the fatal crash in Rhodesia of Secretary-General Dag Hammarskjöld's aircraft flying him on 17 September 1961 from Leopoldville to Elizabethville.

For U.S. and Soviet interests, however, there were on three other continents, as well, overshadowing security issues of great moment in play during this period: the Bay of Pigs invasion and Cuban missile crisis; construction of the Berlin Wall and Soviet challenges to Allied access to Berlin; and a growing U.S. military involvement in Vietnam and Southeast Asia. Within the United States, liberal Democrats and the Civil Rights movement increasingly focused attention on an awakening African continent.

In September 1960, General Joseph-Désiré Mobutu, by then chief-of-staff of the army, seized power from Lumumba and held it for about six months during which Lumumba was murdered under circumstances that remain unclear. Soviet and Soviet bloc representatives were expelled from the Congo, and Cyrille Adoula, a pro-Western friend of the United States, was appointed prime minister by Kasavubu. Soviet influence in the Congo ended; under Adoula the process of reconciliation among Congolese factions could begin. President John F. Kennedy expressed his enthusiastic appreciation and support to Mobutu during a Washington visit. An important and lasting tie thus had been forged.

United Nations forces, numbering 20,000 men from 34 countries at their peak, finally left the Congo in June 1964. A few months later, leftist rebels seized Stanleyville, proclaimed it a peoples republic, and took hundreds of foreign hostages including five U.S. diplomats. President Lyndon B. Johnson provided airlift support to Belgian paratroopers, who succeeded in fragmenting the rebellion. Confident of U.S. backing, an exasperated Mobutu deposed Kasavubu without bloodshed and on 24 November 1965 proclaimed himself president.

Mobutu's rule has been authoritarian, although in general not dependent upon physical coercion of the population. There have been, nonetheless, extrajudicial killings committed by undisciplined and unpaid security forces and countless instances of harassment, wrongful arrest, torture, and other major human rights violations. Mobutu is energetic and charismatic, with a powerful speaking voice, and crowd-pleasing popular appeal. Forceful and canny in his dealings with African and Western interlocutors, Mobutu often has a highly sophisticated and informed strategic view of world developments and knows how he can influence them tactically, although he lacks a realistic appreciation of the political dynamic in the United States.

Despite his firm pro-Western posture in the Cold War, Mobutu established relations with the People's Republic of China in 1972, and a year later visited China and North Korea. He renewed relations with the Soviet Union and bloc states. He launched his "Zairianization" and "authenticity" campaigns, nationalizing many foreign enterprises and driving their previous owners from the country. He prescribed an obligatory national dress for men of Nehru-like jackets, and ordered names to be Africanized, the president himself becoming Marshal Mobutu Sese Seko Kuku Ngbendu wa Za Banga.

The salient attribute of Mobutu's three-decades-long rule, however, is its rooting in kleptocracy: the siphoning off, in staggering amounts, of Zaire's monies and profits from natural resources for Mobutu's personal use and the benefit of many of his close associates, as a way of maintaining power while living in luxury. When world mineral prices, including copper, plunged in 1974, Zaire suffered setbacks from which it has not recovered. Mounting foreign debt and high debt servicing obligations have heavily burdened the economy since then.

Beginning with the administration of President Richard Nixon, the United States, Belgium and France, and other nations concerned about Zaire, worked closely and creatively with the International Monetary Fund (IMF) and World Bank to restructure and reform Zaire's economy, often providing generous debt rescheduling terms. The results were mixed, and ended in failure.

While problems of inflation, poverty, corruption, depletion of natural resources, food shortages, and lack of adequate social services were becoming endemic and largely unaddressed there were also outside challenges to Mobutu's rule. In May 1977 disaffected members of the Lunda-Chokwe ethnic group invaded Shaba from Angola. Mobutu called for help from the newly elected administration of President Jimmy Carter, who was to become an outspoken public advocate of human rights reform globally.

The United States provided only non-lethal support, while Belgium and France sent troops and equipment. Morocco sent 1,500 of its best soldiers. Repelled, the same elements tried again, this time from Angola through Zambia in May 1978, causing great damage to mining installations at Kolwezi. Again, they were turned back with French military assistance, but this time with greater U.S. logistical support, including the subsequent airlifting into Shaba of a stabilizing inter-African force.

In his foreign policy, Mobutu firmly and consistently supported the United States on regional and global issues. Zaire sent 1,800 of its troops to Chad in 1983, with U.S. airlift for French troops as well, to prevent an anticipated Libyan invasion. As a member of the UN Security Council in 1982–1983, Zaire supported U.S. positions on such key issues as Central America and the Soviet downing of a Korean jetliner. It did so again on the Security Council in 1991, as the United States under President George Bush led the West's response to Iraq's invasion of Kuwait. Zaire was also the first African nation to resume diplomatic relations with Israel after the 1967 war, and endorsed the Camp David Accords.

In collaboration with the United States, Mobutu participated actively over many years in overt and covert efforts to counter the Soviet-supported Popular Movement for the Liberation of Angola (MPLA), first by aiding the National Front for the Liberation of Angola (FNLA) of Holden Roberto, and then by supporting Jonas Savimbi and his National Union for the Total Independence of Angola (UNITA). On 3 August 1983 President Ronald W. Reagan proclaimed Mobutu "a faithful friend for twenty years," with the Zairian president at his side.

By 1990, Zaire was well down the road to becoming one of the world's poorest countries. Runaway inflation was rendering its currency worthless, the government deficit was unmanageable, already meager mineral production and exports were in decline, and compliance with U.S.-backed IMF economic reforms became an impossibility.

Social services, including public health programs to counter an AIDS epidemic, had all but disappeared. Neither diagnostic nor preventive procedures were in place to deal with the Ebola-Zaire hemorrhagic fever virus that had first appeared in 1976, and reemerged in 1995. Mobutu proclaimed a transition to democracy, which accomplished little of enduring value. The U.S. Congress ended aid to Zaire. From March 1993 to November 1995 the United States withdrew its ambassador, but maintained diplomatic relations.

A National Conference sanctioned by Mobutu drafted a new constitution and secured the appointment, in 1990, of Etienne Tshisekedi wa Mulumba as prime minister. Tshisekedi, an archfoe of Mobutu, who had lived for many years in vocal exile in Brussels, was the leader of the political party Union for Democracy and Social Progress (UDPS). He was dismissed as prime minister by Mobutu in 1993.

A transition parliament then selected a former prime minister, Kengo wa Dondo, as transition prime minister. Kengo, half-Polish, is a competent manager and skilled financial economist, but a man without a political base in Zaire's tapestry of ethnic entities. The regular armed forces, while generally loyal to Mobutu, are undisciplined, usually unpaid, and frustrated by the economic chaos around them. Mobutu's own position is sustained by the elite Special Presidential Division.

Mobutu's world changed with the end of the Cold War. There are no longer ideological blocs, nor threats of Soviet and Cuban influence in Africa. Whatever social or political promise his leadership held for Zaire evaporated. In the foreign policy of President Bill Clinton, Zaire assumed a low priority, with democratization and humanitarian concerns in the forefront.

BRANDON GROVE, JR.

See also Africa; Belgium; Congo Crisis; Mobutu, Sese Seko

FURTHER READING

Forbarth, Peter. *The River Congo*. New York, 1977.
Kalb, Madeleine G. *The Congo Cables*. New York, 1982.
Weismann, Stephen R. *American Foreign Policy in the Congo: 1960–1964*. Ithaca, N.Y. 1974.
Young, Crawford. *Politics in the Congo: Decolonization and Independence*. Princeton, N.J., 1965.

ZAMBIA

Formerly known as Northern Rhodesia and located in south-central Africa, a landlocked republic bordering Zimbabwe, Zaire, Namibia, Angola, Malawi, Botswana, and Mozambique. Zambia's foreign relations have naturally been heavily influenced by the nations that border it. This is not surprising considering that of the seven countries bordering Zambia, four were involved in long, bloody struggles for independence and a fifth, Zaire, gradually sank into chaos during the 1990s.

Prior to gaining its independence from Great Britain in 1964, the same year in which it established relations with the United States, Zambia had been a member of the Federation of Rhodesia and Nyasaland. Like Malawi, the former Nyasaland, Zambia entered independence under the leadership of a strong president, Dr. Kenneth Kaunda.

Zambia, which was ruled by President Kaunda from 1964–1991, has pursued a policy of nonalignment for most of its independence. Due to its status as a former member of the British Commonwealth and its infrastructural ties to Zimbabwe and South Africa, Zambia has never been in a position to move as far from the West as some other African nations.

The first major crisis Zambia faced was Rhodesia's (now Zimbabwe) unilateral declaration of independence under the white settler government of Ian Smith in 1965. This move was potentially devastating to Zambia since the country's railroad and power lines ran through Rhodesia. Zambia, despite its weak position, enforced the embargo that the United Nations placed on Rhodesia after it declared its independence. Zambia was able to survive due to emergency airlifts of oil and gasoline from the United States and Great Britain. Eventually, Zambia was able to develop rail links through Zaire and Angola; however, the reality of African instability meant that Zambia continued to be at least partially dependent economically on Rhodesia.

Although the United States did come to the aid of Zambia during its initial enforcement of the embargo against Rhodesia, continued U.S. trade with Rhodesia, which was formally legalized with the Byrd Amendment in 1971, served to chill U.S.-Zambian relations during the 1970s. In addition to Rhodesia, South Africa came to directly threaten Zambia during the 1970s once the war of independence in Angola intensified. South African forces, which engaged both Namibian SWAPO (Southwest African Peoples Organization) guerrillas as well as the Marxist MPLA of Angola, often violated Zambian territory. In response to South African and Rhodesian threats, President Kaunda reached an arms deal with the Soviet Union in 1980, which caused tensions in Zambian-U.S. relations.

It is important to note that despite Zambia's arms deal with the USSR, its government continued to pursue a policy of formal nonalignment. This explains why Kaunda was critical of Soviet and Cuban intervention in Angola and Mozambique. Zambia's neutrality helped the country to maintain and even improve its relations with the United States, in the economic realm. For instance, in 1983, Zambia and the United States reached a commodities agreement for the importation of U.S. wheat. Also Zambia's reputation as a stable, moderate country enabled the state to avoid U.S. blockage of its attempts to gain aid from the International Monetary Fund.

In 1990 after more than a quarter century in power, President Kaunda was forced by public pressure to agree to a new constitution with stronger human rights provisions and a schedule for elections. The next year the opposition candidate, labor union leader Frederick Chiluba, was elected president with eighty percent of the vote.

ANTHONY Q. CHEESEBORO

See also Africa; Angola; Zimbabwe

FURTHER READING

Burdette, Marcia. *Zambia: Between Two Worlds.* Boulder, Colo., 1988.
Omer-Cooper, J. D. *History of Southern Africa.* London, 1994.

ZANZIBAR

See Appendix 2

ZHOU ENLAI

(*b.* 5 March 1898; *d.* 8 January 1976)

The prominent Chinese Communist Party (CCP) leader who was, at his death, second in power and prestige only to Chairman Mao Zedong. Born into a lower gentry family, Zhou (Chou) was educated in China, Japan, and France and became one of the earliest members of the CCP. In the communist movement, he distinguished himself by his work with students, workers, intellectuals, and the military. He also developed many ties with the foreign community in China. During World War II he impressed many U.S. diplomats and army officers as an honest, effective leader in the war against Japan, and he was seen as a refreshing contrast to the corrupt and inefficient personnel in the Nationalist government of Jiang Jieshi (Chiang Kai-shek). Zhou participated in 1946 in the unsuccessful effort of General George C. Marshall to mediate an end to the conflict between the Communists and the Nationalists. When the Communists triumphed in 1949 and established the People's Republic of China, Zhou, appointed foreign minister, indicated his government's readiness to talk with the United States about recognition. The administration of President Harry S. Truman was in no rush, however, and China's entry into the Korean War in fall 1950 ended the possibility of normalized relations between the two countries for decades.

In addition to serving as foreign minister from 1949 to 1958, Zhou was premier of the People's Republic of China from 1949 until his death. In this capacity he was responsible for the administration of the government as well as for the implementation of its foreign policy, including the dramatic rapprochement with the United States in the 1970s. Zhou's urbane manner, charm, and intelligence impressed Americans from many walks of life, from the journalist Edgar Snow to President Richard M. Nixon and national security adviser Henry A. Kissinger. Commenting upon Zhou's legendary diplomatic abilities, Kissinger once said that Zhou, possessing "the sense of cultural superiority of an ancient civilization," had the ability to soften "the edges of ideological hostility by an insinuating ease of manner and a seemingly effortless skill to penetrate to the heart of the matter."

GORDON H. CHANG

See also China; Kissinger, Henry Alfred; Mao Zedong; Marshall, George Catlett, Jr.; Nixon, Richard Milhous

FURTHER READING

Wilson, Dick. *Chou: The Story of Zhou Enlai, 1898–1976.* London, 1984.
Suyin, Han. *Eldest Son: Zhou Enlai and the Making of Modern China, 1898–1976.* New York, 1994.

ZIMBABWE

Located in Southern Africa landlocked between South Africa and Zambia, formerly known as Rhodesia (prior to 1980), Zimbabwe is also bordered by Mozambique and Botswana. Zimbabwe began to develop its current cultural and ethnic mix during the latter part of the Bantu migration (circa 1200). The first major civilization to develop in what is now Zimbabwe was Monomotapa, a kingdom dominated by the Shona people. The most famous remnant of this gold-trading society is the stone city of Great Zimbabwe, built around 1400, from which the modern country takes its name.

Modern Zimbabwe began to take shape during the 1890s as part of a plan by Cecil Rhodes, an English businessman who had made his fortune in the diamond mines of South Africa after the 1868 diamond rush. It was his idea to encircle the then independent Afrikaner state of Transvaal (South Africa) with British settlers to the north. The colony was named Rhodesia in honor of Rhodes. After initially arriving at a settlement with King Lobengula of the Ndebele in which the king essentially gave away land without his full understanding, the British eventually went to war with him, killing him, and subjugating his people. When the territory was initially settled by the British, Rhodesia was ruled as an extension of South Africa. This status changed in 1923, when Rhodesia became a separate colony that included both northern Rhodesia (Zambia) and Nyasaland (Malawi) as well as southern Rhodesia (Zimbabwe). Rhodesia was distinguished largely by the fact that it was the only one of these territories with a significant white population.

After World War II, talk of independence or at least increased rights for Africans became common among the indigenous population and the initial strains between Rhodesia and its neighbors began to appear. While the movement towards independence in Northern Rhodesia and Nyasaland (as independent Zambia and Malawi, 1964) generally fit the pattern of black Africa, Rhodesia, like Kenya, had a substantial European population that was hostile to African rule. At first, the white population hoped to maintain Rhodesia's colonial status; Great Britain nonetheless wished to grant independence to a multiracial government. To prevent this change, white Rhodesia, under the leadership of Prime Minister Ian Smith, unilaterally declared its independence in 1965. Within two years of Rhodesia's independence, the UN responded with a series of sanctions against the pariah state.

The United States soon began to play a major role in the history of Rhodesia. Several U.S.-based corporations actively pursued extensive mining operations in Rhodesia, especially for chromium, a metal vital to the defense industry. Rhodesia's metal reserves were the rationale for what became known as the Byrd Amendment of 1971, part of the Armed Forces Procurement Appropriation Authorization Act and written by Virginia senator Harry F. Byrd. The amendment stated that the United States could not ban the importation of defense material from a non-communist nation if that same material was imported from a communist nation. Chromium also was imported from the Soviet Union. After the Byrd Amendment, the United States was forced to veto a measure in the United Nations which would have placed sanctions on any country that continued to trade with Rhodesia. Rhodesia, after its unilateral declaration of independence, received a great deal of support from conservatives in the United States, especially Southerners, who were fighting desegregation. Among those who spoke in favor of white Rhodesia were James Eastland of Mississippi, Strom Thurmond of South Carolina, and Barry Goldwater of Arizona. The National Association for the Advancement of Colored People (NAACP) and prominent civil rights activists, in contrast, strongly supported the embargo against Rhodesia and supported the African liberation movements.

During the period of the Byrd Amendment, the amount of chromium imported from Rhodesia increased rapidly despite the fact that there were several other sources of chromium from non-communist countries. For example, in 1965, the United States imported $500,000 worth of chromium from Rhodesia; however, by 1972, the amount increased to $13,300,000. By 1975, the value of chromium imports had reached $45,000,000. The Byrd Amendment was eventually repealed 15 March 1977, during the administration of President Jimmy Carter.

In 1975, southern Africa changed drastically as the former Portuguese colonies of Angola and Mozambique became independent. Both countries had fought long wars against Portugal and had emerged from their respective conflicts led by openly Marxist governments. Mozambique's independence in particular had a major impact on Rhodesia because the two countries shared a very long border. This meant that African guerrillas of the Patriotic Front under the leadership of Joshua Nkomo and Robert Mugabe could now effectively fight against the Rhodesian government by using Mozambican territory. U.S. diplomats, influenced by their British and South African counterparts, began to increase the intensity of their efforts to find a settlement.

The negotiations leading to the creation of Zimbabwe were likely the most concerted and high profile diplomatic effort ever made by the United States in sub-Saharan Africa. The importance attached to Zimbabwe was largely a reflection of the increasing role of the Cold War in Africa after the marxist revolution in Ethiopia of 1974. The basic goal of the United States was to achieve a settlement that would allow for majority rule while safeguarding white interests. A largely unspoken thought during this period was that the United States and the West had to prove their leadership was capable of providing a fair settlement or else the Soviets would gain a great political advantage in Africa. This Cold War reality and President Carter's dedication to human rights led the Carter administration to actively seek a solution to the Rhodesia conflict.

The primary parties of the negotiations were the leaders of the Patriotic Front, Mugabe and Nkomo, and the white leader, Smith. Negotiations reached fruition on 31 December 1978 and Rhodesia became Zimbabwe by 17 April 1980. The settlement provided that whites would be guaranteed a transitional period and that Zimbabwe would maintain a multiparty system for its first ten years. The United States was the first country to open an embassy in the capital, Harrare. In addition to recognizing Zimbabwe, the United States supported Zimbabwe financially, giving the country more than $200 million during 1980–1984. The United States and Zimbabwe, under the leadership of President Mugabe, have sustained good relations, except for disagreements over the Reagan administration's "constructive engagement" policy towards South Africa. These disagreements, in addition to U.S. criticism of Mugabe's treatment of his political rivals, led to a sharp reduction of U.S. aid after 1984. Despite the chilling of relations, the United States still provided Zimbabwe with $16 million in food relief during an early 1980s drought.

After gaining independence, Zimbabwe pursued policies similar to those of many other countries in Africa. Zimbabwe formally sought to redistribute wealth in the country but showed reluctance to break up successful farms owned by whites. Although this policy has not been popular, it has had some tangible benefits. For example, Zimbabwe has generally been able to feed itself since majority rule and occasionally has been able to export food. Zimbabwe has been an active member of the Southern African Development Cooperation Council (SADCC), an organization of Frontline States (nations bordering South Africa) that has sought to increase economic ties to each other while diminishing their interaction with South Africa. As a member of SADCC, Zimbabwe encouraged the economic isolation of apartheid South Africa, putting Zimbabwe at odds with the U.S. government throughout much of the 1980s. Zimbabwe played an active role in attempting to reach settlements in Mozambique and Namibia during the early 1990s.

ANTHONY Q. CHEESEBORO

See also Africa; Angola; Carter, James Earl; Mozambique; Namibia; Reagan, Ronald Wilson; South Africa

FURTHER READING

Arkhurst, Frederick. *U.S. Policy Toward Africa.* New York, 1975.
Cokorinos, Lee, and James H. Mittelman. "Reagan and Pax Africana." *Journal of Modern African Studies*, vol. 23, no. 4 (1985): 551–574.
Noer, Thomas, J. *Black Liberation: The United States and White Rule in Africa, 1948–1968.* Missouri, 1985.
Omer-Cooper, J. D. *History of Southern Africa.* London, 1994.
Saasa, Oliver. "The Effectiveness of Regional Transport Networks in Southern Africa—Some Post-Apartheid Perspectives." In *Southern Africa After Apartheid*, edited by Bertil Oden. Uppsala, 1993.

ZIMMERMANN TELEGRAM

(1917)

A coded telegram sent by German foreign secretary Arthur Zimmermann to the German ambassador in Mexico, Heinrich von Eckhard at a critical time in World War I. On 17 January 1917 British Naval Intelligence intercepted the telegram. The telegram informed Eckhard that Germany was about to begin unrestricted submarine warfare. If the United States then declared war on Germany, the ambassador was to offer Mexico an alliance on the following basis: "make war together, make peace together, generous financial support, and an understanding on our part that Mexico is to reconquer the lost territory in Texas, New Mexico, and Arizona." In addition, Eckhard was to suggest to the Mexicans that they invite Japan to join the alliance.

Zimmermann's intention was to exploit the tension between the revolutionary government in Mexico and the United States that had led to U.S. military intervention in Mexico in 1914 and 1916. Japanese-American relations were strained because of conflicts over the future of China and because in 1913 California had passed a law prohibiting Asian aliens from owning land in the state. The Germans hoped that even if Mexico and Japan did not actively make war on the United States, concerns about them would strengthen U.S. isolationism and compel the administration of President Woodrow Wilson to keep a large part of its army and navy at home.

To protect the security of their codebreaking methods, the British did not turn over the Zimmermann telegram to the Americans on 17 January but waited until 24 February, when they secured a copy of the slightly modified version of it sent to Mexico by Johann Bernstorff, the German ambassador to the United States. President Woodrow Wilson, who had broken diplomatic relations with Germany on 3 February in response to the German declaration of unrestricted submarine warfare, saw the telegram as further evidence of Germany's hostility and released it to the newspapers, which published it on 1 March. Wilson hoped the telegram would help break the Republican filibuster in the Senate against the administration's bill to arm merchant ships, but although Americans were angered by the telegram, the filibuster continued to the end of the congressional session on 4 March.

On 3 March, Zimmermann foolishly admitted that he had really sent the telegram, and German agents continued their efforts to draw Mexico into an alliance. Nevertheless, on 14 April the Mexican government announced that it would remain neutral. Other issues were more responsible than the Zimmermann telegram for President Wilson's decision to ask Congress on 12 April for a declaration of war against Germany, but the telegram helped unsettle U.S. confidence in its own security and helped confirm American's growing hostility toward Germany, further tilting the president to a hard-line policy toward Germany.

KENDRICK A. CLEMENTS

See also Cryptology; Germany; Mexico; World War I;

FURTHER READING

Doerries, Reinhard R. *Imperial Challenge: Ambassador Count Bernstorff and German-American Relations, 1908–1917.* Chapel Hill, N.C., 1989.
Tuchman, Barbara W. *The Zimmermann Telegram.* New York, 1958.

Appendix 1: Chronology of U.S. Foreign Relations

Compiled by Kurk Dorsey

1754

April–July At the present-day site of Pittsburgh, a clash between French troops and colonial forces under George Washington signals the beginning of the French and Indian War.

19 June–10 July Colonial representatives at the Albany Congress discuss plans for common defensive policy.

1759

13 September James Wolfe defeats the French on the Plains of Abraham outside of Quebec City, guaranteeing British control of North America.

1763

10 February Treaty of Paris ends the French and Indian War; England receives Florida and Canada.

May–November Pontiac rebels against British authority, destroys outposts, and besieges Detroit.

7 October Proclamation of 1763 prevents settlers from moving beyond the crest of the Appalachians.

1764

5 April Parliament passes the Sugar Act with the intention of recouping the costs of the war.

1765

22 March Parliament passes the Stamp Act to cover one-third of the cost of defending North America.

1766

18 March Under pressure from the colonists, Parliament repeals the Stamp Act.

1767

29 June Parliament approves the Townshend Acts to tax imports to the colonies.

1773

16 December To protest the British import tax, Samuel Adams organizes the Boston Tea Party.

1774

March–June Parliament passes the "Intolerable Acts" to regain control of the American colonies.

5 September–26 October Twelve colonies form Continental Congress in Philadelphia to discuss the Intolerable Acts.

18 October The Continental Congress agrees not to import British merchandise.

1775

19 April British troops trying to seize guns and ammunition clash with militia in Lexington and Concord, Massachusetts.

10 May Second Continental Congress meets and adopts a more radical course.

23 August King George III declares a state of rebellion.

August–December Colonial forces under Richard Montgomery and Benedict Arnold invade Canada but are stopped by fierce resistance and bad weather.

29 November Congress establishes the Secret Committees of Correspondence.

1776

10 January Thomas Paine publishes *Common Sense*, urging the colonists to push for independence.

6 April Congress opens colonial ports to ships of all nations.

2 May Louis XVI authorizes the secret transfer of 1 million livres worth of supplies to the Americans.

6 June In Congress, Richard Henry Lee offers a resolution calling for independence.

2 July Congress accepts Thomas Jefferson's Declaration of Independence.

18 July John Adams drafts the Model Treaty.

December Congress modifies the Model Treaty and dispatches John Adams to Holland and Benjamin Franklin to France.

1777

17 October Relying on French arms and munitions, U.S. troops defeat the British at Saratoga, New York.

15 November Congress adopts the Articles of Confederation.

15 December–6 January 1778 British diplomats broach the subject of reconciliation to Franklin.

1778

6 February Count Vergennes and Franklin sign military and commercial treaties in Paris.

29 July French naval units under Comte d'Estaing arrive off Rhode Island.

1779

12 April Hoping to reclaim Gibraltar, Spain agrees to join France in the war against Great Britain.

1780

January John Jay arrives in Madrid and discovers that the Spanish are not prepared to offer support.

28 February Catherine the Great proclaims the League of Armed Neutrality.

11 July French army and naval units under Comte de Rochambeau arrive in the United States.

1781

1 March The Articles of Confederation are finally ratified after four years.

15 June Congress orders Franklin to trade rights to the Mississippi River for more help from Spain and France; Franklin refuses.

19 October At Yorktown, Virginia, Lord Cornwallis surrenders to George Washington and Rochambeau, ending most of the fighting of the revolution.

1782

12 April Jay, Adams, and Franklin open peace negotiations in Paris with British diplomats.

30 November Ignoring Spanish demands and pledges to France, U.S. diplomats accept terms that include independence and most land east of the Mississippi River.

1783

2 July Under Lord Sheffield's direction, Britain restricts U.S. trade with Canada and the West Indies.

3 September France, Spain, Great Britain, and the United States sign the Treaty of Paris.

1784

7 May Congress creates a Department of Foreign Affairs and places Jay at the helm.

21 July Spain closes New Orleans to U.S. trade, threatening the economic security of western states.

30 August The *Empress of China* becomes the first U.S. merchant vessel to reach Asia.

1786

28 June The United States concludes a treaty with Morocco to protect U.S. merchant ships but fails to reach terms with the other Barbary states.

July–August Spanish diplomat Don Diego de Gardoqui and Jay agree to open Spain to U.S. trade in exchange for a thirty-year monopoly on the Mississippi River.

29 August Congress rejects the Jay-Gardoqui agreement.

1787

25 May–17 September Constitutional convention meets in Philadelphia.

13 July Confederation Congress passes Ordinance of 1787 to govern territories.

27 October–2 April 1788 Jay, James Madison, and Alexander Hamilton produce the *Federalist Papers* in support of the new constitution.

1788

December Spain reopens the Mississippi to U.S. commerce.

1789

30 April George Washington is inaugurated as the first president of the United States and appoints Thomas Jefferson to be the first secretary of state.

14 June Outbreak of French Revolution heralds a period of upheaval in Europe and raises questions about the status of Franco-American alliance.

July At Madison's urging, Congress uses its new powers to toughen foreign trade rules.

1790

22 March With reluctance, Jefferson returns from France to become secretary of state.

1791

4 November In the Northwest Territory, Miami chief Little Turtle routs U.S. forces.

1792

11 May A New England merchant and ship captain exploring the Pacific coast names the Columbia River after his vessel.

1793

1 February France declares war on Holland, Austria, and Great Britain, sparking a surge in U.S. agricultural exports to Europe.

8 April "Citizen" Genet arrives with fanfare from France but quickly angers U.S. citizens by trying to draw the country into France's struggle.

22 April Following Hamilton's advice, Washington proclaims U.S. neutrality, thus angering Madison and Jefferson.

1794

2 January Edmund Randolph replaces Jefferson as secretary of state.

26 March Prompted by repeated British seizures of U.S. merchant ships, Madison pushes Congress to cut trade with Great Britain.

18 April The Senate endorses Washington's decision to send Chief Justice Jay to London to resolve the crisis.

20 August General Anthony Wayne defeats the Shawnee in the Battle of Fallen Timbers.

19 November Jay fails to get British concessions on neutral shipping or impressment and settles for opening trade with Great Britain and British abandonment of the northwest forts.

1795

24 June The Senate accepts Jay's Treaty by a thin margin, sparking riots throughout the country.

3 August Twelve Native American tribes agree to the Treaty of Greenville, limiting their holdings in the Ohio Territory.

18 August After much consideration, Washington signs Jay's Treaty.

19 August Washington fires Randolph, believing him guilty of treason; Timothy Pickering becomes the new secretary of state.

27 October In Madrid, Thomas Pinckney signs an agreement to open New Orleans to free U.S. use for three years in exchange for U.S.-Spanish cooperation in stopping Indian attacks.

1796

30 April Washington establishes a precedent by forcing the House of Representatives to appropriate funds to enact Jay's Treaty without releasing secret papers on the matter.

July Angered by Jay's Treaty, France announces that it will no longer regard U.S. merchant ships as neutral; the "undeclared war" begins.

19 September Washington publishes his Farewell Address, warning against "the insidious wiles of foreign influence."

7 December John Adams defeats Thomas Jefferson for the presidency.

1797

4–18 October Charles Pinckney, John Marshall, and Elbridge Gerry arrive in France to resolve the dispute; French agents suggest that a bribe would enhance the negotiations.

1798

25 January–14 July Federalists in Congress pass the Alien and Sedition Acts.

19 May In the aftermath of the XYZ affair, Adams breaks off negotiations with France.

7–16 July Congress authorizes a military build-up and formally withdraws from 1778 treaties as part of the "quasi-war."

1800

12 May Adams fires Pickering for delaying Adams's efforts to negotiate peace with France.

30 September Signing of the Franco-American Treaty of Mortefontaine ends the "quasi-war."

1 October By the Treaty of San Ildefonso, France secretly acquires Louisiana from Spain.

3 December Jefferson defeats Adams soundly in the presidential election.

1801

14 May The Pasha of Tripoli declares war on the United States in order to collect more tribute.

1802

18 April Suspecting a French deal for Louisiana, Jefferson publicly warns that such a move would force the United States into an alliance with Great Britain.

16 October In response to the official transfer of Louisiana to France, Spanish authorities suspend U.S. right to free use of New Orleans.

1803

8 March James Monroe leaves for France with authority to spend $10 million for New Orleans and Florida.

11 April French foreign minister Talleyrand offers to Robert Livingston to sell all of Louisiana for $15 million.

12 April Monroe arrives in France.

30 April Monroe and Livingston accept Talleyrand's offer with the knowledge that Louisiana's borders are very vague.

20 December The United States takes possession of Louisiana, doubling its territory.

1804

14 May Meriwether Lewis and William Clark leave St. Louis on their expedition of exploration.

1805

4 June After the U.S. Navy subdues the pirates, U.S. diplomats reach an accord with Tripoli.

23 July In the *Essex* case, a British judge expands the rights of the Royal Navy to seize U.S. merchant ships trading with France.

7 November Lewis and Clark reach the Oregon coast, strengthening the U.S. claim to that land.

1806

March Shawnee leaders Tecumseh and the Prophet begin to organize tribes in the Ohio Valley.

16 May British Order in Council declares a blockade on Napoleonic Europe, further jeopardizing U.S. merchant ships.

23 September Lewis and Clark return to St. Louis with a wealth of information about the West, Native American tribes, and economic opportunities.

21 November Napoleon issues the Berlin Decree establishing a paper blockade of the British isles; both sides would tighten their rules throughout 1807.

31 December In the Monroe-Pinkney Treaty, Britain agrees to reverse the *Essex* decision and mitigate impressment; a dissatisfied Jefferson refuses to submit the treaty.

1807

22 June H.M.S. *Leopard* defeats the USS *Chesapeake* in U.S. waters; British officers board the ship and remove four crewmen, making impressment a national issue.

2 July Jefferson orders all ports closed to British ships.

22 December Congress passes Jefferson's Embargo Act as a means of retaliating against Great Britain.

1809

1 March Congress replaces the embargo with the less restrictive Non-Intercourse Act.

4 March James Madison is sworn in as the fourth president.

19 April Believing mistakenly that he has an agreement with London, Madison lifts non-intercourse restrictions against Great Britain.

30 May British foreign secretary George Canning repudiates the April agreement, which did not meet his instructions.

9 August Madison reinstates the Non-Intercourse Act against Great Britain.

1810

1 May Macon's Bill Number Two replaces the expired Non-Intercourse Act as U.S. trade policy.

26 September U.S. citizens in West Florida revolt against Spanish rule and declare the Republic of West Florida, which the United States promptly annexes.

2 November Believing mistakenly that France has lifted restrictions on U.S. shipping, Madison reinstates non-intercourse restrictions against Great Britain.

1811

7 November William Henry Harrison gains national fame by defeating Tecumseh at Tippecanoe Creek in Indiana.

1812

1 June Madison sends a war message to Congress specifying British malfeasance on the sea and on the frontier.

16 June Foreign Minister Castlereagh suspends the Orders in Council authorizing British depredations against U.S. shipping.

18 June Unaware of Castlereagh's action, Congress declares war on England.

12 July Initial U.S. forays into Canada fail miserably, placing U.S. forces on the defensive.

1813

5 October At the Battle of the Thames in Ontario, U.S. forces kill Tecumseh and destroy his confederation.

1814

8 August U.S. and British delegates open negotiations at Ghent, which last into December.

24–25 August British troops burn Washington, D.C.

5 October Massachusetts's government calls Hartford Convention to discuss options for revising the Constitution.

24 December The United States and Great Britain reach agreement on a treaty that basically maintains the prewar status quo.

1815

8 January Andrew Jackson salvages some U.S. honor with a victory at New Orleans.

2 March In retaliation for commerce raiding over the previous three years, Congress declares war on Algeria.

May–June Led by Stephen Decatur, U.S. naval forces defeat the Algerian pirates and force the Dey to surrender.

1817

21 March Monroe assumes the presidency, with John Quincy Adams as his secretary of state.

28 April Setting a precedent, President Monroe uses an executive agreement to finalize the Rush-Bagot pact, demilitarizing the Great Lakes.

1818

7 April In pursuit of the Seminole in East Florida, Jackson captures the Spanish fort at St. Marks and orders the executions of two British subjects captured in the region.

28 May Jackson takes Pensacola, completing his sweep of north Florida fortifications; in response, Spain orders Onís to be more conciliatory.

20 October Richard Rush negotiates the Convention of 1818 with London, setting the U.S.-Canadian border to the Rocky Mountains, leaving the Oregon territory open to both sides and temporarily resolving the Newfoundland fisheries dispute.

1819

8 February Four congressional resolutions condemning Jackson go down to defeat.

22 February The United States and Spain agree to the Adams-Onís Treaty, by which the U.S. receives East Florida and a generous western border for the Louisiana Purchase.

1821

22 February Ratifications for the Adams-Onís Treaty are finally exchanged.

12 August Led by Stephen Austin, several hundred U.S. citizens move to Spanish Texas, driven in part by a depression brought about by aggressive British export practices.

4 September The czar issues a ukase claiming the North American coast to the 51st parallel.

1822

8 March With Spanish armies driven from Latin America, Monroe asks Congress for authority to recognize Mexico, Colombia, Peru, Chile, and La Plata.

The on-going Greek revolution against the Turks raises questions about U.S. policy toward revolutionary governments.

1823

16 August British foreign secretary Canning suggests to U.S. minister Richard Rush that the two nations could work in concert to prevent outside encroachment in Spanish America.

7 November Prepared with advice from Jefferson and Madison, Monroe holds a cabinet meeting with the intention of accepting Canning's offer; Adams successfully holds out for an independent course.

2 December In an address to Congress, Monroe lays out the principles that will later be known as the Monroe Doctrine.

1828

19 May Congress passes the Tariff of Abominations.

1830

28 May Congress passes the Indian Removal Act to force Native Americans off of their ancestral lands.

27 September U.S. agents sign the first removal treaty, with the Choctaws of Mississippi.

8 December In a speech to Congress, President Andrew Jackson argues that removal of the Native Americans would be mutually beneficial.

1831

18 March In *Cherokee Nation* v. *the State of Georgia*, the Supreme Court refuses to issue an injunction against the enforcement of the Removal Act.

1832

3 August In Illinois, the Sauk and Fox tribes surrender, ending the Black Hawk war.

1834

January General Antonio Lopez de Santa Anna executes a coup in Mexico and immediately cracks down on the free-wheeling Texans.

1835

October–November Texan leaders establish a provisional government and a militia, which promptly skirmishes with Mexican troops.

29 December The Cherokee finally succumb to Washington's pressure and agree to remove themselves beyond the Mississippi.

1836

6 March Mexican troops capture the Alamo in San Antonio after a two-week siege.

21 April Texans win the Battle of San Jacinto and extract a recognition of independence from Santa Anna.

1837

4 August Texan leaders ask the United States for annexation but are rebuffed.

29 December Canadian soldiers battling insurrectionaries cross into New York and burn the rebel ship *Caroline*.

1838

29 May In retaliation for the *Caroline* incident, New Yorkers burn a Canadian vessel on the St. Lawrence River.

1839

February Tensions on the New Brunswick–Maine border flare briefly into the "Aroostook War," but cool heads in Washington and London prevent an escalation.

1841

November Slaves bound for the United States take control of the slave ship *Creole*, murder a crew member, and receive asylum in the Bahamas.

1842

9 August Old friends Secretary of State Daniel Webster and British minister Lord Ashburton conclude the Webster-Ashburton Treaty finalizing the U.S.-Canadian boundary in the east.

1843

June–July The first major influx of U.S. citizens reaches Oregon and settles in the Willamette Valley.

1844

22 April President John Tyler submits to the Senate a treaty of annexation with Texas.

24 May Samuel Morse invents the telegraph, radically altering the speed of long-distance communication.

8 June The Senate votes 35 to 16 against annexing Texas.

3 July Caleb Cushing finalizes the Treaty of Wangxia with the Chinese government, earning for the United States the same rights that Great Britain had attained after the Opium War.

1845

1 March Tyler annexes Texas through the use of a joint resolution of Congress.

4 March James Polk is sworn in as the eleventh president and proclaims all of Oregon to be U.S. territory.

6 March The Mexican minister leaves Washington to protest U.S. actions.

July John O'Sullivan coins the phrase "Manifest Destiny" to describe the inevitability of U.S. dominance of North America.

12 July Secretary James Buchanan quietly offers to divide Oregon at the 49th parallel, but the British minister quickly rejects the idea.

30 August Polk reverses himself again and takes up the "54°40′ or fight" banner.

2 December In an address to Congress, Polk invokes the Monroe Doctrine in recommending the termination of the joint occupation of Oregon.

6 December Minister John Slidell reaches Mexico City with authorization to purchase New Mexico and California; the government refuses to receive him.

1846

13 January Polk orders Zachary Taylor to lead his troops to the Rio Grande.

24 February Polk learns that London is preparing to send a large naval force to North America and decides that the 49th parallel is adequate.

24 April The first fighting between U.S. and Mexican forces breaks out near Matamoros.

11 May Two days after learning of the fighting near Matamoros, Polk sends a war message to Congress blaming the Mexicans for instigating hostilities.

15 June The United States and Great Britain agree to divide Oregon along the present-day boundary between Washington and British Columbia.

August With U.S. support, Santa Anna returns to Mexico City, takes power, and then reneges on his promise to make peace.

8 August Congressman David Wilmot attaches his proviso to a War Department appropriation bill.

12 December The United States negotiates an agreement with New Granada (Colombia) granting transit rights across the isthmus of Panama.

1847

6 May Polk's emissary, Nicholas Trist, joins the army of General Winfield Scott on its way to Mexico City.

14 September Scott captures Mexico City, fueling the "All-Mexico" movement; Trist begins his search for a government with which he can negotiate.

1848

January In response to the 1846 U.S. accord with New Granada, Great Britain seizes the strategic port of Greytown, Nicaragua.

2 January Prospectors discover gold at Sutter's Mill in California.

2 February Treaty of Guadalupe Hidalgo ends the Mexican War, as the United States agrees to pay approximately $18 million for about 500,000 square miles of land.

10 March The Senate accepts the Treaty of Guadalupe Hidalgo.

1849

September Former Spanish general Narciso Lopez gathers a few hundred veterans to invade Cuba, but the U.S. Navy prevents his departure.

1850

19 April Clayton-Bulwer Pact stipulates that neither the United States nor Great Britain will build or fortify an isthmian canal.

1851

August Lopez and 500 filibusters fail in their effort to conquer Cuba, and the leaders are executed.

1853

4 March In his inaugural address, President Franklin Pierce emphasizes his willingness to annex Cuba.

14 July Commodore Matthew Perry lands in Tokyo Bay to "open" Japan but is rebuffed.

30 December In the Gadsden Purchase, Mexico sells about 30,000 square miles of desert to the United States for $10 million.

1854

February–March In his return visit to Japan, Perry has limited success, negotiating the Treaty of Kanagawa.

April Secretary of State William Marcy instructs the minister in Madrid to buy Cuba for $130 million or work to free it from Spanish control.

5 June Marcy-Elgin Treaty resolves a number of U.S.-Canadian difficulties.

13 July USS *Cyane* bombards Greytown in retaliation for a perceived slight against a U.S. diplomat.

18 October Meeting in Ostend, Belgium, and Aix-la-Chapelle, Germany, three U.S. diplomats produce the Ostend Manifesto, justifying U.S. annexation of Cuba.

1855

June William Walker makes his first of four filibuster attempts at Nicaragua.

1856

14 May Franklin Pierce's administration recognizes Walker's government of Nicaragua, which soon collapses.

1860

6 November Abraham Lincoln is elected president, bringing the sectional crisis to a head.

20 December South Carolina secedes from the Union; by February, six other states join the rebellion.

1861

4 March Abraham Lincoln is inaugurated and appoints William Seward as secretary of state.

16 March Confederate President Jefferson Davis dispatches three ministers to Europe with instructions to use access to cotton as leverage for diplomatic support.

1 April Seward suggests to Lincoln that a foreign war would reunite the Union.

12 April Confederate forces fire on Fort Sumter in South Carolina, starting the Civil War.

19 April At Seward's urging, Lincoln proclaims a blockade of southern ports; the move increases tension between Washington and London.

13 May London declares neutrality but recognizes Confederate belligerency.

14 May U.S. minister Charles Francis Adams reaches London; his strong abolitionist position plays well in England.

21 May Seward pens Dispatch No. 10 threatening war with England, but Lincoln softens the message; upon receipt, Adams ignores it.

21 July Confederates rout Union forces at the first battle of Bull Run.

November Spain, France, and Great Britain land troops at Veracruz, Mexico, ostensibly to encourage Mexico to pay interest on its foreign debts.

8 November Captain Charles Wilkes detains the British ship *Trent* and removes two Confederate agents, James Mason and John Slidell, bound for England, igniting a war scare.

30 November British Cabinet demands a full apology, release of the Confederate agents, and reparations, but Prince Albert tones down the language and averts a crisis.

26 December Choosing to avoid war with Great Britain, Lincoln and Seward agree to release Mason and Slidell.

1862

April Spanish and British troops leave Mexico, but French forces press on to Mexico City.

31 July The CSS *Alabama* leaves Liverpool on its maiden voyage just ahead of London's order to seize the vessel.

22 September With an eye on Great Britain, Lincoln issues the Emancipation Proclamation.

1863

3 February France offers to mediate an end to the war, but Seward quickly rejects the idea.

June–July French troops finally conquer Mexico City and install a new monarchy; Lincoln recalls the U.S. minister.

3–5 July Union victories at Vicksburg and Gettysburg shake European confidence that the South can survive.

September–October Russian Baltic and Pacific fleets pay visits to New York and San Francisco.

3 September Under constant prodding from Adams, the British government confiscates two ships being built in Liverpool to break the blockade.

1864

May The French government seizes two Confederate ships under construction at Nantes.

19 June The USS *Kearsage* sinks the CSS *Alabama* just off the French coast.

1865

9 April The Army of Northern Virginia surrenders at Appomattox Court House, ending the Civil War.

1866

12 February Seward issues an ultimatum demanding the withdrawal of French troops from Mexico.

16 December The Tsar orders his minister in Washington to negotiate the sale of Alaska.

1867

9 April The treaty to buy Alaska for $7.2 million is ratified, and the United States takes possession of the territory in October.

19 June After the departure of French forces, Mexicans execute Maximilian.

1868

28 July The Burlingame Treaty gives the Chinese the right to unlimited immigration.

1869

13 April The Senate rejects the Johnson-Clarendon Convention of January, which was meant to resolve the *Alabama* claims dispute.

1870

30 June The Senate rejects President Ulysses S. Grant's treaty of annexation for Santo Domingo.

1871

8 May The Treaty of Washington establishes an international tribunal of arbitration to resolve all outstanding issues between the United States and Great Britain.

1872

17 February U.S. naval officer signs a treaty with Samoan leaders granting the United States exclusive rights to Pago Pago; the Senate never approves the agreement.

25 August The Treaty of Washington tribunal awards $15.5 million to the United States for the *Alabama* claims.

1873

31 October Spanish authorities in Cuba capture the rebel ship *Virginius*, illegally flying the U.S. flag, and execute some of the crew, including U.S. citizens.

29 November Spain agrees to pay an indemnity to the families of the dead U.S. crewmen of the *Virginius*.

1875

30 January United States and Hawai'i sign a commercial reciprocity deal, and Hawai'i agrees not to grant territory to any third party.

1878

17 January The United States and Samoa agree to a treaty of amity and commerce; the U.S. Navy receives the right to share Pago Pago with other navies.

1880

3 July The United States and European states agree to the Madrid Convention, which restricts the extraterritorial rights of Moroccans.

17 November By the Treaty of 1880, China and the United States agree that Washington has the right to regulate and limit, but not exclude, Chinese immigrants.

1882

6 May Congress passes the Exclusion Act, which severely restricts Asian immigration to the United States.

22 May The United States and Korea sign a treaty of amity and commerce that recognizes Korean independence.

1884

15 November–26 February 1885 At the Congo Conference in Berlin, U.S. delegates push for free trade and the end to slave trade; United States does not ratify the general agreement.

1885

19 June Secretary of State Thomas Bayard proposes a tripartite meeting after the Germans inspire a revolt among Samoans.

25 June–26 July Washington conference on Samoa breaks down when the United States refuses to yield to the Germans.

1 July U.S. termination of the fishing clauses of the Treaty of Washington (1871) leads to confrontations between Canadian authorities and New England fishermen.

1886

July–August U.S. revenue cutters in the Bering Sea seize Canadian schooners used in the pursuit of fur seals; the British government protests.

1887

20 January Ratification of the renewal of the 1875 agreement with Hawai'i occurs after amendment grants the U.S. Navy a base at Pearl Harbor.

22 November–15 February 1888 Anglo-American commission produces a modus vivendi and the Bayard-Chamberlain Treaty to regulate fishing off Newfoundland.

1888

13 July Bayard invites the nations of the Western Hemisphere to a general conference on peace and prosperity.

21 August The Senate rejects the Bayard-Chamberlain Treaty.

1889

15–16 March A hurricane sinks or damages all of the U.S. and German ships at Pago Pago, thereby averting a clash of arms and leading to a tripartite division of the islands.

29 April–14 June At a conference in Berlin, Germany, Great Britain, and the United States agree to an independent Samoa under a tripartite protectorate.

2 October–19 April 1890 Seventeen Latin American nations send delegates to Washington for the International American Conference, which establishes the forerunner of the Pan-American Union.

1890

22 January Secretary of State James Blaine suggests that Canadian actions in the Bering Sea fall just short of piracy.

2 July The United States signs an international agreement to suppress the slave trade from Africa.

1 October Congress passes the McKinley Tariff Act, which ruins the economies of both Cuba and Hawai'i.

1891

14 January Queen Liliuokalani takes power in Hawai'i after overthrowing the pro-American government.

14–31 March The lynch-mob killing of three Italian nationals in New Orleans leads to the withdrawal of the Italian minister to Washington.

16 October In retaliation for U.S. actions during the Chilean civil war, sailors from the USS *Baltimore* are attacked while on shore leave in Valparaiso, Chile.

1892

25 January In response to inflammatory Chilean actions, President Benjamin Harrison sends a message to Congress threatening to go to war; Chile eventually apologizes.

29 February Britain and the United States sign an arbitration treaty regarding the Bering Sea dispute.

1893

16 January With the help from crewmen of the USS *Boston*, white planters in Hawai'i oust Queen Liliuokalani.

14 February U.S. minister agrees with the provisional government of Hawai'i to an annexation treaty.

9 March President Grover Cleveland withdraws Hawai'ian annexation treaty.

30 March The Senate confirms Thomas Bayard as ambassador to Great Britain, the first U.S. citizen to hold that position.

15 August Bering Sea tribunal rules against the United States in almost every area and assesses damages of almost $500,000.

1894

3 December Responding to pleas from Venezuela, President Cleveland calls on Great Britain to submit the Venezuelan boundary dispute to arbitration.

1895

24 February Insurrection breaks out in Cuba, brought about by Spanish oppression and U.S. trade restrictions.

20 July Secretary of State Richard Olney sends a massive note to London threatening to invoke the Monroe Doctrine if Britain does not relax pressure on Venezuela.

26 November In response to Olney's message, Lord Salisbury suggests that the United States should mind its own business.

1896

25 January Concerned about shifts in the global balance of power, Colonial Secretary Joseph Chamberlain announces that war with the United States is unthinkable.

22 May Spain turns down U.S. offer to mediate the dispute between Madrid and the Cuban rebels.

1897

2 February Venezuela and Great Britain agree to submit their dispute to arbitrators.

5 November A new government in Madrid tries to stop the Cuban rebellion with a number of concessions; neither side in Cuba is pleased.

1898

9 February The *New York Journal* publishes a letter by Spanish minister Dupuy de Lome that insults President William McKinley.

15 February A mysterious explosion sinks the USS *Maine* in Havana harbor.

9 March Congress unanimously votes to spend $50 million on defense.

27 March McKinley instructs his minister in Madrid to demand an armistice in Cuba by 1 October.

10 April McKinley learns that the Spanish government will accede to the armistice request but will not accept the other U.S. demands.

11 April McKinley sends Congress a war message calling for armed intervention into the Cuban crisis.

20 April Congress adopts a war resolution including the Teller Amendment, renouncing any claim to Cuba.

21 April Spain breaks diplomatic relations with the United States.

25 April Congress declares war against Spain.

1 May Commodore George Dewey's Asiatic squadron defeats his Spanish counterpart in Manila Bay, effectively putting the Philippines under U.S. control.

16 June The United States finally pays Great Britain the settlement from the 1893 Bering Sea tribunal.

1 July U.S. forces win important land battles in Cuba, including at San Juan Hill.

7 July McKinley annexes Hawai'i through the use of a joint resolution of Congress.

10 December Through the Treaty of Paris, Spain cedes the Philippines, Guam, and Puerto Rico to the United States for $20 million; Cuba gains independence.

1899

18 May–29 July At the first Hague Conference, the United States and 25 other nations establish the Permanent Court of International Arbitration.

6 September Secretary of State John Hay informs U.S. embassies in London, Berlin, and St. Petersburg of the Open Door policy.

3 October Venezuelan boundary tribunal submits a ruling that largely supports British claims.

2 December Germany, Great Britain, and the United States agree to the partition of Samoa.

1900

5 February Signing of Hay-Pauncefote Treaty, through which Great Britain surrenders rights to an isthmian canal, so long as the United States agrees to operate it in a neutral manner.

20 March Despite receiving little international support, Hay declares the Open Door policy "final and definitive."

3 July In response to unrest in China, Hay issues the second Open Door note to reaffirm U.S. opposition to the partition of China.

14 August International expedition reaches Beijing and ends the Boxer revolt.

20 December The Senate amends the Hay-Pauncefote agreement to allow fortification of an isthmian canal; Great Britain will later reject the amended treaty.

1901

12 June The Cuban constitutional convention accepts the Platt Amendment, giving the United States control over Cuban foreign policy.

16 December The Senate accepts a revised Hay-Pauncefote Treaty that allows for fortification of an isthmian canal.

1902

28 June Congress appropriates $40 million dollars to buy the privately-held rights to the Panama Canal project under the condition that Colombia grant perpetual rights to the canal.

1903

22 January Colombia and the United States sign the Hay-Herran Convention, granting a 100-year lease over a canal zone.

24 January Great Britain and the United States agree to a joint tribunal to resolve the Alaska boundary dispute.

12 August The Colombian Senate rejects the Hay-Herran agreement, believing that canal rights are worth substantially more money.

3 September–20 October The Alaska boundary tribunal meets and rules in favor of the United States.

2–13 November With assistance from the United States, Panamanians revolt and declare their independence from Colombia.

18 November Signing of the Hay-Bunau-Varilla Treaty between the United States and Panama establishes the canal zone; Panama receives $10 million plus annual rent.

1904

10 February Outbreak of the Russo-Japanese War threatens stability in the western Pacific.

6 December In his annual message to Congress, President Theodore Roosevelt pronounces the "Roosevelt Corollary" to the Monroe Doctrine.

1905

29 July Under the secret Taft-Katsura agreement, Japan agrees to forswear any interest in the Philippines in exchange for a free hand in Korea.

9 August–5 September In Portsmouth, New Hampshire, Roosevelt leads Russian and Japanese diplomats to a settlement of the Russo-Japanese War.

1906

16 January–7 April The Algeciras Conference, which Roosevelt helps to arrange, resolves the Franco-German dispute over Morocco.

11 October The San Francisco school board creates an international incident by ordering the segregation of Asian children into a separate school.

1907

24 February The Japanese propose the "Gentlemen's Agreement," whereby they promise to restrict emigration in exchange for Roosevelt's intervention in San Francisco.

15 June–15 July The Second Hague Peace Conference accepts the Drago Doctrine in response to earlier efforts by the Germans and the British to collect debts from Venezuela.

14 November–20 December Under Mexican and U.S. auspices, five Central American countries hold a peace conference to end a war among Honduras, El Salvador, and Nicaragua.

16 December–22 February 1909 The Great White Fleet makes its world cruise in part to demonstrate U.S. naval power to Japan.

1908

30 November Root-Takahira agreement commits Japan and United States to maintain the status quo in the Pacific.

1909

27 January Great Britain and the United States agree to submit the Newfoundland fisheries dispute to the Hague Tribunal.

15 July President William Howard Taft appeals to the Chinese government to allow U.S. bankers into a railway-building consortium.

1910

7 September The Hague Tribunal issues a compromise ruling in the Newfoundland fisheries case.

1911

26 January The United States and Canada agree to reciprocal trade, but Canada fails to approve the agreement.

7 February U.S.-Canadian agreement ending pelagic sealing in the Bering Sea leads to a similar agreement with Russia and Japan in July.

20 May U.S., British, German, and French bankers sign a railway-building agreement with China.

25 May Francisco Madero takes power in Mexico and quickly wins recognition from the Taft administration.

6 June Knox-Castrillo Convention gives the United States power to intervene in Nicaragua; although the Senate never accepts the agreement, it sparks unrest in Nicaragua that leads to the landing of U.S. Marines, who stay until 1933.

3 August The Taft administration gets general arbitration treaties with France and Great Britain, but Senate amendments weaken them.

1912

2 August A Senate resolution opposing a major land purchase in Mexico by Japanese investors establishes the Lodge Corollary to the Monroe Doctrine.

1913

22 February After Madero's assassination, Victoriano Huerta takes power in Mexico; Taft does not recognize his government.

4 March New president Woodrow Wilson appoints William Jennings Bryan to be secretary of state; over the next few months he negotiates thirty "cooling off" treaties to prevent war.

5–18 March U.S. bankers pull out of China with the support of the new Wilson administration.

7–24 November The United States calls for Huerta's recognition and then announces its intention to force him from power.

1914

9 April U.S. sailors involved in blockading Mexico are arrested in Tampico; despite a quick apology from the Mexican commander, tension between the two countries increases.

21 April To prevent the delivery of ammunition to Huerta's forces, the U.S. Navy bombards and occupies Veracruz; the occupation lasts into November.

20 May–30 June Argentina, Brazil, and Chile try to mediate the dispute between Wilson, Huerta, and Mexican rebels.

15 July Forces loyal to Venustiano Carranza drive Huerta out of Mexico.

1 August Germany declares war on Russia.

3 August Germany declares war on France and invades Belgium, prompting a British declaration of war against Germany.

4 August In response to the outbreak of war in Europe, Wilson declares U.S. neutrality.

6 August The United States asks the belligerents to honor a broad definition of neutral rights.

15 August The Panama Canal opens.

20 August–23 December In a series of decisions, the British limit neutral rights regarding trade with the Central Powers; the United States protests mildly.

19 October The United States recognizes Carranza as the de facto president of Mexico.

4 November The National City Bank loans France $10 million; U.S. banks will eventually loan $2.3 billion to the Allies.

1915

18 January Japan issues the Twenty-One Demands to China; in May the United States announces that it will not recognize any Japanese gains at China's expense.

February–April Colonel Edward House tours European capitals futilely searching for a possible settlement for the world war.

4 February Germany announces the advent of submarine warfare in the waters around the British Isles and warns neutral vessels to stay out of the area.

10 February The United States warns Germany that it will hold Berlin strictly accountable for actions that destroy U.S. lives or property.

28 March The sinking of the British ship *Falaba* claims the first U.S. citizen's life.

1 May A German submarine sinks the U.S. tanker *Gulflight*.

7 May A German submarine sinks the British liner *Lusitania*, carrying passengers and munitions, killing nearly 1,200 people, including 128 U.S. citizens.

13–28 May Wilson sends the first *Lusitania* note of protest to Germany, demanding an end to unrestricted submarine warfare; two weeks later, the German reply defends their actions.

8 June Disappointed at what he believes is a pro-Allied bias in Wilson's cabinet, Secretary of State Bryan resigns rather than sign another protest note to Germany.

29 July U.S. Marines occupy Haiti, leading to the granting of a U.S. protectorate in September; U.S. occupation lasts until 1934.

1 September In response to the deaths of two U.S. citizens in the sinking of the British liner *Arabic*, German ambassador von Bernstorff issues a pledge to respect the lives of noncombatants.

5 October The German government supports von Bernstorff by offering an apology and indemnity to the United States for the sinking of the *Arabic*.

1916

10 January–9 March Mexican rebels under Francisco "Pancho" Villa kill eighteen U.S. engineers in northern Mexico; later his forces kill seventeen citizens in Columbus, New Mexico.

17 February–7 March Both houses of Congress debate and table resolutions that call on Wilson to prevent U.S. citizens from sailing on belligerent vessels.

18 February The U.S. Senate approves the Bryan-Chamorro Treaty of August 1914, which gives the United States the right to build a canal in Nicaragua.

22 February British foreign secretary Sir Edward Grey and Colonel House, on a second tour of Europe, agree that if the Allies call for a peace conference and the Germans refuse to attend, the United States will probably enter on the Allied side.

15 March General John Pershing leads 15,000 men into northern Mexico in pursuit of Villa but never engages the rebels in battle.

18 April After the German torpedoing of the liner *Sussex* in March, Wilson demands that Germany forgo submarine warfare.

4 May The Germans agree to the *Sussex* demands on the condition, which Wilson ignores, that the United States pressure the Allies to obey international law.

18 July The British announce a list of U.S. companies and individuals who are banned from commercial dealings in the empire because of their assistance to the Central Powers.

30 July German saboteurs destroy an ammunition plant in New Jersey, marking the beginning of a covert effort to limit U.S. military sales to the Allies.

4 August Denmark agrees to sell the Virgin Islands to the United States for $25 million.

29 November After several years of sporadic economic and military control, the United States occupies the Dominican Republic.

12 December Germany proposes peace negotiations which the Allies promptly refuse.

18 December Wilson calls on all combatants to outline their war aims; the Germans refuse, but in January the Allies issue a list of demands.

1917

22 January In a speech to the Senate, Wilson calls for a "peace without victory" in Europe.

31 January Ambassador von Bernstorff informs the United States that unrestricted submarine warfare will begin the next day.

3 February In response to renewed submarine warfare, Wilson severs relations with Germany and warns Berlin of possible U.S. retaliation.

5 February On the same day that Pershing's troops leave Mexico, Carranza proclaims the new Mexican constitution.

24 February British intelligence gives the U.S. government a copy of the Zimmermann Telegram from the German foreign ministry to Mexico, proposing an alliance against the United States.

12 March After twelve senators filibuster Wilson's attempt to arm merchant vessels, the State Department invokes an old law that allows such action.

12 March Czar Nicholas II abdicates and is replaced by the Provisional Government led by Alexander Kerensky.

2 April Wilson asks Congress for a declaration of war against Germany; the Senate and the House pass war resolutions on 4 and 6 April.

26 June The first U.S. soldiers arrive in France under the command of General Pershing.

2 November In the Lansing-Ishii agreement, the United States and Japan formalize their power relationship in the Western Pacific.

6–7 November The Bolsheviks under V. I. Lenin take control of the Russian provisional government and begin publishing details of the Allies' secret treaties.

27 November The Allied and Associated powers form the Supreme War Council.

29 November–3 December At a conference in Paris, the Allies fail to agree upon a statement of war aims to counter Bolshevik calls for revolution.

1918

8 January Wilson proposes to Congress his Fourteen Points as a basis for peace.

19 February Under its new constitution, the Mexican government announces its intent to reclaim title to all lands held by foreign oil companies.

3 March The Treaty of Brest-Litovsk ends the war on the eastern front and allows the Germans to transfer thousands of soldiers to the western front.

21 March Reinforced by troops from the Russian front, German forces in the west begin a series of offensives to crush the Allies before U.S. forces can arrive in numbers.

3 June U.S. forces play their first important role in the war in blunting the German attack at Château-Thierry.

18 July–6 August U.S. forces play a major part in the Second Battle of the Marne, in which the Allies shift to the offensive and begin driving the Germans back.

2 August–June 1919 U.S. troops occupy Archangel with a stated goal of protecting military supplies, although they later assist White Russian forces.

16 August–April 1920 U.S. troops land in Vladivostok for the same reasons.

26 September–11 November More than one million U.S. soldiers participate in the Meuse-Argonne offensive that ends the war.

6–7 October Germany and Austria-Hungary ask the United States to open truce talks based on the Fourteen Points.

5 November The Allies finally accept the Fourteen Points as the basis for talks after Wilson threatens to make a separate peace. Mid-term elections give the Republicans control of Congress.

11 November German and Allied representatives sign an armistice ending the fighting on the western front.

4 December Wilson and his peace commission leave for Paris.

1919

18 January Peace negotiations open in Paris with the Big Four (Wilson, David Lloyd George, Georges Clemenceau, and Vittorio Orlando) in attendance.

14 February Wilson and assistants present the conferees with a draft covenant for the League of Nations, which is to be included as a part of the final treaty.

2–4 March Thirty-nine Senate Republicans sign a round robin rejecting the League of Nations and asking Wilson to defer its creation.

14 March–April The French produce a series of harsh demands on Germany; Wilson's threatened departure causes the French to modify their position.

23 April In response to Italian demands for territorial concessions, Wilson appeals to the Italian public to overrule their leaders; the Italians leave the conference for about two weeks.

28 April In response to Japanese demands, Wilson reluctantly agrees to allow Japan special rights to Shantung.

7 May The victorious powers present Germans with the final peace treaty, which they grudgingly sign in late June.

10 July Wilson presents the Treaty of Versailles to the Senate.

19 August Facing splits in the Senate, Wilson agrees to accept some amendments to the League covenant in order to save the treaty.

4–25 September Wilson undertakes a grueling whistlestop tour to rouse the U.S. public to support the treaty; the tour ends when he collapses in exhaustion and suffers a stroke.

6–18 November Republican Senator Henry Cabot Lodge proposes fourteen reservations to modify the treaty; Wilson rejects them.

19 November The Senate votes down the treaty twice, first with the Republican reservations and then without any amendments.

1920

2 January At the peak of the "Red Scare," U.S. agents under the direction of Attorney General A. Mitchell Palmer arrest about 2,700 suspected subversives.

9 February–19 March Over Wilson's objection, the Senate reconsiders the Treaty of Versailles with the Lodge reservations but fails to get the two-thirds votes necessary.

13 February Wilson fires Lansing, ostensibly for holding unauthorized cabinet meetings during Wilson's illness.

20 May By joint resolution, Congress votes to declare an end to the war, but Wilson vetoes the move.

1921

20 April The Senate accepts a treaty granting Colombia $25 million as compensation for the U.S. role in the Panamanian revolution of 1903.

2 July Congress again uses a joint resolution to end the state of war with Germany and Austria-Hungary.

1 August Through the Balfour Note, Great Britain offers to forgive debts and cancel reparations beyond the amount necessary to repay the United States.

12 November–6 February 1922 The Washington Conference creates limitations on naval building, a power balance in the western Pacific, and official respect for the Open Door and China's integrity.

1922

4 December–7 February 1923 To lessen tension between Honduras and Nicaragua, the Second Central American Conference meets in Washington and creates a Central American court.

1923

11 January French and Belgian troops occupy the Ruhr in response to repeated German inability to pay reparations.

31 August Through the Bucareli Agreement, the United States agrees to recognize the Mexican government in exchange for Mexican acceptance of all subsoil rights granted before 1917.

1924

9 April A U.S. commission headed by Republican businessman Charles Dawes proposes a plan acceptable to Germany, the Allies, and the United States to rescue Germany from insolvency.

1925

14 November The United States cancels 80 percent of the Italian war debt and lowers the interest rate on the rest.

1926

27 January After years of maneuvering, the Senate agrees to U.S. participation in the World Court but includes restrictions that the court can not accept.

29 April The United States cancels 60 percent of the French war debt and lowers the interest rate on the rest.

May U.S. Marines return to Nicaragua, after being gone for just a few months, to stop rebels led by Augusto Sandino.

1927

4 May President Calvin Coolidge sends Henry Stimson to Nicaragua to mediate the civil war and establish elections.

20 June French foreign minister Aristide Briand submits a draft treaty to the United States calling for a bilateral agreement to outlaw war.

20 June–4 August In Geneva, the United States, Great Britain, and Japan discuss limitations on the construction of cruisers, destroyers, and submarines but fail to reach agreement.

28 December Secretary of State Frank Kellogg replies to Briand's proposal by suggesting that the agreement be open to any country.

1928

16 January Most of the nations of the Western Hemisphere meet in Havana and criticize U.S. intervention in Latin America.

27 August In Paris, fourteen nations sign the Kellogg-Briand Pact outlawing war.

19 November Newly elected president Herbert Hoover begins a goodwill tour of eleven Latin American nations.

17 December In a memorandum, J. Reuben Clark of the State Department argues for a repudiation of the Roosevelt Corollary as not in line with the Monroe Doctrine.

1929

11 February At the Committee on German Reparations meeting in Paris, U.S. citizen Owen Young creates a plan to reduce German war debt and extend its time of repayment.

29 October The stock market crashes in New York, providing a symbol of the global economic depression.

9 December President Herbert Hoover authorizes U.S. membership in the World Court after reaching agreement with that body on certain reservations; in 1930 the Senate rejects the pact.

1930

21 January–22 April At the London Naval Conference, Japan, Great Britain, and the United States agree to limits on cruisers, destroyers, and submarines.

1931

17 June Congress passes the Hawley-Smoot Tariff, marking the beginning of a bitter global trade war.

20 June Hoover calls for a one-year moratorium on the repayment of war debts and reparations.

18 September–4 January 1932 The Japanese army takes control of Manchuria in violation of treaty obligations and the League covenant.

21 September The depression forces the Bank of England off the gold standard.

1932

7 January Secretary of State Henry Stimson issues the Stimson Doctrine, that the United States will not recognize Japanese actions in Manchuria.

29 January Japanese forces capture Shanghai and hold it until protests from the League of Nations encourage them to withdraw in May.

2 February–July In Geneva, the major powers hold general disarmament talks at which the United States fails to win support for deep cuts in offensive weaponry.

16 June At the Lausanne Conference, the Allies agree to cancel most of the rest of the German reparations debt.

4 October The League's Lytton Commission proposes a compromise whereby Japan would occupy Manchuria but China would retain sovereignty.

1933

4 March In his inaugural address, President Franklin Delano Roosevelt vows to pursue a Good Neighbor policy toward Latin America; he also begins the process of taking the country off the gold standard.

27 March In response to League endorsement of the Lytton plan, Japan withdraws from the League of Nations.

16 May Roosevelt calls on world leaders to limit armaments and reduce economic warfare.

12 June–27 July At the London Economic Conference, European nations try to create a scheme to stabilize currency, but Roosevelt's refusal to cooperate scuttles the conference.

12 August–20 January 1934 A wave of turmoil in Cuba results in the rise to power of Sgt. Fulgencio Batista, who will rule the country until 1959.

16 November After receiving promises regarding the curtailment of communist activity in the United States, Roosevelt extends diplomatic recognition to the USSR.

26 December In the spirit of the Good Neighbor policy, Secretary of State Cordell Hull gives U.S. consent to a statement opposing intervention drawn up by Latin American nations meeting in Montevideo.

1934

13 April Congress passes the Johnson Debt Default Act to prevent loans to any government that failed to repay its war debts.

29 May In response to both the Good Neighbor policy and Batista's rise to power, the United States and Cuba agree to abrogate the Platt Amendment.

15 June Several countries, including Great Britain and Italy, formally default on their debts owed to the United States.

6 August U.S. Marines leave Haiti after nineteen years.

29 December Japan announces that it will no longer observe the Washington Naval Treaty.

1935

16 January Roosevelt asks the Senate to ratify Hoover's agreement regarding the World Court, but is again refused.

31 August Roosevelt reluctantly signs the Neutrality Act, which places a six-month embargo on the shipment of arms to any belligerent nation; the act is specifically targeted at the Italian-Ethiopian war.

1936

15 January Japan withdraws from the provisions of the London Naval Conference.

29 February Congress extends the Neutrality Act for another fourteen months and adds a prohibition against the extension of loans or credits to warring nations.

2 March The United States and Panama agree to new terms for operation of the Panama canal that require a higher annual rent from the United States and more autonomy for Panama; the Senate ratifies the agreement in 1939.

7 March German forces reoccupy the Rhineland in violation of the Treaty of Versailles.

17 November Germany, Italy, and Japan sign the Anti-Comintern Pact.

1 December At a Pan-American conference in Buenos Aires, delegates agree to consult with each other in case an external power threatens war.

1937

6 January Fearful of being drawn into the Spanish Civil War, Congress passes a joint resolution banning the export of arms to either side.

1 May Congress passes another Neutrality Act, which forbids U.S. citizens from traveling on vessels belonging to belligerents and expands the contraband list.

7 July The Sino-Japanese war begins with Japanese attacks near Beijing; Roosevelt chooses not to apply the Neutrality Act, fearing that it would hurt China.

5 October Surveying the world scene, including aggression in China, Spain, and Ethiopia, Roosevelt calls for a quarantine of aggressor nations.

12–14 December Japanese warplanes in China sink the USS *Panay*, killing two U.S. sailors; the Japanese government quickly apologizes.

1938

11 January Roosevelt proposes to the British a conference on world disarmament that Prime Minister Sir Neville Chamberlain rejects.

1 April In response to an expanded oil-land expropriation scheme started by Mexican President Lazaro Cardenas, the United States halts the purchase of Mexican silver at prices above market value.

29 September France, Great Britain, Germany, and Italy agree in a meeting at Munich to transfer the Sudetenland from Czechoslovakia to Germany.

6 October–31 December The United States and Japan exchange notes in which Washington protests violation of the Open Door policy and Tokyo asserts that the Open Door no longer applies.

24 December A Pan-American conference opens in Lima; U.S. attempts to get a strong declaration of hemispheric unity fail, and Cordell Hull settles for a more reserved Argentine resolution.

1939

9 March In response to unrest and the rise of a strong central government, the United States agrees to provide financial aid to Brazil.

14–15 March The remainder of Czechoslovakia dissolves, as the Germans annex Bohemia and Moravia.

31 March The British and French pledge to aid Poland in case of German aggression.

15 April Roosevelt asks Hitler and Mussolini for guarantees that they will not attack other European or Mediterranean countries.

22 May Germany and Italy sign a military agreement that Hitler calls the Pact of Steel.

25 July The Senate finally ratifies the 1936 U.S.-Panamanian agreement on the Panama canal.

23 August Hitler and Stalin agree to the Nazi-Soviet non-aggression pact.

1 September Germany invades Poland and captures Warsaw in less than four weeks.

3 September Great Britain and France declare war on Germany.

5 September Roosevelt proclaims U.S. neutrality and invokes the provisions of the 1937 Neutrality Act.

17 September The USSR invades Poland from the east.

21 September Roosevelt calls on Congress to repeal the arms embargo against belligerents.

11 October Scientists, most notably Albert Einstein, urge Roosevelt to initiate research into atomic weapons.

14 October The Soviets take advantage of European instability to issue territorial demands on neighboring Finland.

4 November Congress passes the Neutrality Act of 1939, which institutes the "cash and carry" system.

30 November–12 March 1940 After the Finns reject Soviet demands, the Red Army invades Finland and eventually forces a peace settlement on Soviet terms.

1940

26 January The U.S.-Japanese trade agreement expires, but Hull informs Japan that the United States intends to abide by the agreement on an interim basis.

9 April The Germans invade Denmark and Norway; the latter holds out until June

10 May Germany invades France, the Netherlands, Belgium, and Luxembourg.

11 May Chamberlain resigns and leaves Winston Churchill to form a coalition government.

16 May–June In response to the fighting in Europe, Roosevelt calls for an increase in defense appropriations and allows the transfer of surplus war material to the British.

16 June Congress passes the Pittman Resolution, allowing for the sale of war supplies to the countries of the Western Hemisphere.

17 June The USSR conquers Lithuania, Estonia, and Latvia.

20 June Roosevelt appoints Republicans Henry Stimson and Frank Knox to be secretaries of war and navy respectively.

22 June The French and Germans sign an armistice that establishes the Vichy government in the southern portion of the country.

27 June Roosevelt creates the National Defense Research Committee (which evolves a year later into the Office of Scientific Research and Development) under Dr. Vannevar Bush.

20 July Roosevelt signs a bill authorizing a $4 billion naval expansion program.

30 July Meeting at Havana, the Pan-American Union agrees to prevent the transfer of European colonies in the Western Hemisphere to German control.

18 August Roosevelt and Canadian Prime Minister W. L. Mackenzie King, meeting in Ogdensburg, New York, establish the Permanent Joint Board on Defense.

3 September Roosevelt and Churchill complete the destroyers-for-bases deal.

4 September Hull warns the Japanese not to move against French Indochina.

16 September Congress passes the Selective Service Act, creating the first peacetime draft in U.S. history.

22 September Vichy France grants Japan rights to air and naval bases in Indochina.

26 September Roosevelt proclaims an embargo, directed at Japan, on the export of scrap metal.

27 September Japan joins Germany and Italy in a ten-year alliance promising assistance in case of war with a nation not then at war.

31 October The Battle of Britain ends in German defeat, halting Hitler's plan to invade the British Isles.

5 November After a campaign in which both parties support the president's foreign policy, Roosevelt wins an unprecedented third term.

9 December The British open a ground offensive against the Italians in North Africa that gives them their first major victory of the war.

20 December The United States establishes the Office of Production Management, under William Knudsen, to facilitate defense production and the transfer of supplies to Great Britain.

21 December Germany labels U.S. aid to Great Britain "moral aggression."

29 December In a radio address, Roosevelt calls on the United States to make itself the "arsenal of democracy."

1941

6 January In his state of the union address, Roosevelt proclaims the "Four Freedoms."

27 January–29 March British and U.S. staff officers meeting in Washington agree to concentrate on Germany in case of war with both Germany and Japan.

11 March Roosevelt signs the Lend-Lease Act as a means to help any threatened country that the president finds to be vital to U.S. national security.

24 March–1 June A combined German offensive in the Mediterranean drives the British back to Egypt and Malta.

9 April The United States takes over the defense of Greenland.

11 April In the face of effective German submarine tactics, Roosevelt extends U.S. Navy patrols out to 26° West longitude.

13 April Japan and the USSR sign a non-aggression pact.

16 June The United States orders the closing of all German and Italian consulates by 10 July.

22 June Germany invades the Soviet Union; the offensive will reach Moscow and Leningrad before the onset of winter.

24 June Roosevelt promises aid to the USSR.

7 July U.S. forces take control of Iceland to prevent its use as a military base by the Germans.

12 July The British and the Soviets agree not to seek a separate peace with Germany.

24 July The Japanese occupy Indochina, prompting Roosevelt to freeze all Japanese assets and credits in the United States.

9–12 August Churchill and Roosevelt meet on warships in Argentia Bay, Newfoundland, to discuss the war; afterwards they issue the Atlantic Charter as a statement of principles for the post-war order.

12 August By a margin of one vote, the House agrees to extend Selective Service for another eighteen months.

9 September In the face of fierce fighting in the North Atlantic, the U.S. Navy extends its patrol line and convoy duty to Iceland.

18 October Hard-line General Tojo Hideki becomes prime minister of Japan.

30 October A German submarine sinks the USS *Reuben James*, a destroyer on patrol off Iceland; approximately 100 sailors die.

19 November The United States and Mexico settle the dispute about expropriation of oil rights; the deal includes millions of dollars of U.S. support for Mexican development and a joint commission that later establish that Mexico owes $33 million to U.S. oil companies.

20 November Hull and Japanese diplomats open negotiations in Washington to reduce the tension in the Western Pacific, but they have no common ground.

6 December Roosevelt appeals to Emperor Hirohito to preserve peace and withdraw from Indochina.

7 December Japanese forces launch attacks through the Pacific against Pearl Harbor, the Philippines, Guam, Hong Kong, and other Allied bases; Congress declares war on Japan the next day.

11 December Germany and Italy declare war on the United States.

22 December Meeting in Washington, Churchill and Roosevelt agree to a common strategy of victory in Europe first.

1942

1 January Representatives from twenty-six nations, including the USSR, Great Britain, the United States, and China sign the United Nations Declaration, based on the Atlantic Charter.

11 January Japanese forces begin the occupation of the Dutch East Indies.

15–28 January Meeting in Rio de Janeiro, diplomats from all of the American republics except Argentina and Chile vote to break relations with the Axis powers.

15 February British forces surrender Singapore without a fight.

19 February–29 March Acting with authority from Roosevelt, the War Department moves 110,000 people of Japanese ancestry to relocation camps in the western interior.

23 February The United States, Great Britain, Australia, and New Zealand codify the terms of a mutual Lend-Lease agreement.

9 March Japanese forces occupy Rangoon, thus cutting off the Burma Road to China.

6 May Approximately two months after General Douglas MacArthur escapes to Australia, U.S. and Filipino forces on Corregidor surrender.

7–8 May At the Battle of the Coral Sea, U.S. naval forces turn back the Japanese invasion of southern New Guinea, which would have threatened Australia.

29 May Soviet foreign minister V. M. Molotov and U.S. officials agree to comprehensive terms for the U.S.-Soviet Lend-Lease agreement.

3–6 June The U.S. Navy stops the Japanese advance at the Battle of Midway.

7 August U.S. Marines land on Guadalcanal in the Solomon Islands in the first steps towards rolling back Japanese conquests.

12–15 August Churchill and W. Averell Harriman come to Moscow to discuss military strategy in light of the British and U.S. decision not to invade France in 1942.

13 August General Leslie Groves takes over the "Manhattan Project," the secret effort to create an atomic weapon.

17 August The U.S. Air Force carries out its first independent attack on occupied Europe with a raid on Rouen, France.

19 August 6,000 Allied soldiers launch a disastrous raid of Dieppe, France, suggesting the Allies were not ready for a full-scale invasion of France.

13 September German forces reach their high-water mark when they enter Stalingrad, which the Soviets will reconquer in November.

4 November British victory at El Alamein drives the Germans out of Egypt.

8 November U.S. and British troops land in North Africa under the command of General Dwight Eisenhower.

11 November Eisenhower arranges a truce with Admiral Jean Darlan, the Vichy commander in French North Africa, in exchange for recognition of Darlan's leadership of the colonies.

1943

14–24 January Meeting in Casablanca, Churchill and Roosevelt agree to seek the unconditional surrender of the Axis and to invade Italy as soon as possible.

25 April In the wake of the revelation of the Katyn massacre of 1939, the USSR breaks diplomatic relations with the Polish government-in-exile in London.

1 May The Army takes charge of the Manhattan Project.

12–25 May Churchill, Roosevelt, and high-ranking military officers meet in Washington to plan strategy for both theaters, including setting a date of 1 May 1944 for the invasion of France.

13 May The last Axis forces in North Africa surrender.

15 May The Soviets dissolve the Comintern in deference to their allies.

31 May French generals Charles de Gaulle and Henri Giraud join forces to form the French Committee of National Liberation, known as the Free French Forces.

10 July–17 August U.S. and British forces capture Sicily in preparation for an invasion of Italy.

25 July Mussolini resigns and is replaced by Field Marshal Pietro Badoglio.

11–24 August Roosevelt, Churchill, and the Combined Chiefs of Staff meet in Québec and reiterate their plans to invade France while at the same time planning a stronger effort in Southeast Asia.

3 September British troops cross the Straits of Messina from Sicily into Italy.

8 September Italy surrenders unconditionally, but the Germans quickly take control of most of the Italian peninsula.

19–30 October Hull, Molotov, and British foreign minister Anthony Eden meet in Moscow with military leaders to discuss strategy, the status of Poland, and the post-war order.

9 November In Washington, forty-four nations establish the UN Relief and Rehabilitation Agency with power to aid people in liberated Europe and Asia.

10 November The United States and Great Britain establish the Allied Control Commission in Italy, excluding the Soviets.

22–26 November Roosevelt, Churchill, and Jiang Jieshi (Chiang Kai-shek) meet in Cairo and reiterate their commitment to force an unconditional surrender by Japan.

28 November–1 December At the Teheran Conference, Stalin, Churchill, and Roosevelt discuss coordinating their offensives in 1944 and strengthen their plan for a post-war international organization.

4–6 December Back in Cairo, Roosevelt and Churchill name Eisenhower as the Supreme Commander for the invasion of Western Europe.

1944

4 June U.S. troops capture Rome.

6 June The Allies land in Normandy in Operation Overlord, the culmination of years of planning for an effort to liberate Europe.

16 June U.S. warplanes make their first major raid on the Japanese home islands with an attack from China on Kyushu.

1–22 July Meeting at Bretton Woods, New Hampshire, delegates from forty-four countries establish the International Monetary Fund and the World Bank as tools to ensure post-war economic stability; the Soviet Union does not join these organizations.

18 July Tojo resigns as prime minister and military chief of staff.

20 July A plot by German army officers to assassinate Hitler fails.

27 July The USSR recognizes the communist Lublin government of Poland.

2 August Units of the Polish underground in Warsaw launch an offensive against the German garrison, but the Red Army waits outside the city refusing to help.

21 August–7 October At Dumbarton Oaks in Washington, Soviet, U.S., Chinese, and British diplomats outline a tentative charter for the United Nations.

25 August The Allies liberate Paris with Free French troops in the vanguard.

8 September Bulgaria surrenders to the Allies.

11–16 September Churchill and Roosevelt meet in Québec to discuss postwar plans for Germany; Roosevelt temporarily accepts the Morgenthau Plan to strip Germany of its industry.

9–18 October Churchill and Stalin meet in Moscow and carve out their spheres of influence in Eastern Europe.

20 October U.S. forces under MacArthur return to the Philippines.

23–25 October The Battle of Leyte Gulf results in the destruction of Japanese naval power.

28 October After challenging Jiang Jieshi's leadership of China, General Joe Stilwell gets recalled from his position as chief of staff of Allied forces in China.

7 November Roosevelt wins election to his fourth term in the White House after a campaign in which both parties express support for the concept of the United Nations.

16 December The Germans launch the Battle of the Bulge in one last effort to divide the Allies and force a separate peace.

1945

2 January The internment of people of Japanese ancestry ends.

4–11 February Roosevelt, Stalin, and Churchill meet at Yalta and resolve a number of complex issues, including the war against Japan and the shape of postwar Europe.

3 March Through the Act of Chapultepec, the nations of the Pan-American Union, except Argentina, create a security regime for the hemisphere that makes aggression by one state against another an act against all parties.

19 March U.S. forces invade Okinawa, just 360 miles from the home islands; in the fiercest fighting of the war, more than 11,000 U.S. servicemen die.

5 April The Soviets withdraw from their nonaggression pact with Japan.

12 April President Roosevelt dies of a cerebral hemorrhage and is replaced by Vice President Harry S. Truman.

23 April Truman and Molotov have an angry confrontation in the White House over the status of Poland.

24 April Soviet troops reach Berlin; the next day U.S. and Soviet forces meet on the Elbe River.

25 April–26 June Delegates from fifty nations convene in San Francisco and draw up a charter for the United Nations (UN).

8 May V-E Day, the German government accepts an unconditional surrender.

5 June The Allies divide Germany into four occupation zones under an Allied Control Commission.

17 July–2 August Truman, Stalin, and Churchill meet in Potsdam to call for Japan's surrender and to organize the demilitarization of Germany.

26 July Great Britain, China, and the United States demand the unconditional surrender of Japan, warning of the grave consequences of continued fighting; Japan rejects the demand three days later.

28 July Clement Attlee replaces Churchill as prime minister of Great Britain.

28 July The Senate ratifies the UN Charter, which Truman signs ten days later.

6–9 August The United States drops atomic bombs on Hiroshima and Nagasaki, killing approximately 150,000.

8 August Fulfilling his promise from the Yalta conference, Stalin declares war on Japan.

15 August V-J Day arrives as the Japanese agree to surrender on the condition that they retain the institution of the emperor.

2 September Japanese officials sign the surrender agreement on board the USS *Missouri* in Tokyo Bay.

2 September Ho Chi Minh declares Vietnam to be independent.

11 September–2 October Allied foreign ministers in London fail to come to agreement on peace treaties with Italy, Romania, Bulgaria, and Hungary.

20 November–1 October 1946 The International Military Tribunal in Nuremburg tries twenty-four Germans for war crimes; twelve receive death sentences.

16–26 December The Council of Foreign Ministers meets in Moscow to consider proposals for occupied Japan and Europe.

1946

10 January The UN opens with meetings in London that quickly dissolve into a struggle between the western powers and the USSR.

24 January The UN establishes the Atomic Energy Commission (UNAEC) to devise a plan for peaceful control of atomic power.

1 February Norwegian Trygve Lie is elected as the first secretary-general of the UN.

22 February In his "Long Telegram" from the embassy in Moscow, George Kennan describes Soviet leadership in the context of traditional Russian expansionism.

25 February The Soviets announce that they will not remove their troops from northern Iran by 2 March as they had promised.

15 March In a speech in Fulton, Missouri, Churchill calls for closer Anglo-American cooperation in the face of the creation of the Iron Curtain across Eastern Europe.

5 April The Iranians and the Soviets announce an agreement on a timetable for Soviet withdrawal from Iran.

25 April Foreign ministers of France, the USSR, the United States, and Great Britain hold the first of three meetings in Paris that fail to resolve the status of the minor Axis countries.

27 May The United States stops dismantling German industrial assets for shipment to the Soviets for reparations payments.

3 June–12 November 1948 The International Military Tribunal for the Far East tries Japanese leaders on charges of war crimes; more than 700 receive death sentences.

14 June The United States presents the Baruch Plan to the UNAEC, but the Soviets reject it claiming it would allow the U.S. to maintain its nuclear monopoly for some time.

24 June In China, communist rebel Mao Zedong demands of U.S. emissary George Marshall that the United States cut off all aid to the Nationalists.

1 July The United States conducts the first peacetime test of an atomic weapon at the Bikini Atoll in the Pacific.

21 August–11 October In response to Soviet pressure on Turkey, the United States sends two protest notes demanding respect for Turkish sovereignty.

20 September Truman fires Commerce Secretary Henry Wallace for advocating a conciliatory approach to the Soviets.

27 September Soviet ambassador Nikolai Novikov sends his long telegram from Washington to Moscow explaining the sources of U.S. conduct.

11 October With the British planning to pull out of the Greek civil war that started in August, the United States offers the Greek government a credit of $25 million to buy military equipment.

4 November Republicans take control of both houses of Congress, forcing Truman to forge a bipartisan foreign policy.

4 November–12 December Secretary of State James Byrnes and Molotov overcome their differences to work out peace treaties for the minor Axis powers.

December Full-scale guerrilla war breaks out in Vietnam between the Viet Minh and the French.

1947

7 January Marshall leaves China after more than a year of failed mediation efforts.

10 March–24 April In Moscow, Secretary of State George Marshall and British foreign minister Ernest Bevin reject Soviet efforts to punish Germany further.

12 March Formulating what would become known as the Truman Doctrine, the president calls on Congress to provide aid to Greece and Turkey as part of a general U.S. commitment to defend "the free peoples of the world."

23 April–9 May Congress accepts the Truman Doctrine by voting to provide aid to Greece and Turkey.

3 May A revised version of a constitution drawn up by U.S. occupiers becomes law in Japan.

29 May–29 August The U.S. and British militaries loosen restrictions on German economic development in their zones.

5 June Speaking at Harvard University, Secretary of State Marshall outlines an economic assistance program for Europe that becomes known as the Marshall Plan.

27 June–2 July French, Soviet, and British foreign ministers meet to discuss the Marshall Plan, but Molotov withdraws in anger.

July In the journal *Foreign Affairs*, George Kennan, writing under the pseudonym "X," publicly outlines the need for a policy of containment.

26 July The National Security Act merges the War and Navy Departments into the Defense Department and creates the Central Intelligence Agency (CIA) and the National Security Council (NSC).

14–15 August Great Britain grants independence to India and Pakistan.

2 September Most of the Latin American states join the United States in signing the Inter-American Treaty of Reciprocal Assistance, or Rio Pact, in which they pledge to assist one another in case of war.

22 September After two months of discussions, delegates from sixteen European nations call on the United States to provide between $16 and $20 billion in economic aid.

5 October The USSR announces the formation of the Cominform to combat the Marshall Plan and Truman Doctrine.

30 October Twenty-three nations sign the first General Agreement on Tariffs and Trade (GATT) to attack trade restrictions.

25 November–16 December The Council of Foreign Ministers meets in London but dissolves when the Soviets accuse the United States of breaking the Potsdam agreements.

1948

1 January GATT goes into effect.

23 January The Soviets inform the UN that the UN Temporary Commission on Korea is not welcome north of the 38th parallel.

25 February Communists in Czechoslovakia stage a coup d'état.

17 March Luxembourg, the Netherlands, Belgium, France, and Great Britain sign the Brussels Treaty, guaranteeing mutual assistance in case of war in Europe.

2 April Congress approves a creation of the Economic Cooperation Administration with funding of $17 billion to rebuild Europe.

3 April Despite calls from some officials for massive support, Truman signs a bill providing $463 million for the Nationalist Chinese.

1 May In Pyongyang, the North Koreans declare the creation of the People's Democratic Republic of Korea, with authority over the entire peninsula.

2 May The nations of Latin America and the United States sign the Charter of Bogotá, establishing the Organization of American States as a replacement for the Pan-American Union.

14 May Israel declares its independence, and Truman immediately recognizes it; Arab forces attack Israel.

7–18 June The Western Allies begin to unify their zones into the Federal Republic of Germany.

11 June The Senate easily passes the Vandenberg Resolution, encouraging the Truman administration to open talks with European nations regarding a security pact.

24 June The Soviets cut all overland access to West Berlin, prompting the Allies to respond with the Berlin Airlift, which lasts until 12 May 1949.

28 June Yugoslavia's Tito and Stalin publicly split.

3 August Whittaker Chambers accuses Alger Hiss of being a communist, starting a long inquiry that ends in Hiss's conviction for perjury in November 1949.

15 August South Koreans proclaim the Republic of Korea under Syngman Rhee.

17 September Terrorists assassinate the UN mediator for the Arab-Israeli conflict, Swedish Count Folke Bernadotte; his replacement is U.S. citizen Ralph Bunche.

4–25 October Direct talks having failed to produce a settlement, the Western Allies take the Berlin issue to the Security Council, but the Soviets veto the Council's recommendation.

1949

20 January Truman outlines the Point Four Program (so named because it was the fourth point of his inaugural address) to provide assistance to developing nations.

8 March France installs Bao Dai as ruler of an independent Vietnam within the French Union; the United States refuses to recognize the government until February 1950.

4 April Twelve nations sign the North Atlantic Treaty in Washington, establishing the North Atlantic Treaty Organization (NATO).

8 May The United States agrees to provide economic aid and military assistance to French forces in Indochina.

23 May–20 June The Council of Foreign Ministers meets in Paris to discuss German unification, but they cannot agree to a plan.

29 June U.S. forces withdraw from South Korea.

29 July The UNAEC disbands in the face of U.S. and Soviet intransigence.

6 August The State Department releases its white paper declaring that the Nationalist regime is doomed because of its own incompetence.

24 September The United States announces that it has detected evidence that the Soviet Union tested a nuclear weapon.

1 October Mao Zedong proclaims the existence of the People's Republic of China.

27 October The Chinese communists arrest U.S. consul general Angus Ward and hold him for almost two months.

1950

12 January Secretary of State Dean Acheson omits South Korea in his definition of the U.S. security perimeter.

13 January–1 August After the United States blocks the People's Republic of China from taking China's seat at the UN, the USSR boycotts the Security Council.

31 January Truman announces that the United States will build a hydrogen bomb.

9 February Senator Joseph McCarthy tells an audience in West Virginia that the State Department employs dozens of communists.

14 February Mao travels to Moscow and announces an alliance with the Soviet Union.

14 April Truman receives NSC-68, which lays out a policy of increased defense spending and a more aggressive approach toward the Soviets.

25 May Great Britain, France, and the United States issue the Tripartite Declaration, threatening to punish either side that breaks the UN armistice in the Middle East.

25 June North Korean forces invade South Korea; the next day Truman orders U.S. naval and air forces to help South Korea.

27–30 June The UN Security Council authorizes member states to use force to defend South Korea, and U.S. ground troops enter the battle.

7 July The Security Council authorizes the United States to choose a commander for unified forces in South Korea; Truman picks Douglas MacArthur the next day.

9 September Truman calls for increased U.S. ground forces in Western Europe.

15 September MacArthur turns the tide of the Korean War by successfully executing the landing at Inchon; within two weeks UN forces recapture Seoul.

23 September Congress passes the McCarran Act over Truman's veto.

27 September Congress appropriates $27 million for the Point Four Program.

15 October Truman and MacArthur meet on Wake Island to coordinate U.S. efforts in the Korean War.

26 October To fend off a U.S. effort to integrate Germany into NATO, the French call for the creation of a unified Western European army with small German units.

26 November With UN troops nearing the Yalu River, Chinese troops enter the war in force, driving MacArthur south of the 38th parallel.

6 December France and the United States strike a compromise on the integration of Germany into NATO.

19 December NATO foreign ministers choose Dwight Eisenhower to be the organization's supreme military commander.

1951

25 January UN troops open a counteroffensive that pushes the North Korean and Chinese forces back to roughly the current border between North and South Korea.

29 March Julius and Ethel Rosenberg are convicted of espionage and receive death sentences.

4 April After months of debate about the appropriate role of the United States in NATO, the Senate passes a resolution supporting Truman's plan to send more troops to Europe.

11 April Truman fires MacArthur for insubordination, but eight days later MacArthur speaks to a joint session of Congress.

23 June The Soviets suggest a cease-fire and restoration of the border between South and North Korea, which Acheson tentatively accepts.

10 July–26 July 1953 Peace talks take place, first in Kaesong then Panmunjon, which eventually lead to an armistice and a demilitarized zone along the front line.

1 September Australia, New Zealand, and the United States sign a Tripartite Security Treaty.

8 September Forty-nine nations, not including the Soviet Union, sign a peace treaty with Japan; also, the United States and Japan agree that U.S. forces will remain in Japan.

1952

20 February In Lisbon, the NATO Council sets terms for German participation in European defense.

27 May France, West Germany, and Italy form the core of the European Defense Community, and the United States, Britain, and France restore German sovereignty.

3 October The British test their first atomic weapon on islands off Australia.

1 November The United States tests its first hydrogen bomb.

2–5 December President-elect Eisenhower visits Korea, fulfilling a campaign promise.

1953

27 January New Secretary of State John Foster Dulles publicly promises U.S. help to the peoples behind the Iron Curtain.

5 March Stalin dies, leaving the USSR without a strong leader for several years.

18–24 June Food riots break out in East Germany, but the United States maintains a low profile.

27 July Negotiators at Panmunjon sign a truce that ends the Korean War.

19 August With CIA assistance, the Mossadeq regime of Iran is overthrown and the shah restored to power.

20 August The Soviets announce that they have recently tested a hydrogen bomb.

26 September The United States enters into a mutual defense agreement with Francisco Franco's Spain.

30 October The Eisenhower administration produces NSC 162/2, which redefines U.S. foreign policy in his mold.

8 December In a speech to the UN General Assembly, Eisenhower unveils his Atoms for Peace program, which calls for international control of nuclear energy.

1954

12 January Dulles explains the administration's New Look defense policy and its doctrine of "massive retaliation."

25 January–18 February At a foreign ministers conference in Berlin, France and Great Britain reject a Soviet plan for a fifty-year European security agreement that would leave China and the United States as outside observers.

26 February The Senate falls one vote shy of accepting the Bricker Amendment to limit the authority of the president in foreign policy.

16 March The French National Assembly reveals that the United States has paid approximately 80 percent of the costs of the war in Vietnam.

19 March Facing Soviet opposition to the Atoms for Peace proposal, the United States opens negotiations on the plan with South Africa, Australia, and five European nations.

4 April Eisenhower rejects the idea of using U.S. air power to help the beleaguered French garrison at Dienbienphu, which falls a month later.

7 April In a press conference, Eisenhower lends his support to the domino theory of communist expansion.

26 April–20 July At a conference in Geneva, concerned nations reach an accommodation on Vietnam that includes partition at the 17th parallel and the scheduling of elections for 1956.

13 May Congress passes the Wiley-Dondero Act allowing the construction of the St. Lawrence Seaway, which opens in June 1959.

18–29 June With funding from the CIA, rebels under Carlos Castillo Armas overthrow the leftist Guatemalan government of Jacob Arbenz Guzman.

7 August Eisenhower signs a bill creating the Surplus Disposal Program, later called the Food for Peace Program, to distribute U.S. agricultural surpluses to foreign states.

11–17 August After Zhou Enlai (Chou En-lai) warns that the communists will take Taiwan, Eisenhower reiterates that the U.S. 7th Fleet will continue to patrol the waters between Taiwan and the mainland.

30 August Eisenhower signs the Atomic Energy Act regulating the exchange of atomic material and information.

3 September Communist China begins to attack the small, Nationalist offshore islands of Jinmen (Quemoy) and Mazu (Matsu).

8 September Eight nations form the Southeast Asian Treaty Organization (SEATO) to defend the status quo in the region against communist aggression.

23 September The Soviets reverse their position and endorse the Atoms for Peace plan, which then slowly moves through the UN.

27 September The United States and Canada agree to create a Distant Early Warning (DEW) chain of radar stations across Alaska, Greenland, and northern Canada.

30 October In defiance of disapproval from the UN and the Organization of American States (OAS), the United States gives the new government of Guatemala more than $6 million.

17 November South Korea and the United States ratify a mutual defense treaty.

30 December The French National Assembly accepts a British plan, the Brussels Protocol, that finally solves the impasse over the readmission of Germany to the European community.

1955

29 January Eisenhower signs the Formosa Resolution, a purposefully vague statement by Washington that threatens U.S. military intervention in the China crisis.

9 February The Senate overwhelmingly approves a mutual security treaty between the United States and Nationalist China.

23 February The first U.S. military advisors arrive to train the South Vietnamese army.

April Representatives from twenty-nine nations gather at Bandung, Indonesia, to stake out a "non-aligned" position in the Cold War.

6 May The day after the western powers end their occupation, West Germany joins NATO.

15 May The four occupying powers agree to the Austrian State Treaty, which restores Austria to its 1938 borders and neutrality.

16 July–26 October President Ngo Dinh Diem cancels the elections for 1956 and declares himself president of the new Republic of Vietnam.

18–23 July At a summit meeting in Geneva, Eisenhower presents his "Open Skies" proposal to the Soviets but the attendees accomplish little.

1 August Communist Chinese and U.S. diplomats open secret talks in Geneva toward improving relations.

21 November The Baghdad Pact, formed in April under U.S. auspices as a tool of containment in the Middle East, holds its first meeting.

1956

24–25 February At the 20th communist Party Congress, Khrushchev denounces the excesses of Stalin's reign.

7 March Eisenhower denies Israel's request for increased arms sales because he fears sparking an arms race in the Middle East.

17 July Egyptian President Gamal Abdel Nasser accepts $270 million in loans from the United States, Great Britain, and World Bank to build the Aswan High Dam.

19 July Angered by Egypt's growing ties with the USSR, Dulles scuttles the Aswan project, contributing to Nasser's decision to nationalize the Suez Canal one week later.

26 October The USSR, United States, and sixty-eight other nations sign the Statute of the International Atomic Energy Agency (IAEA) after months of negotiations in the UN.

29 October–6 November Armed forces of Israel, Great Britain, and France attack Egypt and take control of the Suez Canal, but they then withdraw under pressure from the U.S. and USSR.

4 November After promising to liberalize its relations with Eastern Europe, the Soviets invade Hungary to smash its reformist government.

1957

5 January The president asks Congress for broad authority to take action in the Middle East in what becomes known as the Eisenhower Doctrine.

7 March The Treaty of Rome creates the European Economic Community (EEC).

3 July Nikita Khrushchev emerges from a four-year power struggle as the undisputed leader of the Soviet Union.

26 August The Soviets announce that they have successfully tested an ICBM.

5 October The Soviets shock the United States by launching *Sputnik*; the next month the secret Gaither report fails to persuade Eisenhower to expand defense spending by 50 percent.

1958

31 March The Soviets announce a temporary unilateral ban on nuclear testing.

7–13 May While on a goodwill tour of Latin America, Vice President Richard Nixon encounters violent protests in Peru and Venezuela.

15 July–25 October The day after leftist elements stage a coup in Lebanon, Eisenhower sends in the Marines to maintain order until the UN can intervene.

23 August–6 October PRC forces bombard Jinmen (Quemoy) and Mazu (Matsu), prompting a cautious response from the Eisenhower administration.

15 October–1 December Twelve nations gather in Washington and produce a convention that delimits Antarctica as a demilitarized continent open to scientific research.

10 November–January 1959 The United States and USSR engage in a verbal duel about the status of West Berlin.

1959

1 January Fulgencio Batista flees Cuba, leaving Fidel Castro's revolutionaries victorious in the three-year civil war.

5 March The United States signs bilateral defense treaties with Iran, Turkey, and Pakistan.

24 March–18 August Following a Baathist Party coup, Iraq pulls out of the Baghdad pact and terminates its agreements with the United States, forcing a name change to the Central Treaty Organization.

25–27 September Khrushchev, after touring the United States, meets with Eisenhower in Washington and agrees to hold a four-power summit on Berlin.

1960

19 January In order to restore some autonomy to Japanese foreign policy, the United States and Japan sign a new ten-year security agreement that limits U.S. authority.

5–11 May After the Soviets shoot down a U.S. spy plane and catch Eisenhower in a lie about the nature of the mission, the president takes personal responsibility for the disaster.

16–17 May The Paris summit on Berlin collapses as Khrushchev chastises Eisenhower for U.S. spying.

29 June–6 July After Cuba nationalizes British and U.S. oil companies, Eisenhower responds by slashing Cuban sugar exports to the United States.

30 June Belgium grants independence to the Congo (Zaire); within two weeks a revolt breaks out that leads to UN intervention into 1964.

9 July Khrushchev and Eisenhower trade threats about the status of Cuba.

14 July The UN Security Council orders Secretary-General Dag Hammarskjöld to send to the Congo a peacekeeping force that eventually includes U.S. units.

28 August Following U.S. leadership, OAS foreign ministers condemn the establishment of a communist regime in the Western Hemisphere.

September Iran, Iraq, Kuwait, Saudi Arabia, and Venezuela form the Organization of Petroleum Exporting Countries (OPEC).

8 November After campaigning on the need for younger, more aggressive foreign policy leadership, John F. Kennedy narrowly defeats Nixon for the presidency.

1961

3 January Eisenhower severs diplomatic relations with Castro's government.

1 March President Kennedy establishes the Peace Corps to send U.S. citizens abroad on humanitarian missions.

13 March Kennedy calls for an "Alliance for Progress" to uplift Latin America's economy.

17 April Thirteen months after Eisenhower authorized the organization of anti-Castro refugees, with Kennedy's approval the ill-fated Bay of Pigs invasion is launched.

11 May Kennedy dispatches 500 military advisors to South Vietnam with authorization to conduct operations against the communists.

17 May At Geneva, the United States proposes a plan to maintain Laotian neutrality through a coalition government, but the Laotian government is hesitant to accept.

3–4 June Kennedy goes to Vienna to meet Khrushchev, who demands a quick settlement of Berlin's status.

13 August Soviet and East German troops seal off West Berlin and begin constructing the Berlin Wall.

4 September Kennedy signs the Foreign Assistance Act to create the U.S. Agency for International Development (USAID).

1962

25 January Kennedy proposes the Trade Expansion Bill to cut tariffs and make the United States more competitive; Congress passes it in October.

6 July After a long civil war, Algeria declares its independence from France.

23 July Delegates from fourteen nations meeting in Geneva sign an accord guaranteeing Laos's neutrality and independence.

22–28 October In the Cuban Missile Crisis, the United States and the USSR come to the brink of nuclear war.

21 December Kennedy and British Prime Minister Harold Macmillan agree that the United States will sell Great Britain Polaris missiles for its nuclear submarine force.

1963

10 June Speaking at the commencement ceremonies of American University, Kennedy signals a willingness to work with the USSR.

20 June The United States and USSR agree to establish a "hot line" to facilitate instant communication between Moscow and Washington.

26 June Standing at the Berlin Wall, Kennedy tells West Berliners that the United States will risk war to defend the city.

15 July–5 August In Moscow, diplomats from Great Britain, the Soviet Union, and the United States complete months of negotiations by agreeing to the Limited Nuclear Test Ban Treaty.

9 October Kennedy approves the sale of 150,000,000 bushels of grain to the USSR.

1 November The United States acquiesces as the South Vietnamese armed forces remove Diem from office and murder him.

22 November Kennedy is assassinated in Dallas; Lyndon B. Johnson becomes president.

1964

9–11 January Riots in the canal zone kill four U.S. soldiers and many civilians and lead to the temporary severing of diplomatic ties between Panama and the United States.

1 February U.S. forces undertake expanded clandestine operations against North Vietnam.

31 March The Brazilian military topples President Joao Goulart from power.

7 August Congress gives a nearly unanimous vote for the Tonkin Gulf Resolution, authorizing President Johnson to take any necessary action to protect U.S. forces.

15 October Aleksei Kosygin and Leonid Brezhnev oust Khrushchev from power.

1965

2–8 March In reprisal for a pair of bombing attacks against U.S. bases in South Vietnam, Johnson orders ground troops into South Vietnam and sustained bombing against the north.

24–25 April Supporters of reformer Juan Bosch seize the government of the Dominican Republic.

28 April–17 May U.S. troops occupy the Dominican Republic as Johnson charges that communists have taken over the government.

13–19 May Johnson orders a bombing pause in order to signal to North Vietnam his willingness to negotiate.

23 May The OAS establishes the Inter-American Peace Force, composed largely of U.S. soldiers, to maintain order in the Dominican Republic.

28 July Johnson announces that he will commit large numbers of combat troops to fight guerrillas in South Vietnam.

31 August The United States installs a provisional government in the Dominican Republic.

10 November Mao launches the decade-long cultural revolution to crush his opponents.

17 December Ferdinand Marcos is elected president of the Philippines.

1966

January–February Senator J. William Fulbright holds televised hearings of the Foreign Relations Committee to criticize Johnson's Vietnam policy.

7–8 February In Honolulu, Johnson meets South Vietnamese Premier Nguyen Cao Ky and reaffirms his commitment to that country.

12 March General Suharto removes Bung Sukarno from power in Indonesia.

1 July Charles de Gaulle announces the withdrawal of France from NATO.

24–25 October Johnson and Ky confer with the leaders of South Korea, Australia, Thailand, the Philippines, and New Zealand in Manila and put forward a "Declaration of Peace."

1967

27 January The United States joins the USSR and fifty-eight other countries in signing a treaty to regulate space exploration and weaponry.

15 April 200,000-300,000 people rally in New York to protest the Vietnam War.

5–10 June Reacting to Egypt's expulsion of the UN peacekeeping force and evidence of coordinated Arab war plans, Israel pre-emptively attacks in the Six-Day War.

23–25 June Johnson and Soviet premier Aleksei Kosygin hold a summit in Glassboro, New Jersey.

3 August Johnson announces that troop strength in South Vietnam will reach 525,000 by the next June.

21–22 October 50,000 protesters march from the Lincoln Memorial to the Pentagon to challenge U.S. policy in Vietnam.

14 December The Harmel report recommends that NATO refocus its efforts on its political responsibilities.

1968

23 January North Korea seizes the USS *Pueblo*, claiming that it was in territorial waters.

30 January Communist forces launch the Tet Offensive in South Vietnam.

13 March Rather than accept his military advisers' call for 200,000 more soldiers, Johnson decides to send only 40,000 reinforcements.

31 March On the same night that he announces that he will not seek reelection, Johnson orders a halt to all U.S. military activity above the 20th parallel.

10 May Peace talks open in Paris between U.S. and North Vietnamese diplomats.

1 July The United States and Soviet Union join sixty other countries in signing the nuclear nonproliferation treaty.

20–21 August Soviet forces invade Czechoslovakia, crushing the Prague Spring reform movement.

31 October In order to further peace talks, Johnson halts all military action against North Vietnam.

22 December North Korea returns the crewmen of the *Pueblo* but keeps the vessel.

27 December The United States announces the sale of fifty advanced warplanes to Israel, marking its new role as the leading provider of high-technology weapons to Israel.

1969

16 January The United States and North Vietnam establish a framework for allowing South Vietnam and the Viet Cong to join the negotiations.

8 June Nixon announces the first troop cuts in Vietnam.

28 July At a speech in Guam, Nixon announces the Nixon Doctrine.

4 August National Security Adviser Henry Kissinger opens secret talks with North Vietnamese diplomats, especially Le Duc Tho.

1 September Muammar al-Qaddafi proclaims the Arab Republic of Libya after overthrowing King Idris.

15 October Protesters around the country participate in "Moratorium Day" against the war.

28 October Newly elected West German Chancellor Willy Brandt officially announces Ostpolitik.

3 November In a speech to the nation, Nixon outlines his plan to withdraw from Indochina as Vietnamization progresses.

17 November–22 December In Helsinki, U.S. and Soviet negotiators establish the framework for Strategic Arms Limitations Talks (SALT).

9 December Secretary of State William Rogers reveals that he has proposed a peace plan for the Middle East whereby Israel will withdraw from the occupied territories in exchange for an Arab peace pledge; both sides reject the plan.

1970

30 April About six weeks after Lon Nol overthrew the neutral Cambodian government, Nixon announces that U.S. troops have recently entered Cambodia to attack communists.

4–14 May Antiwar protests at Kent State University and Jackson State College end with the deaths of demonstrators.

8 May New York City construction workers hold counter-demonstrations.

17–27 September Civil war erupts in Jordan between the government and Palestinian refugees; the government prevails despite Syrian intervention.

31 December Congress repeals the Tonkin Gulf Resolution with Nixon's acquiescence.

1971

8 February-24 March The South Vietnamese Army, with U.S. backing, invades Laos to cut the Ho Chi Minh Trail but fails miserably.

June Newspapers publish the Pentagon Papers.

9–11 July Kissinger makes a secret visit to Beijing to lay the groundwork for Nixon's visit the next year.

3 September The World War II Allies formalize the division of Berlin in the Berlin Treaty.

27 September–25 October At the UN, the United States admits that Beijing should hold China's seat on the Security Council but fails to prevent Taipei's expulsion from the General Assembly.

11 October Kissinger makes a secret peace offer to Le Duc Tho, but progress is slow.

15 October Under threat of unilateral U.S. action, Japan agrees to a 3-year deal to limit textile exports to the United States.

1972

15 February The Senate approves the Seabed Arms Treaty, which prohibits staging nuclear weapons beyond the twelve-mile territorial limit.

21–28 February Nixon visits China and, with Zhou Enlai, issues the Shanghai Communiqué regarding U.S.-China relations and the fate of Taiwan.

30 March North Vietnam launches a major offensive across the demilitarized zone, prompting an escalation of U.S. air raids north of the 17th parallel.

8 May Nixon orders a blockade of North Vietnam and the mining of Haiphong harbor.

22–30 May Nixon travels to Moscow for a summit with Soviet Premier Leonid Brezhnev and signs seven agreements, ranging from arms control to environmental protection.

3 June The United States, France, Great Britain, and the Soviet Union agree to recognize the separate existence of East and West Germany.

13 July Congress authorizes the expenditure of $40 million to help control the international drug trade.

13 July The House of Commons narrowly approves a plan for Great Britain to join the EEC.

13 August The last U.S. combat troops leave South Vietnam.

5 September In the first major incident on international terrorism, members of the Palestine Liberation Organization kill eleven Israeli athletes at the Olympic Games in Munich.

23 September Following unrest in Manila, President Marcos declares martial law.

8–11 October Kissinger and Le Duc Tho reach a tentative agreement on ending the war.

19–23 October Kissinger fails to persuade the South Vietnamese government to accede to his agreement with Le.

20 November–14 December In two separate sets of meetings, Le and Kissinger are unable to reach a final agreement.

1973

8–13 January The peace talks resume, and the negotiators reach a final accord.

27 January The Viet Cong, South Vietnam, North Vietnam, and the United States sign the peace agreements.

22 February The People's Republic of China and the United States announce that they will exchange liaison officers.

17–25 June Brezhnev comes to Washington to further the work of the Moscow Summit.

1 July Nixon signs a bill prohibiting military activity in Indochina.

11 September Chilean army units under Augusto Pinochet overthrow President Salvador Allende.

6 October Egypt and Syria start the Yom Kippur War with a surprise attack on Israel.

15 October To counter Soviet support for Egypt, the United States begins to resupply Israel.

20–21 October Saudi Arabia leads a boycott of oil exports to the United States and price hikes for other nations.

25 October In response to a Soviet offer to enforce unilaterally a UN-sponsored truce in the Middle East, Nixon places U.S. forces on global alert.

7 November Over Nixon's veto, Congress passes the War Powers Resolution.

11 November Egypt and Israel sign an armistice that Kissinger had developed.

1974

11–18 January After several days of shuttle diplomacy, Kissinger works out a permanent agreement between Israel and Egypt to establish a UN buffer between them.

13 February Dissident Aleksandr Solzhenitsyn is expelled from the Soviet Union, symbolizing the human rights abuses that will eventually help to undermine détente.

18 March Most of the Arab and other OPEC countries end their oil embargo.

28 April–31 May Kissinger shuttles among the Middle East capitals and comes out with a truce between Syria and Israel.

27 June–3 July Nixon and Brezhnev meet but fail to move beyond the SALT agreement.

8 August In the face of the Watergate scandal, Nixon announces his resignation effective at noon the next day; Gerald Ford becomes president.

4 September The United States and East Germany establish diplomatic ties.

2 October The Senate accepts the Hughes-Ryan Amendment to restrict CIA clandestine activities.

24 November President Ford and Brezhnev sign the Vladivostok accords on limiting nuclear missiles.

13 December The Senate approves the Jackson-Vanik Amendment, which links trade with the Soviet Union to Soviet emigration policy.

16 December The Senate approves treaties outlawing chemical and biological warfare.

1975

3 January Congress passes the Trade Act to reform U.S. foreign trade; the act includes restrictions on preferences to OPEC nations and the USSR.

9 January–30 April The communist final offensive leads to the surrender of South Vietnam.

17 April The Khmer Rouge force the surrender of the Cambodian government.

29 April One day before the fall of Saigon, U.S. helicopters rescue 6,500 people, including 1,000 U.S. citizens, from the South Vietnamese capital.

13–15 May Cambodian forces seize the merchant vessel *Mayaguez*, spurring a U.S. rescue effort that leaves 41 U.S. servicemen dead.

1 August Thirty-five nations, including the USSR and the United States, sign the Helsinki Accords, which recognize post-World War II boundaries in Europe and require respect for human rights.

4 September Egypt and Israel sign the Sinai Accord that returns part of the region to Egypt in exchange for free passage of the Suez Canal for most Israeli shipping.

25 October Ford and Brezhnev sign the Soviet-American Grain Agreement to regulate grain purchases; American critics call it the "great grain robbery."

10 November The UN General Assembly approves a resolution equating Zionism with racism.

5 December After visiting mainland China, Ford proclaims the Pacific Doctrine, calling for normalization of relations with China and economic cooperation throughout the region.

19 December The Senate approves the Clark Amendment banning covert aid to pro-western guerrillas in Angola.

1976

4 February Under congressional pressure, several major U.S. companies, led by Lockheed Aircraft, admit to bribing foreign officials.

13 April The United States announces that it will extend its exclusive fishing zone from twelve to 200 miles.

27 April In a major policy reversal, Secretary of State Kissinger announces U.S. support for an end to apartheid, independence for Namibia, and black rule in Rhodesia/Zimbabwe.

19 May In response to congressional and executive investigations that revealed a host of illegal CIA activities, the Senate creates a committee to oversee the agency.

28 May Ford and Brezhnev sign the Nuclear Explosion Treaty to limit the size of nuclear tests.

9 September Exactly eight months after the death of Zhou Enlai, Mao Zedong dies, leading to a power struggle in the PRC.

6 October In a campaign debate, Ford asserts that Poland is not under Soviet domination.

November Eugene Rostow, Paul Nitze, Dean Rusk and others form the Committee on the Present Danger to lobby for tougher policy toward the USSR.

1977

20 January Jimmy Carter is sworn in as president and promises to make the defense of human rights a major goal of U.S. foreign policy.

21 January Carter announces a full pardon for any draft evaders who have not committed violent acts.

24 February Secretary of State Cyrus Vance reports that foreign aid to countries with poor human rights records, such as Argentina, will be reduced.

March The new administration opens talks on normalizing relations with Cuba that lead each to open "interests sections" in September 1977.

1 March The Reverend Leon Sullivan proposes the "Sullivan Principles" as guidelines for U.S. firms conducting business in South Africa.

30 March Secretary of State Cyrus Vance, in Moscow, proposes deep cuts in ICBMs as a starting point for renewed SALT; the Soviets quickly reject the idea.

22 May At commencement exercises at Notre Dame University, Carter calls for a new foreign policy free from an "inordinate fear of Communism."

6 June As part of an angry exchange over human rights, the United States attacks the Soviet Union for failing to live up to the Helsinki Accords.

2 July Deng Xiaoping, purged during the Cultural Revolution, emerges as one of the leaders of China.

26 July A U.S. diplomat testifies to Congress that approximately 1.2 million Cambodians have died since the Khmer Rouge took power in April 1975.

7 September The Carter administration signs two Panama Canal treaties that establish a framework for Panamanian control of the canal.

5 October At UN headquarters in New York, Carter signs two controversial treaties on the protection of human rights.

15 November Police use tear gas to break up protests outside the White House against a visit by the Shah of Iran.

19 November Egypt's president, Anwar El-Sadat, travels to Jerusalem to offer peace to the Israeli government.

1978

5 January Iranian police kill at least six Muslim demonstrators in the holy city of Qom.

10 January Newspaper editor Pedro Chamorro is assassinated in Managua, intensifying opposition to the dictatorial Somoza regime.

1 February The Carter administration proposes a new framework for reducing the international arms trade, but foreign competitors refuse to agree.

4 February Somalia reports an attack in Ogaden by Soviet-backed Ethiopian, Cuban, and South Yemeni forces.

25 February State Dept. warns USSR that its action in the Horn of Africa may affect relations and strategic arms agreement.

10 March Carter signs the Nuclear Non-Proliferation Act of 1978.

19 March The United States joins eleven other nations in approving UNSC Resolution 425 (1978) and Resolution 425 (1978), which call for Israeli withdrawal from Lebanon and the creation of a 4,000-man UN Interim Force in Lebanon (UNIFIL).

7 April Under pressure from European allies, Carter decides not to move forward with the neutron bomb.

3 May At a summit meeting, Japan agrees to reduce its trade surplus with the United States.

9 May American and Soviet representatives announce that, except for the issue of verification, they have reached an agreement on a chemical weapons ban.

22 August Sandinista rebels temporarily take over the National Palace in Managua in a demonstration of the power of the Nicaraguan opposition.

5–17 September At the presidential retreat in Maryland, Carter brings Egypt's Sadat and Israel's Menachem Begin to historic agreements toward peace in the Camp David meetings.

6 November The Shah of Iran imposes military rule in an effort to stamp out the rebellion that had been building throughout the year.

8 December Carter explicitly criticizes the USSR, Nicaragua, South Africa, Cambodia and other countries for their human rights records.

15 December Joint communiqués issued in Washington and Beijing announce the establishment of U.S.-PRC diplomatic relations and termination of U.S.-ROC ties and Mutual Defense Treaty.

29 December The Shah of Iran chooses Shahpur Bakhtiar from the opposition to head a civilian government.

1979

1 January The United States formally recognizes the communist regime in Beijing and ends official relations with Taiwan.

16 January Facing revolutionary pressure from Islamic fundamentalists, Shah Reza Pahlavi flees Iran; Ayatollah Khomeini takes power the next month.

17 February PRC troops, backed by air power, invade Vietnam as punishment for the Vietnamese invasion of Cambodia in November 1978; after inflicting 50,000 casualties, Beijing announces success and withdraws by 15 March.

26 March The signing of the Egyptian-Israeli Peace Treaty under Carter's auspices sets terms for transfer of the Sinai peninsula to Egypt and Egyptian recognition of Israel.

6 April The United States terminates aid to Pakistan after learning of that nation's efforts to produce enriched uranium for nuclear weapons.

12 April Negotiators conclude the Tokyo round of the GATT talks, leading to a general, but small, reduction in tariffs and nontariff barriers.

18 June At a summit meeting in Vienna, Carter and Soviet premier Leonid Brezhnev sign SALT II, which limits the each side to 2,400 strategic nuclear delivery vehicles.

19 July The Sandinista rebels capture Managua two days after President Anastasio Somoza Debayle flees Nicaragua.

6 August The United States discloses a July offer to deploy 200 to 600 medium-range Pershing II and cruise missiles capable of reaching Soviet territory for the first time.

15 August Carter fires his UN ambassador, Andrew Young, for secretly meeting with PLO representatives.

31 August The Carter administration accuses the Soviets of slipping a combat brigade into Cuba; the Soviets respond that the brigade has been there for several years.

21 September After two years of discussions, Mexico and the United States agree on a regime for exporting natural gas to the United States.

29 September Congress passes a law requiring the State Department to compile a list of states that support terrorism.

4 October The United States announces NATO High Level Group approval of cruise missile and Pershing II deployment.

15 October Frustrated by the deadlock between leftist rebels and reactionary oligarchs, reformist army officers seize power in El Salvador; within months they choose José Napoleón Duarte as president.

4 November Iranian militants seize sixty-six U.S. citizens as hostages after storming the U.S. embassy in Teheran.

14 November Carter freezes Iranian assets in the United States.

4 December Nicaraguan cabinet resigns and hands power to a five-member Sandinista junta.

12 December Reversing three years of policy, Carter calls for an aggressive defense buildup.

25–27 December Soviet forces enter Afghanistan, ostensibly to reinforce the pro-Soviet government against Islamic fundamentalist rebels.

1980

3–20 January In response to the Soviet invasion of Afghanistan, the Carter administration withdraws SALT II, halts grain shipments to the USSR, and orders a boycott of the Summer Olympics to be held in Moscow.

24 January In his State of the Union Address, the president announces the Carter Doctrine, that the security of the Persian Gulf is vital to U.S. national interest.

7 April Finding no success in diplomatic approaches, the United States severs relations with Iran.

21 April–26 September In the "Mariel boatlift," approximately 120,000 Cuban refugees flee to the United States with Fidel Castro's blessing.

24 April The Carter administration effort to rescue the hostages fails and eight U.S. servicemen die; Secretary of State Cyrus Vance resigns in protest.

19 June Citing treaty obligations, Carter allows the sale of enriched uranium to India.

22 September Hoping to take advantage of revolutionary turmoil, Iraq invades Iran, beginning an eight-year war that will take hundreds of thousands of lives.

17 October The United States agrees to give $75 million in foreign aid to Nicaragua.

1981

20 January Iran releases the last fifty-two hostages on the same day that Ronald Reagan is inaugurated as president after a campaign in which he called for more defense spending and greater exertion of U.S. power abroad.

20 February Indicating a reversal from Carter's policies, the Reagan administration begins to lift sanctions against Chile.

1 April The United States cuts off aid to Nicaragua, citing ties between the Sandinistas and rebels in El Salvador.

21 April Despite tensions with Israel, the Reagan administration agrees to sell eight billion dollars worth of advanced military equipment to Saudi Arabia, notably AWACS.

24 April Citing the damage done to U.S. farmers, Reagan lifts the embargo on grain exports to the USSR.

2–7 June Israeli jets strike PLO targets near Tyre and Tripoli and in Beirut, and they destroy a nuclear reactor at Osirak, Iraq.

19 August U.S. Navy pilots shoot down two Libyan planes over the Gulf of Sidra.

6 October Egyptian President Anwar El-Sadat is assassinated by Moslem extremists during a military parade marking the 1973 war with Israel.

16 November Reagan orders CIA officials to train the Contra rebels who oppose the Sandinistas in Nicaragua.

30 November Intermediate-range Nuclear Forces talks open in Geneva with the United States offering the "zero option," which the Soviets reject.

10–15 December In response to the rise of Solidarity, the Polish army seizes control of the government.

29 December In the wake of the Polish crackdown, the United States imposes economic sanctions on the USSR.

1982

14 January Secretary of State Alexander Haig travels to Egypt and Israel and expresses optimism about establishing Palestinian autonomy.

24 February The Reagan administration announces the Caribbean Basin Initiative in its effort to combat Communism in the region by promoting trade and investment.

26 February The Reagan Administration removes Iraq from the list of terrorist nations, easing trade sanctions.

March The nuclear freeze movement gains support, including from some in Congress, but not enough to change Reagan's policy.

8 March The Reagan administration charges that Soviet troops are using poison gas in their war in Afghanistan.

10 March The United States imposes an embargo on Libyan oil imports and curtails high technology exports to that nation, charging it with supporting terrorist and subversive activities.

28 March In elections boycotted by the Farabundo Marti Front for National Liberation (FMLN), rightists come to power in El Salvador intent on crushing the rebels; killings by death squads continue.

29 March In response to U.S. pressure, Japan says it will restrict automobile exports to the U.S. in the coming year to the previous year's level.

2 April–16 June Argentine forces fail in their attempt to take the disputed Falkland Islands from Great Britain.

6 June Israeli forces invade Lebanon to drive out the PLO, increasing tension with both Syria and the United States.

25 June Citing unspecified policy differences, Haig resigns and is replaced by George Shultz.

29 June Strategic Arms Reduction Talks (START) open in Geneva with a U.S. proposal for deep cuts in ICBMs.

8 July The United States officially rejects the UN Law of the Sea Treaty, which had been completed in April.

19–24 July Thirty-two members of the International Whaling Commission, meeting in England, agree to ban commercial whaling as of 1986.

18 August Mexico announces that it cannot service its foreign debt of $80 billion and opens restructuring talks with foreign banks and the IMF.

25 August Following Israel's invasion of Lebanon, 800 marines land in Beirut as part of an international peacekeeping force; believing their mission accomplished, they withdraw within a few weeks.

September–October Following the assassination of Lebanon's president-elect Bashir Gemayel and the Sabra and Shatila refugee camp massacres, U.S. Marines are redeployed as part of a second mutinational force.

10 November Soviet Premier Leonid Brezhnev dies; former KGB chief Yuri Andropov succeeds him.

8 December Congress prohibits the use of government funds to overthrow the Sandinistas, but the Reagan administration continues to use the CIA to that end.

1983

17 January Ten major industrial nations agree to make available a $20-billion fund to replenish the IMF in order to meet high demand for new loans to the Third World.

10 March The United States claims exclusive economic zones out to 200 miles from shore.

23 March NATO defense ministers reaffirm plans to deploy new U.S. intermediate-range nuclear missiles if no new arms limitation accord is reached by December.

23 March In a national television address, Reagan announces his intent to create a Strategic Defense Initiative (SDI), also known as Star Wars, to defend against nuclear war.

18 April Sixty-three people die in a bomb attack on the U.S. Embassy in Beirut directed at U.S. peacekeepers.

4 May The House votes overwhelmingly in favor of a non-binding resolution calling for a nuclear freeze, but the Senate kills it in November.

23 June The Supreme Court declares unconstitutional a key provision of the 1973 War Powers Act.

18 July Reagan appoints Henry Kissinger to head a commission to study U.S. policy toward Latin America.

1 September Soviet fighters shoot down a South Korean airliner after it passes through Soviet airspace, killing 269 passengers.

8 September The CIA participates in the mining of Nicaraguan harbors in an effort to assist the Contras.

23 October 241 Marines die in a suicide bombing of a barracks building in Beirut.

25 October U.S. forces invade Grenada to depose a Marxist government, protect U.S. students from an alleged threat, and prevent the completion of a potentially strategic airfield.

23 November In response to U.S. deployment of Pershing II missiles in Europe, the Soviets terminate the INF talks.

4 December One U.S. pilot is captured after his plane is shot down during an attack on Syrian positions in Lebanon.

1984

8 January Diplomatic sources report that Cuba has begun withdrawing most of its 10,000 troops in Ethiopia.

23 January The United States formally declares Iran to be a supporter of international terrorism and tightens controls on exports to that country.

7–26 February The United States withdraws its troops from Beirut.

9 February Yuri Andropov dies, and Konstantin Chernenko succeeds him as the leader of the Soviet Union four days later.

10–12 April After the CIA admits to a role in mining Nicaraguan harbors, Congress passes a resolution opposing such action.

26 April–2 May Reversing his earlier pronouncements, Reagan travels to China to strengthen ties.

6 May With help from the CIA, Duarte wins election to the presidency in El Salvador, as the Reagan administration seeks to find a moderate answer to that country's turmoil.

28 September In his first talks with a high-ranking Soviet official, Reagan meets with Soviet Foreign Minister Andrei Gromyko.

November Diplomatic relations restored with Iraq.

1985

8 February In his state of the union address, Reagan announces U.S. support for anti-communist rebels around the world, especially in Nicaragua (the "Reagan Doctrine").

11 March Chernenko dies, and Mikhail Gorbachev comes to power in the USSR and begins a reform process that will lead to the end of the Cold War.

12 March U.S. and Soviet negotiators meet in Geneva to open INF and space weapons talks.

22 March Delegates from 22 nations, meeting in Vienna, sign a preliminary accord mandating protection of the ozone layer.

27 March Despite some official opposition, NATO's nuclear planning group endorses SDI.

20 June Radio Martí begins broadcasting from Florida to Cuba.

August–September Led by Lieutenant Colonel Oliver North, the U.S. government undertakes an effort to funnel profits from arms sales to Iranians (which were meant to lead to the release of U.S. hostages in Lebanon) to the Nicaraguan rebels.

7 October Four members of a militant Palestinian faction hijack the Italian cruise ship, *Achille Lauro*, with more than 400 on board, demand the release of fifty Palestinians from Israeli jails, and murder an American tourist.

23 October Reagan announces a plan to combat "unfair trading practices" abroad, encourage U.S. exports, and start a new round of multilateral trade talks.

19–21 November Reagan and new Soviet premier Mikhail Gorbachev meet in Geneva; although they fail to reach an agreement on nuclear reductions, they form a firm friendship.

27 December Terrorist attacks, linked to Libya, kill seventeen people at the Rome and Zurich airports.

1986

15 January Speaking to a U.S. television audience, Gorbachev proposes a fifteen-year phaseout of nuclear weapons.

7–25 February In a tainted election, Ferdinand Marcos defeats challenger Corazon Aquino for the presidency of the Philippines, leading to demonstrations that force him from power.

18–19 March Reagan and Canadian prime minister Brian Mulroney announces plans to combat acid rain.

20 March The House votes to kill a $100 million dollar aid package for the Contras.

24–25 March U.S. warships enter the Gulf of Sidra to pressure Libyan leader Muammar al-Qaddhafi to halt terrorism and engage in a skirmish with Libyan military units.

5 April A bomb explosion in a discotheque in West Berlin kills one U.S. soldier and injures at least 155.

15 April In response to the terrorist bomb attack in West Berlin, U.S. warplanes bomb Libya.

7 May The Senate votes 95-0 for the Goldwater-Nichols Defense Reorganization Bill in an effort to promote cooperation among the armed services.

22 May NATO defense ministers approve a U.S. plan to resume production of chemical weapons.

27 June The World Court rules that the United States violated international law by funding the Contras, but the United States had declared earlier that it will not accept the ruling.

14 July–November The U.S. military assists Bolivian forces in destroying cocaine labs, signifying an important escalation in the war on drug trafficking.

12 August The U.S. announces that it has suspended its security arrangement with New Zealand after that country refused to allow nuclear vessels or weapons on its territory.

13 August Congress votes $100 million in military and "nonlethal" aid for the Contras.

20 September Trade ministers begin the Uruguay round of the GATT negotiations.

2 October Congress implements strong economic sanctions against South Africa in a repudiation of Reagan's policy of "constructive engagement."

11–12 October Reagan and Gorbachev meet at Reykjavik, Iceland, but Reagan's insistence on SDI prevents an agreement on deep reductions in nuclear weapons.

17 October Congress passes the Immigration Reform and Control Act to crack down on illegal immigration.

3 November A Lebanese magazine reveals that the U.S. government has been funneling arms to Iran in exchange for the hostages in Lebanon.

26 November Reagan appoints former Texas Senator John Tower to head a commission to investigate the Iran-Contra affair.

1987

7 January President Oscar Arias Sanchez of Costa Rica proposes a peace plan for Nicaragua that, despite basic U.S. opposition, forms the basis of sporadic negotiations.

24 January Hostage-taking in Lebanon escalates with the abduction by the Islamic Jihad of three U.S. professors at Beirut University College.

19 February Reagan lifts economic sanctions on Poland, a reward for release of political prisoners and government moves toward reconciliation with Solidarity and the Roman Catholic Church.

20 February After four years of battling mounting debt, Brazil decides not to pay interest to foreign investors, mainly U.S. banks.

26 February The Tower Commission blames Reagan's aides for the Iran-Contra affair but also blame Reagan himself for losing control of U.S. foreign policy.

27 March Attempting to address the growing trade deficit with Japan, the United States imposes restrictions on Japanese imports.

5 May–3 August In Congressional hearings, the full dimensions of the Iran-Contra affair become public knowledge.

17 May Missiles from an Iraqi plane kill thirty-seven on a U.S. warship in the Persian Gulf.

8 June A special panel reports that the new U.S. embassy in Moscow is useless because it is riddled with listening devices.

12 June In a speech at the Brandenburg Gate, Reagan calls on Gorbachev to tear down the Berlin Wall.

28 June At a communist Party Congress, Gorbachev tells Soviet allies that they will have to build socialism on their own, signaling a reduction in foreign aid.

22 July The Reagan administration allows Kuwaiti oil tankers to fly the U.S. flag, and he dispatches naval vessels to the Persian Gulf, in an effort to protect the free passage of oil from Iranian attacks.

4 August The IMF reports that in 1986 West Germany displaced the United States as the world's largest exporter.

16 September In Montreal, the United States and 23 other nations sign a convention to protect the ozone layer by controlling chemical emissions.

3 October The United States and Canada sign a preliminary free-trade agreement.

2 November Gorbachev, launching the celebration of the 70th anniversary of the Bolshevik Revolution, denounces Stalin's historical legacy and defends his program of *perestroika* (restructuring).

13 November Nicaraguan president Daniel Ortega meets with Speaker of the House Jim Wright in Washington, sparking a debate about the role of Congress in foreign policy.

8 December Gorbachev and Reagan meet in Washington and sign the Intermediate-range Nuclear Forces treaty to reduce nuclear weapons in Europe.

1988

29 January The U.S. government announces the end of special duty-free export trade privileges, granted under the GSP, for Hong Kong, Singapore, South Korea, and Taiwan, all countries with which the United States runs a trade deficit.

5 February–25 May In response to indictments against him for drug-related crimes, the United States attempts to oust Panamanian President Manuel Noriega through political and economic pressure.

25 February After arriving in Jerusalem, Secretary of State George Shultz proposes a "land for peace" deal to quell the intifada in the Israeli-occupied West Bank.

14 March Israeli prime minister Shamir fails to endorse Shultz's plan during a visit to Washington, D.C.

14 March The Senate unanimously ratifies the Montreal Protocol on protecting the ozone layer.

16 March Reagan orders 3,200 soldiers into Honduras in response to what he termed a Nicaraguan invasion of that country.

6 April In the face of continued Japanese refusal to accept the power of the International Whaling Commission, the United States closes U.S. waters to Japanese fishing.

14 April Gorbachev accepts a UN plan to withdraw Soviet troops from Afghanistan by early 1989.

12 May Vietnam formally announces it will withdraw 50,000 of its troops from Cambodia by the end of 1988.

1 June The 1987 INF treaty, based on the "zero option," takes effect, and the USSR and United States begin to destroy nuclear weapons in September.

3 July In the Persian Gulf, a U.S. naval vessel destroys an Iranian airliner, which naval personnel mistook for a warplane, killing 290 civilians.

8 August The UN gets Iran and Iraq to sign a truce ending their eight-year war.

23 August Omnibus Trade and Competitiveness Act approved, including the "Super 301" trade barrier retaliatory provision.

15 November U.S. mediators engineer an agreement among Cuba, Angola, and South Africa that brings peace and independence to Namibia and Cuban withdrawal from Angola.

7 December In an address to the U.N. General Assembly, Gorbachev announces plans to cut Soviet military forces by 20 percent, reduce Soviet forces in Eastern Europe, and shift the Soviet military doctrine to a defensive stance.

16 December After getting an explicit commitment from PLO leader Yassir Arafat to pursue peace, the United States makes its first official contact with that organization in Tunisia.

21 December Terrorists destroy Pan Am Flight 103 over Scotland on its way from London to New York, killing more than 250 people.

29–31 December India's Prime Minister Rajiv Gandhi visits Pakistan for Prime Minister Bhutto, and the two agree not to attack each other's nuclear power installations.

1989

4 January In the midst of international tension about Libya's potential to build chemical weapons, U.S. Navy pilots shoot down two Libyan warplanes.

7 January Representatives of 149 nations meet in Paris to reaffirm 1925 Geneva Protocol against the use of chemical weapons; Soviet foreign minister Eduard Shevardnadze announces that the USSR will begin to dismantle its chemical weapons that year.

13–14 February Costa Rica's Arias organizes the "Tesoro Beach Accord," through which the Sandinistas agree to free elections in exchange for the disbanding of the Contras.

10–30 March Facing insurmountable debt loads, Latin American countries and U.S. bankers agree to Treasury Secretary Nicholas Brady's plan of limited debt forgiveness and lower interest rates.

5 April Cambodian premier Hun Sen announces that Vietnam will withdraw all of its 70,000 soldiers in Cambodia by the end of September.

2 May In the first breach in the Iron Curtain, Hungary opens its border with Austria, providing a means for thousands of East Germans to emigrate to West Germany.

2–5 May Meeting in Helsinki, delegates from 79 countries agree to a plan to strengthen the ozone protection accord from the 1987 Montreal protocol.

10 May The Panamanian military under Manuel Noriega declares null the national election of three days earlier that appeared to produce an opposition victory.

12 May Bush states that it is "time to move beyond containment" and "seek the integration of the Soviet Union into the community of nations."

3 June Chinese troops crush prodemocracy demonstrators in Beijing's Tiananmen Square.

4–18 June The Solidarity movement wins control of the Polish Parliament, marking the end of communist domination of that country.

9 November Amidst mounting protests, East Germany opens the Berlin Wall and promises free elections for 1990.

10 November A coup ousts long-time communist leader Todor Zhikov of Bulgaria.

24 November Communist Czechoslovakia collapses in the face of mass protests and the "velvet revolution."

28 November West German chancellor Helmut Kohl proposes his own plan for the reunification of Germany without consulting foreign governments.

2–3 December Gorbachev and Bush meet in Malta to discuss the future of Europe.

9–10 December In China, National Security Affairs Advisor Brent Scowcroft emphasizes the importance of Sino-American trade relations and reaffirms friendship between the two nations.

14 December Christian Democrats win elections in Chile in a defeat for retiring president Pinochet.

20 December More than 20,000 U.S. troops invade Panama to arrest Noriega and install the democratically elected government.

21–25 December The Romanian communist government of Nicolae Ceausescu is overthrown in a violent uprising.

1990

11 February South African leader Nelson Mandela is released after twenty-seven years of imprisonment in South Africa; he begins international visits on 9 June.

13 February East and West Germany, as well as France, the Soviet Union, Great Britain, and the United States, agree on a plan that brings complete reunification by October.

25 February The U.S.-backed National Opposition Union, led by Violeta Chamorro, defeats the Sandinistas in Nicaraguan elections.

11 March The Lithuanian legislature declares independence from the USSR, beginning a process of disintegration that leads to the demise of the Soviet Union in 1991.

13 March The Third Soviet Congress of People's Deputies is convened in Moscow and repeals Soviet constitutional guarantee of communist Party monopoly.

27 May In local elections in Poland, candidates endorsed by Solidarity win more than 40 percent of contested council seats.

31 May–3 June Meeting in Washington, George Bush and Gorbachev agree to liberalize trade relations and to discuss further nuclear arms reductions.

20–30 June Touring the United States, Mandela calls on the world to maintain sanctions against his homeland until the advent of majority rule.

15 July Gorbachev drops objections to German membership in NATO in exchange for economic aid.

16 July Ukraine declares itself sovereign, raising questions about control of the Soviet nuclear arsenal, much of which is in the region.

2 August 140,000 Iraqi troops invade Kuwait as President Saddam Hussein announces his intent to annex the country.

4 August Bush vows to reverse Saddam's actions, begins to build a coalition to defend Saudi Arabia from a similar fate, and deploys U.S. troops under Operation Desert Shield.

3 October East Germany merges with West Germany.

27 October With the exception of Prime Minister Margaret Thatcher, EC leaders meeting in Rome announce their support for the creation of a unified central bank for the EC by 1994.

26–27 November Bush meets with Mexican president Carlos Salinas de Gotari to open talks on liberalizing trade.

1991

12 January After four days of debate, Congress narrowly supports the use of force, under UN auspices, to eject Iraq from Kuwait.

16 January Operation Desert Storm begins with a massive aerial attack against Iraqi forces in Kuwait and Iraq.

21 January Czechoslovakia, Hungary, and Poland all withdraw from the Warsaw Pact leading to its formal dissolution in July.

23 February U.S. and coalition ground forces launch a ground assault that routs the Iraqi army in four days and forces Iraqi acceptance of a UN ceasefire.

7–14 March Secretary of State James Baker makes the first of eight trips to the Middle East to promote bilateral and multilateral Arab-Israeli peace talks which convene in Madrid in October.

17 April The United States sends troops to protect Kurdish refugees in northern Iraq from Iraqi government forces.

30 April Twenty-six nations agree to close Antarctica to most commercial activity for a period of 50 years.

13 May Bush pledges that the United States will not use chemical weapons and that Washington will destroy its entire stockpile once a chemical arms treaty is signed.

12 June Mexico, Canada, and the United States open North American Free Trade Agreement (NAFTA) talks in Toronto.

25 June Yugoslavia dissolves into civil war as Croatia and Slovenia declare their independence in the face of Serb opposition.

10 July Hailing the racial progress in that country, Bush rescinds most of the sanctions against South Africa that have been in place since 1986.

31 July In Moscow, Gorbachev and Bush sign the first Strategic Arms Reduction Treaty (START) that reduces nuclear armaments by half.

18–21 August Russian president Boris Yeltsin helps to blunt a coup by Soviet hardliners against Gorbachev's efforts to decentralize power in the Soviet Union.

30 September Haitian President Jean-Bertrand Aristide is overthrown in a coup d'état led by the Haitian military.

29 October The United States imposes economic sanctions against the Haitian dictators.

25 December The Russian government raises the traditional Russian flag over the Kremlin, marking the official demise of the Soviet Union.

1992

1 January The FMLN and the Salvadoran government agree to a UN-brokered plan for ending the civil war.

3 March Bosnia-Herzegovina declares its independence, sparking a civil war between Orthodox Serbs and Muslim Bosnians.

24 March The United States joins European nations in signing an "Open Skies" accord along the lines first proposed by Eisenhower in 1955.

27 March Iraq accepts a UN plan to destroy its weapons of mass destruction, although it falls well short of actual compliance.

24 April UN establishes UNOSOM I to monitor the ceasefire in Somalia.

23 May Ukraine, Belarus, and Kazakhstan agree to destroy by 1999 the nuclear weapons on their territory.

3–14 June Representatives of more than 175 nations meet at the "Earth Summit" in Rio de Janeiro; the United States signs a treaty on climate change, but not one on biodiversity.

16–17 June Bush and Yeltsin meet in Washington and agree to reduce their nuclear arsenals by two-thirds.

12 August Mexico, Canada, and the United States sign the North American Free Trade Agreement, to become operative on 1 January 1994 .

18–19 November U.S. and European negotiators break a deadlock that had stymied GATT talks.

24 November The last U.S. military base in the Philippines closes.

4 December Bush sends 28,000 U.S. troops to Somalia to assist humanitarian efforts to combat starvation there.

1993

3 January The United States and Russia agree to further deep cuts in nuclear weapons in START II.

13 January In Paris, the UN Conference on Disarmament produces a treaty requiring the destruction of chemical weapons by 2005.

26 February Terrorists from a radical Muslim faction bomb the World Trade Center in New York City, killing five and wounding 1,000.

3–4 April President Bill Clinton meets with Yeltsin in Vancouver and offers him $1.6 billion in economic aid.

16 April The United States and Japan reach agreement on a plan to lower the trade imbalance, but Japan later hesitates to implement the plan.

30 April Clinton signs the biodiversity agreement from the Earth Summit after negotiating a memorandum of understanding with business and environmental leaders.

4 May The UN resumes control of the peacekeeping operation in Somalia.

5 June Gunmen loyal to General Mohammed Aidid kill twenty-four Pakistani soldiers in Somalia, leading to a U.S. effort to capture the warlord.

2 August With Serb forces closing in on Sarajevo, NATO threatens them with air attacks, forcing a temporary withdrawal.

13 September After secret meetings in Norway produce historic breakthroughs, Yassir Arafat and Israeli prime minister Yitzhak Rabin meet in Washington and sign their first peace agreement.

3 October Eighteen U.S. soldiers die in battle with Aidid's forces; television broadcasts pictures of the dead soldiers being dragged through the streets of Mogadishu.

7 October Clinton announces that all U.S. forces will be out of Somalia by 31 March.

12 October The USS *Harlan County*, seeking to land a force of peacekeepers in Haiti, turns back in the face of an angry demonstration.

29 October The ratification of the Maastricht Treaty transforms the European Community into the European Union.

November Congress approves NAFTA.

1994

10–11 January NATO leaders announce their Partnership for Peace program to improve ties with their former Warsaw Pact rivals.

1–25 February The United States demands that North Korea disband its nuclear weapons program and opens negotiations to find a suitable settlement.

3 February The United States ends the ban on trading with Vietnam.

28 February U.S. warplanes destroy several Serbian planes violating the UN "no fly" zone as part of a general effort to push the Serbs back from Sarajevo, but the Serbs continue their advance.

12–14 March With Secretary of State Warren Christopher in Beijing linking trade with human rights, Chinese authorities publicly round up dissidents.

25 March Clinton pulls the last U.S. troops out of Somalia.

15 April The United States signs the "Uruguay Round" of GATT, which establishes a new, more open world trade regime.

4 May Israel and the PLO reach a second agreement.

26 May Clinton explicitly separates human rights and trade when dealing with China as he renews most-favored-nation status.

25 July In Washington, Israel and Jordan declare their intent to sign a peace treaty.

12 August The United States and North Korea reach an agreement on restructuring North Korea's nuclear program.

19 September A mission led by former president Jimmy Carter arranges resignation of Haitian coup leaders; U.S. troops help restore the democratically elected government.

21 October The United States and North Korea reach an agreement to replace North Korean nuclear reactors capable of producing fissionable material.

26 October Israel and Jordan sign peace treaty.

1 December The Senate approves GATT and U.S. participation in the World Trade Organization.

1995

1 January The World Trade Organization replaces GATT as the structure for promoting free trade.

19 January Yeltsin announces that Russia has regained control of the breakaway province of Chechnya, although guerrilla fighting continues.

2 February Talks in Berlin between North Korea and the United States about North Korea's nuclear program reach an impasse.

8 February NATO approves a plan to work with Mideast and North African countries to stem the tide of Islamic fundamentalism.

1 March The last of the UN forces in Somalia leaves with the country still in chaos.

6 March–16 April Canada takes a strong stand against aggressive European Union fishing tactics beyond the 200-mile territorial limit.

4 April Clinton announces a cutoff in CIA funding for the Guatemalan military amid accusations that the agency covered up its knowledge of the murder of a Guatemalan dissident.

30 April In response to efforts to acquire nuclear weapons and continuing support for terrorism, Clinton announces ban on trade with and investment in Iran.

2 May Cuba and the United States reach an agreement on immigration that mandates repatriation of refugees found at sea.

12 May Without a vote, the signatories to the Nuclear Non-proliferation Treaty agree to an indefinite extension of the treaty.

26 May Bosnian Serbs begin taking hundreds of UN soldiers as human shields against NATO bombing.

2–18 June Under pressure from Serbian President Milosevic, who threatens to enforce sanctions, Bosnian Serbs release UN hostages.

7 June Taiwan's president, Lee Teng-hui, attends a reunion at Cornell University, which Beijing denounces as a plot to promote Taiwan's independence.

12 June The United States and North Korea, meeting in Kuala Lumpur, agree on the precise details of implementing their October 1994 agreement on nuclear power.

31 August NATO bombing of Serb positions and a renewed Bosnian-Croatian offensive lead to progress in talks to halt the war in the former Yugoslavia.

4–15 September In Beijing, more than 5,000 delegates from 181 nations attend the Fourth UN World Conference on Women in an atmosphere of tension surrounding China's human rights record.

5 September–February France resumes underground testing of nuclear weapons in the South Pacific despite international opposition.

28 September In a ceremony at the White House, Israel and the PLO agree to "Oslo II," setting terms for the next stage of the peace process.

5 October Twelve nations announce that they have agreed to establish a sixty-day ceasefire in Bosnia to begin in one week.

22–24 October The largest gathering of world leaders ever assembled meets at UN headquarters in New York to celebrate the 50th anniversary of the organization and pledge themselves to improve its ability to promote peace and social development.

30 October Voters in Québec narrowly reject a referendum on seceding from Canada.

4 November A right-wing Israeli extremist assassinates Prime Minister Yitzhak Rabin to protest the Palestinian-Israeli peace process.

14 December Meeting in Dayton, leaders of Bosnia, Serbia, and Croatia agree to end the Bosnian civil war through a treaty that calls for 60,000 NATO troops to serve as peacekeepers.

18 December Advance teams of US soldiers reach Bosnia to begin implementing the peace accord.

1996

5 January Liberal reformer Andrei Kozyrev resigns as Russian foreign minister and is replaced by Yevgeny Primakov.

5 January U.S. troops begin to withdraw from Haiti.

18 January Russia and Azerbaijan sign an agreement opening the way for U.S. and British companies to export Azerbaijani oil.

26 January U.S. Senate ratifies START II, 86-4.

31 January Under U.S. pressure, Greece and Turkey end a dispute over ownership of Aegean islands.

9 February An IRA bombing in London ends a seventeen-month truce and derails the peace talks that the Clinton administration had been encouraging.

19 February Chinese Premier Li Peng exacerbates tensions by warning Taiwan not to declare independence in a March referendum.

24 February Cuban warplanes shoot down two civilian planes flown by Cuban-Americans north of Havana, halting a slow thaw in relations between Cuba and the United States.

27 February In response to the successful fulfillment of the Dayton agreement, the United Nations lifts its economic sanctions on the Bosnian Serbs.

28 February Russia joins the Council of Europe.

29 February In response to Chinese sales of nuclear technology to Pakistan, the United States suspends $10 billion in loans to China.

1 March The United States decertifies Colombia as a country committed to the war on drugs.

8–15 March China stages military exercises in the Taiwan Strait in an effort to intimidate Taiwan on the eve of elections.

11 March The Clinton administration announces that navy vessels will move near Taiwan in response to belligerent Chinese acts.

12 March Clinton signs the controversial Helms-Burton Act to punish Cuba for the destruction of two Cuban-American planes in February.

13 March In response to a series of attacks against Israel, Clinton joins high-ranking representatives from twenty-eight countries in Sharm El-Sheikh, Egypt, in a one-day antiterrorism summit.

15 March In a symbolic gesture, the lower house of the Russian Duma votes to annul the 1991 dissolution of the Soviet Union.

20 March In Prague, Christopher pledges to keep NATO's expansion into Eastern Europe on track.

23 March In national elections, Lee Teng-hui becomes the first democratically elected president of Taiwan.

24 March British, French, and U.S. officials, meeting in Fiji, sign a pact banning nuclear testing in the South Pacific.

31 March 90,000 protestors in Japan call for reduced U.S. presence in their country.

3 April Commerce Secretary Ron Brown and 33 others die in a plane crash near Dubrovnik while on a mission to encourage U.S. investment in the former Yugoslavia.

5–7 April On three consecutive days, North Korean troops cross into the demilitarized zone and then withdraw.

6 April The simmering civil war in Liberia erupts anew, drawing in U.S. Marines to protect the embassy and evacuate U.S. citizens.

9 April Christopher announces that the United States will place environmental issues in the mainstream of its foreign relations.

12–28 April Responding to rocket attacks from Hezbollah guerrillas, Israel invades southern Lebanon.

15 April Clinton and South Korean president Kim Young Sam offer unconditional peace talks with China and North Korea, but China rejects the offer.

20 April North Korean and U.S. diplomats open talks in Berlin on North Korea's nuclear missile program.

20 April In Moscow, Yeltsin and the leaders of the G-7 states pledge to sign a comprehensive nuclear test ban.

24–25 April The PLO officially rescinds its original call for the destruction of Israel, and Israel's Labor Party reciprocates by dropping its objection to a Palestinian state.

1 May Symbolizing his rise in stature, Yassir Arafat visits the White House and meets privately with Clinton.

3 May Negotiators in Geneva sign a treaty curbing the use of land mines, although critics view it as a flawed compromise.

7 May At The Hague, the first war-crimes trial resulting from the Bosnian civil war opens.

14 May The United States announces that it will impose $3 billion in trade sanctions against China in June unless China cracks down on the pirating of intellectual property.

20 May The United Nations and Baghdad agree on an easing of the oil embargo against Iraq in order to fund humanitarian relief in that country.

27 May Russian prime minister Viktor Chernomyrdin and Chechen rebel leader Zelimkhan Yandarbiyev sign a truce agreement to take effect on 31 May.

29 May In Israel, Likud leader Benjamin Netanyahu, who campaigned against key parts of the Oslo agreements, is elected prime minister.

4 June The United States and France agree to collaborate on nuclear weapons research, including sharing data from past tests.

10 June In Belfast, the peace talks open for Northern Ireland with former senator George Mitchell as mediator.

11–15 June UN weapons inspectors surround a military compound after being denied entry by the Iraqi government.

17 June The United States withdraws its threat of sanctions against China after deciding that Beijing was cracking down on copyright infringement.

29 June Using a truck bomb, terrorists, initially believed to be Saudi dissidents, kill nineteen U.S. servicemen at a base in Dharan.

3 July Boris Yeltsin decisively defeats communist Gennady Zyuganov in a run-off election for the Russian presidency.

3-4 September U.S. warplanes bomb military facilities in southern Iraq in retaliation for Iraqi incursions into the Kurdish safe haven in northern Iraq.

10 September The UN General Assembly approves the Comprehensive Test Ban Treaty by a vote of 158-3.

25-26 September Palestinian-Israeli violence flares in Jerusalem, threatening peace process.

Appendix 2: Table of National Data

Compiled by Rebecca Britton

The 185 countries listed are the current members of the United Nations.

Nation	Capital	Date of Independence[1]	U.S. Diplomatic Relations Established[2]	UN Member (* denotes charter member)	Population (million)[3]	Area (thousand sq. km.)[3]	GDP (per capita) US$	Region[4]	Birthrate (per 1,000 population)[3]	Life Expectancy (years at birth)[3]	Infant Mortality (per 1,000 live births)[3]	Literacy Rate (%)[3]
Afghanistan	Kabul	1919	1934	1946	16.9	648	200	South Asia	43.5	44.9	155.8	29
Albania	Tirane	1912, 1920–1939, 1944	1922–1939, 1991	1955	3.4	29	1,100	Southeastern Europe	22.46	73.4	30.0	72
Algeria	Algiers	1962	1962	1962	27.9	2,382	3,300	Northern Africa/Middle East	29.7	67.7	52.1	57
Andorra	Andorra la Vella	—	1995	1993	0.06	0.45	14,500	Western Europe	13.3	78.4	7.9	n/a
Angola	Luanda	1975	1993	1976	9.8	1,247	600	Southern Africa	45.4	45.8	145.4	42
Antigua and Barbuda	Saint John's	1981	1981	1981	0.06	0.44	5,800	Caribbean	17.3	73.1	18.5	89
Argentina	Buenos Aires	1816	1822	1945*	33.91	2,767	5,500	Eastern South America	19.6	71.3	29.4	95
Armenia	Yerevan	1918–1920, 1991	1992	1992	3.5	30	2,040	Southeastern Europe	24.2	72.1	27.1	100
Australia	Canberra	1901	1940	1945	18.08	7,687	19,100	Oceania	14.3	77.6	7.3	100
Austria	Vienna	1918[5]	1838	1955	7.95	84	17,000	Central Europe	11.4	76.7	7.1	99
Azerbaijan	Baku (Baky)	1918–1920, 1991	1992	1992	7.68	87	2,040	Southeastern Europe	23.0	70.9	34.8	100
Bahamas	Nassau	1973	1973	1973	0.27	14	16,500	Caribbean	18.9	71.5	33.5	90
Bahrain	Manama	1971	1971	1971	0.59	0.62	12,000	Middle East	26.6	73.5	19.0	77
Bangladesh	Dhaka	1971	1972	1974	125.15	144	1,000	South Asia	35.0	55.1	106.9	35
Barbados	Bridgetown	1966	1967	1966	0.26	0.43	8,700	Caribbean	15.6	73.8	20.3	99
Belarus	Minsk	1991	1992	1945*[6]	10.4	208	5,890	Eastern Europe	13.1	70.9	18.9	100
Belgium	Brussels	1830	1832	1945	10.06	31	17,700	Western Europe	11.7	77	7.2	99
Belize	Belmopan	1981	1983	1981	0.21	23	2,700	Central America	34.74	68.08	35.6	91
Benin	Porto–Novo	1960	1960	1960	5.34	113	1,200	West Africa	47.7	51.8	110.1	23
Bhutan	Thimphu	1949	No relations[7]	1971	1.7	47	700	South Asia	39.3	50.6	121.1	38
Bolivia	La Paz	1825	1848	1945	7.7	1,099	2,100	Central South America	32.2	63.31	73.7	78

[1] Dates of independence listed only for states that became independent after 1776, the date the United States declared independence.

[2] *Dictionary of American Diplomatic History*, 2nd edition, 1987, John E. Findling ed. (New York: Greenwood Press); United States, Department of State, *Principal Officers of the Department of State and United States Chiefs of Mission, 1778–1990*; Department of State Dispatch, various issues; *Department of State Background Notes*, for various countries.

[3] *Data taken from *World Factbook, 1995–96* (Washington, D.C.: Central Intelligence Agency); *Human Development Report 1996* and *World Development Report 1996* (Washington, D.C.: World Bank); and data provided by the Population Office of the United Nations.

[4] There is no standard system of regionalization used in international publications. The table reflects regional classification based upon a balance of physical, cultural, and political geography features. Some island nations are assigned to the nearest continental region. Sources: *World Factbook 1995–96*; *Atlas of the World 1992* (New York: Oxford University Press); H.J. DeBlij and Peter O. Muller, *Geography Regions and Concepts*, 6th edition (John Wiley and Sons: New York 1992).

[5] Date of overthrow of Hapsburg monarchy, independence from Austro–Hungarian empire and the beginning of the Republic of Austria.

[6] Joined UN as Byelorussian Soviet Socialist Republic (S.S.R.). On September 29, 1991, Byelorussia informed the UN that it had changed its name to Belarus.

[7] Although no formal diplomatic relations exist between the U.S. and Bhutan, informal and friendly contact is maintained by the Bhutanese UN mission in New York, which is accorded consular jurisdiction in the U.S., and the U.S. embassy in New Delhi, which provides consular contact with Bhutan.

Nation	Capital	Date of Independence[1]	U.S. Diplomatic Relations Established[2]	UN Member (* denotes charter member)	Population (million)[3]	Area (thousand sq. km.)[3]	GDP (per capita) US$	Region[4]	Birthrate (per 1,000 population)[3]	Life Expectancy (years at birth)[3]	Infant Mortality (per 1,000 live births)[3]	Literacy Rate (%)[3]
Bosnia and Herzegovina[8]	Sarajevo	1992	1992	1992	4.6	51.2	n/a	Southeastern Europe	13.3	75.13	12.7	93
Botswana	Gaborone	1966	1971	1966	1.3	600	4,500	Southern Africa	32.19	63.05	39.3	72
Brazil	Brasilia	1822	1825	1945*	158.7	8,512	5,000	Eastern South America	21.48	62.25	59.5	81
Brunei Darussalam	Bandar Seri Bangawan	1984	1984	1984	0.28	6	9,000	Southeast Asia	26.18	71.1	25.2	77
Bulgaria	Sofia	1908	1912	1955	8.7	111	3,800	Southeastern Europe	11.71	73.24	12.0	93
Burkina Faso	Ouagadougou	1960	1960	1960	10.1	274	700	Western Africa	48.42	47.03	118.3	18
Burundi	Bujumbura	1962	1962	1962	6.1	28	700	Central Africa	44.02	40.3	113.7	50
Cambodia	Phnom Penh	1953	1950–1965, 1969–1975, 1992	1955	10.2	181	600	Southeast Asia	45.09	49.26	110.6	35
Cameroon	Yaoundé	1960	1960	1960	13.1	475	1,500	Western Africa	40.53	57.07	77.1	54
Canada	Ottawa	1867	1927	1945	28.1	9,976	22,200	Northern North America	14.1	78.13	6.9	99
Cape Verde	Praia	1975	1976	1975	0.42	4	1,070	Western Africa	46.23	62.59	57.7	66
Central African Republic	Bangui	1960	1960	1960	3.1	622	800	Central Africa	42.3	42.59	137.2	27
Chad	N'Djamena	1960	1960	1960	5.4	1,284	500	Central Africa	42.12	40.79	131.8	30
Chile	Santiago	1810	1832	1945*	13.95	757	7,000	Western South America	20.59	74.51	15.1	93
China	Beijing	1912[9]	1912–1949, 1979	1945*[10]	1,190	9,597	2,200	Eastern Asia	18.1	67.91	52.1	78
Colombia	Bogotá	1810	1823	1945	35.57	1,139	5,500	Northern South America	22.64	72.1	28.3	87
Comoros	Moroni	1975	1982	1975	0.53	2	700	Eastern Africa	46.48	57.81	79.6	48
Congo	Brazzaville	1960	1960	1960	2.44	342	2,900	Western Africa	40.27	47.56	111	57
Costa Rica	San Jose	1821	1858	1945	3.34	51	5,900	Central America	25.48	77.8	11	93
Côte d'Ivoire	Yamoussoukro	1960	1960	1960	14.29	323	1,500	Western Africa	46.52	48.92	95	54
Croatia	Zagreb	1991	1992	1992	4.6	57	4,500	Southeastern Europe	11.27	73.6	8.7	93
Cuba	Havana	1898	1902–1961[11]	1945*	11.06	111	1,250	Caribbean	16.59	76.89	10.3	94
Cyprus	Nicosia	1960	1960	1960	0.73	9	11,390	Mediterranean Europe	16.69	76.22	9	94
Czech Republic	Prague	1918,[12] 1993	1919[13]	1945*[14] 1993	10.4	79	7,200	Eastern Europe	13.23	73.08	9.3	n/a
Denmark	Copenhagen	1849[15]	1801	1945*	5.18	43	18,500	Northern Europe	12.45	75.81	6.9	99
Djibouti	Djibouti	1977	1980	1977	0.41	22	1,200	Eastern Africa	42.94	49.23	111	48
Dominica	Roseau	1978	1979	1978	0.08	0.75	2,100	Caribbean	20.46	76.96	10.3	94
Dominican Republic	Santo Domingo	1844	1883	1945*	7.82	49	3,000	Caribbean	24.87	68.35	51.5	83

[8] Some of the data subject to change depending upon full implementation of the Dayton Peace Agreement, signed December 14, 1995.

[9] The Republic of China was established in 1912 and the People's Republic of China in 1949.

[10] The Republic of China was a charter member of the UN. In 1971 its seat was given to the People's Republic of China.

[11] Currently, the U.S. interests section in Havana, which was established in 1977, and the Cuban interests section in Washington, D.C., are under the protection of the Swiss embassy.

[12] In 1918, Czechoslovakia gained independence. In 1993, Czechoslovakia split into two separate nations: the Czech Republic and the Slovak Republic.

[13] On March 21, 1939, the U.S. legation in Czechoslovakia was closed after the occupation of Prague by German forces. Credentials were later presented October 28, 1941.

[14] Czechoslovakia was an original member of the UN. Both the Czech Republic and the Slovak Republic as successor states were admitted to the UN January 19, 1993.

[15] A constitutional monarchy was established in 1849 after 190 years of absolute monarchy.

Nation	Capital	Date of Independence[1]	U.S. Diplomatic Relations Established[2]	UN Member (* denotes charter member)	Population (million)[3]	Area (thousand sq. km.)[3]	GDP (per capita) US$	Region[4]	Birthrate (per 1,000 population)[3]	Life Expectancy (years at birth)[3]	Infant Mortality (per 1,000 live births)[3]	Literacy Rate (%)[3]
Ecuador	Quito	1830	1848	1945	10.67	284	4,000	Western South America	25.82	69.98	39.3	88
Egypt	Cairo	1922	1922	1945*[16]	60.76	1,001	2,400	Northern Africa/Middle East	28.69	60.79	76.4	48
El Salvador	San Salvador	1821	1863	1945*	5.75	21	2,500	Central America	32.81	66.99	40.9	73
Equatorial Guinea	Malabo	1968	1968	1968	0.4	28	700	Western Africa	40.65	52.09	102.6	50
Eritrea	Asmara	1993	1993	1993	3.7	121	500	Eastern Africa	n/a	n/a	n/a	n/a
Estonia	Tallinn	1919–1940, 1991	1922–1940, 1991	1991	1.61	45	5,480	Eastern Europe	13.98	69.96	19.1	100
Ethiopia	Addis Ababa	—	1903	1945	54.92	1,127	400	Eastern Africa	45.01	52.67	106.4	24
Fiji	Suva	1970	1972	1970	0.76	18	4,000	Oceania	24.18	65.14	18.1	86
Finland	Helsinki	1917	1919	1955	5.06	337	16,100	Northern Europe	12.41	75.93	5.3	100
France	Paris	792[17]	1792	1945*	57.84	547	18,200	Western Europe	13.13	78.19	6.6	99
Gabon	Libreville	1960	1960	1960	1.13	268	4,800	Western Africa	28.46	54.67	94.8	61
Gambia	Banjul	1965	1965	1965	0.95	11	800	Western Africa	46.39	50.08	123.5	27
Georgia	T'bilisi	1991	1992	1992	5.6	69	1,390	Southeastern Europe	16.11	72.84	23.4	100
Germany	Berlin	1871, 1949,[18] 1990	1797–1917, 1921–1941, 1955[19]	1973[20]	81.08	357	16,500	Western Europe	11.04	76.34	6.5	99
Ghana	Accra	1957	1957	1957	17.22	239	1,500	Western Africa	44.13	55.52	83.1	60
Greece	Athens	1829	1833	1945	10.56	132	8,900	Southern Europe	10.5	77.71	8.6	93
Grenada	Saint George's	1974	1974	1974	0.09	0.34	3,000	Caribbean	30.28	70.4	12.7	98
Guatemala	Guatemala	1821	1825	1945	10.72	109	3,000	Central America	35.42	64.42	53.9	55
Guinea	Conakry	1958	1959	1958	6.39	246	500	Western Africa	44.08	44.13	139.2	24
Guinea-Bissau	Bissau	1974	1976	1974	1.09	36	800	Western Africa	40.75	47.44	120	36
Guyana	Georgetown	1966	1966	1966	0.72	215	1,900	South America	19.95	64.9	48.5	95
Haiti	Port-au-Prince	1804	1862	1945*	6.49	28	800	Caribbean	39.72	45.11	108.5	53
Honduras	Tegucigalpa	1821	1858	1945	5.31	112	1,950	Central America	34.97	67.6	45.3	73
Hungary	Budapest	1918	1921	1955	10.31	93	5,500	Eastern Europe	12.4	71.3	12.5	99
Iceland	Reykjavik	1944	1944	1946	0.26	103	16,000	Northern Europe	16.4	78.8	4	100
India	New Delhi	1947	1947	1945	919.9	3,288	1,300	South Asia	28.4	58.5	78.4	52
Indonesia	Jakarta	1945	1949	1950[21]	200.4	1,919	2,900	Southeast Asia	24.4	60.7	67.3	77
Iran	Tehran	—	1883–1980	1945*	65.61	1,648	4,780	Middle East	42.4	65.6	60.2	54
Iraq	Baghdad	1932[22]	1931–1967, 1984–1991[23]	1945	19.88	437	2,000	Middle East	44.1	65.7	67.1	60

[16] Egypt and Syria were original members of the UN. In 1958 the United Arab Republic was established by a union of Egypt and Syria and continued as a single member. In 1961 Syria resumed its separate membership in the UN. In 1971, the United Arab Republic changed its name to the Arab Republic of Egypt.

[17] Date of the First French Republic. Dynasties date back to the fifth century.

[18] January 18, 1871, marks the date of unification of the German Empire. In 1945, following World War II, Germany was divided into four zones of occupation (United Kingdom, United States, France, and the Soviet Union). The Federal Republic of Germany (West Germany), including the former U.K., U.S., and French zones, was proclaimed May 23, 1949. The German Democratic Republic (East Germany) included the former U.S.S.R. zone and was proclaimed on October 7, 1949. Unification of West Germany and East Germany took place October 3, 1990.

[19] In 1797, John Quincy Adams was commissioned as minister plenipotentiary to Prussia. In 1871, an envoy was commissioned to the German Empire and, in 1878, to Germany.

[20] The Federal Republic of Germany and the German Democratic Republic were admitted to separate UN seats in 1973. With the accession of the German Democratic Republic to the Federal Republic of Germany in 1990, they now hold a single seat.

[21] Indonesia withdrew from the UN on January 20, 1965, but resumed participation on September 28, 1966.

[22] End of status as British-mandated territory which had been established at the end of World War I.

[23] Iraq broke diplomatic relations with the U.S. during the June 1967 Arab–Israeli war. A U.S. Interests Section in Baghdad under the Belgian flag was established in 1972 and upgraded to embassy status with the resumption of full diplomatic relations in 1984. Diplomatic relations were suspended in January 1991 before the onset of the Persian Gulf War.

Nation	Capital	Date of Independence[1]	U.S. Diplomatic Relations Established[2]	UN Member (* denotes charter member)	Population (million)[3]	Area (thousand sq. km.)[3]	GDP (per capita) US$	Region[4]	Birthrate (per 1,000 population)[3]	Life Expectancy (years at birth)[3]	Infant Mortality (per 1,000 live births)[3]	Literacy Rate (%)[3]
Ireland	Dublin	1921	1927	1955	3.53	70	13,100	Western Europe	14.2	75.6	7.4	98
Israel	Jerusalem	1948	1949	1949	5.05	21	13,350	Middle East	20.5	78	8.6	92
Italy	Rome	1861	1867–1941, 1945	1955	58.14	301	16,700	Southern Europe	10.8	77.6	7.6	97
Jamaica	Kingston	1962	1962	1962	2.55	11	3,200	Caribbean	21.7	74.4	16.8	98
Japan	Tokyo	—	1859–1941, 1952	1956	125.11	378	20,400	Northeast Asia	10.5	79.3	4.3	99
Jordan	Amman	1946	1949	1955	3.96	89	3,000	Middle East	38.8	71.9	32.3	80
Kazakhstan	Almaty	1991	1992	1992	17.27	2,717	3,510	South Asia	19.4	68.0	40.9	100
Kenya	Nairobi	1963	1964	1963	28.24	583	1,200	Eastern Africa	42.4	53.2	74.1	69
Korea, Democratic People's Republic of	P'yongyang	1948	No relations[24]	1991	23.07	121	1,000	Northeast Asia	23.8	69.8	27.7	99
Korea, Republic of	Seoul	1948	1949	1991	45.08	98	9,500	Northeast Asia	15.7	70.6	21.7	96
Kuwait	Kuwait	1961	1961	1963	1.82	18	15,100	Middle East	29.4	75.0	12.5	73
Kyrgyzstan	Bishkek	1991	1992	1992	4.7	198	2,440	South Asia	26.3	67.9	46.8	100
Laos	Vientiane	1949	1950	1955	4.7	237	900	Southeast Asia	43.2	51.7	101.8	64
Latvia	Riga	1918–1940, 1991	1922–1940, 1991	1991	2.75	64	4,810	Eastern Europe	13.8	69.4	21.5	100
Lebanon	Beirut	1941	1942	1945*	3.62	10	1,720	Middle East	27.9	69.4	39.5	80
Lesotho	Maseru	1966	1971	1966	1.94	30	1,500	Southern Africa	34	62.1	69.5	59
Liberia	Monrovia	1847	1863	1945	2.97	111	800	West Africa	43.5	57.7	113.3	40
Libya	Tripoli	1951	1952–1980[25]	1955	5.06	1,760	6,600	Northern Africa/ Middle East	45.3	63.9	63.4	64
Liechtenstein	Vaduz	—	No relations[26]	1990	0.03	0.16	22,300	Western Europe	13.1	77.5	5.3	100
Lithuania	Vilnius	1918–1940, 1991	1922–1940, 1991	1991	3.85	65	3,240	Eastern Europe	14.7	71.2	16.7	100
Luxembourg	Luxembourg	1839	1903	1945*	0.4	3	22,600	Western Europe	12.8	76.7	6.8	100
Macedonia, Former Yugoslav Republic of	Skopje	1991	1995	1993	2.21	25.3	1,000	Southeastern Europe	15.6	73.6	27.8	93
Madagascar	Antananarivo	1960	1960	1960	13.43	587	800	Southeast Africa	45.2	54	89	80
Malawi	Lilongwe	1964	1964	1964	9.73	118	600	Southern Africa	50.42	39.7	141.1	22
Malaysia	Kuala Lumpur	1957	1957	1957[27]	19.28	330	7,500	Southeast Asia	28.45	69.2	25.6	78
Maldives	Male	1965	1965	1965	0.25	0.3	620	South Asia	43.6	64.7	53.8	92
Mali	Bamako	1960	1960	1960	9.11	1,240	650	West Africa	51.8	45.9	106.2	17
Malta	Valletta	1964	1965	1964	0.36	0.32	6,600	Mediterranean Europe	13.6	76.8	7.9	84
Marshall Islands	Majuro	1990	1990	1991	0.05	0.18	1,500	Oceania	46.3	63.1	49.3	93

24 The 1994 U.S.–North Korean agreement included a provision for the opening of liaison offices once other issues are resolved. As of Fall 1996, this had not yet occurred.

25 In 1972, the U.S. withdrew its ambassador from Libya in response to Libyan support for international terrorism. U.S. embassy staff members were withdrawn following a mob attack that set fire to the embassy in December 1979. In 1981, the U.S. government closed the Libyan embassy in Washington, D.C., expelling the staff for conduct contrary to international standards of diplomatic behavior. The U.S. government declared Libya a "state sponsor of terrorism" in December 1979 and due to Libya's continuing support for terrorist activities, relations have not been resumed.

26 The U.S. has no diplomatic or consular mission in Liechtenstein, but the U.S. Consul General at Zurich (Switzerland) has consular accreditation at Vaduz.

27 Originally joined the UN as the Federation of Malaya in 1957, but changed its name to Malaysia in 1963 following admission to the federation of Singapore, Sabah, and Sarawak. Singapore became an independent state and member of the UN in 1965.

Nation	Capital	Date of Independence[1]	U.S. Diplomatic Relations Established[2]	UN Member (* denotes charter member)	Population (million)[3]	Area (thousand sq. km.)[3]	GDP (per capita) US$	Region[4]	Birthrate (per 1,000 population)[3]	Life Expectancy (years at birth)[3]	Infant Mortality (per 1,000 live births)[3]	Literacy Rate (%)[3]
Mauritania	Nouakchott	1960	1960	1961	2.19	1,031	1,050	Northern Africa	47.7	48.1	85.3	34
Mauritius	Port Louis	1968	1968	1968	1.12	2	7,800	Southern Africa	19.3	70.5	18.4	80
Mexico	Mexico	1810	1825	1945	92.2	1,973	8,200	Central America	27.2	72.9	27.4	87
Micronesia, Federated States of	Kolonia	1990	1990	1991	0.12	0.7	1,500	Oceania	28.3	67.6	37.2	90
Moldova, Republic of	Chisinau	1991	1992	1992	4.47	33	3,650	Eastern Europe	16.0	68.1	30.3	100
Monaco	Monaco	—	No relations[28]	1993	0.03	0.001	16,000	Western Europe	10.7	77.7	7.2	99
Mongolia	Ulaanbaatar	1921	1987	1961	2.43	1,565	1,200	East Central Asia	33.0	66.2	43.4	90
Morocco	Rabat	1956	1905	1956	28.56	447	2,500	Northern Africa / Middle East	28.6	68.2	49.6	50
Mozambique	Maputo	1975	1975	1975	17.35	802	600	Southern Africa	45	48.5	128.7	33
Myanmar	Rangoon	1948	1947	1948	44.28	679	950	Southeast Asia	28.5	60	63.7	81
Namibia	Windhoek	1990	1990	1990	1.6	825	2,500	Southern Africa	43.4	61.7	61.8	38
Nepal	Kathmandu	—	1948	1955	21.04	141	1,000	South Asia	37.6	52.5	83.5	26
Netherlands	Amsterdam	1781	1781	1945	15.37	37	17,200	Western Europe	12.62	77.8	6.1	99
New Zealand	Wellington	1907	1942	1945*	3.39	269	15,700	Oceania	15.5	76.4	8.9	99
Nicaragua	Managua	1821	1851	1945*	4.1	130	1,600	Central America	34.7	64.0	52.5	57
Niger	Niamey	1960	1960	1960	8.97	1,267	650	Western Africa	55	44.6	111	28
Nigeria	Abuja	1960	1960	1960	98.09	924	1,000	Western Africa	43.5	55.3	75	51
Norway	Oslo	1905	1905	1945	4.31	324	20,800	Northern Europe	13.3	77.4	6.3	99
Oman	Muscat	1970	1972	1971	1.70	212	10,000	Middle East	40.4	67.8	36.7	41
Pakistan	Islamabad	1947	1947	1947	128.85	804	1,900	South Asia	42.2	57.4	101.9	35
Palau	Koror	1994	1994	1994	0.016	0.46	2,260	Southeast Asia	22.5	71.0	25.0	92
Panama	Panama	1903	1903	1945	2.63	78	4,500	Central America	24.6	74.8	16.5	88
Papua New Guinea	Port Moresby	1975	1975	1975	4.19	462	2,000	Southeast Asia	33.5	56.4	63.3	52
Paraguay	Asuncion	1811	1861	1945*	5.21	407	3,000	Central South America	32	73.2	25.2	90
Peru	Lima	1824	1826	1945	23.65	1,285	3,000	Western South America	25.5	65.6	54.2	85
Philippines	Manila	1946	1946	1945*	69.8	300	2,500	Southeast Asia	27.3	65.3	50.8	90
Poland	Warsaw	1919	1919	1945*	38.65	313	4,680	Central Europe	13.4	72.6	13.1	98
Portugal	Lisbon	—	1791	1955	10.52	92	8,700	Southern Europe	11.6	75.2	9.5	85
Qatar	Doha	1971	1971	1971	0.51	11	17,500	Middle East	18.8	72.6	21.6	76
Romania	Bucharest	1861	1880	1955	23.18	238	2,700	Southeastern Europe	13.6	71.7	19.9	98
Russia	Moscow	1991[29]	1992[29]	1945*[30]	149.6	17,075	5,190	Europe/North Asia	12.6	68.8	27	100
Rwanda	Kigali	1962	1963	1962	8.37	26	800	Central Africa	49.1	40.2	118.7	50
Saint Kitts & Nevis	Basseterre	1983	1984	1983	0.04	0.27	4,000	Caribbean	23.7	66.11	19.9	98
Saint Lucia	Castries	1979	1979	1979	0.14	0.62	3,000	Caribbean	23.1	69.3	18.5	67
Saint Vincent & the Grenadines	Kingstown	1979	1981	1980	0.11	0.34	2,000	Caribbean	20.2	72.2	17.2	96

28 The U.S. maintains no mission in Monaco, but the U.S. Consul General in Marseilles, France, is accredited to Monaco.

29 Russia dates back pre–U.S. independence; the Soviet Union was formed in 1917; it collapsed in 1991 and the Russian Federation emerged as an independent republic. U.S. representatives from 1809–1917 were commissioned to Russia; from 1933–1991 to the Soviet Union.

30 The USSR was an original member of the UN. In 1991 membership of the Soviet Union in the Security Council and all other UN organs was continued by the Russian Federation.

Nation	Capital	Date of Independence[1]	U.S. Diplomatic Relations Established[2]	UN Member (* denotes charter member)	Population (million)[3]	Area (thousand sq. km.)[3]	GDP (per capita) US$	Region[4]	Birthrate (per 1,000 population)[3]	Life Expectancy (years at birth)[3]	Infant Mortality (per 1,000 live births)[3]	Literacy Rate (%)[3]
Samoa	Pago Pago	1962	1971	1976	0.2	3	2,000	Oceania	32.4	67.9	37	97
San Marino	San Marino	—	No relations[31]	1992	0.02	0.06	16,000	Southern Europe	11.1	81.2	5.6	96
São Tomé & Príncipe	São Tomé	1975	1975	1975	0.13	1	450	Western Africa	35.2	63.3	63.5	57
Saudi Arabia	Riyadh	1932	1939	1945*	18.19	1,961	1,100	Middle East	38.2	67.9	52.1	62
Senegal	Dakar	1960	1960	1960	8.73	196	1,400	Western Africa	43.1	56.5	75.7	38
Serbia and Montenegro[32]	Belgrade	—	No relations[33]	—	11.1	102	1,000	Eastern Europe	13.7	79.6	10.8	n/a
Seychelles	Victoria	1976	1976	1976	0.07	0.46	5,900	East Central Africa	21.8	69.6	11.7	58
Sierra Leone	Freetown	1961	1961	1961	4.63	72	1,000	Western Africa	45	46.4	141.9	21
Singapore	Singapore	1965	1966	1965	2.85	0.63	15,000	Southeast Asia	16.51	75.9	5.7	88
Slovak Republic	Bratislava	1918, 1993[12]	1919[13]	1993[14]	5.4	49	5,800	Eastern Europe	14.5	72.8	10.4	n/a
Slovenia	Ljubljana	1991	1992	1992	1.97	20	7,600	Southern Europe	11.8	74.3	8.1	93
Solomon Islands	Honiara	1978	1978	1978	0.38	28	2,500	Oceania	38.9	70.4	27.8	15
Somalia	Mogadishu	1960	1960	1960	6.66	638	500	East Africa	45.9	54.7	125.8	24
South Africa	Pretoria[34]	1910	1929	1945	43.93	1,220	4,000	Southern Africa	33.5	65.11	47.1	76
Spain	Madrid	—	1790	1955	39.3	505	12,700	Southern Europe	11.05	77.7	6.9	95
Sri Lanka	Colombo	1948	1948	1955	18.12	65	3,000	South Asia	18.5	71.9	21.9	88
Sudan	Khartoum	1956	1956–1967, 1971	1956	29.41	2,506	750	East Africa	41.9	54.2	79.5	27
Suriname	Paramaribo	1975	1976	1975	0.42	163	2,800	Northern South America	25.3	69.4	31.3	95
Swaziland	Mbabane[35]	1968	1968	1968	0.93	17	2,500	Southern Africa	43.1	56.3	93.2	67
Sweden	Stockholm	—	1810	1946	8.77	450	17,600	Northern Europe	13.5	78.2	5.7	99
Syria	Damascus	1946	1942	1945*[16]	14.88	185	5,700	Middle East	43.6	66.4	42.5	64
Tajikistan	Dushanbe	1991	1992	1992	5.9	143	1,180	South Asia	34.7	68.7	62	100
Tanzania, United Republic of	Dar es Salaam	1961[36]	1961	1961[37]	27.98	945	600	East Africa	45.4	43.2	109.7	46
Thailand	Bangkok	—	1882	1946	59.5	514	5,500	Southeast Asia	19.4	68.3	37.1	93
Togo	Lome	1960	1960	1960	4.25	57	800	Western Africa	47.3	56.9	88.9	43
Trinidad and Tobago	Port-of-Spain	1962	1962	1962	1.32	5	8,000	Caribbean	19.6	70.7	16.5	95
Tunisia	Tunis	1956	1956	1956	8.72	164	4,000	Northern Africa/Middle East	23.4	72.8	34.1	65
Turkey	Ankara	1923	1827–1917, 1927	1945*	62.15	781	5,100	Southeast Europe/Southwest Asia	25.98	70.9	48.8	81

31 The U.S. maintains no mission in San Marino, but the U.S. Consul General in Florence (Italy) is accredited to San Marino, and has an honorary consulate general from San Marino in the U.S.

32 While listed on this table, Serbia and Montenegro was suspended from UN membership in 1992. It claims the right to the name of Yugoslavia, but the official U.S. position is that the Socialist Federal Republic of Yugoslavia (SFRY) has dissolved and that none of its successor republics represent its continuation.

33 The United States maintained normal diplomatic relations with the former Yugoslavia at the time of its dissolution in 1991. The American mission in Belgrade still exists with a chargé d'affaires as chief of mission although the U.S. has not established normal diplomatic relations with Serbia–Montenegro and the U.S. recalled its ambassador from Belgrade in May 1992 in response to Serbian aggression.

34 Pretoria is the administrative capital, Capetown the legislative capital, and Bloemfontein the judicial capital.

35 Mbabane is the administrative capital, Lobamba the legislative capital.

36 Tanganyika gained independence in 1961, Zanzibar in 1963. The two nations merged in 1964.

37 Tanganyika was a member of the UN from 1961 to 1963. Following the union of Tanganyika and Zanzibar, the United Republic of Tanganyika and Zanzibar continued as a single member, changing its name to the United Republic of Tanzania in 1964.

Nation	Capital	Date of Independence[1]	U.S. Diplomatic Relations Established[2]	UN Member (* denotes charter member)	Population (million)[3]	Area (thousand sq. km.)[3]	GDP (per capita) US$	Region[4]	Birthrate (per 1,000 population)[3]	Life Expectancy (years at birth)[3]	Infant Mortality (per 1,000 live births)[3]	Literacy Rate (%)[3]
Turkmenistan	Ashgabat	1991	1992	1992	3.99	488	3,330	South Asia	30.4	65.1	69.9	100
Uganda	Kampala	1962	1963–1973, 1979	1962	19.12	236	1,200	East Africa	48.8	37.4	112.2	48
Ukraine	Kiev	1917–1919, 1991	1992	1945*	51.8	604	3,960	Eastern Europe	12.3	69.9	20.7	100
United Arab Emirates	Abu Dhabi	1971	1972	1971	2.79	75	24,100	Middle East	27.68	72.2	21.7	68
United Kingdom	London	1801[38]	1785	1945*	58.13	245	16,900	Western Europe	13.3	76.7	7.2	99
United States	Washington, DC	1776	n/a	1945*	260.71	9,373	24,700	North America	15.2	75.9	8.1	97.9
Uruguay	Montevideo	1828	1867	1945	3.19	176	6,000	Eastern South America	17.7	74.0	17.1	96
Uzbekistan	Tashkent	1991	1992	1992	22.6	447	2,430	Central Asia	30	68.5	53.2	100
Vanuatu	Port–Vila	1980	1986	1981	0.16	15	1,050	Oceania	32.2	59.2	68.1	53
Venezuela	Caracas	1811	1835	1945	20.56	912	8,000	Northern South America	25.7	73	27.7	88
Vietnam	Hanoi	1945	1950–1975, 1995	1977	73.1	330	1,000	Southeast Asia	27.13	65.4	45.5	88
Yemen	Sanaa	1990[39]	1946[40]	1947[41]	11.1	528	800	Middle East	50.7	51.4	112.8	38
Zaire	Kinshasa	1960	1960	1960	42.68	2,345	500	Central Africa	48.3	47.4	110.92	72
Zambia	Lusaka	1964	1964	1964	9.18	753	800	Southern Africa	45.9	44.1	85	73
Zimbabwe	Harare	1980	1980	1980	10.9	391	1,400	Southern Africa	37.2	42.0	7.4	67

[38] Date of the formation of the United Kingdom of Great Britain and Ireland. England became a Commonwealth in 1649 and the Kingdom of Great Britain (England, Scotland, and Wales) formed in 1707.

[39] Previously, the Yemen Arab Republic (North Yemen) had become independent from the Ottoman Empire in 1918 and the People's Democratic Republic of Yemen (South Yemen) had become independent from the United Kingdom in 1967.

[40] U.S. representatives were first commissioned to the Kingdom of Yemen. A U.S. embassy was established in 1967 in the Peoples' Democratic Republic of Southern Yemen; relations were severed in 1969. In 1970 the name of the country was changed to the People's Democratic Republic of Yemen and diplomatic relations with the U.S. were resumed in April 1990. In May 1990, the Yemen Arab Republic and the People's Democratic Republic of Yemen united to form the Republic of Yemen.

[41] The Yemen Arab Republic was admitted to UN membership in 1947 and the People's Democratic Republic of Southern Yemen in 1967. In 1990, the two countries merged and have since been represented as one member with the name "Yemen."

Appendix 3: Classified Bibliography of Reference Works

Compiled by Thomas G. Paterson

This bibliography includes only reference works—Annual Surveys (AS), Atlases and Gazetteers (A),
Bibliographies (B), Biographical Aids (BA), Chronologies (C), Documentary Collections and Series (D),
Encyclopedias and Dictionaries (E), and Statistics (S). For historical and contemporary studies of specific
subjects, see the bibliographic lists ("Further Reading") at the end of entries in this encyclopedia.

GENERAL

Annual Surveys (AS)

Facts on File Yearbook (1941–); Freedom House, *Freedom in the World*
(1978); *Keesing's Record of World Events* (also titled *Keesing's Contemporary
Archives*) (1931–); London Institute of World Affairs, *The Yearbook of
World Affairs* (1947–); Alan F. Pater and Jason R. Pater, eds., *What They
Said In ...: The Yearbook of World Opinion* (1971–); *Political Handbook of
the World* (1928–); *The Statesmen's Year-Book World Gazetteer* (1864–).

Atlases and Gazetteers (A)—World

Ewan W. Anderson, *An Atlas of World Political Flashpoints* (1993); Geoffrey Barraclough, ed., *The Times Concise Atlas of World History* (1982);
Andrew Boyd, *An Atlas of World Affairs* (1992); Anna Bramwall, *The Atlas
of Twentieth Century History* (1989); Gerard Chaliand and Jean-Pierre
Rageau, *Strategic Atlas* (1990); *Hammond Atlas of the World* (1992); *The
Harper Atlas of World History* (1992); Michael Kidron and Daniel Smith,
The New State of War and Peace (1991); David Munro, ed., *Chambers
World Gazetteer* (1988); *National Geographic Atlas of the World* (1992);
Richard Natkiel et al., eds., *Atlas of the Twentieth Century* (1982); *The New
York Times Atlas of the World* (1992); *Oxford Atlas of the World* (1992);
Rand McNally, *Today's World* (1992); *The Times Atlas of World History*
(1992); Andrew Wheatcroft, *The World Atlas of Revolutions* (1983).

Atlases and Gazetteers (A)—United States

Rodger Doyle, *Atlas of Contemporary America* (1994); Robert Ferrell and
Richard Natkiel, *Atlas of American History* (1987); Edward W. Fox, *Atlas
of American History* (1964); Kenneth T. Jackson, ed., *Atlas of American
History* (1978); Catherine Mattson and Mark T. Mattson, *Contemporary
Atlas of the United States* (1990); National Geographic Society, *Historical
Atlas of the United States* (1988); U.S. Department of the Interior, *National Atlas of the United States* (1970).

Bibliographies (B)

American Library Association, *Guide to Official Publications of Foreign
Countries* (1990); Dennis A. Barton et al., eds., *A Guide to Manuscripts in
the Presidential Libraries* (1985); Samuel Flagg Bemis and Grace Gardner
Griffin, *Guide to the Diplomatic History of the United States, 1775–1921*
(1935); Richard Dean Burns, ed. *A Guide to American Foreign Relations
Since 1700* (1982); Council on Foreign Relations, *Foreign Affairs Bibliography* (1933–1972); Byron Dexter, ed., *The Foreign Affairs 50–Year Bibliography* (1972); Wilton B. Fowler, *American Diplomatic History Since 1890*
(1975); Frank Freidel, ed., *Harvard Guide to American History* (1974);
Norman A. Graebner, ed., *American Diplomatic History Before 1900*
(1978); Linda Killen and Richard L. Lael, *Versailles and After* (1983);
Gordon Martel, ed., *American Foreign Relations Reconsidered, 1890–1993*
(1994); Mary Beth Norton, ed., *The American Historical Association's
Guide to Historical Literature* (1995); Francis P. Prucha, *Handbook for
Research in American History* (1987). The journal *Diplomatic History* regularly publishes articles that review the historiography of major topics
and periods and provide extensive bibliographical guidance. Journals
such as *Foreign Affairs*, *American Political Science Review*, and *Political
Science Quarterly* regularly publish reviews of recent books; the *Journal
of American History* and *International Security* regularly list recent publications in the field.

Biographical Aids (BA)—World

Robert Benewick and Philip Green, eds., *The Routledge Dictionary of
Twentieth-Century Political Thinkers* (1992); Lucian Boia, ed., *Great Historians of the Modern Age* (1991); Asa Briggs, *A Dictionary of Twentieth Century World Biography* (1990); David Crystal, ed., *The Cambridge Biographical Encyclopedia* (1994); Barry Jones and M. V. Dixon, eds., *The St.
Martin's Press Dictionary of Biography* (1986); *International Who's Who*
(1935–); Magnus Magnuson, ed., *Cambridge Biographical Dictionary*
(1990); Alan Palmer, *Who's Who in Modern History, 1860–1980* (1980);
Profiles of Worldwide Government Leaders (1995–); Philip Rees, *Biographical Dictionary of the Extreme Right Since 1890* (1991); Frank W.
Thackery and John E. Findling, eds., *Statesmen Who Changed the World*
(1993); *Who's Who in the World* (1971–). Also consult the many "Who's
Who" volumes (not listed here) for individual countries.

Biographical Aids (BA)—United States

John S. Bowman, ed., *The Cambridge Dictionary of American Biography*
(1995); *Current Biography* (1940–); *Dictionary of American Biography*
(1928–); John A. Garraty, ed., *Encyclopedia of American Biography*
(1974); *National Cyclopedia of American Biography* (1898–); U.S. Department of State, *Foreign Service List* (1929–); Charles Van Doren, ed.,
Webster's American Biographies (1974); *Webster's Biographical Dictionary*
(1980); *Webster's New Biographical Dictionary* (1988); *Who Was Who in
America* (1963–); *Who's Who in America* (1899–); *Who's Who in American
Politics* (1967–).

Chronologies (C)

Lester H. Brune, *Chronological History of U.S. Foreign Relations* (1985,
1991); Gorton Carruth, *The Encyclopedia of American Facts and Dates*
(1993); Gorton Carruth, *The Encyclopedia of World Facts and Dates*
(1993); Council on Foreign Relations, *Foreign Affairs Chronology,
1978–1989* (1990), and *The United States in World Affairs* (1932–1972);
Robert H. Ferrell and John S. Bowman, eds., *The Twentieth Century*
(1984); Bernard Grun, *The Timetables of History* (1991); John E. Jessup, *A
Chronology of Conflict and Resolution, 1945–1985* (1989); Thomas Parker
and Douglas Nelson, *Day by Day: The Sixties* (1983); Royal Institute of
International Affairs, *Survey of International Affairs, 1920–1963*
(1972–1977).

Documentary Collections and Series (D)

Martin P. Claussen, ed., *The National State Papers of the United States: Texts
of Documents (1789–1817)* (1980–); Council on Foreign Relations, *Documents on American Foreign Relations, 1938/1939–1970* (1939–1973); Royal
Institute of International Affairs, *Documents on International Affairs,
1928–1963* (1929–1973); Arthur M. Schlesinger, Jr., ed., *The Dynamics of
World Power: A Documentary History of U.S. Foreign Policy, 1945–1973*

(1973); U.S. Congress, *American State Papers* (1852–1859); U.S. Department of State, *A Decade of American Foreign Policy: Basic Documents, 1941–1949* (1985), *American Foreign Policy: Basic Documents, 1950–1955* (1957), *American Foreign Policy: Current Documents, 1956– 1967* (1956–1967), *American Foreign Policy: Basic Documents, 1977–1980* (1983–1986), *American Foreign Policy: Current Documents, 1981–* (1984–), *Bulletin* (1938–), *Dispatch* (1990–), *Foreign Relations of United States, 1861–* (1862–), and *Press Conferences of the Secretaries of State, 1922–1974* (n.d.); *Vital Speeches of the Day* (1934–). See also "Treaties."

Encyclopedias and Dictionaries (E)—World

Alan J. Day and Henry W. Degenhardt, eds., *Political Parties of the World* (1984); Henry W. Degenhardt, ed., *Revolutionary and Dissident Movements* (1988); George E. Delury, ed., *World Encyclopedia of Political Systems and Parties* (1987); John Drexel, ed., *The Facts on File Encyclopedia of the 20th Century* (1991); Graham Evans and Jeffrey Newnham, eds., *The Dictionary of World Politics* (1990); *International Encyclopedia of the Social Sciences* (1968–); Joel Krieger et al., eds., *The Oxford Companion to Politics of the World* (1993); John O'Loughlin, ed., *Dictionary of Geopolitics* (1993); Jack C. Plano and Ray Olton, *The International Relations Dictionary* (1988); UNESCO, *World Directory of Social Science Institutions* (1990); Jack E. Vincent, *A Handbook of International Relations* (1968); *Worldmark Encyclopedia of the Nations* (1995).

Encyclopedias and Dictionaries (E)—United States

Alexander DeConde, ed., *Encyclopedia of American Foreign Policy* (1978); Margaret Denning and J. K. Sweeney, *Handbook of American Diplomacy* (1992); John E. Findling, *Dictionary of American Diplomatic History* (1989); Stephen A. Flanders and Carl N. Flanders, *Dictionary of American Foreign Affairs* (1993); Eric Foner and John A. Garraty, eds., *The Reader's Companion to American History* (1991); Stanley Hochman and Eleanor Hochman, *A Dictionary of Contemporary American History* (1993); Stanley I. Kutler, ed., *Encyclopedia of the United States in the Twentieth Century* (1995); Richard B. Morris and Jeffrey B. Morris, eds., *Encyclopedia of American History* (1996).

Statistics (S)—World, General and Political

Thomas T. Makie and Richard Rose, *The International Almanac of Electoral History* (1991); Victor Showers, *World Facts and Figures* (1989); Charles L. Taylor and David A. Jodice, *World Handbook of Political and Social Indicators* (1983); United Nations, *Statistical Yearbook* (1948–); United Nations, *World Statistics in Brief* (1976–); U.S. Central Intelligence Agency, *The World Factbook* (1981–).

Statistics (S)—World, Economic and Social

International Monetary Fund, *International Financial Statistics* (1948–); Nathan Keyfitz and William Flieger, *World Population Growth and Aging* (1990); Timothy S. O'Donnell et al., eds., *World Quality of Life Indicators* (1991); Organisation for Economic Co-operation and Development, *Main Economic Indicators* (1962–); Ruth L. Sivard, *World Military and Social Expenditures* (1974–); The Economist, *One Hundred Years of Economic Statistics* (1989); United Nations, *Demographic Yearbook* (1948–); United Nations, *Report on the World Social Situation* (1952–); United Nations, *World Economic and Social Survey: Current Trends and Policies in the World Economy* (1948–); U. S. Central Intelligence Agency, *Handbook of International Economic Statistics* (1971–); World Bank, *World Tables* (1976–); World Bank, *Social Indicators of Development* (1988–); World Bank, *World Debt Tables* (1974–); World Bank, *World Development Report: Infrastructure for Development* (1978–); World Resources Institute, *World Resources* (1990–).

Statistics (S)—United States

U.S. Bureau of the Census, *Historical Statistics of the United States* (1975); and *Statistical Abstract of the United States* (1878–).

COUNTRIES, REGIONS, AND OTHER PLACES OF THE WORLD[1]

Afghanistan

M. Jamil Hanifi, *Historical and Cultural Dictionary of Afghanistan* (1976) (E)

Africa

Purnima Mehta Bhatt, *Scholar's Guide to Washington, D.C. for African Studies* (1980) (B); Chris Cook and David Killingway, *African Political Facts since 1945* (1991) (E); G. S. P. Freeman-Grenville, *The New Atlas of African History* (1991) (A); Colin Legum, ed., *Africa Contemporary Record* (1968–) (AS); B. R. Mitchell, *International Historical Statistics: Africa, Asia and Oceania, 1750–1988* (1995) (S); Sean Moroney, ed., *Africa* (1989) (E); Thomas P. Ofcansky, *British East Africa, 1865–1963* (1985) (B); Anthony G. Pazzanita and Tony Hodges, *Historical Dictionary of Western Sahara* (1994) (E); Claude S. Phillips, *The African Political Dictionary* (1984) (E); David Shavit, *The United States in Africa* (1989) (E); John Stewart, *African States and Rulers* (1989) (BA and E); U.S. Library of Congress, *The United States and Africa* (1978) (B); U.S. Library of Congress, *The United States and Sub-Saharan Africa* (1984) (B). See also individual countries.

Albania

William B. Bland, *Albania* (1988) (B). See also "Eastern Europe" and "Europe."

Algeria

Alf A. Heggoy, *Historical Dictionary of Algeria* (1981) (E). See also "Africa."

Andorra

See "Europe."

Angola

Richard Black, *Angola* (1992) (B); Susan H. Broadhead, *Historical Dictionary of Angola* (1992) (E). See also "Africa."

Antarctica

Robert Headland, *Chronological List of Antarctic Expeditions and Related Historical Events* (1989) (E and C); John Stewart, *Antarctica* (1990) (E).

Antigua and Barbuda

See "Caribbean."

Arab World

See "Middle East," "Israel, Palestine, and Arab-Israeli Conflict," and individual countries.

Arctic

Clive Holland, *Arctic Exploration and Development* (1993) (E); H. G. R. King, *The Arctic* (1989) (B).

Argentina

Alan Biggs, *Argentina* (1991) (B); Ione S. Wright and Lisa M. Nekhom, *Historical Dictionary of Argentina* (1978) (E). See also "Latin America."

Armenia

Vrej Nerses Neressian, *Armenia* (1993) (B). See also "Russia and the Soviet Union."

Asia and the Pacific

Alexander Besher, *The Pacific Rim Almanac* (1991) (E); Jessica S. Brown et al., eds., *The United States in East Asia* (1985) (B); Norman Douglas and Ngaire Douglas, eds., *Pacific Islands Yearbook* (1932–) (AS); Ainslie T. Embree, ed., *Encyclopedia of Asian History* (1988) (E); Gerald Fry, *Pacific Basin and Oceania* (1987) (B); Haruhiro Fukui, ed., *Political Parties of Asia and the Pacific* (1985) (E); Hong N. Kim, *Scholar's Guide to Washington, D.C., for East Asian Studies* (1979) (B); B. R. Mitchell, *International Historical Statistics: Africa, Asia and Oceania, 1750–1988* (1995)

---

[1] See also U.S. Library of Congress book-length "country studies" which provide extensive historical and current information on most nations.

(S); Gerald Segal, ed., *Political and Economic Encyclopaedia of the Pacific* (1989) (E); David Shavit, *The United States in Asia* (1990) (E). See also individual countries and "Hawai'i."

Australia
Jan Bassett, *The Concise Oxford Dictionary of Australian History* (1986) (E); Alan D. Gilbert and K. S. Ingles, eds., *Australians* (1987) (E). See also "Asia and the Pacific."

Austria
Dengs Salt, *Austria* (1986) (B). See also "Europe."

Azerbaijan
See "Russia and the Soviet Union."

Bahamas
Paul G. Boultbee, *The Bahamas* (1989) (B). See also "Caribbean."

Bahrain
See "Middle East."

Bangladesh
Moh Ābadura Rājjāka, *Bangladesh* (1989) (B). See also "Asia and the Pacific" and "India."

Barbados
Peter B. Potter and Graham M. S. Dann, *Barbados* (1987) (B). See also "Caribbean."

Belarus
See "Russia and the Soviet Union."

Belgium
Raymond C. Riley, *Belgium* (1989) (B). See also "Europe" and "The Netherlands."

Belize
See "Central America" and "Latin America."

Benin
Samuel Decalo, *Historical Dictionary of Benin* (1987) (E). See also "Africa."

Berlin
See "Germany and Berlin."

Bhutan
Ramesh C. Dogra, *Bhutan* (1990) (B). See also "Asia and the Pacific" and "India."

Bolivia
Dwight B. Heath, *Historical Dictionary of Bolivia* (1972) (E); Gertrude M. Yeager, *Bolivia* (1988) (B). See also "Latin America."

Bosnia-Herzegovina
See "Europe" and "Yugoslavia."

Botswana
Fred Morton et al., *Historical Dictionary of Botswana* (1989) (E); John A. Wiseman, *Botswana* (1992) (B). See also "Africa."

Brazil
Solena V. Bryant, *Brazil* (1985) (B); Robert M. Levine, *Historical Dictionary of Brazil* (1979) (E). See also "Latin America."

Brunei Darussalam
See "Middle East."

Bulgaria
Bulgarian Academy of Sciences, *A Short Encyclopaedia of the People's Republic of Bulgaria* (1985) (E); R. J. Crampton, *Bulgaria* (1989) (B). See also "Europe."

Burkina Faso
See "Africa."

Burma
See "Myanmar."

Burundi
Morna Daniels, *Burundi* (1992) (B). See also "Africa."

California
James D. Hart, *A Companion to California* (1987) (E);Doyce B. Nunis, Jr., and Gloria R. Lothrop, eds., *A Guide to the History of California* (1989) (E). See also "Continental Expansion (U.S.)."

Cambodia
See "Vietnam and Southeast Asia."

Cameroon
Mark W. DeLancey, *Cameroon* (1986) (B); Mark W. DeLancey and H. Mbella Mokeba, *Historical Dictionary of Cameroon* (1990) (E). See also "Africa."

Canada
David J. Bercuson and J. L. Granatstein, *The Collins Dictionary of Canadian History: 1867 to the Present* (1988) (E); *The Canadian Encyclopedia* (1988) (E); R. Cole Harris, ed., *Historical Atlas of Canada* (1987–1990) (A); John F. Rooney, Jr., et al., eds., *This Remarkable Continent: An Atlas of United States and Canadian Society and Culture* (1982) (A); Mel Watkins, ed., *Canada* (1993) (E).

Cape Verde
See "Africa."

Caribbean
Roger Hughes, *The Caribbean* (1987) (B). See also "Central America," "Latin America," and individual countries.

Central African Republic
Pierre Kalck, *Historical Dictionary of the Central African Republic* (1992) (E). See also "Africa."

Central America
Tom Barry, *Central America Inside Out* (1991) (C and E); Kenneth J. Grieb, *Central America in the Nineteenth and Twentieth Centuries* (1988) (B); Phil Gunson et al., eds., *The Dictionary of Contemporary Politics of Central America and the Caribbean* (1991) (E); Thomas M. Leonard, *A Guide to Central American Collections in the United States* (1994) (B); Thomas M. Leonard, *Central America and U.S. Policies, 1820s–1980s* (1985) (B). See also "Latin America" and individual countries.

Ceylon
See "Sri Lanka."

Chad
Samuel Decalo, *Historical Dictionary of Chad* (1987) (E). See also "Africa."

Chile
Salvatore Bizzarro, *Historical Dictionary of Chile* (1987) (E); Harold Blakemore, *Chile* (1988) (B). See also "Latin America."

China (and Taiwan)
Wolfgang Bartke, *Biographical Dictionary and Analysis of China's Party Leadership, 1922–1988* (1990) (BA); Wei-chin Lee, *Taiwan* (1990) (B); Colin Mackerras and Amanda Yorke, *The Cambridge Handbook of Contemporary China* (1991) (E); Hugh B. O'Neill, *Companion to Chinese History* (1987) (E); *Republic of China Yearbook* (1989–) (AS). See also "Asia and the Pacific."

Colombia
Robert H. Davis, *Colombia* (1990) (B); Robert H. Davis, *Historical Dictionary of Colombia* (1977) (E). See also "Latin America" and "Colombia."

Comoros

See "Africa."

Congo

Randall Fegley, *The Congo* (1993) (B). See also "Africa."

Costa Rica

Theodore S. Creedman, *Historical Dictionary of Costa Rica* (1991) (E); Charles L. Stansifer, *Costa Rica* (1991) (B). See also "Central America" and "Latin America."

Côte d'Ivoire

Robert J. Mundt, *Historical Dictionary of the Ivory Coast* (1987) (E). See also "Africa."

Croatia

See "Europe" and "Yugoslavia."

Cuba

Ronald H. Chilcote and Sheryl Lutjens, eds., *Cuba, 1953–1978* (1986) (B); Jesse J. Dossick, ed., *Cuba, Cubans, and Cuban-Americans, 1902–1991* (1992) (B); Louis A. Pérez, Jr., *A Guide to Cuban Collections in the United States* (1991) (B), *Cuba* (1988) (B), *Historiography in the Revolution: A Bibliography of Cuban Scholarship, 1959–1979* (1981) (B), and *The Revolutionary War, 1953–1958* (1976) (B); Jaime Suchlicki, *Historical Dictionary of Cuba* (1988) (E). See also "Caribbean," "Latin America," and "Spanish-American-Cuban-Filipino War."

Cyprus

See "Greece" and "Turkey."

Czechoslovakia

David Short, *Czechoslovakia* (1986) (B). See also "Eastern Europe" and "Europe."

Czech Republic

See "Czechoslovakia," "Eastern Europe," and "Europe."

Denmark

Henrik Holtermann, *Danish Foreign Policy* (1988) (B); Kenneth E. Miller, *Denmark* (1987) (B). See also "Europe" and "Scandinavia."

Djibouti

Peter J. Schraeder, *Djibouti* (1991) (B). See also "Africa."

Dominica

Robert Myers, *Dominica* (1987) (B). See also "Caribbean."

Dominican Republic

Kai Schoenhals, *Dominican Republic* (1990) (B). See also "Caribbean" and "Latin America."

Eastern Europe

Kenneth J. Dillon, *Scholar's Guide to Washington, D.C., for Central and East European Studies* (1980) (B); Joyce Moss and George Wilson, *Peoples of the World: Eastern Europe and the Post-Soviet Republics* (1993) (E); Juliusz Stroynowski, *Who's Who in the Socialist Countries of Europe* (1989) (BA). See also individual countries, "Russia and the Soviet Union," and "Europe."

Ecuador

Alan W. Bork and Georg Maier, *Historical Dictionary of Ecuador* (1973) (E); David Corkill, *Ecuador* (1989) (B). See also "Latin America."

Egypt

Ragai N. Makar, *Egypt* (1988) (B); Joan Wucher-King, *Historical Dictionary of Egypt* (1984) (E). See also "Israel, Palestine, and Arab-Israeli Conflict" and "Middle East."

El Salvador

Ralph Lee Woodward, *El Salvador* (1988) (B). See also "Central America" and "Latin America."

Equatorial Guinea

Ronald Fegley, *Equatorial Guinea* (1991) (B); Max Liniger-Goumaz, *Historical Dictionary of Equatorial Guinea* (1988) (E). See also "Africa."

Eritrea

See "Ethiopia."

Estonia

Inese A. Smith and Marita V. Grunts, *The Baltic States* (1993) (B). See also "Russia and the Soviet Union."

Ethiopia

Paulos Milkiss, *Ethiopia* (1989) (B); Chris Prouty and Eugene Rosenfeld, *Historical Dictionary of Ethiopia* (1994) (E). See also "Africa."

Europe

Chris Cook and John Paxton, *European Political Facts, 1918-84* (1986) (E); *The Economist Atlas of the New Europe* (1992) (A); Joan F. Higbee, *Scholar's Guide to Washington, D.C., for Southwest European Studies* (1989) (B); *The Europa World Year Book* (1989–) (AS); B. R. Mitchell, *International Historical Statistics: Europe, 1750–1988* (1992) (S); Francis Nicholson, ed., *Political and Economic Encyclopaedia of Western Europe* (1990) (E); Louis A. Pitschmann, *Scholar's Guide to Washington, D.C., for Northwest European Studies* (1984) (B). See also "Eastern Europe," "North Atlantic Treaty Organization (NATO)," individual countries, and specific wars.

Fiji

See "Asia and the Pacific."

Finland

See "Europe" and "Scandinavia."

France

David S. Bell et al., eds., *Biographical Dictionary of French Political Leaders Since 1870* (1990) (BA); Ronald J. Caldwell, *The Era of Napoleon* (1991) (B); James A. Carr, ed., *American Foreign Policy During the French Revolution-Napoleonic Period, 1789–1815* (1994) (B); Frances Chambers, *France* (1990) (B); *Chronicle of the French Revolution* (1989) (C); Owen Connelly, *Historical Dictionary of Napoleonic France, 1789–1815* (1985) (E); William E. Echard, ed., *Historical Dictionary of the French Second Empire, 1852–1870* (1985) (E); Patrick H. Hutton et al., eds., *Historical Dictionary of the Third French Republic, 1870–1940* (1986) (E); Colin Jones, *The French Revolution* (1988) (E); Edgar Leon Newman, ed., *Historical Dictionary of France from the 1815 Restoration to the Second Empire* (1987) (E). See also "Europe."

Gabon

David E. Gardinier, *Historical Dictionary of Gabon* (1994) (E). See also "Africa."

Gambia

David P. Gamble, *The Gambia* (1988) (B). See also "Africa."

Georgia

See "Russia and the Soviet Union."

Germany and Berlin

Donald S. Detwiler and Ilse E. Detwiler, *West Germany* (1987) (B); Barbara D. Paul, *The Germans After World War II* (1990) (B); Louis L. Snyder, *The Third Reich, 1933–1945* (1987) (B); James Taylor and Warren Shaw, *The Third Reich Almanac* (1988) (E); Ian Wallace, *Berlin* (1993) (B); Ian Wallace, *East Germany* (1987) (B); Christian Zentner and Freidemann Bedürftig, eds., *The Encyclopedia of the Third Reich* (1991) (E). See also "Europe," "Holocaust," "World War I," and "World War II."

Ghana

Daniel M. McFarland, *Historical Dictionary of Ghana* (1985) (E); Robert A. Myers, *Ghana* (1991) (B). See also "Africa."

Great Britain
C. A. Bayly, ed., *Atlas of the British Empire* (1989) (A); David Butler and Gareth Butler, *British Political Facts, 1900–1994* (1994) (E); Peter Catterall, *British History, 1945–1987* (1991) (B); Christopher Haigh, *The Cambridge Historical Encyclopedia of Great Britain and Ireland* (1985) (E); Alfred F. Havighurst, *Modern England, 1901–1984* (1987) (B); David A. Lincove and Gary R. Treadway, eds., *The Anglo-American Relationship* (1988) (B); David Weigall, *Britain & the World, 1815–1986* (1987) (E);. See also "Canada," "Europe," and "War of 1812."

Greece
Henry A. Richter, *Greece and Cyprus Since 1920* (1991) (B). See also "Europe."

Grenada
See "Caribbean."

Guam
See "Asia and the Pacific."

Guatemala
Ralph Lee Woodward, *Guatemala* (1992) (B). See also "Central America" and "Latin America."

Guinea
Thomas E. O'Toole, *Historical Dictionary of Guinea* (1987) (E). See also "Africa."

Guinea-Bissau
Richard Lobban and Joshua Forrest, *Historical Dictionary of the Republic of Guinea-Bissau* (1988) (E); Rosemary E. Galli, *Guinea-Bissau* (1990) (B). See also "Africa."

Guyana
Frances Chambers, *Guyana* (1989) (B). See also "Latin America."

Haiti
Frances Chambers, *Haiti* (1983) (B). See also "Caribbean" and "Latin America."

Hawai'i
Nancy J. Morris and Love Dean, *Hawai'i* (1992) (B). See also "Asia and the Pacific."

Honduras
Colin Danby and Richard Swedberg, *Honduras Bibliography and Research Guide* (1984) (B); Pamela F. Howard-Reguindin, *Honduras* (1992) (B); Harvey K. Meyer and Jessie H. Meyer, *Historical Dictionary of Honduras* (1994) (E). See also "Central America" and "Latin America."

Hong Kong
Ian Scott, *Hong Kong* (1990) (B). See also "China (and Taiwan)" and "Asia and the Pacific."

Hungary
See "Eastern Europe" and "Europe."

Iceland
See "Europe."

India
Pran Nath Chopra, *Encyclopedia of India* (1988) (E); Ashok K. Dutt and M. Margaret Geib, *Atlas of South Asia* (1987) (A); Parshotam Mehra, *A Dictionary of Modern Indian History, 1707–1947* (1987) (E); Francis Robinson, ed., *The Cambridge Encyclopedia of India, Pakistan, Bangladesh, Sri Lanka, Nepal, Bhutan, and the Maldives* (1989) (E); Santosh C. Saha, *Indo-U.S. Relations, 1947–1988* (1990) (B). See also "Asia and the Pacific."

Indian Ocean
Julia J. Gotthold, *Indian Ocean* (1988) (B). See also "Asia and the Pacific" and "India."

Indonesia
Gerald H. Krausse and Sylvia C. Engelen Krausse, *Indonesia* (1994) (B). See also "Asia and the Pacific," "Timor," and "Vietnam and Southeast Asia."

Iran
Sīrūs Ghanī, *Iran and the West* (1987) ı(B); Raza Navabpour, *Iran* (1988) (B); Ehsan Yarshater, ed., *Encyclopaedia Iranica* (1986–) (E). See also "Iraq" and "Middle East."

Iraq
J. Anthony Gardner, *The Iran-Iraq War* (1989) (B). See also "Iran" and "Middle East."

Ireland
J. E. A. Doherty, *A Chronology of Irish History Since 1500* (1990) (C); Michael O. Shannon, *Irish Republic* (1986) (B). See also "Europe" and "Great Britain."

Israel, Palestine, and Arab-Israeli Conflict
Martin Gilbert, *Atlas of the Arab-Israeli Conflict* (1993) (A); *Israel: Yearbook and Almanac* (1948–) (AS); Gregory S. Mahler, *Bibliography of Israeli Politics* (1985) (B); Bernard Reich, *Historical Dictionary of Israel* (1992) (E); Susan H. Rolef, ed., *Political Dictionary of the State of Israel* (1985) (E). See also "Middle East."

Italy
Frank J. Coppa and William Roberts, *Modern Italian History* (1990) (B). See also "Europe."

Ivory Coast
See "Côte d'Ivoire."

Jamaica
See "Caribbean."

Japan
Sadao Asada, ed., *Japan and the World, 1853–1952* (1989) (B); James W. Morley, ed., *Japan's Foreign Policy, 1868–1941* (1974) (B); Rita E. Neri, *U.S. and Japan Foreign Trade* (1988) (B); Frank J. Shulman, *Japan* (1989) (B); William D. Wray, ed., *Japan's Economy* (1995) (B). See also "Asia and the Pacific" and "World War II."

Jordan
See "Israel, Palestine, and Arab-Israeli Conflict" and "Middle East."

Kazakhstan
See "Russia and the Soviet Union."

Kenya
Bethwell A. Ogot, *Historical Dictionary of Kenya* (1981) (E). See also "Africa."

Kiribati
See "Asia and the Pacific."

Korea
Keith D. McFarland, *The Korean War* (1986) (B); James I. Matray, ed., *Historical Dictionary of the Korean War* (1991) (E); Andrew C. Nahm, *Historical Dictionary of the Republic of Korea* (1993) (E); Stanley Sandler, ed., *The Korean War* (1995) (E); Harry G. Summers, Jr., *Korean War Almanac* (1990) (C and E). See also "Asia and the Pacific."

Kuwait
See "Middle East."

Kyrgyzstan
See "Russia and the Soviet Union."

Laos
Helen Cordell, *Laos* (1991) (B); William W. Sage, *Laos* (1986) (B). See also "Vietnam and Southeast Asia."

Latin America

Robert J. Alexander, *Biographical Dictionary of Latin American and Caribbean Political Leaders* (1988) (BA); Leslier Bethell, ed., *The Cambridge Encyclopedia of Latin America*, vol. XI: *Bibliographical Essays* (1995) (B); Simon Collier et al., eds., *The Cambridge Encyclopedia of Latin America and the Caribbean* (1992) (E); Paula H. Covington, ed., *Latin America and the Caribbean* (1992) (B); David W. Dent, ed., *U.S.-Latin American Policymaking* (1995) (B); Liza Gross, *Handbook of Leftist Guerrilla Groups in Latin America and the Caribbean* (1995) (E); Michael Grow, ed., *Scholar's Guide to Washington, D.C. for Latin American and Caribbean Studies* (1979) (B); *Handbook of Latin American Studies* (1935–) (B); Jack W. Hopkins, ed., *Latin America and Caribbean Contemporary Record* (1983–) (AS); Michael C. Meyer, *Supplement to a Bibliography of United States–Latin American Relations Since 1810* (1979) (B); B. R. Mitchell, *International Historical Statistics: The Americas, 1750–1988* (1993) (S); David Shavit, *The United States in Latin America* (1992) (E); Barbara A. Tenenbaum, ed., *Encyclopedia of Latin American History and Culture* (1995) (E); David F. Trask et al., *A Bibliography of United States–Latin American Relations Since 1810* (1979) (B); James W. Wilke, ed., *Statistical Abstract of Latin America* (1955–) (S). See also "Caribbean," "Central America," and individual countries.

Latvia

See "Estonia" and "Russia and the Soviet Union."

Lebanon

C. H. Bleaney, *Lebanon* (1991) (B). See also "Middle East."

Lesotho

Gordon Haliburton, *Historical Dictionary of Lesotho* (1977) (E). See also "Africa" and "South Africa."

Liberia

D. Ellwood Dunn and Svend E. Holsoe, *Historical Dictionary of Liberia* (1985) (E). See also "Africa."

Libya

Lorna Hahn, *Historical Dictionary of Libya* (1981) (E); Richard I. Lawless, *Libya* (1987) (B). See also "Africa" and "Middle East."

Liechtenstein

Regula A. Meier, *Liechtenstein* (1993) (B). See also "Europe."

Lithuania

Jonas Zinkus, ed., *Lithuania* (1986) (E). See also "Estonia" and "Russia and the Soviet Union."

Luxembourg

See "Europe."

Macau

Richard L. Edmonds, *Macau* (1989) (B). See also "Asia and the Pacific," "China," and "Portugal."

Macedonia

See "Eastern Europe," "Europe," and "Yugoslavia."

Madagascar

Hilary Budt, *Madagascar* (1993) (B). See also "Africa."

Malawi

Cynthia A. Crosby, *Historical Dictionary of Malawi* (1993) (E). See also "Africa."

Malaysia

See "Asia and the Pacific" and "Vietnam and Southeast Asia."

Maldives

See "India."

Mali

Pascal J. Imperato, *Historical Dictionary of Mali* (1986) (E). See also "Africa."

Malta

John R. Thackral, *Malta* (1985) (B). See also "Europe."

Marshall Islands

See "Asia and the Pacific."

Mauritania

Simonetta Calderini et al., *Mauritania* (1992) (B). See also "Africa."

Mauritius

Pramila R. Bennett, *Mauritius* (1992) (B); Sydney Selvon, *Historical Dictionary of Mauritius* (1991) (E). See also "Africa."

Mexico

Tom Barry, *Mexico: A Country Guide* (1992) (E); Roderic A. Camp, *Mexican Political Biographies, 1884–1934* (1991) (BA); Roderic A. Camp, *Mexican Political Biographies, 1935–1993* (1995) (BA); *Enciclopedia de México* (1987–1988) (E); Milton H. Jamail and Margo Gutiérrez, *The Border Guide: Institutions and Organizations of the United States–Mexico Borderlands* (1992) (E); David E. Lorey, ed., *United States–Mexico Border Statistics Since 1900* (1990) (S); George D. C. Philip, *Mexico* (1993) (B); Norman E. Tutorow, ed., *The Mexican-American War* (1981) (B); Barbara G. Valk et al., *Borderline* (1988) (B). See also "Latin America."

Micronesia

Nicholas J. Goetzfridt, *Micronesia, 1975–1987* (1989) (B). See also "Asia and the Pacific."

Middle East

Michael Adams, ed., *The Middle East* (1987) (E); Gerald Blake et al., *The Cambridge Atlas of the Middle East and North Africa* (1987) (A); Thomas A. Bryson, *U.S.–Middle East Diplomatic Relations, 1784–1978* (1979) (B); Steven R. Dorr, *Scholar's Guide to Washington, D.C., for Middle Eastern Studies* (1981) (B); John J. Esposito, ed., *The Oxford Encyclopedia of the Modern Islamic World* (1995) (E); Martin Gilbert, *Atlas of the Arab-Israeli Conflict* (1993) (A); Alain Gresh, *An A to Z of the Middle East* (1990) (E); Bruce R. Kuniholm, *The Persian Gulf and United States Policy* (1984) (B); Colin Legum et al., eds., *Middle East Contemporary Survey* (1978–) (AS); Trevor Mostyn, ed., *The Cambridge Encyclopedia of the Middle East and North Africa* (1988) (E); Vincent Ponko, *Britain in the Middle East, 1921–1956* (1990) (B); Bernard Reich, ed., *Political Leaders of the Contemporary Middle East and North Africa* (1990) (BA); David Shavit, *The United States in the Middle East* (1988) (E); Yaacov Shimoni, *Political Dictionary of the Arab World* (1987) (E); Sanford R. Silverburg, *Middle East Bibliography* (1992) (B); Sanford R. Silverburg and Bernard Reich, *United States Foreign Policy and the Middle East/North Africa* (1990) (B); Reeva S. Simon et al., eds., *The Encyclopedia of the Modern Middle East* (1996) (E); Lawrence Ziring, *The Middle East: A Political Dictionary* (1992) (E). See also individual countries.

Moldova

See "Russia and the Soviet Union."

Monaco

See "Europe."

Mongolia

Judith Nordby, *Mongolia* (1993) (M). See also "Asia and the Pacific."

Morocco

William Spencer, *Historical Dictionary of Morocco* (1980) (E). See also "Africa" and "Middle East."

Mozambique

Mario Azevedo, *Historical Dictionary of Mozambique* (1991) (E); Colin Darch and Calisto Pacheleke, *Mozambique* (1987) (B). See also "Africa."

Myanmar

Patricia M. Herbert, *Burma* (1991) (B). See also "Vietnam and Southeast Asia."

Namibia

John J. Grotpeter, *Historical Dictionary of Namibia* (1994) (E); Stanley Schoeman and Elna Schoeman, *Namibia* (1984) (B). See also "Africa" and "South Africa."

Nepal

Basil C. Hedrick and Anne K. Hedrick, *Historical and Cultural Dictionary of Nepal* (1972) (E); John Whelpton, *Nepal* (1990) (B). See also "India."

Netherlands

Peter King and Michael Wintle, *The Netherlands* (1988) (B); Margaret B. Krewson, *The Netherlands and Northern Belgium* (1989) (B). See also "Europe."

New Zealand

John Henderson, *New Zealand Foreign Policy, 1945–1985* (1986) (B); Gordon McLauchlan, ed., *The Illustrated Encyclopedia of New Zealand* (1989) (E). See also "Asia and the Pacific."

Nicaragua

Harvey K. Meyer, *Historical Dictionary of Nicaragua* (1972) (E); Neil Snarr et al., *Sandinista Nicaragua* (1989) (B); Ralph Lee Woodward, *Nicaragua* (1994) (B). See also "Central America" and "Latin America."

Niger

Samuel Decalo, *Historical Dictionary of Niger* (1989) (E). See also "Africa."

Nigeria

Anthony Dyewole, *Historical Dictionary of Nigeria* ((1987) (E); Robert A. Myers, *Nigeria* (1989) (B). See also "Africa."

North Africa

See "Africa," "Middle East," and individual countries.

Northern Ireland

Michael O. Shannon, *Northern Ireland* (1991) (B). See also "Great Britain" and "Ireland."

Norway

Leland B. Sather, *Norway* (1986) (B). See "Scandinavia" and "Europe."

Oceania

See "Asia and the Pacific."

Oman

John D. Anthony, *Historical and Cultural Dictionary of the Sultanate of Oman and the Emirates of Eastern Arabia* (1976) (E); Frank B. Clements, *Oman* (1981) (B). See also "Middle East."

Pakistan

David D. Taylor, *Pakistan* (1990) (B). See also "India."

Palau

See "Asia and the Pacific."

Palestine

See "Israel, Palestine, and Arab-Israeli Conflict" and "Middle East."

Panama and Panama Canal

Basil C. Hedrick and Anne K. Hedrick, *Historical Dictionary of Panama* (1970) (E); Eleanor D. Langstaff, *Panama* (1982) (B); Thomas M. Leonard, ed., *Panama, the Canal, and the United States* (1993) (B). See also "Colombia" and "Latin America."

Papua New Guinea

Alan Butler, *Papua New Guinea* (1988) (B). See also "Asia and the Pacific."

Paraguay

R. Andrew Jackson, *Paraguay* (1987) (B); Charles J. Kolinski, *Historical Dictionary of Paraguay* (1973) (E). See also "Latin America."

Persian Gulf

See "Middle East," "Iran," and "Iraq."

Peru

Marvin Alisky, *Historical Dictionary of Peru* (1979) (E); John R. Fisher, *Peru* (1989) (B). See also "Latin America."

Philippines

Jim Richardson, *Philippines* (1989) (B). See also "Asia and the Pacific," "Spanish-American-Cuban-Filipino War," and "Vietnam and Southeast Asia."

Poland

August G. Kanka, *Poland* (1988) (B); George Sanford and Adrian Gozdecka-Sanford, *Poland* (1993) (B). See also "Eastern Europe" and "Europe."

Polynesia

Robert D. Craig, *Historical Dictionary of Polynesia* (1993) (E). See also "Asia and the Pacific."

Portugal

P. T. H. Unwin, *Portugal* (1987) (B). See also "Europe."

Puerto Rico

Elena E. Cevallos, *Puerto Rico* (1985) (B); Kenneth R. Farr, *Historical Dictionary of Puerto Rico and the U.S. Virgin Islands* (1973) (E). See also "Caribbean" and "Latin America."

Qatar

See "Middle East."

Rivers

Rand McNally Encyclopedia of World Rivers (1980) (E). See also "Continental Expansion (U.S.)."

Romania

Andrea Deletant, *Romania* (1985) (B). See also "Eastern Europe."

Russia and the Soviet Union

N. N. Bolkhovitinov and J. Dane Hartgrove, *Russia and the United States* (1987) (B); Archie Brown et al., eds., *The Cambridge Encyclopedia of Russia and the Soviet Union* (1994) (E); Stephen DeMowbray, *Key Facts in Soviet History* (1990) (C); Steven A. Grant, *Scholar's Guide to Washington, D.C., for Russian/Soviet Studies* (1983) (B); George Jackson, *Dictionary of the Russian Revolution* (1989) (E); James K. Libbey, *American-Russian Economic Relations* (1989) (B); Barbara P. McCrea et al., *The Soviet and East European Political Dictionary* (1984) (E); Joyce Moss and George Wilson, *Peoples of the World: Eastern Europe and the Post-Soviet Republics* (1993) (E); David Shavit, *United States Relations with Russia and the Soviet Union* (1993) (E); Harold Shukman, ed., *The Blackwell Encyclopedia of the Russian Revolution* (1988) (E); Stephen White, ed., *Political and Economic Encyclopedia of the Soviet Union and Eastern Europe* (1990) (E). See also "Cold War," "Communism," "Eastern Europe," and "Europe."

Rwanda

Learthen Dorsey, *Historical Dictionary of Rwanda* (1994) (E); Randall Fegley, *Rwanda* (1993) (B). See also "Africa."

Saint Kitts and Nevis

See "Caribbean."

Saint Lucia

See "Caribbean."

Saint Vincent and the Grenadines

See "Caribbean."

Samoa

See "Asia and the "Pacific."

Samoa (American)

See "Asia and the Pacific."

San Marino

See "Europe" and "Italy."

São Tomé and Príncipe
See "Africa."

Saudi Arabia
Frank Clements, *Saudi Arabia* (1988) (B). See also "Middle East."

Scandinavia
Byron J. Nordstrom, ed., *Dictionary of Scandinavian History* (1986) (E). See also individual countries and "Europe."

Senegal
R. M. Dilley and J. S. Eades, *Senegal* (1994) (B). See also "Africa."

Serbia
See "Eastern Europe," "Europe," and "Yugoslavia."

Seychelles
George Bennett, *Seychelles* (1993) (B). See also "Africa."

Sierra Leone
Cyril P. Foray, *Historical Dictionary of Sierra Leone* (1977) (E). See also Africa."

Singapore
Stella R. Quah, *Singapore* (1988) (B). See also "Vietnam and Southeast Asia."

Slovak Republic
See "Czechoslovakia" and "Eastern Europe."

Slovenia
See "Russia and the Soviet Union."

Solomon Islands
See "Asia and the Pacific."

Somalia
Mark W. DeLancey, *Somalia* (1988) (B). See also "Africa."

South Africa
Jacqueline A. Kalley, *South Africa Under Apartheid* (1989) (B); C. T. Keto, *American-South African Relations, 1784–1980* (1985) (B); Y. G.M. Lulat, *U.S. Relations with South Africa* (1989–1991) (B); Newell M. Stultz, *South Africa* (1989) (B). See also "Africa."

South Asia
See "India" and individual countries.

Southeast Asia
See "Association of Southeast Asian Nations (ASEAN)" and "Vietnam and Southeast Asia."

Soviet Successor States
See "Russia and the Soviet Union."

Soviet Union
See "Russia and the Soviet Union."

Spain
Robert W. Kern, *Historical Dictionary of Modern Spain, 1700–1988* (1990) (E); Graham J. Shields, *Spain* (1985) (B). See also "Europe" and "Spanish-American-Cuban-Filipino War."

Sri Lanka
Vijaya Samaraweera, *Sri Lanka* (1989) (B). See also "Asia and the Pacific" and "India."

Sudan
M. W. Daly, *Sudan* (1992) (B); Carolyn Fluehr-Lobban et al., *Historical Dictionary of Sudan* (1992) (E); Yosa H. Wawa, *Southern Sudan* (1988) (B). See also "Africa."

Suriname
Enid Brown, *Suriname and the Northern Antilles* (1992) (B); Rosemarijn Hoefte, *Suriname* (1990) (B). See also "Caribbean."

Swaziland
John J. Grotpeter, *Historical Dictionary of Swaziland* (1975) (E); Balam Nyeko, *Swaziland* (1982) (B). See also "Africa."

Sweden
Leland B. Sather, *Sweden* (1987) (B). See also "Scandinavia."

Switzerland
Heinz K. Meier, *Switzerland* (1990) (B). See also "Europe."

Syria
Ian J. Seccombe, *Syria* (1987) (B). See also "Middle East."

Taiwan (Formosa)
See "China (and Taiwan)."

Tajikistan
See "Russia and the Soviet Union."

Tanzania, United Republic of
Laura S. Kurtz, *Historical Dictionary of Tanzania* (1978) (E). See also "Africa."

Texas
Walter P. Webb et al., eds., *The Handbook of Texas* (1952, 1976).

Thailand
See "Vietnam and Southeast Asia."

Third World
George T. Kurian, *Atlas of the Third World* (1992) (A); Brian W. W. Welsh and Pavel Butorin, eds., *Dictionary of Development* (1990) (E). See also individual countries and "Development and Developing Nations."

Tibet
John R. Pinfold, *Tibet* (1991) (B). See also "Asia and the Pacific" and "China."

Timor
Ian Rowland, *Timor* (1992) (B). See also "Indonesia."

Togo
Samuel Decalo, *Historical Dictionary of Togo* (1987) (E). See also "Africa."

Tonga
See "Asia and the Pacific."

Trinidad and Tobago
Frances Chambers, *Trinidad and Tobago* (1986) (B). See also "Caribbean."

Tunisia
Kenneth J. Perkins, *Historical Dictionary of Tunisia* (1989) (E). See also "Africa."

Turkey
Meral Güçlü, *Turkey* (1981) (B). See also "Europe."

Turkmenistan
See "Russia and the Soviet Union."

Uganda
Martin Johnson, *Idi Amin and Uganda* (1992) (B). See also "Africa."

Ukraine
Volodymer Kubijouyč, ed., *Encyclopedia of Ukraine* (1984–) (E); Bohdan S. Wynar, *Ukraine* (1990) (B). See also "Russia and the Soviet Union."

United Arab Emirates
Frank Clements, *United Arab Emirates* (1983) (B). See also "Middle East."

United Kingdom
See "Great Britain" and "Northern Ireland."

Uruguay

Henry Finch, *Uruguay* (1989) (B); Jean L. Willis. *Historical Dictionary of Uruguay* (1974) (E). See also "Latin America."

Uzbekistan

See "Russia and the Soviet Union."

Vanuatu

See "Asia and the Pacific."

Vatican City (The Holy See)

See "Europe" and "Italy."

Venezuela

D. A. G. Waddell, *Venezuela* (1990) (B). See also "Latin America," "Organization of Petroleum Exporting Countries (OPEC)," and "Oil."

Vietnam and Southeast Asia

John S. Bowman, ed., *The Vietnam War* (1985) (C); Lester H. Brune and Richard Dean Burns, eds., *America and the Indochina Wars, 1945–1990* (1991) (B); William J. Duiker, *Historical Dictionary of Vietnam* (1989) (E); Caroline D. Harnly, *Agent Orange and Vietnam* (1988) (B); Stanley I. Kutler, ed., *Encyclopedia of the Vietnam War* (1995) (E); David G. Marr, *Vietnam* (1992) (B); Patrick M. Mayerchak, *Scholar's Guide to Washington, D.C., for Southeast Asian Studies* (1983) (B); James S. Olson, *Dictionary of the Vietnam War* (1988) (E), and *The Vietnam War* (1993) (B); Louis A. Peake, *The United States and the Vietnam War* (1986) (B); Harry G. Summers, Jr., *Vietnam War Almanac* (1985) (C); Sandra M. Wittman, *Writing about Vietnam* (1989) (B). See also "Asia and the Pacific," "Association of Southeast Asian Nations (ASEAN)," "Peace Movements," and "Military Affairs, Defense, and Wars."

Virgin Islands and West Indies

Verna Penn Moll, *Virgin Islands* (1991) (B). See also "Caribbean" and "Puerto Rico."

West (U.S.)

See "Continental Expansion (U.S.)."

Western Europe

See "Europe" and individual countries.

Yemen

See "Middle East."

Yugoslavia

John J. Horton, *Yugoslavia* (1990) (B). See also "Eastern Europe" and "Europe."

Zaire

F. Scott Bobb, *Historical Dictionary of Zaire* (1988) (E). See also "Africa."

Zambia

John J. Grotpeter, *Historical Dictionary of Zambia* (1979) (E). See also "Africa."

Zimbabwe

Denis Berens, ed., *A Concise Encyclopedia of Zimbabwe* (1988) (E); *Encyclopedia Zimbabwe* (1987) (E); R. Kent Rasmussen, *Historical Dictionary of Zimbabwe* (1990) (E). See also "Africa."

SUBJECTS

Acquired Immune Deficiency Syndrome (AIDS) Pandemic

Matthew Smallman-Raynor et al., *Atlas of AIDS* (1992) (A and S).

Air Force (U.S.) and Aviation

Charles D. Bright, ed., *Historical Dictionary of the U.S. Air Force* (1992) (E); R. J. Hall and R. D. Campbell, *Dictionary of Aviation* (1991) (E); Michael Taylor, ed., *Brassey's World Aircraft & Systems Directory* (1996) (E); Michael Taylor, *Encyclopedia of the World's Air Forces* (1988) (E); Bruce W. Watson and Susan W. Watson, *The United States Air Force* (1992) (E). See also "Military Affairs, Defense, and Wars" and specific wars.

Alliance for Progress

See "Latin America."

American Civil War

Mark M. Boatner III, *The Civil War Dictionary* (1988) (E); Richard N. Current, ed., *Encyclopedia of the Confederacy* (1993) (E); David C. Roller and Robert W. Twyman, eds., *The Encyclopedia of Southern History* (1979) (E); Jon L. Wakelyn, ed., *Biographical Dictionary of the Confederacy* (1977) (BA).

American Revolution and Colonial Period

Richard L. Blanco, ed., *The American Revolution, 1775–1783* (1993) (E); Richard L. Blanco, *The War of the American Revolution* (1984) (B); Mark M. Boatner III, *Encyclopedia of the American Revolution* (1974) (E); Lester J. Cappon, ed., *Atlas of Early American History: The Revolutionary Era, 1760–1790* (1976) (A); Jacob E. Cooke, ed., *Encyclopedia of the North American Colonies* (1993) (E); John M. Faragher, ed., *The Encyclopedia of Colonial and Revolutionary America* (1990) (E); Jack P. Greene and J. R. Pole, eds., *The Blackwell Encyclopedia of the American Revolution* (1991) (E); Gregory Palmer, ed., *Biographical Sketches of Loyalists of the American Revolution* (1984); John W. Raimo, ed., *Biographical Directory of American Colonial and Revolutionary Governors, 1607–1789* (1980) (BA); *Rand McNally Atlas of the American Revolution* (1974) (A). See also "Military Affairs, Defense, and Wars."

Anti-Communism and McCarthyism

Peter H. Buckingham, *America Sees Red* (1987) (B); John E. Haynes, *Communism and Anti-Communism in the United States* (1987) (B). See also "Cold War" and "Politics (U.S.)."

Arms Control

See "Disarmament and Arms Control" and "Peace Movements."

Army, U.S.

Peter G. Tsouras et al., *The United States Army* (1991) (E). See also "Military Affairs, Defense, and Wars."

Assassination

Carl Sifakis, *Encyclopedia of Assassinations* (1991) (E). See also "Intelligence, CIA, and Covert Action" and "Terrorism."

Association of Southeast Asian Nations (ASEAN)

Patricia Lim, *ASEAN* (1984, 1988) (B). See also "Vietnam and Southeast Asia."

Aviation

See "Air Force (U.S.) and Aviation."

Businesses

Thomas Derdak, ed., *International Directory of Company Histories* (1988) (B); Ankie Hoogvelt, *Multinational Enterprise* (1987) (E); John N. Ingham, *Biographical Dictionary of American Business Leaders* (1983) (BA); John N. Ingham and Lyness B. Feldman, *Contemporary American Business Leaders* (1990) (BA); Wahib Nasrallah, *United States Corporation Histories* (1991) (B); Richard Robinson, *Business History of the World* (1993) (C); Richard Robinson, *United States Business History* (1990) (E); D. C. Stafford and R. H. A. Purkis, *Directory of Multinationals* (1989–1992). See also "Economic Relations," "Shipping," and "Telecommunications Companies."

Central Intelligence Agency (CIA)

See "Intelligence, CIA, and Covert Action."

Chemical Weapons

G. M. Burck and Charles C. Flowerree, *International Handbook on Chemical Weapons Proliferation* (1991) (E). See also "Military Affairs, Defense, and Wars."

Civil War

See "American Civil War."

Cold War

Thomas S. Arms, *Encyclopedia of the Cold War* (1994) (E); Joseph L. Black, *Origins, Evolution, and Nature of the Cold War* (1986) (B). See also "Disarmament and Arms Control," "Nuclear Weapons," and "Russia and the Soviet Union."

Communism

Robert A. Gorman, ed., *Biographical Dictionary of Marxism* (1986) (BA); Robert A. Gorman, ed., *Biographical Dictionary of Neo-Marxism* (1985) (BA); Richard F. Starr et al., eds., *Yearbook on International Communist Affairs* (1966–) (AS). See also "Russia and the Soviet Union."

Confederate States of America

See "American Civil War."

Congress (House and Senate)

Betty Austin, *J. William Fulbright* (1995) (B); Donald C. Brown et al., eds., *The Encyclopedia of the United States Congress* (1994) (E); Congressional Quarterly, *Congress and the Nation, 1945–1984* (1965–1985) (E); Robert U. Goehlert et al., *Members of Congress* (1996) (B); Norman J. Ornstein et al., *Vital Statistics on the United States Congress, 1995–1996* (1995) (S); Joel H. Sibley, ed., *Encyclopedia of the American Legislative System* (1994) (E); U.S. Congress, *Biographical Directory of the United States Congress, 1774–1989* (1989) (BA), *Congresional Globe* (1834–1873) (D), *Congressional Record* (1873–) (D), *The Debates and Proceedings in the Congress of the United States, 1st to 18th Congresses, March 3, 1789-May 27, 1824* (1834–1856) (D), and *Register of Debates in Congress: 18th-25th Congress, 6 December 1824–16 October 1837* (1825–1837) (D).

Constitution

Leonard W. Levy et al., eds., *Encyclopedia of the American Constitution* (1986) (E). See also "Supreme Court."

Containment

See "Cold War."

Continental Expansion (U.S.)

Warren A. Beck and Ynez D. Haase, *Historical Atlas of the American West* (1989) (A); John S. Bowman, ed., *The World Almanac of the American West* (1987) (E); Robert L. Frey, ed., *Railroads in the Nineteenth Century* (1988) (E); William Goetzmann and Glyndwr Williams, *The Atlas of North American Exploration* (1992) (A); J. Norman Heard, *Handbook of the American Frontier* (1987) (E); Adrian Johnson, *America Explored* (1974) (E); Howard R. Lamar, ed., *The Reader's Encyclopedia of the American West* (1977) (E); Clyde A. Milner III et al., eds., *The Oxford History of the American West* (1994) (E); Dan L. Thrapp, *The Encyclopedia of Frontier Biography* (1988–1994) (BA); David Walker, *Biographical Directory of American Territorial Governors* (1984) (BA). See also "California" and "Native Americans."

Counterinsurgency

Benjamin R. Beede, *Intervention and Counterinsurgency* (1984) (B). See also "Intelligence, CIA, and Covert Action."

Crime

Jay R. Nash, *Encyclopedia of World Crime* (1989) (E). See also "Terrorism" and "War Crimes and Trials."

Defense

See "Military Affairs, Defense, and Wars."

Demography

See "Population and Demography."

Department of State, Foreign Service, and Diplomatic Practice

Robert U. Goehlert and Elizabeth Hoffmeister, *The Department of State and American Diplomacy* (1986) (B); Anna K. Nelson, ed., *The State Department Policy Planning Staff Papers, 1947–1949* (1983) (D); U.S. Department of State, *Biographic Register* (1957–) (BA), *Foreign Service List* (1929–1975) (E), *Principal Officers of the Department of State and United States Chiefs of Mission, 1778–1990* (1991) (E), and *Register of the Department of State* (1873- 1937) (E).

Development and Developing Nations

Gerald Fry and Galen R. Martin, *The International Development Dictionary* (1991) (E). See also "Foreign Aid" and "Third World."

Disarmament and Arms Control

Sheikh Rustum Ali, *The Peace and Nuclear War Dictionary* (1989) (E); Stephen E. Atkins, *Arms Control and Disarmament* (1989) (B); Richard Dean Burns, ed., *Encyclopedia of Arms Control and Disarmament* (1993) (E); Jeffrey M. Elliot and Robert Reginald, *The Arms Control, Disarmament, and Military Security Dictionary* (1989) (E); David Scrivener, *Bibliography of Arms Control Verification* (1990) (B); Stockholm International Peace Research Institute, *SIPRI Yearbook: International Armaments and Disarmament* (1969–) (AS and S); United Nations, *Disarmament Yearbook* (1976–) (AS); U.S. Arms Control and Disarmament Agency, *Documents on Disarmament* (1960–) (D). See also "Cold War," "Military Affairs, Defense, and Wars," "Nuclear Weapons," and "Peace Movements."

Drug Trade and Control

Bruce M. Bagley, ed., *Drug Trafficking Research in the Americas* (1995) (B); Scott B. MacDonald and Bruce Zagaris, ed., *International Handbook on Drug Control* (1992) (E).

Earth Summit

See "Environmental Issues."

Economic Relations

Michael Brooke and Peter Buckley, *Handbook of International Trade* (1988) (E); Michael J. Freeman, *Atlas of the World Economy* (1991) (A); Carolyn R. Gipson, *The McGraw-Hill Dictionary of International Trade and Finance* (1994) (E); Douglas Greenwald, *The McGraw-Hill Encyclopedia of Economics* (1994) (E); Peter I. Hajnal, ed., *The Seven-Power Summit* (1989 (D); Thelma Liesner, *One Hundred Years of Economic Statistics* (1989) (S); Timothy O'Donnell et al., eds., *World Economic Data* (1991) (S); James S. Olsen, *Dictionary of United States Economic History* (1992) (E); Bill Orr, *The Global Economy of the '90s* (1992) (S); David W. Pearce, ed., *The MIT Dictionary of Modern Economics* (1992) (E); Glenn Porter, ed., *Encyclopedia of American Economic History* (1980) (E); Donald Rutherford, *Dictionary of Economics* (1992) (E); Dominick Salvatore, ed., *National Trade Policies* (1992) (E); United Nations, *Handbook of International Trade and Development Statistics* (1970–) (AS and S), *International Trade Statistics Yearbook* (1985–) (AS and S), *World Economic Survey* (1955–)(AS and S), and *Yearbook of International Trade Statistics* (1950–1982) (AS and S); Price Waterhouse, *Individual Taxes: A Worldwide Summary* (1993) (E); Leon Zurawicki and Louis Suichnezian, *Global Countertrade* (1991) (B). See also "Businesses," "General Agreement on Tariffs and Trade (GATT)," "Finance," "North American Free Trade Agreement (NAFTA)," and "Tariffs and Protectionism."

Energy

See "Environmental Issues" and "Oil."

Environmental Issues

Lester R. Brown et al., *State of the World* (1984–) (AS); Forest History Society, *Encyclopedia of American Forest and Conservation History* (1983) (E); Irene Franck and David Brownstone, *The Green Encyclopedia* (1992) (E); Fridtjof Nansen Institute (Norway), *Green Globe Yearbook* (1992–) (AS); Stanley P. Johnson, ed., *The Earth Summit* (1993) (D); Robert J. Mason and Mark T. Mattson, *Atlas of United States Environmental Issues* (1990) (A); Organisation for Economic Cooperation and Development, *The State of the Environment* (1991) (E and S); World Resources Institute, *Environmental Almanac* (1993) (E) and *World Resources* (1976–). See also "Law of the Sea."

Espionage

See "Intelligence, CIA, and Covert Action."

Ethnic Groups and Immigration

Gerald Chaliand and Jean-Pierre Rageau, *The Penguin Atlas of Diasporas* (1995) (A); Francesco Cordasco, ed., *Dictionary of American Immigration History* (1990) (E); Stephen Thernstrom, ed., *Harvard Encyclopedia of American Ethnic Groups* (1980) (E); U.S. Congressional Research Service, *Immigration Law and Policy, 1952–1979* (1979) (E). See also "Refugees."

Export Controls

See "Economic Relations" and "Tariffs and Protectionism."

Finance

International Monetary Fund, *Balance of Payments Statistics Yearbook* (1981–) (AS and S); Julian Walmsley, *A Dictionary of International Finance* (1979) (E); *Who's Who in Finance and Industry* (1972–) (BA). See also "Economic Relations" and "International Monetary Fund."

Food Aid and Relief

Nicole Ball, ed., *World Hunger* (1981) (B); UN Food and Agriculture Organization, *Food Aid in Figures* (1983–) (AS and S). See also "Foreign Aid."

Foreign Aid

U.S. Agency for International Development, *United States Overseas Loans and Grants and Assistance from International Organizations, July 1, 1945–Sept. 30, 1990* (1991) (S). See also "Development and Developing Nations" and "Food Aid and Relief."

Foreign Service

See "Department of State, Foreign Service, and Diplomatic Practice."

Foreign Trade

See "Economic Relations," "General Agreement on Tariffs and Trade (GATT)," and "North American Free Trade Agreement (NAFTA)."

French Revolution

See "France."

Frontier (U.S. West)

See "Continental Expansion."

General Agreement on Tariffs and Trade (GATT)

GATT, *Analytical Index: Guide to GATT Law and Practice* (1994). See also "Economic Relations" and "Tariffs and Protectionism."

Genocide

Israel W. Charney, ed., *Genocide* (1988) (B). See also "Holocaust" and "War Crimes and Trials."

Historians

Lucian Boia, ed., *Great Historians of the Modern Age* (1991) (BA).

Holocaust

Harry J. Cargas, *The Holocaust* (1985) (B); Abraham J. Edelheit and Hershel Edelheit, *Bibliography on Holocaust Literature* (1986, 1990) (B); Yisrael Gutman, ed., *Encyclopedia of the Holocaust* (1990) (E); See also "Genocide," "Germany," "Human Rights," "War Crimes and Trials," and "World War II."

Human Rights

America's Watch Staff (periodic reports on Latin American countries); Amnesty International, *The Amnesty International Report* (1977–) (AS); J. A. Andrews and W. D. Hines, *International Protection of Human Rights* (1987) (B); Arie Bloed, ed., *From Helsinki to Vienna* (1990) (D); Albert P. Blaustein et al., *Human Rights Sourcebook* (1987) (E); Ian Brownlie, ed., *Basic Documents on Human Rights* (1992) (D); Jack Donnelly and Rhoda E. Howard, eds., *International Handbook of Human Rights* (1987) (E); Human Rights Watch, *World Report* (1983–) (AS); Charles Humana, *World Human Rights Guide* (1992) (E); Edward Lawson, *Encyclopedia of Human Rights* (1991) (E); Lucille Whalen, *Human Rights* (1989) (E). See also "Holocaust" and "War Crimes and Trials."

Immigration

See "Ethnic Groups and Immigration."

Indians

See "Native Americans."

Intelligence, CIA, and Covert Action

Paul W. Blackstock and Frank L. Schaf, eds., *Intelligence, Espionage, Counterespionage, and Covert Operations* (1978) B); Vincent Buranelli and Nan Buranelli, *Spy/Counterspy: An Encyclopedia of Espionage* (1982) (E); Marjorie W. Cline et al., *Scholar's Guide to Intelligence Literature* (1983) (B); George C. Constantinides, *Intelligence & Espionage* (1983) (B); Larry Langman and David Ebner, *Encyclopedia of American Spy Films* (1990) (E); Harvey Nelsen, "U.S. Intelligence," *Choice* (1992) (B); G. J. A. O'Toole, *The Encyclopedia of American Intelligence and Espionage* (1988) (E); Neal H. Petersen, *American Intelligence, 1775–1990* (1992) (B); Walter Pforzheimer, *Bibliography of Intelligence Literature* (1985) (B); Ronald Seth, *Encyclopedia of Espionage* (1972) (E); Bruce W. Watson et al., eds., *United States Intelligence* (1990) (E). See also "Assassination."

Internationalists

Warren F. Kuehl, ed., *Biographical Dictionary of Internationalists* (1983) (BA). See also "Peace Movements."

International Law

Robert L. Bledsoe and Boleslaw A. Boczek, *The International Law Dictionary* (1987) (E); Francis Déak, ed., *American International Law Cases, 1783–1968* (1971–1978) (D); Ingrid Delupis, ed., *Bibliography of International Law* (1975) (B); James Fox, *Dictionary of International and Comparative Law* (1991) (E); G. H. Hackworth, *Digest of International Law* (1940–1944) (D); Marjorie Whiteman, *Digest of International Law* (1963–1970) (D). See also "Law of the Sea" and "World Court."

International Monetary Fund

Mary Elizabeth Johnson, *The International Monetary Fund, 1944–1992* (1993) (B). See also "Finance" and "International Organizations."

International Organizations

Sheikh Ali, *The International Organization and World Order Dictionary* (1992) (E); George W. Baer, ed., *International Organizations, 1918–1945* (1981) (B); Edward J. Osmanczyk, *The Encyclopedia of the United States and International Organizations* (1990) (E); Giuseppe Schiavone, *International Organizations* (1992) (E); UNESCO, *Guide to the Archives of International Organizations* (1984) (B); Union of International Associations, *Yearbook of International Organizations* (1948–) (AS); U.S. Department of State, *United States Contributions to International Organizations Annual Report* (1952–) (AS). See also specific international organizations.

International Trade

See "Businesses," "Economic Relations," "General Agreement on Tariffs and Trade" and "Tariffs and Protectionism."

Iran-Iraq War

See "Iraq."

Isolationism

Justus D. Doenecke, *Anti-Intervention* (1987) (B); Leroy N. Rieselbach, *The Roots of Isolationism* (1966) (B). See also "Peace Movements."

Journalism

See "Press and Journalism."

Korean War

See "Korea."

Labor

F. John Harper, ed., *Trade Unions of the World* (1987) (E).

Law of the Sea

United Nations, *The Law of the Sea* (1994) (B). See also "Environment" and "International Law."

League of Nations

See "International Organizations."

Low Intensity Warfare

See "Counterinsurgency" and "Intelligence, CIA, and Covert Action."

Loyalists

See "American Revolution and Colonial Period."

Manifest Destiny

Norman A. Graebner, ed., *Manifest Destiny* (1968) (D). See also "Continental Expansion (U.S.)."

Marine Corps

See "Military Affairs, Defense, and Wars" and specific wars.

Marxism

See "Communism."

McCarthyism

See "Anti-Communism and McCarthyism."

Merchant Marine

See "Shipping."

Military Affairs, Defense, and Wars

William M. Arkin et al., *Encyclopedia of the U.S. Military* (1990) (E); Benjamin R. Beede, *Military and Strategic Policy* (1990) (B); Daniel K. Blewett, *American Military History* (1994) (B); C. W. Borkland, *U.S. Defense and Military Fact Book* (1991) (E); Brian Champion, *Advanced Weapons Systems* (1985) (B); *Congress & Defense* (1988–) (AS); Andre Corvisier, ed., *A Dictionary of Military History* (1994); E. Ernest Dupuy and Trevor N. Dupuy, *The Harper Encyclopedia of Military History* (1993) (E); Trevor N. Dupuy et al., *Dictionary of Military Terms* (1986) (E); John C. Fredriksen, *Shield of the Republic, Sword of Empire: A Bibliography of United States Military Affairs, 1783–1846* (1990) (B); Wolfram F. Hanrieder and Lara V. Buel, *Words and Arms: A Dictionary of Security and Defense Terms* (1979) (E); Robin Higham and Doanld J. Mrozek, eds., *A Guide to the Sources of United States Military History* (1975) and *Supplements* (1981, 1986, 1993) (B); International Institute for Strategic Studies, *The Military Balance* (1959/60–) (AS); International Institute for Strategic Studies, *Strategic Survey* (1975–) (AS and C); *International Military and Defense Encyclopedia* (1993) (E); John E. Jessup and Louise B. Ketz, eds., *Encyclopedia of the American Military* (1994) (E); John Keegan and Andrew Wheatcroft, *Who's Who in Military History* (1976) (BA); George C. Kohn, *Dictionary of Wars* (1986) (E); Larry Langman and Egar Borg, *Encyclopedia of American War Films* (1989) (E); Edward Luttwak and Stuart Koehl, *The Dictionary of Modern War* (1991) (E); Kenneth Macksey and William Woodhouse, *The Penguin Encyclopedia of Modern Warfare* (1992); Frank Margiotta, ed., *Brassey's Encyclopedia of Land Forces and Warfare* (1996) (E); Eugene L. Rasor, *General Douglas MacArthur, 1880–1964* (1994) (B); Roger J. Spiller and Joseph G. Dawson III, eds., *Dictionary of American Military Biography* (1984) (BA); Herbert K. Tillema, *International Armed Conflict Since 1945* (1991) (B); U.S. Military Academy, *The West Point Atlas of American Wars, 1689–1953* (1959) (A); Cynthia Watson, *U.S. National Security Policy Groups* (1990) (E); *Webster's American Military Biographies* (1978) (BA). See also "Nuclear Weapons," "Strategic Defense Initiative (SDI)," individual armed services, and specific wars.

Missionaries

Henry Bowden, *Dictionary of American Religious Biography* (1993) (BA).

Multinational Corporations

See "Businesses."

Napoleonic Wars

See "France."

Nationalism

Louis L. Snyder, *Encyclopedia of Nationalism* (1990) (E). See also "Self-Determination."

National Security

See "Military Affairs, Defense, and Wars."

Native Americans

CISCO, *Biographical Dictionary of Indians of the Americas* (1991) (BA); *Handbook of North American Indians* (1978–) (E); J. Norman Heard et al., *Handbook of the American Frontier: Four Centuries of Indian-White Relationships* (1987–) (E); Charles J. Kappler, ed., *Indian Affairs: Law and Treaties* (1904-1941) (D); Barry Klein, ed., *Reference Encyclopedia of the American Indian* (1993) (E); Francis Paul Prucha, *Atlas of American Indian Affairs* (1990) (A); Paul Stuart, *Nation Within a Nation* (1987) (S); Carl Waldman, *Atlas of the North American Indian* (1985) (A); Carl Waldman, *Encyclopedia of Native American Tribes* (1988) (E). See also "Continental Expansion (U.S.)."

Navy (U.S.) and Naval Issues

William B. Cogan, *Dictionary of Admirals of the United States Navy* (1989) (BA); Paolo E. Coletta, *A Selected and Annotated Bibliography of American Naval History* (1988) (B); Paolo E. Coletta et al., eds., *American Secretaries of the Navy* (1980) (BD); John B. Hattendorf and Lynn C. Hattendorf, *A Bibliography of the Works of Alfred Thayer Mahan* (1986) (B); Barbara A. Lynch and John E. Vajda, *United States Naval History* (1993) (B); John V. Noel, Jr., and Edward L. Bruce, *Naval Terms Dictionary* (1988) (E); Jack Sweetman, ed., *American Naval History* (1984) (C); Bruce W. Watson and Susan M. Watson, *The United States Navy* (1991) (E). See also "Military Affairs, Defense, and Wars" and specific wars.

Nobel Peace Prize

Panda McGuire, ed., *Novel Prize Winners* (1992) (B); Tyler Wasson, ed., *Nobel Prize Winners* (1987) (B).

North American Free Trade Agreement (NAFTA)

Jerry M. Rosenberg, *Encyclopedia of the North American Free Trade Agreement, the New American Community, and Latin-American Trade* (1994) (E).

North Atlantic Treaty Organization (NATO)

Augustus R. Norton et al., *NATO* (1985) (B). See also "Cold War," "Europe," "Military Affairs, Defense, and Wars," and "Nuclear Weapons."

Nuclear Weapons

William G. M. Pearson, *The Nuclear Arms Race* (1989) (E); Paul Rogers, *Guide to Nuclear Weapons* (1988) (E); See also "Cold War," "Disarmament and Arms Control," "Military Affairs, Defense, and Wars," and "Space and Satellites."

Oil

Financial Times, *Oil & Gas International Year Book* (1978–) (AS); Paul Stevens, ed., *Oil and Gas Dictionary* (1988) (E); United Nations, *Energy Statistics Yearbook* (1984–) (AS and S); Jim West, ed., *International Petroleum Encyclopedia* (1994) (E). See also "Middle East."

Olympic Games

David Wallechinsky, *The Complete Book of the Olympics* (1992) (E).

Organization of American States

David Sheinin, *The Organization of American States* (1996) (B).

Organization of Petroleum Exporting Countries (OPEC)

See "Oil" and individual countries.

Pan-Americanism

See "Latin America."

Peace Corps
Robert Ridinger, *The Peace Corps* (1989) (B).

Peacekeeping
See "United Nations."

Peace Movements
Marguerite Green, *Peace Archives* (1986) (B); Charles F. Howlett, *The American Peace Movement* (1990) (B); Harold Josephson et al., eds., *Biographical Dictionary of Modern Peace Leaders* (1985) (BA); Elvin Laszlo and Jong Y. Yoo, eds., *World Encyclopedia of Peace* (1986) (E); Robert S. Meyer, *Peace Organizations Past and Present* (1988) (E); Nancy L. Roberts, *American Peace Writers, Editors, and Periodicals* (1991) (BA); Robert A. Seeley, *The Handbook of Non-Violence* (1986) (E). See also "Internationalists" and specific wars.

Pearl Harbor, 1941
Stanley L. Falk, "Pearl Harbor," *Naval History* (1988) (B); Myron J. Smith, Jr., *Pearl Harbor* (1991) (B). See also "Hawai'i" and "World War II."

Petroleum
See "Oil."

Politics (U.S.)
Erik W. Austin and Jerome C. Clubb, *Political Facts of the United States Since 1789* (1986) (E); Mari Jo Buhle et al., eds., *Encyclopedia of the American Left* (1990) (E); Jack P. Greene, ed., *Encyclopedia of American Political History* (1984) (E); Bernard K. Johnpoll and Harvey Klehr, eds., *Biographical Dictionary of the American Left* (1986) (BA); L. Sandy Maisel, ed., *Political Parties and Elections in the United States* (1991) (S); Jay M. Shafritz, *The HarperCollins Dictionary of American Government and Politics* (1992) (E). See also "Congress (House and Senate)," "Presidency (General)," and "Presidents (by Administration)."

Population and Demography
William Petersen and Renee Petersen, *Dictionary of Demography* (1986) (E). See also "Statistics: World, Economic and Social."

Presidency (General)
Norman S. Cohen, *The American Presidents* (1989) (B); Leonard W. Levy and Louis Fisher, eds., *Encyclopedia of the American Presidency* (1993) (E); Robert U. Goehlert and Fenton S. Martin, *The Presidency* (1985) (B); Henry F. Graff, ed., *The Presidents* (1984) (E); Fenton S. Martin and Robert U. Goehlert, *American Presidents* (1987) (B); *Public Papers of the Presidents* (1961–) (D); Lyn Ragsdale, *Vital Statistics on the Presidency* (1995) (S); James D. Richardson, ed., *A Compilation of the Messages and Papers of the Presidents* (1896–1910) (D); Robert Sobel, ed., *Biographical Directory of the United States Executive Branch, 1774–1989* (1990) (BA). See also "Assassination" and "Presidents (by Administration)."

Presidents (by Administration)
Harry Ammon, *James Monroe* (1991) (B); Peter H. Buckingham, *Woodrow Wilson* (1989) (B); Richard Dean Burns, *Harry S. Truman* (1984) (B); John Ferling, *John Adams* (1993) (B); James N. Giglio, *John F. Kennedy* (1995) (B); Otis L. Graham, Jr., and Meghan R. Wander, eds., *Franklin D. Roosevelt* (1985) (E); John R. Greene, *Gerald R. Ford* (1994) (B); Richard S. Kirkendall, ed., *The Harry S. Truman Encyclopedia* (1989) (E); Peter B. Levy, *Encyclopedia of the Reagan-Bush Years* (1996) (E); Mark E. Neely, Jr., *The Abraham Lincoln Encyclopedia* (1982) (BA); Edgar B. Nixon and Donald B. Schewe, eds., *Franklin D. Roosevelt and Foreign Affairs* (1969); Merrill D. Peterson, *Thomas Jefferson* (1986) (E); Robert A. Rutland, ed., *James Madison and the American Nation* (1994) (E). See also "Politics" and "Presidency (General)."

Press and Journalism
Joseph P. McKerns, ed., *Biographical Dictionary of American Journalism* (1989) (BA); William H. Taft, ed., *Encyclopedia of Twentieth-Century Journalists* (1986) (BA).

Protectionism
See "Tariffs and Protectionism."

Public Opinion
Hadley Cantril and Mildred Strunk, eds., *Public Opinion, 1935–1946* (1951) (S); Columbia Broadcast System, *Face the Nation* (1972–) (D); George Gallup, *The Gallup Poll: Public Opinion, 1935–1971* (1972), *1972–1977* (1978), and annual reports (1979–) (AS and S); Survey Research Consultants, *Index to International Public Opinion* (1978–) (AS).

Race and Racism
Jay A. Sigler, ed., *International Handbook on Race and Race Relations* (1987) (E); Meyer Weinberg, *World Racism and Related Inhumanities* (1992) (B). See also "Ethnic Groups and Immigration" and "Genocide."

Refugees
U. S. Committee for Refugees, *World Refugee Survey* (1980–) (AS). See also "Ethnic Groups and Immigration."

Scientists
American Men & Women of Science (1906–) (BA); Charles C. Gillispie, ed., *Dictionary of Scientific Biography* (1970–1980) and *Supplements* (1990) (BA); National Academy of Sciences, *Biographical Memoirs* (1877–) (BA); Roy Porter, ed., *The Biographical Dictionary of Scientists* (1994) (BA). See also "Nuclear Weapons."

Self-Determination
David B. Knight and Maureen Davies, *Self-Determination* (1988) (B). See also "Nationalism."

Shipping
Richard Natkiel, *Atlas of Maritime History* (1986) (A); Rene De La Pedraja, *A Historical Dictionary of the U.S. Merchant Marine and Shipping Industry* (1994) (E); Eric Sullivan, *The Marine Encyclopedic Dictionary* (1988) (E). See also "Businesses."

Slavery and Slave Trade
Randall M. Miller and John D. Smith, eds., *Dictionary of Afro-American Slavery* (1988) (E).

Space and Satellites
Daniel B. Baker, ed., *Explorers and Discoverers of the World* (1993) (BA); Michael Cassutt, *Who's Who in Space* (1987) (BA); Dominick A. Pisano and Cathleen S. Lewis, eds., *Air and Space History* (1988) (B). See also "Nuclear Weapons" and "Strategic Defense Initiative (SDI)."

Spanish-American-Cuban-Filipino War
Benjamin R. Beede, ed., *The War of 1898 and U.S. Interventions, 1899–1934* (1994) (B); Anne C. Venzon, *The Spanish-American War* (1990) (B). See also "Military Affairs, Defense, and Wars."

Strategic Defense Initiative (SDI)
Harry Waldman, *The Dictionary of SDI* (1988) (E). See also "Military Affairs, Defense, and Wars."

Strategy
See "Military Affairs, Defense, and Wars."

Supreme Court
Congressional Quarterly, *The Supreme Court A to Z* (1994) (E); Kermit L. Hall, ed., *The Oxford Companion to the Supreme Court of the United States* (1992) (E); John W. Johnson, ed., *Historic U.S. Court Cases, 1690–1990* (1992) (E); Fenton S. Martin and Robert U. Goehlert, *Supreme Court Bibliography* (1990) (B); Melvin I. Urofsky, ed., *The Supreme Court Justices* (1994) (BA). See also "Constitution" and "International Law."

Tariffs and Protectionism
James M. Lutz, *Protectionism* (1988) (B); United States Trade Representative, *Foreign Trade Barriers* (1986–) (AS). See also "Economic Rela-

tions" and "General Agreement on Tariffs and Trade (GATT)."

Telecommunications Companies
AT&T, *The World's Telephones* (1993) (E). See also "Businesses."

Terrorism
Edward F. Mickolus et al., *International Terrorism in the 1980s* (1989) (C), *Terrorism, 1988–1991* (1993) (C), and *Transnational Terrorism, 1968–1979* (1980) (C); Suzanne R. Ontiveros, *Global Terrorism* (1986) (B); George Rosie, *The Dictionary of International Terrorism* (1986) (E); Alex P. Schmid and Albert J. Jongman, *Political Terrorism* (1988) (E); Jay M. Shafritz et al., *Almanac of Modern Terrorism* (1991) (E); John R. Thackrah, *Encyclopedia of Terrorism and Political Violence* (1987) (E). See also "Crime."

Tourism
Ray Bar-On, *Travel and Tourism Data* (1989) (S). See also "Businesses."

Trade
See "Economic Relations," "General Agreement on Tariffs and Trade (GATT)," and "North American Free Trade Agreement (NAFTA)."

Treaties
M. J. Bowman and D. J. Harris, *Multilateral Treaties: Index and Current Status* (1984) (E); J. A. S. Grenville and Bernard Wasserstein, *The Major International Treaties Since 1945* (1987) (D); Walter Lowrie and Matthew St. C. Clarke, *American State Papers* (1832–1861) (D); D. H. Miller, ed., *Treaties and Other International Acts* (1931–1948) (D); Nicholas Rengger, ed., *Treaties and Alliances of the World* (1990) (E); U.S. Department of State, *Treaties in Force* (1941–) (AS) and *United States Treaties and Other International Agreements, 1951-* (1952–) (D).

United Nations
Joseph P. Baratta, *Strengthening the United Nations* (1987) (B); Blanche Finley, *The Structure of the United Nations General Assembly: An Organizational Approach to Its Work, 1974–1980s* (1988) (E); Stanley R. Greenfield, ed., *Who's Who in the United Nations* (1992) (BA); Kumiko Matsura et al., *Chronology and Fact Book of the United Nations, 1941–1991* (1992) (C); Edmund Jan Osmanczyk, *The Encyclopedia of the United Nations and International Relations* (1990) (E); United Nations, *Basic Facts About the United Nations* (1992) (E), *Everyman's United Nations* (1948–) (AS), *United Nations Handbook* (1985–) (AS), and *Yearbook of the United Nations* (1947–) (AS); U.S. Department of State, *United States Participation in the United Nations* (1984–) (AS). See also "International Organizations."

Vietnam War
See "Vietnam and Southeast Asia."

War Crimes and Trials
John R. Lewis, *Uncertain Judgment* (1979) (B); Norman E. Tutorow, ed., *War Crimes, War Criminals, and War Crimes Trials* (1986) (B). See also "Holocaust" and "Human Rights."

War of 1812
John C. Fredriksen, *Free Trade and Sailors' Rights* (1985) (B); Dwight L. Smith, *The War of 1812* (1985) (B). See also "Military Affairs, Defense, and Wars."

War with Mexico
See "Mexico."

Women and Gender Issues
John A. Edens, *Eleanor Roosevelt* (1994) (B); Edward T. James et al., *Notable American Women, 1607–1950* (1971) (BA); Sally Sheir, ed., *Women's Movements of the World* (1988) (E); Linda Schmittroth, ed., *Statistical Record of Women Worldwide* (1991) (S); Barbara Sicherman and Carol H. Green, eds., *Notable American Women, The Modern Period* (1980) (BA). See also "Peace Movements."

World Court
Shabtai Rosenne, *The World Court* (1989) (E). See also "International Law."

World War I
Arthur Banks, *A Military History Atlas of the First World War* (1975) (A); Martin Gilbert, *Atlas of World War I* (1994) (A); Randall Gray, *Chronicles of the First World War* (1990) (C); Holger H. Herwig and Neil M. Heyman, *Biographical Dictionary of World War I* (1982) (BA); George T. Kurian, *Encyclopedia of the First World War* (1990) (E); Anne C. Venzon, ed., *The United States in the First World War* (1995) (E); David R. Woodward and Robert F. Maddox, eds., *America and World War I* (1985) (B). See also "Military Affairs, Defense, and Wars" and individual armed services.

World War II
Marcel Baudot et al., eds., *The Historical Encyclopedia of World War II* (1980) (E); David G. Chandler and James Lawton Collins, Jr., eds., *The D-Day Encyclopedia* (1993) (E); I. C. B. Dear and M. R. Foot, eds., *The Oxford Companion to World War II* (1995) (E); A. G. S. Enser, *A Subject Bibliography of the Second World War, and Aftermath* (1990) (B); Robert Goralski, *World War II Almanac* (1981) (C); Ian V. Hogg and Bryan Perrett, *Encyclopaedia of the Second World War* (1989) (E); John Keegan, ed., *The Times Atlas of the Second World War* (1989) (A); Warren F. Kimball, ed., *Churchill & Roosevelt* (1984) (D); George T. Kurian, *Encyclopedia of the Second World War* (1991) (E); Thomas Parrish, ed., *The Simon and Schuster Encyclopedia of World War II* (1978) (E); Barrie Pitt and Frances Pitt, *The Month-by-Month Atlas of World War II* (1989) (A); Norman Polmar and Thomas B. Allen, *World War II* (1991) (E); John J. Sbrega, *The War Against Japan* (1989) (B); Louis L. Snyder, *Louis L. Snyder's Historical Guide to World War II* (1982) (E); Ronald Spector, "The Scholarship on World War II," *Journal of Military History* (1991) (B); U.S. Military Academy, *Campaign Atlas to the Second World War* (1980) (A); Elizabeth-Anne Wheal et al., *A Dictionary of the Second World War* (1989) (E); Peter Young, ed., *Atlas of the Second World War* (1973) (A). See also "Military Affairs, Defense, and Wars" and individual armed services.

Index